Quantitative Methods in Business

GBS 220

Waner | Costenoble | Anderson | Sweeney | Williams | Camm | Martin

 CENGAGE
Learning™

Australia • Brazil • Japan • Korea • Mexico • Singapore • Spain • United Kingdom • United States

Quantitative Methods in Business

GBS 220

Sr. Manager, Custom Project Management:
Linda deStefano

Market Development Manager:
Heather Kramer

Sr. Manager, Production & Manufacturing:
Donna M. Brown

Manager Production Editorial:
Kim Fry

Sr. Rights Acquisition Account Manager:
Todd Osborne

Printed in the United States of America

For product information and technology assistance, contact us at
Cengage Learning Customer & Sales Support, 1-800-354-9706
For permission to use material from this text or product,
submit all requests online at **cengage.com/permissions**
Further permissions questions can be emailed to
permissionrequest@cengage.com

This book contains select works from existing Cengage Learning resources and was produced by Cengage Learning Custom Solutions for collegiate use. As such, those adopting and/or contributing to this work are responsible for editorial content accuracy, continuity and completeness.

Compilation © 2013 Cengage Learning

ISBN-13: 978-1-285-88656-5

ISBN-10: 1-285-88656-9

Cengage Learning

5191 Natorp Boulevard
Mason, Ohio 45040
USA
Cengage Learning is a leading provider of customized learning solutions with office locations around the globe, including Singapore, the United Kingdom, Australia, Mexico, Brazil, and Japan. Locate your local office at:
international.cengage.com/region.

Cengage Learning products are represented in Canada by Nelson Education, Ltd.
For your lifelong learning solutions, visit **www.cengage.com/custom.**
Visit our corporate website at **www.cengage.com.**
Visit signature labs online at **cengage.com/canvas.**

Acknowledgements

The content of this text has been adapted from the following product(s):

Source Title: An Introduction to Management Science, Revised (Book Only)
Authors: Anderson/Sweeney/Williams/Camm
ISBN10: 1111532249
ISBN13: 9781111532246

Source Title: Finite Math and Applied Calculus
Authors: Waner/Costenoble
ISBN10: 1439049254
ISBN13: 9781439049259

Table Of Contents

Table of Contents

1

Random Variables and Statistics

Case Study Spotting Tax Fraud with Benford's Law

You are a tax fraud specialist working for the Internal Revenue Service (IRS), and you have just been handed a portion of the tax return from Colossal Conglomerate. The IRS suspects that the portion you were handed may be fraudulent and would like your opinion. Is there any mathematical test, you wonder, that can point to a suspicious tax return based on nothing more than the numbers entered?

age fotostock/SuperStock

Web Site
www.FiniteandCalc.org
At the Web site you will find:

- A detailed chapter summary

- Section by section tutorials

- A true/false quiz

- Additional review exercises

- Histogram, Bernoulli trials, and normal distribution utilities

- The following optional extra sections:

    Sampling Distributions and the Central Limit Theorem

    Confidence Intervals

    Calculus and Statistics

Introduction

Statistics is the branch of mathematics concerned with organizing, analyzing, and interpreting numerical data. For example, given the current annual incomes of 1,000 lawyers selected at random, you might wish to answer some questions: If I become a lawyer, what income am I likely to earn? Do lawyers' salaries vary widely? How widely?

To answer questions like these, it helps to begin by organizing the data in the form of tables or graphs. This is the topic of the first section of the chapter. The second section describes an important class of examples that are applicable to a wide range of situations, from tossing a coin to product testing.

Once the data are organized, the next step is to apply mathematical tools for analyzing the data and answering questions like those posed above. Numbers such as the **mean** and the **standard deviation** can be computed to reveal interesting facts about the data. These numbers can then be used to make predictions about future events.

The chapter ends with a section on one of the most important distributions in statistics, the **normal distribution**. This distribution describes many sets of data and also plays an important role in the underlying mathematical theory.

8.1 Random Variables and Distributions

Random Variables

In many experiments we can assign numerical values to the outcomes. For instance, if we roll a die, each outcome has a value from 1 through 6. If you select a lawyer and ascertain his or her annual income, the outcome is again a number. We call a rule that assigns a number to each outcome of an experiment a **random variable**.

Random Variable

A **random variable** X is a rule that assigns a number, or **value**, to each outcome in the sample space of an experiment.*

* **NOTE** In the language of functions (Chapter 1), a random variable is a *real-valued function* whose domain is the sample space.

Visualizing a Random Variable

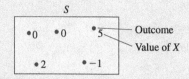

Quick Examples

1. Roll a die; $X =$ the number facing up.
2. Select a mutual fund; $X =$ the number of companies in the fund portfolio.
3. Select a computer; $X =$ the number of megabytes of memory it has.
4. Survey a group of 20 college students; $X =$ the mean SAT.

Discrete and Continuous Random Variables

A **discrete** random variable can take on only specific, isolated numerical values, like the outcome of a roll of a die, or the number of dollars in a randomly chosen bank account. A **continuous** random variable, on the other hand, can take on any values within a continuum or an interval, like the temperature in Central Park, or the height of an athlete in centimeters. Discrete random variables that can take on only finitely many values (like the outcome of a roll of a die) are called **finite** random variables.

Quick Examples

Random Variable	Values	Type
1. Select a mutual fund; $X =$ the number of companies in the fund portfolio.	$\{1, 2, 3, \ldots\}$	Discrete Infinite
2. Take five shots at the goal during a soccer match; $X =$ the number of times you score.	$\{0, 1, 2, 3, 4, 5\}$	Finite
3. Measure the length of an object; $X =$ its length in centimeters.	Any positive real number	Continuous
4. Roll a die until you get a 6; $X =$ the number of times you roll the die.	$\{1, 2, \ldots\}$	Discrete Infinite
5. Bet a whole number of dollars in a race where the betting limit is $100; $X =$ the amount you bet.	$\{0, 1, \ldots, 100\}$	Finite
6. Bet a whole number of dollars in a race where there is no betting limit; $X =$ the amount you bet.	$\{0, 1, \ldots, 100, 101, \ldots\}$	Discrete Infinite

Notes

1. In Chapter 7, the only sample spaces we considered in detail were finite sample spaces. However, in general, sample spaces can be infinite, as in many of the experiments mentioned above.

2. There are some "borderline" situations. For instance, if X is the salary of a factory worker, then X is, strictly speaking, discrete. However, the values of X are so numerous and close together that in some applications it makes sense to model X as a continuous random variable. ■

For the moment, we shall consider only finite random variables.

EXAMPLE 1 **Finite Random Variable**

Let X be the number of heads that come up when a coin is tossed three times. List the value of X for each possible outcome. What are the possible values of X?

Solution First, we describe X as a random variable.

X is the rule that assigns to each outcome the number of heads that come up.

2 Heads ($X = 2$)

We take as the outcomes of this experiment all possible sequences of three heads and tails. Then, for instance, if the outcome is HTH, the value of X is 2. An easy way to list the values of X for all the outcomes is by means of a table.

Web Site
www.FiniteandCalc.org
Go to the Chapter 8 Topic
Summary to find an interactive
simulation based on Example 1.

Outcome	HHH	HHT	HTH	HTT	THH	THT	TTH	TTT
Value of X	3	2	2	1	2	1	1	0

From the table, we also see that the possible values of X are 0, 1, 2, and 3.

➡ **Before we go on...** Remember that X is just a rule we decide on. In Example 1, we could have taken X to be a different rule, such as the number of tails or perhaps the number of heads minus the number of tails. These different rules are examples of different random variables associated with the same experiment. ∎

EXAMPLE 2 Stock Prices

You have purchased $10,000 worth of stock in a biotech company whose newest arthritis drug is awaiting approval by the F.D.A. If the drug is approved this month, the value of the stock will double by the end of the month. If the drug is rejected this month, the stock's value will decline by 80%. If no decision is reached this month, its value will decline by 10%. Let X be the value of your investment at the end of this month. List the value of X for each possible outcome.

Solution There are three possible outcomes: the drug is approved this month, it is rejected this month, and no decision is reached. Once again, we express the random variable as a rule.

The random variable X is the rule that assigns to each outcome the value of your investment at the end of this month.

We can now tabulate the values of X as follows:

Outcome	Approved This Month	Rejected This Month	No Decision
Value of X	$20,000	$2,000	$9,000

Probability Distribution of a Finite Random Variable

Given a random variable X, it is natural to look at certain *events*—for instance, the event that $X = 2$. By this, we mean the event consisting of all outcomes that have an assigned X-value of 2. Looking once again at the chart in Example 1, with X being the number of heads that face up when a coin is tossed three times, we find the following events:

The event that $X = 0$ is {TTT}.

The event that $X = 1$ is {HTT, THT, TTH}.

The event that $X = 2$ is {HHT, HTH, THH}.

The event that $X = 3$ is {HHH}.

The event that $X = 4$ is ∅. There are no outcomes with four heads.

4

Each of these events has a certain probability. For instance, the probability of the event that $X = 2$ is $3/8$ because the event in question consists of three of the eight possible (equally likely) outcomes. We shall abbreviate this by writing

$$P(X = 2) = \frac{3}{8}.$$

The probability that $X = 2$ is $3/8$.

Similarly,

$$P(X = 4) = 0.$$

The probability that $X = 4$ is 0.

When X is a finite random variable, the collection of the probabilities of X equaling each of its possible values is called the **probability distribution** of X. Because the probabilities in a probability distribution can be estimated or theoretical, we shall discuss both *estimated probability distributions* (or *relative frequency distributions*) and *theoretical (modeled) probability distributions* of random variables. (See the next two examples.)

Probability Distribution of a Finite Random Variable

If X is a finite random variable, with values $n_1, n_2, \ldots$ then its **probability distribution** lists the probabilities that $X = n_1, X = n_2, \ldots$ The sum of these probabilities is always 1.

Visualizing the Probability Distribution of a Random Variable

If each outcome in S is equally likely, we get the probability distribution shown for the random variable X.

S
•0 •0 •5
•2 •−1

Probability Distribution of X

x	-1	0	2	5
$P(X = x)$	$\frac{1}{5} = .2$	$\frac{2}{5} = .4$	$\frac{1}{5} = .2$	$\frac{1}{5} = .2$

Here $P(X = x)$ means "the probability that the random variable X has the specific value x."

Quick Example

Roll a fair die; $X =$ the number facing up. Then, the (theoretical) probability that any specific value of X occurs is $\frac{1}{6}$. So, the probability distribution of X is the following (notice that the probabilities add up to 1):

x	1	2	3	4	5	6
$P(X = x)$	$\frac{1}{6}$	$\frac{1}{6}$	$\frac{1}{6}$	$\frac{1}{6}$	$\frac{1}{6}$	$\frac{1}{6}$

Note The distinction between X (upper case) and x (lower case) in the tables above is important; X stands for the random variable in question, whereas x stands for a specific *value* of X (so that x is always a number). Thus, if, say $x = 2$, then $P(X = x)$ means $P(X = 2)$, the probability that X is 2. Similarly, if Y is a random variable, then $P(Y = y)$ is the probability that Y has the specific value y. ∎

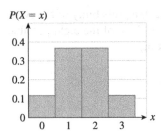

Figure 1

Technology can be used to replicate the histogram in Example 3.

TI-83/84 Plus

STAT EDIT values of *x* in L_1 and probabilities in L_2
WINDOW $0 \leq X \leq 4$, $0 \leq Y \leq 0.5$, Xscl = 1
2ND Y= STAT PLOT on, Histogram icon,
Xlist = L_1 Freq = L_2, then
GRAPH
[More details on page 612.]

Excel

x-values and probabilities in Columns A and B.
Highlight probabilities (column B only) and insert a column chart.
Right click on resulting graph and use Select Data to set the category labels to be the values of *x*.
[More details on page 615.]

Web Site

www.FiniteandCalc.org
Student Home
→ Online Utilities
→ Histogram Utility
Enter the *x*-values and probabilities as shown:

```
0, 1/8
1, 3/8
2, 3/8
3, 1/8
```

Make sure "Show histogram" is checked, and press "Results."

EXAMPLE 3 Probability Distribution

Let *X* be the number of heads that face up in three tosses of a coin. Give the probability distribution of *X*.

Solution *X* is the random variable of Example 1, so its values are 0, 1, 2, and 3. The probability distribution of *X* is given in the following table:

x	0	1	2	3
$P(X = x)$	$\frac{1}{8}$	$\frac{3}{8}$	$\frac{3}{8}$	$\frac{1}{8}$

Notice that the probabilities add to 1, as we might expect.

We can use a bar graph to visualize a probability distribution. Figure 1 shows the bar graph for the probability distribution we obtained. Such a graph is sometimes called a **histogram**.

➡ **Before we go on...** The probabilities in the table in Example 3 are *theoretical* (modeled) probabilities. To obtain a similar table of relative frequencies, we would have to repeatedly toss a coin three times and calculate the fraction of times we got 0, 1, 2, and 3 heads. (See the simulation in the chapter summary at the Web Site.) ■

Note The table of probabilities in Example 3 looks like the probability distribution associated with an experiment, as we studied in Section 7.3. In fact, the probability distribution of a random variable is not really new. Consider the following experiment: toss three coins and count the number of heads. The associated probability distribution (as per Section 7.3) would be this:

Outcome	0	1	2	3
Probability	$\frac{1}{8}$	$\frac{3}{8}$	$\frac{3}{8}$	$\frac{1}{8}$

The difference is that in this chapter we are thinking of 0, 1, 2, and 3 not as the outcomes of the experiment, but as values of the random variable *X*. ■

EXAMPLE 4 Relative Frequency Distribution

The following table shows the (fictitious) income brackets of a sample of 1,000 lawyers in their first year out of law school.

Income Bracket	$20,000–$29,999	$30,000–$39,999	$40,000–$49,999	$50,000–$59,999	$60,000–$69,999	$70,000–$79,999	$80,000–$89,999
Number	20	80	230	400	170	70	30

Think of the experiment of choosing a first-year lawyer at random (all being equally likely) and assign to each lawyer the number *X* that is the midpoint of his or her income bracket. Find the relative frequency distribution of *X*.

Solution Statisticians refer to the income brackets as **measurement classes**. Because the first measurement class contains incomes that are at least $20,000, but less than

6

＊NOTE One might argue that the midpoint should be $(20{,}000 + 29{,}999)/2 = 24{,}999.50$, but we round this to 25,000. So, technically we are using "rounded" midpoints of the measurement classes.

using Technology

Technology can be used to automate the calculations in Example 4. Here is an outline.

TI-83/84 Plus

STAT EDIT values of x in L$_1$ and frequencies in L$_2$.

Home screen:

L$_2$/sum(L$_2$)→L$_3$

[More details on page 612.]

Excel

Headings x, Fr, and $P(X = x)$ in A1–C1

x-values and frequencies in Columns A2–B8

=B2/SUM(B:B) in C2

Copy down column C.

[More details on page 615.]

Web Site

www.FiniteandCalc.org

Student Home

→ Online Utilities

→ Histogram Utility

Enter the x-values and frequencies as shown:

```
25000, 20
35000, 80
45000, 230
55000, 400
65000, 170
75000, 70
85000, 30
```

Make sure "Show probability distribution" is checked, and press "Results." The relative frequency distribution will appear at the bottom of the page.

$30,000, its midpoint is $25,000.＊ Similarly the second measurement class has midpoint $35,000, and so on. We can rewrite the table with the midpoints, as follows:

x	25,000	35,000	45,000	55,000	65,000	75,000	85,000
Frequency	20	80	230	400	170	70	30

We have used the term *frequency* rather than *number*, although it means the same thing. This table is called a **frequency table**. It is *almost* the relative frequency distribution for X, except that we must replace frequencies by relative frequencies. (We did this in calculating relative frequencies in the preceding chapter.) We start with the lowest measurement class. Because 20 of the 1,000 lawyers fall in this group, we have

$$P(X = 25{,}000) = \frac{20}{1{,}000} = .02.$$

We can calculate the remaining relative frequencies similarly to obtain the following distribution:

x	25,000	35,000	45,000	55,000	65,000	75,000	85,000
$P(X = x)$	.02	.08	.23	.40	.17	.07	.03

Note again the distinction between X and x: X stands for the random variable in question, whereas x stands for a specific value (25,000, 35,000, . . . , or 85,000) of X.

EXAMPLE 5 Probability Distribution: Greenhouse Gases

The following table shows per capita emissions of greenhouse gases for the 30 countries with the highest per capita carbon dioxide emissions. (Emissions are rounded to the nearest 5 metric tons.)＊

Country	Per Capita Emissions (metric tons)	Country	Per Capita Emissions (metric tons)
Qatar	70	Estonia	15
Kuwait	40	Faroe Islands	15
United Arab Emirates	40	Saudi Arabia	15
Luxembourg	25	Kazakhstan	15
Trinidad and Tobago	25	Gibraltar	15
Brunei	25	Finland	15
Bahrain	25	Oman	15
Netherlands Antilles	20	Singapore	10
Aruba	20	Palau	10
United States	20	Montserrat	10
Canada	20	Czech Republic	10
Norway	20	Equatorial Guinea	10
Australia	15	New Caledonia	10
Falkland Islands	15	Israel	10
Nauru	15	Russia	10

＊ Figures are based on 2004 data. Source: United Nations Millennium Development Goals Indicators (http://mdgs.un.org/unsd/mdg/Data.aspx).

Consider the experiment in which a country is selected at random from this list, and let X be the per capita carbon dioxide emissions for that country. Find the probability distribution of X and graph it with a histogram. Use the probability distribution to compute $P(X \geq 20)$ (the probability that X is 20 or more) and interpret the result.

Solution The values of X are the possible emissions figures, which we can take to be $0, 5, 10, 15, \ldots, 70$. In the table below, we first compute the frequency of each value of X by counting the number of countries that produce that per capita level of greenhouse gases. For instance, there are seven countries that have $X = 15$. Then, we divide each frequency by the sample size $N = 30$ to obtain the probabilities.*

✱ NOTE Even though we are using the term "frequency," we are really calculating *modeled* probability based on the assumption of equally likely outcomes. In this context, the frequencies are the number of favorable outcomes for each value of X. (See the Q&A discussion at the end of Section 7.3.)

x	0	5	10	15	20	25	30	35	40	45	50	55	60	65	70
Frequency	0	0	8	10	5	4	0	0	2	0	0	0	0	0	1
$P(X = x)$	0	0	$\frac{8}{30}$	$\frac{10}{30}$	$\frac{5}{30}$	$\frac{4}{30}$	0	0	$\frac{2}{30}$	0	0	0	0	0	$\frac{1}{30}$

Figure 2 shows the resulting histogram.

Finally, we compute $P(X \geq 20)$, the probability of the event that X has a value of 20 or more, which is the sum of the probabilities $P(X = 20)$, $P(X = 25)$, and so on. From the table, we obtain

$$P(X \geq 20) = \frac{5}{30} + \frac{4}{30} + \frac{2}{30} + \frac{1}{30} = \frac{12}{30} = .4.$$

Thus, there is a 40% chance that a country randomly selected from the given list produces 20 or more metric tons per capita of carbon dioxide.

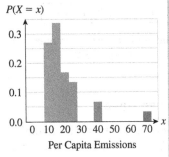

$P(X = x)$

Figure 2

FAQs

Recognizing What to Use as a Random Variable and Deciding on Its Values

Q: *In an application, how, exactly, do I decide what to use as a random variable X?*

A: Be as systematic as possible: First, decide what the experiment is and what its sample space is. Then, based on what is asked for in the application, complete the following sentence: "X assigns ___ to each outcome." For instance, "X assigns the number of flavors to each packet of gummy bears selected," or "X assigns the average faculty salary to each college selected."

Q: *Once I have decided what X should be, how do I decide what values to assign it?*

A: Ask yourself: What are the conceivable values I could get for X? Then choose a collection of values that includes all of these. For instance, if X is the number of heads obtained when a coin is tossed five times, then the possible values of X are 0, 1, 2, 3, 4, and 5. If X is the average faculty salary in dollars, rounded to the nearest $5,000, then possible values of X could be 20,000, 25,000, 30,000, and so on, up to the highest salary in your data.

8.1 EXERCISES

▼ more advanced   ◆ challenging
🤖 indicates exercises that should be solved using technology

In Exercises 1–10, classify each random variable X as finite, discrete infinite, or continuous, and indicate the values that X can take. HINT [See Quick Examples on page 549.]

1. Roll two dice; $X =$ the sum of the numbers facing up.

2. Open a 500-page book on a random page; $X =$ the page number.

3. Select a stock at random; $X =$ your profit, to the nearest dollar, if you purchase one share and sell it one year later.

4. Select an electric utility company at random; $X =$ the exact amount of electricity, in gigawatt hours, it supplies in a year.

5. Look at the second hand of your watch; X is the time it reads in seconds.

6. Watch a soccer game; $X =$ the total number of goals scored.

7. Watch a soccer game; $X =$ the total number of goals scored, up to a maximum of 10.

8. Your class is given a mathematics exam worth 100 points; X is the average score, rounded to the nearest whole number.

9. According to quantum mechanics, the energy of an electron in a hydrogen atom can assume only the values $k/1, k/4, k/9, k/16, \ldots$ for a certain constant value k. $X =$ the energy of an electron in a hydrogen atom.

10. According to classical mechanics, the energy of an electron in a hydrogen atom can assume any positive value. $X =$ the energy of an electron in a hydrogen atom.

In Exercises 11–18, (a) say what an appropriate sample space is; (b) complete the following sentence: "X is the rule that assigns to each . . . "; (c) list the values of X for all the outcomes. HINT [See Example 1.]

11. X is the number of tails that come up when a coin is tossed twice.

12. X is the largest number of consecutive times heads comes up in a row when a coin is tossed three times.

13. X is the sum of the numbers that face up when two dice are rolled.

14. X is the value of the larger number when two dice are rolled.

15. X is the number of red marbles that Tonya has in her hand after she selects four marbles from a bag containing four red marbles and two green ones and then notes how many there are of each color.

16. X is the number of green marbles that Stej has in his hand after he selects four marbles from a bag containing three red marbles and two green ones and then notes how many there are of each color.

17. The mathematics final exam scores for the students in your study group are 89%, 85%, 95%, 63%, 92%, and 80%.

18. The capacities of the hard drives of your dormitory suite mates' computers are 10GB, 15GB, 20GB, 25GB, 30GB, and 35GB.

19. The random variable X has this probability distribution table:

x	2	4	6	8	10
$P(X = x)$	.1	.2	–	–	.1

   a. Assuming $P(X = 8) = P(X = 6)$, find each of the missing values. HINT [See Quick Example on page 551.]
   b. Calculate $P(X \geq 6)$.

20. The random variable X has the probability distribution table shown below:

x	−2	−1	0	1	2
$P(X = x)$	–	–	.4	.1	.1

   a. Calculate $P(X \geq 0)$ and $P(X < 0)$. HINT [See Quick Example on page 551.]
   b. Assuming $P(X = -2) = P(X = -1)$, find each of the missing values.

In Exercises 21–28, give the probability distribution for the indicated random variable and draw the corresponding histogram. HINT [See Example 3.]

21. A fair die is rolled, and X is the number facing up.

22. A fair die is rolled, and X is the square of the number facing up.

23. Three fair coins are tossed, and X is the square of the number of heads showing.

24. Three fair coins are tossed, and X is the number of heads minus the number of tails.

25. A red and a green die are rolled, and X is the sum of the numbers facing up.

26. A red and a green die are rolled, and
$$X = \begin{cases} 0 & \text{If the numbers are the same} \\ 1 & \text{If the numbers are different.} \end{cases}$$

27. ▼ A red and a green die are rolled, and X is the larger of the two numbers facing up.

28. ▼ A red and a green die are rolled, and X is the smaller of the two numbers facing up.

9

APPLICATIONS

29. *Income Distribution up to $100,000* The following table shows the distribution of household incomes for a sample of 1,000 households in the United States with incomes up to $100,000.[1]

Income Bracket	0–19,999	20,000–39,999	40,000–59,999	60,000–79,999	80,000–99,999
Households	240	270	220	160	110

a. Let X be the (rounded) midpoint of a bracket in which a household falls. Find the relative frequency distribution of X and graph its histogram. HINT [See Example 4.]

b. Shade the area of your histogram corresponding to the probability that a U.S. household has a value of X of 50,000 or more. What is this probability?

30. *Income Distribution up to $100,000* Repeat Exercise 29, using the following data for a sample of 1,000 Hispanic households in the U.S.[2]

Income Bracket	0–19,999	20,000–39,999	40,000–59,999	60,000–79,999	80,000–99,999
Households	260	310	210	140	80

31. *Employment in Mexico by Age* The following chart shows the ages of 250 working adults surveyed in Mexico:[3]

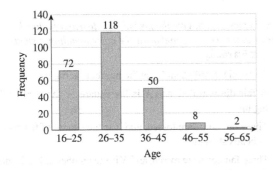

What is the associated random variable? Represent the data as a relative frequency distribution using the (rounded) midpoints of the given measurement classes. HINT [See Example 4.]

32. *Unemployment in Mexico by Age* Repeat the preceding exercise, using the following chart, which shows the ages of 250 unemployed adults surveyed in Mexico:[4]

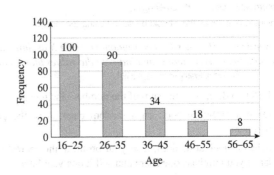

33. *Sport Utility Vehicles—Tow Ratings* The following table shows tow ratings (in pounds) for some popular sports utility vehicles:[5]

Mercedes Grand Marquis V8	2,000
Jeep Wrangler I6	2,000
Ford Explorer V6	3,000
Dodge Dakota V6	4,000
Mitsubishi Montero V6	5,000
Ford Explorer V8	6,000
Dodge Durango V8	6,000
Dodge Ram 1500 V8	8,000
Ford Expedition V8	8,000
Hummer 2-door Hardtop	8,000

Let X be the tow rating of a randomly chosen popular SUV from the list above.

a. What are the values of X?

b. Compute the frequency and probability distributions of X. HINT [See Example 5.]

c. What is the probability that an SUV (from the list above) is rated to tow no more than 5,000 pounds?

34. *Housing Prices* The following table shows the average percentage increase in the price of a house from 1980 to 2001 in nine regions of the United States.[6]

---

[1] Based on the actual household income distribution in 2007. Source: U.S. Census Bureau, Current Population Survey, 2008 Annual Social and Economic Supplement (http://pubdb3.census.gov/macro/032008/hhinc/new06_000.htm).

[2] Ibid.

[3] Based on data from January 2007. Source for data: Instituto Nacional de Estadística y Geografía (INEGI) (www.inegi.org.mx).

[4] Ibid.

[5] Tow rates are for 2000 models and vary considerably within each model. Figures cited are rounded. For more detailed information, consult www.rvsafety.com/towrate2k.htm.

[6] Percentages are rounded to the nearest 25%. Source: Third Quarter 2001 House Price Index, released November 30, 2001 by the Office of Federal Housing Enterprise Oversight; available online at www.ofheo.gov/house/3q01hpi.pdf.

New England	300
Pacific	225
Middle Atlantic	225
South Atlantic	150
Mountain	150
West North Central	125
West South Central	75
East North Central	150
East South Central	125

Let X be the percentage increase in the price of a house in a randomly selected region.

a. What are the values of X?

b. Compute the frequency and probability distribution of X. HINT [See Example 5.]

c. What is the probability that, in a randomly selected region, the percentage increase in the cost of a house exceeded 200%?

35. *Stock Market Gyrations* The following chart shows the day-by-day change, rounded to the nearest 100 points, in the Dow Jones Industrial Average during 20 successive business days around the start of the financial crisis in October 2008:[7]

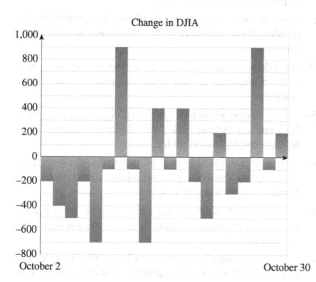

Change in DJIA

October 2 — October 30

Let X be the (rounded) change in the Dow on a randomly selected day.

a. What are the values of X?

b. Compute the frequency and probability distribution of X. HINT [See Example 5.]

c. What is the probability that, on a randomly selected day, the Dow decreased by more than 250 points?

36. *Stock Market Gyrations* Repeat Exercise 35 using the following chart for November–December 2008:[8]

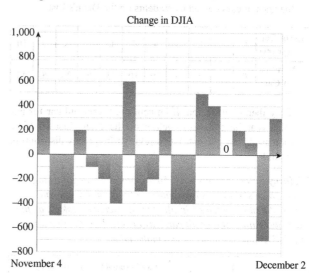

Change in DJIA

November 4 — December 2

37. *Grade Point Averages* The grade point averages of the students in your mathematics class are

3.2, 3.5, 4.0, 2.9, 2.0, 3.3, 3.5, 2.9, 2.5, 2.0,
2.1, 3.2, 3.6, 2.8, 2.5, 1.9, 2.0, 2.2, 3.9, 4.0

Use these raw data to construct a frequency table with the following measurement classes: 1.1–2.0, 2.1–3.0, 3.1–4.0, and find the probability distribution using the (rounded) midpoint values as the values of X. HINT [See Example 5.]

38. *Test Scores* Your scores for the 20 surprise math quizzes last semester were (out of 10)

4.5, 9.5, 10.0, 3.5, 8.0, 9.5, 7.5, 6.5, 7.0, 8.0,
8.0, 8.5, 7.5, 7.0, 8.0, 9.0, 10.0, 8.5, 7.5, 8.0.

Use these raw data to construct a frequency table with the following brackets: 2.1–4.0, 4.1–6.0, 6.1–8.0, 8.1–10.0, and find the probability distribution using the (rounded) midpoint values as the values of X. HINT [See Example 5.]

39. ▼ *Car Purchases* To persuade his parents to contribute to his new car fund, Carmine has spent the last week surveying the ages of 2,000 cars on campus. His findings are reflected in the following frequency table:

Age of Car (years)	0	1	2	3	4	5	6	7	8	9	10
Number of Cars	140	350	450	650	200	120	50	10	5	15	10

Carmine's jalopy is 6 years old. He would like to make the following claim to his parents: "x percent of students have cars newer than mine." Use a relative frequency distribution to find x.

---

[7] Source: http://finance.google.com.

[8] Ibid.

11

40. ▼ *Car Purchases* Carmine's parents, not convinced of his need for a new car, produced the following statistics showing the ages of cars owned by students on the Dean's List:

Age of Car (years)	0	1	2	3	4	5	6	7	8	9	10
Number of Cars	0	2	5	5	10	10	15	20	20	20	40

They then claimed that if he kept his 6-year-old car for another year, his chances of getting on the Dean's List would be increased by x percent. Use a relative frequency distribution to find x.

Highway Safety Exercises 41–50 are based on the following table, which shows crashworthiness ratings for several categories of motor vehicles.[9] In all of these exercises, take X as the crash-test rating of a small car, Y as the crash-test rating for a small SUV, and so on, as shown in the table.

	Number Tested	Overall Frontal Crash Test Rating			
		3 (Good)	2 (Acceptable)	1 (Marginal)	0 (Poor)
Small Cars X	16	1	11	2	2
Small SUVs Y	10	1	4	4	1
Medium SUVs Z	15	3	5	3	4
Passenger Vans U	13	3	0	3	7
Midsize Cars V	15	3	5	0	7
Large Cars W	19	9	5	3	2

41. Compute the relative frequency distribution for X.

42. Compute the relative frequency distribution for Y.

43. Compute $P(X \geq 2)$ and interpret the result.

44. Compute $P(Y \leq 1)$ and interpret the result.

45. Compare $P(Y \geq 2)$ and $P(Z \geq 2)$. What does the result suggest about SUVs?

46. Compare $P(V \geq 2)$ and $P(Z \geq 2)$. What does the result suggest?

47. ▼ Which of the six categories shown has the *lowest* probability of a Good rating?

48. ▼ Which of the six categories shown has the *highest* probability of a Poor rating?

49. ▼ You choose, at random, a small car and a small SUV. What is the probability that both will be rated at least 2?

[9] Ratings are by the Insurance Institute for Highway Safety. Sources: Oak Ridge National Laboratory: "An Analysis of the Impact of Sport Utility Vehicles in the United States," Stacy C. Davis, Lorena F. Truett (August 2000)/Insurance Institute for Highway Safety (www-cta.ornl.gov/Publications/Final SUV report.pdf, www.highwaysafety.org/vehicle_ratings).

50. ▼ You choose, at random, a small car and a midsize car. What is the probability that both will be rated at most 1?

Exercises 51 and 52 assume familiarity with counting arguments and probability (Section 7.4).

51. ▼ *Camping* Kent's Tents has four red tents and three green tents in stock. Karin selects four of them at random. Let X be the number of red tents she selects. Give the probability distribution and find $P(X \geq 2)$.

52. ▼ *Camping* Kent's Tents has five green knapsacks and four yellow ones in stock. Curt selects four of them at random. Let X be the number of green knapsacks he selects. Give the probability distribution and find $P(X \leq 2)$.

53. ◆ *Testing Your Calculator* Use your calculator or computer to generate a sequence of 100 random digits in the range 0–9, and test the random number generator for uniformness by drawing the distribution histogram.

54. ◆ *Testing Your Dice* Repeat Exercise 53, but this time, use a die to generate a sequence of 50 random numbers in the range 1–6.

COMMUNICATION AND REASONING EXERCISES

55. Are all infinite random variables necessarily continuous? Explain.

56. Are all continuous random variables necessarily infinite? Explain.

57. If you are unable to compute the (theoretical) probability distribution for a random variable X, how can you estimate the distribution?

58. What do you expect to happen to the probabilities in a probability distribution as you make the measurement classes smaller?

59. ▼ Give an example of a real-life situation that can be modeled by a random variable with a probability distribution whose histogram is highest on the left.

60. ▼ Give an example of a real-life situation that can be modeled by a random variable with a probability distribution whose histogram is highest on the right.

61. ▼ How wide should the bars in a histogram be so that the area of each bar equals the probability of the corresponding range of values of X?

62. ▼ How wide should the bars in a histogram be so that the probability $P(a \leq X \leq b)$ equals the area of the corresponding portion of the histogram?

63. ▼ Give at least one scenario in which you might prefer to model the number of pages in a randomly selected book using a continuous random variable rather than a discrete random variable.

64. ▼ Give at least one scenario in which you might prefer to model a temperature using a discrete random variable rather than a continuous random variable.

8.2 Bernoulli Trials and Binomial Random Variables

Your electronic production plant produces video game joysticks. Unfortunately, quality control at the plant leaves much to be desired, and 10% of the joysticks the plant produces are defective. A large corporation has expressed interest in adopting your product for its new game console, and today an inspection team will be visiting to test video game joysticks as they come off the assembly line. If the team tests five joysticks, what is the probability that none will be defective? What is the probability that more than one will be defective?

In this scenario we are interested in the following, which is an example of a particular type of finite random variable called a **binomial random variable**: Think of the experiment as a sequence of five "trials" (in each trial the inspection team chooses one joystick at random and tests it) each with two possible outcomes: "success" (a defective joystick) and "failure" (a non-defective one).* If we now take X to be the number of successes (defective joysticks) the inspection team finds, we can recast the questions above as follows: Find $P(X = 0)$ and $P(X > 1)$.

✳ NOTE These are customary names for the two possible outcomes, and often do not indicate actual success or failure at anything. "Success" is the label we give the outcome of interest—in this case, finding a defective joystick.

† NOTE Jakob Bernoulli (1654–1705) was one of the pioneers of probability theory.

Bernoulli Trial

A **Bernoulli**[†] **trial** is an experiment that has two possible outcomes, called **success** and **failure**. If the probability of success is p then the probability of failure is $q = 1 - p$.

Visualizing a Bernoulli Trial

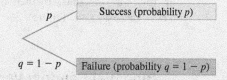

Tossing a coin three times is an example of a **sequence of independent Bernoulli trials**: a sequence of Bernoulli trials in which the outcomes in any one trial are independent (in the sense of the preceding chapter) of those in any other trial, and in which the probability of success is the same for all the trials.

Quick Examples

1. Roll a die, and take success to be the event that you roll a 6. Then $p = 1/6$ and $q = 5/6$. Rolling the die 10 times is then an example of a sequence of 10 independent Bernoulli trials.

2. Provide a property with flood insurance for 20 years, and take success to be the event that the property is flooded during a particular year. Observing whether or not the property is flooded each year for 20 years is then an example of 20 independent Bernoulli trials (assuming that the occurrence of flooding one year is independent of whether there was flooding in earlier years).

✳ NOTE Choosing a "loser" (a fund that will depreciate next year) slightly depletes the pool of "losers" and hence slightly decreases the probability of choosing another one. However, the fact that the pool of funds is very large means that this decrease is extremely small. Hence, p is very nearly constant.

3. You know that 60% of all bond funds will depreciate in value next year. Take success to be the event that a randomly chosen fund depreciates next year. Then $p = .6$ and $q = .4$. Choosing five funds at random for your portfolio from a very large number of possible funds is, approximately,* an example of five independent Bernolli trials.

4. Suppose that E is an event in an experiment with sample space S. Then we can think of the experiment as a Bernoulli trial with two outcomes; success if E occurs, and failure if E' occurs. The probability of success is then

$$p = P(E)$$ Success is the occurrence of E.

and the probability of failure is

$$q = P(E') = 1 - P(E) = 1 - p.$$ Failure is the occurrence of E'.

Repeating the experiment 30 times, say, is then an example of 30 independent Bernoulli trials.

Note Quick Example 4 above tells us that Bernoulli trials are not very special kinds of experiments; in fact, we are performing a Bernoulli trial every time we repeat *any* experiment and observe whether a specific event E occurs. Thinking of an experiment in this way amounts, mathematically, to thinking of $\{E, E'\}$ as our sample space (E = success, E' = failure). ∎

Binomial Random Variable

A **binomial random variable** is one that counts the number of successes in a sequence of independent Bernoulli trials, where the number of trials is fixed.

Visualizing a Binomial Random Variable

X = Number of Successes

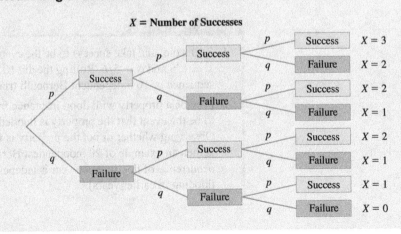

14

> ### Quick Examples
>
> 1. Roll a die ten times; X is the number of times you roll a 6.
> 2. Provide a property with flood insurance for 20 years; X is the number of years, during the 20-year period, during which the property is flooded (assuming that the occurrence of flooding one year is independent of whether there was flooding in earlier years).
> 3. You know that 60% of all bond funds will depreciate in value next year, and you randomly select four from a very large number of possible choices; X is the number of bond funds you hold that will depreciate next year. (X is approximately binomial; see the margin note on p. 560.)

EXAMPLE 1 Probability Distribution of a Binomial Random Variable

Suppose that we have a possibly unfair coin with the probability of heads p and the probability of tails $q = 1 - p$.

a. Let X be the number of heads you get in a sequence of five tosses. Find $P(X = 2)$.

b. Let X be the number of heads you get in a sequence of n tosses. Find $P(X = x)$.

Solution

a. We are looking for the probability of getting exactly two heads in a sequence of five tosses. Let's start with a simpler question: What is the probability that we will get the sequence HHTTT?

The probability that the first toss will come up heads is p.

The probability that the second toss will come up heads is also p.

The probability that the third toss will come up tails is q.

The probability that the fourth toss will come up tails is q.

The probability that the fifth toss will come up tails is q.

The probability that the first toss will be heads *and* the second will be heads *and* the third will be tails *and* the fourth will be tails *and* the fifth will be tails equals the probability of the *intersection* of these five events. Because these are independent events, the probability of the intersection is the product of the probabilities, which is

$$p \times p \times q \times q \times q = p^2 q^3.$$

Now HHTTT is only one of several outcomes with two heads and three tails. Two others are HTHTT and TTTHH. How many such outcomes are there altogether? This is the number of "words" with two H's and three T's, and we know from Chapter 6 that the answer is $C(5, 2) = 10$.

Each of the 10 outcomes with two H's and three T's has the same probability: $p^2 q^3$. (Why?) Thus, the probability of getting one of these 10 outcomes is the probability of the union of all these (mutually exclusive) events, and we saw in the preceding chapter that this is just the sum of the probabilities. In other words, the probability we are after is

$$P(X = 2) = p^2 q^3 + p^2 q^3 + \cdots + p^2 q^3 \qquad C(5, 2) \text{ times}$$
$$= C(5, 2) p^2 q^3.$$

15

The structure of this formula is as follows:

Number of heads   Number of tails

$$P(X = 2) = C(5, 2)p^2 q^3$$

Number of tosses   Probability of tails
Number of heads   Probability of heads

b. What we did using the numbers 5 and 2 in part (a) works as well in general. For the general case, with n tosses and x heads, replace 5 with n and replace 2 with x to get:

$$P(X = x) = C(n, x)p^x q^{n-x}.$$

(Note that the coefficient of q is the number of tails, which is $n - x$.)

The calculation in Example 1 applies to any binomial random variable, so we can say the following:

Probability Distribution of Binomial Random Variables

If X is the number of successes in a sequence of n independent Bernoulli trials, then

$$P(X = x) = C(n, x)p^x q^{n-x}$$

where

n = number of trials
p = probability of success
q = probability of failure = $1 - p$.

Quick Example

If you roll a fair die five times, the probability of throwing exactly two 6s is

$$P(X = 2) = C(5, 2)\left(\frac{1}{6}\right)^2 \left(\frac{5}{6}\right)^3 = 10 \times \frac{1}{36} \times \frac{125}{216} \approx .1608.$$

Here, we used $n = 5$ and $p = 1/6$, the probability of rolling a 6 on one roll of the die.

EXAMPLE 2 Aging

By 2030, the probability that a randomly chosen resident in the United States will be 65 years old or older is projected to be .2.*

a. What is the probability that, in a randomly selected sample of six U.S. residents, exactly four of them will be 65 or older?

b. If X is the number of people aged 65 or older in a sample of six, construct the probability distribution of X and plot its histogram.

---

* Source: U.S. Census Bureau, Decennial Census, Population Estimates and Projections (www.agingstats.gov/agingstatsdotnet/Main_Site/Data/2008_Documents/Population.aspx).

c. Compute $P(X \le 2)$.

d. Compute $P(X \ge 2)$.

Solution

a. The experiment is a sequence of Bernoulli trials; in each trial we select a person and ascertain his or her age. If we take "success" to mean selection of a person aged 65 or older, then the probability distribution is

$$P(X = x) = C(n, x)p^x q^{n-x}$$

where n = number of trials = 6

p = probability of success = .2
q = probability of failure = .8

So,

$$P(X = 4) = C(6, 4)(.2)^4(.8)^2$$
$$= 15 \times .0016 \times .64 = .01536$$

b. We have already computed $P(X = 4)$. Here are all the calculations:

$$P(X = 0) = C(6, 0)(.2)^0(.8)^6$$
$$= 1 \times 1 \times .262144 = .262144$$

$$P(X = 1) = C(6, 1)(.2)^1(.8)^5$$
$$= 6 \times .2 \times .32768 = .393216$$

$$P(X = 2) = C(6, 2)(.2)^2(.8)^4$$
$$= 15 \times .04 \times .4096 = .24576$$

$$P(X = 3) = C(6, 3)(.2)^3(.8)^3$$
$$= 20 \times .008 \times .512 = .08192$$

$$P(X = 4) = C(6, 4)(.2)^4(.8)^2$$
$$= 15 \times .0016 \times .64 = .01536$$

$$P(X = 5) = C(6, 5)(.2)^5(.8)^1$$
$$= 6 \times .00032 \times .8 = .001536$$

$$P(X = 6) = C(6, 6)(.2)^6(.8)^0$$
$$= 1 \times .000064 \times 1 = .000064.$$

The probability distribution is therefore as follows:

x	0	1	2	3	4	5	6
$P(X = x)$	.262144	.393216	.24576	.08192	.01536	.001536	.000064

Figure 3 shows its histogram.

c. $P(X \le 2)$—the probability that the number of people selected who are at least 65 years old is either 0, 1, or 2—is the probability of the union of these events and is thus the sum of the three probabilities:

$$P(X \le 2) = P(X = 0) + P(X = 1) + P(X = 2)$$
$$= .262144 + .393216 + .24576$$
$$= .90112.$$

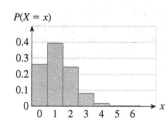

$P(X = x)$

Figure 3

using Technology

Technology can be used to replicate the histogram in Example 2.

TI-83/84 Plus

Y= screen: Y₁=6 nCr
X*0.2^X*0.8^(6-X)
[2ND] [TBLSET] Set Indpt to Ask.
[2ND] [TABLE] Enter x-values
0, 1, ..., 6.
[More details on page 612.]

Excel

Headings x and $P(X = x)$ in A1, B1

x-values 0, 1, ..., 6 in A2–A8

`=BINOMDIST(A2,6,0,.2,0)` in B2

Copy down to B6.

[More details on page 615.]

Web Site

www.FiniteandCalc.org

Student Home

→ Online Utilities

→ Binomial Distribution Utility

Enter $n = 6$ and $p = .2$ and press "Generate Distribution."

d. To compute $P(X \geq 2)$, we *could* compute the sum

$$P(X \geq 2) = P(X = 2) + P(X = 3) + P(X = 4) + P(X = 5) + P(X = 6)$$

but it is far easier to compute the probability of the complement of the event:

$$P(X < 2) = P(X = 0) + P(X = 1)$$
$$= .262144 + .393216 = .65536$$

and then subtract the answer from 1:

$$P(X \geq 2) = 1 - P(X < 2)$$
$$= 1 - .65536 = .34464.$$

FAQs

Terminology and Recognizing When to Use the Binomial Distribution

Q: *What is the difference between Bernoulli trials and a binomial random variable?*

A: A Bernoulli trial is a type of experiment, whereas a binomial random variable is the resulting kind of random variable. More precisely, if your experiment consists of performing a sequence of n Bernoulli trials (think of throwing a dart n times at random points on a dartboard hoping to hit the bull's eye), then the random variable X that counts the number of successes (the number of times you actually hit the bull's eye) is a binomial random variable.

Q: *How do I recognize when a situation gives a binomial random variable?*

A: Make sure that the experiment consists of a sequence of independent Bernoulli trials; that is, a sequence of a fixed number of trials of an experiment that has two outcomes, where the outcome of each trial does not depend on the outcomes in previous trials, and where the probability of success is the same for all the trials. For instance, repeatedly throwing a dart at a dartboard hoping to hit the bull's eye does not constitute a sequence of Bernoulli trials if you adjust your aim each time depending on the outcome of your previous attempt. This dart-throwing experiment can be modeled by a sequence of Bernoulli trials if you make no adjustments after each attempt and your aim does not improve (or deteriorate) with time.

8.2 EXERCISES

▼ more advanced   ◆ challenging

🔲 indicates exercises that should be solved using technology

In Exercises 1–10, you are performing 5 independent Bernoulli trials with $p = .1$ and $q = .9$. Calculate the probability of each of the stated outcomes. Check your answer using technology. HINT [See Quick Example on page 562.]

1. Two successes

2. Three successes

3. No successes

4. No failures

5. All successes

6. All failures

7. At most two successes

8. At least four successes

9. At least three successes

10. At most three successes

In Exercises 11–18, X is a binomial variable with $n = 6$ and $p = .4$. Compute the given probabilities. Check your answer using technology. HINT [See Example 2.]

11. $P(X = 3)$

12. $P(X = 4)$

13. $P(X \leq 2)$

14. $P(X \leq 1)$

15. $P(X \geq 5)$

16. $P(X \geq 4)$

17. $P(1 \leq X \leq 3)$

18. $P(3 \leq X \leq 5)$

In Exercises 19 and 20, graph the histogram of the given binomial distribution. Check your answer using technology.

19. $n = 5, p = \frac{1}{4}, q = \frac{3}{4}$

20. $n = 5, p = \frac{1}{3}, q = \frac{2}{3}$

In Exercises 21 and 22, graph the histogram of the given binomial distribution and compute the given quantity, indicating the corresponding region on the graph.

21. $n = 4, p = \frac{1}{3}, q = \frac{2}{3}; P(X \le 2)$

22. $n = 4, p = \frac{1}{4}, q = \frac{3}{4}; P(X \le 1)$

APPLICATIONS

23. *Internet Addiction* The probability that a randomly chosen person in the Netherlands connects to the Internet immediately upon waking is approximately .25.[10] What is the probability that, in a randomly selected sample of five people, two connect to the Internet immediately upon waking? HINT [See Example 2.]

24. *Alien Retirement* The probability that a randomly chosen citizen-entity of Cygnus is of pension age[11] is approximately .8. What is the probability that, in a randomly selected sample of four citizen-entities, all of them are of pension age? HINT [See Example 2.]

25. *'90s Internet Stock Boom* According to a July, 1999, article in the *New York Times*,[12] venture capitalists had this "rule of thumb": The probability that an Internet start-up company will be a "stock market success" resulting in "spectacular profits for early investors" is .2. If you were a venture capitalist who invested in 10 Internet start-up companies, what was the probability that at least 1 of them would be a stock market success? (Round your answer to four decimal places.)

26. *'90s Internet Stock Boom* According to the article cited in Exercise 25, 13.5% of Internet stocks that entered the market in 1999 ended up trading below their initial offering prices. If you were an investor who purchased five Internet stocks at their initial offering prices, what was the probability that at least four of them would end up trading at or above their initial offering price? (Round your answer to four decimal places.)

27. *Job Training* *(from the GRE Exam in Economics)* In a large on-the-job training program, half of the participants are female and half are male. In a random sample of three participants, what is the probability that an investigator will draw at least one male?

28. *Job Training* *(based on a question from the GRE Exam in Economics)* In a large on-the-job training program, half of the participants are female and half are male. In a random sample of five participants, what is the probability that an investigator will draw at least two males?

29. *Manufacturing* Your manufacturing plant produces air bags, and it is known that 10% of them are defective. Five air bags are tested.
   a. Find the probability that three of them are defective.
   b. Find the probability that at least two of them are defective.

30. *Manufacturing* Compute the probability distribution of the binomial variable described in the preceding exercise, and use it to compute the probability that if five air bags are tested, at least one will be defective and at least one will not.

31. *Teenage Pastimes* According to a study,[13] the probability that a randomly selected teenager watched a rented video at least once during a week was .71. What is the probability that at least 8 teenagers in a group of 10 watched a rented movie at least once last week?

32. *Other Teenage Pastimes* According to the study cited in the preceding exercise, the probability that a randomly selected teenager studied at least once during a week was only .52. What is the probability that less than half of the students in your study group of 10 have studied in the last week?

33. *Subprime Mortgages* In November 2008 the probability that a randomly selected subprime home mortgage in Florida was in foreclosure was .24.[14] Choose 10 subprime home mortgages at random.
   a. What is the probability that exactly five of them were in foreclosure?
   b. Use technology to generate the probability distribution for the associated binomial random variable.
   c. Fill in the blank: If 10 subprime home mortgages were chosen at random, the number of them most likely to have been in foreclosure was _____.

34. *Subprime Mortgages* In November 2008 the probability that a randomly selected subprime home mortgage in Texas was current in its payments was .67.[15] Choose 10 subprime home mortgages at random.
   a. What is the probability that exactly four of them were current?
   b. Use technology to generate the probability distribution for the associated binomial random variable.
   c. Fill in the blank: If 10 subprime home mortgages were chosen at random, the number of them most likely to have been current was _____.

35. ▽ *Triple Redundancy* In order to ensure reliable performance of vital computer systems, aerospace engineers sometimes employ the technique of "triple redundancy," in which three identical computers are installed in a space vehicle. If one of the three computers gives results different from the other two,

---

[10] Source: *Webwereld* November 17, 2008 (http://webwereld.nl/article/view/id/53599).

[11] The retirement age in Cygnus is 12,000 bootlags, which is equivalent to approximately 20 minutes Earth time.

[12] "Not All Hit It Rich in the Internet Gold Rush," *The New York Times*, July 20, 1999, p. A1.

[13] Sources: Rand Youth Poll/Teen-age Research Unlimited/*The New York Times*, March 14, 1998, p. D1.

[14] Source: Federal Reserve Bank of New York (www.newyorkfed.org/regional/subprime.html).

[15] Ibid.

it is assumed to be malfunctioning and it is ignored. This technique will work as long as no more than one computer malfunctions. Assuming that an onboard computer is 99% reliable (that is, the probability of its failing is .01), what is the probability that at least two of the three computers will malfunction?

36. ▼ *IQ Scores* Mensa is a club for people who have high IQ scores. To qualify, your IQ must be at least 132, putting you in the top 2% of the general population. If a group of 10 people are chosen at random, what is the probability that at least 2 of them qualify for Mensa?

37. 🔲 ▼ *Standardized Tests* Assume that on a standardized test of 100 questions, a person has a probability of 80% of answering any particular question correctly. Find the probability of answering between 75 and 85 questions, inclusive, correctly. (Assume independence, and round your answer to four decimal places.)

38. 🔲 ▼ *Standardized Tests* Assume that on a standardized test of 100 questions, a person has a probability of 80% of answering any particular question correctly. Find the probability of answering at least 90 questions correctly. (Assume independence, and round your answer to four decimal places.)

39. 🔲 ▼ *Product Testing* It is known that 43% of all the ZeroFat hamburger patties produced by your factory actually contain more than 10 grams of fat. Compute the probability distribution for $n = 50$ Bernoulli trials.

   a. What is the most likely value for the number of burgers in a sample of 50 that contain more than 10 grams of fat?

   b. Complete the following sentence: There is an approximately 71% chance that a batch of 50 ZeroFat patties contains ____ or more patties with more than 10 grams of fat.

   c. Compare the graphs of the distributions for $n = 50$ trials and $n = 20$ trials. What do you notice?

40. 🔲 ▼ *Product Testing* It is known that 65% of all the ZeroCal hamburger patties produced by your factory actually contain more than 1,000 calories. Compute the probability distribution for $n = 50$ Bernoulli trials.

   a. What is the most likely value for the number of burgers in a sample of 50 that contain more than 1,000 calories?

   b. Complete the following sentence: There is an approximately 73% chance that a batch of 50 ZeroCal patties contains ____ or more patties with more than 1,000 calories.

   c. Compare the graphs of the distributions for $n = 50$ trials and $n = 20$ trials. What do you notice?

41. 🔲 ▼ *Quality Control* A manufacturer of light bulbs chooses bulbs at random from its assembly line for testing. If the probability of a bulb's being bad is .01, how many bulbs do they need to test before the probability of finding at least one bad one rises to more than .5? (You may have to use trial and error to solve this.)

42. 🔲 ▼ *Quality Control* A manufacturer of light bulbs chooses bulbs at random from its assembly line for testing. If the probability of a bulb's being bad is .01, how many bulbs do they need to test before the probability of finding at least two bad ones rises to more than .5? (You may have to use trial and error to solve this.)

43. ▼ *Highway Safety* According to a study,[16] a male driver in the United States will average 562 accidents per 100 million miles. Regard an n-mile trip as a sequence of n Bernoulli trials with "success" corresponding to having an accident during a particular mile. What is the probability that a male driver will have an accident in a one-mile trip?

44. ▼ *Highway Safety*: According to the study cited in the preceding exercise, a female driver in the United States will average 611 accidents per 100 million miles. Regard an n-mile trip as a sequence of n Bernoulli trials with "success" corresponding to having an accident during a particular mile. What is the probability that a female driver will have an accident in a one-mile trip?

45. ◆ *Mad Cow Disease* In March 2004, the U.S. Agriculture Department announced plans to test approximately 243,000 slaughtered cows per year for mad cow disease (bovine spongiform encephalopathy).[17] When announcing the plan, the Agriculture Department stated that "by the laws of probability, that many tests should detect mad cow disease even if it is present in only 5 cows out of the 45 million in the nation."[18] Test the Department's claim by computing the probability that, if only 5 out of 45 million cows had mad cow disease, at least 1 cow would test positive in a year (assuming the testing was done randomly).

46. ◆ *Mad Cow Disease* According to the article cited in Exercise 45, only 223,000 of the cows being tested for bovine spongiform encephalopathy were to be "downer cows"; cows unable to walk to their slaughter. Assuming that just one downer cow in 500,000 is infected on average, use a binomial distribution to find the probability that 2 or more cows would test positive in a year. Your associate claims that "by the laws of probability, that many tests should detect at least two cases of mad cow disease even if it is present in only 2 cows out of a million downers." Comment on that claim.

COMMUNICATION AND REASONING EXERCISES

47. A soccer player is more likely to score on his second shot if he was successful on his first. Can we model a succession of shots a player takes as a sequence of Bernoulli trials? Explain.

---

[16] Data based on a report by National Highway Traffic Safety Administration released in January, 1996. Source for data: U.S. Department of Transportation/*The New York Times*, April 9, 1999, p. F1.

[17] Source: *The New York Times*, March 17, 2004, p. A19.

[18] As stated in the *New York Times* article.

48. A soccer player takes repeated shots on goal. What assumption must we make if we want to model a succession of shots by a player as a sequence of Bernoulli trials?

49. Your friend just told you that "misfortunes always occur in threes." If life is just a sequence of Bernoulli trials, is this possible? Explain.

50. Suppose an experiment consists of repeatedly (every week) checking whether your graphing calculator battery has died. Is this a sequence of Bernoulli trials? Explain.

51. In an experiment with sample space S, a certain event E has a probability p of occurring. What has this scenario to do with Bernoulli trials?

52. An experiment consists of removing a gummy bear from a bag originally containing 10, and then eating it. Regard eating a lime flavored bear as success. Repeating the experiment five times is a sequence of Bernoulli trials, right?

53. ▼ Why is the following not a binomial random variable? Select, without replacement, five marbles from a bag containing six red marbles and two blue ones, and let X be the number of red marbles you have selected.

54. ▼ By contrast with Exercise 53, why can the following be modeled by a binomial random variable? Select, without replacement, 5 electronic components from a batch of 10,000 in which 1,000 are defective, and let X be the number of defective components you select.

8.3 Measures of Central Tendency

Mean, Median, and Mode of a Set of Data

One day you decide to measure the popularity rating of your statistics instructor, Mr. Pelogrande. Ideally, you should poll all of Mr. Pelogrande's students, which is what statisticians would refer to as the **population**. However, it would be difficult to poll all the members of the population in question (Mr. Pelogrande teaches more than 400 students). Instead, you decide to survey 10 of his students, chosen at random, and ask them to rate Mr. Pelogrande on a scale of 0–100. The survey results in the following set of data:

60, 50, 55, 0, 100, 90, 40, 20, 40, 70.

Such a collection of data is called a **sample**, because the 10 people polled represent only a (small) sample of Mr. Pelogrande's students. We should think of the individual scores 60, 50, 55, ... as values of a random variable: Choose one of Mr. Pelogrande's students at random and let X be the rating the student gives to Mr. Pelogrande.

How do we distill a single measurement, or **statistic**, from this sample that would describe Mr. Pelogrande's popularity? Perhaps the most commonly used statistic is the **average**, or **mean**, which is computed by adding the scores and dividing the sum by the number of scores in the sample:

$$\text{Sample Mean} = \frac{60 + 50 + 55 + 0 + 100 + 90 + 40 + 20 + 40 + 70}{10} = \frac{525}{10} = 52.5.$$

We might then conclude, based on the sample, that Mr. Pelogrande's average popularity rating is about 52.5. The usual notation for the sample mean is $\bar{x}$, and the formula we use to compute it is

$$\bar{x} = \frac{x_1 + x_2 + \cdots + x_n}{n}$$

where $x_1, x_2, \ldots, x_n$ are the values of X in the sample.

A convenient way of writing the sum that appears in the numerator is to use **summation** or **sigma notation**. We write the sum $x_1 + x_2 + \cdots + x_n$ as

$$\sum_{i=1}^{n} x_i.$$

$\displaystyle\sum_{i=1}^{n}$ by itself stands for "the sum, from $i = 1$ to n."

$\displaystyle\sum_{i=1}^{n} x_i$ stands for "the sum of the x_i, from $i = 1$ to n."

We think of i as taking on the values $1, 2, \ldots, n$ in turn, making x_i equal $x_1, x_2, \ldots, x_n$ in turn, and we then add up these values.

Sample and Mean

A **sample** is a sequence of values (or scores) of a random variable X. (The process of collecting such a sequence is sometimes called **sampling** X.) The **sample mean** is the average of the values, or **scores**, in the sample. To compute the sample mean, we use the following formula:

$$\bar{x} = \frac{x_1 + x_2 + \cdots + x_n}{n} = \frac{\sum_{i=1}^{n} x_i}{n}$$

or simply

$$\bar{x} = \frac{\sum_i x_i}{n}. \qquad \sum_i \text{ stands for "sum over all } i\text{."}^{*}$$

Here, n is the **sample size** (number of scores), and $x_1, x_2, \ldots, x_n$ are the individual values.

If the sample $x_1, x_2, \ldots, x_n$ consists of all the values of X from the entire population[†] (for instance, the ratings given Mr. Pelogrande by *all* of his students), we refer to the mean as the **population mean**, and write it as μ (Greek "mu") instead of $\bar{x}$.

Visualizing the Mean

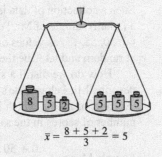

$$\bar{x} = \frac{8 + 5 + 2}{3} = 5$$

* **NOTE** In Section 1.4 we simply wrote $\sum x$ for the sum of all the x_i, but here we will use the subscripts to make it easier to interpret formulas in this and the next section.

† **NOTE** When we talk about *populations*, the understanding is that the underlying experiment consists of selecting a member of a given population and ascertaining the value of X.

Quick Examples

1. The mean of the sample 1, 2, 3, 4, 5 is $\bar{x} = 3$.

2. The mean of the sample −1, 0, 2 is $\bar{x} = \dfrac{-1 + 0 + 2}{3} = \dfrac{1}{3}$.

3. The mean of the population −3, −3, 0, 0, 1 is

$$\mu = \frac{-3 - 3 + 0 + 0 + 1}{5} = -1.$$

Note: Sample Mean versus Population Mean
Determining a population mean can be difficult or even impossible. For instance, computing the mean household income for the United States would entail recording the income of every single household in the United States. Instead of attempting to do this, we usually use sample means instead. The larger the sample used, the more accurately we expect the sample mean to approximate the population mean. Estimating how accurately a sample mean based on a given sample size approximates the population mean is possible, but we will not go into that in this book. ■

The mean $\bar{x}$ is an attempt to describe where the "center" of the sample is. It is therefore called a **measure of central tendency**. There are two other common measures of central tendency: the "middle score," or **median**, and the "most frequent score," or **mode**. These are defined as follows.

Median and Mode

The **sample median** m is the middle score (in the case of an odd-size sample), or average of the two middle scores (in the case of an even-size sample) when the scores in a sample are arranged in ascending order.

A **sample mode** is a score that appears most often in the collection. (There may be more than one mode in a sample.)

Visualizing the Median and Mode

Median = Middle Score = 4

Mode = Most Frequent Score = 2

As before, we refer to the **population median** and **population mode** if the sample consists of the data from the entire population.

Quick Examples

1. The sample median of 2, –3, –1, 4, 2 is found by first arranging the scores in ascending order: –3, –1, 2, 2, 4 and then selecting the middle (third) score: $m = 2$. The sample mode is also 2 because this is the score that appears most often.
2. The sample 2, 5, 6, –1, 0, 6 has median $m = (2 + 5)/2 = 3.5$ and mode 6.

The mean tends to give more weight to scores that are further away from the center than does the median. For example, if you take the largest score in a collection of more than two numbers and make it larger, the mean will increase but the median will remain the same. For this reason the median is often preferred for collections that contain a wide range of scores. The mode can sometimes lie far from the center and is thus used less often as an indication of where the "center" of a sample lies.

EXAMPLE 1 Teenage Spending in the '90s

A 10-year survey of spending patterns of U.S. teenagers in the 1990s yielded the following figures (in billions of dollars spent in a year):* 90, 90, 85, 80, 80, 80, 80, 85, 90, 100. Compute and interpret the mean, median, and mode, and illustrate the data on a graph.

Solution The *mean* is given by

$$\bar{x} = \frac{\sum_i x_i}{n}$$

$$= \frac{90 + 90 + 85 + 80 + 80 + 80 + 80 + 85 + 90 + 100}{10} = \frac{860}{10} = 86.$$

Thus, spending by teenagers averaged $86 billion per year.

For the *median*, we arrange the sample data in ascending order:

80, 80, 80, 80, 85, 85, 90, 90, 90, 100.

We then take the average of the two middle scores:

$$m = \frac{85 + 85}{2} = 85.$$

This means that in half the years in question, teenagers spent $85 billion or less, and in half they spent $85 billion or more.

For the *mode* we choose the score (or scores) that occurs most frequently: $80 billion. Thus, teenagers spent $80 billion per year more often than any other amount.

The frequency histogram in Figure 4 illustrates these three measures.

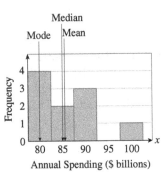

Figure 4

---

* Spending figures are rounded, and cover the years 1988 through 1997. Source: Rand Youth Poll/Teenage Research Unlimited/*The New York Times*, March 14, 1998, p. D1.

➡️ **Before we go on...** There is a nice geometric interpretation of the difference between the median and mode: The median line shown in Figure 4 divides the total area of the histogram into two equal pieces, whereas the mean line passes through its "center of gravity"; if you placed the histogram on a knife-edge along the mean line, it would balance. ■

Expected Value of a Finite Random Variable

Now, instead of looking at a sample of values of a given random variable, let us look at the probability distribution of the random variable itself and see if we can predict the sample mean without actually taking a sample. This prediction is what we call the *expected value* of the random variable.

EXAMPLE 2 Expected Value of a Random Variable

Suppose you roll a fair die a large number of times. What do you expect to be the average of the numbers that face up?

Solution Suppose we take a sample of n rolls of the die (where n is large). Because the probability of rolling a 1 is 1/6, we would expect that we would roll a 1 one sixth of the time, or $n/6$ times. Similarly, each other number should also appear $n/6$ times. The frequency table should then look like this:

x	1	2	3	4	5	6
Number of Times x Is Rolled (frequency)	$\frac{n}{6}$	$\frac{n}{6}$	$\frac{n}{6}$	$\frac{n}{6}$	$\frac{n}{6}$	$\frac{n}{6}$

Note that we would not really expect the scores to be evenly distributed in practice, although for very large values of n we would expect the frequencies to vary only by a small percentage. To calculate the sample mean, we would add up all the scores and divide by the sample size. Now, the table tells us that there are $n/6$ ones, $n/6$ twos, $n/6$ threes, and so on, up to $n/6$ sixes. Adding these all up gives

$$\sum_i x_i = \frac{n}{6} \cdot 1 + \frac{n}{6} \cdot 2 + \frac{n}{6} \cdot 3 + \frac{n}{6} \cdot 4 + \frac{n}{6} \cdot 5 + \frac{n}{6} \cdot 6.$$

(Notice that we can obtain this number by multiplying the frequencies by the values of X and then adding.) Thus, the mean is

$$\bar{x} = \frac{\sum_i x_i}{n}$$

$$= \frac{\frac{n}{6} \cdot 1 + \frac{n}{6} \cdot 2 + \frac{n}{6} \cdot 3 + \frac{n}{6} \cdot 4 + \frac{n}{6} \cdot 5 + \frac{n}{6} \cdot 6}{n}$$

$$= \frac{1}{6} \cdot 1 + \frac{1}{6} \cdot 2 + \frac{1}{6} \cdot 3 + \frac{1}{6} \cdot 4 + \frac{1}{6} \cdot 5 + \frac{1}{6} \cdot 6 \qquad \text{Divide top and bottom by } n.$$

$$= 3.5.$$

This is the average value we expect to get after a large number of rolls or, in short, the **expected value** of a roll of the die. More precisely, we say that this is the expected value of the random variable X whose value is the number we get by rolling a die. Notice that n, the number of rolls, does not appear in the expected value. In fact, we could redo the calculation more simply by dividing the frequencies in the table by n *before* adding. Doing this replaces the frequencies with the *probabilities*, $1/6$. That is, it *replaces the frequency distribution with the probability distribution*.

x	1	2	3	4	5	6
$P(X=x)$	$\frac{1}{6}$	$\frac{1}{6}$	$\frac{1}{6}$	$\frac{1}{6}$	$\frac{1}{6}$	$\frac{1}{6}$

The expected value of X is then the sum of the products $x \cdot P(X = x)$. This is how we shall compute it from now on.

Expected Value of a Finite Random Variable

If X is a finite random variable that takes on the values $x_1, x_2, \ldots, x_n$, then the **expected value** of X, written $E(X)$ or μ, is

$$\mu = E(X) = x_1 \cdot P(X = x_1) + x_2 \cdot P(X = x_2) + \cdots + x_n \cdot P(X = x_n)$$
$$= \sum_i x_i \cdot P(X = x_i).$$

To obtain the expected value, multiply the values of X by their probabilities, and then add the results.

In Words

To compute the expected value from the probability distribution of X, we multiply the values of X by their probabilities and add up the results.

Interpretation

We interpret the expected value of X as a *prediction* of the mean of a large random sample of measurements of X; in other words, it is what we "expect" the mean of a large number of scores to be. (The larger the sample, the more accurate this prediction will tend to be.)

Quick Example

If X has the distribution shown,

x	−1	0	4	5
$P(X = x)$	.3	.5	.1	.1

then $\mu = E(X) = -1(.3) + 0(.5) + 4(.1) + 5(.1) = -.3 + 0 + .4 + .5 = .6$.

EXAMPLE 3 Sports Injuries

According to historical data, the number of injuries that a member of the Enormous State University women's soccer team will sustain during a typical season is given by the following probability distribution table:

Injuries	0	1	2	3	4	5	6
Probability	.20	.20	.22	.20	.15	.01	.02

If X denotes the number of injuries sustained by a player during one season, compute $E(X)$ and interpret the result.

Solution We can compute the expected value using the following tabular approach: take the probability distribution table, add another row in which we compute the product $x P(X = x)$, and then add these products together.

x	0	1	2	3	4	5	6	
$P(X = x)$	.20	.20	.22	.20	.15	.01	.02	**Total:**
$xP(X = x)$	0	.20	.44	.60	.60	.05	.12	2.01

The total of the entries in the bottom row is the expected value. Thus,

$$E(X) = 2.01.$$

We interpret the result as follows: If many soccer players are observed for a season, we predict that the average number of injuries each will sustain is about two.

using Technology

Technology can be used to compute the expected values in Example 3.

TI-83/84 Plus

STAT EDIT values of X in L_1 and probabilities in L_2.
Home screen: sum(L_1*L_2)
[More details on page 613.]

Excel

Headings x and $P(X = x)$ in A1, B1.
x-values and probabilities in A2–B8.
=A2*B2 in C2, copied down to B6.
=SUM(C2:C8) in C9.
[More details on page 616.]

Web Site
www.FiniteandCalc.org

Student Home

→ Online Utilities

→ Histogram Utility

Enter the *x*-values and frequencies as shown:

```
0, .2
1, .2
2, .22
3, .2
4, .15
5, .01
6, .02
```

Make sure "Show expected value and standard deviation" is checked, and press "Results." The results will appear at the bottom of the page.

EXAMPLE 4 Roulette

A roulette wheel (of the kind used in the United States) has the numbers 1 through 36, 0 and 00. A bet on a single number pays 35 to 1. This means that if you place a $1 bet on a single number and win (your number comes up), you get your $1 back plus $35 (that is, you gain $35). If your number does not come up, you lose the $1 you bet. What is the expected gain from a $1 bet on a single number?

Solution The probability of winning is 1/38, so the probability of losing is 37/38. Let X be the gain from a $1 bet. X has two possible values: $X = -1$ if you lose and $X = 35$ if you win. $P(X = -1) = 37/38$ and $P(X = 35) = 1/38$. This probability distribution and the calculation of the expected value are given in the following table:

x	-1	35	
$P(X = x)$	$\frac{37}{38}$	$\frac{1}{38}$	**Total:**
$xP(X = x)$	$-\frac{37}{38}$	$\frac{35}{38}$	$-\frac{2}{38}$

So, we expect to average a small loss of $2/38 \approx \$0.0526$ on each spin of the wheel.

➡ **Before we go on...** Of course, you cannot actually lose the expected $0.0526 on one spin of the roulette wheel in Example 4. However, if you play many times, this is what you expect your *average* loss per bet to be. For example, if you played 100 times, you could expect to lose about $100 \times 0.0526 = \$5.26$. ∎

A betting game in which the expected value is zero is called a **fair game**. For example, if you and I flip a coin, and I give you $1 each time it comes up heads but you give me $1 each time it comes up tails, then the game is fair. Over the long run, we expect to come out even. On the other hand, a game like roulette in which the expected value is not zero is **biased**. Most casino games are slightly biased in favor of the house.* Thus, most gamblers will lose only a small amount and many gamblers will actually win something (and return to play some more). However, when the earnings are averaged over the huge numbers of people playing, the house is guaranteed to come out ahead. This is how casinos make (lots of) money.

✱ **NOTE** Only rarely are games not biased in favor of the house. However, blackjack played without continuous shuffle machines can be beaten by card counting.

Expected Value of a Binomial Random Variable

Suppose you guess all the answers to the questions on a multiple-choice test. What score can you expect to get? This scenario is an example of a sequence of Bernoulli trials (see the preceding section), and the number of correct guesses is therefore a binomial random variable whose expected value we wish to know. There is a simple formula for the expected value of a binomial random variable.

Expected Value of Binomial Random Variable

If X is the binomial random variable associated with n independent Bernoulli trials, each with probability p of success, then the expected value of X is

$$\mu = E(X) = np.$$

> ### Quick Examples
>
> 1. If X is the number of successes in 20 Bernoulli trials with $p = .7$, then the expected number of successes is $\mu = E(X) = (20)(.7) = 14$.
> 2. If an event F in some experiment has $P(F) = .25$, the experiment is repeated 100 times, and X is the number of times F occurs, then $E(X) = (100)(.25) = 25$ is the number of times we expect F to occur.

Where does this formula come from? We *could* use the formula for expected value and compute the sum

$$E(X) = 0C(n, 0)p^0q^n + 1C(n, 1)p^1q^{n-1} + 2C(n, 2)p^2q^{n-2} + \cdots + nC(n, n)p^nq^0$$

directly (using the binomial theorem), but this is one of the many places in mathematics where a less direct approach is much easier. X is the number of successes in a sequence of n Bernoulli trials, each with probability p of success. Thus, p is the fraction of time we expect a success, so out of n trials we expect np successes. Because X counts successes, we expect the value of X to be np. (With a little more effort, this can be made into a formal proof that the sum above equals np.)

EXAMPLE 5 Guessing on an Exam

An exam has 50 multiple-choice questions, each having four choices. If a student randomly guesses on each question, how many correct answers can he or she expect to get?

Solution Each guess is a Bernoulli trial with probability of success 1 in 4, so $p = .25$. Thus, for a sequence of $n = 50$ trials,

$$\mu = E(X) = np = (50)(.25) = 12.5.$$

Thus, the student can expect to get about 12.5 correct answers.

Q: *Wait a minute. How can a student get a fraction of a correct answer?*

A: Remember that the expected value is the average number of correct answers a student will get if he or she guesses on a large number of such tests. Or, we can say that if many students use this strategy of guessing, they will average about 12.5 correct answers each.

Estimating the Expected Value from a Sample

It is not always possible to know the probability distribution of a random variable. For instance, if we take X to be the income of a randomly selected lawyer, one could not be expected to know the probability distribution of X. However, we can still obtain a good *estimate* of the expected value of X (the average income of all lawyers) by using the relative frequency distribution based on a large random sample.

EXAMPLE 6 **Estimating an Expected Value**

The following table shows the (fictitious) incomes of a random sample of 1,000 lawyers in the United States in their first year out of law school.

Income Bracket	$20,000–$29,999	$30,000–$39,999	$40,000–$49,999	$50,000–$59,999	$60,000–$69,999	$70,000–$79,999	$80,000–$89,999
Number	20	80	230	400	170	70	30

Estimate the average of the incomes of all lawyers in their first year out of law school.

Solution We first interpret the question in terms of a random variable. Let X be the income of a lawyer selected at random from among all currently practicing first-year lawyers in the United States. We are given a sample of 1,000 values of X, and we are asked to find the expected value of X. First, we use the midpoints of the income brackets to set up a relative frequency distribution for X:

x	25,000	35,000	45,000	55,000	65,000	75,000	85,000
$P(X = x)$	.02	.08	.23	.40	.17	.07	.03

Our estimate for $E(X)$ is then

$$E(X) = \sum_i x_i \cdot P(X = x_i)$$

$$= (25,000)(.02) + (35,000)(.08) + (45,000)(.23) + (55,000)(.40)$$
$$+ (65,000)(.17) + (75,000)(.07) + (85,000)(.03) = \$54,500.$$

Thus, $E(X)$ is approximately $54,500. That is, the average income of all currently practicing first-year lawyers in the United States is approximately $54,500.

FAQ

Recognizing When to Compute the Mean and When to Compute the Expected Value

Q: *When am I supposed to compute the mean (add the values of X and divide by n) and when am I supposed to use the expected value formula?*

A: The formula for the mean (adding and dividing by the number of observations) is used to compute the mean of a sequence of random scores, or sampled values of X. If, on the other hand, you are given the probability distribution for X (even if it is only an estimated probability distribution) then you need to use the expected value formula.

8.3 EXERCISES

▼ more advanced   ◆ challenging
□ indicates exercises that should be solved using technology

Compute the mean, median, and mode of the data samples in Exercises 1–8. HINT [See Quick Examples on pages 568 and 569.]

1. $-1, 5, 5, 7, 14$

2. $2, 6, 6, 7, -1$

3. $2, 5, 6, 7, -1, -1$

4. $3, 1, 6, -3, 0, 5$

5. $\frac{1}{2}, \frac{3}{2}, -4, \frac{5}{4}$

6. $-\frac{3}{2}, \frac{3}{8}, -1, \frac{5}{2}$

7. $2.5, -5.4, 4.1, -0.1, -0.1$

8. $4.2, -3.2, 0, 1.7, 0$

9. ▼ Give a sample of six scores with mean 1 and with median $\neq$ mean. (Arrange the scores in ascending order.)

10. ▼ Give a sample of five scores with mean 100 and median 1. (Arrange the scores in ascending order.)

In Exercises 11–16, calculate the expected value of X for the given probability distribution. HINT [See Quick Example on page 572.]

11.

x	0	1	2	3
$P(X=x)$	.5	.2	.2	.1

12.

x	1	2	3	4
$P(X=x)$	.1	.2	.5	.2

13.

x	10	20	30	40
$P(X=x)$	$\frac{15}{50}$	$\frac{20}{50}$	$\frac{10}{50}$	$\frac{5}{50}$

14.

x	2	4	6	8
$P(X=x)$	$\frac{1}{20}$	$\frac{15}{20}$	$\frac{2}{20}$	$\frac{2}{20}$

15.

x	-5	-1	0	2	5	10
$P(X=x)$	.2	.3	.2	.1	.2	0

16.

x	-20	-10	0	10	20	30
$P(X=x)$	.2	.4	.2	.1	0	.1

In Exercises 17–28, calculate the expected value of the given random variable X. [Exercises 23, 24, 27, and 28 assume familiarity with counting arguments and probability (Section 7.4).] HINT [See Quick Example page 572.]

17. X is the number that faces up when a fair die is rolled.

18. X is a number selected at random from the set $\{1, 2, 3, 4\}$.

19. X is the number of tails that come up when a coin is tossed twice.

20. X is the number of tails that come up when a coin is tossed three times.

21. ▼ X is the higher number when two dice are rolled.

22. ▼ X is the lower number when two dice are rolled.

23. ▼ X is the number of red marbles that Suzan has in her hand after she selects four marbles from a bag containing four red marbles and two green ones.

24. ▼ X is the number of green marbles that Suzan has in her hand after she selects four marbles from a bag containing three red marbles and two green ones.

25. ▼ 20 darts are thrown at a dartboard. The probability of hitting a bull's-eye is .1. Let X be the number of bull's-eyes hit.

26. ▼ 30 darts are thrown at a dartboard. The probability of hitting a bull's-eye is $\frac{1}{5}$. Let X be the number of bull's-eyes hit.

27. □ ▼ Select five cards without replacement from a standard deck of 52, and let X be the number of queens you draw.

28. □ ▼ Select five cards without replacement from a standard deck of 52, and let X be the number of red cards you draw.

APPLICATIONS

29. *Stock Market Gyrations* Following is a sample of the day-by-day change, rounded to the nearest 100 points, in the Dow Jones Industrial Average during 10 successive business days around the start of the financial crisis in October 2008:[19]

$-400, -500, -200, -700, -100, 900, -100, -700, 400, -100$

Compute the mean and median of the given sample. Fill in the blank: There were as many days with a change in the Dow above _____ points as there were with changes below that. HINT [See Quick Examples on pages 568 and 569.]

30. *Stock Market Gyrations* Following is a sample of the day-by-day change, rounded to the nearest 100 points, in the Dow Jones Industrial Average during 10 successive business days around the start of the financial crisis in October 2008:[20]

$-100, 400, -200, -500, 200, -300, -200, 900, -100, 200$

Compute the mean and median of the given sample. Fill in the blank: There were as many days with a change in the Dow above _____ points as there were with changes below that. HINT [See Quick Examples on pages 568 and 569.]

31. *Gold* The following figures show the price of gold per ounce, in dollars, for the 10-business day period Feb. 2–Feb. 13, 2009:[21]

$918, 905, 905, 920, 913, 895, 910, 938, 943, 936$

---

[19] Source: http://finance.google.com.

[20] Ibid.

[21] Prices rounded to the nearest $1. Source: www.kitco.com/gold.londonfix.html.

Find the sample mean, median, and mode(s). What do your answers tell you about the price of gold?

32. *Silver* The following figures show the price of silver per ounce, in dollars, for the 10-business day period Feb. 2–Feb. 13, 2009:[22]

12.4, 12.4, 12.4, 12.8, 12.9, 13.0, 13.0, 13.4, 13.3, 13.4

Find the sample mean, median, and mode(s). What do your answers tell you about the price of silver?

33. *Supermarkets* A survey of 52 U.S. supermarkets yielded the following relative frequency table, where X is the number of checkout lanes at a randomly chosen supermarket.[23]

x	1	2	3	4	5	6	7	8	9	10
$P(X=x)$	.01	.04	.04	.08	.10	.15	.25	.20	.08	.05

a. Compute $\mu = E(X)$ and interpret the result. HINT [See Example 3.]

b. Which is larger, $P(X < \mu)$ or $P(X > \mu)$? Interpret the result.

34. *Video Arcades* Your company, Sonic Video, Inc., has conducted research that shows the following probability distribution, where X is the number of video arcades in a randomly chosen city with more than 500,000 inhabitants.

x	0	1	2	3	4	5	6	7	8	9
$P(X=x)$	.07	.09	.35	.25	.15	.03	.02	.02	.01	.01

a. Compute $\mu = E(X)$ and interpret the result. HINT [See Example 3.]

b. Which is larger, $P(X < \mu)$ or $P(X > \mu)$? Interpret the result.

35. *School Enrollment* The following table shows the approximate numbers of school goers in the United States (residents who attended some educational institution) in 1998, broken down by age group.[24]

Age	3–6.9	7–12.9	13–16.9	17–22.9	23–26.9	27–42.9
Population (millions)	12	24	15	14	2	5

Use the rounded midpoints of the given measurement classes to compute the probability distribution of the age X of a school goer. (Round probabilities to two decimal places.) Hence compute the expected value of X. What information does the expected value give about residents enrolled in schools?

36. *School Enrollment* Repeat Exercise 35, using the following data from 1980.[25]

Age	3–6.9	7–12.9	13–16.9	17–22.9	23–26.9	27–42.9
Population (millions)	8	20	11	13	1	3

37. *Employment in Mexico by Age* The following chart shows the ages of a survey of 250 working adults in Mexico:[26]

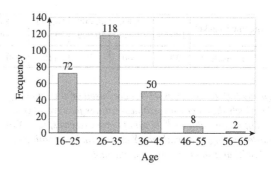

Use the estimated probability distribution based on the (rounded) midpoints of the given measurement classes to obtain an estimate of the expected age of a working adult in Mexico. HINT [See Example 6.]

38. *Unemployment in Mexico by Age* Repeat the preceding exercise, using the following chart, which shows the ages of a survey of 250 unemployed adults in Mexico:[27]

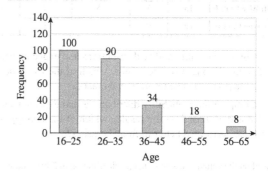

[22] Prices rounded to the nearest $1. Source: www.kitco.com/gold.londonfix.html.

[23] Sources: J.T. McClave, P.G. Benson, T. Sincich, Statistics for Business and Economics, 7th Ed. (Prentice Hall, 1998) p. 177, W. Chow *et al.* "A model for predicting a supermarket's annual sales per square foot," Graduate School of Management, Rutgers University.

[24] Data are approximate, Source: Statistical Abstract of the United States: 2000.

[25] Ibid.

[26] Based on data from through January 2007. Source for data: Instituto Nacional de Estadística y Geografía (INEGI) (www.inegi.org.mx).

[27] Ibid.

39. 🖼 *Income Distribution up to $100,000* The following table shows the distribution of household incomes for a sample of 1,000 households in the United States with incomes up to $100,000.[28]

Income Bracket	0–19,999	20,000–39,999	40,000–59,999	60,000–79,999	80,000–99,999
Households	270	280	200	150	100

Use this information to estimate, to the nearest $1,000, the average household income for such households. HINT [See Example 6.]

40. 🖼 *Income Distribution up to $100,000* Repeat Exercise 39, using the following data for a sample of 1,000 Hispanic households in the United States.[29]

Income Bracket	0–19,999	20,000–39,999	40,000–59,999	60,000–79,999	80,000–99,999
Households	300	340	190	110	60

Highway Safety Exercises 41–44 are based on the following table, which shows crashworthiness ratings for several categories of motor vehicles.[30] In all of these exercises, take X as the crash-test rating of a small car, Y as the crash-test rating for a small SUV, and so on as shown in the table.

	Number Tested	Overall Frontal Crash-Test Rating			
		3 (Good)	2 (Acceptable)	1 (Marginal)	0 (Poor)
Small Cars X	16	1	11	2	2
Small SUVs Y	10	1	4	4	1
Medium SUVs Z	15	3	5	3	4
Passenger Vans U	13	3	0	3	7
Midsize Cars V	15	3	5	0	7
Large Cars W	19	9	5	3	2

41. ▼ Compute the probability distributions and expected values of X and Y. Based on the results, which of the two types of vehicle performed better in frontal crashes?

42. ▼ Compute the probability distributions and expected values of Z and V. Based on the results, which of the two types of vehicle performed better in frontal crashes?

43. 🖼 ▼ Based on expected values, which of the following categories performed best in crash tests: small cars, midsize cars, or large cars?

44. 🖼 ▼ Based on expected values, which of the following categories performed best in crash tests: small SUVs, medium SUVs, or passenger vans?

45. ▼ *Roulette* A roulette wheel has the numbers 1 through 36, 0, and 00. Half of the numbers from 1 through 36 are red, and a bet on red pays even money (that is, if you win, you will get back your $1 plus another $1). How much do you expect to win with a $1 bet on red? HINT [See Example 4.]

46. ▼ *Roulette* A roulette wheel has the numbers 1 through 36, 0, and 00. A bet on two numbers pays 17 to 1 (that is, if one of the two numbers you bet comes up, you get back your $1 plus another $17). How much do you expect to win with a $1 bet on two numbers? HINT [See Example 4.]

47. *Teenage Pastimes* According to a study,[31] the probability that a randomly selected teenager shopped at a mall at least once during a week was .63. How many teenagers in a randomly selected group of 40 would you expect to shop at a mall during the next week? HINT [See Example 5.]

48. *Other Teenage Pastimes* According to the study referred to in the preceding exercise, the probability that a randomly selected teenager played a computer game at least once during a week was .48. How many teenagers in a randomly selected group of 30 would you expect to play a computer game during the next seven days? HINT [See Example 5.]

49. ▼ *Manufacturing* Your manufacturing plant produces air bags, and it is known that 10% of them are defective. A random collection of 20 air bags is tested.

   a. How many of them would you expect to be defective?

   b. In how large a sample would you expect to find 12 defective airbags?

50. ▼ *Spiders* Your pet tarantula, Spider, has a .12 probability of biting an acquaintance who comes into contact with him. Next week, you will be entertaining 20 friends (all of whom will come into contact with Spider).

   a. How many guests should you expect Spider to bite?

   b. At your last party, Spider bit 6 of your guests. Assuming that Spider bit the expected number of guests, how many guests did you have?

Exercises 51 and 52 assume familiarity with counting arguments and probability (Section 7.4).

51. ▼ *Camping* Kent's Tents has four red tents and three green tents in stock. Karin selects four of them at random. Let X be the number of red tents she selects. Give the probability distribution of X and find the expected number of red tents selected.

52. ▼ *Camping* Kent's Tents has five green knapsacks and four yellow ones in stock. Curt selects four of them at random. Let X be the number of green knapsacks he selects. Give the

---

[28] Based on the actual household income distribution in 2003. Source: U.S. Census Bureau, Current Population Survey, 2004 Annual Social and Economic Supplement (http://pubdb3.census.gov/macro/032004/hhinc/new06_000.htm).

[29] Ibid.

[30] Ratings are by the Insurance Institute for Highway Safety. Sources: Oak Ridge National Laboratory: "An Analysis of the Impact of Sport Utility Vehicles in the United States" Stacy C. Davis, Lorena F. Truett, August 2000, Insurance Institute for Highway Safety (www-cta.ornl.gov/Publications/Final SUV report.pdf, www.highwaysafety.org/vehicle_ratings).

[31] Source: Rand Youth Poll/Teen-age Research Unlimited/*The New York Times*, March 14, 1998, p. D1.

probability distribution of X, and find the expected number of green knapsacks selected.

53. ⓘ ▼ *Stock Portfolios* You are required to choose between two stock portfolios, FastForward Funds and SolidState Securities. Stock analysts have constructed the following probability distributions for next year's rate of return for the two funds.

FastForward Funds

Rate of Return	−.4	−.3	−.2	−.1	0	.1	.2	.3	.4
Probability	.015	.025	.043	.132	.289	.323	.111	.043	.019

SolidState Securities

Rate of Return	−.4	−.3	−.2	−.1	0	.1	.2	.3	.4
Probability	.012	.023	.050	.131	.207	.330	.188	.043	.016

Which of the two funds gives the higher expected rate of return?

54. ⓘ ▼ *Risk Management* Before making your final decision whether to invest in FastForward Funds or SolidState Securities (see Exercise 53), you consult your colleague in the risk management department of your company. She informs you that, in the event of a stock market crash, the following probability distributions for next year's rate of return would apply:

FastForward Funds

Rate of Return	−.8	−.7	−.6	−.5	−.4	−.2	−.1	0	.1
Probability	.028	.033	.043	.233	.176	.230	.111	.044	.102

SolidState Securities

Rate of Return	−.8	−.7	−.6	−.5	−.4	−.2	−.1	0	.1
Probability	.033	.036	.038	.167	.176	.230	.211	.074	.035

Which of the two funds offers the lowest risk in case of a market crash?

55. ◆ *Insurance Schemes* The Acme Insurance Company is launching a drive to generate greater profits, and it decides to insure racetrack drivers against wrecking their cars. The company's research shows that, on average, a racetrack driver races four times a year and has a 1 in 10 chance of wrecking a vehicle, worth an average of $100,000, in every race. The annual premium is $5,000, and Acme automatically drops any driver who is involved in an accident (after paying for a new car), but does not refund the premium. How much profit (or loss) can the company expect to earn from a typical driver in a year? HINT [Use a tree diagram to compute the probabilities of the various outcomes.]

56. ◆ *Insurance* The Blue Sky Flight Insurance Company insures passengers against air disasters, charging a prospective passenger $20 for coverage on a single plane ride. In the event of a fatal air disaster, it pays out $100,000 to the named beneficiary. In the event of a nonfatal disaster, it pays out an average of $25,000 for hospital expenses. Given that the probability of a plane's crashing on a single trip is .00000087,[32] and that a passenger involved in a plane crash has a .9 chance of being killed, determine the profit (or loss) per passenger that the insurance company expects to make on each trip. HINT [Use a tree to compute the probabilities of the various outcomes.]

COMMUNICATION AND REASONING EXERCISES

57. In a certain set of scores, there are as many values above the mean as below it. It follows that

(A) The median and mean are equal.
(B) The mean and mode are equal.
(C) The mode and median are equal.
(D) The mean, mode, and median are all equal.

58. In a certain set of scores, the median occurs more often than any other score. It follows that

(A) The median and mean are equal.
(B) The mean and mode are equal.
(C) The mode and median are equal.
(D) The mean, mode, and median are all equal.

59. Your friend Charlesworth claims that the median of a collection of data is always close to the mean. Is he correct? If so, say why; if not, give an example to prove him wrong.

60. Your other friend Imogen asserts that Charlesworth is wrong and that it is the mode and the median that are always close to each other. Is she correct? If so, say why; if not, give an example to prove her wrong.

61. Must the expected number of times you hit a bull's-eye after 50 attempts always be a whole number? Explain.

62. Your statistics instructor tells you that the expected score of the upcoming midterm test is 75%. That means that 75% is the most likely score to occur, right?

63. ▼ Your grade in a recent midterm was 80%, but the class average was 83%. Most people in the class scored better than you, right?

64. ▼ Your grade in a recent midterm was 80%, but the class median was 100%. Your score was lower than the average score, right?

65. ▼ Slim tells you that the population mean is just the mean of a suitably large sample. Is he correct? Explain.

66. ▼ Explain how you can use a sample to estimate an expected value.

67. ▼ Following is an excerpt from a full-page ad by **MoveOn.org** in the *New York Times* criticizing President G.W. Bush:[33]

On Tax Cuts:

George Bush: ". . . Americans will keep, this year, an average of almost $1,000 more of their own money."

The Truth: Nearly half of all taxpayers get less than $100. And 31% of all taxpayers get nothing at all.

The statements referred to as "The Truth" contradict the statement attributed to President Bush, right? Explain.

---

[32] This was the probability of a passenger plane crashing per departure in 1990. (Source: National Transportation Safety Board.)

[33] Source: Full-page ad in the *New York Times*, September 17, 2003, p. A25.

68. ▼ Following is an excerpt from a five-page ad by WeissneggerForGov.org in *The Martian Enquirer* criticizing Supreme Martian Administrator, Gov. Red Davis:

On Worker Accommodation:

Gov. Red Davis: "The median size of Government worker habitats in Valles Marineris is at least 400 square feet."

Weissnegger: "The average size of a Government worker habitat in Valles Marineris is a mere 150 square feet."

The statements attributed to Weissnegger do not contradict the statement attributed to Gov. Davis, right? Explain.

69. ▼ Sonia has just told you that the expected household income in the United States is the same as the population mean of all U.S. household incomes. Clarify her statement by describing an experiment and an associated random variable X so that the expected household income is the expected value of X.

70. ▼ If X is a random variable, what is the difference between a sample mean of measurements of X and the expected value of X? Illustrate by means of an example.

8.4 Measures of Dispersion

Variance and Standard Deviation of a Set of Scores

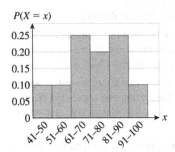

Figure 5(a)

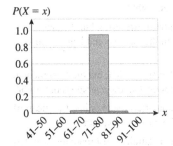

Figure 5(b)

Your grade on a recent midterm was 68%; the class average was 72%. How do you stand in comparison with the rest of the class? If the grades were widely scattered, then your grade may be close to the mean and a fair number of people may have done a lot worse than you (Figure 5a). If, on the other hand, almost all the grades were within a few points of the average, then your grade may not be much higher than the lowest grade in the class (Figure 5b).

This scenario suggests that it would be useful to have a way of measuring not only the central tendency of a set of scores (mean, median or mode) but also the amount of "scatter" or "dispersion" of the data.

If the scores in our set are $x_1, x_2, \ldots, x_n$ and their mean is $\bar{x}$ (or μ in the case of a population mean), we are really interested in the distribution of the differences $x_i - \bar{x}$. We could compute the *average* of these differences, but this average will always be 0. (Why?) It is really the *sizes* of these differences that interest us, so we might try computing the average of the absolute values of the differences. This idea is reasonable, but it leads to technical difficulties that are avoided by a slightly different approach: The statistic we use is based on the average of the *squares* of the differences, as explained in the following definitions.

Population Variance and Standard Deviation

If the values $x_1, x_2, \ldots, x_n$ are all the measurements of X in the entire population, then the **population variance** is given by

$$\sigma^2 = \frac{(x_1 - \mu)^2 + (x_2 - \mu)^2 + \cdots + (x_n - \mu)^2}{n} = \frac{\sum_{i=1}^{n} (x_i - \mu)^2}{n}.$$

(Remember that μ is the symbol we use for the *population* mean.) The **population standard deviation** is the square root of the population variance:

$$\sigma = \sqrt{\sigma^2}.$$

Sample Variance and Standard Deviation

The **sample variance** of a sample $x_1, x_2, \ldots, x_n$ of n values of X is given by

$$s^2 = \frac{(x_1 - \bar{x})^2 + (x_2 - \bar{x})^2 + \cdots + (x_n - \bar{x})^2}{n - 1} = \frac{\sum_{i=1}^{n} (x_i - \bar{x})^2}{n - 1}.$$

34

The **sample standard deviation** is the square-root of the sample variance:

$$s = \sqrt{s^2}.$$

Visualizing Small and Large Variance

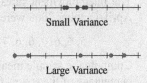

Small Variance

Large Variance

Quick Examples

1. The sample variance of the scores 1, 2, 3, 4, 5 is the sum of the squares of the differences between the scores and the mean $\bar{x} = 3$, divided by $n - 1 = 4$:

$$s^2 = \frac{(1-3)^2 + (2-3)^2 + (3-3)^2 + (4-3)^2 + (5-3)^2}{4} = \frac{10}{4} = 2.5$$

so

$$s = \sqrt{2.5} \approx 1.58.$$

2. The population variance of the scores 1, 2, 3, 4, 5 is the sum of the squares of the differences between the scores and the mean $\mu = 3$, divided by $n = 5$:

$$\sigma^2 = \frac{(1-3)^2 + (2-3)^2 + (3-3)^2 + (4-3)^2 + (5-3)^2}{5} = \frac{10}{5} = 2$$

so

$$\sigma = \sqrt{2} \approx 1.41.$$

Q: *The population variance is the average of the squares of the differences between the values and the mean. But why do we divide by n − 1 instead of n when calculating the sample variance?*

A: In real-life applications, we would like the variance we calculate from a sample to approximate the variance of the whole population. In statistical terms, we would like the expected value of the sample variance s^2 to be the same as the population variance σ^2. The sample variance s^2 as we have defined it is the "unbiased estimator" of the population variance σ^2 that accomplishes this task; if, instead, we divided by n in the formula for s^2, we would, on average, tend to underestimate the population variance. (See the online text on Sampling Distributions at the Web site for further discussion of unbiased estimators.) Note that as the sample size gets larger and larger, the discrepancy between the formulas for s^2 and σ^2 becomes negligible; dividing by n gives almost the same answer as dividing by $n - 1$. It is traditional, nonetheless, to use the sample variance in preference to the population variance when working with samples, and we do that here. In practice we should not try to draw conclusions about the entire population from samples so small that the difference between the two formulas matters. As one book puts it, "If the difference between n and $n - 1$ ever matters to you, then you are probably up to no good anyway—e.g., trying to substantiate a questionable hypothesis with marginal data."[34]

---

[34] Press, W.H., Teukolsky, S.A., Vetterling, W.T., and Flannery, B.P., *Numerical Recipes: The Art of Scientific Computing*, Cambridge University Press, 2007.

using Technology

Technology can be used to compute the mean and standard deviation in Example 1.

TI-83/84 Plus

STAT EDIT values of x in L_1.

STAT CALC 1-Var Stats

ENTER .

[More details on page 613.]

Excel

x-values in A1–A7

=AVERAGE(A1:A7) in A8

=STDEV(A1:A7) in A9

[More details on page 616.]

Here's a simple example of calculating standard deviation.

EXAMPLE 1 Unemployment

The unemployment rates (in percentage points) in the United States for the months April–October 2008 were:*

5, 6, 6, 6, 6, 6, 7.

Compute the sample mean and standard deviation, rounded to one decimal place. What percentage of the scores fall within one standard deviation of the mean? What percentage fall within two standard deviations of the mean?

Solution The sample mean is

$$\bar{x} = \frac{\sum_i x_i}{n} = \frac{5 + 6 + 6 + 6 + 6 + 6 + 7}{7} = \frac{42}{7} = 6.$$

The sample variance is

$$
\begin{aligned}
s^2 &= \frac{\sum_{i=1}^{n} (x_i - \bar{x})^2}{n - 1} \\
&= \frac{(5-6)^2 + (6-6)^2 + (6-6)^2 + (6-6)^2 + (6-6)^2 + (6-6)^2 + (7-6)^2}{6} \\
&= \frac{1 + 0 + 0 + 0 + 0 + 0 + 1}{6} = \frac{1}{3}.
\end{aligned}
$$

Thus, the sample standard deviation is

$$s = \sqrt{\frac{1}{3}} \approx 0.6. \qquad \text{Rounded to one decimal place}$$

To ask which scores fall "within one standard deviation of the mean" is to ask which scores fall in the interval $[\bar{x} - s, \bar{x} + s]$, or $[6 - 0.6, 6 + 0.6] = [5.4, 6.6]$. Five out of the seven scores (the five 6s) fall in this interval, so the percentage of scores that fall within one standard deviation of the mean is $5/7 \approx 71\%$.

For two standard deviations, the interval in question is $[\bar{x} - 2s, \bar{x} + 2s] \approx [6 - 1.2, 6 + 1.2] = [4.8, 7.2]$, which includes all of the scores. In other words, 100% of the scores fall within two standard deviations of the mean.

---

*Figures are rounded. Source: Bureau of Labor Statistics (www.bls.gov).

Q: *In Example 1, 71% of the scores fell within one standard deviation of the mean and all of them fell within two standard deviations of the mean. Is this typical?*

A: Actually, the percentage of scores within a number of standard deviations of the mean depends a great deal on the way the scores are distributed. There are two useful methods for *estimating* the percentage of scores that fall within any number of standard deviations of the mean. The first method applies to any set of data, and is due to P.L. Chebyshev (1821–1894), while the second applies to "nice" sets of data, and is based on the "normal distribution," which we shall discuss in Section 5.

Chebyshev's Rule

For any set of data, the following statements are true:

At least 3/4 of the scores fall within two standard deviations of the mean (within the interval $[\bar{x} - 2s, \bar{x} + 2s]$ for samples or $[\mu - 2\sigma, \mu + 2\sigma]$ for populations).

At least 8/9 of the scores fall within three standard deviations of the mean (within the interval $[\bar{x} - 3s, \bar{x} + 3s]$ for samples or $[\mu - 3\sigma, \mu + 3\sigma]$ for populations).

At least 15/16 of the scores fall within four standard deviations of the mean (within the interval $[\bar{x} - 4s, \bar{x} + 4s]$ for samples or $[\mu - 4\sigma, \mu + 4\sigma]$ for populations).

. . .

At least $1 - 1/k^2$ of the scores fall within k standard deviations of the mean (within the interval $[\bar{x} - ks, \bar{x} + ks]$ for samples or $[\mu - k\sigma, \mu + k\sigma]$ for populations).

Visualizing Chebyshev's Rule

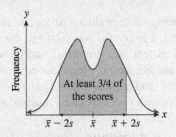
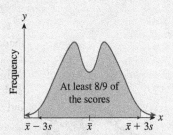

Empirical Rule*

For a set of data whose frequency distribution is "bell-shaped" and symmetric (see Figure 6), the following is true:

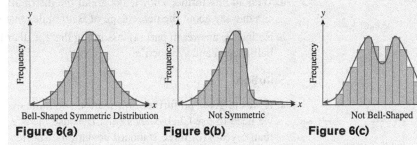

Bell-Shaped Symmetric Distribution · Not Symmetric · Not Bell-Shaped

Figure 6(a)   **Figure 6(b)**   **Figure 6(c)**

✱ **NOTE** Unlike Chebyshev's rule, which is a precise theorem, the empirical rule is a "rule of thumb" that is intentionally vague about what exactly is meant by a "bell-shaped distribution" and "approximately such-and-such %." (As a result, the rule is often stated differently in different textbooks.) We will see in Section 8.5 that if the distribution is a *normal* one, the empirical rule translates to a precise statement.

Approximately 68% of the scores fall within one standard deviation of the mean (within the interval $[\bar{x} - s, \bar{x} + s]$ for samples or $[\mu - \sigma, \mu + \sigma]$ for populations).

Approximately 95% of the scores fall within two standard deviations of the mean (within the interval $[\bar{x} - 2s, \bar{x} + 2s]$ for samples or $[\mu - 2\sigma, \mu + 2\sigma]$ for populations).

Approximately 99.7% of the scores fall within three standard deviations of the mean (within the interval $[\bar{x} - 3s, \bar{x} + 3s]$ for samples or $[\mu - 3\sigma, \mu + 3\sigma]$ for populations).

Visualizing the Empirical Rule

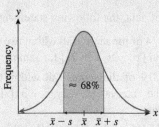
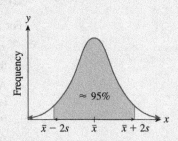

1. If the mean of a sample is 20 with standard deviation $s = 2$, then at least $15/16 = 93.75\%$ of the scores lie within four standard deviations of the mean—that is, in the interval $[12, 28]$.

2. If the mean of a sample with a bell-shaped symmetric distribution is 20 with standard deviation $s = 2$, then approximately 95% of the scores lie in the interval $[16, 24]$.

The empirical rule could not be applied in Example 1. The distribution was not bell-shaped (sketch it to see for yourself) and the fact that there were only six scores limits the accuracy further. The empirical rule is, however, accurate in distributions that are bell-shaped and symmetric, even if not perfectly so. Chebyshev's rule, on the other hand, is always valid (and applies in Example 1 in particular) but tends to be "overcautious" and in practice underestimates how much of a distribution lies in a given interval.

EXAMPLE 2 Automobile Life

The average life span of a Batmobile is 9 years, with a standard deviation of 2 years. My own Batmobile lasted less than 3 years before being condemned to the bat-junkyard.

a. Without any further knowledge about the distribution of Batmobile life spans, what can one say about the percentage of Batmobiles that last less than 3 years?

b. Refine the answer in part (a), assuming that the distribution of Batmobile life spans is bell-shaped and symmetric.

Solution

a. If we are given no further information about the distribution of Batmobile life spans, we need to use Chebyshev's rule. Because the life span of my Batmobile was more than 6 years (or three standard deviations) shorter than the mean, it lies outside the range $[\mu - 3\sigma, \mu + 3\sigma] = [3, 15]$. Because *at least* 8/9 of the life spans of all Batmobiles lie in this range, *at most* 1/9, or 11%, of the life spans lie outside this range (see Figure 7). Some of these, like the life span of my own Batmobile, are less than 3 years, while the rest are more than $\mu + 3\sigma = 15$ years.

b. Because we know more about the distribution now than we did in part (a), we can use the empirical rule and obtain sharper results. The empirical rule predicts that approximately 99.7% of the life spans of Batmobiles lie in the range $[\mu - 3\sigma, \mu + 3\sigma] = [3, 15]$. Thus, approximately $1 - 99.7\% = 0.3\%$ of them lie outside that range. Because the distribution is symmetric, however, more can be said: half of that 0.3%, or 0.15% of Batmobiles will last longer than 15 years, while the other 0.15% are, like my own ill-fated Batmobile, doomed to a life span of less than 3 years (see Figure 8).

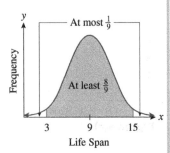

Figure 7

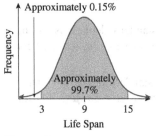

Figure 8

Variance and Standard Deviation of a Finite Random Variable

Recall that the expected value of a random variable X is a prediction of the average of a large sample of values of X. Can we similarly predict the variance of a large sample? Suppose we have a sample $x_1, x_2, \ldots, x_n$. If n is large, the sample and population variances are essentially the same, so we concentrate on the population variance, which is the average of the numbers $(x_i - \bar{x})^2$. This average can be predicted using $E([X - \mu]^2)$ the expected value of $(X - \mu)^2$. In general, we make the following definition.

Variance and Standard Deviation of a Finite Random Variable

If X is a finite random variable taking on values $x_1, x_2, \ldots, x_n$, then the **variance** of X is

$$\sigma^2 = E([X - \mu]^2)$$
$$= (x_1 - \mu)^2 P(X = x_1) + (x_2 - \mu)^2 P(X = x_2) + \cdots + (x_n - \mu)^2 P(X = x_n)$$
$$= \sum_i (x_i - \mu)^2 P(X = x_i).$$

The **standard deviation** of X is then the square root of the variance:

$$\sigma = \sqrt{\sigma^2}.$$

To compute the variance from the probability distribution of X, first compute the expected value μ and then compute the expected value of $(X - \mu)^2$.

Quick Example

The following distribution has expected value $\mu = E(X) = 2$:

x	-1	2	3	10
$P(X = x)$	.3	.5	.1	.1

The variance of X is

$$\sigma^2 = (x_1 - \mu)^2 P(X = x_1) + (x_2 - \mu)^2 P(X = x_2) + \cdots + (x_n - \mu)^2 P(X = x_n)$$
$$= (-1 - 2)^2(.3) + (2 - 2)^2(.5) + (3 - 2)^2(.1) + (10 - 2)^2(.1) = 9.2.$$

The standard deviation of X is

$$\sigma = \sqrt{9.2} \approx 3.03.$$

Note We can interpret the variance of X as the number we expect to get for the variance of a large sample of values of X, and similarly for the standard deviation. ∎

We can calculate the variance and standard deviation of a random variable using a tabular approach just as when we calculated the expected value in Example 3 in the preceding section.

using Technology

Technology can be used to automate the calculations of Example 3.

TI-83/84 Plus

STAT EDIT values of x in L_1, probabilities in L_2.
Home screen: sum(L_1*L_2)
$\rightarrow$ M
Then sum((L_1–M)^2*L_2)
[More details on page 613.]

Excel

x-values in A2–A7, probabilities in B2–B7
=A2*B2 in C2; copy down to C7.
=SUM(C2:C7) in C8
=(A2–$C$8)^2*B2 in D2; copy down to D7.
=SUM(D2:D7) in D8
[More details on page 616.]

Web Site

www.FiniteandCalc.org

Student Home

$\rightarrow$ Online Utilities

$\rightarrow$ Histogram Utility

Enter the x-values and probabilities as shown:

```
10, .2
20, .2
30, .3
40, .1
50, .1
60, .1
```

Make sure "Show expected value and standard deviation" is checked, and press "Results."

EXAMPLE 3 Variance of a Random Variable

Compute the variance and standard deviation for the following probability distribution.

x	10	20	30	40	50	60
$P(X = x)$	.2	.2	.3	.1	.1	.1

Solution We first compute the expected value, μ, in the usual way:

x	10	20	30	40	50	60	
$P(X = x)$	.2	.2	.3	.1	.1	.1	
$xP(X = x)$	2	4	9	4	5	6	$\mu = 30$

Next, we add an extra three rows:

- a row for the differences $(x - \mu)$, which we get by subtracting μ from the values of X
- a row for the squares $(x - \mu)^2$, which we obtain by squaring the values immediately above
- a row for the products $(x - \mu)^2 P(X = x)$, which we obtain by multiplying the values in the second and the fifth rows.

x	10	20	30	40	50	60	
$P(X = x)$	.2	.2	.3	.1	.1	.1	
$xP(X = x)$	2	4	9	4	5	6	$\mu = 30$
$x - \mu$	−20	−10	0	10	20	30	
$(x - \mu)^2$	400	100	0	100	400	900	
$(x - \mu)^2 P(X = x)$	80	20	0	10	40	90	$\sigma^2 = 240$

The sum of the values in the last row is the variance. The standard deviation is then the square root of the variance:

$$\sigma = \sqrt{240} \approx 15.49.$$

Note Chebyshev's rule and the empirical rule apply to random variables just as they apply to samples and populations, as we illustrate in the following example. ∎

EXAMPLE 4 Internet Commerce

Your newly launched company, CyberPromo, Inc., sells computer games on the Internet.

a. Statistical research indicates that the lifespan of an Internet marketing company such as yours is symmetrically distributed with an expected value of 30 months and standard deviation of 4 months. Complete the following sentence:

There is (at least/at most/approximately)_____ a _____ percent chance that CyberPromo will still be around for more than 3 years.

b. How would the answer to part (a) be affected if the distribution of lifespans was not known to be symmetric?

Solution

a. Do we use Chebyshev's rule or the empirical rule? Because the empirical rule requires that the distribution be both symmetric and bell-shaped—not just symmetric—we cannot conclude that it applies here, so we are forced to use Chebyshev's rule instead.

Let X be the lifespan of an Internet commerce site. The expected value of X is 30 months, and the hoped-for lifespan of CyberPromo, Inc., is 36 months, which is 6 months, or $6/4 = 1.5$ standard deviations, above the mean. Chebyshev's rule tells us that X is within $k = 1.5$ standard deviations of the mean at least $1 - 1/k^2$ of the time; that is,

$$P(24 \leq X \leq 36) \geq 1 - \frac{1}{k^2} = 1 - \frac{1}{1.5^2} \approx .56.$$

In other words, at least 56% of all Internet marketing companies have life spans in the range of 24 to 36 months. Thus, *at most* 44 % have life spans outside this range. Because the distribution is symmetric, at most 22% have life spans longer than 36 months. Thus we can complete the sentence as follows:

There is at most a 22% chance that CyberPromo will still be around for more than 3 years.

b. If the given distribution was not known to be symmetric, how would this affect the answer? We saw above that regardless of whether the distribution is symmetric or not, at most 44% have lifespans outside the range 24 to 36 months. Because the distribution is not symmetric, we cannot conclude that at most half of the 44% have lifespans longer than 36 months, and all we can say is that *no more than 44% can possibly have life spans longer than 36 years*. In other words:

There is at most a 44% chance that CyberPromo will still be around for more than 3 years.

Variance and Standard Deviation of a Binomial Random Variable

We saw that there is an easy formula for the expected value of a binomial random variable: $\mu = np$, where n is the number of trials and p is the probability of success. Similarly, there is a simple formula for the variance and standard deviation.

Variance and Standard Deviation of a Binomial Random Variable

If X is a binomial random variable associated with n independent Bernoulli trials, each with probability p of success, then the variance and standard deviation of X are given by

$$\sigma^2 = npq \quad \text{and} \quad \sigma = \sqrt{npq}$$

where $q = 1 - p$ is the probability of failure.

Quick Example

If X is the number of successes in 20 Bernoulli trials with $p = .7$, then the standard deviation is $\sigma = \sqrt{npq} = \sqrt{(20)(.7)(.3)} \approx 2.05$.

NOTE Remember that the empirical rule only gives an *estimate* of probabilities. In Section 8.5 we give a more accurate approximation that takes into account the fact that the binomial distribution is not continuous.

For values of p near $1/2$ and large values of n, a binomial distribution is bell-shaped and (nearly) symmetric, hence the empirical rule applies. One rule of thumb is that we can use the empirical rule when both $np \geq 10$ and $nq \geq 10$.*

EXAMPLE 5 Internet Commerce

You have calculated that there is a 40% chance that a hit on your Web page results in a fee paid to your company CyberPromo, Inc. Your Web page receives 25 hits per day. Let X be the number of hits that result in payment of the fee ("successful hits").

a. What are the expected value and standard deviation of X?

b. Complete the following: On approximately 95 out of 100 days, I will get between ___ and ___ successful hits.

Solution

a. The random variable X is binomial with $n = 25$ and $p = .4$. To compute μ and σ, we use the formulas

$$\mu = np = (25)(.4) = 10 \text{ successful hits}$$

$$\sigma = \sqrt{npq} = \sqrt{(25)(.4)(.6)} \approx 2.45 \text{ hits.}$$

b. Because $np = 10 \geq 10$ and $nq = (25)(.6) = 15 \geq 10$, we can use the empirical rule, which tells us that there is an approximately 95% probability that the number of successful hits is within two standard deviations of the mean—that is, in the interval

$$[\mu - 2\sigma, \mu + 2\sigma] = [10 - 2(2.45), 10 + 2(2.45)] = [5.1, 14.9].$$

Thus, on approximately 95 out of 100 days, I will get between <u>5.1</u> and <u>14.9</u> successful hits.

FAQ

Recognizing When to Use the Empirical Rule or Chebyshev's Rule

Q: *How do I decide whether to use Chebyshev's rule or the empirical rule?*

A: Check to see whether the probability distribution you are considering is both symmetric and bell-shaped. If so, you can use the empirical rule. If not, then you must use Chebyshev's rule. Thus, for instance, if the distribution is symmetric but not known to be bell-shaped, you must use Chebyshev's rule.

8.4 EXERCISES

▼ more advanced   ◆ challenging

🔲 indicates exercises that should be solved using technology

Compute the (sample) variance and standard deviation of the data samples given in Exercises 1–8. (You calculated the means in the last exercise set. Round all answers to two decimal places.) HINT [See Quick Examples on page 581.]

1. $-1, 5, 5, 7, 14$ **2.** $2, 6, 6, 7, -1$

3. $2, 5, 6, 7, -1, -1$ **4.** $3, 1, 6, -3, 0, 5$

5. $\dfrac{1}{2}, \dfrac{3}{2}, -4, \dfrac{5}{4}$ **6.** $-\dfrac{3}{2}, \dfrac{3}{8}, -1, \dfrac{5}{2}$

7. $2.5, -5.4, 4.1, -0.1, -0.1$ **8.** $4.2, -3.2, 0, 1.7, 0$

In Exercises 9–14, calculate the standard deviation of X for each probability distribution. (You calculated the expected values in the last exercise set. Round all answers to two decimal places.) HINT [See Quick Examples on page 585.]

9.

x	0	1	2	3
$P(X = x)$	.5	.2	.2	.1

10.

x	1	2	3	4
$P(X = x)$	.1	.2	.5	.2

11.

x	10	20	30	40
$P(X = x)$	$\frac{3}{10}$	$\frac{2}{5}$	$\frac{1}{5}$	$\frac{1}{10}$

12.

x	2	4	6	8
$P(X = x)$	$\frac{1}{20}$	$\frac{15}{20}$	$\frac{2}{20}$	$\frac{2}{20}$

13.

x	−5	−1	0	2	5	10
$P(X = x)$	.2	.3	.2	.1	.2	0

14.

x	−20	−10	0	10	20	30
$P(X = x)$	.2	.4	.2	.1	0	.1

In Exercises 15–24, calculate the expected value, the variance, and the standard deviation of the given random variable X. (You calculated the expected values in the last exercise set. Round all answers to two decimal places.)

15. X is the number that faces up when a fair die is rolled.

16. X is the number selected at random from the set $\{1, 2, 3, 4\}$.

17. X is the number of tails that come up when a coin is tossed twice.

18. X is the number of tails that come up when a coin is tossed three times.

19. ▼ X is the higher number when two dice are rolled.

20. ▼ X is the lower number when two dice are rolled.

21. ▼ X is the number of red marbles that Suzan has in her hand after she selects four marbles from a bag containing four red marbles and two green ones.

22. ▼ X is the number of green marbles that Suzan has in her hand after she selects four marbles from a bag containing three red marbles and two green ones.

23. ▼ Twenty darts are thrown at a dartboard. The probability of hitting a bull's-eye is .1. Let X be the number of bull's-eyes hit.

24. ▼ Thirty darts are thrown at a dartboard. The probability of hitting a bull's-eye is $\frac{1}{5}$. Let X be the number of bull's-eyes hit.

APPLICATIONS

25. *Popularity Ratings* In your bid to be elected class representative, you have your election committee survey five randomly chosen students in your class and ask them to rank you on a scale of 0–10. Your rankings are 3, 2, 0, 9, 1.

   a. Find the sample mean and standard deviation. (Round your answers to two decimal places.) HINT [See Example 1 and Quick Examples on page 581.]

   b. Assuming the sample mean and standard deviation are indicative of the class as a whole, in what range does the empirical rule predict that approximately 68% of the class

will rank you? What other assumptions must we make to use the rule?

26. *Popularity Ratings* Your candidacy for elected class representative is being opposed by Slick Sally. Your election committee has surveyed six of the students in your class and had them rank Sally on a scale of 0–10. The rankings were 2, 8, 7, 10, 5, 8.

   a. Find the sample mean and standard deviation. (Round your answers to two decimal places.) HINT [See Example 1 and Quick Examples on page 581.]

   b. Assuming the sample mean and standard deviation are indicative of the class as a whole, in what range does the empirical rule predict that approximately 95% of the class will rank Sally? What other assumptions must we make to use the rule?

27. *Unemployment* Following is a sample of unemployment rates (in percentage points) in the United States sampled from the period 1990–2004:[35]

   4.2, 4.7, 5.4, 5.8, 4.9.

   a. Compute the mean and standard deviation of the given sample. (Round your answers to one decimal place.)

   b. Assuming the distribution of unemployment rates in the population is symmetric and bell-shaped, 95% of the time, the unemployment rate is between ____ and ____ percent.

28. *Unemployment* Following is a sample of unemployment rates among Hispanics (in percentage points) in the US sampled from the period 1990–2004:[36]

   7.7, 7.5, 9.3, 6.9, 8.6

   a. Compute the mean and standard deviation of the given sample. (Round your answers to one decimal place.)

   b. Assuming the distribution of unemployment rates in the population of interest is symmetric and bell-shaped, 68% of the time, the unemployment rate is between ____ and ____ percent.

29. *Stock Market Gyrations* Following is a sample of the day-by-day change, rounded to the nearest 100 points, in the Dow Jones Industrial Average during 10 successive business days around the start of the financial crisis in October 2008:[37]

−400, −500, −200, −700, −100, 900, −100, −700, 400, −100

   a. Compute the mean and standard deviation of the given sample. (Round your answers to the nearest whole number.)

   b. Assuming the distribution of day-by-day changes of the Dow during financial crises is symmetric and bell-shaped, then the Dow falls by more than ____ points 16% of the time. What is the percentage of times in the sample that the Dow actually fell by more than that amount? HINT [See Example 2(b).]

---

[35] Sources for data: Bureau of Labor Statistics (BLS) (www.bls.gov).
[36] Ibid.
[37] Source: http://finance.google.com.

30. Stock Market Gyrations Following is a sample of the day-by-day change, rounded to the nearest 100 points, in the Dow Jones Industrial Average during 10 successive business days around the start of the financial crisis in October 2008:[38]

−100, 400, −200, −500, 200, −300, −200, 900, −100, 200.

a. Compute the mean and standard deviation of the given sample. (Round your answers to the nearest whole number.)

b. Assuming the distribution of day-by-day changes of the Dow during financial crises is symmetric and bell-shaped, then the Dow rises by more than ___ points 2.5% of the time. What is the percentage of times in the sample that the Dow actually rose by more than that amount? HINT [See Example 2(b).]

31. ⬛ **Sport Utility Vehicles** Following are highway driving gas mileages of a selection of medium-sized sport utility vehicles (SUVs):[39]

17, 18, 17, 18, 21, 16, 21, 18, 16, 14, 15, 22, 17, 19, 17, 18.

a. Find the sample standard deviation (rounded to two decimal places).

b. In what gas mileage range does Chebyshev's inequality predict that at least 8/9 (approximately 89%) of the selection will fall?

c. What is the actual percentage of SUV models of the sample that fall in the range predicted in part (b)? Which gives the more accurate prediction of this percentage: Chebyshev's rule or the empirical rule?

32. ⬛ **Sport Utility Vehicles** Following are the city driving gas mileages of a selection of sport utility vehicles (SUVs):[40]

14, 15, 14, 15, 13, 16, 12, 14, 19, 18, 16, 16, 12, 15, 15, 13.

a. Find the sample standard deviation (rounded to two decimal places).

b. In what gas mileage range does Chebyshev's inequality predict that at least 75% of the selection will fall?

c. What is the actual percentage of SUV models of the sample that fall in the range predicted in part (b)? Which gives the more accurate prediction of this percentage: Chebyshev's rule or the empirical rule?

33. Shopping Malls A survey of all the shopping malls in your region yields the following probability distribution, where X is the number of movie theater screens in a selected mall:

Number of Movie Screens	0	1	2	3	4
Probability	.4	.1	.2	.2	.1

Compute the expected value μ and the standard deviation σ of X. (Round answers to two decimal places.) What percentage of malls have a number of movie theater screens within two standard deviations of μ?

34. Pastimes A survey of all the students in your school yields the following probability distribution, where X is the number of movies that a selected student has seen in the past week:

Number of Movies	0	1	2	3	4
Probability	.5	.1	.2	.1	.1

Compute the expected value μ and the standard deviation σ of X. (Round answers to two decimal places.) For what percentage of students is X within two standard deviations of μ?

35. ⬛ **Income Distribution up to $100,000** The following table shows the distribution of household incomes for a sample of 1,000 households in the United States with incomes up to $100,000.[41]

2000 Income (thousands)	$10	$30	$50	$70	$90
Households	270	280	200	150	100

Compute the expected value μ and the standard deviation σ of the associated random variable X. If we define a "lower income" family as one whose income is more than one standard deviation below the mean, and a "higher income" family as one whose income is at least one standard deviation above the mean, what is the income gap between higher- and lower-income families in the United States? (Round your answers to the nearest $1,000.)

36. ⬛ **Income Distribution up to $100,000** Repeat Exercise 35, using the following data for a sample of 1,000 Hispanic households in the United States.[42]

2000 Income (thousands)	$10	$30	$50	$70	$90
Households	300	340	190	110	60

37. Hispanic Employment: Male The following table shows the approximate number of males of Hispanic origin employed in the United States in 2005, broken down by age group.[43]

Age	15–24.9	25–54.9	55–64.9
Employment (thousands)	16,000	13,000	1,600

---

[38] Source: http://finance.google.com.

[39] Figures are the low-end of ranges for 1999 models tested. Source: Oak Ridge National Laboratory: "An Analysis of the Impact of Sport Utility Vehicles in the United States" Stacy C. Davis, Lorena F. Truett (August 2000)/Insurance Institute for Highway Safety (http://cta.ornl.gov/cta/Publications/pdf/ORNL_TM_2000_147.pdf).

[40] Ibid.

[41] Based on the actual household income distribution in 2003. Source: U.S. Census Bureau, Current Population Survey, 2004 Annual Social and Economic Supplement (http://pubdb3.census.gov/macro/032004/hhinc/new06_000.htm).

[42] Ibid.

[43] Figures are rounded. Bounds for the age groups for the first and third categories were adjusted for computational convenience. Source: Bureau of Labor Statistics (ftp://ftp.bls.gov/pub/suppl/empsit.cpseed15.txt).

a. Use the rounded midpoints of the given measurement classes to compute the expected value and the standard deviation of the age X of a male Hispanic worker in the United States. (Round all probabilities and intermediate calculations to two decimal places.)

b. In what age interval does the empirical rule predict that 68% of all male Hispanic workers will fall? (Round answers to the nearest year.)

38. *Hispanic Employment: Female* Repeat Exercise 37, using the corresponding data for females of Hispanic origin.[44]

Age	15–24.9	25–54.9	55–64.9
Employment (thousands)	1,200	5,000	600

a. Use the rounded midpoints of the given measurement classes to compute the expected value and the standard deviation of the age X of a female Hispanic worker in the United States. (Round all probabilities and intermediate calculations to two decimal places.)

b. In what age interval does the empirical rule predict that 68% of all female Hispanic workers will fall? (Round answers to the nearest year.)

39. *Commerce* You have been told that the average life span of an Internet-based company is 2 years, with a standard deviation of 0.15 years. Further, the associated distribution is highly skewed (not symmetric). Your Internet company is now 2.6 years old. What percentage of all Internet-based companies have enjoyed a life span at least as long as yours? Your answer should contain one of the following phrases: *At least; At most; Approximately.* HINT [See Example 2.]

40. *Commerce* You have been told that the average life span of a car-compounding service is 3 years, with a standard deviation of 0.2 years. Further, the associated distribution is symmetric but not bell-shaped. Your car-compounding service is exactly 2.6 years old. What fraction of car-compounding services last at most as long as yours? Your answer should contain one of the following phrases: *At least; At most; Approximately.* HINT [See Example 2.]

41. *Batmobiles* The average life span of a Batmobile is 9 years, with a standard deviation of 2 years.[45] Further, the probability distribution of the life spans of Batmobiles is symmetric, but not known to be bell-shaped.

Because my old Batmobile has been sold as bat-scrap, I have decided to purchase a new one. According to the above information, there is

(A) At least **(B)** At most **(C)** Approximately

a ____ percent chance that my new Batmobile will last 13 years or more.

42. *Spiderman Coupés* The average life span of a Spiderman Coupé is 8 years, with a standard deviation of 2 years. Further, the probability distribution of the life spans of Spiderman Coupés is not known to be bell-shaped or symmetric. I have just purchased a brand-new Spiderman Coupé. According to the above information, there is

(A) At least **(B)** At most **(C)** Approximately

a ____ percent chance that my new Spiderman Coupé will last for less than 4 years.

43. *Teenage Pastimes* According to a study,[46] the probability that a randomly selected teenager shopped at a mall at least once during a week was .63. Let X be the number of students in a randomly selected group of 40 that will shop at a mall during the next week.

a. Compute the expected value and standard deviation of X. (Round answers to two decimal places.) HINT [See Example 5.]

b. Fill in the missing quantity: There is an approximately 2.5% chance that ___ or more teenagers in the group will shop at a mall during the next week.

44. *Other Teenage Pastimes* According to the study referred to in the preceding exercise, the probability that a randomly selected teenager played a computer game at least once during a week was .48. Let X be the number of teenagers in a randomly selected group of 30 who will play a computer game during the next 7 days.

a. Compute the expected value and standard deviation of X. (Round answers to two decimal places.) HINT [See Example 5.]

b. Fill in the missing quantity: There is an approximately 16% chance that ___ or more teenagers in the group will play a computer game during the next 7 days.

45. ▼ *Teenage Marketing* In 2000, 22% of all teenagers in the United States had checking accounts.[47] Your bank, TeenChex Inc., is interested in targeting teenagers who do not already have a checking account.

a. If TeenChex selects a random sample of 1,000 teenagers, what number of teenagers *without* checking accounts can it expect to find? What is the standard deviation of this number? (Round the standard deviation to one decimal place.)

b. Fill in the missing quantities: There is an approximately 95% chance that between ___ and ___ teenagers in the sample will not have checking accounts. (Round answers to the nearest whole number.)

[44] Figures are rounded. Bounds for the age groups for the first and third categories were adjusted for computational convenience. Source: Bureau of Labor Statistics (ftp://ftp.bls.gov/pub/suppl/empsit.cpseed15.txt).

[45] See Example 2.

[46] Source: Rand Youth Poll/Teenage Research Unlimited/*The New York Times*, March 14, 1998, p. D1.

[47] Source: Teenage Research Unlimited, January 25, 2001 (www.teenresearch.com).

46. ▼ *Teenage Marketing* In 2000, 18% of all teenagers in the United States owned stocks or bonds.[48] Your brokerage company, TeenStox Inc., is interested in targeting teenagers who do not already own stocks or bonds.

   a. If TeenStox selects a random sample of 2,000 teenagers, what number of teenagers who *do not* own stocks or bonds can it expect to find? What is the standard deviation of this number? (Round the standard deviation to one decimal place.)

   b. Fill in the missing quantities: There is an approximately 99.7% chance that between ___ and ___ teenagers in the sample will not own stocks or bonds. (Round answers to the nearest whole number.)

47. ▯ ▼ *Supermarkets* A survey of supermarkets in the United States yielded the following relative frequency table, where X is the number of checkout lanes at a randomly chosen supermarket:[49]

x	1	2	3	4	5	6	7	8	9	10
$P(X = x)$	.01	.04	.04	.08	.10	.15	.25	.20	.08	.05

   a. Compute the mean, variance, and standard deviation (accurate to one decimal place).

   b. As financial planning manager at Express Lane Mart, you wish to install a number of checkout lanes that is in the range of at least 75% of all supermarkets. What is this range according to Chebyshev's inequality? What is the *least* number of checkout lanes you should install so as to fall within this range?

48. ▯ ▼ *Video Arcades* Your company, Sonic Video, Inc., has conducted research that shows the following probability distribution, where X is the number of video arcades in a randomly chosen city with more than 500,000 inhabitants:

x	0	1	2	3	4	5	6	7	8	9
$P(X = x)$	.07	.09	.35	.25	.15	.03	.02	.02	.01	.01

   a. Compute the mean, variance, and standard deviation (accurate to one decimal place).

   b. As CEO of Startrooper Video Unlimited, you wish to install a chain of video arcades in Sleepy City, U.S.A. The city council regulations require that the number of arcades be within the range shared by at least 75% of all cities. What is this range? What is the *largest* number of video arcades you should install so as to comply with this regulation?

Distribution of Wealth If we model after-tax household income by a normal distribution, then the figures of a 1995 study imply the information in the following table, which should be used for Exercises 49–60.[50] Assume that the distribution of incomes in each country is bell-shaped and symmetric.

Country	United States	Canada	Switzerland	Germany	Sweden
Mean Household Income	$38,000	$35,000	$39,000	$34,000	$32,000
Standard Deviation	$21,000	$17,000	$16,000	$14,000	$11,000

49. If we define a "poor" household as one whose after-tax income is at least 1.3 standard deviations below the mean, what is the household income of a poor family in the United States?

50. If we define a "poor" household as one whose after-tax income is at least 1.3 standard deviations below the mean, what is the household income of a poor family in Switzerland?

51. If we define a "rich" household as one whose after-tax income is at least 1.3 standard deviations above the mean, what is the household income of a rich family in the United States?

52. If we define a "rich" household as one whose after-tax income is at least 1.3 standard deviations above the mean, what is the household income of a rich family in Sweden?

53. ▼ Refer to Exercise 49. Which of the five countries listed has the poorest households (i.e., the lowest cutoff for considering a household poor)?

54. ▼ Refer to Exercise 52. Which of the five countries listed has the wealthiest households (i.e., the highest cutoff for considering a household rich)?

55. ▼ Which of the five countries listed has the largest gap between rich and poor?

56. ▼ Which of the five countries listed has the smallest gap between rich and poor?

57. What percentage of U.S. families earned an after-tax income of $17,000 or less?

58. What percentage of U.S. families earned an after-tax income of $80,000 or more?

59. What is the after-tax income range of approximately 99.7% of all Germans?

60. What is the after-tax income range of approximately 99.7% of all Swedes?

---

[48] Source: Teenage Research Unlimited, January 25, 2001 (www.teenresearch.com).

[49] Source: J.T. McClave, P.G. Benson, T. Sincich, *Statistics for Business and Economics*, 7th Ed. (Prentice Hall, 1998) p. 177, W. Chow *et al.* "A model for predicting a supermarket's annual sales per square foot," Graduate School of Management, Rutgers University.

[50] The data are rounded to the nearest $1,000 and based on a report published by the Luxembourg Income Study. The report shows after-tax income, including government benefits (such as food stamps) of households with children. Our figures were obtained from the published data by assuming a normal distribution of incomes. All data were based on constant 1991 U.S. dollars and converted foreign currencies (adjusted for differences in buying power). Source: Luxembourg Income Study/*The New York Times*, August 14, 1995, p. A9.

Aging Exercises 61–66 are based on the following list, which shows the percentage of aging population (residents of age 65 and older) in each of the 50 states in 1990 and 2000:[51]

2000

> 6, 9, 10, 10, 10, 11, 11, 11, 11, 11,
> 11, 11, 12, 12, 12, 12, 12, 12, 12, 12,
> 12, 12, 12, 13, 13, 13, 13, 13, 13, 13,
> 13, 13, 13, 13, 13, 13, 13, 14, 14, 14,
> 14, 14, 14, 14, 15, 15, 15, 15, 16, 18

1990

> 4, 9, 10, 10, 10, 10, 10, 11, 11, 11,
> 11, 11, 11, 11, 11, 12, 12, 12, 12, 12,
> 12, 13, 13, 13, 13, 13, 13, 13, 13, 13,
> 13, 13, 13, 13, 14, 14, 14, 14, 14,
> 14, 14, 14, 15, 15, 15, 15, 15, 15, 18.

61. Compute the population mean and standard deviation for the 2000 data.

62. Compute the population mean and standard deviation for the 1990 data.

63. Compare the actual percentage of states whose aging population in 2000 was within one standard deviation of the mean to the percentage predicted by the empirical rule. Comment on your answer.

64. Compare the actual percentage of states whose aging population in 1990 was within one standard deviation of the mean to the percentage predicted by the empirical rule. Comment on your answer.

65. What was the actual percentage of states whose aging population in 1990 was within two standard deviations of the mean? Is Chebyshev's rule valid? Explain.

66. What was the actual percentage of states whose aging population in 2000 was within two standard deviations of the mean? Is Chebyshev's rule valid? Explain.

67. ▼ *Electric Grid Stress* The following chart shows the approximate standard deviation of the power grid frequency, in 1/1,000 cycles per second, taken over six-month periods. (0.9 is the average standard deviation.)[52]

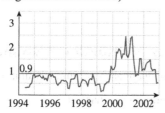

[51] Percentages are rounded and listed in ascending order. Source: U.S. Census Bureau, Census 2000 Summary File 1 (www.census.gov/prod/2001pubs/c2kbr01-10.pdf).

[52] Source Robert Blohm, energy consultant and adviser to the North American Electric Reliability Council/*The New York Times*, August 20, 2003, p. A16.

Which of the following statements are true? (More than one may be true.)

(A) The power grid frequency was at or below the mean until late 1999.

(B) The power grid frequency was more stable in mid-1999 than in 1995.

(C) The power grid frequency was more stable in mid-2002 than in mid-1999.

(D) The greatest fluctuations in the power grid frequency occurred in 2000–2001.

(E) The power grid frequency was more stable around January 1995 than around January 1999.

68. ▼ *Electric Grid Stress* The following chart shows the approximate monthly means of the power grid frequency, in 1/1,000 cycles per second. 0.0 represents the desired frequency of exactly 60 cycles per second.[53]

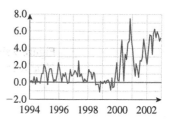

Which of the following statements are true? (More than one may be true.)

(A) Both the mean and the standard deviation show an upward trend from 2000 on.

(B) The mean, but not the standard deviation, shows an upward trend from 2000 on.

(C) The demand for electric power peaked in the second half of 2001.

(D) The standard deviation was larger in the second half of 2002 than in the second half of 1999.

(E) The mean of the monthly means in 2000 was lower than that for 2002, but the standard deviation of the monthly means was higher.

COMMUNICATION AND REASONING EXERCISES

69. Which is greater: the sample standard deviation or the population standard deviation? Explain.

70. Suppose you take larger and larger samples of a given population. Would you expect the sample and population standard deviations to get closer or further apart? Explain.

71. In one Finite Math class, the average grade was 75 and the standard deviation of the grades was 5. In another Finite Math class, the average grade was 65 and the standard deviation of the grades was 20. What conclusions can you draw about the distributions of the grades in each class?

[53] Ibid.

72. You are a manager in a precision manufacturing firm and you must evaluate the performance of two employees. You do so by examining the quality of the parts they produce. One particular item should be 50.0 ± 0.3 mm long to be usable. The first employee produces parts that are an average of 50.1 mm long with a standard deviation of 0.15 mm. The second employee produces parts that are an average of 50.0 mm long with a standard deviation of 0.4 mm. Which employee do you rate higher? Why? (Assume that the empirical rule applies.)

73. ▼ If a finite random variable has an expected value of 10 and a standard deviation of 0, what must its probability distribution be?

74. ▼ If the values of X in a population consist of an equal number of 1s and −1s, what is its standard deviation?

75. ◆ Find an algebraic formula for the population standard deviation of a sample $\{x, y\}$ of two scores $(x \le y)$.

76. ◆ Find an algebraic formula for the sample standard deviation of a sample $\{x, y\}$ of two scores $(x \le y)$.

8.5 Normal Distributions

Continuous Random Variables

Figure 9 shows the probability distributions for the number of successes in sequences of 10 and 15 independent Bernoulli trials, each with probability of success $p = .5$.

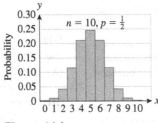

Figure 9(a)   **Figure 9(b)**

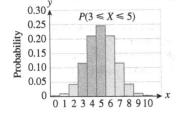

Figure 10

Because each column is 1 unit wide, its area is numerically equal to its height. Thus, the area of each rectangle can be interpreted as a probability. For example, in Figure 9(a) the area of the rectangle over $X = 3$ represents $P(X = 3)$. If we want to find $P(3 \le X \le 5)$, we can add up the areas of the three rectangles over 3, 4, and 5, shown shaded in Figure 10. Notice that if we add up the areas of *all* the rectangles in Figure 9(a), the total is 1 because $P(0 \le X \le 10) = 1$. We can summarize these observations.

Properties of the Probability Distribution Histogram

In a probability distribution histogram where each column is 1 unit wide:

• The total area enclosed by the histogram is 1 square unit.

• $P(a \le X \le b)$ is the area enclosed by the rectangles lying between and including $X = a$ and $X = b$.

This discussion is motivation for considering another kind of random variable, one whose probability distribution is specified not by a bar graph, as above, but by the graph of a function.

Continuous Random Variable; Probability Density Function

A **continuous random variable** X may take on any real value whatsoever. The probabilities $P(a \leq X \leq b)$ are defined by means of a **probability density function**, a function whose graph lies above the x-axis with the total area between the graph and the x-axis being 1. The probability $P(a \leq X \leq b)$ is defined to be the area enclosed by the curve, the x-axis, and the lines $x = a$ and $x = b$ (see Figure 11).

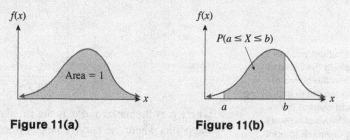

Figure 11(a)   **Figure 11(b)**

Notes

1. In Chapter 7, we defined probability distributions only for *finite* sample spaces. Because continuous random variables have infinite sample spaces, we need the definition above to give meaning to $P(a \leq X \leq b)$ if X is a continuous random variable.

2. If $a = b$, then $P(X = a) = P(a \leq X \leq a)$ is the area under the curve between the lines $x = a$ and $x = a$—no area at all! Thus, when X is a continuous random variable, $P(X = a) = 0$ for every value of a.

3. Whether we take the region in Figure 11(b) to include the boundary or not does not affect the area. The probability $P(a < X < b)$ is defined as the area strictly between the vertical lines $x = a$ and $x = b$, but is, of course, the same as $P(a \leq X \leq b)$, because the boundary contributes nothing to the area. When we are calculating probabilities associated with a continuous random variable,

$$P(a \leq X \leq b) = P(a < X \leq b) = P(a \leq X < b) = P(a < X < b). \quad \blacksquare$$

Normal Density Functions

Among all the possible probability density functions, there is an important class of functions called **normal density functions**, or **normal distributions**. The graph of a normal density function is bell-shaped and symmetric, as the following figure shows. The formula for a normal density function is rather complicated looking:

$$f(x) = \frac{1}{\sigma\sqrt{2\pi}} e^{-\frac{(x-\mu)^2}{2\sigma^2}}.$$

The quantity μ is called the **mean** and can be any real number. The quantity σ is called the **standard deviation** and can be any positive real number. The number $e = 2.7182\ldots$ is a useful constant that shows up many places in mathematics, much as the constant π does. Finally, the constant $1/(\sigma\sqrt{2\pi})$ that appears in front is there to make the total area come out to be 1. We rarely use the actual formula in computations; instead, we use tables or technology.

Normal Density Function; Normal Distribution

A **normal density function**, or **normal distribution**, is a function of the form

$$f(x) = \frac{1}{\sigma\sqrt{2\pi}}e^{-\frac{(x-\mu)^2}{2\sigma^2}}.$$

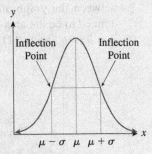

where μ is the mean and σ is the standard deviation. The "inflection points" are the points where the curve changes from bending in one direction to bending in another.*

✳ NOTE Pretend you were driving along the curve in a car. Then the points of inflection are the points where you would change the direction in which you are steering (from left to right or right to left).

using Technology

The graphs in Figure 12 can be drawn on a TI-83/84 Plus or the Web site grapher.

TI-83/84 Plus
Figure 12(a):
`Y₁=normalpdf(x,2,1)`
Figure 12(b):
`Y₁=normalpdf(x,0,2)`
Figure 12(c):
`Y₁=normalpdf(x)`

Web Site
www.FiniteandCalc.org
  Student Home
    → Online Utilities
    → Function Evaluator and
       Grapher
Figure 12(a):
`normalpdf(x,2,1)`
Figure 12(b):
`normalpdf(x,0,2)`
Figure 12(c):
`normalpdf(x)`

Figure 12 shows the graph of several normal density functions. The third of these has mean 0 and standard deviation 1, and is called the **standard normal distribution**. We use Z rather than X to refer to the standard normal variable.

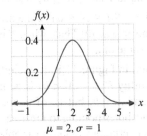

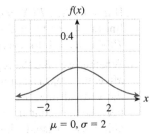

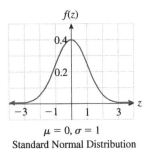

Figure 12(a)   **Figure 12(b)**   **Figure 12(c)**

Calculating Probabilities Using the Standard Normal Distribution

The standard normal distribution has $\mu = 0$ and $\sigma = 1$. The corresponding variable is called the **standard normal variable**, which we always denote by Z. Recall that to calculate the probability $P(a \leq Z \leq b)$, we need to find the area under the distribution curve between the vertical lines $z = a$ and $z = b$. We can use the table in the Appendix to look up these areas, or we can use technology. Here is an example.

EXAMPLE 1 Standard Normal Distribution

Let Z be the standard normal variable. Calculate the following probabilities:

a. $P(0 \leq Z \leq 2.4)$

b. $P(0 \leq Z \leq 2.43)$

c. $P(-1.37 \leq Z \leq 2.43)$

d. $P(1.37 \leq Z \leq 2.43)$

Solution

a. We are asking for the shaded area under the standard normal curve shown in Figure 13. We can find this area, correct to four decimal places, by looking at the table in the Appendix, which lists the area under the standard normal curve from $Z = 0$ to $Z = b$ for any value of b between 0 and 3.09. To use the table, write 2.4 as 2.40, and read the entry in the row labeled 2.4 and the column labeled .00 ($2.4 + .00 = 2.40$). Here is the relevant portion of the table:

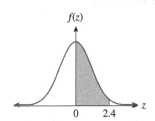

Figure 13

Z	.00	.01	.02	.03
2.3	.4893	.4896	.4898	.4901
→ 2.4	.4918	.4920	.4922	.4925
2.5	.4938	.4940	.4941	.4943

Thus, $P(0 \leq Z \leq 2.40) = .4918$.

b. The area we require can be read from the same portion of the table shown above. Write 2.43 as $2.4 + .03$, and read the entry in the row labeled 2.4 and the column labeled .03:

Z	.00	.01	.02	.03
2.3	.4893	.4896	.4898	.4901
→ 2.4	.4918	.4920	.4922	.4925
2.5	.4938	.4940	.4941	.4943

Thus, $P(0 \leq Z \leq 2.43) = .4925$.

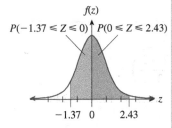

Figure 14

c. Here we cannot use the table directly because the range $-1.37 \leq Z \leq 2.43$ does not start at 0. But we can break the area up into two smaller areas that start or end at 0:

$$P(-1.37 \leq Z \leq 2.43) = P(-1.37 \leq Z \leq 0) + P(0 \leq Z \leq 2.43).$$

In terms of the graph, we are splitting the desired area into two smaller areas (Figure 14).

We already calculated the area of the right-hand piece in part (b):

$$P(0 \leq Z \leq 2.43) = .4925.$$

For the left-hand piece, the symmetry of the normal curve tells us that

$$P(-1.37 \leq Z \leq 0) = P(0 \leq Z \leq 1.37).$$

This we can find on the table. Look at the row labeled 1.3 and the column labeled .07, and read

$$P(-1.37 \leq Z \leq 0) = P(0 \leq Z \leq 1.37) = .4147.$$

Thus,

$$P(-1.37 \leq Z \leq 2.43) = P(-1.37 \leq Z \leq 0) + P(0 \leq Z \leq 2.43)$$
$$= .4147 + .4925$$
$$= .9072.$$

using Technology

Technology can be used to calculate the probabilities in Example 1. For instance, the calculation for part (c) is as follows:

TI-83/84 Plus
Home Screen:
`normalcdf(-1.37, 2.43)`
(`normalcdf` is in `2ND` `VARS`.)
[More details on page 614.]

Excel
`=NORMSDIST(2.43)`
`-NORMSDIST(-1.37)`
[More details on page 616.]

Web Site
www.FiniteandCalc.org

Student Home

→ Online Utilities

→ Normal Distribution
   Utility

Set up as shown and press
"Calculate Probability."

d. The range $1.37 \leq Z \leq 2.43$ does not contain 0, so we cannot use the technique of part (c). Instead, the corresponding area can be computed as the *difference* of two areas:

$$P(1.37 \leq Z \leq 2.43) = P(0 \leq Z \leq 2.43) - P(0 \leq Z \leq 1.37)$$
$$= .4925 - .4147$$
$$= .0778.$$

Calculating Probabilities for Any Normal Distribution

Although we have tables to compute the area under the *standard* normal curve, there are no readily available tables for nonstandard distributions. For example, If $\mu = 2$ and $\sigma = 3$, then how would we calculate $P(0.5 \leq X \leq 3.2)$? The following conversion formula provides a method for doing so:

Standardizing a Normal Distribution

If X has a normal distribution with mean μ and standard deviation σ, and if Z is the standard normal variable, then

$$P(a \leq X \leq b) = P\left(\frac{a - \mu}{\sigma} \leq Z \leq \frac{b - \mu}{\sigma}\right).$$

Quick Example

If $\mu = 2$ and $\sigma = 3$, then

$$P(0.5 \leq X \leq 3.2) = P\left(\frac{0.5 - 2}{3} \leq Z \leq \frac{3.2 - 2}{3}\right)$$
$$= P(-0.5 \leq Z \leq 0.4) = .1915 + .1554 = .3469.$$

To completely justify the above formula requires more mathematics than we shall discuss here. However, here is the main idea: if X is normal with mean μ and standard deviation σ, then $X - \mu$ is normal with mean 0 and standard deviation still σ, while $(X - \mu)/\sigma$ is normal with mean 0 and standard deviation 1. In other words, $(X - \mu)/\sigma = Z$. Therefore,

$$P(a \leq X \leq b) = P\left(\frac{a - \mu}{\sigma} \leq \frac{X - \mu}{\sigma} \leq \frac{b - \mu}{\sigma}\right) = P\left(\frac{a - \mu}{\sigma} \leq Z \leq \frac{b - \mu}{\sigma}\right).$$

EXAMPLE 2 Quality Control

Pressure gauges manufactured by Precision Corp. must be checked for accuracy before being placed on the market. To test a pressure gauge, a worker uses it to measure the pressure of a sample of compressed air known to be at a pressure of exactly 50 pounds per square inch. If the gauge reading is off by more than 1% (0.5 pounds), it is rejected. Assuming that the reading of a pressure gauge under these circumstances is a normal random variable with mean 50 and standard deviation 0.4, find the percentage of gauges rejected.

using Technology

Technology can be used to calculate the probability $P(49.5 \leq X \leq 50.5)$ in Example 2:

TI-83/84 Plus
Home Screen:
`normalcdf(49.5, 50.5, 50, 0.4)`
(`normalcdf` is in 2ND VARS.)
[More details on page 614.]

Excel
`=NORMDIST(50.5,50, 0.4,1)`
`-NORMDIST(49.5, 50,0.4,1)`
[More details on page 617.]

Web Site
www.FiniteandCalc.org
Student Home
 → Online Utilities
 → Normal Distribution Utility
Set up as shown and press "Calculate Probability."

Solution If X is the reading of the gauge, then X has a normal distribution with $\mu = 50$ and $\sigma = 0.4$. We are asking for $P(X < 49.5$ or $X > 50.5) = 1 - P(49.5 \leq X \leq 50.5)$. We calculate

$$P(49.5 \leq X \leq 50.5) = P\left(\frac{49.5 - 50}{0.4} \leq Z \leq \frac{50.5 - 50}{0.4}\right) \quad \text{Standardize}$$

$$= P(-1.25 \leq Z \leq 1.25)$$
$$= 2 \cdot P(0 \leq Z \leq 1.25)$$
$$= 2(.3944) = .7888.$$

So, $P(X < 49.5$ or $X > 50.5) = 1 - P(49.5 \leq X \leq 50.5)$
$$= 1 - .7888 = .2112.$$

In other words, about 21% of the gauges will be rejected.

In many applications, we need to know the probability that a value of a normal random variable will lie within one standard deviation of the mean, or within two standard deviations, or within some number of standard deviations. To compute these probabilities, we first notice that, if X has a normal distribution with mean μ and standard deviation σ, then

$$P(\mu - k\sigma \leq X \leq \mu + k\sigma) = P(-k \leq Z \leq k)$$

by the standardizing formula. We can compute these probabilities for various values of k using the table in the Appendix, and we obtain the following results.

Probability of a Normal Distribution Being within k Standard Deviations of Its Mean

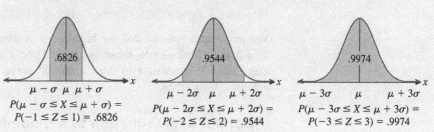

$P(\mu - \sigma \leq X \leq \mu + \sigma) =$ $\quad P(\mu - 2\sigma \leq X \leq \mu + 2\sigma) =$ $\quad P(\mu - 3\sigma \leq X \leq \mu + 3\sigma) =$
$P(-1 \leq Z \leq 1) = .6826$ $\quad P(-2 \leq Z \leq 2) = .9544$ $\quad P(-3 \leq Z \leq 3) = .9974$

Now you can see where the empirical rule comes from! Notice also that the probabilities above are a good deal larger than the lower bounds given by Chebyshev's rule. Chebyshev's rule must work for distributions that are skew or any shape whatsoever.

EXAMPLE 3 Loans

The values of mortgage loans made by a certain bank one year were normally distributed with a mean of $120,000 and a standard deviation of $40,000.

a. What is the probability that a randomly selected mortgage loan was in the range of $40,000–$200,000?

b. You would like to state in your annual report that 50% of all mortgage loans were in a certain range with the mean in the center. What is that range?

Solution

a. We are asking for the probability that a loan was within two standard deviations ($80,000) of the mean. By the calculation done previously, this probability is .9544.

b. We look for the k such that

$$P(120{,}000 - k \cdot 40{,}000 \leq X \leq 120{,}000 + k \cdot 40{,}000) = .5.$$

Because

$$P(120{,}000 - k \cdot 40{,}000 \leq X \leq 120{,}000 + k \cdot 40{,}000) = P(-k \leq Z \leq k)$$

we look in the Appendix to see for which k we have

$$P(0 \leq Z \leq k) = .25$$

so that $P(-k \leq Z \leq k) = .5$. That is, we look *inside* the table to see where 0.25 is, and find the corresponding k. We find

$$P(0 \leq Z \leq 0.67) = .2486$$

and $\quad P(0 \leq Z \leq 0.68) = .2517.$

Therefore, the k we want is about half-way between 0.67 and 0.68, call it 0.675. This tells us that 50% of all mortgage loans were in the range

$$120{,}000 - 0.675 \cdot 40{,}000 = \$93{,}000$$

to $\quad 120{,}000 + 0.675 \cdot 40{,}000 = \$147{,}000.$

Normal Approximation to a Binomial Distribution

You might have noticed that the histograms of some of the binomial distributions we have drawn (for example, those in Figure 1) have a very rough bell shape. In fact, in many cases it is possible to draw a normal curve that closely approximates a given binomial distribution.

Normal Approximation to a Binomial Distribution

If X is the number of successes in a sequence of n independent Bernoulli trials, with probability p of success in each trial, and if the range of values of X within three standard deviations of the mean lies entirely within the range 0 to n (the possible values of X), then

$$P(a \leq X \leq b) \approx P(a - 0.5 \leq Y \leq b + 0.5)$$

where Y has a normal distribution with the same mean and standard deviation as X; that is, $\mu = np$ and $\sigma = \sqrt{npq}$, where $q = 1 - p$.

Notes

1. The condition that $0 \leq \mu - 3\sigma < \mu + 3\sigma \leq n$ is satisfied if n is sufficiently large and p is not too close to 0 or 1; it ensures that most of the normal curve lies in the range 0 to n.

2. In the formula $P(a \leq X \leq b) \approx P(a - 0.5 \leq Y \leq b + 0.5)$, we assume that a and b are integers. The use of $a - 0.5$ and $b + 0.5$ is called the **continuity correction**. To see that it is necessary, think about what would happen if you wanted to approximate, say, $P(X = 2) = P(2 \leq X \leq 2)$. Should the answer be 0? ■

Figures 15 and 16 show two binomial distributions with their normal approximations superimposed, and illustrate how closely the normal approximation fits the binomial distribution.

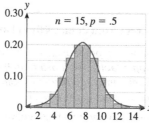

Figure 15

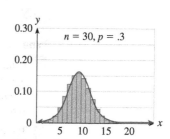

Figure 16

EXAMPLE 4 Coin Tosses

a. If you flip a fair coin 100 times, what is the probability of getting more than 55 heads or fewer than 45 heads?

b. What number of heads (out of 100) would make you suspect that the coin is not fair?

Solution

a. We are asking for

$$P(X < 45 \text{ or } X > 55) = 1 - P(45 \leq X \leq 55).$$

We *could* compute this by calculating

$$1 - [C(100, 45)(.5)^{45}(.5)^{55} + C(100, 46)(.5)^{46}(.5)^{54} + \cdots + C(100, 55)(.5)^{55}(.5)^{45}]$$

but we can much more easily *approximate* it by looking at a normal distribution with mean $\mu = 50$ and standard deviation $\sigma = \sqrt{(100)(.5)(.5)} = 5$. (Notice that three standard deviations above and below the mean is the range 35 to 65, which is well within the range of possible values for X, which is 0 to 100, so the approximation should be a good one.) Let Y have this normal distribution. Then

$$P(45 \leq X \leq 55) \approx P(44.5 \leq Y \leq 55.5)$$
$$= P(-1.1 \leq Z \leq 1.1)$$
$$= .7286.$$

Therefore,

$$P(X < 45 \text{ or } X > 55) \approx 1 - .7286 = .2714.$$

b. This is a deep question that touches on the concept of **statistical significance**: What evidence is strong enough to overturn a reasonable assumption (the assumption that the coin is fair)? Statisticians have developed sophisticated ways of answering this question, but we can look at one simple test now. Suppose we tossed a coin 100 times and got 66 heads. If the coin were fair, then $P(X > 65) \approx P(Y > 65.5) = P(Z > 3.1) \approx .001$. This is small enough to raise a reasonable doubt that the coin is fair. However, we should not be too surprised if we threw 56 heads because we can calculate $P(X > 55) \approx .1357$, which is not such a small probability. As we said, the actual tests of statistical significance are more sophisticated than this, but we shall not go into them.

FAQ

When to Subtract from .5 and When Not To

Q: *When computing probabilities like, say $P(Z \leq 1.2)$, $P(Z \geq 1.2)$, or $P(1.2 \leq Z \leq 2.1)$ using a table, just looking up the given values (1.2, 2.1, or whatever) is not enough. Sometimes you have to subtract from .5, sometimes not. Is there a simple rule telling me what to do when?*

A: The simplest—and also most instructive—way of knowing what to do is to draw a picture of the standard normal curve, and shade in the area you are looking for. Drawing pictures also helps one come up with the following mechanical rules:

1. To compute $P(a \leq Z \leq b)$, look up the areas corresponding to $|a|$ and $|b|$ in the table. If a and b have opposite signs, add these areas. Otherwise, subtract the smaller area from the larger.

2. To compute $P(Z \leq a)$, look up the area corresponding to $|a|$. If a is positive, add .5. Otherwise, subtract from .5.

3. To compute $P(Z \geq a)$, look up the area corresponding to $|a|$. If a is positive, subtract from .5. Otherwise, add .5.

8.5 EXERCISES

▼ more advanced ◆ challenging

🔲 indicates exercises that should be solved using technology

Note: Answers for Section 8.5 were computed using the 4-digit table in the Appendix, and may differ slightly from the more accurate answers generated using technology.

In Exercises 1–8, Z is the standard normal distribution. Find the indicated probabilities. HINT [See Example 1.]

1. $P(0 \leq Z \leq 0.5)$

2. $P(0 \leq Z \leq 1.5)$

3. $P(-0.71 \leq Z \leq 0.71)$

4. $P(-1.71 \leq Z \leq 1.71)$

5. $P(-0.71 \leq Z \leq 1.34)$

6. $P(-1.71 \leq Z \leq 0.23)$

7. $P(0.5 \leq Z \leq 1.5)$

8. $P(0.71 \leq Z \leq 1.82)$

In Exercises 9–14, X has a normal distribution with the given mean and standard deviation. Find the indicated probabilities. HINT [See Quick Example on page 598.]

9. $\mu = 50$, $\sigma = 10$, find $P(35 \leq X \leq 65)$

10. $\mu = 40$, $\sigma = 20$, find $P(35 \leq X \leq 45)$

11. $\mu = 50$, $\sigma = 10$, find $P(30 \leq X \leq 62)$

12. $\mu = 40$, $\sigma = 20$, find $P(30 \leq X \leq 53)$

13. $\mu = 100$, $\sigma = 15$, find $P(110 \leq X \leq 130)$

14. $\mu = 100$, $\sigma = 15$, find $P(70 \leq X \leq 80)$

15. ▼ Find the probability that a normal variable takes on values within 0.5 standard deviations of its mean.

16. ▼ Find the probability that a normal variable takes on values within 1.5 standard deviations of its mean.

17. ▼ Find the probability that a normal variable takes on values more than $\frac{2}{3}$ standard deviations away from its mean.

18. ▼ Find the probability that a normal variable takes on values more than $\frac{5}{3}$ standard deviations away from its mean.

19. If you roll a die 100 times, what is the approximate probability that you will roll between 10 and 15 ones, inclusive? (Round your answer to two decimal places.) HINT [See Example 4.]

20. If you roll a die 100 times, what is the approximate probability that you will roll between 15 and 20 ones, inclusive? (Round your answer to two decimal places.) HINT [See Example 4.]

21. If you roll a die 200 times, what is the approximate probability that you will roll fewer than 25 ones, inclusive? (Round your answer to two decimal places.)

22. If you roll a die 200 times, what is the approximate probability that you will roll more than 40 ones? (Round your answer to two decimal places.)

APPLICATIONS

23. *SAT Scores* SAT test scores are normally distributed with a mean of 500 and a standard deviation of 100. Find the probability that a randomly chosen test-taker will score between 450 and 550. HINT [See Example 3.]

24. *SAT Scores* SAT test scores are normally distributed with a mean of 500 and a standard deviation of 100. Find the probability that a randomly chosen test-taker will score 650 or higher. HINT [See Example 3.]

25. *LSAT Scores* LSAT test scores are normally distributed with a mean of 500 and a standard deviation of 100. Find the probability that a randomly chosen test-taker will score between 300 and 550.

26. *LSAT Scores* LSAT test scores are normally distributed with a mean of 500 and a standard deviation of 100. Find the probability that a randomly chosen test-taker will score 250 or lower.

27. *IQ Scores* IQ scores (as measured by the Stanford-Binet intelligence test) are normally distributed with a mean of 100 and a standard deviation of 16. What percentage of the population has an IQ score between 110 and 140? (Round your answer to the nearest percentage point.)

28. *IQ Scores* Refer to Exercise 27. What percentage of the population has an IQ score between 80 and 90? (Round your answer to the nearest percentage point.)

29. *IQ Scores* Refer to Exercise 27. Find the approximate number of people in the United States (assuming a total population of 280,000,000) with an IQ higher than 120.

30. *IQ Scores* Refer to Exercise 27. Find the approximate number of people in the United States (assuming a total population of 280,000,000) with an IQ higher than 140.

31. *Baseball* The mean batting average in major league baseball is about 0.250. Supposing that batting averages are normally distributed, that the standard deviation in the averages is 0.03, and that there are 250 batters, what is the expected number of batters with an average of at least 0.400?

32. *Baseball* The mean batting average in major league baseball is about 0.250. Supposing that batting averages are normally distributed, that the standard deviation in the averages is 0.05, and that there are 250 batters, what is the expected number of batters with an average of at least 0.400?[54]

33. *Marketing* Your pickle company rates its pickles on a scale of spiciness from 1 to 10. Market research shows that customer preferences for spiciness are normally distributed, with a mean of 7.5 and a standard deviation of 1. Assuming that you sell 100,000 jars of pickles, how many jars with a spiciness of 9 or above do you expect to sell?

34. *Marketing* Your hot sauce company rates its sauce on a scale of spiciness of 1 to 20. Market research shows that customer preferences for spiciness are normally distributed, with a mean of 12 and a standard deviation of 2.5. Assuming that you sell 300,000 bottles of sauce, how many bottles with a spiciness below 9 do you expect to sell?

Distribution of Wealth If we model after-tax household income with a normal distribution, then the figures of a 1995 study imply the information in the following table, which should be used for Exercises 35–40.[55] Assume that the distribution of incomes in each country is normal, and round all percentages to the nearest whole number.

Country	United States	Canada	Switzerland	Germany	Sweden
Mean Household Income	$38,000	$35,000	$39,000	$34,000	$32,000
Standard Deviation	$21,000	$17,000	$16,000	$14,000	$11,000

35. What percentage of U.S. households had an income of $50,000 or more?

36. What percentage of German households had an income of $50,000 or more?

37. What percentage of Swiss households are either very wealthy (income at least $100,000) or very poor (income at most $12,000)?

38. What percentage of Swedish households are either very wealthy (income at least $100,000) or very poor (income at most $12,000)?

39. Which country has a higher proportion of very poor families (income $12,000 or less): the United States or Canada?

40. Which country has a higher proportion of very poor families (income $12,000 or less): Canada or Switzerland?

41. ▼ *Comparing IQ Tests* IQ scores as measured by both the Stanford-Binet intelligence test and the Wechsler intelligence test have a mean of 100. The standard deviation for the Stanford-Binet test is 16, while that for the Wechsler test is

---

[54] The last time that a batter ended the year with an average above 0.400 was in 1941. The batter was Ted Williams of the Boston Red Sox, and his average was 0.406. Over the years, as pitching and batting have improved, the standard deviation in batting averages has declined from around 0.05 when professional baseball began to around 0.03 by the end of the twentieth century. For a very interesting discussion of statistics in baseball and in evolution, see Stephen Jay Gould, *Full House: The Spread of Excellence from Plato to Darwin*, Random House, 1997.

[55] The data are rounded to the nearest $1,000 and is based on a report published by the Luxembourg Income Study. The report shows after-tax income, including government benefits (such as food stamps) of households with children. Our figures were obtained from the published data by assuming a normal distribution of incomes. All data were based on constant 1991 U.S. dollars and converted foreign currencies (adjusted for differences in buying power). Source: Luxembourg Income Study/ *The New York Times*, August 14, 1995, p. A9.

15. For which test do a smaller percentage of test-takers score less than 80? Why?

42. ▼ *Comparing IQ Tests* Referring to Exercise 41, for which test do a larger percentage of test-takers score more than 120?

43. ▼ *Product Repairs* The new copier your business bought lists a mean time between failures of 6 months, with a standard deviation of 1 month. One month after a repair, it breaks down again. Is this surprising? (Assume that the times between failures are normally distributed.)

44. ▼ *Product Repairs* The new computer your business bought lists a mean time between failures of 1 year, with a standard deviation of 2 months. Ten months after a repair, it breaks down again. Is this surprising? (Assume that the times between failures are normally distributed.)

Software Testing Exercises 45–50 are based on the following information, gathered from student testing of a statistical software package called MODSTAT.[56] Students were asked to complete certain tasks using the software, without any instructions. The results were as follows. (Assume that the time for each task is normally distributed.)

Task	Mean Time (minutes)	Standard Deviation
Task 1: Descriptive Analysis of Data	11.4	5.0
Task 2: Standardizing Scores	11.9	9.0
Task 3: Poisson Probability Table	7.3	3.9
Task 4: Areas under Normal Curve	9.1	5.5

45. Find the probability that a student will take at least 10 minutes to complete Task 1.

46. Find the probability that a student will take at least 10 minutes to complete Task 3.

47. ▼ Assuming that the time it takes a student to complete each task is independent of the others, find the probability that a student will take at least 10 minutes to complete each of Tasks 1 and 2.

48. ▼ Assuming that the time it takes a student to complete each task is independent of the others, find the probability that a student will take at least 10 minutes to complete each of Tasks 3 and 4.

49. ◆ It can be shown that if X and Y are independent normal random variables with means μ_X and μ_Y and standard deviations σ_X and σ_Y respectively, then their sum $X + Y$ is also normally distributed and has mean $\mu = \mu_X + \mu_Y$ and standard deviation $\sigma = \sqrt{\sigma_X^2 + \sigma_Y^2}$. Assuming that the time it takes a student to complete each task is independent of the others, find the

probability that a student will take at least 20 minutes to complete both Tasks 1 and 2.

50. ◆ Referring to Exercise 49, compute the probability that a student will take at least 20 minutes to complete both Tasks 3 and 4.

51. *Computers* In 2001, 51% of all households in the United States had a computer.[57] Find the probability that in a small town with 800 households, at least 400 had a computer in 2001. HINT [See Example 4.]

52. *Television Ratings* Based on data from Nielsen Research, there is a 15% chance that any television that is turned on during the time of the evening newscasts will be tuned to ABC's evening news show.[58] Your company wishes to advertise on a small local station carrying ABC that serves a community with 2,500 households that regularly tune in during this time slot. Find the approximate probability that at least 400 households will be tuned in to the show. HINT [See Example 4.]

53. *Aviation* The probability of a plane crashing on a single trip in 1989 was .00000165.[59] Find the approximate probability that in 100,000,000 flights, there will be fewer than 180 crashes.

54. *Aviation* The probability of a plane crashing on a single trip in 1990 was .00000087. Find the approximate probability that in 100,000,000 flights, there will be more than 110 crashes.

55. ▼ *Insurance* Your company issues flight insurance. You charge $2 and in the event of a plane crash, you will pay out $1 million to the victim or his or her family. In 1989, the probability of a plane crashing on a single trip was .00000165. If ten people per flight buy insurance from you, what was your approximate probability of losing money over the course of 100 million flights in 1989? HINT [First determine how many crashes there must be for you to lose money.]

56. ▼ *Insurance* Refer back to the preceding exercise. What is your approximate probability of losing money over the course of 10 million flights?

57. ◆ *Polls* In a certain political poll, each person polled has a 90% probability of telling his or her real preference. Suppose that 55% of the population really prefer candidate Goode, and 45% prefer candidate Slick. First find the probability that a person polled will say that he or she prefers Goode. Then find the approximate probability that, if 1,000 people are polled, more than 52% will say they prefer Goode.

58. ◆ *Polls* In a certain political poll, each person polled has a 90% probability of telling his or her real preference. Suppose that 1,000 people are polled and 51% say that they prefer candidate Goode, while 49% say that they prefer candidate

---

[56] Data are rounded to one decimal place. Source: *Student Evaluations of MODSTAT*, by Joseph M. Nowakowski, Muskingum College, New Concord, OH, 1997 (http://members.aol.com/rcknodt/pubpage.htm).

[57] Source: NTIA and ESA, U.S. Department of Commerce, using U.S. Bureau of the Census Current Population Survey supplements.

[58] Source: Nielsen Media Research/ABC Network/*New York Times*, March 18, 2002, p. C1.

[59] Source for this exercise and the following three: National Transportation Safety Board.

Slick. Find the approximate probability that Goode could do at least this well if, in fact, only 49% prefer Goode.

59. ◆ *IQ Scores* Mensa is a club for people with high IQs. To qualify, you must be in the top 2% of the population. One way of qualifying is by having an IQ of at least 148, as measured by the Cattell intelligence test. Assuming that scores on this test are normally distributed with a mean of 100, what is the standard deviation? HINT [Use the table in the Appendix "backwards."]

60. ◆ *SAT Scores* Another way to qualify for Mensa (see the previous exercise) is to score at least 1,250 on the SAT [combined Critical Reading (Verbal, before March 2005) and Math scores], which puts you in the top 2%. Assuming that SAT scores are normally distributed with a mean of 1,000, what is the standard deviation? [See the hint for the previous exercise.]

COMMUNICATION AND REASONING EXERCISES

61. Under what assumptions are the estimates in the empirical rule exact?

62. If X is a continuous random variable, what values can the quantity $P(X = a)$ have?

63. Which is larger for a continuous random variable, $P(X \leq a)$ or $P(X < a)$?

64. Which of the following is greater: $P(X \leq b)$ or $P(a \leq X \leq b)$?

65. ▽ A uniform continuous distribution is one with a probability density curve that is a horizontal line. If X takes on values between the numbers a and b with a uniform distribution, find the height of its probability density curve.

66. ▽ Which would you expect to have the greater variance: the standard normal distribution or the uniform distribution taking values between -1 and 1? Explain.

67. ◆ Which would you expect to have a density curve that is higher at the mean: the standard normal distribution, or a normal distribution with standard deviation 0.5? Explain.

68. ◆ Suppose students must perform two tasks: Task 1 and Task 2. Which of the following would you expect to have a smaller standard deviation?

   (A) The time it takes a student to perform both tasks if the time it takes to complete Task 2 is independent of the time it takes to complete Task 1.

   (B) The time it takes a student to perform both tasks if students will perform similarly in both tasks.

   Explain.

CHAPTER 8 REVIEW

KEY CONCEPTS

Web Site www.FiniteandCalc.org
Go to the student Web site at www.FiniteandCalc.org to find a comprehensive and interactive Web-based summary of Chapter 8.

8.1 Random Variables and Distributions

Random variable; discrete vs continuous random variable *p. 549*
Probability distribution of a finite random variable *p. 551*
Using measurement classes *p. 552*

8.2 Bernoulli Trials and Binomial Random Variables

Bernoulli trial; binomial random variable *pp. 559, 560*
Probability distribution of binomial random variable:
$P(X = x) = C(n, x)p^x q^{n-x}$
p. 562

8.3 Measures of Central Tendency

Sample, sample mean; population, population mean *p. 567*
Sample median, sample mode *p. 569*
Expected value of a random variable:
$\mu = E(X) = \sum_i x_i \cdot P(X = x_i)$
p. 571
Expected value of a binomial random variable: $\mu = E(X) = np$ *p. 573*

8.4 Measures of Dispersion

Population variance:
$\sigma^2 = \dfrac{\sum_{i=1}^{n}(x_i - \mu)^2}{n}$
Population standard deviation:
$\sigma = \sqrt{\sigma^2}$ *p. 580*
Sample variance:
$s^2 = \dfrac{\sum_{i=1}^{n}(x_i - \bar{x})^2}{n - 1}$
Sample standard deviation:
$s = \sqrt{s^2}$ *p. 580*

Chebyshev's Rule *p. 583*
Empirical Rule *p. 583*
Variance of a random variable:
$\sigma^2 = \sum_i(x_i - \mu)^2 P(X = x_i)$ *p. 585*
Standard deviation of X: $\sigma = \sqrt{\sigma^2}$ *p. 585*
Variance and standard deviation of a binomial random variable:
$\sigma^2 = npq, \sigma = \sqrt{npq}$ *p. 587*

8.5 Normal Distributions

Probability density function *p. 595*
Normal density function; normal distribution; standard normal distribution *p. 595*
Calculating probabilities based on the standard normal distribution *p. 596*
Standardizing a normal distribution *p. 596*
Calculating probabilities based on non-standard normal distributions *p. 598*
Normal approximation to a binomial distribution *p. 600*

REVIEW EXERCISES

In Exercises 1–6, find the probability distribution for the given random variable and draw a histogram.

1. A couple has two children; $X =$ the number of boys. (Assume an equal likelihood of a child being a boy or a girl.)

2. A couple has three children; $X =$ the number of girls. (Assume an equal likelihood of a child being a boy or a girl.)

3. A four-sided die (with sides numbered 1 through 4) is rolled twice in succession; $X =$ the sum of the two numbers.

4. 48.2% of *Xbox* players are in their teens, 38.6% are in their twenties, 11.6% are in their thirties, and the rest are in their forties; $X =$ age of an *Xbox* player. (Use the midpoints of the measurement classes.)

5. From a bin that contains 20 defective joysticks and 30 good ones, 3 are chosen at random; $X =$ the number of defective joysticks chosen. (Round all probabilities to four decimal places.)

6. Two dice are weighted so that each number 2, 3, 4, and 5 is half as likely to face up as each 1 and 6; $X =$ the number of 1s that face up when both are thrown.

7. Use any method to calculate the sample mean, median, and standard deviation of the following sample of scores: $-1, 2, 0, 3, 6$.

8. Use any method to calculate the sample mean, median, and standard deviation of the following sample of scores: $4, 4, 5, 6, 6$.

9. Give an example of a sample of four scores with mean 1, and median 0. (Arrange them in ascending order.)

10. Give an example of a sample of six scores with sample standard deviation 0 and mean 2.

11. Give an example of a population of six scores with mean 0 and population standard deviation 1.

12. Give an example of a sample of five scores with mean 0 and sample standard deviation 1.

A die is constructed in such a way that rolling a 6 is twice as likely as rolling each other number. That die is rolled four times. Let X be the number of times a 6 is rolled. Evaluate the probabilities in Exercises 13–20.

13. $P(X = 1)$

14. $P(X = 3)$

15. The probability that 6 comes up at most twice

16. The probability that 6 comes up at most once

17. The probability that X is more than 3

18. The probability that X is at least 2

19. $P(1 \leq X \leq 3)$

20. $P(X \leq 3)$

21. A couple has three children; $X =$ the number of girls. (Assume an equal likelihood of a child being a boy or a girl.) Find the expected value and standard deviation of X, and complete the following sentence with the smallest possible whole number: All values of X lie within ___ standard deviations of the expected value.

22. A couple has four children; $X =$ the number of boys. (Assume only a 25% chance of a child being a boy.) Find the standard deviation of X, and complete the following sentence with the smallest possible whole number: All values of X lie within ___ standard deviations of the expected value.

23. A random variable X has the following frequency distribution.

x	-3	-2	-1	0	1	2	3
$fr(X = x)$	1	2	3	4	3	2	1

Find the probability distribution, expected value, and standard deviation of X, and complete the following sentence: 87.5% (or 14/16) of the time, X is within ___ (round to one decimal place) standard deviations of the expected value.

24. A random variable X has the following frequency distribution.

x	-4	-2	0	2	4	6
$fr(X = x)$	3	3	4	5	3	2

Find the probability distribution, expected value, and standard deviation of X, and complete the following sentence: ___ percent of the values of X lie within one standard deviation of the expected value.

25. A random variable X has expected value $\mu = 100$ and standard deviation $\sigma = 16$. Use Chebyshev's rule to find an interval in which X is guaranteed to lie with a probability of at least 90%.

26. A random variable X has a symmetric distribution and an expected value $\mu = 200$ and standard deviation $\sigma = 5$. Use Chebyshev's rule to find a value that X is guaranteed to exceed with a probability of at most 10%.

27. A random variable X has a bell-shaped, symmetric distribution, with expected value $\mu = 200$ and standard deviation $\sigma = 20$. The empirical rule tells us that X has a value greater than ___ approximately 0.15% of the time.

28. A random variable X has a bell-shaped, symmetric distribution, with expected value $\mu = 100$ and standard deviation $\sigma = 30$. Use the empirical rule to give an interval in which X lies approximately 95% of the time.

In Exercises 29–34 the mean and standard deviation of a normal variable X are given. Find the indicated probability.

29. X is the standard normal variable Z; $P(0 \le X \le 1.5)$.

30. X is the standard normal variable Z; $P(X \le -1.5)$.

31. X is the standard normal variable Z; $P(|X| \ge 2.1)$.

32. $\mu = 100$, $\sigma = 16$; $P(80 \le X \le 120)$

33. $\mu = 0$, $\sigma = 2$; $P(X \le -1)$

34. $\mu = -1$, $\sigma = 0.5$; $P(X \ge 1)$

APPLICATIONS

Marketing As a promotional gimmick, OHaganBooks.com has been selling copies of the Encyclopædia Galactica at an extremely low price that is changed each week at random in a nationally televised drawing. Exercises 35–40 are based on the following table, which summarizes the anticipated sales.

Price	$5.50	$10	$12	$15
Frequency (weeks)	1	2	3	4
Weekly sales	6,200	3,500	3,000	1,000

35. What is the expected value of the price of *Encyclopædia Galactica*?

36. What are the expected weekly sales of *Encyclopædia Galactica*?

37. What is the expected weekly revenue from sales of *Encyclopædia Galactica*? (Revenue = Price per copy sold × Number of copies sold.)

38. OHaganBooks.com originally paid Duffin Press $20 per copy for the *Encyclopædia Galactica*. What is the expected weekly loss from sales of the encyclopædia? (Loss = Loss per copy sold × Number of copies sold.)

39. True or false? If X and Y are two random variables, then $E(XY) = E(X)E(Y)$ (the expected value of the product of two random variables is the product of the expected values). Support your claim by referring to the answers of Exercises 35, 36, and 37.

40. True or false? If X and Y are two random variables, then $E(X/Y) = E(X)/E(Y)$ (the expected value of the ratio of two random variables is the ratio of the expected values). Support your claim by referring to the answers of Exercises 36 and 38.

41. *Online Sales* The following table shows the number of online orders at OHaganBooks.com per million residents in 100 U.S. cities during one month:

Orders (per million residents)	1–2.9	3–4.9	5–6.9	7–8.9	9–10.9
Number of Cities	25	35	15	15	10

a. Let X be the number of orders per million residents in a randomly chosen U.S. city (use rounded midpoints of the given measurement classes). Construct the probability distribution for X and hence compute the expected value μ of X and standard deviation σ. (Round answers to four decimal places.)

b. What range of orders per million residents does the empirical rule predict from approximately 68% of all cities? Would you judge that the empirical rule applies? Why?

c. The actual percentage of cities from which you obtain between 3 and 8 orders per million residents is (choose the correct answer that gives the most specific information):

(A) Between 50% and 65% (B) At least 65%
(C) At least 50% (D) 57.5%

42. *Pollen* Marjory Duffin is planning a joint sales meeting with OHaganBooks.com in Atlanta at the end of March, but is extremely allergic to pollen, so she went online to find pollen counts for the period. The following table shows the results of her search:

Pollen Count	0–1.9	2–3.9	4–5.9	6–7.9	8–8.9	10–11.9
Number of Days	3	5	7	2	1	2

a. Let X be the pollen count on a given day (use rounded midpoints of the given measurement classes). Construct the probability distribution for X and hence compute the expected value μ of X and standard deviation σ. (Round answers to four decimal places.)

b. What range of pollen counts does the empirical rule predict on approximately 95% of the days? Would you judge that the empirical rule applies? Why?

c. The actual percentage of days on which the pollen count is between 2 and 7 is (choose the correct answer that gives the most specific information):

  (A) Between 50% and 60%   **(B)** At least 60%

  (C) At most 70%   **(D)** Between 60% and 70%

Mac vs. Windows On average, 5% of all hits by Mac OS users and 10% of all hits by Windows users result in orders for books at OHaganBooks.com. Due to online promotional efforts, the site traffic is approximately 10 hits per hour by Mac OS users, and 20 hits per hour by Windows users. Compute the probabilities in Exercises 43–48. (Round all answers to three decimal places.)

43. What is the probability that exactly three Windows users will order books in the next hour?

44. What is the probability that at most three Windows users will order books in the next hour?

45. What is the probability that exactly one Mac OS user and three Windows users will order books in the next hour?

46. What assumption must you make to justify your calculation in Exercise 45?

47. How many orders for books can OHaganBooks.com expect in the next hour from Mac OS users?

48. How many orders for books can OHaganBooks.com expect in the next hour from Windows users?

Online Cosmetics OHaganBooks.com has launched a subsidiary, GnuYou.com, which sells beauty products online. Most products sold by GnuYou.com are skin creams and hair products. Exercises 49–52 are based on the following table, which shows monthly revenues earned through sales of these products. (Assume a normal distribution. Round all answers to three decimal places.)

Product	*Skin Creams*	*Hair Products*
Mean Monthly Revenue	$38,000	$34,000
Standard Deviation	$21,000	$14,000

49. What is the probability that GnuYou.com will sell *at least* $50,000 worth of skin cream next month?

50. What is the probability that GnuYou.com will sell *at most* $50,000 worth of hair products next month?

51. What is the probability that GnuYou.com will sell less than $12,000 of skin creams next month?

52. What is the probability that GnuYou.com will sell less than $12,000 of hair products next month?

53. *Intelligence* Billy-Sean O'Hagan, now a senior at Suburban State University, has done exceptionally well and has just joined Mensa, a club for people with high IQs. Within Mensa is a group called the Three Sigma Club because their IQ scores are at least three standard deviations higher than the United States mean. Assuming a U.S. population of 280,000,000, how many people in the United States are qualified for the Three Sigma Club? (Round your answer to the nearest 1,000 people.)

54. *Intelligence* To join Mensa (not necessarily the Three Sigma Club), one needs an IQ of at least 132, corresponding to the top 2% of the population. Assuming that scores on this test are normally distributed with a mean of 100, what is the standard deviation? (Round your answer to the nearest whole number.)

55. *Intelligence* Based on the information given in Exercises 53 and 54, what score must Billy-Sean have to get into the Three Sigma Club? (Assume that IQ scores are normally distributed with a mean of 100, and use the rounded standard deviation.)

Case Study   Spotting Tax Fraud with Benford's Law[60]

You are a tax fraud specialist working for the Internal Revenue Service (IRS), and you have just been handed a portion of the tax return from Colossal Conglomerate. The IRS suspects that the portion you were handed may be fraudulent, and would like your opinion. Is there any mathematical test, you wonder, that can point to a suspicious tax return based on nothing more than the numbers entered?

---

[60] The discussion is based on the article "Following Benford's Law, or Looking Out for No. 1" by Malcolm W. Browne, *The New York Times*, August 4, 1998, p. F4. The use of Benford's Law in detecting tax evasion is discussed in a Ph.D. dissertation by Dr. Mark J. Nigrini (Southern Methodist University, Dallas).

You decide, on an impulse, to make a list of the first digits of all the numbers entered in the portion of the Colossal Conglomerate tax return (there are 625 of them). You reason that, if the tax return is an honest one, the first digits of the numbers should be uniformly distributed. More precisely, if the experiment consists of selecting a number at random from the tax return, and the random variable X is defined to be the first digit of the selected number, then X should have the following probability distribution:

x	1	2	3	4	5	6	7	8	9
$P(X = x)$	$\frac{1}{9}$	$\frac{1}{9}$	$\frac{1}{9}$	$\frac{1}{9}$	$\frac{1}{9}$	$\frac{1}{9}$	$\frac{1}{9}$	$\frac{1}{9}$	$\frac{1}{9}$

You then do a quick calculation based on this probability distribution, and find an expected value of $E(X) = 5$. Next, you turn to the Colossal Conglomerate tax return data and calculate the relative frequency (estimated probability) of the actual numbers in the tax return. You find the following results.

Colossal Conglomerate Return

y	1	2	3	4	5	6	7	8	9
$P(Y = y)$	.29	.1	.04	.15	.31	.08	.01	.01	.01

It certainly does look suspicious! For one thing, the digits 1 and 5 seem to occur a lot more often than any of the other digits, and roughly three times what you predicted. Moreover, when you compute the expected value, you obtain $E(Y) = 3.48$, considerably lower than the value of 5 you predicted. Gotcha! you exclaim.

You are about to file a report recommending a detailed audit of Colossal Conglomerate when you recall an article you once read about first digits in lists of numbers. The article dealt with a remarkable discovery in 1938 by Dr. Frank Benford, a physicist at General Electric. What Dr. Benford noticed was that the pages of logarithm tables that listed numbers starting with the digits 1 and 2 tended to be more soiled and dog-eared than the pages that listed numbers starting with higher digits—say, 8. For some reason, numbers that start with low digits seemed more prevalent than numbers that start with high digits. He subsequently analyzed more than 20,000 sets of numbers, such as tables of baseball statistics, listings of widths of rivers, half-lives of radioactive elements, street addresses, and numbers in magazine articles. The result was always the same: Inexplicably, numbers that start with low digits tended to appear more frequently than those that start with high ones, with numbers beginning with the digit 1 most prevalent of all.[61] Moreover, the expected value of the first digit was not the expected 5, but 3.44.

Because the first digits in Colossal Conglomerate's return have an expected value of 3.48, very close to Benford's value, it might appear that your suspicion was groundless after all. (Back to the drawing board . . .)

Out of curiosity, you decide to investigate Benford's discovery more carefully. What you find is that Benford did more than simply observe a strange phenomenon in lists of numbers. He went further and derived the following formula for the probability distribution of first digits in lists of numbers:

$$P(X = x) = \log(1 + 1/x) \qquad (x = 1, 2, \ldots, 9).$$

---

[61] This does not apply to all lists of numbers. For instance, a list of randomly chosen numbers between 100 and 999 will have first digits uniformly distributed between 1 and 9.

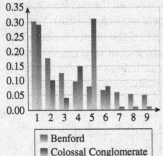

Figure 17

You compute these probabilities, and find the following distribution (the probabilities are all rounded, and thus do not add to exactly 1).

x	1	2	3	4	5	6	7	8	9
$P(X=x)$	.30	.18	.12	.10	.08	.07	.06	.05	.05

You then enter these data along with the Colossal Conglomerate tax return data in your spreadsheet program and obtain the graph shown in Figure 17.

The graph shows something awfully suspicious happening with the digit 5. The percentage of numbers in the Colossal Conglomerate return that begin with 5 far exceeds Benford's prediction that approximately 8% of all numbers should begin with 5.

Now it seems fairly clear that you are justified in recommending Colossal Conglomerate for an audit, after all.

Q: *Because no given set of data can reasonably be expected to satisfy Benford's Law exactly, how can I be certain that the Colossal Conglomerate data is not simply due to chance?*

A: You can never be 100% certain. It is certainly conceivable that the tax figures just happen to result in the "abnormal" distribution in the Colossal Conglomerate tax return. However—and this is the subject of "inferential statistics"—there is a method for deciding whether you can be, say "95% certain" that the anomaly reflected in the data is not due to chance. To check, you must first compute a statistic that determines how far a given set of data deviates from satisfying a theoretical prediction (Benford's Law, in this case). This statistic is called a **sum-of-squares error**, and given by the following formula (reminiscent of the variance):

$$ \text{SSE} = n\left[\frac{[P(y_1) - P(x_1)]^2}{P(x_1)} + \frac{[P(y_2) - P(x_2)]^2}{P(x_2)} + \cdots + \frac{[P(y_9) - P(x_9)]^2}{P(x_9)} \right]. $$

Here, n is the sample size: 625 in the case of Colossal Conglomerate. The quantities $P(x_i)$ are the theoretically predicted probabilities according to Benford's Law, and the $P(y_i)$ are the probabilities in the Colossal Conglomerate return. Notice that if the Colossal Conglomerate return probabilities had exactly matched the theoretically predicted probabilities, then SSE would have been zero. Notice also the effect of multiplying by the sample size n: The larger the sample, the more likely that the discrepancy between the $P(x_i)$ and the $P(y_i)$ is not due to chance. Substituting the numbers gives

$$ \text{SSE} \approx 625\left[\frac{[.29 - .30]^2}{.30} + \frac{[.1 - .18]^2}{.18} + \cdots + \frac{[.01 - .05]^2}{.05} \right] $$

$$ \approx 552.^{[62]} $$

Q: *The value of SSE does seem quite large. But how can I use this figure in my report? I would like to say something impressive, such as "Based on the portion of the Colossal Conglomerate tax return analyzed, one can be 95% certain that the figures are anomalous."*

A: The error SSE is used by statisticians to answer exactly such a question. What they would do is compare this figure to the largest SSE we would have expected to get by

---

[62] If you use more accurate values for the probabilities in Benford's distribution, the value is approximately 560.

chance in 95 out of 100 selections of data that *do* satisfy Benford's law. This "biggest error" is computed using a "Chi-Squared" distribution and can be found in Excel by entering

=CHIINV(0.05, 8).

Here, the 0.05 is $1 - 0.95$, encoding the "95% certainty," and the 8 is called the "number of degrees of freedom" = number of outcomes (9) minus 1.

You now find, using Excel, that the chi-squared figure is 15.5, meaning that the largest SSE that you could have expected purely by chance is 15.5. Because Colossal Conglomerate's error is much larger at 552, you can now justifiably say in your report that there is a 95% certainty that the figures are anomalous.[63]

EXERCISES

Which of the following lists of data would you expect to follow Benford's law? If the answer is "no," give a reason.

1. Distances between cities in France, measured in kilometers.
2. Distances between cities in France, measured in miles.
3. The grades (0–100) in your math instructor's grade book.
4. The Dow Jones averages for the past 100 years.
5. Verbal SAT scores of college-bound high school seniors.
6. Life spans of companies.

Use technology to determine whether the given distribution of first digits fails, with 95% certainty, to follow Benford's law.

7. Good Neighbor Inc.'s tax return ($n = 1,000$)

y	1	2	3	4	5	6	7	8	9
$P(Y = y)$	.31	.16	.13	.11	.07	.07	.05	.06	.04

8. Honest Growth Funds Stockholder Report ($n = 400$)

y	1	2	3	4	5	6	7	8	9
$P(Y = y)$	.28	.16	.1	.11	.07	.09	.05	.07	.07

[63] What this actually means is that, if you were to do a similar analysis on a large number of tax returns, and you designated as "not conforming to Benford's Law" all of those whose value of SSE was larger than 15.5, you would be justified in 95% of the cases.

TI-83/84 Plus **Technology Guide**

Section 8.1

Example 3 (page 552) Let X be the number of heads that face up in three tosses of a coin. We obtained the following probability distribution of X in the text:

x	0	1	2	3
$P(X = x)$	$\frac{1}{8}$	$\frac{3}{8}$	$\frac{3}{8}$	$\frac{1}{8}$

Use technology to obtain the corresponding histogram.

Solution with Technology

1. In the TI-83/84 Plus, you can enter a list of probabilities as follows: press $\boxed{\text{STAT}}$, choose EDIT, and then press $\boxed{\text{ENTER}}$. Clear columns L_1 and L_2 if they are not already cleared. (Select the heading of a column and press $\boxed{\text{CLEAR}}$ $\boxed{\text{ENTER}}$ to clear it.) Enter the values of X in the column under L_1 (pressing $\boxed{\text{ENTER}}$ after each entry) and enter the frequencies in the column under L_2.

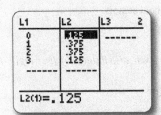

2. To graph the data as in Figure 1, first set the $\boxed{\text{WINDOW}}$ to $0 \le X \le 4$, $0 \le Y \le 0.5$, and Xscl $= 1$ (the width of the bars). Then turn STAT PLOT on ([2nd] $\boxed{\text{Y=}}$), and configure it by selecting the histogram icon, setting Xlist $= L_1$ and Freq $= L_2$. Then hit $\boxed{\text{GRAPH}}$.

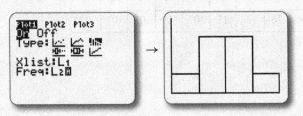

Example 4 (page 552) We obtained the following frequency table in the text:

x	25,000	35,000	45,000	55,000	65,000	75,000	85,000
Frequency	20	80	230	400	170	70	30

Find the probability distribution of X.

Solution with Technology

We need to divide each frequency by the sum. Although the computations in this example (dividing the seven frequencies by 1,000) are simple to do by hand, they could become tedious in general, so technology is helpful.

1. On the TI-83/84 Plus, press $\boxed{\text{STAT}}$, select EDIT, enter the values of X in the L_1 list, and enter the frequencies in the L_2 list as in Example 3.

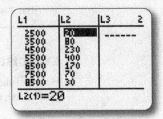

2. Then, on the home screen, enter

$$L_2/1{,}000 \to L_3$$ L_2 is $\boxed{\text{2nd}}$ $\boxed{\text{2}}$, L_3 is $\boxed{\text{2nd}}$ $\boxed{\text{3}}$.

or, better yet,

$$L_2/\text{sum}(L_2) \to L_3$$ Sum is found in $\boxed{\text{2nd}}$ $\boxed{\text{STAT}}$, under MATH.

3. After pressing $\boxed{\text{ENTER}}$ you can now go back to the $\boxed{\text{STAT}}$ EDIT screen, and you will find the probabilities displayed in L_3 as shown.

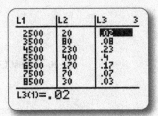

Section 8.2

Example 2(b) (page 562) By 2030, the probability that a randomly chosen resident in the United States will be 65 years old or older is projected to be .2. If X is the number of people aged 65 or older in a sample of 6, construct the probability distribution of X.

Solution with Technology

In the "Y=" screen, you can enter the binomial distribution formula

$$Y_1 = 6 \text{ nCr } X*0.2^X*0.8^{(6-X)}$$

directly (to get nCr, press MATH and select PRB), and hit TABLE. You can then replicate the table in the text by choosing $X = 0, 1, \ldots, 6$ (use the TBLSET screen to set "Indpnt" to "Ask" if you have not already done so).

The TI-83/84 Plus also has a built-in binomial distribution function that you can use in place of the explicit formula:

$Y_1 = $ binompdf(6, 0.2, X)   Press 2nd VARS 0.

The TI-83/84 Plus function binompcf (directly following binompdf) gives the value of the *cumulative* distribution function, $P(0 \le X \le x)$.

To graph the resulting probability distribution on your calculator, follow the instructions for graphing a histogram in Section 8.1.

Section 8.3

Example 3 (page 572) According to historical data, the number of injuries that a member of the Enormous State University women's soccer team will sustain during a typical season is given by the following probability distribution table:

Injuries	0	1	2	3	4	5	6
Probability	.2	.2	.22	.2	.15	.01	.02

If X denotes the number of injuries sustained by a player during one season, compute $E(X)$.

Solution with Technology

To obtain the expected value of a probability distribution on the TI-83/84 Plus, press STAT, select EDIT, and then press ENTER, and enter the values of X in the L_1 list and the probabilities in the column in the L_2 list. Then, on the home screen, you can obtain the expected value as

sum $(L_1 * L_2)$ L_1 is 2nd 1 L_2 is 2nd 2
    Sum is found in 2nd STAT, under MATH

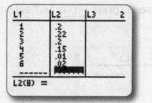

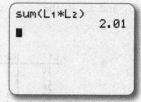

Section 8.4

Example 1 (page 582) The unemployment rates (in percentage points) in the U.S. for the months April–October 2008 were[64]

5, 6, 6, 6, 6, 6, 7.

Compute the sample mean and standard deviation.

Solution with Technology

On the TI-83/84 Plus, enter the sample scores in list L_1 on the STAT/EDIT screen, then go to STAT/CALC, select 1-Var Stats, and hit ENTER. The resulting display shows, among other statistics, the sample standard deviation s as "Sx" as well as the population standard deviation σ as "σx."

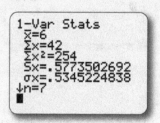

Example 3 (page 586) Compute the variance and standard deviation for the following probability distribution.

x	10	20	30	40	50	60
$P(X = x)$	.2	.2	.3	.1	.1	.1

Solution with Technology

1. As in Example 3 in the preceding section, begin by entering the probability distribution of X into columns

[64] Figures are rounded. Sources: Bureau of Labor Statistics (BLS) (www.bls.gov).

L_1 and L_2 in the LIST screen (press $\boxed{\text{STAT}}$ and select EDIT).

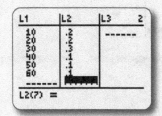

2. Then, on the home screen, enter

sum(L_1*L_2)$\rightarrow$M   Stores the value of μ as M
                               Sum is found in $\boxed{\text{2nd}}$ $\boxed{\text{STAT}}$,
                               under MATH.

3. To obtain the variance, enter the following.

sum((L_1-M)^2*L_2)   Computation of
                          $\sum(x - \mu)^2 P(X = x)$

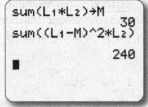

Section 8.5

Example 1(b), (c) (page 596) Let Z be the standard normal variable. Calculate the following probabilities.
b. $P(0 \leq Z \leq 2.43)$
c. $P(-1.37 \leq Z \leq 2.43)$

Solution with Technology

On the TI-83/84 Plus, press $\boxed{\text{2nd}}$ $\boxed{\text{VARS}}$ to obtain the selection of distribution functions. The first function, normalpdf, gives the values of the normal density function (whose graph is the normal curve). The second, normalcdf, gives $P(a \leq Z \leq b)$. For example, to compute $P(0 \leq Z \leq 2.43)$, enter

    normalcdf(0, 2.43)

To compute $P(-1.37 \leq Z \leq 2.43)$, enter

    normalcdf(-1.37, 2.43)

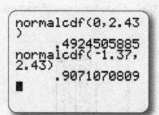

Example 2 (page 598) Pressure gauges manufactured by Precision Corp. must be checked for accuracy before being placed on the market. To test a pressure gauge, a worker uses it to measure the pressure of a sample of compressed air known to be at a pressure of exactly 50 pounds per square inch. If the gauge reading is off by more than 1% (0.5 pounds), it is rejected. Assuming that the reading of a pressure gauge under these circumstances is a normal random variable with mean 50 and standard deviation 0.4, find the percentage of gauges rejected.

Solution with Technology

As seen in the text, we need to compute $1 - P(49.5 \leq X \leq 50.5)$ with $\mu = 50$ and $\sigma = 0.4$. On the TI-83/84 Plus, the built-in normalcdf function permits us to compute $P(a \leq X \leq b)$ for nonstandard normal distributions as well. The format is

    normalcdf(a, b, μ, σ) $P(a \leq X \leq b)$

For example, we can compute $P(49.5 \leq X \leq 50.5)$ by entering

    normalcdf(49.5, 50.5, 50, 0.4)

Then subtract it from 1 to obtain the answer:

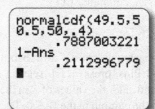

EXCEL Technology Guide

Section 8.1

Example 3 (page 552) Let *X* be the number of heads that face up in three tosses of a coin. We obtained the following probability distribution of *X* in the text:

x	0	1	2	3
P(X = x)	$\frac{1}{8}$	$\frac{3}{8}$	$\frac{3}{8}$	$\frac{1}{8}$

Use technology to obtain the corresponding histogram.

Solution with Technology

1. In Excel, enter the values of *X* in one column and the probabilities in another.

	A	B
1	x	P(X=x)
2	0	0.125
3	1	0.375
4	2	0.375
5	3	0.125

2. Next, select *only* the column of probabilities (B2–B5) and then choose Insert → Column Chart. (Select the first type of column chart that appears.) Right-click on the resulting chart and choose "Select Data." In the resulting dialog box, click on "Edit" under "Horizontal (Category) Axis Labels," highlight the values of *x* (A2–A8 in Example 4), then click OK. To adjust the width of the bars, right-click on a bar, select "Format Data Series," and adjust the gap width to your liking. Here is a possible result (gap width zero):

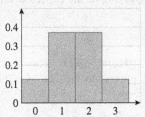

Example 4 (page 552) We obtained the following frequency table in the text:

x	25,000	35,000	45,000	55,000	65,000	75,000	85,000
Frequency	20	80	230	400	170	70	30

Find the probability distribution of *X*.

Solution with Technology

We need to divide each frequency by the sum. Although the computations in this example (dividing the seven frequencies by 1,000) are simple to do by hand, they could become tedious in general, so technology is helpful. Excel manipulates lists with ease. Set up your spreadsheet as shown.

	A	B	C
1	x	Fr	P(X=x)
2	25000	20	=B2/SUM(B:B)
3	35000	80	
4	45000	230	
5	55000	400	
6	65000	170	
7	75000	70	
8	85000	30	

↓

	A	B	C
1	x	Fr	P(X=x)
2	25000	20	0.02
3	35000	80	0.08
4	45000	230	0.23
5	55000	400	0.4
6	65000	170	0.17
7	75000	70	0.07
8	85000	30	0.03

The formula SUM(B:B) gives the sum of all the numerical entries in Column B. You can now change the frequencies to see the effect on the probabilities. You can also add new values and frequencies to the list if you copy the formula in column C further down the column.

Section 8.2

Example 2(b) (page 562) By 2030, the probability that a randomly chosen resident in the United States will be 65 years old or older is projected to be .2. If *X* is the number of people aged 65 or older in a sample of 6, construct the probability distribution of *X*.

Solution with Technology

You can generate the binomial distribution as follows in Excel:

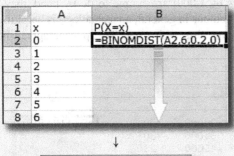

The values of X are shown in column A, and the probabilities are computed in column B. The arguments of the BINOMDIST function are as follows:

BINOMDIST(x, n, p, Cumulative (0 = no, 1 = yes)).

Setting the last argument to 0 (as shown) gives $P(X = x)$. Setting it to 1 gives $P(X \le x)$.

To graph the resulting probability distribution using Excel, follow the instructions for graphing a histogram in Section 8.1.

Section 8.3

Example 3 (page 572) According to historical data, the number of injuries that a member of the Enormous State University women's soccer team will sustain during a typical season is given by the following probability distribution table:

Injuries	0	1	2	3	4	5	6
Probability	.2	.2	.22	.2	.15	.01	.02

If X denotes the number of injuries sustained by a player during one season, compute $E(X)$.

Solution with Technology

As the method we used suggests, the calculation of the expected value from the probability distribution is particularly easy to do using a spreadsheet program such as Excel. The following worksheet shows one way to do it. (The first two columns contain the probability distribution of X; the quantities $xP(X = x)$ are summed in cell C9.)

An alternative is to use the SUMPRODUCT function in Excel: Once we enter the first two columns above, the formula

=SUMPRODUCT(A2:A8,B2:B8)

computes the sum of the products of corresponding entries in the columns, giving us the expected value.

Section 8.4

Example 1 (page 582) The unemployment rates (in percentage points) in the U.S. for the months April–October 2008 were[65]

5, 6, 6, 6, 6, 6, 7.

Compute the sample mean and standard deviation.

---

[65] Figures are rounded. Sources: Bureau of Labor Statistics (BLS) (www.bls.gov).

Solution with Technology

To compute the sample mean and standard deviation of a collection of scores in Excel, set up your spreadsheet as follows:

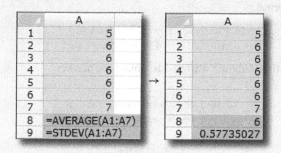

For the population standard deviation, use

=STDEVP(A1:A6)

Example 3 (page 586) Compute the variance and standard deviation for the following probability distribution.

x	10	20	30	40	50	60
$P(X=x)$	.2	.2	.3	.1	.1	.1

Solution with Technology

As in Example 3 in the preceding section, begin by entering the probability distribution into columns A and B, and then proceed as shown:

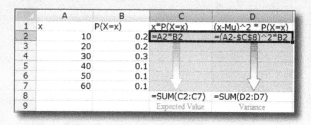

The variance then appears in cell D8:

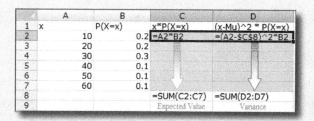

Section 8.5

Example 1(b), (c) (page 596) Let Z be the standard normal variable. Calculate the following probabilities.
b. $P(0 \leq Z \leq 2.43)$
c. $P(-1.37 \leq Z \leq 2.43)$

Solution with Technology

In Excel, the function NORMSDIST (Normal Standard Distribution) gives the area shown on the left in Figure 18. (Tables such as the one in the Appendix give the area shown on the right.)

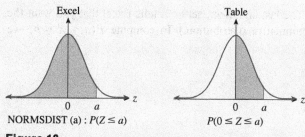

Figure 18

To compute a general area, $P(a \leq Z \leq b)$ in Excel, subtract the cumulative area to a from that to b:

=NORMSDIST(b)-NORMSDIST(a) $P(a \leq Z \leq b)$

In particular, to compute $P(0 \leq Z \leq 2.43)$, use

=NORMSDIST(2.43)-NORMSDIST(0)

and to compute $P(-1.37 \leq Z \leq 2.43)$, use

=NORMSDIST(2.43)-NORMSDIST(-1.37)

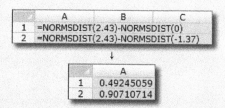

Example 2 (page 598) Pressure gauges manufactured by Precision Corp. must be checked for accuracy before being placed on the market. To test a pressure gauge, a worker uses it to measure the pressure of a sample of compressed air known to be at a pressure of exactly 50 pounds

71

per square inch. If the gauge reading is off by more than 1% (0.5 pounds), it is rejected. Assuming that the reading of a pressure gauge under these circumstances is a normal random variable with mean 50 and standard deviation 0.4, find the percentage of gauges rejected.

Solution with Technology

In Excel, we use the function NORMDIST instead of NORMSDIST. Its format is similar to NORMSDIST, but includes extra arguments as shown.

$$=\text{NORMDIST}(a, \mu, \sigma, 1) \quad P(X \leq a)$$

(The last argument, set to 1, tells Excel that you want the cumulative distribution.) To compute $P(a \leq X \leq b)$ we enter the following in any vacant cell:

$$=\text{NORMDIST}(b, \mu, \sigma, 1)$$
$$-\text{NORMDIST}(a, \mu, \sigma, 1) \quad P(a \leq X \leq b)$$

For example, we can compute $P(49.5 \leq X \leq 50.5)$ by entering

```
=NORMDIST(50.5,50,0.4,1)
  -NORMDIST(49.5,50,0.4,1)
```

We then subtract it from 1 to obtain the answer:

	A	B	C	D
1	=NORMDIST(50.5,50,0.4,1)-NORMDIST(49.5,50,0.4,1)			
2	=1-A1			

↓

	A
1	0.78870045
2	0.21129955

Answers to Selected Exercises

Section 8.1

1. Finite; $\{2, 3, \ldots, 12\}$ **3.** Discrete infinite; $\{0, 1, -1,$
$2, -2, \ldots\}$ (negative profits indicate loss)   **5.** Continuous; X
can assume any value between 0 and 60.   **7.** Finite; $\{0, 1,$
$2, \ldots, 10\}$ **9.** Discrete infinite $\{k/1, k/4, k/9, k/16, \ldots\}$
11. a. $S = \{HH, HT, TH, TT\}$
b. X is the rule that assigns to each outcome the number of tails.
c.

Outcome	HH	HT	TH	TT
Value of X	0	1	1	2

13. a. $S = \{(1, 1), (1, 2), \ldots, (1, 6), (2, 1), (2, 2), \ldots, (6, 6)\}$
b. X is the rule that assigns to each outcome the sum of the two
numbers.
c.

Outcome	(1, 1)	(1, 2)	(1, 3)	...	(6, 6)
Value of X	2	3	4	...	12

15. a. $S = \{(4, 0), (3, 1), (2, 2)\}$ (listed in order (red, green))
b. X is the rule that assigns to each outcome the number of red
marbles.
c.

Outcome	(4, 0)	(3, 1)	(2, 2)
Value of X	4	3	2

73

17. a. S = the set of students in the study group.
b. X is the rule that assigns to each student his or her final exam score. **c.** The values of X, in the order given, are 89%, 85%, 95%, 63%, 92%, 80%. **19. a.** $P(X = 8) = P(X = 6) = .3$ **b.** .7

21.

x	1	2	3	4	5	6
$P(X = x)$	$\frac{1}{6}$	$\frac{1}{6}$	$\frac{1}{6}$	$\frac{1}{6}$	$\frac{1}{6}$	$\frac{1}{6}$

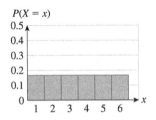

23.

x	0	1	4	9
$P(X = x)$	$\frac{1}{8}$	$\frac{3}{8}$	$\frac{3}{8}$	$\frac{1}{8}$

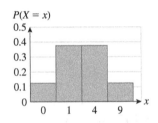

25.

x	2	3	4	5	6	7	8	9	10	11	12
$P(X = x)$	$\frac{1}{36}$	$\frac{2}{36}$	$\frac{3}{36}$	$\frac{4}{36}$	$\frac{5}{36}$	$\frac{6}{36}$	$\frac{5}{36}$	$\frac{4}{36}$	$\frac{3}{36}$	$\frac{2}{36}$	$\frac{1}{36}$

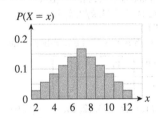

27.

x	1	2	3	4	5	6
$P(X = x)$	$\frac{1}{36}$	$\frac{3}{36}$	$\frac{5}{36}$	$\frac{7}{36}$	$\frac{9}{36}$	$\frac{11}{36}$

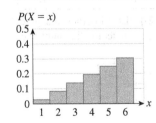

29. a.

x	10,000	30,000	50,000	70,000	90,000
$P(X = x)$	.24	.27	.22	.16	.11

b. .27 Histogram:

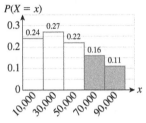

31. The random variable is X = age of a working adult in Mexico.

x	20	30	40	50	60
$P(X = x)$	.288	.472	.200	.032	.008

33. a. 2,000, 3,000, 4,000, 5,000, 6,000, 7,000, 8,000 (7,000 is optional)
b.

x	2,000	3,000	4,000	5,000	6,000	7,000	8,000
Freq.	2	1	1	1	2	0	3
$P(X = x)$	.2	.1	.1	.1	.2	0	.3

c. $P(X \le 5,000) = .5$ **35. a.** $-700, -600, -500, -400,$ $-300, -200, -100, 0, 100, 200, 300, 400, 500, 600, 700, 800,$ 900 ($-600, 0, 100, 300, 500, 600, 700,$ and 800 are optional.)
b.

x	-700	-600	-500	-400	-300	-200	-100	0
Freq.	2	0	2	1	1	4	4	0
$P(X = x)$	.1	0	.1	.05	.05	.2	.2	0

x	100	200	300	400	500	600	700	800	900
Freq.	0	2	0	2	0	0	0	0	2
$P(X = x)$	0	.1	0	.1	0	0	0	0	.1

c. .3

37.

Class	1.1 − 2.0	2.1 − 3.0	3.1 − 4.0
Freq.	4	7	9

x	1.5	2.5	3.5
$P(X = x)$	.20	.35	.45

39. 95.5%

41.

x	3	2	1	0
$P(X = x)$	.0625	.6875	.125	.125

43. .75 The probability that a randomly selected small car is rated Good or Acceptable is .75. **45.** $P(Y \ge 2) = .50$, $P(Z \ge 2) \approx .53$, suggesting that medium SUVs are safer than small SUVs in frontal crashes **47.** Small cars **49.** .375

51.

x	1	2	3	4
$P(X = x)$	$\frac{4}{35}$	$\frac{18}{35}$	$\frac{12}{35}$	$\frac{1}{35}$

$P(X \geq 2) = 31/35 \approx .886$

53. Answers will vary.   **55.** No; for instance, if X is the number of times you must toss a coin until heads comes up, then X is infinite but not continuous.   **57.** By measuring the values of X for a large number of outcomes, and then using the estimated probability (relative frequency)   **59.** Here is an example: Let X be the number of days a diligent student waits before beginning to study for an exam scheduled in 10 days' time.   **61.** The bars should be 1 unit wide, so that their height is numerically equal to their area.   **63.** Answers may vary. If we are interested in exact page counts, then the number of possible values is very large and the values are (relatively speaking) close together, so using a continuous random variable might be advantageous. In general, the finer and more numerous the measurement classes, the more likely it becomes that a continuous random variable could be advantageous.

Section 8.2

1. .0729   **3.** .59049   **5.** .00001   **7.** .99144   **9.** .00856   **11.** .27648   **13.** .54432   **15.** .04096   **17.** .77414

19. $P(X = x)$

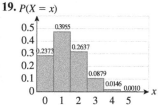

21. $P(X = x)$

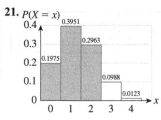

$P(X \leq 2) = .8889$

23. .2637   **25.** .8926   **27.** .875   **29. a.** .0081   **b.** .08146   **31.** .41   **33. a.** .0509   **b.** Probability distribution (entries rounded to four decimal places):

x	0	1	2	3	4
$P(X = x)$	.0643	.2030	.2885	.2429	.1343
5	6	7	8	9	10
.0509	.0134	.0024	.0003	.0000	.0000

c. 2   **35.** .000298   **37.** .8321   **39. a.** 21   **b.** 20   **c.** The graph for $n = 50$ trials is more widely distributed than the graph for $n = 20$.   **41.** 69 trials   **43.** $.562 \times 10^{-5}$ **45.** .0266; because there is only a 2.66% chance of detecting the disease in a given year, the government's claim seems dubious.   **47.** No; in a

sequence of Bernoulli trials, the occurrence of one success does not affect the probability of success on the next attempt.   **49.** No; if life is a sequence of Bernoulli trials, then the occurrence of one misfortune ("success") does not affect the probability of a misfortune on the next trial. Hence, misfortunes may very well not "occur in threes."   **51.** Think of performing the experiment as a Bernoulli trial with "success" being the occurrence of E. Performing the experiment n times independently in succession would then be a sequence of n Bernoulli trials.   **53.** The probability of selecting a red marble changes after each selection, as the number of marbles left in the bag decreases. This violates the requirement that, in a sequence of Bernoulli trials, the probability of "success" does not change.

Section 8.3

1. $\bar{x} = 6$, median $= 5$, mode $= 5$ **3.** $\bar{x} = 3$, median $= 3.5$, mode $= -1$ **5.** $\bar{x} = -0.1875$, median $= 0.875$, every value is a mode   **7.** $\bar{x} = 0.2$, median $= -0.1$, mode $= -0.1$ **9.** Answers may vary. Two examples are: 0, 0, 0, 0, 0, 6 and 0, 0, 0, 1, 2, 3   **11.** 0.9   **13.** 21   **15.** -0.1 **17.** 3.5   **19.** 1   **21.** 4.472   **23.** 2.667   **25.** 2   **27.** 0.385   **29.** $\bar{x} = -150$, $m = -150$; -150 **31.** $\bar{x} = \$918.30$, median $= \$915.50$, mode $= \$905$. Over the 10-business day period sampled, the price of gold averaged $915.30 per ounce. It was above $915.50 as many times as it was below that, and stood at $905 more often than any other price.   **33. a.** 6.5; there was an average of 6.5 checkout lanes in each supermarket that was surveyed.   **b.** $P(X < \mu) = .42$; $P(X > \mu) = .58$, and is thus larger. Most supermarkets have more than the average number of checkout lanes.

35.

X	5	10	15	20	25	35
$P(X)$	.17	.33	.21	.19	.03	.07

$E(X) = 14.3$;

the average age of a school goer in 1998 was 14.3.   **37.** 30   **39.** $41,000

41.

x	3	2	1	0
$P(X = x)$	.0625	.6875	.125	.125

$E(X) = 1.6875$

y	3	2	1	0
$P(Y = y)$	.1	.4	.4	.1

$E(Y) = 1.5$;

small cars

43. Large cars   **45.** Expect to lose 5.3¢.   **47.** 25.2 students   **49. a.** Two defective airbags   **b.** 120 airbags

51.

x	1	2	3	4
$P(X = x)$	$\frac{4}{35}$	$\frac{18}{35}$	$\frac{12}{35}$	$\frac{1}{35}$

$E(X) = 16/7 \approx 2.2857$ tents

53. FastForward: 3.97%; SolidState: 5.51%; SolidState gives the higher expected return.   **55.** A loss of $29,390   **57.** (A)   **59.** He is wrong; for example, the collection 0, 0, 300 has mean 100

and median 0.   **61.** No. The expected number of times you will hit the dart-board is the average number of times you will hit the bull's eye per 50 shots; the average of a set of whole numbers need not be a whole number.   **63.** Wrong. It might be the case that only a small fraction of people in the class scored better than you but received exceptionally high scores that raised the class average. Suppose, for instance, that there are 10 people in the class. Four received 100%, you received 80%, and the rest received 70%. Then the class average is 83%, 5 people have lower scores than you, but only 4 have higher scores.
65. No; the mean of a very large sample is only an *estimate* of the population mean. The means of larger and larger samples *approach* the population mean as the sample size increases.
67. Wrong. The statement attributed to President Bush asserts that the mean tax refund would be $1,000, whereas the statements referred to as "The Truth" suggest that the *median* tax refund would be close to $100 [and that the 31st percentile would be zero].   **69.** Select a U.S. household at random, and let X be the income of that household. The expected value of X is then the population mean of all U.S. household incomes.

Section 8.4

1. $s^2 = 29$; $s = 5.39$ **3.** $s^2 = 12.4$; $s = 3.52$
5. $s^2 = 6.64$; $s = 2.58$ **7.** $s^2 = 13.01$; $s = 3.61$ **9.** 1.04
11. 9.43   **13.** 3.27   **15.** Expected value = 3.5, variance = 2.918, standard deviation = 1.71   **17.** Expected value = 1, variance = 0.5, standard deviation = 0.71
19. Expected value = 4.47, variance = 1.97, standard deviation = 1.40   **21.** Expected value = 2.67, variance = 0.36, standard deviation = 0.60
23. Expected value = 2, variance = 1.8, standard deviation = 1.34   **25. a.** $\bar{x} = 3$, $s = 3.54$ **b.** [0, 6.54] We must assume that the population distribution is bell-shaped and symmetric.   **27. a.** $\bar{x} = 5.0$, $s = 0.6$ **b.** 3.8, 6.2
29. a. $\bar{x} = -150$, $s \approx 495$ **b.** 645, 20%   **31. a.** 2.18
b. [11.22, 24.28] **c.** 100%; Empirical rule   **33.** $\mu = 1.5$, $\sigma = 1.43$; 100%   **35.** $\mu = 40.6$, $\sigma \approx 26$; $52,000
37. a. $\mu \approx 30.2$ yrs. old, $\sigma = 11.78$ years **b.** 18–42   **39.** At most 6.25%   **41.** At most; 12.5%   **43. a.** $\mu = 25.2$, $\sigma = 3.05$ **b.** 31
45. a. $\mu = 780$, $\sigma \approx 13.1$ **b.** 754, 806   **47. a.** $\mu = 6.5$, $\sigma^2 = 4.0$, $\sigma = 2.0$ **b.** [2.5, 10.5]; three checkout lanes
49. $10,700 or less   **51.** $65,300 or more   **53.** U.S.   **55.** U.S.
57. 16%   **59.** 0–$76,000   **61.** $\mu = 12.56\%$, $\sigma \approx 1.8885\%$
63. 78%; the empirical rule predicts 68%. The associated probability distribution is roughly bell-shaped but not symmetric.
65. 96%. Chebyshev's rule is valid, since it predicts that *at least* 75% of the scores are in this range.   **67.** (B), (D)   **69.** The sample standard deviation is bigger; the formula for sample standard deviation involves division by the smaller term $n - 1$ instead of n, which makes the resulting number larger.   **71.** The grades in the first class were clustered fairly close to 75. By Chebyshev's inequality, at least 88% of the class had grades in the range 60–90. On the other hand, the grades in the second class were widely dispersed. The second class had a much wider spread of ability than did the first class.   **73.** The variable must take on only the value 10, with probability 1.   **75.** $(y - x)/2$

Section 8.5

1. .1915   **3.** .5222   **5.** .6710   **7.** .2417   **9.** .8664
11. .8621   **13.** .2286   **15.** .3830   **17.** .5028   **19.** .35
21. .05   **23.** .3830   **25.** .6687   **27.** 26%   **29.** 29,600,000
31. 0   **33.** About 6,680   **35.** 28%   **37.** 5%   **39.** The U.S.
41. Wechsler. As this test has a smaller standard deviation, a greater percentage of scores fall within 20 points of the mean.
43. This is surprising, because the time between failures was more than five standard deviations away from the mean, which happens with an extremely small probability.   **45.** .6103
47. .6103 × .5832 ≈ .3559   **49.** .6255   **51.** .7257   **53.** .8708
55. .0029   **57.** Probability that a person will say Goode = .54. Probability that Goode polls more than 52% ≈ .8925.
59. 23.4   **61.** When the distribution is normal   **63.** Neither. They are equal.   **65.** $1/(b - a)$ **67.** A normal distribution with standard deviation 0.5, because it is narrower near the mean, but must enclose the same amount of area as the standard curve, and so it must be higher.

Chapter 8 Review

1.

x	0	1	2
$P(X = x)$	1/4	1/2	1/4

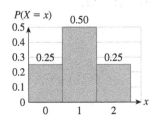

3.

x	2	3	4	5	6	7	8
$P(X = x)$	1/16	2/16	3/16	4/16	3/16	2/16	1/16

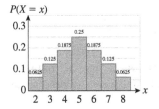

5.

x	0	1	2	3
$P(X = x)$	.2071	.4439	.2908	.0582

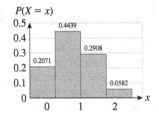

7. $\bar{x} = 2, m = 2, s \approx 2.7386$ **9.** Two examples are: 0, 0, 0, 4 and $-1, -1, 1, 5$ **11.** An example is $-1, -1, -1, 1, 1, 1$
13. .4165   **15.** .9267   **17.** .0067   **19.** .7330   **21.** $\mu = 1.5$, $\sigma = 0.8660$; 2
23.

x	-3	-2	-1	0	1	2	3
$P(X = x)$	1/16	2/16	3/16	4/16	3/16	2/16	1/16

$\mu = 0, \sigma = 1.5811$; within 1.3 standard deviations of the mean
25. [49.4, 150.6]   **27.** 260   **29.** .4332   **31.** .0358   **33.** .3085
35. \$12.15   **37.** \$27,210   **39.** False; let $X =$ price and $Y =$ weekly sales. Then weekly Revenue $= XY$. However, $27,210 \neq 12.15 \times 2,620$. In other words, $E(XY) \neq E(X)E(Y)$.
41. a.

x	2	4	6	8	10
$P(X = x)$	.25	.35	.15	.15	.1

$\mu = 5, \sigma = 2.5690$ **b.** Between 2.431 and 7.569 orders per million residents; the empirical rule does not apply because the distribution is not symmetric. **c.** (A)   **43.** .190   **45.** .060
47. 0.5   **49.** .284   **51.** .108   **53.** Using normal distribution table: 364,000 people. More accurate answer: 378,000 people.
55. 148

2

Techniques of Differentiation with Applications

Case Study Projecting Market Growth

You are on the board of directors at Fullcourt Academic Press. The sales director of the high school division has just burst into your office with a proposal for an expansion strategy based on the assumption that the number of high school seniors in the United States will be growing at a rate of at least 5,600 per year through the year 2015. Because the figures actually appear to be leveling off, you are suspicious about this estimate. You would like to devise a model that predicts this trend before tomorrow's scheduled board meeting.

How do you go about doing this?

Yuri Arcurs, 2009/Used under license from Shutterstock.com

Web Site

At the Web site you will find:

- Section by section tutorials, including game tutorials with randomized quizzes

- A detailed chapter summary

- A true/false quiz

- Additional review exercises

- Graphers, Excel tutorials, and other resources

- The following extra topic:

  Linear Approximation and Error Estimation

Introduction

In Chapter 10 we studied the concept of the derivative of a function, and we saw some of the applications for which derivatives are useful. However, computing the derivative of a function algebraically seemed to be a time-consuming process, forcing us to restrict attention to fairly simply functions.

In this chapter we develop shortcut techniques that will allow us to write down the derivative of a function directly without having to calculate any limit. These techniques will also enable us to differentiate any closed-form function—that is, any function, no matter how complicated, that can be specified by a formula involving powers, radicals, absolute values, exponents, and logarithms. (In a later chapter, we will discuss how to add trigonometric functions to this list.) We also show how to find the derivatives of functions that are only specified *implicitly*—that is, functions for which we are not given an explicit formula for y in terms of x but only an equation relating x and y.

algebra Review

For this chapter, you should be familiar with the algebra reviewed in **Chapter 0, Sections 3 and 4.**

11.1 Derivatives of Powers, Sums, and Constant Multiples

Up to this point we have approximated derivatives using difference quotients, and we have done exact calculations using the definition of the derivative as the limit of a difference quotient. In general, we would prefer to have an exact calculation, and it is also very useful to have a formula for the derivative function when we can find one. However, the calculation of a derivative as a limit is often tedious, so it would be nice to have a quicker method. We discuss the first of the shortcut rules in this section. By the end of this chapter, we will be able to find fairly quickly the derivative of almost any function we can write.

Shortcut Formula: The Power Rule

If you look at Examples 2 and 3 in Section 10.6, you may notice a pattern:

$$f(x) = x^2 \implies f'(x) = 2x$$
$$f(x) = x^3 \implies f'(x) = 3x^2$$

This pattern generalizes to any power of x:

Theorem 11.1 The Power Rule

If n is any constant and $f(x) = x^n$, then

$$f'(x) = nx^{n-1}.$$

Quick Examples

1. If $f(x) = x^2$, then $f'(x) = 2x^1 = 2x$.
2. If $f(x) = x^3$, then $f'(x) = 3x^2$.
3. If $f(x) = x$, rewrite as $f(x) = x^1$, so $f'(x) = 1x^0 = 1$.
4. If $f(x) = 1$, rewrite as $f(x) = x^0$, so $f'(x) = 0x^{-1} = 0$.

Web Site
www.FiniteandCalc.org
At the Web site you can find
a proof of the power rule by
following:

Everything for Calculus
→ Chapter 11
→ Proof of the Power Rule

✱ NOTE See the section on exponents in the algebra review to brush up on negative and fractional exponents.

The proof of the power rule involves first studying the case when n is a positive integer, and then studying the cases of other types of exponents (negative integer, rational number, irrational number). You can find a proof at the Web site.

EXAMPLE 1 Using the Power Rule for Negative and Fractional Exponents

Calculate the derivatives of the following:

a. $f(x) = \dfrac{1}{x}$ **b.** $f(x) = \dfrac{1}{x^2}$ **c.** $f(x) = \sqrt{x}$

Solution

a. Rewrite* as $f(x) = x^{-1}$. Then $f'(x) = (-1)x^{-2} = -\dfrac{1}{x^2}$.

b. Rewrite as $f(x) = x^{-2}$. Then $f'(x) = (-2)x^{-3} = -\dfrac{2}{x^3}$.

c. Rewrite as $f(x) = x^{0.5}$. Then $f'(x) = 0.5x^{-0.5} = \dfrac{0.5}{x^{0.5}}$. Alternatively, rewrite $f(x)$

as $x^{1/2}$, so that $f'(x) = \dfrac{1}{2}x^{-1/2} = \dfrac{1}{2x^{1/2}} = \dfrac{1}{2\sqrt{x}}$.

By rewriting the given functions in Example 1 before taking derivatives, we converted them from **rational** or **radical form** (as in, say, $\dfrac{1}{x^2}$ and $\sqrt{x}$) to **exponent form** (as in x^{-2} and $x^{0.5}$; see the Algebra Review, Section 0.2) to enable us to use the power rule. (See the Caution below.)

Caution

We cannot apply the power rule to terms in the denominators or under square roots. For example:

1. The derivative of $\dfrac{1}{x^2}$ is **NOT** $\dfrac{1}{2x}$; it is $-\dfrac{2}{x^3}$.   See Example 1(b).

2. The derivative of $\sqrt{x^3}$ is **NOT** $\sqrt{3x^2}$; it is $1.5x^{0.5}$.   Rewrite $\sqrt{x^3}$ as $x^{3/2}$ or $x^{1.5}$ and apply the power rule.

Table 1 Table of Derivative Formulas

$f(x)$	$f'(x)$
1	0
x	1
x^2	$2x$
x^3	$3x^2$
x^n	nx^{n-1}
$\dfrac{1}{x}$	$-\dfrac{1}{x^2}$
$\dfrac{1}{x^2}$	$-\dfrac{2}{x^3}$
$\sqrt{x}$	$\dfrac{1}{2\sqrt{x}}$

Some of the derivatives in Example 1 are very useful to remember, so we summarize them in Table 1. We suggest that you add to this table as you learn more derivatives. It is *extremely* helpful to remember the derivatives of common functions such as $1/x$ and $\sqrt{x}$, even though they can be obtained by using the power rule as in the above example.

Another Notation: Differential Notation

Here is a useful notation based on the "d-notation" we discussed in Section 10.5. **Differential notation** is based on an abbreviation for the phrase "the derivative with respect to x." For example, we learned that if $f(x) = x^3$, then $f'(x) = 3x^2$. When we say "$f'(x) = 3x^2$," we mean the following:

The derivative of x^3 with respect to x equals $3x^2$.

✳ **NOTE** This may seem odd in the case of $f(x) = x^3$ because there are no other variables to worry about. But in expressions like st^3 that involve variables other than x, it is necessary to specify just what the variable of the function is. This is the same reason that we write "$f(x) = x^3$" rather than just "$f = x^3$."

You may wonder why we sneaked in the words "with respect to x." All this means is that the variable of the function is x, and not any other variable.✳ Because we use the phrase "the derivative with respect to x" often, we use the following abbreviation.

Differential Notation; Differentiation

$\dfrac{d}{dx}$ means "the derivative with respect to x."

Thus, $\dfrac{d}{dx}[f(x)]$ is the same thing as $f'(x)$, the derivative of $f(x)$ with respect to x. If y is a function of x, then the derivative of y with respect to x is

$$\frac{d}{dx}(y) \qquad \text{or, more compactly,} \qquad \frac{dy}{dx}$$

To **differentiate** a function $f(x)$ with respect to x means to take its derivative with respect to x.

Quick Examples

In Words	**Formula**
1. The derivative with respect to x of x^3 is $3x^2$.	$\dfrac{d}{dx}(x^3) = 3x^2$
2. The derivative with respect to t of $\dfrac{1}{t}$ is $-\dfrac{1}{t^2}$.	$\dfrac{d}{dt}\left(\dfrac{1}{t}\right) = -\dfrac{1}{t^2}$
3. If $y = x^4$, then $\dfrac{dy}{dx} = 4x^3$.	
4. If $u = \dfrac{1}{t^2}$, then $\dfrac{du}{dt} = -\dfrac{2}{t^3}$.	

Notes

1. $\dfrac{dy}{dx}$ is Leibniz' notation for the derivative we discussed in Section 10.5. (See the discussion before Example 3 there.)

2. Leibniz notation illustrates units nicely: units of $\dfrac{dy}{dx}$ are units of y per unit of x. ∎

The Rules for Sums and Constant Multiples

We can now find the derivatives of more complicated functions, such as polynomials, using the following rules:

Theorem 11.2 Derivatives of Sums, Differences, and Constant Multiples

If $f(x)$ and $g(x)$ are any two differentiable functions, and if c is any constant, then the functions $f(x) + g(x)$ and $cf(x)$ are differentiable, and

$$[f(x) \pm g(x)]' = f'(x) \pm g'(x) \qquad \text{Sum Rule}$$

$$[cf(x)]' = cf'(x). \qquad \text{Constant Multiple Rule}$$

In Words:

- The derivative of a sum is the sum of the derivatives, and the derivative of a difference is the difference of the derivatives.
- The derivative of c times a function is c times the derivative of the function.

Differential Notation:

$$\frac{d}{dx}[f(x) \pm g(x)] = \frac{d}{dx}f(x) \pm \frac{d}{dx}g(x)$$

$$\frac{d}{dx}[cf(x)] = c\frac{d}{dx}f(x)$$

Quick Examples

1. $\dfrac{d}{dx}[x^2 - x^4] = \dfrac{d}{dx}[x^2] - \dfrac{d}{dx}[x^4] = 2x - 4x^3$

2. $\dfrac{d}{dx}[7x^3] = 7\dfrac{d}{dx}[x^3] = 7(3x^2) = 21x^3$

   In other words, we multiply the coefficient (7) by the exponent (3), and then decrease the exponent by 1.

3. $\dfrac{d}{dx}[12x] = 12\dfrac{d}{dx}[x] = 12(1) = 12$

   In other words, the derivative of a constant times x is that constant.

4. $\dfrac{d}{dx}[-x^{0.5}] = \dfrac{d}{dx}[(-1)x^{0.5}] = (-1)\dfrac{d}{dx}[x^{0.5}] = (-1)(0.5)x^{-0.5}$

   $= -0.5x^{-0.5}$

5. $\dfrac{d}{dx}[12] = \dfrac{d}{dx}[12(1)] = 12\dfrac{d}{dx}[1] = 12(0) = 0.$

   In other words, the derivative of a constant is zero.

6. If my company earns twice as much (annual) revenue as yours and the derivative of your revenue function is the curve on the left, then the derivative of my revenue function is the curve on the right.

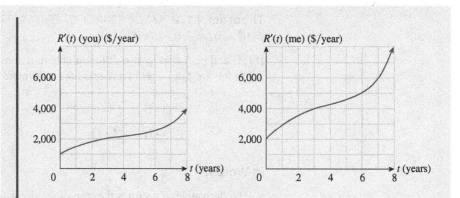

7. Suppose that a company's revenue R and cost C are changing with time. Then so is the profit, $P(t) = R(t) - C(t)$, and the rate of change of the profit is

$$P'(t) = R'(t) - C'(t).$$

In words: *The derivative of the profit is the derivative of revenue minus the derivative of cost.*

Proof of the Sum Rule

By the definition of the derivative of a function,

$$\frac{d}{dx}[f(x) + g(x)] = \lim_{h \to 0} \frac{[f(x+h) + g(x+h)] - [f(x) + g(x)]}{h}$$

$$= \lim_{h \to 0} \frac{[f(x+h) - f(x)] + [g(x+h) - g(x)]}{h}$$

$$= \lim_{h \to 0} \left[\frac{f(x+h) - f(x)}{h} + \frac{g(x+h) - g(x)}{h} \right]$$

$$= \lim_{h \to 0} \frac{f(x+h) - f(x)}{h} + \lim_{h \to 0} \frac{g(x+h) - g(x)}{h}$$

$$= \frac{d}{dx}[f(x)] + \frac{d}{dx}[g(x)].$$

The next-to-last step uses a property of limits: the limit of a sum is the sum of the limits. Think about why this should be true. The last step uses the definition of the derivative again (and the fact that the functions are differentiable).

The proof of the rule for constant multiples is similar.

EXAMPLE 2 **Combining the Sum and Constant Multiple Rules, and Dealing with *x* in the Denominator**

Find the derivatives of the following:

a. $f(x) = 3x^2 + 2x - 4$ **b.** $f(x) = \dfrac{2x}{3} - \dfrac{6}{x} + \dfrac{2}{3x^{0.2}} - \dfrac{x^4}{2}$

84

Solution

a. $\dfrac{d}{dx}(3x^2 + 2x - 4) = \dfrac{d}{dx}(3x^2) + \dfrac{d}{dx}(2x - 4)$ Rule for sums

$$= \dfrac{d}{dx}(3x^2) + \dfrac{d}{dx}(2x) - \dfrac{d}{dx}(4)$$ Rule for differences

$$= 3(2x) + 2(1) - 0$$ See Quick Example 2.

$$= 6x + 2$$

b. Notice that f has x and powers of x in the denominator. We deal with these terms the same way we did in Example 1, by rewriting them in exponent form (that is, in the form constant × power of x):

$$f(x) = \frac{2x}{3} - \frac{6}{x} + \frac{2}{3x^{0.2}} - \frac{x^4}{2}$$ Rational form

$$= \frac{2}{3}x - 6x^{-1} + \frac{2}{3}x^{-0.2} - \frac{1}{2}x^4$$ Exponent form

We are now ready to take the derivative:

$$f'(x) = \frac{2}{3}(1) - 6(-1)x^{-2} + \frac{2}{3}(-0.2)x^{-1.2} - \frac{1}{2}(4x^3)$$

$$= \frac{2}{3} + 6x^{-2} - \frac{0.4}{3}x^{-1.2} - 2x^3$$ Exponent form

$$= \frac{2}{3} + \frac{6}{x^2} - \frac{0.4}{3x^{1.2}} - 2x^3$$ Rational form

Notice that in Example 2(a) we had three terms in the expression for $f(x)$, not just two. By applying the rule for sums and differences twice, we saw that the derivative of a sum or difference of three terms is the sum or difference of the derivatives of the terms. (One of those terms had zero derivative, so the final answer had only two terms.) In fact, the derivative of a sum or difference of any number of terms is the sum or difference of the derivatives of the terms. Put another way, to take the derivative of a sum or difference of any number of terms, we take derivatives term by term.

Note Nothing forces us to use only x as the independent variable when taking derivatives (although it is traditional to give x preference). For instance, part (a) in Example 2 can be rewritten as

$$\frac{d}{dt}(3t^2 + 2t - 4) = 6t + 2$$ $\frac{d}{dt}$ means "derivative with respect to t."

or

$$\frac{d}{du}(3u^2 + 2u - 4) = 6u + 2.$$ $\frac{d}{du}$ means "derivative with respect to u." ∎

In the previous examples, we saw instances of the following important facts. (Think about these graphically to see why they must be true.)

The Derivative of a Constant Times *x* and the Derivative of a Constant

If c is any constant, then:

Rule	Quick Examples	
$\dfrac{d}{dx}(cx) = c$	$\dfrac{d}{dx}(6x) = 6$	$\dfrac{d}{dx}(-x) = -1$
$\dfrac{d}{dx}(c) = 0$	$\dfrac{d}{dx}(5) = 0$	$\dfrac{d}{dx}(\pi) = 0$

In Example 5 of Section 10.6 we saw that $f(x) = |x|$ fails to be differentiable at $x = 0$. In the next example we use the power rule and find more functions not differentiable at a point.

EXAMPLE 3 Functions Not Differentiable at a Point

Find the natural domains of the derivatives of $f(x) = x^{1/3}$ and $g(x) = x^{2/3}$, and $h(x) = |x|$.

Solution Let's first look at the functions f and g. By the power rule,

$$f'(x) = \frac{1}{3}x^{-2/3} = \frac{1}{3x^{2/3}}$$

and

$$g'(x) = \frac{2}{3}x^{-1/3} = \frac{2}{3x^{1/3}}.$$

$f'(x)$ and $g'(x)$ are defined only for nonzero values of x, and their natural domains consist of all real numbers except 0. Thus, the derivatives f' and g' do not exist at $x = 0$. In other words, f and g are not differentiable at $x = 0$. If we look at Figure 1, we notice why these functions fail to be differentiable at $x = 0$: The graph of f has a vertical tangent line at 0. Because a vertical line has undefined slope, the derivative is undefined at that point. The graph of g comes to a sharp point (called a **cusp**) at 0, so it is not meaningful to speak about a tangent line at that point; therefore, the derivative of g is not defined there. (Actually, there is a reasonable candidate for the tangent line at $x = 0$, but it is the vertical line again.)

We can also detect this nondifferentiability by computing some difference quotients numerically. In the case of $f(x) = x^{1/3}$, we get the following table:

h	± 1	± 0.1	± 0.01	± 0.001	± 0.0001
$\dfrac{f(0 + h) - f(0)}{h}$	1	4.6416	21.544	100	464.16

suggesting that the difference quotients $[f(0 + h) - f(0)]/h$ grow large without bound rather than approach any fixed number as h approaches 0. (Can you see how the behavior of the difference quotients in the table is reflected in the graph?)

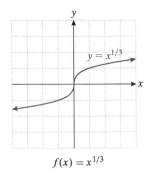

$f(x) = x^{1/3}$

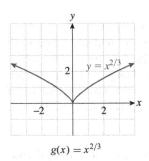

$g(x) = x^{2/3}$

Figure 1

using Technology

If you try to graph the function $f(x) = x^{2/3}$ using the format

```
X^(2/3)
```

you may get only the right-hand portion of Figure 1 because graphing utilities are (often) not programmed to raise negative numbers to fractional exponents. (However, many will handle `X^(1/3)` correctly, as a special case they recognize.) To avoid this difficulty, you can take advantage of the identity

$$x^{2/3} = (x^2)^{1/3}$$

so that it is always a nonnegative number that is being raised to a fractional exponent. Thus, use the format

```
(X^2)^(1/3)
```

to obtain both portions of the graph.

Now we return to the function $h(x) = |x|$ discussed in Example 5 of Section 10.6. We saw there that $|x|$ is not differentiable at $x = 0$. What about values of x *other than* 0? For such values, we can write:

$$|x| = \begin{cases} -x & \text{if } x < 0 \\ x & \text{if } x > 0 \end{cases}$$

Hence, by the power rule (think of x as x^1):

$$f'(x) = \begin{cases} -1 & \text{if } x < 0 \\ 1 & \text{if } x > 0 \end{cases}$$

Q : *So does that mean there is no single formula for the derivative of $|x|$?*

A : Actually, there *is* a convenient formula. Consider the ratio

$$\frac{|x|}{x}.$$

If x is positive, then $|x| = x$, so $|x|/x = x/x = 1$. On the other hand, if x is negative then $|x| = -x$, so $|x|/x = -x/x = -1$. In other words,

$$\frac{|x|}{x} = \begin{cases} -1 & \text{if } x < 0 \\ 1 & \text{if } x > 0 \end{cases},$$

which is exactly the formula we obtained for $f'(x)$. In other words:

Derivative of |x|

$$\frac{d}{dx}|x| = \frac{|x|}{x}$$

Note that the derivative does not exist when $x = 0$.

Quick Example

$$\frac{d}{dx}[3|x| + x] = 3\frac{|x|}{x} + 1$$

APPLICATION

The next Example is similar to Example 3 in Section 10.4, but this time we analyze the curve using the derivative.

EXAMPLE 4 Gold Price

You are a commodities trader and you monitor the price of gold on the New York Spot Market very closely during an active morning. Suppose you find that the price of an ounce of gold can be approximated by the function

$$G(t) = -8t^2 + 144t + 150 \text{ dollars} \quad (7.5 \le t \le 10.5)$$

where t is time in hours. (See Figure 2. $t = 8$ represents 8:00 AM.)

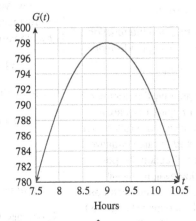

Source: www.kitco.com (August 15, 2008) $G(t) = -8t^2 + 144t + 150$

Figure 2

a. According to the model, how fast was the price of gold changing at 10:00 AM?

b. According to the model, the price of gold

   (A) increased at a faster and faster rate

   (B) increased at a slower and slower rate

   (C) decreased at a faster and faster rate

   (D) decreased at a slower and slower rate

   between 9:30 and 10:30 AM.

Solution

a. Differentiating the given function with respect to t gives

$$G'(t) = -16t + 144.$$

Because 10:00 AM corresponds to $t = 10$, we obtain

$$G'(10) = -16(10) + 144 = -16.$$

The units of the derivative are dollars per hour, so we conclude that, at 10:00 AM, the price of gold was dropping at a rate of $16 per hour.

b. From the graph, we can see that, between 9:30 and 10:30 AM (the interval [9.5, 10.5]), the price of gold was decreasing. Also from the graph, we see that the slope of the tangent becomes more and more negative as t increases, so the price of gold is decreasing at a faster and faster rate (choice (C)).

We can also see this algebraically from the derivative, $G'(t) = -16t + 144$: For values of t larger than 9, $G'(t)$ is negative; that is, the rate of change of G is negative, so the price of gold is decreasing. Further, as t increases, $G'(t)$ becomes more and more negative, so the price of gold is decreasing at a faster and faster rate, confirming that choice (C) is the correct one.

An Application to Limits: L'Hospital's Rule

The limits that caused us some trouble in Sections 10.1–10.3 are those of the form $\lim_{x \to a} f(x)$ in which substituting $x = a$ gave us an indeterminate form, such as

$$\lim_{x \to 2} \frac{x^3 - 8}{x - 2}$$ Substituting $x = 2$ yields $\frac{0}{0}$.

$$\lim_{x \to +\infty} \frac{2x - 4}{x - 1}$$ Substituting $x = +\infty$ yields $\frac{\infty}{\infty}$.

L'Hospital's rule gives us an alternate way of computing limits such as these without the need to do any preliminary simplification. It also allows us to compute some limits for which algebraic simplification does not work.[*]

✱ **NOTE** Guillaume François Antoine, Marquis de l'Hospital (1661–1704) wrote the first textbook on calculus, *Analyse des infiniment petits pour l'intelligence des lignes courbes*, in 1692. The rule now known as l'Hospital's Rule appeared first in this book.

Theorem 11.3 L'Hospital's Rule

If f and g are two differentiable functions such that substituting $x = a$ in the expression $\dfrac{f(x)}{g(x)}$ gives the indeterminate form $\dfrac{0}{0}$ or $\dfrac{\infty}{\infty}$, then

$$\lim_{x \to a} \frac{f(x)}{g(x)} = \lim_{x \to a} \frac{f'(x)}{g'(x)}$$

That is, we can replace $f(x)$ and $g(x)$ with their *derivatives* and try again to take the limit.

Quick Examples

1. Substituting $x = 2$ in $\dfrac{x^3 - 8}{x - 2}$ yields $\dfrac{0}{0}$. Therefore, l'Hospital's rule applies and

$$\lim_{x \to 2} \frac{x^3 - 8}{x - 2} = \lim_{x \to 2} \frac{3x^2}{1} = \frac{3(2)^2}{1} = 12.$$

2. Substituting $x = +\infty$ in $\dfrac{2x - 4}{x - 1}$ yields $\dfrac{\infty}{\infty}$. Therefore, l'Hospital's rule applies and

$$\lim_{x \to +\infty} \frac{2x - 4}{x - 1} = \lim_{x \to +\infty} \frac{2}{1} = 2.$$

✱ **NOTE** A proof of l'Hospital's rule can be found in most advanced calculus textbooks.

The proof of l'Hospital's rule is beyond the scope of this text.[*]

EXAMPLE 5 Applying L'Hospital's Rule

Check whether l'Hospital's rule applies to each of the following limits. If it does, use it to evaluate the limit. Otherwise, use some other method to evaluate the limit.

a. $\displaystyle \lim_{x \to 1} \frac{x^2 - 2x + 1}{4x^3 - 3x^2 - 6x + 5}$

b. $\displaystyle \lim_{x \to +\infty} \frac{2x^2 - 4x}{5x^3 - 3x + 5}$

c. $\lim\limits_{x \to 1} \dfrac{x-1}{x^3 - 3x^2 + 3x - 1}$ 　　　　　**d.** $\lim\limits_{x \to 1} \dfrac{x}{x^3 - 3x^2 + 3x - 1}$

Solution

a. Setting $x = 1$ yields

$$\frac{1 - 2 + 1}{4 - 3 - 6 + 5} = \frac{0}{0}.$$

Therefore, l'Hospital's rule applies and

$$\lim_{x \to 1} \frac{x^2 - 2x + 1}{4x^3 - 3x^2 - 6x + 5} = \lim_{x \to 1} \frac{2x - 2}{12x^2 - 6x - 6}.$$

We are left with a closed-form function. However, we cannot substitute $x = 1$ to find the limit because the function $(2x - 2)/(12x^2 - 6x - 6)$ is still not defined at $x = 1$. In fact, if we set $x = 1$, we again get $0/0$. Thus, l'Hospital's rule applies again, and

$$\lim_{x \to 1} \frac{2x - 2}{12x^2 - 6x - 6} = \lim_{x \to 1} \frac{2}{24x - 6}.$$

Once again we have a closed-form function, but this time it is defined when $x = 1$, giving

$$\frac{2}{24 - 6} = \frac{1}{9}.$$

Thus,

$$\lim_{x \to 1} \frac{x^2 - 2x + 1}{4x^3 - 3x^2 - 6x + 5} = \frac{1}{9}.$$

b. Setting $x = +\infty$ yields $\dfrac{\infty}{\infty}$, so

$$\lim_{x \to +\infty} \frac{2x^2 - 4x}{5x^3 - 3x + 5} = \lim_{x \to +\infty} \frac{4x - 4}{15x^2 - 3}.$$

Setting $x = +\infty$ again yields $\dfrac{\infty}{\infty}$, so we can apply the rule again to obtain

$$\lim_{x \to +\infty} \frac{4x - 4}{15x^2 - 3} = \lim_{x \to +\infty} \frac{4}{30x}.$$

Note that we cannot apply l'Hospital's rule a third time because setting $x = +\infty$ yields the *determinate* form $4/\infty = 0$ (see the discussion at the end of Section 10.3). Thus, the limit is 0.

c. Setting $x = 1$ yields $0/0$ so, by l'Hospital's rule,

$$\lim_{x \to 1} \frac{x-1}{x^3 - 3x^2 + 3x - 1} = \lim_{x \to 1} \frac{1}{3x^2 - 6x + 3}.$$

We are left with a closed-form function that is still not defined at $x = 1$. Further, l'Hospital's rule no longer applies because putting $x = 1$ yields the determinate form $1/0$. To investigate this limit, we refer to the discussion at the end of Section 10.3 and find

$$\lim_{x \to 1} \frac{1}{3x^2 - 6x + 3} = \lim_{x \to 1} \frac{1}{3(x-1)^2} = +\infty. \qquad \frac{1}{0^+} = +\infty$$

d. Setting $x = 1$ in the expression yields the determinate form $1/0$, so l'Hospital's rule does not apply here. Using the methods of Section 10.3 again, we find that the limit does not exist.

90

FAQs

Using the Rules and Recognizing When a Function is Not Differentiable

Q: I would *like* to say that the derivative of $5x^2 - 8x + 4$ is just $10x - 8$ without having to go through all that stuff about derivatives of sums and constant multiples. Can I simply forget about all the rules and write down the answer?

A: We developed the rules for sums and constant multiples precisely for that reason: so that we could simply write down a derivative without having to think about it too hard. So, you are perfectly justified in simply writing down the derivative without going through the rules, but bear in mind that what you are really doing is applying the power rule, the rule for sums, and the rule for multiples over and over.

Q: Is there a way of telling from its formula whether a function f is not differentiable at a point?

A: Here are some indicators to look for in the formula for f:

- The absolute value of some expression; f may not be differentiable at points where that expression is zero.

  Example: $f(x) = 3x^2 - |x - 4|$ is not differentiable at $x = 4$.

- A fractional power smaller than 1 of some expression; f may not be differentiable at points where that expression is zero.

  Example: $f(x) = (x^2 - 16)^{2/3}$ is not differentiable at $x = \pm 4$.

11.1 EXERCISES

▼ more advanced   ◆ challenging
🔲 indicates exercises that should be solved using technology

*In Exercises 1–10, use the shortcut rules to **mentally** calculate the derivative of the given function.* HINT [See Examples 1 and 2.]

1. $f(x) = x^5$

2. $f(x) = x^4$

3. $f(x) = 2x^{-2}$

4. $f(x) = 3x^{-1}$

5. $f(x) = -x^{0.25}$

6. $f(x) = -x^{-0.5}$

7. $f(x) = 2x^4 + 3x^3 - 1$

8. $f(x) = -x^3 - 3x^2 - 1$

9. $f(x) = -x + \dfrac{1}{x} + 1$

10. $f(x) = \dfrac{1}{x} + \dfrac{1}{x^2}$

In Exercises 11–16, obtain the derivative dy/dx and state the rules that you use. HINT [See Example 2.]

11. $y = 10$

12. $y = x^3$

13. $y = x^2 + x$

14. $y = x - 5$

15. $y = 4x^3 + 2x - 1$

16. $y = 4x^{-1} - 2x - 10$

In Exercises 17–40, find the derivative of each function. HINT [See Examples 1 and 2.]

17. $f(x) = x^2 - 3x + 5$

18. $f(x) = 3x^3 - 2x^2 + x$

19. $f(x) = x + x^{0.5}$

20. $f(x) = x^{0.5} + 2x^{-0.5}$

21. $g(x) = x^{-2} - 3x^{-1} - 2$

22. $g(x) = 2x^{-1} + 4x^{-2}$

23. $g(x) = \dfrac{1}{x} - \dfrac{1}{x^2}$

24. $g(x) = \dfrac{1}{x^2} + \dfrac{1}{x^3}$

25. $h(x) = \dfrac{2}{x^{0.4}}$

26. $h(x) = -\dfrac{1}{2x^{0.2}}$

27. $h(x) = \dfrac{1}{x^2} + \dfrac{2}{x^3}$

28. $h(x) = \dfrac{2}{x} - \dfrac{2}{x^3} + \dfrac{1}{x^4}$

29. $r(x) = \dfrac{2}{3x} - \dfrac{1}{2x^{0.1}}$

30. $r(x) = \dfrac{4}{3x^2} + \dfrac{1}{x^{3.2}}$

31. $r(x) = \dfrac{2x}{3} - \dfrac{x^{0.1}}{2} + \dfrac{4}{3x^{1.1}} - 2$

32. $r(x) = \dfrac{4x^2}{3} + \dfrac{x^{3.2}}{6} - \dfrac{2}{3x^2} + 4$

33. $t(x) = |x| + \dfrac{1}{x}$

34. $t(x) = 3|x| - \sqrt{x}$

35. $s(x) = \sqrt{x} + \dfrac{1}{\sqrt{x}}$

36. $s(x) = x + \dfrac{7}{\sqrt{x}}$

HINT [For Exercises 37–40, first expand the given function.]

37. ▼ $s(x) = x \left(x^2 - \dfrac{1}{x} \right)$ **38.** ▼ $s(x) = x^{-1} \left(x - \dfrac{2}{x} \right)$

39. ▼ $t(x) = \dfrac{x^2 - 2x^3}{x}$ **40.** ▼ $t(x) = \dfrac{2x + x^2}{x}$

In Exercises 41–46, evaluate the given expression.

41. $\dfrac{d}{dx}(2x^{1.3} - x^{-1.2})$ **42.** $\dfrac{d}{dx}(2x^{4.3} + x^{0.6})$

43. ▼ $\dfrac{d}{dx}[1.2(x - |x|)]$ **44.** ▼ $\dfrac{d}{dx}[4(x^2 + 3|x|)]$

45. ▼ $\dfrac{d}{dt}(at^3 - 4at)$;   (a constant)

46. ▼ $\dfrac{d}{dt}(at^2 + bt + c)$;   (a, b, c constant)

In Exercises 47–52, find the indicated derivative.

47. $y = \dfrac{x^{10.3}}{2} + 99x^{-1}$; $\dfrac{dy}{dx}$ **48.** $y = \dfrac{x^{1.2}}{3} - \dfrac{x^{0.9}}{2}$; $\dfrac{dy}{dx}$

49. $s = 2.3 + \dfrac{2.1}{t^{1.1}} - \dfrac{t^{0.6}}{2}$; $\dfrac{ds}{dt}$ **50.** $s = \dfrac{2}{t^{1.1}} + t^{-1.2}$; $\dfrac{ds}{dt}$

51. ▼ $V = \dfrac{4}{3}\pi r^3$; $\dfrac{dV}{dr}$ **52.** ▼ $A = 4\pi r^2$; $\dfrac{dA}{dr}$

In Exercises 53–58, find the slope of the tangent to the graph of the given function at the indicated point. HINT [Recall that the slope of the tangent to the graph of f at x = a is f'(a).]

53. $f(x) = x^3$; $(-1, -1)$ **54.** $g(x) = x^4$; $(-2, 16)$

55. $f(x) = 1 - 2x$; $(2, -3)$ **56.** $f(x) = \dfrac{x}{3} - 1$; $(-3, -2)$

57. $g(t) = \dfrac{1}{t^5}$; $(1, 1)$ **58.** $s(t) = \dfrac{1}{t^3}$; $\left(-2, -\dfrac{1}{8}\right)$

In Exercises 59–64, find the equation of the tangent line to the graph of the given function at the point with the indicated x-coordinate. In each case, sketch the curve together with the appropriate tangent line.

59. ▼ $f(x) = x^3$; $x = -1$ **60.** ▼ $f(x) = x^2$; $x = 0$

61. ▼ $f(x) = x + \dfrac{1}{x}$; $x = 2$ **62.** ▼ $f(x) = \dfrac{1}{x^2}$; $x = 1$

63. ▼ $f(x) = \sqrt{x}$; $x = 4$ **64.** ▼ $f(x) = 2x + 4$; $x = -1$

In Exercises 65–70, find all values of x (if any) where the tangent line to the graph of the given equation is horizontal. HINT [The tangent line is horizontal when its slope is zero.]

65. ▼ $y = 2x^2 + 3x - 1$ **66.** ▼ $y = -3x^2 - x$

67. ▼ $y = 2x + 8$ **68.** ▼ $y = -x + 1$

69. ▼ $y = x + \dfrac{1}{x}$ **70.** ▼ $y = x - \sqrt{x}$

71. ◆ Write out the proof that $\dfrac{d}{dx}(x^4) = 4x^3$.

72. ◆ Write out the proof that $\dfrac{d}{dx}(x^5) = 5x^4$.

🔲 In Exercises 73–76, use technology to graph the derivative of the given function for the given range of values of x. Then use your graph to estimate all values of x (if any) where **(a)** the given function is not differentiable, and **(b)** the tangent line to the graph of the given function is horizontal. Round answers to one decimal place.

73. ▼ $h(x) = |x - 3|$; $-5 \le x \le 5$

74. ▼ $h(x) = 2x + (x - 3)^{1/3}$; $-5 \le x \le 5$

75. ▼ $f(x) = x - 5(x - 1)^{2/5}$; $-4 \le x \le 6$

76. ▼ $f(x) = |2x + 5| - x^2$; $-4 \le x \le 4$

🔲 In Exercises 77–80, investigate the differentiability of the given function at the given points numerically (that is, use a table of values). If f'(a) exists, give its approximate value. HINT [See Example 3.]

77. $f(x) = x^{1/3}$ **a.** $a = 1$ **b.** $a = 0$

78. $f(x) = x + |1 - x|$ **a.** $a = 1$ **b.** $a = 0$

79. ▼ $f(x) = [x(1 - x)]^{1/3}$ **a.** $a = 1$ **b.** $a = 0$

80. ▼ $f(x) = (1 - x)^{2/3}$ **a.** $a = -1$ **b.** $a = 1$

In Exercises 81–92 say whether l'Hospital's rule applies. If is does, use it to evaluate the given limit. If not, use some other method.

81. $\displaystyle\lim_{x \to 1} \dfrac{x^2 - 2x + 1}{x^2 - x}$ **82.** $\displaystyle\lim_{x \to -1} \dfrac{x^2 + 3x + 2}{x^2 + x}$

83. $\displaystyle\lim_{x \to 2} \dfrac{x^3 - 8}{x - 2}$ **84.** $\displaystyle\lim_{x \to 0} \dfrac{x^3 + 8}{x^2 + 3x + 2}$

85. $\displaystyle\lim_{x \to 1} \dfrac{x^2 + 3x + 2}{x^2 + x}$ **86.** $\displaystyle\lim_{x \to -2} \dfrac{x^3 + 8}{x^2 + 3x + 2}$

87. $\displaystyle\lim_{x \to -\infty} \dfrac{3x^2 + 10x - 1}{2x^2 - 5x}$ **88.** $\displaystyle\lim_{x \to -\infty} \dfrac{6x^2 + 5x + 100}{3x^2 - 9}$

89. $\displaystyle\lim_{x \to -\infty} \dfrac{10x^2 + 300x + 1}{5x + 2}$ **90.** $\displaystyle\lim_{x \to -\infty} \dfrac{2x^4 + 20x^3}{1000x^3 + 6}$

91. $\displaystyle\lim_{x \to -\infty} \dfrac{x^3 - 100}{2x^2 + 500}$ **92.** $\displaystyle\lim_{x \to -\infty} \dfrac{x^2 + 30x}{2x^6 + 10x}$

APPLICATIONS

93. *Crude Oil Prices* The price per barrel of crude oil in constant 2008 dollars can be approximated by

$$P(t) = 0.45t^2 - 12t + 105 \text{ dollars} \quad (0 \le t \le 28)$$

where t is time in years since the start of 1980.[1] Find $P'(t)$ and $P'(20)$. What does the answer tell you about the price of crude oil? HINT [See Example 2.]

94. *Median Home Price* The median home price in the United States over the period 2004–2009 can be approximated by

$$P(t) = -5t^2 + 75t - 30 \text{ thousand dollars} \quad (4 \le t \le 9)$$

where t is time in years since the start of 2000.[2] Find $P'(t)$ and $P'(6)$. What does the answer tell you about home prices? HINT [See Example 2.]

95. *College Basketball: Men* The number of NCAA men's college basketball teams in the United States can be modeled by:

$$n(t) = -0.56t^2 + 14t + 930 \quad (0 \le t \le 8)$$

where t is time in years since 2000.[3]

Men's Basketball Teams

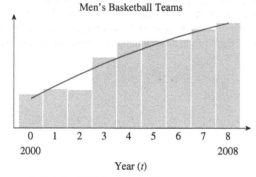

Year (t)

a. Find $n'(t)$. HINT [See Example 2.]

b. How fast (to the nearest whole number) was the number of men's college basketball teams increasing in 2006?

c. According to the model, did the rate of increase of the number of teams increase or decrease with time? Explain. HINT [See Example 4.]

96. *College Basketball: Women* The number of NCAA women's college basketball teams in the United States can be modeled by:

$$n(t) = -0.98t^2 + 32t + 1{,}850 \quad (0 \le t \le 8)$$

where t is time in years since 2000.[4]

Women's basketball teams

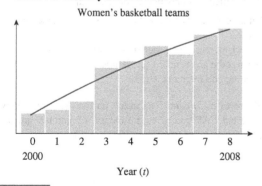

Year (t)

a. Find $n'(t)$. HINT [See Example 2.]

b. How fast (to the nearest whole number) was the number of women's college basketball teams increasing in 2005?

c. According to the model, did the rate of increase of the number of teams increase or decrease with time? Explain. HINT [See Example 4.]

97. *Food Versus Education* The following equation shows the approximate relationship between the percentage y of total personal consumption spent on food and the corresponding percentage x spent on education.[5]

$$y = \frac{35}{x^{0.35}} \text{ percentage points} \quad (6.5 \le x \le 17.5)$$

According to the model, spending on food is decreasing at a rate of _____ percentage points per one percentage point increase in spending on education when 10% of total consumption is spent on education. (Answer should be rounded to two significant digits.) HINT [See Example 2(b).]

98. *Food Versus Recreation* The following equation shows the approximate relationship between the percentage y of total personal consumption spent on food and the corresponding percentage x spent on recreation.[6]

$$y = \frac{33}{x^{0.63}} \text{ percentage points} \quad (2.5 \le x \le 4.5)$$

According to the model, spending on food is decreasing at a rate of _____ percentage points per one percentage point increase in spending on recreation when 3% of total consumption is spent on recreation. (Answer should be rounded to two significant digits.) HINT [See Example 2(b).]

99. *Velocity* If a stone is dropped from a height of 400 feet, its height s after t seconds is given by $s(t) = 400 - 16t^2$, with s in feet.

a. Compute $s'(t)$ and hence find its velocity at times $t = 0$, 1, 2, 3, and 4 seconds.

b. When does it reach the ground, and how fast is it traveling when it hits the ground? HINT [It reaches the ground when $s(t) = 0$.]

100. *Velocity* If a stone is thrown down at 120 ft/s from a height of 1,000 feet, its height s after t seconds is given by $s(t) = 1{,}000 - 120t - 16t^2$, with s in feet.

a. Compute $s'(t)$ and hence find its velocity at times $t = 0$, 1, 2, 3, and 4 seconds.

b. When does it reach the ground, and how fast is it traveling when it hits the ground? HINT [It reaches the ground when $s(t) = 0$.]

[1] Source for data: www.inflationdata.com.

[2] Source for data: www.investmenttools.com.

[3] 2007 and 2008 figures are estimates. Source: The 2008 Statistical Abstract, www.census.gov/.

[4] Ibid.

[5] Model based on historical and projected data from 1908–2010. Sources: Historical data, Bureau of Economic Analysis; projected data, Bureau of Labor Statistics/*New York Times*, December 1, 2003, p. C2.

[6] Ibid.

101. *iPhone Sales* iPhone sales from the 2nd quarter in 2007 through the 2nd quarter in 2008 can be approximated by

$$S(t) = -390t^2 + 3{,}300t - 4{,}800 \text{ thousand phones}$$
$$(2 \le t \le 6)$$

in quarter t. ($t = 1$ represents the start of the first quarter of 2007.)[7]

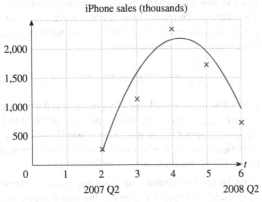

iPhone sales (thousands)

a. Compute $S'(t)$. How fast were iPhone sales changing in the first quarter of 2008 ($t = 5$)? (Be careful to give correct units of measurement.)

b. According to the model, iPhone sales

(A) increased at a faster and faster rate
(B) increased at a slower and slower rate
(C) decreased at a faster and faster rate
(D) decreased at a slower and slower rate

during the first two quarters shown (the interval [2, 4]). Justify your answer in two ways: geometrically, reasoning entirely from the graph; and algebraically, reasoning from the derivative of S. HINT [See Example 4.]

102. *Facebook Membership* The number of **Facebook** members from the start of 2006 to mid-2008 can be approximated by

$$S(t) = 15t^2 - 76t + 101 \text{ million members} \quad (2 \le t \le 4.5)$$

in year t ($t = 0$ represents the start of 2004).[8]

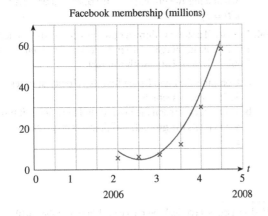

Facebook membership (millions)

a. Compute $S'(t)$. According to the model, how fast was **Facebook** membership changing at the start of 2008 ($t = 4$)? (Be careful to give correct units of measurement.)

b. According to the model, **Facebook** membership

(A) increased at a faster and faster rate
(B) increased at a slower and slower rate
(C) decreased at a faster and faster rate
(D) decreased at a slower and slower rate

during 2007 (the interval [3, 4]). Justify your answer in two ways: geometrically, reasoning entirely from the graph; and algebraically, reasoning from the derivative of S. HINT [See Example 4.]

103. *Ecology* Increasing numbers of manatees ("sea sirens") have been killed by boats off the Florida coast. The following graph shows the relationship between the number of boats registered in Florida and the number of manatees killed each year.

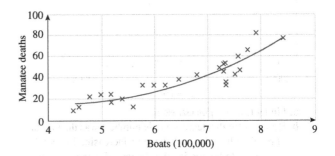

The regression curve shown is given by

$$f(x) = 3.55x^2 - 30.2x + 81 \quad (4.5 \le x \le 8.5)$$

where x is the number of boats (hundreds of thousands) registered in Florida in a particular year and $f(x)$ is the number of manatees killed by boats in Florida that year.[9]

a. Compute $f'(x)$. What are the units of measurement of $f'(x)$?

b. Is $f'(x)$ increasing or decreasing with increasing x? Interpret the answer. HINT [See Example 4.]

c. Compute and interpret $f'(8)$.

104. *SAT Scores by Income* The graph on the next page shows U.S. verbal SAT scores as a function of parents' income level.[10]

---

[7] The model is the authors'. Source for data: Apple financial statements, www.apple.com.

[8] The model is the authors'. Sources for data: www.facebook.com/, http://insidehighered.com (Some data are interpolated.)

[9] Regression model is based on data from 1976 to 2000. Sources for data: Florida Department of Highway Safety & Motor Vehicles, Florida Marine Institute/*New York Times*, February 12, 2002, p. F4.

[10] Based on 1994 data. Source: The College Board/*New York Times*, March 5, 1995, p. E16.

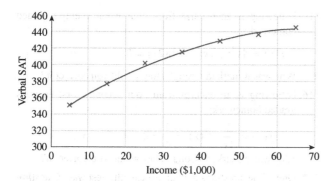

The regression curve shown is given by

$$f(x) = -0.021x^2 + 3.0x + 336 \quad (5 \le x \le 65)$$

where $f(x)$ is the average SAT verbal score of a student whose parents earn x thousand dollars per year.[11]

a. Compute $f'(x)$. What are the units of measurement of $f'(x)$?

b. Is $f'(x)$ increasing or decreasing with increasing x? Interpret the answer. HINT [See Example 4.]

c. Compute and interpret $f'(30)$.

105. *ISP Market Share* The following graph shows approximate market shares, in percentage points, of Microsoft's MSN Internet service provider, and the combined shares of MSN, Comcast, Earthlink, and AOL for the period 1999–2004.[12]

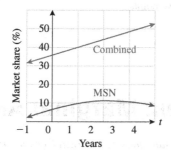

Here, t is time in years since June 2000. Let $c(t)$ be the combined market share at time t, and let $m(t)$ be MSN's share at time t.

a. What does the function $c(t) - m(t)$ measure? What does $c'(t) - m'(t)$ measure?

b. Based on the graphs shown, $c(t) - m(t)$ is

(A) increasing
(B) decreasing
(C) increasing, then decreasing
(D) decreasing, then increasing

on the interval [3, 4].

c. Based on the graphs shown, $c'(t) - m'(t)$ is

(A) positive
(B) negative
(C) positive, then negative
(D) negative, then positive

on the interval [3, 4].

d. The two market shares are approximated by

MSN: $m(t) = -0.83t^2 + 3.8t + 6.8 \quad (-1 \le t \le 4)$
Combined: $c(t) = 4.2t + 36 \qquad (-1 \le t \le 4)$

Compute $c'(2) - m'(2)$. Interpret your answer.

106. ▼ *ISP Revenue* The following graph shows the approximate total revenue, in millions of dollars, of Microsoft's MSN Internet service provider, as well as the portion of the revenue due to advertising for the period June 2001–January 2004.[13]

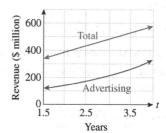

Here, t is time in years since January 2000. Let $s(t)$ be the total revenue at time t, and let $a(t)$ be revenue due to advertising at time t.

a. What does the function $s(t) - a(t)$ measure? What does $s'(t) - a'(t)$ measure?

b. Based on the graphs shown, $s(t) - a(t)$ is

(A) increasing
(B) decreasing
(C) increasing, then decreasing
(D) decreasing, then increasing

on the interval [2, 4].

c. Based on the graphs shown, $s'(t) - a'(t)$ is

(A) positive
(B) negative
(C) positive, then negative
(D) negative, then positive

on the interval [2, 4].

d. The two revenue curves are approximated by

Advertising: $a(t) = 20t^2 - 27t + 120 \quad (1.5 \le t \le 4)$
Total: $s(t) = 96t + 190 \qquad (1.5 \le t \le 4)$

Compute $a'(2)$, $s'(2)$, and hence $s'(2) - a'(2)$. Interpret your answer.

---

[11] Regression model is based on 1994 data. Source: The College Board/*New York Times*, March 5, 1995, p. E16.

[12] The curves are regression models. Source for data: Solomon Research, Morgan Stanley/*New York Times*, July 19, 2004.

[13] Ibid.

COMMUNICATION AND REASONING EXERCISES

107. What instructions would you give to a fellow student who wanted to accurately graph the tangent line to the curve $y = 3x^2$ at the point $(-1, 3)$?

108. What instructions would you give to a fellow student who wanted to accurately graph a line at right angles to the curve $y = 4/x$ at the point where $x = 0.5$?

109. Consider $f(x) = x^2$ and $g(x) = 2x^2$. How do the slopes of the tangent lines of f and g at the same x compare?

110. Consider $f(x) = x^3$ and $g(x) = x^3 + 3$. How do the slopes of the tangent lines of f and g compare?

111. Suppose $g(x) = -f(x)$. How do the derivatives of f and g compare?

112. Suppose $g(x) = f(x) - 50$. How do the derivatives of f and g compare?

113. Following is an excerpt from your best friend's graded homework:

$$3x^4 + 11x^5 = 12x^3 + 55x^4 \quad \text{✗ WRONG} \quad -8$$

Why was it marked wrong? How would you correct it?

114. Following is an excerpt from your second best friend's graded homework:

$$f(x) = \frac{3}{4x^2}; f'(x) = \frac{3}{8x} \quad \text{✗ WRONG} \quad -10$$

Why was it marked wrong? How would you correct it?

115. Following is an excerpt from your worst enemy's graded homework:

$$f(x) = 4x^2; f'(x) = (0)(2x) = 0 \quad \text{✗ WRONG} \quad -6$$

Why was it marked wrong? How would you correct it?

116. Following is an excerpt from your second worst enemy's graded homework:

$$f(x) = \frac{3}{4x}; f'(x) = \frac{0}{4} = 0 \quad \text{✗ WRONG} \quad -10$$

Why was it marked wrong? How would you correct it?

117. One of the questions in your last calculus test was "**Question 1(a)** Give the definition of the derivative of a function f." Following is your answer and the grade you received:

$$nx^{n-1} \quad \text{✗ WRONG} \quad -10$$

Why was it marked wrong? What is the correct answer?

118. ▽ How would you respond to an acquaintance who says, "I finally understand what the derivative is: It is nx^{n-1}! Why weren't we taught that in the first place instead of the difficult way using limits?"

119. ▽ Sketch the graph of a function whose derivative is undefined at exactly two points but which has a tangent line at all but one point.

120. ▽ Sketch the graph of a function that has a tangent line at each of its points, but whose derivative is undefined at exactly two points.

11.2 A First Application: Marginal Analysis

In Chapter 1, we considered linear *cost functions* of the form $C(x) = mx + b$, where C is the total cost, x is the number of items, and m and b are constants. The slope m is the *marginal cost*. It measures the *cost of one more item*. Notice that the derivative of $C(x) = mx + b$ is $C'(x) = m$. In other words, for a linear cost function, *the marginal cost is the derivative of the cost function*.

In general, we make the following definition.

Marginal Cost

A **cost function** specifies the total cost C as a function of the number of items x. In other words, $C(x)$ is the total cost of x items. The **marginal cost function** is the derivative $C'(x)$ of the cost function $C(x)$. It measures the rate of change of cost with respect to x.

Units

The units of marginal cost are units of cost (dollars, say) per item.

Interpretation

We interpret $C'(x)$ as the approximate cost of one more item.[*]

* **NOTE** See Example 1.

Quick Example

If $C(x) = 400x + 1,000$ dollars, then the marginal cost function is $C'(x) = \$400$ per item (a constant).

EXAMPLE 1 Marginal Cost

Suppose that the cost in dollars to manufacture portable CD players is given by

$$C(x) = 150,000 + 20x - 0.0001x^2$$

where x is the number of CD players manufactured.[*] Find the marginal cost function $C'(x)$ and use it to estimate the cost of manufacturing the 50,001st CD player.

Solution Since

$$C(x) = 150,000 + 20x - 0.0001x^2$$

the marginal cost function is

$$C'(x) = 20 - 0.0002x.$$

The units of $C'(x)$ are units of C (dollars) per unit of x (CD players). Thus, $C'(x)$ is measured in dollars per CD player.

The cost of the 50,001st CD player is the amount by which the total cost would rise if we increased production from 50,000 CD players to 50,001. Thus, we need to know the rate at which the total cost rises as we increase production. This rate of change is measured by the derivative, or marginal cost, which we just computed. At $x = 50,000$, we get

$$C'(50,000) = 20 - 0.0002(50,000) = \$10 \text{ per CD player}.$$

In other words, we estimate that the 50,001st CD player will cost approximately $10.

* **NOTE** You might well ask where on Earth this formula came from. There are two approaches to obtaining cost functions in real life: analytical and empirical. The analytical approach is to calculate the cost function from scratch. For example, in the above situation, we might have fixed costs of $150,000, plus a production cost of $20 per CD player. The term $0.0001x^2$ may reflect a cost saving for high levels of production, such as a bulk discount in the cost of electronic components. In the empirical approach, we first obtain the cost at several different production levels by direct observation. This gives several points on the (as yet unknown) cost versus production level graph. Then find the equation of the curve that best fits these points, usually using regression.

➡ **Before we go on...** In Example 1, the marginal cost is really only an *approximation* to the cost of the 50,001st CD player:

$$C'(50,000) \approx \frac{C(50,001) - C(50,000)}{1} \quad \text{Set } h = 1 \text{ in the definition of the derivative.}$$

$$= C(50,001) - C(50,000)$$

$$= \text{cost of the 50,001st CD player}$$

97

The exact cost of the 50,001st CD player is

$$C(50,001) - C(50,000) = [150,000 + 20(50,001) - 0.0001(50,001)^2]$$
$$- [150,000 + 20(50,000) - 0.0001(50,000)^2]$$
$$= \$9.9999$$

So, the marginal cost is a good approximation to the actual cost.

Graphically, we are using the tangent line to approximate the cost function near a production level of 50,000. Figure 3 shows the graph of the cost function together with the tangent line at $x = 50,000$. Notice that the tangent line is essentially indistinguishable from the graph of the function for some distance on either side of 50,000.

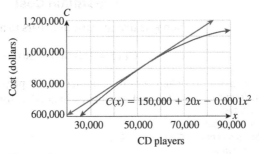

Figure 3

■

Notes

1. In general, the difference quotient $[C(x + h) - C(x)]/h$ gives the **average cost per item** to produce h more items at a current production level of x items. (Why?)

2. Notice that $C'(x)$ is much easier to calculate than $[C(x + h) - C(x)]/h$. (Try it.)

We can extend the idea of marginal cost to include other functions, like revenue and profit:

Marginal Revenue and Profit

A **revenue** or **profit function** specifies the total revenue R or profit P as a function of the number of items x. The derivatives, $R'(x)$ and $P'(x)$ of these functions are called the **marginal revenue** and **marginal profit** functions. They measure the rate of change of revenue and profit with respect to x.

Units
The units of marginal revenue and profit are the same as those of marginal cost: dollars (or euros, pesos, etc.) per item.

Interpretation
We interpret $R'(x)$ and $P'(x)$ as the approximate revenue and profit from the sale of one more item.

EXAMPLE 2 Marginal Revenue and Profit

You operate an *iPod* customizing service (a typical customized iPod might have a custom color case with blinking lights and a personalized logo). The cost to refurbish x iPods in a month is calculated to be

$$C(x) = 0.25x^2 + 40x + 1,000 \text{ dollars.}$$

You charge customers $80 per iPod for the work.

a. Calculate the marginal revenue and profit functions. Interpret the results.

b. Compute the revenue and profit, and also the marginal revenue and profit, if you have refurbished 20 units this month. Interpret the results.

c. For which value of x is the marginal profit zero? Interpret your answer.

Solution

a. We first calculate the revenue and profit functions:

$$R(x) = 80x \qquad \text{Revenue} = \text{Price} \times \text{Quantity}$$

$$P(x) = R(x) - C(x) \qquad \text{Profit} = \text{Revenue} - \text{Cost}$$

$$= 80x - (0.25x^2 + 40x + 1,000)$$

$$P(x) = -0.25x^2 + 40x - 1,000.$$

The marginal revenue and profit functions are then the derivatives:

$$\text{Marginal revenue} = R'(x) = 80$$

$$\text{Marginal profit} = P'(x) = -0.5x + 40.$$

Interpretation: $R'(x)$ gives the approximate revenue from the refurbishing of one more item, and $P'(x)$ gives the approximate profit from the refurbishing of one more item. Thus, if x iPods have been refurbished in a month, you will earn a revenue of $80 and make a profit of approximately $(-0.5x + 40)$ if you refurbish one more that month.

Notice that the marginal revenue is a constant, so you earn the same revenue ($80) for each iPod you refurbish. However, the marginal profit, $(-0.5x + 40)$, decreases as x increases, so your additional profit is about 50¢ less for each additional iPod you refurbish.

b. From part (a), the revenue, profit, marginal revenue, and marginal profit functions are

$$R(x) = 80x$$

$$P(x) = -0.25x^2 + 40x - 1,000$$

$$R'(x) = 80$$

$$P'(x) = -0.5x + 40$$

Because you have refurbished $x = 20$ iPods this month, $x = 20$, so

$R(20) = 80(20) = \$1,600$	Total revenue from 20 iPods
$P(20) = -0.25(20)^2 + 40(20) - 1,000 = -\$300$	Total profit from 20 iPods
$R'(20) = \$80$ per unit	Approximate revenue from the 21st iPod
$P'(20) = -0.5(20) + 40 = \$30$ per unit	Approximate profit from the 21st iPod

Interpretation: If you refurbish 20 iPods in a month, you will earn a total revenue of $160 and a profit of –$300 (indicating a loss of $300). Refurbishing one more iPod that month will earn you an additional revenue of $80 and an additional profit of about $30.

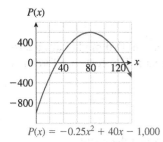

$P(x) = -0.25x^2 + 40x - 1,000$

Figure 4

c. The marginal profit is zero when $P'(x) = 0$:

$$-0.5x + 40 = 0$$

$$x = \frac{40}{0.5} = 80 \text{ iPods}$$

Thus, if you refurbish 80 iPods in a month, refurbishing one more will get you (approximately) zero additional profit. To understand this further, let us take a look at the graph of the profit function, shown in Figure 4. Notice that the graph is a parabola (the profit function is quadratic) with vertex at the point $x = 80$, where $P'(x) = 0$, so the profit is a maximum at this value of x.

➡ **Before we go on...** In general, setting $P'(x) = 0$ and solving for x will always give the exact values of x for which the profit peaks as in Figure 4, assuming there is such a value. We recommend that you graph the profit function to check whether the profit is indeed a maximum at such a point. ■

EXAMPLE 3 Marginal Product

A consultant determines that Precision Manufacturers' annual profit (in dollars) is given by

$$P(n) = -200,000 + 400,000n - 4,600n^2 - 10n^3 \qquad (10 \le n \le 50)$$

where n is the number of assembly-line workers it employs.

a. Compute $P'(n)$. $P'(n)$ is called the **marginal product** at the employment level of n assembly-line workers. What are its units?

b. Calculate $P(20)$ and $P'(20)$, and interpret the results.

c. Precision Manufacturers currently employs 20 assembly-line workers and is considering laying off some of them. What advice would you give the company's management?

Solution

a. Taking the derivative gives

$$P'(n) = 400,000 - 9,200n - 30n^2.$$

The units of $P'(n)$ are profit (in dollars) per worker.

b. Substituting into the formula for $P(n)$, we get

$$P(20) = -200,000 + 400,000(20) - 4,600(20)^2 - 10(20)^3 = \$5,880,000.$$

Thus, Precision Manufacturer will make an annual profit of $5,880,000 if it employs 20 assembly-line workers. On the other hand,

$$P'(20) = 400,000 - 9,200(20) - 30(20)^2 = \$204,000/\text{worker}.$$

Thus, at an employment level of 20 assembly-line workers, annual profit is increasing at a rate of $204,000 per additional worker. In other words, if the company were to employ one more assembly-line worker, its annual profit would increase by approximately $204,000.

c. Because the marginal product is positive, profits will increase if the company increases the number of workers and will decrease if it decreases the number of workers, so your advice would be to hire additional assembly-line workers. Downsizing their assembly-line workforce would reduce their annual profits.

100

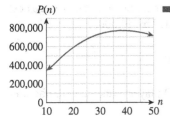

Figure 5

Before we go on... In Example 3, it would be interesting for Precision Manufacturers to ascertain how many additional assembly-line workers they should hire to obtain the *maximum* annual profit. Taking our cue from Example 2, we suspect that such a value of n would correspond to a point where $P'(n) = 0$. Figure 5 shows the graph of P, and on it we see that the highest point of the graph is indeed a point where the tangent line is horizontal; that is, $P'(n) = 0$, and occurs somewhere between $n = 35$ and 40. To compute this value of n more accurately, set $P'(n) = 0$ and solve for n:

$$P'(n) = 400,000 - 9,200n - 30n^2 = 0 \quad \text{or} \quad 40,000 - 920n - 3n^2 = 0.$$

We can now obtain n using the quadratic formula:

$$n = \frac{-b \pm \sqrt{b^2 - 4ac}}{2a} = \frac{920 \pm \sqrt{920^2 - 4(-3)(40,000)}}{2(-3)}$$

$$= \frac{920 \pm \sqrt{1,326,400}}{-6} \approx -345.3 \text{ or } 38.6.$$

The only meaningful solution is the positive one, $n \approx 38.6$ workers, and we conclude that the company should employ between 38 and 39 assembly-line workers for a maximum profit. To see which gives the larger profit, 38 or 39, we check:

$$P(38) = \$7,808,880$$

while

$$P(39) = \$7,810,210.$$

This tells us that the company should employ 39 assembly-line workers for a maximum profit. Thus, instead of laying off any of its 20 assembly-line workers, the company should hire 19 additional assembly line workers for a total of 39. ∎

Average Cost

EXAMPLE 4 Average Cost

Suppose the cost in dollars to manufacture portable CD players is given by

$$C(x) = 150,000 + 20x - 0.0001x^2$$

where x is the number of CD players manufactured. (This is the cost equation we saw in Example 1.)

a. Find the average cost per CD player if 50,000 CD players are manufactured.

b. Find a formula for the average cost per CD player if x CD players are manufactured. This function of x is called the **average cost function, $\bar{C}(x)$**.

Solution

a. The total cost of manufacturing 50,000 CD players is given by

$$C(50,000) = 150,000 + 20(50,000) - 0.0001(50,000)^2$$

$$= \$900,000.$$

Because 50,000 CD players cost a total of $900,000 to manufacture, the average cost of manufacturing one CD player is this total cost divided by 50,000:

$$\bar{C}(50,000) = \frac{900,000}{50,000} = \$18.00 \text{ per CD player.}$$

Thus, if 50,000 CD players are manufactured, each CD player costs the manufacturer an average of $18.00 to manufacture.

b. If we replace 50,000 by x, we get the general formula for the average cost of manufacturing x CD players:

$$\bar{C}(x) = \frac{C(x)}{x}$$

$$= \frac{1}{x}(150,000 + 20x - 0.0001x^2)$$

$$= \frac{150,000}{x} + 20 - 0.0001x. \qquad \text{Average cost function}$$

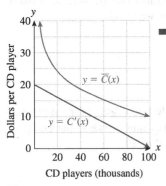

Dollars per CD player

CD players (thousands)

Figure 6

➡ **Before we go on...** Average cost and marginal cost convey different but related information. The average cost $\bar{C}(50,000) = \$18$ that we calculated in Example 4 is the cost per item of manufacturing the first 50,000 CD players, whereas the marginal cost $C'(50,000) = \$10$ that we calculated in Example 1 gives the (approximate) cost of manufacturing the *next* CD player. Thus, according to our calculations, the first 50,000 CD players cost an average of $18 to manufacture, but it costs only about $10 to manufacture the next one. Note that the marginal cost at a production level of 50,000 CD players is lower than the average cost. This means that the average cost to manufacture CDs is going down with increasing volume. (Think about why.)

Figure 6 shows the graphs of average and marginal cost. Notice how the decreasing marginal cost seems to pull the average cost down with it. ◼

To summarize:

Average Cost

Given a cost function C, the **average cost** of the first x items is given by

$$\bar{C}(x) = \frac{C(x)}{x}.$$

The average cost is distinct from the **marginal cost** $C'(x)$, which tells us the approximate cost of the *next* item.

Quick Example

For the cost function $C(x) = 20x + 100$ dollars

Marginal Cost $= C'(x) = \$20$ per additional item.

Average Cost $= \bar{C}(x) = \dfrac{C(x)}{x} = \dfrac{20x + 100}{x} = \$(20 + 100/x)$ per item.

11.2 EXERCISES

▼ more advanced   ◆ challenging
🔲 indicates exercises that should be solved using technology

In Exercises 1–4, for each cost function, find the marginal cost at the given production level x, and state the units of measurement. (All costs are in dollars.) HINT [See Example 1.]

1. $C(x) = 10,000 + 5x - 0.0001x^2$; $x = 1,000$

2. $C(x) = 20,000 + 7x - 0.00005x^2$; $x = 10,000$

3. $C(x) = 15,000 + 100x + \dfrac{1,000}{x}$; $x = 100$

4. $C(x) = 20,000 + 50x + \dfrac{10,000}{x}$; $x = 100$

In Exercises 5 and 6, find the marginal cost, marginal revenue, and marginal profit functions, and find all values of x for which the marginal profit is zero. Interpret your answer.
HINT [See Example 2.]

5. $C(x) = 4x$; $R(x) = 8x - 0.001x^2$

6. $C(x) = 5x^2$; $R(x) = x^3 + 7x + 10$

7. ▼ A certain cost function has the following graph:

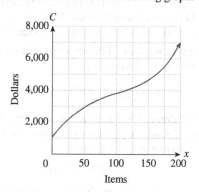

Items

a. The associated marginal cost is

   (A) increasing, then decreasing
   (B) decreasing, then increasing
   (C) always increasing
   (D) always decreasing

b. The marginal cost is least at approximately

   (A) $x = 0$ **(B)** $x = 50$ **(C)** $x = 100$ **(D)** $x = 150$

c. The cost of 50 items is

   (A) approximately $20, and increasing at a rate of about $3,000 per item
   (B) approximately $0.50, and increasing at a rate of about $3,000 per item
   (C) approximately $3,000, and increasing at a rate of about $20 per item
   (D) approximately $3,000, and increasing at a rate of about $0.50 per item

8. ▼ A certain cost function has the following graph:

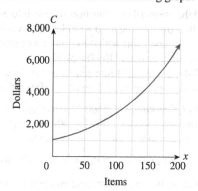

Items

a. The associated marginal cost is

   (A) increasing, then decreasing
   (B) decreasing, then increasing
   (C) always increasing
   (D) always decreasing

b. When $x = 100$, the marginal cost is

   (A) greater than the average cost
   (B) less than the average cost
   (C) approximately equal to the average cost

c. The cost of 150 items is

   (A) approximately $4,400, and increasing at a rate of about $40 per item
   (B) approximately $40, and increasing at a rate of about $4,400 per item
   (C) approximately $4,400, and increasing at a rate of about $1 per item
   (D) approximately $1, and increasing at a rate of about $4,400 per item

APPLICATIONS

9. *Advertising Costs* The cost, in thousands of dollars, of airing x television commercials during a Super Bowl game is given by[14]

$$C(x) = 150 + 2,250x - 0.02x^2.$$

a. Find the marginal cost function and use it to estimate how fast the cost is increasing when $x = 4$. Compare this with the exact cost of airing the fifth commercial. HINT [See Example 1.]

b. Find the average cost function $\bar{C}$, and evaluate $\bar{C}(4)$. What does the answer tell you? HINT [See Example 4.]

---

[14]CBS charged an average of $2.25 million per 30-second television spot during the 2004 Super Bowl game. This explains the coefficient of x in the cost function. Source: Advertising Age Research, www.AdAge.com/.

10. *Marginal Cost and Average Cost* The cost of producing x teddy bears per day at the Cuddly Companion Co. is calculated by their marketing staff to be given by the formula

$$C(x) = 100 + 40x - 0.001x^2.$$

a. Find the marginal cost function and use it to estimate how fast the cost is going up at a production level of 100 teddy bears. Compare this with the exact cost of producing the 101st teddy bear. HINT [See Example 1.]

b. Find the average cost function $\bar{C}$, and evaluate $\bar{C}(100)$. What does the answer tell you? HINT [See Example 4.]

11. *Marginal Revenue and Profit* Your college newspaper, *The Collegiate Investigator*, sells for 90¢ per copy, The cost of producing x copies of an edition is given by

$$C(x) = 70 + 0.10x + 0.001x^2 \text{ dollars.}$$

a. Calculate the marginal revenue and profit functions. HINT [See Example 2.]

b. Compute the revenue and profit, and also the marginal revenue and profit, if you have produced and sold 500 copies of the latest edition. Interpret the results.

c. For which value of x is the marginal profit zero? Interpret your answer.

12. *Marginal Revenue and Profit* The Audubon Society at Enormous State University (ESU) is planning its annual fundraising "Eatathon." The society will charge students $1.10 per serving of pasta. The society estimates that the total cost of producing x servings of pasta at the event will be

$$C(x) = 350 + 0.10x + 0.002x^2 \text{ dollars.}$$

a. Calculate the marginal revenue and profit functions. HINT [See Example 2.]

b. Compute the revenue and profit, and also the marginal revenue and profit, if you have produced and sold 200 servings of pasta. Interpret the results.

c. For which value of x is the marginal profit zero? Interpret your answer.

13. *Marginal Profit* Suppose $P(x)$ represents the profit on the sale of x DVDs. If $P(1,000) = 3,000$ and $P'(1,000) = -3$, what do these values tell you about the profit?

14. *Marginal Loss* An automobile retailer calculates that its loss on the sale of type M cars is given by $L(50) = 5,000$ and $L'(50) = -200$, where $L(x)$ represents the loss on the sale of x type M cars. What do these values tell you about losses?

15. *Marginal Profit* Your monthly profit (in dollars) from selling magazines is given by

$$P = 5x + \sqrt{x}$$

where x is the number of magazines you sell in a month. If you are currently selling $x = 50$ magazines per month, find your profit and your marginal profit. Interpret your answers.

16. *Marginal Profit* Your monthly profit (in dollars) from your newspaper route is given by

$$P = 2n - \sqrt{n}$$

where n is the number of subscribers on your route. If you currently have 100 subscribers, find your profit and your marginal profit. Interpret your answers.

17. ▼ *Marginal Revenue: Pricing Tuna* Assume that the demand function for tuna in a small coastal town is given by

$$p = \frac{20,000}{q^{1.5}} \qquad (200 \le q \le 800)$$

where p is the price (in dollars) per pound of tuna, and q is the number of pounds of tuna that can be sold at the price p in one month.

a. Calculate the price that the town's fishery should charge for tuna in order to produce a demand of 400 pounds of tuna per month.

b. Calculate the monthly revenue R as a function of the number of pounds of tuna q.

c. Calculate the revenue and marginal revenue (derivative of the revenue with respect to q) at a demand level of 400 pounds per month, and interpret the results.

d. If the town fishery's monthly tuna catch amounted to 400 pounds of tuna, and the price is at the level in part (a), would you recommend that the fishery raise or lower the price of tuna in order to increase its revenue?

18. ▼ *Marginal Revenue: Pricing Tuna* Repeat Exercise 17, assuming a demand equation of

$$p = \frac{60}{q^{0.5}} \qquad (200 \le q \le 800).$$

19. *Marginal Product* A car wash firm calculates that its daily profit (in dollars) depends on the number n of workers it employs according to the formula

$$P = 400n - 0.5n^2.$$

Calculate the marginal product at an employment level of 50 workers, and interpret the result. HINT [See Example 3.]

20. *Marginal Product* Repeat the preceding exercise using the formula

$$P = -100n + 25n^2 - 0.005n^4.$$

HINT [See Example 3.]

21. *Average and Marginal Cost* The daily cost to manufacture generic trinkets for gullible tourists is given by the cost function

$$C(x) = -0.001x^2 + 0.3x + 500 \text{ dollars}$$

where x is the number of trinkets.

a. As x increases, the marginal cost
(A) increases   (B) decreases   (C) increases, then decreases   (D) decreases, then increases

b. As x increases, the average cost

  (A) increases   **(B)** decreases   **(C)** increases, then decreases   **(D)** decreases, then increases

c. The marginal cost is

  (A) greater than   **(B)** equal to   **(C)** less than the average cost when $x = 100$. HINT [See Example 4.]

22. *Average and Marginal Cost* Repeat Exercise 21, using the following cost function for imitation oil paintings (x is the number of "oil paintings" manufactured):

$$C(x) = 0.1x^2 - 3.5x + 500 \text{ dollars.}$$

HINT [See Example 4.]

23. *Advertising Cost* Your company is planning to air a number of television commercials during the ABC Television Network's presentation of the Academy Awards. ABC is charging your company $1.6 million per 30-second spot.[15] Additional fixed costs (development and personnel costs) amount to $500,000, and the network has agreed to provide a discount of $10,000\sqrt{x}$ for x television spots.

a. Write down the cost function C, marginal cost function C', and average cost function $\bar{C}$.

b. Compute $C'(3)$ and $\bar{C}(3)$. (Round all answers to three significant digits.) Use these two answers to say whether the average cost is increasing or decreasing as x increases.

24. *Housing Costs* The cost C of building a house is related to the number k of carpenters used and the number x of electricians used by the formula[16]

$$C = 15,000 + 50k^2 + 60x^2.$$

a. Assuming that 10 carpenters are currently being used, find the cost function C, marginal cost function C', and average cost function $\bar{C}$, all as functions of x.

b. Use the functions you obtained in part (a) to compute $C'(15)$ and $\bar{C}(15)$. Use these two answers to say whether the average cost is increasing or decreasing as the number of electricians increases.

25. ▼ *Emission Control* The cost of controlling emissions at a firm rises rapidly as the amount of emissions reduced increases. Here is a possible model:

$$C(q) = 4,000 + 100q^2$$

where q is the reduction in emissions (in pounds of pollutant per day) and C is the daily cost (in dollars) of this reduction.

a. If a firm is currently reducing its emissions by 10 pounds each day, what is the marginal cost of reducing emissions further?

b. Government clean-air subsidies to the firm are based on the formula

$$S(q) = 500q$$

where q is again the reduction in emissions (in pounds per day) and S is the subsidy (in dollars). At what reduction level does the marginal cost surpass the marginal subsidy?

c. Calculate the net cost function, $N(q) = C(q) - S(q)$, given the cost function and subsidy above, and find the value of q that gives the lowest net cost. What is this lowest net cost? Compare your answer to that for part (b) and comment on what you find.

26. ▼ *Taxation Schemes* Here is a curious proposal for taxation rates based on income:

$$T(i) = 0.001i^{0.5}$$

where i represents total annual income in dollars and $T(i)$ is the income tax rate as a percentage of total annual income. (Thus, for example, an income of $50,000 per year would be taxed at about 22%, while an income of double that amount would be taxed at about 32%.)[17]

a. Calculate the after-tax (net) income $N(i)$ an individual can expect to earn as a function of income i.

b. Calculate an individual's marginal after-tax income at income levels of $100,000 and $500,000.

c. At what income does an individual's marginal after-tax income become negative? What is the after-tax income at that level, and what happens at higher income levels?

d. What do you suspect is the most anyone can earn after taxes? (See NOTE at the bottom of this page.)

27. ▼ *Fuel Economy* Your Porsche's gas mileage (in miles per gallon) is given as a function $M(x)$ of speed x in miles per hour. It is found that

$$M'(x) = \frac{3,600x^{-2} - 1}{(3,600x^{-1} + x)^2}.$$

Estimate $M'(10)$, $M'(60)$, and $M'(70)$. What do the answers tell you about your car?

28. ▼ *Marginal Revenue* The estimated marginal revenue for sales of ESU soccer team T-shirts is given by

$$R'(p) = \frac{(8 - 2p)e^{-p^2 + 8p}}{10,000,000}$$

---

[15] ABC charged an average of $1.6 million for a 30-second spot during the 2005 Academy Awards presentation. Source: CNN/Reuters, www.cnn.com, February 9, 2005.

[16] Based on an exercise in *Introduction to Mathematical Economics* by A. L. Ostrosky, Jr., and J. V. Koch (Waveland Press, Prospect Heights, Illinois, 1979).

[17] This model has the following interesting feature: An income of $1 million per year would be taxed at 100%, leaving the individual penniless!

where p is the price (in dollars) that the soccer players charge for each shirt. Estimate $R'(3)$, $R'(4)$, and $R'(5)$. What do the answers tell you?

29. ◆ **Marginal Cost** *(from the GRE Economics Test)* In a multi-plant firm in which the different plants have different and continuous cost schedules, if costs of production for a given output level are to be minimized, which of the following is essential?

(A) Marginal costs must equal marginal revenue.
(B) Average variable costs must be the same in all plants.
(C) Marginal costs must be the same in all plants.
(D) Total costs must be the same in all plants.
(E) Output per worker per hour must be the same in all plants.

30. ◆ **Study Time** *(from the GRE economics test)* A student has a fixed number of hours to devote to study and is certain of the relationship between hours of study and the final grade for each course. Grades are given on a numerical scale (0 to 100), and each course is counted equally in computing the grade average. In order to maximize his or her grade average, the student should allocate these hours to different courses so that

(A) the grade in each course is the same.
(B) the marginal product of an hour's study (in terms of final grade) in each course is zero.
(C) the marginal product of an hour's study (in terms of final grade) in each course is equal, although not necessarily equal to zero.
(D) the average product of an hour's study (in terms of final grade) in each course is equal.
(E) the number of hours spent in study for each course is equal.

31. ◆ **Marginal Product** *(from the GRE Economics Test)* Assume that the marginal product of an additional senior professor is 50% higher than the marginal product of an additional junior professor and that junior professors are paid one-half the amount that senior professors receive. With a fixed overall budget, a university that wishes to maximize its quantity of output from professors should do which of the following?

(A) Hire equal numbers of senior professors and junior professors.
(B) Hire more senior professors and junior professors.
(C) Hire more senior professors and discharge junior professors.
(D) Discharge senior professors and hire more junior professors.
(E) Discharge all senior professors and half of the junior professors.

32. ◆ **Marginal Product** *(based on a question from the GRE Economics Test)* Assume that the marginal product of an additional senior professor is twice the marginal product of an additional junior professor and that junior professors are paid two-thirds the amount that senior professors receive. With a fixed overall budget, a university that wishes to maximize its quantity of output from professors should do which of the following?

(A) Hire equal numbers of senior professors and junior professors.
(B) Hire more senior professors and junior professors.
(C) Hire more senior professors and discharge junior professors.
(D) Discharge senior professors and hire more junior professors.
(E) Discharge all senior professors and half of the junior professors.

COMMUNICATION AND REASONING EXERCISES

33. The marginal cost of producing the 1,001st item is

(A) equal to
(B) approximately equal to
(C) always slightly greater than

the actual cost of producing the 1,001st item.

34. For the cost function $C(x) = mx + b$, the marginal cost of producing the 1,001st item is,

(A) equal to
(B) approximately equal to
(C) always slightly greater than

the actual cost of producing the 1,001st item.

35. What is a cost function? Carefully explain the difference between *average cost* and *marginal cost* in terms of (a) their mathematical definition, (b) graphs, and (c) interpretation.

36. The cost function for your grand piano manufacturing plant has the property that $\bar{C}(1,000) = \$3,000$ per unit and $C'(1,000) = \$2,500$ per unit. Will the average cost increase or decrease if your company manufactures a slightly larger number of pianos? Explain your reasoning.

37. If the average cost to manufacture one grand piano increases as the production level increases, which is greater, the marginal cost or the average cost?

38. If your analysis of a manufacturing company yielded positive marginal profit but negative profit at the company's current production levels, what would you advise the company to do?

39. ▼ If the marginal cost is decreasing, is the average cost necessarily decreasing? Explain.

40. ▼ If the average cost is decreasing, is the marginal cost necessarily decreasing? Explain.

41. ◆ If a company's marginal average cost is zero at the current production level, positive for a slightly higher production level, and negative for a slightly lower production level, what should you advise the company to do?

42. ◆ The **acceleration** of cost is defined as the derivative of the marginal cost function: that is, the derivative of the derivative—or *second derivative*—of the cost function. What are the units of acceleration of cost, and how does one interpret this measure?

11.3 The Product and Quotient Rules

We know how to find the derivatives of functions that are sums of powers, such as polynomials. In general, if a function is a sum or difference of functions whose derivatives we know, then we know how to find its derivative. But what about *products and quotients* of functions whose derivatives we know? For instance, how do we calculate the derivative of something like $x^2/(x+1)$? The derivative of $x^2/(x+1)$ is not, as one might suspect, $2x/1 = 2x$. That calculation is based on an assumption that the derivative of a quotient is the quotient of the derivatives. But it is easy to see that this assumption is false: For instance, the derivative of $1/x$ is not $0/1 = 0$, but $-1/x^2$. Similarly, the derivative of a product is not the product of the derivatives: For instance, the derivative of $x = 1 \cdot x$ is not $0 \cdot 1 = 0$, but 1.

To identify the correct method of computing the derivatives of products and quotients, let's look at a simple example. We know that the daily revenue resulting from the sale of q items per day at a price of p dollars per item is given by the product, $R = pq$ dollars. Suppose you are currently selling wall posters on campus. At this time your daily sales are 50 posters, and sales are increasing at a rate of 4 per day. Furthermore, you are currently charging $10 per poster, and you are also raising the price at a rate of $2 per day. Let's use this information to estimate how fast your daily revenue is increasing. In other words, let us estimate the rate of change, dR/dt, of the revenue R.

There are two contributions to the rate of change of daily revenue: the increase in daily sales and the increase in the unit price. We have

$\dfrac{dR}{dt}$ due to increasing price: $2 per day $\times$ 50 posters = $100 per day

$\dfrac{dR}{dt}$ due to increasing sales: $10 per poster $\times$ 4 posters per day = $40 per day

Thus, we estimate the daily revenue to be increasing at a rate of $100 + $40 = $140 per day. Let us translate what we have said into symbols:

$\dfrac{dR}{dt}$ due to increasing price: $\dfrac{dp}{dt} \times q$

$\dfrac{dR}{dt}$ due to increasing sales: $p \times \dfrac{dq}{dt}$

Thus, the rate of change of revenue is given by

$$\frac{dR}{dt} = \frac{dp}{dt}q + p\frac{dq}{dt}.$$

Because $R = pq$, we have discovered the following rule for differentiating a product:

$$\frac{d}{dt}(pq) = \frac{dp}{dt}q + p\frac{dq}{dt}$$ The derivative of a product is the derivative of the first times the second, plus the first times the derivative of the second.

This rule and a similar rule for differentiating quotients are given next, and also a discussion of how these results are proved rigorously.

Product Rule

If $f(x)$ and $g(x)$ are differentiable functions of x, then so is their product $f(x)g(x)$, and

$$\frac{d}{dx}[f(x)g(x)] = f'(x)g(x) + f(x)g'(x).$$

Product Rule in Words

The derivative of a product is the derivative of the first times the second, plus the first times the derivative of the second.

> ### Quick Example
>
> $f(x) = x^2$ and $g(x) = 3x - 1$ are both differentiable functions of x, and so their product $x^2(3x - 1)$ is differentiable, and
>
> $$\frac{d}{dx}[x^2(3x - 1)] = 2x \cdot (3x - 1) + x^2 \cdot (3).$$
>
>   ↑   ↑   ↑ ↑
>
>   Derivative of first   Second First Derivative of second

Quotient Rule

If $f(x)$ and $g(x)$ are differentiable functions of x, then so is their quotient $f(x)/g(x)$ (provided $g(x) \neq 0$), and

$$\frac{d}{dx}\left(\frac{f(x)}{g(x)}\right) = \frac{f'(x)g(x) - f(x)g'(x)}{[g(x)]^2}.$$

Quotient Rule in Words

The derivative of a quotient is the derivative of the top times the bottom, minus the top times the derivative of the bottom, all over the bottom squared.

> ### Quick Example
>
> $f(x) = x^3$ and $g(x) = x^2 + 1$ are both differentiable functions of x, and so their quotient $x^3/(x^2 + 1)$ is differentiable, and
>
>   Derivative of top   Bottom   Top   Derivative of bottom
>   ↓   ↓   ↓   ↓
>
> $$\frac{d}{dx}\left(\frac{x^3}{x^2 + 1}\right) = \frac{3x^2(x^2 + 1) - x^3 \cdot 2x}{(x^2 + 1)^2}$$
>
>   ↑
>   Bottom squared

Notes

1. Don't try to remember the rules by the symbols we have used, but remember them in words. (The slogans are easy to remember, even if the terms are not precise.)

2. One more time: *The derivative of a product is* NOT *the product of the derivatives, and the derivative of a quotient is* NOT *the quotient of the derivatives.* To find the derivative of a product, you must use the product rule, and to find the derivative of a quotient, you must use the quotient rule.*

* NOTE Leibniz made this mistake at first, too, so you would be in good company if you forgot to use the product or quotient rule.

Q: *Wait a minute! The expression $2x^3$ is a product, and we already know that its derivative is $6x^2$. Where did we use the product rule?*

A: To differentiate functions such as $2x^3$, we have used the rule from Section 10.4:

The derivative of c times a function is c times the derivative of the function.

However, the product rule gives us the same result:

Derivative of first Second   First Derivative of second

$$\frac{d}{dx}(2x^3) = (0)(x^3) \quad + \quad (2)(3x^2) = 6x^2 \qquad \text{Product rule}$$

$$\frac{d}{dx}(2x^3) = (2)(3x^2) = 6x^2 \qquad \text{Derivative of a constant times a function}$$

We do not recommend that you use the product rule to differentiate functions such as $2x^3$; continue to use the simpler rule when one of the factors is a constant.

Derivation of the Product Rule

Before we look at more examples of using the product and quotient rules, let's see why the product rule is true. To calculate the derivative of the product $f(x)g(x)$ of two differentiable functions, we go back to the definition of the derivative:

$$\frac{d}{dx}[f(x)g(x)] = \lim_{h \to 0} \frac{f(x+h)g(x+h) - f(x)g(x)}{h}.$$

✱ NOTE Adding an appropriate form of zero is an age-old mathematical ploy.

We now rewrite this expression so that we can evaluate the limit: Notice that the numerator reflects a simultaneous change in f [from $f(x)$ to $f(x+h)$] and g [from $g(x)$ to $g(x+h)$]. To separate the two effects, we add and subtract a quantity in the numerator that reflects a change in only one of the functions:

$$\frac{d}{dx}[f(x)g(x)] = \lim_{h \to 0} \frac{f(x+h)g(x+h) - f(x)g(x)}{h}$$

$$= \lim_{h \to 0} \frac{f(x+h)g(x+h) - f(x)g(x+h) + f(x)g(x+h) - f(x)g(x)}{h} \qquad \text{We subtracted and added the quantity✱ } f(x)g(x+h).$$

$$= \lim_{h \to 0} \frac{[f(x+h) - f(x)]\,g(x+h) + f(x)[g(x+h) - g(x)]}{h} \qquad \text{Common factors}$$

$$= \lim_{h \to 0} \left(\frac{f(x+h) - f(x)}{h}\right) g(x+h) + \lim_{h \to 0} f(x)\left(\frac{g(x+h) - g(x)}{h}\right) \qquad \text{Limit of sum}$$

$$= \lim_{h \to 0} \left(\frac{f(x+h) - f(x)}{h}\right) \lim_{h \to 0} g(x+h) + \lim_{h \to 0} f(x)\lim_{h \to 0}\left(\frac{g(x+h) - g(x)}{h}\right) \qquad \text{Limit of product}$$

Web Site
www.FiniteandCalc.org
For a proof of the fact that, if g is differentiable, it must be continuous, go to the Web site and follow the path

Everything for Calculus

→ Chapter 11

→ Continuity and
   Differentiability

Now we already know the following four limits:

$$\lim_{h \to 0} \frac{f(x+h) - f(x)}{h} = f'(x) \qquad \text{Definition of derivative of } f; f \text{ is differentiable.}$$

$$\lim_{h \to 0} \frac{g(x+h) - g(x)}{h} = g'(x) \qquad \text{Definition of derivative of } g; g \text{ is differentiable.}$$

$$\lim_{h \to 0} g(x+h) = g(x) \qquad \text{If } g \text{ is differentiable, it must be continuous.}$$

$$\lim_{h \to 0} f(x) = f(x) \qquad \text{Limit of a constant}$$

Web Site
www.FiniteandCalc.org
The quotient rule can be
proved in a very similar way.
Go to the Web site and follow
the path

Everything for Calculus
→ Chapter 11
→ Proof of Quotient Rule

Putting these limits into the one we're calculating, we get

$$\frac{d}{dx}[f(x)g(x)] = f'(x)g(x) + f(x)g'(x)$$

which is the product rule.

EXAMPLE 5 **Using the Product Rule**

Compute the following derivatives.

a. $\frac{d}{dx}[(x^{3.2} + 1)(1 - x)]$ Simplify the answer.

b. $\frac{d}{dx}[(x + 1)(x^2 + 1)(x^3 + 1)]$ Do not expand the answer.

Solution

a. We can do the calculation in two ways.

Using the Product Rule:

$$\frac{d}{dx}[(x^{3.2} + 1)(1 - x)] = \underset{\downarrow}{(3.2x^{2.2})}\underset{\downarrow}{(1 - x)} + \underset{\downarrow}{(x^{3.2} + 1)}\underset{\downarrow}{(-1)}$$

Derivative of first, Second, First, Derivative of second

$$= 3.2x^{2.2} - 3.2x^{3.2} - x^{3.2} - 1 \quad \text{Expand the answer.}$$

$$= -4.2x^{3.2} + 3.2x^{2.2} - 1$$

Not Using the Product Rule: First, expand the given expression.

$$(x^{3.2} + 1)(1 - x) = -x^{4.2} + x^{3.2} - x + 1$$

Thus,

$$\frac{d}{dx}[(x^{3.2} + 1)(1 - x)] = \frac{d}{dx}(-x^{4.2} + x^{3.2} - x + 1)$$

$$= -4.2x^{3.2} + 3.2x^{2.2} - 1$$

In this example the product rule saves us little or no work, but in later sections we shall see examples that can be done in no other way. Learn how to use the product rule now!

b. Here we have a product of *three* functions, not just two. We can find the derivative by using the product rule twice:

$$\frac{d}{dx}[(x + 1)(x^2 + 1)(x^3 + 1)]$$

$$= \frac{d}{dx}(x + 1) \cdot [(x^2 + 1)(x^3 + 1)] + (x + 1) \cdot \frac{d}{dx}[(x^2 + 1)(x^3 + 1)]$$

$$= (1)(x^2 + 1)(x^3 + 1) + (x + 1)[(2x)(x^3 + 1) + (x^2 + 1)(3x^2)]$$

$$= (1)(x^2 + 1)(x^3 + 1) + (x + 1)(2x)(x^3 + 1) + (x + 1)(x^2 + 1)(3x^2)$$

We can see here a more general product rule:

$$(fgh)' = f'gh + fg'h + fgh'$$

Notice that every factor has a chance to contribute to the rate of change of the product. There are similar formulas for products of four or more functions.

EXAMPLE 6 Using the Quotient Rule

Compute the derivatives **a.** $\dfrac{d}{dx}\left[\dfrac{1 - 3.2x^{-0.1}}{x + 1}\right]$ **b.** $\dfrac{d}{dx}\left[\dfrac{(x + 1)(x + 2)}{x - 1}\right]$

Solution

a.
$$\dfrac{d}{dx}\left[\dfrac{1 - 3.2x^{-0.1}}{x + 1}\right] = \dfrac{\overset{\text{Derivative of top}}{\downarrow}\,\overset{\text{Bottom}}{\downarrow}\;\overset{\text{Top}}{\downarrow}\;\overset{\text{Derivative of bottom}}{\downarrow}}{\underset{\uparrow}{(x + 1)^2}}$$

$$= \dfrac{(0.32x^{-1.1})(x + 1) - (1 - 3.2x^{-0.1})(1)}{(x + 1)^2}$$

Bottom squared

$$= \dfrac{0.32x^{-0.1} + 0.32x^{-1.1} - 1 + 3.2x^{-0.1}}{(x + 1)^2}$$ Expand the numerator.

$$= \dfrac{3.52x^{-0.1} + 0.32x^{-1.1} - 1}{(x + 1)^2}$$

b. Here we have both a product and a quotient. Which rule do we use, the product or the quotient rule? Here is a way to decide. Think about how we would calculate, step by step, the value of $(x + 1)(x + 2)/(x - 1)$ for a specific value of x—say $x = 11$. Here is how we would probably do it:

1. Calculate $(x + 1)(x + 2) = (11 + 1)(11 + 2) = 156$.

2. Calculate $x - 1 = 11 - 1 = 10$.

3. Divide 156 by 10 to get 15.6.

Now ask: *What was the last operation we performed?* The last operation we performed was division, so we can regard the whole expression as a *quotient*—that is, as $(x + 1)(x + 2)$ *divided by* $(x - 1)$. Therefore, we should use the quotient rule.

The first thing the quotient rule tells us to do is to take the derivative of the numerator. Now, the numerator is a product, so we must use the product rule to take its derivative. Here is the calculation:

$$\dfrac{d}{dx}\left[\dfrac{(x + 1)(x + 2)}{x - 1}\right] = \dfrac{\overbrace{[(1)(x + 2) + (x + 1)(1)]}^{\text{Derivative of top}}(x - 1) - \overbrace{[(x + 1)(x + 2)]}^{\text{Top}}(1)}{(x - 1)^2}$$

Bottom squared

$$= \dfrac{(2x + 3)(x - 1) - (x + 1)(x + 2)}{(x - 1)^2}$$

$$= \dfrac{x^2 - 2x - 5}{(x - 1)^2}$$

What is important is to determine the *order of operations* and, in particular, to determine the last operation to be performed. Pretending to do an actual calculation reminds us of the order of operations; we call this technique the **calculation thought experiment**.

➡ **Before we go on...** We used the quotient rule in Example 6 because the function was a quotient; we used the product rule to calculate the derivative of the numerator because the numerator was a product. Get used to this: Differentiation rules usually must be used in combination.

Here is another way we could have done this problem: Our calculation thought experiment could have taken the following form.

1. Calculate $(x + 1)/(x - 1) = (11 + 1)/(11 - 1) = 1.2$.

2. Calculate $x + 2 = 11 + 2 = 13$.

3. Multiply 1.2 by 13 to get 15.6.

We would have then regarded the expression as a *product*—the product of the factors $(x + 1)/(x - 1)$ and $(x + 2)$—and used the product rule instead. We can't escape the quotient rule, however: We need to use it to take the derivative of the first factor, $(x + 1)/(x - 1)$. Try this approach for practice and check that you get the same answer. ■

Calculation Thought Experiment

The **calculation thought experiment** is a technique to determine whether to treat an algebraic expression as a product, quotient, sum, or difference. Given an expression, consider the steps you would use in computing its value. If the last operation is multiplication, treat the expression as a product; if the last operation is division, treat the expression as a quotient; and so on.

Quick Examples

1. $(3x^2 - 4)(2x + 1)$ can be computed by first calculating the expressions in parentheses and then multiplying. Because the last step is multiplication, we can treat the expression as a product.

2. $\dfrac{2x - 1}{x}$ can be computed by first calculating the numerator and denominator and then dividing one by the other. Because the last step is division, we can treat the expression as a quotient.

3. $x^2 + (4x - 1)(x + 2)$ can be computed by first calculating x^2, then calculating the product $(4x - 1)(x + 2)$, and finally adding the two answers. Thus, we can treat the expression as a sum.

4. $(3x^2 - 1)^5$ can be computed by first calculating the expression in parentheses and then raising the answer to the fifth power. Thus, we can treat the expression as a power. (We shall see how to differentiate powers of expressions in Section 11.4.)

5. The expression $(x + 1)(x + 2)/(x - 1)$ can be treated as either a quotient or a product: We can write it as a quotient: $\dfrac{(x + 1)(x + 2)}{x - 1}$ or as a product: $(x + 1)\left(\dfrac{x + 2}{x - 1}\right)$. (See Example 6(b).)

EXAMPLE 7 **Using the Calculation Thought Experiment**

Find $\dfrac{d}{dx}\left[6x^2 + 5\left(\dfrac{x}{x-1}\right)\right]$.

Solution The calculation thought experiment tells us that the expression we are asked to differentiate can be treated as a *sum*. Because the derivative of a sum is the sum of the derivatives, we get

$$\frac{d}{dx}\left[6x^2 + 5\left(\frac{x}{x-1}\right)\right] = \frac{d}{dx}(6x^2) + \frac{d}{dx}\left[5\left(\frac{x}{x-1}\right)\right].$$

In other words, we must take the derivatives of $6x^2$ and $5\left(\dfrac{x}{x-1}\right)$ separately and then add the answers. The derivative of $6x^2$ is $12x$. There are two ways of taking the derivative of $5\left(\dfrac{x}{x-1}\right)$: We could either first multiply the expression $\left(\dfrac{x}{x-1}\right)$ by 5 to get $\left(\dfrac{5x}{x-1}\right)$ and then take its derivative using the quotient rule, or we could pull the 5 out, as we do next.

$$\frac{d}{dx}\left(6x^2 + 5\left(\frac{x}{x-1}\right)\right) = \frac{d}{dx}(6x^2) + \frac{d}{dx}\left[5\left(\frac{x}{x-1}\right)\right] \quad \text{Derivative of sum}$$

$$= 12x + 5\frac{d}{dx}\left(\frac{x}{x-1}\right) \quad \text{Constant} \times \text{Function}$$

$$= 12x + 5\left(\frac{(1)(x-1) - (x)(1)}{(x-1)^2}\right) \quad \text{Quotient rule}$$

$$= 12x + 5\left(\frac{-1}{(x-1)^2}\right)$$

$$= 12x - \frac{5}{(x-1)^2}$$

APPLICATIONS

In the next example, we return to a scenario similar to the one discussed at the start of this section.

EXAMPLE 8 **Applying the Product and Quotient Rules: Revenue and Average Cost**

Sales of your newly launched miniature wall posters for college dorms, *iMiniPosters,* are really taking off. (Those old-fashioned large wall posters no longer fit in today's "downsized" college dorm rooms.) Monthly sales to students at the start of this year were 1,500 iMiniPosters, and since that time, sales have been increasing by 300 posters each month, even though the price you charge has also been going up.

a. The price you charge for iMiniPosters is given by:

$$p(t) = 10 + 0.05t^2 \text{ dollars per poster,}$$

where t is time in months since the start of January of this year. Find a formula for the monthly revenue, and then compute its rate of change at the beginning of March.

b. The number of students who purchase iMiniPosters in a month is given by

$$n(t) = 800 + 0.2t,$$

where t is as in part (a). Find a formula for the average number of posters each student buys, and hence estimate the rate at which this number was growing at the beginning of March.

Solution

a. To compute monthly revenue as a function of time t, we use

$$R(t) = p(t)q(t). \qquad \text{Revenue = Price} \times \text{Quantity}$$

We already have a formula for $p(t)$. The function $q(t)$ measures sales, which were 1,500 posters/month at time $t = 0$, and rising by 300 per month:

$$q(t) = 1,500 + 300t.$$

Therefore, the formula for revenue is

$$R(t) = p(t)q(t)$$
$$R(t) = (10 + 0.05t^2)(1,500 + 300t).$$

Rather than expand this expression, we shall leave it as a product so that we can use the product rule in computing its rate of change:

$$R'(t) = p'(t)q(t) + p(t)q'(t)$$
$$= [0.10t][1,500 + 300t] + [10 + 0.05t^2][300].$$

Because the beginning of March corresponds to $t = 2$, we have

$$R'(2) = [0.10(2)][1,500 + 300(2)] + [10 + 0.05(2)^2][300]$$
$$= (0.2)(2,100) + (10.2)(300) = \$3,480 \text{ per month.}$$

Therefore, your monthly revenue was increasing at a rate of \$3,480 per month at the beginning of March.

b. The average number of posters sold to each student is

$$k(t) = \frac{\text{Number of posters}}{\text{Number of students}}$$

$$k(t) = \frac{q(t)}{n(t)} = \frac{1,500 + 300t}{800 + 0.2t}.$$

The rate of change of $k(t)$ is computed with the quotient rule:

$$k'(t) = \frac{q'(t)n(t) - q(t)n'(t)}{n(t)^2}$$

$$= \frac{(300)(800 + 0.2t) - (1,500 + 300t)(0.2)}{(800 + 0.2t)^2}$$

so that

$$k'(2) = \frac{(300)[800 + 0.2(2)] - [1,500 + 300(2)](0.2)}{[800 + 0.2(2)]^2}$$

$$= \frac{(300)(800.4) - (2,100)(0.2)}{800.4^2} \approx 0.37 \text{ posters/student per month.}$$

Therefore, the average number of posters sold to each student was increasing at a rate of about 0.37 posters/student per month.

11.3 EXERCISES

▼ more advanced   ◆ challenging

⊤ indicates exercises that should be solved using technology

In Exercises 1–12:

a. Calculate the derivative of the given function without using either the product or quotient rule.

b. Use the product or quotient rule to find the derivative. Check that you obtain the same answer. HINT [See Quick Examples on page 810.]

1. $f(x) = 3x$ **2.** $f(x) = 2x^2$

3. $g(x) = x \cdot x^2$ **4.** $g(x) = x \cdot x$

5. $h(x) = x(x + 3)$ **6.** $h(x) = x(1 + 2x)$

7. $r(x) = 100x^{2.1}$ **8.** $r(x) = 0.2x^{-1}$ **9.** $s(x) = \dfrac{2}{x}$

10. $t(x) = \dfrac{x}{3}$ **11.** $u(x) = \dfrac{x^2}{3}$ **12.** $s(x) = \dfrac{3}{x^2}$

Calculate $\dfrac{dy}{dx}$ in Exercises 13–20. Simplify your answer.
HINT [See Example 5.]

13. $y = 3x(4x^2 - 1)$ **14.** $y = 3x^2(2x + 1)$

15. $y = x^3(1 - x^2)$ **16.** $y = x^5(1 - x)$

17. $y = (2x + 3)^2$ **18.** $y = (4x - 1)^2$

19. $x\sqrt{x}$ **20.** $x^2\sqrt{x}$

Calculate $\dfrac{dy}{dx}$ in Exercises 21–50. You need not expand your answers.

21. $y = (x + 1)(x^2 - 1)$

22. $y = (4x^2 + x)(x - x^2)$

23. $y = (2x^{0.5} + 4x - 5)(x - x^{-1})$

24. $y = (x^{0.7} - 4x - 5)(x^{-1} + x^{-2})$

25. $y = (2x^2 - 4x + 1)^2$

26. $y = (2x^{0.5} - x^2)^2$

27. $y = \left(\dfrac{x}{3.2} + \dfrac{3.2}{x}\right)(x^2 + 1)$

28. $y = \left(\dfrac{x^{2.1}}{7} + \dfrac{2}{x^{2.1}}\right)(7x - 1)$

29. $x^2(2x + 3)(7x + 2)$ HINT [See Example 5b.]

30. $x(x^2 - 3)(2x^2 + 1)$ HINT [See Example 5b.]

31. $(5.3x - 1)(1 - x^{2.1})(x^{-2.3} - 3.4)$

32. $(1.1x + 4)(x^{2.1} - x)(3.4 - x^{-2.1})$

33. ▼ $y = (\sqrt{x} + 1)\left(\sqrt{x} + \dfrac{1}{x^2}\right)$

34. ▼ $y = (4x^2 - \sqrt{x})\left(\sqrt{x} - \dfrac{2}{x^2}\right)$

35. $y = \dfrac{2x + 4}{3x - 1}$ HINT [See Example 6.]

36. $y = \dfrac{3x - 9}{2x + 4}$ HINT [See Example 6.]

37. $y = \dfrac{2x^2 + 4x + 1}{3x - 1}$ **38.** $y = \dfrac{3x^2 - 9x + 11}{2x + 4}$

39. $y = \dfrac{x^2 - 4x + 1}{x^2 + x + 1}$ **40.** $y = \dfrac{x^2 + 9x - 1}{x^2 + 2x - 1}$

41. $y = \dfrac{x^{0.23} - 5.7x}{1 - x^{-2.9}}$ **42.** $y = \dfrac{8.43x^{-0.1} - 0.5x^{-1}}{3.2 + x^{2.9}}$

43. ▼ $y = \dfrac{\sqrt{x} + 1}{\sqrt{x} - 1}$ **44.** ▼ $y = \dfrac{\sqrt{x} - 1}{\sqrt{x} + 1}$

45. ▼ $y = \dfrac{\left(\dfrac{1}{x} + \dfrac{1}{x^2}\right)}{x + x^2}$ **46.** ▼ $y = \dfrac{\left(1 - \dfrac{1}{x^2}\right)}{x^2 - 1}$

47. $y = \dfrac{(x + 3)(x + 1)}{3x - 1}$ HINT [See Example 6b.]

48. $y = \dfrac{x}{(x - 5)(x - 4)}$ HINT [See Example 6b.]

49. $y = \dfrac{(x + 3)(x + 1)(x + 2)}{3x - 1}$

50. $y = \dfrac{3x - 1}{(x - 5)(x - 4)(x - 1)}$

In Exercises 51–56, compute the derivatives.

51. $\dfrac{d}{dx}[(x^2 + x)(x^2 - x)]$

52. $\dfrac{d}{dx}[(x^2 + x^3)(x + 1)]$

53. $\dfrac{d}{dx}[(x^3 + 2x)(x^2 - x)]\Big|_{x=2}$

54. $\dfrac{d}{dx}[(x^2 + x)(x^2 - x)]\Big|_{x=1}$

55. $\dfrac{d}{dt}[(t^2 - t^{0.5})(t^{0.5} + t^{-0.5})]\Big|_{t=1}$

56. $\dfrac{d}{dt}[(t^2 + t^{0.5})(t^{0.5} - t^{-0.5})]\Big|_{t=1}$

In Exercises 57–64 use the calculation thought experiment to say whether the expression is written as a sum, difference, scalar multiple, product, or quotient. Then use the appropriate rules to find its derivative. HINT [See Quick Examples on page 814 and Example 7.]

115

57. $y = x^4 - (x^2 + 120)(4x - 1)$

58. $y = x^4 - \dfrac{x^2 + 120}{4x - 1}$

59. $y = x + 1 + 2\left(\dfrac{x}{x + 1}\right)$

60. $y = (x + 2) - 4(x^2 - x)\left(x + \dfrac{1}{x}\right)$

(Do not simplify the answer.)

61. $y = (x + 2)\left(\dfrac{x}{x + 1}\right)$

(Do not simplify the answer.)

62. $y = \dfrac{(x + 2)x}{x + 1}$

(Do not simplify the answer.)

63. $y = (x + 1)(x - 2) - 2\left(\dfrac{x}{x + 1}\right)$

64. $y = \dfrac{x + 2}{x + 1} + (x + 1)(x - 2)$

In Exercises 65–70, find the equation of the line tangent to the graph of the given function at the point with the indicated x-coordinate.

65. $f(x) = (x^2 + 1)(x^3 + x); x = 1$

66. $f(x) = (x^{0.5} + 1)(x^2 + x); x = 1$

67. $f(x) = \dfrac{x + 1}{x + 2}; x = 0$ **68.** $f(x) = \dfrac{\sqrt{x} + 1}{\sqrt{x} + 2}; x = 4$

69. $f(x) = \dfrac{x^2 + 1}{x}; x = -1$ **70.** $f(x) = \dfrac{x}{x^2 + 1}; x = 1$

APPLICATIONS

71. Revenue The monthly sales of **Sunny Electronics'** new sound system are given by $q(t) = 2,000t - 100t^2$ units per month, t months after its introduction. The price Sunny charges is $p(t) = 1,000 - t^2$ dollars per sound system, t months after introduction. Find the rate of change of monthly sales, the rate of change of the price, and the rate of change of monthly revenue five months after the introduction of the sound system. Interpret your answers. HINT [See Example 8(a).]

72. Revenue The monthly sales of **Sunny Electronics'** new *iSun* walkman is given by $q(t) = 2,000t - 100t^2$ units per month, t months after its introduction. The price Sunny charges is $p(t) = 100 - t^2$ dollars per *iSun*, t months after introduction. Find the rate of change of monthly sales, the rate of change of the price, and the rate of change of monthly revenue six months after the introduction of the *iSun*. Interpret your answers. HINT [See Example 8(a).]

73. Saudi Oil Revenues The spot price of crude oil during the period 2000–2005 can be approximated by

$$P(t) = 5t + 25 \text{ dollars per barrel} \quad (0 \le t \le 5)$$

in year t, where $t = 0$ represents 2000. Saudi Arabia's crude oil production over the same period can be approximated by

$$Q(t) = 0.082t^2 - 0.22t + 8.2 \text{ million barrels per day.}[18]$$
$$(0 \le t \le 5)$$

Use these models to estimate Saudi Arabia's daily oil revenue and also its rate of change in 2001. (Round your answers to the nearest $1 million.)

74. Russian Oil Revenues Russia's crude oil production during the period 2000–2005 can be approximated by

$$Q(t) = -0.066t^2 + 0.96t + 6.1 \text{ million barrels per day}[19]$$
$$(0 \le t \le 5)$$

in year t, where $t = 0$ represents 2000. Use the model for the spot price in Exercise 73 to estimate Russia's daily oil revenue and also its rate of change in 2001.

75. Revenue Dorothy Wagner is currently selling 20 "I ♥ Calculus" T-shirts per day, but sales are dropping at a rate of 3 per day. She is currently charging $7 per T-shirt, but to compensate for dwindling sales, she is increasing the unit price by $1 per day. How fast, and in what direction is her daily revenue currently changing?

76. Pricing Policy Let us turn Exercise 75 around a little: Dorothy Wagner is currently selling 20 "I ♥ Calculus" T-shirts per day, but sales are dropping at a rate of 3 per day. She is currently charging $7 per T-shirt, and she wishes to increase her daily revenue by $10 per day. At what rate should she increase the unit price to accomplish this (assuming that the price increase does not affect sales)?

77. Bus Travel Thoroughbred Bus Company finds that its monthly costs for one particular year were given by $C(t) = 10,000 + t^2$ dollars after t months. After t months the company had $P(t) = 1,000 + t^2$ passengers per month. How fast is its cost per passenger changing after 6 months? HINT [See Example 8(b).]

78. Bus Travel Thoroughbred Bus Company finds that its monthly costs for one particular year were given by $C(t) = 100 + t^2$ dollars after t months. After t months, the company had $P(t) = 1,000 + t^2$ passengers per month. How fast is its cost per passenger changing after 6 months? HINT [See Example 8(b).]

79. Fuel Economy Your muscle car's gas mileage (in miles per gallon) is given as a function $M(x)$ of speed x in mph, where

$$M(x) = \dfrac{3,000}{x + 3,600x^{-1}}.$$

Calculate $M'(x)$, and then $M'(10)$, $M'(60)$, and $M'(70)$. What do the answers tell you about your car?

---

[18] Source for data: EIA/Saudi British Bank (www.sabb.com). 2004 figures are based on mid-year data, and 2005 data are estimates.

[19] Source for data: Energy Information Administration (www.eia.doe.gov), Pravda (http://english.pravda.ru). 2004 figures are based on mid-year data, and 2005 data are estimates.

80. *Fuel Economy* Your used Chevy's gas mileage (in miles per gallon) is given as a function $M(x)$ of speed x in mph, where

$$M(x) = \frac{4{,}000}{x + 3{,}025x^{-1}}.$$

Calculate $M'(x)$ and hence determine *the sign* of each of the following: $M'(40)$, $M'(55)$, and $M'(60)$. Interpret your results.

81. ▽*Oil Imports from Mexico* Daily oil production in Mexico and daily U.S. oil imports from Mexico during 2005–2009 can be approximated by

$$P(t) = 3.9 - 0.10t \text{ million barrels} \quad (5 \le t \le 9)$$
$$I(t) = 2.1 - 0.11t \text{ million barrels} \quad (5 \le t \le 9)$$

where t is time in years since the start of 2000.[20]

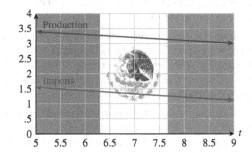

a. What are represented by the functions $P(t) - I(t)$ and $I(t)/P(t)$?

b. Compute $\left.\dfrac{d}{dt}\left[\dfrac{I(t)}{P(t)}\right]\right|_{t=8}$ to two significant digits. What

does the answer tell you about oil imports from Mexico?

82. ▽*Oil Imports from Mexico* Daily oil production in Mexico and daily U.S. oil imports from Mexico during 2000–2004 can be approximated by

$$P(t) = 3.0 + 0.13t \text{ million barrels} \quad (0 \le t \le 4)$$
$$I(t) = 1.4 + 0.06t \text{ million barrels} \quad (0 \le t \le 4)$$

where t is time in years since the start of 2000.[21]

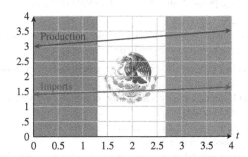

a. What are represented by the functions $P(t) - I(t)$ and $I(t)/P(t)$?

b. Compute $\left.\dfrac{d}{dt}\left[\dfrac{I(t)}{P(t)}\right]\right|_{t=3}$ to two significant digits. What

does the answer tell you about oil imports from Mexico?

83. ▽*Military Spending* The annual cost per active-duty armed service member in the United States increased from \$80,000 in 1995 to a projected \$120,000 in 2007. In 1995, there were 1.5 million armed service personnel, and this number was projected to decrease to 1.4 million in 2003.[22] Use linear models for annual cost and personnel to estimate, to the nearest \$10 million, the rate of change of total military personnel costs in 2002.

84. ▽*Military Spending in the 1990s* The annual cost per active-duty armed service member in the United States increased from \$80,000 in 1995 to \$90,000 in 2000. In 1990, there were 2 million armed service personnel and this number decreased to 1.5 million in 2000.[23] Use linear models for annual cost and personnel to estimate, to the nearest \$10 million, the rate of change of total military personnel costs in 1995.

85. ▽*Biology—Reproduction* The Verhulst model for population growth specifies the reproductive rate of an organism as a function of the total population according to the following formula:

$$R(p) = \frac{r}{1 + kp}$$

where p is the total population in thousands of organisms, r and k are constants that depend on the particular circumstances and the organism being studied, and $R(p)$ is the reproduction rate in thousands of organisms per hour.[24] If $k = 0.125$ and $r = 45$, find $R'(p)$ and then $R'(4)$. Interpret the result.

86. ▽*Biology—Reproduction* Another model, the predator satiation model for population growth, specifies that the reproductive rate of an organism as a function of the total population varies according to the following formula:

$$R(p) = \frac{rp}{1 + kp}$$

where p is the total population in thousands of organisms, r and k are constants that depend on the particular circumstances and the organism being studied, and $R(p)$ is the reproduction rate in new organisms per hour.[25] Given that $k = 0.2$ and $r = 0.08$, find $R'(p)$ and $R'(2)$. Interpret the result.

---

[20] Source for data: Energy Information Administration (www.eia.doe.gov)/Pemex.

[21] Ibid.

[22] Annual costs are adjusted for inflation. Sources: Department of Defense, Stephen Daggett, military analyst, Congressional Research Service/*New York Times*, April 19, 2002, p. A21.

[23] Ibid.

[24] Source: *Mathematics in Medicine and the Life Sciences* by F. C. Hoppensteadt and C. S. Peskin (Springer-Verlag, New York, 1992) pp. 20–22.

[25] Ibid.

87. ▼Embryo Development Bird embryos consume oxygen from the time the egg is laid through the time the chick hatches. For a typical galliform bird egg, the oxygen consumption (in milliliters) t days after the egg was laid can be approximated by[26]

$$C(t) = -0.016t^4 + 1.1t^3 - 11t^2 + 3.6t. \quad (15 \le t \le 30)$$

(An egg will usually hatch at around $t = 28$.) Suppose that at time $t = 0$ you have a collection of 30 newly laid eggs and that the number of eggs decreases linearly to zero at time $t = 30$ days. How fast is the total oxygen consumption of your collection of embryos changing after 25 days? (Round your answers to two significant digits.) Comment on the result. HINT [Total oxygen consumption = Oxygen consumption per egg × Number of eggs.]

88. ▼Embryo Development Turkey embryos consume oxygen from the time the egg is laid through the time the chick hatches. For a brush turkey, the oxygen consumption (in milliliters) t days after the egg was laid can be approximated by[27]

$$C(t) = -0.0071t^4 + 0.95t^3 - 22t^2 + 95t. \quad (25 \le t \le 50)$$

(An egg will typically hatch at around $t = 50$.) Suppose that at time $t = 0$ you have a collection of 100 newly laid eggs and that the number of eggs decreases linearly to zero at time $t = 50$ days. How fast is the total oxygen consumption of your collection of embryos changing after 40 days? (Round your answer to two significant digits.) Interpret the result. HINT [Total oxygen consumption = Oxygen consumption per egg × Number of eggs.]

COMMUNICATION AND REASONING EXERCISES

89. If f and g are functions of time, and at time $t = 3$, f equals 5 and is rising at a rate of 2 units per second, and g equals 4 and is rising at a rate of 5 units per second, then the product fg equals _____ and is rising at a rate of _____ units per second.

90. If f and g are functions of time, and at time $t = 2$, f equals 3 and is rising at a rate of 4 units per second, and g equals 5 and is rising at a rate of 6 units per second, then fg equals _____ and is rising at a rate of _____ units per second.

91. If f and g are functions of time, and at time $t = 3$, f equals 5 and is rising at a rate of 2 units per second, and g equals 4 and is rising at a rate of 5 units per second, then f/g equals _____ and is changing at a rate of _____ units per second.

92. If f and g are functions of time, and at time $t = 2$, f equals 3 and is rising at a rate of 4 units per second, and g equals 5 and is rising at a rate of 6 units per second, then f/g equals _____ and is changing at a rate of _____ units per second.

---

[26] The model is derived from graphical data published in the article "The Brush Turkey" by Roger S. Seymour, *Scientific American*, December, 1991, pp. 108–114.

[27] Ibid.

93. You have come across the following in a newspaper article: "Revenues of HAL Home Heating Oil Inc. are rising by $4.2 million per year. This is due to an annual increase of 70¢ per gallon in the price HAL charges for heating oil and an increase in sales of 6 million gallons of oil per year." Comment on this analysis.

94. Your friend says that because average cost is obtained by dividing the cost function by the number of units x, it follows that the derivative of average cost is the same as marginal cost because the derivative of x is 1. Comment on this analysis.

95. ▼Find a demand function $q(p)$ such that, at a price per item of $p = \$100$, revenue will rise if the price per item is increased.

96. ▼What must be true about a demand function $q(p)$ so that, at a price per item of $p = \$100$, revenue will decrease if the price per item is increased?

97. ▼You and I are both selling a steady 20 T-shirts per day. The price I am getting for my T-shirts is increasing twice as fast as yours, but your T-shirts are currently selling for twice the price of mine. Whose revenue is increasing faster: yours, mine, or neither? Explain.

98. ▼You and I are both selling T-shirts for a steady $20 per shirt. Sales of my T-shirts are increasing at twice the rate of yours, but you are currently selling twice as many as I am. Whose revenue is increasing faster: yours, mine, or neither? Explain.

99. ◆*Marginal Product (from the GRE Economics Test)* Which of the following statements about average product and marginal product is correct?

(A) If average product is decreasing, marginal product must be less than average product.

(B) If average product is increasing, marginal product must be increasing.

(C) If marginal product is decreasing, average product must be less than marginal product.

(D) If marginal product is increasing, average product must be decreasing.

(E) If marginal product is constant over some range, average product must be constant over that range.

100. ◆*Marginal Cost (based on a question from the GRE Economics Test)* Which of the following statements about average cost and marginal cost is correct?

(A) If average cost is increasing, marginal cost must be increasing.

(B) If average cost is increasing, marginal cost must be decreasing.

(C) If average cost is increasing, marginal cost must be more than average cost.

(D) If marginal cost is increasing, average cost must be increasing.

(E) If marginal cost is increasing, average cost must be larger than marginal cost.

11.4 The Chain Rule

We can now find the derivatives of expressions involving powers of x combined using addition, subtraction, multiplication, and division, but we still cannot take the derivative of an expression like $(3x + 1)^{0.5}$. For this we need one more rule. The function $h(x) = (3x + 1)^{0.5}$ is not a sum, difference, product, or quotient. To find out what it is, we can use the calculation thought experiment and think about the last operation we would perform in calculating $h(x)$.

1. Calculate $3x + 1$.

2. Take the 0.5 power (square root) of the answer.

The last operation is "take the 0.5 power." We do not yet have a rule for finding the derivative of the 0.5 power of a quantity other than x.

There is a way to build $h(x) = (3x + 1)^{0.5}$ out of two simpler functions: $u(x) = 3x + 1$ (the function that corresponds to the first step in the calculation above) and $f(x) = x^{0.5}$ (the function that corresponds to the second step):

$$h(x) = (3x + 1)^{0.5}$$
$$= [u(x)]^{0.5} \qquad u(x) = 3x + 1$$
$$= f(u(x)) \qquad f(x) = x^{0.5}$$

We say that h is the **composite** of f and u. We read $f(u(x))$ as "f of u of x."

To compute $h(1)$, say, we first compute $3 \cdot 1 + 1 = 4$ and then take the square root of 4, giving $h(1) = 2$. To compute $f(u(1))$ we follow exactly the same steps: First compute $u(1) = 4$ and then $f(u(1)) = f(4) = 2$. We always compute $f(u(x))$ numerically from the inside out: Given x, first compute $u(x)$ and then $f(u(x))$.

Now, f and u are functions *whose derivatives we know*. The *chain rule* allows us to use our knowledge of the derivatives of f and u to find the derivative of $f(u(x))$. For the purposes of stating the rule, let us avoid some of the nested parentheses by abbreviating $u(x)$ as u. Thus, we write $f(u)$ instead of $f(u(x))$ and remember that u is a function of x.

Chain Rule

If f is a differentiable function of u and u is a differentiable function of x, then the composite $f(u)$ is a differentiable function of x, and

$$\frac{d}{dx}[f(u)] = f'(u)\frac{du}{dx} \qquad \text{Chain Rule}$$

In words *The derivative of f(quantity) is the derivative of f, evaluated at that quantity, times the derivative of the quantity.*

Quick Examples

1. Take $f(u) = u^2$. Then

$$\frac{d}{dx}[u^2] = 2u\frac{du}{dx} \qquad \text{Because } f'(u) = 2u$$

The derivative of a quantity squared is two times the quantity, times the derivative of the quantity.

2. Take $f(u) = u^{0.5}$. Then

$$\frac{d}{dx}[u^{0.5}] = 0.5u^{-0.5}\frac{du}{dx} \qquad \text{Because } f'(u) = 0.5u^{-0.5}$$

The derivative of a quantity raised to the 0.5 is 0.5 times the quantity raised to the −0.5, times the derivative of the quantity.

As the quick examples illustrate, for every power of a function u whose derivative we know, we now get a "generalized" differentiation rule. The following table gives more examples.

Original Rule	Generalized Rule	In Words
$\dfrac{d}{dx}[x^2] = 2x$	$\dfrac{d}{dx}[u^2] = 2u\dfrac{du}{dx}$	The derivative of a quantity squared is twice the quantity, times the derivative of the quantity.
$\dfrac{d}{dx}[x^3] = 3x^2$	$\dfrac{d}{dx}[u^3] = 3u^2\dfrac{du}{dx}$	The derivative of a quantity cubed is 3 times the quantity squared, times the derivative of the quantity.
$\dfrac{d}{dx}\left(\dfrac{1}{x}\right) = -\dfrac{1}{x^2}$	$\dfrac{d}{dx}\left(\dfrac{1}{u}\right) = -\dfrac{1}{u^2}\dfrac{du}{dx}$	The derivative of 1 over a quantity is negative 1 over the quantity squared, times the derivative of the quantity.
Power Rule	**Generalized Power Rule**	**In Words**
$\dfrac{d}{dx}[x^n] = nx^{n-1}$	$\dfrac{d}{dx}[u^n] = nu^{n-1}\dfrac{du}{dx}$	The derivative of a quantity raised to the n is n times the quantity raised to the n − 1, times the derivative of the quantity.

To motivate the chain rule, let us see why it is true in the special case when $f(u) = u^3$, where the chain rule tells us that

$$\frac{d}{dx}[u^3] = 3u^2\frac{du}{dx} \qquad \text{Generalized Power Rule with } n = 3$$

But we could have done this using the product rule instead:

$$\frac{d}{dx}[u^3] = \frac{d}{dx}[u \cdot u \cdot u] = \frac{du}{dx}u \cdot u + u\frac{du}{dx}u + u \cdot u\frac{du}{dx} = 3u^2\frac{du}{dx}$$

Web Site

www.FiniteandCalc.org

Everything for Calculus

→ Chapter 11

→ Proof of Chain Rule

which gives us the same result. A similar argument works for $f(u) = u^n$ where $n = 2, 3, 4, \ldots$ We can then use the quotient rule and the chain rule for positive powers to verify the generalized power rule for *negative* powers as well. For the case of a general differentiable function f, the proof of the chain rule is beyond the scope of this book, but you can find one on the Web site by the path shown in the margin.

EXAMPLE 1 **Using the Chain Rule**

Compute the following derivatives.

a. $\dfrac{d}{dx}[(2x^2 + x)^3]$ **b.** $\dfrac{d}{dx}[(x^3 + x)^{100}]$ **c.** $\dfrac{d}{dx}\sqrt{3x + 1}$

Solution

a. Using the calculation thought experiment, we see that the last operation we would perform in calculating $(2x^2 + x)^3$ is that of *cubing*. Thus we think of $(2x^2 + x)^3$ as *a quantity cubed*. There are two similar methods we can use to calculate its derivative.

Method 1: Using the formula We think of $(2x^2 + x)^3$ as u^3, where $u = 2x^2 + x$. By the formula,

$$\frac{d}{dx}[u^3] = 3u^2 \frac{du}{dx} \qquad \text{Generalized Power Rule}$$

Now substitute for u:

$$\frac{d}{dx}[(2x^2 + x)^3] = 3(2x^2 + x)^2 \frac{d}{dx}(2x^2 + x)$$
$$= 3(2x^2 + x)^2(4x + 1)$$

Method 2: Using the verbal form If we prefer to use the verbal form, we get:

The derivative of $(2x^2 + x)$ cubed is three times $(2x^2 + x)$ squared, times the derivative of $(2x^2 + x)$.

In symbols,

$$\frac{d}{dx}[(2x^2 + x)^3] = 3(2x^2 + x)^2(4x + 1),$$

as we obtained above.

b. First, the calculation thought experiment: If we were computing $(x^3 + x)^{100}$, the last operation we would perform is *raising a quantity to the power* 100. Thus we are dealing with *a quantity raised to the power* 100, and so we must again use the generalized power rule. According to the verbal form of the generalized power rule, the derivative of a quantity raised to the power 100 is 100 times that quantity to the power 99, times the derivative of that quantity. In symbols,

$$\frac{d}{dx}[(x^3 + x)^{100}] = 100(x^3 + x)^{99}(3x^2 + 1).$$

c. We first rewrite the expression $\sqrt{3x + 1}$ as $(3x + 1)^{0.5}$ and then use the generalized power rule as in parts (a) and (b):

The derivative of a quantity raised to the 0.5 is 0.5 times the quantity raised to the −0.5, times the derivative of the quantity.

Thus,

$$\frac{d}{dx}[(3x + 1)^{0.5}] = 0.5(3x + 1)^{-0.5} \cdot 3 = 1.5(3x + 1)^{-0.5}.$$

➡ **Before we go on...** The following are examples of common errors in solving Example 1(b):

$$\text{"}\frac{d}{dx}[(x^3 + x)^{100}] = 100(3x^2 + 1)^{99}\text{"} \qquad \text{✗} \quad \textit{WRONG!}$$

$$\text{"}\frac{d}{dx}[(x^3 + x)^{100}] = 100(x^3 + x)^{99}\text{"} \qquad \text{✗} \quad \textit{WRONG!}$$

Remember that the generalized power rule says that the derivative of a quantity to the power 100 is 100 times *that same quantity* raised to the power 99, *times the derivative of that quantity*. ∎

Q : *It seems that there are now two formulas for the derivative of an nth power:*

1. $\dfrac{d}{dx}[x^n] = nx^{n-1}$

2. $\dfrac{d}{dx}[u^n] = nu^{n-1}\dfrac{du}{dx}$

Which one do I use?

A : Formula 1 is the original power rule, which applies only to a power of *x*. For instance, it applies to x^{10}, but it does not apply to $(2x+1)^{10}$ because the quantity that is being raised to a power is not *x*. Formula 2 applies to a power of any *function of x*, such as $(2x+1)^{10}$. It can even be used in place of the original power rule. For example, if we take $u = x$ in Formula 2, we obtain

$$\dfrac{d}{dx}[x^n] = nx^{n-1}\dfrac{dx}{dx}$$

$$= nx^{n-1} \qquad \text{The derivative of } x \text{ with respect to } x \text{ is 1.}$$

Thus, the generalized power rule really *is* a generalization of the original power rule, as its name suggests.

EXAMPLE 2 More Examples Using the Chain Rule

Find: **a.** $\dfrac{d}{dx}[(2x^5 + x^2 - 20)^{-2/3}]$ **b.** $\dfrac{d}{dx}\left[\dfrac{1}{\sqrt{x+2}}\right]$ **c.** $\dfrac{d}{dx}\left[\dfrac{1}{x^2+x}\right]$

Solution Each of the given functions is, or can be rewritten as, a power of a function whose derivative we know. Thus, we can use the method of Example 1.

a. $\dfrac{d}{dx}[(2x^5 + x^2 - 20)^{-2/3}] = -\dfrac{2}{3}(2x^5 + x^2 - 20)^{-5/3}(10x^4 + 2x)$

b. $\dfrac{d}{dx}\left[\dfrac{1}{\sqrt{x+2}}\right] = \dfrac{d}{dx}(x+2)^{-1/2} = -\dfrac{1}{2}(x+2)^{-3/2} \cdot 1 = -\dfrac{1}{2(x+2)^{3/2}}$

c. $\dfrac{d}{dx}\left[\dfrac{1}{x^2+x}\right] = \dfrac{d}{dx}(x^2+x)^{-1} = -(x^2+x)^{-2}(2x+1) = -\dfrac{2x+1}{(x^2+x)^2}$

➡ **Before we go on...** In Example 2(c), we could have used the quotient rule instead of the generalized power rule. We can think of the quantity $1/(x^2+x)$ in two different ways using the calculation thought experiment:

1. As 1 divided by something—in other words, as a quotient

2. As something raised to the -1 power

Of course, we get the same derivative using either approach. ■

We now look at some more complicated examples.

122

EXAMPLE 3 Harder Examples Using the Chain Rule

Find $\dfrac{dy}{dx}$ in each case.   **a.** $y = [(x + 1)^{-2.5} + 3x]^{-3}$ **b.** $y = (x + 10)^3 \sqrt{1 - x^2}$

Solution

a. The calculation thought experiment tells us that the last operation we would perform in calculating y is raising the quantity $[(x + 1)^{-2.5} + 3x]$ to the power -3. Thus, we use the generalized power rule.

$$\frac{dy}{dx} = -3[(x + 1)^{-2.5} + 3x]^{-4} \frac{d}{dx}[(x + 1)^{-2.5} + 3x]$$

We are not yet done; we must still find the derivative of $(x + 1)^{-2.5} + 3x$. Finding the derivative of a complicated function in several steps helps to keep the problem manageable. Continuing, we have

$$\frac{dy}{dx} = -3[(x + 1)^{-2.5} + 3x]^{-4} \frac{d}{dx}[(x + 1)^{-2.5} + 3x]$$

$$= -3[(x + 1)^{-2.5} + 3x]^{-4} \left[\frac{d}{dx}[(x + 1)^{-2.5}] + \frac{d}{dx}(3x) \right] \quad \text{Derivative of a sum}$$

Now we have two derivatives left to calculate. The second of these we know to be 3, and the first is the derivative of a quantity raised to the -2.5 power. Thus

$$\frac{dy}{dx} = -3[(x + 1)^{-2.5} + 3x]^{-4}[-2.5(x + 1)^{-3.5} \cdot 1 + 3].$$

b. The expression $(x + 10)^3 \sqrt{1 - x^2}$ is a product, so we use the product rule:

$$\frac{d}{dx}[(x + 10)^3 \sqrt{1 - x^2}] = \left(\frac{d}{dx}[(x + 10)^3] \right) \sqrt{1 - x^2} + (x + 10)^3 \left(\frac{d}{dx} \sqrt{1 - x^2} \right)$$

$$= 3(x + 10)^2 \sqrt{1 - x^2} + (x + 10)^3 \frac{1}{2\sqrt{1 - x^2}}(-2x)$$

$$= 3(x + 10)^2 \sqrt{1 - x^2} - \frac{x(x + 10)^3}{\sqrt{1 - x^2}}$$

APPLICATIONS

The next example is a new treatment of Example 3 from Section 11.2.

EXAMPLE 4 Marginal Product

Precision Manufacturers is informed by a consultant that its annual profit is given by

$$P = -200{,}000 + 4{,}000q - 0.46q^2 - 0.00001q^3$$

where q is the number of surgical lasers it sells each year. The consultant also informs Precision that the number of surgical lasers it can manufacture each year depends on the number n of assembly line workers it employs according to the equation

$$q = 100n \qquad \text{Each worker contributes 100 lasers per year.}$$

Use the chain rule to find the marginal product $\dfrac{dP}{dn}$.

123

Solution We could calculate the marginal product by substituting the expression for q in the expression for P to obtain P as a function of n (as given in Example 3 from Section 11.2) and then finding dP/dn. Alternatively—and this will simplify the calculation—we can use the chain rule. To see how the chain rule applies, notice that P is a function of q, where q in turn is given as a function of n. By the chain rule,

$$\frac{dP}{dn} = P'(q)\frac{dq}{dn} \qquad \text{Chain Rule}$$

$$= \frac{dP}{dq}\frac{dq}{dn} \qquad \text{Notice how the "quantities" } dq \text{ appear to cancel.}$$

Now we compute

$$\frac{dP}{dq} = 4{,}000 - 0.92q - 0.00003q^2$$

and $\quad \dfrac{dq}{dn} = 100.$

Substituting into the equation for $\dfrac{dP}{dn}$ gives

$$\frac{dP}{dn} = (4{,}000 - 0.92q - 0.00003q^2)(100)$$

$$= 400{,}000 - 92q - 0.003q^2$$

Notice that the answer has q as a variable. We can express dP/dn as a function of n by substituting $100n$ for q:

$$\frac{dP}{dn} = 400{,}000 - 92(100n) - 0.003(100n)^2$$

$$= 400{,}000 - 9{,}200n - 30n^2$$

The equation

$$\frac{dP}{dn} = \frac{dP}{dq}\frac{dq}{dn}$$

in the example above is an appealing way of writing the chain rule because it suggests that the "quantities" dq cancel. In general, we can write the chain rule as follows.

Chain Rule in Differential Notation

If y is a differentiable function of u, and u is a differentiable function of x, then

$$\frac{dy}{dx} = \frac{dy}{du}\frac{du}{dx}$$

Notice how the units cancel:

$$\frac{\text{Units of } y}{\text{Units of } x} = \frac{\text{Units of } y}{\text{Units of } u}\frac{\text{Units of } u}{\text{Units of } x}$$

1. If $y = u^3$, where $u = 4x + 1$, then

$$\frac{dy}{dx} = \frac{dy}{du}\frac{du}{dx} = 3u^2 \cdot 4 = 12u^2 = 12(4x + 1)^2.$$

2. If $q = 43p^2$ where p (and hence q also) is a differentiable function of t, then

$$\frac{dq}{dt} = \frac{dq}{dp}\frac{dp}{dt}$$

$$= 86p\frac{dp}{dt}. \qquad p \text{ is not specified, so we leave } dp/dt \text{ as is.}$$

You can see one of the reasons we still use Leibniz differential notation: The chain rule looks like a simple "cancellation" of du terms.

EXAMPLE 5 Marginal Revenue

Suppose a company's weekly revenue R is given as a function of the unit price p, and p in turn is given as a function of weekly sales q (by means of a demand equation). If

$$\left.\frac{dR}{dp}\right|_{q=1,000} = \$40 \text{ per } \$1 \text{ increase in price}$$

and

$$\left.\frac{dp}{dq}\right|_{q=1,000} = -\$20 \text{ per additional item sold per week}$$

find the marginal revenue when sales are 1,000 items per week.

Solution The marginal revenue is $\dfrac{dR}{dq}$. By the chain rule, we have

$$\frac{dR}{dq} = \frac{dR}{dp}\frac{dp}{dq} \qquad \begin{array}{l}\text{Units: Revenue per item}\\ = \text{Revenue per \$1 price increase} \times \text{price increase per additional item}\end{array}$$

Because we are interested in the marginal revenue at a demand level of 1,000 items per week, we have

$$\left.\frac{dR}{dq}\right|_{q=1,000} = (40)(-20) = -\$800 \text{ per additional item sold.}$$

Thus, if the price is lowered to increase the demand from 1,000 to 1,001 items per week, the weekly revenue will drop by approximately \$800.

Look again at the way the terms "du" appeared to cancel in the differential formula $\dfrac{dy}{dx} = \dfrac{dy}{du}\dfrac{du}{dx}$. In fact, the chain rule tells us more:

125

Manipulating Derivatives in Differential Notation

1. Suppose y is a function of x. Then, thinking of x as a function of y (as, for instance, when we can solve for x)* one has

✳ **NOTE** The notion of "thinking of x as a function of y" will be made more precise in Section 11.4.

$$\frac{dx}{dy} = \frac{1}{\left(\dfrac{dy}{dx}\right)}, \text{ provided } \frac{dy}{dx} \neq 0.$$ Notice again how $\frac{dy}{dx}$ behaves like a fraction.

Quick Example

In the demand equation $q = -0.2p - 8$, we have $\dfrac{dq}{dp} = -0.2$. Therefore,

$$\frac{dp}{dq} = \frac{1}{\left(\dfrac{dq}{dp}\right)} = \frac{1}{-0.2} = -5.$$

2. Suppose x and y are functions of t. Then, thinking of y as a function of x (as, for instance, when we can solve for t as a function of x, and hence obtain y as a function of x) one has

$$\frac{dy}{dx} = \frac{dy/dt}{dx/dt}.$$ The terms dt appear to cancel.

Quick Example

If $x = 3 - 0.2t$ and $y = 6 + 6t$, then

$$\frac{dy}{dx} = \frac{dy/dt}{dx/dt} = \frac{6}{-0.2} = -30.$$

To see why the above formulas work, notice that the second formula,

$$\frac{dy}{dx} = \frac{\left(\dfrac{dy}{dt}\right)}{\left(\dfrac{dx}{dt}\right)}$$

can be written as

$$\frac{dy}{dx}\frac{dx}{dt} = \frac{dy}{dt},$$ Multiply both sides by $\frac{dx}{dt}$.

which is just the differential form of the chain rule. For the first formula, use the second formula with y playing the role of t:

$$\frac{dy}{dx} = \frac{dy/dy}{dx/dy}$$

$$= \frac{1}{dx/dy}.$$ $\frac{dy}{dy} = \frac{d}{dy}[y] = 1$

126

FAQs

Using the Chain Rule

Q: *How do I decide whether or not to use the chain rule when taking a derivative?*

A: Use the calculation thought experiment (Section 11.3): Given an expression, consider the steps you would use in computing its value.

- If the last step is *raising a quantity to a power*, as in $\left(\dfrac{x^2 - 1}{x + 4}\right)^4$, then the first step to use is the chain rule (in the form of the generalized power rule):

$$\frac{d}{dx}\left(\frac{x^2 - 1}{x + 4}\right)^4 = 4\left(\frac{x^2 - 1}{x + 4}\right)^3 \frac{d}{dx}\left(\frac{x^2 - 1}{x + 4}\right).$$

Then use the appropriate rules to finish the computation. You may need to again use the calculation thought experiment to decide on the next step (here the quotient rule):

$$= 4\left(\frac{x^2 - 1}{x + 4}\right)^3 \frac{(2x)(x + 4) - (x^2 - 1)(1)}{(x + 4)^2}.$$

- If the last step is *division*, as in $\dfrac{(x^2 - 1)}{(3x + 4)^4}$, then the first step to use is the quotient rule:

$$\frac{d}{dx}\frac{(x^2 - 1)}{(3x + 4)^4} = \frac{(2x)(3x + 4)^4 - (x^2 - 1)\dfrac{d}{dx}(3x + 4)^4}{(3x + 4)^8}.$$

Then use the appropriate rules to finish the computation (here the chain rule):

$$= \frac{(2x)(3x + 4)^4 - (x^2 - 1)4(3x + 4)^3(3)}{(3x + 4)^8}.$$

- If the last step is *multiplication, addition, subtraction, or multiplication by a constant,* then the first rule to use is the product rule, or the rule for sums, differences, or constant multiples as appropriate.

Q: *Every time I compute a derivative, I leave something out. How do I make sure I am really done when taking the derivative of a complicated-looking expression?*

A: Until you are an expert at taking derivatives, the key is to use one rule at a time and write out each step, rather than trying to compute the derivative in a single step.

To illustrate this, try computing the derivative of $(x + 10)^3\sqrt{1 - x^2}$ in Example 3(b) in two ways: First try to compute it in a single step, and then compute it by writing out each step as shown in the example. How do your results compare? For more practice, try Exercises 83 and 84 following.

11.4 EXERCISES

▼ more advanced ◆ challenging
▣ indicates exercises that should be solved using technology

Calculate the derivatives of the functions in Exercises 1–46.
HINT [See Example 1.]

1. $f(x) = (2x + 1)^2$

2. $f(x) = (3x - 1)^2$

3. $f(x) = (x - 1)^{-1}$

4. $f(x) = (2x - 1)^{-2}$

5. $f(x) = (2 - x)^{-2}$

6. $f(x) = (1 - x)^{-1}$

7. $f(x) = (2x + 1)^{0.5}$

8. $f(x) = (-x + 2)^{1.5}$

9. $f(x) = (4x - 1)^{-1}$

10. $f(x) = (x + 7)^{-2}$

11. $f(x) = \dfrac{1}{3x - 1}$

12. $f(x) = \dfrac{1}{(x + 1)^2}$

13. $f(x) = (x^2 + 2x)^4$

14. $f(x) = (x^3 - x)^3$

15. $f(x) = (2x^2 - 2)^{-1}$

16. $f(x) = (2x^3 + x)^{-2}$

17. $g(x) = (x^2 - 3x - 1)^{-5}$

18. $g(x) = (2x^2 + x + 1)^{-3}$

19. $h(x) = \dfrac{1}{(x^2 + 1)^3}$

20. $h(x) = \dfrac{1}{(x^2 + x + 1)^2}$

HINT [See Example 2.]   HINT [See Example 2.]

21. $r(x) = (0.1x^2 - 4.2x + 9.5)^{1.5}$

22. $r(x) = (0.1x - 4.2x^{-1})^{0.5}$

23. $r(s) = (s^2 - s^{0.5})^4$

24. $r(s) = (2s + s^{0.5})^{-1}$

25. $f(x) = \sqrt{1 - x^2}$

26. $f(x) = \sqrt{x + x^2}$

27. $h(x) = 2[(x + 1)(x^2 - 1)]^{-1/2}$ HINT [See Example 3.]

28. $h(x) = 3[(2x - 1)(x - 1)]^{-1/3}$ HINT [See Example 3.]

29. $h(x) = (3.1x - 2)^2 - \dfrac{1}{(3.1x - 2)^2}$

30. $h(x) = \left[3.1x^2 - 2 - \dfrac{1}{3.1x - 2}\right]^2$

31. $f(x) = [(6.4x - 1)^2 + (5.4x - 2)^3]^2$

32. $f(x) = (6.4x - 3)^{-2} + (4.3x - 1)^{-2}$

33. $f(x) = (x^2 - 3x)^{-2}(1 - x^2)^{0.5}$

34. $f(x) = (3x^2 + x)(1 - x^2)^{0.5}$

35. $s(x) = \left(\dfrac{2x + 4}{3x - 1}\right)^2$

36. $s(x) = \left(\dfrac{3x - 9}{2x + 4}\right)^3$

37. $g(z) = \left(\dfrac{z}{1 + z^2}\right)^3$

38. $g(z) = \left(\dfrac{z^2}{1 + z}\right)^2$

39. $f(x) = [(1 + 2x)^4 - (1 - x)^2]^3$

40. $f(x) = [(3x - 1)^2 + (1 - x)^5]^2$

41. $t(x) = [2 + (x + 1)^{-0.1}]^{4.3}$

42. $t(x) = [(x + 1)^{0.1} - 4x]^{-5.1}$

43. ▼ $r(x) = \left(\sqrt{2x + 1} - x^2\right)^{-1}$

44. ▼ $r(x) = \left(\sqrt{x + 1} + \sqrt{x}\right)^3$

45. ▼ $f(x) = (1 + (1 + (1 + 2x)^3)^3)^3$

46. ▼ $f(x) = 2x + (2x + (2x + 1)^3)^3$

Find the indicated derivatives in Exercises 47–54. In each case, the independent variable is a (unspecified) function of t.
HINT [See Quick Example 2 on page 827.]

47. $y = x^{100} + 99x^{-1}$. Find $\dfrac{dy}{dt}$.

48. $y = x^{0.5}(1 + x)$. Find $\dfrac{dy}{dt}$.

49. $s = \dfrac{1}{r^3} + r^{0.5}$. Find $\dfrac{ds}{dt}$.

50. $s = r + r^{-1}$. Find $\dfrac{ds}{dt}$.

51. $V = \dfrac{4}{3}\pi r^3$. Find $\dfrac{dV}{dt}$.

52. $A = 4\pi r^2$. Find $\dfrac{dA}{dt}$.

53. ▼ $y = x^3 + \dfrac{1}{x}$, $x = 2$ when $t = 1$, $\left.\dfrac{dx}{dt}\right|_{t=1} = -1$

Find $\left.\dfrac{dy}{dt}\right|_{t=1}$.

54. ▼ $y = \sqrt{x} + \dfrac{1}{\sqrt{x}}$, $x = 9$ when $t = 1$, $\left.\dfrac{dx}{dt}\right|_{t=1} = -1$

Find $\left.\dfrac{dy}{dt}\right|_{t=1}$.

In Exercises 55–60, compute the indicated derivative using the chain rule. HINT [See Quick Examples on page 828.]

55. $y = 3x - 2$; $\dfrac{dx}{dy}$

56. $y = 8x + 4$; $\dfrac{dx}{dy}$

57. $x = 2 + 3t$, $y = -5t$; $\dfrac{dy}{dx}$

58. $x = 1 - t/2$, $y = 4t - 1$; $\dfrac{dy}{dx}$

59. $y = 3x^2 - 2x$; $\left.\dfrac{dx}{dy}\right|_{x=1}$

60. $y = 3x - \dfrac{2}{x}$; $\left.\dfrac{dx}{dy}\right|_{x=2}$

APPLICATIONS

61. *Marginal Product* Paramount Electronics has an annual profit given by

$$P = -100{,}000 + 5{,}000q - 0.25q^2$$

where q is the number of laptop computers it sells each year. The number of laptop computers it can make and sell each year depends on the number n of electrical engineers Paramount employs, according to the equation

$$q = 30n + 0.01n^2.$$

Use the chain rule to find $\left.\dfrac{dP}{dn}\right|_{n=10}$ and interpret the result. HINT [See Example 3.]

62. Marginal Product Refer back to Exercise 61. The average profit $\bar{P}$ per computer is given by dividing the total profit P by q:

$$\bar{P} = -\frac{100{,}000}{q} + 5{,}000 - 0.25q.$$

Determine the **marginal average product**, $d\bar{P}/dn$ at an employee level of 10 engineers. Interpret the result. HINT [See Example 3.]

63. Food Versus Education The percentage y (of total personal consumption) an individual spends on food is approximately

$$y = 35x^{-0.25} \text{ percentage points} \quad (6.5 \le x \le 17.5)$$

where x is the percentage the individual spends on education.[28] An individual finds that she is spending

$$x = 7 + 0.2t$$

percent of her personal consumption on education, where t is time in months since January 1. Use direct substitution to express the percentage y as a function of time t (do not simplify the expression) and then use the chain rule to estimate how fast the percentage she spends on food is changing on November 1. Be sure to specify the units.

64. Food Versus Recreation The percentage y (of total personal consumption) an individual spends on food is approximately

$$y = 33x^{-0.63} \text{ percentage points} \quad (2.5 \le x \le 4.5)$$

where x is the percentage the individual spends on recreation.[29] A college student finds that he is spending

$$x = 3.5 + 0.1t$$

percent of his personal consumption on recreation, where t is time in months since January 1. Use direct substitution to express the percentage y as a function of time t (do not simplify the expression) and then use the chain rule to estimate how fast the percentage he spends on food is changing on November 1. Be sure to specify the units.

65. Marginal Revenue The weekly revenue from the sale of rubies at **Royal Ruby Retailers (RRR)** is increasing at a rate of $40 per $1 increase in price, and the price is decreasing at a rate of $0.75 per additional ruby sold. What is the marginal revenue? (Be sure to state the units of measurement.) Interpret the result. HINT [See Example 5.]

66. Marginal Revenue The weekly revenue from the sale of emeralds at **Eduardo's Emerald Emporium (EEE)** is decreasing at a rate of €500 per €1 increase in price, and the price is decreasing at a rate of €0.45 per additional emerald sold.

What is the marginal revenue? (Be sure to state the units of measurement.) Interpret the result. HINT [See Example 5.]

67. Crime Statistics The murder rate in large cities (over 1 million residents) can be related to that in smaller cities (500,000–1,000,000 residents) by the following linear model:[30]

$$y = 1.5x - 1.9 \quad (15 \le x \le 25)$$

where y is the murder rate (in murders per 100,000 residents each year) in large cities and x is the murder rate in smaller cities. During the period 1991–1998, the murder rate in small cities was decreasing at an average rate of 2 murders per 100,000 residents each year. Use the chain rule to estimate how fast the murder rate was changing in larger cities during that period. (Show how you used the chain rule in your answer.)

68. Crime Statistics Following is a quadratic model relating the murder rates described in the preceding exercise:

$$y = 0.1x^2 - 3x + 39 \quad (15 \le x \le 25)$$

In 1996, the murder rate in smaller cities was approximately 22 murders per 100,000 residents each year and was decreasing at a rate of approximately 2.5 murders per 100,000 residents each year. Use the chain rule to estimate how fast the murder rate was changing for large cities. (Show how you used the chain rule in your answer.)

69. Existing Home Sales The following graph shows the approximate value of home prices and existing home sales in 2006–2010 as a percentage change from 2003, together with quadratic approximations.[31]

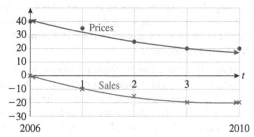

Home prices and sales of existing homes

The quadratic approximations are given by

Home Prices: $P(t) = t^2 - 10t + 41 \quad (0 \le t \le 4)$

Existing Home Sales: $S(t) = 1.5t^2 - 11t \quad (0 \le t \le 4)$

where t is time in years since the start of 2006. Use the chain rule to estimate $\left.\dfrac{dS}{dP}\right|_{t=2}$. What does the answer tell you about home sales and prices? HINT [See Quick Example 2 on page 828.]

[28] Model based on historical and projected data from 1908–2010. Sources: Historical data, Bureau of Economic Analysis; projected data, Bureau of Labor Statistics/*New York Times*, December 1, 2003, p. C2.
[29] Ibid.

[30] The model is a linear regression model. Source for data: Federal Bureau of Investigation, Supplementary Homicide Reports/*New York Times*, May 29, 2000, p. A12.
[31] Sources: Standard & Poors/Bloomberg Financial Markets/*New York Times*, September 29, 2007, p. C3. Projection is the authors'.

70. *Existing Home Sales* The following graph shows the approximate value of home prices and existing home sales in 2004–2007 as a percentage change from 2003, together with quadratic approximations.[32]

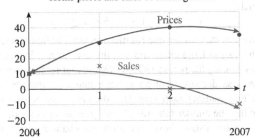

Home prices and sales of existing homes

The quadratic approximations are given by

Home Prices: $P(t) = -6t^2 + 27t + 10$ $(0 \le t \le 3)$

Existing Home Sales: $S(t) = -4t^2 + 4t + 11$ $(0 \le t \le 3)$

where t is time in years since the start of 2004. Use the chain rule to estimate $\left.\dfrac{dS}{dP}\right|_{t=2}$. What does the answer tell you about home sales and prices? HINT [See Quick Example 2 on page 828.]

71. ▼ *Pollution* An offshore oil well is leaking oil and creating a circular oil slick. If the radius of the slick is growing at a rate of 2 miles/hour, find the rate at which the area is increasing when the radius is 3 miles. (The area of a disc of radius r is $A = \pi r^2$.) HINT [See Quick Example 2 on page 828.]

72. ▼ *Mold* A mold culture in a dorm refrigerator is circular and growing. The radius is growing at a rate of 0.3 cm/day. How fast is the area growing when the culture is 4 centimeters in radius? (The area of a disc of radius r is $A = \pi r^2$.) HINT [See Quick Example 2 on page 828.]

73. ▼ *Budget Overruns* The Pentagon is planning to build a new, spherical satellite. As is typical in these cases, the specifications keep changing, so that the size of the satellite keeps growing. In fact, the radius of the planned satellite is growing 0.5 feet per week. Its cost will be $1,000 per cubic foot. At the point when the plans call for a satellite 10 feet in radius, how fast is the cost growing? (The volume of a solid sphere of radius r is $V = \frac{4}{3}\pi r^3$.)

74. ▼ *Soap Bubbles* The soap bubble I am blowing has a radius that is growing at a rate of 4 cm/s. How fast is the surface area growing when the radius is 10 cm? (The surface area of a sphere of radius r is $S = 4\pi r^2$.)

75. ▣ ▼ *Revenue Growth* The demand for the Cyberpunk II arcade video game is modeled by the logistic curve

$$q(t) = \frac{10{,}000}{1 + 0.5e^{-0.4t}}$$

where $q(t)$ is the total number of units sold t months after its introduction.

a. Use technology to estimate $q'(4)$.

b. Assume that the manufacturers of Cyberpunk II sell each unit for $800. What is the company's marginal revenue dR/dq?

c. Use the chain rule to estimate the rate at which revenue is growing 4 months after the introduction of the video game.

76. ▣ ▼ *Information Highway* The amount of information transmitted each month in the early years of the Internet (1988 to 1994) can be modeled by the equation

$$q(t) = \frac{2e^{0.69t}}{3 + 1.5e^{-0.4t}} \qquad (0 \le t \le 6)$$

where q is the amount of information transmitted each month in billions of data packets and t is the number of years since the start of 1988.[33]

a. Use technology to estimate $q'(2)$.

b. Assume that it costs $5 to transmit a million packets of data. What is the marginal cost $C'(q)$?

c. How fast was the cost increasing at the start of 1990?

Money Stock *Exercises 77–80 are based on the following demand function for money (taken from a question on the GRE Economics Test):*

$$M_d = 2 \times y^{0.6} \times r^{-0.3} \times p$$

where

$M_d = $ *demand for nominal money balances (money stock)*
$y = $ *real income*
$r = $ *an index of interest rates*
$p = $ *an index of prices*

*These exercises also use the idea of **percentage rate of growth**:*

$$\text{Percentage Rate of Growth of } M = \frac{\text{Rate of Growth of } M}{M}$$
$$= \frac{dM/dt}{M}$$

77. ◆ (from the GRE Economics Test) If the interest rate and price level are to remain constant while real income grows at 5 percent per year, the money stock must grow at what percent per year?

78. ◆ (from the GRE Economics Test) If real income and price level are to remain constant while the interest rate grows at 5 percent per year, the money stock must change by what percent per year?

79. ◆ (from the GRE Economics Test) If the interest rate is to remain constant while real income grows at 5 percent per year

---

[32] Sources: Standard & Poors /Bloomberg Financial Markets/*New York Times*, September 29, 2007, p. C3. Projection is the authors'.

[33] This is the authors' model, based on figures published in *New York Times*, Nov. 3, 1993.

and the price level rises at 5 percent per year, the money stock must grow at what percent per year?

80. ◆ (from the GRE Economics Test) If real income grows by 5 percent per year, the interest rate grows by 2 percent per year, and the price level drops by 3 percent per year, the money stock must change by what percent per year?

COMMUNICATION AND REASONING EXERCISES

81. Complete the following: The derivative of 1 over a glob is -1 over . . . .

82. Complete the following: The derivative of the square root of a glob is 1 over . . . .

83. Say why the following was marked wrong and give the correct answer.

$$\frac{d}{dx}[(3x^3 - x)^3] = 3(9x^2 - 1)^2 \quad ✗ \quad WRONG!$$

84. Say why the following was marked wrong and give the correct answer.

$$\frac{d}{dx}\left[\left(\frac{3x^2 - 1}{2x - 2}\right)^3\right] = 3\left(\frac{3x^2 - 1}{2x - 2}\right)^2\left(\frac{6x}{2}\right) \quad ✗ \quad WRONG!$$

85. Name two major errors in the following graded test question and give the correct answer.

$$\frac{d}{dx}\left[\left(\frac{3x^2 - 1}{2x - 2}\right)^3\right] = 3\left(\frac{6x}{2}\right)^2 \quad ✗ \quad WRONG! SEE ME!$$

86. Name two major errors in the following graded test question and give the correct answer.

$$\frac{d}{dx}[(3x^3 - x)(2x + 1)]^4 = 4[(9x^2 - 1)(2)]^3 \quad ✗ \quad WRONG! SEE ME!$$

87. ▼ Formulate a simple procedure for deciding whether to apply first the chain rule, the product rule, or the quotient rule when finding the derivative of a function.

88. ▼ Give an example of a function f with the property that calculating $f'(x)$ requires use of the following rules in the given order: (1) the chain rule, (2) the quotient rule, and (3) the chain rule.

89. ◆ Give an example of a function f with the property that calculating $f'(x)$ requires use of the chain rule five times in succession.

90. ◆ What can you say about composites of linear functions?

11.5 Derivatives of Logarithmic and Exponential Functions

At this point, we know how to take the derivative of any algebraic expression in x (involving powers, radicals, and so on). We now turn to the derivatives of logarithmic and exponential functions.

Derivative of the Natural Logarithm

$$\frac{d}{dx}[\ln x] = \frac{1}{x} \qquad \text{Recall that } \ln x = \log_e x.$$

Quick Examples

1. $\dfrac{d}{dx}[3 \ln x] = 3 \cdot \dfrac{1}{x} = \dfrac{3}{x}$ Derivative of a constant times a function

2. $\dfrac{d}{dx}[x \ln x] = 1 \cdot \ln x + x \cdot \dfrac{1}{x}$ Product rule, because $x \ln x$ is a product

       $= \ln x + 1.$

131

The above simple formula works only for the natural logarithm (the logarithm with base e). For logarithms with bases other than e, we have the following:

Derivative of the Logarithm with Base b

$$\frac{d}{dx}[\log_b x] = \frac{1}{x \ln b}$$ Notice that, if $b = e$, we get the same formula as previously.

Quick Examples

1. $\dfrac{d}{dx}[\log_3 x] = \dfrac{1}{x \ln 3} \approx \dfrac{1}{1.0986x}$

2. $\dfrac{d}{dx}[\log_2(x^4)] = \dfrac{d}{dx}(4\log_2 x)$ We used the logarithm identity $\log_b(x^r) = r\log_b x$.

$$= 4 \cdot \frac{1}{x \ln 2} \approx \frac{4}{0.6931x}$$

Derivation of the formulas $\dfrac{d}{dx}[\ln x] = \dfrac{1}{x}$ and $\dfrac{d}{dx}[\log_b x] = \dfrac{1}{x \ln b}$

To compute $\dfrac{d}{dx}[\ln x]$, we need to use the definition of the derivative. We also use properties of the logarithm to help evaluate the limit.

$$\frac{d}{dx}[\ln x] = \lim_{h \to 0} \frac{\ln(x+h) - \ln x}{h}$$ Definition of the derivative

$$= \lim_{h \to 0} \frac{1}{h}[\ln(x+h) - \ln x]$$ Algebra

$$= \lim_{h \to 0} \frac{1}{h} \ln\left(\frac{x+h}{x}\right)$$ Properties of the logarithm

$$= \lim_{h \to 0} \frac{1}{h} \ln\left(1 + \frac{h}{x}\right)$$ Algebra

$$= \lim_{h \to 0} \ln\left(1 + \frac{h}{x}\right)^{1/h}$$ Properties of the logarithm

which we rewrite as

$$\lim_{h \to 0} \ln\left[\left(1 + \frac{1}{(x/h)}\right)^{x/h}\right]^{1/x}.$$

As $h \to 0^+$, the quantity x/h is getting large and positive, and so the quantity in brackets is approaching e (see the definition of e in Section 9.2), which leaves us with

$$\ln[e]^{1/x} = \frac{1}{x} \ln e = \frac{1}{x}$$

NOTE We actually used the fact that the logarithm function is continuous when we took the limit.

which is the derivative we are after.* What about the limit as $h \to 0^-$? We will glide over that case and leave it for the interested reader to pursue.†

The rule for the derivative of $\log_b x$ follows from the fact that $\log_b x = \ln x / \ln b$.

If we were to take the derivative of the natural logarithm of a *quantity* (a function of x), rather than just x, we would need to use the chain rule:

†NOTE Here is an outline of the argument for negative h. Because x must be positive for $\ln x$ to be defined, we find that $x/h \to -\infty$ as $h \to 0^-$, and so we must consider the quantity $(1 + 1/m)^m$ for large negative m. It turns out the limit is still e (check it numerically!) and so the computation above still works.

Derivatives of Logarithms of Functions

Original Rule	*Generalized Rule*	*In Words*
$\frac{d}{dx}[\ln x] = \frac{1}{x}$	$\frac{d}{dx}[\ln u] = \frac{1}{u}\frac{du}{dx}$	The derivative of the natural logarithm of a quantity is 1 over that quantity, times the derivative of that quantity.
$\frac{d}{dx}[\log_b x] = \frac{1}{x \ln b}$	$\frac{d}{dx}[\log_b u] = \frac{1}{u \ln b}\frac{du}{dx}$	The derivative of the log to base b of a quantity is 1 over the product of $\ln b$ and that quantity, times the derivative of that quantity.

Quick Examples

§ NOTE If we were to evaluate $\ln(x^2 + 1)$, the last operation we would perform would be to take the natural logarithm of a quantity. Thus, the calculation thought experiment tells us that we are dealing with $\ln$ *of a quantity*, and so we need the generalized logarithm rule as stated above.

1. $\dfrac{d}{dx}\ln[x^2 + 1] = \dfrac{1}{x^2+1}\dfrac{d}{dx}(x^2+1)$ $u = x^2 + 1$ (See the margin note.§)

$$= \frac{1}{x^2+1}(2x) = \frac{2x}{x^2+1}$$

2. $\dfrac{d}{dx}\log_2[x^3 + x] = \dfrac{1}{(x^3+x)\ln 2}\dfrac{d}{dx}(x^3+x)$ $u = x^3 + x$

$$= \frac{1}{(x^3+x)\ln 2}(3x^2+1) = \frac{3x^2+1}{(x^3+x)\ln 2}$$

EXAMPLE 1 Derivative of Logarithmic Function

Find $\dfrac{d}{dx}[\ln\sqrt{x+1}]$.

Solution The calculation thought experiment tells us that we have the natural logarithm of a quantity, so

$$\frac{d}{dx}[\ln\sqrt{x+1}] = \frac{1}{\sqrt{x+1}}\frac{d}{dx}\sqrt{x+1} \qquad \frac{d}{dx}\ln u = \frac{1}{u}\frac{du}{dx}$$

$$= \frac{1}{\sqrt{x+1}}\cdot\frac{1}{2\sqrt{x+1}} \qquad \frac{d}{dx}\sqrt{u} = \frac{1}{2\sqrt{u}}\frac{du}{dx}$$

$$= \frac{1}{2(x+1)}.$$

➡ **Before we go on...** What happened to the square root in Example 1? As with many problems involving logarithms, we could have done this one differently and with less bother if we had simplified the expression $\ln\sqrt{x+1}$ using the properties of logarithms *before* differentiating. Doing this, we get

$$\ln\sqrt{x+1} = \ln(x+1)^{1/2} = \frac{1}{2}\ln(x+1). \qquad \text{Simplify the logarithm first.}$$

Thus,

$$\frac{d}{dx}[\ln\sqrt{x+1}] = \frac{d}{dx}\left[\frac{1}{2}\ln(x+1)\right]$$

$$= \frac{1}{2}\left(\frac{1}{x+1}\right)\cdot 1 = \frac{1}{2(x+1)},$$

the same answer as above. ∎

EXAMPLE 2 **Derivative of a Logarithmic Function**

Find $\dfrac{d}{dx}[\ln[(1+x)(2-x)]]$.

Solution This time, we simplify the expression $\ln[(1+x)(2-x)]$ before taking the derivative.

$$\ln[(1+x)(2-x)] = \ln(1+x) + \ln(2-x) \qquad \text{Simplify the logarithm first.}$$

Thus,

$$\frac{d}{dx}[\ln[(1+x)(2-x)]] = \frac{d}{dx}[\ln(1+x)] + \frac{d}{dx}\ln(2-x)]$$

$$= \frac{1}{1+x} - \frac{1}{2-x} \qquad \text{Because } \frac{d}{dx}\ln(2-x) = -\frac{1}{2-x}$$

$$= \frac{1-2x}{(1+x)(2-x)}.$$

➡ **Before we go on...** For practice, try doing Example 2 without simplifying first. What other differentiation rule do you need to use? ∎

EXAMPLE 3 Logarithm of an Absolute Value

Find $\dfrac{d}{dx}[\ln|x|]$.

Solution Before we start, we note that $\ln x$ is defined only for positive values of x, so its domain is the set of positive real numbers. The domain of $\ln|x|$, on the other hand, is the set of *all* nonzero real numbers. For example, $\ln|-2| = \ln 2 \approx 0.6931$. For this reason, $\ln|x|$ often turns out to be more useful than the ordinary logarithm function.

Now we'll get to work. The calculation thought experiment tells us that $\ln|x|$ is the natural logarithm of a quantity, so we use the chain rule:

$$\frac{d}{dx}[\ln|x|] = \frac{1}{|x|}\frac{d}{dx}|x| \qquad u = |x|$$

$$= \frac{1}{|x|}\frac{|x|}{x} \qquad \text{Recall that } \frac{d}{dx}|x| = \frac{|x|}{x}.$$

$$= \frac{1}{x}.$$

➡ **Before we go on...** Figure 7(a) shows the graphs of $y = \ln|x|$ and $y = 1/x$. Figure 7(b) shows the graphs of $y = \ln|x|$ and $y = 1/|x|$. You should be able to see from these graphs why the derivative of $\ln|x|$ is $1/x$ and not $1/|x|$.

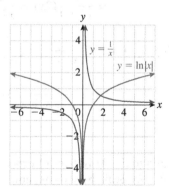

Figure 7(a)

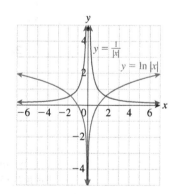

Figure 7(b)

This last example, in conjunction with the chain rule, gives us the following formulas.

Derivative of Logarithms of Absolute Values

Original Rule	Generalized Rule	In Words
$\dfrac{d}{dx}[\ln|x|] = \dfrac{1}{x}$	$\dfrac{d}{dx}[\ln|u|] = \dfrac{1}{u}\dfrac{du}{dx}$	The derivative of the natural logarithm of the absolute value of a quantity is 1 over that quantity, times the derivative of that quantity.
$\dfrac{d}{dx}[\log_b|x|] = \dfrac{1}{x\ln b}$	$\dfrac{d}{dx}[\log_b|u|] = \dfrac{1}{u\ln b}\dfrac{du}{dx}$	The derivative of the log to base b of the absolute value of a quantity is 1 over the product of $\ln b$ and that quantity, times the derivative of that quantity.

Note: Compare the above formulas with those on page 835. They tell us that we can simply ignore the absolute values in $\ln|u|$ or $\log_b|u|$ when taking the derivative.

Quick Examples

1. $\dfrac{d}{dx}[\ln|x^2 + 1|] = \dfrac{1}{x^2+1}\dfrac{d}{dx}(x^2+1)$ $u = x^2+1$

$$= \dfrac{1}{x^2+1}(2x) = \dfrac{2x}{x^2+1}$$

2. $\dfrac{d}{dx}[\log_2|x^3 + x|] = \dfrac{1}{(x^3+x)\ln 2}\dfrac{d}{dx}(x^3+x)$ $u = x^3 + x$

$$= \dfrac{1}{(x^3+x)\ln 2}(3x^2+1) = \dfrac{3x^2+1}{(x^3+x)\ln 2}$$

We now turn to the derivatives of *exponential* functions—that is, functions of the form $f(x) = b^x$. We begin by showing how *not* to differentiate them.

Caution The derivative of b^x is *not* xb^{x-1}. The power rule applies only to *constant* exponents. In this case the exponent is decidedly *not* constant, and so the power rule does not apply.

The following shows the correct way of differentiating b^x, beginning with a special case.

Derivative of e^x

$$\frac{d}{dx}[e^x] = e^x$$

Quick Examples

1. $\dfrac{d}{dx}[3e^x] = 3\dfrac{d}{dx}[e^x] = 3e^x$

2. $\dfrac{d}{dx}\left[\dfrac{e^x}{x}\right] = \dfrac{e^x x - e^x(1)}{x^2}$ Quotient rule

$$= \frac{e^x(x-1)}{x^2}$$

✱ NOTE There is another—very simple—function that is its own derivative. What is it?

Thus, e^x has the amazing property that its derivative is itself!✱ For bases other than e, we have the following generalization:

Derivative of b^x

If b is any positive number, then

$$\frac{d}{dx}[b^x] = b^x \ln b.$$

Note that if $b = e$, we obtain the previous formula.

Quick Example

$$\frac{d}{dx}[3^x] = 3^x \ln 3$$

Derivation of the formula $\dfrac{d}{dx}[e^x] = e^x$

✱ NOTE This shortcut is an example of a technique called *logarithmic differentiation*, which is occasionally useful. We will see it again in the next section.

To find the derivative of e^x we use a shortcut.✱ Write $g(x) = e^x$. Then

$$\ln g(x) = x.$$

Take the derivative of both sides of this equation to get

$$\frac{g'(x)}{g(x)} = 1$$

or

$$g'(x) = g(x) = e^x.$$

In other words, the exponential function with base e is its own derivative. The rule for exponential functions with other bases follows from the equality $b^x = e^{x \ln b}$ (why?) and the chain rule. (Try it.)

If we were to take the derivative of e raised to a *quantity*, not just x, we would need to use the chain rule, as follows.

Derivatives of Exponentials of Functions

Original Rule	*Generalized Rule*	*In Words*
$\dfrac{d}{dx}[e^x] = e^x$	$\dfrac{d}{dx}[e^u] = e^u \dfrac{du}{dx}$	*The derivative of e raised to a quantity is e raised to that quantity, times the derivative of that quantity.*
$\dfrac{d}{dx}[b^x] = b^x \ln b$	$\dfrac{d}{dx}[b^u] = b^u \ln b \dfrac{du}{dx}$	*The derivative of b raised to a quantity is b raised to that quantity, times ln b, times the derivative of that quantity.*

Quick Examples

✳ **NOTE** The calculation thought experiment tells us that we have e raised to a quantity.

1. $\dfrac{d}{dx}\left[e^{x^2+1}\right] = e^{x^2+1} \dfrac{d}{dx}\left[x^2 + 1\right]$ $\quad u = x^2 + 1$ (See margin note.✳)

   $= e^{x^2+1}(2x) = 2x\, e^{x^2+1}$

2. $\dfrac{d}{dx}[2^{3x}] = 2^{3x} \ln 2 \dfrac{d}{dx}[3x]$ $\quad u = 3x$

   $= 2^{3x}(\ln 2)(3) = (3 \ln 2)2^{3x}$

3. $\dfrac{d}{dt}[30e^{1.02t}] = 30e^{1.02t}(1.02) = 30.6e^{1.02t}$ $\quad u = 1.02t$

4. If \$1,000 is invested in an account earning 5% per year compounded continuously, then the rate of change of the account balance after t years is

   $$\frac{d}{dt}[1,000e^{0.05t}] = 1,000(0.05)e^{0.05t} = 50e^{0.05t} \text{ dollars/year.}$$

APPLICATIONS

EXAMPLE 4 Epidemics

In the early stages of the AIDS epidemic during the 1980s, the number of cases in the United States was increasing by about 50% every 6 months. By the start of 1983, there were approximately 1,600 AIDS cases in the United States.✳ Had this trend continued, how many new cases per year would have been occurring by the start of 1993?

✳ Data based on regression of 1982–1986 figures. Source for data: Centers for Disease Control and Prevention. HIV/AIDS Surveillance Report, 2000;12 (No. 2).

Solution To find the answer, we must first model this exponential growth using the methods of Chapter 9. Referring to Example 4 in Section 9.2, we find that t years after the start of 1983 the number of cases is

$$A = 1,600(2.25^t).$$

We are asking for the number of new cases each year. In other words, we want the rate of change, dA/dt:

$$\frac{dA}{dt} = 1,600(2.25)^t \ln 2.25 \text{ cases per year.}$$

At the start of 1993, $t = 10$, so the number of new cases per year is

$$\left.\frac{dA}{dt}\right|_{r=10} = 1,600(2.25)^{10} \ln 2.25 \approx 4,300,000 \text{ cases per year.}$$

➡ **Before we go on...** In Example 4, the figure for the number of new cases per year is so large because we assumed that exponential growth—the 50% increase every six months—would continue. A more realistic model for the spread of a disease is the logistic model. (See Section 9.4, as well as the next example.) ■

Photononstop/Superstock

EXAMPLE 5 Sales Growth

The sales of the Cyberpunk II video game can be modeled by the logistic curve

$$q(t) = \frac{10,000}{1 + 0.5e^{-0.4t}}$$

where $q(t)$ is the total number of units sold t months after its introduction. How fast is the game selling 2 years after its introduction?

Solution We are asked for $q'(24)$. We can find the derivative of $q(t)$ using the quotient rule, or we can first write

$$q(t) = 10,000(1 + 0.5e^{-0.4t})^{-1}$$

and then use the generalized power rule:

$$q'(t) = -10,000(1 + 0.5e^{-0.4t})^{-2}(0.5e^{-0.4t})(-0.4)$$
$$= \frac{2,000e^{-0.4t}}{(1 + 0.5e^{-0.4t})^2}.$$

Thus,

$$q'(24) = \frac{2,000e^{-0.4(24)}}{(1 + 0.5e^{-0.4(24)})^2} \approx 0.135 \text{ units per month.}$$

So, after 2 years, sales are quite slow.

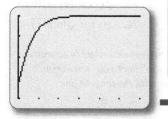

Figure 8

➡ **Before we go on...** We can check the answer in Example 5 graphically. If we plot the total sales curve for $0 \le t \le 30$ and $6,000 \le q \le 10,000$, on a TI-83/84 Plus, for example, we get the graph shown in Figure 8. Notice that total sales level off at about

* NOTE We can also say this using limits:
$$\lim_{t \to +\infty} q(t) = 10,000.$$

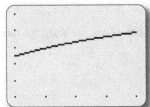

Figure 9

10,000 units.* We computed $q'(24)$, which is the slope of the curve at the point with t-coordinate 24. If we zoom in to the portion of the curve near $t = 24$, we obtain the graph shown in Figure 9, with $23 \le t \le 25$ and $9{,}999 \le q \le 10{,}000$. The curve is almost linear in this range. If we use the two endpoints of this segment of the curve, $(23, 9{,}999.4948)$ and $(25, 9{,}999.7730)$, we can approximate the derivative as

$$\frac{9{,}999.7730 - 9{,}999.4948}{25 - 23} = 0.1391$$

which is accurate to two decimal places. ∎

11.5 EXERCISES

▼ more advanced ◆ challenging
⬚ indicates exercises that should be solved using technology

Find the derivatives of the functions in Exercises 1–76. HINT [See Quick Examples on page 835.]

1. $f(x) = \ln(x - 1)$
2. $f(x) = \ln(x + 3)$
3. $f(x) = \log_2 x$
4. $f(x) = \log_3 x$
5. $g(x) = \ln|x^2 + 3|$
6. $g(x) = \ln|2x - 4|$
7. $h(x) = e^{x+3}$
   HINT [See Quick Examples on page 840.]
8. $h(x) = e^{x^2}$
   HINT [See Quick Examples on page 840.]
9. $f(x) = e^{-x}$
10. $f(x) = e^{1-x}$
11. $g(x) = 4^x$
12. $g(x) = 5^x$
13. $h(x) = 2^{x^2-1}$
14. $h(x) = 3^{x^2-x}$
15. $f(x) = x \ln x$
16. $f(x) = 3 \ln x$
17. $f(x) = (x^2 + 1) \ln x$
18. $f(x) = (4x^2 - x) \ln x$
19. $f(x) = (x^2 + 1)^5 \ln x$
20. $f(x) = (x + 1)^{0.5} \ln x$
21. $g(x) = \ln|3x - 1|$
22. $g(x) = \ln|5 - 9x|$
23. $g(x) = \ln|2x^2 + 1|$
24. $g(x) = \ln|x^2 - x|$
25. $g(x) = \ln(x^2 - 2.1x^{0.3})$
26. $g(x) = \ln(x - 3.1x^{-1})$
27. $h(x) = \ln[(-2x + 1)(x + 1)]$
28. $h(x) = \ln[(3x + 1)(-x + 1)]$
29. $h(x) = \ln\left(\dfrac{3x + 1}{4x - 2}\right)$
30. $h(x) = \ln\left(\dfrac{9x}{4x - 2}\right)$
31. $r(x) = \ln\left|\dfrac{(x + 1)(x - 3)}{-2x - 9}\right|$
32. $r(x) = \ln\left|\dfrac{-x + 1}{(3x - 4)(x - 9)}\right|$
33. $s(x) = \ln(4x - 2)^{1.3}$
34. $s(x) = \ln(x - 8)^{-2}$
35. $s(x) = \ln\left|\dfrac{(x + 1)^2}{(3x - 4)^3(x - 9)}\right|$
36. $s(x) = \ln\left|\dfrac{(x + 1)^2(x - 3)^4}{2x + 9}\right|$
37. $h(x) = \log_2(x + 1)$
38. $h(x) = \log_3(x^2 + x)$

39. $r(t) = \log_3(t + 1/t)$
40. $r(t) = \log_3\left(t + \sqrt{t}\right)$
41. $f(x) = (\ln|x|)^2$
42. $f(x) = \dfrac{1}{\ln|x|}$
43. $r(x) = \ln(x^2) - [\ln(x - 1)]^2$
44. $r(x) = (\ln(x^2))^2$
45. $f(x) = xe^x$
46. $f(x) = 2e^x - x^2 e^x$
47. $r(x) = \ln(x + 1) + 3x^3 e^x$
48. $r(x) = \ln|x + e^x|$
49. $f(x) = e^x \ln|x|$
50. $f(x) = e^x \log_2|x|$
51. $f(x) = e^{2x+1}$
52. $f(x) = e^{4x-5}$
53. $h(x) = e^{x^2-x+1}$
54. $h(x) = e^{2x^2-x+1/x}$
55. $s(x) = x^2 e^{2x-1}$
56. $s(x) = \dfrac{e^{4x-1}}{x^3 - 1}$
57. $r(x) = (e^{2x-1})^2$
58. $r(x) = (e^{2x^2})^3$
59. $t(x) = 3^{2x-4}$
60. $t(x) = 4^{-x+5}$
61. $v(x) = 3^{2x+1} + e^{3x+1}$
62. $v(x) = e^{2x} 4^{2x}$
63. $u(x) = \dfrac{3^{x^2}}{x^2 + 1}$
64. $u(x) = (x^2 + 1)4^{x^2-1}$
65. $g(x) = \dfrac{e^x + e^{-x}}{e^x - e^{-x}}$
66. $g(x) = \dfrac{1}{e^x + e^{-x}}$
67. ▼ $g(x) = e^{3x-1} e^{x-2} e^x$
68. ▼ $g(x) = e^{-x+3} e^{2x-1} e^{-x+11}$
69. ▼ $f(x) = \dfrac{1}{x \ln x}$
70. ▼ $f(x) = \dfrac{e^{-x}}{xe^x}$
71. ▼ $f(x) = [\ln(e^x)]^2 - \ln[(e^x)^2]$
72. ▼ $f(x) = e^{\ln x} - e^{2\ln(x^2)}$
73. ▼ $f(x) = \ln|\ln x|$
74. ▼ $f(x) = \ln|\ln|\ln x||$
75. ▼ $s(x) = \ln\sqrt{\ln x}$
76. ▼ $s(x) = \sqrt{\ln(\ln x)}$

Find the equations of the straight lines described in Exercises 77–82. Use graphing technology to check your answers by plotting the given curve together with the tangent line.

77. Tangent to $y = e^x \log_2 x$ at the point $(1, 0)$
78. Tangent to $y = e^x + e^{-x}$ at the point $(0, 2)$
79. Tangent to $y = \ln\sqrt{2x + 1}$ at the point where $x = 0$
80. Tangent to $y = \ln\sqrt{2x^2 + 1}$ at the point where $x = 1$

140

81. At right angles to $y = e^{x^2}$ at the point where $x = 1$

82. At right angles to $y = \log_2(3x + 1)$ at the point where $x = 1$

APPLICATIONS

83. ***Research and Development: Industry*** The total spent on research and development by industry in the United States during 1995–2007 can be approximated by

$$S(t) = 57.5 \ln t + 31 \text{ billion dollars} \quad (5 \le t \le 19)$$

where t is the year since 1990.[34] What was the total spent in 2000 ($t = 10$) and how fast was it increasing? HINT [See Quick Examples on page 833.]

84. ***Research and Development: Federal*** The total spent on research and development by the federal government in the United States during 1995–2007 can be approximated by

$$S(t) = 7.4 \ln t + 3 \text{ billion dollars} \quad (5 \le t \le 19)$$

where t is the year since 1990.[35] What was the total spent in 2005 ($t = 15$) and how fast was it increasing? HINT [See Quick Examples on page 833.]

85. ***Research and Development: Industry*** The function $S(t)$ in Exercise 83 can also be written (approximately) as

$$S(t) = 57.5 \ln (1.71t + 17.1) \text{ billion dollars}$$
$$(-5 \le t \le 9)$$

where this time t is the year since 2000. Use this alternative formula to estimate the amount spent in 2000 and its rate of change, and check your answers by comparing it with those in Exercise 83.

86. ***Research and Development: Federal*** The function $S(t)$ in Exercise 84 can also be written (approximately) as

$$S(t) = 7.4 \ln (1.5t + 15) \text{ billion dollars}$$
$$(-5 \le t \le 9)$$

where this time t is the year since 2000. Use this alternative formula to estimate the amount spent in 2005 and its rate of change, and check your answers by comparing it with those in Exercise 84.

87. ▼ ***Carbon Dating*** The age in years of a specimen that originally contained 10g of carbon 14 is given by

$$y = \log_{0.999879}(0.1x)$$

where x is the amount of carbon 14 it currently contains. Compute $\dfrac{dy}{dx}\bigg|_{x=5}$ and interpret your answer. HINT [For the calculation, see Quick Examples on page 835.]

88. ▼ ***Iodine Dating*** The age in years of a specimen that originally contained 10g of iodine 131 is given by

$$y = \log_{0.999567}(0.1x)$$

where x is the amount of iodine 131 it currently contains. Compute $\dfrac{dy}{dx}\bigg|_{x=8}$ and interpret your answer. HINT [For the calculation, see Quick Examples on page 835.]

89. ***New York City Housing Costs: Downtown*** The average price of a two-bedroom apartment in downtown New York City during the real estate boom from 1994 to 2004 can be approximated by

$$p(t) = 0.33e^{0.16t} \text{ million dollars} \quad (0 \le t \le 10)$$

where t is time in years ($t = 0$ represents 1994).[36] What was the average price of a two-bedroom apartment in downtown New York City in 2003, and how fast was it increasing? (Round your answers to two significant digits.) HINT [See Quick Example 3 on page 840.]

90. ***New York City Housing Costs: Uptown*** The average price of a two-bedroom apartment in uptown New York City during the real estate boom from 1994 to 2004 can be approximated by

$$p(t) = 0.14e^{0.10t} \text{ million dollars} \quad (0 \le t \le 10)$$

where t is time in years ($t = 0$ represents 1994).[37] What was the average price of a two-bedroom apartment in uptown New York City in 2002, and how fast was it increasing? (Round your answers to two significant digits.) HINT [See Quick Example 3 on page 840.]

91. ***Big Brother*** The following chart shows the total number of wiretaps authorized each year by U.S. state and federal courts from 1990 to 2007 ($t = 0$ represents 1990):[38]

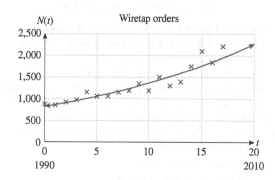

These data can be approximated with the model (shown on the graph)

$$N(t) = 820e^{0.051t}. \quad (0 \le t \le 17)$$

[34] Spending is in constant 2000 dollars. Source for data through 2006: National Science Foundation, Division of Science Resources Statistics, National Patterns of R&D Resources (www.nsf.gov/statistics) August 2008.

[35] Federal funding excluding grants to industry and nonprofit organizations. Spending is in constant 2000 dollars. Source for data through 2006: National Science Foundation, Division of Science Resources Statistics, National Patterns of R&D Resources (www.nsf.gov/statistics) August 2008.

[36] Model is based on a exponential regression. Source for data: Miller Samuel/*New York Times*, March 28, 2004, p. RE 11.

[37] Ibid.

[38] Source for data: 2007 Wiretap Report, Administrative Office of the United States Courts (www.uscourts.gov/wiretap07/2007WTText.pdf).

a. Find $N(15)$ and $N'(15)$. Be sure to state the units of measurement. To how many significant digits should we round the answers? Why?

b. The number of people whose communications are intercepted averages around 100 per wiretap order.[39] What does the answer to part (a) tell you about the number of people whose communications were intercepted?[40]

c. According to the model, the number of wiretaps orders each year (choose one):

(A) increased at a linear rate
(B) decreased at a quadratic rate
(C) increased at an exponential rate
(D) increased at a logarithmic rate

over the period shown.

92. *Big Brother* The following chart shows the number of wiretaps authorized each year by U.S. state courts from 1990 to 2007 ($t = 0$ represents 1990):[41]

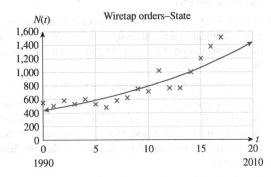

Wiretap orders–State

These data can be approximated with the model (shown on the graph)

$$N(t) = 440e^{0.06t}. \quad (0 \le t \le 17)$$

a. Find $N(10)$ and $N'(10)$. Be sure to state the units of measurement. To how many significant digits should we round the answers? Why?

b. The number of people whose communications are intercepted averages around 100 per wiretap order.[42] What does the answer to part (a) tell you about the number of people whose communications were intercepted?[43]

c. According to the model, the number of wiretaps orders each year (choose one)

(A) increased at a linear rate
(B) decreased at a quadratic rate

(C) increased at an exponential rate
(D) increased at a logarithmic rate

over the period shown.

93. *Investments* If $10,000 is invested in a savings account offering 4% per year, compounded continuously, how fast is the balance growing after 3 years?

94. *Investments* If $20,000 is invested in a savings account offering 3.5% per year, compounded continuously, how fast is the balance growing after 3 years?

95. *Investments* If $10,000 is invested in a savings account offering 4% per year, compounded semiannually, how fast is the balance growing after 3 years?

96. *Investments* If $20,000 is invested in a savings account offering 3.5% per year, compounded semiannually, how fast is the balance growing after 3 years?

97. *SARS* In the early stages of the deadly SARS (Severe Acute Respiratory Syndrome) epidemic in 2003, the number of cases was increasing by about 18% each day.[44] On March 17, 2003 (the first day for which statistics were reported by the World Health Organization) there were 167 cases. Find an exponential model that predicts the number of people infected t days after March 17, 2003, and use it to estimate how fast the epidemic was spreading on March 31, 2003. (Round your answer to the nearest whole number of new cases per day.) HINT [See Example 4.]

98. *SARS* A few weeks into the deadly SARS (Severe Acute Respiratory Syndrome) epidemic in 2003, the number of cases was increasing by about 4% each day.[45] On April 1, 2003 there were 1,804 cases. Find an exponential model that predicts the number $A(t)$ of people infected t days after April 1, 2003, and use it to estimate how fast the epidemic was spreading on April 30, 2003. (Round your answer to the nearest whole number of new cases per day.) HINT [See Example 4.]

99. ▼ *SAT Scores by Income* The following chart shows United State verbal SAT scores as a function of parents' income level:[46]

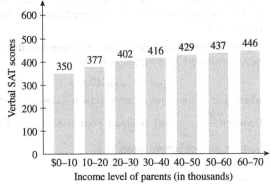

a. The data can best be modeled by which of the following?

(A) $S(x) = 470 - 136e^{-0.0000264x}$
(B) $S(x) = 136e^{-0.0000264x}$

---

[39] Source for data: 2007 Wiretap Report, Administrative Office of the United States Courts (www.uscourts.gov/wiretap07/2007WTText.pdf).

[40] Assume there is no significant overlap between the people whose communications are intercepted in different wiretap orders.

[41] Source for data: 2007 Wiretap Report, Administrative Office of the United States Courts (www.uscourts.gov/wiretap07/2007WTText.pdf).

[42] Ibid.

[43] Assume there is no significant overlap between the people whose communications are intercepted in different wiretap orders.

[44] World Health Organization (www.who.int).

[45] Ibid.

[46] Source: The College Board/*New York Times*, March 5, 1995, p. E16.

(C) $S(x) = 355(1.000004^x)$

(D) $S(x) = 470 - 355(1.000004^x)$

($S(x)$ is the average verbal SAT score of students whose parents earn \$$x$ per year.)

b. Use $S'(x)$ to predict how a student's verbal SAT score is affected by a \$1,000 increase in parents' income for a student whose parents earn \$45,000.

c. Does $S'(x)$ increase or decrease as x increases? Interpret your answer.

100. ▼ *SAT Scores by Income* The following chart shows U.S. average math SAT scores as a function of parents' income level:[47]

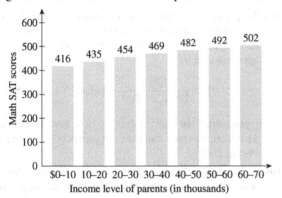

a. The data can best be modeled by which of the following?

(A) $S(x) = 535 - 415(1.000003^x)$

(B) $S(x) = 535 - 136e^{0.0000213x}$

(C) $S(x) = 535 - 136e^{-0.0000213x}$

(D) $S(x) = 415(1.000003^x)$

($S(x)$ is the average math SAT score of students whose parents earn \$$x$ per year.)

b. Use $S'(x)$ to predict how a student's math SAT score is affected by a \$1,000 increase in parents' income for a student whose parents earn \$45,000.

c. Does $S'(x)$ increase or decrease as x increases? Interpret your answer.

101. ▼ *Demographics: Average Age and Fertility* The following graph shows a plot of average age of a population versus fertility rate (the average number of children each woman has in her lifetime) in the United States and Europe over the period 1950–2005.[48]

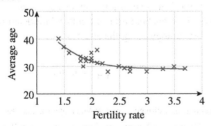

---

[47] Source: The College Board/*New York Times*, March 5, 1995, p. E16.

[48] The separate data for Europe and the United States are collected in the same graph. 2005 figures are estimates. Source: United Nations World Population Division/*New York Times*, June 29, 2003, p. 3.

The equation of the accompanying curve is

$$a = 28.5 + 120(0.172)^x \quad (1.4 \le x \le 3.7)$$

where a is the average age (in years) of the population and x is the fertility rate.

a. Compute $a'(2)$. What does the answer tell you about average age and fertility rates?

b. Use the answer to part (a) to estimate how much the fertility rate would need to increase from a level of 2 children per woman to lower the average age of a population by about 1 year.

102. ▼ *Demographics: Average Age and Fertility* The following graph shows a plot of average age of a population versus fertility rate (the average number of children each woman has in her lifetime) in Europe over the period 1950–2005.[49]

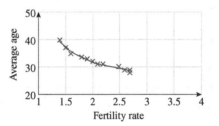

The equation of the accompanying curve is

$$g = 27.6 + 128(0.181)^x \quad (1.4 \le x \le 3.7)$$

where g is the average age (in years) of the population and x is the fertility rate.

a. Compute $g'(2.5)$. What does the answer tell you about average age and fertility rates?

b. Referring to the model that combines the data for Europe and the United States in Exercise 101, which population's average age is affected more by a changing fertility rate at the level of 2.5 children per woman?

103. *Epidemics* A flu epidemic described in Example 1 in Section 9.4 approximately followed the curve

$$P = \frac{150}{1 + 15,000e^{-0.35t}} \text{ million people}$$

where P is the number of people infected and t is the number of weeks after the start of the epidemic. How fast is the epidemic growing (that is, how many new cases are there each week) after 20 weeks? After 30 weeks? After 40 weeks? (Round your answers to two significant digits.) HINT [See Example 5.]

104. *Epidemics* Another epidemic follows the curve

$$P = \frac{200}{1 + 20,000e^{-0.549t}} \text{ million people}$$

---

[49] All European countries including the Russian Federation. 2005 figures are estimates. Source: United Nations World Population Division/*New York Times*, June 29, 2003, p. 3.

where t is in years. How fast is the epidemic growing after 10 years? After 20 years? After 30 years? (Round your answers to two significant digits.) HINT [See Example 5.]

105. *Subprime Mortgages* The percentage of mortgages issued in the United States that are subprime (normally classified as risky) can be approximated by

$$A(t) = \frac{15.0}{1 + 8.6e^{-0.59t}} \text{ percent} \quad (0 \le t \le 8)$$

t years after the start of 2000.[50]

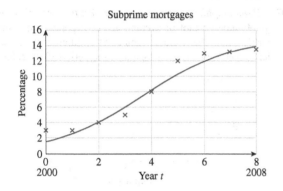

Subprime mortgages

How fast, to the nearest 0.1 percent, was the percentage increasing at the start of 2003? How would you check that the answer is approximately correct by looking at the graph?

106. *Subprime Mortgage Debt* The approximate value of subprime (normally classified as risky) mortgage debt outstanding in the United States can be approximated by

$$A(t) = \frac{1,350}{1 + 4.2e^{-0.53t}} \text{ \$ billion} \quad (0 \le t \le 8)$$

t years after the start of 2000.[51]

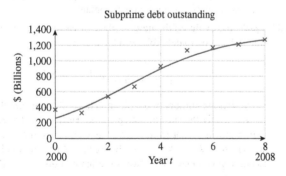

Subprime debt outstanding

How fast, to the nearest \$1 billion, was the subprime mortgage debt increasing at the start of 2005? How would you

check that the answer is approximately correct by looking at the graph?

107. *Subprime Mortgages* (Compare Exercise 105.) The percentage of mortgages issued in the United States that are subprime (normally classified as risky) can be approximated by

$$A(t) = \frac{15.0}{1 + 8.6(1.8)^{-t}} \text{ percent} \quad (0 \le t \le 8)$$

t years after the start of 2000.[52] How fast, to the nearest 0.1 percent, was the percentage increasing at the start of 2003?

108. *Subprime Mortgage Debt* (Compare Exercise 106.) The approximate value of subprime (normally classified as risky) mortgage debt outstanding in the United States can be approximated by

$$A(t) = \frac{1,350}{1 + 4.2(1.7)^{-t}} \text{ \$ billion} \quad (0 \le t \le 8)$$

t years after the start of 2000.[53] How fast, to the nearest \$1 billion, was the subprime mortgage debt increasing at the start of 2005?

109. ▼ *Population Growth* The population of Lower Anchovia was 4,000,000 at the start of 2010 and was doubling every 10 years. How fast was it growing per year at the start of 2010? (Round your answer to three significant digits.) HINT [Use the method of Example 2 in Section 9.2 to obtain an exponential model for the population.]

110. ▼ *Population Growth* The population of Upper Anchovia was 3,000,000 at the start of 2011 and doubling every 7 years. How fast was it growing per year at the start of 2011? (Round your answer to three significant digits.) HINT [Use the method of Example 2 in Section 9.2 to obtain an exponential model for the population.]

111. ▼ *Radioactive Decay* Plutonium 239 has a half-life of 24,400 years. How fast is a lump of 10 grams decaying after 100 years?

112. ▼ *Radioactive Decay* Carbon 14 has a half-life of 5,730 years. How fast is a lump of 20 grams decaying after 100 years?

113. ▢ ▼ *Diffusion of New Technology* Numeric control is a technology whereby the operation of machines is controlled by numerical instructions on disks, tapes, or cards. In a study, E. Mansfield and associates[54] modeled the growth of this technology using the equation

$$p(t) = \frac{0.80}{1 + e^{4.46 - 0.477t}}$$

[50] 2009 figure is an estimate. Sources: Mortgage Bankers Association, UBS.

[51] 2008–2009 figures are estimates. Source: www.data360.org/dataset.aspx? Data_Set_Id=9549.

[52] 2009 figure is an estimate. Sources: Mortgage Bankers Association, UBS.

[53] 2008–2009 figures are estimates. Source: www.data360.org/dataset.aspx? Data_Set_Id=9549.

[54] Source: "The Diffusion of a Major Manufacturing Innovation," in *Research and Innovation in the Modern Corporation* (W.W. Norton and Company, Inc., New York, 1971, pp. 186–205).

where $p(t)$ is the fraction of firms using numeric control in year t.

a. Graph this function for $0 \leq t \leq 20$ and estimate $p'(10)$ graphically. Interpret the result.

b. Use your graph to estimate $\displaystyle\lim_{t \to +\infty} p(t)$ and interpret the result.

c. Compute $p'(t)$, graph it, and again find $p'(10)$.

d. Use your graph to estimate $\displaystyle\lim_{t \to +\infty} p'(t)$ and interpret the result.

114. ▽ *Diffusion of New Technology* Repeat Exercise 113 using the revised formula

$$p(t) = \frac{0.90e^{-0.1t}}{1 + e^{4.50 - 0.477t}}$$

which takes into account that in the long run this new technology will eventually become outmoded and will be replaced by a newer technology. Draw your graphs using the range $0 \leq t \leq 40$.

115. ◆ *Cell Phone Revenues* The number of cell phone subscribers in China for the period 2000–2005 was projected to follow the equation[55]

$$N(t) = 39t + 68 \text{ million subscribers}$$

in year t ($t = 0$ represents 2000). The average annual revenue per cell phone user was $350 in 2000. Assuming that, due to competition, the revenue per cell phone user decreases continuously at an annual rate of 10%, give a formula for the annual revenue in year t. Hence, project the annual revenue and its rate of change in 2002. Round all answers to the nearest billion dollars or billion dollars per year.

116. ◆ *Cell Phone Revenues* The annual revenue for cell phone use in China for the period 2000–2005 was projected to follow the equation[56]

$$R(t) = 14t + 24 \text{ billion dollars}$$

in year t ($t = 0$ represents 2000). At the same time, there were approximately 68 million subscribers in 2000. Assuming that the number of subscribers increases continuously at an annual rate of 10%, give a formula for the annual revenue per subscriber in year t. Hence, project to the nearest dollar the annual revenue per subscriber and its rate of change in 2002. (Be careful with units!)

---

[55] Based on a regression of projected figures (coefficients are rounded). Source: Intrinsic Technology/*New York Times*, Nov. 24, 2000, p. C1.

[56] Not allowing for discounting due to increased competition. Source: Ibid.

COMMUNICATION AND REASONING EXERCISES

117. Complete the following: The derivative of e raised to a glob is . . . .

118. Complete the following: The derivative of the natural logarithm of a glob is . . . .

119. Complete the following: The derivative of 2 raised to a glob is . . . .

120. Complete the following: The derivative of the base 2 logarithm of a glob is . . . .

121. What is wrong with the following?

$$\frac{d}{dx} \ln |3x + 1| = \frac{3}{|3x + 1|} \qquad ✗ \quad \textit{WRONG!}$$

122. What is wrong with the following?

$$\frac{d}{dx} 2^{2x} = (2)2^{2x} \qquad ✗ \quad \textit{WRONG!}$$

123. What is wrong with the following?

$$\frac{d}{dx} 3^{2x} = (2x)3^{2x-1} \qquad ✗ \quad \textit{WRONG!}$$

124. What is wrong with the following?

$$\frac{d}{dx} \ln(3x^2 - 1) = \frac{1}{6x} \qquad ✗ \quad \textit{WRONG!}$$

125. ▽ The number N of music downloads on campus is growing exponentially with time. Can $N'(t)$ grow linearly with time? Explain.

126. ▽ The number N of graphing calculators sold on campus is decaying exponentially with time. Can $N'(t)$ grow with time? Explain.

*The **percentage rate of change** or **fractional rate of change** of a function is defined to be the ratio $f'(x)/f(x)$. (It is customary to express this as a percentage when speaking about percentage rate of change.)*

127. ◆ Show that the fractional rate of change of the exponential function e^{kx} is equal to k, which is often called its **fractional growth rate**.

128. ◆ Show that the fractional rate of change of $f(x)$ is the rate of change of $\ln(f(x))$.

129. ◆ Let $A(t)$ represent a quantity growing exponentially. Show that the percentage rate of change, $A'(t)/A(t)$, is constant.

130. ◆ Let $A(t)$ be the amount of money in an account that pays interest which is compounded some number of times per year. Show that the percentage rate of growth, $A'(t)/A(t)$, is constant. What might this constant represent?

11.6 Implicit Differentiation

Consider the equation $y^5 + y + x = 0$, whose graph is shown in Figure 10.

How did we obtain this graph? We did not solve for y as a function of x; that is impossible. In fact, we solved for x in terms of y to find points to plot. Nonetheless, the graph in Figure 10 is the graph of a function because it passes the vertical line test: Every vertical line crosses the graph no more than once, so for each value of x there is no more than one corresponding value of y. Because we cannot solve for y explicitly in terms of x, we say that the equation $y^5 + y + x = 0$ determines y as an **implicit function** of x.

Now, suppose we want to find the slope of the tangent line to this curve at, say, the point $(2, -1)$ (which, you should check, is a point on the curve). In the following example we find, surprisingly, that it is possible to obtain a formula for dy/dx without having to first solve the equation for y.

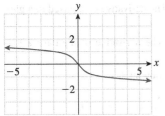

Figure 10

EXAMPLE 1 Implicit Differentiation

Find $\dfrac{dy}{dx}$, given that $y^5 + y + x = 0$.

Solution We use the chain rule and a little cleverness. Think of y as a function of x and take the derivative with respect to x of both sides of the equation:

$$y^5 + y + x = 0 \qquad\qquad \text{Original equation}$$

$$\frac{d}{dx}[y^5 + y + x] = \frac{d}{dx}[0] \qquad \text{Derivative with respect to } x \text{ of both sides}$$

$$\frac{d}{dx}[y^5] + \frac{d}{dx}[y] + \frac{d}{dx}[x] = 0 \qquad \text{Derivative rules}$$

Now we must be careful. The derivative *with respect to x* of y^5 is *not* $5y^4$. Rather, because y is a function of x, we must use the chain rule, which tells us that

$$\frac{d}{dx}[y^5] = 5y^4 \frac{dy}{dx}.$$

Thus, we get

$$5y^4 \frac{dy}{dx} + \frac{dy}{dx} + 1 = 0.$$

We want to find dy/dx, so we *solve for it*:

$$(5y^4 + 1)\frac{dy}{dx} = -1 \qquad \text{Isolate } dy/dx \text{ on one side.}$$

$$\frac{dy}{dx} = -\frac{1}{5y^4 + 1} \qquad \text{Divide both sides by } 5y^4 + 1.$$

➡ **Before we go on...** Note that we should not expect to obtain dy/dx as an explicit function of x if y was not an explicit function of x to begin with. For example, the formula we found in Example 1 for dy/dx is not a function of x because there is a y in it. However, the result is still useful because we can evaluate the derivative at any point on the graph. For instance, at the point $(2, -1)$ on the graph, we get

$$\frac{dy}{dx} = -\frac{1}{5y^4 + 1} = -\frac{1}{5(-1)^4 + 1} = -\frac{1}{6}.$$

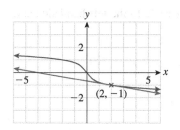

Figure 11

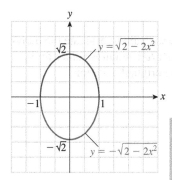

Figure 12

Thus, the slope of the tangent line to the curve $y^5 + y + x = 0$ at the point $(2, -1)$ is $-1/6$. Figure 11 shows the graph and this tangent line. ■

This procedure we just used—differentiating an equation to find dy/dx without first solving the equation for y—is called **implicit differentiation.**

In Example 1 we were given an equation in x and y that determined y as an (implicit) function of x, even though we could not solve for y. But an equation in x and y need not always determine y as a function of x. Consider, for example, the equation

$$2x^2 + y^2 = 2.$$

Solving for y yields $y = \pm\sqrt{2 - 2x^2}$. The $\pm$ sign reminds us that for some values of x there are two corresponding values for y. We can graph this equation by superimposing the graphs of

$$y = \sqrt{2 - 2x^2} \qquad \text{and} \qquad y = -\sqrt{2 - 2x^2}.$$

The graph, an *ellipse*, is shown in Figure 12.

The graph of $y = \sqrt{2 - 2x^2}$ constitutes the top half of the ellipse, and the graph of $y = -\sqrt{2 - 2x^2}$ constitutes the bottom half.

EXAMPLE 2 Slope of Tangent Line

Refer to Figure 12. Find the slope of the tangent line to the ellipse $2x^2 + y^2 = 2$ at the point $(1/\sqrt{2}, 1)$.

Solution Because $(1/\sqrt{2}, 1)$ is on the top half of the ellipse in Figure 12, we *could* differentiate the function $y = \sqrt{2 - 2x^2}$, to obtain the result, but it is actually easier to apply implicit differentiation to the original equation.

$$2x^2 + y^2 = 2 \qquad\qquad \text{Original equation}$$

$$\frac{d}{dx}[2x^2 + y^2] = \frac{d}{dx}[2] \qquad \text{Derivative with respect to } x \text{ of both sides}$$

$$4x + 2y\frac{dy}{dx} = 0$$

$$2y\frac{dy}{dx} = -4x \qquad\qquad \text{Solve for } dy/dx.$$

$$\frac{dy}{dx} = -\frac{4x}{2y} = -\frac{2x}{y}$$

To find the slope at $(1/\sqrt{2}, 1)$ we now substitute for x and y:

$$\frac{dy}{dx}\bigg|_{(1/\sqrt{2},1)} - \frac{2/\sqrt{2}}{1} = -\sqrt{2}.$$

Thus, the slope of the tangent to the ellipse at the point $(1/\sqrt{2}, 1)$ is $-\sqrt{2} \approx -1.414$.

EXAMPLE 3 Tangent Line for an Implicit Function

Find the equation of the tangent line to the curve $\ln y = xy$ at the point where $y = 1$.

Solution First, we use implicit differentiation to find dy/dx:

$$\frac{d}{dx}[\ln y] = \frac{d}{dx}[xy] \qquad \text{Take } d/dx \text{ of both sides.}$$

$$\frac{1}{y}\frac{dy}{dx} = (1)y + x\frac{dy}{dx}. \qquad \text{Chain rule on left, product rule on right}$$

147

To solve for dy/dx, we bring all the terms containing dy/dx to the left-hand side and all terms not containing it to the right-hand side:

$$\frac{1}{y}\frac{dy}{dx} - x\frac{dy}{dx} = y \qquad \text{Bring the terms with } dy/dx \text{ to the left.}$$

$$\frac{dy}{dx}\left(\frac{1}{y} - x\right) = y \qquad \text{Factor out } dy/dx.$$

$$\frac{dy}{dx}\left(\frac{1 - xy}{y}\right) = y$$

$$\frac{dy}{dx} = y\left(\frac{y}{1 - xy}\right) = \frac{y^2}{1 - xy}. \qquad \text{Solve for } dy/dx.$$

The derivative gives the slope of the tangent line, so we want to evaluate the derivative at the point where $y = 1$. However, the formula for dy/dx requires values for both x and y. We get the value of x by substituting $y = 1$ in the original equation:

$$\ln y = xy$$

$$\ln(1) = x \cdot 1$$

But $\ln(1) = 0$, and so $x = 0$ for this point. Thus,

$$\left.\frac{dy}{dx}\right|_{(0,1)} = \frac{1^2}{1 - (0)(1)} = 1.$$

Therefore, the tangent line is the line through $(x, y) = (0, 1)$ with slope 1, which is

$$y = x + 1.$$

➡ **Before we go on...** Example 3 presents an instance of an implicit function in which it is simply not possible to solve for y. Try it. ∎

Sometimes, it is easiest to differentiate a complicated function of x by first taking the logarithm and then using implicit differentiation—a technique called **logarithmic differentiation**.

EXAMPLE 4 **Logarithmic Differentiation**

Find $\dfrac{d}{dx}\left[\dfrac{(x + 1)^{10}(x^2 + 1)^{11}}{(x^3 + 1)^{12}}\right]$ without using the product or quotient rules.

Solution Write

$$y = \frac{(x + 1)^{10}(x^2 + 1)^{11}}{(x^3 + 1)^{12}}$$

and then take the natural logarithm of both sides:

$$\ln y = \ln\left[\frac{(x + 1)^{10}(x^2 + 1)^{11}}{(x^3 + 1)^{12}}\right].$$

We can use properties of the logarithm to simplify the right-hand side:

$$\ln y = \ln(x + 1)^{10} + \ln(x^2 + 1)^{11} - \ln(x^3 + 1)^{12}$$

$$= 10\ln(x + 1) + 11\ln(x^2 + 1) - 12\ln(x^3 + 1).$$

Now we can find $\dfrac{dy}{dx}$ using implicit differentiation:

$$\frac{1}{y}\frac{dy}{dx} = \frac{10}{x+1} + \frac{22x}{x^2+1} - \frac{36x^2}{x^3+1} \qquad \text{Take } d/dx \text{ of both sides.}$$

$$\frac{dy}{dx} = y\left(\frac{10}{x+1} + \frac{22x}{x^2+1} - \frac{36x^2}{x^3+1}\right) \qquad \text{Solve for } dy/dx.$$

$$= \frac{(x+1)^{10}(x^2+1)^{11}}{(x^3+1)^{12}}\left(\frac{10}{x+1} + \frac{22x}{x^2+1} - \frac{36x^2}{x^3+1}\right). \qquad \text{Substitute for } y.$$

➡ **Before we go on...** Redo Example 4 using the product and quotient rules (and the chain rule) instead of logarithmic differentiation and compare the answers. Compare also the amount of work involved in both methods. ■

APPLICATION

Productivity usually depends on both labor and capital. Suppose, for example, you are managing a surfboard manufacturing company. You can measure its productivity by counting the number of surfboards the company makes each year. As a measure of labor, you can use the number of employees, and as a measure of capital you can use its operating budget. The so-called *Cobb-Douglas* model uses a function of the form:

$$P = Kx^a y^{1-a} \qquad \text{Cobb-Douglas model for productivity}$$

where P stands for the number of surfboards made each year, x is the number of employees, and y is the operating budget. The numbers K and a are constants that depend on the particular situation studied, with a between 0 and 1.

David Samuel Robbins/CORBIS

EXAMPLE 5 **Cobb-Douglas Production Function**

The surfboard company you own has the Cobb-Douglas production function

$$P = x^{0.3}y^{0.7}$$

where P is the number of surfboards it produces per year, x is the number of employees, and y is the daily operating budget (in dollars). Assume that the production level P is constant.

a. Find $\dfrac{dy}{dx}$.

b. Evaluate this derivative at $x = 30$ and $y = 10,000$, and interpret the answer.

Solution

a. We are given the equation $P = x^{0.3}y^{0.7}$, in which P is constant. We find $\dfrac{dy}{dx}$ by implicit differentiation

$$0 = \frac{d}{dx}[x^{0.3}y^{0.7}] \qquad d/dx \text{ of both sides}$$

$$0 = 0.3x^{-0.7}y^{0.7} + x^{0.3}(0.7)y^{-0.3}\frac{dy}{dx} \qquad \text{Product and chain rules}$$

$$-0.7x^{0.3}y^{-0.3}\frac{dy}{dx} = 0.3x^{-0.7}y^{0.7} \qquad \text{Bring term with } dy/dx \text{ to left.}$$

$$\frac{dy}{dx} = -\frac{0.3x^{-0.7}y^{0.7}}{0.7x^{0.3}y^{-0.3}} \qquad \text{Solve for } dy/dx.$$

$$= -\frac{3y}{7x}. \qquad \text{Simplify.}$$

b. Evaluating this derivative at $x = 30$ and $y = 10,000$ gives

$$\frac{dy}{dx}\bigg|_{x=30,\ y=10,000} = -\frac{3(10,000)}{7(30)} \approx -143.$$

To interpret this result, first look at the units of the derivative: We recall that the units of dy/dx are units of y per unit of x. Because y is the daily budget, its units are dollars; because x is the number of employees, its units are employees. Thus,

$$\frac{dy}{dx}\bigg|_{x=30,\ y=10,000} \approx -\$143 \text{ per employee.}$$

Next, recall that dy/dx measures the rate of change of y as x changes. Because the answer is negative, the daily budget to maintain production at the fixed level is decreasing by approximately \$143 per additional employee at an employment level of 30 employees and a daily operating budget of \$10,000. In other words, increasing the workforce by one worker will result in a savings of approximately \$143 per day. Roughly speaking, *a new employee is worth \$143 per day* at the current levels of employment and production.

11.6 EXERCISES

▼ more advanced   ◆ challenging

Ⓣ indicates exercises that should be solved using technology

In Exercises 1–10, find dy/dx, using implicit differentiation. In each case, compare your answer with the result obtained by first solving for y as a function of x and then taking the derivative.
HINT [See Example 1.]

1. $2x + 3y = 7$ **2.** $4x - 5y = 9$

3. $x^2 - 2y = 6$ **4.** $3y + x^2 = 5$

5. $2x + 3y = xy$ **6.** $x - y = xy$

7. $e^x y = 1$ **8.** $e^x y - y = 2$

9. $y \ln x + y = 2$ **10.** $\dfrac{\ln x}{y} = 2 - x$

In Exercises 11–30, find the indicated derivative using implicit differentiation. HINT [See Example 1.]

11. $x^2 + y^2 = 5; \dfrac{dy}{dx}$ **12.** $2x^2 - y^2 = 4; \dfrac{dy}{dx}$

13. $x^2 y - y^2 = 4; \dfrac{dy}{dx}$ **14.** $xy^2 - y = x; \dfrac{dy}{dx}$

15. $3xy - \dfrac{y}{3} = \dfrac{2}{x}; \dfrac{dy}{dx}$ **16.** $\dfrac{xy}{2} - y^2 = 3; \dfrac{dy}{dx}$

17. $x^2 - 3y^2 = 8; \dfrac{dx}{dy}$ **18.** $(xy)^2 + y^2 = 8; \dfrac{dx}{dy}$

19. $p^2 - pq = 5p^2 q^2; \dfrac{dp}{dq}$ **20.** $q^2 - pq = 5p^2 q^2; \dfrac{dp}{dq}$

21. $xe^y - ye^x = 1; \dfrac{dy}{dx}$ **22.** $x^2 e^y - y^2 = e^x; \dfrac{dy}{dx}$

23. ▼ $e^{st} = s^2; \dfrac{ds}{dt}$ **24.** ▼ $e^{s^2 t} - st = 1; \dfrac{ds}{dt}$

25. ▼ $\dfrac{e^x}{y^2} = 1 + e^y; \dfrac{dy}{dx}$ **26.** ▼ $\dfrac{x}{e^y} + xy = 9y; \dfrac{dy}{dx}$

27. ▼ $\ln(y^2 - y) + x = y; \dfrac{dy}{dx}$ **28.** ▼ $\ln(xy) - x \ln y = y; \dfrac{dy}{dx}$

29. ▼ $\ln(xy + y^2) = e^y; \dfrac{dy}{dx}$ **30.** ▼ $\ln(1 + e^{xy}) = y; \dfrac{dy}{dx}$

In Exercises 31–42, use implicit differentiation to find (a) the slope of the tangent line, and (b) the equation of the tangent line at the indicated point on the graph. (Round answers to four decimal places as needed.) If only the x-coordinate is given, you must also find the y-coordinate.) HINT [See Examples 2, 3.]

31. $4x^2 + 2y^2 = 12, (1, -2)$ **32.** $3x^2 - y^2 = 11, (-2, 1)$

33. $2x^2 - y^2 = xy, (-1, 2)$ **34.** $2x^2 + xy = 3y^2, (-1, -1)$

35. $x^2y - y^2 + x = 1, (1, 0)$

36. $(xy)^2 + xy - x = 8, (-8, 0)$

37. $xy - 2000 = y, x = 2$

38. $x^2 - 10xy = 200, x = 10$

39. ▼ $\ln(x + y) - x = 3x^2, x = 0$

40. ▼ $\ln(x - y) + 1 = 3x^2, x = 0$

41. ▼ $e^{xy} - x = 4x, x = 3$

42. ▼ $e^{-xy} + 2x = 1, x = -1$

In Exercises 43–52, use logarithmic differentiation to find dy/dx. Do not simplify the result. HINT [See Example 4.]

43. $y = \dfrac{2x + 1}{4x - 2}$ **44.** $y = (3x + 2)(8x - 5)$

45. $y = \dfrac{(3x + 1)^2}{4x(2x - 1)^3}$ **46.** $y = \dfrac{x^2(3x + 1)^2}{(2x - 1)^3}$

47. $y = (8x - 1)^{1/3}(x - 1)$ **48.** $y = \dfrac{(3x + 2)^{2/3}}{3x - 1}$

49. $y = (x^3 + x)\sqrt{x^3 + 2}$ **50.** $y = \sqrt{\dfrac{x - 1}{x^2 + 2}}$

51. ▼ $y = x^x$ **52.** ▼ $y = x^{-x}$

APPLICATIONS

53. *Productivity* The number of CDs per hour that Snappy Hardware can manufacture at its plant is given by

$$P = x^{0.6}y^{0.4}$$

where x is the number of workers at the plant and y is the monthly budget (in dollars). Assume P is constant, and compute $\dfrac{dy}{dx}$ when $x = 100$ and $y = 200,000$. Interpret the result. HINT [See Example 5.]

54. *Productivity* The number of cell-phone accessory kits (neon lights, matching covers, and earpods) per day that USA Cellular Makeover Inc. can manufacture at its plant in Cambodia is given by

$$P = x^{0.5}y^{0.5}$$

where x is the number of workers at the plant and y is the monthly budget (in dollars). Assume P is constant, and compute $\dfrac{dy}{dx}$ when $x = 200$ and $y = 100,000$. Interpret the result. HINT [See Example 5.]

55. *Demand* The demand equation for soccer tournament T-shirts is

$$xy - 2,000 = y$$

where y is the number of T-shirts the Enormous State University soccer team can sell at a price of $\$x$ per shirt. Find $\dfrac{dy}{dx}\bigg|_{x=5}$, and interpret the result.

56. *Cost Equations* The cost y (in cents) of producing x gallons of Ectoplasm hair gel is given by the cost equation

$$y^2 - 10xy = 200.$$

Evaluate $\dfrac{dy}{dx}$ at $x = 1$ and interpret the result.

57. *Housing Costs*[57] The cost C (in dollars) of building a house is related to the number k of carpenters used and the number e of electricians used by the formula

$$C = 15,000 + 50k^2 + 60e^2.$$

If the cost of the house is fixed at $\$200,000$, find $\dfrac{dk}{de}\bigg|_{e=15}$ and interpret your result.

58. *Employment* An employment research company estimates that the value of a recent MBA graduate to an accounting company is

$$V = 3e^2 + 5g^3$$

where V is the value of the graduate, e is the number of years of prior business experience, and g is the graduate school grade-point average. If V is fixed at 200, find $\dfrac{de}{dg}$ when $g = 3.0$ and interpret the result.

59. ▼ *Grades*[58] A productivity formula for a student's performance on a difficult English examination is

$$g = 4tx - 0.2t^2 - 10x^2 \quad (t < 30)$$

where g is the score the student can expect to obtain, t is the number of hours of study for the examination, and x is the student's grade-point average.

a. For how long should a student with a 3.0 grade-point average study in order to score 80 on the examination?

b. Find $\dfrac{dt}{dx}$ for a student who earns a score of 80, evaluate it when $x = 3.0$, and interpret the result.

60. ▼ *Grades* Repeat the preceding exercise using the following productivity formula for a basket-weaving examination:

$$g = 10tx - 0.2t^2 - 10x^2 \quad (t < 10).$$

Comment on the result.

_____
[57] Based on an Exercise in *Introduction to Mathematical Economics* by A. L. Ostrosky Jr., and J. V. Koch (Waveland Press, Springfield, Illinois, 1979).

[58] Ibid.

Exercises 61 and 62 are based on the following demand function for money (taken from a question on the GRE Economics Test):

$$M_d = (2) \times (y)^{0.6} \times (r)^{-0.3} \times (p)$$

where

M_d = *demand for nominal money balances (money stock)*

y = *real income*

r = *an index of interest rates*

p = *an index of prices.*

61. ◆ *Money Stock* If real income grows while the money stock and the price level remain constant, the interest rate must change at what rate? (First find dr/dy, then dr/dt; your answers will be expressed in terms of r, y, and $\dfrac{dy}{dt}$.)

62. ◆ *Money Stock* If real income grows while the money stock and the interest rate remain constant, the price level must change at what rate?

COMMUNICATION AND REASONING EXERCISES

63. Fill in the missing terms: The equation $x = y^3 + y - 3$ specifies ___ as a function of ___, and ___ as an implicit function of ___.

64. Fill in the missing terms: When $x \neq 0$ in the equation $xy = x^3 + 4$, it is possible to specify ___ as a function of ___. However, ___ is only an implicit function of ___.

65. ▼ Use logarithmic differentiation to give another proof of the product rule.

66. ▼ Use logarithmic differentiation to give a proof of the quotient rule.

67. ▼ If y is given explicitly as a function of x by an equation $y = f(x)$, compare finding dy/dx by implicit differentiation to finding it explicitly in the usual way.

68. ▼ Explain why one should not expect dy/dx to be a function of x if y is not a function of x.

69. ◆ If y is a function of x and $dy/dx \neq 0$ at some point, regard x as an implicit function of y and use implicit differentiation to obtain the equation

$$\frac{dx}{dy} = \frac{1}{dy/dx}.$$

70. ◆ If you are given an equation in x and y such that dy/dx is a function of x only, what can you say about the graph of the equation?

CHAPTER 11 REVIEW

KEY CONCEPTS

Web Site www.FiniteandCalc.org
Go to the student Web site at
www.FiniteandCalc.org to find a
comprehensive and interactive
Web-based summary of Chapter 11.

11.1 Derivatives of Powers, Sums, and Constant Multiples

Power Rule: If n is any constant and
$f(x) = x^n$, then $f'(x) = nx^{n-1}$.
p. 782

Using the power rule for negative and
fractional exponents p. 783

Sums, differences, and constant multiples
p. 785

Combining the rules p. 786

$\frac{d}{dx}(cx) = c$, $\frac{d}{dx}(c) = 0$ p. 788

$f(x) = x^{1/3}$ and $g(x) = x^{2/3}$ are not
differentiable at $x = 0$. p. 788

Derivative of $f(x) = |x|$: $\frac{d}{dx}|x| = \frac{|x|}{x}$
p. 789

L'Hospital's Rule p. 791

11.2 A First Application: Marginal Analysis

Marginal cost function $C'(x)$ p. 798

Marginal revenue and profit functions
$R'(x)$ and $P'(x)$ p. 800

What it means when the marginal profit
is zero p. 801

Marginal product p. 802

Average cost of the first x items:

$\bar{C}(x) = \frac{C(x)}{x}$ p. 803

11.3 The Product and Quotient Rules

Product rule: $\frac{d}{dx}[f(x)g(x)] =$

$\quad f'(x)g(x) + f(x)g'(x)$ p. 809

Quotient rule: $\frac{d}{dx}\left[\frac{f(x)}{g(x)}\right] =$

$\quad \dfrac{f'(x)g(x) - f(x)g'(x)}{[g(x)]^2}$ p. 810

Using the product rule p. 812
Using the quotient rule p. 813
Calculation thought experiment p. 814
Application to revenue and average
cost p. 815

11.4 The Chain Rule

Chain rule: $\frac{d}{dx}[f(u)] = f'(u)\frac{du}{dx}$ p. 821

Generalized power rule:

$\quad \frac{d}{dx}[u^n] = nu^{n-1}\frac{du}{dx}$ p. 822

Using the chain rule p. 822
Application to marginal product p. 825
Chain rule in differential notation:

$\quad \frac{dy}{dx} = \frac{dy}{du}\frac{du}{dx}$ p. 826

Manipulating derivatives in differential
notation p. 828

11.5 Derivatives of Logarithmic and Exponential Functions

Derivative of the natural logarithm:

$\quad \frac{d}{dx}[\ln x] = \frac{1}{x}$ p. 833

Derivative of logarithm with base b:

$\quad \frac{d}{dx}[\log_b x] = \frac{1}{x \ln b}$ p. 834

Derivatives of logarithms of functions:

$\quad \frac{d}{dx}[\ln u] = \frac{1}{u}\frac{du}{dx}$

$\quad \frac{d}{dx}[\log_b u] = \frac{1}{u \ln b}\frac{du}{dx}$ p. 835

Derivatives of logarithms of absolute
values:

$\quad \frac{d}{dx}[\ln|x|] = \frac{1}{x}$ $\quad \frac{d}{dx}[\ln|u|] = \frac{1}{u}\frac{du}{dx}$

$\quad \frac{d}{dx}[\log_b|x|] = \frac{1}{x \ln b}$

$\quad \frac{d}{dx}[\log_b|u|] = \frac{1}{u \ln b}\frac{du}{dx}$ p. 838

Derivative of e^x: $\frac{d}{dx}[e^x] = e^x$ p. 839

Derivative of b^x: $\frac{d}{dx}[b^x] = b^x \ln b$ p. 839

Derivatives of exponential functions
p. 840

Application to epidemics p. 840

Application to sales growth (logistic
function) p. 841

11.6 Implicit Differentiation

Implicit function of x p. 848
Implicit differentiation p. 848
Using implicit differentiation p. 848
Finding a tangent line p. 849
Logarithmic differentiation p. 850

REVIEW EXERCISES

In Exercises 1–20 find the derivative of the given function.

1. $f(x) = 10x^5 + \frac{1}{2}x^4 - x + 2$

2. $f(x) = \frac{10}{x^5} + \frac{1}{2x^4} - \frac{1}{x} + 2$

3. $f(x) = 3x^3 + 3\sqrt[3]{x}$

4. $f(x) = \frac{2}{x^{2.1}} - \frac{x^{0.1}}{2}$

5. $f(x) = x + \frac{1}{x^2}$

6. $f(x) = 2x - \frac{1}{x}$

7. $f(x) = \frac{4}{3x} - \frac{2}{x^{0.1}} + \frac{x^{1.1}}{3.2} - 4$

8. $f(x) = \frac{4}{x} + \frac{x}{4} - |x|$

9. $f(x) = e^x(x^2 - 1)$

10. $f(x) = \frac{x^2 + 1}{x^2 - 1}$

11. $f(x) = (x^2 - 1)^{10}$

12. $f(x) = \frac{1}{(x^2 - 1)^{10}}$

13. $f(x) = e^x(x^2 + 1)^{10}$

14. $f(x) = \left[\frac{x - 1}{3x + 1}\right]^3$

15. $f(x) = \frac{3^x}{x - 1}$

16. $f(x) = 4^{-x}(x + 1)$

17. $f(x) = e^{x^2 - 1}$

18. $f(x) = (x^2 + 1)e^{x^2 - 1}$

19. $f(x) = \ln(x^2 - 1)$

20. $f(x) = \frac{\ln(x^2 - 1)}{x^2 - 1}$

153

In Exercises 21–28 find all values of x (if any) where the tangent line to the graph of the given equation is horizontal.

21. $y = -3x^2 + 7x - 1$ **22.** $y = 5x^2 - 2x + 1$

23. $y = \dfrac{x}{2} + \dfrac{2}{x}$ **24.** $y = \dfrac{x^2}{2} - \dfrac{8}{x^2}$

25. $y = x - e^{2x-1}$ **26.** $y = e^{x^2}$

27. $y = \dfrac{x}{x+1}$ **28.** $y = \sqrt{x}(x - 1)$

In Exercises 29–34, find dy/dx for the given equation.

29. $x^2 - y^2 = x$ **30.** $2xy + y^2 = y$

31. $e^{xy} + xy = 1$ **32.** $\ln\left(\dfrac{y}{x}\right) = y$

33. $y = \dfrac{(2x - 1)^4(3x + 4)}{(x + 1)(3x - 1)^3}$ **34.** $y = x^{x-1}3^x$

In Exercises 35–40 find the equation of the tangent line to the graph of the given equation at the specified point.

35. $y = (x^2 - 3x)^{-2}$; $x = 1$ **36.** $y = (2x^2 - 3)^{-3}$; $x = -1$

37. $y = x^2 e^{-x}$; $x = -1$ **38.** $y = \dfrac{x}{1 + e^x}$; $x = 0$

39. $xy - y^2 = x^2 - 3$; $(-1, 1)$ **40.** $\ln(xy) + y^2 = 1$; $(-1, -1)$

APPLICATIONS

41. Sales OHaganBooks.com fits the cubic curve

$$w(t) = -3.7t^3 + 74.6t^2 + 135.5t + 6{,}300$$

to its weekly sales figures (see Chapter 10 Review Exercise 47), as shown in the following graph:

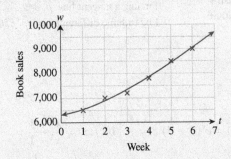

a. According to the cubic model, what was the rate of increase of sales at the beginning of the second week ($t = 1$)? (Round your answer to the nearest unit.)

b. If we extrapolate the model, what would be the rate of increase of weekly sales at the beginning of the 8th week ($t = 7$)?

c. Graph the function w for $0 \le t \le 20$. Would it be realistic to use the function to predict sales through week 20? Why?

d. By examining the graph, say why the choice of a quadratic model would result in radically different long-term predictions of sales.

42. Rising Sea Level Marjory Duffin fit the cubic curve

$$L(t) = -0.0001t^3 + 0.02t^2 + 2.2t \text{ mm}$$

to the New York sea level figures she had seen after purchasing a beachfront condominium in New York (see Chapter 10 Review Exercise 48; t is time in years since 1900). The curve and data are shown in the following graph:

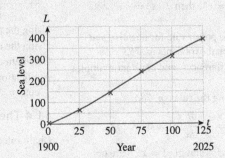

Sea Level Change since 1900

a. According to the cubic model, what was the rate at which the sea level was rising in 2000 ($t = 100$)? (Round your answer to two significant digits.)

b. If we extrapolate the model, what would be the rate at which the sea level is rising in 2025 ($t = 125$)?

c. Graph the function L for $0 \le t \le 200$. Why is it not realistic to use the function to predict the sea level through 2100?

d. James Stewart, a summer intern at Duffin House Publishers, differs. As he puts it, "The cubic curve came from doing regression on the actual data, and thus reflects the actual trend of the data. We can't argue against reality!" Comment on this assertion.

43. Cost As OHaganBooks.com's sales increase, so do its costs. If we take into account volume discounts from suppliers and shippers, the weekly cost of selling x books is

$$C(x) = -0.00002x^2 + 3.2x + 5{,}400 \text{ dollars}$$

a. What is the marginal cost at a sales level of 8,000 books per week?

b. What is the average cost per book at a sales level of 8,000 books per week?

c. What is the marginal average cost ($d\bar{C}/dx$) at a sales level of 8,000 books per week?

d. Interpret the results of parts (a)–(c).

44. Cost OHaganBooks.com has been experiencing a run of bad luck with its summer college intern program in association with Party Central University (begun as a result of a suggestion by Marjory Duffin over dinner one evening). The frequent errors in filling orders, charges from movie download sites and dating sites, and beverages spilled on computer equipment have resulted in an estimated weekly cost to the company of

$$C(x) = 25x^2 - 5.2x + 4,000 \text{ dollars}$$

where x is the number of college interns employed.

a. What is the marginal cost at a level of 10 interns?
b. What is the average cost per intern at a level of 10 interns?
c. What is the marginal average cost at a level of 10 interns?
d. Interpret the results of parts (a)–(c).

45. Revenue At the moment, OHaganBooks.com is selling 1,000 books per week and its sales are rising at a rate of 200 books per week. Also, it is now selling all its books for $20 each, but its price is dropping at a rate of $1 per week.

a. At what rate is OHaganBooks.com's weekly revenue rising or falling?
b. John O'Hagan would like to see the company's weekly revenue increase at a rate of $5,000 per week. At what rate would sales have to have been increasing to accomplish that goal, assuming all the other information is as given above?

46. Revenue Due to ongoing problems with its large college intern program, OHaganBooks.com has decided to offer to transfer its interns to its competitor JungleBooks.com (whose headquarters happens to be across the road) for a small fee. At the moment, it is transferring 5 students per week, and this number is rising at a rate of 4 students per week. Also, it is now charging JungleBooks $400 per intern, but this amount is decreasing at a rate of $20 per week.

a. At what rate is OHaganBooks.com's weekly revenue from this transaction rising or falling?
b. Flush with success of the transfer program, John O'Hagan would like to see the company's resulting revenue increase at a rate of $3,900 per week. At what rate would the transfer of interns have to increase to accomplish that goal, assuming all the other information is as given above?

47. Percentage Rate of Change of Revenue The percentage rate of change of a quantity Q is Q'/Q. Why is the percentage rate of change of revenue always equal to the sum of the percentage rates of change of unit price and weekly sales?

48. P/E Ratios At the beginning of last week, OHaganBooks.com stock was selling for $100 per share, rising at a rate of $50 per year. Its earnings amounted to $1 per share, rising at a rate of $0.10 per year. At what rate was its price-to-earnings (P/E) ratio, the ratio of its stock price to its earnings per share, rising or falling?

49. P/E Ratios Refer to Exercise 48. Curt Hinrichs, who recently invested in OHaganBooks.com stock, would have liked to see the P/E ratio increase at a rate of 100 points per year. How fast would the stock have to have been rising, assuming all the other information is as given in Exercise 48?

50. Percentage Rate of Change of P/E Ratios The percentage rate of change of a quantity Q is Q'/Q. Why is the percentage rate of change of P/E always equal to the percentage rate of change of unit price minus the percentage rate of change of earnings?

51. Sales OHaganBooks.com decided that the cubic curve in Exercise 41 was not suitable for extrapolation, so instead it tried

$$s(t) = 6,000 + \frac{4,500}{1 + e^{-0.55(t-4.8)}}$$

as shown in the following graph:

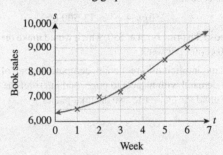

a. Compute $s'(t)$ and use the answer to estimate the rate of increase of weekly sales at the beginning of the 7th week ($t = 6$). (Round your answer to the nearest unit.)
b. Compute $\lim_{t \to +\infty} s'(t)$ and interpret the answer.

52. Rising Sea Level Upon some reflection, Marjory Duffin decided that the curve in Exercise 42 was not suitable for extrapolation, so instead she tried

$$L(t) = \frac{418}{1 + 17.2e^{-0.041t}} \qquad (0 \le t \le 125)$$

(t is time in years since 1900) as shown in the following graph:

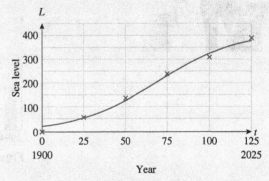

a. Compute $L'(t)$ and use the answer to estimate the rate at which the sea level was rising in 2000 ($t = 100$). (Round your answer to two decimal places.)
b. Compute $\lim_{t \to +\infty} L'(t)$ and interpret the answer.

53. Web Site Activity The number of "hits" on OHaganBooks.com's Web site was 1,000 per day at the beginning of the year, and was growing at a rate of 5% per week. If this growth rate continued for the whole year (52 weeks), find the rate of increase (in hits per day per week) at the end of the year.

155

54. Web Site Activity The number of "hits" on ShadyDownload .net during the summer intern program at OHaganBooks.com was 100 per day at the beginning of the intern program, and was growing at a rate of 15% per day. If this growth rate continued for the duration of the whole summer intern program (85 days), find the rate of increase (in hits per day per day) at the end of the program.

55. Demand and Revenue The price p that OHaganBooks.com charges for its latest leather-bound gift edition of *The Complete Harry Potter* is related to the demand q in weekly sales by the equation

$$250pq + q^2 = 13,500,000$$

Suppose the price is set at $50, which would make the demand 1,000 copies per week.

a. Using implicit differentiation, compute the rate of change of demand with respect to price, and interpret the result. (Round the answer to two decimal places.)

b. Use the result of part (a) to compute the rate of change of revenue with respect to price. Should the price be raised or lowered to increase revenue?

56. Demand and Revenue The price p that OHaganBooks.com charges for its latest leather-bound gift edition of *The Lord of the Rings* is related to the demand q in weekly sales by the equation

$$100pq + q^2 = 5,000,000.$$

Suppose the price is set at $40, which would make the demand 1,000 copies per week.

a. Using implicit differentiation, compute the rate of change of demand with respect to price, and interpret the result. (Round the answer to two decimal places.)

b. Use the result of part (a) to compute the rate of change of revenue with respect to price. Should the price be raised or lowered to increase revenue?

Case Study   Projecting Market Growth

You are on the board of directors at Fullcourt Academic Press, a major textbook supplier to private schools, and TJM, the sales director of the high school division, has just burst into your office with data showing the number of private high school graduates each year over the past 14 years (Figure 13).[59]

Private high school graduates (thousands)

243 246 245 254 265 273 279 279 285 296 299 304 309 311 315

1994   1996   1998   2000   2002   2004   2006   2008

Figure 13

TJM is pleased that the figures appear to support a basic premise of his recent proposal for an expansion strategy: The number of high school seniors in private schools in the United States will be growing at a rate of at least 5,600 per year through the year 2015. TJM points out that the rate of increase predicted by the regression line (see Figure 14) based on the data since 1994 is around 5.6 thousand students per year, so it would not be overly optimistic to assume that the trend will continue—at least for the next 7 years.

---

[59] Source: National Center for Educational Statistics (http://nces.ed.gov/).

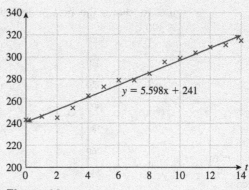

Figure 14

Although you are tempted to support TJM's proposal at the next board meeting, you would like to estimate first whether the 5,600 figure is a realistic expectation, especially because the graph suggests that the number of graduates began to "level off" (in the language of calculus, the *derivative appears to be decreasing*) toward the end of the period. Moreover, you recall reading somewhere that the numbers of students in the lower grades have also begun to level off, so it is safe to predict that the slowing of growth in the senior class will continue over the next few years. You really need precise data about numbers in the lower grades in order to make a meaningful prediction, but TJM's report is scheduled to be presented tomorrow and you would like a quick and easy way of "extending the curve to the right" by then.

It would certainly be helpful if you had a mathematical model of the data in Figure 13 that you could use to project the current trend. But what kind of model should you use? A linear model would be no good because it would not show any change in the derivative (the derivative of a linear function is constant). In addition, best-fit polynomial and exponential functions do not accurately reflect the leveling off, as you realize after trying to fit a few of them (Figure 15).

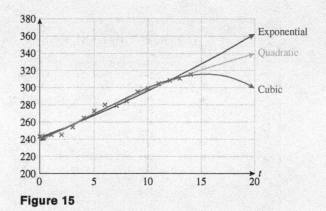

Figure 15

You then recall that a logistic curve can model the leveling-off property you desire, and so you try fitting a curve of the form

$$y = \frac{N}{1 + Ab^{-t}}.$$

157

Figure 16 shows the best-fit logistic curve, which eventually levels off at around $N = 390$.

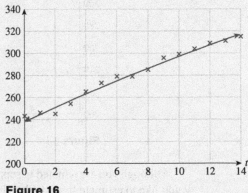

Figure 16

✳ NOTE There is another, more
mathematical, reason for not
using logistic regression to
predict long-term leveling off:
The regression value of the
long-term level N is extremely
sensitive to the values of the
other coefficients. As a result,
there can be good fits to the
same set of data with a wide
variety of values of N.

Web Site
www.FiniteandCalc.org
Follow the path

Chapter 1

→ New Functions from Old:
   Scaled and Shifted
   Functions

to find a detailed treatment of
scaled and shifted functions.

You are slightly troubled by the shape of the regression curve: It doesn't seem to "follow
the s-shape" of the data very convincingly. Moreover, the curve doesn't appear to fit the
data significantly more snugly than the quadratic or cubic models.✳ To reassure yourself,
you decide to look for another kind of s-shaped model as a backup.

After flipping through a calculus book, you stumble across a function that is slightly
more general than the one you have:

$$y = c + \frac{N}{1 + Ab^{-t}} \qquad \text{Shifted Logistic Curve}$$

The added term c has the effect of shifting the graph up c units. Turning once again to
your calculus book (see the discussion of logistic regression in Section 9.4), you see that
a best-fit curve is one that minimizes the sum-of-squares error. Here is an Excel spreadsheet showing the errors for $c = 200, N = 100, A = 3$, and $b = 1.2$.

	A	B	C	D	E	F	G	H
1	t (Year)	y (Observed)	y (Predicted)	residual^2	N	A	b	c
2	0	243	225	324	100	3	1.2	200
3	1	246	228.5714286	303.755102				
4	2	245	232.4324324	157.9437546	SSE:	11120.4856		
5	3	254	236.5482234	304.5645082				
6	4	265	240.8703879	582.2381806				
7	5	273	245.3384642	765.1605612				
8	6	279	249.8829265	847.8039683				
9	7	279	254.4293239	603.7181244				
10	8	285	258.9030791	681.0492791				
11	9	296	263.2343045	1073.590803				
12	10	299	267.3619884	1000.963778				
13	11	304	271.2370477	1073.411042				
14	12	309	274.8239786	1168.000439				
15	13	311	278.1011037	1082.337379				
16	14	315	281.0596311	1151.94864				

The formula for the function in cell C2 is

$$\texttt{=\$H\$2+\$E\$2/(1+\$F\$2*\$G\$2\^(-A2))} \qquad c + \frac{N}{1 + Ab^{-t}}$$

158

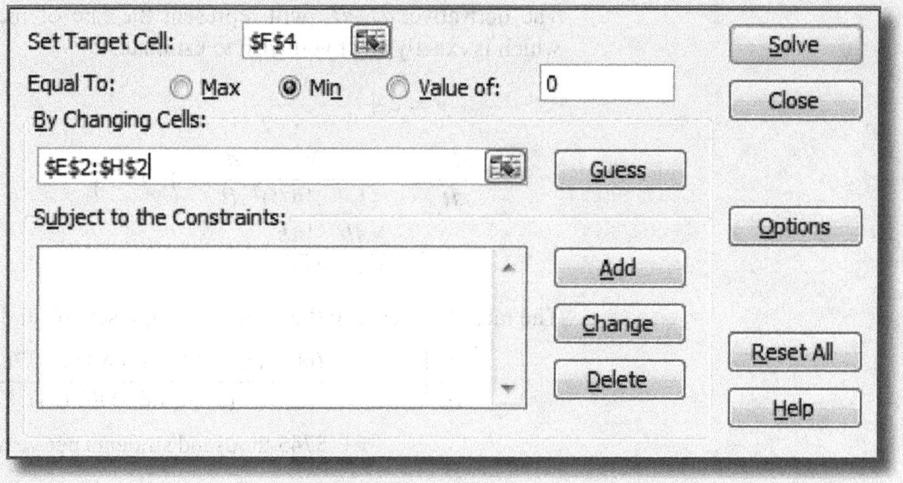

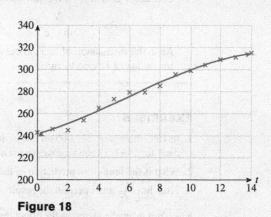

Figure 17

Figure 17 shows how to set up Solver to find the best values for *N, A, b,* and *c* for the setup used in this spreadsheet. The Target Cell, $F$4, contains the value of SSE, which is to be minimized. The Changing Cells are the cells containing the values of the constants *N, A, b,* and *c* that we want to change. That's it.

Now click "Solve." After thinking about it for a few seconds, Excel gives the optimal values of *N, A, b,* and *c* in cells E2–H2, and the minimum value of SSE in cell F4.* You find

$$N = 108.248027, \quad A = 3.85006915, \quad b = 1.27688839, \quad c = 218.351709$$

with SSE $\approx$ 101.2, which is a better fit than the unshifted logistic regression curve (SSE $\approx$ 129.8). Figure 18 shows that not only does this choice of model and constants give a good fit, but that the curve seems to follow the "s-shape" more convincingly than the unshifted logistic curve.

✻ NOTE Depending on the settings in Solver, you may need to run the utility twice in succession to reach the minimum value of SSE.

Figure 18

159

The derivative, dy/dt, will represent the rate of increase of high school graduates, which is exactly what you wish to estimate:

$$y = c + \frac{N}{1 + Ab^{-t}}$$

$$\frac{dy}{dt} = -\frac{N}{(1 + Ab^{-t})^2}\frac{d}{dt}\left[1 + Ab^{-t}\right]$$

$$= \frac{NAb^{-t}\ln b}{(1 + Ab^{-t})^2}$$

The rate of increase in the number of high school students in 2015 ($t = 21$) is given by

$$\frac{dy}{dt}\bigg|_{t=21} = \frac{(108.248027)(3.85006915)1.27688839^{-21}\ln 1.27688839}{(1 + (3.85006915)1.27688839^{-21})^2}$$

$$\approx 0.5745 \text{ thousand students per year}$$

or 570 students per year—far less than the optimistic estimate of 5,600 in the proposal!

You now conclude that TJM's prediction is suspect and that further research will have to be done before the board can support the proposal.

Q: *How accurately does the model predict the number of high school graduates?*

A: Using a regression curve-fitting model to make long-term predictions is always risky. A more accurate model would have to take into account such factors as the birth rate and current school populations at all levels.

Q: *Which values of the constants should I use as starting values when using Excel to find the best-fit curve?*

A: If the starting values of the constants are far from the optimal values, Solver may find a nonoptimal solution. Thus, you need to obtain some rough initial estimate of the constants by examining the graph. Figure 19 shows some important features of the curve that you can use to obtain estimates of N, A, b, and c by inspecting the graph.

From the graph, c is the lower asymptote (in a graph showing only the right-hand portion of the curve in Figure 19 we need to mentally extend the curve to the left), and N is the vertical distance between the upper and lower asymptotes. Once we have estimates for c and N, we can estimate A from the y-intercept m using

$$A = 1 - \frac{N}{m - c}. \qquad m = y\text{-intercept}$$

As in the discussion of logistic curves in Chapter 9, b is the base of exponential growth for values of t close to zero.

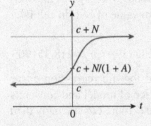

Figure 19

EXERCISES

1. In 1993 there were 247,000 private high school graduates. What does the regression model "predict" for 1993? (Round answer to the nearest 1,000.) What is the residual ($y_{observed} - y_{predicted}$)?

2. What is the long-term prediction of the model? (Round answer to the nearest 1,000.)

3. Find $\lim\limits_{t\to\infty} \dfrac{dy}{dt}$ and interpret the result.

4. ⓘ You receive a memo to the effect that the 2007 and 2008 figures are not accurate. Use Excel Solver to re-estimate the best-fit constants N, a, b, and c in the absence of this data and obtain new estimates for the 2007 and 2008 data. What does the new model predict the rate of change in the number of high school seniors will be in 2015?

5. **Another Model** Using the original data, find the best-fit shifted *predator-prey satiation curve* of the form

$$f(t) = y = c + b\frac{a(t-m)}{1+a|t-m|}. \quad (a, b, c, m \text{ constant})$$

Its graph is shown below:

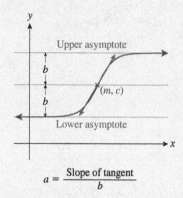

$$a = \frac{\text{Slope of tangent}}{b}$$

(Start with the following values: $a = 0.05$, $b = 160$, $c = 250$, $m = 5$. You might have to run Solver twice in succession to minimize SSE.) Graph the data together with the model. What is SSE? Is the model as accurate a fit as the model used in the text? What does this model predict will be the growth rate of the number of high school graduates in 2015? Comment on the answer. (Round the coefficients in the model and all answers to four decimal places.)

6. **Demand for Freon** The demand for chlorofluorocarbon-12 (CFC-12)—the ozone-depleting refrigerant commonly known as Freon[60]—has been declining significantly in response to regulation and concern about the ozone layer. The chart below shows the projected demand for CFC-12 for the period 1994–2005.[61]

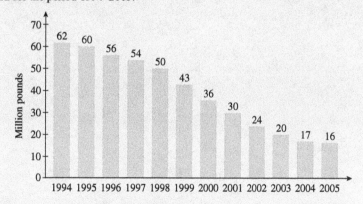

a. Use Excel Solver to obtain the best-fit equation of the form

$$f(t) = c + b\frac{a(t-m)}{1+a|t-m|}$$

where $t =$ years since 1990. Use your function to estimate the total demand for CFC-12 from the start of the year 2000 to the start of 2010. (Start with the following values: $a = 1$, $b = -25$, $c = 35$, and $m = 10$, and round your answers to four decimal places.)

b. According to your model, how fast is the demand for Freon declining in 2000?

---

[60] The name given to it by Du Pont.

[61] Source: The Automobile Consulting Group (*New York Times*, December 26, 1993, p. F23). The exact figures were not given, and the chart is a reasonable facsimile of the chart that appeared in *New York Times*.

Answers to Selected Exercises

Section 11.1

1. $5x^4$ **3.** $-4x^{-3}$ **5.** $-0.25x^{-0.75}$ **7.** $8x^3 + 9x^2$

9. $-1 - 1/x^2$ **11.** $\dfrac{dy}{dx} = 10(0) = 0$ (constant multiple and

power rule)   **13.** $\dfrac{dy}{dx} = \dfrac{d}{dx}(x^2) + \dfrac{d}{dx}(x)$ (sum rule) $= 2x + 1$

(power rule)   **15.** $\dfrac{dy}{dx} = \dfrac{d}{dx}(4x^3) + \dfrac{d}{dx}(2x) - \dfrac{d}{dx}(1)$ (sum
and difference)

17. $f'(x) = 2x - 3$ **19.** $f'(x) = 1 + 0.5x^{-0.5}$

21. $g'(x) = -2x^{-3} + 3x^{-2}$ **23.** $g'(x) = -\dfrac{1}{x^2} + \dfrac{2}{x^3}$

25. $h'(x) = -\dfrac{0.8}{x^{1.4}}$ **27.** $h'(x) = -\dfrac{2}{x^3} - \dfrac{6}{x^4}$

29. $r'(x) = -\dfrac{2}{3x^2} + \dfrac{0.1}{2x^{1.1}}$ **31.** $r'(x) = \dfrac{2}{3} - \dfrac{0.1}{2x^{0.9}} - \dfrac{4.4}{3x^{2.1}}$

33. $t'(x) = |x|/x - 1/x^2$ **35.** $s'(x) = \dfrac{1}{2\sqrt{x}} - \dfrac{1}{2x\sqrt{x}}$

37. $s'(x) = 3x^2$ **39.** $t'(x) = 1 - 4x$ **41.** $2.6x^{0.3} + 1.2x^{-2.2}$
43. $1.2(1 - |x|/x)$ **45.** $3at^2 - 4a$ **47.** $5.15x^{9.3} - 99x^{-2}$
49. $-\dfrac{2.31}{t^{2.1}} - \dfrac{0.3}{t^{0.4}}$ **51.** $4\pi r^2$ **53.** 3 **55.** -2 **57.** -5
59. $y = 3x + 2$ **61.** $y = \dfrac{3}{4}x + 1$

 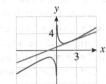

63. $y = \dfrac{1}{4}x + 1$ **65.** $x = -3/4$

67. No such values
69. $x = 1, -1$

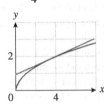

73.

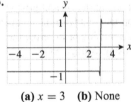

(a) $x = 3$ **(b)** None

75.

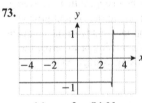

(a) $x = 1$ **(b)** $x = 4.2$

77. a. $f'(1) = 1/3$ **b.** Not differentiable at 0
79. a. Not differentiable at 1 **b.** Not differentiable at 0
81. Yes; 0 **83.** Yes; 12 **85.** No; 3 **87.** Yes; 3/2
89. Yes; diverges to $-\infty$ **91.** Yes; diverges to $-\infty$
93. $P'(t) = 0.9t - 12$; $P'(20) = 6$; the price of a barrel of crude oil was increasing at a rate of \$6 per year in 2000.

95. a. $n'(t) = -1.12t + 14$ **b.** 7 teams/year **c.** Decreases; $n'(t)$ is a linear function with negative slope, so it decreases with increasing t. **97.** 0.55 **99. a.** $s'(t) = -32t$; 0, -32, -64, -96, -128 ft/s **b.** 5 seconds; downward at 160 ft/s
101. a. $S'(t) = -780t + 3{,}300$; dropping at a rate of 600,000 iPhones per quarter. **b.** (B); geometrically: The graph is rising but less steeply, over [2, 4]. Algebraically: The slope is the derivative: $-780t + 3{,}300$, which is positive but decreasing over [2, 4]. **103. a.** $f'(x) = 7.1x - 30.2$ manatees per 100,000 boats. **b.** Increasing; the number of manatees killed per additional 100,000 boats increases as the number of boats increases. **c.** $f'(8) = 26.6$ manatees per 100,000 additional boats. At a level of 800,000 boats, the number of manatee deaths is increasing at a rate of 26.6 manatees per 100,000 additional boats. **105. a.** $c(t) - m(t)$ measures the combined market share of the other three providers (Comcast, Earthlink, and AOL); $c'(t) - m'(t)$ measures the rate of change of the combined market share of the other three providers. **b.** (A) **c.** (A) **d.** 3.72% per year. In 1992, the combined market share of the other three providers was increasing at a rate of about 3.72 percentage points per year. **107.** After graphing the curve $y = 3x^2$, draw the line passing through $(-1, 3)$ with slope -6.
109. The slope of the tangent line of g is twice the slope of the tangent line of f. **111.** $g'(x) = -f'(x)$ **113.** The left-hand side is not equal to the right-hand side. The *derivative* of the left-hand side is equal to the right-hand side, so your friend should have written $\dfrac{d}{dx}\left(3x^4 + 11x^5\right) = 12x^3 + 55x^4$.

115. The derivative of a constant times a function is the constant times the derivative of the function, so that $f'(x) = (2)(2x) = 4x$. Your enemy mistakenly computed the *derivative* of the constant times the derivative of the function. (The derivative of a product of two functions is not the product of the derivative of the two functions. The rule for taking the derivative of a product is discussed later in the chapter.).
117. For a general function f, the derivative of f is defined to be $f'(x) = \lim\limits_{h \to 0} \dfrac{f(x + h) - f(x)}{h}$. One then finds by calculation that the derivative of the specific function x^n is nx^{n-1}. In short, nx^{n-1} is the derivative of a specific function: $f(x) = x^n$, it is not the *definition* of the derivative of a general function or even the definition of the derivative of the function $f(x) = x^n$.
119. Answers may vary.

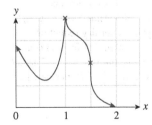

Section 11.2

1. $C'(1,000) = \$4.80$ per item   **3.** $C'(100) = \$99.90$ per item
5. $C'(x) = 4$; $R'(x) = 8 - x/500$; $P'(x) = 4 - x/500$;
$P'(x) = 0$ when $x = 2,000$. Thus, at a production level of 2,000, the profit is stationary (neither increasing nor decreasing) with respect to the production level. This may indicate a maximum profit at a production level of 2,000.   **7. a.** (B) **b.** (C) **c.** (C)
9. a. $C'(x) = 2,250 - 0.04x$. The cost is going up at a rate of $2,249,840 per television commercial. The exact cost of airing the fifth television commercial is $C(5) - C(4) = \$2,249,820$.
b. $\bar{C}(x) = 150/x + 2,250 - 0.02x$; $\bar{C}(4) = \$2,287,420$ per television commercial. The average cost of airing the first four television commercials is $2,287,420.   **11. a.** $R'(x) = 0.90$, $P'(x) = 0.80 - 0.002x$ **b.** Revenue: $450, Profit: $80, Marginal revenue: $0.90, Marginal profit: $-\$0.20$. The total revenue from the sale of 500 copies is $450. The profit from the production and sale of 500 copies is $80. Approximate revenue from the sale of the 501st copy is 90¢. Approximate loss from the sale of the 501st copy is 20¢. **c.** $x = 400$. The profit is a maximum when you produce and sell 400 copies.   **13.** The profit on the sale of 1,000 DVDs is $3,000, and is decreasing at a rate of $3 per additional DVD sold.   **15.** $P \approx \$257.07$ and $dP/dx \approx 5.07$. Your current profit is $257.07 per month, and this would increase at a rate of $5.07 per additional magazine in sales.   **17. a.** $2.50 per pound **b.** $R(q) = 20,000/q^{0.5}$
c. $R(400) = \$1,000$. This is the monthly revenue that will result from setting the price at $2.50 per pound. $R'(400) = -\$1.25$ per pound of tuna. Thus, at a demand level of 400 pounds per month, the revenue is decreasing at a rate of $1.25 per pound. **d.** The fishery should raise the price (to reduce the demand).   **19.** $P'(50) = \$350$. This means that, at an employment level of 50 workers, the firm's daily profit will increase at a rate of $350 per additional worker it hires.
21. a. (B) **b.** (B) **c.** (C)
23. a. $C(x) = 500,000 + 1,600,000x - 100,000\sqrt{x}$;

$$C'(x) = 1,600,000 - \frac{50,000}{\sqrt{x}};$$

$$\bar{C}(x) = \frac{500,000}{x} + 1,600,000 - \frac{100,000}{\sqrt{x}}$$

b. $C'(3) \approx \$1,570,000$ per spot, $\bar{C}(3) \approx \$1,710,000$ per spot. The average cost will decrease as x increases.
25. a. $C'(q) = 200q$; $C'(10) = \$2,000$ per one-pound reduction in emissions. **b.** $S'(q) = 500$. Thus $S'(q) = C'(q)$ when $500 = 200q$, or $q = 2.5$ pounds per day reduction.
c. $N(q) = C(q) - S(q) = 100q^2 - 500q + 4,000$. This is a parabola with lowest point (vertex) given by $q = 2.5$. The net cost at this production level is $N(2.5) = \$3,375$ per day. The

value of q is the same as that for part (b). The net cost to the firm is minimized at the reduction level for which the cost of controlling emissions begins to increase faster than the subsidy. This is why we get the answer by setting these two rates of increase equal to each other.   **27.** $M'(10) \approx 0.0002557$ mpg/mph. This means that, at a speed of 10 mph, the fuel economy is increasing at a rate of 0.0002557 miles per gallon per 1-mph increase in speed. $M'(60) = 0$ mpg/mph. This means that, at a speed of 60 mph, the fuel economy is neither increasing nor decreasing with increasing speed. $M'(70) \approx -0.00001799$. This means that, at 70 mph, the fuel economy is decreasing at a rate of 0.00001799 miles per gallon per 1-mph increase in speed. Thus 60 mph is the most fuel-efficient speed for the car.
29. (C)   **31.** (D)   **33.** (B)   **35.** Cost is often measured as a function of the number of items x. Thus, $C(x)$ is the cost of producing (or purchasing, as the case may be) x items.
a. The average cost function $\bar{C}(x)$ is given by $\bar{C}(x) = C(x)/x$. The marginal cost function is the derivative, $C'(x)$, of the cost function. **b.** The average cost $\bar{C}(r)$ is the slope of the line through the origin and the point on the graph where $x = r$. The marginal cost of the rth unit is the slope of the tangent to the graph of the cost function at the point where $x = r$.
c. The average cost function $\bar{C}(x)$ gives the average cost of producing the first x items. The marginal cost function $C'(x)$ is the rate at which cost is changing with respect to the number of items x, or the incremental cost per item, and approximates the cost of producing the $(x + 1)$st item.   **37.** The marginal cost
39. Not necessarily. For example, it may be the case that the marginal cost of the 101st item is larger than the average cost of the first 100 items (even though the marginal cost is decreasing). Thus, adding this additional item will *raise* the average cost.   **41.** The circumstances described suggest that the average cost function is at a relatively low point at the current production level, and so it would be appropriate to advise the company to maintain current production levels; raising or lowering the production level will result in increasing average costs.

Section 11.3

1. 3   **3.** $3x^2$ **5.** $2x + 3$ **7.** $210x^{1.1}$ **9.** $-2/x^2$
11. $2x/3$ **13.** $3(4x^2 - 1) + 3x(8x) = 36x^2 - 3$
15. $3x^2(1 - x^2) + x^3(-2x) = 3x^2 - 5x^4$
17. $2(2x + 3) + (2x + 3)(2) = 8x + 12$ **19.** $3\sqrt{x}/2$
21. $(x^2 - 1) + 2x(x + 1) = (x + 1)(3x - 1)$
23. $(x^{-0.5} + 4)(x - x^{-1}) + (2x^{0.5} + 4x - 5)(1 + x^{-2})$
25. $8(2x^2 - 4x + 1)(x - 1)$
27. $(1/3.2 - 3.2/x^2)(x^2 + 1) + 2x(x/3.2 + 3.2/x)$
29. $2x(2x + 3)(7x + 2) + 2x^2(7x + 2) + 7x^2(2x + 3)$

31. $5.3(1 - x^{2.1})(x^{-2.3} - 3.4) - 2.1x^{1.1}(5.3x - 1)(x^{-2.3} - 3.4) - 2.3x - 3.3(5.3x - 1)(1 - x^{2.1})$

33. $\dfrac{1}{2\sqrt{x}}\left(\sqrt{x} + \dfrac{1}{x^2}\right) + (\sqrt{x} + 1)\left(\dfrac{1}{2\sqrt{x}} - \dfrac{2}{x^3}\right)$ **35.** $\dfrac{2(3x - 1) - 3(2x + 4)}{(3x - 1)^2} = -14/(3x - 1)^2$

37. $\dfrac{(4x + 4)(3x - 1) - 3(2x^2 + 4x + 1)}{(3x - 1)^2} = (6x^2 - 4x - 7)/(3x - 1)^2$

39. $\dfrac{(2x - 4)(x^2 + x + 1) - (x^2 - 4x + 1)(2x + 1)}{(x^2 + x + 1)^2} = (5x^2 - 5)/(x^2 + x + 1)^2$

41. $\dfrac{(0.23x^{-0.77} - 5.7)(1 - x^{-2.9}) - 2.9x^{-3.9}(x^{0.23} - 5.7x)}{(1 - x^{-2.9})^2}$ **43.** $\dfrac{\frac{1}{2}x^{-1/2}(x^{1/2} - 1) - \frac{1}{2}x^{-1/2}(x^{1/2} + 1)}{(x^{1/2} - 1)^2} = \dfrac{-1}{\sqrt{x}\left(\sqrt{x} - 1\right)^2}$

45. $-3/x^4$ **47.** $\dfrac{[(x + 1) + (x + 3)](3x - 1) - 3(x + 3)(x + 1)}{(3x - 1)^2} = (3x^2 - 2x - 13)/(3x - 1)^2$

49. $\dfrac{[(x + 1)(x + 2) + (x + 3)(x + 2) + (x + 3)(x + 1)](3x - 1) - 3(x + 3)(x + 1)(x + 2)}{(3x - 1)^2}$

51. $4x^3 - 2x$ **53.** 64 **55.** 3
57. Difference; $4x^3 - 12x^2 + 2x - 480$
59. Sum; $1 + 2/(x + 1)^2$
61. Product; $\left[\dfrac{x}{x + 1}\right] + (x + 2)\dfrac{1}{(x + 1)^2}$

63. Difference; $2x - 1 - 2/(x + 1)^2$ **65.** $y = 12x - 8$
67. $y = x/4 + 1/2$ **69.** $y = -2$ **71.** $q'(5) = 1,000$ units/month (sales are increasing at a rate of 1,000 units per month); $p'(5) = -\$10$/month (the price of a sound system is dropping at a rate of \$10 per month); $R'(5) = 900,000$ (revenue is increasing at a rate of \$900,000 per month).   **73.** \$242 million; increasing at a rate of \$39 million per year.   **75.** Decreasing at a rate of \$1 per day   **77.** Decreasing at a rate of approximately \$0.10 per month

79. $M'(x) = \dfrac{3,000(3,600x^{-2} - 1)}{(x + 3,600x^{-1})^2}$; $M'(10) \approx 0.7670$ mpg/mph.
This means that, at a speed of 10 mph, the fuel economy is increasing at a rate of 0.7670 miles per gallon per one mph increase in speed. $M'(60) = 0$ mpg/mph. This means that, at a speed of 60 mph, the fuel economy is neither increasing nor decreasing with increasing speed. $M'(70) \approx -0.0540$. This means that, at 70 mph, the fuel economy is decreasing at a rate of 0.0540 miles per gallon per one mph increase in speed. 60 mph is the most fuel-efficient speed for the car. (In the next chapter we shall discuss how to locate largest values in general.)
81. a. $P(t) - I(t)$ represents the daily production of oil in Mexico that was not exported to the United States. $I(t)/P(t)$ represents U.S. imports of oil from Mexico as a fraction of the total produced there.   **b.** -0.023 per year; at the start of 2008, the fraction of oil produced in Mexico that was imported by the United States was decreasing at a rate of 0.023 (or 2.3 percentage points) per year.   **83.** Increasing at a rate of about \$3,420 million per year.

85. $R'(p) = -\dfrac{5.625}{(1 + 0.125p)^2}$; $R'(4) = -2.5$ thousand organisms per hour, per 1,000 organisms. This means that the reproduction rate of organisms in a culture containing 4,000 organisms is declining at a rate of 2,500 organisms per hour, per 1,000 additional organisms.   **87.** Oxygen consumption is decreasing at a rate of 1,600 milliliters per day. This is due to the fact that the number of eggs is decreasing, because $C'(25)$ is positive.   **89.** 20; 33   **91.** $5/4$; $-17/16$ **93.** The analysis is suspect, as it seems to be asserting that the annual increase in revenue, which we can think of as dR/dt, is the product of the annual increases, dp/dt in price, and dq/dt in sales. However, because $R = pq$, the product rule implies that dR/dt is not the product of dp/dt and dq/dt, but is instead

$$\frac{dR}{dt} = \frac{dp}{dt} \cdot q + p \cdot \frac{dq}{dt}.$$ **95.** Answers will vary.

$q = -p + 1,000$ is one example.   **97.** Mine; it is increasing twice as fast as yours. The rate of change of revenue is given by $R'(t) = p'(t)q(t)$ because $q'(t) = 0$. Thus, $R'(t)$ does not depend on the selling price $p(t)$.   **99.** (A)

Section 11.4
1. $4(2x + 1)$ **3.** $-(x - 1)^{-2}$ **5.** $2(2 - x)^{-3}$
7. $(2x + 1)^{-0.5}$ **9.** $-4(4x - 1)^{-2}$ **11.** $-3/(3x - 1)^2$
13. $4(x^2 + 2x)^3(2x + 2)$ **15.** $-4x(2x^2 - 2)^{-2}$
17. $-5(2x - 3)(x^2 - 3x - 1)^{-6}$ **19.** $-6x/(x^2 + 1)^4$
21. $1.5(0.2x - 4.2)(0.1x^2 - 4.2x + 9.5)^{0.5}$
23. $4(2s - 0.5s^{-0.5})(s^2 - s^{0.5})^3$ **25.** $-x/\sqrt{1 - x^2}$
27. $-[(x + 1)(x^2 - 1)]^{-3/2}(3x - 1)(x + 1)$
29. $6.2(3.1x - 2) + 6.2/(3.1x - 2)^3$
31. $2[(6.4x - 1)^2 + (5.4x - 2)^3][12.8(6.4x - 1) + 16.2(5.4x - 2)^2]$ **33.** $-2(x^2 - 3x)^{-3}(2x - 3)(1 - x^2)^{0.5}$
$-x(x^2 - 3x)^{-2}(1 - x^2)^{-0.5}$

35. $-56(x+2)/(3x-1)^3$ **37.** $3z^2(1-z^2)/(1+z^2)^4$
39. $3[(1+2x)^4-(1-x)^2]^2[8(1+2x)^3+2(1-x)]$
41. $-0.43(x+1)^{-1.1}[2+(x+1)^{-0.1}]^{3.3}$

43. $-\dfrac{\left(\dfrac{1}{\sqrt{2x+1}}-2x\right)}{(\sqrt{2x+1}-x^2)^2}$

45. $54(1+2x)^2\left(1+(1+2x)^3\right)^2\left(1+\left(1+(1+2x)^3\right)^3\right)^2$

47. $(100x^{99}-99x^{-2})dx/dt$ **49.** $(-3r^{-4}+0.5r^{-0.5})dr/dt$
51. $4\pi r^2 dr/dt$ **53.** $-47/4$ **55.** $1/3$ **57.** $-5/3$ **59.** $1/4$

61. $\dfrac{dP}{dn}\Big|_{n=10}=146{,}454.9.$ At an employment level of

10 engineers, Paramount will increase its profit at a rate of $146,454.90 per additional engineer hired.
63. $y=35(7+0.2t)^{-0.25}$; -0.11 percentage points per month.
65. $-$30 per additional ruby sold. The revenue is decreasing at a rate of $30 per additional ruby sold.
67. $\dfrac{dy}{dt}=\dfrac{dy}{dx}\dfrac{dx}{dt}=(1.5)(-2)=-3$ murders per 100,000

residents/yr each year.   **69.** $5/6\approx0.833$; relative to the 2003 levels, home sales were changing at a rate of 0.833 percentage points per percentage point change in price. (Equivalently, home sales in 2008 were dropping at a rate of 0.833 percentage points per percentage point drop in price.)   **71.** 12π mi^2/h
73. $200,000\pi$/week $\approx$ $628,000/week   **75. a.** $q'(4)\approx333$ units per month   **b.** $dR/dq=$ $800/unit   **c.** $dR/dt\approx$ $267,000 per month   **77.** 3% per year   **79.** 8% per year   **81.** The glob squared, times the derivative of the glob.   **83.** The derivative of a quantity cubed is three times the *original quantity* squared, times the derivative of the quantity, not three times the derivative of the quantity squared. Thus, the correct answer is $3(3x^3-x)^2(9x^2-1)$.   **85.** First, the derivative of a quantity cubed is three times the *original quantity* squared times the derivative of the quantity, not three times the derivative of the quantity squared. Second, the derivative of a quotient is not the quotient of the derivatives; the quotient rule needs to be used in calculating the derivative of $\dfrac{3x^2-1}{2x-2}$.
Thus, the correct result (before simplifying) is

$$3\left(\frac{3x^2-1}{2x-2}\right)^2\left(\frac{6x(2x-2)-(3x^2-1)(2)}{(2x-2)^2}\right).$$

87. Following the calculation thought experiment, pretend that you were evaluating the function at a specific value of x. If the last operation you would perform is addition or subtraction, look at each summand separately. If the last operation is multiplication, use the product rule first; if it is division, use the quotient rule first; if it is any other operation (such as raising a quantity to a power or taking a radical of a quantity) then use the chain rule first.   **89.** An example is

$$f(x)=\sqrt{x+\sqrt{x+\sqrt{x+\sqrt{x+\sqrt{x+1}}}}}.$$

Section 11.5

1. $1/(x-1)$ **3.** $1/(x\ln2)$ **5.** $2x/(x^2+3)$ **7.** e^{x+3}
9. $-e^{-x}$ **11.** $4^x\ln4$ **13.** $2^{x^2-1}2x\ln2$ **15.** $1+\ln x$
17. $2x\ln x+(x^2+1)/x$ **19.** $10x(x^2+1)^4\ln x+(x^2+1)^5/x$
21. $3/(3x-1)$ **23.** $4x/(2x^2+1)$
25. $(2x-0.63x^{-0.7})/(x^2-2.1x^{0.3})$
27. $-2/(-2x+1)+1/(x+1)$ **29.** $3/(3x+1)-4/(4x-2)$
31. $1/(x+1)+1/(x-3)-2/(2x+9)$ **33.** $5.2/(4x-2)$
35. $2/(x+1)-9/(3x-4)-1/(x-9)$
37. $\dfrac{1}{(x+1)\ln2}$ **39.** $\dfrac{1-1/t^2}{(t+1/t)\ln3}$ **41.** $\dfrac{2\ln|x|}{x}$
43. $\dfrac{2}{x}-\dfrac{2\ln(x-1)}{x-1}$ **45.** $e^x(1+x)$
47. $1/(x+1)+3e^x(x^3+3x^2)$ **49.** $e^x(\ln|x|+1/x)$
51. $2e^{2x+1}$ **53.** $(2x-1)e^{x^2-x+1}$ **55.** $2xe^{2x-1}(1+x)$
57. $4(e^{2x-1})^2$ **59.** $2\cdot3^{2x-4}\ln3$ **61.** $2\cdot3^{2x+1}\ln3+3e^{3x+1}$
63. $\dfrac{2x3^{x^2}[(x^2+1)\ln3-1]}{(x^2+1)^2}$ **65.** $-4/(e^x-e^{-x})^2$
67. $5e^{5x-3}$ **69.** $-\dfrac{\ln x+1}{(x\ln x)^2}$ **71.** $2(x-1)$ **73.** $\dfrac{1}{x\ln x}$
75. $\dfrac{1}{2x\ln x}$ **77.** $y=(e/\ln2)(x-1)\approx3.92(x-1)$

79. $y=x$ **81.** $y=-[1/(2e)](x-1)+e$ **83.** $163 billion and increasing at a rate of $5.75 billion per year   **85.** $163 billion and increasing at a rate of $5.75 billion per year.
87. $-1,653$ years per gram; the age of the specimen is decreasing at a rate of about 1,653 years per additional one gram of carbon 14 present in the sample. (Equivalently, the age of the specimen is increasing at a rate of about 1,653 years per additional one gram less of carbon 14 in the sample.)   **89.** Average price: $1.4 million; increasing at a rate of about $220,000 per year.   **91. a.** $N(15)\approx1,762\approx1,800$ (rounded to 2 significant digits) wiretap orders; $N'(15)\approx89.87\approx90$ wiretap orders per year (rounded to 2 significant digits). The constants in the model are specified to 2 significant digits, so we cannot expect the answer to be accurate to more than 2 digits.   **b.** In 2005, the number of people whose communications were intercepted was about 180,000 and increasing at a rate of about 9,000 people per year.   **c.** (C)   **93.** $451.00 per year   **95.** $446.02 per year
97. $A(t)=167(1.18)^t$; 280 new cases per day   **99. a.** (A)
b. The verbal SAT increases by approximately 1 point.
c. $S'(x)$ decreases with increasing x, so that as parental income increases, the effect on SAT scores decreases.   **101. a.** -6.25 years/child; when the fertility rate is 2 children per woman, the average age of a population is dropping at a rate of 6.25 years per one-child increase in the fertility rate.   **b.** 0.160
103. 3,300,000 cases/week; 11,000,000 cases/week; 640,000 cases/week   **105.** 2.1 percentage points per year; the rate of change is the slope of the tangent at $t=3$. This is also approximately the average rate of change over [2, 4], which is about $4/2=2$, in approximate agreement with the answer.
107. 2.1 percentage points per year   **109.** 277,000 people per year   **111.** 0.000283 g/yr

113. a.

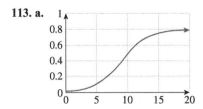

$p'(10) \approx 0.09$, so the percentage of firms using numeric control is increasing at a rate of 9 percentage points per year after 10 years. **b.** 0.80. Thus, in the long run, 80% of all firms will be using numeric control.

c. $p'(t) = 0.3816e^{4.46-0.477t}/(1 + e^{4.46-0.477t})^2$. $p'(10) = 0.0931$.
Graph:

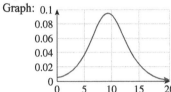

115. $R(t) = 350e^{-0.1t}(39t + 68)$ million dollars; $R(2) \approx$ $42 billion; $R'(2) \approx $7 billion per year **117.** e raised to the glob, times the derivative of the glob. **119.** 2 raised to the glob, times the derivative of the glob, times the natural logarithm of 2. **121.** The derivative of $\ln |u|$ is not $\dfrac{1}{|u|}\dfrac{du}{dx}$; it is $\dfrac{1}{u}\dfrac{du}{dx}$.

Thus, the correct derivative is $\dfrac{3}{3x+1}$. **123.** The power rule does not apply when the exponent is not constant. The derivative of 3 raised to a quantity is 3 raised to the quantity, times the derivative of the quantity, times $\ln 3$. Thus, the correct answer is $3^{2x} 2 \ln 3$. **125.** No. If $N(t)$ is exponential, so is its derivative. **127.** If $f(x) = e^{kx}$, then the fractional rate of change is $\dfrac{f'(x)}{f(x)} = \dfrac{ke^{kx}}{e^{kx}} = k$, the fractional growth rate.

129. If $A(t)$ is growing exponentially, then $A(t) = A_0 e^{kt}$ for constants A_0 and k. Its percentage rate of change is then

$$\frac{A'(t)}{A(t)} = \frac{kA_0 e^{kt}}{A_0 e^{kt}} = k, \text{ a constant.}$$

Section 11.6

1. $-2/3$ **3.** x **5.** $(y-2)/(3-x)$ **7.** $-y$

9. $-\dfrac{y}{x(1+\ln x)}$ **11.** $-x/y$ **13.** $-2xy/(x^2 - 2y)$

15. $-(6+9x^2 y)/(9x^3 - x^2)$ **17.** $3y/x$

19. $(p + 10p^2 q)/(2p - q - 10pq^2)$

21. $(ye^x - e^y)/(xe^y - e^x)$ **23.** $se^{st}/(2s - te^{st})$

25. $ye^x/(2e^x + y^3 e^y)$ **27.** $(y - y^2)/(-1 + 3y - y^2)$

29. $-y/(x + 2y - xye^y - y^2 e^y)$ **31. a.** 1 **b.** $y = x - 3$

33. a. -2 **b.** $y = -2x$ **35. a.** -1 **b.** $y = -x + 1$

37. a. $-2,000$ **b.** $y = -2,000x + 6,000$ **39. a.** 0

b. $y = 1$ **41. a.** -0.1898 **b.** $y = -0.1898x + 1.4721$

43. $\dfrac{2x+1}{4x-2}\left[\dfrac{2}{2x+1} - \dfrac{4}{4x-2}\right]$

45. $\dfrac{(3x+1)^2}{4x(2x-1)^3}\left[\dfrac{6}{3x+1} - \dfrac{1}{x} - \dfrac{6}{2x-1}\right]$

47. $(8x-1)^{1/3}(x-1)\left[\dfrac{8}{3(8x-1)} + \dfrac{1}{x-1}\right]$

49. $(x^3+x)\sqrt{x^3+2}\left[\dfrac{3x^2+1}{x^3+x} + \dfrac{1}{2}\dfrac{3x^2}{x^3+2}\right]$

51. $x^x(1 + \ln x)$ **53.** $-$3,000 per worker. The monthly budget to maintain production at the fixed level P is decreasing by approximately $3,000 per additional worker at an employment level of 100 workers and a monthly operating budget of $200,000. **55.** -125 T-shirts per dollar; when the price is set at $5, the demand is dropping by 125 T-shirts per $1 increase in price. **57.** $\dfrac{dk}{de}\Big|_{e=15} = -0.307$ carpenters per electrician. This means that, for a $200,000 house whose construction employs 15 electricians, adding one more electrician would cost as much as approximately 0.307 additional carpenters. In other words, one electrician is worth approximately 0.307 carpenters.

59. a. 22.93 hours. (The other root is rejected because it is larger than 30.) **b.** $\dfrac{dt}{dx} = \dfrac{4t - 20x}{0.4t - 4x}$; $\dfrac{dt}{dx}\Big|_{x=3.0} \approx -11.2$ hours per grade point. This means that, for a 3.0 student who scores 80 on the examination, 1 grade point is worth approximately 11.2 hours.

61. $\dfrac{dr}{dy} = 2\dfrac{r}{y}$, so $\dfrac{dr}{dt} = 2\dfrac{r}{y}\dfrac{dy}{dt}$ by the chain rule.

63. x, y, y, x **65.** Let $y = f(x)g(x)$.
Then $\ln y = \ln f(x) + \ln g(x)$, and

$$\frac{1}{y}\frac{dy}{dx} = \frac{f'(x)}{f(x)} + \frac{g'(x)}{g(x)}, \text{ so } \frac{dy}{dx} = y\left(\frac{f'(x)}{f(x)} + \frac{g'(x)}{g(x)}\right) =$$

$$f(x)g(x)\left(\frac{f'(x)}{f(x)} + \frac{g'(x)}{g(x)}\right) = f'(x)g(x) + f(x)g'(x).$$

67. Writing $y = f(x)$ specifies y as an explicit function of x. This can be regarded as an equation giving y as an *implicit* function of x. The procedure of finding dy/dx by implicit differentiation is then the same as finding the derivative of y as an explicit function of x: We take d/dx of both sides.

69. Differentiate both sides of the equation $y = f(x)$ with respect to y to get $1 = f'(x) \cdot \dfrac{dx}{dy}$, giving $\dfrac{dx}{dy} = \dfrac{1}{f'(x)} = \dfrac{1}{dy/dx}$.

Chapter 11 Review

1. $50x^4 + 2x^3 - 1$ **3.** $9x^2 + x^{-2/3}$ **5.** $1 - 2/x^3$

7. $-\dfrac{4}{3x^2} + \dfrac{0.2}{x^{1.1}} + \dfrac{1.1x^{0.1}}{3.2}$ **9.** $e^x(x^2 + 2x - 1)$

11. $20x(x^2 - 1)^9$ **13.** $e^x(x^2 + 1)^9(x^2 + 20x + 1)$

15. $3^x[(x-1)\ln 3 - 1]/(x-1)^2$ **17.** $2xe^{x^2 - 1}$

19. $2x/(x^2 - 1)$ **21.** $x = 7/6$ **23.** $x = \pm 2$

25. $x = (1 - \ln 2)/2$ **27.** None **29.** $\dfrac{2x-1}{2y}$ **31.** $-y/x$

33. $\dfrac{(2x-1)^4(3x+4)}{(x+1)(3x-1)^3}\left[\dfrac{8}{2x-1}+\dfrac{3}{3x+4}-\dfrac{1}{x+1}-\dfrac{9}{3x-1}\right]$

35. $y=-x/4+1/2$ **37.** $y=-3ex-2e$ **39.** $y=x+2$
41. a. 274 books per week **b.** 636 books per week **c.** The
function w begins to decrease more and more rapidly after
$t=14$ Graph:

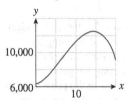

d. Because the data suggest an upward curving parabola, the
long-term prediction of sales for a quadratic model would be
that sales will increase without bound, in sharp contrast to (c)
43. a. \$2.88 per book **b.** \$3.715 per book **c.** Approximately
$-\$0.000104$ per book, per additional book sold. **d.** At a sales
level of 8,000 books per week, the cost is increasing at a rate of
\$2.88 per book (so that the 8,001st book costs approximately
\$2.88 to sell), and it costs an average of \$3.715 per book to sell
the first 8,000 books. Moreover, the average cost is decreasing at
a rate of \$0.000104 per book, per additional book sold.
45. a. \$3,000 per week (rising) **b.** 300 books per week

47. $R=pq$ gives $R'=p'q+pq'$. Thus, $R'/R=R'/(pq)=$
$(p'q+pq')/pq=p'/p+q'/q$ **49.** \$110 per year

51. a. $s'(t)=\dfrac{2{,}475e^{-0.55(t-4.8)}}{(1+e^{-0.55(t-4.8)})^2}$; 556 books per week

b. 0; In the long term, the rate of increase of weekly sales slows
to zero. **53.** 616.8 hits per day per week.
55. a. -17.24 copies per \$1. The demand for the gift edition
of *The Complete Harry Potter* is dropping at a rate of about
17.24 copies per \$1 increase in the price. **b.** \$138 per dollar is
positive, so the price should be raised.

3

Further Applications of the Derivative

Case Study Production Lot Size Management

Your publishing company is planning the production of its latest best seller, which it predicts will sell 100,000 copies each month over the coming year. The book will be printed in several batches of the same number, evenly spaced throughout the year. Each print run has a setup cost of $5,000, a single book costs $1 to produce, and monthly storage costs for books awaiting shipment average 1¢ per book. **To meet the anticipated demand at minimum total cost to your company, how many printing runs should you plan?**

SUNNYphotography.com/Alamy

Web Site

At the Web site you will find:

- Section by section tutorials, including game tutorials with randomized quizzes

- A detailed chapter summary

- A true/false quiz

- Additional review exercises

- Graphers, Excel tutorials, and other resources

- The following extra topic:

  Linear Approximation and Error Estimation

Introduction

In this chapter we begin to see the power of calculus as an optimization tool. In Chapter 9 we saw how to price an item in order to get the largest revenue when the demand function is linear. Using calculus, we can handle nonlinear functions, which are much more general. In Section 12.1 we show how calculus can be used to solve the problem of finding the values of a variable that lead to a maximum or minimum value of a given function. In Section 12.2 we show how this helps us in various real-world applications.

Another theme in this chapter is that calculus can help us to draw and understand the graph of a function. By the time you have completed the material in Section 12.1, you will be able to locate and sketch some of the important features of a graph, such as where it rises and where it falls. In Section 12.3 we look at the *second derivative,* the derivative of the derivative function, and what it tells us about how the graph *curves.* In Section 12.4 we put a number of ideas together that help to explain what you see in a graph (drawn, for example, using graphing technology) and to locate its most important points.

We also include sections on related rates and elasticity of demand. The first of these (Section 12.5) examines further the concept of the derivative as a rate of change. The second (Section 12.6) returns to the problem of optimizing revenue based on the demand equation, looking at it in a new way that leads to an important idea in economics—elasticity.

algebra Review

For this chapter, you should be familiar with the algebra reviewed in **Chapter 0**, **sections 5 and 6**.

12.1 Maxima and Minima

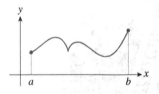

Figure 1

Figure 1 shows the graph of a function f whose domain is the closed interval $[a, b]$. A mathematician sees lots of interesting things going on here. There are hills and valleys, and even a small chasm (called a *cusp*) near the center. For many purposes, the important features of this curve are the highs and lows. Suppose, for example, you know that the price of the stock of a certain company will follow this graph during the course of a week. Although you would certainly make a handsome profit if you bought at time a and sold at time b, your best strategy would be to follow the old adage to "buy low and sell high," buying at all the lows and selling at all the highs.

Figure 2 shows the graph once again with the highs and lows marked. Mathematicians have names for these points: the highs (at the x-values p, r, and b) are referred to as **relative maxima**, and the lows (at the x-values a, q, and s) are referred to as **relative minima**. Collectively, these highs and lows are referred to as **relative extrema**. (A point of language: The singular forms of the plurals *minima, maxima,* and *extrema* are *minimum, maximum,* and *extremum.*)

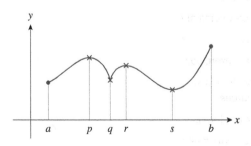

Figure 2

Why do we refer to these points as relative extrema? Take a look at the point corresponding to $x = r$. It is the highest point of the graph *compared to other points nearby.*

170

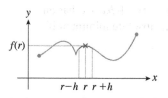

Figure 3

If you were an extremely nearsighted mountaineer standing at the point where $x = r$, you would *think* that you were at the highest point of the graph, not being able to see the distant peaks at $x = p$ and $x = b$.

Let's translate into mathematical terms. We are talking about the heights of various points on the curve. The height of the curve at $x = r$ is $f(r)$, so we are saying that $f(r)$ is greater than or equal to $f(x)$ for every x near r. In other words, $f(r)$ *is the greatest value that $f(x)$ has for all choices of x between $r - h$ and $r + h$* for some (possibly small) h. (See Figure 3.)

We can phrase the formal definition as follows.

Relative Extrema

f has a **relative maximum** at $x = r$ if there is some interval $(r - h, r + h)$ (even a very small one) for which $f(r) \geq f(x)$ for all x in $(r - h, r + h)$ for which $f(x)$ is defined.

f has a **relative minimum** at $x = r$ if there is some interval $(r - h, r + h)$ (even a very small one) for which $f(r) \leq f(x)$ for all x in $(r - h, r + h)$ for which $f(x)$ is defined.

Quick Examples

In Figure 2, f has the following relative extrema:

1. Relative maxima at p and r.

2. A relative maximum at b. (See Figure 4.) Note that $f(x)$ is not defined for $x > b$. However, $f(b) \geq f(x)$ for every x in the interval $(b - h, b + h)$ *for which $f(x)$ is defined*—that is, for every x in $(b - h, b]$.

3. Relative minima at a, q, and s.

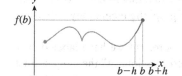

Figure 4

Note Our definition of relative extremum allows f to have a relative extremum at an endpoint of its domain; the definitions used in some books do not. In view of examples like the stock-market investing strategy mentioned above, we find it more useful to allow endpoints as relative extrema. ■

Looking carefully at Figure 2, we can see that the lowest point on the whole graph is where $x = s$ and the highest point is where $x = b$. This means that $f(s)$ is the least value of f on the whole domain of f (the interval $[a, b]$) and $f(b)$ is the greatest value. We call these the *absolute* minimum and maximum.

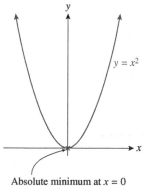

$y = x^2$

Absolute minimum at $x = 0$

Absolute Extrema

f has an **absolute maximum** at r if $f(r) \geq f(x)$ for every x in the domain of f.

f has an **absolute minimum** at r if $f(r) \leq f(x)$ for every x in the domain of f.

Quick Examples

1. In Figure 2, f has an absolute maximum at b and an absolute minimum at s.

2. If $f(x) = x^2$ then $f(x) \geq f(0)$ for every real number x. Therefore, $f(x) = x^2$ has an absolute minimum at $x = 0$. (See the figure.)

3. Generalizing (2), every quadratic function $f(x) = ax^2 + bx + c$ has an absolute extremum at its vertex $x = -b/(2a)$, an absolute minimum if $a > 0$, and an absolute maximum if $a < 0$.

Some graphs have no absolute extrema at all (think of the graph of $y = x$), while others might have an absolute maximum but no absolute minimum (like $y = x^2$), or vice versa. When f does have an absolute maximum, there is only one absolute maximum *value* of f, but this value may occur at different values of x. (See Figure 5.)

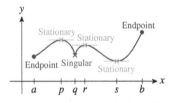

Absolute maxima at $x = a$ and $x = b$

Figure 5

Q: *At how many different values of x can f take on its absolute maximum value?*

A: An extreme case is that of a constant function; because we use $\geq$ in the definition of absolute maximum, a constant function has an absolute maximum (and minimum) at every point in its domain.

Now, how do we go about locating extrema? In many cases we can get a good idea by using graphing technology to zoom in on a maximum or minimum and approximate its coordinates. However, calculus gives us a way to find the exact locations of the extrema and at the same time to understand why the graph of a function behaves the way it does. In fact, it is often best to combine the powers of graphing technology with those of calculus, as we shall see.

In Figure 6 we see the graph from Figure 1 once more, but we have labeled each extreme point as one of three types. At the points labeled "Stationary," the tangent lines to the graph are horizontal, and so have slope 0, so f' (which gives the slope) is 0. Any time $f'(x) = 0$, we say that f has a **stationary point** at x because the rate of change of f is zero there. We call an extremum that occurs at a stationary point a **stationary extremum**. In general, to find the exact location of each stationary point, we need to solve the equation $f'(x) = 0$.

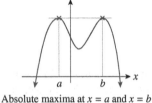

Figure 6

There is a relative minimum in Figure 6 at $x = q$, but there is no horizontal tangent there. In fact, there is no tangent line at all; $f'(q)$ is not defined. (Recall a similar situation with the graph of $f(x) = |x|$ at $x = 0$.) When $f'(x)$ does not exist for some x in the domain of f, we say that f has a **singular point** at x. We shall call an extremum that occurs at a singular point a **singular extremum**. The points that are either stationary or singular we call collectively the **critical points** of f.

The remaining two extrema are at the **endpoints** of the domain.* As we see in the figure, they are (almost) always either relative maxima or relative minima.

We bring all the above information together in Figure 7:

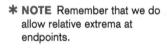

✱ NOTE Remember that we do allow relative extrema at endpoints.

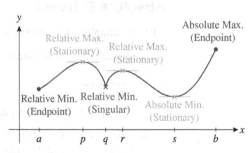

Figure 7

✱ NOTE Here is an outline of the argument. Suppose *f* has a relative maximum, say, at *x* = *a*, at a point other than an endpoint of the domain. Then either *f* is differentiable there, or it is not. If it is not, then we have a singular point. If *f* is differentiable at *x* = *a*, then consider the slope of the secant line through the points where *x* = *a* and *x* = *a* + *h* for small positive *h*. Because *f* has a relative maximum at *x* = *a*, it is falling (or level) to the right of *x* = *a*, and so the slope of this secant line must be ≤ 0. Thus, we must have $f'(a) \leq 0$ in the limit as $h \to 0$. On the other hand, if *h* is small and *negative*, then the corresponding secant line must have slope ≥ 0 because *f* is also falling (or level) as we move left from *x* = *a*, and so $f'(a) \geq 0$. Because $f'(a)$ is both ≥ 0 and ≤ 0, it must be zero, and so we have a stationary point at *x* = *a*.

Q : *Are there any other types of relative extrema?*

A : No; relative extrema of a function always occur at critical points or endpoints. (A rigorous proof is beyond the scope of this book.)✱

Locating Candidates for Relative Extrema

If *f* is a real valued function, then its relative extrema occur among the following types of points:

1. **Stationary Points:** *f* has a stationary point at *x* if *x* is in the domain and $f'(x) = 0$. To locate stationary points, set $f'(x) = 0$ and solve for *x*.

2. **Singular Points:** *f* has a singular point at *x* if *x* is in the domain and $f'(x)$ is not defined. To locate singular points, find values of *x* where $f'(x)$ is *not* defined, but $f(x)$ *is* defined.

3. **Endpoints:** The *x*-coordinates of endpoints are endpoints of the domain, if any. Recall that closed intervals contain endpoints, but open intervals do not.

Once we have the *x*-coordinates of a candidate for a relative extremum, we find the corresponding *y*-coordinate using $y = f(x)$.

Quick Examples

1. **Stationary Points:** Let $f(x) = x^3 - 12x$. Then to locate the stationary points, set $f'(x) = 0$ and solve for *x*. This gives $3x^2 - 12 = 0$, so *f* has stationary points at $x = \pm 2$. Thus, the stationary points are $(-2, f(-2)) = (-2, 16)$ and $(2, f(2)) = (2, -16)$.

2. **Singular points:** Let $f(x) = 3(x - 1)^{1/3}$. Then $f'(x) = (x - 1)^{-2/3} = 1/(x - 1)^{2/3}$. $f'(1)$ is not defined, although $f(1)$ *is* defined. Thus, the (only) singular point occurs at $x = 1$. Its coordinates are $(1, f(1)) = (1, 0)$.

3. **Endpoints:** Let $f(x) = 1/x$, with domain $(-\infty, 0) \cup [1, +\infty)$. Then the only endpoint in the domain of *f* occurs when $x = 1$ and has coordinates $(1, 1)$. The natural domain of $1/x$ has no endpoints.

Remember, though, that these are only *candidates* for relative extrema. It is quite possible, as we shall see, to have a stationary point or a singular point that is neither a relative maximum nor a relative minimum. (It is also possible for an endpoint to be neither a maximum nor a minimum, but only in functions whose graphs are rather bizarre—see Exercise 65.)

Now let's look at some examples of finding maxima and minima. In all of these examples, we will use the following procedure: First, we find the derivative, which we examine to find the stationary points and singular points. Next, we make a table listing the *x*-coordinates of the critical points and endpoints, together with their *y*-coordinates. We use this table to make a rough sketch of the graph. From the table and rough sketch, we usually have enough data to be able to say where the extreme points are and what kind they are.

EXAMPLE 1 Maxima and Minima

Find the relative and absolute maxima and minima of

$$f(x) = x^2 - 2x$$

on the interval $[0, 4]$.

Solution We first calculate $f'(x) = 2x - 2$. We use this derivative to locate the critical points (stationary and singular points).

Stationary Points To locate the stationary points, we solve the equation $f'(x) = 0$, or

$$2x - 2 = 0,$$

getting $x = 1$. The domain of the function is $[0, 4]$, so $x = 1$ is in the domain. Thus, the only candidate for a stationary relative extremum occurs when $x = 1$.

Singular Points We look for points where the derivative is not defined. However, the derivative is $2x - 2$, which is defined for every x. Thus, there are no singular points and hence no candidates for singular relative extrema.

Endpoints The domain is $[0, 4]$, so the endpoints occur when $x = 0$ and $x = 4$.

We record these values of x in a table, together with the corresponding y-coordinates (values of f):

x	0	1	4
$f(x) = x^2 - 2x$	0	-1	8

This gives us three points on the graph, $(0, 0)$, $(1, -1)$, and $(4, 8)$, which we plot in Figure 8. We remind ourselves that the point $(1, -1)$ is a stationary point of the graph by drawing in a part of the horizontal tangent line. Connecting these points must give us a graph something like that in Figure 9. Notice that the graph has a horizontal tangent line at $x = 1$ but not at either of the endpoints because the endpoints are not stationary points.

From Figure 9 we can see that f has the following extrema:

x	$y = x^2 - 2x$	*Classification*
0	0	Relative maximum (endpoint)
1	-1	Absolute minimum (stationary point)
4	8	Absolute maximum (endpoint)

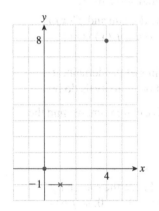

Figure 8

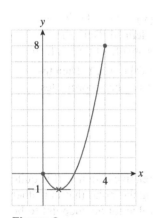

Figure 9

➡ **Before we go on...** A little terminology: If the point (a, b) on the graph of f represents a maximum (or minimum) of f, we sometimes say that **f has a maximum (or minimum) value of b at $x = a$.** Thus, in the above example, we could have said the following:

- f has a relative maximum value of 0 at $x = 0$.
- f has an absolute minimum value of -1 at $x = 1$.
- f has an absolute maximum value of 8 at $x = 4$.

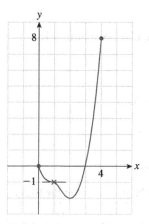

Figure 10

✱ NOTE Why "first" derivative test? To distinguish it from a test based on the **second derivative** of a function, which we shall discuss in Section 12.3.

Q : *How can we be sure that the graph in Example 1 doesn't look like Figure 10?*

A : If it did, there would be another critical point somewhere between $x = 1$ and $x = 4$. But we already know that there aren't any other critical points. The table we made listed all of the possible extrema; there can be no more.

First Derivative Test

The **first derivative test**✱ gives another, very systematic, way of checking whether a critical point is a relative maximum or minimum. To motivate the first derivative test, consider again the critical point $x = 1$ in Example 1. If we look at some values of $f'(x)$ to the left and right of the critical point, we obtain the information shown in the following table:

	Point to the Left	Critical Point	Point to the Right
x	0	1	2
$f'(x) = 2x - 2$	-2	0	2
Direction of Graph	↘	→	↗

At $x = 0$ (to the left of the critical point) we see that $f'(0) = -2 < 0$, so the graph has negative slope and f is decreasing. We note this with the downward pointing arrow. At $x = 2$ (to the right of the critical point), we find $f'(2) = 2 > 0$, so the graph has positive slope and f is increasing. In fact, because $f'(x) = 0$ only at $x = 1$, we know that $f'(x) < 0$ for all x in $[0, 1)$, and we can say that f is decreasing on the interval $[0, 1]$. Similarly, f is increasing on $[1, 4]$.

So, starting at $x = 0$, the graph of f goes down until we reach $x = 1$ and then it goes back up, telling us that $x = 1$ must be a relative minimum. Notice how the relative minimum is suggested by the arrows to the left and right.

First Derivative Test for Relative Extrema

Suppose that c is a critical point of the continuous function f, and that its derivative is defined for x close to, and on both sides of, $x = c$. Then, determine the sign of the derivative to the left and right of $x = c$.

1. If $f'(x)$ is positive to the left of $x = c$ and negative to the right, then f has a relative maximum at $x = c$.
2. If $f'(x)$ is negative to the left of $x = c$ and positive to the right, then f has a relative minimum at $x = c$.
3. If $f'(x)$ has the same sign on both sides of $x = c$, then f has neither a relative maximum nor a relative minimum at $x = c$.

Quick Examples

1. In Example 1 above, we saw that $f(x) = x^2 - 2x$ has a critical point at $x = 1$ with $f'(x)$ negative to the left of $x = 1$ and positive to the right (see the table). Therefore, f has a relative minimum at $x = 1$.

2. Here is a graph showing a function f with a singular point at $x = 1$:

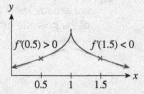

The graph gives us the information shown in the table:

	Point to the Left	Critical Point	Point to the Right
x	0.5	1	1.5
$f'(x)$	+	Undefined	−
Direction of Graph	↗		↘

Since $f'(x)$ is positive to the left of $x = 1$ and negative to the right, we see that f has a relative maximum at $x = 1$. (Notice again how this is suggested by the direction of the arrows.)

EXAMPLE 2 Unbounded Interval

Find all extrema of $f(x) = 3x^4 - 4x^3$ on $[-1, \infty)$.

Solution We first calculate $f'(x) = 12x^3 - 12x^2$.

Stationary points We solve the equation $f'(x) = 0$, which is

$12x^3 - 12x^2 = 0$ or
$12x^2(x - 1) = 0$.

There are two solutions, $x = 0$ and $x = 1$, and both are in the domain. These are our candidates for the x-coordinates of stationary relative extrema.

Singular points There are no points where $f'(x)$ is not defined, so there are no singular points.

Endpoints The domain is $[-1, \infty)$, so there is one endpoint, at $x = -1$.

We record these points in a table with the corresponding y-coordinates:

x	−1	0	1
$f(x) = 3x^4 - 4x^3$	7	0	−1

We will illustrate three methods we can use to determine which are minima, which are maxima, and which are neither:

1. Plot these points and sketch the graph by hand.

2. Use the First Derivative Test.

3. Use technology to help us.

Use the method you find most convenient.

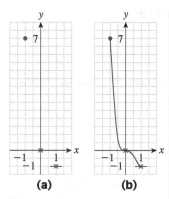

(a)   (b)

Figure 11

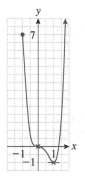

Figure 12

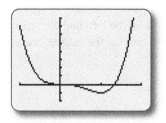

Figure 13

Using a Hand Plot: If we plot these points by hand, we obtain Figure 11(a), which suggests Figure 11(b).

We can't be sure what happens to the right of $x = 1$. Does the curve go up, or does it go down? To find out, let's plot a "test point" to the right of $x = 1$. Choosing $x = 2$, we obtain $y = 3(2)^4 - 4(2)^3 = 16$, so $(2, 16)$ is another point on the graph. Thus, it must turn upward to the right of $x = 1$, as shown in Figure 12.

From the graph, we find that f has the following extrema:

A relative (endpoint) maximum at $(-1, 7)$

An absolute (stationary) minimum at $(1, -1)$

Using the First Derivative Test: List the critical and endpoints in a table, and add additional points as necessary so that each critical point has a noncritical point on either side. Then compute the derivative at each of these points, and draw an arrow to indicate the direction of the graph.

	End Point	Critical Point		Critical Point	
x	-1	0	0.5	1	2
$f'(x) = 12x^3 - 12x^2$	-24	0	-1.5	0	48
Direction of Graph	$\searrow$	$\rightarrow$	$\searrow$	$\rightarrow$	$\nearrow$

Notice that the arrows now suggest the shape of the curve in Figure 12. The first derivative test tells us that the function has a relative maximum at $x = -1$, neither a maximum nor a minimum at $x = 0$, and a relative minimum at $x = 1$. Deciding which of these extrema are absolute and which are relative requires us to compute y-coordinates and plot the corresponding points on the graph by hand, as we did in the first method.

---

using Technology

If we use technology to show the graph, we should choose the viewing window so that it contains the three interesting points we found: $x = -1$, $x = 0$, and $x = 1$. Again, we can't be sure yet what happens to the right of $x = 1$; does the graph go up or down from that point? If we set the viewing window to an interval of $[-1, 2]$ for x and $[-2, 8]$ for y, we will leave enough room to the right of $x = 1$ and below $y = -1$ to see what the graph will do. The result will be something like Figure 13.

Now we can tell what happens to the right of $x = 1$: the function increases. We know that it cannot later decrease again because if it did, there would have to be another critical point where it turns around, and we found that there are no other critical points. ■

➡ **Before we go on...** Notice that the stationary point at $x = 0$ in Example 2 is neither a relative maximum nor a relative minimum. It is simply a place where the graph of f flattens out for a moment before it continues to fall. Notice also that f has no absolute maximum because $f(x)$ increases without bound as x gets large. ■

EXAMPLE 3 Singular Point

Find all extrema of $f(t) = t^{2/3}$ on $[-1, 1]$.

Solution First, $f'(t) = \dfrac{2}{3}t^{-1/3}$.

Stationary points We need to solve

$$\frac{2}{3}t^{-1/3} = 0.$$

We can rewrite this equation without the negative exponent:

$$\frac{2}{3t^{1/3}} = 0.$$

Now, the only way that a fraction can equal 0 is if the numerator is 0, so this fraction can never equal 0. Thus, there are no stationary points.

Singular points The derivative

$$f'(t) = \frac{2}{3t^{1/3}}$$

is not defined for $t = 0$. However, f itself *is* defined at $t = 0$, so 0 is in the domain. Thus, f has a singular point at $t = 0$.

Endpoints There are two endpoints, -1 and 1.

We now put these three points in a table with the corresponding y-coordinates:

t	-1	0	1
$f(t)$	1	0	1

Using a Hand Plot: The derivative, $f'(t) = 2/(3t^{1/3})$, is not defined at the singular point $t = 0$. To help us sketch the graph, let's use limits to investigate what happens to the derivative as we approach 0 from either side:

$$\lim_{t\to 0^-} f'(t) = \lim_{t\to 0^-} \frac{2}{3t^{1/3}} = -\infty$$

$$\lim_{t\to 0^+} f'(t) = \lim_{t\to 0^+} \frac{2}{3t^{1/3}} = +\infty.$$

Thus, the graph decreases very steeply, approaching $t = 0$ from the left, and then rises very steeply as it leaves to the right. It would make sense to say that the tangent line at $x = 0$ is vertical, as seen in Figure 14.

From this graph, we find the following extrema for f:

    An absolute (endpoint) maximum at $(-1, 1)$

    An absolute (singular) minimum at $(0, 0)$

    An absolute (endpoint) maximum at $(1, 1)$.

Notice that the absolute maximum value of f is achieved at two values of t: $t = -1$ and $t = 1$.

First Derivative Test: Here is the corresponding table for the first derivative test.

	t	-1	0	1
$f'(t) = \dfrac{2}{3t^{1/3}}$		$-\dfrac{2}{3}$	Undefined	$\dfrac{2}{3}$
Direction of Graph		↘	↕	↗

(We drew a vertical arrow at $t = 0$ to indicate a vertical tangent.) Again, notice how the arrows suggest the shape of the curve in Figure 14, and the first derivative test confirms that we have a relative minimum at $x = 0$.

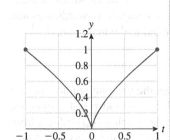

Figure 14

* NOTE Many graphing calculators will give you only the right-hand half of the graph shown in Figure 14 because fractional powers of negative numbers are not, in general, real numbers. To obtain the whole curve, enter the formula as Y=(x^2)^(1/3), a fractional power of the non-negative function x^2.

using Technology

Because there is only one critical point, at $t = 0$, it is clear from this table that f must decrease from $t = -1$ to $t = 0$ and then increase from $t = 0$ to $t = 1$. To graph f using technology, choose a viewing window with an interval of $[-1, 1]$ for t and $[0, 1]$ for y. The result will be something like Figure 14.* ▪

In Examples 1 and 3, we could have found the absolute maxima and minima without doing any graphing. In Example 1, after finding the critical points and endpoints, we created the following table:

x	0	1	4
$f(x)$	0	−1	8

From this table we can see that f must decrease from its value of 0 at $x = 0$ to -1 at $x = 1$, and then increase to 8 at $x = 4$. The value of 8 must be the largest value it takes on, and the value of -1 must be the smallest, on the interval $[0, 4]$. Similarly, in Example 3 we created the following table:

t	−1	0	1
$f(t)$	1	0	1

From this table we can see that the largest value of f on the interval $[-1, 1]$ is 1 and the smallest value is 0. We are taking advantage of the following fact, the proof of which uses some deep and beautiful mathematics (alas, beyond the scope of this book):

Extreme Value Theorem

If f is *continuous* on a *closed interval* $[a, b]$, then it will have an absolute maximum and an absolute minimum value on that interval. Each absolute extremum must occur at either an endpoint or a critical point. Therefore, the absolute maximum is the largest value in a table of the values of f at the endpoints and critical points, and the absolute minimum is the smallest value.

Quick Example

The function $f(x) = 3x - x^3$ on the interval $[0, 2]$ has one critical point at $x = 1$. The values of f at the critical point and the endpoints of the interval are given in the following table:

	Endpoint	Critical point	Endpoint
x	0	1	2
$f(x)$	0	2	−2

From this table we can say that the absolute maximum value of f on $[0, 2]$ is 2, which occurs at $x = 1$, and the absolute minimum value of f is -2, which occurs at $x = 2$.

As we can see in Example 2 and the following examples, if the domain is not a closed interval then f may not have an absolute maximum and minimum, and a table of values as above is of little help in determining whether it does.

EXAMPLE 4 **Domain Not a Closed Interval**

Find all extrema of $f(x) = x + \dfrac{1}{x}$.

Solution Because no domain is specified, we take the domain to be as large as possible. The function is not defined at $x = 0$ but is at all other points, so we take its domain to be $(-\infty, 0) \cup (0, +\infty)$. We calculate

$$f'(x) = 1 - \frac{1}{x^2}.$$

Stationary Points Setting $f'(x) = 0$, we solve

$$1 - \frac{1}{x^2} = 0$$

to find $x = \pm 1$. Calculating the corresponding values of f, we get the two stationary points $(1, 2)$ and $(-1, -2)$.

Singular Points The only value of x for which $f'(x)$ is not defined is $x = 0$, but then f is not defined there either, so there are no singular points in the domain.

Endpoints The domain, $(-\infty, 0) \cup (0, +\infty)$, has no endpoints.

From this scant information, it is hard to tell what f does. If we are sketching the graph by hand, or using the first derivative test, we will need to plot additional "test points" to the left and right of the stationary points $x = \pm 1$.

▦ using Technology

For the technology approach, let's choose a viewing window with an interval of $[-3, 3]$ for x and $[-4, 4]$ for y, which should leave plenty of room to see how f behaves near the stationary points. The result is something like Figure 15.

From this graph we can see that f has:

A relative (stationary) maximum at $(-1, -2)$

A relative (stationary) minimum at $(1, 2)$

Curiously, the relative maximum is lower than the relative minimum! Notice also that, because of the break in the graph at $x = 0$, the graph did not need to rise to get from $(-1, -2)$ to $(1, 2)$. ▪

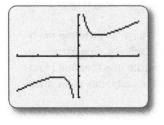

Figure 15

So far we have been solving the equation $f'(x) = 0$ to obtain our candidates for stationary extrema. However, it is often not easy—or even possible—to solve equations analytically. In the next example, we show a way around this problem by using graphing technology.

EXAMPLE 5 ▦ **Finding Approximate Extrema Using Technology**

Graph the function $f(x) = (x - 1)^{2/3} - \dfrac{x^2}{2}$ with domain $[-2, +\infty)$. Also graph its derivative and hence locate and classify all extrema of f, with coordinates accurate to two decimal places.

Solution In Example 4 of Section 10.5, we saw how to draw the graphs of f and f' using technology. Note that the technology formula to use for the graph of f is

```
((x-1)^2)^(1/3)-0.5*x^2
```

instead of

```
(x-1)^(2/3)-0.5*x^2.
```

(Why?)

Figure 16 shows the resulting graphs of f and f'.

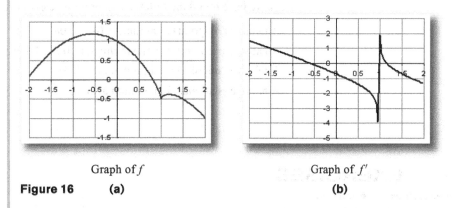

Graph of f Graph of f'

Figure 16   **(a)**   **(b)**

If we extend Xmax beyond $x = 2$, we find that the graph continues downward, apparently without any further interesting behavior.

Stationary Points The graph of f shows two stationary points, both maxima, at around $x = -0.6$ and $x = 1.2$. Notice that the graph of f' is zero at precisely these points. Moreover, it is easier to locate these values accurately on the graph of f' because it is easier to pinpoint where a graph crosses the x-axis than to locate a stationary point. Zooming in to the stationary point at $x \approx -0.6$ results in Figure 17.

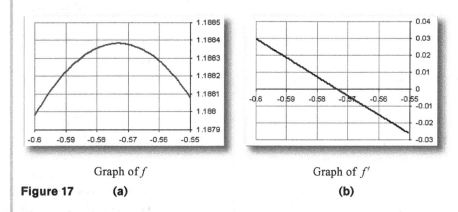

Graph of f Graph of f'

Figure 17   **(a)**   **(b)**

From the graph of f, we can see that the stationary point is somewhere between -0.58 and -0.57. The graph of f' shows more clearly that the zero of f', hence the stationary point of f lies somewhat closer to -0.57 than to -0.58. Thus, the stationary point occurs at $x \approx -0.57$, rounded to two decimal places.

In a similar way, we find the second stationary point at $x \approx 1.18$.

Singular Points Going back to Figure 16, we notice what appears to be a cusp (singular point) at the relative minimum around $x = 1$, and this is confirmed by a glance at the graph of f', which seems to take a sudden jump at that value. Zooming in closer suggests that the singular point occurs at exactly $x = 1$. In fact, we can calculate

$$f'(x) = \frac{2}{3(x-1)^{1/3}} - x.$$

From this formula we see clearly that $f'(x)$ is defined everywhere except at $x = 1$.

Endpoints The only endpoint in the domain is $x = -2$, which gives a relative minimum.

Thus, we have found the following approximate extrema for f:

A relative (endpoint) minimum at $(-2, 0.08)$

An absolute (stationary) maximum at $(-0.57, 1.19)$

A relative (singular) minimum at $(1, -0.5)$

A relative (stationary) maximum at $(1.18, -0.38)$.

12.1 EXERCISES

▼ more advanced ◆ challenging

 indicates exercises that should be solved using technology

In Exercises 1–12, locate and classify all extrema in each graph. (By classifying the extrema, we mean listing whether each extremum is a relative or absolute maximum or minimum.) Also, locate any stationary points or singular points that are not relative extrema. HINT [See Figure 7.]

1.
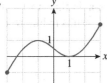

2.
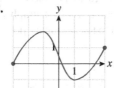

3.
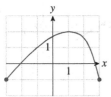

4.
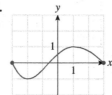

5.
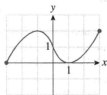

6.
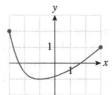

7.
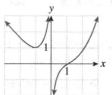

8.
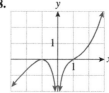

9.
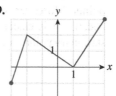

10.
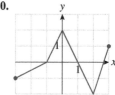

11.
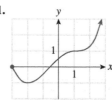

12.
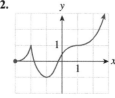

Find the exact location of all the relative and absolute extrema of each function in Exercises 13–44. HINT [See Example 1.]

13. $f(x) = x^2 - 4x + 1$ with domain $[0, 3]$

14. $f(x) = 2x^2 - 2x + 3$ with domain $[0, 3]$

15. $g(x) = x^3 - 12x$ with domain $[-4, 4]$

16. $g(x) = 2x^3 - 6x + 3$ with domain $[-2, 2]$

17. $f(t) = t^3 + t$ with domain $[-2, 2]$

18. $f(t) = -2t^3 - 3t$ with domain $[-1, 1]$

19. $h(t) = 2t^3 + 3t^2$ with domain $[-2, +\infty)$ HINT [See Example 2.]

20. $h(t) = t^3 - 3t^2$ with domain $[-1, +\infty)$ HINT [See Example 2.]

21. $f(x) = x^4 - 4x^3$ with domain $[-1, +\infty)$

22. $f(x) = 3x^4 - 2x^3$ with domain $[-1, +\infty)$

23. $g(t) = \frac{1}{4}t^4 - \frac{2}{3}t^3 + \frac{1}{2}t^2$ with domain $(-\infty, +\infty)$

24. $g(t) = 3t^4 - 16t^3 + 24t^2 + 1$ with domain $(-\infty, +\infty)$

25. $h(x) = (x - 1)^{2/3}$ with domain $[0, 2]$ HINT [See Example 3.]

26. $h(x) = (x + 1)^{2/5}$ with domain $[-2, 0]$ HINT [See Example 3.]

27. $k(x) = \frac{2x}{3} + (x + 1)^{2/3}$ with domain $(-\infty, 0]$

28. $k(x) = \frac{2x}{5} - (x - 1)^{2/5}$ with domain $[0, +\infty)$

29. ▼ $f(t) = \frac{t^2 + 1}{t^2 - 1}; -2 \le t \le 2, t \ne \pm 1$

30. ▼ $f(t) = \frac{t^2 - 1}{t^2 + 1}$ with domain $[-2, 2]$

31. ▼ $f(x) = \sqrt{x}(x - 1); x \ge 0$

32. ▼ $f(x) = \sqrt{x}(x + 1); x \ge 0$

33. ▼ $g(x) = x^2 - 4\sqrt{x}$

34. ▼ $g(x) = \frac{1}{x} - \frac{1}{x^2}$

35. ▼ $g(x) = \frac{x^3}{x^2 + 3}$

36. ▼ $g(x) = \frac{x^3}{x^2 - 3}$

37. ▼ $f(x) = x - \ln x$ with domain $(0, +\infty)$

38. ▼ $f(x) = x - \ln x^2$ with domain $(0, +\infty)$

39. ▼ $g(t) = e^t - t$ with domain $[-1, 1]$

40. ▼ $g(t) = e^{-t^2}$ with domain $(-\infty, +\infty)$

41. ▼ $f(x) = \frac{2x^2 - 24}{x + 4}$

42. ▼ $f(x) = \frac{x - 4}{x^2 + 20}$

43. ▼ $f(x) = xe^{1-x^2}$

44. ▼ $f(x) = x \ln x$ with domain $(0, +\infty)$

In Exercises 45–48, use graphing technology and the method in Example 5 to find the x-coordinates of the critical points, accurate to two decimal places. Find all relative and absolute maxima and minima. HINT [See Example 5.]

45. ⬚ $y = x^2 + \frac{1}{x - 2}$ with domain $(-3, 2) \cup (2, 6)$

46. ⬚ $y = x^2 - 10(x - 1)^{2/3}$ with domain $(-4, 4)$

47. ⬚ $f(x) = (x - 5)^2(x + 4)(x - 2)$ with domain $[-5, 6]$

48. ⬚ $f(x) = (x + 3)^2(x - 2)^2$ with domain $[-5, 5]$

In Exercises 49–56, the graph of the derivative *of a function f is shown. Determine the x-coordinates of all stationary and singular points of f, and classify each as a relative maximum, relative minimum, or neither. (Assume that f(x) is defined and continuous everywhere in $[-3, 3]$.)* HINT [See Example 5.]

49. ▼

50. ▼
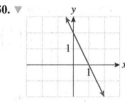

51. ▼
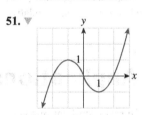

52. ▼
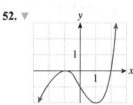

53. ▼
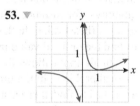

54. ▼
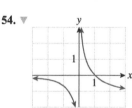

55. ▼
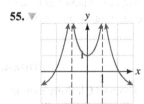

56. ▼
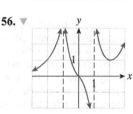

COMMUNICATION AND REASONING EXERCISES

57. Draw the graph of a function f with domain the set of all real numbers, such that f is not linear and has no relative extrema.

58. Draw the graph of a function g with domain the set of all real numbers, such that g has a relative maximum and minimum but no absolute extrema.

59. Draw the graph of a function that has stationary and singular points but no relative extrema.

60. Draw the graph of a function that has relative, not absolute, maxima and minima, but has no stationary or singular points.

61. If a stationary point is not a relative maximum, then must it be a relative minimum? Explain your answer.

62. If one endpoint is a relative maximum, must the other be a relative minimum? Explain your answer.

63. ▽ We said that if f is continuous on a closed interval $[a, b]$, then it will have an absolute maximum and an absolute minimum. Draw the graph of a function with domain $[0, 1]$ having an absolute maximum but no absolute minimum.

64. ▽ Refer to Exercise 63. Draw the graph of a function with domain $[0, 1]$ having no absolute extrema.

65. ⊡ ▽ Must endpoints always be extrema? Consider the following function (based on the trigonometric sine function—see Chapter 16 for a discussion of its properties):

$$f(x) = \begin{cases} x \sin\left(\dfrac{1}{x}\right) & \text{if } x > 0 \\ 0 & \text{if } x = 0 \end{cases}.$$

Technology formula: x*sin(1/x)

Graph this function using the technology formula above for $0 \le x \le h$, choosing smaller and smaller values of h, and decide whether f has a either a relative maximum or relative

minimum at the endpoint $x = 0$. Explain your answer. (Note: Very few graphers can draw this curve accurately; the grapher that comes with Mac computers is probably among the best, while the TI-83/84 Plus is probably among the worst.)

66. ⊡ ▽ Refer to the preceding exercise, and consider the function

$$f(x) = \begin{cases} x^2 \sin\left(\dfrac{1}{x}\right) & \text{if } x \neq 0 \\ 0 & \text{if } x = 0 \end{cases}.$$

Technology formula: x^2*sin(1/x)

Graph this function using the technology formula above for $0 \le x \le h$, choosing smaller and smaller values of h, and decide **(a)** whether $x = 0$ is a stationary point, and **(b)** whether f has either a relative maximum or a relative minimum at $x = 0$. [For part (a), use technology to estimate the derivative at $x = 0$.] Explain your answers.

12.2 Applications of Maxima and Minima

In many applications we would like to find the largest or smallest possible value of some quantity—for instance, the greatest possible profit or the lowest cost. We call this the *optimal* (best) value. In this section we consider several such examples and use calculus to find the optimal value in each.

In all applications the first step is to translate a written description into a mathematical problem. In the problems we look at in this section, there are *unknowns* that we are asked to find, there is an expression involving those unknowns that must be made as large or as small as possible—the **objective function**—and there may be **constraints**—equations or inequalities relating the variables.*

✳ **NOTE** If you have studied linear programming, you will notice a similarity here, but unlike the situation in linear programming, neither the objective function nor the constraints need be linear.

EXAMPLE 1 Minimizing Average Cost

Gymnast Clothing manufactures expensive hockey jerseys for sale to college bookstores in runs of up to 500. Its cost (in dollars) for a run of x hockey jerseys is

$$C(x) = 2{,}000 + 10x + 0.2x^2.$$

How many jerseys should Gymnast produce per run in order to minimize average cost?*

Solution Here is the procedure we will follow to solve problems like this.

1. *Identify the unknown(s).* There is one unknown: x, the number of hockey jerseys Gymnast should produce per run. (We know this because the question is, How many jerseys . . . ?)

2. *Identify the objective function.* The objective function is the quantity that must be made as small (in this case) as possible. In this example it is the average cost, which is given by

$$\bar{C}(x) = \frac{C(x)}{x} = \frac{2{,}000 + 10x + 0.2x^2}{x}$$

$$= \frac{2{,}000}{x} + 10 + 0.2x \text{ dollars/jersey.}$$

✳ **NOTE** Why don't we seek to minimize total cost? The answer would be uninteresting; to minimize total cost, we would make *no* jerseys at all. Minimizing the average cost is a more practical objective.

3. *Identify the constraints (if any).* At most 500 jerseys can be manufactured in a run. Also, $\bar{C}(0)$ is not defined. Thus, x is constrained by

$$0 < x \le 500.$$

Put another way, the domain of the objective function $\bar{C}(x)$ is $(0, 500]$.

4. *State and solve the resulting optimization problem.* Our optimization problem is:

$$\text{Minimize } \bar{C}(x) = \frac{2{,}000}{x} + 10 + 0.2x \qquad \text{Objective function}$$

$$\text{subject to } 0 < x \le 500. \qquad \text{Constraint}$$

We now solve this problem as in Section 12.1. We first calculate

$$\bar{C}'(x) = -\frac{2{,}000}{x^2} + 0.2.$$

We solve $\bar{C}'(x) = 0$ to find $x = \pm 100$. We reject $x = -100$ because -100 is not in the domain of $\bar{C}$ (and makes no sense), so we have one stationary point, at $x = 100$. There, the average cost is $\bar{C}(100) = \$50$ per jersey.

The only point at which the formula for $\bar{C}'$ is not defined is $x = 0$, but that is not in the domain of $\bar{C}$, so we have no singular points. We have one endpoint in the domain, at $x = 500$. There, the average cost is $\bar{C}(500) = \$114$.

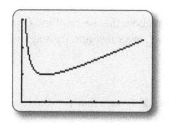

Figure 18

---

using Technology

Let's plot $\bar{C}$ in a viewing window with the intervals $[0, 500]$ for x and $[0, 150]$ for y, which will show the whole domain and the two interesting points we've found so far. The result is Figure 18.

From the graph of $\bar{C}$, we can see that the stationary point at $x = 100$ gives the absolute minimum. We can therefore say that Gymnast Clothing should produce 100 jerseys per run, for a lowest possible average cost of $\$50$ per jersey. ■

EXAMPLE 2 Maximizing Area

Slim wants to build a rectangular enclosure for his pet rabbit, Killer, against the side of his house, as shown in Figure 19. He has bought 100 feet of fencing. What are the dimensions of the largest area that he can enclose?

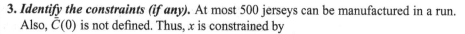

Figure 19

Solution

1. *Identify the unknown(s).* To identify the unknown(s), we look at the question: What are the *dimensions* of the largest area he can enclose? Thus, the unknowns are the dimensions of the fence. We call these x and y, as shown in Figure 20.

2. *Identify the objective function.* We look for what it is that we are trying to maximize (or minimize). The phrase "largest area" tells us that our object is to *maximize the area*, which is the product of length and width, so our objective function is

$$A = xy, \text{ where } A \text{ is the area of the enclosure.}$$

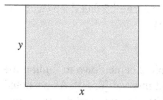

Figure 20

3. *Identify the constraints (if any).* What stops Slim from making the area as large as he wants? He has only 100 feet of fencing to work with. Looking again at Figure 20, we see that the sum of the lengths of the three sides must equal 100, so

$$x + 2y = 100.$$

One more point: Because x and y represent the lengths of the sides of the enclosure, neither can be a negative number.

4. *State and solve the resulting optimization problem.* Our mathematical problem is:

Maximize $A = xy$ Objective function

subject to $x + 2y = 100$, $x \geq 0$, and $y \geq 0$.   Constraints

We know how to find maxima and minima of a function of one variable, but A appears to depend on two variables. We can remedy this by using a constraint to express one variable in terms of the other. Let's take the constraint $x + 2y = 100$ and solve for x in terms of y:

$$x = 100 - 2y.$$

Substituting into the objective function gives

$$A = xy = (100 - 2y)y = 100y - 2y^2$$

and we have eliminated x from the objective function. What about the inequalities? One says that $x \geq 0$, but we want to eliminate x from this as well. We substitute for x again, getting

$$100 - 2y \geq 0.$$

Solving this inequality for y gives $y \leq 50$. The second inequality says that $y \geq 0$. Now, we can restate our problem with x eliminated:

Maximize $A(y) = 100y - 2y^2$ subject to $0 \leq y \leq 50$.

We now proceed with our usual method of solving such problems. We calculate $A'(y) = 100 - 4y$. Solving $100 - 4y = 0$, we get one stationary point at $y = 25$. There, $A(25) = 1{,}250$. There are no points at which $A'(y)$ is not defined, so there are no singular points. We have two endpoints, at $y = 0$ and $y = 50$. The corresponding areas are $A(0) = 0$ and $A(50) = 0$. We record the three points we found in a table:

y	0	25	50
$A(y)$	0	1,250	0

It's clear now how A must behave: It increases from 0 at $y = 0$ to 1,250 at $y = 25$ and then decreases back to 0 at $y = 50$. Thus, the largest possible value of A is 1,250 square feet, which occurs when $y = 25$. To completely answer the question that was asked, we need to know the corresponding value of x. We have $x = 100 - 2y$, so $x = 50$ when $y = 25$. Thus, Slim should build his enclosure 50 feet across and 25 feet deep (with the "missing" 50-foot side being formed by part of the house).

➡ **Before we go on...** Notice that the problem in Example 2 came down to finding the absolute maximum value of A on the closed and bounded interval $[0, 50]$. As we noted in the preceding section, the table of values of A at its critical points and the endpoints of the interval gives us enough information to find the absolute maximum. ∎

Let's stop for a moment and summarize the steps we've taken in these two examples.

Solving an Optimization Problem

1. **Identify the unknown(s), possibly with the aid of a diagram.** These are usually the quantities asked for in the problem.

2. **Identify the objective function.** This is the quantity you are asked to maximize or minimize. You should name it explicitly, as in "Let S = surface area."

3. **Identify the constraint(s).** These can be equations relating variables or inequalities expressing limitations on the values of variables.

4. **State the optimization problem.** This will have the form "Maximize [minimize] the objective function subject to the constraint(s)."

5. **Eliminate extra variables.** If the objective function depends on several variables, solve the constraint equations to express all variables in terms of one particular variable. Substitute these expressions into the objective function to rewrite it as a function of a single variable. Substitute the expressions into any inequality constraints to help determine the domain of the objective function.

6. **Find the absolute maximum (or minimum) of the objective function.** Use the techniques of the preceding section.

Now for some further examples.

EXAMPLE 3 Maximizing Revenue

Cozy Carriage Company builds baby strollers. Using market research, the company estimates that if it sets the price of a stroller at p dollars, then it can sell $q = 300{,}000 - 10p^2$ strollers per year. What price will bring in the greatest annual revenue?

Solution The question we are asked identifies our main unknown, the price p. However, there is another quantity that we do not know, q, the number of strollers the company will sell per year. The question also identifies the objective function, revenue, which is

$$R = pq.$$

Including the equality constraint given to us, that $q = 300{,}000 - 10p^2$, and the "reality" inequality constraints $p \geq 0$ and $q \geq 0$, we can write our problem as

Maximize $R = pq$ subject to $q = 300{,}000 - 10p^2$, $p \geq 0$, and $q \geq 0$.

We are given q in terms of p, so let's substitute to eliminate q:

$$R = pq = p(300{,}000 - 10p^2) = 300{,}000p - 10p^3$$

Substituting in the inequality $q \geq 0$, we get

$$300{,}000 - 10p^2 \geq 0.$$

Thus, $p^2 \leq 30{,}000$, which gives $-100\sqrt{3} \leq p \leq 100\sqrt{3}$. When we combine this with $p \geq 0$, we get the following restatement of our problem:

Maximize $R(p) = 300{,}000p - 10p^3$ such that $0 \leq p \leq 100\sqrt{3}$.

187

We solve this problem in much the same way we did the preceding one. We calculate $R'(p) = 300,000 - 30p^2$. Setting $300,000 - 30p^2 = 0$, we find one stationary point at $p = 100$. There are no singular points and we have the endpoints $p = 0$ and $p = 100\sqrt{3}$. Putting these points in a table and computing the corresponding values of R, we get the following:

p	0	100	$100\sqrt{3}$
$R(p)$	0	20,000,000	0

Thus, Cozy Carriage should price its strollers at $100 each, which will bring in the largest possible revenue of $20,000,000.

EXAMPLE 4 Optimizing Resources

The Metal Can Company has an order to make cylindrical cans with a volume of 250 cubic centimeters. What should be the dimensions of the cans in order to use the least amount of metal in their production?

Solution We are asked to find the dimensions of the cans. It is traditional to take as the dimensions of a cylinder the height h and the radius of the base r, as in Figure 21.

We are also asked to minimize the amount of metal used in the can, which is the area of the surface of the cylinder. We can look up the formula or figure it out ourselves: Imagine removing the circular top and bottom and then cutting vertically and flattening out the hollow cylinder to get a rectangle, as shown in Figure 22.

Figure 21

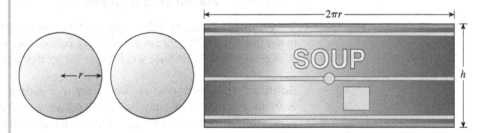

Figure 22

Our objective function is the (total) surface area S of the can. The area of each disc is πr^2, while the area of the rectangular piece is $2\pi r h$. Thus, our objective function is

$$S = 2\pi r^2 + 2\pi r h.$$

As usual, there is a constraint: The volume must be exactly 250 cubic centimeters. The formula for the volume of a cylinder is $V = \pi r^2 h$, so

$$\pi r^2 h = 250.$$

It is easiest to solve this constraint for h in terms of r:

$$h = \frac{250}{\pi r^2}.$$

Substituting in the objective function, we get

$$S = 2\pi r^2 + 2\pi r \frac{250}{\pi r^2} = 2\pi r^2 + \frac{500}{r}.$$

Now r cannot be negative or 0, but it can become very large (a very wide but very short can could have the right volume). We therefore take the domain of $S(r)$ to be $(0, +\infty)$, so our mathematical problem is as follows:

$$\text{Minimize } S(r) = 2\pi r^2 + \frac{500}{r} \text{ subject to } r > 0.$$

Now we calculate

$$S'(r) = 4\pi r - \frac{500}{r^2}.$$

To find stationary points, we set this equal to 0 and solve:

$$4\pi r - \frac{500}{r^2} = 0$$

$$4\pi r = \frac{500}{r^2}$$

$$4\pi r^3 = 500$$

$$r^3 = \frac{125}{\pi}.$$

So

$$r = \sqrt[3]{\frac{125}{\pi}} = \frac{5}{\sqrt[3]{\pi}} \approx 3.41.$$

The corresponding surface area is approximately $S(3.41) \approx 220$. There are no singular points or endpoints in the domain.

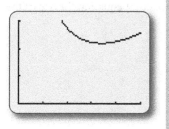

Figure 23

:::: **using** Technology

To see how S behaves near the one stationary point, let's graph it in a viewing window with interval $[0, 5]$ for r and $[0, 300]$ for S. The result is Figure 23.

From the graph we can clearly see that the smallest surface area occurs at the stationary point at $r \approx 3.41$. The height of the can will be

$$h = \frac{250}{\pi r^2} \approx 6.83.$$

Thus, the can that uses the least amount of metal has a height of approximately 6.83 centimeters and a radius of approximately 3.41 centimeters. Such a can will use approximately 220 square centimeters of metal.

➡ **Before we go on...** We obtained the value of r in Example 4 by solving the equation

$$4\pi r = \frac{500}{r^2}.$$

This time, let us do things differently: Divide both sides by 4π to obtain

$$r = \frac{500}{4\pi r^2} = \frac{125}{\pi r^2}$$

189

and compare what we got with the expression for h:

$$h = \frac{250}{\pi r^2}$$

which we see is exactly twice the expression for r. Put another way, the height is exactly equal to the diameter so that the can looks square when viewed from the side. Have you ever seen cans with that shape? Why do you think most cans do not have this shape? ∎

EXAMPLE 5 Allocation of Labor

The Gym Sock Company manufactures cotton athletic socks. Production is partially automated through the use of robots. Daily operating costs amount to $50 per laborer and $30 per robot. The number of pairs of socks the company can manufacture in a day is given by a Cobb-Douglas* production formula

✱ **NOTE** Cobb-Douglas production formulas were discussed in Section 11.6.

$$q = 50n^{0.6}r^{0.4}$$

where q is the number of pairs of socks that can be manufactured by n laborers and r robots. Assuming that the company wishes to produce 1,000 pairs of socks per day at a minimum cost, how many laborers and how many robots should it use?

Solution The unknowns are the number of laborers n and the number of robots r. The objective is to minimize the daily cost:

$$C = 50n + 30r.$$

The constraints are given by the daily quota

$$1,000 = 50n^{0.6}r^{0.4}$$

and the fact that n and r are nonnegative. We solve the constraint equation for one of the variables; let's solve for n:

$$n^{0.6} = \frac{1,000}{50r^{0.4}} = \frac{20}{r^{0.4}}.$$

Taking the $1/0.6$ power of both sides gives

$$n = \left(\frac{20}{r^{0.4}}\right)^{1/0.6} = \frac{20^{1/0.6}}{r^{0.4/0.6}} = \frac{20^{5/3}}{r^{2/3}} \approx \frac{147.36}{r^{2/3}}.$$

Substituting in the objective equation gives us the cost as a function of r:

$$C(r) \approx 50\left(\frac{147.36}{r^{2/3}}\right) + 30r$$

$$= 7{,}368r^{-2/3} + 30r.$$

The only remaining constraint on r is that $r > 0$. To find the minimum value of $C(r)$, we first take the derivative:

$$C'(r) \approx -4{,}912r^{-5/3} + 30.$$

Setting this equal to zero, we solve for r:

$$r^{-5/3} \approx 0.006107$$

$$r \approx (0.006107)^{-3/5} \approx 21.3.$$

The corresponding cost is $C(21.3) \approx \$1{,}600$. There are no singular points or endpoints in the domain of C.

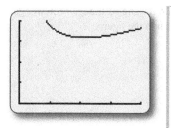

Figure 24

using Technology

To see how C behaves near its stationary point, let's draw its graph in a viewing window with an interval of $[0, 40]$ for r and $[0, 2,000]$ for C. The result is Figure 24.

From the graph we can see that C does have its minimum at the stationary point. The corresponding value of n is

$$n \approx \frac{147.36}{r^{2/3}} \approx 19.2.$$

At this point, our solution appears to be this: Use (approximately) 19.2 laborers and (approximately) 21.3 robots to meet the manufacturing quota at a minimum cost. However, we are not interested in fractions of robots or people, so we need to find integer solutions for n and r. If we round these numbers, we get the solution $(n, r) = (19, 21)$. However, a quick calculation shows that

$$q = 50(19)^{0.6}(21)^{0.4} \approx 989 \text{ pairs of socks,}$$

which fails to meet the quota of 1,000. Thus, we need to round at least one of the quantities n and r *upward* in order to meet the quota. The three possibilities, with corresponding values of q and C, are as follows:

$$(n, r) = (20, 21), \text{ with } q \approx 1,020 \text{ and } C = \$1,630$$
$$(n, r) = (19, 22), \text{ with } q \approx 1,007 \text{ and } C = \$1,610$$
$$(n, r) = (20, 22), \text{ with } q \approx 1,039 \text{ and } C = \$1,660.$$

Of these, the solution that meets the quota at a minimum cost is $(n, r) = (19, 22)$. Thus, the Gym Sock Co. should use 19 laborers and 22 robots, at a cost of $50 \times 19 + 30 \times 22 = \$1,610$, to manufacture $50 \times 19^{0.6} \times 22^{0.4} \approx 1,007$ pairs of socks.

12.2 EXERCISES

▼ more advanced   ◆ challenging

🖳 indicates exercises that should be solved using technology

Solve the optimization problems in Exercises 1–8. HINT [See Example 2.]

1. Maximize $P = xy$ with $x + y = 10$.

2. Maximize $P = xy$ with $x + 2y = 40$.

3. Minimize $S = x + y$ with $xy = 9$ and both x and $y > 0$.

4. Minimize $S = x + 2y$ with $xy = 2$ and both x and $y > 0$.

5. Minimize $F = x^2 + y^2$ with $x + 2y = 10$.

6. Minimize $F = x^2 + y^2$ with $xy^2 = 16$.

7. Maximize $P = xyz$ with $x + y = 30$ and $y + z = 30$, and x, y, and $z \geq 0$.

8. Maximize $P = xyz$ with $x + z = 12$ and $y + z = 12$, and x, y, and $z \geq 0$.

9. For a rectangle with perimeter 20 to have the largest area, what dimensions should it have?

10. For a rectangle with area 100 to have the smallest perimeter, what dimensions should it have?

APPLICATIONS

11. *Average Cost: iPods* Assume that it costs **Apple** approximately

$$C(x) = 22,500 + 100x + 0.01x^2$$

dollars to manufacture x 30-gigabyte video iPods in a day.[1] How many iPods should be manufactured in order to minimize average cost? What is the resulting average cost of an iPod? (Give your answer to the nearest dollar.) HINT [See Example 1.]

12. *Average Cost: Xboxes* Assume that it costs **Microsoft** approximately

$$C(x) = 14,400 + 550x + 0.01x^2$$

---

[1] Not the actual cost equation; the authors do not know Apple's actual cost equation. The marginal cost in the model given is in rough agreement with the actual marginal cost for reasonable values of x. Source for cost data: *Manufacturing & Technology News*, July 31, 2007 Volume 14, No. 14 (www.manufacturingnews.com).

dollars to manufacture x Xbox 360s in a day.[2] How many Xboxes should be manufactured in order to minimize average cost? What is the resulting average cost of an Xbox? (Give your answer to the nearest dollar.) HINT [See Example 1.]

13. **Pollution Control** The cost of controlling emissions at a firm rises rapidly as the amount of emissions reduced increases. Here is a possible model:

$$C(q) = 4{,}000 + 100q^2$$

where q is the reduction in emissions (in pounds of pollutant per day) and C is the daily cost to the firm (in dollars) of this reduction. What level of reduction corresponds to the lowest average cost per pound of pollutant, and what would be the resulting average cost to the nearest dollar?

14. **Pollution Control** Repeat the preceding exercise using the following cost function:

$$C(q) = 2{,}000 + 200q^2.$$

15. **Pollution Control** (Compare Exercise 13.) The cost of controlling emissions at a firm is given by

$$C(q) = 4{,}000 + 100q^2$$

where q is the reduction in emissions (in pounds of pollutant per day) and C is the daily cost to the firm (in dollars) of this reduction. Government clean-air subsidies amount to $500 per pound of pollutant removed. How many pounds of pollutant should the firm remove each day in order to minimize *net* cost (cost minus subsidy)?

16. **Pollution Control** (Compare Exercise 14.) Repeat the preceding exercise, using the following cost function:

$$C(q) = 2{,}000 + 200q^2$$

with government subsidies amounting to $100 per pound of pollutant removed per day.

17. **Fences** I would like to create a rectangular vegetable patch. The fencing for the east and west sides costs $4 per foot, and the fencing for the north and south sides costs only $2 per foot. I have a budget of $80 for the project. What are the dimensions of the vegetable patch with the largest area I can enclose? HINT [See Example 2.]

18. **Fences** I would like to create a rectangular orchid garden that abuts my house so that the house itself forms the northern boundary. The fencing for the southern boundary costs $4 per foot, and the fencing for the east and west sides costs $2 per foot. If I have a budget of $80 for the project, what are the dimensions of the garden with the largest area I can enclose? HINT [See Example 2.]

19. **Fences** You are building a right-angled triangular flower garden along a stream as shown in the figure.

The fencing of the left border costs $5 per foot, while the fencing of the lower border costs $1 per foot. (No fencing is required along the river.) You want to spend $100 and enclose as much area as possible. What are the dimensions of your garden, and what area does it enclose? [The area of a right-triangle is given by $A = xy/2$.]

20. **Fences** Repeat Exercise 19, this time assuming that the fencing of the left border costs $8 per foot, while the fencing of the lower border costs $2 per foot, and that you can spend $400.

21. ▼ **Fences** (Compare Exercise 17.) For tax reasons, I need to create a rectangular vegetable patch with an area of exactly 242 sq. ft. The fencing for the east and west sides costs $4 per foot, and the fencing for the north and south sides costs only $2 per foot. What are the dimensions of the vegetable patch with the least expensive fence? HINT [Compare Exercise 3.]

22. ▼ **Fences** (Compare Exercise 18.) For reasons too complicated to explain, I need to create a rectangular orchid garden with an area of exactly 324 sq. ft. abutting my house so that the house itself forms the northern boundary. The fencing for the southern boundary costs $4 per foot, and the fencing for the east and west sides costs $2 per foot. What are the dimensions of the orchid garden with the least expensive fence? HINT [Compare Exercise 4.]

23. **Revenue** Hercules Films is deciding on the price of the video release of its film *Son of Frankenstein*. Its marketing people estimate that at a price of p dollars, it can sell a total of $q = 200{,}000 - 10{,}000p$ copies. What price will bring in the greatest revenue? HINT [See Example 3.]

24. **Profit** Hercules Films is also deciding on the price of the video release of its film *Bride of the Son of Frankenstein*. Again, marketing estimates that at a price of p dollars, it can sell $q = 200{,}000 - 10{,}000p$ copies, but each copy costs $4 to make. What price will give the greatest *profit*?

25. **Revenue: Cell Phones** Worldwide quarterly sales of **Nokia** cell phones were approximately $q = -p + 156$ million phones

---

[2] Not the actual cost equation; the authors do not know Microsoft's actual cost equation. The marginal cost in the model given is in rough agreement with the actual marginal cost for reasonable values of x. Source for estimate of marginal cost: iSuppli (www.isuppli.com).

when the wholesale price was $\$p$. At what wholesale price should **Nokia** have sold its phones to maximize its quarterly revenue? What would have been the resulting revenue?[3]

26. *Revenue: Cell Phones* Worldwide annual sales of all cell phones were approximately $-10p + 1,600$ million phones when the wholesale price was $\$p$. At what wholesale price should cell phones have been sold to maximize annual revenue? What would have been the resulting revenue?[4]

27. *Revenue: Monorail Service* The demand, in rides per day, for monorail service in Las Vegas in 2005 can be approximated by $q = -4,500p + 41,500$ when the fare was $\$p$. What price should have been charged to maximize total revenue?[5]

28. *Demand for Monorail Service, Mars* The demand, in rides per day, for monorail service in the three urbynes (or districts) of Utarek, Mars, can be approximated by $q = -2p + 24$ million riders when the fare is $\bar{\bar{Z}}p$. What price should be charged to maximize total revenue?[6]

29. ▽ *Revenue* Assume that the demand for tuna in a small coastal town is given by

$$p = \frac{500,000}{q^{1.5}}$$

where q is the number of pounds of tuna that can be sold in a month at p dollars per pound. Assume that the town's fishery wishes to sell at least 5,000 pounds of tuna per month.

a. How much should the town's fishery charge for tuna in order to maximize monthly revenue? HINT [See Example 3, and don't neglect endpoints.]

b. How much tuna will it sell per month at that price?

c. What will be its resulting revenue?

30. ▽ *Revenue* Economist Henry Schultz devised the following demand function for corn:

$$p = \frac{6,570,000}{q^{1.3}}$$

where q is the number of bushels of corn that could be sold at p dollars per bushel in one year.[7] Assume that at least 10,000 bushels of corn per year must be sold.

a. How much should farmers charge per bushel of corn to maximize annual revenue? HINT [See Example 3, and don't neglect endpoints.]

b. How much corn can farmers sell per year at that price?

c. What will be the farmers' resulting revenue?

31. ▽ *Revenue* The wholesale price for chicken in the United States fell from 25¢ per pound to 14¢ per pound, while per capita chicken consumption rose from 22 pounds per year to 27.5 pounds per year.[8] Assuming that the demand for chicken depends linearly on the price, what wholesale price for chicken maximizes revenues for poultry farmers, and what does that revenue amount to?

32. ▽ *Revenue* Your underground used-book business is booming. Your policy is to sell all used versions of *Calculus and You* at the same price (regardless of condition). When you set the price at $10, sales amounted to 120 volumes during the first week of classes. The following semester, you set the price at $30 and sold not a single book. Assuming that the demand for books depends linearly on the price, what price gives you the maximum revenue, and what does that revenue amount to?

33. *Profit: Cell Phones* (Compare Exercise 25.) Worldwide quarterly sales of **Nokia** cell phones were approximately $q = -p + 156$ million phones when the wholesale price was $\$p$. Assuming that it cost **Nokia** $40 to manufacture each cell phone, at what wholesale price should **Nokia** have sold its phones to maximize its quarterly profit? What would have been the resulting profit?[9] (The actual wholesale price was $105 in the fourth quarter of 2004.) HINT [See Example 3, and recall that Profit = Revenue − Cost.]

34. *Profit: Cell Phones* (Compare Exercise 26.) Worldwide annual sales of all cell phones were approximately $-10p + 1,600$ million phones when the wholesale price was $\$p$. Assuming that it costs $30 to manufacture each cell phone, at what wholesale price should cell phones have been sold to maximize annual profit? What would have been the resulting profit?[10] HINT [See Example 3, and recall that Profit = Revenue − Cost.]

35. ▽ *Profit* The demand equation for your company's virtual reality video headsets is

$$p = \frac{1,000}{q^{0.3}}$$

where q is the total number of headsets that your company can sell in a week at a price of p dollars. The total manufacturing and shipping cost amounts to $100 per headset.

a. What is the greatest profit your company can make in a week, and how many headsets will your company sell at this level of profit? (Give answers to the nearest whole number.)

b. How much, to the nearest $1, should your company charge per headset for the maximum profit?

[3] Demand equation based on second- and fourth-quarter sales. Source: Embedded.com/Company reports December, 2004.

[4] Demand equation based on estimated 2004 sales and projected 2008 sales. Source: I-Stat/NDR, December 2004.

[5] Source for ridership data: *New York Times*, February 10, 2007, p. A9.

[6] $\bar{\bar{Z}}$ designates Zonars, the official currency in Mars. See www.marsnext .com for details of the Mars colony, its commerce, and its culture.

[7] Based on data for the period 1915–1929. Source: Henry Schultz, *The Theory and Measurement of Demand*, (as cited in *Introduction to Mathematical Economics* by A. L. Ostrosky, Jr., and J. V. Koch, Waveland Press, Prospect Heights, Illinois, 1979).

[8] Data are provided for the years 1951–1958. Source: U.S. Department of Agriculture, *Agricultural Statistics*.

[9] Source: Embedded.com/Company reports, December 2004.

[10] Wholesale price projections are the authors'. Source for sales prediction: I-Stat/NDR, December 2004.

36. ▼ Profit Due to sales by a competing company, your company's sales of virtual reality video headsets have dropped, and your financial consultant revises the demand equation to

$$p = \frac{800}{q^{0.35}}$$

where q is the total number of headsets that your company can sell in a week at a price of p dollars. The total manufacturing and shipping cost still amounts to $100 per headset.

a. What is the greatest profit your company can make in a week, and how many headsets will your company sell at this level of profit? (Give answers to the nearest whole number.)

b. How much, to the nearest $1, should your company charge per headset for the maximum profit?

37. Paint Cans A company manufactures cylindrical paint cans with open tops with a volume of 27,000 cubic centimeters. What should be the dimensions of the cans in order to use the least amount of metal in their production? HINT [See Example 4.]

38. Metal Drums A company manufactures cylindrical metal drums with open tops with a volume of 1 cubic meter. What should be the dimensions of the drum in order to use the least amount of metal in their production? HINT [See Example 4.]

39. Tin Cans A company manufactures cylindrical tin cans with closed tops with a volume of 250 cubic centimeters. The metal used to manufacture the cans costs $0.01 per square cm for the sides and $0.02 per square cm for the (thicker) top and bottom. What should be the dimensions of the cans in order to minimize the cost of metal in their production? What is the ratio height/radius? HINT [See Example 4.]

40. Metal Drums A company manufactures cylindrical metal drums with open tops with a volume of 2 cubic meters. The metal used to manufacture the cans costs $2 per square meter for the sides and $3 per square meter for the (thicker) bottom. What should be the dimensions of the drums in order to minimize the cost of metal in their production? What is the ratio height/radius? HINT [See Example 4.]

41. ▼ Box Design Chocolate Box Company is going to make open-topped boxes out of 6×16-inch rectangles of cardboard by cutting squares out of the corners and folding up the sides. What is the largest volume box it can make this way?

42. ▼ Box Design Vanilla Box Company is going to make open-topped boxes out of 12×12-inch rectangles of cardboard by cutting squares out of the corners and folding up the sides. What is the largest volume box it can make this way?

43. ▼ Box Design A packaging company is going to make closed boxes, with square bases, that hold 125 cubic centimeters. What are the dimensions of the box that can be built with the least material?

44. ▼ Box Design A packaging company is going to make open-topped boxes, with square bases, that hold 108 cubic centimeters. What are the dimensions of the box that can be built with the least material?

45. ▼ Luggage Dimensions American Airlines requires that the total outside dimensions (length + width + height) of a checked bag not exceed 62 inches.[11] Suppose you want to check a bag whose height equals its width. What is the largest volume bag of this shape that you can check on an **American** flight?

46. ▼ Luggage Dimensions American Airlines requires that the total outside dimensions (length + width + height) of a carry-on bag not exceed 45 inches.[12] Suppose you want to carry on a bag whose length is twice its height. What is the largest volume bag of this shape that you can carry on an **American** flight?

47. ▼ Luggage Dimensions Fly-by-Night Airlines has a peculiar rule about luggage: The length and width of a bag must add up to at most 45 inches, and the width and height must also add up to 45 inches. What are the dimensions of the bag with the largest volume that Fly-by-Night will accept?

48. ▼ Luggage Dimensions Fair Weather Airlines has a similar rule. It will accept only bags for which the sum of the length and width is at most 36 inches, while the sum of length, height, and twice the width is at most 72 inches. What are the dimensions of the bag with the largest volume that Fair Weather will accept?

49. ▼ Package Dimensions The **U.S. Postal Service (USPS)** will accept packages only if the length plus girth is no more than 108 inches.[13] (See the figure.)

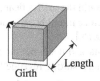

Girth Length

Assuming that the front face of the package (as shown in the figure) is square, what is the largest volume package that the **USPS** will accept?

50. ▼ Package Dimensions United Parcel Service (UPS) will accept only packages with a length of no more than 108 inches and length plus girth of no more than 165 inches.[14] (See figure for the preceding exercise.) Assuming that the front face of the package (as shown in the figure) is square, what is the largest volume package that **UPS** will accept?

51. ▼ Cell Phone Revenues The number of cell phone subscribers in China in the years 2000–2005 was projected to follow the equation $N(t) = 39t + 68$ million subscribers in year t ($t = 0$ represents January 2000). The average annual revenue per cell phone user was $350 in 2000.[15] If we assume

[11] According to information on its Web site (www.aa.com/).

[12] Ibid.

[13] The requirement for packages sent other than Parcel Post, as of September 2008 (www.usps.com/).

[14] The requirement as of September 2008 (www.ups.com/).

[15] Based on a regression of projected figures (coefficients are rounded). Source: Intrinsic Technology/New York Times, Nov. 24, 2000, p. C1.

that due to competition the revenue per cell phone user decreases continuously at an annual rate of 30%, we can model the annual revenue as

$$R(t) = 350(39t + 68)e^{-0.3t} \text{ million dollars.}$$

Determine **a.** when to the nearest 0.1 year the revenue was projected to peak and **b.** the revenue, to the nearest $1 million, at that time.

52. ▼ *Cell Phone Revenues* (Refer to Exercise 51.) If we assume instead that the revenue per cell phone user decreases continuously at an annual rate of 20%, we obtain the revenue model

$$R(t) = 350(39t + 68)e^{-0.2t} \text{ million dollars.}$$

Determine **a.** when to the nearest 0.1 year the revenue was projected to peak and **b.** the revenue, to the nearest $1 million, at that time.

53. ▼ *Research and Development* Spending on research and development by drug companies in the United States t years after 1970 can be modeled by

$$S(t) = 2.5e^{0.08t} \text{ billion dollars.} \quad (0 \le t \le 31)$$

The number of new drugs approved by the Federal Drug Administration (FDA) over the same period can be modeled by

$$D(t) = 10 + t \text{ drugs per year.}^{16} \quad (0 \le t \le 31)$$

When was the function $D(t)/S(t)$ at a maximum? What is the maximum value of $D(t)/S(t)$? What does the answer tell you about the cost of developing new drugs?

54. ▼ *Research and Development* (Refer to Exercise 53.) If the number of new drugs approved by the FDA had been $10 + 2t$ new drugs each year, when would the function $D(t)/S(t)$ have reached a maximum? What does the answer tell you about the cost of developing new drugs?

55. ▼ *Asset Appreciation* As the financial consultant to a classic auto dealership, you estimate that the total value (in dollars) of its collection of 1959 Chevrolets and Fords is given by the formula

$$v = 300,000 + 1,000t^2 \quad (t \ge 5)$$

where t is the number of years from now. You anticipate a continuous inflation rate of 5% per year, so that the discounted (present) value of an item that will be worth $\$v$ in t years' time is

$$p = ve^{-0.05t}.$$

When would you advise the dealership to sell the vehicles to maximize their discounted value?

56. ▼ *Plantation Management* The value of a fir tree in your plantation increases with the age of the tree according to the formula

$$v = \frac{20t}{1 + 0.05t}$$

where t is the age of the tree in years. Given a continuous inflation rate of 5% per year, the discounted (present) value of a newly planted seedling is

$$p = ve^{-0.05t}.$$

At what age (to the nearest year) should you harvest your trees in order to ensure the greatest possible discounted value?

57. ▼ *Marketing Strategy* FeatureRich Software Company has a dilemma. Its new program, Doors-X 10.27, is almost ready to go on the market. However, the longer the company works on it, the better it can make the program and the more it can charge for it. The company's marketing analysts estimate that if it delays t days, it can set the price at $100 + 2t$ dollars. On the other hand, the longer it delays, the more market share they will lose to their main competitor (see the next exercise) so that if it delays t days it will be able to sell $400,000 - 2,500t$ copies of the program. How many days should FeatureRich delay the release in order to get the greatest revenue?

58. ▼ *Marketing Strategy* FeatureRich Software's main competitor (see previous exercise) is Moon Systems, and Moon is in a similar predicament. Its product, Walls-Y 11.4, could be sold now for $200, but for each day Moon delays, it could increase the price by $4. On the other hand, it could sell 300,000 copies now, but each day it waits will cut sales by 1,500. How many days should Moon delay the release in order to get the greatest revenue?

59. ▼ *Average Profit* The FeatureRich Software Company sells its graphing program, Dogwood, with a volume discount. If a customer buys x copies, then he or she pays[17] $\$500\sqrt{x}$. It cost the company $10,000 to develop the program and $2 to manufacture each copy. If a single customer were to buy all the copies of Dogwood, how many copies would the customer have to buy for FeatureRich Software's average profit per copy to be maximized? How are average profit and marginal profit related at this number of copies?

60. ▼ *Average Profit* Repeat the preceding exercise with the charge to the customer $\$600\sqrt{x}$ and the cost to develop the program $9,000.

61. *Resource Allocation* Your company manufactures automobile alternators, and production is partially automated through the use of robots. Daily operating costs amount to $100 per laborer and $16 per robot. In order to meet production deadlines, the company calculates that the numbers of laborers and robots must satisfy the constraint

$$xy = 10,000$$

---

[16] The exponential model for R&D is based on the 1970 and 2001 spending in constant 2001 dollars, while the linear model for new drugs approved is based on the 6-year moving average from data from 1970–2000. Source for data: Pharmaceutical Research and Manufacturers of America, FDA/*New York Times*, April 19, 2002, p. C1.

[17] This is similar to the way site licenses have been structured for the program Maple®.

where x is the number of laborers and y is the number of robots. Assuming that the company wishes to meet production deadlines at a minimum cost, how many laborers and how many robots should it use? HINT [See Example 5.]

62. *Resource Allocation* Your company is the largest sock manufacturer in the solar system, and production is automated through the use of androids and robots. Daily operating costs amount to ᵺ200 per android and ᵺ8 per robot.[18] In order to meet production deadlines, the company calculates that the numbers of androids and robots must satisfy the constraint

$$xy = 1{,}000{,}000$$

where x is the number of androids and y is the number of robots. Assuming that the company wishes to meet production deadlines at a minimum cost, how many androids and how many robots should it use? HINT [See Example 5.]

63. ▼ *Resource Allocation* Your automobile assembly plant has a Cobb-Douglas production function given by

$$q = x^{0.4}y^{0.6}$$

where q is the number of automobiles it produces per year, x is the number of employees, and y is the daily operating budget (in dollars). Annual operating costs amount to an average of \$20,000 per employee plus the operating budget of \$365y. Assume that you wish to produce 1,000 automobiles per year at a minimum cost. How many employees should you hire? HINT [See Example 5.]

64. ▼ *Resource Allocation* Repeat the preceding exercise using the production formula

$$q = x^{0.5}y^{0.5}.$$

HINT [See Example 5.]

65. ▼ *Incarceration Rate* The incarceration rate (the number of persons in prison per 100,000 residents) in the United States can be approximated by

$$N(t) = 0.04t^3 - 2t^2 + 40t + 460 \quad (0 \le t \le 18)$$

(t is the year since 1990).[19] When, to the nearest year, was the incarceration rate increasing most rapidly? When was it increasing least rapidly? HINT [You are being asked to find the extreme values of the rate of change of the incarceration rate.]

66. ▼ *Prison Population* The prison population in the United States can be approximated by

$$N(t) = 0.02t^3 - 2t^2 + 100t + 1{,}100 \text{ thousand people}$$
$$(0 \le t \le 18)$$

(t is the year since 1990).[20] When, to the nearest year, was the prison population increasing most rapidly? When was it increasing least rapidly? HINT [You are being asked to find the extreme values of the rate of change of the prison population.]

67. ▼ *Embryo Development* The oxygen consumption of a bird embryo increases from the time the egg is laid through the time the chick hatches. In a typical galliform bird, the oxygen consumption can be approximated by

$$c(t) = -0.065t^3 + 3.4t^2 - 22t + 3.6 \text{ milliliters per day}$$
$$(8 \le t \le 30)$$

where t is the time (in days) since the egg was laid.[21] (An egg will typically hatch at around $t = 28$.) When, to the nearest day, is $c'(t)$ a maximum? What does the answer tell you?

68. ▼ *Embryo Development* The oxygen consumption of a turkey embryo increases from the time the egg is laid through the time the chick hatches. In a brush turkey, the oxygen consumption can be approximated by

$$c(t) = -0.028t^3 + 2.9t^2 - 44t + 95 \text{ milliliters per day}$$
$$(20 \le t \le 50)$$

where t is the time (in days) since the egg was laid.[22] (An egg will typically hatch at around $t = 50$.) When, to the nearest day, is $c'(t)$ a maximum? What does the answer tell you?

69. ▦ ▼ *Subprime Mortgages* The percentage of U.S.-issued mortgages that are subprime can be approximated by

$$A(t) = \frac{15.0}{1 + 8.6(1.8)^{-t}} \text{ percent} \quad (0 \le t \le 8)$$

t years after the start of 2000.[23] Graph the *derivative* of $A(t)$ and determine the year during which this derivative had an absolute maximum and also its value at that point. What does the answer tell you?

70. ▦ ▼ *Subprime Mortgage Debt* The approximate value of subprime (normally classified as risky) mortgage debt outstanding in the United States can be approximated by

$$A(t) = \frac{1{,}350}{1 + 4.2(1.7)^{-t}} \text{ billion dollars} \quad (0 \le t \le 8)$$

t years after the start of 2000.[24] Graph the *derivative* of $A(t)$ and determine the year during which this derivative had an absolute maximum and also its value at that point. What does the answer tell you?

71. ▦ ▼ *Asset Appreciation* You manage a small antique company that owns a collection of Louis XVI jewelry boxes. Their value v is increasing according to the formula

$$v = \frac{10{,}000}{1 + 500e^{-0.5t}}$$

---

[18] ᵺ are Standard Solar Units of currency.

[19] Source for data: Sourcebook of Criminal Justice Statistics Online (www.albany.edu/sourcebook).

[20] Ibid.

[21] The model approximates graphical data published in the article "The Brush Turkey" by Roger S. Seymour, *Scientific American,* December, 1991, pp. 108–114.

[22] Ibid.

[23] Sources: Mortgage Bankers Association, UBS.

[24] Source: www.data360.org/dataset.aspx?Data_Set_Id=9549.

where t is the number of years from now. You anticipate an inflation rate of 5% per year, so that the present value of an item that will be worth $\$v$ in t years' time is given by

$$p = v(1.05)^{-t}.$$

When (to the nearest year) should you sell the jewelry boxes to maximize their present value? How much (to the nearest constant dollar) will they be worth at that time?

72. ▣ ▼ *Harvesting Forests* The following equation models the approximate volume in cubic feet of a typical Douglas fir tree of age t years.[25]

$$V = \frac{22,514}{1 + 22,514t^{-2.55}}$$

The lumber will be sold at $10 per cubic foot, and you do not expect the price of lumber to appreciate in the foreseeable future. On the other hand, you anticipate a general inflation rate of 5% per year, so that the present value of an item that will be worth $\$v$ in t years' time is given by

$$p = v(1.05)^{-t}.$$

At what age (to the nearest year) should you harvest a Douglas fir tree in order to maximize its present value? How much (to the nearest constant dollar) will a Douglas fir tree be worth at that time?

73. ◆ *Agriculture* The fruit yield per tree in an orchard containing 50 trees is 100 pounds per tree each year. Due to crowding, the yield decreases by 1 pound per season for every additional tree planted. How may additional trees should be planted for a maximum total annual yield?

74. ◆ *Agriculture* Two years ago your orange orchard contained 50 trees and the total yield was 75 bags of oranges. Last year you removed ten of the trees and noticed that the total yield increased to 80 bags. Assuming that the yield per tree depends linearly on the number of trees in the orchard, what should you do this year to maximize your total yield?

75. ◆ *Revenue* (based on a question on the GRE Economics Test[26]) If total revenue (*TR*) is specified by $TR = a + bQ - cQ^2$, where Q is quantity of output and a, b, and c are positive parameters, then *TR* is maximized for this firm when it produces Q equal to:

(A) $b/2ac$ (B) $b/4c$ (C) $(a+b)/c$ (D) $b/2c$ (E) $c/2b$

76. ◆ *Revenue* (based on a question on the GRE Economics Test) If total demand (*Q*) is specified by $Q = -aP + b$, where P is unit price and a and b are positive parameters, then

total revenue is maximized for this firm when it charges P equal to:

(A) $b/2a$ (B) $b/4a$ (C) a/b (D) $a/2b$ (E) $-b/2a$

COMMUNICATION AND REASONING EXERCISES

77. You are interested in knowing the height of the tallest condominium complex that meets the city zoning requirements that the height H should not exceed eight times the distance D from the road and that it must provide parking for at least 50 cars. The objective function of the associated optimization problem is then:

(A) H (B) $H - 8D$ (C) D (D) $D - 8H$

One of the constraints is:

(A) $8H = D$ (B) $8D = H$
(C) $H'(D) = 0$ (D) $D'(H) = 0$

78. You are interested in building a condominium complex with a height H of at least 8 times the distance D from the road and parking area of at least 1,000 sq ft. at the cheapest cost C. The objective function of the associated optimization problem is then:

(A) H (B) D (C) C (D) $H + D - C$

One of the constraints is:

(A) $H - 8D = 0$ (B) $H + D - C = 0$
(C) $C'(D) = 0$ (D) $8H = D$

79. Explain why the following problem is uninteresting: A packaging company wishes to make cardboard boxes with open tops by cutting square pieces from the corners of a square sheet of cardboard and folding up the sides. What is the box with the least surface area it can make this way?

80. Explain why finding the production level that minimizes a cost function is frequently uninteresting. What would a more interesting objective be?

81. Your friend Margo claims that all you have to do to find the absolute maxima and minima in applications is set the derivative equal to zero and solve. "All that other stuff about endpoints and so-on is a waste of time just to make life hard for us," according to Margo. Explain why she is wrong, and find at least one exercise in this exercise set to illustrate your point.

82. You are having a hard time persuading your friend Marco that maximizing revenue is not the same as maximizing profit. "How on earth can you expect to obtain the largest profit if you are not taking in the largest revenue?" Explain why he is wrong, and find at least one exercise in this exercise set to illustrate your point.

83. ▼ If demand q decreases as price p increases, what does the minimum value of dq/dp measure?

84. ▼ Explain how you would solve an optimization problem of the following form. Maximize $P = f(x, y, z)$ subject to $z = g(x, y)$ and $y = h(x)$.

[25] The model is the authors' and is based on data in *Environmental and Natural Resource Economics* by Tom Tietenberg, Third Edition, (New York: HarperCollins, 1992), p. 282.

[26] Source: GRE Economics Test, by G. Gallagher, G. E. Pollock, W. J. Simeone, G. Yohe (Piscataway, NJ: Research and Education Association, 1989).

12.3 Higher Order Derivatives: Acceleration and Concavity

The **second derivative** is simply the derivative of the derivative function. To explain why we would be interested in such a thing, we start by discussing one of its interpretations.

Acceleration

Recall that if $s(t)$ represents the position of a car at time t, then its velocity is given by the derivative: $v(t) = s'(t)$. But one rarely drives a car at a constant speed; the velocity itself is changing. The rate at which the velocity is changing is the **acceleration**. Because the derivative measures the rate of change, acceleration is the derivative of velocity: $a(t) = v'(t)$. Because v is the derivative of s, we can express the acceleration in terms of s:

$$a(t) = v'(t) = (s')'(t) = s''(t)$$

That is, a is the derivative of the derivative of s, in other words, the second derivative of s, which we write as s''. (In this context you will often hear the derivative s' referred to as the **first derivative**.)

Second Derivative, Acceleration

If a function f has a derivative that is in turn differentiable, then its **second derivative** is the derivative of the derivative of f, written as f''. If $f''(a)$ exists, we say that f is **twice differentiable at** $x = a$.

Quick Examples

1. If $f(x) = x^3 - x$, then $f'(x) = 3x^2 - 1$, so $f''(x) = 6x$ and $f''(-2) = -12$.
2. If $f(x) = 3x + 1$, then $f'(x) = 3$, so $f''(x) = 0$.
3. If $f(x) = e^x$, then $f'(x) = e^x$, so $f''(x) = e^x$ as well.

The **acceleration** of a moving object is the derivative of its velocity—that is, the second derivative of the position function.

Quick Example

If t is time in hours and the position of a car at time t is $s(t) = t^3 + 2t^2$ miles, then the car's velocity is $v(t) = s'(t) = 3t^2 + 4t$ miles per hour and its acceleration is $a(t) = s''(t) = v'(t) = 6t + 4$ miles per hour per hour.

Differential Notation for the Second Derivative

We have written the second derivative of $f(x)$ as $f''(x)$. We could also use differential notation:

$$f''(x) = \frac{d^2f}{dx^2}$$

This notation comes from writing the second derivative as the derivative of the derivative in differential notation:

$$f''(x) = \frac{d}{dx}\left[\frac{df}{dx}\right] = \frac{d^2f}{dx^2}$$

Similarly, if $y = f(x)$, we write $f''(x)$ as $\dfrac{d}{dx}\left[\dfrac{dy}{dx}\right] = \dfrac{d^2y}{dx^2}$. For example, if $y = x^3$, then $\dfrac{d^2y}{dx^2} = 6x$.

An important example of acceleration is the acceleration due to gravity.

EXAMPLE 1 Acceleration Due to Gravity

According to the laws of physics, the height of an object near the surface of the earth falling in a vacuum from an initial rest position 100 feet above the ground under the influence of gravity is approximately

$$s(t) = 100 - 16t^2 \text{ feet}$$

in t seconds. Find its acceleration.

Solution The velocity of the object is

$$v(t) = s'(t) = -32t \text{ ft/s.} \qquad \text{Differential notation: } v = \frac{ds}{dt} = -32t \text{ ft/s.}$$

The reason for the negative sign is that the height of the object is decreasing with time, so its velocity is negative. Hence, the acceleration is

$$a(t) = s''(t) = -32 \text{ ft/s}^2. \qquad \text{Differential notation: } a = \frac{d^2s}{dt^2} = -32 \text{ ft/s}^2.$$

(We write ft/s^2 as an abbreviation for feet/second/second—that is, feet per second per second. It is often read "feet per second squared.") Thus, the *downward* velocity is increasing by 32 ft/s every second. We say that 32 ft/s^2 is the **acceleration due to gravity**. If we ignore air resistance, all falling bodies near the surface of the earth, no matter what their weight, will fall with this acceleration.*

* NOTE On other planets the acceleration due to gravity is different. For example, on Jupiter, it is about three times as large as on Earth.

† NOTE An interesting aside: Galileo's experiments depended on getting extremely accurate timings. Because the timepieces of his day were very inaccurate, he used the most accurate time measurement he could: He sang and used the beat as his stopwatch.

§ NOTE A true story: The point was made again during the Apollo 15 mission to the moon (July 1971) when astronaut David R. Scott dropped a feather and a hammer from the same height. The moon has no atmosphere, so the two hit the surface of the moon simultaneously.

➡ **Before we go on...** In very careful experiments using balls rolling down inclined planes, Galileo made one of his most important discoveries—that the acceleration due to gravity is constant and does not depend on the weight or composition of the object falling.† A famous, though probably apocryphal, story has him dropping cannonballs of different weights off the Leaning Tower of Pisa to prove his point.§ ∎

EXAMPLE 2 Acceleration of Sales

For the first 15 months after the introduction of a new video game, the total sales can be modeled by the curve

$$S(t) = 20e^{0.4t} \text{ units sold}$$

where t is the time in months since the game was introduced. After about 25 months total sales follow more closely the curve

$$S(t) = 100{,}000 - 20e^{17-0.4t}$$

How fast are total sales accelerating after 10 months? How fast are they accelerating after 30 months? What do these numbers mean?

Solution By acceleration we mean the rate of change of the rate of change, which is the second derivative. During the first 15 months, the first derivative of sales is

$$\frac{dS}{dt} = 8e^{0.4t}$$

and so the second derivative is

$$\frac{d^2S}{dt^2} = 3.2e^{0.4t}$$

Thus, after 10 months the acceleration of sales is

$$\left.\frac{d^2S}{dt^2}\right|_{t=10} = 3.2e^4 \approx 175 \text{ units/month/month, or units/month}^2$$

We can also compute total sales

$$S(10) = 20e^4 \approx 1,092 \text{ units}$$

and the rate of change of sales

$$\left.\frac{dS}{dt}\right|_{t=10} = 8e^4 \approx 437 \text{ units/month.}$$

What do these numbers mean? By the end of the tenth month, a total of 1,092 video games have been sold. At that time the game is selling at the rate of 437 units per month. This rate of sales is increasing by 175 units per month per month. More games will be sold each month than the month before.

To analyze the sales after 30 months is similar, using the formula

$$S(t) = 100,000 - 20e^{17-0.4t}.$$

The derivative is

$$\frac{dS}{dt} = 8e^{17-0.4t}$$

and the second derivative is

$$\frac{d^2S}{dt^2} = -3.2e^{17-0.4t}.$$

After 30 months,

$$S(30) = 100,000 - 20e^{17-12} \approx 97,032 \text{ units}$$

$$\left.\frac{dS}{dt}\right|_{t=30} = 8e^{17-12} \approx 1,187 \text{ units/month}$$

$$\left.\frac{d^2S}{dt^2}\right|_{t=30} = -3.2e^{17-12} \approx -475 \text{ units/month}^2.$$

By the end of the 30th month, 97,032 video games have been sold, the game is selling at a rate of 1,187 units per month, and the rate of sales is *decreasing* by 475 units per month. Fewer games are sold each month than the month before.

Geometric Interpretation of Second Derivative: Concavity

The first derivative of f tells us where the graph of f is rising [where $f'(x) > 0$] and where it is falling [where $f'(x) < 0$]. The second derivative tells in what direction the graph of f *curves* or *bends*. Consider the graphs in Figures 25 and 26.

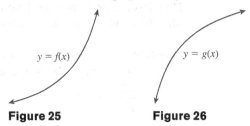

Figure 25   **Figure 26**

Think of a car driving from left to right along each of the roads shown in the two figures. A car driving along the graph of *f* in Figure 25 will turn to the left (upward); a car driving along the graph of *g* in Figure 26 will turn to the right (downward). We say that the graph of *f* is **concave up** and the graph of *g* is **concave down**. Now think about the derivatives of *f* and *g*. The derivative $f'(x)$ starts small but *increases* as the graph gets steeper. Because $f'(x)$ is increasing, its derivative $f''(x)$ must be positive. On the other hand, $g'(x)$ *decreases* as we go to the right. Because $g'(x)$ is decreasing, its derivative $g''(x)$ must be negative. Summarizing, we have the following.

Concavity and the Second Derivative

A curve is **concave up** if its slope is increasing, in which case the second derivative is positive. A curve is **concave down** if its slope is decreasing, in which case the second derivative is negative. A point in the domain of *f* where the graph of *f* changes concavity, from concave up to concave down or vice versa, is called a **point of inflection**. At a point of inflection, the second derivative is either zero or undefined.

Locating Points of Inflection

To locate possible points of inflection, list points where $f''(x) = 0$ and also points where $f''(x)$ is not defined.

Quick Examples

1. The graph of the function *f* shown in Figure 27 is concave up when $1 < x < 3$, so $f''(x) > 0$ for $1 < x < 3$. It is concave down when $x < 1$ and $x > 3$, so $f''(x) < 0$ when $x < 1$ and $x > 3$. It has points of inflection at $x = 1$ and $x = 3$.

2. Consider $f(x) = x^3 - 3x$, whose graph is shown in Figure 28. $f''(x) = 6x$ is negative when $x < 0$ and positive when $x > 0$. The graph of *f* is concave down when $x < 0$ and concave up when $x > 0$. *f* has a point of inflection at $x = 0$, where the second derivative is 0.

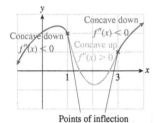

Figure 27

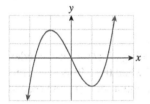

Figure 28

The following example shows one of the reasons it's useful to look at concavity.

EXAMPLE 3 Inflation

Figure 29 shows the value of the U.S. Consumer Price Index (CPI) from January 2007 through June 2008.*

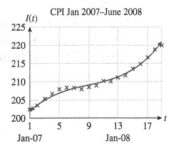

Figure 29

The approximating curve shown on the figure is given by

$$I(t) = 0.0075t^3 - 0.2t^2 + 2.2t + 200 \qquad (1 \le t \le 19)$$

---

*The CPI is compiled by the Bureau of Labor Statistics and is based upon a 1982 value of 100. For instance, a CPI of 200 means the CPI has doubled since 1982. Source: InflationData.com (www.inflationdata.com).

where t is time in months ($t = 1$ represents January 2007). When the CPI is increasing, the U.S. economy is **experiencing inflation**. In terms of the model, this means that the derivative is positive: $I'(t) > 0$. Notice that $I'(t) > 0$ for the entire period shown (the graph is sloping upward), so the U.S. economy experienced inflation for $1 \leq t \leq 19$. We could measure **inflation** by the first derivative $I'(t)$ of the CPI, but we traditionally measure it as a ratio:

$$\text{Inflation rate} = \frac{I'(t)}{I(t)}, \quad \text{Relative rate of change of the CPI}$$

expressed as a percentage per unit time (per month in this case).

a. Use the model to estimate the inflation rate in January 2008.

b. Was inflation slowing or speeding up in January 2008?

c. When was inflation slowing? When was inflation speeding up? When was inflation slowest?

Solution

a. We need to compute $I'(t)$:

$$I'(t) = 0.0225t^2 - 0.4t + 2.2$$

Thus, the inflation rate in January 2008 was given by

$$\text{Inflation rate} = \frac{I'(13)}{I(13)} = \frac{0.0225(13)^2 - 0.4(13) + 2.2}{0.0075(13)^3 - 0.2(13)^2 + 2.2(13) + 200}$$

$$= \frac{0.8025}{211.2775} \approx 0.00380,$$

or 0.38% per month.*

* **NOTE** The 0.38% monthly inflation rate corresponds to a $12 \times 0.38 = 4.56\%$ annual inflation rate. This result could be obtained directly by changing the units of the t-axis from months to years and then redoing the calculation.

b. We say that inflation is "slowing" when the CPI is decelerating ($I''(t) < 0$; the index rises at a slower rate). Similarly, inflation is "speeding up" when the CPI is accelerating ($I''(t) > 0$; the index rises at a faster rate). From the formula for $I'(t)$, the second derivative is

$$I''(t) = 0.045t - 0.4$$
$$I''(13) = 0.045(13) - 0.4 = 0.185.$$

Because this quantity is positive, we conclude that inflation was speeding up in January 2008.

c. When inflation is slowing, $I''(t)$ is negative, so the graph of the CPI is concave down. When inflation is speeding up, it is concave up. At the point at which it switches, there is point of inflection (Figure 30).

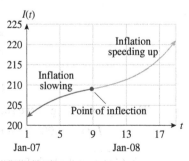

Figure 30

202

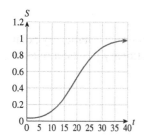

(a) Graph of S

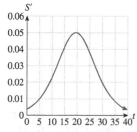

(b) Graph of S'

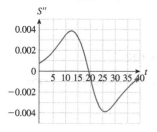

(c) Graph of S''

Figure 31

 using Technology

We can use a TI-83/84 Plus or a downloadable Excel sheet at the Web site to graph the second derivative of the function in Example 4:

TI-83/84 Plus
```
Y₁=1/(1+50*e^(-0.2X))
Y₂=nDeriv(Y₁,X,X)
Y₃=nDeriv(Y₂,X,X)
```

Web Site
www.FiniteandCalc.org

Student Web Site

→ Online Utilities

→ Excel First and Second
   Derivative Graphing Utility

Function:
```
1/(1+50*exp(-0.2*x))
```

The point of inflection occurs when $I''(t) = 0$; that is,

$$0.045t - 0.4 = 0$$

$$t = \frac{0.4}{0.45} \approx 8.9.$$

Thus, inflation was slowing when $t < 8.9$ (that is, until the end of August), and speeding up when $t > 8.9$ (after that time). Inflation was slowest at the point when it stopped slowing down and began to speed up, $t \approx 8.9$; notice that the graph has the least slope at that point.

EXAMPLE 4 The Point of Diminishing Returns

After the introduction of a new video game, the total worldwide sales are modeled by the curve

$$S(t) = \frac{1}{1 + 50e^{-0.2t}} \text{ million units sold}$$

where t is the time in months since the game was introduced (compare Example 2). The graphs of $S(t)$, $S'(t)$, and $S''(t)$ are shown in Figure 31. Where is the graph of S concave up, and where is it concave down? Where are any points of inflection? What does this all mean?

Solution Look at the graph of S. We see that the graph of S is concave up in the early months and then becomes concave down later. The point of inflection, where the concavity changes, is somewhere between 15 and 25 months.

Now look at the graph of S''. This graph crosses the t-axis very close to $t = 20$, is positive before that point, and negative after that point. Because positive values of S'' indicate S is concave up and negative values concave down, we conclude that the graph of S is concave up for about the first 20 months; that is, for $0 < t < 20$ and concave down for $20 < t < 40$. The concavity switches at the point of inflection, which occurs at about $t = 20$ (when $S''(t) = 0$; a more accurate answer is $t \approx 19.56$).

What does this all mean? Look at the graph of S', which shows sales per unit time, or monthly sales. From this graph we see that monthly sales are increasing for $t < 20$: more units are being sold each month than the month before. Monthly sales reach a peak of 0.05 million = 50,000 games per month at the point of inflection $t = 20$ and then begin to drop off. Thus, the point of inflection occurs at the time when monthly sales stop increasing and start to fall off; that is, the time when monthly sales peak. The point of inflection is sometimes called the **point of diminishing returns**. Although the total sales figure continues to rise (see the graph of S: game units continue to be sold), the *rate* at which units are sold starts to drop. (See Figure 32.)

Figure 32

The Second Derivative Test for Relative Extrema

The second derivative often gives us a way of knowing whether or not a stationary point is a relative extremum. Figure 33 shows a graph with two stationary points: a relative maximum at $x = a$ and a relative minimum at $x = b$.

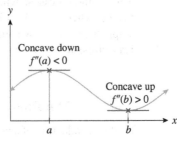

Concave down
$f''(a) < 0$

Concave up
$f''(b) > 0$

Figure 33

Notice that the curve is *concave down* at the relative maximum ($x = a$), so that $f''(a) < 0$, and *concave up* at the relative minimum ($x = b$), so that $f''(b) > 0$. This suggests the following (compare the First Derivative Test in Section 12.1).

Second Derivative Test for Relative Extrema

Suppose that the function f has a stationary point at $x = c$, and that $f''(c)$ exists. Determine the sign of $f''(c)$.

1. If $f''(c) > 0$ then f has a relative minimum at $x = c$.

2. If $f''(c) < 0$ then f has a relative maximum at $x = c$.

If $f''(c) = 0$ then the test is inconclusive and you need to use one of the methods of Section 12.1 (such as the first derivative test) to determine whether or not f has a relative extremum at $x = c$.

Quick Examples

1. $f(x) = x^2 - 2x$ has $f'(x) = 2x - 2$ and hence a stationary point at $x = 1$. $f''(x) = 2$, and so $f''(1) = 2$, which is positive, so f has a relative minimum at $x = 1$.

2. Let $f(x) = x^3 - 3x^2 - 9x$. Then
$$f'(x) = 3x^2 - 6x - 9 = 3(x + 1)(x - 3)$$
Stationary points at $x = -1, x = 3$
$$f''(x) = 6x - 6$$
$f''(-1) = -12$, so there is a relative maximum at $x = -1$
$f''(3) = 12$, so there is a relative minimum at $x = 3$.

3. $f(x) = x^4$ has $f'(x) = 4x^3$ and hence a stationary point at $x = 0$. $f''(x) = 12x^2$ and so $f''(0) = 0$, telling us that the second derivative test is inconclusive. However, we can see from the graph of f or the first derivative test that f has a minimum at $x = 0$.

Higher Order Derivatives

There is no reason to stop at the second derivative; we could once again take the *derivative* of the second derivative to obtain the **third derivative**, f''', and we could take the derivative once again to obtain the **fourth derivative**, written $f^{(4)}$, and then continue to obtain $f^{(5)}$, $f^{(6)}$, and so on (assuming we get a differentiable function at each stage).

Higher Order Derivatives

We define

$$f'''(x) = \frac{d}{dx}[f''(x)]$$

$$f^{(4)}(x) = \frac{d}{dx}[f'''(x)]$$

$$f^{(5)}(x) = \frac{d}{dx}[f^{(4)}(x)],$$

and so on, assuming all these derivatives exist.

Different Notations

$$f'(x), f''(x), f'''(x), f^{(4)}(x), \ldots, f^{(n)}(x), \ldots$$

$$\frac{df}{dx}, \frac{d^2f}{dx^2}, \frac{d^3f}{dx^3}, \frac{d^4f}{dx^4}, \ldots, \frac{d^nf}{dx^n}, \ldots$$

$$\frac{dy}{dx}, \frac{d^2y}{dx^2}, \frac{d^3y}{dx^3}, \frac{d^4y}{dx^4}, \ldots, \frac{d^ny}{dx^n}, \ldots \qquad \text{When } y = f(x)$$

$$y, y', y'', y''', y^{(4)}, \ldots, y^{(n)}, \ldots \qquad \text{When } y = f(x)$$

Quick Examples

1. If $f(x) = x^3 - x$, then $f'(x) = 3x^2 - 1$, $f''(x) = 6x$, $f'''(x) = 6$, $f^{(4)}(x) = f^{(5)}(x) = \cdots = 0$.
2. If $f(x) = e^x$, then $f'(x) = e^x$, $f''(x) = e^x$, $f'''(x) = e^x$, $f^{(4)}(x) = f^{(5)}(x) = \cdots = e^x$.

Q: *We know that the second derivative can be interpreted as acceleration. How do we interpret the third derivative; and the fourth, fifth, and so on?*

A: Think of a car traveling down the road (with position $s(t)$ at time t) in such a way that its acceleration $\dfrac{d^2s}{dt^2}$ is changing with time (for instance, the driver may be slowly increasing pressure on the accelerator, causing the car to accelerate at a greater and greater rate). Then $\dfrac{d^3s}{dt^3}$ is the rate of change of acceleration. $\dfrac{d^4s}{dt^4}$ would then be the *acceleration* of the acceleration, and so on.

Q: *How are these higher order derivatives reflected in the graph of a function f?*

A: Because the concavity is measured by f'', its derivative f''' tells us the rate of change of concavity. Similarly, $f^{(4)}$ would tell us the *acceleration* of concavity, and so on. These properties are very subtle and hard to discern by simply looking at the curve; the higher the order, the more subtle the property. There is a remarkable theorem by Taylor* that tells us that, for a large class of functions (including polynomial, exponential, logarithmic, and trigonometric functions) the values of all orders of derivative $f(a)$, $f'(a)$, $f''(a)$, $f'''(a)$, and so on at the single point $x = a$ are enough to describe the entire graph (even at points very far from $x = a$)! In other words, the smallest piece of a graph near any point *a* contains sufficient information to "clone" the entire graph!

* **NOTE** Brook Taylor (1685–1731) was an English mathematician.

FAQs

Interpreting Points of Inflection and Using the Second Derivative Test

Q: *It says in Example 4 that monthly sales reach a maximum at the point of inflection (second derivative is zero), but the Second Derivative test says that, for a maximum, the second derivative must be positive. What is going on here?*

A: What is a maximum in Example 4 is the *rate of change of* sales: which is measured in sales per unit time (monthly sales in the example). In other words, it is the *derivative* of the total sales function that is a maximum, so we located the maximum by setting its derivative (which is the *second* derivative of total sales) equal to zero. In general: To find relative (stationary) extrema of the *original* function, set $f'(x)$ equal to zero and solve for *x* as usual. The second derivative test can then be used to test the stationary point obtained. To find relative (stationary) extrema of the *rate of change of f*, set $f''(x) = 0$ and solve for *x*.

Q: *I used the second derivative test and it was inconclusive. That means that there is neither a relative maximum nor a relative minimum at $x = a$, right?*

A: Wrong. If (as is often the case) the second derivative is zero at a stationary point, all it means is that the second derivative test itself cannot determine whether the given point is a relative maximum, minimum, or neither. For instance, $f(x) = x^4$ has a stationary minimum at $x = 0$, but the second derivative test is inconclusive. In such cases, one should use another test (such as the first derivative test) to decide if the point is a relative maximum, minimum, or neither.

12.3 EXERCISES

▼ more advanced ◆ challenging

⏹ indicates exercises that should be solved using technology

In Exercises 1–10, calculate $\dfrac{d^2y}{dx^2}$. HINT [See Quick Examples on page 894.]

1. $y = 3x^2 - 6$

2. $y = -x^2 + x$

3. $y = \dfrac{2}{x}$

4. $y = -\dfrac{2}{x^2}$

5. $y = 4x^{0.4} - x$

6. $y = 0.2x^{-0.1}$

7. $y = e^{-(x-1)} - x$

8. $y = e^{-x} + e^x$

9. $y = \dfrac{1}{x} - \ln x$

10. $y = x^{-2} + \ln x$

In Exercises 11–16, the position s of a point (in feet) is given as a function of time t (in seconds). Find (a) its acceleration as a function of t and (b) its acceleration at the specified time. HINT [See Example 1.]

11. $s = 12 + 3t - 16t^2$; $t = 2$

12. $s = -12 + t - 16t^2$; $t = 2$

13. $s = \dfrac{1}{t} + \dfrac{1}{t^2}$; $t = 1$ **14.** $s = \dfrac{1}{t} - \dfrac{1}{t^2}$; $t = 2$

15. $s = \sqrt{t} + t^2$; $t = 4$ **16.** $s = 2\sqrt{t} + t^3$; $t = 1$

In Exercises 17–24, the graph of a function is given. Find the approximate coordinates of all points of inflection of each function (if any). HINT [See Quick Examples on page 897.]

17. 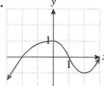   **18.**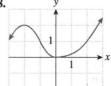

19. 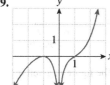   **20.**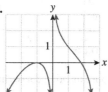

21. 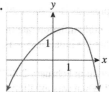   **22.**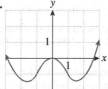

23. 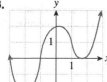   **24.**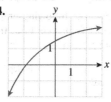

In Exercises 25–28, the graph of the derivative, $f'(x)$, is given. Determine the x-coordinates of all points of inflection of $f(x)$, if any. (Assume that $f(x)$ is defined and continuous everywhere in $[-3, 3]$.) HINT [See the **Before we go on** discussion in Example 4.]

25. 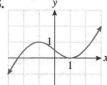   **26.**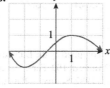

27. 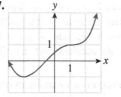   **28.**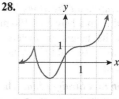

In Exercises 29–32, the graph of the second derivative, $f''(x)$, is given. Determine the x-coordinates of all points of inflection of $f(x)$, if any. (Assume that $f(x)$ is defined and continuous everywhere in $[-3, 3]$.)

29. 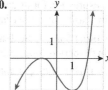   **30.**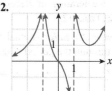

31. 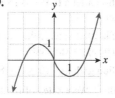   **32.**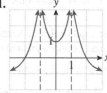

In Exercises 33–44, find the x-coordinates of all critical points of the given function. Determine whether each critical point is a relative maximum, minimum, or neither by first applying the second derivative test, and, if the test fails, by some other method. HINT [See Quick Examples on page 900.]

33. $f(x) = x^2 - 4x + 1$ **34.** $f(x) = 2x^2 - 2x + 3$

35. $g(x) = x^3 - 12x$ **36.** $g(x) = 2x^3 - 6x + 3$

37. $f(t) = t^3 - t$ **38.** $f(t) = -2t^3 + 3t$

39. $f(x) = x^4 - 4x^3$ **40.** $f(x) = 3x^4 - 2x^3$

41. $f(x) = e^{-x^2}$ **42.** $f(x) = e^{2-x^2}$

43. $f(x) = xe^{1-x^2}$ **44.** $f(x) = xe^{-x^2}$

In Exercises 45–54, calculate the derivatives of all orders: $f'(x), f''(x), f'''(x), f^{(4)}(x), \ldots, f^{(n)}(x), \ldots$ HINT [See Quick Examples on page 901.]

45. $f(x) = 4x^2 - x + 1$ **46.** $f(x) = -3x^3 + 4x$

47. $f(x) = -x^4 + 3x^2$ **48.** $f(x) = x^4 + x^3$

49. $f(x) = (2x + 1)^4$ **50.** $f(x) = (-2x + 1)^3$

51. $f(x) = e^{-x}$ **52.** $f(x) = e^{2x}$

53. $f(x) = e^{3x-1}$ **54.** $f(x) = 2e^{-x+3}$

APPLICATIONS

55. _Acceleration on Mars_ If a stone is dropped from a height of 40 meters above the Martian surface, its height in meters after t seconds is given by $s = 40 - 1.9t^2$. What is its acceleration? HINT [See Example 1.]

56. Acceleration on the Moon If a stone is thrown up at 10 m per second from a height of 100 meters above the surface of the Moon, its height in meters after t seconds is given by $s = 100 + 10t - 0.8t^2$. What is its acceleration? HINT [See Example 1.]

57. Motion in a Straight Line The position of a particle moving in a straight line is given by $s = t^3 - t^2$ ft after t seconds. Find an expression for its acceleration after a time t. Is its velocity increasing or decreasing when $t = 1$?

58. Motion in a Straight Line The position of a particle moving in a straight line is given by $s = 3e^t - 8t^2$ ft after t seconds. Find an expression for its acceleration after a time t. Is its velocity increasing or decreasing when $t = 1$?

59. Bottled Water Sales Annual sales of bottled water in the United States in the period 2000–2008 can be approximated by

$$R(t) = 12t^2 + 500t + 4{,}700 \text{ million gallons} \quad (0 \le t \le 8)$$

where t is time in years since 2000.[27] Were sales of bottled water accelerating or decelerating in 2004? How quickly? HINT [See Example 2.]

60. Bottled Water Sales Annual U.S. per capita sales of bottled water through the period 2000–2008 can be approximated by

$$Q(t) = 0.04t^2 + 1.5t + 17 \text{ gallons} \quad (0 \le t \le 8)$$

where t is time in years since 2000.[28] Were U.S. per capita sales of bottled water accelerating or decelerating in 2006? How quickly?

61. Embryo Development The daily oxygen consumption of a bird embryo increases from the time the egg is laid through the time the chick hatches. In a typical galliform bird, the oxygen consumption can be approximated by

$$c(t) = -0.065t^3 + 3.4t^2 - 22t + 3.6 \text{ ml} \quad (8 \le t \le 30)$$

where t is the time (in days) since the egg was laid.[29] (An egg will typically hatch at around $t = 28$.) Use the model to estimate the following (give the units of measurement for each answer and round all answers to two significant digits):

a. The daily oxygen consumption 20 days after the egg was laid

b. The rate at which the oxygen consumption is changing 20 days after the egg was laid

c. The rate at which the oxygen consumption is accelerating 20 days after the egg was laid

62. Embryo Development The daily oxygen consumption of a turkey embryo increases from the time the egg is laid through the time the chick hatches. In a brush turkey, the oxygen consumption can be approximated by

$$c(t) = -0.028t^3 + 2.9t^2 - 44t + 95 \text{ ml} \quad (20 \le t \le 50)$$

where t is the time (in days) since the egg was laid.[30] (An egg will typically hatch at around $t = 50$.) Use the model to estimate the following (give the units of measurement for each answer and round all answers to two significant digits):

a. The daily oxygen consumption 40 days after the egg was laid

b. The rate at which the oxygen consumption is changing 40 days after the egg was laid

c. The rate at which the oxygen consumption is accelerating 40 days after the egg was laid

63. Inflation The following graph shows the approximate value of the United States Consumer Price Index (CPI) from December 2006 through July 2007.[31]

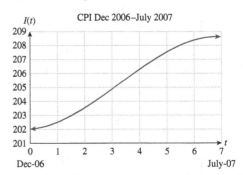

The approximating curve shown on the figure is given by

$$I(t) = -0.04t^3 + 0.4t^2 + 0.1t + 202 \quad (0 \le t \le 7)$$

where t is time in months ($t = 0$ represents December 2006).

a. Use the model to estimate the monthly inflation rate in February 2007 ($t = 2$). [Recall that the inflation *rate* is $I'(t)/I(t)$.]

b. Was inflation slowing or speeding up in February 2007?

c. When was inflation speeding up? When was inflation slowing? HINT [See Example 3.]

64. Inflation The following graph shows the approximate value of the U.S. Consumer Price Index (CPI) from September 2004 through November 2005.[32]

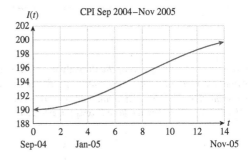

---

[27] Source for data: Beverage Marketing Corporation (www.bottledwater.org).

[28] Ibid.

[29] The model approximates graphical data published in the article "The Brush Turkey" by Roger S. Seymour, *Scientific American,* December, 1991, pp. 108–114.

[30] Ibid.

[31] The CPI is compiled by the Bureau of Labor Statistics and is based upon a 1982 value of 100. For instance, a CPI of 200 means the CPI has doubled since 1982. Source: InflationData.com (www.inflationdata.com).

[32] Ibid.

The approximating curve shown on the figure is given by

$$I(t) = -0.005t^3 + 0.12t^2 - 0.01t + 190 \quad (0 \le t \le 14)$$

where t is time in months ($t = 0$ represents September 2004).

a. Use the model to estimate the monthly inflation rate in July 2005 ($t = 10$). [Recall that the inflation *rate* is $I'(t)/I(t)$.]

b. Was inflation slowing or speeding up in July 2005?

c. When was inflation speeding up? When was inflation slowing? HINT [See Example 3.]

65. *Inflation* The following graph shows the approximate value of the U.S. Consumer Price Index (CPI) from July 2005 through March 2006.[33]

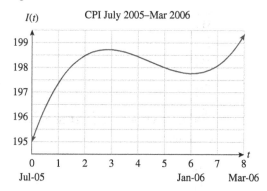

The approximating curve shown on the figure is given by

$$I(t) = 0.06t^3 - 0.8t^2 + 3.1t + 195 \quad (0 \le t \le 8)$$

where t is time in months ($t = 0$ represents July 2005).

a. Use the model to estimate the monthly inflation rates in December 2005 and February 2006 ($t = 5$ and $t = 7$).

b. Was inflation slowing or speeding up in February 2006?

c. When was inflation decreasing? When was inflation increasing?

66. *Inflation* The following graph shows the approximate value of the U.S. Consumer Price Index (CPI) from March 2006 through May 2007.[34]

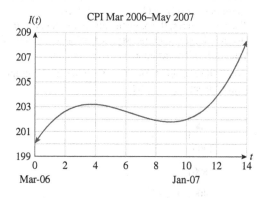

The approximating curve shown on the figure is given by

$$I(t) = 0.02t^3 - 0.38t^2 + 2t + 200 \quad (0 \le t \le 14)$$

where t is time in months ($t = 0$ represents March, 2006).

a. Use the model to estimate the monthly inflation rates in September 2006 and January 2007 ($t = 6$ and $t = 10$).

b. Was inflation slowing or speeding up in January 2007?

c. When was inflation decreasing? When was inflation increasing?

67. *Scientific Research* The percentage of research articles in the prominent journal *Physical Review* that were written by researchers in the United States during the years 1983–2003 can be modeled by

$$P(t) = 25 + \frac{36}{1 + 0.06(0.7)^{-t}}$$

where t is time in years since 1983.[35] The graphs of P, P', and P'' are shown here:

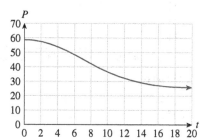

Graph of P

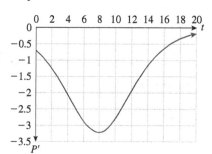

Graph of P'

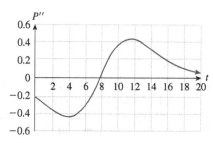

Graph of P''

---

[33] The CPI is compiled by the Bureau of Labor Statistics and is based upon a 1982 value of 100. For instance, a CPI of 200 means the CPI has doubled since 1982. Source: InflationData.com (www.inflationdata.com).

[34] Ibid.

[35] Source: The American Physical Society/*New York Times*, May 3, 2003, p. A1.

Determine, to the nearest whole number, the values of t for which the graph of P is concave up, and where it is concave down, and locate any points of inflection. What does the point of inflection tell you about science articles? HINT [See Example 4.]

68. *Scientific Research* The number of research articles in the prominent journal *Physical Review* that were written by researchers in Europe during the years 1983–2003 can be modeled by

$$P(t) = \frac{7.0}{1 + 5.4(1.2)^{-t}}$$

where t is time in years since 1983.[36] The graphs of P, P', and P'' are shown here:

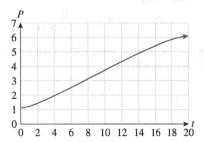

Graph of P

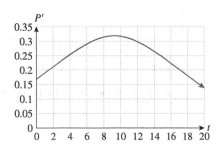

Graph of P'

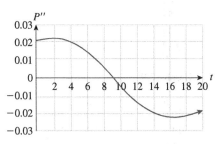

Graph of P''

Determine, to the nearest whole number, the values of t for which the graph of P is concave up, and where it is concave down, and locate any points of inflection. What does the point of inflection tell you about science articles?

69. *Embryo Development* Here are sketches of the graphs of c, c', and c'' from Exercise 61:

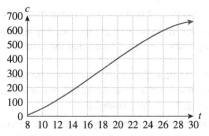

Graph of c

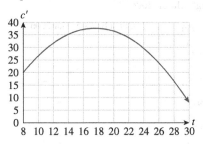

Graph of c'

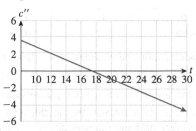

Graph of c''

Multiple choice:

a. The graph of c' **(A)** has a point of inflection **(B)** has no points of inflection in the range shown.

b. At around 18 days after the egg is laid, daily oxygen consumption is: **(A)** at a maximum, **(B)** increasing at a maximum rate, or **(C)** just beginning to decrease.

c. For $t > 18$ days, the oxygen consumption is **(A)** increasing at a decreasing rate, **(B)** decreasing at an increasing rate, or **(C)** increasing at an increasing rate.

70. *Embryo Development* Here are sketches of the graphs of c, c', and c'' from Exercise 62:

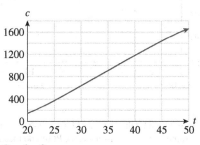

Graph of c

210

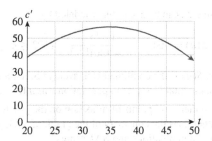

Graph of c'

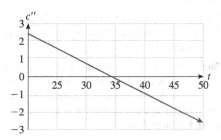

Graph of c''

Multiple choice:

a. The graph of c: **(A)** has points of inflection, **(B)** has no points of inflection, or **(C)** may or may not have a point of inflection, but the graphs do not provide enough information.

b. At around 35 days after the egg is laid, the rate of change of daily oxygen consumption is: **(A)** at a maximum, **(B)** increasing at a maximum rate, or **(C)** just becoming negative.

c. For $t < 35$ days, the oxygen consumption is: **(A)** increasing at an increasing rate, **(B)** increasing at a decreasing rate, or **(C)** decreasing at an increasing rate.

71. ▊ *Subprime Mortgages* The percentage of U.S.-issued mortgages that are subprime can be approximated by

$$A(t) = \frac{15.0}{1 + 8.6(1.8)^{-t}} \text{ percent} \quad (0 \leq t \leq 8)$$

t years after the start of 2000.[37] Graph the function as well as its first and second derivatives. Determine, to the nearest whole number, the values of t for which the graph of A is concave up and concave down, and the t-coordinate of any points of inflection. What does the point of inflection tell you about subprime mortgages? HINT [To graph the second derivative, see the note in the margin on page 899.]

72. ▊ *Subprime Mortgage Debt* The approximate value of subprime (normally classified as risky) mortgage debt outstanding in the United States can be approximated by

$$A(t) = \frac{1{,}350}{1 + 4.2(1.7)^{-t}} \text{ billion dollars} \quad (0 \leq t \leq 8)$$

t years after the start of 2000.[38] Graph the function as well as its first and second derivatives. Determine, to the nearest whole number, the values of t for which the graph of A is concave up and concave down, and the t-coordinate of any points of inflection. What does the point of inflection tell you about subprime mortgages? HINT [To graph the second derivative, see the note in the margin on page 899.]

73. *Epidemics* The following graph shows the total number n of people (in millions) infected in an epidemic as a function of time t (in years):

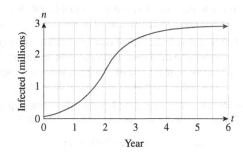

a. When to the nearest year was the rate of new infection largest?

b. When could the Centers for Disease Control and Prevention announce that the rate of new infection was beginning to drop? HINT [See Example 4.]

74. *Sales* The following graph shows the total number of Pomegranate Q4 computers sold since their release (t is in years):

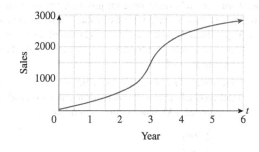

a. When were the computers selling fastest?

b. Explain why this graph might look as it does. HINT [See Example 4.]

---

[37] Sources: Mortgage Bankers Association, UBS.

[38] 2008 figure is an estimate.
Source: www.data360.org/dataset.aspx?Data_Set_Id=9549.

75. Industrial Output The following graph shows the yearly industrial output (measured in billions of zonars) of the Republic of Mars over a seven-year period:

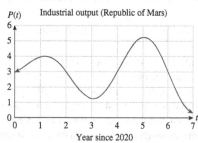

Industrial output (Republic of Mars)

Year since 2020

a. When to the nearest year did the rate of change of yearly industrial output reach a maximum?

b. When to the nearest year did the rate of change of yearly industrial output reach a minimum?

c. When to the nearest year does the graph first change from concave down to concave up? The result tells you that:

  (A) In that year the rate of change of industrial output reached a minimum compared with nearby years.

  (B) In that year the rate of change of industrial output reached a maximum compared with nearby years.

76. Profits The following graph shows the yearly profits of Gigantic Conglomerate, Inc. (GCI) from 2020 to 2035:

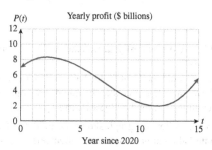

Yearly profit ($ billions)

Year since 2020

a. Approximately when were the profits rising most rapidly?

b. Approximately when were the profits falling most rapidly?

c. Approximately when could GCI's board of directors legitimately tell stockholders that they had "turned the company around"?

77. ▼ Education and Crime The following graph shows a striking relationship between the total prison population and the average combined SAT score in the United States:

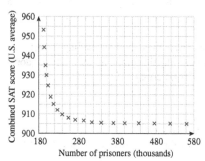

Number of prisoners (thousands)

These data can be accurately modeled by

$$S(n) = 904 + \frac{1{,}326}{(n - 180)^{1.325}}. \quad (192 \le n \le 563)$$

Here, $S(n)$ is the combined U.S. average SAT score at a time when the total U.S. prison population was n thousand.[39]

a. Are there any points of inflection on the graph of S?

b. What does the concavity of the graph of S tell you about prison populations and SAT scores?

78. ▼ Education and Crime Refer back to the model in the preceding exercise.

a. Are there any points of inflection on the graph of S'?

b. When is S'' a maximum? Interpret your answer in terms of prisoners and SAT scores.

79. ▼ Patents In 1965, the economist F. M. Scherer modeled the number, n, of patents produced by a firm as a function of the size, s, of the firm (measured in annual sales in millions of dollars). He came up with the following equation based on a study of 448 large firms:[40]

$$n = -3.79 + 144.42s - 23.86s^2 + 1.457s^3.$$

a. Find $\left.\dfrac{d^2n}{ds^2}\right|_{s=3}$. Is the rate at which patents are produced as the size of a firm goes up increasing or decreasing with size when $s = 3$? Comment on Scherer's words, "... we find diminishing returns dominating."

b. Find $\left.\dfrac{d^2n}{ds^2}\right|_{s=7}$ and interpret the answer.

c. Find the s-coordinate of any points of inflection and interpret the result.

80. ▼ Returns on Investments A company finds that the number of new products it develops per year depends on the size of its annual R&D budget, x (in thousands of dollars), according to the formula

$$n(x) = -1 + 8x + 2x^2 - 0.4x^3.$$

a. Find $n''(1)$ and $n''(3)$, and interpret the results.

b. Find the size of the budget that gives the largest rate of return as measured in new products per dollar (again, called the point of diminishing returns).

81. ▢ ▼ Oil Imports from Mexico Daily oil production in Mexico and daily U.S. oil imports from Mexico during 2005–2009 can be approximated by

$$P(t) = 3.9 - 0.10t \text{ million barrels} \quad (5 \le t \le 9)$$
$$I(t) = 2.1 - 0.11t \text{ million barrels} \quad (5 \le t \le 9)$$

---

[39] The model is the authors' based on data for the years 1967–1989. Sources: *Sourcebook of Criminal Justice Statistics*, 1990, p. 604/ Educational Testing Service.

[40] Source: F. M. Scherer, "Firm Size, Market Structure, Opportunity, and the Output of Patented Inventions," *American Economic Review* 55 (December 1965): pp. 1097–1125.

where t is time in years since the start of 2000.[41]

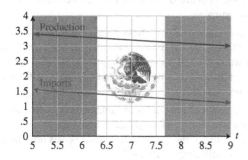

Graph the function $I(t)/P(t)$ and its derivative. Is the graph of $I(t)/P(t)$ concave up or concave down? The concavity of $I(t)/P(t)$ tells you that:

(A) The percentage of oil produced in Mexico that was exported to the United States was decreasing.

(B) The percentage of oil produced in Mexico that was not exported to the United States was increasing.

(C) The percentage of oil produced in Mexico that was exported to the United States was decreasing at a slower rate.

(D) The percentage of oil produced in Mexico that was exported to the United States was decreasing at a faster rate.

82. ▢ ▼ *Oil Imports from Mexico* Repeat Exercise 81 using instead the models for 2000–2004 shown below:

$$P(t) = 3.0 + 0.13t \text{ million barrels} \quad (0 \le t \le 4)$$
$$I(t) = 1.4 + 0.06t \text{ million barrels} \quad (0 \le t \le 4)$$

(t is time in years since the start of 2000).[42]

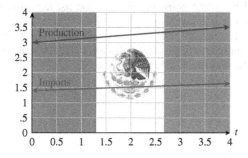

83. ◆ *Logistic Models* Let

$$f(x) = \frac{N}{1 + Ab^{-x}}$$

for constants N, A, and b (A and b positive and $b \ne 1$). Show that f has a single point of inflection at $x = \ln A / \ln b$.

84. ◆ *Logistic Models* Let

$$f(x) = \frac{N}{1 + Ae^{-kx}}$$

for constants N, A, and k (A and k positive). Show that f has a single point of inflection at $x = \ln A/k$.

85. ▢ *Population: Puerto Rico* The population of Puerto Rico in 1950–2025 can be approximated by

$$P(t) = \frac{4{,}500}{1 + 1.1466 \, (1.0357)^{-t}} \text{ thousand people} \quad (0 \le t \le 75)$$

(t is the year since 1950).[43] Use the result of Exercise 83 to find the location of the point of inflection in the graph of P. What does the result tell you about the population of Puerto Rico?

86. ▢ *Population: Virgin Islands* The population of the Virgin Islands can be approximated by

$$P(t) = \frac{110}{1 + 2.3596 \, (1.0767)^{-t}} \text{ thousand people} \quad (0 \le t \le 75)$$

(t is the year since 1950).[44] Use the result of Exercise 83 to find the location of the point of inflection in the graph of P. What does the result tell you about the population of the Virgin Islands?

87. ▢ ▼ *Asset Appreciation* You manage a small antique store that owns a collection of Louis XVI jewelry boxes. Their value v is increasing according to the formula

$$v = \frac{10{,}000}{1 + 500e^{-0.5t}}$$

where t is the number of years from now. You anticipate an inflation rate of 5% per year, so that the present value of an item that will be worth $\$v$ in t years' time is given by

$$p = v(1.05)^{-t}.$$

What is the greatest rate of increase of the value of your antiques, and when is this rate attained?

88. ▢ ▼ *Harvesting Forests* The following equation models the approximate volume in cubic feet of a typical Douglas fir tree of age t years[45]:

$$V = \frac{22{,}514}{1 + 22{,}514 t^{-2.55}}.$$

The lumber will be sold at $10 per cubic foot, and you do not expect the price of lumber to appreciate in the foreseeable future. On the other hand, you anticipate a general inflation

---

[41] Source for data: Energy Information Administration/Pemex (http://www.eia.doe.gov)

[42] Ibid.

[43] Figures from 2010 on are U.S. census projections. Source for data: The 2008 Statistical Abstract (www.census.gov/).

[44] Ibid.

[45] The model is the authors', and is based on data in *Environmental and Natural Resource Economics* by Tom Tietenberg, Third Edition (New York: HarperCollins, 1992), p. 282.

rate of 5% per year, so that the present value of an item that will be worth v in t years time is given by

$$p = v(1.05)^{-t}.$$

What is the largest rate of increase of the value of a fir tree, and when is this rate attained?

89. ▼ *Asset Appreciation* As the financial consultant to a classic auto dealership, you estimate that the total value of its collection of 1959 Chevrolets and Fords is given by the formula

$$v = 300,000 + 1,000t^2$$

where t is the number of years from now. You anticipate a continuous inflation rate of 5% per year, so that the discounted (present) value of an item that will be worth v in t years' time is given by

$$p = ve^{-0.05t}.$$

When is the value of the collection of classic cars increasing most rapidly? When is it decreasing most rapidly?

90. ▼ *Plantation Management* The value of a fir tree in your plantation increases with the age of the tree according to the formula

$$v = \frac{20t}{1 + 0.05t}$$

where t is the age of the tree in years. Given a continuous inflation rate of 5% per year, the discounted (present) value of a newly planted seedling is

$$p = ve^{-0.05t}.$$

When is the discounted value of a tree increasing most rapidly? Decreasing most rapidly?

COMMUNICATION AND REASONING EXERCISES

91. Complete the following: If the graph of a function is concave up on its entire domain, then its second derivative is _____ on the domain.

92. Complete the following: If the graph of a function is concave up on its entire domain, then its first derivative is _____ on the domain.

93. Daily sales of Kent's Tents reached a maximum in January 2002 and declined to a minimum in January 2003 before starting to climb again. The graph of daily sales shows a point of inflection at June 2002. What is the significance of the point of inflection?

94. The graph of daily sales of Luddington's Wellington boots is concave down, although sales continue to increase. What properties of the graph of daily sales versus time are reflected in the following behaviors?

a. a point of inflection next year
b. a horizontal asymptote

95. ▼ Company A's profits satisfy $P(0) = \$1$ million, $P'(0) = \$1$ million per year, and $P''(0) = -\$1$ million per year per year. Company B's profits satisfy $P(0) = \$1$ million, $P'(0) = -\$1$ million per year, and $P''(0) = \$1$ million per year per year. There are no points of inflection in either company's profit curve. Sketch two pairs of profit curves: one in which Company A ultimately outperforms Company B and another in which Company B ultimately outperforms Company A.

96. ▼ Company C's profits satisfy $P(0) = \$1$ million, $P'(0) = \$1$ million per year, and $P''(0) = -\$1$ million per year per year. Company D's profits satisfy $P(0) = \$0$ million, $P'(0) = \$0$ million per year, and $P''(0) = \$1$ million per year per year. There are no points of inflection in either company's profit curve. Sketch two pairs of profit curves: one in which Company C ultimately outperforms Company D and another in which Company D ultimately outperforms Company C.

97. ▼ Explain geometrically why the derivative of a function has a relative extremum at a point of inflection, if it is defined there. Which points of inflection give rise to relative maxima in the derivative?

98. ▼ If we regard position, s, as a function of time, t, what is the significance of the *third* derivative, $s'''(t)$? Describe an everyday scenario in which this arises.

12.4 Analyzing Graphs

Mathematical curves are beautiful—their subtle form can be imitated by only the best of artists—and calculus gives us the tools we need to probe their secrets. While it is easy to use graphing technology to draw a graph, we must use calculus to understand what we are seeing. Following is a list of some of the most interesting features of the graph of a function.

Features of a Graph

1. *The x- and y-intercepts:* If $y = f(x)$, find the x-intercept(s) by setting $y = 0$ and solving for x; find the y-intercept by setting $x = 0$ and solving for y:

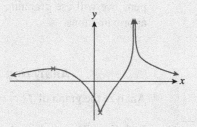

2. *Extrema:* Use the techniques of Section 12.1 to locate the maxima and minima:

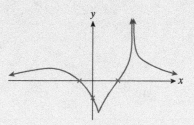

3. *Points of inflection:* Use the techniques of Section 12.2 to locate the points of inflection:

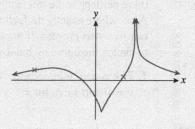

4. *Behavior near points where the function is not defined:* If $f(x)$ is not defined at $x = a$, consider $\lim_{x \to a^-} f(x)$ and $\lim_{x \to a^+} f(x)$ to see how the graph of f behaves as x approaches a:

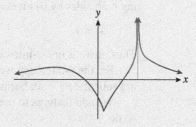

5. *Behavior at infinity:* Consider $\lim_{x \to -\infty} f(x)$ and $\lim_{x \to +\infty} f(x)$ if appropriate, to see how the graph of f behaves far to the left and right:

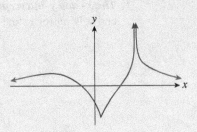

Note It is sometimes difficult or impossible to solve all of the equations that come up in Steps 1, 2, and 3 of the previous analysis. As a consequence, we might not be able to say exactly where the x-intercept, extrema, or points of inflection are. When this happens, we will use graphing technology to assist us in determining accurate numerical approximations. ∎

$-50 \le x \le 50, -20 \le y \le 20$

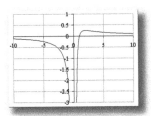

$-10 \le x \le 10, -3 \le y \le 1$

Figure 34

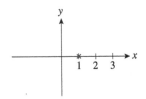

Figure 35

EXAMPLE 1 Analyzing a Graph

Analyze the graph of $f(x) = \dfrac{1}{x} - \dfrac{1}{x^2}$.

Solution The graph, as drawn using graphing technology, is shown in Figure 34, using two different viewing windows. (Note that $x = 0$ is not in the domain of f.) The second window in Figure 34 seems to show the features of the graph better than the first. Does the second viewing window include *all* the interesting features of the graph? Or are there perhaps some interesting features to the right of $x = 10$ or to the left of $x = -10$? Also, where exactly do features like maxima, minima, and points of inflection occur? In our five-step process of analyzing the interesting features of the graph, we will be able to sketch the curve by hand, and also answer these questions.

1. *The x- and y-intercepts:* We consider $y = \dfrac{1}{x} - \dfrac{1}{x^2}$. To find the x-intercept(s), we set $y = 0$ and solve for x:

$$0 = \frac{1}{x} - \frac{1}{x^2}$$

$$\frac{1}{x} = \frac{1}{x^2}.$$

Multiplying both sides by x^2 (we know that x cannot be zero, so we are not multiplying both sides by 0) gives

$$x = 1.$$

Thus, there is one x-intercept (which we can see in Figure 34) at $x = 1$.

For the y-intercept, we would substitute $x = 0$ and solve for y. However, we cannot substitute $x = 0$; because $f(0)$ is not defined, the graph does not meet the y-axis.

We add features to our freehand sketch as we go. Figure 35 shows what we have so far.

2. Relative extrema: We calculate $f'(x) = -\dfrac{1}{x^2} + \dfrac{2}{x^3}$. To find any stationary points, we set the derivative equal to 0 and solve for x:

$$-\frac{1}{x^2} + \frac{2}{x^3} = 0$$

$$\frac{1}{x^2} = \frac{2}{x^3}$$

$$x = 2.$$

Thus, there is one stationary point, at $x = 2$. We can use a test point to the right to determine that this stationary point is a relative maximum:

x	1 (Intercept)	2	3 (Test point)
$y = \dfrac{1}{x} - \dfrac{1}{x^2}$	0	$\dfrac{1}{4}$	$\dfrac{2}{9}$

The only possible singular point is at $x = 0$ because $f'(0)$ is not defined. However, $f(0)$ is not defined either, so there are no singular points. Figure 36 shows our graph so far.

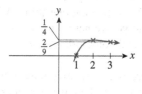

Figure 36

3. Points of inflection: We calculate $f''(x) = \dfrac{2}{x^3} - \dfrac{6}{x^4}$. To find points of inflection, we set the second derivative equal to 0 and solve for x:

$$\frac{2}{x^3} - \frac{6}{x^4} = 0$$

$$\frac{2}{x^3} = \frac{6}{x^4}$$

$$2x = 6$$

$$x = 3.$$

Figure 34 confirms that the graph of f changes from being concave down to being concave up at $x = 3$, so this is a point of inflection. $f''(x)$ is not defined at $x = 0$, but that is not in the domain, so there are no other points of inflection. In particular, the graph must be concave down in the whole region $(-\infty, 0)$, as we can see by calculating the second derivative at any one point in that interval: $f''(-1) = -8 < 0$.

Figure 37 shows our graph so far (we extended the curve near $x = 3$ to suggest a point of inflection at $x = 3$).

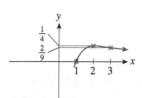

Figure 37

4. Behavior near points where f is not defined: The only point where $f(x)$ is not defined is $x = 0$. From the graph, $f(x)$ appears to go to $-\infty$ as x approaches 0 from either side. To calculate these limits, we rewrite $f(x)$:

$$f(x) = \frac{1}{x} - \frac{1}{x^2} = \frac{x-1}{x^2}$$

Now, if x is close to 0 (on either side), the numerator $x - 1$ is close to -1 and the denominator is a very small but positive number. The quotient is therefore a negative number of very large magnitude. Therefore,

$$\lim_{x \to 0^-} f(x) = -\infty$$

and

$$\lim_{x \to 0^+} f(x) = -\infty.$$

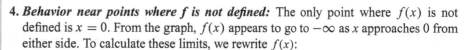

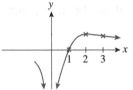

Figure 38

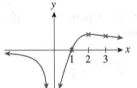

Figure 39

From these limits, we see the following:

(1) Immediately to the *left* of $x = 0$, the graph plunges down toward $-\infty$.

(2) Immediately to the *right* of $x = 0$, the graph also plunges down toward $-\infty$.

Figure 38 shows our graph with these features added. We say that f has a **vertical asymptote** at $x = 0$, meaning that the points on the graph of f get closer and closer to points on a vertical line (the y-axis in this case) further and further from the origin.

5. *Behavior at infinity:* Both $1/x$ and $1/x^2$ go to 0 as x goes to $-\infty$ or $+\infty$; that is,

$$\lim_{x \to -\infty} f(x) = 0$$

and

$$\lim_{x \to +\infty} f(x) = 0.$$

Thus, on the extreme left and right of our picture, the height of the curve levels off toward zero. Figure 39 shows the completed freehand sketch of the graph.

We say that f has a **horizontal asymptote** at $y = 0$. (Notice another thing: We haven't plotted a single point to the left of the y-axis, and yet we have a pretty good idea of what the curve looks like there! Compare the technology-drawn curve in Figure 34.)

In summary, there is one x-intercept at $x = 1$; there is one relative maximum (which, we can now see, is also an absolute maximum) at $x = 2$; there is one point of inflection at $x = 3$, where the graph changes from being concave down to concave up. There is a vertical asymptote at $x = 0$, on both sides of which the graph goes down toward $-\infty$, and a horizontal asymptote at $y = 0$.

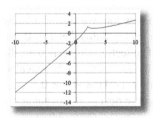

Technology:
2*x/3-((x-2)^2)^(1/3)

Figure 40

EXAMPLE 2 Analyzing a Graph

Analyze the graph of $f(x) = \dfrac{2x}{3} - (x - 2)^{2/3}$.

Solution Figure 40 shows a technology-generated version of the graph. Note that in the technology formulation $(x - 2)^{2/3}$ is written as $[(x - 2)^2]^{1/3}$ to avoid problems with some graphing calculators and Excel.

Let us now recreate this graph by hand, and in the process identify the features we see in Figure 40.

1. *The x- and y-intercepts:* We consider $y = \dfrac{2x}{3} - (x - 2)^{2/3}$. For the y-intercept, we set $x = 0$ and solve for y:

$$y = \frac{2(0)}{3} - (0 - 2)^{2/3} = -2^{2/3} \approx -1.59.$$

To find the x-intercept(s), we set $y = 0$ and solve for x. However, if we attempt this, we will find ourselves with a cubic equation that is hard to solve. (Try it!) Following the advice in the note on page 912, we use graphing technology to locate the x-intercept we see in Figure 40 by zooming in (Figure 41). From Figure 41, we find $x \approx 1.24$. We shall see in the discussion to follow that there can be no other x-intercepts.

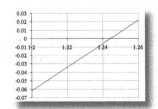

Figure 41

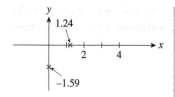

Figure 42

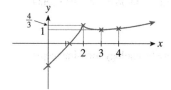

Figure 43

Figure 42 shows our freehand sketch so far.

2. *Relative extrema:* We calculate

$$f'(x) = \frac{2}{3} - \frac{2}{3}(x - 2)^{-1/3}$$

$$= \frac{2}{3} - \frac{2}{3(x - 2)^{1/3}}.$$

To find any stationary points, we set the derivative equal to 0 and solve for x:

$$\frac{2}{3} - \frac{2}{3(x - 2)^{1/3}} = 0$$

$$(x - 2)^{1/3} = 1$$

$$x - 2 = 1^3 = 1$$

$$x = 3.$$

To check for singular points, look for points where $f(x)$ is defined and $f'(x)$ is not defined. The only such point is $x = 2$: $f'(x)$ is not defined at $x = 2$, whereas $f(x)$ is defined there, so we have a singular point at $x = 2$.

x	2 (Singular point)	3 (Stationary point)	4 (Test point)
$y = \dfrac{2x}{3} - (x - 2)^{2/3}$	$\dfrac{4}{3}$	1	1.079

Figure 43 shows our graph so far.

We see that there is a singular relative maximum at $(2, 4/3)$ (we will confirm that the graph eventually gets higher on the right) and a stationary relative minimum at $x = 3$.

3. *Points of inflection:* We calculate

$$f''(x) = \frac{2}{9(x - 2)^{4/3}}.$$

To find points of inflection, we set the second derivative equal to 0 and solve for x. But the equation

$$0 = \frac{2}{9(x - 2)^{4/3}}$$

has no solution for x, so there are no points of inflection on the graph.

4. *Behavior near points where f is not defined:* Because $f(x)$ is defined everywhere, there are no such points to consider. In particular, there are no vertical asymptotes.

5. *Behavior at infinity:* We estimate the following limits numerically:

$$\lim_{x \to -\infty} \left[\frac{2x}{3} - (x - 2)^{2/3} \right] = -\infty$$

and

$$\lim_{x \to +\infty} \left[\frac{2x}{3} - (x - 2)^{2/3} \right] = +\infty.$$

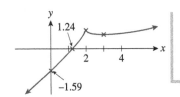

Figure 44

Thus, on the extreme left the curve goes down toward $-\infty$, and on the extreme right the curve rises toward $+\infty$. In particular, there are no horizontal asymptotes. (There can also be no other x-intercepts.)

Figure 44 shows the completed graph.

12.4 EXERCISES

▼ more advanced   ◆ challenging

indicates exercises that should be solved using technology

In Exercises 1–26, sketch the graph of the given function, indicating (a) x- and y-intercepts, (b) extrema, (c) points of inflection, (d) behavior near points where the function is not defined, and (e) behavior at infinity. Where indicated, technology should be used to approximate the intercepts, coordinates of extrema, and/or points of inflection to one decimal place. Check your sketch using technology. HINT [See Example 1.]

1. $f(x) = x^2 + 2x + 1$

2. $f(x) = -x^2 - 2x - 1$

3. $g(x) = x^3 - 12x$, domain $[-4, 4]$

4. $g(x) = 2x^3 - 6x$, domain $[-4, 4]$

5. $h(x) = 2x^3 - 3x^2 - 36x$ [Use technology for x-intercepts.]

6. $h(x) = -2x^3 - 3x^2 + 36x$ [Use technology for x-intercepts.]

7. $f(x) = 2x^3 + 3x^2 - 12x + 1$ [Use technology for x-intercepts.]

8. $f(x) = 4x^3 + 3x^2 + 2$ [Use technology for x-intercepts.]

9. $k(x) = -3x^4 + 4x^3 + 36x^2 + 10$ [Use technology for x-intercepts.]

10. $k(x) = 3x^4 + 4x^3 - 36x^2 - 10$ [Use technology for x-intercepts.]

11. $g(t) = \frac{1}{4}t^4 - \frac{2}{3}t^3 + \frac{1}{2}t^2$

12. $g(t) = 3t^4 - 16t^3 + 24t^2 + 1$

13. $f(x) = x + \dfrac{1}{x}$

14. $f(x) = x^2 + \dfrac{1}{x^2}$

15. $g(x) = x^3/(x^2 + 3)$

16. $g(x) = x^3/(x^2 - 3)$

17. $f(t) = \dfrac{t^2 + 1}{t^2 - 1}$, domain $[-2, 2]$, $t \neq \pm 1$

18. $f(t) = \dfrac{t^2 - 1}{t^2 + 1}$, domain $[-2, 2]$

19. $k(x) = \dfrac{2x}{3} + (x + 1)^{2/3}$ [Use technology for x-intercepts.

HINT [See Example 2.]

20. $k(x) = \dfrac{2x}{5} - (x - 1)^{2/5}$ [Use technology for x-intercepts.

HINT [See Example 2.]

21. $f(x) = x - \ln x$, domain $(0, +\infty)$

22. $f(x) = x - \ln x^2$, domain $(0, +\infty)$

23. $f(x) = x^2 + \ln x^2$ [Use technology for x-intercepts.]

24. $f(x) = 2x^2 + \ln x$ [Use technology for x-intercepts.]

25. $g(t) = e^t - t$, domain $[-1, 1]$

26. $g(t) = e^{-t^2}$

In Exercises 27–30, use technology to sketch the graph of the given function, labeling all relative and absolute extrema and points of inflection, and vertical and horizontal asymptotes. The coordinates of the extrema and points of inflection should be accurate to two decimal places. HINT [To locate extrema accurately, plot the first derivative; to locate points of inflection accurately, plot the second derivative.]

27. ▼ $f(x) = x^4 - 2x^3 + x^2 - 2x + 1$

28. ▼ $f(x) = x^4 + x^3 + x^2 + x + 1$

29. ▼ $f(x) = e^x - x^3$

30. ▼ $f(x) = e^x - \dfrac{x^4}{4}$

APPLICATIONS

31. *Home Prices* The following graph shows the approximate value of the home price index as a percentage change from 2003. The locations of the maximum and the point of inflection are indicated on the graph (t is time in years since the start of 2004).[46]

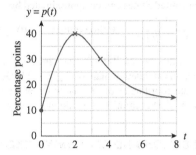

Analyze the graph's important features and interpret each feature in terms of the home price index.

32. *Existing Home Sales* The following graph shows the approximate value of existing home sales as a percentage change from 2003. The locations of the maximum and the point of inflection are indicated on the graph (t is time in years since the start of 2004).[47]

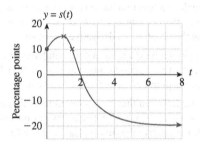

Analyze the graph's important features and interpret each feature in terms of the existing home sales.

33. *Consumer Price Index* The following graph shows the approximate value of the U.S. Consumer Price Index (CPI) from July 2005 through March 2006.[48]

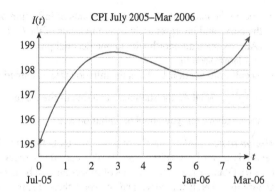

The approximating curve shown on the figure is given by

$$I(t) = 0.06t^3 - 0.8t^2 + 3.1t + 195 \quad (0 \le t \le 8)$$

where t is time in months ($t = 0$ represents July 2005).

a. Locate the intercepts, extrema, and points of inflection of the curve and interpret each feature in terms of the CPI. (Approximate all coordinates to one decimal place.) HINT [See Example 1.]

b. Recall from Section 12.2 that the inflation rate is defined to be $\dfrac{I'(t)}{I(t)}$. What do the stationary extrema of the curve shown above tell you about the inflation rate?

34. *Inflation* The following graph shows the approximate value of the U.S. Consumer Price Index (CPI) from March 2006 through May 2007.[49]

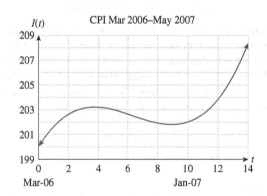

The approximating curve shown on the figure is given by

$$I(t) = 0.02t^3 - 0.38t^2 + 2t + 200 \quad (0 \le t \le 14)$$

where t is time in months ($t = 0$ represents March, 2006).

[46] 2008–2012 data are the authors' projections. Source for data: S&P/Case-Shiller Home Price Index. Source: Standard & Poors/*New York Times*, September 29, 2007, p. C3.

[47] 2008–2012 data are the authors' projections. Source for data: Bloomberg Finiancial Markets/*New York Times*, September 29, 2007, p. C3.

[48] The CPI is compiled by the Bureau of Labor Statistics and is based upon a 1982 value of 100. For instance, a CPI of 200 means the CPI has doubled since 1982. Source: InflationData.com (www.inflationdata.com).

[49] Ibid.

a. Locate the intercepts, extrema, and points of inflection of the curve and interpret each feature in terms of the CPI. (Approximate all coordinates to one decimal place.) HINT [See Example 1.]

b. Recall from Section 12.2 that the inflation rate is defined to be $\dfrac{I'(t)}{I(t)}$. What do the stationary extrema of the curve shown above tell you about the inflation rate?

35. *Motion in a Straight Line* The distance of a UFO from an observer is given by $s = 2t^3 - 3t^2 + 100$ feet after t seconds ($t \geq 0$). Obtain the extrema, points of inflection, and behavior at infinity. Sketch the curve and interpret these features in terms of the movement of the UFO.

36. *Motion in a Straight Line* The distance of the Mars orbiter from your location in Utarek, Mars is given by $s = 2(t - 1)^3 -3(t - 1)^2 + 100$ km after t seconds ($t \geq 0$). Obtain the extrema, points of inflection, and behavior at infinity. Sketch the curve and interpret these features in terms of the movement of the Mars orbiter.

37. *Average Cost: iPods* Assume that it costs **Apple** approximately

$$C(x) = 22{,}500 + 100x + 0.01x^2$$

dollars to manufacture x 30-gigabyte video iPods in a day.[50] Obtain the average cost function, sketch its graph, and analyze the graph's important features. Interpret each feature in terms of iPods. HINT [Recall that the average cost function is $\bar{C}(x) = C(x)/x$.]

38. *Average Cost: Xboxes* Assume that it costs **Microsoft** approximately

$$C(x) = 14{,}400 + 550x + 0.01x^2$$

dollars to manufacture x Xbox 360s in a day.[51] Obtain the average cost function, sketch its graph, and analyze the graph's important features. Interpret each feature in terms of Xboxes. HINT [Recall that the average cost function is $\bar{C}(x) = C(x)/x$.]

39. 🔲 ▼ ***Subprime Mortgages*** The percentage of U.S.-issued mortgages that were subprime can be approximated by

$$A(t) = \frac{15.0}{1 + 8.6(1.8)^{-t}} \text{ percent} \qquad (0 \leq t \leq 8)$$

---

[50] Not the actual cost equation; the authors do not know Apple's actual cost equation. The marginal cost in the model given is in rough agreement with the actual marginal cost for reasonable values of x. Source for cost data: Manufacturing & Technology News, July 31, 2007 Volume 14, No. 14 (www.manufacturingnews.com).

[51] Not the actual cost equation; the authors do not know Microsoft's actual cost equation. The marginal cost in the model given is in rough agreement with the actual marginal cost for reasonable values of x. Source for estimate of marginal cost: iSuppli: (www.isuppli.com/news/xbox/).

t years after the start of 2000.[52] Graph the *derivative $A'(t)$* of $A(t)$ using an extended domain of $0 \leq t \leq 15$. Determine the approximate coordinates of the maximum and determine the behavior of $A'(t)$ at infinity. What do the answers tell you?

40. 🔲 ▼ ***Subprime Mortgage Debt*** The approximate value of subprime (normally classified as risky) mortgage debt outstanding in the United States can be approximated by

$$A(t) = \frac{1{,}350}{1 + 4.2(1.7)^{-t}} \text{ billion dollars} \qquad (0 \leq t \leq 8)$$

t years after the start of 2000.[53] Graph the *derivative $A'(t)$* of $A(t)$ using an extended domain of $0 \leq t \leq 15$. Determine the approximate coordinates of the maximum and determine the behavior of $A'(t)$ at infinity. What do the answers tell you?

COMMUNICATION AND REASONING EXERCISES

41. A function is *bounded* if its entire graph lies between two horizontal lines. Can a bounded function have vertical asymptotes? Can a bounded function have horizontal asymptotes? Explain.

42. A function is *bounded above* if its entire graph lies below some horizontal line. Can a bounded above function have vertical asymptotes? Can a bounded above function have horizontal asymptotes? Explain.

43. If the graph of a function has a vertical asymptote at $x = a$ in such a way that y increases to $+\infty$ as $x \to a$, what can you say about the graph of its derivative? Explain.

44. If the graph of a function has a horizontal asymptote at $y = a$ in such a way that y decreases to a as $x \to +\infty$, what can you say about the graph of its derivative? Explain.

45. Your friend tells you that he has found a continuous function defined on $(-\infty, +\infty)$ with exactly two critical points, each of which is a relative maximum. Can he be right?

46. Your other friend tells you that she has found a continuous function with two critical points, one a relative minimum and one a relative maximum, and no point of inflection between them. Can she be right?

47. ▼ By thinking about extrema, show that, if $f(x)$ is a polynomial, then between every pair of zeros (x-intercepts) of $f(x)$ there is a zero of $f'(x)$.

48. ▼ If $f(x)$ is a polynomial of degree 2 or higher, show that between every pair of relative extrema of $f(x)$ there is a point of inflection of $f(x)$.

---

[52] 2009 figure is an estimate. Sources: Mortgage Bankers Association, UBS.

[53] 2008–2009 figure are estimates. Source: www.data360.org/dataset.aspx?Data_Set_Id=9549.

12.5 Related Rates

We start by recalling some basic facts about the rate of change of a quantity:

Rate of Change of Q

If Q is a quantity changing over time t, then the derivative dQ/dt is the rate at which Q changes over time.

Quick Examples

1. If A is the area of an expanding circle, then dA/dt is the rate at which the area is increasing.
2. *Words:* The radius r of a sphere is currently 3 cm and increasing at a rate of 2 cm/s.

   Symbols: $r = 3$ cm and $dr/dt = 2$ cm/s.

In this section we are concerned with what are called **related rates** problems. In such a problem we have two (sometimes more) related quantities, we know the rate at which one is changing, and we wish to find the rate at which another is changing. A typical example is the following.

EXAMPLE 1 The Expanding Circle

The radius of a circle is increasing at a rate of 10 cm/s. How fast is the area increasing at the instant when the radius has reached 5 cm?

Solution We have two related quantities: the radius of the circle, r, and its area, A. The first sentence of the problem tells us that r is increasing at a certain rate. When we see a sentence referring to speed or change, it is very helpful to rephrase the sentence using the phrase "the rate of change of." Here, we can say

> *The rate of change of r is* 10 cm/s.

Because the rate of change is the derivative, we can rewrite this sentence as the equation

$$\frac{dr}{dt} = 10.$$

Similarly, the second sentence of the problem asks how A is changing. We can rewrite that question:

> *What is the rate of change of A when the radius is 5 cm?*

Using mathematical notation, the question is:

> *What is* $\dfrac{dA}{dt}$ *when* $r = 5$?

Thus, knowing one rate of change, dr/dt, we wish to find a related rate of change, dA/dt. To find exactly how these derivatives are related, we need the equation relating the variables, which is

$$A = \pi r^2.$$

223

To find the relationship between the derivatives, we take the derivative of both sides of this equation *with respect to t*. On the left we get dA/dt. On the right we need to remember that r is a function of t and use the chain rule. We get

$$\frac{dA}{dt} = 2\pi r \frac{dr}{dt}.$$

Now we substitute the given values $r = 5$ and $dr/dt = 10$. This gives

$$\frac{dA}{dt}\bigg|_{r=5} = 2\pi(5)(10) = 100\pi \approx 314 \text{ cm}^2/\text{s}.$$

Thus, the area is increasing at the rate of $314 \text{ cm}^2/\text{s}$ when the radius is 5 cm.

We can organize our work as follows:

Solving a Related Rates Problem

A. The Problem

1. List the related, changing quantities.
2. Restate the problem in terms of rates of change. Rewrite the problem using mathematical notation for the changing quantities and their derivatives.

B. The Relationship

1. Draw a diagram, if appropriate, showing the changing quantities.
2. Find an equation or equations relating the changing quantities.
3. Take the derivative with respect to time of the equation(s) relating the quantities to get the **derived equation(s)**, which relate the rates of change of the quantities.

C. The Solution

1. Substitute into the derived equation(s) the given values of the quantities and their derivatives.
2. Solve for the derivative required.

We can illustrate the procedure with the "ladder problem" found in almost every calculus textbook.

EXAMPLE 2 The Falling Ladder

Jane is at the top of a 5-foot ladder when it starts to slide down the wall at a rate of 3 feet per minute. Jack is standing on the ground behind her. How fast is the base of the ladder moving when it hits him if Jane is 4 feet from the ground at that instant?

Solution The first sentence talks about (the top of) the ladder sliding down the wall. Thus, one of the changing quantities is the height of the top of the ladder. The question asked refers to the motion of the base of the ladder, so another changing quantity is the distance of the base of the ladder from the wall. Let's record these variables and follow the outline above to obtain the solution.

A. The Problem

1. The changing quantities are

h = height of the top of the ladder
b = distance of the base of the ladder from the wall

2. We rephrase the problem in words, using the phrase "rate of change":

The rate of change of the height of the top of the ladder is −3 feet per minute. What is the rate of change of the distance of the base from the wall when the top of the ladder is 4 feet from the ground?

We can now rewrite the problem mathematically:

$$\frac{dh}{dt} = -3. \text{ Find } \frac{db}{dt} \text{ when } h = 4.$$

B. The Relationship

1. Figure 45 shows the ladder and the variables h and b. Notice that we put in the figure the fixed length, 5, of the ladder, but any changing quantities, like h and b, we leave as variables. We shall not use any specific values for h or b until the very end.

2. From the figure, we can see that h and b are related by the Pythagorean theorem:

$$h^2 + b^2 = 25.$$

3. Taking the derivative with respect to time of the equation above gives us the derived equation:

$$2h\frac{dh}{dt} + 2b\frac{db}{dt} = 0.$$

C. The Solution

1. We substitute the known values $dh/dt = -3$ and $h = 4$ into the derived equation:

$$2(4)(-3) + 2b\frac{db}{dt} = 0.$$

We would like to solve for db/dt, but first we need the value of b, which we can determine from the equation $h^2 + b^2 = 25$, using the value $h = 4$:

$$16 + b^2 = 25$$
$$b^2 = 9$$
$$b = 3.$$

Substituting into the derived equation, we get

$$-24 + 2(3)\frac{db}{dt} = 0.$$

2. Solving for db/dt gives

$$\frac{db}{dt} = \frac{24}{6} = 4.$$

Thus, the base of the ladder is sliding away from the wall at 4 ft/min when it hits Jack.

Figure 45

AFP/Getty Images

EXAMPLE 3 **Average Cost**

The cost to manufacture x cell phones in a day is

$$C(x) = 10,000 + 20x + \frac{x^2}{10,000} \text{ dollars.}$$

The daily production level is currently $x = 5,000$ cell phones and is increasing at a rate of 100 units per day. How fast is the average cost changing?

Solution

A. The Problem

1. The changing quantities are the production level x and the average cost, $\bar{C}$.

2. We rephrase the problem as follows:

The daily production level is $x = 5,000$ units and the rate of change of x is 100 units/ day. What is the rate of change of the average cost, $\bar{C}$?

In mathematical notation,

$$x = 5,000 \text{ and } \frac{dx}{dt} = 100. \text{ Find } \frac{d\bar{C}}{dt}.$$

B. The Relationship

1. In this example the changing quantities cannot easily be depicted geometrically.

2. We are given a formula for the *total* cost. We get the *average* cost by dividing the total cost by x:

$$\bar{C} = \frac{C}{x}.$$

So,

$$\bar{C} = \frac{10,000}{x} + 20 + \frac{x}{10,000}.$$

3. Taking derivatives with respect to t of both sides, we get the derived equation:

$$\frac{d\bar{C}}{dt} = \left(-\frac{10,000}{x^2} + \frac{1}{10,000} \right) \frac{dx}{dt}.$$

C. The Solution

Substituting the values from part A into the derived equation, we get

$$\frac{d\bar{C}}{dt} = \left(-\frac{10,000}{5,000^2} + \frac{1}{10,000} \right) 100$$

$$= -0.03 \text{ dollars/day.}$$

Thus, the average cost is decreasing by 3¢ per day.

The scenario in the following example is similar to Example 5 in Section 12.2.

226

EXAMPLE 4 Allocation of Labor

The Gym Sock Company manufactures cotton athletic socks. Production is partially automated through the use of robots. The number of pairs of socks the company can manufacture in a day is given by a Cobb-Douglas production formula:

$$q = 50n^{0.6}r^{0.4}$$

where q is the number of pairs of socks that can be manufactured by n laborers and r robots. The company currently produces 1,000 pairs of socks each day and employs 20 laborers. It is bringing one new robot on line every month. At what rate are laborers being laid off, assuming that the number of socks produced remains constant?

Solution

A. The Problem

1. The changing quantities are the number of laborers n and the number of robots r.

2. $\dfrac{dr}{dt} = 1$. Find $\dfrac{dn}{dt}$ when $n = 20$.

B. The Relationship

1. No diagram is appropriate here.

2. The equation relating the changing quantities:

$$1,000 = 50n^{0.6}r^{0.4}$$

or

$$20 = n^{0.6}r^{0.4}.$$

(Productivity is constant at 1,000 pairs of socks each day.)

3. The derived equation is

$$0 = 0.6n^{-0.4}\left(\frac{dn}{dt}\right)r^{0.4} + 0.4n^{0.6}r^{-0.6}\left(\frac{dr}{dt}\right)$$

$$= 0.6\left(\frac{r}{n}\right)^{0.4}\left(\frac{dn}{dt}\right) + 0.4\left(\frac{n}{r}\right)^{0.6}\left(\frac{dr}{dt}\right).$$

We solve this equation for dn/dt because we shall want to find dn/dt below and because the equation becomes simpler when we do this:

$$0.6\left(\frac{r}{n}\right)^{0.4}\left(\frac{dn}{dt}\right) = -0.4\left(\frac{n}{r}\right)^{0.6}\left(\frac{dr}{dt}\right)$$

$$\frac{dn}{dt} = -\frac{0.4}{0.6}\left(\frac{n}{r}\right)^{0.6}\left(\frac{n}{r}\right)^{0.4}\left(\frac{dr}{dt}\right)$$

$$= -\frac{2}{3}\left(\frac{n}{r}\right)\left(\frac{dr}{dt}\right).$$

C. The Solution

Substituting the numbers in A into the last equation in B, we get

$$\frac{dn}{dt} = -\frac{2}{3}\left(\frac{20}{r}\right)(1).$$

227

We need to compute r by substituting the known value of n in the original formula:

$$20 = n^{0.6}r^{0.4}$$

$$20 = 20^{0.6}r^{0.4}$$

$$r^{0.4} = \frac{20}{20^{0.6}} = 20^{0.4}$$

$$r = 20.$$

Thus,

$$\frac{dn}{dt} = -\frac{2}{3}\left(\frac{20}{20}\right)(1) = -\frac{2}{3} \text{ laborers per month.}$$

The company is laying off laborers at a rate of $2/3$ per month, or two every three months. We can interpret this result as saying that, at the current level of production and number of laborers, one robot is as productive as $2/3$ of a laborer, or 3 robots are as productive as 2 laborers.

12.5 EXERCISES

▼ more advanced   ◆ challenging

▒ indicates exercises that should be solved using technology

Rewrite the statements and questions in Exercises 1–8 in mathematical notation. HINT [See Quick Examples on page 919.]

1. The population P is currently 10,000 and growing at a rate of 1,000 per year.

2. There are presently 400 cases of Bangkok flu, and the number is growing by 30 new cases every month.

3. The annual revenue of your tie-dye T-shirt operation is currently $7,000 but is decreasing by $700 each year. How fast are annual sales changing?

4. A ladder is sliding down a wall so that the distance between the top of the ladder and the floor is decreasing at a rate of 3 feet per second. How fast is the base of the ladder receding from the wall?

5. The price of shoes is rising $5 per year. How fast is the demand changing?

6. Stock prices are rising $1,000 per year. How fast is the value of your portfolio increasing?

7. The average global temperature is 60°F and rising by 0.1°F per decade. How fast are annual sales of Bermuda shorts increasing?

8. The country's population is now 260,000,000 and is increasing by 1,000,000 people per year. How fast is the annual demand for diapers increasing?

APPLICATIONS

9. **Sun Spots** The area of a circular sun spot is growing at a rate of 1,200 km²/s.

   a. How fast is the radius growing at the instant when it equals 10,000 km? HINT [See Example 1.]
   b. How fast is the radius growing at the instant when the sun spot has an area of 640,000 km²? HINT [Use the area formula to determine the radius at that instant.]

10. **Puddles** The radius of a circular puddle is growing at a rate of 5 cm/s.

   a. How fast is its area growing at the instant when the radius is 10 cm? HINT [See Example 1.]
   b. How fast is the area growing at the instant when it equals 36 cm²? HINT [Use the area formula to determine the radius at that instant.]

11. **Balloons** A spherical party balloon is being inflated with helium pumped in at a rate of 3 cubic feet per minute. How fast is the radius growing at the instant when the radius has reached 1 foot? (The volume of a sphere of radius r is $V = \frac{4}{3}\pi r^3$.) HINT [See Example 1.]

12. **More Balloons** A rather flimsy spherical balloon is designed to pop at the instant its radius has reached 10 centimeters. Assuming the balloon is filled with helium at a rate of 10 cubic centimeters per second, calculate how fast the radius is growing at the instant it pops. (The volume of a sphere of radius r is $V = \frac{4}{3}\pi r^3$.) HINT [See Example 1.]

13. Sliding Ladders The base of a 50-foot ladder is being pulled away from a wall at a rate of 10 feet per second. How fast is the top of the ladder sliding down the wall at the instant when the base of the ladder is 30 feet from the wall? HINT [See Example 2.]

14. Sliding Ladders The top of a 5-foot ladder is sliding down a wall at a rate of 10 feet per second. How fast is the base of the ladder sliding away from the wall at the instant when the top of the ladder is 3 feet from the ground? HINT [See Example 2.]

15. Average Cost The average cost function for the weekly manufacture of portable CD players is given by

$$\bar{C}(x) = 150,000x^{-1} + 20 + 0.0001x \text{ dollars per player,}$$

where x is the number of CD players manufactured that week. Weekly production is currently 3,000 players and is increasing at a rate of 100 players per week. What is happening to the average cost? HINT [See Example 3.]

16. Average Cost Repeat the preceding exercise, using the revised average cost function

$$\bar{C}(x) = 150,000x^{-1} + 20 + 0.01x \text{ dollars per player.}$$

HINT [See Example 3.]

17. Demand Demand for your tie-dyed T-shirts is given by the formula

$$q = 500 - 100p^{0.5}$$

where q is the number of T-shirts you can sell each month at a price of p dollars. If you currently sell T-shirts for $15 each and you raise your price by $2 per month, how fast will the demand drop? (Round your answer to the nearest whole number.)

18. Supply The number of portable CD players you are prepared to supply to a retail outlet every week is given by the formula

$$q = 0.1p^2 + 3p$$

where p is the price it offers you. The retail outlet is currently offering you $40 per CD player. If the price it offers decreases at a rate of $2 per week, how will this affect the number you supply?

19. Revenue You can now sell 50 cups of lemonade per week at 30¢ per cup, but demand is dropping at a rate of 5 cups per week each week. Assuming that raising the price does not affect demand, how fast do you have to raise your price if you want to keep your weekly revenue constant? HINT [Revenue = Price × Quantity.]

20. Revenue You can now sell 40 cars per month at $20,000 per car, and demand is increasing at a rate of 3 cars per month each month. What is the fastest you could drop your price before your monthly revenue starts to drop? HINT [Revenue = Price × Quantity.]

21. ▼ **Oil Revenues** Daily oil production by **Pemex**, Mexico's national oil company, can be approximated by

$$q(t) = -0.022t^2 + 0.2t + 2.9 \text{ million barrels} \quad (1 \le t \le 9)$$

where t is time in years since the start of 2000.[54]

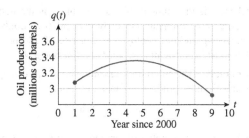

At the start of 2008 the price of oil was $90 per barrel and increasing at a rate of $80 per year.[55] How fast was **Pemex**'s oil (daily) revenue changing at that time?

22. ▼ **Oil Expenditures** Daily oil imports to the United States from Mexico can be approximated by

$$q(t) = -0.015t^2 + 0.1t + 1.4 \text{ million barrels} \quad (0 \le t \le 8)$$

where t is time in years since the start of 2000.[56]

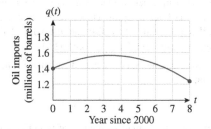

At the start of 2004 the price of oil was $30 per barrel and increasing at a rate of $40 per year.[57] How fast was (daily) oil expenditure for imports from Mexico changing at that time?

23. Resource Allocation Your company manufactures automobile alternators, and production is partially automated through the use of robots. In order to meet production deadlines, your company calculates that the numbers of laborers and robots must satisfy the constraint

$$xy = 10,000$$

where x is the number of laborers and y is the number of robots. Your company currently uses 400 robots and is increasing robot deployment at a rate of 16 per month. How fast is it laying off laborers? HINT [See Example 4.]

24. Resource Allocation Your company is the largest sock manufacturer in the solar system, and production is automated through the use of androids and robots. In order to meet production deadlines, your company calculates that the numbers of androids and robots must satisfy the constraint

$$xy = 1,000,000$$

[54] Source for data: Energy Information Administration/Pemex (http://www.eia.doe.gov).

[55] Based on NYMEX crude oil futures; average rate of change during January–June, 2008.

[56] Source for data: Energy Information Administration/Pemex (http://www.eia.doe.gov).

[57] Based on NYMEX crude oil futures; average rate of change during 2004–2005.

where x is the number of androids and y is the number of robots. Your company currently uses 5000 androids and is increasing android deployment at a rate of 200 per month. How fast is it scrapping robots? HINT [See Example 4.]

25. *Production* The automobile assembly plant you manage has a Cobb-Douglas production function given by

$$P = 10x^{0.3}y^{0.7}$$

where P is the number of automobiles it produces per year, x is the number of employees, and y is the daily operating budget (in dollars). You maintain a production level of 1,000 automobiles per year. If you currently employ 150 workers and are hiring new workers at a rate of 10 per year, how fast is your daily operating budget changing? HINT [See Example 4.]

26. *Production* Refer back to the Cobb-Douglas production formula in the preceding exercise. Assume that you maintain a constant work force of 200 workers and wish to increase production in order to meet a demand that is increasing by 100 automobiles per year. The current demand is 1000 automobiles per year. How fast should your daily operating budget be increasing? HINT [See Example 4.]

27. *Demand* Assume that the demand equation for tuna in a small coastal town is

$$pq^{1.5} = 50,000$$

where q is the number of pounds of tuna that can be sold in one month at the price of p dollars per pound. The town's fishery finds that the demand for tuna is currently 900 pounds per month and is increasing at a rate of 100 pounds per month each month. How fast is the price changing?

28. *Demand* The demand equation for rubies at Royal Ruby Retailers is

$$q + \frac{4}{3}p = 80$$

where q is the number of rubies RRR can sell per week at p dollars per ruby. RRR finds that the demand for its rubies is currently 20 rubies per week and is dropping at a rate of one ruby per week. How fast is the price changing?

29. ▼ *Ships Sailing Apart* The H.M.S. Dreadnaught is 40 miles north of Montauk and steaming due north at 20 miles/hour, while the U.S.S. Mona Lisa is 50 miles east of Montauk and steaming due east at an even 30 miles/hour. How fast is their distance apart increasing?

30. ▼ *Near Miss* My aunt and I were approaching the same intersection, she from the south and I from the west. She was traveling at a steady speed of 10 miles/hour, while I was approaching the intersection at 60 miles/hour. At a certain instant in time, I was one-tenth of a mile from the intersection, while she was one-twentieth of a mile from it. How fast were we approaching each other at that instant?

31. ▼ *Baseball* A baseball diamond is a square with side 90 ft.

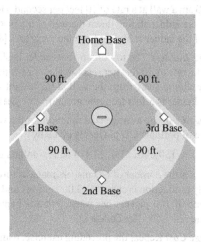

A batter at home base hits the ball and runs toward first base with a speed of 24 ft/s. At what rate is his distance from third base increasing when he is halfway to first base?

32. ▼ *Baseball* Refer to Exercise 31. Another player is running from third base to home at 30 ft/s. How fast is her distance from second base increasing when she is 60 feet from third base?

33. ▼ *Movement along a Graph* A point on the graph of $y = 1/x$ is moving along the curve in such a way that its x-coordinate is increasing at a rate of 4 units per second. What is happening to the y-coordinate at the instant the y-coordinate is equal to 2?

34. ▼ *Motion around a Circle* A point is moving along the circle $x^2 + (y - 1)^2 = 8$ in such a way that its x-coordinate is decreasing at a rate of 1 unit per second. What is happening to the y-coordinate at the instant when the point has reached $(-2, 3)$?

35. ▼ *Education* In 1991, the expected income of an individual depended on his or her educational level according to the following formula:

$$I(n) = 2928.8n^3 - 115,860n^2 + 1,532,900n - 6,760,800.$$
$$(12 \leq n \leq 15)$$

Here, n is the number of school years completed and $I(n)$ is the individual's expected income.[58] You have completed 13 years of school and are currently a part-time student. Your schedule is such that you will complete the equivalent of one year of college every three years. Assuming that your salary is linked to the above model, how fast is your income going up? (Round your answer to the nearest $1.)

_____

[58] The model is a best-fit cubic based on Table 358, U.S. Department of Education, *Digest of Education Statistics, 1991*, Washington, DC: Government Printing Office, 1991.

36. ▼ *Education* Refer back to the model in the preceding exercise. Assume that someone has completed 14 years of school and that her income is increasing by $10,000 per year. How much schooling per year is this rate of increase equivalent to?

37. ▼ *Employment* An employment research company estimates that the value of a recent MBA graduate to an accounting company is

$$V = 3e^2 + 5g^3$$

where V is the value of the graduate, e is the number of years of prior business experience, and g is the graduate school grade point average. A company that currently employs graduates with a 3.0 average wishes to maintain a constant employee value of $V = 200$, but finds that the grade point average of its new employees is dropping at a rate of 0.2 per year. How fast must the experience of its new employees be growing in order to compensate for the decline in grade point average?

38. ▼ *Grades*[59] A production formula for a student's performance on a difficult English examination is given by

$$g = 4hx - 0.2h^2 - 10x^2$$

where g is the grade the student can expect to obtain, h is the number of hours of study for the examination, and x is the student's grade point average. The instructor finds that students' grade point averages have remained constant at 3.0 over the years, and that students currently spend an average of 15 hours studying for the examination. However, scores on the examination are dropping at a rate of 10 points per year. At what rate is the average study time decreasing?

39. ▼ *Cones* A right circular conical vessel is being filled with green industrial waste at a rate of 100 cubic meters per second. How fast is the level rising after 200π cubic meters have been poured in? The cone has a height of 50 m and a radius of 30 m at its brim. (The volume of a cone of height h and cross-sectional radius r at its brim is given by $V = \frac{1}{3}\pi r^2 h$.)

40. ▼ *More Cones* A circular conical vessel is being filled with ink at a rate of 10 cm³/s. How fast is the level rising after 20 cm³ have been poured in? The cone has height 50 cm and radius 20 cm at its brim. (The volume of a cone of height h and cross-sectional radius r at its brim is given by $V = \frac{1}{3}\pi r^2 h$.)

41. ▼ *Cylinders* The volume of paint in a right cylindrical can is given by $V = 4t^2 - t$ where t is time in seconds and V is the volume in cm³. How fast is the level rising when the height is 2 cm? The can has a height of 4 cm and a radius of 2 cm. HINT [To get h as a function of t, first solve the volume $V = \pi r^2 h$ for h.]

42. ▼ *Cylinders* A cylindrical bucket is being filled with paint at a rate of 6 cm³ per minute. How fast is the level rising when the bucket starts to overflow? The bucket has a radius of 30 cm and a height of 60 cm.

43. ▼ *Computers vs. Income* The demand for personal computers in the home goes up with household income. For a given community, we can approximate the average number of computers in a home as

$$q = 0.3454 \ln x - 3.047 \quad 10,000 \le x \le 125,000$$

where x is mean household income.[60] Your community has a mean income of $30,000, increasing at a rate of $2,000 per year. How many computers per household are there, and how fast is the number of computers in a home increasing? (Round your answer to four decimal places.)

44. ▼ *Computers vs. Income* Refer back to the model in the preceding exercise. The average number of computers per household in your town is 0.5 and is increasing at a rate of 0.02 computers per household per year. What is the average household income in your town, and how fast is it increasing? (Round your answers to the nearest $10.)

Education and Crime The following graph shows a striking relationship between the total prison population and the average combined SAT score in the U.S.

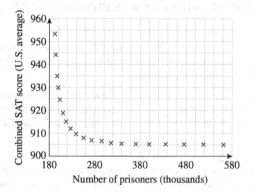

Exercises 45 and 46 are based on the following model for these data:

$$S(n) = 904 + \frac{1,326}{(n-180)^{1.325}}. \quad (192 \le n \le 563)$$

Here, $S(n)$ is the combined average SAT score at a time when the total prison population is n thousand.[61]

45. ▼ In 1985, the U.S. prison population was 475,000 and increasing at a rate of 35,000 per year. What was the average SAT score, and how fast, and in what direction, was it changing? (Round your answers to two decimal places.)

---

[59] Based on an Exercise in *Introduction to Mathematical Economics* by A.L. Ostrosky Jr. and J.V. Koch (Waveland Press, Illinois, 1979.)

[60] The model is a regression model. Source for data: Income distribution: Computer data: Forrester Research/*The New York Times*, August 8, 1999, p. BU4.

[61] The model is the authors' based on data for the years 1967–1989. Sources: Sourcebook of Criminal Justice Statistics, 1990, p. 604/ Educational Testing Service.

231

Chapter 3: Further Applications of the Derivative

46. ▼ In 1970, the U.S. combined SAT average was 940 and dropping by 10 points per year. What was the U.S. prison population, and how fast, and in what direction, was it changing? (Round your answers to the nearest 100.)

Divorce Rates A study found that the divorce rate d (given as a percentage) appears to depend on the ratio r of available men to available women.[62] *This function can be approximated by*

$$d(r) = \begin{cases} -40r + 74 & \text{if } r \leq 1.3 \\ \dfrac{130r}{3} - \dfrac{103}{3} & \text{if } r > 1.3 \end{cases}.$$

Exercises 47 and 48 are based on this model.

47. ◆ There are currently 1.1 available men per available woman in Littleville, and this ratio is increasing by 0.05 per year. What is happening to the divorce rate?

48. ◆ There are currently 1.5 available men per available woman in Largeville, and this ratio is decreasing by 0.03 per year. What is happening to the divorce rate?

COMMUNICATION AND REASONING EXERCISES

49. Why is this section titled "related rates"?

50. If you know how fast one quantity is changing and need to compute how fast a second quantity is changing, what kind of information do you need?

51. In a related rates problem, there is no limit to the number of changing quantities we can consider. Illustrate this by creating a related rates problem with four changing quantities.

---

[62] The cited study, by Scott J. South and associates, appeared in the *American Sociological Review* (February, 1995). Figures are rounded. Source: *The New York Times*, February 19, 1995, p. 40.

52. If three quantities are related by a single equation, how would you go about computing how fast one of them is changing based on a knowledge of the other two?

53. ▼ The demand and unit price for your store's checkered T-shirts are changing with time. Show that the percentage rate of change of revenue equals the sum of the percentage rates of change of price and demand. (The percentage rate of change of a quantity Q is $Q'(t)/Q(t)$.)

54. ▼ The number N of employees and the total floor space S of your company are both changing with time. Show that the percentage rate of change of square footage per employee equals the percentage rate of change of S minus the percentage rate of change of N. (The percentage rate of change of a quantity Q is $Q'(t)/Q(t)$.)

55. ▼ In solving a related rates problem, a key step is solving the derived equation for the unknown rate of change (once we have substituted the other values into the equation). Call the unknown rate of change X. The derived equation is what kind of equation in X?

56. ▼ On a recent exam, you were given a related rates problem based on an algebraic equation relating two variables x and y. Your friend told you that the correct relationship between dx/dt and dy/dt was given by

$$\left(\frac{dx}{dt}\right) = \left(\frac{dy}{dt}\right)^2.$$

Could he be correct?

57. ▼ Transform the following into a mathematical statement about derivatives: If my grades are improving at twice the speed of yours, then your grades are improving at half the speed of mine.

58. ▼ If two quantities x and y are related by a linear equation, how are their rates of change related?

12.6 Elasticity

You manufacture an extremely popular brand of sneakers and want to know what will happen if you increase the selling price. Common sense tells you that demand will drop as you raise the price. But will the drop in demand be enough to cause your revenue to fall? Or will it be small enough that your revenue will rise because of the higher selling price? For example, if you raise the price by 1%, you might suffer only a 0.5% loss in sales. In this case, the loss in sales will be more than offset by the increase in price and your revenue will rise. In such a case, we say that the demand is **inelastic**, because it is not very sensitive to the increase in price. On the other hand, if your 1% price increase results in a 2% drop in demand, then raising the price will cause a drop in revenues. We then say that the demand is **elastic** because it reacts strongly to a price change.

❋ NOTE Coming up with a good demand equation is not always easy. We saw in Chapter 1 that it is possible to find a linear demand equation if we know the sales figures at two different prices. However, such an equation is only a first approximation. To come up with a more accurate demand equation, we might need to gather data corresponding to sales at several different prices and use curve-fitting techniques like regression. Another approach would be an analytic one, based on mathematical modeling techniques that an economist might use.

We can use calculus to measure the response of demand to price changes if we have a demand equation for the item we are selling.❋ We need to know the *percentage drop in demand per percentage increase in price*. This ratio is called the **elasticity of demand**, or **price elasticity of demand**, and is usually denoted by E. Let's derive a formula for E in terms of the demand equation.

Assume that we have a demand equation

$$q = f(p)$$

where q stands for the number of items we would sell (per week, per month, or what have you) if we set the price per item at p. Now suppose we increase the price p by a very small amount, Δp. Then our percentage increase in price is $(\Delta p/p) \times 100\%$. This increase in p will presumably result in a decrease in the demand q. Let's denote this corresponding decrease in q by $-\Delta q$ (we use the minus sign because, by convention, Δq stands for the *increase* in demand). Thus, the percentage decrease in demand is $(-\Delta q/q) \times 100\%$.

Now E is the ratio

$$E = \frac{\text{Percentage decrease in demand}}{\text{Percentage increase in price}}$$

so

$$E = \frac{-\dfrac{\Delta q}{q} \times 100\%}{\dfrac{\Delta p}{p} \times 100\%}.$$

Canceling the 100%s and reorganizing, we get

$$E = -\frac{\Delta q}{\Delta p} \cdot \frac{p}{q}.$$

Q : *What small change in price will we use for Δp?*

A : It should probably be pretty small. If, say, we increased the price of sneakers to \$1 million per pair, the sales would likely drop to zero. But knowing this tells us nothing about how the market would respond to a modest increase in price. In fact, we'll do the usual thing we do in calculus and let Δp approach 0.

In the expression for E, if we let Δp go to 0, then the ratio $\Delta q/\Delta p$ goes to the derivative dq/dp. This gives us our final and most useful definition of the elasticity.

Price Elasticity of Demand

The **price elasticity of demand** E is the percentage rate of decrease of demand per percentage increase in price. E is given by the formula

$$E = -\frac{dq}{dp} \cdot \frac{p}{q}.$$

We say that the demand is **elastic** if $E > 1$, is **inelastic** if $E < 1$, and has **unit elasticity** if $E = 1$.

Quick Example

Suppose that the demand equation is $q = 20,000 - 2p$ where p is the price in dollars. Then

$$E = -(-2)\frac{p}{20,000 - 2p} = \frac{p}{10,000 - p}.$$

If $p = \$2,000$, then $E = 1/4$, and demand is inelastic at this price.

If $p = \$8,000$, then $E = 4$, and demand is elastic at this price.

If $p = \$5,000$, then $E = 1$, and the demand has unit elasticity at this price.

We are generally interested in the price that maximizes revenue and, in ordinary cases, the price that maximizes revenue must give unit elasticity. One way of seeing this is as follows:[*] If the demand is inelastic (which ordinarily occurs at a low unit price) then raising the price by a small percentage—1% say—results in a smaller percentage drop in demand. For example, in the Quick Example above, if $p = \$2,000$, d then the demand would drop by only $\frac{1}{4}$% for every 1% increase in price. To see the effect on revenue, we use the fact[*] that, for small changes in price,

Percentage change in revenue $\approx$ Percentage change in price
+ Percentage change in demand

$$= 1 + \left(-\frac{1}{4}\right) = \frac{3}{4}\%.$$

Thus, the revenue will increase by about $3/4$%. Put another way:

If the demand is inelastic, raising the price increases revenue.

On the other hand, if the price is elastic (which ordinarily occurs at a high unit price), then increasing the price slightly will lower the revenue, so:

If the demand is elastic, lowering the price increases revenue.

The price that results in the largest revenue must therefore be at unit elasticity.

✳ NOTE For another—more rigorous—argument, see Exercise 27.

✳ NOTE See, for example, Exercise 53 in Section 12.4.

EXAMPLE 1 Price Elasticity of Demand: Dolls

Suppose that the demand equation for Bobby Dolls is given by $q = 216 - p^2$, where p is the price per doll in dollars and q is the number of dolls sold per week.

a. Compute the price elasticity of demand when $p = \$5$ and $p = \$10$, and interpret the results.

b. Find the ranges of prices for which the demand is elastic and the range for which the demand is inelastic

c. Find the price at which the weekly revenue is maximized. What is the maximum weekly revenue?

Solution

a. The price elasticity of demand is

$$E = -\frac{dq}{dp} \cdot \frac{p}{q}.$$

Taking the derivative and substituting for q gives

$$E = 2p \cdot \frac{p}{216 - p^2} = \frac{2p^2}{216 - p^2}.$$

When $p = \$5$,

$$E = \frac{2(5)^2}{216 - 5^2} = \frac{50}{191} \approx 0.26.$$

Thus, when the price is set at \$5, the demand is dropping at a rate of 0.26% per 1% increase in the price. Because $E < 1$, the demand is inelastic at this price, so raising the price will increase revenue.

When $p = \$10$,

$$E = \frac{2(10)^2}{216 - 10^2} = \frac{200}{116} \approx 1.72.$$

Thus, when the price is set at \$10, the demand is dropping at a rate of 1.72% per 1% increase in the price. Because $E > 1$, demand is elastic at this price, so raising the price will decrease revenue; lowering the price will increase revenue.

b. and c. We answer part (c) first. Setting $E = 1$, we get

$$\frac{2p^2}{216 - p^2} = 1$$
$$p^2 = 72.$$

Thus, we conclude that the maximum revenue occurs when $p = \sqrt{72} \approx \$8.49$. We can now answer part (b): The demand is elastic when $p > \$8.49$ (the price is too high), and the demand is inelastic when $p < \$8.49$ (the price is too low). Finally, we calculate the maximum weekly revenue, which equals the revenue corresponding to the price of \$8.49:

$$R = qp = (216 - p^2)p = (216 - 72)\sqrt{72} = 144\sqrt{72} \approx \$1,222.$$

The concept of elasticity can be applied in other situations. In the following example we consider *income* elasticity of demand—the percentage increase in demand for a particular item per percentage increase in personal income.

EXAMPLE 2 Income Elasticity of Demand: Porsches

You are the sales director at Suburban Porsche and have noticed that demand for Porsches depends on income according to

$$q = 0.005e^{-0.05x^2 + x}. \qquad (1 \le x \le 10)$$

Here, x is the income of a potential customer in hundreds of thousands of dollars and q is the probability that the person will actually purchase a Porsche.[*] The **income elasticity of demand** is

$$E = \frac{dq}{dx}\frac{x}{q}.$$

Compute and interpret E for $x = 2$ and 9.

using Technology

See the Technology Guides at the end of the chapter to find out how to automate computations like those in part (a) of Example 1 using a graphing calculator or Excel. Here is an outline for the TI-83/84 Plus:

TI-83/84 Plus
$Y_1 = 216 - X^2$
$Y_2 = -$nDeriv$(Y_1, X, X) * X / Y_1$
[2ND] [TABLE] Enter $x = 5$
[More details on page 944.]

Excel
Enter values of p: 4.9, 4.91, ..., 5.0, 5.01, ..., 5.1 in A5–A25.
In B5 enter `216-A5^2` and copy down to B25.
In C5 enter `=(A6-A5)/A5` and paste the formula in C5–D24.
In E5 enter `=-D5/C5` and copy down to E24. This column contains the values of E for the values of p in column A.
[More details on page 944.]

✱ NOTE In other words, q is the fraction of visitors to your showroom having income x who actually purchase a Porsche.

Solution

Q: *Why is there no negative sign in the formula?*

A: Because we anticipate that the demand will increase as income increases, the ratio

$$\frac{\text{Percentage increase in demand}}{\text{Percentage increase in income}}$$

will be positive, so there is no need to introduce a negative sign.

Turning to the calculation, since $q = 0.005e^{-0.05x^2+x}$,

$$\frac{dq}{dx} = 0.005e^{-0.05x^2+x}(-0.1x + 1)$$

and so

$$E = \frac{dq}{dx}\frac{x}{q}$$

$$= 0.005e^{-0.05x^2+x}(-0.1x + 1)\frac{x}{0.005e^{-0.05x^2+x}}$$

$$= x(-0.1x + 1).$$

When $x = 2$, $E = 2[-0.1(2) + 1] = 1.6$. Thus, at an income level of \$200,000, the probability that a customer will purchase a Porsche increases at a rate of 1.6% per 1% increase in income.

When $x = 9$, $E = 9[-0.1(9) + 1)] = 0.9$. Thus, at an income level of \$900,000, the probability that a customer will purchase a Porsche increases at a rate of 0.9% per 1% increase in income.

12.6 EXERCISES

▼ more advanced ◆ challenging
▒ indicates exercises that should be solved using technology

APPLICATIONS

1. *Demand for Oranges* The weekly sales of Honolulu Red Oranges is given by $q = 1,000 - 20p$. Calculate the price elasticity of demand when the price is \$30 per orange (yes, \$30 per orange[63]). Interpret your answer. Also, calculate the price that gives a maximum weekly revenue, and find this maximum revenue. HINT [See Example 1.]

2. *Demand for Oranges* Repeat the preceding exercise for weekly sales of $1,000 - 10p$. HINT [See Example 1.]

3. *Tissues* The consumer demand equation for tissues is given by $q = (100 - p)^2$, where p is the price per case of tissues and q is the demand in weekly sales.

a. Determine the price elasticity of demand E when the price is set at \$30, and interpret your answer.

b. At what price should tissues be sold in order to maximize the revenue?

c. Approximately how many cases of tissues would be demanded at that price?

4. *Bodybuilding* The consumer demand curve for Professor Stefan Schwarzenegger dumbbells is given by $q = (100 - 2p)^2$, where p is the price per dumbbell, and q is the demand in weekly sales. Find the price Professor Schwarzenegger should charge for his dumbbells in order to maximize revenue.

5. *T-Shirts* The Physics Club sells $E = mc^2$ T-shirts at the local flea market. Unfortunately, the club's previous administration has been losing money for years, so you decide to do an analysis of the sales. A quadratic regression based on old sales data reveals the following demand equation for the T-shirts:

$$q = -2p^2 + 33p. \quad (9 \le p \le 15)$$

---

[63] They are very hard to find, and their possession confers considerable social status.

Here, p is the price the club charges per T-shirt, and q is the number it can sell each day at the flea market.

a. Obtain a formula for the price elasticity of demand for $E = mc^2$ T-shirts.

b. Compute the elasticity of demand if the price is set at $10 per shirt. *Interpret the result.*

c. How much should the Physics Club charge for the T-shirts in order to obtain the maximum daily revenue? What will this revenue be?

6. *Comics* The demand curve for original *Iguanawoman* comics is given by

$$q = \frac{(400 - p)^2}{100} \quad (0 \le p \le 400)$$

where q is the number of copies the publisher can sell per week if it sets the price at p.

a. Find the price elasticity of demand when the price is set at $40 per copy.

b. Find the price at which the publisher should sell the books in order to maximize weekly revenue.

c. What, to the nearest $1, is the maximum weekly revenue the publisher can realize from sales of *Iguanawoman* comics?

7. *College Tuition* A study of about 1,800 U.S. colleges and universities resulted in the demand equation $q = 9,900 - 2.2p$, where q is the enrollment at a college or university, and p is the average annual tuition (plus fees) it charges.[64]

a. The study also found that the average tuition charged by universities and colleges was $2,900. What is the corresponding price elasticity of demand? Is the price elastic or inelastic? Should colleges charge more or less on average to maximize revenue?

b. Based on the study, what would you advise a college to charge its students in order to maximize total revenue, and what would the revenue be?

8. *Demand for Fried Chicken* A fried chicken franchise finds that the demand equation for its new roast chicken product, "Roasted Rooster," is given by

$$p = \frac{40}{q^{1.5}}$$

where p is the price (in dollars) per quarter-chicken serving and q is the number of quarter-chicken servings that can be sold per hour at this price. Express q as a function of p and find the price elasticity of demand when the price is set at $4 per serving. Interpret the result.

9. *Paint-By-Number* The estimated monthly sales of *Mona Lisa* paint-by-number sets is given by the formula $q = 100e^{-3p^2+p}$,

where q is the demand in monthly sales and p is the retail price in yen.

a. Determine the price elasticity of demand E when the retail price is set at ¥3 and interpret your answer.

b. At what price will revenue be a maximum?

c. Approximately how many paint-by-number sets will be sold per month at the price in part (b)?

10. *Paint-By-Number* Repeat the previous exercise using the demand equation $q = 100e^{p-3p^2/2}$.

11. ▼ *Linear Demand Functions* A general linear demand function has the form $q = mp + b$ (m and b constants, $m \neq 0$).

a. Obtain a formula for the price elasticity of demand at a unit price of p.

b. Obtain a formula for the price that maximizes revenue.

12. ▼ *Exponential Demand Functions* A general exponential demand function has the form $q = Ae^{-bp}$ (A and b nonzero constants).

a. Obtain a formula for the price elasticity of demand at a unit price of p.

b. Obtain a formula for the price that maximizes revenue.

13. ▼ *Hyperbolic Demand Functions* A general hyperbolic demand function has the form $q = \dfrac{k}{p^r}$ (r and k nonzero constants).

a. Obtain a formula for the price elasticity of demand at unit price p.

b. How does E vary with p?

c. What does the answer to part (b) say about the model?

14. ▼ *Quadratic Demand Functions* A general quadratic demand function has the form $q = ap^2 + bp + c$ (a, b, and c constants with $a \neq 0$).

a. Obtain a formula for the price elasticity of demand at a unit price p.

b. Obtain a formula for the price or prices that could maximize revenue.

15. ▼ *Modeling Linear Demand* You have been hired as a marketing consultant to Johannesburg Burger Supply, Inc., and you wish to come up with a unit price for its hamburgers in order to maximize its weekly revenue. To make life as simple as possible, you assume that the demand equation for Johannesburg hamburgers has the linear form $q = mp + b$, where p is the price per hamburger, q is the demand in weekly sales, and m and b are certain constants you must determine.

a. Your market studies reveal the following sales figures: When the price is set at $2.00 per hamburger, the sales amount to 3,000 per week, but when the price is set at $4.00 per hamburger, the sales drop to zero. Use these data to calculate the demand equation.

b. Now estimate the unit price that maximizes weekly revenue and predict what the weekly revenue will be at that price.

---

[64] Based on a study by A.L. Ostrosky Jr. and J.V. Koch , as cited in their book, *Introduction to Mathematical Economics* (Waveland Press, Illinois, 1979) p. 133.

16. ▼ *Modeling Linear Demand* You have been hired as a marketing consultant to Big Book Publishing, Inc., and you have been approached to determine the best selling price for the hit calculus text by Whiner and Istanbul entitled *Fun with Derivatives*. You decide to make life easy and assume that the demand equation for *Fun with Derivatives* has the linear form $q = mp + b$, where p is the price per book, q is the demand in annual sales, and m and b are certain constants you'll have to figure out.

a. Your market studies reveal the following sales figures: when the price is set at $50.00 per book, the sales amount to 10,000 per year; when the price is set at $80.00 per book, the sales drop to 1000 per year. Use these data to calculate the demand equation.

b. Now estimate the unit price that maximizes annual revenue and predict what Big Book Publishing, Inc.'s annual revenue will be at that price.

17. *Income Elasticity of Demand: Live Drama* The likelihood that a child will attend a live theatrical performance can be modeled by

$$q = 0.01(-0.0078x^2 + 1.5x + 4.1) \quad (15 \le x \le 100)$$

Here, q is the fraction of children with annual household income x thousand dollars who will attend a live dramatic performance at a theater during the year.[65] Compute the income elasticity of demand at an income level of $20,000 and interpret the result. (Round your answer to two significant digits.) HINT [See Example 2.]

18. *Income Elasticity of Demand: Live Concerts* The likelihood that a child will attend a live musical performance can be modeled by

$$q = 0.01(0.0006x^2 + 0.38x + 35). \quad (15 \le x \le 100)$$

Here, q is the fraction of children with annual household income x who will attend a live musical performance during the year.[66] Compute the income elasticity of demand at an income level of $30,000 and interpret the result. HINT [See Example 2.]

19. *Income Elasticity of Demand: Computer Usage* The demand for personal computers in the home goes up with household income. The following graph shows some data on computer usage together with the logarithmic model $q = 0.3454 \ln(x) - 3.047$, where q is the probability that a household with annual income x will have a computer.[67]

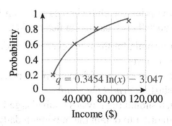

$q = 0.3454 \ln(x) - 3.047$

a. Compute the income elasticity of demand for computers, to two decimal places, for a household income of $60,000 and interpret the result.

b. As household income increases, how is income elasticity of demand affected?

c. How reliable is the given model of demand for incomes well above $120,000? Explain.

d. What can you say about E for incomes much larger than those shown?

20. *Income Elasticity of Demand: Internet Usage* The demand for Internet connectivity also goes up with household income. The following graph shows some data on Internet usage, together with the logarithmic model $q = 0.2802 \ln(x) - 2.505$, where q is the probability that a home with annual household income x will have an Internet connection.[68]

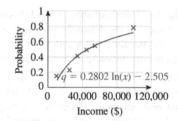

$q = 0.2802 \ln(x) - 2.505$

a. Compute the income elasticity of demand to two decimal places for a household income of $60,000 and interpret the result.

b. As household income increases, how is income elasticity of demand affected?

c. The logarithmic model shown above is not appropriate for incomes well above $100,000. Suggest a model that might be more appropriate.

d. In the model you propose, how does E behave for very large incomes?

21. ▼ *Income Elasticity of Demand (based on a question on the GRE Economics Test)* If $Q = a P^\alpha Y^\beta$ is the individual's demand function for a commodity, where P is the (fixed) price of the commodity, Y is the individual's income, and a, α, and β are parameters, explain why β can be interpreted as the income elasticity of demand.

---

[65] Based on a quadratic regression of data from a 2001 survey. Source for data: New York Foundation of the Arts (www.nyfa.org/culturalblueprint/).

[66] Ibid.

[67] All figures are approximate. The model is a regression model, and x measures the probability that a given household will have one or more computers. Source: Income distribution computer data: Forrester Research/*The New York Times*, August 8, 1999, p. BU4.

[68] All figures are approximate, and the model is a regression model. The Internet connection figures were actually quoted as "share of consumers who use the Internet, by household income." Sources: Luxembourg Income Study/*The New York Times*, August 14, 1995, p. A9, Commerce Department, Deloitte & Touche Survey/*The New York Times*, November 24, 1999, p. C1.

22. ▼ *College Tuition (from the GRE Economics Test)* A time-series study of the demand for higher education, using tuition charges as a price variable, yields the following result:

$$\frac{dq}{dp} \cdot \frac{p}{q} = -0.4$$

where p is tuition and q is the quantity of higher education. Which of the following is suggested by the result?

(A) As tuition rises, students want to buy a greater quantity of education.

(B) As a determinant of the demand for higher education, income is more important than price.

(C) If colleges lowered tuition slightly, their total tuition receipts would increase.

(D) If colleges raised tuition slightly, their total tuition receipts would increase.

(E) Colleges cannot increase enrollments by offering larger scholarships.

23. ▼ *Modeling Exponential Demand* As the new owner of a supermarket, you have inherited a large inventory of unsold imported Limburger cheese, and you would like to set the price so that your revenue from selling it is as large as possible. Previous sales figures of the cheese are shown in the following table:

Price per Pound, p	$3.00	$4.00	$5.00
Monthly Sales in Pounds, q	407	287	223

a. Use the sales figures for the prices $3 and $5 per pound to construct a demand function of the form $q = Ae^{-bp}$, where A and b are constants you must determine. (Round A and b to two significant digits.)

b. Use your demand function to find the price elasticity of demand at each of the prices listed.

c. At what price should you sell the cheese in order to maximize monthly revenue?

d. If your total inventory of cheese amounts to only 200 pounds, and it will spoil one month from now, how should you price it in order to receive the greatest revenue? Is this the same answer you got in part (c)? If not, give a brief explanation.

24. ▼ *Modeling Exponential Demand* Repeat the preceding exercise, but this time use the sales figures for $4 and $5 per pound to construct the demand function.

COMMUNICATION AND REASONING EXERCISES

25. Complete the following: When demand is inelastic, revenue will decrease if ____ .

26. Complete the following: When demand has unit elasticity, revenue will decrease if ____ .

27. ▼ Given that the demand q is a differentiable function of the unit price p, show that the revenue $R = pq$ has a stationary point when

$$q + p\frac{dq}{dp} = 0.$$

Deduce that the stationary points of R are the same as the points of unit price elasticity of demand. (Ordinarily, there is only one such stationary point, corresponding to the absolute maximum of R.) HINT [Differentiate R with respect to p.]

28. ▼ Given that the demand q is a differentiable function of income x, show that the quantity $R = q/x$ has a stationary point when

$$q - x\frac{dq}{dx} = 0.$$

Deduce that stationary points of R are the same as the points of unit income elasticity of demand. HINT [Differentiate R with respect to x.]

29. ◆ Your calculus study group is discussing price elasticity of demand, and a member of the group asks the following question: "Since elasticity of demand measures the response of demand to change in unit price, what is the difference between elasticity of demand and the quantity $-dq/dp$?" How would you respond?

30. ◆ Another member of your study group claims that unit price elasticity of demand need not always correspond to maximum revenue. Is he correct? Explain your answer.

CHAPTER 12 REVIEW

KEY CONCEPTS

Web Site www.FiniteandCalc.org
Go to the student Web site at
www.FiniteandCalc.org to find a
comprehensive and interactive
Web-based summary of Chapter 12.

12.1 Maxima and Minima

Relative maximum, relative minimum
p. 867

Absolute maximum, absolute
minimum p. 867

Stationary points, singular points,
endpoints p. 869

Finding and classifying maxima
and minima p. 869

First derivative test for relative
extrema p. 871

Extreme value theorem p. 875

Using technology to locate approximate
extrema p. 876

12.2 Applications of Maxima and Minima

Minimizing average cost p. 880

Maximizing area p. 881

Steps in solving optimization
problems p. 883

Maximizing revenue p. 883

Optimizing resources p. 884

Allocation of labor p. 886

12.3 Higher Order Derivatives: Acceleration and Concavity

The second derivative of a function f is
the derivative of the derivative of f,
written as f'' p. 894

The acceleration of a moving object is
the second derivative of the position
function p. 894

Acceleration due to gravity p. 895

Acceleration of sales p. 895

Concave up, concave down, point of
inflection p. 896

Locating points of inflection p. 897

Application to inflation p. 897

Second derivative test for relative
extrema p. 900

Higher order derivatives p. 901

12.4 Analyzing Graphs

Features of a graph: x- and y-intercepts,
relative extrema, points of inflection;
behavior near points where the

function is not defined, behavior at
infinity p. 911

Analyzing a graph p. 912

12.5 Related Rates

If Q is a quantity changing over time t,
then the derivative dQ/dt is the rate at
which Q changes over time p. 919

The expanding circle p. 919

Steps in solving related rates
problems p. 920

The falling ladder p. 920

Average cost p. 922

Allocation of labor p. 923

12.6 Elasticity

Price elasticity of demand
$E = -\dfrac{dq}{dp} \cdot \dfrac{p}{q}$; demand is elastic
if $E > 1$, inelastic if $E < 1$, has unit
elasticity if $E = 1$ p. 929

Computing and interpreting elasticity,
and maximizing revenue p. 929

Using technology to compute
elasticity p. 931

Income elasticity of demand p. 931

REVIEW EXERCISES

In Exercises 1–8, find all the relative and absolute extrema of
the given functions on the given domain (if supplied) or on the
largest possible domain (if no domain is supplied).

1. $f(x) = 2x^3 - 6x + 1$ on $[-2, +\infty)$

2. $f(x) = x^3 - x^2 - x - 1$ on $(-\infty, \infty)$

3. $g(x) = x^4 - 4x$ on $[-1, 1]$

4. $f(x) = \dfrac{x+1}{(x-1)^2}$ on $[-2, 1) \cup (1, 2]$

5. $g(x) = (x-1)^{2/3}$ **6.** $g(x) = x^2 + \ln x$ on $(0, +\infty)$

7. $h(x) = \dfrac{1}{x} + \dfrac{1}{x^2}$ **8.** $h(x) = e^{x^2} + 1$

In Exercises 9–12, the graph of the function f or its derivative is
given. Find the approximate x-coordinates of all relative extrema
and points of inflection of the original function f (if any).

9. Graph of f:

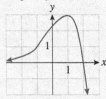

10. Graph of f:

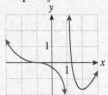

11. Graph of f':

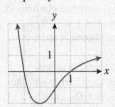

12. Graph of f':

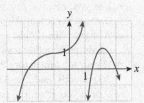

In Exercises 13 and 14, the graph of the second derivative of a
function f is given. Find the approximate x-coordinates of all
points of inflection of the original function f (if any).

13. Graph of f'':

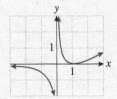

14. Graph of f'':

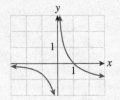

In Exercises 15 and 16, the position s of a point (in meters) is given as a function of time t (in seconds). Find **(a)** its acceleration as a function of t and **(b)** its acceleration at the specified time.

15. $s = \dfrac{2}{3t^2} - \dfrac{1}{t}; t = 1$ **16.** $s = \dfrac{4}{t^2} - \dfrac{3t}{4}; t = 2$

In Exercises 17–22, sketch the graph of the given function, indicating all relative and absolute extrema and points of inflection. Find the coordinates of these points exactly, where possible. Also indicate any horizontal and vertical asymptotes.

17. $f(x) = x^3 - 12x$ on $[-2, +\infty)$

18. $g(x) = x^4 - 4x$ on $[-1, 1]$

19. $f(x) = \dfrac{x^2 - 3}{x^3}$

20. $f(x) = (x - 1)^{2/3} + \dfrac{2x}{3}$

21. $g(x) = (x - 3)\sqrt{x}$

22. $g(x) = (x + 3)\sqrt{x}$

APPLICATIONS

23. *Revenue* Demand for the latest best-seller at OHaganBooks.com, *A River Burns Through It*, is given by

$$q = -p^2 + 33p + 9 \quad (18 \le p \le 28)$$

copies sold per week when the price is p dollars. What price should the company charge to obtain the largest revenue?

24. *Revenue* Demand for *The Secret Loves of John O*, a romance novel by Margó Dufón that flopped after two weeks on the market, is given by

$$q = -2p^2 + 5p + 6 \quad (0 \le p \le 3.3)$$

copies sold per week when the price is p dollars. What price should OHaganBooks charge to obtain the largest revenue?

25. *Profit* Taking into account storage and shipping, it costs OHaganBooks.com

$$C = 9q + 100$$

dollars to sell q copies of *A River Burns Through It* in a week (see Exercise 23).

a. If demand is as in Exercise 23, express the weekly profit earned by OHaganBooks.com from the sale of *A River Burns Through It* as a function of unit price p.

b. What price should the company charge to get the largest weekly profit? What is the maximum possible weekly profit?

c. Compare your answer in part (b) with the price the company should charge to obtain the largest revenue (Exercise 23). Explain any difference.

26. *Profit* Taking into account storage and shipping, it costs OHaganBooks.com

$$C = 3q$$

dollars to sell q copies of Margó Dufón's *The Secret Loves of John O* in a week (see Exercise 24).

a. If demand is as in Exercise 24, express the weekly profit earned by OHaganBooks.com from the sale of *The Secret Loves of John O* as a function of unit price p.

b. What price should the company charge to get the largest weekly profit? What is the maximum possible weekly profit?

c. Compare your answer in part (b) with the price the company should charge to obtain the largest revenue (Exercise 24). Explain any difference.

27. *Box Design* The sales department at OHaganBooks.com, which has decided to send chocolate lobsters to each of its customers, is trying to design a shipping box with a square base. It has a roll of cardboard 36 inches wide from which to make the boxes. Each box will be obtained by cutting out corners from a rectangle of cardboard as shown in the following diagram:

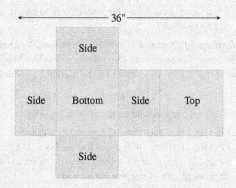

(Notice that the top and bottom of each box will be square, but the sides will not necessarily be square.) What are the dimensions of the boxes with the largest volume that can be made in this way? What is the maximum volume?

28. *Box Redesign* The sales department at OHaganBooks.com was not pleased with the result of the box design in the preceding exercise; the resulting box was too large for the chocolate lobsters, so, following a suggestion by a math major student intern, the department decided to redesign the boxes to meet the following specifications: As in Exercise 27, each box would be obtained by cutting out corners from a rectangle of cardboard as shown in the following diagram:

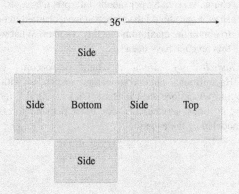

(Notice that the top and bottom of each box would be square, but not necessarily the sides.) The dimensions would be such that the total surface area of the sides plus the bottom of the box would be as large as possible. What are the dimensions of the boxes with the largest area that can be made in this way? How does this box compare with that obtained in Exercise 27?

29. **Elasticity of Demand** (Compare Exercise 23). Demand for the latest best-seller at OHaganBooks.com, *A River Burns Through It*, is given by

$$q = -p^2 + 33p + 9 \qquad (18 \le p \le 28)$$

copies sold per week when the price is p dollars.

   a. Find the price elasticity of demand as a function of p.
   b. Find the elasticity of demand for this book at a price of $20 and at a price of $25. (Round your answers to two decimal places.) Interpret the answers.
   c. What price should the company charge to obtain the largest revenue?

30. **Elasticity of Demand** (Compare Exercise 24). Demand for *The Secret Loves of John O*, a romance novel by Margó Dufón that flopped after two weeks on the market, is given by

$$q = -2p^2 + 5p + 6 \qquad (0 \le p \le 3.3)$$

copies sold per week when the price is p dollars.

   a. Find the price elasticity of demand as a function of p.
   b. Find the elasticity of demand for this book at a price of $1 and at a price of $3. (Round your answers to two decimal places.) Interpret the answers.
   c. What price should the company charge to obtain the largest revenue?

31. **Elasticity of Demand** Last year OHaganBooks.com experimented with an online subscriber service, Red On Line (ROL), for its electronic book service. The consumer demand for ROL was modeled by the equation

$$q = 1,000e^{-p^2+p}$$

where p was the monthly access charge and q is the number of subscribers.

   a. Obtain a formula for the price elasticity of demand, E, for ROL services.
   b. Compute the elasticity of demand if the monthly access charge is set at $2 per month. Interpret the result.
   c. How much should the company have charged in order to obtain the maximum monthly revenue? What would this revenue have been?

32. **Elasticity of Demand** JungleBooks.com (one of OHaganBooks' main competitors) responded with its own online subscriber service, Better On Line (BOL), for its electronic book service. The consumer demand for BOL was modeled by the equation

$$q = 2,000e^{-3p^2+2p}$$

where p was the monthly access charge and q is the number of subscribers.

   a. Obtain a formula for the price elasticity of demand, E, for BOL services.
   b. Compute the elasticity of demand if the monthly access charge is set at $2 per month. Interpret the result.
   c. How much should the company have charged in order to obtain the maximum monthly revenue? What would this revenue have been?

33. **Sales** OHaganBooks.com modeled its weekly sales over a period of time with the function

$$s(t) = 6,053 + \frac{4,474}{1 + e^{-0.55(t-4.8)}}$$

where t is the time in weeks. Following are the graphs of s, s', and s'':

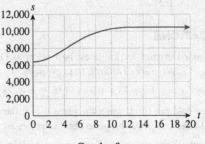

Graph of s

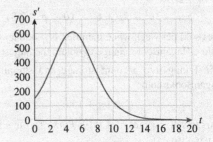

Graph of s'

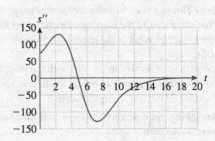

Graph of s''

a. Estimate when, to the nearest week, the weekly sales were growing fastest.

b. To what features on the graphs of s, s', and s'' does your answer to part (a) correspond?

c. The graph of s has a horizontal asymptote. What is the approximate value (s-coordinate) of this asymptote, and what is its significance in terms of weekly sales at OHaganBooks.com?

d. The graph of s' has a horizontal asymptote. What is the value (s'-coordinate) of this asymptote, and what is its significance in terms of weekly sales at OHaganBooks.com?

34. *Sales* The quarterly sales of OHagan χPods (OHaganBooks' answer to the *iPod*; a portable audio book unit with an incidental music feature) from the fourth quarter of 2009 can be roughly approximated by the function

$$N(t) = \frac{1{,}100}{1 + 9(1.8)^{-t}} \quad (t \geq 0)$$

where t is time in quarters since the fourth quarter of 2009. Following are the graphs of N, N', and N'':

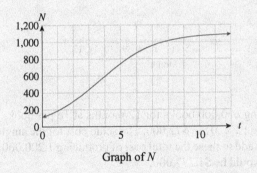

Graph of N

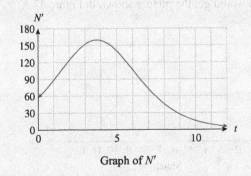

Graph of N'

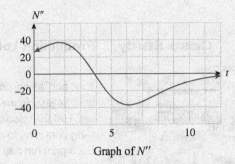

Graph of N''

a. Estimate when, to the nearest quarter, the quarterly sales were growing fastest.

b. To what features on the graphs of N, N', and N'' does your answer to part (a) correspond?

c. The graph of N has a horizontal asymptote. What is the approximate value (N-coordinate) of this asymptote, and what is its significance in terms of quarterly sales of χPods?

d. The graph of N' has a horizontal asymptote. What is the value (N'-coordinate) of this asymptote, and what is its significance in terms of quarterly sales of χPods?

35. *Chance Encounter* Marjory Duffin is walking north towards the corner entrance of OHaganBooks.com company headquarters at 5 ft/s, while John O'Hagan is walking west toward the same entrance, also at 5 ft/s. How fast is their distance apart decreasing when:

a. Each of them is 2 ft from the corner?

b. Each of them is 1 ft. from the corner?

c. Each of them is h ft. from the corner?

d. They collide on the corner?

36. *Company Logos* OHaganBooks.com's Web site has an animated graphic with its name in a rectangle whose height and width change; on either side of the rectangle are semicircles, as in the figure, whose diameters are the same as the height of the rectangle.

For reasons too complicated to explain, the designer wanted the combined area of the rectangle and semicircles to remain constant. At one point during the animation, the width of the rectangle is 1 inch, growing at a rate of 0.5 inches per second, while the height is 3 inches. How fast is the height changing?

SUNY/Productophotography/Alamy

Case Study   Production Lot Size Management

Your publishing company, Knockem Dead Paperbacks, Inc., is about to release its next best-seller, *Henrietta's Heaving Heart* by Celestine A. Lafleur. The company expects to sell 100,000 books each month in the next year. You have been given the job of scheduling print runs to meet the anticipated demand and minimize total costs to the company. Each print run has a setup cost of $5,000, each book costs $1 to produce, and monthly storage costs for books awaiting shipment average 1¢ per book. What will you do?

If you decide to print all 1,200,000 books (the total demand for the year, 100,000 books per month for 12 months) in a single run at the start of the year and sales run as predicted, then the number of books in stock would begin at 1,200,000 and decrease to zero by the end of the year, as shown in Figure 46.

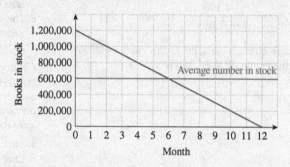

Figure 46

On average, you would be storing 600,000 books for 12 months at 1¢ per book, giving a total storage cost of $600,000 \times 12 \times .01 = \$72,000$. The setup cost for the single print run would be $5,000. When you add to these the total cost of producing 1,200,000 books at $1 per book, your total cost would be $1,277,000.

If, on the other hand, you decide to cut down on storage costs by printing the book in two runs of 600,000 each, you would get the picture shown in Figure 47.

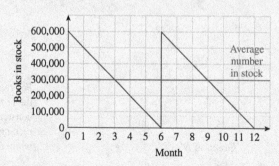

Figure 47

Now, the storage cost would be cut in half because on average there would be only 300,000 books in stock. Thus, the total storage cost would be $36,000, and the setup cost would double to $10,000 (because there would now be two runs). The production costs would be the same: 1,200,000 books @ $1 per book. The total cost would therefore be reduced to $1,246,000, a savings of $31,000 compared to your first scenario.

244

"Aha!" you say to yourself, after doing these calculations. "Why not drastically cut costs by setting up a run every month?" You calculate that the setup costs alone would be $12 \times \$5,000 = \$60,000$, which is already more than the setup plus storage costs for two runs, so a run every month will cost too much. Perhaps, then, you should investigate three runs, four runs, and so on, until you find the lowest cost. This strikes you as too laborious a process, especially considering that you will have to do it all over again when planning for Lafleur's sequel, *Lorenzo's Lost Love,* due to be released next year. Realizing that this is an optimization problem, you decide to use some calculus to help you come up with a *formula* that you can use for all future plans. So you get to work.

Instead of working with the number 1,200,000, you use the letter N so that you can be as flexible as possible. (What if *Lorenzo's Lost Love* sells more copies?) Thus, you have a total of N books to be produced for the year. You now calculate the total cost of using x print runs per year. Because you are to produce a total of N books in x print runs, you will have to produce N/x books in each print run. N/x is called the **lot size**. As you can see from the diagrams above, the average number of books in storage will be half that amount, $N/(2x)$.

Now you can calculate the total cost for a year. Write P for the setup cost of a single print run ($P = \$5,000$ in your case) and c for the *annual* cost of storing a book (to convert all of the time measurements to years; $c = \$0.12$ here). Finally, write b for the cost of producing a single book ($b = \$1$ here). The costs break down as follows.

Setup Costs: x print runs @ P dollars per run: Px

Storage Costs: $N/(2x)$ books stored @ c dollars per year: $cN/(2x)$

Production Costs: N books @ b dollars per book: Nb

Total Cost: $Px + \dfrac{cN}{2x} + Nb$

Remember that P, N, c, and b are all constants and x is the only variable. Thus, your cost function is

$$C(x) = Px + \frac{cN}{2x} + Nb$$

and you need to find the value of x that will minimize $C(x)$. But that's easy! All you need to do is find the relative extrema and select the absolute minimum (if any).

The domain of $C(x)$ is $(0, +\infty)$ because there is an x in the denominator and x can't be negative. To locate the extrema, you start by locating the critical points:

$$C'(x) = P - \frac{cN}{2x^2}.$$

The only singular point would be at $x = 0$, but 0 is not in the domain. To find stationary points, you set $C'(x) = 0$ and solve for x:

$$P - \frac{cN}{2x^2} = 0$$

$$2x^2 = \frac{cN}{P}$$

so

$$x = \sqrt{\frac{cN}{2P}}.$$

There is only one stationary point, and there are no singular points or endpoints. To graph the function you will need to put in numbers for the various constants. Substituting $N = 1{,}200{,}000$, $P = 5{,}000$, $c = 0.12$, and $b = 1$, you get

$$C(x) = 5{,}000x + \frac{72{,}000}{x} + 1{,}200{,}000$$

with the stationary point at

$$x = \sqrt{\frac{(0.12)(1{,}200{,}000)}{2(5000)}} \approx 3.79.$$

The total cost at the stationary point is

$$C(3.79) \approx 1{,}240{,}000.$$

You now graph $C(x)$ in a window that includes the stationary point, say, $0 \le x \le 12$ and $1{,}100{,}000 \le C \le 1{,}500{,}000$, getting Figure 48.

From the graph, you can see that the stationary point is an absolute minimum. In the graph it appears that the graph is always concave up, which also tells you that your stationary point is a minimum. You can check the concavity by computing the second derivative:

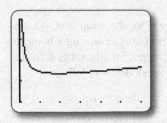

$$C''(x) = \frac{cN}{x^3} > 0.$$

Figure 48

The second derivative is always positive because c, N, and x are all positive numbers, so indeed the graph is always concave up. Now you also know that it works regardless of the particular values of the constants.

So now you are practically done! You know that the absolute minimum cost occurs when you have $x \approx 3.79$ print runs per year. Don't be disappointed that the answer is not a whole number; whole number solutions are rarely found in real scenarios. What the answer (and the graph) do indicate is that either 3 or 4 print runs per year will cost the least money. If you take $x = 3$, you get a total cost of

$$C(3) = \$1{,}239{,}000$$

If you take $x = 4$, you get a total cost of

$$C(4) = \$1{,}238{,}000$$

So, four print runs per year will allow you to minimize your total costs.

EXERCISES

1. *Lorenzo's Lost Love* will sell 2,000,000 copies in a year. The remaining costs are the same. How many print runs should you use now?
2. In general, what happens to the number of runs that minimizes cost if both the setup cost and the total number of books are doubled?
3. In general, what happens to the number of runs that minimizes cost if the setup cost increases by a factor of 4?
4. Assuming that the total number of copies and storage costs are as originally stated, find the setup cost that would result in a single print run.
5. Assuming that the total number of copies and setup cost are as originally stated, find the storage cost that would result in a print run each month.

6. In Figure 47 we assumed that all the books in each run were manufactured in a very short time; otherwise the figure might have looked more like Figure 49, which shows the inventory, assuming a slower rate of production.

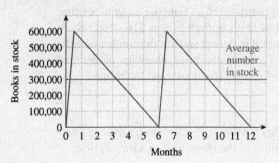

Figure 49

How would this affect the answer?

7. Referring to the general situation discussed in the text, find the cost as a function of the total number of books produced, assuming that the number of runs is chosen to minimize total cost. Also find the average cost per book.

8. Let $\bar{C}$ be the average cost function found in the preceding exercise. Calculate $\lim_{N \to +\infty} \bar{C}(N)$ and interpret the result.

TI-83/84 Plus | **Technology Guide**

Section 12.6

Example 1(a) (page 930) Suppose that the demand equation for Bobby Dolls is given by $q = 216 - p^2$, where p is the price per doll in dollars and q is the number of dolls sold per week. Compute the price elasticity of demand when $p = \$5$ and $p = \$10$, and interpret the results.

Solution with Technology

The TI-83/84 Plus function nDeriv can be used to compute approximations of the elasticity E at various prices.

1. Set

> $Y_1 = 216 - X^2$ Demand equation
>
> $Y_2 = -nDeriv(Y_1, X, X) * X/Y_1$ Formula for E

EXCEL | **Technology Guide**

Section 12.6

Example 1(a) (page 930) Suppose that the demand equation for Bobby Dolls is given by $q = 216 - p^2$, where p is the price per doll in dollars and q is the number of dolls sold per week. Compute the price elasticity of demand when $p = \$5$ and $p = \$10$, and interpret the results.

Solution with Technology

To approximate E in Excel, we can use the following approximation of E.

$$E \approx \frac{\text{Percentage decrease in demand}}{\text{Percentage increase in price}} \approx -\frac{\left(\dfrac{\Delta q}{q}\right)}{\left(\dfrac{\Delta p}{p}\right)}$$

The smaller Δp is, the better the approximation. Let's use $\Delta p = 1\cent$, or 0.01 (which is small compared with the typical prices we consider—around \$5 to \$10).

1. We start by setting up our worksheet to list a range of prices, in increments of Δp, on either side of a price in which we are interested, such as $p_0 = \$5$:

2. Use the table feature to list the values of elasticity for a range of prices. For part (a) we chose values of X close to 5:

We start in cell A5 with the formula for $p_0 - 10\Delta p$ and then successively add Δp going down column A. You will find that the value $p_0 = 5$ appears midway down the list.

2. Next, we compute the corresponding values for the demand q in Column B.

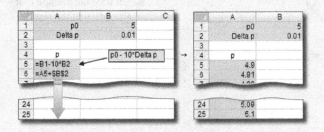

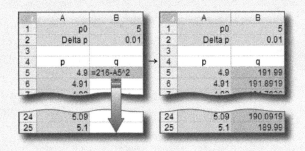

3. We add two new columns for the percentage changes in *p* and *q*. The formula shown in cell C5 is copied down columns C and D, to Row 24. (Why not Row 25?)

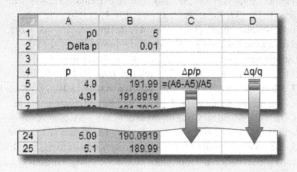

	A	B	C	D
1	p0	5		
2	Delta p	0.01		
3				
4	p	q	Δp/p	Δq/q
5	4.9	191.99	=(A6-A5)/A5	
6	4.91	191.8919		
7				
24	5.09	190.0919		
25	5.1	189.99		

4. The elasticity can now be computed in column E as shown:

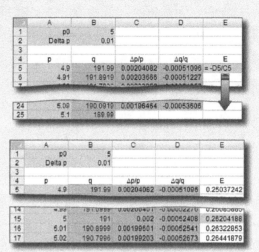

	A	B	C	D	E
1	p0	5			
2	Delta p	0.01			
3					
4	p	q	Δp/p	Δq/q	E
5	4.9	191.99	0.00204082	-0.00051096	= -D5/C5
6	4.91	191.8919	0.00203666	-0.00051227	
24	5.09	190.0919	0.00196464	-0.00053606	
25	5.1	189.99			

	A	B	C	D	E
1	p0	5			
2	Delta p	0.01			
3					
4	p	q	Δp/p	Δq/q	E
5	4.9	191.99	0.00204082	-0.00051096	0.25037242
14	4.99	191.0999	0.00200401	-0.00052276	0.26065865
15	5	191	0.002	-0.00052408	0.26204188
16	5.01	190.8999	0.00199601	-0.00052541	0.26322853
17	5.02	190.7996	0.00199203	-0.00052673	0.26441879

$(-2, -1/3)$, relative minimum at $(-1, -2/3)$, absolute maximum at $(0, 1)$ **29.** Relative min: $(-2, 5/3)$, relative max: $(0, -1)$, relative min: $(2, 5/3)$ **31.** Relative max: $(0, 0)$; absolute min: $(1/3, -2\sqrt{3}/9)$ **33.** Relative max: $(0, 0)$, absolute min: $(1, -3)$ **35.** No relative extrema   **37.** Absolute min: $(1, 1)$ **39.** Relative max: $(-1, 1 + 1/e)$, absolute min: $(0, 1)$, absolute max: $(1, e - 1)$ **41.** Relative max: $(-6, -24)$, relative min: $(-2, -8)$ **43.** Absolute max $(1/\sqrt{2}, \sqrt{e/2})$, absolute min: $(-1/\sqrt{2}, -\sqrt{e/2})$ **45.** Relative min at $(0.15, -0.52)$ and $(2.45, 8.22)$, relative max at $(1.40, 0.29)$ **47.** Absolute max at $(-5, 700)$, relative max at $(3.10, 28.19)$ and $(6, 40)$, absolute min at $(-2.10, -392.69)$ and relative min at $(5, 0)$.   **49.** Stationary minimum at $x = -1$ **51.** Stationary minima at $x = -2$ and $x = 2$, stationary maximum at $x = 0$ **53.** Singular minimum at $x = 0$, stationary non-extreme point at $x = 1$ **55.** Stationary minimum at $x = -2$, singular non-extreme points at $x = -1$ and $x = 1$, stationary maximum at $x = 2$

57. Answers will vary.   **59.** Answers will vary.

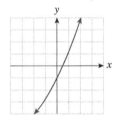   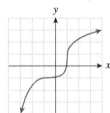

61. Not necessarily; it could be neither a relative maximum nor a relative minimum, as in the graph of $y = x^3$ at the origin.
63. Answers will vary.

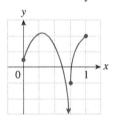

Answers to Selected Exercises

Section 12.1

1. Absolute min: $(-3, -1)$, relative max: $(-1, 1)$, relative min: $(1, 0)$, absolute max: $(3, 2)$ **3.** Absolute min: $(3, -1)$ and $(-3, -1)$, absolute max: $(1, 2)$ **5.** Absolute min: $(-3, 0)$ and $(1, 0)$, absolute max: $(-1, 2)$ and $(3, 2)$ **7.** Relative min: $(-1, 1)$ **9.** Absolute min: $(-3, -1)$, relative max: $(-2, 2)$, relative min: $(1, 0)$, absolute max: $(3, 3)$ **11.** Relative max: $(-3, 0)$, absolute min: $(-2, -1)$, stationary non-extreme point: $(1, 1)$ **13.** Absolute max: $(0, 1)$, absolute min: $(2, -3)$, relative max: $(3, -2)$ **15.** Absolute min: $(-4, -16)$, absolute max: $(-2, 16)$, absolute min: $(2, -16)$, absolute max: $(4, 16)$ **17.** Absolute min: $(-2, -10)$, absolute max: $(2, 10)$ **19.** Absolute min: $(-2, -4)$, relative max: $(-1, 1)$, relative min: $(0, 0)$ **21.** Relative max: $(-1, 5)$, absolute min: $(3, -27)$ **23.** Absolute min: $(0, 0)$ **25.** Absolute maxima at $(0, 1)$ and $(2, 1)$, absolute min at $(1, 0)$ **27.** Relative maximum at

65. The graph oscillates faster and faster above and below zero as it approaches the end-point at 0, so 0 cannot be either a relative minimum or maximum.

Section 12.2

1. $x = y = 5$; $P = 25$ **3.** $x = y = 3$; $S = 6$ **5.** $x = 2$, $y = 4$; $F = 20$ **7.** $x = 20$, $y = 10$, $z = 20$; $P = 4,000$ **9.** 5×5 **11.** 1,500 per day for an average cost of $130 per iPod   **13.** $\sqrt{40} \approx 6.32$ pounds of pollutant per day, for an average cost of about $1,265 per pound   **15.** 2.5 lb   **17.** 5×10 **19.** 50×10 for an area of 250 sq. ft.   **21.** 11×22 **23.** $10   **25.** $78 for a quarterly revenue of $6,084 million, or $6.084 billion   **27.** $4.61 for a daily revenue of $95,680.55   **29. a.** $1.41 per pound   **b.** 5,000 pounds **c.** $7,071.07 per month   **31.** 34.5¢ per pound, for an annual (per capita) revenue of $5.95   **33.** $98 for an annual profit of $3,364 million, or $3.364 billion   **35. a.** 656 headsets, for a profit of $28,120 **b.** $143 per headset   **37.** Height = Radius of base ≈ 20.48 cm.   **39.** Height ≈ 10.84 cm; Radius ≈ 2.71 cm; Height/Radius = 4   **41.** $13\frac{1}{3}$ in × $3\frac{1}{3}$ in × $1\frac{1}{3}$ in for a volume of 1,600/27 ≈ 59 cubic inches   **43.** 5 × 5 × 5 cm   **45.** $l = w = h ≈ 20.67$ in, volume ≈ 8,827 in^3 **47.** $l = 30$ in, $w = 15$ in, $h = 30$ in   **49.** $l = 36$ in, $w = h = 18$ in, $V = 11,664$ in^3 **51. a.** 1.6 years, or year 2001.6;   **b.** R_{max} = $28,241 million   **53.** $t = 2.5$ or midway through 1972; $D(2.5)/S(2.5) ≈ 4.09$. The number of new (approved) drugs per $1 billion of spending on research and development reached a high of around four approved drugs per $1 billion midway through 1972.   **55.** 30 years from now   **57.** 55 days   **59.** 1,600 copies. At this value of x, average profit equals marginal profit; beyond this the marginal profit is smaller than the average.   **61.** 40 laborers and 250 robots   **63.** 71 employees   **65.** Increasing most rapidly in 1990; increasing least rapidly in 2007   **67.** Maximum when $t = 17$ days. This means that the embryo's oxygen consumption is increasing most rapidly 17 days after the egg is laid.   **69.** Graph of derivative:

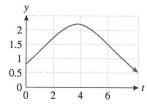

The absolute maximum occurs at approximately (3.7, 2.2) during the year 2003. The percentage of mortgages that were subprime was increasing most rapidly during 2003, when it increased at a rate of around 2.2 percentage points per year.   **71.** You should sell them in 17 years' time, when they will be worth approximately $3,960.   **73.** 25 additional trees   **75.** (D)   **77.** (A); (B)   **79.** The problem is uninteresting because the company can accomplish the objective by cutting away the entire sheet of cardboard, resulting in a box with surface area zero.   **81.** Not all absolute extrema occur at stationary points; some may occur at an endpoint or singular point of the domain, as in Exercises 29, 30, 65, and 66.   **83.** The minimum of dq/dp is the fastest that the demand is dropping in response to increasing price.

Section 12.3
1. 6   **3.** $4/x^3$ **5.** $-0.96x^{-1.6}$ **7.** $e^{-(x-1)}$ **9.** $2/x^3 + 1/x^2$ **11. a.** $a = -32$ ft/s^2 **b.** $a = -32$ ft/s^2 **13. a.** $a = 2/t^3 + 6/t^4$ ft/s^2 **b.** $a = 8$ ft/s^2 **15. a.** $a = -1/(4t^{3/2}) + 2$ ft/s^2 **b.** $a = 63/32$ ft/s^2 **17.** (1, 0)   **19.** (1, 0)   **21.** None   **23.** (−1, 0), (1, 1)   **25.** Points of inflection at $x = -1$ and $x = 1$ **27.** One point of inflection, at $x = -2$ **29.** Points of inflection at $x = -2, x = 0, x = 2$ **31.** Points of inflection at $x = -2$ and $x = 2$ **33.** $x = 2$; minimum   **35.** Maximum at $x = -2$, minimum at $x = 2$ **37.** Maximum at $t = -1/\sqrt{3}$, minimum at $t = 1/\sqrt{3}$ **39.** Non-extreme stationary point at $x = 0$ minimum at $x = 3$ **41.** Maximum at $x = 0$ **43.** Minimum at

$x = -1/\sqrt{2}$; maximum at $x = 1/\sqrt{2}$ **45.** $f'(x) = 8x - 1$; $f''(x) = 8$; $f'''(x) = f^{(4)}(x) = \ldots = f^{(n)}(x) = 0$ **47.** $f'(x) = -4x^3 + 6x$; $f''(x) = -12x^2 + 6$; $f'''(x) = -24x$; $f^{(4)}(x) = -24$; $f^{(5)}(x) = f^{(6)}(x) = \ldots = f^{(n)}(x) = 0$ **49.** $f'(x) = 8(2x + 1)^3$; $f''(x) = 48(2x + 1)^2$; $f'''(x) = 192(2x + 1)$; $f^{(4)}(x) = 384$; $f^{(5)}(x) = f^{(6)}(x) = \ldots = f^{(n)}(x) = 0$ **51.** $f'(x) = -e^{-x}$; $f''(x) = e^{-x}$; $f'''(x) = -e^{-x}$; $f^{(4)}(x) = e^{-x}$; $f^{(n)}(x) = (-1)^n e^{-x}$ **53.** $f'(x) = 3e^{3x-1}$; $f''(x) = 9e^{3x-1}$; $f'''(x) = 27e^{3x-1}$; $f^{(4)}(x) = 81e^{3x-1}$; $f^{(n)}(x) = 3^n e^{3x-1}$ **55.** -3.8 m/s^2 **57.** $6t - 2$ ft/s^2; increasing   **59.** Accelerating by 24 million gals/yr^2 **61. a.** 400 ml   **b.** 36 ml/day   **c.** -1 ml/day^2 **63. a.** 0.6%   **b.** Speeding up   **c.** Speeding up for $t < 3.33$ (prior to 1/3 of the way through March) and slowing for $t > 3.33$ (after that time)   **65. a.** December 2005: -0.202% (deflation rate of 0.202%) February 2006: 0.363%   **b.** Speeding up   **c.** Decreasing for $t < 4.44$ (prior to mid-November) and increasing for $t > 4.44$ (after that time).   **67.** Concave up for $8 < t < 20$, concave down for $0 < t < 8$, point of inflection around $t = 8$. The percentage of articles written by researchers in the United States was decreasing most rapidly at around $t = 8$ (1991).   **69. a.** (B)   **b.** (B)   **c.** (A)   **71.** Graphs:

$A(t)$:

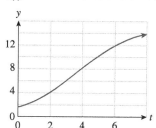

$A'(t)$:

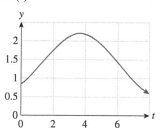

$A''(t)$:

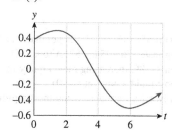

Concave up when $t < 4$; concave down when $t > 4$; point of inflection when $t \approx 4$. The percentage of U.S. mortgages that were subprime was increasing fastest at the beginning of 2004. **73. a.** 2 years into the epidemic **b.** 2 years into the epidemic **75. a.** 2024 **b.** 2026 **c.** 2022; (A) **77. a.** There are no points of inflection in the graph of S. **b.** Because the graph is concave up, the derivative of S is increasing, and so the rate of *decrease* of SAT scores with increasing numbers of prisoners is diminishing. In other words, the apparent effect of more prisoners is diminishing. **79. a.** $\dfrac{d^2n}{ds^2}\Big|_{s=3} = -21.494$. Thus, for a firm

with annual sales of \$3 million, the rate at which new patents are produced decreases with increasing firm size. This means that the returns (as measured in the number of new patents per increase of \$1 million in sales) are diminishing as the firm size

increases. **b.** $\dfrac{d^2n}{ds^2}\Big|_{s=7} = 13.474$. Thus, for a firm with annual

sales of \$7 million, the rate at which new patents are produced increases with increasing firm size by 13.474 new patents per \$1 million increase in annual sales. **c.** There is a point of inflection when $s \approx 5.4587$, so that in a firm with sales of \$5,458,700 per year, the number of new patents produced per additional \$1 million in sales is a minimum.
81. Graphs:

$I(t)/P(t)$:

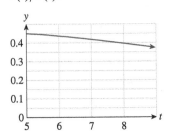

$[I(t)/P(t)]'$:

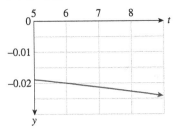

Concave down; (D)   **83.** (Proof)   **85.** $t \approx 4$; the population of Puerto Rico was increasing fastest in 1954.   **87.** About \$570 per year, after about 12 years   **89.** Increasing most rapidly in 17.64 years, decreasing most rapidly now (at $t = 0$)
91. Non-negative   **93.** Daily sales were decreasing most rapidly in June 2002.

95.

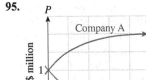

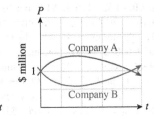

97. At a point of inflection, the graph of a function changes either from concave up to concave down, or vice versa. If it changes from concave up to concave down, then the derivative changes from increasing to decreasing, and hence has a relative maximum. Similarly, if it changes from concave down to concave up, the derivative has a relative minimum.

Section 11.4
1. a. x-intercept: -1; y-intercept: 1 **b.** Absolute min at $(-1, 0)$ **c.** None **d.** None **e.** $y \to +\infty$ as $x \to \pm\infty$
Graph:

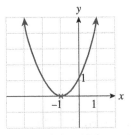

3. a. x-intercepts: $-\sqrt{12}$, 0, $\sqrt{12}$; y-intercept: 0 **b.** Absolute min at $(-4, -16)$ and $(2, -16)$, absolute max at $(-2, 16)$ and $(4, 16)$ **c.** $(0, 0)$ **d.** None **e.** None
Graph:

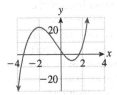

5. a. x-intercepts: -3.6, 0, 5.1; y-intercept: 0 **b.** Relative max at $(-2, 44)$, relative min at $(3, -81)$ **c.** $(0.5, -18.5)$ **d.** None **e.** $y \to -\infty$ as $x \to -\infty$; $y \to +\infty$ as $x \to +\infty$
Graph:

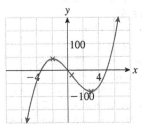

7. a. x-intercepts: 0.1, 1.8; y-intercept: 1 **b.** Relative max at $(-2, 21)$, relative min at $(1, -6)$ **c.** $(-1/2, 15/2)$ **d.** None **e.** $y \to -\infty$ as $x \to -\infty$; $y \to +\infty$ as $x \to +\infty$
Graph:

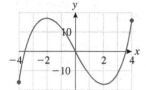

9. a. x-intercepts: -2.9, 4.2; y-intercept: 10 **b.** Relative max at $(-2, 74)$, relative min at $(0, 10)$, absolute max at $(3, 199)$ **c.** $(-1.12, 44.8)$, $(1.79, 117.3)$ **d.** None **e.** $y \to -\infty$ as $x \to -\infty$; $y \to -\infty$ as $x \to +\infty$
Graph:

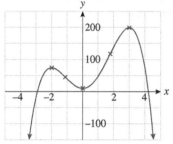

11. a. x-intercepts: None; y-intercept: 0 **b.** Absolute min at $(0, 0)$ **c.** $(1/3, 11/324)$ and $(1, 1/12)$ **d.** None **e.** $y \to +\infty$ as $x \to -\infty$; $y \to +\infty$ as $x \to +\infty$
Graph:

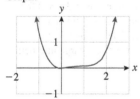

13. a. x-intercepts: None; y-intercept: None **b.** Relative min at $(1, 2)$, relative max at $(-1, -2)$ **c.** None **d.** $y \to -\infty$ as $x \to 0^-$; $y \to +\infty$ as $x \to 0^+$, so there is a vertical asymptote at $x = 0$. **e.** $y \to -\infty$ as $x \to -\infty$; $y \to +\infty$ as $x \to +\infty$
Graph:

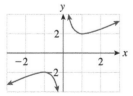

15. a. x-intercept: 0; y-intercept: 0 **b.** None **c.** $(0, 0)$, $(-3, -9/4)$, and $(3, 9/4)$ **d.** None **e.** $y \to -\infty$ as $x \to -\infty$; $y \to +\infty$ as $x \to +\infty$

Graph:

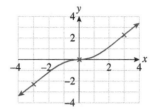

17. a. t-intercepts: None; y-intercept: -1 **b.** Relative min at $(-2, 5/3)$ and $(2, 5/3)$, relative max at $(0, -1)$ **c.** None **d.** $y \to +\infty$ as $t \to -1^-$; $y \to -\infty$ as $t \to -1^+$; $y \to -\infty$ as $t \to 1^-$; $y \to +\infty$ as $t \to 1^+$; so there are vertical asymptotes at $t = \pm 1$. **e.** None
Graph:

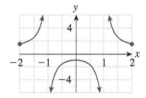

19. a. x-intercepts: -0.6; y-intercept: 1 **b.** Relative maximum at $(-2, -1/3)$, relative minimum at $(-1, -2/3)$ **c.** None **d.** None. **e.** $y \to -\infty$ as $x \to -\infty$; $y \to +\infty$ as $x \to +\infty$
Graph:

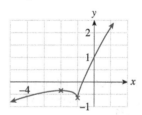

21. a. x-intercepts: None; y-intercept: None **b.** Absolute min at $(1, 1)$ **c.** None **d.** Vertical asymptote at $x = 0$ **e.** $y \to +\infty$ as $x \to +\infty$
Graph:

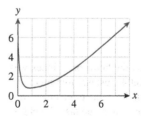

23. a. x-intercepts: ± 0.8; x-intercept: None **b.** None **c.** $(1, 1)$ and $(-1, 1)$ **d.** $y \to -\infty$ as $x \to 0$; vertical asymptote at $x = 0$ **e.** $y \to +\infty$ as $x \to \pm\infty$

Graph:

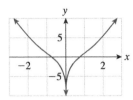

25. a. t-intercepts: None; y-intercept: 1 **b.** Absolute min at $(0, 1)$. Absolute max at $(1, e - 1)$, relative max at $(-1, e^{-1} + 1)$. **c.** None **e.** None
Graph:

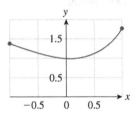

27. Absolute min at $(1.40, -1.49)$; points of inflection: $(0.21, 0.61)$, $(0.79, -0.55)$
Graph:

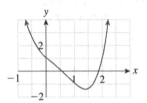

29. $f(x) = e^x - x^3$. Relative min at $(-0.46, 0.73)$, relative max at $(0.91, 1.73)$, absolute min at $(3.73, -10.22)$; points of inflection at $(0.20, 1.22)$ and $(2.83, -5.74)$
Graph:

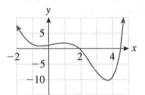

31. y-intercept: 10; t-intercepts: None; the home price index was 10 percentage points at the start of 2004; absolute minimum at $(0, 10)$; absolute maximum at $(2, 40)$; the home price index was lowest in 2004 when it stood at 10 percentage points. The index was at its highest in 2006 at 40 points. Point of inflection at $(3.5, 30)$; the home price index was decreasing most rapidly midway through 2007 when it stood at 30 percentage points. As $t \to +\infty$, $y \to 15$; assuming the trend shown in the graph continues indefinitely, the home price index will approach a value of 15 percentage points in the long term. **33. a.** Intercepts: No t-intercept; y-intercept at $I(0) = 195$. The CPI was never zero

during the given period; in July 2005 the CPI was 195. Absolute min at $(0, 195)$, absolute max at $(8, 199.3)$, relative max at $(2.9, 198.7)$, relative min at $(6.0, 197.8)$. The CPI was at a low of 195 in July 2005, rose to 198.7 around October 2005, dipped to 197.8 around January 2006, and then rose to a high of 199.3 in March 2006. There is a point of inflection at $(4.4, 198.2)$. The rate of change of the CPI (inflation) reached a minimum around mid-November 2005 when the CPI was 198.2.
b. The inflation rate was zero at around October 2005 and January 2006. **35.** Extrema: Relative max at $(0, 100)$, absolute min at $(1, 99)$; point of inflection $(0.5, 99.5)$; $s \to +\infty$ as $t \to +\infty$. At time $t = 0$ seconds, the UFO is stationary, 100 feet away from the observer, and begins to move closer. At time $t = 0.5$ seconds, when the UFO is 99.5 feet away, its distance is decreasing most rapidly (it is moving toward the observer most rapidly). It then slows down to a stop at $t = 1$ second when it is at its closest point (99 feet away) and then begins to move further and further away.
Graph:

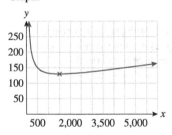

37. Intercepts: None; Absolute minimum at $(1,500, 130)$; No points of inflection; vertical asymptote at $x = 0$. As $x \to +\infty$, $y \to +\infty$. The average cost is never zero, nor is it defined for zero iPods. The average cost is a minimum (\$130) when 1,500 iPods are manufactured per day. The average cost becomes extremely large for very small or very large numbers of iPods.
Graph:

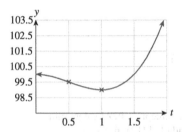

39. Graph of derivative:

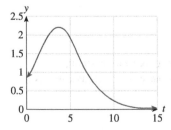

The absolute maximum occurs at approximately (3.7, 2.2); during the year 2003. The percentage of mortgages that were subprime was increasing most rapidly during 2003, when it increased at a rate of around 2.2 percentage points per year. As $t \to +\infty$, $A'(t) \to 0$; In the long term, assuming the trend shown in the model continues, the rate of change of the percentage of mortgages that were subprime approaches zero; that is, the percentage of mortgages that were subprime approaches a constant value. **41.** No; yes. Near a vertical asymptote the value of y increases without bound, and so the graph could not be included between two horizontal lines; hence, no vertical asymptotes are possible. Horizontal asymptotes are possible, as for instance in the graph in Exercise 31. **43.** It too has a vertical asymptote at $x = a$; the magnitude of the derivative increases without bound as $x \to a$. **45.** No. If the leftmost critical point is a relative maximum, the function will decrease from there until it reaches the rightmost critical point, so can't have a relative maximum there. **47.** Between every pair of zeros of $f(x)$ there must be a local extremum, which must be a stationary point of $f(x)$, hence a zero of $f'(x)$.

Section 12.5

1. $P = 10,000$; $\dfrac{dP}{dt} = 1,000$ **3.** Let R be the annual revenue of my company, and let q be annual sales. $R = 7,000$ and $\dfrac{dR}{dt} = -700$. Find $\dfrac{dq}{dt}$. **5.** Let p be the price of a pair of shoes, and let q be the demand for shoes. $\dfrac{dp}{dt} = 5$. Find $\dfrac{dq}{dt}$.

7. Let T be the average global temperature, and let q be the number of Bermuda shorts sold per year. $T = 60$ and $\dfrac{dT}{dt} = 0.1$. Find $\dfrac{dq}{dt}$. **9. a.** $6/(100\pi) \approx 0.019$ km/sec **b.** $6/(8\sqrt{\pi}) \approx 0.4231$ km/sec **11.** $3/(4\pi) \approx 0.24$ ft/min **13.** 7.5 ft/s **15.** Decreasing at a rate of $1.66 per player per week **17.** Monthly sales will drop at a rate of 26 T-shirts per month. **19.** Raise the price by 3¢ per week. **21.** Increasing at a rate of $233.68 million per year **23.** 1 laborer per month **25.** The daily operating budget is dropping at a rate of $2.40 per year. **27.** The price is decreasing at a rate of approximately 31¢ per pound per month. **29.** $2,300/\sqrt{4,100} \approx 36$ miles/hour. **31.** 10.7 ft/s **33.** The y coordinate is decreasing at a rate of 16 units per second. **35.** $1,814 per year **37.** Their prior experience must increase at a rate of approximately 0.97 years every year. **39.** $\dfrac{2,500}{9\pi} \left(\dfrac{3}{5,000} \right)^{2/3} \approx 0.63$ m/sec

41. $\dfrac{\sqrt{1 + 128\pi}}{4\pi} \approx 1.6$ cm/sec **43.** 0.5137 computers per household, and increasing at a rate of 0.0230 computers per household per year. **45.** The average SAT score was 904.71 and decreasing at a rate of 0.11 per year. **47.** Decreasing by 2 percentage points per year **49.** The section is called "related rates" because the goal is to compute the rate of change of a quantity based on a knowledge of the rate of change of a related quantity. **51.** Answers may vary: A rectangular solid has

dimensions 2 cm $\times$ 5 cm $\times$ 10 cm, and each side is expanding at a rate of 3 cm/second. How fast is the volume increasing? **53.** (Proof) **55.** Linear **57.** Let $x =$ my grades and $y =$ your grades. If $dx/dt = 2\, dy/dt$, then $dy/dt = (1/2)\, dx/dt$.

Section 12.6

1. $E = 1.5$; the demand is going down 1.5% per 1% increase in price at that price level; revenue is maximized when $p = \$25$; weekly revenue at that price is $12,500. **3. a.** $E = 6/7$; the demand is going down 6% per 7% increase in price at that price level; thus, a price increase is in order. **b.** Revenue is maximized when $p = 100/3 \approx \$33.33$ **c.** Demand would be $(100 - 100/3)^2 = (200/3)^2 \approx 4,444$ cases per week. **5. a.** $E = (4p - 33)/(-2p + 33)$ **b.** 0.54; the demand for $E = mc^2$ T-shirts is going down by about 0.54% per 1% increase in the price. **c.** $11 per shirt for a daily revenue of $1,331 **7. a.** $E = 1.81$. Thus, the demand is elastic at the given tuition level, showing that a decrease in tuition will result in an increase in revenue. **b.** They should charge an average of $2,250 per student, and this will result in an enrollment of about 4,950 students, giving a revenue of about $11,137,500. **9. a.** $E = 51$; the demand is going down 51% per 1% increase in price at that price level; thus, a large price decrease is advised. **b.** Revenue is maximized when $p = ¥0.50$. **c.** Demand would be $100e^{-3/4 + 1/2} \approx 78$ paint-by-number sets per month. **11. a.** $E = -\dfrac{mp}{mp + b}$ **b.** $p = -\dfrac{b}{2m}$ **13. a.** $E = r$ **b.** E is independent of p. **c.** If $r = 1$, then the revenue is not affected by the price. If $r > 1$, then the revenue is always elastic, while if $r < 1$, the revenue is always inelastic. This is an unrealistic model because there should always be a price at which the revenue is a maximum. **15. a.** $q = -1,500p + 6,000$. **b.** $2 per hamburger, giving a total weekly revenue of $6,000. **17.** $E \approx 0.77$. At a family income level of $20,000, the fraction of children attending a live theatrical performance is increasing by 0.77% per 1% increase in household income. **19. a.** $E \approx 0.46$. The demand for computers is increasing by 0.46% per one percent increase in household income. **b.** E decreases as income increases. **c.** Unreliable; it predicts a likelihood greater than 1 at incomes of $123,000 and above. In a more appropriate model, one would expect the curve to level off at or below 1. **d.** $E \approx 0$ **21.** $\dfrac{Y}{Q} \cdot \dfrac{dQ}{dY} = \beta$. An increase in income of x% will result in an increase in demand of βx%. (Note that we do *not* take the negative here, because we expect an increase in income to produce an *increase* in demand.) **23. a.** $q = 1,000e^{-0.30p}$ **b.** At $p = \$3$, $E = 0.9$; at $p = \$4$, $E = 1.2$; at $p = \$5$, $E = 1.5$ **c.** $p = \$3.33$ **d.** $p = \$5.36$. Selling at a lower price would increase demand, but you cannot sell more than 200 pounds anyway. You should charge as much as you can and still be able to sell all 200 pounds. **25.** The price is lowered. **27.** Start with $R = pq$, and differentiate with respect to p to obtain $\dfrac{dR}{dp} = q + p\dfrac{dq}{dp}$.

For a stationary point, $dR/dp = 0$, and so $q + p\dfrac{dq}{dp} = 0$.

Rearranging this result gives $p\dfrac{dq}{dp} = -q$, and hence $-\dfrac{dq}{dp}\cdot\dfrac{p}{q} = 1$, or $E = 1$, showing that stationary points of R correspond to points of unit elasticity.   **29.** The distinction is best illustrated by an example. Suppose that q is measured in weekly sales and p is the unit price in dollars. Then the quantity $-dq/dp$ measures the drop in weekly sales per \$1 increase in price. The elasticity of demand E, on the other hand, measures the *percentage* drop in sales per *one percent* increase in price. Thus, $-dq/dp$ measures absolute change, while E measures fractional, or percentage, change.

Chapter 12 Review

1. Relative max: $(-1, 5)$, absolute min: $(-2, -3)$ and $(1, -3)$
3. Absolute max: $(-1, 5)$, absolute min: $(1, -3)$
5. Absolute min: $(1, 0)$ **7.** Absolute min: $(-2, -1/4)$
9. Relative max at $x = 1$, point of inflection at $x = -1$
11. Relative max at $x = -2$, relative min at $x = 1$, point of inflection at $x = -1$ **13.** One point of inflection, at $x = 0$
15. a. $a = 4/t^4 - 2/t^3$ m/sec^2 **b.** 2 m/sec^2 **17.** Relative max: $(-2, 16)$; absolute min: $(2, -16)$; point of inflection: $(0, 0)$; no horizontal or vertical asymptotes

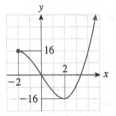

19. Relative min: $(-3, -2/9)$; relative max: $(3, 2/9)$; inflection: $(-3\sqrt{2}, -5\sqrt{2}/36)$, $(3\sqrt{2}, 5\sqrt{2}/36)$; vertical asymptote: $x = 0$; horizontal asymptote: $y = 0$

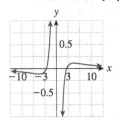

21. Relative max at $(0, 0)$, absolute min at $(1, -2)$, no asymptotes

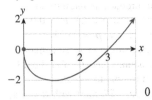

23. \$22.14 per book   **25. a.** Profit $= -p^3 + 42p^2 - 288p - 181$
b. \$24 per copy; \$3,275 **c.** For maximum revenue, the company should charge \$22.14 per copy. At this price, the cost per book is decreasing with increasing price, while the revenue is not

decreasing (its derivative is zero). Thus, the profit is increasing with increasing price, suggesting that the maximum profit will occur at a higher price. **27.** 12 in $\times$ 12 in $\times$ 6 in, for a volume of 864 in^3 **29. a.** $E = \dfrac{2p^2 - 33p}{-p^2 + 33p + 9}$ **b.** 0.52, 2.03; when the price is \$20, demand is dropping at a rate of 0.52% per 1% increase in the price; when the price is \$25, demand is dropping at a rate of 2.03% per 1% increase in the price.
c. \$22.14 per book   **31. a.** $E = 2p^2 - p$ **b.** 6; the demand is dropping at a rate of 6% per 1% increase in the price. **c.** \$1.00, for a monthly revenue of \$1,000   **33. a.** week 5 **b.** Point of inflection on the graph of s; maximum on the graph of s', t-intercept in the graph of s''. **c.** 10,500; if weekly sales continue as predicted by the model, they will level off at around 10,500 books per week in the long term. **d.** 0; if weekly sales continue as predicted by the model, the rate of change of sales approaches zero in the long term.   **35. a.–d.** $10/\sqrt{2}$ ft/s

4

Functions of Several Variables

Web Site
www.FiniteandCalc.org
At the Web site you will find:

- A detailed chapter summary

- A true/false quiz

- A surface grapher

- An Excel surface grapher

- A linear multiple regression utility

- The following optional extra sections:

    Maxima and Minima: Boundaries and the Extreme Value Theorem

    The Chain Rule for Functions of Several Variables

Case Study Modeling College Population

College Malls Inc. is planning to build a national chain of shopping malls in college neighborhoods. The company is planning to lease only to stores that target the specific age demographics of the national college student population. To decide which age brackets to target, the company has asked you, a paid consultant, for an analysis of the college population by student age, and of its trends over time. **How can you analyze the relevant data?**

David Pearson/Alamy

Introduction

We have studied functions of a single variable extensively. But not every useful function is a function of only one variable. In fact, most are not. For example, if you operate an online bookstore in competition with **Amazon.com**, **BN.com**, and Booksamillion.com, your sales may depend on those of your competitors. Your company's daily revenue might be modeled by a function such as

$$R(x, y, z) = 10{,}000 - 0.01x - 0.02y - 0.01z + 0.00001yz$$

where x, y, and z are the online daily revenues of **Amazon.com**, **BN.com**, and Booksamillion.com, respectively. Here, R is a function of three variables because it *depends on x, y*, and z. As we shall see, the techniques of calculus extend readily to such functions. Among the applications we shall look at is optimization: finding, where possible, the maximum or minimum of a function of two or more variables.

15.1 Functions of Several Variables from the Numerical, Algebraic, and Graphical Viewpoints

Numerical and Algebraic Viewpoints

Recall that a function of one variable is a rule for manufacturing a new number $f(x)$ from a single independent variable x. A function of two or more variables is similar, but the new number now depends on more than one independent variable.

Function of Several Variables

A **real-valued function**, f, **of** $x, y, z, \ldots$ is a rule for manufacturing a new number, written $f(x, y, z, \ldots)$, from the values of a sequence of independent variables $(x, y, z, \ldots)$. The function f is called a **real-valued function of two variables** if there are two independent variables, a **real-valued function of three variables** if there are three independent variables, and so on.

Quick Examples

1. $f(x, y) = x - y$ Function of two variables

     $f(1, 2) = 1 - 2 = -1$ Substitute 1 for x and 2 for y.

     $f(2, -1) = 2 - (-1) = 3$ Substitute 2 for x and -1 for y.

     $f(y, x) = y - x$ Substitute y for x and x for y.

2. $g(x, y) = x^2 + y^2$ Function of two variables

     $g(-1, 3) = (-1)^2 + 3^2 = 10$ Substitute -1 for x and 3 for y.

3. $h(x, y, z) = x + y + xz$ Function of three variables

     $h(2, 2, -2) = 2 + 2 + 2(-2) = 0$ Substitute 2 for x, 2 for y, and -2 for z.

Note It is often convenient to use $x_1, x_2, x_3, \ldots$ for the independent variables, so that, for instance, the third example above would be $h(x_1, x_2, x_3) = x_1 + x_2 + x_1x_3$. ∎

Figure 1 illustrates the concept of a function of two variables: In goes a pair of numbers and out comes a single number.

$$(x, y) \longrightarrow \boxed{g} \longrightarrow x^2 + y^2 \qquad (2, -1) \longrightarrow \boxed{g} \longrightarrow 5$$

Figure 1

As with functions of one variable, functions of several variables can be represented numerically (using a table of values), algebraically (using a formula as in the above examples), and sometimes graphically (using a graph).

Let's now look at a number of examples of interesting functions of several variables.

EXAMPLE 1 **Cost Function**

You own a company that makes two models of speakers: the Ultra Mini and the Big Stack. Your total monthly cost (in dollars) to make x Ultra Minis and y Big Stacks is given by

$$C(x, y) = 10{,}000 + 20x + 40y.$$

What is the significance of each term in this formula?

Solution The terms have meanings similar to those we saw for linear cost functions of a single variable. Let us look at the terms one at a time.

Constant Term Consider the monthly cost of making no speakers at all ($x = y = 0$). We find

$$C(0, 0) = 10{,}000. \qquad \text{Cost of making no speakers is \$10,000.}$$

Thus, the constant term 10,000 is the **fixed cost**, the amount you have to pay each month even if you make no speakers.

Coefficients of x and y Suppose you make a certain number of Ultra Minis and Big Stacks one month and the next month you increase production by one Ultra Mini. The costs are

$$C(x, y) = 10{,}000 + 20x + 40y \qquad \text{First month}$$
$$C(x + 1, y) = 10{,}000 + 20(x + 1) + 40y \qquad \text{Second month}$$
$$= 10{,}000 + 20x + 20 + 40y$$
$$= C(x, y) + 20.$$

Thus, each Ultra Mini adds $20 to the total cost. We say that $20 is the **marginal cost** of each Ultra Mini. Similarly, because of the term $40y$, each Big Stack adds $40 to the total cost. The marginal cost of each Big Stack is $40.

This cost function is an example of a *linear function of two variables*. The coefficients of x and y play roles similar to that of the slope of a line. In particular, they give the rates of change of the function as each variable increases while the other stays constant (think about it). We shall say more about linear functions below.

using Technology

See the Technology Guides at the end of the chapter to see how you can use a TI-83/84 Plus and Excel to display various values of $C(x, y)$ in Example 1. Here is an outline:

TI-83/84 Plus

Y_1=10000+20X+40Y

To evaluate C(10, 30):

10 → X

30 → Y

Y_1 [More details on page 1142.]

Excel

x-values down column A starting in A2

y-values down column B starting in B2

=10000+20*A2+40*B2 in C2; copy down column C. [More details on page 1142.]

259

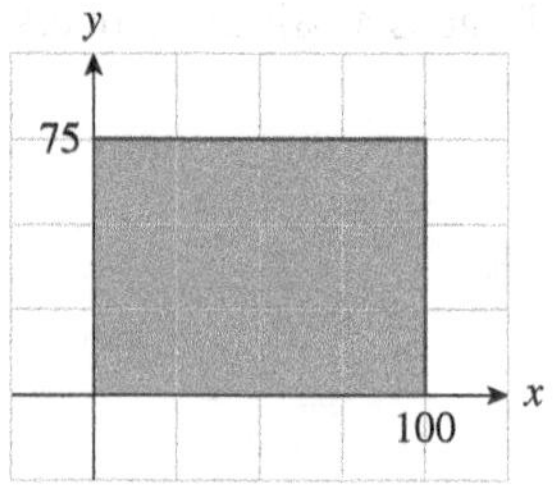

Figure 2

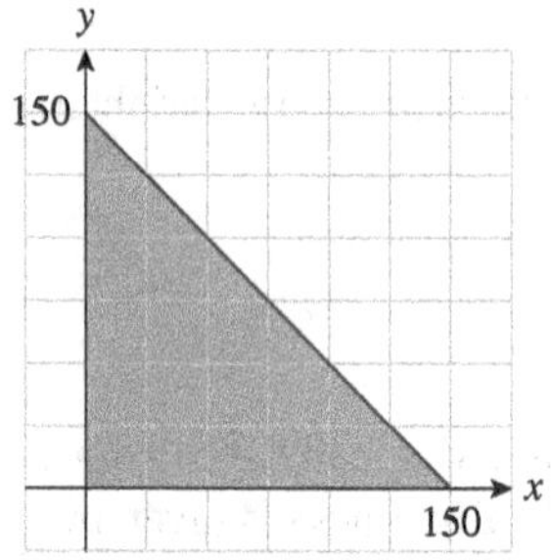

Figure 3

➡ **Before we go on...** In Example 1 which values of x and y may we substitute into $C(x, y)$? Certainly we must have $x \geq 0$ and $y \geq 0$ because it makes no sense to speak of manufacturing a negative number of speakers. Also, there is certainly some upper bound to the number of speakers that can be made in a month. The bound might take one of several forms. The number of each model may be bounded—say $x \leq 100$ and $y \leq 75$. The inequalities $0 \leq x \leq 100$ and $0 \leq y \leq 75$ describe the region in the plane shaded in Figure 2.

Another possibility is that the *total* number of speakers is bounded—say, $x + y \leq 150$. This, together with $x \geq 0$ and $y \geq 0$, describes the region shaded in Figure 3.

In either case, the region shown represents the pairs (x, y) for which $C(x, y)$ is defined. Just as with a function of one variable, we call this region the **domain** of the function. As before, when the domain is not given explicitly, we agree to take the largest domain possible. ■

EXAMPLE 2 Faculty Salaries

David Katz came up with the following function for the salary of a professor with 10 years of teaching experience in a large university.

$$S(x, y, z) = 13{,}005 + 230x + 18y + 102z$$

Here, S is the salary in 1969–1970 in dollars per year, x is the number of books the professor has published, y is the number of articles published, and z is the number of "excellent" articles published.* What salary do you expect that a professor with 10 years' experience earned in 1969–1970 if she published 2 books, 20 articles, and 3 "excellent" articles?

Solution All we need to do is calculate

$$S(2, 20, 3) = 13{,}005 + 230(2) + 18(20) + 102(3)$$
$$= \$14{,}131.$$

---

*David A. Katz, "Faculty Salaries, Promotions and Productivity at a Large University," *American Economic Review*, June 1973, pp. 469–477. Prof. Katz's equation actually included other variables, such as the number of dissertations supervised; our equation assumes that all of these are zero.

➡ **Before we go on...** In Example 1, we gave a linear function of two variables. In Example 2 we have a linear function of three variables. Katz came up with his model by surveying a large number of faculty members and then finding the linear function "best" fitting the data. Such models are called **multiple linear regression** models. In the Case Study at the end of this chapter, we shall see a spreadsheet method of finding the coefficients of a multiple regression model from a set of observed data.

What does this model say about the value of a single book or a single article? If a book takes 15 times as long to write as an article, how would you recommend that a professor spend her writing time? ■

Here are two simple kinds of functions of several variables.

Linear Function

A function f of n variables is **linear** if f has the property that

$$f(x_1, x_2, \ldots, x_n) = a_0 + a_1 x_1 + \cdots + a_n x_n. \qquad (a_0, a_1, a_2, \ldots, a_n \text{ constants})$$

260

Quick Examples

1. $f(x, y) = 3x - 5y$ Linear function of x and y
2. $C(x, y) = 10,000 + 20x + 40y$ Example 1
3. $S(x_1, x_2, x_3) = 13,005 + 230x_1 + 18x_2 + 102x_3$ Example 2

Interaction Function

If we add to a linear function one or more terms of the form $bx_i x_j$ (b a nonzero constant and $i \neq j$), we get a **second-order interaction function**.

Quick Examples

1. $C(x, y) = 10,000 + 20x + 40y + 0.1xy$
2. $R(x_1, x_2, x_3) = 10,000 - 0.01x_1 - 0.02x_2 - 0.01x_3 + 0.00001x_2 x_3$

So far, we have been specifying functions of several variables **algebraically**—by using algebraic formulas. If you have ever studied statistics, you are probably familiar with statistical tables. These tables may also be viewed as representing functions **numerically**, as the next example shows.

EXAMPLE 3 Function Represented Numerically: Body Mass Index

The following table lists some values of the "body mass index," which gives a measure of the massiveness of your body, taking height into account.* The variable w represents your weight in pounds, and h represents your height in inches. An individual with a body mass index of 25 or above is generally considered overweight.

* **NOTE** It is interesting that weight-lifting competitions are usually based on weight, rather than body mass index. As a consequence, taller people are at a significant disadvantage in these competitions because they must compete with shorter, stockier people of the same weight. (An extremely thin, very tall person can weigh as much as a muscular short person, although his body mass index would be significantly lower.)

$w \rightarrow$

		130	140	150	160	170	180	190	200	210
h	60	25.2	27.1	29.1	31.0	32.9	34.9	36.8	38.8	40.7
$\downarrow$	61	24.4	26.2	28.1	30.0	31.9	33.7	35.6	37.5	39.4
	62	23.6	25.4	27.2	29.0	30.8	32.7	34.5	36.3	38.1
	63	22.8	24.6	26.4	28.1	29.9	31.6	33.4	35.1	36.9
	64	22.1	23.8	25.5	27.2	28.9	30.7	32.4	34.1	35.8
	65	21.5	23.1	24.8	26.4	28.1	29.7	31.4	33.0	34.7
	66	20.8	22.4	24.0	25.6	27.2	28.8	30.4	32.0	33.6
	67	20.2	21.8	23.3	24.9	26.4	28.0	29.5	31.1	32.6
	68	19.6	21.1	22.6	24.1	25.6	27.2	28.7	30.2	31.7
	69	19.0	20.5	22.0	23.4	24.9	26.4	27.8	29.3	30.8
	70	18.5	19.9	21.4	22.8	24.2	25.6	27.0	28.5	29.9
	71	18.0	19.4	20.8	22.1	23.5	24.9	26.3	27.7	29.1
	72	17.5	18.8	20.2	21.5	22.9	24.2	25.6	26.9	28.3
	73	17.0	18.3	19.6	20.9	22.3	23.6	24.9	26.2	27.5
	74	16.6	17.8	19.1	20.4	21.7	22.9	24.2	25.5	26.7
	75	16.1	17.4	18.6	19.8	21.1	22.3	23.6	24.8	26.0
	76	15.7	16.9	18.1	19.3	20.5	21.7	22.9	24.2	25.4

using Technology

See the Technology Guides at the end of the chapter to see how to use Excel to create the table in Example 3. Here is an outline:

Excel

w-values 130 to 210 in B1–J1

h-values 60 to 76 in A2–A18

```
=0.45*B$1/
(0.0254*$A2)^2
```

in B2; copy down and across through J18. [More details on page 1142.]

As the table shows, the value of the body mass index depends on two quantities: w and h. Let us write $M(w, h)$ for the body mass index function. What are $M(140, 62)$ and $M(210, 63)$?

Solution We can read the answers from the table:

$$M(140, 62) = 25.4 \qquad w = 140 \text{ lb}, h = 62 \text{ in}$$

and

$$M(210, 63) = 36.9. \qquad w = 210 \text{ lb}, h = 63 \text{ in}$$

The function $M(w, h)$ is actually given by the formula

$$M(w, h) = \frac{0.45w}{(0.0254h)^2}.$$

[The factor 0.45 converts the weight to kilograms, and 0.0254 converts the height to meters. If w is in kilograms and h is in meters, the formula is simpler: $M(w, h) = w/h^2$.]

Geometric Viewpoint: Three-Dimensional Space and the Graph of a Function of Two Variables

Just as functions of a single variable have graphs, so do functions of two or more variables. Recall that the graph of $f(x)$ consists of all points $(x, f(x))$ in the xy-plane. By analogy, we would like to say that the graph of a function of *two* variables, $f(x, y)$, consists of all points of the form $(x, y, f(x, y))$. Thus, we need three axes: the x-, y-, and z-axes. In other words, our graph will live in **three-dimensional space**, or **3-space**.*

Just as we had two mutually perpendicular axes in two-dimensional space (the xy-plane; see Figure 4(a)), so we have three mutually perpendicular axes in three-dimensional space (Figure 4(b)).

* **NOTE** If we were dealing instead with a function of *three* variables, then we would need to go to *four-dimensional* space. Here we run into visualization problems (to say the least!) so we won't discuss the graphs of functions of three or more variables in this text.

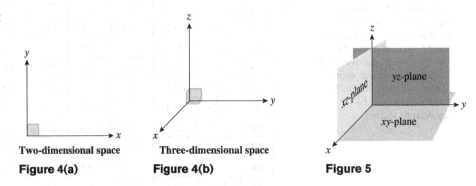

Two-dimensional space	Three-dimensional space	
Figure 4(a)	**Figure 4(b)**	**Figure 5**

In both 2-space and 3-space, the axis labeled with the last letter goes up. Thus, the z-direction is the "up" direction in 3-space, rather than the y-direction.

Three important planes are associated with these axes: the xy-plane, the yz-plane, and the xz-plane. These planes are shown in Figure 5. Any two of these planes intersect in one of the axes (for example, the xy- and xz-planes intersect in the x-axis) and all three meet at the origin. Notice that the xy-plane consists of all points with z-coordinate zero, the xz-plane consists of all points with $y = 0$, and the yz-plane consists of all points with $x = 0$.

In 3-space, each point has *three* coordinates, as you might expect: the x-coordinate, the y-coordinate, and the z-coordinate. To see how this works, look at the following examples.

The z-coordinate of a point is its height above the xy-plane.

EXAMPLE 4 **Plotting Points in Three Dimensions**

Locate the points $P(1, 2, 3)$, $Q(-1, 2, 3)$, $R(1, -1, 0)$, and $S(1, 2, -2)$ in 3-space.

Solution To locate P, the procedure is similar to the one we used in 2-space: Start at the origin, proceed one unit in the x direction, then proceed two units in the y direction, and finally, proceed three units in the z direction. We wind up at the point P shown in Figures 6(a) and 6(b).

Here is another, extremely useful way of thinking about the location of P. First, look at the x- and y-coordinates, obtaining the point $(1, 2)$ in the xy-plane. The point we want is then three units vertically above the point $(1, 2)$ because the z-coordinate of a point is just its height above the xy-plane. This strategy is shown in Figure 6(c).

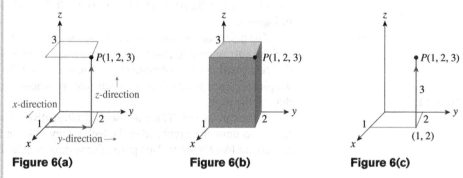

Figure 6(a)   **Figure 6(b)**   **Figure 6(c)**

Plotting the points Q, R, and S is similar, using the convention that negative coordinates correspond to moves back, left, or down. (See Figure 7.)

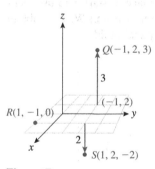

Figure 7

Our next task is to describe the graph of a function $f(x, y)$ of two variables.

Graph of a Function of Two Variables

The **graph of the function f of two variables** is the set of all points $(x, y, f(x, y))$ in three-dimensional space, where we restrict the values of (x, y) to lie in the domain of f. In other words, the graph is the set of all the points (x, y, z) with $z = f(x, y)$.

For *every* point (x, y) in the domain of f, the z-coordinate of the corresponding point on the graph is given by evaluating the function at (x, y). Thus, there will be a point on the graph above *every* point in the domain of f, so that the graph is usually a *surface* of some sort.

EXAMPLE 5 **Graph of a Function of Two Variables**

Describe the graph of $f(x, y) = x^2 + y^2$.

Solution Your first thought might be to make a table of values. You could choose some values for x and y and then, for each such pair, calculate $z = x^2 + y^2$. For example, you might get the following table:

	$x \rightarrow$		
$y \downarrow$	**−1**	**0**	**1**
−1	2	1	2
0	1	0	1
1	2	1	2

$$f(x, y) = x^2 + y^2$$

This gives the following nine points on the graph of f: $(-1, -1, 2), (-1, 0, 1), (-1, 1, 2),$ $(0, -1, 1), (0, 0, 0), (0, 1, 1), (1, -1, 2), (1, 0, 1),$ and $(1, 1, 2)$. These points are shown in Figure 8.

The points on the xy-plane we chose for our table are the grid points in the xy-plane, and the corresponding points on the graph are marked with solid dots. The problem is that this small number of points hardly tells us what the surface looks like, and even if we plotted more points, it is not clear that we would get anything more than a mass of dots on the page.

What can we do? There are several alternatives. One place to start is to use technology to draw the graph. (See the technology note on the next page.) We then obtain something like Figure 9. This particular surface is called a **paraboloid**.

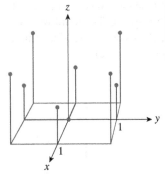

Figure 8

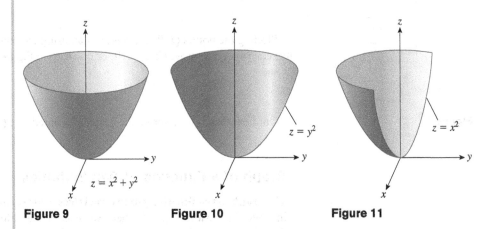

Figure 9　　　　**Figure 10**　　　　**Figure 11**

If we slice vertically through this surface along the yz-plane, we get the picture in Figure 10. The shape of the front edge, where we cut, is a parabola. To see why, note that the yz-plane is the set of points where $x = 0$. To get the intersection of $x = 0$ and $z = x^2 + y^2$, we substitute $x = 0$ in the second equation, getting $z = y^2$. This is the equation of a parabola in the yz-plane.

Similarly, we can slice through the surface with the xz-plane by setting $y = 0$. This gives the parabola $z = x^2$ in the xz-plane (Figure 11).

✻ **NOTE** See Section 0.7 for a discussion of equations of circles.

using Technology

We can use technology to obtain the graph of the function in Example 5:

Excel

Table of values:

x-values −3 to 3 in B1–H1
y-values −3 to 3 in A2–A8
=B1^2+A2^2

in B2; copy down and across through H8.
Graph: Highlight A1 through H8 and insert a Surface chart.
[More details on page 1143.]

Web Site

www.FiniteandCalc.org

Everything for Calculus

→ Chapter 15

→ Math Tools (Surface Graphing Utility)

Enter x^2+y^2 for $f(x, y)$
Set xMin = −3, xMax = 3,
yMin = −3, yMax = 3
Press "Graph."

We can also look at horizontal slices through the surface, that is, slices by planes parallel to the xy-plane. These are given by setting $z = c$ for various numbers c. For example, if we set $z = 1$, we will see only the points with height 1. Substituting in the equation $z = x^2 + y^2$ gives the equation

$$1 = x^2 + y^2,$$

which is the equation of a circle of radius 1.✻ If we set $z = 4$, we get the equation of a circle of radius 2:

$$4 = x^2 + y^2.$$

In general, if we slice through the surface at height $z = c$, we get a circle (of radius $\sqrt{c}$). Figure 12 shows several of these circles.

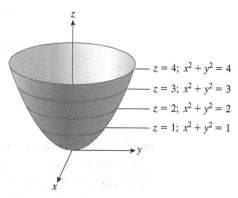

— $z = 4$; $x^2 + y^2 = 4$
— $z = 3$; $x^2 + y^2 = 3$
— $z = 2$; $x^2 + y^2 = 2$
— $z = 1$; $x^2 + y^2 = 1$

Figure 12

Looking at these circular slices, we see that this surface is the one we get by taking the parabola $z = x^2$ and spinning it around the z-axis. This is an example of what is known as a **surface of revolution**.

➡ **Before we go on...** The graph of any function of the form $f(x, y) = Ax^2 + By^2 + Cxy + Dx + Ey + F$ ($A, B, \ldots, F$ constants), with $4AB - C^2$ positive, can be shown to be a paraboloid of the same general shape as that in Example 5 if A and B are positive, or upside-down if A and B are negative. If $A \neq B$, the horizontal slices will be ellipses rather than circles.

Notice that each horizontal slice through the surface in Example 5 was obtained by putting $z = constant$. This gave us an equation in x and y that described a curve. These curves are called the **level curves** of the surface $z = f(x, y)$. In Example 5, the equations are of the form $x^2 + y^2 = c$ (c constant), and so the level curves are circles. Figure 13 shows the level curves for $c = 0, 1, 2, 3,$ and 4.

The level curves give a contour map or topographical map of the surface. Each curve shows all of the points on the surface at a particular height c. You can use this contour map to visualize the shape of the surface. Imagine moving the contour at $c = 1$ to a height of 1 unit above the xy-plane, the contour at $c = 2$ to a height of 2 units above the xy-plane, and so on. You will end up with something like Figure 12. ■

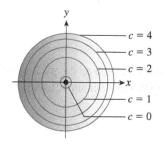

— $c = 4$
— $c = 3$
— $c = 2$
— $c = 1$
— $c = 0$

Level curves of the paraboloid
$z = x^2 + y^2$

Figure 13

The following summary includes the techniques we have just used plus some additional ones:

Analyzing the Graph of a Function of Two Variables

If possible, use technology to render the graph of a given function $z = f(x, y)$. Given the function $z = f(x, y)$, you can analyze its graph as follows:

Step 1 Obtain the **x-, y-, and z-intercepts** (the places where the surface crosses the coordinate axes).

x-Intercept(s): Set $y = 0$ and $z = 0$ and solve for x.

y-Intercept(s): Set $x = 0$ and $z = 0$ and solve for y.

z-Intercept: Set $x = 0$ and $y = 0$ and compute z.

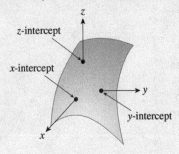

Step 2 Slice the surface along planes parallel to the xy-, yz-, and xz-planes.

$z = constant$ Set $z = constant$ and analyze the resulting curves.
(level curves) These are the curves resulting from horizontal slices.

$x = constant$ Set $x = constant$ and analyze the resulting curves.
These are the curves resulting from slices parallel to the yz-plane.

$y = constant$ Set $y = constant$ and analyze the resulting curves.
These are the curves resulting from slices parallel to the xz-plane.

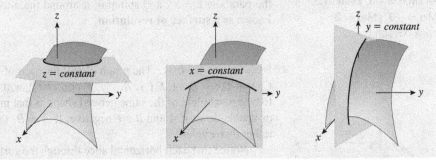

Spreadsheets often have built-in features to render surfaces such as the paraboloid in Example 5. In the following example, we use Excel to graph another surface and then analyze it as above.

EXAMPLE 6 Analyzing a Surface

Describe the graph of $f(x, y) = x^2 - y^2$.

Solution First we obtain a picture of the graph using technology. Figure 14 shows two graphs obtained using resources at the Web site.

266

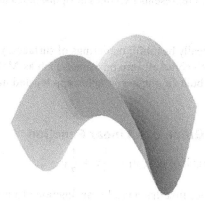

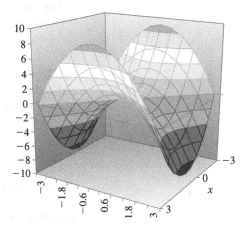

Figure 14

See the Technology Guides at the end of the chapter to find out how to obtain a similar graph from scratch on an ordinary Excel sheet.

The graph shows an example of a "saddle point" at the origin. (We return to this idea in Section 15.3.) To analyze the graph for the features shown in the box above, replace $f(x, y)$ by z to obtain

$$z = x^2 - y^2.$$

Step 1: *Intercepts* Setting any two of the variables x, y, and z equal to zero results in the third also being zero, so the x-, y-, and z-intercepts are all 0. In other words, the surface touches all three axes in exactly one point, the origin.

Step 1: *Slices* Slices in various directions show more interesting features.

Slice by $x = c$ This gives $z = c^2 - y^2$, which is the equation of a parabola that opens downward. You can see two of these slices ($c = -3, c = 3$) as the front and back edges of the surface in Figure 14. (More are shown in Figure 15(a).)

Slice by $y = c$ This gives $z = x^2 - c^2$, which is the equation of a parabola once again—this time, opening upward. You can see two of these slices ($c = -3, c = 3$) as the left and right edges of the surface in Figure 14. (More are shown in Figure 15(b).)

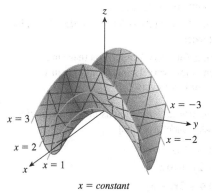

x = constant

Figure 15(a)

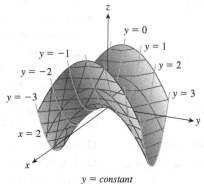

y = constant

Figure 15(b)

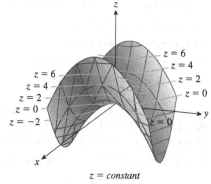

z = constant

Figure 15(c)

Slice by $z = c$ This gives $x^2 - y^2 = c$, which is a hyperbola. The level curves for various values of c are visible in Figure 14 as the horizontal slices. (See Figure 15(c).) The case $c = 0$ is interesting: The equation $x^2 - y^2 = 0$ can be rewritten as $x = \pm y$ (why?), which represents two lines at right-angles to each other.

To obtain really beautiful renderings of surfaces, you could use one of the commercial computer algebra software packages, such as Mathematica® or Maple®, or, if you use a Mac, the built-in grapher (grapher.app located in the Utilities folder).

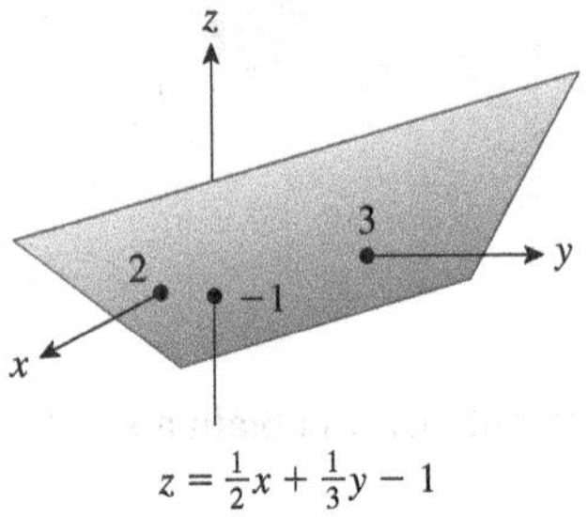

EXAMPLE 7 Graph of a Linear Function

Describe the graph of $g(x, y) = \dfrac{1}{2}x + \dfrac{1}{3}y - 1$.

Solution Notice first that g is a linear function of x and y. Figure 16 shows a portion of the graph, which is a plane.

We can get a good idea of what plane this is by looking at the x-, y-, and z-intercepts.

x-intercept Set $y = z = 0$, which gives $x = 2$.

y-intercept Set $x = z = 0$, which gives $y = 3$.

z-intercept Set $x = y = 0$, which gives $z = -1$.

Three points are enough to define a plane, so we can say that the plane is the one passing through the three points $(2, 0, 0)$, $(0, 3, 0)$, and $(0, 0, -1)$.

$z = \frac{1}{2}x + \frac{1}{3}y - 1$

Figure 16

Note It can be shown that the graph of every linear function of two variables is a plane. What do the level curves look like? ∎

15.1 EXERCISES

▼ more advanced   ◆ challenging

🔲 indicates exercises that should be solved using technology

For each function in Exercises 1–4, evaluate **(a)** $f(0, 0)$;
(b) $f(1, 0)$; **(c)** $f(0, -1)$; **(d)** $f(a, 2)$; **(e)** $f(y, x)$;
(f) $f(x + h, y + k)$ HINT [See Quick Examples page 1080.]

1. $f(x, y) = x^2 + y^2 - x + 1$

2. $f(x, y) = x^2 - y - xy + 1$

3. $f(x, y) = 0.2x + 0.1y - 0.01xy$

4. $f(x, y) = 0.4x - 0.5y - 0.05xy$

For each function in Exercises 5–8, evaluate **(a)** $g(0, 0, 0)$;
(b) $g(1, 0, 0)$; **(c)** $g(0, 1, 0)$; **(d)** $g(z, x, y)$;
(e) $g(x + h, y + k, z + l)$, *provided such a value exists.*

5. $g(x, y, z) = e^{x+y+z}$ **6.** $g(x, y, z) = \ln(x + y + z)$

7. $g(x, y, z) = \dfrac{xyz}{x^2 + y^2 + z^2}$ **8.** $g(x, y, z) = \dfrac{e^{xyz}}{x + y + z}$

9. Let $f(x, y, z) = 1.5 + 2.3x - 1.4y - 2.5z$. Complete the following sentences. HINT [See Example 1.]

a. f ___ by ___ units for every 1 unit of increase in x.
b. f ___ by ___ units for every 1 unit of increase in y.
c. _____ by 2.5 units for every _____.

10. Let $g(x, y, z) = 0.01x + 0.02y - 0.03z - 0.05$. Complete the following sentences.

a. g ___ by ___ units for every 1 unit of increase in z.
b. g ___ by ___ units for every 1 unit of increase in x.
c. _____ by 0.02 units for every _____.

In Exercises 11–18, classify each function as linear, interaction, or neither. HINT [See Quick Examples page 1083.]

11. $L(x, y) = 3x - 2y + 6xy - 4y^2$

12. $L(x, y, z) = 3x - 2y + 6xz$

13. $P(x_1, x_2, x_3) = 0.4 + 2x_1 - x_3$

14. $Q(x_1, x_2) = 4x_2 - 0.5x_1 - x_1^2$

15. $f(x, y, z) = \dfrac{x + y - z}{3}$

16. $g(x, y, z) = \dfrac{xz - 3yz + z^2}{4z}$ $\quad (z \neq 0)$

17. $g(x, y, z) = \dfrac{xz - 3yz + z^2 y}{4z}$ $\quad (z \neq 0)$

18. $f(x, y) = x + y + xy + x^2 y$

In Exercises 19 and 20, use the given tabular representation of the function f to compute the quantities asked for. HINT **[See Example 3.]**

19.

$x \rightarrow$		10	20	30	40
y ↓	10	−1	107	162	−3
	20	−6	194	294	−14
	30	−11	281	426	−25
	40	−16	368	558	−36

a. $f(20, 10)$ **b.** $f(40, 20)$ **c.** $f(10, 20) - f(20, 10)$

20.

$x \rightarrow$		10	20	30	40
y ↓	10	162	107	−5	−7
	20	294	194	−22	−30
	30	426	281	−39	−53
	40	558	368	−56	−76

a. $f(10, 30)$ **b.** $f(20, 10)$ **c.** $f(10, 40) + f(10, 20)$

▣ *In Exercises 21 and 22, use a spreadsheet or some other method to complete the given tables.*

21. $P(x, y) = x - 0.3y + 0.45xy$

$x \rightarrow$		10	20	30	40
y ↓	10				
	20				
	30				
	40				

22. $Q(x, y) = 0.4x + 0.1y - 0.06xy$

$x \rightarrow$		10	20	30	40
y ↓	10				
	20				
	30				
	40				

23. ▣ ▼ The following statistical table lists some values of the "Inverse F distribution" ($\alpha = 0.5$):

$n \rightarrow$										
	1	**2**	**3**	**4**	**5**	**6**	**7**	**8**	**9**	**10**
d ↓ **1**	161.4	199.5	215.7	224.6	230.2	234.0	236.8	238.9	240.5	241.9
2	18.51	19.00	19.16	19.25	19.30	19.33	19.35	19.37	19.39	19.40
3	10.13	9.552	9.277	9.117	9.013	8.941	8.887	8.812	8.812	8.785
4	7.709	6.944	6.591	6.388	6.256	6.163	6.094	5.999	5.999	5.964
5	6.608	5.786	5.409	5.192	5.050	4.950	4.876	4.772	4.772	4.735
6	5.987	5.143	4.757	4.534	4.387	4.284	4.207	4.099	4.099	4.060
7	5.591	4.737	4.347	4.120	3.972	3.866	3.787	3.677	3.677	3.637
8	5.318	4.459	4.066	3.838	3.688	3.581	3.500	3.388	3.388	3.347
9	5.117	4.256	3.863	3.633	3.482	3.374	3.293	3.179	3.179	3.137
10	4.965	4.103	3.708	3.478	3.326	3.217	3.135	3.020	3.020	2.978

In Excel, you can compute the value of this function at (n, d) by the formula

$=$ FINV (0.05, n, d)   The 0.05 is the value of alpha (α).

Use Excel to re-create this table.

24. ▣ ▼ The formula for body mass index $M(w, h)$, if w is given in kilograms and h is given in meters, is

$$M(w, h) = \frac{w}{h^2} \quad \text{See Example 3.}$$

Use this formula to complete the following table in Excel:

$w \rightarrow$		70	80	90	100	110	120	130
h ↓	1.8							
	1.85							
	1.9							
	1.95							
	2							
	2.05							
	2.1							
	2.15							
	2.2							
	2.25							
	2.3							

In Exercises 25–28, use either a graphing calculator or a spreadsheet to complete each table. Express all your answers as decimals rounded to four decimal places.

25.

x	y	$f(x, y) = x^2\sqrt{1 + xy}$
3	1	
1	15	
0.3	0.5	
56	4	

26.

x	y	$f(x, y) = x^2 e^y$
0	2	
−1	5	
1.4	2.5	
11	9	

27.

x	y	$f(x, y) = x \ln(x^2 + y^2)$
3	1	
1.4	−1	
e	0	
0	e	

28.

x	y	$f(x, y) = \dfrac{x}{x^2 - y^2}$
−1	2	
0	0.2	
0.4	2.5	
10	0	

29. ▽ Brand Z's annual sales are affected by the sales of related products X and Y as follows: Each $1 million increase in sales of brand X causes a $2.1 million decline in sales of brand Z, whereas each $1 million increase in sales of brand Y results in an increase of $0.4 million in sales of brand Z. Currently, brands X, Y, and Z are each selling $6 million per year. Model the sales of brand Z using a linear function.

30. ▽ Let $f(x, y, z) = 43.2 - 2.3x + 11.3y - 4.5z$. Complete the following: An increase of 1 in the value of y causes the value of f to ___ by ___, whereas increasing the value of x by 1 and ___ the value of z by ___ causes a decrease of 11.3 in the value of f.

31. Sketch the cube with vertices $(0, 0, 0)$, $(1, 0, 0)$, $(0, 1, 0)$, $(0, 0, 1)$, $(1, 1, 0)$, $(1, 0, 1)$, $(0, 1, 1)$, and $(1, 1, 1)$. HINT [See Example 4.]

32. Sketch the cube with vertices $(-1, -1, -1)$, $(1, -1, -1)$, $(-1, 1, -1)$, $(-1, -1, 1)$, $(1, 1, -1)$, $(1, -1, 1)$, $(-1, 1, 1)$, and $(1, 1, 1)$. HINT [See Example 4.]

33. Sketch the pyramid with vertices $(1, 1, 0)$, $(1, -1, 0)$, $(-1, 1, 0)$, $(-1, -1, 0)$, and $(0, 0, 2)$.

34. Sketch the solid with vertices $(1, 1, 0)$, $(1, -1, 0)$, $(-1, 1, 0)$, $(-1, -1, 0)$, $(0, 0, -1)$, and $(0, 0, 1)$.

Sketch the planes in Exercises 35–40.

35. $z = -2$ **36.** $z = 4$

37. $y = 2$ **38.** $y = -3$

39. $x = -3$ **40.** $x = 2$

Match each equation in Exercises 41–48 with one of the graphs below. (If necessary, use technology to render the surfaces.) HINT [See Examples 5, 6, and 7.]

41. $f(x, y) = 1 - 3x + 2y$ **42.** $f(x, y) = 1 - \sqrt{x^2 + y^2}$

43. $f(x, y) = 1 - (x^2 + y^2)$ **44.** $f(x, y) = y^2 - x^2$

45. $f(x, y) = -\sqrt{1 - (x^2 + y^2)}$

46. $f(x, y) = 1 + (x^2 + y^2)$

47. $f(x, y) = \dfrac{1}{x^2 + y^2}$ **48.** $f(x, y) = 3x - 2y + 1$

(A)   (B)

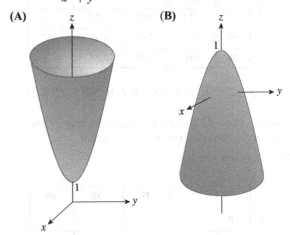

(C)   (D)

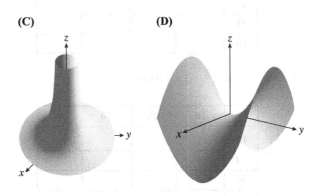

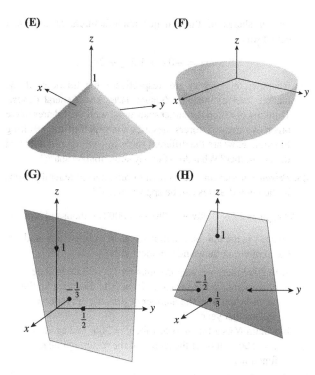

(E)

(F)

(G)

(H)

In Exercises 49–54 sketch the level curves $f(x, y) = c$ for the given function and values of c. HINT [See Example 5.]

49. $f(x, y) = 2x^2 + 2y^2$; $c = 0, 2, 18$

50. $f(x, y) = 3x^2 + 3y^2$; $c = 0, 3, 27$

51. $f(x, y) = y + 2x^2$; $c = -2, 0, 2$

52. $f(x, y) = 2y - x^2$; $c = -2, 0, 2$

53. $f(x, y) = 2xy - 1$; $c = -1, 0, 1$

54. $f(x, y) = 2 + xy$; $c = -2, 0, 2$

Sketch the graphs of the functions in Exercises 55–76. HINT [See Example 7.]

55. $f(x, y) = 1 - x - y$ **56.** $f(x, y) = x + y - 2$

57. $g(x, y) = 2x + y - 2$ **58.** $g(x, y) = 3 - x + 2y$

59. $h(x, y) = x + 2$ **60.** $h(x, y) = 3 - y$

61. $r(x, y) = x + y$ **62.** $r(x, y) = x - y$

🖳 Use of technology is suggested in Exercises 63–76. HINT [See Example 6.]

63. $s(x, y) = 2x^2 + 2y^2$. Show cross sections at $z = 1$ and $z = 2$.

64. $s(x, y) = -(x^2 + y^2)$. Show cross sections at $z = -1$ and $z = -2$.

65. $t(x, y) = x^2 + 2y^2$. Show cross sections at $x = 0$ and $z = 1$.

66. $t(x, y) = \frac{1}{2}x^2 + y^2$. Show cross sections at $x = 0$ and $z = 1$.

67. $f(x, y) = 2 + \sqrt{x^2 + y^2}$. Show cross sections at $z = 3$ and $y = 0$.

68. $f(x, y) = 2 - \sqrt{x^2 + y^2}$. Show cross sections at $z = 0$ and $y = 0$.

69. $f(x, y) = -2\sqrt{x^2 + y^2}$. Show cross sections at $z = -4$ and $y = 1$.

70. $f(x, y) = 2 + 2\sqrt{x^2 + y^2}$. Show cross sections at $z = 4$ and $y = 1$.

71. $f(x, y) = y^2$ **72.** $g(x, y) = x^2$

73. $h(x, y) = \dfrac{1}{y}$ **74.** $k(x, y) = e^y$

75. $f(x, y) = e^{-(x^2+y^2)}$ **76.** $g(x, y) = \dfrac{1}{\sqrt{x^2 + y^2}}$

APPLICATIONS

77. *Marginal Cost* Your weekly cost (in dollars) to manufacture x cars and y trucks is

$$C(x, y) = 240{,}000 + 6{,}000x + 4{,}000y.$$

  a. What is the marginal cost of a car? Of a truck? HINT [See Example 1.]

  b. Describe the graph of the cost function C. HINT [See Example 7.]

  c. Describe the slice $x = 10$. What cost function does this slice describe?

  d. Describe the level curve $z = 480{,}000$. What does this curve tell you about costs?

78. *Marginal Cost* Your weekly cost (in dollars) to manufacture x bicycles and y tricycles is

$$C(x, y) = 24{,}000 + 60x + 20y.$$

  a. What is the marginal cost of a bicycle? Of a tricycle? HINT [See Example 1.]

  b. Describe the graph of the cost function C. HINT [See Example 7.]

  c. Describe the slice by $y = 100$. What cost function does this slice describe?

  d. Describe the level curve $z = 72{,}000$. What does this curve tell you about costs?

79. *Marginal Cost* Your sales of online video and audio clips are booming. Your Internet provider, Moneydrain.com, wants to get in on the action and has offered you unlimited technical assistance and consulting if you agree to pay Moneydrain 3¢ for every video clip and 4¢ for every audio clip you sell on the site. Further, Moneydrain agrees to charge you only $10 per month to host your site. Set up a (monthly) cost function for the scenario, and describe each variable.

80. *Marginal Cost* Your Cabaret nightspot "Jazz on Jupiter" has become an expensive proposition: You are paying monthly costs of $50,000 just to keep the place running. On top of that, your regular cabaret artist is charging you $3,000 per performance, and your jazz ensemble is charging you $1,000 per hour. Set up a (monthly) cost function for the scenario, and describe each variable.

271

81. *Scientific Research* In each year from 1983 to 2003, the percentage y of research articles in *Physical Review* written by researchers in the United States can be approximated by

$$y = 82 - 0.78t - 1.02x \text{ percentage points} \quad (0 \le t \le 20)$$

where t is the year since 1983 and x is the percentage of articles written by researchers in Europe.[1]

a. In 2003, researchers in Europe wrote 38% of the articles published by the journal that year. What percentage was written by researchers in the United States?

b. In 1983, researchers in the United States wrote 61% of the articles published that year. What percentage was written by researchers in Europe?

c. What are the units of measurement of the coefficient of t?

82. *Scientific Research* The number z of research articles in *Physical Review* that were written by researchers in the United States from 1993 through 2003 can be approximated by

$$z = 5{,}960 - 0.71x + 0.50y \quad (3{,}000 \le x, y \le 6{,}000)$$

articles each year, where x is the number of articles written by researchers in Europe and y is the number written by researchers in other countries (excluding Europe and the United States).[2]

a. In the year 2000, approximately 5,500 articles were written by researchers in Europe, and 4,500 by researchers in other countries. How many (to the nearest 100) were written by researchers in the United States?

b. According to the model, if 5,000 articles were written in Europe and an equal number by researchers in the United States and other countries, what would that number be?

c. What is the significance of the fact that the coefficient of x is negative?

83. *Market Share in the 1900s:* **Chrysler, Ford, General Motors** In the late 1900s, the relationship between the domestic market shares of three major U.S. manufacturers of cars and light trucks could be modeled by

$$x_3 = 0.66 - 2.2x_1 - 0.02x_2$$

where x_1, x_2, and x_3 are, respectively, the fractions of the market held by **Chrysler, Ford,** and **General Motors**.[3] Thinking of **General Motors'** market share as a function of the shares of the other two manufacturers, describe the graph of the resulting function. How are the different slices by $x_1 = constant$ related to one another? What does this say about market share?

84. *Market Share in the 1900s:* **Kellogg, General Mills, General Foods** In the late 1900s, the relationship among the domestic market shares of three major manufacturers of breakfast cereal was

$$x_1 = -0.4 + 1.2x_2 + 2x_3$$

where x_1, x_2, and x_3 are, respectively, the fractions of the market held by **Kellogg, General Mills,** and **General Foods**.[4] Thinking of **Kellogg's** market share as a function of shares of the other two manufacturers, describe the graph of the resulting function. How are the different slices by $x_2 = constant$ related to one another? What does this say about market share?

85. *Prison Population* The number of prisoners in federal prisons in the United States can be approximated by

$$N(x, y) = 27 - 0.08x + 0.08y + 0.0002xy \text{ thousand inmates}$$

where x is the number, in thousands, in state prisons, and y is the number, in thousands, in local jails.[5]

a. In 2007 there were approximately 1.3 million in state prisons and 781 thousand in local jails. Estimate, to the nearest thousand, the number of prisoners in federal prisons that year.

b. Obtain N as a function of x for $y = 300$, and again for $y = 500$. Interpret the slopes of the resulting linear functions.

86. *Prison Population* The number of prisoners in state prisons in the United States can be approximated by

$$N(x, y) = -260 + 7x + 2y - 0.009xy \text{ thousand inmates}$$

where x is the number, in thousands, in federal prisons, and y is the number, in thousands, in local jails.[6]

a. In 2007 there were approximately 189 thousand in federal prisons and 781 thousand in local jails. Estimate, to the nearest 0.1 million, the number of prisoners in state prisons that year.

b. Obtain N as a function of y for $x = 80$, and again for $x = 100$. Interpret the slopes of the resulting linear functions.

87. *Marginal Cost (Interaction Model)* Your weekly cost (in dollars) to manufacture x cars and y trucks is

$$C(x, y) = 240{,}000 + 6{,}000x + 4{,}000y - 20xy.$$

(Compare with Exercise 77.)

a. Describe the slices $x = $ constant and $y = $ constant.

b. Is the graph of the cost function a plane? How does your answer relate to part (a)?

c. What are the slopes of the slices $x = 10$ and $x = 20$? What does this say about cost?

[1] Source: The American Physical Society/*New York Times*, May 3, 2003, p. A1.

[2] Ibid.

[3] The model is based on a linear regression. Source of data: Ward's AutoInfoBank/*The New York Times*, July 29, 1998, p. D6.

[4] The models are based on a linear regression. Source of data: Bloomberg Financial Markets/*The New York Times*, November 28, 1998, p. C1.

[5] Source for data: Sourcebook of Criminal Justice Statistics Online (www.albany.edu/sourcebook/wk1/t6132007.wk1).

[6] Ibid.

88. *Marginal Cost (Interaction Model)* Repeat the preceding exercise using the weekly cost to manufacture x bicycles and y tricycles given by

$$C(x, y) = 24,000 + 60x + 20y + 0.3xy.$$

(Compare with Exercise 78.)

89. ▼ *Online Revenue* Let us look once again at the example we used to introduce the chapter. Your major online bookstore is in direct competition with **Amazon.com**, **BN.com**, and **Borders.com**. Your company's daily revenue in dollars is given by

$$R(x, y, z) = 10,000 - 0.01x - 0.02y - 0.01z + 0.00001yz,$$

where x, y, and z are the online daily revenues of **Amazon.com**, **BN.com**, and **Borders.com** respectively.

a. If, on a certain day, **Amazon.com** shows revenue of $12,000, while **BN.com** and **Borders.com** each show $5,000, what does the model predict for your company's revenue that day?

b. If **Amazon.com** and **BN.com** each show daily revenue of $5,000, give an equation showing how your daily revenue depends on that of **Borders.com**.

90. ▼ *Online Revenue* Repeat the preceding exercise, using the revised revenue function

$$R(x, y, z) = 20,000 - 0.02x - 0.04y - 0.01z + 0.00001yz.$$

91. ▼ *Profits:* Walmart, Target The following table shows the approximate net earnings, in billions of dollars, of **Walmart** and **Target** in 2000, 2004, and 2008.[7]

	2000	2004	2008
Walmart	160	250	370
Target	27	42	62

Model **Walmart**'s net earnings as a function of **Target**'s net earnings and time, using a linear function of the form

$$f(x, t) = Ax + Bt + C \quad (A, B, C \text{ constants})$$

where f is **Walmart**'s net earnings (in billions of dollars), x is **Target**'s net earnings (in billions of dollars), and t is time in years since 2000. In 2006 **Target**'s net earnings were about $52.5 billion. What does your model estimate as **Walmart**'s net earnings that year?

92. ▼ *Profits:* Nintendo, Nokia The following table shows the approximate net earnings of **Nintendo** (in billions of yen) and **Nokia** (in billions of euro) in 2000, 2004, and 2008.[8]

	2000	2004	2008
Nintendo	530	510	1700
Nokia	30	30	52

Model **Nintendo**'s net earnings as a function of **Nokia**'s net earnings and time, using a linear function of the form

$$f(x, t) = Ax + Bt + C \quad (A, B, C \text{ constants})$$

where f is **Nintendo**'s net earnings (in billions of yen), x is **Nokia**'s net earnings (in billions of euro), and t is time in years since 2000. In 2007 **Nokia**'s net earnings were about €50 billion. What does your model estimate as **Nokia**'s net earnings that year?

93. ▼ *Utility* Suppose your newspaper is trying to decide between two competing desktop publishing software packages, Macro Publish and Turbo Publish. You estimate that if you purchase x copies of Macro Publish and y copies of Turbo Publish, your company's daily productivity will be

$$U(x, y) = 6x^{0.8}y^{0.2} + x$$

where $U(x, y)$ is measured in pages per day (U is called a *utility function*). If $x = y = 10$, calculate the effect of increasing x by one unit, and interpret the result.

94. ▼ *Housing Costs*[9] The cost C (in dollars) of building a house is related to the number k of carpenters used and the number e of electricians used by

$$C(k, e) = 15,000 + 50k^2 + 60e^2.$$

If $k = e = 10$, compare the effects of increasing k by one unit and of increasing e by one unit. Interpret the result.

95. ▼ *Volume* The volume of an ellipsoid with cross-sectional radii a, b, and c is $V(a, b, c) = \frac{4}{3}\pi abc$.

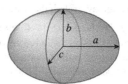

a. Find at least two sets of values for a, b, and c such that $V(a, b, c) = 1$.
b. Find the value of a such that $V(a, a, a) = 1$, and describe the resulting ellipsoid.

96. ▼ *Volume* The volume of a right elliptical cone with height h and radii a and b of its base is $V(a, b, h) = \frac{1}{3}\pi abh$.

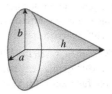

a. Find at least two sets of values for a, b, and h such that $V(a, b, h) = 1$.
b. Find the value of a such that $V(a, a, a) = 1$, and describe the resulting cone.

---

[7] Sources: www.walmartstores.com/Investors, www.investors.target.com
[8] Sources: www.nintendo.com/corp/, www.investors.nokia.com
[9] Based on an Exercise in *Introduction to Mathematical Economics* by A. L. Ostrosky Jr. and J. V. Koch (Waveland Press, Illinois, 1979).

Exercises 97–100 involve "Cobb-Douglas" productivity functions. These functions have the form

$$P(x, y) = Kx^a y^{1-a}$$

where P stands for the number of items produced per year, x is the number of employees, and y is the annual operating budget. (The numbers K and a are constants that depend on the situation we are looking at, with $0 \le a \le 1$.)

97. Productivity How many items will be produced per year by a company with 100 employees and an annual operating budget of \$500,000 if $K = 1,000$ and $a = 0.5$? (Round your answer to one significant digit.)

98. Productivity How many items will be produced per year by a company with 50 employees and an annual operating budget of \$1,000,000 if $K = 1,000$ and $a = 0.5$? (Round your answer to one significant digit.)

99. ▼ Modeling Production with Cobb-Douglas Two years ago my piano manufacturing plant employed 1,000 workers, had an operating budget of \$1 million, and turned out 100 pianos. Last year, I slashed the operating budget to \$10,000, and production dropped to 10 pianos.

  a. Use the data for each of the two years and the Cobb-Douglas formula to obtain two equations in K and a.

  b. Take logs of both sides in each equation and obtain two linear equations in a and log K.

  c. Solve these equations to obtain values for a and K.

  d. Use these values in the Cobb-Douglas formula to predict production if I increase the operating budget back to \$1 million but lay off half the work force.

100. ▼ Modeling Production with Cobb-Douglas Repeat the preceding exercise using the following data: Two years ago—1,000 employees, \$1 million operating budget, 100 pianos; last year—1,000 employees, \$100,000 operating budget, 10 pianos.

101. ▼ Pollution The burden of man-made aerosol sulfate in the earth's atmosphere, in grams per square meter, is

$$B(x, n) = \frac{xn}{A}$$

where x is the total weight of aerosol sulfate emitted into the atmosphere per year and n is the number of years it remains in the atmosphere. A is the surface area of the earth, approximately 5.1×10^{14} square meters.[10]

  a. Calculate the burden, given the 1995 estimated values of $x = 1.5 \times 10^{14}$ grams per year, and $n = 5$ days.

  b. What does the function $W(x, n) = xn$ measure?

102. ▼ Pollution The amount of aerosol sulfate (in grams) was approximately 45×10^{12} grams in 1940 and has been increasing exponentially ever since, with a doubling time of approximately 20 years.[11] Use the model from the preceding exercise to give a formula for the atmospheric burden of aerosol sulfate as a function of the time t in years since 1940 and the number of years n it remains in the atmosphere.

103. ▼ Alien Intelligence Frank Drake, an astronomer at the University of California at Santa Cruz, devised the following equation to estimate the number of planet-based civilizations in our Milky Way galaxy willing and able to communicate with Earth:[12]

$$N(R, f_p, n_e, f_l, f_i, f_c, L) = Rf_p n_e f_l f_i f_c L$$

  $R = $ the number of new stars formed in our galaxy each year

  $f_p = $ the fraction of those stars that have planetary systems

  $n_e = $ the average number of planets in each such system that can support life

  $f_l = $ the fraction of such planets on which life actually evolves

  $f_i = $ the fraction of life-sustaining planets on which intelligent life evolves

  $f_c = $ the fraction of intelligent-life-bearing planets on which the intelligent beings develop the means and the will to communicate over interstellar distances

  $L = $ the average lifetime of such technological civilizations (in years)

  a. What would be the effect on N if any one of the variables were doubled?

  b. How would you modify the formula if you were interested only in the number of intelligent-life-bearing planets in the galaxy?

  c. How could one convert this function into a linear function?

  d. (For discussion) Try to come up with an estimate of N.

104. ▼ More Alien Intelligence The formula given in the preceding exercise restricts attention to planet-based civilizations in our galaxy. Give a formula that includes intelligent planet-based aliens from the galaxy Andromeda. (Assume that all the variables used in the formula for the Milky Way have the same values for Andromeda.)

COMMUNICATION AND REASONING EXERCISES

105. Let $f(x, y) = \dfrac{x}{y}$. How are $f(x, y)$ and $f(y, x)$ related?

106. Let $f(x, y) = x^2 y^3$. How are $f(x, y)$ and $f(-x, -y)$ related?

[10] Source: Robert J. Charlson and Tom M. L. Wigley, "Sulfate Aerosol and Climatic Change," *Scientific American*, February, 1994, pp. 48–57.

[11] Ibid.

[12] Source: "First Contact" (Plume Books/Penguin Group)/*The New York Times*, October 6, 1992, p. C1.

107. Give an example of a function of the two variables x and y with the property that interchanging x and y has no effect.

108. Give an example of a function f of the two variables x and y with the property that $f(x, y) = -f(y, x)$.

109. Give an example of a function f of the three variables x, y, and z with the property that $f(x, y, z) = f(y, x, z)$ and $f(-x, -y, -z) = -f(x, y, z)$.

110. Give an example of a function f of the three variables x, y, and z with the property that $f(x, y, z) = f(y, x, z)$ and $f(-x, -y, -z) = f(x, y, z)$.

111. Illustrate by means of an example how a real-valued function of the two variables x and y gives different real-valued functions of one variable when we restrict y to be different constants.

112. Illustrate by means of an example how a real-valued function of one variable x gives different real-valued functions of the two variables y and z when we substitute for x suitable functions of y and z.

113. ▼ If f is a linear function of x and y, show that if we restrict y to be a fixed constant, then the resulting function of x is linear. Does the slope of this linear function depend on the choice of y?

114. ▼ If f is an interaction function of x and y, show that if we restrict y to be a fixed constant, then the resulting function of x is linear. Does the slope of this linear function depend on the choice of y?

115. ▼ Suppose that $C(x, y)$ represents the cost of x CDs and y cassettes. If $C(x, y + 1) < C(x + 1, y)$ for every $x \geq 0$ and $y \geq 0$, what does this tell you about the cost of CDs and cassettes?

116. ▼ Suppose that $C(x, y)$ represents the cost of renting x DVDs and y video games. If $C(x + 2, y) < C(x, y + 1)$ for every $x \geq 0$ and $y \geq 0$, what does this tell you about the cost of renting DVDs and video games?

117. Complete the following: The graph of a linear function of two variables is a _____ .

118. Complete the following: The level curves of a linear function of two variables are _____ .

119. ▼ **Heat-Seeking Missiles** The following diagram shows some level curves of the temperature, in degrees Fahrenheit, of a region in space, as well as the location, on the 100-degree curve, of a heat-seeking missile moving through the region. (These level curves are called **isotherms**.) In which of the three directions shown should the missile be traveling so as to experience the fastest rate of increase in temperature at the given point? Explain your answer.

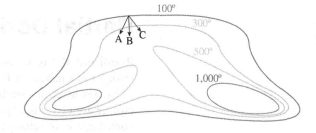

120. ▼ **Hiking** The following diagram shows some level curves of the altitude of a mountain valley, as well as the location, on the 2,000-ft curve, of a hiker. The hiker is currently moving at the greatest possible rate of descent. In which of the three directions shown is he moving? Explain your answer.

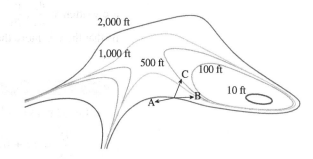

121. Your study partner Slim claims that because the surface $z = f(x, y)$ you have been studying is a plane, it follows that all the slices $x = constant$ and $y = constant$ are straight lines. Do you agree or disagree? Explain.

122. Your other study partner Shady just told you that the surface $z = xy$ you have been trying to graph must be a plane because you've already found that the slices $x = constant$ and $y = constant$ are all straight lines. Do you agree or disagree? Explain.

123. Why do we not sketch the graphs of functions of three or more variables?

124. The surface of a mountain can be thought of as the graph of what function?

125. Why is three-dimensional space used to represent the graph of a function of two variables?

126. Why is it that we can sketch the graphs of functions of two variables on the two-dimensional flat surfaces of these pages?

15.2 Partial Derivatives

Recall that if f is a function of x, then the derivative df/dx measures how fast f changes as x increases. If f is a function of two or more variables, we can ask how fast f changes as each variable increases while the others remain fixed. These rates of change are called the "partial derivatives of f," and they measure how each variable contributes to the change in f. Here is a more precise definition.

Partial Derivatives

The **partial derivative of f with respect to x** is the derivative of f with respect to x, when all other variables are treated as constant. Similarly, the **partial derivative of f with respect to y** is the derivative of f with respect to y, with all other variables treated as constant, and so on for other variables. The partial derivatives are written as $\dfrac{\partial f}{\partial x}$, $\dfrac{\partial f}{\partial y}$, and so on. The symbol ∂ is used (instead of d) to remind us that there is more than one variable and that we are holding the other variables fixed.

Quick Examples

1. Let $f(x, y) = x^2 + y^2$.

$$\frac{\partial f}{\partial x} = 2x + 0 = 2x \qquad \text{Because } y^2 \text{ is treated as a constant}$$

$$\frac{\partial f}{\partial y} = 0 + 2y = 2y \qquad \text{Because } x^2 \text{ is treated as a constant}$$

2. Let $z = x^2 + xy$.

$$\frac{\partial z}{\partial x} = 2x + y \qquad \frac{\partial}{\partial x}(xy) = \frac{\partial}{\partial x}(x \cdot \text{constant}) = \text{constant} = y$$

$$\frac{\partial z}{\partial y} = 0 + x \qquad \frac{\partial}{\partial y}(xy) = \frac{\partial}{\partial x}(\text{constant} \cdot y) = \text{constant} = x$$

3. Let $f(x, y) = x^2y + y^2x - xy + y$.

$$\frac{\partial f}{\partial x} = 2xy + y^2 - y \qquad y \text{ is treated as a constant.}$$

$$\frac{\partial f}{\partial y} = x^2 + 2xy - x + 1 \qquad x \text{ is treated as a constant.}$$

Interpretation

$\dfrac{\partial f}{\partial x}$ is the rate at which f changes as x changes, for a fixed (constant) y.

$\dfrac{\partial f}{\partial y}$ is the rate at which f changes as y changes, for a fixed (constant) x.

EXAMPLE 1 Marginal Cost: Linear Model

We return to Example 1 from Section 15.1. Suppose that you own a company that makes two models of speakers, the Ultra Mini and the Big Stack. Your total monthly cost (in dollars) to make x Ultra Minis and y Big Stacks is given by

$$C(x, y) = 10,000 + 20x + 40y.$$

What is the significance of $\dfrac{\partial C}{\partial x}$ and of $\dfrac{\partial C}{\partial y}$?

Solution First we compute these partial derivatives:

$$\frac{\partial C}{\partial x} = 20$$

$$\frac{\partial C}{\partial y} = 40.$$

We interpret the results as follows: $\dfrac{\partial C}{\partial x} = 20$ means that the cost is increasing at a rate of \$20 per additional Ultra Mini (if production of Big Stacks is held constant); $\dfrac{\partial C}{\partial y} = 40$ means that the cost is increasing at a rate of \$40 per additional Big Stack (if production of Ultra Minis is held constant). In other words, these are the **marginal costs** of each model of speaker.

➡ **Before we go on...** How much does the cost rise if you increase x by Δx and y by Δy? In Example 1, the change in cost is given by

$$\Delta C = 20\Delta x + 40\Delta y = \frac{\partial C}{\partial x}\Delta x + \frac{\partial C}{\partial y}\Delta y.$$

This suggests the **chain rule for several variables**. Part of this rule says that if x and y are both functions of t, then C is a function of t through them, and the rate of change of C with respect to t can be calculated as

$$\frac{dC}{dt} = \frac{\partial C}{\partial x} \cdot \frac{dx}{dt} + \frac{\partial C}{\partial y} \cdot \frac{dy}{dt}.$$

See the optional section on the chain rule for several variables for further discussion and applications of this interesting result. ■

EXAMPLE 2 Marginal Cost: Interaction Model

Another possibility for the cost function in the preceding example is the interaction model

$$C(x, y) = 10,000 + 20x + 40y + 0.1xy.$$

a. *Now* what are the marginal costs of the two models of speakers?

b. What is the marginal cost of manufacturing Big Stacks at a production level of 100 Ultra Minis and 50 Big Stacks per month?

Solution

a. We compute the partial derivatives:

$$\frac{\partial C}{\partial x} = 20 + 0.1y$$

$$\frac{\partial C}{\partial y} = 40 + 0.1x.$$

Thus, the marginal cost of manufacturing Ultra Minis increases by \$0.1 or 10¢ for each Big Stack that is manufactured. Similarly, the marginal cost of manufacturing Big Stacks increases by 10¢ for each Ultra Mini that is manufactured.

b. From part (a), the marginal cost of manufacturing Big Stacks is

$$\frac{\partial C}{\partial y} = 40 + 0.1x.$$

At a production level of 100 Ultra Minis and 50 Big Stacks per month, we have $x = 100$ and $y = 50$. Thus, the marginal cost of manufacturing Big Stacks at these production levels is

$$\left.\frac{\partial C}{\partial y}\right|_{(100,50)} = 40 + 0.1(100) = \$50 \text{ per Big Stack}.$$

Partial derivatives of functions of three variables are obtained in the same way as those for functions of two variables, as the following example shows.

EXAMPLE 3 Function of Three Variables

Calculate $\dfrac{\partial f}{\partial x}$, $\dfrac{\partial f}{\partial y}$, and $\dfrac{\partial f}{\partial z}$ if $f(x, y, z) = xy^2z^3 - xy$.

Solution Although we now have three variables, the calculation remains the same: $\partial f/\partial x$ is the derivative of f with respect to x, with *both* other variables, y and z, held constant:

$$\frac{\partial f}{\partial x} = y^2z^3 - y.$$

Similarly, $\partial f/\partial y$ is the derivative of f with respect to y, with both x and z held constant:

$$\frac{\partial f}{\partial y} = 2xyz^3 - x.$$

Finally, to find $\partial f/\partial z$, we hold both x and y constant and take the derivative with respect to z.

$$\frac{\partial f}{\partial z} = 3xy^2z^2.$$

Note The procedure for finding a partial derivative is the same for any number of variables: To get the partial derivative with respect to any one variable, we treat all the others as constants. ■

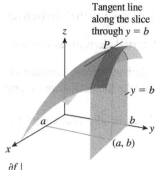

Tangent line along the slice through $y = b$

$\left.\dfrac{\partial f}{\partial x}\right|_{(a,b)}$ is the slope of the tangent line at the point $P(a, b, f(a, b))$ along the slice through $y = b$.

Figure 17

Geometric Interpretation of Partial Derivatives

Recall that if f is a function of one variable x, then the derivative df/dx gives the slopes of the tangent lines to its graph. Now, suppose that f is a function of x and y. By definition, $\partial f/\partial x$ is the derivative of the function of x we get by holding y fixed. If we evaluate this derivative at the point (a, b), we are holding y fixed at the value b, taking the ordinary derivative of the resulting function of x, and evaluating this at $x = a$. Now, holding y fixed at b amounts to slicing through the graph of f along the plane $y = b$, resulting in a curve. Thus, the partial derivative is the slope of the tangent line to this curve at the point where $x = a$ and $y = b$, along the plane $y = b$ (Figure 17). This fits with our interpretation of $\partial f/\partial x$ as the rate of increase of f with increasing x when y is held fixed at b.

The other partial derivative, $\partial f/\partial y|_{(a,b)}$ is, similarly, the slope of the tangent line at the same point $P(a, b, f(a, b))$ but along the slice by the plane $x = a$. You should draw the corresponding picture for this on your own.

Second-Order Partial Derivatives

Just as for functions of a single variable, we can calculate second derivatives. Suppose, for example, that we have a function of x and y, say, $f(x, y) = x^2 - x^2 y^2$. We know that

$$\frac{\partial f}{\partial x} = 2x - 2xy^2.$$

If we take the partial derivative with respect to x once again, we obtain

$$\frac{\partial}{\partial x}\left(\frac{\partial f}{\partial x}\right) = 2 - 2y^2. \qquad \text{Take } \frac{\partial}{\partial x} \text{ of } \frac{\partial f}{\partial x}.$$

(The symbol $\partial/\partial x$ means "the partial derivative with respect to x," just as d/dx stands for "the derivative with respect to x.") This is called the **second-order partial derivative** and is written $\dfrac{\partial^2 f}{\partial x^2}$. We get the following derivatives similarly:

$$\frac{\partial f}{\partial y} = -2x^2 y$$

$$\frac{\partial^2 f}{\partial y^2} = -2x^2. \qquad \text{Take } \frac{\partial}{\partial y} \text{ of } \frac{\partial f}{\partial y}.$$

Now what if we instead take the partial derivative with respect to y of $\partial f/\partial x$?

$$\frac{\partial^2 f}{\partial y \partial x} = \frac{\partial}{\partial y}\left(\frac{\partial f}{\partial x}\right) \qquad \text{Take } \frac{\partial}{\partial y} \text{ of } \frac{\partial f}{\partial x}.$$

$$= \frac{\partial}{\partial y}[2x - 2xy^2] = -4xy.$$

Here, $\dfrac{\partial^2 f}{\partial y \partial x}$ means "first take the partial derivative with respect to x and then with respect to y," and is called a **mixed partial derivative**. If we differentiate in the opposite order, we get

$$\frac{\partial^2 f}{\partial x \partial y} = \frac{\partial}{\partial x}\left(\frac{\partial f}{\partial y}\right) = \frac{\partial}{\partial x}[-2x^2 y] = -4xy,$$

the same expression as $\dfrac{\partial^2 f}{\partial y \partial x}$. This is no coincidence: The mixed partial derivatives $\dfrac{\partial^2 f}{\partial x \partial y}$ and $\dfrac{\partial^2 f}{\partial y \partial x}$ are always the same as long as the first partial derivatives are both differentiable functions of x and y and the mixed partial derivatives are continuous. Because all the functions we shall use are of this type, we can take the derivatives in any order we like when calculating mixed derivatives.

Here is another notation for partial derivatives that is especially convenient for second-order partial derivatives:

$$f_x \text{ means } \frac{\partial f}{\partial x}$$

$$f_y \text{ means } \frac{\partial f}{\partial y}$$

$$f_{xy} \text{ means } (f_x)_y = \frac{\partial^2 f}{\partial y \partial x} \quad \text{(Note the order in which the derivatives are taken.)}$$

$$f_{yx} \text{ means } (f_y)_x = \frac{\partial^2 f}{\partial x \partial y}.$$

15.2 EXERCISES

▼ more advanced   ◆ challenging
🔲 indicates exercises that should be solved using technology

In Exercises 1–18, calculate $\dfrac{\partial f}{\partial x}, \dfrac{\partial f}{\partial y}, \dfrac{\partial f}{\partial x}\Big|_{(1,-1)}$, *and* $\dfrac{\partial f}{\partial y}\Big|_{(1,-1)}$

when defined. HINT [See Quick Examples page 1098.]

1. $f(x, y) = 10{,}000 - 40x + 20y$
2. $f(x, y) = 1{,}000 + 5x - 4y$
3. $f(x, y) = 3x^2 - y^3 + x - 1$
4. $f(x, y) = x^{1/2} - 2y^4 + y + 6$
5. $f(x, y) = 10{,}000 - 40x + 20y + 10xy$
6. $f(x, y) = 1{,}000 + 5x - 4y - 3xy$
7. $f(x, y) = 3x^2 y$
8. $f(x, y) = x^4 y^2 - x$
9. $f(x, y) = x^2 y^3 - x^3 y^2 - xy$
10. $f(x, y) = x^{-1} y^2 + xy^2 + xy$
11. $f(x, y) = (2xy + 1)^3$ 12. $f(x, y) = \dfrac{1}{(xy+1)^2}$
13. ▼ $f(x, y) = e^{x+y}$ 14. ▼ $f(x, y) = e^{2x+y}$
15. ▼ $f(x, y) = 5x^{0.6} y^{0.4}$ 16. ▼ $f(x, y) = -2x^{0.1} y^{0.9}$
17. ▼ $f(x, y) = e^{0.2xy}$ 18. ▼ $f(x, y) = xe^{xy}$

In Exercises 19–28, find $\dfrac{\partial^2 f}{\partial x^2}, \dfrac{\partial^2 f}{\partial y^2}, \dfrac{\partial^2 f}{\partial x \partial y}$, *and* $\dfrac{\partial^2 f}{\partial y \partial x}$, *and evaluate them all at* $(1, -1)$ *if possible.* HINT [See Discussion on page 1101.]

19. $f(x, y) = 10{,}000 - 40x + 20y$
20. $f(x, y) = 1{,}000 + 5x - 4y$

21. $f(x, y) = 10{,}000 - 40x + 20y + 10xy$
22. $f(x, y) = 1{,}000 + 5x - 4y - 3xy$
23. $f(x, y) = 3x^2 y$ 24. $f(x, y) = x^4 y^2 - x$
25. ▼ $f(x, y) = e^{x+y}$ 26. ▼ $f(x, y) = e^{2x+y}$
27. ▼ $f(x, y) = 5x^{0.6} y^{0.4}$ 28. ▼ $f(x, y) = -2x^{0.1} y^{0.9}$

In Exercises 29–40, find $\dfrac{\partial f}{\partial x}, \dfrac{\partial f}{\partial y}, \dfrac{\partial f}{\partial z}$, *and their values at* $(0, -1, 1)$

if possible. HINT [See Example 3.]

29. $f(x, y, z) = xyz$
30. $f(x, y, z) = xy + xz - yz$
31. ▼ $f(x, y, z) = -\dfrac{4}{x + y + z^2}$
32. ▼ $f(x, y, z) = \dfrac{6}{x^2 + y^2 + z^2}$
33. ▼ $f(x, y, z) = xe^{yz} + ye^{xz}$
34. ▼ $f(x, y, z) = xye^z + xe^{yz} + e^{xyz}$
35. ▼ $f(x, y, z) = x^{0.1} y^{0.4} z^{0.5}$
36. ▼ $f(x, y, z) = 2x^{0.2} y^{0.8} + z^2$
37. ▼ $f(x, y, z) = e^{xyz}$
38. ▼ $f(x, y, z) = \ln(x + y + z)$
39. ▼ $f(x, y, z) = \dfrac{2{,}000z}{1 + y^{0.3}}$
40. ▼ $f(x, y, z) = \dfrac{e^{0.2x}}{1 + e^{-0.1y}}$

APPLICATIONS

41. **Marginal Cost (Linear Model)** Your weekly cost (in dollars) to manufacture x cars and y trucks is

$$C(x, y) = 240,000 + 6,000x + 4,000y.$$

Calculate and interpret $\dfrac{\partial C}{\partial x}$ and $\dfrac{\partial C}{\partial y}$. HINT [See Example 1.]

42. **Marginal Cost (Linear Model)** Your weekly cost (in dollars) to manufacture x bicycles and y tricycles is

$$C(x, y) = 24,000 + 60x + 20y.$$

Calculate and interpret $\dfrac{\partial C}{\partial x}$ and $\dfrac{\partial C}{\partial y}$.

43. **Scientific Research** In each year from 1983 to 2003, the percentage y of research articles in *Physical Review* written by researchers in the United States can be approximated by

$$y = 82 - 0.78t - 1.02x \text{ percentage points} \quad (0 \leq t \leq 20)$$

where t is the year since 1983 and x is the percentage of articles written by researchers in Europe.[13] Calculate and interpret $\dfrac{\partial y}{\partial t}$ and $\dfrac{\partial y}{\partial x}$.

44. **Scientific Research** The number z of research articles in *Physical Review* that were written by researchers in the United States from 1993 through 2003 can be approximated by

$$z = 5,960 - 0.71x + 0.50y \quad (3,000 \leq x, y \leq 6,000)$$

articles each year, where x is the number of articles written by researchers in Europe and y is the number written by researchers in other countries (excluding Europe and the United States).[14] Calculate and interpret $\dfrac{\partial z}{\partial x}$ and $\dfrac{\partial z}{\partial y}$.

45. **Marginal Cost (Interaction Model)** Your weekly cost (in dollars) to manufacture x cars and y trucks is

$$C(x, y) = 240,000 + 6,000x + 4,000y - 20xy.$$

(Compare with Exercise 77.) Compute the marginal cost of manufacturing cars at a production level of 10 cars and 20 trucks. HINT [See Example 2.]

46. **Marginal Cost (Interaction Model)** Your weekly cost (in dollars) to manufacture x bicycles and y tricycles is

$$C(x, y) = 24,000 + 60x + 20y + 0.3xy.$$

(Compare with Exercise 78.) Compute the marginal cost of manufacturing tricycles at a production level of 10 bicycles and 20 tricycles. HINT [See Example 2.]

47. **Brand Loyalty: Mazda** The fraction of **Mazda** car owners who chose another new **Mazda** can be modeled by the following function:[15]

$$M(c, f, g, h, t) = 1.1 - 3.8c + 2.2f + 1.9g - 1.7h - 1.3t.$$

Here, c is the fraction of **Chrysler** car owners who remained loyal to **Chrysler**, f is the fraction of **Ford** car owners remaining loyal to **Ford**, g the corresponding figure for **General Motors**, h the corresponding figure for **Honda**, and t for **Toyota**.

   a. Calculate $\dfrac{\partial M}{\partial c}$ and $\dfrac{\partial M}{\partial f}$ and interpret the answers.

   b. One year it was observed that $c = 0.56$, $f = 0.56$, $g = 0.72$, $h = 0.50$, and $t = 0.43$. According to the model, what percentage of **Mazda** owners remained loyal to **Mazda**? (Round your answer to the nearest percentage point.)

48. **Brand Loyalty** The fraction of **Mazda** car owners who chose another new **Mazda** can be modeled by the following function:[16]

$$M(c, f) = 9.4 + 7.8c + 3.6c^2 - 38f - 22cf + 43f^2$$

where c is the fraction of **Chrysler** car owners who remained loyal to **Chrysler** and f is the fraction of **Ford** car owners remaining loyal to **Ford**.

   a. Calculate $\dfrac{\partial M}{\partial c}$ and $\dfrac{\partial M}{\partial f}$ evaluated at the point (0.7, 0.7), and interpret the answers.

   b. One year it was observed that $c = 0.56$, and $f = 0.56$. According to the model, what percentage of **Mazda** owners remained loyal to **Mazda**? (Round your answer to the nearest percentage point.)

49. ▼ **Income Gap** The following model is based on data on the median family incomes of Hispanic and white families in the United States for the period 1980–2008:[17]

$$z(t, x) = 31,200 + 270t + 13,500x + 140xt$$

where

$$z(t, x) = \text{median family income}$$
$$t = \text{year } (t = 0 \text{ represents } 1980)$$
$$x = \begin{cases} 0 & \text{if the income was for a Hispanic family} \\ 1 & \text{if the income was for a white family.} \end{cases}$$

---

[13] Source: The American Physical Society/*New York Times*, May 3, 2003, p. A1.

[14] Ibid.

[15] The model is an approximation of a linear regression based on data from the period 1988–1995. Source for data: Chrysler, Maritz Market Research, Consumer Attitude Research, and Strategic Vision/*The New York Times*, November 3, 1995, p. D2.

[16] The model is an approximation of a second order regression based on data from the period 1988–1995. Source for data: Chrysler, Maritz Market Research, Consumer Attitude Research, and Strategic Vision/*The New York Times*, November 3, 1995, p. D2.

[17] Incomes are in 2007 dollars. Source for data: U.S. Census Bureau (www.census.gov).

a. Use the model to estimate the median income of a Hispanic family and of a white family in 2000.

b. According to the model, how fast was the median income for a Hispanic family increasing in 2000? How fast was the median income for a white family increasing in 2000?

c. Do the answers in part (b) suggest that the income gap between white and Hispanic families was widening or narrowing during the given period?

d. What does the coefficient of xt in the formula for $z(t, x)$ represent in terms of the income gap?

50. ▼ *Income Gap* The following model is based on data on the median family incomes of black and white families in the United States for the period 1980–2008:[18]

$$z(t, x) = 24,500 + 390t + 20,200x + 20xt$$

where

$z(t, x)$ = median family income

t = year ($t = 0$ represents 1980)

$$x = \begin{cases} 0 & \text{if the income was for a black family} \\ 1 & \text{if the income was for a white family.} \end{cases}$$

a. Use the model to estimate the median income of a black family and of a white family in 2000.

b. According to the model, how fast was the median income for a black family increasing in 2000? How fast was the median income for a white family increasing in 2000?

c. Do the answers in part (b) suggest that the income gap between white and black families was widening or narrowing during the given period?

d. What does the coefficient of xt in the formula for $z(t, x)$ represent in terms of the income gap?

51. ▼ *Marginal Cost* Your weekly cost (in dollars) to manufacture x cars and y trucks is

$$C(x, y) = 200,000 + 6,000x + 4,000y - 100,000e^{-0.01(x+y)}.$$

What is the marginal cost of a car? Of a truck? How do these marginal costs behave as total production increases?

52. ▼ *Marginal Cost* Your weekly cost (in dollars) to manufacture x bicycles and y tricycles is

$$C(x, y) = 20,000 + 60x + 20y + 50\sqrt{xy}.$$

What is the marginal cost of a bicycle? Of a tricycle? How do these marginal costs behave as x and y increase?

53. ▼ *Average Cost* If you average your costs over your total production, you get the **average cost**, written $\bar{C}$:

$$\bar{C}(x, y) = \frac{C(x, y)}{x + y}.$$

Find the average cost for the cost function in Exercise 51. Then find the marginal average cost of a car and the marginal average cost of a truck at a production level of 50 cars and 50 trucks. Interpret your answers.

[18] Incomes are in 2007 dollars. Source for data: U.S. Census Bureau (www.census.gov).

54. ▼ *Average Cost* Find the average cost for the cost function in Exercise 52. (See the preceding exercise.) Then find the marginal average cost of a bicycle and the marginal average cost of a tricycle at a production level of five bicycles and five tricycles. Interpret your answers.

55. ▼ *Marginal Revenue* As manager of an auto dealership, you offer a car rental company the following deal: You will charge $15,000 per car and $10,000 per truck, but you will then give the company a discount of $5,000 times the square root of the total number of vehicles it buys from you. Looking at your marginal revenue, is this a good deal for the rental company?

56. ▼ *Marginal Revenue* As marketing director for a bicycle manufacturer, you come up with the following scheme: You will offer to sell a dealer x bicycles and y tricycles for

$$R(x, y) = 3,500 - 3,500e^{-0.02x - 0.01y} \text{ dollars.}$$

Find your marginal revenue for bicycles and for tricycles. Are you likely to be fired for your suggestion?

57. ▼ *Research Productivity* Here we apply a variant of the Cobb-Douglas function to the modeling of research productivity. A mathematical model of research productivity at a particular physics laboratory is

$$P = 0.04x^{0.4}y^{0.2}z^{0.4}$$

where P is the annual number of groundbreaking research papers produced by the staff, x is the number of physicists on the research team, y is the laboratory's annual research budget, and z is the annual National Science Foundation subsidy to the laboratory. Find the rate of increase of research papers per government-subsidy dollar at a subsidy level of $1,000,000 per year and a staff level of 10 physicists if the annual budget is $100,000.

58. ▼ *Research Productivity* A major drug company estimates that the annual number P of patents for new drugs developed by its research team is best modeled by the formula

$$P = 0.3x^{0.3}y^{0.4}z^{0.3}$$

where x is the number of research biochemists on the payroll, y is the annual research budget, and z is the size of the bonus awarded to discoverers of new drugs. Assuming that the company has 12 biochemists on the staff, has an annual research budget of $500,000 and pays $40,000 bonuses to developers of new drugs, calculate the rate of growth in the annual number of patents per new research staff member.

59. ▼ *Utility* Your newspaper is trying to decide between two competing desktop publishing software packages, Macro Publish and Turbo Publish. You estimate that if you purchase x copies of Macro Publish and y copies of Turbo Publish, your company's daily productivity will be

$$U(x, y) = 6x^{0.8}y^{0.2} + x.$$

$U(x, y)$ is measured in pages per day.

a. Calculate $\left.\dfrac{\partial U}{\partial x}\right|_{(10,5)}$ and $\left.\dfrac{\partial U}{\partial y}\right|_{(10,5)}$ to two decimal places, and interpret the results.

b. What does the ratio $\left.\dfrac{\partial U}{\partial x}\right|_{(10,5)} \Big/ \left.\dfrac{\partial U}{\partial y}\right|_{(10,5)}$ tell about the usefulness of these products?

60. ▼ *Grades*[19] A production formula for a student's performance on a difficult English examination is given by

$$g(t, x) = 4tx - 0.2t^2 - x^2$$

where g is the grade the student can expect to get, t is the number of hours of study for the examination, and x is the student's grade point average.

a. Calculate $\left.\dfrac{\partial g}{\partial t}\right|_{(10,3)}$ and $\left.\dfrac{\partial g}{\partial x}\right|_{(10,3)}$ and interpret the results.

b. What does the ratio $\left.\dfrac{\partial g}{\partial t}\right|_{(10,3)} \Big/ \left.\dfrac{\partial g}{\partial x}\right|_{(10,3)}$ tell about the relative merits of study and grade point average?

61. ▼ *Electrostatic Repulsion* If positive electric charges of Q and q coulombs are situated at positions (a, b, c) and (x, y, z) respectively, then the force of repulsion they experience is given by

$$F = K \frac{Qq}{(x-a)^2 + (y-b)^2 + (z-c)^2}$$

where $K \approx 9 \times 10^9$, F is given in newtons, and all positions are measured in meters. Assume that a charge of 10 coulombs is situated at the origin, and that a second charge of 5 coulombs is situated at $(2, 3, 3)$ and moving in the y-direction at one meter per second. How fast is the electrostatic force it experiences decreasing? (Round the answer to one significant digit.)

62. ▼ *Electrostatic Repulsion* Repeat the preceding exercise, assuming that a charge of 10 coulombs is situated at the origin and that a second charge of 5 coulombs is situated at $(2, 3, 3)$ and moving in the negative z direction at one meter per second. (Round the answer to one significant digit.)

63. ▼ *Investments* Recall that the compound interest formula for annual compounding is

$$A(P, r, t) = P(1 + r)^t$$

where A is the future value of an investment of P dollars after t years at an interest rate of r.

a. Calculate $\dfrac{\partial A}{\partial P}$, $\dfrac{\partial A}{\partial r}$, and $\dfrac{\partial A}{\partial t}$, all evaluated at $(100, 0.10, 10)$. (Round your answers to two decimal places.) Interpret your answers.

b. What does the function $\left.\dfrac{\partial A}{\partial P}\right|_{(100,0.10,t)}$ of t tell about your investment?

64. ▼ *Investments* Repeat the preceding exercise, using the formula for continuous compounding:

$$A(P, r, t) = Pe^{rt}$$

65. ▼ *Modeling with the Cobb-Douglas Production Formula* Assume you are given a production formula of the form

$$P(x, y) = Kx^a y^b \quad (a + b = 1).$$

a. Obtain formulas for $\dfrac{\partial P}{\partial x}$ and $\dfrac{\partial P}{\partial y}$, and show that $\dfrac{\partial P}{\partial x} = \dfrac{\partial P}{\partial y}$ precisely when $x/y = a/b$.

b. Let x be the number of workers a firm employs and let y be its monthly operating budget in thousands of dollars. Assume that the firm currently employs 100 workers and has a monthly operating budget of \$200,000. If each additional worker contributes as much to productivity as each additional \$1,000 per month, find values of a and b that model the firm's productivity.

66. ▼ *Housing Costs*[20] The cost C of building a house is related to the number k of carpenters used and the number e of electricians used by

$$C(k, e) = 15{,}000 + 50k^2 + 60e^2.$$

If three electricians are currently employed in building your new house and the marginal cost per additional electrician is the same as the marginal cost per additional carpenter, how many carpenters are being used? (Round your answer to the nearest carpenter.)

67. ▼ *Nutrient Diffusion* Suppose that one cubic centimeter of nutrient is placed at the center of a circular petri dish filled with water. We might wonder how the nutrient is distributed after a time of t seconds. According to the classical theory of diffusion, the concentration of nutrient (in parts of nutrient per part of water) after a time t is given by

$$u(r, t) = \frac{1}{4\pi Dt} e^{-\frac{r^2}{4Dt}}.$$

Here D is the *diffusivity*, which we will take to be 1, and r is the distance from the center in centimeters. How fast is the concentration increasing at a distance of 1 cm from the center 3 seconds after the nutrient is introduced?

68. ▼ *Nutrient Diffusion* Refer back to the preceding exercise. How fast is the concentration increasing at a distance of 4 cm from the center 4 seconds after the nutrient is introduced?

COMMUNICATION AND REASONING EXERCISES

69. Given that $f(a, b) = r$, $f_x(a, b) = s$, and $f_y(a, b) = t$, complete the following: _____ is increasing at a rate of _____ units per unit of x, _____ is increasing at a rate of _____ units per unit of y, and the value of _____ is _____ when $x =$ _____ and $y =$ _____.

70. A firm's productivity depends on two variables, x and y. Currently, $x = a$ and $y = b$, and the firm's productivity is 4,000 units. Productivity is increasing at a rate of 400 units per unit *decrease* in x, and is decreasing at a rate of 300 units per unit increase in y. What does all of this information tell you about the firm's productivity function $g(x, y)$?

71. Complete the following: Let $f(x, y, z)$ be the cost to build a development of x cypods (one-bedroom units) in the city-state of Utarek, Mars, y argaats (two-bedroom units) and z orbici

---

[19] Based on an Exercise in *Introduction to Mathematical Economics* by A. L. Ostrosky Jr. and J. V. Koch (Waveland Press, Illinois, 1979).

[20] Ibid.

(singular: orbicus; three-bedroom units) in $\overline{\overline{Z}}$ (zonars, the designated currency in Utarek).[21] Then $\dfrac{\partial f}{\partial z}$ measures _____ and has units _____ .

72. Complete the following: Let $f(t, x, y)$ be the projected number of citizens of the Principality State of Voodice, Luna[22] in year t since its founding, assuming the presence of x lunar vehicle factories and y domed settlements. Then $\dfrac{\partial f}{\partial x}$ measures _____ and has units _____ .

73. Give an example of a function $f(x, y)$ with $f_x(1, 1) = -2$ and $f_y(1, 1) = 3$.

74. Give an example of a function $f(x, y, z)$ that has all of its partial derivatives equal to nonzero constants.

---

[21] Source: www.marsnext.com/comm/zonars.html

[22] Source: www.voodice.info

75. ▼ The graph of $z = b + mx + ny$ (b, m, and n constants) is a plane.

   a. Explain the geometric significance of the numbers b, m, and n.

   b. Show that the equation of the plane passing through (h, k, l) with slope m in the x direction (in the sense of $\partial/\partial x$) and slope n in the y direction is

$$z = l + m(x - h) + n(y - k).$$

76. ▼ The **tangent plane** to the graph of $f(x, y)$ at $P(a, b, f(a, b))$ is the plane containing the lines tangent to the slice through the graph by $y = b$ (as in Figure 17) and the slice through the graph by $x = a$. Use the result of the preceding exercise to show that the equation of the tangent plane is

$$z = f(a, b) + f_x(a, b)(x - a) + f_y(a, b)(y - b).$$

15.3 Maxima and Minima

In Chapter 12, on applications of the derivative, we saw how to locate relative extrema of a function of a single variable. In this section we extend our methods to functions of two variables. Similar techniques work for functions of three or more variables.

Figure 18 shows a portion of the graph of the function $f(x, y) = 2(x^2 + y^2) - (x^4 + y^4) + 1$. The graph in Figure 18 resembles a "flying carpet," and several interesting points, marked a, b, c, and d are shown.

1. The point a has coordinates $(0, 0, f(0, 0))$, is directly above the origin $(0, 0)$, and is the lowest point in its vicinity; water would puddle there. We say that f has a **relative minimum** at $(0, 0)$ because $f(0, 0)$ is smaller than $f(x, y)$ for any (x, y) near $(0, 0)$.

2. Similarly, the point b is higher than any point in its vicinity. Thus, we say that f has a **relative maximum** at $(1, 1)$.

3. The points c and d represent a new phenomenon and are called **saddle points**. They are neither relative maxima nor relative minima but seem to be a little of both.

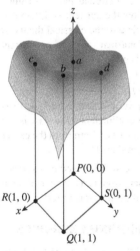

Figure 18

To see more clearly what features a saddle point has, look at Figure 19, which shows a portion of the graph near the point d.

If we slice through the graph along $y = 1$, we get a curve on which d is the *lowest* point. Thus, d looks like a relative minimum along this slice. On the other hand, if we slice through the graph along $x = 0$, we get another curve, on which d is the *highest* point, so d looks like a relative maximum along this slice. This kind of behavior characterizes a saddle point: f has a **saddle point** at (r, s) if f has a relative minimum at (r, s) along some slice through that point and a relative maximum along another slice through that point. If you look at the other saddle point, c, in Figure 18, you see the same characteristics.

While numerical information can help us locate the approximate positions of relative extrema and saddle points, calculus permits us to locate these points accurately, as we did for functions of a single variable. Look once again at Figure 18, and notice the following:

• The points P, Q, R, and S are all in the **interior** of the domain of f; that is, none lie on the boundary of the domain. Said another way, we can move some distance in any direction from any of these points without leaving the domain of f.

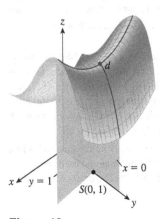

Figure 19

- The tangent lines along the slices through these points parallel to the x- and y-axes are *horizontal*. Thus, the partial derivatives $\partial f/\partial x$ and $\partial f/\partial y$ are zero when evaluated at any of the points P, Q, R, and S. This gives us a way of locating candidates for relative extrema and saddle points.

The following summary generalizes and also expands on some of what we have just said:

* **NOTE** For $(x, y, \ldots)$ to be near $(r, s, \ldots)$ we mean that x is in some open interval $(r - h_1, r + h_1)$ centered at r, y is in some open interval $(s - h_2, s + h_2)$ centered at s, and so on.

Relative and Absolute Maxima and Minima

The function f of n variables has a **relative maximum** at $(x_1, x_2, \ldots, x_n) = (r_1, r_2, \ldots, r_n)$ if $f(r_1, r_2, \ldots, r_n) \geq f(x_1, x_2, \ldots, x_n)$ for every point $(x_1, x_2, \ldots, x_n)$ near* $(r_1, r_2, \ldots, r_n)$ in the domain of f. We say that f has an **absolute maximum** at $(r_1, r_2, \ldots, r_n)$ if $f(r_1, r_2, \ldots, r_n) \geq f(x_1, x_2, \ldots, x_n)$ for every point $(x_1, x_2, \ldots, x_n)$ in the domain of f. The terms **relative minimum** and **absolute minimum** are defined in a similar way.

Locating Candidates for Relative Extrema and Saddle Points in the Interior of the Domain of f:

- Set $\dfrac{\partial f}{\partial x_1} = 0, \dfrac{\partial f}{\partial x_2} = 0, \ldots, \dfrac{\partial f}{\partial x_n} = 0$, simultaneously, and solve for $x_1, x_2, \ldots, x_n$.

- Check that the resulting points $(x_1, x_2, \ldots, x_n)$ are in the interior of the domain of f.

Points at which all the partial derivatives of f are zero are called **critical points**. The critical points are the only candidates for relative extrema and saddle points in the interior of the domain of f, assuming that its partial derivatives are defined at every point.*

* **NOTE** One can use the techniques of the next section to find extrema on the *boundary* of the domain of a function; for a complete discussion, see the optional extra section: *Maxima and Minima: Boundaries and the Extreme Value Theorem*. (We shall not consider the analogs of the singular points.)

Quick Examples

In each of the following Quick Examples, the domain is the whole Cartesian plane, and the partial derivatives are defined at every point, so the critical points give us the only candidates for relative extrema and saddle points:

1. Let $f(x, y) = x^3 + (y - 1)^2$. Then $\dfrac{\partial f}{\partial x} = 3x^2$ and $\dfrac{\partial f}{\partial y} = 2(y - 1)$. Thus, we solve the system

   $$3x^2 = 0 \quad \text{and} \quad 2(y - 1) = 0.$$

   The first equation gives $x = 0$, and the second gives $y = 1$. Thus, the only critical point is $(0, 1)$.

2. Let $f(x, y) = x^2 - 4xy + 8y$. Then $\dfrac{\partial f}{\partial x} = 2x - 4y$ and $\dfrac{\partial f}{\partial y} = -4x + 8$.

   Thus, we solve

   $$2x - 4y = 0 \quad \text{and} \quad -4x + 8 = 0.$$

   The second equation gives $x = 2$, and the first then gives $y = 1$. Thus, the only critical point is $(2, 1)$.

3. Let $f(x, y) = e^{-(x^2+y^2)}$. Taking partial derivatives and setting them equal to zero gives

$$-2xe^{-(x^2+y^2)} = 0 \qquad \text{We set } \frac{\partial f}{\partial x} = 0.$$

$$-2ye^{-(x^2+y^2)} = 0. \qquad \text{We set } \frac{\partial f}{\partial y} = 0.$$

The first equation implies that $x = 0$,* and the second implies that $y = 0$. Thus, the only critical point is $(0, 0)$.

✳ NOTE Recall that if a product of two numbers is zero, then one or the other must be zero. In this case the number $e^{-(x^2+y^2)}$ can't be zero (because e^u is never zero), which gives the result claimed.

In the next example we first locate all critical points, and then classify each one as a relative maximum, minimum, saddle point, or none of these.

EXAMPLE 1 Locating and Classifying Critical Points

Locate all critical points of $f(x, y) = x^2y - x^2 - 2y^2$. Graph the function to classify the critical points as relative maxima, minima, saddle points, or none of these.

Solution The partial derivatives are

$$f_x = 2xy - 2x = 2x(y - 1)$$
$$f_y = x^2 - 4y.$$

Setting these equal to zero gives

$$x = 0 \text{ or } y = 1$$
$$x^2 = 4y.$$

We get a solution by choosing either $x = 0$ or $y = 1$ and substituting into $x^2 = 4y$.

Case 1: x = 0 Substituting into $x^2 = 4y$ gives $0 = 4y$ and hence $y = 0$. Thus, the critical point for this case is $(x, y) = (0, 0)$.

Case 2: y = 1 Substituting into $x^2 = 4y$ gives $x^2 = 4$ and hence $x = \pm 2$. Thus, we get two critical points for this case: $(2, 1)$ and $(-2, 1)$.

We now have three critical points altogether: $(0, 0)$, $(2, 1)$, and $(-2, 1)$. Because the domain of f is the whole Cartesian plane and the partial derivatives are defined at every point, these critical points are the only candidates for relative extrema and saddle points. We get the corresponding points on the graph by substituting for x and y in the equation for f to get the z-coordinates. The points are $(0, 0, 0)$, $(2, 1, -2)$, and $(-2, 1, -2)$.

ℹ️ *Classifying the Critical Points Graphically* To classify the critical points graphically, we look at the graph of f shown in Figure 20.

Examining the graph carefully, we see that the point $(0, 0, 0)$ is a relative maximum. As for the other two critical points, are they saddle points or are they relative maxima? They are relative maxima along the y-direction, but they are relative minima along the lines $y = \pm x$ (see the top edge of the picture, which shows a dip at $(-2, 1, 2)$) and so they are saddle points. If you don't believe this, we will get more evidence following and in a later example.

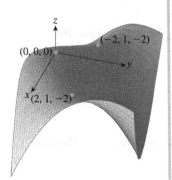

Figure 20

Ⅰ *Classifying the Critical Points Numerically*   We can use a tabular representation of the function to classify the critical points numerically. The following tabular representation of the function can be obtained using Excel. (See the Excel Technology Guide discussion of Section 15.1 Example 3 at the end of the chapter for information on using Excel to generate such a table.)

		$x \rightarrow$						
		−3	**−2**	**−1**	**0**	**1**	**2**	**3**
y	**−3**	−54	−34	−22	−18	−22	−34	−54
$\downarrow$	**−2**	−35	−20	−11	−8	−11	−20	−35
	−1	−20	−10	−4	−2	−4	−10	−20
	0	−9	−4	−1	0	−1	−4	−9
	1	−2	−2	−2	−2	−2	−2	−2
	2	1	−4	−7	−8	−7	−4	1
	3	0	−10	−16	−18	−16	−10	0

The shaded and colored cells show rectangular neighborhoods of the three critical points $(0, 0)$, $(2, 1)$, and $(−2, 1)$. (Notice that they overlap.) The values of f at the points are at the centers of these rectangles. Looking at the gray neighborhood of $(x, y) = (0, 0)$, we see that $f(0, 0) = 0$ is the largest value of f in the shaded cells, suggesting that f has a maximum at $(0, 0)$. The shaded neighborhood of $(2, 1)$ on the right shows $f(2, 1) = −2$ as the maximum along some slices (e.g., the vertical slice), and a minimum along the diagonal slice from top left to bottom right. This is what results in a saddle point on the graph. The point $(−2, 1)$ is similar, and thus f also has a saddle point at $(−2, 1)$.

Q : *Is there an algebraic way of deciding whether a given point is a relative maximum, relative minimum, or saddle point?*

A : There is a "second derivative test" for functions of two variables, stated as follows.

Second Derivative Test for Functions of Two Variables

Suppose (a, b) is a critical point in the interior of the domain of the function f of two variables. Let H be the quantity

$$H = f_{xx}(a, b) f_{yy}(a, b) - [f_{xy}(a, b)]^2. \qquad \text{\textit{H} is called the \textit{Hessian}.}$$

Then, if H is *positive*,

- f has a relative minimum at (a, b) if $f_{xx}(a, b) > 0$.
- f has a relative maximum at (a, b) if $f_{xx}(a, b) < 0$.

If H is *negative*,

- f has a saddle point at (a, b).

If $H = 0$, the test tells us nothing, so we need to look at the graph or a numerical table to see what is going on.

Quick Examples

1. Let $f(x, y) = x^2 - y^2$. Then

$$f_x = 2x \quad \text{and} \quad f_y = -2y,$$

which gives $(0, 0)$ as the only critical point. Also,

$$f_{xx} = 2, f_{xy} = 0, \quad \text{and} \quad f_{yy} = -2, \qquad \text{Note that these are constant.}$$

which gives $H = (2)(-2) - 0^2 = -2$. Because H is negative, we have a saddle point at $(0, 0)$.

2. Let $f(x, y) = x^2 + 2y^2 + 2xy + 4x$. Then

$$f_x = 2x + 2y + 4 \quad \text{and} \quad f_y = 2x + 4y.$$

Setting these equal to zero gives a system of two linear equations in two unknowns:

$$x + y = -2$$
$$x + 2y = 0.$$

This system has solution $(-4, 2)$, so this is our only critical point. The second partial derivatives are $f_{xx} = 2$, $f_{xy} = 2$, and $f_{yy} = 4$, so $H = (2)(4) - 2^2 = 4$. Because $H > 0$ and $f_{xx} > 0$, we have a relative minimum at $(-4, 2)$.

Note There is a second derivative test for functions of three or more variables, but it is considerably more complicated. We stick with functions of two variables for the most part in this book. The justification of the second derivative test is beyond the scope of this book. ∎

EXAMPLE 2 Using the Second Derivative Test

Use the second derivative test to analyze the function $f(x, y) = x^2 y - x^2 - 2y^2$ discussed in Example 1, and confirm the results we got there.

Solution We saw in Example 1 that the first-order derivatives are

$$f_x = 2xy - 2x = 2x(y - 1)$$
$$f_y = x^2 - 4y$$

and the critical points are $(0, 0)$, $(2, 1)$, and $(-2, 1)$. We also need the second derivatives:

$$f_{xx} = 2y - 2$$
$$f_{xy} = 2x$$
$$f_{yy} = -4.$$

The point (0, 0): $f_{xx}(0, 0) = -2$, $f_{xy}(0, 0) = 0$, $f_{yy}(0, 0) = -4$, so $H = 8$. Because $H > 0$ and $f_{xx}(0, 0) < 0$, the second derivative test tells us that f has a relative maximum at $(0, 0)$.

The point (2, 1): $f_{xx}(2, 1) = 0$, $f_{xy}(2, 1) = 4$ and $f_{yy}(2, 1) = -4$, so $H = -16$. Because $H < 0$, we know that f has a saddle point at $(2, 1)$.

The point (−2, 1): $f_{xx}(-2, 1) = 0$, $f_{xy}(-2, 1) = -4$ and $f_{yy}(-2, 1) = -4$, so once again $H = -16$, and f has a saddle point at $(-2, 1)$.

288

Deriving the Regression Formulas

Back in Section 1.4, we presented the following set of formulas for the **regression** or **best-fit** line associated with a given set of data points (x_1, y_1), (x_2, y_2), ..., (x_n, y_n).

Regression Line

The line that best fits the n data points (x_1, y_1), (x_2, y_2), ..., (x_n, y_n) has the form

$$y = mx + b$$

where

$$m = \frac{n\left(\sum xy\right) - \left(\sum x\right)\left(\sum y\right)}{n\left(\sum x^2\right) - \left(\sum x\right)^2}$$

$$b = \frac{\sum y - m\left(\sum x\right)}{n}$$

n = number of data points.

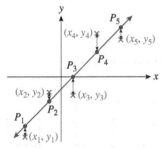

Figure 21

Derivation of the Regression Line Formulas

Recall that the regression line is defined to be the line that minimizes the sum of the squares of the **residuals**, measured by the vertical distances shown in Figure 21, which shows a regression line associated with $n = 5$ data points. In the figure, the points $P_1, \ldots, P_n$ on the regression line have coordinates $(x_1, mx_1 + b)$, $(x_2, mx_2 + b)$, ..., $(x_n, mx_n + b)$. The residuals are the quantities $y_{\text{Observed}} - y_{\text{Predicted}}$:

$$y_1 - (mx_1 + b), y_2 - (mx_2 + b), \ldots, y_n - (mx_n + b).$$

The sum of the squares of the residuals is therefore

$$S(m, b) = [y_1 - (mx_1 + b)]^2 + [y_2 - (mx_2 + b)]^2 + \cdots + [y_n - (mx_n + b)]^2$$

and this is the quantity we must minimize by choosing m and b. Because we reason that there is a line that minimizes this quantity, there must be a relative minimum at that point. We shall see in a moment that the function S has at most one critical point, which must therefore be the desired absolute minimum. To obtain the critical points of S, we set the partial derivatives equal to zero and solve:

$$S_m = 0: \qquad -2x_1[y_1 - (mx_1 + b)] - \cdots - 2x_n[y_n - (mx_n + b)] = 0$$
$$S_b = 0: \qquad -2[y_1 - (mx_1 + b)] - \cdots - 2[y_n - (mx_n + b)] = 0.$$

Dividing by -2 and gathering terms allows us to rewrite the equations as

$$m\left(x_1^2 + \cdots + x_n^2\right) + b(x_1 + \cdots + x_n) = x_1 y_1 + \cdots + x_n y_n$$
$$m(x_1 + \cdots + x_n) + nb \qquad\qquad = y_1 + \cdots + y_n.$$

We can rewrite these equations more neatly using $\sum$-notation:

$$m\left(\sum x^2\right) + b\left(\sum x\right) = \sum xy$$
$$m\left(\sum x\right) + nb \qquad = \sum y.$$

This is a system of two linear equations in the two unknowns m and b. It may or may not have a unique solution. When there is a unique solution, we can conclude that the best fit line is given by solving these two equations for m and b. Alternatively, there is a general formula for the solution of any system of two equations in two unknowns, and if we apply this formula to our two equations, we get the regression formulas above.

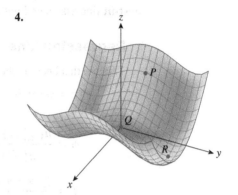

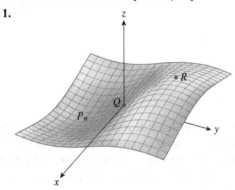

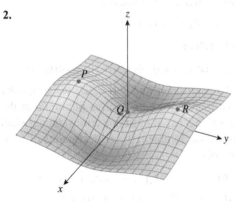

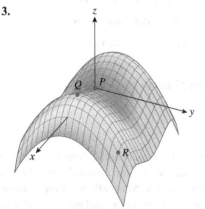

15.3 EXERCISES

▼ more advanced   ◆ challenging

🚹 indicates exercises that should be solved using technology

In Exercises 1–4, classify each labeled point on the graph as one of the following:

    a. a relative maximum

    b. a relative minimum

    c. a saddle point

    d. a critical point but neither a relative extremum nor a saddle point

    e. none of the above HINT [See Example 1.]

1.

2.

3.

4.

In Exercises 5–10, classify the shaded value in each table as one of the following:

    a. a relative maximum

    b. a relative minimum

    c. a saddle point

    d. neither a relative extremum nor a saddle point

5. $x \rightarrow$

$y \downarrow$	−3	−2	−1	0	1	2
−3	10	5	2	1	2	5
−2	9	4	1	0	1	4
−1	10	5	2	1	2	5
0	13	8	5	4	5	8
1	18	13	10	9	10	13
2	25	20	17	16	17	20
3	34	29	26	25	26	29

6. $x \rightarrow$

$y \downarrow$	−3	−2	−1	0	1	2
−3	5	0	−3	−4	−3	0
−2	8	3	0	−1	0	3
−1	9	4	1	0	1	4
0	8	3	0	−1	0	3
1	5	0	−3	−4	−3	0
2	0	−5	−8	−9	−8	−5
3	−7	−12	−15	−16	−15	−12

7.

$x \rightarrow$

$y \downarrow$		**-3**	**-2**	**-1**	**0**	**1**	**2**
	-3	5	0	-3	-4	-3	0
	-2	8	3	0	-1	0	3
	-1	9	4	1	0	1	4
	0	8	3	0	-1	0	3
	1	5	0	-3	-4	-3	0
	2	0	-5	-8	-9	-8	-5
	3	-7	-12	-15	-16	-15	-12

8.

$x \rightarrow$

$y \downarrow$		**-3**	**-2**	**-1**	**0**	**1**	**2**
	-3	2	3	2	-1	-6	-13
	-2	3	4	3	0	-5	-12
	-1	2	3	2	-1	-6	-13
	0	-1	0	-1	-4	-9	-16
	1	-6	-5	-6	-9	-14	-21
	2	-13	-12	-13	-16	-21	-28
	3	-22	-21	-22	-25	-30	-37

9.

$x \rightarrow$

$y \downarrow$		**-3**	**-2**	**-1**	**0**	**1**	**2**
	-3	4	5	4	1	-4	-11
	-2	3	4	3	0	-5	-12
	-1	4	5	4	1	-4	-11
	0	7	8	7	4	-1	-8
	1	12	13	12	9	4	-3
	2	19	20	19	16	11	4
	3	28	29	28	25	20	13

10.

$x \rightarrow$

$y \downarrow$		**-3**	**-2**	**-1**	**0**	**1**	**2**
	-3	100	101	100	97	92	85
	-2	99	100	99	96	91	84
	-1	98	99	98	95	90	83
	0	91	92	91	88	83	76
	1	72	73	72	69	64	57
	2	35	36	35	32	27	20
	3	-26	-25	-26	-29	-34	-41

Locate and classify all the critical points of the functions in Exercises 11–36. HINT [See Example 2.]

11. $f(x, y) = x^2 + y^2 + 1$

12. $f(x, y) = 4 - (x^2 + y^2)$

13. $g(x, y) = 1 - x^2 - x - y^2 + y$

14. $g(x, y) = x^2 + x + y^2 - y - 1$

15. $k(x, y) = x^2 - 3xy + y^2$

16. $k(x, y) = x^2 - xy + 2y^2$

17. $f(x, y) = x^2 + 2xy + 2y^2 - 2x + 4y$

18. $f(x, y) = x^2 + xy - y^2 + 3x - y$

19. $g(x, y) = -x^2 - 2xy - 3y^2 - 3x - 2y$

20. $g(x, y) = -x^2 - 2xy + y^2 + x - 4y$

21. $h(x, y) = x^2 y - 2x^2 - 4y^2$

22. $h(x, y) = x^2 + y^2 - y^2 x - 4$

23. $f(x, y) = x^2 + 2xy^2 + 2y^2$

24. $f(x, y) = x^2 + x^2 y + y^2$

25. $s(x, y) = e^{x^2 + y^2}$ **26.** $s(x, y) = e^{-(x^2 + y^2)}$

27. $t(x, y) = x^4 + 8xy^2 + 2y^4$ **28.** $t(x, y) = x^3 - 3xy + y^3$

29. $f(x, y) = x^2 + y - e^y$ **30.** $f(x, y) = xe^y$

31. $f(x, y) = e^{-(x^2 + y^2 + 2x)}$ **32.** $f(x, y) = e^{-(x^2 + y^2 - 2x)}$

33. ▼ $f(x, y) = xy + \dfrac{2}{x} + \dfrac{2}{y}$ **34.** ▼ $f(x, y) = xy + \dfrac{4}{x} + \dfrac{2}{y}$

35. ▼ $g(x, y) = x^2 + y^2 + \dfrac{2}{xy}$ **36.** ▼ $g(x, y) = x^3 + y^3 + \dfrac{3}{xy}$

37. ▼ Refer back to Exercise 11. Which (if any) of the critical points of $f(x, y) = x^2 + y^2 + 1$ are absolute extrema?

38. ▼ Refer back to Exercise 12. Which (if any) of the critical points of $f(x, y) = 4 - (x^2 + y^2)$ are absolute extrema?

39. ⬛▼ Refer back to Exercise 21. Which (if any) of the critical points of $h(x, y) = x^2 y - 2x^2 - 4y^2$ are absolute extrema?

40. ⬛▼ Refer back to Exercise 22. Which (if any) of the critical points of $h(x, y) = x^2 + y^2 - y^2 x - 4$ are absolute extrema?

APPLICATIONS

41. *Brand Loyalty* Suppose the fraction of **Mazda** car owners who chose another new **Mazda** can be modeled by the following function:[23]

$$M(c, f) = 11 + 8c + 4c^2 - 40f - 20cf + 40f^2$$

where c is the fraction of **Chrysler** car owners who remained loyal to **Chrysler** and f is the fraction of **Ford** car owners

---

[23] This model is not accurate, although it was inspired by an approximation of a second order regression based on data from the period 1988–1995. Source for original data: Chrysler, Maritz Market Research, Consumer Attitude Research, and Strategic Vision/*The New York Times*, November 3, 1995, p. D2.

remaining loyal to **Ford**. Locate and classify all the critical points and interpret your answer. HINT [See Example 2.]

42. *Brand Loyalty* Repeat the preceding exercise using the function:

$$M(c, f) = -10 - 8f - 4f^2 + 40c + 20fc - 40c^2$$

HINT [See Example 2.]

43. ▼ *Pollution Control* The cost of controlling emissions at a firm goes up rapidly as the amount of emissions reduced goes up. Here is a possible model:

$$C(x, y) = 4,000 + 100x^2 + 50y^2$$

where x is the reduction in sulfur emissions, y is the reduction in lead emissions (in pounds of pollutant per day), and C is the daily cost to the firm (in dollars) of this reduction. Government clean-air subsidies amount to $500 per pound of sulfur and $100 per pound of lead removed. How many pounds of pollutant should the firm remove each day in order to minimize *net* cost (cost minus subsidy)?

44. ▼ *Pollution Control* Repeat the preceding exercise using the following information:

$$C(x, y) = 2,000 + 200x^2 + 100y^2$$

with government subsidies amounting to $100 per pound of sulfur and $500 per pound of lead removed per day.

45. ▼ *Revenue* Your company manufactures two models of speakers, the Ultra Mini and the Big Stack. Demand for each depends partly on the price of the other. If one is expensive, then more people will buy the other. If p_1 is the price of the Ultra Mini, and p_2 is the price of the Big Stack, demand for the Ultra Mini is given by

$$q_1(p_1, p_2) = 100,000 - 100p_1 + 10p_2$$

where q_1 represents the number of Ultra Minis that will be sold in a year. The demand for the Big Stack is given by

$$q_2(p_1, p_2) = 150,000 + 10p_1 - 100p_2.$$

Find the prices for the Ultra Mini and the Big Stack that will maximize your total revenue.

46. ▼ *Revenue* Repeat the preceding exercise, using the following demand functions:

$$q_1(p_1, p_2) = 100,000 - 100p_1 + p_2$$
$$q_2(p_1, p_2) = 150,000 + p_1 - 100p_2.$$

47. ▼ *Luggage Dimensions: American Airlines* American Airlines requires that the total outside dimensions (length + width + height) of a checked bag not exceed 62 inches.[24] What are the dimensions of the largest volume bag that you can check on an American flight?

48. ▼ *Carry-on Bag Dimensions: American Airlines* American Airlines requires that the total outside dimensions (length + width + height) of a carry-on bag not exceed 45 inches.[25] What are the dimensions of the largest volume bag that you can carry on an American flight?

49. ▼ *Package Dimensions: USPS* The U.S. Postal Service (USPS) will accept only packages with a length plus girth no more than 108 inches.[26] (See the figure.)

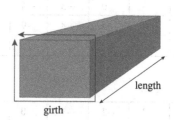

What are the dimensions of the largest volume package that the **USPS** will accept? What is its volume?

50. ▼ *Package Dimensions: UPS* United Parcel Service (UPS) will accept only packages with length no more than 108 inches and length plus girth no more than 165 inches.[27] (See figure for the preceding exercise.) What are the dimensions of the largest volume package that UPS will accept? What is its volume?

COMMUNICATION AND REASONING EXERCISES

51. Sketch the graph of a function that has one extremum and no saddle points.

52. Sketch the graph of a function that has one saddle point and one extremum.

53. ▼ Sketch the graph of a function that has one relative extremum, no absolute extrema, and no saddle points.

54. ▼ Sketch the graph of a function that has infinitely many absolute maxima.

55. Let $H = f_{xx}(a, b)f_{yy}(a, b) - f_{xy}(a, b)^2$. What condition on H guarantees that f has a relative extremum at the point (a, b)?

56. Let H be as in the preceding exercise. Give an example to show that it is possible to have $H = 0$ and a relative minimum at (a, b).

57. ▼ Suppose that when the graph of $f(x, y)$ is sliced by a vertical plane through (a, b) parallel to either the xz-plane or the yz-plane, the resulting curve has a relative maximum at (a, b). Does this mean that f has a relative maximum at (a, b)? Explain your answer.

[24] According to information on its Web site (www.aa.com).

[25] Ibid.

[26] The requirement for packages sent other than Parcel Post, as of September 2008 (www.usps.com).

[27] The requirement as of September 2008 (www.ups.com).

58. ▽ Suppose that f has a relative maximum at (a, b). Does it follow that, if the graph of f is sliced by a vertical plane parallel to either the xz-plane or the yz-plane, the resulting curve has a relative maximum at (a, b)? Explain your answer.

59. ▽ *Average Cost* Let $C(x, y)$ be any cost function. Show that when the average cost is minimized, the marginal costs C_x and C_y both equal the average cost. Explain why this is reasonable.

60. ▽ *Average Profit* Let $P(x, y)$ be any profit function. Show that when the average profit is maximized, the marginal

profits P_x and P_y both equal the average profit. Explain why this is reasonable.

61. ◆ The tangent plane to a graph was introduced in Exercise 76 in the preceding section. Use the equation of the tangent plane given there to explain why the tangent plane is parallel to the xy-plane at a relative maximum or minimum of $f(x, y)$.

62. ◆ Use the equation of the tangent plane given in Exercise 76 in the preceding section to explain why the tangent plane is parallel to the xy-plane at a saddle point of $f(x, y)$.

15.4 Constrained Maxima and Minima and Applications

So far we have looked only at the relative extrema of functions with no constraints. However, in Section 12.2 we saw examples in which we needed to find the maximum or minimum of an objective function subject to one or more constraints on the independent variables. For instance, consider the following problem:

$$\text{Minimize } S = xy + 2xz + 2yz \quad \text{subject to } xyz = 4 \text{ with } x > 0, \, y > 0, \, z > 0.$$

One strategy for solving such problems is essentially the same as the strategy we used earlier: Solve the constraint equation for one of the variables, substitute into the objective function, and then optimize the resulting function using the methods of the preceding section. We will call this the *substitution method.* An alternative method, called the *method of Lagrange multipliers*, is useful when it is difficult or impossible to solve the constraint equation for one of the variables, and even when it is possible to do so.

Substitution Method

EXAMPLE 1 **Using Substitution**

Minimize $S = xy + 2xz + 2yz$ subject to $xyz = 4$ with $x > 0$, $y > 0$, $z > 0$.

Solution As suggested in the above discussion, we proceed as follows:

Solve the constraint equation for one of the variables and then substitute in the objective function. The constraint equation is $xyz = 4$. Solving for z gives

$$z = \frac{4}{xy}.$$

The objective function is $S = xy + 2xz + 2yz$, so substituting $z = 4/xy$ gives

$$S = xy + 2x\frac{4}{xy} + 2y\frac{4}{xy}$$

$$= xy + \frac{8}{y} + \frac{8}{x}.$$

Minimize the resulting function of two variables. We use the method in Section 15.4 to find the minimum of $S = xy + \dfrac{8}{y} + \dfrac{8}{x}$ for $x > 0$ and $y > 0$. We look for critical points:

$$S_x = y - \frac{8}{x^2} \qquad S_y = x - \frac{8}{y^2}$$

$$S_{xx} = \frac{16}{x^3} \qquad S_{xy} = 1 \qquad S_{yy} = \frac{16}{y^3}.$$

We now equate the first partial derivatives to zero:

$$y = \frac{8}{x^2} \qquad \text{and} \qquad x = \frac{8}{y^2}.$$

To solve for x and y, we substitute the first of these equations in the second, getting

$$x = \frac{x^4}{8}$$

$$x^4 - 8x = 0$$

$$x(x^3 - 8) = 0.$$

The two solutions are $x = 0$, which we reject because x cannot be zero, and $x = 2$. Substituting $x = 2$ in $y = 8/x^2$ gives $y = 2$ also. Thus, the only critical point is $(2, 2)$. To apply the second derivative test, we compute

$$S_{xx}(2, 2) = 2 \qquad S_{xy}(2, 2) = 1 \qquad S_{yy}(2, 2) = 2$$

and find that $H = 3 > 0$, so we have a relative minimum at $(2, 2)$.

The corresponding value of z is given by the constraint equation:

$$z = \frac{4}{xy} = \frac{4}{4} = 1.$$

The corresponding value of the objective function is

$$S = xy + \frac{8}{y} + \frac{8}{x} = 4 + \frac{8}{2} + \frac{8}{2} = 12.$$

Figure 22 shows a portion of the graph of $S = xy + \dfrac{8}{y} + \dfrac{8}{x}$ for positive x and y (drawn using the Excel Surface Grapher in the Chapter 15 utilities at the Web site), and suggests that there is a single absolute minimum, which must be at our only candidate point $(2, 2)$.

We conclude that the minimum of S is 12 and occurs at $(2, 2, 1)$.

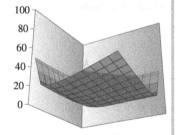

Graph of $S = xy + \dfrac{8}{y} + \dfrac{8}{x}$

$(0.2 \le x \le 5, 0.2 \le y \le 5)$

Figure 22

The Method of Lagrange Multipliers

As we mentioned above, the method of Lagrange multipliers has the advantage that it can be used in constrained optimization problems when it is difficult or impossible to solve a constraint equation for one of the variables. We restrict attention to the case of a single constraint equation, although the method also generalizes to any number of constraint equations.

Locating Relative Extrema Using the Method of Lagrange Multipliers

To locate the candidates for relative extrema of a function $f(x, y, \ldots)$ subject to the constraint $g(x, y, \ldots) = 0$:

1. Construct the **Lagrangian function**

$$L(x, y, \ldots) = f(x, y, \ldots) - \lambda g(x, y, \ldots)$$

where λ is a new unknown called a **Lagrange multiplier.**

2. The candidates for the relative extrema occur at the critical points of $L(x, y, \ldots)$. To find them, set all the partial derivatives of $L(x, y, \ldots)$ equal to zero and solve the resulting system, together with the constraint equation $g(x, y, \ldots) = 0$, for the unknowns $x, y, \ldots$ and λ.

The points $(x, y, \ldots)$ that occur in solutions are then the candidates for the relative extrema of f subject to $g = 0$.

Although the justification for the method of Lagrange multipliers is beyond the scope of this text (a derivation can be found in many vector calculus textbooks), we will demonstrate by example how it is used.

EXAMPLE 2 Using Lagrange Multipliers

Use the method of Lagrange multipliers to find the maximum value of $f(x, y) = 2xy$ subject to $x^2 + 4y^2 = 32$.

Solution We start by rewriting the problem with the constraint in the form $g(x, y) = 0$:

Maximize $f(x, y) = 2xy$ subject to $x^2 + 4y^2 - 32 = 0$.

Here, $g(x, y) = x^2 + 4y^2 - 32$, and the Lagrangian function is

$$\begin{aligned} L(x, y) &= f(x, y) - \lambda g(x, y) \\ &= 2xy - \lambda(x^2 + 4y^2 - 32). \end{aligned}$$

The system of equations we need to solve is thus

$$\begin{aligned} L_x = 0: &\quad 2y - 2\lambda x = 0 \\ L_y = 0: &\quad 2x - 8\lambda y = 0 \\ g = 0: &\quad x^2 + 4y^2 - 32 = 0. \end{aligned}$$

It is often convenient to solve such a system by first solving one of the equations for λ and then substituting in the remaining equations. Thus, we start by solving the first equation to obtain

$$\lambda = \frac{y}{x}.$$

(A word of caution: Because we divided by x, we made the implicit assumption that $x \neq 0$, so before continuing we should check what happens if $x = 0$. But if $x = 0$, then the first equation, $2y = 2\lambda x$, tells us that $y = 0$ as well, and this contradicts the third equation: $x^2 + 4y^2 - 32 = 0$. Thus, we can rule out the possibility that $x = 0$.) Substituting the value of λ in the second equation gives

$$2x - 8\left(\frac{y}{x}\right)y = 0 \quad \text{or} \quad x^2 = 4y^2.$$

We can now substitute $x^2 = 4y^2$ in the constraint equation, obtaining

$$4y^2 + 4y^2 - 32 = 0$$
$$8y^2 = 32$$
$$y = \pm 2.$$

We now substitute back to obtain

$$x^2 = 4y^2 = 16,$$
$$\text{or} \qquad x = \pm 4.$$

We don't need the value of λ, so we won't solve for it. Thus, the candidates for relative extrema are given by $x = \pm 4$ and $y = \pm 2$, that is, the four points $(-4, -2)$, $(-4, 2)$, $(4, -2)$, and $(4, 2)$. Recall that we are seeking the values of x and y that give the maximum value for $f(x, y) = 2xy$. Because we now have only four points to choose from, we compare the values of f at these four points and conclude that the maximum value of f occurs when $(x, y) = (-4, -2)$ or $(4, 2)$.

Something is suspicious in Example 2. We didn't check to see whether these candidates were relative extrema to begin with, let alone absolute extrema! How do we justify this omission? One of the difficulties with using the method of Lagrange multipliers is that it does not provide us with a test analogous to the second derivative test for functions of several variables. However, if you grant that the function in question does have an absolute maximum, then we require no test, because one of the candidates must give this maximum.

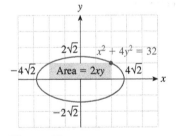

Figure 23

Q : *But how do we know that the given function has an absolute maximum?*

A : The best way to see this is by giving a geometric interpretation. The constraint $x^2 + 4y^2 = 32$ tells us that the point (x, y) must lie on the ellipse shown in Figure 23. The function $f(x, y) = 2xy$ gives the area of the rectangle shaded in Figure 23. There must be a largest such rectangle, because the area varies continuously from 0 when (x, y) is on the x-axis, to positive when (x, y) is in the first quadrant, to 0 again when (x, y) is on the y-axis, so f must have an absolute maximum for at least one pair of coordinates (x, y).

We now show how to use Lagrange multipliers to solve the minimization problem in Example 1:

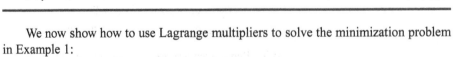

EXAMPLE 3 Using Lagrange Multipliers: Function of Three Variables

Use the method of Lagrange multipliers to find the minimum value of $S = xy + 2xz + 2yz$ subject to $xyz = 4$ with $x > 0$, $y > 0$, $z > 0$.

Solution We start by rewriting the problem in standard form:

Maximize $f(x, y, z) = xy + 2xz + 2yz$

subject to $xyz - 4 = 0$ (with $x > 0$, $y > 0$, $z > 0$).

Here, $g(x, y, z) = xyz - 4$, and the Lagrangian function is

$$L(x, y, z) = f(x, y, z) - \lambda g(x, y, z)$$
$$= xy + 2xz + 2yz - \lambda(xyz - 4).$$

The system of equations we need to solve is thus

$$\begin{aligned} L_x = 0: & \quad y + 2z - \lambda yz = 0 \\ L_y = 0: & \quad x + 2z - \lambda xz = 0 \\ L_z = 0: & \quad 2x + 2y - \lambda xy = 0 \\ g = 0: & \quad xyz - 4 = 0. \end{aligned}$$

As in the last example, we solve one of the equations for λ and substitute in the others. The first equation gives

$$\lambda = \frac{1}{z} + \frac{2}{y}.$$

Substituting this into the second equation gives

$$x + 2z = x + \frac{2xz}{y}$$

or

$$2 = \frac{2x}{y}, \qquad \text{Subtract } x \text{ from both sides and then divide by } z.$$

giving

$$y = x.$$

Substituting the expression for λ into the third equation gives

$$2x + 2y = \frac{xy}{z} + 2x$$

or

$$2 = \frac{x}{z}, \qquad \text{Subtract } 2x \text{ from both sides and then divide by } y.$$

giving

$$z = \frac{x}{2}.$$

Now we have both y and z in terms of x. We substitute these values in the last (constraint) equation:

$$x(x)\left(\frac{x}{2}\right) - 4 = 0$$
$$x^3 = 8$$
$$x = 2.$$

Thus, $y = x = 2$, and $z = \frac{x}{2} = 1$. Therefore, the only critical point occurs at $(2, 2, 1)$ as we found in Example 1, and the corresponding value of S is

$$S = xy + 2xz + 2yz = (2)(2) + 2(2)(1) + 2(2)(1) = 12.$$

➡ **Before we go on...** Again, the method of Lagrange multipliers does not tell us whether the critical point in Example 3 is a maximum, minimum, or neither. However, if you grant that the function in question does have an absolute minimum, then the values we found must give this minimum value. ■

APPLICATIONS

EXAMPLE 4 **Minimizing Area**

Find the dimensions of an open-top rectangular box that has a volume of 4 cubic feet and the smallest possible surface area.

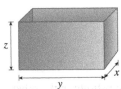

Figure 24

Solution Our first task is to rephrase this request as a mathematical optimization problem. Figure 24 shows a picture of the box with dimensions x, y, and z. We want to minimize the total surface area, which is given by

$$S = xy + 2xz + 2yz. \qquad \text{Base + Sides + Front and Back}$$

This is our objective function. We can't simply choose x, y, and z to all be zero, however, because the enclosed volume must be 4 cubic feet. So,

$$xyz = 4. \qquad \text{Constraint}$$

This is our constraint equation. Other unstated constraints are $x > 0$, $y > 0$, and $z > 0$, because the dimensions of the box must be positive. We now restate the problem as follows:

Minimize $S = xy + 2xz + 2yz$ subject to $xyz = 4$, $x > 0$, $y > 0$, $z > 0$.

But this is exactly the problem in Examples 1 and 3, and has a solution $x = 2$, $y = 2$, $z = 1$, $S = 12$. Thus, the required dimensions of the box are

$$x = 2 \text{ ft}, y = 2 \text{ ft}, z = 1 \text{ ft},$$

requiring a total surface area of 12 ft^2.

Q: *In Example 1 we checked that we had a relative minimum at* $(x, y) = (2, 2)$ *and we were persuaded graphically that this was probably an absolute minimum. Can we be sure that this relative minimum is an absolute minimum?*

A: Yes. There must be a least surface area among all boxes that hold 4 cubic feet. (Why?) Because this would give a relative minimum of S and because the only possible relative minimum of S occurs at (2, 2), this is the absolute minimum.

EXAMPLE 5 **Maximizing productivity**

An electric motor manufacturer uses workers and robots on its assembly line, and has a Cobb-Douglas productivity function[*] of the form

$$P(x, y) = 10x^{0.2}y^{0.8} \text{ motors manufactured per day}$$

***NOTE** Cobb-Douglas production formulas were discussed in Section 11.6.

Fredrik Persson/AP Photo

where x is the number of assembly-line workers and y is the number of robots. Daily operating costs amount to \$100 per worker and \$16 per robot. How many workers and robots should be used to maximize productivity if the manufacturer has a daily budget of \$4,000?

Solution Our objective function is the productivity $P(x, y)$, and the constraint is

$$100x + 16y = 4,000.$$

So, the optimization problem is:

Maximize $P(x, y) = 10x^{0.2}y^{0.8}$ subject to $100x + 16y = 4{,}000$ ($x \geq 0$, $y \geq 0$).

Here, $g(x, y) = 100x + 16y - 4{,}000$, and the Lagrangian function is

$$L(x, y) = P(x, y) - \lambda g(x, y)$$
$$= 10x^{0.2}y^{0.8} - \lambda(100x + 16y - 4{,}000).$$

The system of equations we need to solve is thus

$$L_x = 0: \quad 2x^{-0.8}y^{0.8} - 100\lambda = 0$$
$$L_y = 0: \quad 8x^{0.2}y^{-0.2} - 16\lambda = 0$$
$$g = 0: \quad 100x + 16y = 4{,}000.$$

We can rewrite the first two equations as:

$$2\left(\frac{y}{x}\right)^{0.8} = 100\lambda \qquad 8\left(\frac{x}{y}\right)^{0.2} = 16\lambda.$$

Dividing the first by the second to eliminate λ gives

$$\frac{1}{4}\left(\frac{y}{x}\right)^{0.8}\left(\frac{y}{x}\right)^{0.2} = \frac{100}{16}$$

that is,
$$\frac{1}{4}\frac{y}{x} = \frac{25}{4},$$

giving
$$y = 25x.$$

Substituting this result into the constraint equation gives

$$100x + 16(25x) = 4{,}000$$
$$500x = 4{,}000$$

so $\quad x = 8$ workers, $\quad y = 25x = 200$ robots

for a productivity of

$$P(8, 200) = 10(8)^{0.2}(200)^{0.8} \approx 1{,}051 \text{ motors manufactured per day.}$$

FAQ

When to Use Lagrange Multipliers

Q: *When can I use the method of Lagrange multipliers? When should I use it?*

A: We have discussed the method only when there is a single equality constraint. There is a generalization, which we have not discussed, that works when there are more equality constraints (we need to introduce one multiplier for each constraint). So, if you have a problem with more than one equality constraint, or with any inequality constraints, you must use the substitution method. On the other hand, if you have one equality constraint, and it would be difficult to solve it for one of the variables, then you should use Lagrange multipliers.

15.4 EXERCISES

▼ more advanced   ◆ challenging
🅣 indicates exercises that should be solved using technology

In Exercises 1–6, solve the given optimization problem by using substitution. HINT [See Example 1.]

1. Find the maximum value of $f(x, y, z) = 1 - x^2 - y^2 - z^2$ subject to $z = 2y$. Also find the corresponding point(s) (x, y, z).

2. Find the minimum value of $f(x, y, z) = x^2 + y^2 + z^2 - 2$ subject to $x = y$. Also find the corresponding point(s) (x, y, z).

3. Find the maximum value of $f(x, y, z) = 1 - x^2 - x - y^2 + y - z^2 + z$ subject to $3x = y$. Also find the corresponding point(s) (x, y, z).

4. Find the maximum value of $f(x, y, z) = 2x^2 + 2x + y^2 - y + z^2 - z - 1$ subject to $z = 2y$. Also find the corresponding point(s) (x, y, z).

5. Minimize $S = xy + 4xz + 2yz$ subject to $xyz = 1$ with $x > 0$, $y > 0$, $z > 0$.

6. Minimize $S = xy + xz + yz$ subject to $xyz = 2$ with $x > 0$, $y > 0$, $z > 0$.

In Exercises 7–18, use Lagrange multipliers to solve the given optimization problem. HINT [See Example 2.]

7. Find the maximum value of $f(x, y) = xy$ subject to $x + 2y = 40$. Also find the corresponding point(s) (x, y).

8. Find the maximum value of $f(x, y) = xy$ subject to $3x + y = 60$. Also find the corresponding point(s) (x, y).

9. Find the maximum value of $f(x, y) = 4xy$ subject to $x^2 + y^2 = 8$. Also find the corresponding point(s) (x, y).

10. Find the maximum value of $f(x, y) = xy$ subject to $y = 3 - x^2$. Also find the corresponding point(s) (x, y).

11. Find the minimum value of $f(x, y) = x^2 + y^2$ subject to $x + 2y = 10$. Also find the corresponding point(s) (x, y).

12. Find the minimum value of $f(x, y) = x^2 + y^2$ subject to $xy^2 = 16$. Also find the corresponding point(s) (x, y).

13. The problem in Exercise 1. HINT [See Example 3.]

14. The problem in Exercise 2. HINT [See Example 3.]

15. The problem in Exercise 3.

16. The problem in Exercise 4.

17. The problem in Exercise 5.

18. The problem in Exercise 6.

APPLICATIONS

Exercises 19–22 were solved in Section 12.2. This time, use the method of Lagrange multipliers to solve them.

19. **Fences** I want to fence in a rectangular vegetable patch. The fencing for the east and west sides costs $4 per foot, and the fencing for the north and south sides costs only $2 per foot.

I have a budget of $80 for the project. What is the largest area I can enclose?

20. **Fences** My orchid garden abuts my house so that the house itself forms the northern boundary. The fencing for the southern boundary costs $4 per foot, and the fencing for the east and west sides costs $2 per foot. If I have a budget of $80 for the project, what is the largest area I can enclose?

21. **Revenue** Hercules Films is deciding on the price of the video release of its film *Son of Frankenstein*. Its marketing people estimate that at a price of p dollars, it can sell a total of $q = 200{,}000 - 10{,}000p$ copies. What price will bring in the greatest revenue?

22. **Profit** Hercules Films is also deciding on the price of the video release of its film *Bride of the Son of Frankenstein*. Again, marketing estimates that at a price of p dollars it can sell $q = 200{,}000 - 10{,}000p$ copies, but each copy costs $4 to make. What price will give the greatest *profit*?

23. **Geometry** At what points on the sphere $x^2 + y^2 + z^2 = 1$ is the product xyz a maximum? (The method of Lagrange multipliers can be used.)

24. **Geometry** At what point on the surface $z = (x^2 + x + y^2 + 4)^{1/2}$ is the quantity $x^2 + y^2 + z^2$ a minimum? (The method of Lagrange multipliers can be used.)

25. ▼ **Geometry** What point on the surface $z = x^2 + y - 1$ is closest to the origin? HINT [Minimize the square of the distance from (x, y, z) to the origin.]

26. ▼ **Geometry** What point on the surface $z = x + y^2 - 3$ is closest to the origin? HINT [Minimize the square of the distance from (x, y, z) to the origin.]

27. ▼ **Geometry** Find the point on the plane $-2x + 2y + z - 5 = 0$ closest to $(-1, 1, 3)$. HINT [Minimize the square of the distance from the given point to a general point on the plane.]

28. ▼ **Geometry** Find the point on the plane $2x - 2y - z + 1 = 0$ closest to $(1, 1, 0)$.

29. **Construction Cost** A closed rectangular box is made with two kinds of materials. The top and bottom are made with heavy-duty cardboard costing 20¢ per square foot, and the sides are made with lightweight cardboard costing 10¢ per square foot. Given that the box is to have a capacity of 2 cubic feet, what should its dimensions be if the cost is to be minimized? HINT [See Example 4.]

30. **Construction Cost** Repeat the preceding exercise assuming that the heavy-duty cardboard costs 30¢ per square foot, the lightweight cardboard costs 5¢ per square foot, and the box is to have a capacity of 6 cubic feet. HINT [See Example 4.]

31. **Package Dimensions: USPS** The U.S. Postal Service (USPS) will accept only packages with a length plus girth no more than 108 inches.[28] (See the figure.)

---

[28] The requirement for packages sent other than Parcel Post, as of September 2008 (www.usps.com).

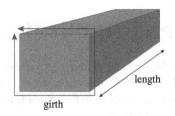

length

girth

What are the dimensions of the largest volume package that the **USPS** will accept? What is its volume? (This exercise is the same as Exercise 49 in the preceding section. This time, solve it using Lagrange multipliers.)

32. *Package Dimensions: UPS* **United Parcel Service** (**UPS**) will accept only packages with length no more than 108 inches and length plus girth no more than 165 inches.[29] (See figure for the preceding exercise.) What are the dimensions of the largest volume package that **UPS** will accept? What is its volume? (This exercise is the same as Exercise 50 in the preceding section. This time, solve it using Lagrange multipliers.)

33. ▼ *Construction Cost* My company wishes to manufacture boxes similar to those described in Exercise 29 as cheaply as possible, but unfortunately the company that manufactures the cardboard is unable to give me price quotes for the heavy-duty and lightweight cardboard. Find formulas for the dimensions of the box in terms of the price per square foot of heavy-duty and lightweight cardboard.

34. ▼ *Construction Cost* Repeat the preceding exercise, assuming that only the bottoms of the boxes are to be made using heavy-duty cardboard.

35. ▼ *Geometry* Find the dimensions of the rectangular box with largest volume that can be inscribed above the xy-plane and under the paraboloid $z = 1 - (x^2 + y^2)$.

36. ▼ *Geometry* Find the dimensions of the rectangular box with largest volume that can be inscribed above the xy-plane and under the paraboloid $z = 2 - (2x^2 + y^2)$.

37. *Productivity* The Gym Shirt Company manufactures cotton socks. Production is partially automated through the use of robots. Daily operating costs amount to $150 per laborer and $60 per robot. The number of pairs of socks the company can manufacture in a day is given by a Cobb-Douglas production formula

$$q = 50n^{0.6}r^{0.4}$$

where q is the number of pairs of socks that can be manufactured by n laborers and r robots. Assuming that the company has a daily operating budget of $1,500 and wishes to maximize productivity, how many laborers and how many robots should it use? What is the productivity at these levels? HINT [See Example 5.]

29 The requirement as of September 2008 (www.ups.com).

38. *Productivity* Your automobile assembly plant has a Cobb-Douglas production function given by

$$q = 100x^{0.3}y^{0.7}$$

where q is the number of automobiles it produces per year, x is the number of employees, and y is the monthly assembly-line budget (in thousands of dollars). Annual operating costs amount to an average of $60 thousand per employee plus the operating budget of $12y$ thousand. Your annual budget is $1,200,000. How many employees should you hire and what should your assembly-line budget be to maximize productivity? What is the productivity at these levels?

COMMUNICATION AND REASONING EXERCISES

39. Outline two methods of solution of the problem "*Maximize $f(x, y, z)$ subject to $g(x, y, z) = 0$*" and give an advantage and disadvantage of each.

40. Suppose we know that $f(x, y)$ has both partial derivatives in its domain $D: x > 0$, $y > 0$, and that (a, b) is the only point in D such that $f_x(a, b) = f_y(a, b) = 0$. Must it be the case that, if f has an absolute maximum, it occurs at (a, b)? Explain.

41. Under what circumstances would it be necessary to use the method of Lagrange multipliers?

42. Under what circumstances would the method of Lagrange multipliers not apply?

43. Restate the following problem as a maximization problem of the form *Maximize $f(x, y)$ subject to $g(x, y) = 0$*":

Find the maximum value of $h(x) = 1 - 2x^2$.

44. Restate the following problem as a maximization problem of the form *Maximize $f(x, y, z)$ subject to $g(x, y, z) = 0$*":

Find the maximum value of $h(x, y) = 1 - 2(x^2 + y^2)$.

45. ▼ If the partial derivatives of a function of several variables are never 0, is it possible for the function to have relative extrema on some domain? Explain your answer.

46. ◆ A **linear programming problem in two variables** is a problem of the form: *Maximize (or minimize) $f(x, y)$ subject to constraints of the form $C(x, y) \geq 0$ or $C(x, y) \leq 0$*. Here, the objective function f and the constraints C are linear functions. There may be several linear constraints in one problem. Explain why the solution cannot occur in the interior of the domain of f.

47. ◆ Refer back to Exercise 46. Explain why the solution will actually be at a corner of the domain of f (where two or more of the line segments that make up the boundary meet). This result—or rather a slight generalization of it—is known as the Fundamental Theorem of Linear Programming.

15.5 Double Integrals and Applications

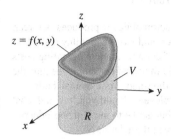

Figure 25

When discussing functions of one variable, we computed the area under a graph by integration. The analog for the graph of a function of two variables is the *volume V* under the graph, as in Figure 25. Think of the region R in the xy-plane as the "shadow" under the portion of the surface $z = f(x, y)$ shown.

By analogy with the definite integral of a function of one variable, we make the following definition:

Geometric Definition of the Double Integral

The **double integral of $f(x, y)$ over the region R in the xy-plane** is defined as

(Volume *above* the region R and under the graph of f)

$-$ (Volume *below* the region R and above the graph of f)

We denote the double integral of $f(x, y)$ over the region R by $\iint_R f(x, y)\, dx\, dy$.

Quick Example

Take $f(x, y) = 2$ and take R to be the rectangle $0 \le x \le 1$, $0 \le y \le 1$. Then the graph of f is a flat horizontal surface $z = 2$, and

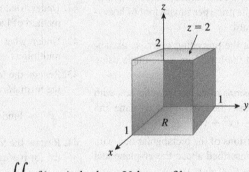

$$\iint_R f(x, y)\, dx\, dy = \text{Volume of box}$$
$$= \text{Width} \times \text{Length} \times \text{Height} = 1 \times 1 \times 2 = 2.$$

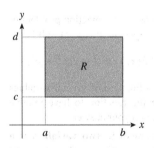

Figure 26

As we saw in the case of the definite integral of a function of one variable, we also desire *numerical* and *algebraic* definitions for two reasons: (1) to make the mathematical definition more precise, so as not to rely on the notion of "volume," and (2) for direct computation of the integral using technology or analytical tools.

We start with the simplest case, when the region R is a rectangle $a \le x \le b$ and $c \le y \le d$. (See Figure 26.) To compute the volume over R, we mimic what we did to find the area under the graph of a function of one variable. We break up the interval $[a, b]$ into m intervals all of width $\Delta x = (b - a)/m$, and we break up $[c, d]$ into n intervals all of width $\Delta y = (d - c)/n$. Figure 27 shows an example with $m = 4$ and $n = 5$.

This gives us mn rectangles defined by $x_{i-1} \le x \le x_i$ and $y_{j-1} \le y \le y_j$. Over one of these rectangles, f is approximately equal to its value at one corner—say $f(x_i, y_j)$. The volume under f over this small rectangle is then approximately the volume of the

Figure 27

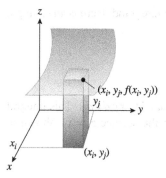

Figure 28

rectangular brick (size exaggerated) shown in Figure 28. This brick has height $f(x_i, y_j)$, and its base is Δx by Δy. Its volume is therefore $f(x_i, y_j) \Delta x \, \Delta y$. Adding together the volumes of all of the bricks over the small rectangles in R, we get

$$\iint_R f(x, y) \, dx \, dy \approx \sum_{j=1}^{n} \sum_{i=1}^{m} f(x_i, y_j) \Delta x \, \Delta y.$$

This double sum is called a **double Riemann sum**. We define the double integral to be the limit of the Riemann sums as m and n go to infinity.

Algebraic Definition of the Double Integral

$$\iint_R f(x, y) \, dx \, dy = \lim_{n \to \infty} \lim_{m \to \infty} \sum_{j=1}^{n} \sum_{i=1}^{m} f(x_i, y_j) \Delta x \, \Delta y$$

Note This definition is adequate (the limit exists) when f is continuous. More elaborate definitions are needed for general functions. ■

This definition also gives us a clue about how to compute a double integral. The innermost sum is $\sum_{i=1}^{m} f(x_i, y_j) \Delta x$, which is a Riemann sum for $\int_a^b f(x, y_j) \, dx$. The innermost limit is therefore

$$\lim_{m \to \infty} \sum_{i=1}^{m} f(x_i, y_j) \Delta x = \int_a^b f(x, y_j) \, dx.$$

The outermost limit is then also a Riemann sum, and we get the following way of calculating double integrals:

Computing the Double Integral over a Rectangle

If R is the rectangle $a \le x \le b$ and $c \le y \le d$, then

$$\iint_R f(x, y) \, dx \, dy = \int_c^d \left(\int_a^b f(x, y) \, dx \right) dy = \int_a^b \left(\int_c^d f(x, y) \, dy \right) dx.$$

The second formula comes from switching the order of summation in the double sum.

Quick Example

If R is the rectangle $1 \le x \le 2$ and $1 \le y \le 3$, then

$$\iint_R 1 \, dx \, dy = \int_1^3 \left(\int_1^2 1 \, dx \right) dy$$

$$= \int_1^3 \left[x \right]_{x=1}^2 dy \qquad \text{Evaluate the inner integral.}$$

$$= \int_1^3 1 \, dy \qquad \qquad \left[x \right]_{x=1}^2 = 2 - 1 = 1.$$

$$= \left[y \right]_{y=1}^3 = 3 - 1 = 2.$$

The Quick Example used a constant function for the integrand. Here is an example in which the integrand is not constant.

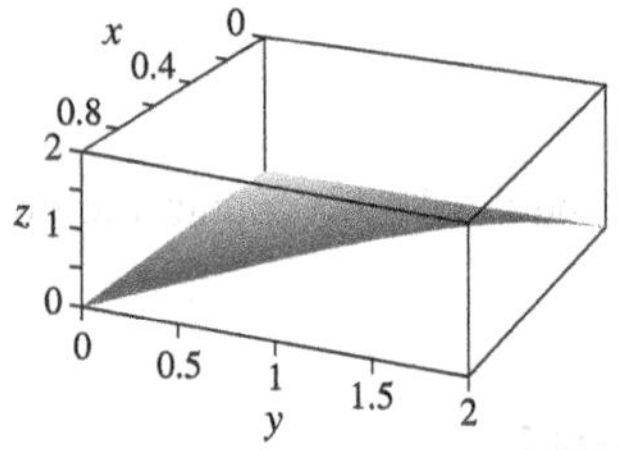

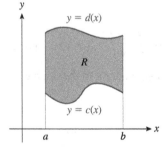

$z = xy, 0 \le x \le 1$ and $0 \le y \le 2$

Figure 29

EXAMPLE 1 Double Integral over a Rectangle

Let R be the rectangle $0 \le x \le 1$ and $0 \le y \le 2$. Compute $\iint_R xy\,dx\,dy$. This integral gives the volume of the part of the boxed region under the surface $z = xy$ shown in Figure 29.

Solution

$$\iint_R xy\,dx\,dy = \int_0^2 \int_0^1 xy\,dx\,dy$$

(We usually drop the parentheses around the inner integral like this.) As in the Quick Example, we compute this **iterated integral** from the inside out. First we compute

$$\int_0^1 xy\,dx.$$

To do this computation, we do as we did when finding partial derivatives: We treat y as a constant. This gives

$$\int_0^1 xy\,dx = \left[\frac{x^2}{2} \cdot y\right]_{x=0}^1 = \frac{1}{2}y - 0 = \frac{y}{2}.$$

We can now calculate the outer integral.

$$\int_0^2 \int_0^1 xy\,dx\,dy = \int_0^2 \frac{y}{2}\,dy = \left[\frac{y^2}{4}\right]_0^2 = 1$$

➡ **Before we go on...** We could also reverse the order of integration in Example 1.

$$\int_0^1 \int_0^2 xy\,dy\,dx = \int_0^1 \left(\left[x \cdot \frac{y^2}{2}\right]_{y=0}^2\right) dx = \int_0^1 2x\,dx = \left[x^2\right]_0^1 = 1 \qquad \blacksquare$$

Often we need to integrate over regions R that are not rectangular. There are two cases that come up. The first is a region like the one shown in Figure 30. In this region, the bottom and top sides are defined by functions $y = c(x)$ and $y = d(x)$, respectively, so that the whole region can be described by the inequalities $a \le x \le b$ and $c(x) \le y \le d(x)$. To evaluate a double integral over such a region, we have the following formula:

Figure 30

Computing the Double Integral over a Nonrectangular Region

If R is the region $a \le x \le b$ and $c(x) \le y \le d(x)$ (Figure 30), then we integrate over R according to the following equation:

$$\iint_R f(x, y)\,dx\,dy = \int_a^b \int_{c(x)}^{d(x)} f(x, y)\,dy\,dx.$$

304

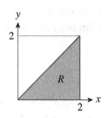

Figure 31

EXAMPLE 2 Double Integral over a Nonrectangular Region

R is the triangle shown in Figure 31. Compute $\iint_R x \, dx \, dy$.

Solution R is the region described by $0 \le x \le 2, 0 \le y \le x$. We have

$$\iint_R x \, dx \, dy = \int_0^2 \int_0^x x \, dy \, dx$$

$$= \int_0^2 [xy]_{y=0}^x \, dx$$

$$= \int_0^2 x^2 \, dx$$

$$= \left[\frac{x^3}{3}\right]_0^2 = \frac{8}{3}.$$

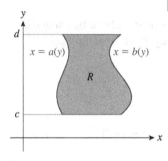

Figure 32

The second type of region is shown in Figure 32. This is the region described by $c \le y \le d$ and $a(y) \le x \le b(y)$. To evaluate a double integral over such a region, we have the following formula:

Double Integral over a Nonrectangular Region (continued)

If R is the region $c \le y \le d$ and $a(y) \le x \le b(y)$ (Figure 32), then we integrate over R according to the following equation:

$$\iint_R f(x, y) \, dx \, dy = \int_c^d \int_{a(y)}^{b(y)} f(x, y) \, dx \, dy.$$

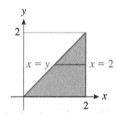

Figure 33

EXAMPLE 3 Double Integral over a Nonrectangular Region

Redo Example 2, integrating in the opposite order.

Solution We can integrate in the opposite order if we can describe the region in Figure 31 in the way shown in Figure 32. In fact, it is the region $0 \le y \le 2$ and $y \le x \le 2$. To see this, we draw a horizontal line through the region, as in Figure 33. The line extends from $x = y$ on the left to $x = 2$ on the right, so $y \le x \le 2$. The possible heights for such a line are $0 \le y \le 2$. We can now compute the integral:

$$\iint_R x \, dx \, dy = \int_0^2 \int_y^2 x \, dx \, dy$$

$$= \int_0^2 \left[\frac{x^2}{2}\right]_{x=y}^2 \, dy$$

$$= \int_0^2 \left(2 - \frac{y^2}{2}\right) dy$$

$$= \left[2y - \frac{y^3}{6}\right]_0^2 = \frac{8}{3}.$$

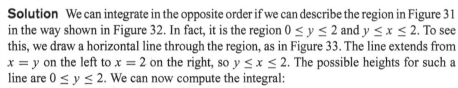

Note Many regions can be described in two different ways, as we saw in Examples 2 and 3. Sometimes one description will be much easier to work with than the other, so it pays to consider both. ■

APPLICATIONS

There are many applications of double integrals besides finding volumes. For example, we can use them to find *averages*. Remember that the average of $f(x)$ on $[a, b]$ is given by $\int_a^b f(x)\,dx$ divided by $(b - a)$, the length of the interval.

Average of a Function of Two Variables

The average of $f(x, y)$ on the region R is

$$\bar{f} = \frac{1}{A} \iint_R f(x, y)\,dx\,dy.$$

Here, A is the area of R. We can compute the area A geometrically, or by using the techniques from the chapter on applications of the integral, or by computing

$$A = \iint_R 1\,dx\,dy.$$

Quick Example

The average value of $f(x, y) = xy$ on the rectangle given by $0 \le x \le 1$ and $0 \le y \le 2$ is

$$\bar{f} = \frac{1}{2} \iint_R xy\,dx\,dy \qquad \text{The area of the rectangle is 2.}$$

$$= \frac{1}{2} \int_0^2 \int_0^1 xy\,dx\,dy$$

$$= \frac{1}{2} \cdot 1 = \frac{1}{2}. \qquad \text{We calculated the integral in Example 1.}$$

EXAMPLE 4 **Average Revenue**

Your company is planning to price its new line of subcompact cars at between $10,000 and $15,000. The marketing department reports that if the company prices the cars at p dollars per car, the demand will be between $q = 20,000 - p$ and $q = 25,000 - p$ cars sold in the first year. What is the average of all the possible revenues your company could expect in the first year?

Solution Revenue is given by $R = pq$ as usual, and we are told that

$$10,000 \le p \le 15,000$$

and $\quad 20,000 - p \le q \le 25,000 - p.$

This domain D of prices and demands is shown in Figure 34.

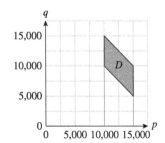

Figure 34

306

To average the revenue R over the domain D, we need to compute the area A of D. Using either calculus or geometry, we get $A = 25,000,000$. We then need to integrate R over D:

$$\iint_D pq\,dp\,dq = \int_{10,000}^{15,000} \int_{20,000-p}^{25,000-p} pq\,dq\,dp$$

$$= \int_{10,000}^{15,000} \left[\frac{pq^2}{2}\right]_{q=20,000-p}^{25,000-p} dp$$

$$= \frac{1}{2}\int_{10,000}^{15,000} [p(25,000-p)^2 - p(20,000-p)^2]\,dp$$

$$= \frac{1}{2}\int_{10,000}^{15,000} [225,000,000p - 10,000p^2]\,dp$$

$$\approx 3,072,900,000,000,000.$$

The average of all the possible revenues your company could expect in the first year is therefore

$$\bar{R} = \frac{3,072,900,000,000,000}{25,000,000} \approx \$122,900,000.$$

➡ **Before we go on...** To check that the answer obtained in Example 4 is reasonable, notice that the revenues at the corners of the domain are $100,000,000 per year, $150,000,000 per year (at two corners), and $75,000,000 per year. Some of these are smaller than the average and some larger, as we would expect. ∎

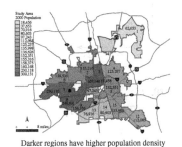

Another useful application of the double integral comes about when we consider density. For example, suppose that $P(x, y)$ represents the population density (in people per square mile, say) in the city of Houston, shown in Figure 35.

If we break the city up into small rectangles (for example, city blocks), then the population in the small rectangle $x_{i-1} \leq x \leq x_i$ and $y_{j-1} \leq y \leq y_j$ is approximately $P(x_i, y_j)\Delta x\,\Delta y$. Adding up all of these population estimates, we get

$$\text{Total population} \approx \sum_{j=1}^{n}\sum_{i=1}^{m} P(x_i, y_j)\,\Delta x\,\Delta y.$$

Darker regions have higher population density

Figure 35

Because this is a double Riemann sum, when we take the limit as m and n go to infinity, we get the following calculation of the population of the city:

$$\text{Total population} = \iint_{\text{City}} P(x, y)\,dx\,dy.$$

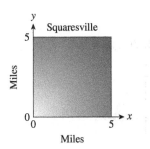

Figure 36

EXAMPLE 5 Population

Squaresville is a city in the shape of a square 5 miles on a side. The population density at a distance of x miles east and y miles north of the southwest corner is $P(x, y) = x^2 + y^2$ thousand people per square mile. Find the total population of Squaresville.

Solution Squaresville is pictured in Figure 36, in which we put the origin in the southwest corner of the city.

To compute the total population, we integrate the population density over the city S.

$$\text{Total population} = \iint_{\text{Squaresville}} P(x, y)\, dx\, dy$$

$$= \int_0^5 \int_0^5 (x^2 + y^2)\, dx\, dy$$

$$= \int_0^5 \left[\frac{x^3}{3} + xy^2 \right]_{x=0}^5 dy$$

$$= \int_0^5 \left[\frac{125}{3} + 5y^2 \right] dy$$

$$= \frac{1{,}250}{3} \approx 417 \text{ thousand people}$$

➡ **Before we go on...** Note that the average population density is the total population divided by the area of the city, which is about 17,000 people per square mile. Compare this calculation with the calculations of averages in the previous two examples. ■

15.5 EXERCISES

▼ more advanced   ◆ challenging

⊤ indicates exercises that should be solved using technology

Compute the integrals in Exercises 1–16. HINT [See Example 1.]

1. $\displaystyle\int_0^1 \int_0^1 (x - 2y)\, dx\, dy$

2. $\displaystyle\int_{-1}^1 \int_0^2 (2x + 3y)\, dx\, dy$

3. $\displaystyle\int_0^1 \int_0^2 (ye^x - x - y)\, dx\, dy$

4. $\displaystyle\int_1^2 \int_2^3 \left(\frac{1}{x} + \frac{1}{y} \right) dx\, dy$

5. $\displaystyle\int_0^2 \int_0^3 e^{x+y}\, dx\, dy$

6. $\displaystyle\int_0^1 \int_0^1 e^{x-y}\, dx\, dy$

7. $\displaystyle\int_0^1 \int_0^{2-y} x\, dx\, dy$

8. $\displaystyle\int_0^1 \int_0^{2-y} y\, dx\, dy$

9. $\displaystyle\int_{-1}^1 \int_{y-1}^{y+1} e^{x+y}\, dx\, dy$

10. $\displaystyle\int_0^1 \int_y^{y+2} \frac{1}{\sqrt{x + y}}\, dx\, dy$

HINT [See Example 2.]   HINT [See Example 2.]

11. $\displaystyle\int_0^1 \int_{-x^2}^{x^2} x\, dy\, dx$

12. $\displaystyle\int_1^4 \int_{-\sqrt{x}}^{\sqrt{x}} \frac{1}{x}\, dy\, dx$

13. $\displaystyle\int_0^1 \int_0^x e^{x^2}\, dy\, dx$

14. $\displaystyle\int_0^1 \int_0^{x^2} e^{x^3+1}\, dy\, dx$

15. $\displaystyle\int_0^2 \int_{1-x}^{8-x} (x + y)^{1/3}\, dy\, dx$

16. $\displaystyle\int_1^2 \int_{1-2x}^{x^2} \frac{x + 1}{(2x + y)^3}\, dy\, dx$

In Exercises 17–24, find $\iint_R f(x, y)\, dx\, dy$, where R is the indicated domain. (Remember that you often have a choice as to the order of integration.) HINT [See Example 2.]

17. $f(x, y) = 2$

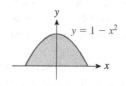

18. $f(x, y) = x$

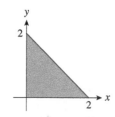

19. $f(x, y) = 1 + y$
HINT [See Example 3.]

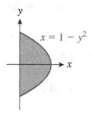

20. $f(x, y) = e^{x+y}$
HINT [See Example 3.]

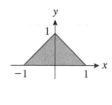

21. $f(x, y) = xy^2$

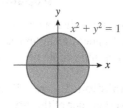

22. $f(x, y) = xy^2$

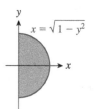

23. $f(x, y) = x^2 + y^2$

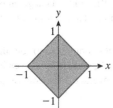

24. $f(x, y) = x^2$

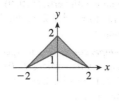

In Exercises 25–30, find the average value of the given function over the indicated domain. HINT [See Quick Examples page 1128.]

25. $f(x, y) = y$

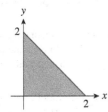

26. $f(x, y) = 2 + x$

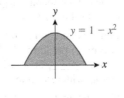

$y = 1 - x^2$

27. $f(x, y) = e^y$

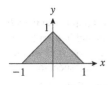

28. $f(x, y) = y$

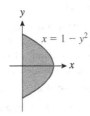

$x = 1 - y^2$

29. $f(x, y) = x^2$

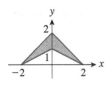

30. $f(x, y) = x^2 + y^2$

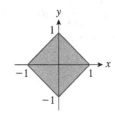

In Exercises 31–36, sketch the region over which you are integrating, and then write down the integral with the order of integration reversed (changing the limits of integration as necessary).

31. ▼ $\displaystyle\int_0^1 \int_0^{1-y} f(x, y)\, dx\, dy$ **32.** ▼ $\displaystyle\int_{-1}^1 \int_0^{1+y} f(x, y)\, dx\, dy$

33. ▼ $\displaystyle\int_{-1}^1 \int_0^{\sqrt{1+y}} f(x, y)\, dx\, dy$ **34.** ▼ $\displaystyle\int_{-1}^1 \int_0^{\sqrt{1-y}} f(x, y)\, dx\, dy$

35. ▼ $\displaystyle\int_1^2 \int_1^{4/x^2} f(x, y)\, dy\, dx$ **36.** ▼ $\displaystyle\int_1^{e^2} \int_0^{\ln x} f(x, y)\, dy\, dx$

37. Find the volume under the graph of $z = 1 - x^2$ over the region $0 \le x \le 1$ and $0 \le y \le 2$.

38. Find the volume under the graph of $z = 1 - x^2$ over the triangle $0 \le x \le 1$ and $0 \le y \le 1 - x$.

39. ▼ Find the volume of the tetrahedron shown in the figure. Its corners are $(0, 0, 0)$, $(1, 0, 0)$, $(0, 1, 0)$, and $(0, 0, 1)$.

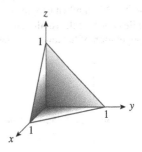

40. ▼ Find the volume of the tetrahedron with corners at $(0, 0, 0)$, $(a, 0, 0)$, $(0, b, 0)$, and $(0, 0, c)$.

APPLICATIONS

41. *Productivity* A productivity model at the Handy Gadget Company is

$$P = 10{,}000 x^{0.3} y^{0.7}$$

where P is the number of gadgets the company turns out per month, x is the number of employees at the company, and y is the monthly operating budget in thousands of dollars. Because the company hires part-time workers, it uses anywhere between 45 and 55 workers each month, and its operating budget varies from \$8,000 to \$12,000 per month. What is the average of the possible numbers of gadgets it can turn out per month? (Round the answer to the nearest 1,000 gadgets.) HINT [See Quick Examples page 1128.]

42. *Productivity* Repeat the preceding exercise using the productivity model

$$P = 10{,}000 x^{0.7} y^{0.3}.$$

43. *Revenue* Your latest CD-ROM of clip art is expected to sell between $q = 8{,}000 - p^2$ and $q = 10{,}000 - p^2$ copies if priced at p dollars. You plan to set the price between \$40 and \$50. What is the average of all the possible revenues you can make? HINT [See Example 4.]

44. *Revenue* Your latest DVD drive is expected to sell between $q = 180{,}000 - p^2$ and $q = 200{,}000 - p^2$ units if priced at p dollars. You plan to set the price between \$300 and \$400. What is the average of all the possible revenues you can make? HINT [See Example 4.]

45. *Revenue* Your self-published novel has demand curves between $p = 15{,}000/q$ and $p = 20{,}000/q$. You expect to sell between 500 and 1,000 copies. What is the average of all the possible revenues you can make?

46. *Revenue* Your self-published book of poetry has demand curves between $p = 80,000/q^2$ and $p = 100,000/q^2$. You expect to sell between 50 and 100 copies. What is the average of all the possible revenues you can make?

47. *Population Density* The town of West Podunk is shaped like a rectangle 20 miles from west to east and 30 miles from north to south. (See the figure.) It has a population density of $P(x, y) = e^{-0.1(x+y)}$ hundred people per square mile x miles east and y miles north of the southwest corner of town. What is the total population of the town? HINT [See Example 5.]

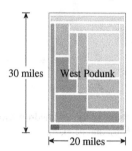

30 miles — West Podunk — 20 miles

48. *Population Density* The town of East Podunk is shaped like a triangle with an east-west base of 20 miles and a north-south height of 30 miles. (See the figure.) It has a population density of $P(x, y) = e^{-0.1(x+y)}$ hundred people per square mile x miles east and y miles north of the southwest corner of town. What is the total population of the town? HINT [See Example 5.]

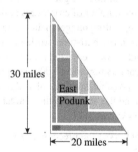

30 miles — East Podunk — 20 miles

49. *Temperature* The temperature at the point (x, y) on the square with vertices $(0, 0)$, $(0, 1)$, $(1, 0)$, and $(1, 1)$ is given by $T(x, y) = x^2 + 2y^2$. Find the average temperature on the square.

50. *Temperature* The temperature at the point (x, y) on the square with vertices $(0, 0)$, $(0, 1)$, $(1, 0)$, and $(1, 1)$ is given by $T(x, y) = x^2 + 2y^2 - x$. Find the average temperature on the square.

COMMUNICATION AND REASONING EXERCISES

51. Explain how double integrals can be used to compute the area between two curves in the xy plane.

52. Explain how double integrals can be used to compute the volume of solids in 3-space.

53. Complete the following: The first step in calculating an integral of the form $\int_a^b \int_{r(x)}^{s(x)} f(x, y) \, dy \, dx$ is to evaluate the integral _____, obtained by holding ___ constant and integrating with respect to ___ .

54. If the units of $f(x, y)$ are zonars per square meter, and x and y are given in meters, what are the units of $\int_a^b \int_{r(x)}^{s(x)} f(x, y) \, dy \, dx$?

55. If the units of $\int_a^b \int_{r(x)}^{s(x)} f(x, y) \, dy \, dx$ are paintings, the units of x are picassos, and the units of y are dalis, what are the units of $f(x, y)$?

56. Complete the following: If the region R is bounded on the left and right by vertical lines and on the top and bottom by the graphs of functions of x, then we integrate over R by first integrating with respect to _____ and then with respect to ___.

57. ▽ Show that if a, b, c, and d are constant, then $\int_a^b \int_c^d f(x) g(y) \, dx \, dy = \int_c^d f(x) \, dx \int_a^b g(y) \, dy$. Test this result on the integral $\int_0^1 \int_1^2 y e^x \, dx \, dy$.

58. ▽ Refer to Exercise 57. If a, b, c, and d are constants, can $\int_a^b \int_c^d \frac{f(x)}{g(y)} \, dx \, dy$ be expressed as a product of two integrals? Explain.

310

CHAPTER 15 REVIEW

KEY CONCEPTS

Web Site www.FiniteandCalc.org
Go to the student Web site at www.FiniteandCalc.org to find a comprehensive and interactive Web-based summary of Chapter 15.

15.1 Functions of Several Variables from the Numerical, Algebraic, and Graphical Viewpoints

A real-valued function, f, of $x, y, z, \ldots$ p. 1080
Cost functions p. 1081
A linear function of the variables $x_1, x_2, \ldots, x_n$ is a function of the form
$f(x_1, x_2, \ldots, x_n) = a_0 + a_1 x_1 + \ldots + a_n x_n$ ($a_0, a_1, \ldots, a_n$ constants) p. 1082
Representing functions of two variables numerically p. 1083
Using Excel to represent a function of two variables p. 1084
Plotting points in three dimensions p. 1085
Graph of a function of two variables p. 1086
Analyzing the graph of a function of two variables p. 1088
Graph of a linear function p. 1090

15.2 Partial Derivatives

Definition of partial derivatives p. 1098

Application to marginal cost: linear cost function p. 1099
Application to marginal cost: interaction cost function p. 1099
Geometric interpretation of partial derivatives p. 1101
Second order partial derivatives p. 1101

15.3 Maxima and Minima

Definition of relative maximum and minimum p. 1107
Locating candidates for relative maxima and minima p. 1107
Classifying critical points graphically p. 1108
Classifying critical points numerically p. 1109
Second derivative test for a function of two variables p. 1109
Using the second derivative test p. 1110
Deriving the regression formulas:
$$m = \frac{n\left(\sum xy\right) - \left(\sum x\right)\left(\sum y\right)}{n\left(\sum x^2\right) - \left(\sum x\right)^2}$$
$$b = \frac{\sum y - m\left(\sum x\right)}{n}$$
n = number of data points p. 1111

15.4 Constrained Maxima and Minima and Applications

Constrained maximum and minimum problem p. 1115
Solving constrained maxima and minima problems using substitution p. 1115
The method of Lagrange multipliers p. 1116
Using Lagrange multipliers p. 1117

15.5 Double Integrals and Applications

Geometric definition of the double integral p. 1124
Algebraic definition of the double integral
$$\iint_R f(x, y)\, dx\, dy =$$
$$\lim_{n \to \infty} \lim_{m \to \infty} \sum_{j=1}^{n} \sum_{i=1}^{m} f(x_i, y_j)\Delta x \Delta y$$
p. 1125
Computing the double integral over a rectangle p. 1125
Computing the double integral over nonrectangular regions p. 1126
Average of $f(x, y)$ on the region R:
$$\bar{f} = \frac{1}{A} \iint_R f(x, y)\, dx\, dy \quad \text{p. 1128}$$

REVIEW EXERCISES

1. Let $f(x, y, z) = \dfrac{x}{y + xz} + x^2 y$. Evaluate $f(0, 1, 1), f(2, 1, 1), f(-1, 1, -1), f(z, z, z)$, and $f(x + h, y + k, z + l)$.

2. Let $g(x, y, z) = xy(x + y - z) + x^2$. Evaluate $g(0, 0, 0), g(1, 0, 0), g(0, 1, 0), g(x, x, x)$, and $g(x, y + k, z)$.

3. Let $f(x, y, z) = 2.72 - 0.32x - 3.21y + 12.5z$. Complete the following: f ___ by ___ units for every 1 unit of increase in x, and ___ by ___ units for every unit of increase in z.

4. Let $g(x, y, z) = 2.16x + 11y - 1.53z + 31.4$. Complete the following: g ___ by ___ units for every 1 unit of increase in y, and ___ by ___ units for every unit of increase in z.

In Exercises 5–6 complete the given table for values for $h(x, y) = 2x^2 + xy - x$.

5.

	$x \to$		
		−1	0	1
y	−1			
↓	0			
	1			

6.

	$x \to$		
		−2	2	3
y	−2			
↓	2			
	3			

7. Give a formula for a (single) function f with the property that $f(x, y) = -f(y, x)$ and $f(1, -1) = 3$.

8. Let $f(x, y) = x^2 + (y + 1)^2$. Show that $f(y, x) = f(x + 1, y - 1)$.

In Exercises 9–14, compute the partial derivatives shown for the given function.

9. $f(x, y) = x^2 + xy$; find f_x, f_y, and f_{yy}

10. $f(x, y) = \dfrac{6}{xy} + \dfrac{xy}{6}$; find f_x, f_y, and f_{yy}

11. $f(x, y) = 4x + 5y - 6xy$; find $f_{xx}(1, 0) - f_{xx}(3, 2)$

12. $f(x, y) = e^{xy} + e^{3x^2 - y^2}$; find $\dfrac{\partial f}{\partial x}$ and $\dfrac{\partial^2 f}{\partial x \partial y}$

311

13. $f(x, y, z) = \dfrac{x}{x^2 + y^2 + z^2}$; find $\dfrac{\partial f}{\partial x}$, $\dfrac{\partial f}{\partial y}$, $\dfrac{\partial f}{\partial z}$ and $\dfrac{\partial f}{\partial x}\bigg|_{(0,1,0)}$

14. $f(x, y, z) = x^2 + y^2 + z^2 + xyz$; find $f_{xx} + f_{yy} + f_{zz}$

In Exercises 15–19, locate and classify all critical points.

15. $f(x, y) = (x - 1)^2 + (2y - 3)^2$

16. $g(x, y) = (x - 1)^2 - 3y^2 + 9$

17. $h(x, y) = e^{xy}$

18. $j(x, y) = xy + x^2$

19. $f(x, y) = \ln(x^2 + y^2) - (x^2 + y^2)$

In Exercises 20–23, solve the following constrained optimization problems by using substitution to eliminate a variable. (Do not use Lagrange multipliers.)

20. Find the minimum value of $f(x, y, z) = x^2 + y^2 + z^2 - 1$ subject to $x = y + z$. Also find the corresponding point(s) (x, y, z).

21. Find the largest value of xyz subject to $x + y + z = 1$ with $x > 0, y > 0, z > 0$. Also find the corresponding point(s) (x, y, z).

22. Minimize $S = xy + x^2 z^2 + 4yz$ subject to $xyz = 1$ with $x > 0, y > 0, z > 0$.

23. Find the point on the surface $z = \sqrt{x^2 + 2(y - 3)^2}$ closest to the origin.

In Exercises 24–28, use Lagrange multipliers to solve the given optimization problem.

24. Find the maximum value of $f(x, y) = xy$ subject to $y = e^{-x}$. Also find the corresponding point(s) (x, y).

25. Find the minimum value of $f(x, y) = x^2 + y^2$ subject to $xy = 2$. Also find the corresponding point(s) (x, y).

26. The problem in Exercise 20.

27. The problem in Exercise 22.

28. The problem in Exercise 23.

In Exercises 29–34, compute the given quantities.

29. $\displaystyle\int_0^1 \int_0^2 (2xy)\, dx\, dy$

30. $\displaystyle\int_1^2 \int_0^1 xye^{x+y}\, dx\, dy$

31. $\displaystyle\int_0^2 \int_0^{2x} \frac{1}{x^2 + 1}\, dy\, dx$

32. The average value of xye^{x+y} over the rectangle $0 \le x \le 1$, $1 \le y \le 2$

33. $\iint_R (x^2 - y^2)\, dx\, dy$, where R is the region shown in the figure

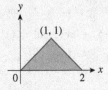

34. The volume under the graph of $z = 1 - y$ over the region in the xy plane between the parabola $y = 1 - x^2$ and the x-axis.

APPLICATIONS

35. *Web Site Traffic* OHaganBooks.com has two principal competitors: JungleBooks.com and FarmerBooks.com. Current Web site traffic at OHaganBooks.com is estimated at 5,000 hits per day. This number is predicted to decrease by 0.8 for every new customer of JungleBooks.com and by 0.6 for every new customer of FarmerBooks.com.

  a. Use this information to model the daily Web site traffic at OHaganBooks.com as a linear function of the new customers of its two competitors.

  b. According to the model, if Junglebooks.com gets 100 new customers and OHaganBooks.com traffic drops to 4,770 hits per day, how many new customers has FarmerBooks.com obtained?

  c. The model in part (a) did not take into account the growth of the total online consumer base. OHaganBooks.com expects to get approximately one additional hit per day for every 10,000 new Internet shoppers. Modify your model in part (a) so as to include this information using a new independent variable.

  d. How many new Internet shoppers would it take to offset the effects on traffic at OHaganBooks.com of 100 new customers at each of its competitor sites?

36. *Productivity* Billy-Sean O'Hagan is writing up his Ph.D. thesis in biophysics but finds that his productivity is affected by the temperature and the number of text messages he receives per hour. On a brisk winter's day when the temperature is $0°C$ and there are no text messages, Billy-Sean can produce 15 pages of his thesis. His productivity goes down by 0.3 pages per degree Celsius increase in the temperature and by 1.2 pages for each additional text message per hour.

  a. Use this information to model Billy-Sean's productivity p as a function of the temperature and the hourly rate of text messages.

  b. The other day the temperature was $20°C$ and Billy-Sean managed to produce only three pages of his thesis. What was the hourly rate of incoming text messages?

  c. Billy reasons that each cup of coffee he drinks per hour can counter the effect on his productivity of two text messages per hour. Modify the model in part (a) to take consumption of coffee into account.

  d. What would the domain of your function look like to ensure that p is never negative?

37. *Internet Advertising* To increase business at OHaganBooks.com, you have purchased banner ads at well-known Internet portals and have advertised on television. The following interaction model shows the average number h of hits per day as a function of monthly expenditures x on banner ads and y on television advertising (x and y are in dollars).

$$h(x, y) = 1{,}800 + 0.05x + 0.08y + 0.00003xy$$

a. Based on your model, how much traffic can you anticipate if you spend $2,000 per month for banner ads and $3,000 per month on television advertising?

b. Evaluate $\dfrac{\partial h}{\partial y}$, specify its units of measurement, and indicate whether it increases or decreases with increasing x.

c. How much should the company spend on banner ads to obtain 1 hit per day for each $5 spent per month on television advertising?

38. Company Retreats Their companies having recently been bailed out by the government at taxpayer expense, Marjory Duffin and John O'Hagan are planning a joint winter business retreat in Cancun, but they are not sure how many sales reps to take along. The following interaction model shows the estimated cost C to their companies (in dollars) as a function of the number of sales reps x and the length of time t in days.

$$C(x, t) = 20,000 - 100x + 600t + 300xt$$

a. Based on the model, how much would it cost to take five sales reps along for a 10-day retreat?

b. Evaluate $\dfrac{\partial C}{\partial t}$, specify its units of measurement, and indicate whether it increases or decreases with increasing x.

c. How many reps should they take along if they wish to limit the marginal daily cost to $1,200?

39. Internet Advertising Refer to the model in Exercise 37. One or more of the following statements is correct. Identify which one(s).

(A) If nothing is spent on television advertising, one more dollar spent per month in banner ads will buy approximately 0.05 hits per day at OHaganBooks.com.

(B) If nothing is spent on television advertising, one more hit per day at OHaganBooks.com will cost the company about 5¢ per month in banner ads.

(C) If nothing is spent on banner ads, one more hit per day at OHaganBooks.com will cost the company about 5¢ per month in banner ads.

(D) If nothing is spent on banner ads, one more dollar spent per month in banner ads will buy approximately 0.05 hits per day at OHaganBooks.com.

(E) Hits at OHaganBooks.com cost approximately 5¢ per month spent on banner ads, and this cost increases at a rate of 0.003¢ per month, per hit.

40. Company Retreats Refer to the model in Exercise 38. One or more of the following statements is correct. Identify which one(s).

(A) If the retreat lasts for 10 days, the daily cost per sales rep is $400.

(B) If the retreat lasts for 10 days, each additional day will cost the company $2,900.

(C) If the retreat lasts for 10 days, each additional sales rep will cost the company $800.

(D) If the retreat lasts for 10 days, the daily cost per sales rep is $2,900.

(E) If the retreat lasts for 10 days, each additional sales rep will cost the company $2,900.

41. Productivity The holiday season is now at its peak and OHaganBooks.com has been understaffed and swamped with orders. The current backlog (orders unshipped for two or more days) has grown to a staggering 50,000, and new orders are coming in at a rate of 5,000 per day. Research based on productivity data at OHaganBooks.com results in the following model:

$$P(x, y) = 1,000x^{0.9}y^{0.1} \text{ additional orders filled per day}$$

where x is the number of additional personnel hired and y is the daily budget (excluding salaries) allocated to eliminating the backlog.

a. How many additional orders will be filled per day if the company hires 10 additional employees and budgets an additional $1,000 per day? (Round the answer to the nearest 100.)

b. In addition to the daily budget, extra staffing costs the company $150 per day for every new staff member hired. In order to fill at least 15,000 additional orders per day at a minimum total daily cost, how many new staff members should the company hire? (Use the method of Lagrange multipliers.)

42. Productivity The holiday season has now ended, and orders at OHaganBooks.com have plummeted, leaving staff members in the shipping department with little to do besides spend their time on their Facebook pages, so the company is considering laying off a number of personnel and slashing the shipping budget. Research based on productivity data at OHaganBooks.com results in the following model:

$$C(x, y) = 1,000x^{0.8}y^{0.2} \text{ fewer orders filled per day}$$

where x is the number of personnel laid off and y is the cut in the shipping budget (excluding salaries).

a. How many fewer orders will be filled per day if the company lays off 15 additional employees and cuts the budget by an additional $2,000 per day? (Round the answer to the nearest 100.)

b. In addition to the cut in the shipping budget, the layoffs will save the company $200 per day for every new staff member laid off. The company needs to meet a target of 20,000 fewer orders per day but, for tax reasons, it must minimize the total resulting savings. How many new staff members should the company lay off? (Use the method of Lagrange multipliers.)

43. Profit If OHaganBooks.com sells x paperback books and y hardcover books per week, it will make an average weekly profit of

$$P(x, y) = 3x + 10y \text{ dollars.}$$

If it sells between 1,200 and 1,500 paperback books and between 1,800 and 2,000 hardcover books per week, what is the average of all its possible weekly profits?

44. *Cost* It costs Duffin publishers

$$C(x, y) = x^2 + 2y \text{ dollars}$$

to produce x coffee table art books and y paperback books per week. If it produces between 100 and 120 art books and between 800 and 1,000 paperbacks per week, what is the average of all its possible weekly costs?

David Pearson/Alamy

Case Study   Modeling College Population

College Malls, Inc. is planning to build a national chain of shopping malls in college neighborhoods. However, malls in general have been experiencing large numbers of store closings due to, among other things, misjudgments of the shopper demographics. As a result, the company is planning to lease only to stores that target the specific age demographics of the national college student population.

As a marketing consultant to College Malls, you will be providing the company with a report that addresses the following specific issues:

- A quick way of estimating the number of students of any specified age and in any particular year, and the effect of increasing age on the college population
- The ages that correspond to relatively high and low college populations
- How fast the 20-year-old and 25-year-old student populations are increasing
- Some near-term projections of the student population trend

You decide that a good place to start would be with a visit to the Census Bureau's Web site at www.census.gov. After some time battling with search engines, all you can find is some data on college enrollment for three age brackets for the period 1980–2005, as shown in the following table:[30]

College Enrollment (thousands)

Year	1980	1985	1990	1995	1999	2000	2001	2002	2003	2004	2005
18–24	7,229	7,537	7,964	8,541	9,260	9,451	9,629	10,033	10,364	10,608	10,831
25–34	2,703	3,063	3,161	3,349	3,095	3,207	3,422	3,401	3,494	3,695	3,601
35–41	1,207	1,661	2,318	2,669	2,699	2,507	2,684	2,868	2,630	2,883	2,857

The data are inadequate for several reasons: The data are given only for certain years, and in age brackets rather than year-by-year; nor is it obvious as to how you would project the figures. However, you notice that the table is actually a numerical representation of a function of two variables: year and age. Since the age brackets are of different sizes, you "normalize" the data by dividing each figure by the number of years represented in the corresponding age bracket; for instance, you divide the 1980 figure for the first age group by 7 in order to obtain the average enrollment for each year of age in that group.

---

[30] Source: Bureau of the Census, 2008 (www.census.gov/population/www/socdemo/school.html).

You then rewrite the resulting table representing the years by values of t and each age bracket by the age x at its center (enrollment values are rounded):

$t \rightarrow$	0	5	10	15	19	20	21	22	23	24	25
21	1,033	1,077	1,138	1,220	1,323	1,350	1,376	1,433	1,481	1,515	1,547
29.5	270	306	316	335	310	321	342	340	349	370	360
38	172	237	331	381	386	358	383	410	376	412	408

(x axis label on left: $x \downarrow$)

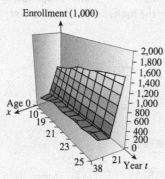

Figure 37

In order to see a visual representation of what the data are saying, you use Excel to graph the data as a surface (Figure 37). It is important to notice that Excel does not scale the t-axis as you would expect: It uses one subdivision for each year shown in the chart, and the result is an uneven scaling of the t-axis. Despite this drawback, you do see two trends after looking at views of the graph from various angles. First, enrollment of 38-year-olds (the front edge of the graph) seems to be increasing faster than enrollment of 21-year-olds. Second, the enrollment for all ages seem to be increasing approximately linearly with time since 1999, although at different rates for different age groups; for instance, the front and rear edges rise more-or-less linearly, but do not seem to be parallel.

At this point you realize that a mathematical model of these data would be useful; not only would it "smooth out the bumps" but it would give you a way to estimate enrollment N at each specific age, project the enrollments, and thereby complete the project for College Malls. Although technology can give you a regression model for data such as this, it is up to you to decide on the form of the model. It is in choosing an appropriate model that your analysis of the graph comes in handy. Because N should vary linearly with time t for each value of x, you would like

$$N = mt + k$$

for each value of x. Also, because there are three values of x for every value of time, you try a quadratic model for N as a function of x:

$$N = a + bx + cx^2$$

Putting these together, you get the following candidate model

$$N(t, x) = a_1 + a_2t + a_3x + a_4x^2$$

where a_1, a_2, a_3, and a_4 are constants. However, for each specific age $x = k$, you get

$$N(t, k) = a_1 + a_2t + a_3k + a_4k^2 = \text{Constant} + a_2t$$

with the same slope a_2 for every choice of the age k, contrary to your observation that enrollment for different age groups is rising at different rates, so you will need a more elaborate model. You recall from your applied calculus course that interaction functions give a way to model the effect of one variable on the rate of change of another, so, as an experiment, you try adding interaction terms to your model:

Model 1: $N(t, x) = a_1 + a_2t + a_3x + a_4x^2 + a_5xt$ Second order model

Model 2: $N(t, x) = a_1 + a_2t + a_3x + a_4x^2 + a_5xt + a_6x^2t$.   Third order model

(Model 1 is referred to as a second order model because it contains no products of more than two independent variables, whereas Model 2 contains the third order term $x^2t = x \cdot x \cdot t$.) If you study these two models for specific values k of x you get:

Model 1: $N = \text{Constant} + (a_2 + a_5k)t$ Slope depends linearly on age

Model 2: $N = \text{Constant} + (a_2 + a_5k + a_6k^2)t$.   Slope depends quadratically on age

315

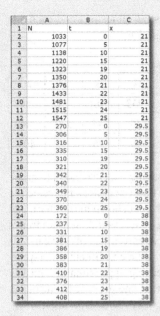

Figure 38

This is encouraging: Both models show different slopes for different ages. Model 1 would predict that the slope either increases with increasing age (a_5 positive) or decreases with increasing age (a_5 negative). However, the graph suggests that the slope is larger for both younger and older students, but smaller for students of intermediate age, contrary to what Model 1 predicts. So you decide to go with the more flexible Model 2, which permits the slope to decrease and then increase with increasing age. This is exactly what you observe on the graph.

You decide to use Excel to generate your model. However, the data as shown in the table are not in a form Excel can use for regression. The data need to be organized into columns: Column A for the dependent variable N and Columns B–C for the independent variables, as shown in Figure 38. You then add columns for the higher order terms x^2, xt, and $x^2 t$ as shown below:

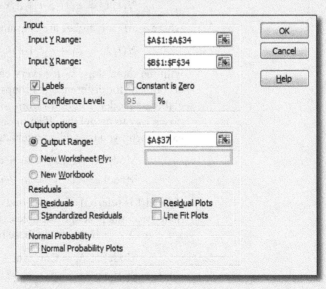

Next, in the "Analysis" section of the Data tab, choose "Data analysis." (If this command is not available, you will need to load the Analysis ToolPak add-in.) Choose "Regression" from the list that appears, and in the resulting dialogue box enter the location of the data and where you want to put the results as shown in Figure 39; identify where the dependent and independent variables are (A1–A34 for the Y range, and B1–F34 for the X range), check "Labels," and click "OK."

Figure 39

316

A portion of the output is shown below, with some of the important statistics highlighted.

37	SUMMARY OUTPUT					
38						
39	*Regression Statistics*					
40	Multiple R	0.99807463				
41	R Square	0.99615297				
42	Adjusted R Square	0.99544056				
43	Standard Error	32.4693397				
44	Observations	33				
45						
46	ANOVA					
47		*df*	*SS*	*MS*	*F*	*Significance F*
48	Regression	5	7370748.67	1474149.73	1398.28173	1.0623E-31
49	Residual	27	28464.96658	1054.25802		
50	Total	32	7399213.636			
51						
52		*Coefficients*	*Standard Error*	*t Stat*	*P-value*	*Lower 95%*
53	Intercept	5317.742	324.3264401	16.3962642	1.4646E-15	4652.279561
54	t	165.703742	17.52824924	9.45352497	4.6746E-10	129.7387692
55	x	-296.5247	22.98384198	-12.901442	4.6484E-13	-343.6836131
56	x^2	4.26166483	0.38821602	10.9775605	1.8505E-11	3.465111887
57	x*t	-10.325579	1.242163638	-8.3125755	6.3811E-09	-12.87428658
58	x^2*t	0.16304663	0.020981167	7.77109439	2.3426E-08	0.119996859

The desired constants a_1, a_2, a_3, a_4, and a_5 appear in the coefficients column at the bottom left, in the correct order: a_1 is the "intercept," a_2 is the coefficient of t, and so on. Thus, if we round to five significant digits, we have

$$a_1 = 5{,}317.7 \quad a_2 = 165.70 \quad a_3 = -296.52$$
$$a_4 = 4.2617 \quad a_5 = -10.326 \quad a_6 = 0.16305$$

which gives our regression model:

$$N(t, x) = 5{,}317.7 + 165.70t - 296.52x + 4.2617x^2 - 10.326xt + 0.16305x^2t.$$

Fine, you say to yourself, now you have the model, but how good a fit is it to the data? That is where the "Multiple R" at the top of the data analysis comes in. R is called the **multiple coefficient of correlation,** and generalizes the coefficient of correlation discussed in the section on regression in Chapter 1: The closer R is to 1, the better the fit. We can interpret its square, given in the table as "R Square" with value 0.996, as indicating that approximately 99.6% of the variation in college enrollment is explained by the regression model, indicating an excellent fit. The "P-values" at bottom right are also indicators of the appropriateness of the model; a P-value close to zero indicates a high degree of confidence that the corresponding independent variable contributes significantly to the value of the college enrollment (a P-value less than 0.05 would indicate, for example, that the corresponding coefficient is statistically significant at a level of more than 95% confidence) whereas a P-value close to 1 indicates low confidence; there is a P-value for each coefficient. Because all the values are extremely tiny, you are confident indeed that the model is an appropriate one. Another statistical indicator is the value of "F" on the right—an indicator of confidence in the model as a whole. The fact that it too is large and its "Significance F" is tiny is yet another good sign.*

As comforting as these statistics are, nothing can be quite as persuasive as a graph. You turn to the graphing software of your choice and notice that the graph of the model appears to be a faithful representation of the data. (See Figure 40.)

✱ **NOTE** We are being deliberately vague about the exact meaning of these statistics, which are discussed fully in many applied statistics texts.

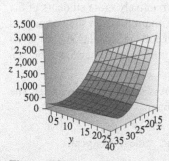

Figure 40

Now you get to work, using the model to address the questions posed by College Malls.

1. *A quick way of estimating the number of students of any specified age and in any particular year, and the effect of increasing age on the college population.* You already have a quantitative relationship in the form of the regression model. As for the second part of the question, the rate of change of college enrollment with respect to age is given by the partial derivative:

$$\frac{\partial N}{\partial x} = -296.52 + 8.5234x - 10.326t + 0.32610xt \text{ thousand students per}$$
$$\text{additional year of age.}$$

Thus, for example, with $x = 20$ in 2004 ($t = 24$), we have

$$\frac{\partial N}{\partial x} = -296.52 + 8.5234(20) - 10.326(24) + 0.32610(20)(24)$$

$$\approx -217 \text{ thousand students per additional year of age,}$$

so there were about 217,000 fewer students of age 21 than age 20 in 2004.
On the other hand, when $x = 38$ in the same year, one has

$$\frac{\partial N}{\partial x} = -296.52 + 8.5234(38) - 10.326(24) + 0.32610(38)(24)$$

$$\approx 77 \text{ thousand students per additional year of age,}$$

so there were about 77,000 more students of age 39 than age 38 that year.

2. *The ages that correspond to relatively high and low college populations.* Although a glance at the graph shows you that there are no relative maxima, holding t constant (that is, on any given year) gives a parabola along the corresponding slice and hence a minimum somewhere along the slice.

$$\frac{\partial N}{\partial x} = 0$$

when $$-296.52 + 8.5234x - 10.326t + 0.32610xt = 0,$$

which gives $$x = \frac{296.52 + 10.326t}{8.5234 + 0.32610t} \text{ years of age.}$$

For instance, in 2000 ($t = 20$), the age at which there are the fewest students (in the given range) is 33.4 years of age. The relative maxima for each slice occur at the front and back edges of the surface, meaning that there are relatively more students of the lowest and highest ages represented. The absolute maximum for each slice occurs, as expected, at the lowest age. In short, a mall catering to college students should focus mostly on freshman-age students, least on 33-year-olds, and somewhat more on people around age 40.

3. *How fast the 20-year-old and 25-year-old student populations are increasing.* The rate of change of student population with respect to time is

$$\frac{\partial N}{\partial t} = 165.70 - 10.326x + 0.16305x^2 \text{ thousand students per year.}$$

318

For the three age groups in question, we obtain

$$x = 20: 165.70 - 10.326(20) + 0.16305(20)^2 = 24.4 \text{ thousand students/year}$$

$$x = 25: 165.70 - 10.326(25) + 0.16305(25)^2 \approx 9.5 \text{ thousand students/year}.$$

(Note that these rates of change are independent of time as we chose a model that is linear in time.)

4. *Some near-term projections of the student population trend.* As we have seen throughout the book, extrapolation can be a risky venture; however, *near-term* extrapolation from a good model can be reasonable. You enter the model in an Excel spreadsheet to obtain the following predicted college enrollments (in thousands) for the years 2006–2010:

x ↓	$t \rightarrow$				
	26	**27**	**28**	**29**	**30**
21	1,510	1,531	1,551	1,572	1,593
29.5	357	359	362	365	368
38	431	440	449	458	467

EXERCISES

1. Use Excel to obtain Model 1:

$$N(t, x) = a_1 + a_2 t + a_3 x + a_4 x^2 + a_5 xt.$$

Compare the fit of this model with that of the quadratic model above. Comment on the result.

2. How much is there to be gained by adding an additional term of the form $a_7 t^2$ to the original model? (Perform the regression and analyze the result by referring to the P-value for the resulting coefficient of t^2.) How does the addition of this term affect the slices $x = $ constant?

3. Compute and interpret $\left.\dfrac{\partial N}{\partial t}\right|_{(10,18)}$ and $\left.\dfrac{\partial^2 N}{\partial t \partial x}\right|_{(10,18)}$ for the model in the text. What are their units of measurement?

4. Notice that the derivatives in the preceding exercise do not depend on time. What additional polynomial term(s) would make both $\partial N/\partial t$ and $\partial^2 N/\partial t \partial x$ depend on time? (Write down the entire model.) Of what order is your model?

5. Test the model you constructed in the preceding question by discussing the P-values of the additional coefficients.

TI-83/84 Plus Technology Guide

Section 15.1

Example 1 (page 1081) You own a company that makes two models of speakers: the Ultra Mini and the Big Stack. Your total monthly cost (in dollars) to make x Ultra Minis and y Big Stacks is given by

$$C(x, y) = 10{,}000 + 20x + 40y.$$

Compute several values of this function.

Solution with Technology

You can have a TI-83/84 Plus compute $C(x, y)$ numerically as follows:

1. In the "Y=" screen, enter

$$Y_1 = 10000 + 20X + 40Y$$

2. To evaluate, say, $C(10, 30)$ (the cost to make 10 Ultra Minis and 30 Big Stacks), enter

$$10 \rightarrow X$$
$$30 \rightarrow Y$$
$$Y_1$$

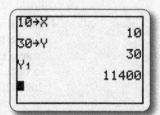

and the calculator will evaluate the function and give the answer $C(10, 30) = 11{,}400$.

This procedure is too laborious if you want to calculate $f(x, y)$ for a large number of different values of x and y.

EXCEL Technology Guide

Section 15.1

Example 1 (page 1081) You own a company that makes two models of speakers: the Ultra Mini and the Big Stack. Your total monthly cost (in dollars) to make x Ultra Minis and y Big Stacks is given by

$$C(x, y) = 10{,}000 + 20x + 40y.$$

Compute several values of this function.

Solution with Technology

Excel handles functions of several variables easily. The following setup shows how a table of values of C can be created, using values of x and y you enter:

	A	B	C
1	x	y	C(x, y)
2	10	30	=10000+20*A2+40*B2
3	20	30	
4	15	0	
5	0	30	
6	30	30	

↓

	A	B	C
1	x	y	C(x, y)
2	10	30	11400
3	20	30	11600
4	15	0	10300
5	0	30	11200
6	30	30	11800

A disadvantage of this layout is that it's not easy to enter values of x and y systematically in two columns. Can you find a way to remedy this? (See Example 3 for one method.)

Example 3 (page 1083) Use technology to create a table of values of the body mass index

$$M(w, h) = \frac{0.45w}{(0.0254h)^2}.$$

Solution with Technology

We can use this formula to recreate a table in Excel, as follows:

	A	B	C	D
1		130	140	150
2	60	=0.45*B$1/(0.0254*$A2)^2		
3	61			
4	62			
5	63			
6	64			
7	65			
8	66			
9	67			

In the formula in cell B2 we have used B$1 instead of B1 for the w-coordinate because we want all references to w to use the same row (1). Similarly, we want all references to h to refer to the same column (A), so we used $A2 instead of A2.

We copy the formula in cell B2 to all of the red shaded area to obtain the desired table:

	A	B	C	D	
1		130	140	150	
2	60	25.18755038	27.12505425	29.06255813	3
3	61	24.36849808	26.24299793	28.11749778	29.9
4	62	23.58875685	25.40327661	27.21779637	29.0
5	63	22.84585068	24.60322381	26.36059694	28.1
6	64	22.13749545	23.84037971	25.54326398	27.2
7	65	21.46158138	23.11247226	24.76336314	26.4
8	66	20.81615733	22.41740021	24.01864308	25.6
9	67	20.19941665	21.75321793	23.30701921	24.8

Example 5 (page 1086)   Obtain the graph of $f(x, y) = x^2 + y^2$.

Solution with Technology

1. Set up a table showing a range of values of x and y and the corresponding values of the function (see Example 3):

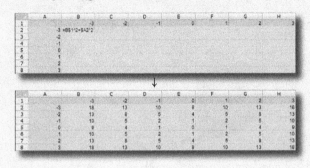

2. Select the cells with the values (B2: H8) and insert a chart, with the "Surface" option selected and "Series in Columns" selected as the data option, to obtain a graph like the following:

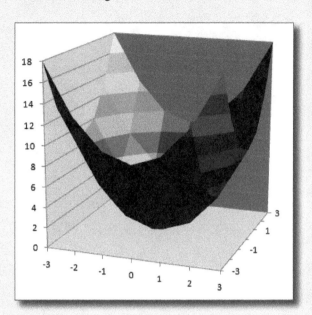

31.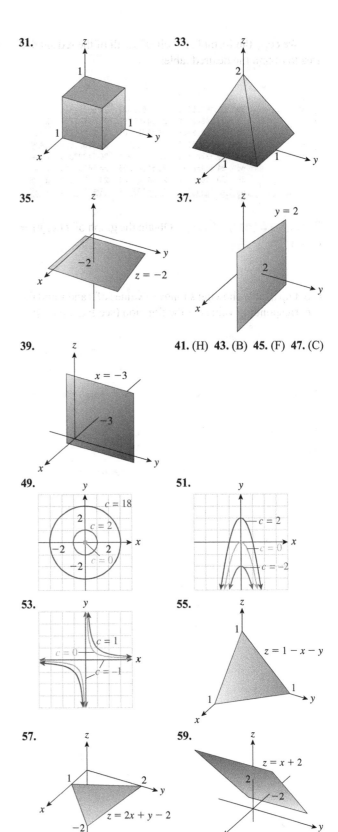

33.

35.

37.

39.

41. (H) **43.** (B) **45.** (F) **47.** (C)

49.

51.

53.

55.

57.

59.

Answers to Selected Exercises

Section 15.1

1. a. 1 **b.** 1 **c.** 2 **d.** $a^2 - a + 5$ **e.** $y^2 + x^2 - y + 1$
f. $(x + h)^2 + (y + k)^2 - (x + h) + 1$ **3. a.** 0 **b.** 0.2
c. -0.1 **d.** $0.18a + 0.2$ **e.** $0.1x + 0.2y - 0.01xy$
f. $0.2(x + h) + 0.1(y + k) - 0.01(x + h)(y + k)$ **5. a.** 1
b. e **c.** e **d.** e^{x+y+z} **e.** $e^{x+h+y+k+z+l}$ **7. a.** Does not exist
b. 0 **c.** 0 **d.** $xyz/(x^2 + y^2 + z^2)$ **e.** $(x + h)(y + k)(z + l)/$
$[(x + h)^2 + (y + k)^2 + (z + l)^2]$ **9. a.** Increases; 2.3
b. Decreases; 1.4 **c.** Decreases; 1 unit increase in z
11. Neither **13.** Linear **15.** Linear **17.** Interaction
19. a. 107 **b.** -14 **c.** -113

21.

	$x \to$			
	10	**20**	**30**	**40**
y **10**	52	107	162	217
$\downarrow$ **20**	94	194	294	394
30	136	281	426	571
40	178	368	558	748

25. 18, 4, 0.0965, 47,040 **27.** 6.9078, 1.5193, 5.4366, 0
29. Let $z =$ annual sales of Z (in millions of dollars),
$x =$ annual sales of X, and $y =$ annual sales of Y. The model is
$z = -2.1x + 0.4y + 16.2$.

322

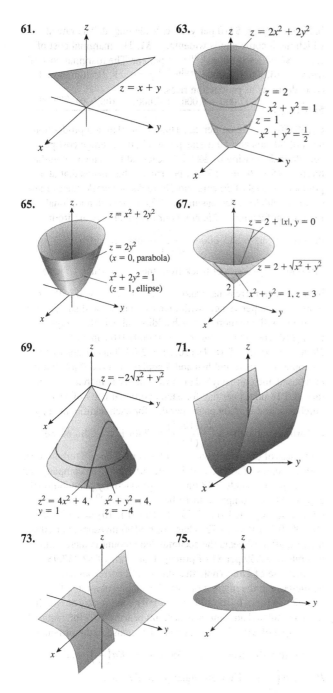

61. $z = x + y$

63. $z = 2x^2 + 2y^2$; $z = 2$; $x^2 + y^2 = 1$; $z = 1$; $x^2 + y^2 = \frac{1}{2}$

65. $z = x^2 + 2y^2$; $z = 2y^2$ ($x = 0$, parabola); $x^2 + 2y^2 = 1$ ($z = 1$, ellipse)

67. $z = 2 + |x|, y = 0$; $z = 2 + \sqrt{x^2 + y^2}$; $x^2 + y^2 = 1, z = 3$

69. $z = -2\sqrt{x^2 + y^2}$; $z^2 = 4x^2 + 4$, $y = 1$; $x^2 + y^2 = 4$, $z = -4$

71.

73.

75.

77. a. The marginal cost of cars is $6,000 per car. The marginal cost of trucks is $4,000 per truck. **b.** The graph is a plane with x-intercept -40, y-intercept -60, and z-intercept $240,000$. **c.** The slice $x = 10$ is the straight line with equation $z = 300,000 + 4,000y$. It describes the cost function for the manufacture of trucks if car production is held fixed at 10 cars per week. **d.** The level curve $z = 480,000$ is the straight line $6,000x + 4,000y = 240,000$. It describes the number of cars and trucks you can manufacture to maintain weekly costs at $480,000. **79.** $C(x, y) = 10 + 0.03x + 0.04y$ where C is the cost in dollars, $x = $ # video clips sold per month, $y = $ # audio clips sold per month **81. a.** 28% **b.** 21% **c.** Percentage points per year **83.** The graph is a plane with x_1-intercept 0.3, x_2-intercept 33, and x_3-intercept 0.66. The slices by $x_1 = $ constant are straight lines that are parallel to each other. Thus, the rate of change of **General Motors'** share as a function of **Ford**'s share does not depend on **Chrysler**'s share. Specifically, GM's share decreases by 0.02 percentage points per one percentage-point increase in **Ford**'s market share, regardless of **Chrysler**'s share. **85. a.** 189 thousand prisoners **b.** $y = 300$: $N = -0.02x + 51$; $y = 500$: $N = 0.02x + 67$; when there are 300,000 prisoners in local jails, the number in federal prisons decreases by 20 per 1,000 additional prisoners in state prisons. When there are 500,000 prisoners in local jails, the number in federal prisons increases by 20 per 1,000 additional prisoners in state prisons. **87. a.** The slices $x = $ constant and $y = $ constant are straight lines. **b.** No. Even though the slices $x = $ constant and $y = $ constant are straight lines, the level curves are not, and so the surface is not a plane. **c.** The slice $x = 10$ has a slope of 3,800. The slice $x = 20$ has a slope of 3,600. Manufacturing more cars lowers the marginal cost of manufacturing trucks. **89. a.** $9,980 **b.** $R(z) = 9,850 + 0.04z$ **91.** $f(x, t) = 6x - 2$; $313 billion **93.** $U(11, 10) - U(10, 10) \approx 5.75$. This means that, if your company now has 10 copies of Macro Publish and 10 copies of Turbo Publish, then the purchase of one additional copy of Macro Publish will result in a productivity increase of approximately 5.75 pages per day. **95.** Answers will vary. $(a, b, c) = (3, 1/4, 1/\pi)$; $(a, b, c) = (1/\pi, 3, 1/4)$. **97.** 7,000,000 **99. a.** $100 = K(1,000)^a(1,000,000)^{1-a}$; $10 = K(1,000)^a(10,000)^{1-a}$ **b.** $\log K - 3a = -4$; $\log K - a = -3$ **c.** $P = 71$ pianos (to the nearest piano) **101. a.** 4×10^{-3} gram per square meter **b.** The total weight of sulfates in the earth's atmosphere **103. a.** The value of N would be doubled. **b.** $N(R, f_p, n_e, f_l, f_i, L) = R f_p n_e f_l f_i L$, where here L is the average lifetime of an intelligent civilization **c.** Take the logarithm of both sides, since this would yield the linear function $\ln(N) = \ln(R) + \ln(f_p) + \ln(n_e) + \ln(f_l) + \ln(f_i) + \ln(f_c) + \ln(L)$. **105.** They are reciprocals of each other. **107.** For example, $f(x, y) = x^2 + y^2$. **109.** For example, $f(x, y, z) = xyz$ **111.** For example, take $f(x, y) = x + y$. Then setting $y = 3$ gives $f(x, 3) = x + 3$. This can be viewed as a function of the single variable x. Choosing other values for y gives other functions of x. **113.** The slope is independent of the choice of $y = k$. **115.** That CDs cost more than cassettes **117.** Plane **119. (B)** Traveling in the direction B results in the shortest trip to nearby isotherms, and hence the fastest rate of increase in temperature. **121.** Agree: Any slice through a plane is a straight line. **123.** The graph of a function of three or more variables lives in four-dimensional (or higher) space, which makes it difficult to draw and visualize.

Section 15.2

1. $f_x(x, y) = -40$; $f_y(x, y) = 20$; $f_x(1, -1) = -40$; $f_y(1, -1) = 20$ **3.** $f_x(x, y) = 6x + 1$; $f_y(x, y) = -3y^2$; $f_x(1, -1) = 7$; $f_y(1, -1) = -3$ **5.** $f_x(x, y) = -40 + 10y$; $f_y(x, y) = 20 + 10x$; $f_x(1, -1) = -50$; $f_y(1, -1) = 30$

7. $f_x(x, y) = 6xy$; $f_y(x, y) = 3x^2$; $f_x(1, -1) = -6$; $f_y(1, -1) = 3$ **9.** $f_x(x, y) = 2xy^3 - 3x^2y^2 - y$; $f_y(x, y) = 3x^2y^2 - 2x^3y - x$; $f_x(1, -1) = -4$; $f_y(1, -1) = 4$ **11.** $f_x(x, y) = 6y(2xy + 1)^2$; $f_y(x, y) = 6x(2xy + 1)^2$; $f_x(1, -1) = -6$; $f_y(1, -1) = 6$ **13.** $f_x(x, y) = e^{x+y}$; $f_y(x, y) = e^{x+y}$; $f_x(1, -1) = 1$; $f_y(1, -1) = 1$ **15.** $f_x(x, y) = 3x^{-0.4}y^{0.4}$; $f_y(x, y) = 2x^{0.6}y^{-0.6}$; $f_x(1, -1)$ undefined; $f_y(1, -1)$ undefined **17.** $f_x(x, y) = 0.2ye^{0.2xy}$; $f_y(x, y) = 0.2xe^{0.2xy}$; $f_x(1, -1) = -0.2e^{-0.2}$; $f_y(1, -1) = 0.2e^{-0.2}$ **19.** $f_{xx}(x, y) = 0$; $f_{yy}(x, y) = 0$; $f_{xy}(x, y) = f_{yx}(x, y) = 0$; $f_{xx}(1, -1) = 0$; $f_{yy}(1, -1) = 0$; $f_{xy}(1, -1) = f_{yx}(1, -1) = 0$ **21.** $f_{xx}(x, y) = 0$; $f_{yy}(x, y) = 0$; $f_{xy}(x, y) = f_{yx}(x, y) = 10$; $f_{xx}(1, -1) = 0$; $f_{yy}(1, -1) = 0$; $f_{xy}(1, -1) = f_{yx}(1, -1) = 10$ **23.** $f_{xx}(x, y) = 6y$; $f_{yy}(x, y) = 0$; $f_{xy}(x, y) = f_{yx}(x, y) = 6x$; $f_{xx}(1, -1) = -6$; $f_{yy}(1, -1) = 0$; $f_{xy}(1, -1) = f_{yx}(1, -1) = 6$ **25.** $f_{xx}(x, y) = e^{x+y}$; $f_{yy}(x, y) = e^{x+y}$; $f_{xy}(x, y) = f_{yx}(x, y) = e^{x+y}$; $f_{xx}(1, -1) = 1$; $f_{yy}(1, -1) = 1$; $f_{xy}(1, -1) = f_{yx}(1, -1) = 1$ **27.** $f_{xx}(x, y) = -1.2x^{-1.4}y^{0.4}$; $f_{yy}(x, y) = -1.2x^{0.6}y^{-1.6}$; $f_{xy}(x, y) = f_{yx}(x, y) = 1.2x^{-0.4}y^{-0.6}$; $f_{xx}(1, -1)$ undefined; $f_{yy}(1, -1)$ undefined; $f_{xy}(1, -1)$ & $f_{yx}(1, -1)$ undefined **29.** $f_x(x, y, z) = yz$; $f_y(x, y, z) = xz$; $f_z(x, y, z) = xy$; $f_x(0, -1, 1) = -1$; $f_y(0, -1, 1) = 0$; $f_z(0, -1, 1) = 0$ **31.** $f_x(x, y, z) = 4/(x + y + z^2)^2$; $f_y(x, y, z) = 4/(x + y + z^2)^2$; $f_z(x, y, z) = 8z/(x + y + z^2)^2$; $f_x(0, -1, 1)$ undefined; $f_y(0, -1, 1)$ undefined; $f_z(0, -1, 1)$ undefined **33.** $f_x(x, y, z) = e^{yz} + yze^{xz}$; $f_y(x, y, z) = xze^{yz} + e^{xz}$; $f_z(x, y, z) = xy(e^{yz} + e^{xz})$; $f_x(0, -1, 1) = e^{-1} - 1$; $f_y(0, -1, 1) = 1$; $f_z(0, -1, 1) = 0$ **35.** $f_x(x, y, z) = 0.1x^{-0.9}y^{0.4}z^{0.5}$; $f_y(x, y, z) = 0.4x^{0.1}y^{-0.6}z^{0.5}$; $f_z(x, y, z) = 0.5x^{0.1}y^{0.4}z^{-0.5}$; $f_x(0, -1, 1)$ undefined; $f_y(0, -1, 1)$ undefined; $f_z(0, -1, 1)$ undefined **37.** $f_x(x, y, z) = yze^{xyz}$, $f_y(x, y, z) = xze^{xyz}$, $f_z(x, y, z) = xye^{xyz}$; $f_x(0, -1, 1) = -1$; $f_y(0, -1, 1) = f_z(0, -1, 1) = 0$ **39.** $f_x(x, y, z) = 0$; $f_y(x, y, z) = -\dfrac{600z}{y^{0.7}(1 + y^{0.3})^2}$; $f_z(x, y, z) = \dfrac{2,000}{1 + y^{0.3}}$; $f_x(0, -1, 1)$ undefined; $f_y(0, -1, 1)$ undefined; $f_z(0, -1, 1)$ undefined **41.** $\partial C/\partial x = 6,000$, the marginal cost to manufacture each car is $6,000. $\partial C/\partial y = 4,000$, the marginal cost to manufacture each truck is $4,000. **43.** $\partial y/\partial t = -0.78$. The number of articles written by researchers in the United States was decreasing at a rate of 0.78 percentage points per year. $\partial y/\partial x = -1.02$. The number of articles written by researchers in the United States was decreasing at a rate of 1.02 percentage points per one percentage point increase in articles written in Europe. **45.** $5,600 per car **47. a.** $\partial M/\partial c = -3.8$, $\partial M/\partial f = 2.2$. For every 1 point increase in the percentage of **Chrysler** owners who remain loyal, the percentage of **Mazda** owners who remain loyal decreases by 3.8 points. For every 1 point increase in the percentage of **Ford** owners who remain loyal, the percentage of **Mazda** owners who remain loyal increases by 2.2 points. **b.** 16% **49. a.** $36,600; $52,900

b. $270 per year; $410 per year **c.** Widening **d.** The rate at which the income gap is widening **51.** The marginal cost of cars is $6,000 + 1,000e^{-0.01(x+y)}$ per car. The marginal cost of trucks is $4,000 + 1,000e^{-0.01(x+y)}$ per truck. Both marginal costs decrease as production rises. **53.** $\bar{C}(x, y) = \dfrac{200,000 + 6,000x + 4,000y - 100,000e^{-0.01(x+y)}}{x + y}$; $\bar{C}_x(50, 50) = -$2.64$ per car. This means that at a production level of 50 cars and 50 trucks per week, the average cost per vehicle is decreasing by $2.64 for each additional car manufactured. $\bar{C}_y(50, 50) = -$22.64$ per truck. This means that at a production level of 50 cars and 50 trucks per week, the average cost per vehicle is decreasing by $22.64 for each additional truck manufactured. **55.** No; your marginal revenue from the sale of cars is $15,000 - \dfrac{2,500}{\sqrt{x + y}}$ per car and $10,000 - \dfrac{2,500}{\sqrt{x + y}}$ per truck from the sale of trucks. These increase with increasing x and y. In other words, you will earn more revenue per vehicle with increasing sales, and so the rental company will pay more for each additional vehicle it buys. **57.** $P_z(10, 100,000, 1,000,000) \approx 0.0001010$ papers/$ **59. a.** $U_x(10, 5) = 5.18$, $U_y(10, 5) = 2.09$. This means that if 10 copies of Macro Publish and 5 copies of Turbo Publish are purchased, the company's daily productivity is increasing at a rate of 5.18 pages per day for each additional copy of Macro purchased and by 2.09 pages per day for each additional copy of Turbo purchased. **b.** $\dfrac{U_x(10, 5)}{U_y(10, 5)} \approx 2.48$ is the ratio of the usefulness of one additional copy of Macro to one of Turbo. Thus, with 10 copies of Macro and 5 copies of Turbo, the company can expect approximately 2.48 times the productivity per additional copy of Macro compared to Turbo. **61.** 6×10^9 N/sec **63. a.** $A_P(100, 0.1, 10) = 2.59$; $A_r(100, 0.1, 10) = 2,357.95$; $A_t(100, 0.1, 10) = 24.72$. Thus, for a $100 investment at 10% interest, after 10 years the accumulated amount is increasing at a rate of $2.59 per $1 of principal, at a rate of $2,357.95 per increase of 1 in r (note that this would correspond to an increase in the interest rate of 100%), and at a rate of $24.72 per year. **b.** $A_P(100, 0.1, t)$ tells you the rate at which the accumulated amount in an account bearing 10% interest with a principal of $100 is growing per $1 increase in the principal, t years after the investment. **65. a.** $P_x = Ka\left(\dfrac{y}{x}\right)^b$ and $P_y = Kb\left(\dfrac{x}{y}\right)^a$. They are equal precisely when $\dfrac{a}{b} = \left(\dfrac{x}{y}\right)^b \left(\dfrac{x}{y}\right)^a$. Substituting $b = 1 - a$ now gives $\dfrac{a}{b} = \dfrac{x}{y}$. **b.** The given information implies that $P_x(100, 200) = P_y(100, 200)$. By part (a), this occurs precisely when $a/b = x/y = 100/200 = 1/2$. But $b = 1 - a$, so $a/(1 - a) = 1/2$, giving $a = 1/3$ and $b = 2/3$. **67.** Decreasing at 0.0075 parts of nutrient per part of water/sec **69.** f is increasing at a rate of s units per unit of x, f is increasing at a rate of t units per unit of y, and the value of

324

f is $\underline{r}$ when $x = \underline{a}$ and $y = \underline{b}$ **71.** The marginal cost of building an additional orbicus; zonars per unit.   **73.** Answers will vary. One example is $f(x, y) = -2x + 3y$. Others are $f(x, y) = -2x + 3y + 9$ and $f(x, y) = xy - 3x + 2y + 10$.
75. a. b is the z-intercept of the plane. m is the slope of the intersection of the plane with the xz-plane. n is the slope of the intersection of the plane with the yz-plane. **b.** Write $z = b + rx + sy$. We are told that $\partial z / \partial x = m$, so $r = m$. Similarly, $s = n$. Thus, $z = b + mx + ny$. We are also told that the plane passes through (h, k, l). Substituting gives $l = b + mh + nk$. This gives b as $l - mh - nk$. Substituting in the equation for z therefore gives $z = l - mh - nk + mx + ny = l + m(x - h) + n(y - k)$, as required.

Section 15.3

1. P: relative minimum; Q: none of the above; R: relative maximum   **3.** P: saddle point; Q: relative maximum; R: none of the above   **5.** Relative minimum   **7.** Neither   **9.** Saddle point   **11.** Relative minimum at $(0, 0, 1)$ **13.** Relative maximum at $(-1/2, 1/2, 3/2)$ **15.** Saddle point at $(0, 0, 0)$
17. Minimum at $(4, -3, -10)$ **19.** Maximum at $(-7/4, 1/4, 19/8)$ **21.** Relative maximum at $(0, 0, 0)$, saddle points at $(\pm 4, 2, -16)$ **23.** Relative minimum at $(0, 0, 0)$, saddle points at $(-1, \pm 1, 1)$ **25.** Relative minimum at $(0, 0, 1)$
27. Relative minimum at $(-2, \pm 2, -16)$, $(0, 0)$ a critical point that is not a relative extremum   **29.** Saddle point at $(0, 0, -1)$
31. Relative maximum at $(-1, 0, e)$ **33.** Relative minimum at $(2^{1/3}, 2^{1/3}, 3(2^{2/3}))$ **35.** Relative minimum at $(1, 1, 4)$ and $(-1, -1, 4)$ **37.** Absolute minimum at $(0, 0, 1)$ **39.** None; the relative maximum at $(0, 0, 0)$ is not absolute. (Look at, say, $(10, 10)$.)   **41.** Minimum of $1/3$ at $(c, f) = (2/3, 2/3)$. Thus, at least $1/3$ of all **Mazda** owners would choose another new **Mazda**, and this lowest loyalty occurs when $2/3$ of **Chrysler** and **Ford** owners remain loyal to their brands.   **43.** It should remove 2.5 pounds of sulfur and 1 pound of lead per day.   **45.** You should charge $\$580.81$ for the Ultra Mini and $\$808.08$ for the Big Stack   **47.** $l = w = h \approx 20.67$ in, volume $\approx 8,827$ cubic inches   **49.** 18 in $\times$ 18 in $\times$ 36 in, volume $= 11,664$ cubic inches

51.   **53.** Continues up indefinitely

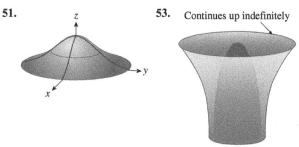

Continues down indefinitely
Function not defined on circle

55. H must be positive.   **57.** No. In order for there to be a relative maximum at (a, b), *all* vertical planes through (a, b) should yield a curve with a relative maximum at (a, b). It could happen that a slice by another vertical plane through (a, b) (such as

$x - a = y - b$) does not yield a curve with a relative maximum at (a, b). [An example is $f(x, y) = x^2 + y^2 - \sqrt{xy}$, at the point $(0, 0)$. Look at the slices through $x = 0$, $y = 0$ and $y = x$.]
59. $\bar{C}_x = \dfrac{\partial}{\partial x}\left(\dfrac{C}{x + y}\right) = \dfrac{(x + y)C_x - C}{(x + y)^2}$. If this is zero, then
$(x + y)C_x = C$, or $C_x = \dfrac{C}{x + y} = \bar{C}$. Similarly, if $\bar{C}_y = 0$ then
$C_y = \bar{C}$. This is reasonable because if the average cost is decreasing with increasing x, then the average cost is greater than the marginal cost C_x. Similarly, if the average cost is increasing with increasing x, then the average cost is less than the marginal cost C_x. Thus, if the average cost is stationary with increasing x, then the average cost equals the marginal cost C_x. (The situation is similar for the case of increasing y.)
61. The equation of the tangent plane at the point (a, b) is $z = f(a, b) + f_x(a, b)(x - a) + f_y(a, b)(y - b)$. If f has a relative extremum at (a, b), then $f_x(a, b) = 0 = f_y(a, b)$. Substituting these into the equation of the tangent plane gives $z = f(a, b)$, a constant. But the graph of $z = constant$ is a plane parallel to the xy-plane.

Section 15.4

1. 1; $(0, 0, 0)$ **3.** 1.35; $(1/10, 3/10, 1/2)$ **5.** Minimum value $= 6$ at $(1, 2, 1/2)$ **7.** 200; $(20, 10)$ **9.** 16; $(2, 2)$ and $(-2, -2)$
11. 20; $(2, 4)$ **13.** 1; $(0, 0, 0)$ **15.** 1.35; $(1/10, 3/10, 1/2)$
17. Minimum value $= 6$ at $(1, 2, 1/2)$ **19.** $5 \times 10 = 50$ sq. ft.
21. $\$10$ **23.** $(1/\sqrt{3}, 1/\sqrt{3}, 1/\sqrt{3})$, $(-1/\sqrt{3}, -1/\sqrt{3}, 1/\sqrt{3})$, $(1/\sqrt{3}, -1/\sqrt{3}, -1/\sqrt{3})$, $(-1/\sqrt{3}, 1/\sqrt{3}, -1/\sqrt{3})$
25. $(0, 1/2, -1/2)$ **27.** $(-5/9, 5/9, 25/9)$ **29.** $l \times w \times h = 1 \times 1 \times 2$ **31.** 18 in $\times$ 18 in $\times$ 36 in, volume $= 11,664$ cubic inches   **33.** $(2l/h)^{1/3} \times (2l/h)^{1/3} \times 2^{1/3}(h/l)^{2/3}$, where $l =$ cost of lightweight cardboard and $h =$ cost of heavy-duty cardboard per square foot   **35.** $1 \times 1 \times 1/2$ **37.** 6 laborers, 10 robots for a productivity of 368 pairs of socks per day
39. Method 1: Solve $g(x, y, z) = 0$ for one of the variables and substitute in $f(x, y, z)$. Then find the maximum value of the resulting function of 2 variables. Advantage (answers may vary): We can use the second derivative test to check whether the resulting critical points are maxima, minima, saddle points, or none of these. Disadvantage (answers may vary): We may not be able to solve $g(x, y, z) = 0$ for one of the variables. Method 2: Use the method of Lagrange multipliers. Advantage (answers may vary): We do not need to solve the constraint equation for one of the variables. Disadvantage (answers may vary): The method does not tell us whether the critical points obtained are maxima, minima, points of inflection, or none of these.
41. If the only constraint is an equality constraint, and if it is impossible to eliminate one of the variables in the objective function by substitution (solving the constraint equation for a variable or some other method).   **43.** Answers may vary: Maximize $f(x, y) = 1 - x^2 - y^2$ subject to $x = y$.
45. Yes. There may be relative extrema at points on the boundary of the domain of the function. The partial derivatives of the function need not be 0 at such points.   **47.** If the solution were located in the interior of one of the line segments making up the

boundary of the domain of f, then the derivative of a certain function would be 0. This function is obtained by substituting the linear equation $C(x, y) = 0$ in the linear objective function. But since the result would again be a linear function, it is either constant, or its derivative is a non-zero constant. In either event, extrema lie on the boundary of that line segment; that is, at one of the corners of the domain.

Section 15.5

1. $-1/2$ **3.** $e^2/2 - 7/2$ **5.** $(e^3 - 1)(e^2 - 1)$ **7.** $7/6$
9. $[e^3 - e - e^{-1} + e^{-3}]/2$ **11.** $1/2$ **13.** $(e - 1)/2$ **15.** $45/2$
17. $8/3$ **19.** $4/3$ **21.** 0 **23.** $2/3$ **25.** $2/3$ **27.** $2(e - 2)$
29. $2/3$

31. $\displaystyle\int_0^1 \int_0^{1-x} f(x, y)\, dy\, dx$ **33.** $\displaystyle\int_0^1 \int_0^{1-x} f(x, y)\, dy\, dx$

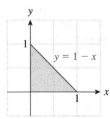
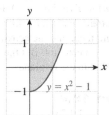

35. $\displaystyle\int_1^4 \int_1^{2/\sqrt{y}} f(x, y)\, dx\, dy$

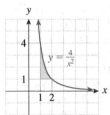

37. $4/3$ **39.** $1/6$ **41.** $162{,}000$ gadgets **43.** $\$312{,}750$
45. $\$17{,}500$ **47.** $8{,}216$ **49.** 1 degree **51.** The area between the curves $y = r(x)$ and $y = s(x)$ and the vertical lines $x = a$ and $x = b$ is given by $\int_a^b \int_{r(x)}^{s(x)} dy\, dx$ assuming that $r(x) \le s(x)$ for $a \le x \le b$. **53.** The first step in calculating an integral of the form $\int_a^b \int_{r(x)}^{s(x)} f(x, y)\, dy\, dx$ is to evaluate the integral $\int_{r(x)}^{s(x)} f(x, y)\, dy$, obtained by holding x constant and integrating with respect to y. **55.** Paintings per picasso per dali **57.** Left-hand side is $\int_a^b \int_c^d f(x) g(y)\, dx\, dy = \int_a^b \left(g(y) \int_c^d f(x)\, dx \right) dy$ (because $g(y)$ is treated as a constant in the inner integral) $= \left(\int_c^d f(x)\, dx \right) \int_a^b g(y)\, dy$ (because $\int_c^d f(x)\, dx$ is a constant and can therefore be taken outside the integral).
$\displaystyle\int_0^1 \int_1^2 y e^x\, dx\, dy = \frac{1}{2}(e^2 - e)$ no matter how we compute it.

Chapter 15 Review

1. 0; $14/3$; $1/2$; $\dfrac{1}{1+z} + z^3$; $\dfrac{x+h}{y+k+(x+h)(z+l)} +$
$(x+h)^2(y+k)$ **3.** Decreases by 0.32 units; increases by 12.5 units **5.** Reading left to right, starting at the top: $4, 0, 0, 3,$

$0, 1, 2, 0, 2$ **7.** Answers may vary; two examples are $f(x, y) = 3(x - y)/2$ and $f(x, y) = 3(x - y)^3/8$. **9.** $f_x = 2x + y,$
$f_y = x$, $f_{yy} = 0$ **11.** 0 **13.** $\dfrac{\partial f}{\partial x} = \dfrac{-x^2 + y^2 + z^2}{(x^2 + y^2 + z^2)^2}$, $\dfrac{\partial f}{\partial y} =$
$\dfrac{2xy}{(x^2 + y^2 + z^2)^2}$, $\dfrac{\partial f}{\partial z} = -\dfrac{2xz}{(x^2 + y^2 + z^2)^2}$, $\dfrac{\partial f}{\partial x}\Big|_{(0,1,0)} = 1$
15. Absolute minimum at $(1, 3/2)$ **17.** Saddle point at $(0, 0)$
19. Absolute maximum at each point on the circle $x^2 + y^2 = 1$
21. $1/27$ at $(1/3, 1/3, 1/3)$ **23.** $(0, 2, \sqrt{2})$ **25.** 4; $(\sqrt{2}, \sqrt{2})$
and $(-\sqrt{2}, -\sqrt{2})$ **27.** Minimum value $= 5$ at $(2, 1, 1/2)$
29. 2 **31.** $\ln 5$ **33.** 1 **35. a.** $h(x, y) = 5{,}000 - 0.8x - 0.6y$
hits per day ($x =$ number of new customers at JungleBooks.com, $y =$ number of new customers at FarmerBooks.com) **b.** 250
c. $h(x, y, z) = 5{,}000 - 0.8x - 0.6y + 0.0001z$ ($z =$ number of new Internet shoppers) **d.** 1.4 million **37. a.** $2{,}320$ hits per day
b. $0.08 + 0.00003x$ hits (daily) per dollar spent on television advertising per month; increases with increasing x **c.** $\$4{,}000$ per month **39.** (A) **41. a.** About $15{,}800$ additional orders per day
b. 11 **43.** $\$23{,}050$

Appendix A **Logic**

Introduction

Logic is the underpinning of all reasoned argument. The ancient Greeks recognized its role in mathematics and philosophy, and studied it extensively. Aristotle, in his *Organon*, wrote the first systematic treatise on logic. His work had a heavy influence on philosophy, science and religion through the Middle Ages.

But Aristotle's logic was expressed in ordinary language, so was subject to the ambiguities of ordinary language. Philosophers came to want to express logic more formally and symbolically, more like the way that mathematics is written (Leibniz, in the 17th century, was probably the first to envision and call for such a formalism). It was with the publication in 1847 of G. Boole's *The Mathematical Analysis of Logic* and A. DeMorgan's *Formal Logic* that **symbolic logic** came into being, and logic became recognized as part of mathematics. Since Boole and DeMorgan, logic and mathematics have been inextricably intertwined. Logic is part of mathematics, but at the same time it is the language of mathematics.

The study of symbolic logic is usually broken into several parts. The first and most fundamental is the **propositional logic**. Built on top of this is the **predicate logic**, which is the language of mathematics. In this appendix we give an introduction to propositional logic.

A.1 **Statements and Logical Operators**

Propositional logic is the study of *propositions*. A **statement**, or **proposition**, is any declarative sentence which is either true (T) or false (F). We refer to T or F as the **truth value** of the statement.

For a much more extensive interactive treatment of logic, including discussion of proofs, rules of inference, and an introduction to the predicate calculus, go online and follow:

Online Text

→ Online Topics in Finite Mathematics

→ Introduction to Logic

EXAMPLE 1 **Statements**

a. "$2 + 2 = 4$" is a statement because it can be either true or false.* Because it happens to be a true statement, its truth value is T.

b. "$1 = 0$" is also a statement, but its truth value is F.

c. "It will rain tomorrow" is a statement. To determine its truth value, we shall have to wait for tomorrow.

d. "Solve the following equation for x" is not a statement, because it cannot be assigned any truth value whatsoever. It is an imperative, or command, rather than a declarative sentence.

e. "The number 5" is not a statement, because it is not even a complete sentence.

---

*Is "$2 + 2 = 4$" a sentence? Read it aloud: "Two plus two equals four," is a perfectly respectable English sentence.

f. "This statement is false" gets us into a bind: If it were true, then, because it is declaring itself to be false, it must be false. On the other hand, if it were false, then its declaring itself false is a lie, so it is true! In other words, if it is true, then it is false, and if it is false, then it is true, and we go around in circles. We get out of this bind by saying that because the sentence cannot be either true or false, we refuse to call it a statement. An equivalent pseudo-statement is: "I am lying," so this sentence is known as **the liar's paradox**.

Note Sentences that refer to themselves, or *self-referential sentences*, as illustrated in Example 1(f), are not permitted to be statements. This eliminates the liar's paradox and several similar problems. ■

We shall use letters like p, q, r and so on to stand for statements. Thus, for example, we might decide that p should stand for the statement "the moon is round." We write

p: "the moon is round" p is the statement that the moon is round

to express this.

We can form new statements from old ones in several different ways. For example, starting with p: "I am an Anchovian," we can form the **negation** of p: "It is not the case that I am an Anchovian" or simply "I am not an Anchovian."

Negation of a Statement

If p is a statement, then its **negation** is the statement "not p" and is denoted by $\sim p$. We mean by this that, if p is true, then $\sim p$ is false, and vice versa.

Quick Examples

1. If p: "$2 + 2 = 4$," then $\sim p$: "It is not the case that $2 + 2 = 4$," or, more simply, $\sim p$: "$2 + 2 \neq 4$."
2. If q: "$1 = 0$," then $\sim q$: "$1 \neq 0$."
3. If r: "Diamonds are a pearl's best friend," then $\sim r$: "Diamonds are not a pearl's best friend."
4. If s: "All politicians are crooks," then $\sim s$: "Not all politicians are crooks."
5. **Double Negation:** If p is any statement, then the negation of $\sim p$ is $\sim(\sim p)$: "not (not p)," or, in other words, p. Thus $\sim(\sim p)$ has the same meaning as p.

Notes

1. Notice in Quick Example 1 above that $\sim p$ is false, because p is true. However, in Quick Example 2, $\sim q$ is true, because q is false. A statement of the form $\sim q$ can very well be true; it is a common mistake to think it must be false.

2. Saying that not all politicians are crooks is not the same as saying that no politicians are crooks, but is the same as saying that some (meaning one or more) politicians are not crooks.

3. The symbol $\sim$ is our first example of a **logical operator**.

4. When we say in Quick Example 5 above that $\sim(\sim p)$ has the same meaning as p, we mean that they are *logically equivalent*—a notion we will make precise below. ■

Here is another way we can form a new statement from old ones. Starting with p: "I am wise," and q: "I am strong," we can form the statement "I am wise and I am strong." We denote this new statement by $p \wedge q$, read "p and q." In order for $p \wedge q$ to be true, *both p and q* must be true. Thus, for example, if I am wise but not strong, then $p \wedge q$ is false. The symbol $\wedge$ is another logical operator. The statement $p \wedge q$ is called the **conjunction** of p and q.

Conjunction

The **conjunction** of p and q is the statement $p \wedge q$, which we read "p and q." It can also be said in a number of different ways, such as "p even though q." The statement $p \wedge q$ is true when both p and q are true and false otherwise.

Quick Examples

1. If p: "This galaxy will ultimately disappear into a black hole" and q: "$2 + 2 = 4$," then $p \wedge q$ is the statement "Not only will this galaxy ultimately disappear into a black hole, but $2 + 2 = 4$!"

2. If p: "$2 + 2 = 4$" and q: "$1 = 0$," then $p \wedge q$: "$2 + 2 = 4$ and $1 = 0$." Its truth value is F because q is F.

3. With p and q as in Quick Example 1, the statement $p \wedge (\sim q)$ says: "This galaxy will ultimately disappear into a black hole and $2 + 2 \neq 4$," or, more colorfully, as "Contrary to your hopes, this galaxy is doomed to disappear into a black hole; moreover, two plus two is decidedly *not* equal to four!"

Notes

1. We sometimes use the word "but" as an emphatic form of "and." For instance, if p: "It is hot," and q: "It is not humid," then we can read $p \wedge q$ as "It is hot but not humid." There are always many ways of saying essentially the same thing in a natural language; one of the purposes of symbolic logic is to strip away the verbiage and record the underlying logical structure of a statement.

2. A **compound statement** is a statement formed from simpler statements via the use of logical operators. Examples are $\sim p$, $(\sim p) \wedge (q \wedge r)$ and $p \wedge (\sim p)$. A statement that cannot be expressed as a compound statement is called an **atomic statement**.[1] For example, "I am clever" is an atomic statement. In a compound statement such as $(\sim p) \wedge (q \wedge r)$, we refer to p, q and r as the **variables** of the statement. Thus, for example, $\sim p$ is a compound statement in the single variable p. ∎

Before discussing other logical operators, we pause for a moment to talk about **truth tables**, which give a convenient way to analyze compound statements.

Truth Table

The **truth table** for a compound statement shows, for each combination of possible truth values of its variables, the corresponding truth value of the statement.

---

[1]"Atomic" comes from the Greek for "not divisible." Atoms were originally thought to be the indivisible components of matter, but the march of science proved that wrong. The name stuck, though.

Quick Examples

1. The truth table for negation, that is, for $\sim p$, is:

p	$\sim p$
T	F
F	T

Each row shows a possible truth value for p and the corresponding value of $\sim p$.

2. The truth table for conjunction, that is, for $p \wedge q$, is:

p	q	$p \wedge q$
T	T	T
T	F	F
F	T	F
F	F	F

Each row shows a possible combination of truth values of p and q and the corresponding value of $p \wedge q$.

EXAMPLE 2 Construction of Truth Tables

Construct truth tables for the following compound statements.

a. $\sim(p \wedge q)$ **b.** $(\sim p) \wedge q$

Solution

a. Whenever we encounter a complex statement, we work from the inside out, just as we might do if we had to evaluate an algebraic expression like $-(a + b)$. Thus, we start with the p and q columns, then construct the $p \wedge q$ column, and finally, the $\sim(p \wedge q)$ column.

p	q	$p \wedge q$	$\sim(p \wedge q)$
T	T	T	F
T	F	F	T
F	T	F	T
F	F	F	T

Notice how we get the $\sim(p \wedge q)$ column from the $p \wedge q$ column: we reverse all the truth values.

b. Because there are two variables, p and q, we again start with the p and q columns. We then evaluate $\sim p$, and finally take the conjunction of the result with q.

p	q	$\sim p$	$(\sim p) \wedge q$
T	T	F	F
T	F	F	F
F	T	T	T
F	F	T	F

Because we are "and-ing" $\sim p$ with q, we look at the values in the $\sim p$ and q columns and combine these according to the instructions for "and." Thus, for example, in the first row we have $F \wedge T = F$ and in the third row we have $T \wedge T = T$.

Here is a third logical operator. Starting with p: "You are over 18" and q: "You are accompanied by an adult," we can form the statement "You are over 18 or are accompanied by an adult," which we write symbolically as $p \vee q$, read "p or q." Now in English the word "or" has several possible meanings, so we have to agree on which one we want here. Mathematicians have settled on the **inclusive or:** $p \vee q$ means p is true or q is true *or both are true*.[2] With p and q as above, $p \vee q$ stands for "You are over 18 or are accompanied by an adult, or both." We shall sometimes include the phrase "or both" for emphasis, but even if we leave it off we still interpret "or" as inclusive.

Disjunction

The **disjunction** of p and q is the statement $p \vee q$, which we read "p or q." Its truth value is defined by the following truth table.

p	q	$p \vee q$
T	T	T
T	F	T
F	T	T
F	F	F

This is the **inclusive** or, so $p \vee q$ is true when p is true or q is true *or both* are true.

Quick Examples

1. Let p: "The butler did it" and let q: "The cook did it." Then $p \vee q$: "Either the butler or the cook did it."
2. Let p: "The butler did it," and let q: "The cook did it," and let r: "The lawyer did it." Then $(p \vee q) \wedge (\sim r)$: "Either the butler or the cook did it, but not the lawyer."

Note The only way for $p \vee q$ to be false is for *both* p and q to be false. For this reason, we can say that $p \vee q$ also means "p and q are not both false." ∎

To introduce our next logical operator, we ask you to consider the following statement: "If you earn an A in logic, then I'll buy you a new car." It seems to be made up out of two simpler statements,

p: "You earn an A in logic," and
q: "I will buy you a new car."

---

[2]There is also the **exclusive or:** "*p or q but not both.*" This can be expressed as $(p \vee q) \wedge \sim(p \wedge q)$. Do you see why?

The original statement says: *if p is true, then q is true*, or, more simply, **if p, then** q. We can also phrase this as p **implies** q, and we write the statement symbolically as $p \rightarrow q$.

Now let us suppose for the sake of argument that the original statement: "If you earn an A in logic, then I'll buy you a new car," is true. This does *not* mean that you *will* earn an A in logic. All it says is that *if* you do so, then I will buy you that car. Thinking of this as a promise, the only way that it can be broken is if you *do* earn an A and I do *not* buy you a new car. With this in mind, we define the logical statement $p \rightarrow q$ as follows.

Conditional

The **conditional** $p \rightarrow q$, which we read "if p, then q" or "p implies q," is defined by the following truth table:

p	q	$p \rightarrow q$
T	T	T
T	F	F
F	T	T
F	F	T

The arrow "$\rightarrow$" is the **conditional** operator, and in $p \rightarrow q$ the statement p is called the **antecedent,** or **hypothesis,** and q is called the **consequent,** or **conclusion.** A statement of the form $p \rightarrow q$ is also called an **implication.**

Quick Examples

1. "If $1 + 1 = 2$ then the sun rises in the east" has the form $p \rightarrow q$ where p: "$1 + 1 = 2$" is true and q: "the sun rises in the east." is also true. Therefore the statement is true.

2. "If the moon is made of green cheese, then I am Arnold Schwartzenegger" has the form $p \rightarrow q$ where p is false. From the truth table, we see that $p \rightarrow q$ is therefore true, regardless of whether or not I am Arnold Schwartzenegger.

3. "If $1 + 1 = 2$ then $0 = 1$" has the form $p \rightarrow q$ where this time p is true but q is false. Therefore, by the truth table, the given statement is false.

Notes

1. The only way that $p \rightarrow q$ can be false is if p is true and q is false—this is the case of the "broken promise" in the car example above.

2. If you look at the last two rows of the truth table, you see that we say that "$p \rightarrow q$" is true when p is false, *no matter what the truth value of q.* Think again about the promise—if you don't get that A, then whether or not I buy you a new car, I have not broken my promise. It may seem strange at first to say that F → T is T and F → F is also T, but, as they did in choosing to say that "or" is always inclusive, mathematicians agreed that the truth table above gives the most useful definition of the conditional. ■

It is usually misleading to think of "if p then q" as meaning that p *causes* q. For instance, tropical weather conditions cause hurricanes, but one cannot claim that if there are tropical weather conditions, then there are (always) hurricanes. Here is a list of some English phrases that *do* have the same meaning as $p \rightarrow q$.

Some Phrasings of the Conditional

We interpret each of the following as equivalent to the conditional $p \to q$.

If p then q.	p implies q.
q follows from p.	Not p unless q.
q if p.	p only if q.
Whenever p, q.	q whenever p.
p is sufficient for q.	q is necessary for p.
p is a sufficient condition for q.	q is a necessary condition for p.

Quick Example

"If it's Tuesday, this must be Belgium" can be rephrased in several ways as follows:

"Its being Tuesday implies that this is Belgium."
"This is Belgium if it's Tuesday."
"It's Tuesday only if this is Belgium."
"It can't be Tuesday unless this is Belgium."
"Its being Tuesday is sufficient for this to be Belgium."
"That this is Belgium is a necessary condition for its being Tuesday."

Notice the difference between "if" and "only if." We say that "p only if q" means $p \to q$ because, assuming that $p \to q$ is true, p can be true only if q is also. In other words, the only line of the truth table that has $p \to q$ true and p true also has q true. The phrasing "p is a sufficient condition for q" says that it suffices to know that p is true to be able to conclude that q is true. For example, it is sufficient that you get an A in logic for me to buy you a new car. Other things might induce me to buy you the car, but an A in logic would suffice. The phrasing "q is necessary for p" says that for p to be true, q must be true (just as we said for "p only if q").

Q: *Does the commutative law hold for the conditional? In other words, is $p \to q$ the same as $q \to p$?*

A: No, as we can see in the following truth table:

p	q	$p \to q$	$q \to p$
T	T	T	T
T	F	F	T
F	T	T	F
F	F	T	T

not the same

Converse and Contrapositive

The statement $q \to p$ is called the **converse** of the statement $p \to q$. A conditional and its converse are *not* the same.

The statement $\sim q \to \sim p$ is the **contrapositive** of the statement $p \to q$. A conditional and its contrapositive are logically equivalent in the sense we define below: they have the same truth value for all possible values of p and q.

333

EXAMPLE 3 Converse and Contrapositive

Give the converse and contrapositive of the statement "If you earn an A in logic, then I'll buy you a new car."

Solution This statement has the form $p \to q$ where p: "you earn an A" and q: "I'll buy you a new car." The converse is $q \to p$. In words, this is "If I buy you a new car then you earned an A in logic."

The contrapositive is $(\sim q) \to (\sim p)$. In words, this is "If I don't buy you a new car, then you didn't earn an A in logic."

Assuming that the original statement is true, notice that the converse is not necessarily true. There is nothing in the original promise that prevents me from buying you a new car if you do not earn the A. On the other hand, the contrapositive is true. If I don't buy you a new car, it must be that you didn't earn an A; otherwise I would be breaking my promise.

It sometimes happens that we do want both a conditional and its converse to be true. The conjunction of a conditional and its converse is called a **biconditional**.

Biconditional

The **biconditional,** written $p \leftrightarrow q$, is defined to be the statement $(p \to q) \wedge (q \to p)$. Its truth table is the following:

p	q	$p \leftrightarrow q$
T	T	T
T	F	F
F	T	F
F	F	T

Phrasings of the Biconditional

We interpret each of the following as equivalent to $p \leftrightarrow q$.

p if and only if q.
p is necessary and sufficient for q.
p is equivalent to q.

Quick Example

"I teach math if and only if I am paid a large sum of money." can be rephrased in several ways as follows:

"I am paid a large sum of money if and only if I teach math."
"My teaching math is necessary and sufficient for me to be paid a large sum of money."
"For me to teach math, it is necessary and sufficient that I be paid a large sum of money."

A.2 Logical Equivalence

We mentioned above that we say that two statements are **logically equivalent** if for all possible truth values of the variables involved the two statements always have the same truth values. If s and t are equivalent, we write $s \equiv t$. This is *not* another logical statement. It is simply the claim that the two statements s and t are logically equivalent. Here are some examples.

EXAMPLE 4 Logical Equivalence

Use truth tables to show the following:

a. $p \equiv \sim(\sim p)$. This is called **double negation**.

b. $\sim(p \wedge q) \equiv (\sim p) \vee (\sim q)$. This is one of **DeMorgan's Laws**.

Solution

a. To demonstrate the logical equivalence of these two statements, we construct a truth table with columns for both p and $\sim(\sim p)$.

same

p	$\sim p$	$\sim(\sim p)$
T	F	T
F	T	F

Because the p and $\sim(\sim p)$ columns contain the same truth values in all rows, the two statements are logically equivalent.

b. We construct a truth table showing both $\sim(p \wedge q)$ and $(\sim p) \vee (\sim q)$.

same

p	q	$p \wedge q$	$\sim(p \wedge q)$	$\sim p$	$\sim q$	$(\sim p) \vee (\sim q)$
T	T	T	F	F	F	F
T	F	F	T	F	T	T
F	T	F	T	T	F	T
F	F	F	T	T	T	T

Because the $\sim(p \wedge q)$ column and $(\sim p) \vee (\sim q)$ column agree, the two statements are equivalent.

➡ **Before we go on...** The statement $\sim(p \wedge q)$ can be read as "It is not the case that both p and q are true" or "p and q are not both true." We have just shown that this is equivalent to "Either p is false or q is false." ∎

Here are the two equivalences known as DeMorgan's Laws.

DeMorgan's Laws

If p and q are statements, then

$$\sim(p \wedge q) \equiv (\sim p) \vee (\sim q)$$
$$\sim(p \vee q) \equiv (\sim p) \wedge (\sim q)$$

Quick Example

Let p: "the President is a Democrat," and q: "the President is a Republican." Then the following two statements say the same thing:

$\sim(p \wedge q)$: "the President is not both a Democrat and a Republican."

$(\sim p) \vee (\sim q)$: "either the President is not a Democrat, or he is not a Republican (or he is neither)."

Here is a list of some important logical equivalences, some of which we have already encountered. All of them can be verified using truth tables as in Example 4. (The verifications of some of these are in the exercise set.)

Important Logical Equivalences

$\sim(\sim p) \equiv p$	the Double Negative Law
$p \wedge q \equiv q \wedge p$	the Commutative Law for Conjunction.
$p \vee q \equiv q \vee p$	the Commutative Law for Disjunction.
$(p \wedge q) \wedge r \equiv p \wedge (q \wedge r)$	the Associative Law for Conjunction.
$(p \vee q) \vee r \equiv p \vee (q \vee r)$	the Associative Law for Disjunction.
$\sim(p \vee q) \equiv (\sim p) \wedge (\sim q)$	DeMorgan's Laws
$\sim(p \wedge q) \equiv (\sim p) \vee (\sim q)$	
$p \wedge (q \vee r) \equiv (p \wedge q) \vee (p \wedge r)$	the Distributive Laws
$p \vee (q \wedge r) \equiv (p \vee q) \wedge (p \vee r)$	
$p \wedge p \equiv p$	Absorption Laws
$p \vee p \equiv p$	
$p \to q \equiv (\sim q) \to (\sim p)$	Contrapositive Law

Note that these logical equivalences apply to *any* statement. The ps, qs and rs can stand for atomic statements or compound statements, as we see in the next example.

EXAMPLE 5 Applying Logical Equivalences

a. Apply DeMorgan's law (once) to the statement $\sim([p \wedge (\sim q)] \wedge r)$.

b. Apply the distributive law to the statement $(\sim p) \wedge [q \vee (\sim r)]$.

c. Consider: "You will get an A if either you are clever and the sun shines, or you are clever and it rains." Rephrase the condition more simply using the distributive law.

Solution

a. We can analyze the given statement from the outside in. It is first of all a negation, but further, it is the negation $\sim(A \wedge B)$, where A is the compound statement $[p \wedge (\sim q)]$ and B is r:

$$\sim(\quad \overbrace{A} \quad \wedge \quad B)$$
$$\sim(\; [p \wedge (\sim q)] \wedge \quad r)$$

336

Now one of DeMorgan's laws is

$$\sim(A \wedge B) \equiv (\sim A) \vee (\sim B)$$

Applying this equivalence gives

$$\sim([p \wedge (\sim q)] \wedge r) \equiv (\sim[p \wedge (\sim q)]) \vee (\sim r)$$

b. The given statement has the form $A \wedge [B \vee C]$, where $A = (\sim p)$, $B = q$, and $C = (\sim r)$. So, we apply the distributive law $A \wedge [B \vee C], \equiv [A \wedge B] \vee [A \wedge C]$:

$$(\sim p) \wedge [q \vee (\sim r)] \equiv [(\sim p) \wedge q] \vee [(\sim p) \wedge (\sim r)]$$

(We need not stop here: The second expression on the right is just begging for an application of DeMorgan's law. . .)

c. The condition is "either you are clever and the sun shines, or you are clever and it rains." Let's analyze this symbolically: Let p: "You are clever," q: "The sun shines," and r: "It rains." The condition is then $(p \wedge q) \vee (p \wedge r)$. We can "factor out" the p using one of the distributive laws in reverse, getting

$$(p \wedge q) \vee (p \wedge r) \equiv p \wedge (q \vee r)$$

We are taking advantage of the fact that the logical equivalences we listed can be read from right to left as well as from left to right. Putting $p \wedge (q \vee r)$ back into English, we can rephrase the sentence as "You will get an A if you are clever and either the sun shines or it rains."

➡ **Before we go on...** In part (a) of Example 5 we could, if we wanted, apply DeMorgan's law again, this time to the statement $\sim[p \wedge (\sim q)]$ that is part of the answer. Doing so gives

$$\sim[p \wedge (\sim q)] \equiv (\sim p) \vee \sim(\sim q) \equiv (\sim p) \vee q$$

Notice that we've also used the double negative law. Therefore, the original expression can be simplified as follows:

$$\sim([p \wedge (\sim q)] \wedge r) \equiv (\sim[p \wedge (\sim q)]) \vee (\sim r) \equiv ((\sim p) \vee q) \vee (\sim r)$$

which we can write as

$$(\sim p) \vee q \vee (\sim r)$$

because the associative law tells us that it does not matter which two expressions we "or" first. ∎

A.3 Tautologies, Contradictions, and Arguments

Tautologies and Contradictions

A compound statement is a **tautology** if its truth value is always T, regardless of the truth values of its variables. It is a **contradiction** if its truth value is always F, regardless of the truth values of its variables.

337

Quick Examples

1. $p \vee (\sim p)$ has truth table

p	$\sim p$	$p \vee (\sim p)$
T	F	T
F	T	T

— all T's

and is therefore a tautology.

2. $p \wedge (\sim p)$ has truth table

p	$\sim p$	$p \wedge (\sim p)$
T	F	F
F	T	F

and is therefore a contradiction.

When a statement is a tautology, we also say that the statement is **tautological**. In common usage this sometimes means simply that the statement is self-evident. In logic it means something stronger: that the statement is always true, under all circumstances. In contrast, a contradiction, or **contradictory** statement, is *never* true, under any circumstances.

Some of the most important tautologies are the **tautological implications**, tautologies that have the form of implications. We look at two of them: Direct Reasoning, and Indirect Reasoning:

Modus Ponens or Direct Reasoning

The following tautology is called *modus ponens* or **direct reasoning**:

$$[(p \rightarrow q) \wedge p] \rightarrow q$$

In Words
If an implication and its antecedent (p) are both true, then so is its consequent (q).

Quick Example

If my loving math implies that I will pass this course, and if I do love math, then I will pass this course.

Note You can check that the statement $[(p \rightarrow q) \wedge p] \rightarrow q$ is a tautology by drawing its truth table. ∎

Tautological implications are useful mainly because they allow us to check the validity of **arguments**.

Argument

An **argument** is a list of statements called **premises** followed by a statement called the **conclusion.** If the premises are $P_1, P_2, \ldots, P_n$ and the conclusion is C, then we say that the argument is **valid** if the statement $(P_1 \wedge P_2 \wedge \ldots \wedge P_n) \rightarrow C$ is a tautology. In other words, an argument is valid if the truth of all its premises logically implies the truth of its conclusion.

Quick Examples

1. The following is a valid argument:

$$p \rightarrow q$$
$$\underline{p}$$
$$\therefore \quad q$$

(This is the traditional way of writing an argument: We list the premises above a line and then put the conclusion below; the symbol "$\therefore$" stands for the word "therefore.") This argument is valid because the statement $[(p \rightarrow q) \wedge p] \rightarrow q$ is a tautology, namely *modus ponens*.

2. The following is an invalid argument:

$$p \rightarrow q$$
$$\underline{q}$$
$$\therefore \quad p$$

The argument is invalid because the statement $[(p \rightarrow q) \wedge q] \rightarrow p$ is not a tautology. In fact, if p is F and q is T, then the whole statement is F.

The argument in Quick Example 2 above is known as the *fallacy of affirming the consequent*. It is a common invalid argument and not always obviously flawed at first sight, so is often exploited by advertisers. For example, consider the following claim: All Olympic athletes drink Boors, so you should too. The suggestion is that, if you drink Boors, you will be an Olympic athlete:

If you are an Olympic Athlete you drink Boors.	Premise (Let's pretend this is True)
You drink Boors.	Premise (True)
$\therefore$ You are an Olympic Athlete.	Conclusion (May be false!)

This is an error that Boors hopes you will make!

There is, however, a correct argument in which we *deny* the consequent:

Modus Tollens or Indirect Reasoning

The following tautology is called *modus tollens* or **indirect reasoning:**

$$[(p \rightarrow q) \wedge (\sim q)] \rightarrow (\sim p)$$

In Words
If an implication is true but its consequent (q) is false, then its antecedent (p) is false.

In Argument Form

$$p \rightarrow q$$
$$\sim q$$
$$\therefore \ \sim q$$

Quick Example

If my loving math implies that I will pass this course, and if I do not pass the course, then it must be the case that I do not love math.
In argument form:

If I love math, then I will pass this course.

I will not pass the course.

Therefore, I do not love math.

Note This argument is not as direct as *modus ponens;* it contains a little twist: "If I loved math I would pass this course. However, I will not pass this course. Therefore, it must be that I don't love math (else I *would* pass this course)." Hence the name "indirect reasoning."

Note that, again, there is a similar, but fallacious argument to avoid, for instance: "If I were an Olympic athlete then I would drink Boors ($p \rightarrow q$). However, I am not an Olympic athlete ($\sim p$). Therefore, I won't drink Boors. ($\sim q$)." This is a mistake Boors certainly hopes you do *not* make! ■

There are other interesting tautologies that we can use to justify arguments. We mention one more and refer the interested reader to the website for more examples and further study.

For an extensive list of tautologies go online and follow:

Chapter L Logic

→ List of Tautologies and Tautological Implications

Disjunctive Syllogism or "One or the Other"

The following tautologies are both known as the **disjunctive syllogism** or **one-or-the-other:**

$$[(p \vee q) \wedge (\sim p)] \rightarrow q \qquad [(p \vee q) \wedge (\sim q)] \rightarrow p$$

In Words
If one or the other of two statements is true, but one is known to be false, then the other must be true.

In Argument Form

$$p \vee q \qquad\qquad p \vee q$$
$$\sim p \qquad\qquad\quad \sim q$$
$$\therefore \ q \qquad\qquad\quad \therefore \ p$$

Quick Example

The butler or the cook did it. The butler didn't do it. Therefore, the cook did it.
In argument form:

The butler or the cook did it.

The butler did not do it.

Therefore, the cook did it.

A EXERCISES

Which of Exercises 1–10 are statements? Comment on the truth values of all the statements you encounter. If a sentence fails to be a statement, explain why. HINT [See Example 1.]

1. All swans are white. **2.** The fat cat sat on the mat.

3. Look in thy glass and tell whose face thou viewest.[3]

4. My glass shall not persuade me I am old.[4]

5. There is no largest number.

6. 1,000,000,000 is the largest number.

7. Intelligent life abounds in the universe.

8. There may or may not be a largest number.

9. This is exercise number 9. **10.** This sentence no verb.[5]

Let p: "Our mayor is trustworthy," q: "Our mayor is a good speller," and r = "Our mayor is a patriot." Express each of the statements in Exercises 11–16 in logical form: HINT [See Quick Examples on pp. A2, A3, A5.]

11. Although our mayor is not trustworthy, he is a good speller.

12. Either our mayor is trustworthy, or he is a good speller.

13. Our mayor is a trustworthy patriot who spells well.

14. While our mayor is both trustworthy and patriotic, he is not a good speller.

15. It may or may not be the case that our mayor is trustworthy.

16. Our mayor is either not trustworthy or not a patriot, yet he is an excellent speller.

Let p: "Willis is a good teacher," q: "Carla is a good teacher," r: "Willis' students hate math," s: "Carla's students hate math." Express the statements in Exercises 17–24 in words.

17. $p \wedge (\sim r)$ **18.** $(\sim p) \wedge (\sim q)$

19. $q \vee (\sim q)$ **20.** $((\sim p) \wedge (\sim s)) \vee q$

21. $r \wedge (\sim r)$ **22.** $(\sim s) \vee (\sim r)$

23. $\sim (q \vee s)$ **24.** $\sim (p \wedge r)$

Assume that it is true that "Polly sings well," it is false that "Quentin writes well," and it is true that "Rita is good at math." Determine the truth of each of the statements in Exercises 25–32.

25. Polly sings well and Quentin writes well.

26. Polly sings well or Quentin writes well.

27. Polly sings poorly and Quentin writes well.

28. Polly sings poorly or Quentin writes poorly.

29. Either Polly sings well and Quentin writes poorly, or Rita is good at math.

30. Either Polly sings well and Quentin writes poorly, or Rita is not good at math.

31. Either Polly sings well or Quentin writes well, or Rita is good at math.

32. Either Polly sings well and Quentin writes well, or Rita is bad at math.

Find the truth value of each of the statements in Exercises 33–48. HINT [See Quick Examples on p. A6.]

33. "If $1 = 1$, then $2 = 2$." **34.** "If $1 = 1$, then $2 = 3$."

35. "If $1 \neq 0$, then $2 \neq 2$." **36.** "If $1 = 0$, then $1 = 1$."

37. "A sufficient condition for 1 to equal 2 is $1 = 3$."

38. "$1 = 1$ is a sufficient condition for 1 to equal 0."

39. "$1 = 0$ is a necessary condition for 1 to equal 1."

40. "$1 = 1$ is a necessary condition for 1 to equal 2."

41. "If I pay homage to the great Den, then the sun will rise in the east."

42. "If I fail to pay homage to the great Den, then the sun will still rise in the east."

43. "In order for the sun to rise in the east, it is necessary that it sets in the west."

44. "In order for the sun to rise in the east, it is sufficient that it sets in the west."

45. "The sun rises in the west only if it sets in the west."

46. "The sun rises in the east only if it sets in the east."

47. "In order for the sun to rise in the east, it is necessary and sufficient that it sets in the west."

48. "In order for the sun to rise in the west, it is necessary and sufficient that it sets in the east."

Construct the truth tables for the statements in Exercises 49–62. HINT [See Example 2.]

49. $p \wedge (\sim q)$ **50.** $p \vee (\sim q)$

51. $\sim (\sim p) \vee p$ **52.** $p \wedge (\sim p)$

53. $(\sim p) \wedge (\sim q)$ **54.** $(\sim p) \vee (\sim q)$

55. $(p \wedge q) \wedge r$ **56.** $p \wedge (q \wedge r)$

57. $p \wedge (q \vee r)$ **58.** $(p \wedge q) \vee (p \wedge r)$

59. $p \rightarrow (q \vee p)$ **60.** $(p \vee q) \rightarrow \sim p$

61. $p \leftrightarrow (p \vee q)$ **62.** $(p \wedge q) \leftrightarrow \sim p$

Use truth tables to verify the logical equivalences given in Exercises 63–72.

63. $p \wedge p \equiv p$ **64.** $p \vee p \equiv p$

65. $p \vee q \equiv q \vee p$ **66.** $p \wedge q \equiv q \wedge p$
(Commutative law for disjunction) (Commutative law for conjunction)

---

[3] William Shakespeare Sonnet 3

[4] Ibid., Sonnet 22.

[5] From *Metamagical Themas: Questing for the Essence of Mind and Pattern* by Douglas R. Hofstadter (Bantam Books, New York 1986)

67. $\sim(p \vee q) \equiv (\sim p) \wedge (\sim q)$ **68.** $\sim(p \wedge (\sim q)) \equiv (\sim p) \vee q$

69. $(p \wedge q) \wedge r \equiv p \wedge (q \wedge r)$ **70.** $(p \vee q) \vee r \equiv p \vee (q \vee r)$
(Associative law for conjunction)   (Associative law for disjunction)

71. $p \rightarrow q \equiv (\sim q) \rightarrow (\sim p)$ **72.** $\sim(p \rightarrow q) \equiv p \wedge (\sim q)$

In Exercises 73–78, use truth tables to check whether the given statement is a tautology, a contradiction, or neither. HINT [See Quick Examples on p. A11.]

73. $p \wedge (\sim p)$ **74.** $p \wedge p$

75. $p \wedge \sim(p \vee q)$ **76.** $p \vee \sim(p \vee q)$

77. $p \vee \sim(p \wedge q)$ **78.** $q \vee \sim(p \wedge (\sim p))$

Apply the stated logical equivalence to the given statement in Exercises 79–84. HINT [See Example 5a, b.]

79. $p \vee (\sim p)$; the commutative law

80. $p \wedge (\sim q)$; the commutative law

81. $\sim(p \wedge (\sim q))$; DeMorgan's law

82. $\sim(q \vee (\sim p))$; DeMorgan's law

83. $p \vee ((\sim p) \wedge q)$; the distributive law

84. $(\sim q) \wedge ((\sim p) \vee q)$; the distributive law.

In Exercises 85–88, use the given logical equivalence to rewrite the given sentence. HINT [See Example 5c.]

85. It is not true that both I am Julius Caesar and you are a fool. DeMorgan's law.

86. It is not true that either I am Julius Caesar or you are a fool. DeMorgan's law.

87. Either it is raining and I have forgotten my umbrella, or it is raining and I have forgotten my hat. The distributive law.

88. I forgot my hat or my umbrella, and I forgot my hat or my glasses. The distributive law.

Give the contrapositive and converse of each of the statements in Exercises 89 and 90, phrasing your answers in words.

89. "If I think, then I am."

90. "If these birds are of a feather, then they flock together."

Exercises 91 and 92 are multiple choice. Indicate which statement is equivalent to the given statement, and say why that statement is equivalent to the given one.

91. "In order for you to worship Den, it is necessary for you to sacrifice beasts of burden."
   (A) "If you are not sacrificing beasts of burden, then you are not worshiping Den."
   (B) "If you are sacrificing beasts of burden, then you are worshiping Den."
   (C) "If you are not worshiping Den, then you are not sacrificing beasts of burden."

92. "In order to read the Tarot, it is necessary for you to consult the Oracle."
   (A) "In order to consult the Oracle, it is necessary to read the Tarot."
   (B) "In order not to consult the Oracle, it is necessary not to read the Tarot."
   (C) "In order not to read the Tarot, it is necessary not to read the Oracle."

In Exercises 93–102, write the given argument in symbolic form (use the underlined letters to represent the statements containing them), then decide whether it is valid or not, If it is valid, name the validating tautology. HINT [See Quick Examples on pp. A12, A13, A14.]

93. If I am <u>h</u>ungry I am also <u>t</u>hirsty. I am hungry. Therefore, I am thirsty.

94. If I am not <u>h</u>ungry, then I certainly am not <u>t</u>hirsty either. I am not thirsty, and so I cannot be hungry.

95. For me to bring my <u>u</u>mbrella, it's sufficient that it <u>r</u>ain. It is not raining. Therefore, I will not bring my umbrella.

96. For me to bring my <u>u</u>mbrella, it's necessary that it <u>r</u>ain. But it is not raining. Therefore, I will not bring my umbrella.

97. For me to pass <u>m</u>ath, it is sufficient that I have a good <u>t</u>eacher. I will not pass math. Therefore, I have a bad teacher.

98. For me to pass <u>m</u>ath, it is necessary that I have a good <u>t</u>eacher. I will pass math. Therefore, I have a good teacher.

99. I will either pass <u>m</u>ath or I have a <u>b</u>ad teacher. I have a good teacher. Therefore, I will pass math.

100. Either <u>r</u>oses are not red or <u>v</u>iolets are not blue. But roses are red. Therefore, violets are not blue.

101. I am either <u>s</u>mart or <u>a</u>thletic, and I am athletic. So I must not be smart.

102. The president is either <u>w</u>ise or <u>s</u>trong. She is strong. Therefore, she is not wise.

In Exercises 103–108, use the stated tautology to complete the argument.

103. If John is a swan, it is necessary that he is green. John is indeed a swan. Therefore, _____. (*Modus ponens.*)

104. If Jill had been born in Texas, then she would be able to ride horses. But Jill cannot ride horses. Therefore, ___. (*Modus tollens.*)

105. If John is a swan, it is necessary that he is green. But John is not green. Therefore, _____. (*Modus tollens.*)

106. If Jill had been born in Texas, then she would be able to ride horses. Jill was born in Texas. Therefore, ___ (*Modus ponens.*)

107. Peter is either a scholar or a gentleman. He is not, however, a scholar. Therefore, ___. (*Disjunctive syllogism.*)

108. Pam is either a plumber or an electrician. She is not, however, an electrician. Therefore, ___ (*Disjunctive syllogism.*)

342

COMMUNICATION AND REASONING EXERCISES

109. If two statements are logically equivalent, what can be said about their truth tables?

110. If a proposition is neither a tautology nor a contradiction, what can be said about its truth table?

111. If A and B are two compound statements such that $A \vee B$ is a contradiction, what can you say about A and B?

112. If A and B are two compound statements such that $A \wedge B$ is a tautology, what can you say about A and B?

113. Give an example of an instance where $p \to q$ means that q causes p.

114. Complete the following. If $p \to q$, then its converse, ___ , is the statement that ___ and (is/is not) logically equivalent to $p \to q$.

115. Give an instance of a biconditional $p \leftrightarrow q$ where neither one of p or q causes the other. Answers may vary.

Appendix B **Area Under a Normal Curve**

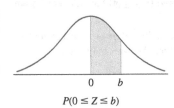

$P(0 \le Z \le b)$

Z	0.00	0.01	0.02	0.03
2.3	.4893	.4896	.4898	.4901
→ 2.4	.4918	.4920	.4922	.4925
2.5	.4938	.4940	.4941	.4943

The table below gives the probabilities $P(0 \le Z \le b)$ where Z is a standard normal variable. For example, to find $P(0 \le Z \le 2.43)$, write 2.43 as $2.4 + 0.03$, and read the entry in the row labeled 2.4 and the column labeled 0.03. From the portion of the table shown at left, you will see that $P(0 \le Z \le 2.43) = .4925$.

Z	0.00	0.01	0.02	0.03	0.04	0.05	0.06	0.07	0.08	0.09
0.0	.0000	.0040	.0080	.0120	.0160	.0199	.0239	.0279	.0319	.0359
0.1	.0398	.0438	.0478	.0517	.0557	.0596	.0636	.0675	.0714	.0753
0.2	.0793	.0832	.0871	.0910	.0948	.0987	.1026	.1064	.1103	.1141
0.3	.1179	.1217	.1255	.1293	.1331	.1368	.1406	.1443	.1480	.1517
0.4	.1554	.1591	.1628	.1664	.1700	.1736	.1772	.1808	.1844	.1879
0.5	.1915	.1950	.1985	.2019	.2054	.2088	.2123	.2157	.2190	.2224
0.6	.2257	.2291	.2324	.2357	.2389	.2422	.2454	.2486	.2517	.2549
0.7	.2580	.2611	.2642	.2673	.2704	.2734	.2764	.2794	.2823	.2852
0.8	.2881	.2910	.2939	.2967	.2995	.3023	.3051	.3078	.3106	.3133
0.9	.3159	.3186	.3212	.3238	.3264	.3289	.3315	.3340	.3365	.3389
1.0	.3413	.3438	.3461	.3485	.3508	.3531	.3554	.3577	.3599	.3621
1.1	.3643	.3665	.3686	.3708	.3729	.3749	.3770	.3790	.3810	.3830
1.2	.3849	.3869	.3888	.3907	.3925	.3944	.3962	.3980	.3997	.4015
1.3	.4032	.4049	.4066	.4082	.4099	.4115	.4131	.4147	.4162	.4177
1.4	.4192	.4207	.4222	.4236	.4251	.4265	.4279	.4292	.4306	.4319
1.5	.4332	.4345	.4357	.4370	.4382	.4394	.4406	.4418	.4429	.4441
1.6	.4452	.4463	.4474	.4484	.4495	.4505	.4515	.4525	.4535	.4545
1.7	.4554	.4564	.4573	.4582	.4591	.4599	.4608	.4616	.4625	.4633
1.8	.4641	.4649	.4656	.4664	.4671	.4678	.4686	.4693	.4699	.4706
1.9	.4713	.4719	.4726	.4732	.4738	.4744	.4750	.4756	.4761	.4767
2.0	.4772	.4778	.4783	.4788	.4793	.4798	.4803	.4808	.4812	.4817
2.1	.4821	.4826	.4830	.4834	.4838	.4842	.4846	.4850	.4854	.4857
2.2	.4861	.4864	.4868	.4871	.4875	.4878	.4881	.4884	.4887	.4890
2.3	.4893	.4896	.4898	.4901	.4904	.4906	.4909	.4911	.4913	.4916
2.4	.4918	.4920	.4922	.4925	.4927	.4929	.4931	.4932	.4934	.4936
2.5	.4938	.4940	.4941	.4943	.4945	.4946	.4948	.4949	.4951	.4952
2.6	.4953	.4955	.4956	.4957	.4959	.4960	.4961	.4962	.4963	.4964
2.7	.4965	.4966	.4967	.4968	.4969	.4970	.4971	.4972	.4973	.4974
2.8	.4974	.4975	.4976	.4977	.4977	.4978	.4979	.4979	.4980	.4981
2.9	.4981	.4982	.4982	.4983	.4984	.4984	.4985	.4985	.4986	.4986
3.0	.4987	.4987	.4987	.4988	.4988	.4989	.4989	.4989	.4990	.4990

An Introduction to Linear Programming

CONTENTS

Linear programming is a problem-solving approach developed to help managers make decisions. Numerous applications of linear programming can be found in today's competitive business environment. For instance, Eastman Kodak uses linear programming to determine where to manufacture products throughout their worldwide facilities, and GE Capital uses linear programming to help determine optimal lease structuring. Marathon Oil Company uses linear programming for gasoline blending and to evaluate the economics of a new terminal or pipeline. The Management Science in Action, Timber Harvesting Model at MeadWestvaco Corporation, provides another example of the use of linear programming. Later in the chapter another Management Science in Action illustrates how the Hanshin Expressway Public Corporation uses linear programming for traffic control on an urban toll expressway in Osaka, Japan.

To illustrate some of the properties that all linear programming problems have in common, consider the following typical applications:

1. A manufacturer wants to develop a production schedule and an inventory policy that will satisfy sales demand in future periods. Ideally, the schedule and policy will enable the company to satisfy demand and at the same time *minimize* the total production and inventory costs.

2. A financial analyst must select an investment portfolio from a variety of stock and bond investment alternatives. The analyst would like to establish the portfolio that *maximizes* the return on investment.

3. A marketing manager wants to determine how best to allocate a fixed advertising budget among alternative advertising media such as radio, television, newspaper, and magazine. The manager would like to determine the media mix that *maximizes* advertising effectiveness.

4. A company has warehouses in a number of locations throughout the United States. For a set of customer demands, the company would like to determine how much each warehouse should ship to each customer so that total transportation costs are *minimized*.

MANAGEMENT SCIENCE IN ACTION

TIMBER HARVESTING MODEL AT MEADWESTVACO CORPORATION*

MeadWestvaco Corporation is a major producer of premium papers for periodicals, books, commercial printing, and business forms. The company also produces pulp and lumber, designs and manufactures packaging systems for beverage and other consumables markets, and is a world leader in the production of coated board and shipping containers. Quantitative analyses at MeadWestvaco are developed and implemented by the company's Decision Analysis Department. The department assists decision makers by providing them with analytical tools of quantitative methods as well as personal analysis and recommendations.

MeadWestvaco uses quantitative models to assist with the long-range management of the company's timberland. Through the use of large-scale linear programs, timber harvesting plans are developed to cover a substantial time horizon. These models consider wood market conditions,

mill pulpwood requirements, harvesting capacities, and general forest management principles. Within these constraints, the model arrives at an optimal harvesting and purchasing schedule based on discounted cash flow. Alternative schedules reflect changes in the various assumptions concerning forest growth, wood availability, and general economic conditions.

Quantitative methods are also used in the development of the inputs for the linear programming models. Timber prices and supplies as well as mill requirements must be forecast over the time horizon, and advanced sampling techniques are used to evaluate land holdings and to project forest growth. The harvest schedule is then developed using quantitative methods.

*Based on information provided by Dr. Edward P. Winkofsky.

Linear programming was initially referred to as "programming in a linear structure." In 1948 Tjalling Koopmans suggested to George Dantzig that the name was much too long; Koopmans suggested shortening it to linear programming. George Dantzig agreed and the field we now know as linear programming was named.

These examples are only a few of the situations in which linear programming has been used successfully, but they illustrate the diversity of linear programming applications. A close scrutiny reveals one basic property they all have in common. In each example, we were concerned with *maximizing* or *minimizing* some quantity. In example 1, the manufacturer wanted to minimize costs; in example 2, the financial analyst wanted to maximize return on investment; in example 3, the marketing manager wanted to maximize advertising effectiveness; and in example 4, the company wanted to minimize total transportation costs. *In all linear programming problems, the maximization or minimization of some quantity is the objective.*

All linear programming problems also have a second property: restrictions, or **constraints,** that limit the degree to which the objective can be pursued. In example 1, the manufacturer is restricted by constraints requiring product demand to be satisfied and by the constraints limiting production capacity. The financial analyst's portfolio problem is constrained by the total amount of investment funds available and the maximum amounts that can be invested in each stock or bond. The marketing manager's media selection decision is constrained by a fixed advertising budget and the availability of the various media. In the transportation problem, the minimum-cost shipping schedule is constrained by the supply of product available at each warehouse. *Thus, constraints are another general feature of every linear programming problem.*

2.1 A SIMPLE MAXIMIZATION PROBLEM

Par, Inc., is a small manufacturer of golf equipment and supplies whose management has decided to move into the market for medium- and high-priced golf bags. Par's distributor is enthusiastic about the new product line and has agreed to buy all the golf bags Par produces over the next three months.

After a thorough investigation of the steps involved in manufacturing a golf bag, management determined that each golf bag produced will require the following operations:

1. Cutting and dyeing the material
2. Sewing
3. Finishing (inserting umbrella holder, club separators, etc.)
4. Inspection and packaging

The director of manufacturing analyzed each of the operations and concluded that if the company produces a medium-priced standard model, each bag will require $7/10$ hour in the cutting and dyeing department, $1/2$ hour in the sewing department, 1 hour in the finishing department, and $1/10$ hour in the inspection and packaging department. The more expensive deluxe model will require 1 hour for cutting and dyeing, $5/6$ hour for sewing, $2/3$ hour for finishing, and $1/4$ hour for inspection and packaging. This production information is summarized in Table 2.1.

Par's production is constrained by a limited number of hours available in each department. After studying departmental workload projections, the director of manufacturing estimates that 630 hours for cutting and dyeing, 600 hours for sewing, 708 hours for finishing, and 135 hours for inspection and packaging will be available for the production of golf bags during the next three months.

The accounting department analyzed the production data, assigned all relevant variable costs, and arrived at prices for both bags that will result in a profit contribution[1] of $10 for

---

[1]From an accounting perspective, profit contribution is more correctly described as the contribution margin per bag; for example, overhead and other shared costs have not been allocated.

TABLE 2.1 PRODUCTION REQUIREMENTS PER GOLF BAG

Department	Production Time (hours)	
	Standard Bag	**Deluxe Bag**
Cutting and Dyeing	$7/10$	1
Sewing	$1/2$	$5/6$
Finishing	1	$2/3$
Inspection and Packaging	$1/10$	$1/4$

It is important to understand that we are maximizing profit contribution, not profit. Overhead and other shared costs must be deducted before arriving at a profit figure.

every standard bag and $9 for every deluxe bag produced. Let us now develop a mathematical model of the Par, Inc., problem that can be used to determine the number of standard bags and the number of deluxe bags to produce in order to maximize total profit contribution.

Problem Formulation

Problem formulation, or **modeling,** is the process of translating the verbal statement of a problem into a mathematical statement. Formulating models is an art that can only be mastered with practice and experience. Even though every problem has some unique features, most problems also have common features. As a result, *some* general guidelines for model formulation can be helpful, especially for beginners. We will illustrate these general guidelines by developing a mathematical model for the Par, Inc., problem.

Understand the Problem Thoroughly We selected the Par, Inc., problem to introduce linear programming because it is easy to understand. However, more complex problems will require much more thinking in order to identify the items that need to be included in the model. In such cases, read the problem description quickly to get a feel for what is involved. Taking notes will help you focus on the key issues and facts.

Describe the Objective The objective is to maximize the total contribution to profit.

Describe Each Constraint Four constraints relate to the number of hours of manufacturing time available; they restrict the number of standard bags and the number of deluxe bags that can be produced.

Constraint 1: Number of hours of cutting and dyeing time used must be less than or equal to the number of hours of cutting and dyeing time available.

Constraint 2: Number of hours of sewing time used must be less than or equal to the number of hours of sewing time available.

Constraint 3: Number of hours of finishing time used must be less than or equal to the number of hours of finishing time available.

Constraint 4: Number of hours of inspection and packaging time used must be less than or equal to the number of hours of inspection and packaging time available.

Define the Decision Variables The controllable inputs for Par, Inc., are (1) the number of standard bags produced, and (2) the number of deluxe bags produced. Let

$$S = \text{number of standard bags}$$
$$D = \text{number of deluxe bags}$$

In linear programming terminology, S and D are referred to as the **decision variables.**

Write the Objective in Terms of the Decision Variables Par's profit contribution comes from two sources: (1) the profit contribution made by producing S standard bags, and (2) the profit contribution made by producing D deluxe bags. If Par makes $10 for every standard bag, the company will make $10S$ if S standard bags are produced. Also, if Par makes $9 for every deluxe bag, the company will make $9D$ if D deluxe bags are produced. Thus, we have

$$\text{Total Profit Contribution} = 10S + 9D$$

Because the objective—maximize total profit contribution—is a function of the decision variables S and D, we refer to $10S + 9D$ as the *objective function*. Using "Max" as an abbreviation for maximize, we write Par's objective as follows:

$$\text{Max } 10S + 9D$$

Write the Constraints in Terms of the Decision Variables

Constraint 1:

$$\binom{\text{Hours of cutting and}}{\text{dyeing time used}} \leq \binom{\text{Hours of cutting and}}{\text{dyeing time available}}$$

Every standard bag Par produces will use $^7/_{10}$ hour cutting and dyeing time; therefore, the total number of hours of cutting and dyeing time used in the manufacture of S standard bags is $^7/_{10}S$. In addition, because every deluxe bag produced uses 1 hour of cutting and dyeing time, the production of D deluxe bags will use $1D$ hours of cutting and dyeing time. Thus, the total cutting and dyeing time required for the production of S standard bags and D deluxe bags is given by

$$\text{Total hours of cutting and dyeing time used} = {}^7/_{10}S + 1D$$

The units of measurement on the left-hand side of the constraint must match the units of measurement on the right-hand side.

The director of manufacturing stated that Par has at most 630 hours of cutting and dyeing time available. Therefore, the production combination we select must satisfy the requirement

$$^7/_{10}S + 1D \leq 630 \tag{2.1}$$

Constraint 2:

$$\binom{\text{Hours of sewing}}{\text{time used}} \leq \binom{\text{Hours of sewing}}{\text{time available}}$$

From Table 2.1, we see that every standard bag manufactured will require $^1/_2$ hour for sewing, and every deluxe bag will require $^5/_6$ hour for sewing. Because 600 hours of sewing time are available, it follows that

$$^1/_2 S + {}^5/_6 D \leq 600 \tag{2.2}$$

Constraint 3:

$$\left(\begin{array}{c}\text{Hours of finishing} \\ \text{time used}\end{array}\right) \leq \left(\begin{array}{c}\text{Hours of finishing} \\ \text{time available}\end{array}\right)$$

Every standard bag manufactured will require 1 hour for finishing, and every deluxe bag will require $\frac{2}{3}$ hour for finishing. With 708 hours of finishing time available, it follows that

$$1S + \frac{2}{3}D \leq 708 \tag{2.3}$$

Constraint 4:

$$\left(\begin{array}{c}\text{Hours of inspection and} \\ \text{packaging time used}\end{array}\right) \leq \left(\begin{array}{c}\text{Hours of inspection and} \\ \text{packaging time available}\end{array}\right)$$

Every standard bag manufactured will require $\frac{1}{10}$ hour for inspection and packaging, and every deluxe bag will require $\frac{1}{4}$ hour for inspection and packaging. Because 135 hours of inspection and packaging time are available, it follows that

$$\frac{1}{10}S + \frac{1}{4}D \leq 135 \tag{2.4}$$

We have now specified the mathematical relationships for the constraints associated with the four departments. Have we forgotten any other constraints? Can Par produce a negative number of standard or deluxe bags? Clearly, the answer is no. Thus, to prevent the decision variables S and D from having negative values, two constraints,

$$S \geq 0 \quad \text{and} \quad D \geq 0 \tag{2.5}$$

must be added. These constraints ensure that the solution to the problem will contain nonnegative values for the decision variables and are thus referred to as the **nonnegativity constraints.** Nonnegativity constraints are a general feature of all linear programming problems and may be written in the abbreviated form:

$$S, D \geq 0$$

Try Problem 24(a) to test your ability to formulate a mathematical model for a maximization linear programming problem with less-than-or-equal-to constraints.

Mathematical Statement of the Par, Inc., Problem

The mathematical statement or mathematical formulation of the Par, Inc., problem is now complete. We succeeded in translating the objective and constraints of the problem into a set of mathematical relationships referred to as a **mathematical model.** The complete mathematical model for the Par problem is as follows:

$$\text{Max} \quad 10S + 9D$$

subject to (s.t.)

$$\frac{7}{10}S + 1D \leq 630 \quad \text{Cutting and dyeing}$$
$$\frac{1}{2}S + \frac{5}{6}D \leq 600 \quad \text{Sewing}$$
$$1S + \frac{2}{3}D \leq 708 \quad \text{Finishing}$$
$$\frac{1}{10}S + \frac{1}{4}D \leq 135 \quad \text{Inspection and packaging}$$
$$S, D \geq 0 \tag{2.6}$$

Our job now is to find the product mix (i.e., the combination of S and D) that satisfies all the constraints and, at the same time, yields a value for the objective function that is greater than or equal to the value given by any other feasible solution. Once these values are calculated, we will have found the optimal solution to the problem.

This mathematical model of the Par problem is **a linear programming model,** or **linear program.** The problem has the objective and constraints that, as we said earlier, are common properties of all *linear* programs. But what is the special feature of this mathematical model that makes it a linear program? The special feature that makes it a linear program is that the objective function and all constraint functions are linear functions of the decision variables.

Mathematical functions in which each variable appears in a separate term and is raised to the first power are called **linear functions.** The objective function $(10S + 9D)$ is linear because each decision variable appears in a separate term and has an exponent of 1. The amount of production time required in the cutting and dyeing department $(\frac{7}{10}S + 1D)$ is also a linear function of the decision variables for the same reason. Similarly, the functions on the left-hand side of all the constraint inequalities (the constraint functions) are linear functions. Thus, the mathematical formulation of this problem is referred to as a linear program.

Try Problem 1 to test your ability to recognize the types of mathematical relationships that can be found in a linear program.

Linear *programming* has nothing to do with computer programming. The use of the word *programming* here means "choosing a course of action." Linear programming involves choosing a course of action when the mathematical model of the problem contains only linear functions.

NOTES AND COMMENTS

1. The three assumptions necessary for a linear programming model to be appropriate are proportionality, additivity, and divisibility. *Proportionality* means that the contribution to the objective function and the amount of resources used in each constraint are proportional to the value of each decision variable. *Additivity* means that the value of the objective function and the total resources used can be found by summing the objective function contribution and the resources used for all decision variables. *Divisibility* means that the decision variables are continuous. The divisibility assumption plus the nonnegativity constraints mean that decision variables can take on any value greater than or equal to zero.

2. Management scientists formulate and solve a variety of mathematical models that contain an objective function and a set of constraints. Models of this type are referred to as *mathematical programming models.* Linear programming models are a special type of mathematical programming model in that the objective function and all constraint functions are linear.

2.2　GRAPHICAL SOLUTION PROCEDURE

A linear programming problem involving only two decision variables can be solved using a graphical solution procedure. Let us begin the graphical solution procedure by developing a graph that displays the possible solutions (S and D values) for the Par problem. The graph (Figure 2.1) will have values of S on the horizontal axis and values of D on the vertical axis. Any point on the graph can be identified by the S and D values, which indicate the position of the point along the horizontal and vertical axes, respectively. Because every point (S, D) corresponds to a possible solution, every point on the graph is called a *solution point*. The solution point where $S = 0$ and $D = 0$ is referred to as the origin. Because S and D must be nonnegative, the graph in Figure 2.1 only displays solutions where $S \geq 0$ and $D \geq 0$.

Earlier, we saw that the inequality representing the cutting and dyeing constraint is

$$\tfrac{7}{10}S + 1D \leq 630$$

To show all solution points that satisfy this relationship, we start by graphing the solution points satisfying the constraint as an equality. That is, the points where $\tfrac{7}{10}S + 1D = 630$. Because the graph of this equation is a line, it can be obtained by identifying two points that satisfy the equation and then drawing a line through the points. Setting $S = 0$ and solving for D, we see that the point ($S = 0$, $D = 630$) satisfies the equation. To find a second point satisfying this equation, we set $D = 0$ and solve for S. By doing so, we obtain

FIGURE 2.1　SOLUTION POINTS FOR THE TWO-VARIABLE PAR, INC., PROBLEM

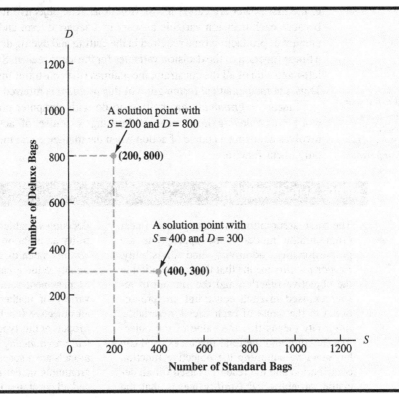

$\frac{7}{10}S + 1(0) = 630$, or $S = 900$. Thus, a second point satisfying the equation is ($S = 900$, $D = 0$). Given these two points, we can now graph the line corresponding to the equation

$$\frac{7}{10}S + 1D = 630$$

This line, which will be called the cutting and dyeing *constraint line,* is shown in Figure 2.2. We label this line "C & D" to indicate that it represents the cutting and dyeing constraint line.

Recall that the inequality representing the cutting and dyeing constraint is

$$\frac{7}{10}S + 1D \leq 630$$

Can you identify all of the solution points that satisfy this constraint? Because all points on the line satisfy $\frac{7}{10}S + 1D = 630$, we know any point on this line must satisfy the constraint. But where are the solution points satisfying $\frac{7}{10}S + 1D < 630$? Consider two solution points: ($S = 200$, $D = 200$) and ($S = 600$, $D = 500$). You can see from Figure 2.2 that the first solution point is below the constraint line and the second is above the constraint line. Which of these solutions will satisfy the cutting and dyeing constraint? For the point ($S = 200$, $D = 200$), we see that

$$\frac{7}{10}S + 1D = \frac{7}{10}(200) + 1(200) = 340$$

FIGURE 2.2   THE CUTTING AND DYEING CONSTRAINT LINE

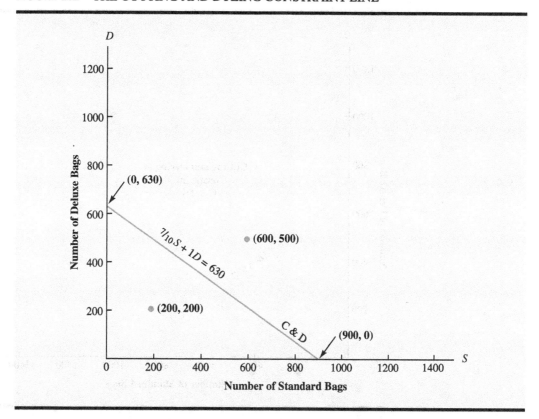

Because the 340 hours is less than the 630 hours available, the ($S = 200$, $D = 200$) production combination, or solution point, satisfies the constraint. For the point ($S = 600$, $D = 500$), we have

$$^{7}\!/_{10}S + 1D = ^{7}\!/_{10}(600) + 1(500) = 920$$

The 920 hours is greater than the 630 hours available, so the ($S = 600$, $D = 500$) solution point does not satisfy the constraint and is thus not feasible.

Can you graph a constraint line and find the solution points that are feasible? Try Problem 2.

If a solution point is not feasible for a particular constraint, then all other solution points on the same side of that constraint line are not feasible. If a solution point is feasible for a particular constraint, then all other solution points on the same side of the constraint line are feasible for that constraint. Thus, one has to evaluate the constraint function for only one solution point to determine which side of a constraint line is feasible. In Figure 2.3 we indicate all points satisfying the cutting and dyeing constraint by the shaded region.

We continue by identifying the solution points satisfying each of the other three constraints. The solutions that are feasible for each of these constraints are shown in Figure 2.4.

Four separate graphs now show the feasible solution points for each of the four constraints. In a linear programming problem, we need to identify the solution points that satisfy *all* the constraints *simultaneously*. To find these solution points, we can draw all four constraints on one graph and observe the region containing the points that do in fact satisfy all the constraints simultaneously.

FIGURE 2.3 FEASIBLE SOLUTIONS FOR THE CUTTING AND DYEING CONSTRAINT, REPRESENTED BY THE SHADED REGION

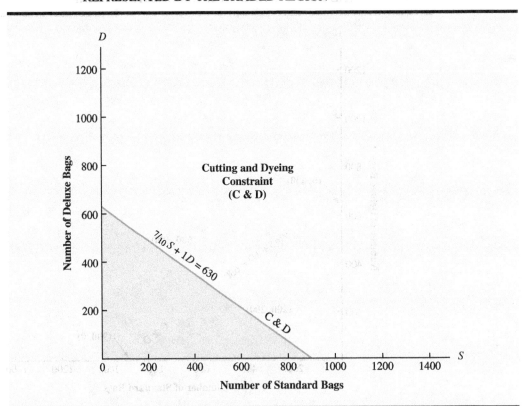

FIGURE 2.4 FEASIBLE SOLUTIONS FOR THE SEWING, FINISHING, AND INSPECTION AND PACKAGING CONSTRAINTS, REPRESENTED BY THE SHADED REGIONS

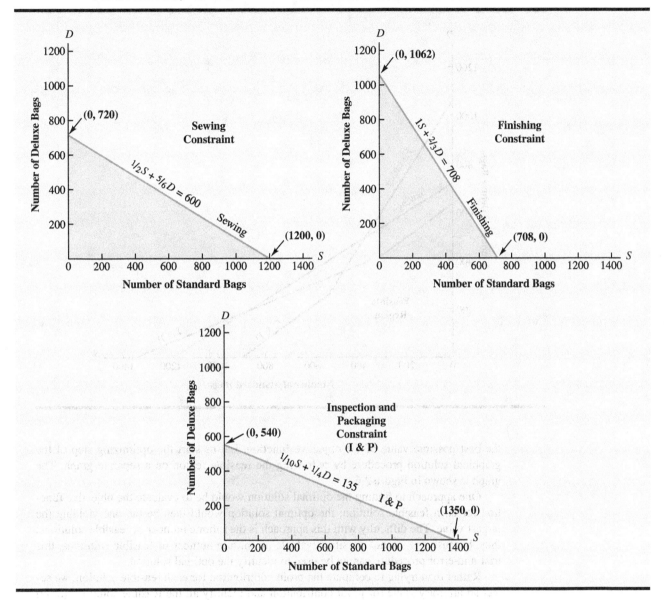

Try Problem 7 to test your ability to find the feasible region given several constraints.

The graphs in Figures 2.3 and 2.4 can be superimposed to obtain one graph with all four constraints. This combined-constraint graph is shown in Figure 2.5. The shaded region in this figure includes every solution point that satisfies all the constraints simultaneously. Solutions that satisfy all the constraints are termed **feasible solutions,** and the shaded region is called the feasible solution region, or simply the **feasible region.** Any solution point on the boundary of the feasible region or within the feasible region is a *feasible solution point.*

Now that we have identified the feasible region, we are ready to proceed with the graphical solution procedure and find the optimal solution to the Par, Inc., problem. Recall that the optimal solution for a linear programming problem is the feasible solution that provides

355

FIGURE 2.5 COMBINED-CONSTRAINT GRAPH SHOWING THE FEASIBLE REGION
FOR THE PAR, INC., PROBLEM

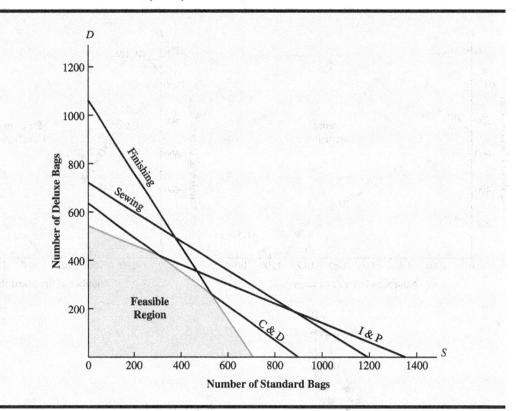

the best possible value of the objective function. Let us start the optimizing step of the
graphical solution procedure by redrawing the feasible region on a separate graph. The
graph is shown in Figure 2.6.

One approach to finding the optimal solution would be to evaluate the objective function for each feasible solution; the optimal solution would then be the one yielding the
largest value. The difficulty with this approach is the infinite number of feasible solutions;
thus, because one cannot possibly evaluate an infinite number of feasible solutions, this
trial-and-error procedure cannot be used to identify the optimal solution.

Rather than trying to compute the profit contribution for each feasible solution, we select an arbitrary value for profit contribution and identify all the feasible solutions (S, D)
that yield the selected value. For example, which feasible solutions provide a profit contribution of $1800? These solutions are given by the values of S and D in the feasible region
that will make the objective function

$$10S + 9D = 1800$$

This expression is simply the equation of a line. Thus, all feasible solution points
(S, D) yielding a profit contribution of $1800 must be on the line. We learned earlier in this
section how to graph a constraint line. The procedure for graphing the profit or objective
function line is the same. Letting $S = 0$, we see that D must be 200; thus, the solution

FIGURE 2.6 FEASIBLE REGION FOR THE PAR, INC., PROBLEM

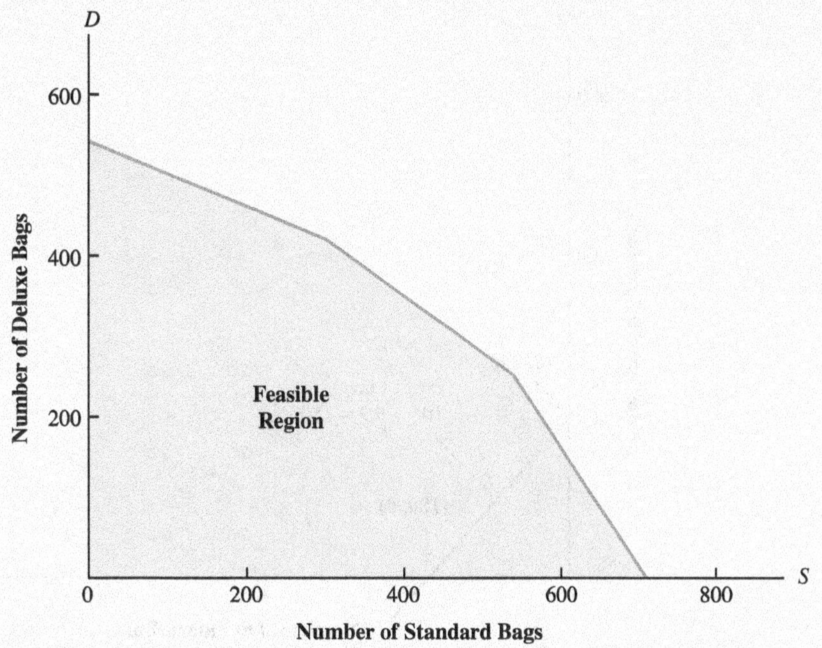

point ($S = 0$, $D = 200$) is on the line. Similarly, by letting $D = 0$, we see that the solution point ($S = 180$, $D = 0$) is also on the line. Drawing the line through these two points identifies all the solutions that have a profit contribution of $1800. A graph of this profit line is presented in Figure 2.7.

Because the objective is to find the feasible solution yielding the largest profit contribution, let us proceed by selecting higher profit contributions and finding the solutions yielding the selected values. For instance, let us find all solutions yielding profit contributions of $3600 and $5400. To do so, we must find the S and D values that are on the following lines:

$$10S + 9D = 3600$$

and

$$10S + 9D = 5400$$

Using the previous procedure for graphing profit and constraint lines, we draw the $3600 and $5400 profit lines as shown on the graph in Figure 2.8. Although not all solution points on the $5400 profit line are in the feasible region, at least some points on the line are, and it is therefore possible to obtain a feasible solution that provides a $5400 profit contribution.

Can we find a feasible solution yielding an even higher profit contribution? Look at Figure 2.8, and see what general observations you can make about the profit lines already drawn. Note the following: (1) the profit lines are *parallel* to each other, and (2) higher

FIGURE 2.7 $1800 PROFIT LINE FOR THE PAR, INC., PROBLEM

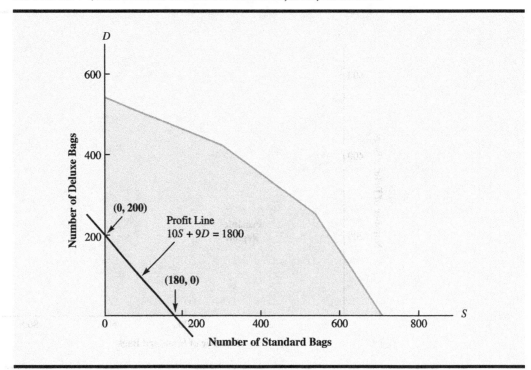

FIGURE 2.8   SELECTED PROFIT LINES FOR THE PAR, INC., PROBLEM

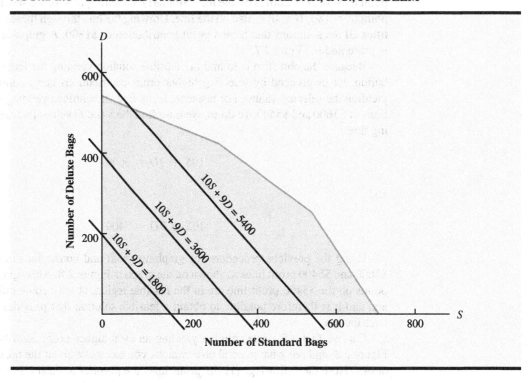

profit lines are obtained as we move farther from the origin. These observations can also be expressed algebraically. Let P represent total profit contribution. The objective function is

$$P = 10S + 9D$$

Solving for D in terms of S and P, we obtain

$$9D = -10S + P$$
$$D = -\tfrac{10}{9}S + \tfrac{1}{9}P \qquad (2.7)$$

Equation (2.7) is the *slope-intercept form* of the linear equation relating S and D. The coefficient of S, $-\tfrac{10}{9}$, is the slope of the line, and the term $\tfrac{1}{9}P$ is the D intercept (i.e., the value of D where the graph of equation (2.7) crosses the D axis). Substituting the profit contributions of $P = 1800$, $P = 3600$, and $P = 5400$ into equation (2.7) yields the following slope-intercept equations for the profit lines shown in Figure 2.8:

For $P = 1800$,

$$D = -\tfrac{10}{9}S + 200$$

For $P = 3600$,

$$D = -\tfrac{10}{9}S + 400$$

For $P = 5400$,

$$D = -\tfrac{10}{9}S + 600$$

Can you graph the profit line for a linear program? Try Problem 6.

The slope $(-\tfrac{10}{9})$ is the same for each profit line because the profit lines are parallel. Further, we see that the D intercept increases with larger profit contributions. Thus, higher profit lines are farther from the origin.

Because the profit lines are parallel and higher profit lines are farther from the origin, we can obtain solutions that yield increasingly larger values for the objective function by continuing to move the profit line farther from the origin in such a fashion that it remains parallel to the other profit lines. However, at some point we will find that any further outward movement will place the profit line completely outside the feasible region. Because solutions outside the feasible region are unacceptable, the point in the feasible region that lies on the highest profit line is the optimal solution to the linear program.

You should now be able to identify the optimal solution point for this problem. Use a ruler or the edge of a piece of paper, and move the profit line as far from the origin as you can. What is the last point in the feasible region that you reach? This point, which is the optimal solution, is shown graphically in Figure 2.9.

The optimal values of the decision variables are the S and D values at the optimal solution. Depending on the accuracy of the graph, you may or may not be able to determine the *exact* S and D values. Based on the graph in Figure 2.9, the best we can do is conclude that the optimal production combination consists of approximately 550 standard bags (S) and approximately 250 deluxe bags (D).

FIGURE 2.9 OPTIMAL SOLUTION FOR THE PAR, INC., PROBLEM

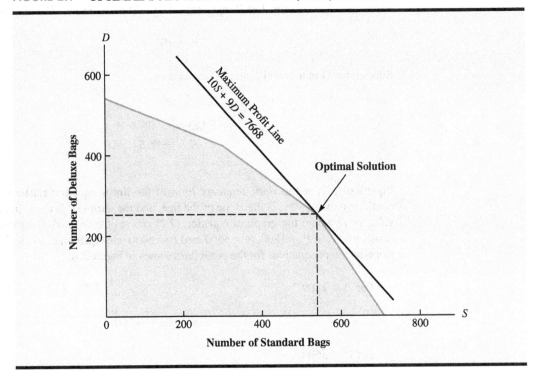

A closer inspection of Figures 2.5 and 2.9 shows that the optimal solution point is at the intersection of the cutting and dyeing and the finishing constraint lines. That is, the optimal solution point is on both the cutting and dyeing constraint line

$$\tfrac{7}{10}S + 1D = 630 \qquad (2.8)$$

and the finishing constraint line

$$1S + \tfrac{2}{3}D = 708 \qquad (2.9)$$

Thus, the optimal values of the decision variables S and D must satisfy both equations (2.8) and (2.9) simultaneously. Using equation (2.8) and solving for S gives

$$\tfrac{7}{10}S = 630 - 1D$$

or

$$S = 900 - \tfrac{10}{7}D \qquad (2.10)$$

Substituting this expression for S into equation (2.9) and solving for D provides the following:

$$1(900 - {}^{10}\!\!/_7 D) + {}^2\!\!/_3 D = 708$$
$$900 - {}^{10}\!\!/_7 D + {}^2\!\!/_3 D = 708$$
$$900 - {}^{30}\!\!/_{21} D + {}^{14}\!\!/_{21} D = 708$$
$$-{}^{16}\!\!/_{21} D = -192$$
$$D = \frac{192}{{}^{16}\!\!/_{21}} = 252$$

Using $D = 252$ in equation (2.10) and solving for S, we obtain

$$S = 900 - {}^{10}\!\!/_7 (252)$$
$$= 900 - 360 = 540$$

Although the optimal solution to the Par, Inc., problem consists of integer values for the decision variables, this result will not always be the case.

The exact location of the optimal solution point is $S = 540$ and $D = 252$. Hence, the optimal production quantities for Par, Inc., are 540 standard bags and 252 deluxe bags, with a resulting profit contribution of $10(540) + 9(252) = \$7668$.

For a linear programming problem with two decision variables, the exact values of the decision variables can be determined by first using the graphical solution procedure to identify the optimal solution point and then solving the two simultaneous constraint equations associated with it.

A Note on Graphing Lines

Try Problem 10 to test your ability to use the graphical solution procedure to identify the optimal solution and find the exact values of the decision variables at the optimal solution.

An important aspect of the graphical method is the ability to graph lines showing the constraints and the objective function of the linear program. The procedure we used for graphing the equation of a line is to find any two points satisfying the equation and then draw the line through the two points. For the Par, Inc., constraints, the two points were easily found by first setting $S = 0$ and solving the constraint equation for D. Then we set $D = 0$ and solved for S. For the cutting and dyeing constraint line

$$^7\!\!/_{10} S + 1D = 630$$

this procedure identified the two points ($S = 0$, $D = 630$) and ($S = 900$, $D = 0$). The cutting and dyeing constraint line was then graphed by drawing a line through these two points.

All constraints and objective function lines in two-variable linear programs can be graphed if two points on the line can be identified. However, finding the two points on the line is not always as easy as shown in the Par, Inc., problem. For example, suppose a company manufactures two models of a small handheld computer: the Assistant (A) and the Professional (P). Management needs 50 units of the Professional model for its own sales-force, and expects sales of the Professional to be at most one-half of the sales of the Assistant. A constraint enforcing this requirement is

$$P - 50 \leq \tfrac{1}{2} A$$

or

$$2P - 100 \leq A$$

or

$$2P - A \leq 100$$

Using the equality form and setting $P = 0$, we find the point ($P = 0, A = -100$) is on the constraint line. Setting $A = 0$, we find a second point ($P = 50, A = 0$) on the constraint line. If we have drawn only the nonnegative ($P \geq 0, A \geq 0$) portion of the graph, the first point ($P = 0, A = -100$) cannot be plotted because $A = -100$ is not on the graph. Whenever we have two points on the line but one or both of the points cannot be plotted in the nonnegative portion of the graph, the simplest approach is to enlarge the graph. In this example, the point ($P = 0, A = -100$) can be plotted by extending the graph to include the negative A axis. Once both points satisfying the constraint equation have been located, the line can be drawn. The constraint line and the feasible solutions for the constraint $2P - A \leq 100$ are shown in Figure 2.10.

As another example, consider a problem involving two decision variables, R and T. Suppose that the number of units of R produced had to be at least equal to the number of units of T produced. A constraint enforcing this requirement is

$$R \geq T$$

or

$$R - T \geq 0$$

FIGURE 2.10   FEASIBLE SOLUTIONS FOR THE CONSTRAINT $2P - A \leq 100$

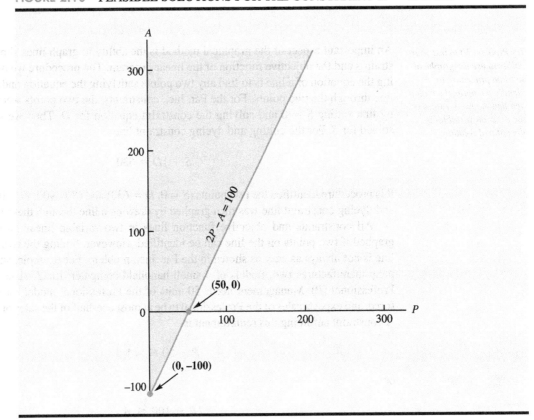

Can you graph a constraint line when the origin is on the constraint line? Try Problem 5.

To find all solutions satisfying the constraint as an equality, we first set $R = 0$ and solve for T. This result shows that the origin ($T = 0$, $R = 0$) is on the constraint line. Setting $T = 0$ and solving for R provides the same point. However, we can obtain a second point on the line by setting T equal to any value other than zero and then solving for R. For instance, setting $T = 100$ and solving for R, we find that the point ($T = 100$, $R = 100$) is on the line. With the two points ($R = 0$, $T = 0$) and ($R = 100$, $T = 100$), the constraint line $R - T = 0$ and the feasible solutions for $R - T \geq 0$ can be plotted as shown in Figure 2.11.

Summary of the Graphical Solution Procedure for Maximization Problems

For additional practice in using the graphical solution procedure, try Problem 24(b), 24(c), and 24(d).

As we have seen, the graphical solution procedure is a method for solving two-variable linear programming problems such as the Par, Inc., problem. The steps of the graphical solution procedure for a maximization problem are summarized here:

1. Prepare a graph of the feasible solutions for each of the constraints.
2. Determine the feasible region by identifying the solutions that satisfy all the constraints simultaneously.
3. Draw an objective function line showing the values of the decision variables that yield a specified value of the objective function.
4. Move parallel objective function lines toward larger objective function values until further movement would take the line completely outside the feasible region.
5. Any feasible solution on the objective function line with the largest value is an optimal solution.

FIGURE 2.11 FEASIBLE SOLUTIONS FOR THE CONSTRAINT $R - T \geq 0$

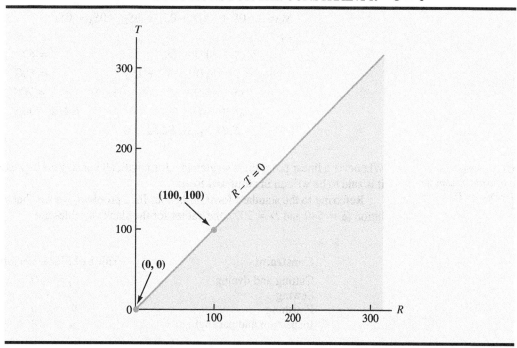

Slack Variables

In addition to the optimal solution and its associated profit contribution, Par's management will probably want information about the production time requirements for each production operation. We can determine this information by substituting the optimal solution values ($S = 540$, $D = 252$) into the constraints of the linear program.

Constraint	Hours Required for $S = 540$ and $D = 252$	Hours Available	Unused Hours
Cutting and dyeing	$\frac{7}{10}(540) + 1(252) = 630$	630	0
Sewing	$\frac{1}{2}(540) + \frac{5}{6}(252) = 480$	600	120
Finishing	$1(540) + \frac{2}{3}(252) = 708$	708	0
Inspection and packaging	$\frac{1}{10}(540) + \frac{1}{4}(252) = 117$	135	18

Thus, the complete solution tells management that the production of 540 standard bags and 252 deluxe bags will require all available cutting and dyeing time (630 hours) and all available finishing time (708 hours), while $600 - 480 = 120$ hours of sewing time and $135 - 117 = 18$ hours of inspection and packaging time will remain unused. The 120 hours of unused sewing time and 18 hours of unused inspection and packaging time are referred to as *slack* for the two departments. In linear programming terminology, any unused capacity for a $\leq$ constraint is referred to as the *slack* associated with the constraint.

Can you identify the slack associated with a constraint? Try Problem 24(e).

Often variables, called **slack variables,** are added to the formulation of a linear programming problem to represent the slack, or idle capacity. Unused capacity makes no contribution to profit; thus, slack variables have coefficients of zero in the objective function. After the addition of four slack variables, denoted S_1, S_2, S_3, and S_4, the mathematical model of the Par, Inc., problem becomes

$$\text{Max} \quad 10S + 9D + 0S_1 + 0S_2 + 0S_3 + 0S_4$$

s.t.

$$
\begin{aligned}
\tfrac{7}{10}S + 1D + 1S_1 \qquad\qquad\qquad\quad &= 630 \\
\tfrac{1}{2}S + \tfrac{5}{6}D \quad + 1S_2 \qquad\qquad\quad &= 600 \\
1S + \tfrac{2}{3}D \qquad\quad + 1S_3 \qquad &= 708 \\
\tfrac{1}{10}S + \tfrac{1}{4}D \qquad\qquad\qquad + 1S_4 &= 135 \\
S, D, S_1, S_2, S_3, S_4 &\geq 0
\end{aligned}
$$

Can you write a linear program in standard form? Try Problem 18.

Whenever a linear program is written in a form with all constraints expressed as equalities, it is said to be written in **standard form.**

Referring to the standard form of the Par, Inc., problem, we see that at the optimal solution ($S = 540$ and $D = 252$), the values for the slack variables are

Constraint	Value of Slack Variable
Cutting and dyeing	$S_1 = 0$
Sewing	$S_2 = 120$
Finishing	$S_3 = 0$
Inspection and packaging	$S_4 = 18$

Could we have used the graphical solution to provide some of this information? The answer is yes. By finding the optimal solution point on Figure 2.5, we can see that the cutting and dyeing and the finishing constraints restrict, or *bind*, the feasible region at this point. Thus, this solution requires the use of all available time for these two operations. In other words, the graph shows us that the cutting and dyeing and the finishing departments will have zero slack. On the other hand, the sewing and the inspection and packaging constraints are not binding the feasible region at the optimal solution, which means we can expect some unused time or slack for these two operations.

As a final comment on the graphical analysis of this problem, we call your attention to the sewing capacity constraint as shown in Figure 2.5. Note, in particular, that this constraint did not affect the feasible region. That is, the feasible region would be the same whether the sewing capacity constraint were included or not, which tells us that enough sewing time is available to accommodate any production level that can be achieved by the other three departments. The sewing constraint does not affect the feasible region and thus cannot affect the optimal solution; it is called a **redundant constraint.**

NOTES AND COMMENTS

1. In the standard-form representation of a linear programming model, the objective function coefficients for slack variables are zero. This zero coefficient implies that slack variables, which represent unused resources, do not affect the value of the objective function. However, in some applications, unused resources can be sold and contribute to profit. In such cases, the corresponding slack variables become decision variables representing the amount of unused resources to be sold. For each of these variables, a nonzero coefficient in the objective function would reflect the profit associated with selling a unit of the corresponding resource.

2. Redundant constraints do not affect the feasible region; as a result, they can be removed from a linear programming model without affecting the optimal solution. However, if the linear programming model is to be re-solved later, changes in some of the data might make a previously redundant constraint a binding constraint. Thus, we recommend keeping all constraints in the linear programming model even though at some point in time one or more of the constraints may be redundant.

2.3 EXTREME POINTS AND THE OPTIMAL SOLUTION

Suppose that the profit contribution for Par's standard golf bag is reduced from $10 to $5 per bag, while the profit contribution for the deluxe golf bag and all the constraints remain unchanged. The complete linear programming model of this new problem is identical to the mathematical model in Section 2.1, except for the revised objective function:

$$\text{Max } 5S + 9D$$

How does this change in the objective function affect the optimal solution to the Par, Inc., problem? Figure 2.12 shows the graphical solution of this new problem with the revised objective function. Note that without any change in the constraints, the feasible region does not change. However, the profit lines have been altered to reflect the new objective function.

By moving the profit line in a parallel manner toward higher profit values, we find the optimal solution as shown in Figure 2.12. The values of the decision variables at this point

FIGURE 2.12 OPTIMAL SOLUTION FOR THE PAR, INC., PROBLEM WITH AN OBJECTIVE FUNCTION OF $5S + 9D$

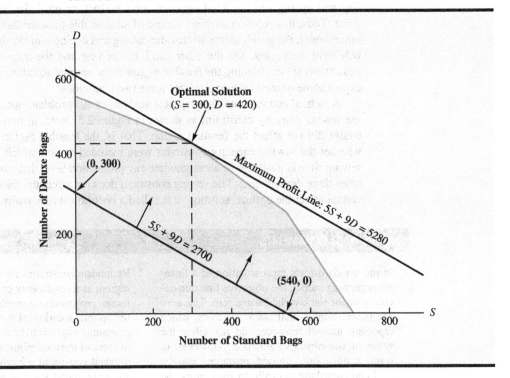

are $S = 300$ and $D = 420$. The reduced profit contribution for the standard bag caused a change in the optimal solution. In fact, as you may have suspected, we are cutting back the production of the lower-profit standard bags and increasing the production of the higher-profit deluxe bags.

What observations can you make about the location of the optimal solutions in the two linear programming problems solved thus far? Look closely at the graphical solutions in Figures 2.9 and 2.12. Notice that the optimal solutions occur at one of the vertices, or "corners," of the feasible region. In linear programming terminology, these vertices are referred to as the **extreme points** of the feasible region. The Par, Inc., feasible region has five vertices, or five extreme points (see Figure 2.13). We can now formally state our observation about the location of optimal solutions as follows:

For additional practice in identifying the extreme points of the feasible region and determining the optimal solution by computing and comparing the objective function value at each extreme point, try Problem 13.

> The optimal solution to a linear program can be found at an extreme point of the feasible region.[2]

This property means that if you are looking for the optimal solution to a linear program, you do not have to evaluate all feasible solution points. In fact, you have to consider

---

[2]We will discuss in Section 2.6 the two special cases (infeasibility and unboundedness) in linear programming that have no optimal solution, and for which this statement does not apply.

FIGURE 2.13 THE FIVE EXTREME POINTS OF THE FEASIBLE REGION
FOR THE PAR, INC., PROBLEM

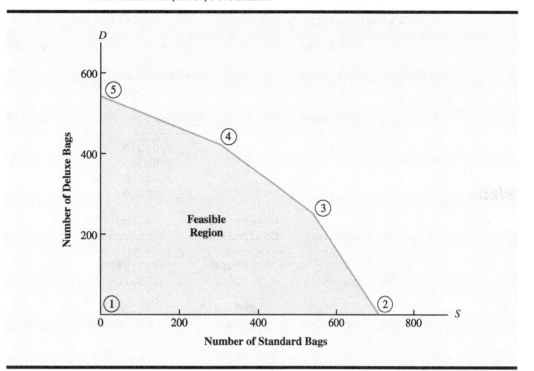

only the feasible solutions that occur at the extreme points of the feasible region. Thus, for the Par, Inc., problem, instead of computing and comparing the profit contributions for all feasible solutions, we can find the optimal solution by evaluating the five extreme-point solutions and selecting the one that provides the largest profit contribution. Actually, the graphical solution procedure is nothing more than a convenient way of identifying an optimal extreme point for two-variable problems.

2.4 COMPUTER SOLUTION OF THE PAR, INC., PROBLEM

In January 1952 the first successful computer solution of a linear programming problem was performed on the SEAC (Standards Eastern Automatic Computer). The SEAC, the first digital computer built by the National Bureau of Standards under U.S. Air Force sponsorship, had a 512-word memory and magnetic tape for external storage.

Computer programs designed to solve linear programming problems are now widely available. After a short period of familiarization with the specific features of the package, users are able to solve linear programming problems with few difficulties. Problems involving thousands of variables and thousands of constraints are now routinely solved with computer packages. Some of the leading commercial packages include CPLEX, Gurobi, LINGO, MOSEK, Risk Solver for Excel, and Xpress-MP. Packages are also available for free download. A good example is Clp (COIN-OR linear programming).

The solution to Par, Inc. is shown in Figure 2.14. The authors have chosen to make this book flexible and not rely on a specific linear programming package. Hence, the output in Figure 2.14 is generic and is not an actual printout from a particular software package. The output provided in Figure 2.14 is typical of most linear programming packages. We use this output format throughout the text. At the website for this course two linear programming packages are provided. A description of the packages is provided in the appendices. In Appendix 2.1 we show how to solve the Par, Inc., problem using LINGO. In Appendix 2.2 we

367

FIGURE 2.14 THE SOLUTION FOR THE PAR, INC., PROBLEM

```
Optimal Objective Value =              7668.00000

     Variable              Value            Reduced Cost
    ------------         ------------       ------------
        S                540.00000            0.00000
        D                252.00000            0.00000

    Constraint         Slack/Surplus          Dual Value
    ------------         ------------       ------------
        1                  0.00000            4.37500
        2                120.00000            0.00000
        3                  0.00000            6.93750
        4                 18.00000            0.00000
```

WEB file

Par

```
                      Objective        Allowable         Allowable
     Variable         Coefficient       Increase          Decrease
    ----------       ------------      ----------        ----------
        S              10.00000         3.50000           3.70000
        D               9.00000         5.28571           2.33333

                         RHS            Allowable         Allowable
    Constraint          Value           Increase          Decrease
    ----------       ------------      ----------        ----------
        1              630.00000        52.36364          134.40000
        2              600.00000        Infinite          120.00000
        3              708.00000        192.00000         128.00000
        4              135.00000        Infinite           18.00000
```

show how to formulate a spreadsheet model for the Par, Inc., problem and use Excel Solver to solve the problem.

Interpretation of Computer Output

Let us look more closely at the output in Figure 2.14 and interpret the computer solution provided for the Par, Inc., problem. The optimal solution to this problem will provide a profit of $7668. Directly below the objective function value, we find the values of the decision variables at the optimal solution. We have $S = 540$ standard bags and $D = 252$ deluxe bags as the optimal production quantities.

Recall that the Par, Inc., problem had four less-than-or-equal-to constraints corresponding to the hours available in each of four production departments. The information shown in the Slack/Surplus column provides the value of the slack variable for each of the departments. This information is summarized here:

Constraint Number	Constraint Name	Slack
1	Cutting and dyeing	0
2	Sewing	120
3	Finishing	0
4	Inspection and packaging	18

368

From this information, we see that the binding constraints (the cutting and dyeing and the finishing constraints) have zero slack at the optimal solution. The sewing department has 120 hours of slack or unused capacity, and the inspection and packaging department has 18 hours of slack or unused capacity.

The rest of the output in Figure 2.14 can be used to determine how changes in the input data impact the optimal solution. We shall defer discussion of reduced costs, dual values, allowable increases and decreases of objective function coefficients and right-hand-side values until Chapter 3, when we study the topic of sensitivity analysis.

NOTES AND COMMENTS

Linear programming solvers are now a standard feature of most spreadsheet packages. In Appendix 2.2 we show how spreadsheets can be used to solve linear programs by using Excel to solve the Par, Inc., problem.

2.5 A SIMPLE MINIMIZATION PROBLEM

M&D Chemicals produces two products that are sold as raw materials to companies manufacturing bath soaps and laundry detergents. Based on an analysis of current inventory levels and potential demand for the coming month, M&D's management specified that the combined production for products A and B must total at least 350 gallons. Separately, a major customer's order for 125 gallons of product A must also be satisfied. Product A requires 2 hours of processing time per gallon and product B requires 1 hour of processing time per gallon. For the coming month, 600 hours of processing time are available. M&D's objective is to satisfy these requirements at a minimum total production cost. Production costs are $2 per gallon for product A and $3 per gallon for product B.

To find the minimum-cost production schedule, we will formulate the M&D Chemicals problem as a linear program. Following a procedure similar to the one used for the Par, Inc., problem, we first define the decision variables and the objective function for the problem. Let

$$A = \text{number of gallons of product A}$$
$$B = \text{number of gallons of product B}$$

With production costs at $2 per gallon for product A and $3 per gallon for product B, the objective function that corresponds to the minimization of the total production cost can be written as

$$\text{Min } 2A + 3B$$

Next, consider the constraints placed on the M&D Chemicals problem. To satisfy the major customer's demand for 125 gallons of product A, we know A must be at least 125. Thus, we write the constraint

$$1A \geq 125$$

For the combined production for both products, which must total at least 350 gallons, we can write the constraint

$$1A + 1B \geq 350$$

Finally, for the limitation of 600 hours on available processing time, we add the constraint

$$2A + 1B \leq 600$$

After adding the nonnegativity constraints $(A, B \geq 0)$, we arrive at the following linear program for the M&D Chemicals problem:

Min $2A + 3B$

s.t.

$1A$	≥ 125	Demand for product A
$1A + 1B$	≥ 350	Total production
$2A + 1B$	≤ 600	Processing time
A, B	≥ 0	

Because the linear programming model has only two decision variables, the graphical solution procedure can be used to find the optimal production quantities. The graphical solution procedure for this problem, just as in the Par problem, requires us to first graph the constraint lines to find the feasible region. By graphing each constraint line separately and then checking points on either side of the constraint line, the feasible solutions for each constraint can be identified. By combining the feasible solutions for each constraint on the same graph, we obtain the feasible region shown in Figure 2.15.

FIGURE 2.15   THE FEASIBLE REGION FOR THE M&D CHEMICALS PROBLEM

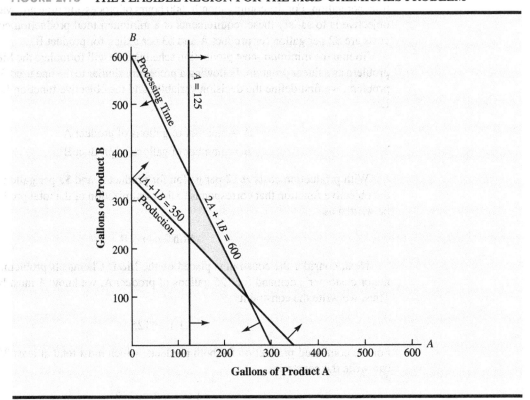

To find the minimum-cost solution, we now draw the objective function line corresponding to a particular total cost value. For example, we might start by drawing the line $2A + 3B = 1200$. This line is shown in Figure 2.16. Clearly, some points in the feasible region would provide a total cost of $1200. To find the values of A and B that provide smaller total cost values, we move the objective function line in a lower left direction until, if we moved it any farther, it would be entirely outside the feasible region. Note that the objective function line $2A + 3B = 800$ intersects the feasible region at the extreme point $A = 250$ and $B = 100$. This extreme point provides the minimum-cost solution with an objective function value of 800. From Figures 2.15 and 2.16, we can see that the total production constraint and the processing time constraint are binding. Just as in every linear programming problem, the optimal solution occurs at an extreme point of the feasible region.

Summary of the Graphical Solution Procedure for Minimization Problems

Can you use the graphical solution procedure to determine the optimal solution for a minimization problem? Try Problem 31.

The steps of the graphical solution procedure for a minimization problem are summarized here:

1. Prepare a graph of the feasible solutions for each of the constraints.
2. Determine the feasible region by identifying the solutions that satisfy all the constraints simultaneously.

FIGURE 2.16   GRAPHICAL SOLUTION FOR THE M&D CHEMICALS PROBLEM

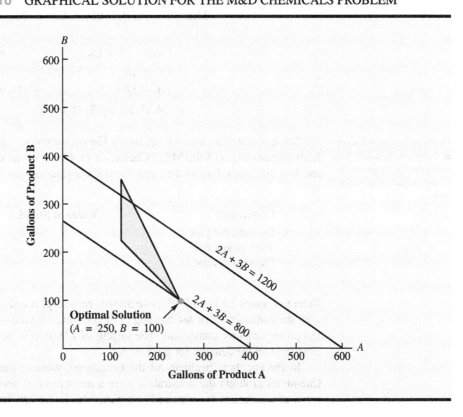

3. Draw an objective function line showing the values of the decision variables that yield a specified value of the objective function.
4. Move parallel objective function lines toward smaller objective function values until further movement would take the line completely outside the feasible region.
5. Any feasible solution on the objective function line with the smallest value is an optimal solution.

Surplus Variables

The optimal solution to the M&D Chemicals problem shows that the desired total production of $A + B = 350$ gallons has been achieved by using all available processing time of $2A + 1B = 2(250) + 1(100) = 600$ hours. In addition, note that the constraint requiring that product A demand be met has been satisfied with $A = 250$ gallons. In fact, the production of product A exceeds its minimum level by $250 - 125 = 125$ gallons. This excess production for product A is referred to as *surplus*. In linear programming terminology, any excess quantity corresponding to a $\geq$ constraint is referred to as surplus.

Recall that with a $\leq$ constraint, a slack variable can be added to the left-hand side of the inequality to convert the constraint to equality form. With a $\geq$ constraint, a **surplus variable** can be subtracted from the left-hand side of the inequality to convert the constraint to equality form. Just as with slack variables, surplus variables are given a coefficient of zero in the objective function because they have no effect on its value. After including two surplus variables, S_1 and S_2, for the $\geq$ constraints and one slack variable, S_3, for the $\leq$ constraint, the linear programming model of the M&D Chemicals problem becomes

$$
\begin{aligned}
\text{Min} \quad & 2A + 3B + 0S_1 + 0S_2 + 0S_3 \\
\text{s.t.} \quad & \\
& 1A \quad\quad\ - 1S_1 \quad\quad\quad\quad\quad = 125 \\
& 1A + 1B \quad\quad\ - 1S_2 \quad\quad\quad = 350 \\
& 2A + 1B \quad\quad\quad\quad\quad + 1S_3 = 600 \\
& A, B, S_1, S_2, S_3 \geq 0
\end{aligned}
$$

Try Problem 35 to test your ability to use slack and surplus variables to write a linear program in standard form.

All the constraints are now equalities. Hence, the preceding formulation is the standard-form representation of the M&D Chemicals problem. At the optimal solution of $A = 250$ and $B = 100$, the values of the surplus and slack variables are as follows:

Constraint	Value of Surplus or Slack Variables
Demand for product A	$S_1 = 125$
Total production	$S_2 = 0$
Processing time	$S_3 = 0$

Refer to Figures 2.15 and 2.16. Note that the zero surplus and slack variables are associated with the constraints that are binding at the optimal solution—that is, the total production and processing time constraints. The surplus of 125 units is associated with the nonbinding constraint on the demand for product A.

In the Par, Inc., problem all the constraints were of the $\leq$ type, and in the M&D Chemicals problem the constraints were a mixture of $\geq$ and $\leq$ types. The number and types of constraints encountered in a particular linear programming problem depend on the specific conditions existing in the problem. Linear programming problems may have some $\leq$ constraints, some $=$ constraints, and some $\geq$ constraints. For an equality constraint, feasible solutions must lie directly on the constraint line.

An example of a linear program with two decision variables, G and H, and all three constraint forms is given here:

Try Problem 34 to practice solving a linear program with all three constraint forms.

$$\text{Min} \quad 2G + 2H$$
$$\text{s.t.}$$
$$1G + 3H \leq 12$$
$$3G + 1H \geq 13$$
$$1G - 1H = 3$$
$$G, H \geq 0$$

The standard-form representation of this problem is

$$\text{Min} \quad 2G + 2H + 0S_1 + 0S_2$$
$$\text{s.t.}$$
$$1G + 3H + 1S_1 \qquad = 12$$
$$3G + 1H \qquad - 1S_2 = 13$$
$$1G - 1H \qquad = 3$$
$$G, H, S_1, S_2 \geq 0$$

The standard form requires a slack variable for the $\leq$ constraint and a surplus variable for the $\geq$ constraint. However, neither a slack nor a surplus variable is required for the third constraint because it is already in equality form.

When solving linear programs graphically, it is not necessary to write the problem in its standard form. Nevertheless, you should be able to compute the values of the slack and surplus variables and understand what they mean, because the values of slack and surplus variables are included in the computer solution of linear programs.

A final point: The standard form of the linear programming problem is equivalent to the original formulation of the problem. That is, the optimal solution to any linear programming problem is the same as the optimal solution to the standard form of the problem. The standard form has not changed the basic problem; it has only changed how we write the constraints for the problem.

Computer Solution of the M&D Chemicals Problem

The optimal solution to M&D is given in Figure 2.17. The computer output shows that the minimum-cost solution yields an objective function value of $800. The values of the decision variables show that 250 gallons of product A and 100 gallons of product B provide the minimum-cost solution.

The Slack/Surplus column shows that the $\geq$ constraint corresponding to the demand for product A (see constraint 1) has a surplus of 125 units. This column tells us that production of product A in the optimal solution exceeds demand by 125 gallons. The Slack/Surplus values are zero for the total production requirement (constraint 2) and the processing time limitation (constraint 3), which indicates that these constraints are binding at the optimal solution. We will discuss the rest of the computer output that appears in Figure 2.17 in Chapter 3 when we study the topic of sensitivity analysis.

FIGURE 2.17 THE SOLUTION FOR THE M&D CHEMICALS PROBLEM

```
Optimal Objective Value =            800.00000

        Variable             Value            Reduced Cost
     --------------     --------------     ----------------

          A                250.00000             0.00000
          B                100.00000             0.00000

       Constraint       Slack/Surplus         Dual Value
     --------------     --------------     ----------------

          1                125.00000             0.00000
          2                  0.00000             4.00000
          3                  0.00000            -1.00000

                         Objective         Allowable          Allowable
        Variable        Coefficient        Increase           Decrease
     --------------     ------------      -----------        -----------

          A               2.00000          1.00000            Infinite
          B               3.00000          Infinite           1.00000

                            RHS            Allowable          Allowable
       Constraint         Value           Increase           Decrease
     --------------     ------------      -----------        -----------

          1              125.00000         125.00000          Infinite
          2              350.00000         125.00000          50.00000
          3              600.00000         100.00000          125.00000
```

WEB file

M&D

2.6   SPECIAL CASES

In this section we discuss three special situations that can arise when we attempt to solve linear programming problems.

Alternative Optimal Solutions

From the discussion of the graphical solution procedure, we know that optimal solutions can be found at the extreme points of the feasible region. Now let us consider the special case in which the optimal objective function line coincides with one of the binding constraint lines on the boundary of the feasible region. We will see that this situation can lead to the case of **alternative optimal solutions;** in such cases, more than one solution provides the optimal value for the objective function.

To illustrate the case of alternative optimal solutions, we return to the Par, Inc., problem. However, let us assume that the profit for the standard golf bag (S) has been decreased to $6.30. The revised objective function becomes $6.3S + 9D$. The graphical solution of this problem is shown in Figure 2.18. Note that the optimal solution still occurs at an extreme point. In fact, it occurs at two extreme points: extreme point ④ ($S = 300$, $D = 420$) and extreme point ③ ($S = 540$, $D = 252$).

The objective function values at these two extreme points are identical; that is,

$$6.3S + 9D = 6.3(300) + 9(420) = 5670$$

374

FIGURE 2.18   PAR, INC., PROBLEM WITH AN OBJECTIVE FUNCTION OF $6.3S + 9D$ (ALTERNATIVE OPTIMAL SOLUTIONS)

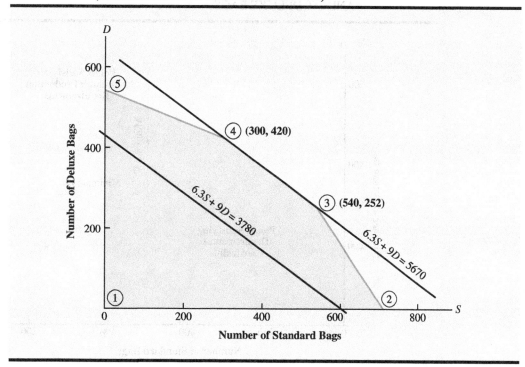

and

$$6.3S + 9D = 6.3(540) + 9(252) = 5670$$

Furthermore, any point on the line connecting the two optimal extreme points also provides an optimal solution. For example, the solution point ($S = 420$, $D = 336$), which is halfway between the two extreme points, also provides the optimal objective function value of

$$6.3S + 9D = 6.3(420) + 9(336) = 5670$$

A linear programming problem with alternative optimal solutions is generally a good situation for the manager or decision maker. It means that several combinations of the decision variables are optimal and that the manager can select the most desirable optimal solution. Unfortunately, determining whether a problem has alternative optimal solutions is not a simple matter.

Infeasibility

Infeasibility means that no solution to the linear programming problem satisfies all the constraints, including the nonnegativity conditions. Graphically, infeasibility means that a feasible region does not exist; that is, no points satisfy all the constraints and the nonnegativity conditions simultaneously. To illustrate this situation, let us look again at the problem faced by Par, Inc.

Problems with no feasible solution do arise in practice, most often because management's expectations are too high or because too many restrictions have been placed on the problem.

Suppose that management specified that at least 500 of the standard bags and at least 360 of the deluxe bags must be manufactured. The graph of the solution region may now be constructed to reflect these new requirements (see Figure 2.19). The shaded area in the lower

FIGURE 2.19   NO FEASIBLE REGION FOR THE PAR, INC., PROBLEM WITH
MINIMUM PRODUCTION REQUIREMENTS OF 500 STANDARD
AND 360 DELUXE BAGS

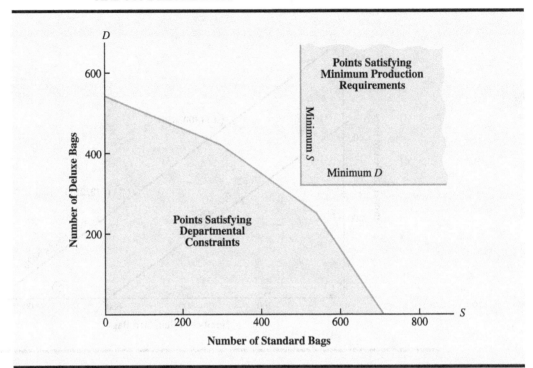

left-hand portion of the graph depicts those points satisfying the departmental constraints on the availability of time. The shaded area in the upper right-hand portion depicts those points satisfying the minimum production requirements of 500 standard and 360 deluxe bags. But no points satisfy both sets of constraints. Thus, we see that if management imposes these minimum production requirements, no feasible region exists for the problem.

How should we interpret infeasibility in terms of this current problem? First, we should tell management that given the resources available (i.e., production time for cutting and dyeing, sewing, finishing, and inspection and packaging), it is not possible to make 500 standard bags and 360 deluxe bags. Moreover, we can tell management exactly how much of each resource must be expended to make it possible to manufacture 500 standard and 360 deluxe bags. Table 2.2 shows the minimum amounts of resources that must be available, the amounts currently available, and additional amounts that would be required to accomplish this level of production. Thus, we need 80 more hours for cutting and dyeing, 32 more hours for finishing, and 5 more hours for inspection and packaging to meet management's minimum production requirements.

If, after reviewing this information, management still wants to manufacture 500 standard and 360 deluxe bags, additional resources must be provided. Perhaps by hiring another person to work in the cutting and dyeing department, transferring a person from elsewhere in the plant to work part-time in the finishing department, or having the sewing people help out periodically with the inspection and packaging, the resource requirements can be met. As you can see, many possibilities are available for corrective management action, once we discover the lack of a feasible solution. The important thing to realize is that linear programming

TABLE 2.2 RESOURCES NEEDED TO MANUFACTURE 500 STANDARD BAGS AND 360 DELUXE BAGS

Operation	Minimum Required Resources (hours)	Available Resources (hours)	Additional Resources Needed (hours)
Cutting and dyeing	$\frac{7}{10}(500) + 1(360) = 710$	630	80
Sewing	$\frac{1}{2}(500) + \frac{5}{6}(360) = 550$	600	None
Finishing	$1(500) + \frac{2}{3}(360) = 740$	708	32
Inspection and packaging	$\frac{1}{10}(500) + \frac{1}{4}(360) = 140$	135	5

analysis can help determine whether management's plans are feasible. By analyzing the problem using linear programming, we are often able to point out infeasible conditions and initiate corrective action.

Whenever you attempt to solve a problem that is infeasible using either LINGO or Excel Solver, you will get an error message indicating that the problem is infeasible. In this case you know that no solution to the linear programming problem will satisfy all constraints, including the nonnegativity conditions. Careful inspection of your formulation is necessary to try to identify why the problem is infeasible. In some situations, the only reasonable approach is to drop one or more constraints and re-solve the problem. If you are able to find an optimal solution for this revised problem, you will know that the constraint(s) that was omitted, in conjunction with the others, is causing the problem to be infeasible.

Unbounded

The solution to a maximization linear programming problem is **unbounded** if the value of the solution may be made infinitely large without violating any of the constraints; for a minimization problem, the solution is unbounded if the value may be made infinitely small. This condition might be termed *managerial utopia;* for example, if this condition were to occur in a profit maximization problem, the manager could achieve an unlimited profit.

However, in linear programming models of real problems, the occurrence of an unbounded solution means that the problem has been improperly formulated. We know it is not possible to increase profits indefinitely. Therefore, we must conclude that if a profit maximization problem results in an unbounded solution, the mathematical model doesn't represent the real-world problem sufficiently. Usually, what has happened is that a constraint has been inadvertently omitted during problem formulation.

As an illustration, consider the following linear program with two decision variables, X and Y:

$$\text{Max} \quad 20X + 10Y$$
$$\text{s.t.}$$
$$1X \qquad \geq 2$$
$$1Y \leq 5$$
$$X, Y \geq 0$$

In Figure 2.20 we graphed the feasible region associated with this problem. Note that we can only indicate part of the feasible region because the feasible region extends indefinitely in the direction of the X axis. Looking at the objective function lines in Figure 2.20, we see that the solution to this problem may be made as large as we desire. That is, no matter what solution we pick, we will always be able to reach some feasible solution with a larger value. Thus, we say that the solution to this linear program is *unbounded.*

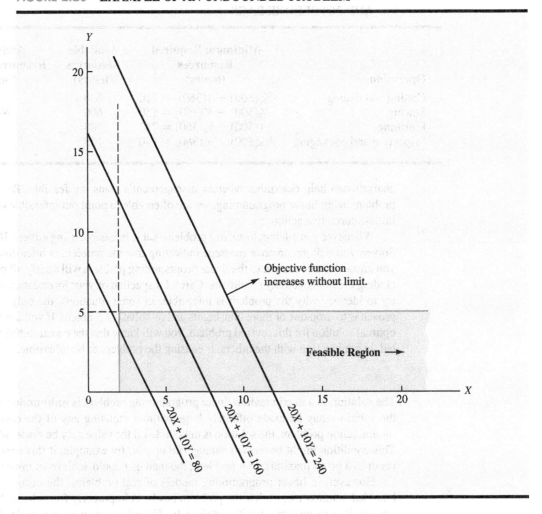

FIGURE 2.20 EXAMPLE OF AN UNBOUNDED PROBLEM

Can you recognize whether a linear program involves alternative optimal solutions or infeasibility, or is unbounded? Try Problems 42 and 43.

Whenever you attempt to solve a problem that is unbounded using either LINGO or Excel Solver you will get a message telling you that the problem is unbounded. Because unbounded solutions cannot occur in real problems, the first thing you should do is to review your model to determine whether you incorrectly formulated the problem. In many cases, this error is the result of inadvertently omitting a constraint during problem formulation.

NOTES AND COMMENTS

1. Infeasibility is independent of the objective function. It exists because the constraints are so restrictive that no feasible region for the linear programming model is possible. Thus, when you encounter infeasibility, making changes in the coefficients of the objective function will not help; the problem will remain infeasible.

2. The occurrence of an unbounded solution is often the result of a missing constraint. However, a change in the objective function may cause a previously unbounded problem to become bounded with an optimal solution. For example, the graph in Figure 2.20 shows an unbounded solution for the objective function Max $20X + 10Y$. However, changing the objective function to Max $-20X - 10Y$ will provide the optimal solution $X = 2$ and $Y = 0$ even though no changes have been made in the constraints.

In this chapter we showed how to formulate linear programming models for the Par, Inc., and M&D Chemicals problems. To formulate a linear programming model of the Par, Inc., problem we began by defining two decision variables: S = number of standard bags and D = number of deluxe bags. In the M&D Chemicals problem, the two decision variables were defined as A = number of gallons of product A and B = number of gallons of product B. We selected decision-variable names of S and D in the Par, Inc., problem and A and B in the M&D Chemicals problem to make it easier to recall what these decision variables represented in the problem. Although this approach works well for linear programs involving a small number of decision variables, it can become difficult when dealing with problems involving a large number of decision variables.

A more general notation that is often used for linear programs uses the letter x with a subscript. For instance, in the Par, Inc., problem, we could have defined the decision variables as follows:

$$x_1 = \text{number of standard bags}$$
$$x_2 = \text{number of deluxe bags}$$

In the M&D Chemicals problem, the same variable names would be used, but their definitions would change:

$$x_1 = \text{number of gallons of product A}$$
$$x_2 = \text{number of gallons of product B}$$

A disadvantage of using general notation for decision variables is that we are no longer able to easily identify what the decision variables actually represent in the mathematical model. However, the advantage of general notation is that formulating a mathematical model for a problem that involves a large number of decision variables is much easier. For instance, for a linear programming model with three decision variables, we would use variable names of x_1, x_2, and x_3; for a problem with four decision variables, we would use variable names of x_1, x_2, x_3, and x_4, and so on. Clearly, if a problem involved 1000 decision variables, trying to identify 1000 unique names would be difficult. However, using the general linear programming notation, the decision variables would be defined as $x_1, x_2, x_3, \ldots, x_{1000}$.

To illustrate the graphical solution procedure for a linear program written using general linear programming notation, consider the following mathematical model for a maximization problem involving two decision variables:

$$\text{Max} \quad 3x_1 + 2x_2$$
$$\text{s.t.}$$
$$2x_1 + 2x_2 \leq 8$$
$$1x_1 + 0.5x_2 \leq 3$$
$$x_1, x_2 \geq 0$$

We must first develop a graph that displays the possible solutions (x_1 and x_2 values) for the problem. The usual convention is to plot values of x_1 along the horizontal axis and values of x_2 along the vertical axis. Figure 2.21 shows the graphical solution for this two-variable problem. Note that for this problem the optimal solution is $x_1 = 2$ and $x_2 = 2$, with an objective function value of 10.

FIGURE 2.21   GRAPHICAL SOLUTION OF A TWO-VARIABLE LINEAR PROGRAM
WITH GENERAL NOTATION

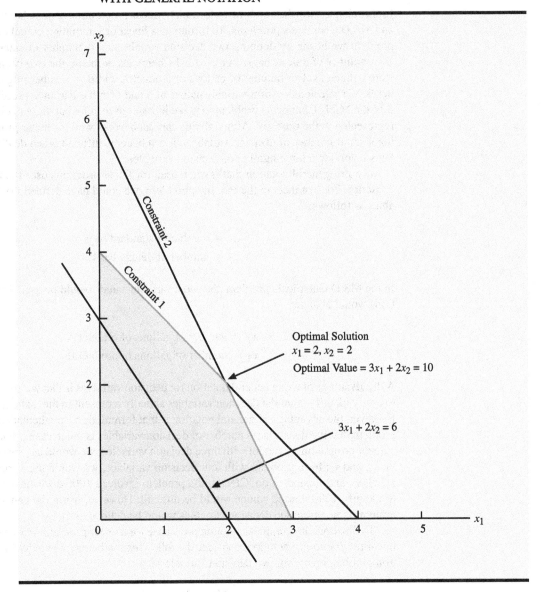

Using general linear programming notation, we can write the standard form of the preceding linear program as follows:

$$\text{Max} \quad 3x_1 + 2x_2 + 0s_1 + 0s_2$$

s.t.

$$2x_1 + 2x_2 + 1s_1 \qquad = 8$$
$$1x_1 + 0.5x_2 + \qquad 1s_2 = 3$$
$$x_1, x_2, s_1, s_2 \geq 0$$

Thus, at the optimal solution $x_1 = 2$ and $x_2 = 2$; the values of the slack variables are $s_1 = s_2 = 0$.

SUMMARY

We formulated linear programming models for two problems: the Par, Inc., maximization problem and the M&D Chemicals minimization problem. For both problems we showed a graphical solution procedure and provided a computer solution to the problem in a generic solution table. In formulating a mathematical model of these problems, we developed a general definition of a linear programming model.

A linear programming model is a mathematical model with the following characteristics:

1. A linear objective function that is to be maximized or minimized
2. A set of linear constraints
3. Variables that are all restricted to nonnegative values

Slack variables may be used to write less-than-or-equal-to constraints in equality form and surplus variables may be used to write greater-than-or-equal-to constraints in equality form. The value of a slack variable can usually be interpreted as the amount of unused resource, whereas the value of a surplus variable indicates the amount over and above some stated minimum requirement. When all constraints have been written as equalities, the linear program has been written in its standard form.

If the solution to a linear program is infeasible or unbounded, no optimal solution to the problem can be found. In the case of infeasibility, no feasible solutions are possible, whereas, in the case of an unbounded solution, the objective function can be made infinitely large for a maximization problem and infinitely small for a minimization problem. In the case of alternative optimal solutions, two or more optimal extreme points exist, and all the points on the line segment connecting them are also optimal.

This chapter concludes with a section showing how to write a linear program using general linear programming notation. The Management Science in Action, Using Linear Programming for Traffic Control, provides another example of the widespread use of linear programming. In the next two chapters we will see many more applications of linear programming.

MANAGEMENT SCIENCE IN ACTION

USING LINEAR PROGRAMMING FOR TRAFFIC CONTROL*

The Hanshin Expressway was the first urban toll expressway in Osaka, Japan. Although in 1964 its length was only 2.3 kilometers, today it is a large-scale urban expressway network of 200 kilometers. The Hanshin Expressway provides service for the Hanshin (Osaka-Kobe) area, the second-most populated area in Japan. An average of 828,000 vehicles use the expressway each day, with daily traffic sometimes exceeding 1 million vehicles. In 1990, the Hanshin Expressway Public Corporation started using an automated traffic control system in order to maximize the number of vehicles flowing into the expressway network.

The automated traffic control system relies on two control methods: (1) limiting the number of cars that enter the expressway at each entrance ramp; and (2) providing drivers with up-to-date and accurate traffic information, including expected travel times and information about accidents. The approach used to limit the number of vehicles depends upon whether the expressway is in a normal or steady state of operation, or whether some type of unusual event, such as an accident or a breakdown, has occurred.

In the first phase of the steady-state case, the Hanshin system uses a linear programming model to maximize the total number of vehicles entering the system, while preventing traffic congestion and adverse effects on surrounding road networks. The data that drive the linear programming model are collected from detectors installed every 500 meters along the expressway and at all entrance and exit ramps. Every five minutes the real-time data collected from the detectors are used to update the model coefficients, and a new linear program computes the maximum number of vehicles the expressway can accommodate.

The automated traffic control system has been successful. According to surveys, traffic control decreased the length of congested portions of the expressway by 30% and the duration by 20%. It proved to be extremely cost effective, and drivers consider it an indispensable service.

*Based on T. Yoshino, T. Sasaki, and T. Hasegawa, "The Traffic-Control System on the Hanshin Expressway," *Interfaces* (January/February 1995): 94–108.

GLOSSARY

Constraint   An equation or inequality that rules out certain combinations of decision variables as feasible solutions.

Problem formulation   The process of translating the verbal statement of a problem into a mathematical statement called the *mathematical model.*

Decision variable   A controllable input for a linear programming model.

Nonnegativity constraints   A set of constraints that requires all variables to be nonnegative.

Mathematical model   A representation of a problem where the objective and all constraint conditions are described by mathematical expressions.

Linear programming model   A mathematical model with a linear objective function, a set of linear constraints, and nonnegative variables.

Linear program   Another term for linear programming model.

Linear functions   Mathematical expressions in which the variables appear in separate terms and are raised to the first power.

Feasible solution   A solution that satisfies all the constraints.

Feasible region   The set of all feasible solutions.

Slack variable   A variable added to the left-hand side of a less-than-or-equal-to constraint to convert the constraint into an equality. The value of this variable can usually be interpreted as the amount of unused resource.

Standard form   A linear program in which all the constraints are written as equalities. The optimal solution of the standard form of a linear program is the same as the optimal solution of the original formulation of the linear program.

Redundant constraint   A constraint that does not affect the feasible region. If a constraint is redundant, it can be removed from the problem without affecting the feasible region.

Extreme point   Graphically speaking, extreme points are the feasible solution points occurring at the vertices or "corners" of the feasible region. With two-variable problems, extreme points are determined by the intersection of the constraint lines.

Surplus variable   A variable subtracted from the left-hand side of a greater-than-or-equal-to constraint to convert the constraint into an equality. The value of this variable can usually be interpreted as the amount over and above some required minimum level.

Alternative optimal solutions   The case in which more than one solution provides the optimal value for the objective function.

Infeasibility   The situation in which no solution to the linear programming problem satisfies all the constraints.

Unbounded   If the value of the solution may be made infinitely large in a maximization linear programming problem or infinitely small in a minimization problem without violating any of the constraints, the problem is said to be unbounded.

PROBLEMS

1. Which of the following mathematical relationships could be found in a linear programming model, and which could not? For the relationships that are unacceptable for linear programs, state why.
   a. $-1A + 2B \leq 70$
   b. $2A - 2B = 50$
   c. $1A - 2B^2 \leq 10$
   d. $3\sqrt{A} + 2B \geq 15$
   e. $1A + 1B = 6$
   f. $2A + 5B + 1AB \leq 25$

2. Find the solutions that satisfy the following constraints:
   a. $4A + 2B \leq 16$
   b. $4A + 2B \geq 16$
   c. $4A + 2B = 16$

3. Show a separate graph of the constraint lines and the solutions that satisfy each of the following constraints:
   a. $3A + 2B \leq 18$
   b. $12A + 8B \geq 480$
   c. $5A + 10B = 200$

4. Show a separate graph of the constraint lines and the solutions that satisfy each of the following constraints:
   a. $3A - 4B \geq 60$
   b. $-6A + 5B \leq 60$
   c. $5A - 2B \leq 0$

5. Show a separate graph of the constraint lines and the solutions that satisfy each of the following constraints:
   a. $A \geq 0.25 (A + B)$
   b. $B \leq 0.10 (A + B)$
   c. $A \leq 0.50 (A + B)$

6. Three objective functions for linear programming problems are $7A + 10B$, $6A + 4B$, and $-4A + 7B$. Show the graph of each for objective function values equal to 420.

7. Identify the feasible region for the following set of constraints:

$$0.5A + 0.25B \geq 30$$
$$1A + 5B \geq 250$$
$$0.25A + 0.5B \leq 50$$
$$A, B \geq 0$$

8. Identify the feasible region for the following set of constraints:

$$2A - 1B \leq 0$$
$$-1A + 1.5B \leq 200$$
$$A, B \geq 0$$

9. Identify the feasible region for the following set of constraints:

$$3A - 2B \geq 0$$
$$2A - 1B \leq 200$$
$$1A \leq 150$$
$$A, B \geq 0$$

10. For the linear program

$$\text{Max} \quad 2A + 3B$$
$$\text{s.t.}$$
$$1A + 2B \le 6$$
$$5A + 3B \le 15$$
$$A, B \ge 0$$

find the optimal solution using the graphical solution procedure. What is the value of the objective function at the optimal solution?

11. Solve the following linear program using the graphical solution procedure:

$$\text{Max} \quad 5A + 5B$$
$$\text{s.t.}$$
$$1A \qquad \le 100$$
$$1B \le 80$$
$$2A + 4B \le 400$$
$$A, B \ge 0$$

12. Consider the following linear programming problem:

$$\text{Max} \quad 3A + 3B$$
$$\text{s.t.}$$
$$2A + 4B \le 12$$
$$6A + 4B \le 24$$
$$A, B \ge 0$$

a. Find the optimal solution using the graphical solution procedure.
b. If the objective function is changed to $2A + 6B$, what will the optimal solution be?
c. How many extreme points are there? What are the values of A and B at each extreme point?

13. Consider the following linear program:

$$\text{Max} \quad 1A + 2B$$
$$\text{s.t.}$$
$$1A \qquad \le 5$$
$$1B \le 4$$
$$2A + 2B = 12$$
$$A, B \ge 0$$

a. Show the feasible region.
b. What are the extreme points of the feasible region?
c. Find the optimal solution using the graphical procedure.

14. RMC, Inc., is a small firm that produces a variety of chemical products. In a particular production process, three raw materials are blended (mixed together) to produce two products: a fuel additive and a solvent base. Each ton of fuel additive is a mixture of ⅖ ton of material 1 and ⅗ of material 3. A ton of solvent base is a mixture of ½ ton of material 1, ⅕ ton of material 2, and ³⁄₁₀ ton of material 3. After deducting relevant costs, the profit contribution is $40 for every ton of fuel additive produced and $30 for every ton of solvent base produced.

384

RMC's production is constrained by a limited availability of the three raw materials. For the current production period, RMC has available the following quantities of each raw material:

Raw Material	Amount Available for Production
Material 1	20 tons
Material 2	5 tons
Material 3	21 tons

Assuming that RMC is interested in maximizing the total profit contribution, answer the following:

a. What is the linear programming model for this problem?

b. Find the optimal solution using the graphical solution procedure. How many tons of each product should be produced, and what is the projected total profit contribution?

c. Is there any unused material? If so, how much?

d. Are any of the constraints redundant? If so, which ones?

15. Refer to the Par, Inc., problem described in Section 2.1. Suppose that Par's management encounters the following situations:

a. The accounting department revises its estimate of the profit contribution for the deluxe bag to $18 per bag.

b. A new low-cost material is available for the standard bag, and the profit contribution per standard bag can be increased to $20 per bag. (Assume that the profit contribution of the deluxe bag is the original $9 value.)

c. New sewing equipment is available that would increase the sewing operation capacity to 750 hours. (Assume that $10A + 9B$ is the appropriate objective function.) If each of these situations is encountered separately, what is the optimal solution and the total profit contribution?

16. Refer to the feasible region for Par, Inc., problem in Figure 2.13.

a. Develop an objective function that will make extreme point ⑤ the optimal extreme point.

b. What is the optimal solution for the objective function you selected in part (a)?

c. What are the values of the slack variables associated with this solution?

SELF test   17. Write the following linear program in standard form:

$$\text{Max} \quad 5A + 2B$$
$$\text{s.t.}$$
$$1A - 2B \le 420$$
$$2A + 3B \le 610$$
$$6A - 1B \le 125$$
$$A, B \ge 0$$

18. For the linear program

$$\text{Max} \quad 4A + 1B$$
$$\text{s.t.}$$
$$10A + 2B \le 30$$
$$3A + 2B \le 12$$
$$2A + 2B \le 10$$
$$A, B \ge 0$$

a. Write this problem in standard form.
b. Solve the problem using the graphical solution procedure.
c. What are the values of the three slack variables at the optimal solution?

19. Given the linear program

$$\text{Max} \quad 3A + 4B$$
$$\text{s.t.}$$
$$-1A + 2B \leq 8$$
$$1A + 2B \leq 12$$
$$2A + 1B \leq 16$$
$$A, B \geq 0$$

a. Write the problem in standard form.
b. Solve the problem using the graphical solution procedure.
c. What are the values of the three slack variables at the optimal solution?

20. For the linear program

$$\text{Max} \quad 3A + 2B$$
$$\text{s.t.}$$
$$A + B \geq 4$$
$$3A + 4B \leq 24$$
$$A \qquad \geq 2$$
$$A - B \leq 0$$
$$A, B \geq 0$$

a. Write the problem in standard form.
b. Solve the problem.
c. What are the values of the slack and surplus variables at the optimal solution?

21. Consider the following linear program:

$$\text{Max} \quad 2A + 3B$$
$$\text{s.t.}$$
$$5A + 5B \leq 400 \quad \text{Constraint 1}$$
$$-1A + 1B \leq 10 \quad \text{Constraint 2}$$
$$1A + 3B \geq 90 \quad \text{Constraint 3}$$
$$A, B \geq 0$$

Figure 2.22 shows a graph of the constraint lines.
a. Place a number (1, 2, or 3) next to each constraint line to identify which constraint it represents.
b. Shade in the feasible region on the graph.
c. Identify the optimal extreme point. What is the optimal solution?
d. Which constraints are binding? Explain.
e. How much slack or surplus is associated with the nonbinding constraint?

22. Reiser Sports Products wants to determine the number of All-Pro (A) and College (C) footballs to produce in order to maximize profit over the next four-week planning horizon. Constraints affecting the production quantities are the production capacities in three departments: cutting and dyeing; sewing; and inspection and packaging. For

FIGURE 2.22 GRAPH OF THE CONSTRAINT LINES FOR EXERCISE 21

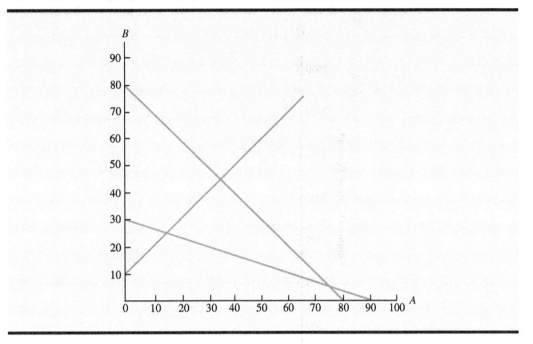

the four-week planning period, 340 hours of cutting and dyeing time, 420 hours of sewing time, and 200 hours of inspection and packaging time are available. All-Pro footballs provide a profit of $5 per unit and College footballs provide a profit of $4 per unit. The linear programming model with production times expressed in minutes is as follows:

$$\text{Max} \quad 5A + 4C$$
s.t.
$$12A + 6C \leq 20{,}400 \quad \text{Cutting and dyeing}$$
$$9A + 15C \leq 25{,}200 \quad \text{Sewing}$$
$$6A + 6C \leq 12{,}000 \quad \text{Inspection and packaging}$$
$$A, C \geq 0$$

A portion of the graphical solution to the Reiser problem is shown in Figure 2.23.

a. Shade the feasible region for this problem.

b. Determine the coordinates of each extreme point and the corresponding profit. Which extreme point generates the highest profit?

c. Draw the profit line corresponding to a profit of $4000. Move the profit line as far from the origin as you can in order to determine which extreme point will provide the optimal solution. Compare your answer with the approach you used in part (b).

d. Which constraints are binding? Explain.

e. Suppose that the values of the objective function coefficients are $4 for each All-Pro model produced and $5 for each College model. Use the graphical solution procedure to determine the new optimal solution and the corresponding value of profit.

FIGURE 2.23   PORTION OF THE GRAPHICAL SOLUTION FOR EXERCISE 22

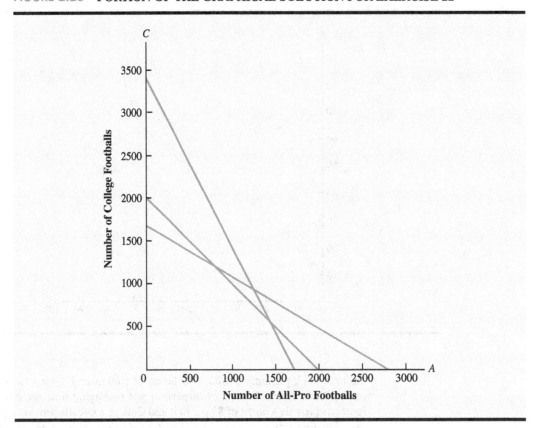

23. Embassy Motorcycles (EM) manufacturers two lightweight motorcycles designed for easy handling and safety. The EZ-Rider model has a new engine and a low profile that make it easy to balance. The Lady-Sport model is slightly larger, uses a more traditional engine, and is specifically designed to appeal to women riders. Embassy produces the engines for both models at its Des Moines, Iowa, plant. Each EZ-Rider engine requires 6 hours of manufacturing time and each Lady-Sport engine requires 3 hours of manufacturing time. The Des Moines plant has 2100 hours of engine manufacturing time available for the next production period. Embassy's motorcycle frame supplier can supply as many EZ-Rider frames as needed. However, the Lady-Sport frame is more complex and the supplier can only provide up to 280 Lady-Sport frames for the next production period. Final assembly and testing requires 2 hours for each EZ-Rider model and 2.5 hours for each Lady-Sport model. A maximum of 1000 hours of assembly and testing time are available for the next production period. The company's accounting department projects a profit contribution of $2400 for each EZ-Rider produced and $1800 for each Lady-Sport produced.

   a. Formulate a linear programming model that can be used to determine the number of units of each model that should be produced in order to maximize the total contribution to profit.
   b. Solve the problem graphically. What is the optimal solution?
   c. Which constraints are binding?

388

24. Kelson Sporting Equipment, Inc., makes two different types of baseball gloves: a regular model and a catcher's model. The firm has 900 hours of production time available in its cutting and sewing department, 300 hours available in its finishing department, and 100 hours available in its packaging and shipping department. The production time requirements and the profit contribution per glove are given in the following table:

| | Production Time (hours) | | | |
Model	Cutting and Sewing	Finishing	Packaging and Shipping	Profit/Glove
Regular model	1	$\frac{1}{2}$	$\frac{1}{8}$	$5
Catcher's model	$\frac{3}{2}$	$\frac{1}{3}$	$\frac{1}{4}$	$8

Assuming that the company is interested in maximizing the total profit contribution, answer the following:

a. What is the linear programming model for this problem?

b. Find the optimal solution using the graphical solution procedure. How many gloves of each model should Kelson manufacture?

c. What is the total profit contribution Kelson can earn with the given production quantities?

d. How many hours of production time will be scheduled in each department?

e. What is the slack time in each department?

25. George Johnson recently inherited a large sum of money; he wants to use a portion of this money to set up a trust fund for his two children. The trust fund has two investment options: (1) a bond fund and (2) a stock fund. The projected returns over the life of the investments are 6% for the bond fund and 10% for the stock fund. Whatever portion of the inheritance he finally decides to commit to the trust fund, he wants to invest at least 30% of that amount in the bond fund. In addition, he wants to select a mix that will enable him to obtain a total return of at least 7.5%.

a. Formulate a linear programming model that can be used to determine the percentage that should be allocated to each of the possible investment alternatives.

b. Solve the problem using the graphical solution procedure.

26. The Sea Wharf Restaurant would like to determine the best way to allocate a monthly advertising budget of $1000 between newspaper advertising and radio advertising. Management decided that at least 25% of the budget must be spent on each type of media, and that the amount of money spent on local newspaper advertising must be at least twice the amount spent on radio advertising. A marketing consultant developed an index that measures audience exposure per dollar of advertising on a scale from 0 to 100, with higher values implying greater audience exposure. If the value of the index for local newspaper advertising is 50 and the value of the index for spot radio advertising is 80, how should the restaurant allocate its advertising budget in order to maximize the value of total audience exposure?

a. Formulate a linear programming model that can be used to determine how the restaurant should allocate its advertising budget in order to maximize the value of total audience exposure.

b. Solve the problem using the graphical solution procedure.

27. Blair & Rosen, Inc. (B&R), is a brokerage firm that specializes in investment portfolios designed to meet the specific risk tolerances of its clients. A client who contacted B&R this past week has a maximum of $50,000 to invest. B&R's investment advisor decides to recommend a portfolio consisting of two investment funds: an Internet fund and a Blue

Chip fund. The Internet fund has a projected annual return of 12%, whereas the Blue Chip fund has a projected annual return of 9%. The investment advisor requires that at most $35,000 of the client's funds should be invested in the Internet fund. B&R services include a risk rating for each investment alternative. The Internet fund, which is the more risky of the two investment alternatives, has a risk rating of 6 per thousand dollars invested. The Blue Chip fund has a risk rating of 4 per thousand dollars invested. For example, if $10,000 is invested in each of the two investment funds, B&R's risk rating for the portfolio would be 6(10) + 4(10) = 100. Finally, B&R developed a questionnaire to measure each client's risk tolerance. Based on the responses, each client is classified as a conservative, moderate, or aggressive investor. Suppose that the questionnaire results classified the current client as a moderate investor. B&R recommends that a client who is a moderate investor limit his or her portfolio to a maximum risk rating of 240.

a. What is the recommended investment portfolio for this client? What is the annual return for the portfolio?

b. Suppose that a second client with $50,000 to invest has been classified as an aggressive investor. B&R recommends that the maximum portfolio risk rating for an aggressive investor is 320. What is the recommended investment portfolio for this aggressive investor? Discuss what happens to the portfolio under the aggressive investor strategy.

c. Suppose that a third client with $50,000 to invest has been classified as a conservative investor. B&R recommends that the maximum portfolio risk rating for a conservative investor is 160. Develop the recommended investment portfolio for the conservative investor. Discuss the interpretation of the slack variable for the total investment fund constraint.

28. Tom's, Inc., produces various Mexican food products and sells them to Western Foods, a chain of grocery stores located in Texas and New Mexico. Tom's, Inc., makes two salsa products: Western Foods Salsa and Mexico City Salsa. Essentially, the two products have different blends of whole tomatoes, tomato sauce, and tomato paste. The Western Foods Salsa is a blend of 50% whole tomatoes, 30% tomato sauce, and 20% tomato paste. The Mexico City Salsa, which has a thicker and chunkier consistency, consists of 70% whole tomatoes, 10% tomato sauce, and 20% tomato paste. Each jar of salsa produced weighs 10 ounces. For the current production period, Tom's, Inc., can purchase up to 280 pounds of whole tomatoes, 130 pounds of tomato sauce, and 100 pounds of tomato paste; the price per pound for these ingredients is $0.96, $0.64, and $0.56, respectively. The cost of the spices and the other ingredients is approximately $0.10 per jar. Tom's, Inc., buys empty glass jars for $0.02 each, and labeling and filling costs are estimated to be $0.03 for each jar of salsa produced. Tom's contract with Western Foods results in sales revenue of $1.64 for each jar of Western Foods Salsa and $1.93 for each jar of Mexico City Salsa.

a. Develop a linear programming model that will enable Tom's to determine the mix of salsa products that will maximize the total profit contribution.

b. Find the optimal solution.

29. AutoIgnite produces electronic ignition systems for automobiles at a plant in Cleveland, Ohio. Each ignition system is assembled from two components produced at AutoIgnite's plants in Buffalo, New York, and Dayton, Ohio. The Buffalo plant can produce 2000 units of component 1, 1000 units of component 2, or any combination of the two components each day. For instance, 60% of Buffalo's production time could be used to produce component 1 and 40% of Buffalo's production time could be used to produce component 2; in this case, the Buffalo plant would be able to produce 0.6(2000) = 1200 units of component 1 each day and 0.4(1000) = 400 units of component 2 each day. The Dayton plant can produce 600 units of component 1, 1400 units of component 2, or any combination of the two components each day. At the end of each day, the component production at Buffalo and Dayton is sent to Cleveland for assembly of the ignition systems on the following workday.

a. Formulate a linear programming model that can be used to develop a daily production schedule for the Buffalo and Dayton plants that will maximize daily production of ignition systems at Cleveland.
b. Find the optimal solution.

30. A financial advisor at Diehl Investments identified two companies that are likely candidates for a takeover in the near future. Eastern Cable is a leading manufacturer of flexible cable systems used in the construction industry, and ComSwitch is a new firm specializing in digital switching systems. Eastern Cable is currently trading for $40 per share, and ComSwitch is currently trading for $25 per share. If the takeovers occur, the financial advisor estimates that the price of Eastern Cable will go to $55 per share and ComSwitch will go to $43 per share. At this point in time, the financial advisor has identified ComSwitch as the higher risk alternative. Assume that a client indicated a willingness to invest a maximum of $50,000 in the two companies. The client wants to invest at least $15,000 in Eastern Cable and at least $10,000 in ComSwitch. Because of the higher risk associated with ComSwitch, the financial advisor has recommended that at most $25,000 should be invested in ComSwitch.

a. Formulate a linear programming model that can be used to determine the number of shares of Eastern Cable and the number of shares of ComSwitch that will meet the investment constraints and maximize the total return for the investment.
b. Graph the feasible region.
c. Determine the coordinates of each extreme point.
d. Find the optimal solution.

31. Consider the following linear program:

$$\text{Min} \quad 3A + 4B$$
s.t.
$$1A + 3B \geq 6$$
$$1A + 1B \geq 4$$
$$A, B \geq 0$$

Identify the feasible region and find the optimal solution using the graphical solution procedure. What is the value of the objective function?

32. Identify the three extreme-point solutions for the M&D Chemicals problem (see Section 2.5). Identify the value of the objective function and the values of the slack and surplus variables at each extreme point.

33. Consider the following linear programming problem:

$$\text{Min} \quad A + 2B$$
s.t.
$$A + 4B \leq 21$$
$$2A + B \geq 7$$
$$3A + 1.5B \leq 21$$
$$-2A + 6B \geq 0$$
$$A, B \geq 0$$

a. Find the optimal solution using the graphical solution procedure and the value of the objective function.
b. Determine the amount of slack or surplus for each constraint.
c. Suppose the objective function is changed to max $5A + 2B$. Find the optimal solution and the value of the objective function.

34. Consider the following linear program:

$$\text{Min} \quad 2A + 2B$$

s.t.

$$1A + 3B \leq 12$$
$$3A + 1B \geq 13$$
$$1A - 1B = 3$$
$$A, B \geq 0$$

a. Show the feasible region.
b. What are the extreme points of the feasible region?
c. Find the optimal solution using the graphical solution procedure.

35. For the linear program

$$\text{Min} \quad 6A + 4B$$

s.t.

$$2A + 1B \geq 12$$
$$1A + 1B \geq 10$$
$$1B \leq 4$$
$$A, B \geq 0$$

a. Write the problem in standard form.
b. Solve the problem using the graphical solution procedure.
c. What are the values of the slack and surplus variables?

36. As part of a quality improvement initiative, Consolidated Electronics employees complete a three-day training program on teaming and a two-day training program on problem solving. The manager of quality improvement has requested that at least 8 training programs on teaming and at least 10 training programs on problem solving be offered during the next six months. In addition, senior-level management has specified that at least 25 training programs must be offered during this period. Consolidated Electronics uses a consultant to teach the training programs. During the next quarter, the consultant has 84 days of training time available. Each training program on teaming costs $10,000 and each training program on problem solving costs $8000.
   a. Formulate a linear programming model that can be used to determine the number of training programs on teaming and the number of training programs on problem solving that should be offered in order to minimize total cost.
   b. Graph the feasible region.
   c. Determine the coordinates of each extreme point.
   d. Solve for the minimum cost solution.

37. The New England Cheese Company produces two cheese spreads by blending mild cheddar cheese with extra sharp cheddar cheese. The cheese spreads are packaged in 12-ounce containers, which are then sold to distributors throughout the Northeast. The Regular blend contains 80% mild cheddar and 20% extra sharp, and the Zesty blend contains 60% mild cheddar and 40% extra sharp. This year, a local dairy cooperative offered to provide up to 8100 pounds of mild cheddar cheese for $1.20 per pound and up to 3000 pounds of extra sharp cheddar cheese for $1.40 per pound. The cost to blend and package the cheese spreads, excluding the cost of the cheese, is $0.20 per container. If each container of Regular is sold for $1.95 and each container of Zesty is sold for $2.20, how many containers of Regular and Zesty should New England Cheese produce?

38. Applied Technology, Inc. (ATI), produces bicycle frames using two fiberglass materials that improve the strength-to-weight ratio of the frames. The cost of the standard grade material is $7.50 per yard and the cost of the professional grade material is $9.00 per yard. The standard and professional grade materials contain different amounts of fiberglass, carbon fiber, and Kevlar as shown in the following table:

	Standard Grade	**Professional Grade**
Fiberglass	84%	58%
Carbon fiber	10%	30%
Kevlar	6%	12%

ATI signed a contract with a bicycle manufacturer to produce a new frame with a carbon fiber content of at least 20% and a Kevlar content of not greater than 10%. To meet the required weight specification, a total of 30 yards of material must be used for each frame.

a. Formulate a linear program to determine the number of yards of each grade of fiberglass material that ATI should use in each frame in order to minimize total cost. Define the decision variables and indicate the purpose of each constraint.

b. Use the graphical solution procedure to determine the feasible region. What are the coordinates of the extreme points?

c. Compute the total cost at each extreme point. What is the optimal solution?

d. The distributor of the fiberglass material is currently overstocked with the professional grade material. To reduce inventory, the distributor offered ATI the opportunity to purchase the professional grade for $8 per yard. Will the optimal solution change?

e. Suppose that the distributor further lowers the price of the professional grade material to $7.40 per yard. Will the optimal solution change? What effect would an even lower price for the professional grade material have on the optimal solution? Explain.

39. Innis Investments manages funds for a number of companies and wealthy clients. The investment strategy is tailored to each client's needs. For a new client, Innis has been authorized to invest up to $1.2 million in two investment funds: a stock fund and a money market fund. Each unit of the stock fund costs $50 and provides an annual rate of return of 10%; each unit of the money market fund costs $100 and provides an annual rate of return of 4%.

The client wants to minimize risk subject to the requirement that the annual income from the investment be at least $60,000. According to Innis's risk measurement system, each unit invested in the stock fund has a risk index of 8, and each unit invested in the money market fund has a risk index of 3; the higher risk index associated with the stock fund simply indicates that it is the riskier investment. Innis's client also specified that at least $300,000 be invested in the money market fund.

a. Determine how many units of each fund Innis should purchase for the client to minimize the total risk index for the portfolio.

b. How much annual income will this investment strategy generate?

c. Suppose the client desires to maximize annual return. How should the funds be invested?

40. Photo Chemicals produces two types of photographic developing fluids. Both products cost Photo Chemicals $1 per gallon to produce. Based on an analysis of current inventory levels and outstanding orders for the next month, Photo Chemicals' management specified that at least 30 gallons of product 1 and at least 20 gallons of product 2 must be produced during the next two weeks. Management also stated that an existing inventory of highly perishable raw material required in the production of both fluids must be used within the

next two weeks. The current inventory of the perishable raw material is 80 pounds. Although more of this raw material can be ordered if necessary, any of the current inventory that is not used within the next two weeks will spoil—hence, the management requirement that at least 80 pounds be used in the next two weeks. Furthermore, it is known that product 1 requires 1 pound of this perishable raw material per gallon and product 2 requires 2 pounds of the raw material per gallon. Because Photo Chemicals' objective is to keep its production costs at the minimum possible level, the firm's management is looking for a minimum cost production plan that uses all the 80 pounds of perishable raw material and provides at least 30 gallons of product 1 and at least 20 gallons of product 2. What is the minimum cost solution?

41. Southern Oil Company produces two grades of gasoline: regular and premium. The profit contributions are $0.30 per gallon for regular gasoline and $0.50 per gallon for premium gasoline. Each gallon of regular gasoline contains 0.3 gallons of grade A crude oil and each gallon of premium gasoline contains 0.6 gallons of grade A crude oil. For the next production period, Southern has 18,000 gallons of grade A crude oil available. The refinery used to produce the gasolines has a production capacity of 50,000 gallons for the next production period. Southern Oil's distributors have indicated that demand for the premium gasoline for the next production period will be at most 20,000 gallons.

    a. Formulate a linear programming model that can be used to determine the number of gallons of regular gasoline and the number of gallons of premium gasoline that should be produced in order to maximize total profit contribution.

    b. What is the optimal solution?

    c. What are the values and interpretations of the slack variables?

    d. What are the binding constraints?

42. Does the following linear program involve infeasibility, unbounded, and/or alternative optimal solutions? Explain.

$$\text{Max} \quad 4A + 8B$$
$$\text{s.t.}$$
$$2A + 2B \le 10$$
$$-1A + 1B \ge 8$$
$$A, B \ge 0$$

43. Does the following linear program involve infeasibility, unbounded, and/or alternative optimal solutions? Explain.

$$\text{Max} \quad 1A + 1B$$
$$\text{s.t.}$$
$$8A + 6B \ge 24$$
$$2B \ge 4$$
$$A, B \ge 0$$

44. Consider the following linear program:

$$\text{Max} \quad 1A + 1B$$
$$\text{s.t.}$$
$$5A + 3B \le 15$$
$$3A + 5B \le 15$$
$$A, B \ge 0$$

a. What is the optimal solution for this problem?

b. Suppose that the objective function is changed to $1A + 2B$. Find the new optimal solution.

45. Consider the following linear program:

$$\text{Max} \quad 1A - 2B$$
$$\text{s.t.}$$
$$-4A + 3B \leq 3$$
$$1A - 1B \leq 3$$
$$A, B \geq 0$$

a. Graph the feasible region for the problem.

b. Is the feasible region unbounded? Explain.

c. Find the optimal solution.

d. Does an unbounded feasible region imply that the optimal solution to the linear program will be unbounded?

46. The manager of a small independent grocery store is trying to determine the best use of her shelf space for soft drinks. The store carries national and generic brands and currently has 200 square feet of shelf space available. The manager wants to allocate at least 60% of the space to the national brands and, regardless of the profitability, allocate at least 10% of the space to the generic brands. How many square feet of space should the manager allocate to the national brands and the generic brands under the following circumstances?

a. The national brands are more profitable than the generic brands.

b. Both brands are equally profitable.

c. The generic brand is more profitable than the national brand.

47. Discuss what happens to the M&D Chemicals problem (see Section 2.5) if the cost per gallon for product A is increased to $3.00 per gallon. What would you recommend? Explain.

48. For the M&D Chemicals problem in Section 2.5, discuss the effect of management's requiring total production of 500 gallons for the two products. List two or three actions M&D should consider to correct the situation you encounter.

49. PharmaPlus operates a chain of 30 pharmacies. The pharmacies are staffed by licensed pharmacists and pharmacy technicians. The company currently employs 85 full-time equivalent pharmacists (combination of full time and part time) and 175 full-time equivalent technicians. Each spring management reviews current staffing levels and makes hiring plans for the year. A recent forecast of the prescription load for the next year shows that at least 250 full-time equivalent employees (pharmacists and technicians) will be required to staff the pharmacies. The personnel department expects 10 pharmacists and 30 technicians to leave over the next year. To accommodate the expected attrition and prepare for future growth, management stated that at least 15 new pharmacists must be hired. In addition, PharmaPlus's new service quality guidelines specify no more than two technicians per licensed pharmacist. The average salary for licensed pharmacists is $40 per hour and the average salary for technicians is $10 per hour.

a. Determine a minimum-cost staffing plan for PharmaPlus. How many pharmacists and technicians are needed?

b. Given current staffing levels and expected attrition, how many new hires (if any) must be made to reach the level recommended in part (a)? What will be the impact on the payroll?

50. Expedition Outfitters manufactures a variety of specialty clothing for hiking, skiing, and mountain climbing. Its management decided to begin production on two new parkas designed

395

for use in extremely cold weather: the Mount Everest Parka and the Rocky Mountain Parka. The manufacturing plant has 120 hours of cutting time and 120 hours of sewing time available for producing these two parkas. Each Mount Everest Parka requires 30 minutes of cutting time and 45 minutes of sewing time, and each Rocky Mountain Parka requires 20 minutes of cutting time and 15 minutes of sewing time. The labor and material cost is $150 for each Mount Everest Parka and $50 for each Rocky Mountain Parka, and the retail prices through the firm's mail order catalog are $250 for the Mount Everest Parka and $200 for the Rocky Mountain Parka. Because management believes that the Mount Everest Parka is a unique coat that will enhance the image of the firm, they specified that at least 20% of the total production must consist of this model. Assuming that Expedition Outfitters can sell as many coats of each type as it can produce, how many units of each model should it manufacture to maximize the total profit contribution?

51. English Motors, Ltd. (EML), developed a new all-wheel-drive sports utility vehicle. As part of the marketing campaign, EML produced a video tape sales presentation to send to both owners of current EML four-wheel-drive vehicles as well as to owners of four-wheel-drive sports utility vehicles offered by competitors; EML refers to these two target markets as the current customer market and the new customer market. Individuals who receive the new promotion video will also receive a coupon for a test drive of the new EML model for one weekend. A key factor in the success of the new promotion is the response rate, the percentage of individuals who receive the new promotion and test drive the new model. EML estimates that the response rate for the current customer market is 25% and the response rate for the new customer market is 20%. For the customers who test drive the new model, the sales rate is the percentage of individuals that make a purchase. Marketing research studies indicate that the sales rate is 12% for the current customer market and 20% for the new customer market. The cost for each promotion, excluding the test drive costs, is $4 for each promotion sent to the current customer market and $6 for each promotion sent to the new customer market. Management also specified that a minimum of 30,000 current customers should test drive the new model and a minimum of 10,000 new customers should test drive the new model. In addition, the number of current customers who test drive the new vehicle must be at least twice the number of new customers who test drive the new vehicle. If the marketing budget, excluding test drive costs, is $1.2 million, how many promotions should be sent to each group of customers in order to maximize total sales?

52. Creative Sports Design (CSD) manufactures a standard-size racket and an oversize racket. The firm's rackets are extremely light due to the use of a magnesium-graphite alloy that was invented by the firm's founder. Each standard-size racket uses 0.125 kilograms of the alloy and each oversize racket uses 0.4 kilograms; over the next two-week production period only 80 kilograms of the alloy are available. Each standard-size racket uses 10 minutes of manufacturing time and each oversize racket uses 12 minutes. The profit contributions are $10 for each standard-size racket and $15 for each oversize racket, and 40 hours of manufacturing time are available each week. Management specified that at least 20% of the total production must be the standard-size racket. How many rackets of each type should CSD manufacture over the next two weeks to maximize the total profit contribution? Assume that because of the unique nature of their products, CSD can sell as many rackets as they can produce.

53. Management of High Tech Services (HTS) would like to develop a model that will help allocate their technicians' time between service calls to regular contract customers and new customers. A maximum of 80 hours of technician time is available over the two-week planning period. To satisfy cash flow requirements, at least $800 in revenue (per technician) must be generated during the two-week period. Technician time for regular customers generates $25 per hour. However, technician time for new customers only

generates an average of $8 per hour because in many cases a new customer contact does not provide billable services. To ensure that new customer contacts are being maintained, the technician time spent on new customer contacts must be at least 60% of the time spent on regular customer contacts. Given these revenue and policy requirements, HTS would like to determine how to allocate technician time between regular customers and new customers so that the total number of customers contacted during the two-week period will be maximized. Technicians require an average of 50 minutes for each regular customer contact and 1 hour for each new customer contact.

    a.   Develop a linear programming model that will enable HTS to allocate technician time between regular customers and new customers.

    b.   Find the optimal solution.

54.   Jackson Hole Manufacturing is a small manufacturer of plastic products used in the automotive and computer industries. One of its major contracts is with a large computer company and involves the production of plastic printer cases for the computer company's portable printers. The printer cases are produced on two injection molding machines. The M-100 machine has a production capacity of 25 printer cases per hour, and the M-200 machine has a production capacity of 40 cases per hour. Both machines use the same chemical material to produce the printer cases; the M-100 uses 40 pounds of the raw material per hour and the M-200 uses 50 pounds per hour. The computer company asked Jackson Hole to produce as many of the cases during the upcoming week as possible; it will pay $18 for each case Jackson Hole can deliver. However, next week is a regularly scheduled vacation period for most of Jackson Hole's production employees; during this time, annual maintenance is performed for all equipment in the plant. Because of the downtime for maintenance, the M-100 will be available for no more than 15 hours, and the M-200 will be available for no more than 10 hours. However, because of the high setup cost involved with both machines, management requires that, each machine must be operated for at least 5 hours. The supplier of the chemical material used in the production process informed Jackson Hole that a maximum of 1000 pounds of the chemical material will be available for next week's production; the cost for this raw material is $6 per pound. In addition to the raw material cost, Jackson Hole estimates that the hourly cost of operating the M-100 and the M-200 are $50 and $75, respectively.

    a.   Formulate a linear programming model that can be used to maximize the contribution to profit.

    b.   Find the optimal solution.

55.   The Kartick Company is trying to determine how much of each of two products to produce over the coming planning period. There are three departments, A, B and C, with limited labor hours available in each department. Each product must be processed by each department and the per-unit requirements for each product, labor hours available, and per-unit profit are as shown below.

	Labor required in each department		
	Product (hrs./unit)		**Labor Hours**
Department	**Product 1**	**Product 2**	**Available**
A	1.00	0.30	100
B	0.30	0.12	36
C	0.15	0.56	50
Profit Contribution	$33.00	$24.00	

A linear program for this situation is as follows:

Let x_1 = the amount of product 1 to produce

x_2 = the amount of product 2 to produce

Maximize $33\,x_1 + 24\,x_2$

s.t.

$$1.0\,x_1 + .30\,x_2 \le 100 \quad \text{Department A}$$
$$.30\,x_1 + .12\,x_2 \le 36 \quad \text{Department B}$$
$$.15\,x_1 + .56\,x_2 \le 50 \quad \text{Department C}$$
$$x_1, x_2 \ge 0$$

Mr. Kartick (the owner) used trial and error with a spreadsheet model to arrive at a solution. His proposed solution is $x_1 = 75$ and $x_2 = 60$, as shown below in Figure 2.24. He said he felt his proposed solution is optimal.

Is his solution optimal? Without solving the problem, explain why you believe this solution is optimal or not optimal.

FIGURE 2.24   MR. KARTICK'S TRIAL-AND-ERROR MODEL

	A	B	C	D	E
1	**Kartick**				
2	**Data**				
3				Hours	
4	Department	Prod 1	Prod 2	Available	
5	A	1.00	0.30	100	
6	B	0.30	0.12	36	
7	C	0.15	0.56	50	
8	Per unit				
9	Contribution	$33.00	$24.00		
10					
11	**Decisions**				
12					
13		Prod 1	Prod 2		
14	Quantity	75	60		
15					
16					
17	**Model**				
18		Hours	Unused		
19	Department	Used	Hours		
20	A	93	7		
21	B	29.7	6.3		
22	C	44.85	5.15		
23					
24	Contribution	$3,915.00			

56. Assume you are given a minimization linear program that has an optimal solution. The problem is then modified by changing an equality constraint in the problem to a less-than-or-equal-to constraint. Is it possible that the modified problem is infeasible? Answer yes or no and justify.

57. Assume you are given a minimization linear program that has an optimal solution. The problem is then modified by changing a greater-than-or-equal-to constraint in the problem to a less-than-or-equal-to constraint. Is it possible that the modified problem is infeasible? Answer yes or no and justify.

58. A consultant was hired to build an optimization model for a large marketing research company. The model is based on a consumer survey that was taken in which each person was asked to rank 30 new products in descending order based on their likelihood of purchasing the product. The consultant was assigned the task of building a model that selects the minimum number of products (which would then be introduced into the marketplace) such that the first, second, and third choice of every subject in the survey is included in the list of selected products. While building a model to figure out which products to introduce, the consultant's boss walked up to her and said: "Look, if the model tells us we need to introduce more than 15 products, then add a constraint which limits the number of new products to 15 or less. It's too expensive to introduce more than 15 new products." Evaluate this statement in terms of what you have learned so far about constrained optimization models.

Case Problem 1   WORKLOAD BALANCING

Digital Imaging (DI) produces photo printers for both the professional and consumer markets. The DI consumer division recently introduced two photo printers that provide color prints rivaling those produced by a professional processing lab. The DI-910 model can produce a 4" × 6" borderless print in approximately 37 seconds. The more sophisticated and faster DI-950 can even produce a 13" × 19" borderless print. Financial projections show profit contributions of $42 for each DI-910 and $87 for each DI-950.

The printers are assembled, tested, and packaged at DI's plant located in New Bern, North Carolina. This plant is highly automated and uses two manufacturing lines to produce the printers. Line 1 performs the assembly operation with times of 3 minutes per DI-910 printer and 6 minutes per DI-950 printer. Line 2 performs both the testing and packaging operations. Times are 4 minutes per DI-910 printer and 2 minutes per DI-950 printer. The shorter time for the DI-950 printer is a result of its faster print speed. Both manufacturing lines are in operation one 8-hour shift per day.

Managerial Report

Perform an analysis for Digital Imaging in order to determine how many units of each printer to produce. Prepare a report to DI's president presenting your findings and recommendations. Include (but do not limit your discussion) a consideration of the following:

1. The recommended number of units of each printer to produce to maximize the total contribution to profit for an 8-hour shift. What reasons might management have for not implementing your recommendation?

2. Suppose that management also states that the number of DI-910 printers produced must be at least as great as the number of DI-950 units produced. Assuming that the objective is to maximize the total contribution to profit for an 8-hour shift, how many units of each printer should be produced?

3. Does the solution you developed in part (2) balance the total time spent on line 1 and the total time spent on line 2? Why might this balance or lack of it be a concern to management?

4. Management requested an expansion of the model in part (2) that would provide a better balance between the total time on line 1 and the total time on line 2. Management wants to limit the difference between the total time on line 1 and the total time on line 2 to 30 minutes or less. If the objective is still to maximize the total contribution to profit, how many units of each printer should be produced? What effect does this workload balancing have on total profit in part (2)?

5. Suppose that in part (1) management specified the objective of maximizing the total number of printers produced each shift rather than total profit contribution. With this objective, how many units of each printer should be produced per shift? What effect does this objective have on total profit and workload balancing?

For each solution that you develop, include a copy of your linear programming model and graphical solution in the appendix to your report.

Case Problem 2 PRODUCTION STRATEGY

Better Fitness, Inc. (BFI), manufactures exercise equipment at its plant in Freeport, Long Island. It recently designed two universal weight machines for the home exercise market. Both machines use BFI-patented technology that provides the user with an extremely wide range of motion capability for each type of exercise performed. Until now, such capabilities have been available only on expensive weight machines used primarily by physical therapists.

At a recent trade show, demonstrations of the machines resulted in significant dealer interest. In fact, the number of orders that BFI received at the trade show far exceeded its manufacturing capabilities for the current production period. As a result, management decided to begin production of the two machines. The two machines, which BFI named the BodyPlus 100 and the BodyPlus 200, require different amounts of resources to produce.

The BodyPlus 100 consists of a frame unit, a press station, and a pec-dec station. Each frame produced uses 4 hours of machining and welding time and 2 hours of painting and finishing time. Each press station requires 2 hours of machining and welding time and 1 hour of painting and finishing time, and each pec-dec station uses 2 hours of machining and welding time and 2 hours of painting and finishing time. In addition, 2 hours are spent assembling, testing, and packaging each BodyPlus 100. The raw material costs are $450 for each frame, $300 for each press station, and $250 for each pec-dec station; packaging costs are estimated to be $50 per unit.

The BodyPlus 200 consists of a frame unit, a press station, a pec-dec station, and a leg-press station. Each frame produced uses 5 hours of machining and welding time and 4 hours of painting and finishing time. Each press station requires 3 hours machining and welding time and 2 hours of painting and finishing time, each pec-dec station uses 2 hours of machining and welding time and 2 hours of painting and finishing time, and each leg-press station requires 2 hours of machining and welding time and 2 hours of painting and finishing time. In addition, 2 hours are spent assembling, testing, and packaging each Body-Plus 200. The raw material costs are $650 for each frame, $400 for each press station, $250 for each pec-dec station, and $200 for each leg-press station; packaging costs are estimated to be $75 per unit.

For the next production period, management estimates that 600 hours of machining and welding time, 450 hours of painting and finishing time, and 140 hours of assembly, testing, and packaging time will be available. Current labor costs are $20 per hour for machining and welding time, $15 per hour for painting and finishing time, and $12 per hour for assembly, testing, and packaging time. The market in which the two machines must compete suggests a retail price of $2400 for the BodyPlus 100 and $3500 for the BodyPlus 200, although some flexibility may be available to BFI because of the unique capabilities of the new machines. Authorized BFI dealers can purchase machines for 70% of the suggested retail price.

BFI's president believes that the unique capabilities of the BodyPlus 200 can help position BFI as one of the leaders in high-end exercise equipment. Consequently, he has stated that the number of units of the BodyPlus 200 produced must be at least 25% of the total production.

Managerial Report

Analyze the production problem at Better Fitness, Inc., and prepare a report for BFI's president presenting your findings and recommendations. Include (but do not limit your discussion to) a consideration of the following items:

1. What is the recommended number of BodyPlus 100 and BodyPlus 200 machines to produce?
2. How does the requirement that the number of units of the BodyPlus 200 produced be at least 25% of the total production affect profits?
3. Where should efforts be expended in order to increase profits?

Include a copy of your linear programming model and graphical solution in an appendix to your report.

Case Problem 3   HART VENTURE CAPITAL

Hart Venture Capital (HVC) specializes in providing venture capital for software development and Internet applications. Currently HVC has two investment opportunities: (1) Security Systems, a firm that needs additional capital to develop an Internet security software package, and (2) Market Analysis, a market research company that needs additional capital to develop a software package for conducting customer satisfaction surveys. In exchange for Security Systems stock, the firm has asked HVC to provide $600,000 in year 1, $600,000 in year 2, and $250,000 in year 3 over the coming three-year period. In exchange for their stock, Market Analysis has asked HVC to provide $500,000 in year 1, $350,000 in year 2, and $400,000 in year 3 over the same three-year period. HVC believes that both investment opportunities are worth pursuing. However, because of other investments, they are willing to commit at most $800,000 for both projects in the first year, at most $700,000 in the second year, and $500,000 in the third year.

HVC's financial analysis team reviewed both projects and recommended that the company's objective should be to maximize the net present value of the total investment in Security Systems and Market Analysis. The net present value takes into account the estimated value of the stock at the end of the three-year period as well as the capital outflows that are necessary during each of the three years. Using an 8% rate of return, HVC's financial analysis team estimates that 100% funding of the Security Systems project has a net present value of $1,800,000, and 100% funding of the Market Analysis project has a net present value of $1,600,000.

HVC has the option to fund any percentage of the Security Systems and Market Analysis projects. For example, if HVC decides to fund 40% of the Security Systems

401

project, investments of 0.40($600,000) = $240,000 would be required in year 1, 0.40($600,000) = $240,000 would be required in year 2, and 0.40($250,000) = $100,000 would be required in year 3. In this case, the net present value of the Security Systems project would be 0.40($1,800,000) = $720,000. The investment amounts and the net present value for partial funding of the Market Analysis project would be computed in the same manner.

Managerial Report

Perform an analysis of HVC's investment problem and prepare a report that presents your findings and recommendations. Include (but do not limit your discussion to) a consideration of the following items:

1. What is the recommended percentage of each project that HVC should fund and the net present value of the total investment?
2. What capital allocation plan for Security Systems and Market Analysis for the coming three-year period and the total HVC investment each year would you recommend?
3. What effect, if any, would HVC's willingness to commit an additional $100,000 during the first year have on the recommended percentage of each project that HVC should fund?
4. What would the capital allocation plan look like if an additional $100,000 is made available?
5. What is your recommendation as to whether HVC should commit the additional $100,000 in the first year?

Provide model details and relevant computer output in a report appendix.

Appendix 2.1 SOLVING LINEAR PROGRAMS WITH LINGO

LINGO is a product of LINDO Systems. It was developed by Linus E. Schrage and Kevin Cunningham at the University of Chicago.

In this appendix we describe how to use LINGO to solve the Par, Inc., problem. When you start LINGO, two windows are immediately displayed. The outer or main frame window contains all the command menus and the command toolbar. The smaller window is the model window; this window is used to enter and edit the linear programming model you want to solve. The first item we enter into the model window is the objective function. Recall that the objective function for the Par, Inc., problem is Max $10S + 9D$. Thus, in the first line of the LINGO model window, we enter the following expression:

$$\text{MAX} = 10*S + 9*D;$$

Note that in LINGO the symbol * is used to denote multiplication and that the objective function line ends with a semicolon. In general, each mathematical expression (objective function and constraints) in LINGO is terminated with a semicolon.

Next, we press the enter key to move to a new line. The first constraint in the Par, Inc., problem is $0.7S + 1D \leq 630$. Thus, in the second line of the LINGO model window we enter the following expression:

$$0.7*S + 1*D <= 630$$

Note that LINGO interprets the $<=$ symbol as $\leq$. Alternatively, we could enter $<$ instead of $<=$. As was the case when entering the objective function, a semicolon is required at the end of the first constraint. Pressing the enter key moves us to a new line as we continue the process by entering the remaining constraints as shown here:

$$0.5*S + \tfrac{5}{6}*D <= 600$$
$$1*S + \tfrac{2}{3}*D <= 708$$
$$0.1*S + 0.25*D <= 135$$

The model window will now appear as follows:

$$\text{MAX} = 10*S + 9*D$$
$$0.7*S + 1*D <= 630$$
$$0.5*S + \tfrac{5}{6}*D <= 600$$
$$1*S + \tfrac{2}{3}*D <= 708$$
$$0.1*S + 0.25*D <= 135$$

When entering a fraction into LINGO it is not necessary to convert the fraction into an equivalent or rounded decimal number. For example, simply enter the fraction $\tfrac{2}{3}$ into LINGO as $\tfrac{2}{3}$ and do not worry about converting to a decimal or how many decimal places to use. Enter $\tfrac{7}{10}$ either as $\tfrac{7}{10}$ or .7. Let LINGO act as a calculator for you.

LINGO is very flexible about the format of an equation and it is not necessary to have the variables on the left hand side of an equation and the constant term on the right. For example,

$$0.7*S + 1*D <= 630$$

could also be entered as

$$0.7*S <= 630 - 1*D$$

This feature will be very useful later when writing models in a clear and understandable form. Finally, note that although we have expressly included a coefficient of 1 on the variable D above, this is not necessary. In LINGO, 1*D and D are equivalent.

If you make an error in entering the model, you can correct it at any time by simply positioning the cursor where you made the error and entering the necessary correction.

To solve the model, select the Solve command from the LINGO menu or press the Solve button on the toolbar at the top of the main frame window. LINGO will begin the solution process by determining whether the model conforms to all syntax requirements. If the LINGO model doesn't pass these tests, you will be informed by an error message. If LINGO does not find any errors in the model input, it will begin to solve the model. As part of the solution process, LINGO displays a Solver Status window that allows you to monitor the progress of the solver. LINGO displays the solution in a new window titled "Solution Report." The output that appears in the Solution Report window for the Par, Inc., problem is shown in Figure 2.25.

The first part of the output shown in Figure 2.25 indicates that an optimal solution has been found and that the value of the objective function is 7668. We see that the optimal solution is $S = 540$ and $D = 252$, and that the slack variables for the four constraints (rows 2–5) are 0, 120, 0, and 18. We will discuss the use of the information in the Reduced Cost column and the Dual Price column in Chapter 3 when we study the topic of sensitivity analysis.

FIGURE 2.25   PAR, INC., SOLUTION REPORT USING LINGO

```
Global optimal solution found.
Objective value:                         7668.000
Total solver iterations:                        2

          Variable             Value        Reduced Cost
       ---------------   ---------------   ----------------
                 S           540.0000           0.000000
                 D           252.0000           0.000000

          Row          Slack or Surplus        Dual Price
       ---------------   ---------------   ----------------
                 1           7668.000           1.000000
                 2           0.000000           4.375000
                 3           120.0000           0.000000
                 4           0.000000           6.937500
                 5           18.00000           0.000000
```

Appendix 2.2   SOLVING LINEAR PROGRAMS WITH EXCEL

In this appendix we will use an Excel worksheet to solve the Par, Inc., linear programming problem. We will enter the problem data for the Par problem in the top part of the worksheet and develop the linear programming model in the bottom part of the worksheet.

Formulation

Whenever we formulate a worksheet model of a linear program, we perform the following steps:

Step 1. Enter the problem data in the top part of the worksheet.
Step 2. Specify cell locations for the decision variables.
Step 3. Select a cell and enter a formula for computing the value of the objective function.
Step 4. Select a cell and enter a formula for computing the left-hand side of each constraint.
Step 5. Select a cell and enter a formula for computing the right-hand side of each constraint.

The formula worksheet that we developed for the Par, Inc., problem using these five steps is shown in Figure 2.26. Note that the worksheet consists of two sections: a data section and a model section. The four components of the model are screened, and the cells reserved for the decision variables are enclosed in a boldface box. Figure 2.26 is called a formula worksheet because it displays the formulas that we have entered and not the values computed from those formulas. In a moment we will see how Excel's Solver is used to find the optimal solution to the Par, Inc., problem. But first, let's review each of the preceding steps as they apply to the Par, Inc., problem.

Step 1. Enter the problem data in the top part of the worksheet.
Cells B5:C8 show the production requirements per unit for each product. Note that in cells C6 and C7, we have entered the exact fractions. That is, in cell C6 we have entered $=5/6$ and in cell C7 we have entered $=2/3$.

404

FIGURE 2.26 FORMULA WORKSHEET FOR THE PAR, INC., PROBLEM

	A	B	C	D
1	Par, Inc.			
2				
3		**Production Time**		
4	**Operation**	**Standard**	**Deluxe**	**Time Available**
5	Cutting and Dyeing	0.7	1	630
6	Sewing	0.5	0.83333	600
7	Finishing	1	0.66667	708
8	Inspection and Packaging	0.1	0.25	135
9	**Profit Per Bag**	10	9	
10				
11				
12	**Model**			
13				
14		**Decision Variables**		
15		**Standard**	**Deluxe**	
16	**Bags Produced**			
17				
18	**Maximize Total Profit**	=B9*B16+C9*C16		
19				
20	**Constraints**	**Hours Used (LHS)**		**Hours Available (RHS)**
21	Cutting and Dyeing	=B5*B16+C5*C16	<=	=D5
22	Sewing	=B6*B16+C6*C16	<=	=D6
23	Finishing	=B7*B16+C7*C16	<=	=D7
24	Inspection and Packaging	=B8*B16+C8*C16	<=	=D8

Cells B9:C9 show the profit contribution per unit for the two products.

Cells D5:D8 show the number of hours available in each department.

Step 2. Specify cell locations for the decision variables.

Cell B16 will contain the number of standard bags produced, and cell C16 will contain the number of deluxe bags produced.

Step 3. Select a cell and enter a formula for computing the value of the objective function.

Cell B18: =B9*B16+C9*C16

Step 4. Select a cell and enter a formula for computing the left-hand side of each constraint.

With four constraints, we have

Cell B21: =B5*B16+C5*C16

Cell B22: =B6*B16+C6*C16

Cell B23: =B7*B16+C7*C16

Cell B24: =B8*B16+C8*C16

Step 5. Select a cell and enter a formula for computing the right-hand side of each constraint.

With four constraints, we have

Cell D21: =D5

Cell D22: =D6

Cell D23: =D7

Cell D24: =D8

Note that descriptive labels make the model section of the worksheet easier to read and understand. For example, we added "Standard," "Deluxe," and "Bags Produced" in rows 15 and 16 so that the values of the decision variables appearing in cells B16 and C16 can be easily interpreted. In addition, we entered "Maximize Total Profit" in cell A18 to indicate that the value of the objective function appearing in cell B18 is the maximum profit contribution. In the constraint section of the worksheet we added the constraint names as well as the " $<=$ " symbols to show the relationship that exists between the left-hand side and the right-hand side of each constraint. Although these descriptive labels are not necessary to use Excel Solver to find a solution to the Par, Inc., problem, the labels make it easier for the user to understand and interpret the optimal solution.

Appendix A provides a discussion of how to properly build and structure a good spreadsheet model.

Excel Solution

The standard Excel Solver developed by Frontline Systems can be used to solve all of the linear programming problems presented in this text.

The following steps describe how Excel Solver can be used to obtain the optimal solution to the Par, Inc., problem:

Step 1. Select the **Data tab** on the **Ribbon**

Step 2. Select **Solver** from the **Analysis Group**

Step 3. When the **Solver Parameters** dialog box appears (see Figure 2.27):
Enter B18 into the **Set Objective** box
Select the **To: Max** option
Enter B16:C16 into the **By Changing Variable Cells** box

Step 4. Select **Add**
When the **Add Constraint** dialog box appears:
Enter B21:B24 in the left-hand box of the **Cell Reference** area
Select <= from the middle drop-down button.
Enter D21:D24 in the **Constraint** area
Click **OK**

Step 5. When the **Solver Parameters** dialog box reappears:
Select the checkbox, **Make Unconstrained Variables Non-Negative**

Step 6. Select the **Select a Solving Method** drop-down button
Select **Simplex LP**

Step 7. Choose **Solve**

Step 8. When the **Solver Results** dialog box appears:
Select **Keep Solver Solution**
Click **OK**

Figure 2.27 shows the completed **Solver Parameters** dialog box, and Figure 2.28 shows the optimal solution in the worksheet. The optimal solution of 540 standard bags and 252 deluxe bags is the same as we obtained using the graphical solution procedure. In addition to the output information shown in Figure 2.28, Solver has an option to provide sensitivity analysis information. We discuss sensitivity analysis in Chapter 3.

In Step 5 we selected the **Make Unconstrained Variables Non-Negative** checkbox to avoid having to enter nonnegativity constraints for the decision variables. In general, whenever we want to solve a linear programming model in which the decision variables are all restricted to be nonnegative, we will select this option. In addition, in Step 4 we entered all four less-than-or-equal-to constraints simultaneously by entering B21:B24 in the left-hand

FIGURE 2.27 SOLVER PARAMETERS DIALOG BOX FOR THE PAR, INC., PROBLEM

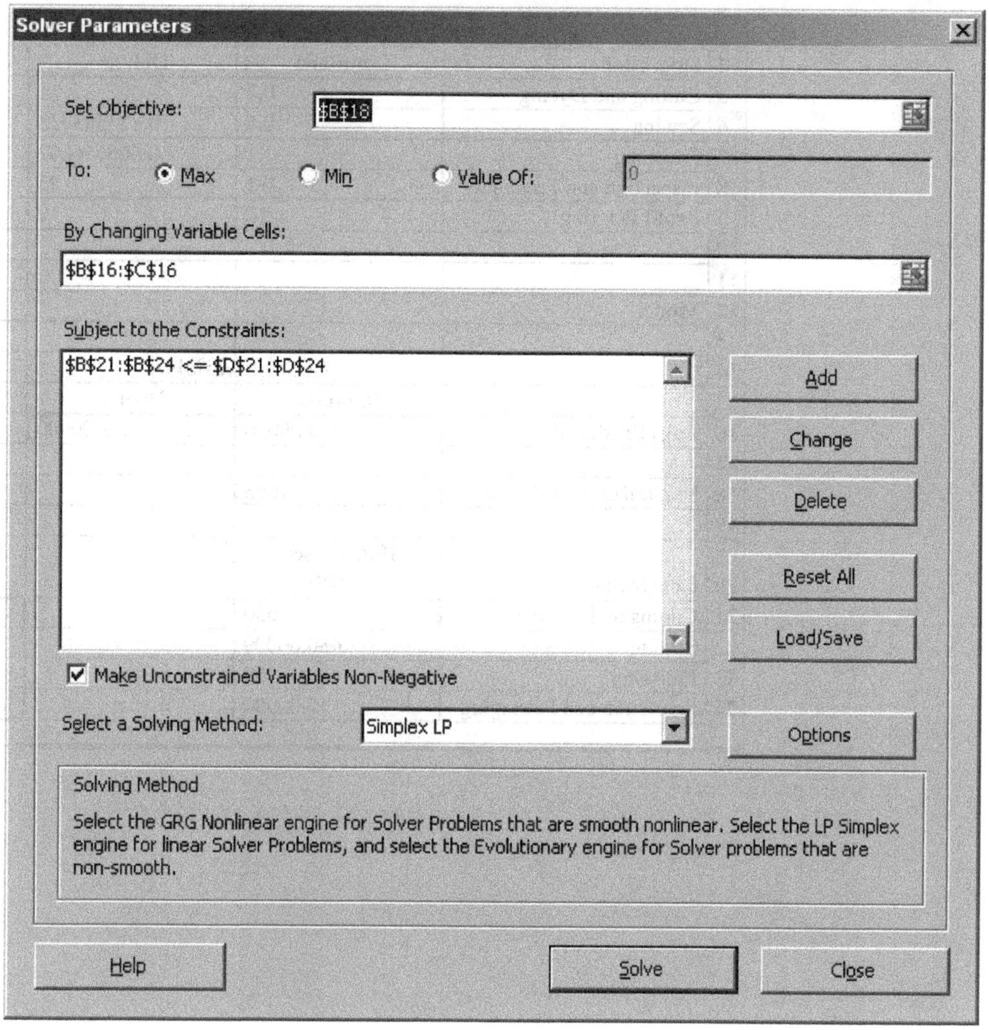

box of the **Cell Reference** area, selecting $\leq=$, and entering D21:D24 in the right-hand box. Alternatively, we could have entered the four constraints one at a time.

As a reminder, when entering a fraction into Excel, it is not necessary to convert the fraction into an equivalent or rounded decimal number. For example, simply enter the fraction $2/3$ into Excel as $=2/3$ and do not worry about converting to a decimal or how many decimal places to use. Enter $7/10$ either as $=7/10$ or $=.7$. When entering a fraction, the "$=$" sign is necessary; otherwise, Excel will treat the fraction as text rather than a number.

FIGURE 2.28   EXCEL SOLUTION FOR THE PAR, INC., PROBLEM

	A	B	C	D
4	Operation	Standard	Deluxe	Time Available
5	Cutting and Dyeing	0.7	1	630
6	Sewing	0.5	0.833333333	600
7	Finishing	1	0.666666667	708
8	Inspection and Packaging	0.1	0.25	135
9	Profit Per Bag	10	9	
10				
11				
12	Model			
13				
14		Decision Variables		
15		Standard	Deluxe	
16	Bags Produced	540.00000	252.00000	
17				
18	Maximize Total Profit	7668		
19				
20	Constraints	Hours Used (LHS)		Hours Available (RHS)
21	Cutting and Dyeing	630	<=	630
22	Sewing	480.00000	<=	600
23	Finishing	708	<=	708
24	Inspection and Packaging	117.00000	<=	135

References and Bibliography

Ahuja, R. K., T. L. Magnanti, and J. B. Orlin. *Network Flows, Theory, Algorithms, and Applications.* Prentice Hall, 1993.

Bazarra, M. S., J. J. Jarvis, and H. D. Sherali. *Linear Programming and Network Flows,* 2d ed. Wiley, 1990.

Carino, H. F., and C. H. Le Noir, Jr. "Optimizing Wood Procurement in Cabinet Manufacturing," *Interfaces* (March/April 1988): 10–19.

Dantzig, G. B. *Linear Programming and Extensions.* Princeton University Press, 1963.

Davis, Morton D. *Game Theory: A Nontechnical Introduction.* Dover, 1997.

Evans, J. R., and E. Minieka. *Optimization Algorithms for Networks and Graphs,* 2d ed. Marcel Dekker, 1992.

Ford, L. R., and D. R. Fulkerson. *Flows and Networks.* Princeton University Press, 1962.

Geoffrion, A., and G. Graves. "Better Distribution Planning with Computer Models," *Harvard Business Review* (July/August 1976).

Greenberg, H. J. "How to Analyze the Results of Linear Programs—Part 1: Preliminaries," *Interfaces* 23, no. 4 (July/August 1993): 56–67.

Greenberg, H. J. "How to Analyze the Results of Linear Programs—Part 2: Price Interpretation," *Interfaces* 23, no. 5 (September/October 1993): 97–114.

Greenberg, H. J. "How to Analyze the Results of Linear Programs—Part 3: Infeasibility Diagnosis," *Interfaces* 23, no. 6 (November/December 1993): 120–139.

Lillien, G., and A. Rangaswamy. *Marketing Engineering: Computer-Assisted Marketing Analysis and Planning.* Addison-Wesley, 1998.

Martin, R. K. *Large Scale Linear and Integer Optimization: A Unified Approach.* Kluwer Academic Publishers, 1999.

McMillian, John. *Games, Strategies, and Managers.* Oxford University Press, 1992.

Myerson, Roger B. *Game Theory: Analysis of Conflict.* Harvard University Press, 1997.

Nemhauser, G. L., and L. A. Wolsey. *Integer and Combinatorial Optimization.* Wiley, 1999.

Osborne, Martin J. *An Introduction to Game Theory.* Oxford University Press, 2004.

Schrage, Linus. *Optimization Modeling with LINDO,* 4th ed. LINDO Systems Inc., 2000.

Sherman, H. D. "Hospital Efficiency Measurement and Evaluation," *Medical Care* 22, no. 10 (October 1984): 922–938.

Winston, W. L., and S. C. Albright. *Practical Management Science,* 2d ed. Duxbury Press, 2001.

Self-Test Solutions and Answers to Even-Numbered Problems

1. Parts (a), (b), and (e) are acceptable linear programming relationships.

   Part (c) is not acceptable because of $-2x_2^2$.

   Part (d) is not acceptable because of $3\sqrt{x_1}$.

   Part (f) is not acceptable because of $1x_1x_2$.

   Parts (c), (d), and (f) could not be found in a linear programming model because they contain nonlinear terms.

2. a.

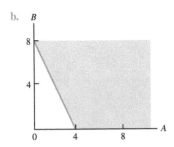

b.

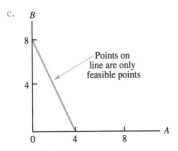

c.

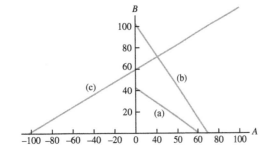

6. $7A + 10B = 420$
   $6A + 4B = 420$
   $-4A + 7B = 420$

7.

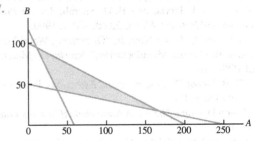

10.

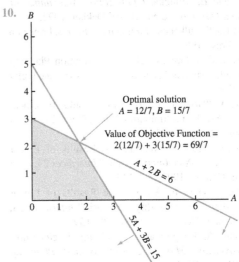

Optimal solution
$A = 12/7, B = 15/7$

Value of Objective Function = $2(12/7) + 3(15/7) = 69/7$

$A + 2B = 6$

$5A + 3B = 15$

	$A + 2B =$ 6	(1)
	$5A + 3B =$ 15	(2)
Equation (1) times 5:	$5A + 10B = 30$	(3)
Equation (2) minus equation (3):	$-7B = -15$	
	$B = 15/7$	
From equation (1):	$A = 6 - 2(15/7)$	
	$= 6 - 30/7 = 12/7$	

12. a. $A = 3, B = 1.5$; value of optimal solution = 13.5
    b. $A = 0, B = 3$; value of optimal solution = 18
    c. Four: (0, 0), (4, 0), (3, 1.5), and (0.3)

13. a.

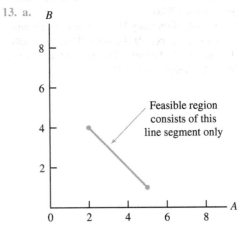

Feasible region consists of this line segment only

410

b. The extreme points are (5, 1) and (2, 4).

c.

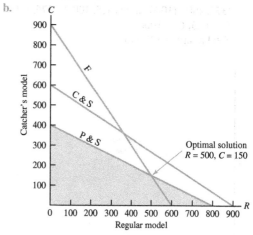

14. a. Let F = number of tons of fuel additive
    S = number of tons of solvent base

    Max $40F + 30S$

    s.t.

    $\frac{2}{5}F + \frac{1}{2}S \leq 20$ Material 1

    $\frac{1}{5}S \leq 5$ Material 2

    $\frac{3}{5}F + \frac{3}{10}S \leq 21$ Material 3

    $F, S \geq 0$

   b. $F = 25, S = 20$

   c. Material 2:4 tons are used; 1 ton is unused.

   d. No redundant constraints

16. a. $3S + 9D$

   b. (0, 540)

   c. 90, 150, 348, 0

17. Max $5A + 2B + 0s_1 + 0s_2 + 0s_3$

    s.t.

    $1A - 2B + 1s_1 \qquad\qquad = 420$

    $2A + 3B - \qquad + 1s_2 \qquad = 610$

    $6A - 1B + \qquad\qquad + 1s_3 = 125$

    $A, B, s_1, s_2, s_3 \geq 0$

18. b. $A = 18/7, B = 15/7$

   c. 0, 0, 4/7

20. b. $A = 3.43, B = 3.43$

   c. 2.86, 0, 1.43, 0

22. b.

Extreme Point	Coordinates	Profit ($)
1	(0, 0)	0
2	(1700, 0)	8500
3	(1400, 600)	9400
4	(800, 1200)	8800
5	(0, 1680)	6720

Extreme point 3 generates the highest profit.

c. $A = 1400, C = 600$

d. Cutting and dyeing constraint and the packaging constraint

e. $A = 800, C = 1200$; profit = $9200

24. a. Let R = number of units of regular model
    C = number of units of catcher's model

    Max $5R + 8C$

    $1R + \frac{3}{2}C \leq 900$ Cutting and sewing

    $\frac{1}{2}R + \frac{1}{3}C \leq 300$ Finishing

    $\frac{1}{8}R + \frac{1}{4}C \leq 100$ Packaging and shipping

    $R, C \geq 0$

   b.

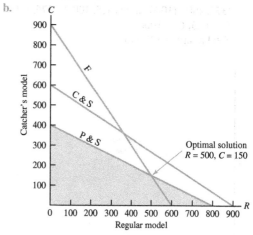

   c. $5(500) + 8(150) = \$3700$

   d. C & S $\quad 1(500) + \frac{3}{2}(150) = 725$

   F $\qquad\quad \frac{1}{2}(500) + \frac{1}{3}(150) = 300$

   P & S $\quad \frac{1}{8}(500) + \frac{1}{4}(150) = 100$

   e.

Department	Capacity	Usage	Slack
Cutting and sewing	900	725	175 hours
Finishing	300	300	0 hours
Packaging and shipping	100	100	0 hours

26. a. Max $50N + 80R$

    s.t.

    $N + R = 1000$

    $N \qquad\quad \geq 250$

    $R \geq 250$

    $N - 2R \geq 0$

    $N, R \geq 0$

   b. $N = 666.67, R = 333.33$; Audience exposure = 60,000

28. a. Max $1W + 1.25M$

    s.t.

    $5W + 7M \leq 4480$

    $3W + 1M \leq 2080$

    $2W + 2M \leq 1600$

    $W, M \geq 0$

   b. $W = 560, M = 240$; Profit = 860

411

30. a. Max $15E + 18C$
   s.t.
   $$40E + 25C \leq 50{,}000$$
   $$40E \qquad\quad \geq 15{,}000$$
   $$25C \geq 10{,}000$$
   $$25C \leq 25{,}000$$
   $$E, C \geq 0$$

   c. $(375, 400); (1000, 400); (625, 1000); (375, 1000)$
   d. $E = 625, C = 1000$
      Total return $= \$27{,}375$

31.

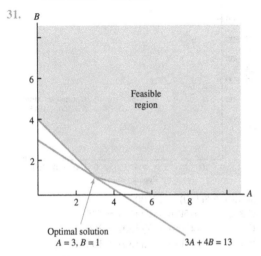

Objective function value $= 13$

32.

Extreme Points	Objective Function Value	Surplus Demand	Surplus Total Production	Slack Processing Time
(250, 100)	800	125	—	—
(125, 225)	925	—	—	125
(125, 350)	1300	—	125	—

34. a.

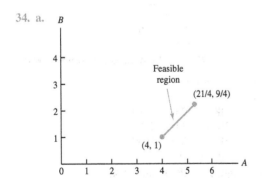

   b. The two extreme points are
      $(A = 4, B = 1)$ and $(A = 21/4, B = 9/4)$
   c. The optimal solution (see part (a)) is $A = 4, B = 1$.

35. a. Min $6A + 4B + 0s_1 + 0s_2 + 0s_3$
   s.t.
   $$2A + 1B - s_1 \qquad\qquad = 12$$
   $$1A + 1B \qquad - s_2 \qquad = 10$$
   $$1B \qquad\qquad + s_3 = 4$$
   $$A, B, s_1, s_2, s_3 \geq 0$$

   b. The optimal solution is $A = 6, B = 4$.
   c. $s_1 = 4, s_2 = 0, s_3 = 0$

36. a. Min $10{,}000T + 8{,}000P$
   s.t.
   $$T \qquad\qquad \geq 8$$
   $$P \geq 10$$
   $$T + \qquad P \geq 25$$
   $$3T + \qquad 2P \leq 84$$

   c. $(15, 10); (21.33, 10); (8, 30); (8, 17)$
   d. $T = 8, P = 17$
      Total cost $= \$216{,}000$

38. a. Min $7.50S + 9.00P$
   s.t.
   $$0.10S + 0.30P \geq 6$$
   $$0.06S + 0.12P \leq 3$$
   $$S + \quad P = 30$$
   $$S, P \geq 0$$

   c. Optional solution is $S = 15, P = 15$.
   d. No
   e. Yes

40. $P_1 = 30, P_2 = 25;$ Cost $= \$55$

42.

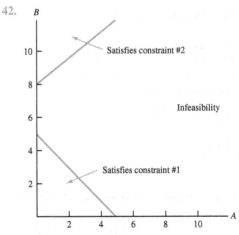

43.

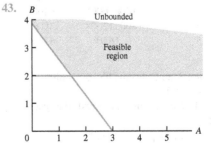

412

44. a. $A = {}^{30}\!/_{16}, B = {}^{30}\!/_{16}$; Value of optimal solution $= {}^{60}\!/_{16}$
    b. $A = 0, B = 3$; Value of optimal solution $= 6$

46. a. 180, 20
    b. Alternative optimal solutions
    c. 120, 80

48. No feasible solution

50. $M = 65.45, R = 261.82$; Profit $= \$45,818$

52. $S = 384, O = 80$

54. a. Max $\quad 160M_1 + 345M_2$
    s.t.
$$
\begin{array}{rcl}
M_1 & \leq & 15 \\
M_2 & \leq & 10 \\
M_1 & \geq & 5 \\
M_2 & \geq & 5 \\
40M_1 + 50M_2 & \leq & 1000 \\
M_1, M_2 & \geq & 0
\end{array}
$$

    b. $M_1 = 12.5, M_2 = 10$

56. No, this could not make the problem infeasible. Changing an equality constraint to an inequality constraint can only make the feasible region larger, not smaller. No solutions have been eliminated and anything that was feasible before is still feasible.

58. The statement by the boss shows a fundamental misunderstanding of optimization models. If there were an optimal solution with 15 or less products, the model would find it, because it is trying to minimize. If there is no solution with 15 or less, adding this constraint will make the model infeasible.

7

Linear Programming Applications in Marketing, Finance, and Operations Management

CONTENTS

Linear programming has proven to be one of the most successful quantitative approaches to decision making. Applications have been reported in almost every industry. These applications include production scheduling, media selection, financial planning, capital budgeting, transportation, distribution system design, product mix, staffing, and blending.

The wide variety of Management Science in Actions presented in Chapters 2 and 3 illustrated the use of linear programming as a flexible problem-solving tool. The Management Science in Action, A Marketing Planning Model at Marathon Oil Company, provides another example of the use of linear programming by showing how Marathon uses a large-scale linear programming model to solve a wide variety of planning problems. Later in the chapter other Management Science in Action features illustrate how GE Capital uses linear programming for optimal lease structuring; how Jeppesen Sanderson uses linear programming to optimize production of flight manuals; and how the Kellogg Company uses a large-scale linear programming model to integrate production, distribution, and inventory planning.

In this chapter we present a variety of applications from the traditional business areas of marketing, finance, and operations management. Modeling, computer solution, and interpretation of output are emphasized. A mathematical model is developed for each problem studied, and solutions are presented for most of the applications. In the chapter appendix we illustrate the use of Excel Solver by solving a financial planning problem.

MANAGEMENT SCIENCE IN ACTION

A MARKETING PLANNING MODEL AT MARATHON OIL COMPANY*

Marathon Oil Company has four refineries within the United States, operates 50 light products terminals, and has product demand at more than 95 locations. The Supply and Transportation Division faces the problem of determining which refinery should supply which terminal and, at the same time, determining which products should be transported via pipeline, barge, or tanker to minimize cost. Product demand must be satisfied, and the supply capability of each refinery must not be exceeded. To help solve this difficult problem, Marathon Oil developed a marketing planning model.

The marketing planning model is a large-scale linear programming model that takes into account sales not only at Marathon product terminals but also at all exchange locations. An exchange contract is an agreement with other oil product marketers that involves exchanging or trading Marathon's products for theirs at different locations. All pipelines, barges, and tankers within Marathon's marketing area are also represented in the linear programming model.

The objective of the model is to minimize the cost of meeting a given demand structure, taking into account sales price, pipeline tariffs, exchange contract costs, product demand, terminal operating costs, refining costs, and product purchases.

The marketing planning model is used to solve a wide variety of planning problems that vary from evaluating gasoline blending economics to analyzing the economics of a new terminal or pipeline. With daily sales of about 10 million gallons of refined light product, a savings of even one-thousandth of a cent per gallon can result in significant long-term savings. At the same time, what may appear to be a savings in one area, such as refining or transportation, may actually add to overall costs when the effects are fully realized throughout the system. The marketing planning model allows a simultaneous examination of this total effect.

*Based on information provided by Robert W. Wernert at Marathon Oil Company, Findlay, Ohio.

4.1 MARKETING APPLICATIONS

Applications of linear programming in marketing are numerous. In this section we discuss applications in media selection and marketing research.

Media Selection

In Section 2.1 we provided some general guidelines for modeling linear programming problems. You may want to review Section 2.1 before proceeding with the linear programming applications in this chapter.

Media selection applications of linear programming are designed to help marketing managers allocate a fixed advertising budget to various advertising media. Potential media include newspapers, magazines, radio, television, and direct mail. In these applications, the objective is to maximize reach, frequency, and quality of exposure. Restrictions on the allowable allocation usually arise during consideration of company policy, contract requirements, and media availability. In the application that follows, we illustrate how a media selection problem might be formulated and solved using a linear programming model.

Relax-and-Enjoy Lake Development Corporation is developing a lakeside community at a privately owned lake. The primary market for the lakeside lots and homes includes all middle- and upper-income families within approximately 100 miles of the development. Relax-and-Enjoy employed the advertising firm of Boone, Phillips, and Jackson (BP&J) to design the promotional campaign.

After considering possible advertising media and the market to be covered, BP&J recommended that the first month's advertising be restricted to five media. At the end of the month, BP&J will then reevaluate its strategy based on the month's results. BP&J collected data on the number of potential customers reached, the cost per advertisement, the maximum number of times each medium is available, and the exposure quality rating for each of the five media. The quality rating is measured in terms of an exposure quality unit, a measure of the relative value of one advertisement in each of the media. This measure, based on BP&J's experience in the advertising business, takes into account factors such as audience demographics (age, income, and education of the audience reached), image presented, and quality of the advertisement. The information collected is presented in Table 4.1.

Relax-and-Enjoy provided BP&J with an advertising budget of $30,000 for the first month's campaign. In addition, Relax-and-Enjoy imposed the following restrictions on how BP&J may allocate these funds: At least 10 television commercials must be used, at least 50,000 potential customers must be reached, and no more than $18,000 may be spent on television advertisements. What advertising media selection plan should be recommended?

TABLE 4.1 ADVERTISING MEDIA ALTERNATIVES FOR THE RELAX-AND-ENJOY LAKE DEVELOPMENT CORPORATION

Advertising Media	Number of Potential Customers Reached	Cost ($) per Advertisement	Maximum Times Available per Month*	Exposure Quality Units
1. Daytime TV (1 min), station WKLA	1000	1500	15	65
2. Evening TV (30 sec), station WKLA	2000	3000	10	90
3. Daily newspaper (full page), *The Morning Journal*	1500	400	25	40
4. Sunday newspaper magazine (½ page color), *The Sunday Press*	2500	1000	4	60
5. Radio, 8:00 A.M. or 5:00 P.M. news (30 sec), station KNOP	300	100	30	20

*The maximum number of times the medium is available is either the maximum number of times the advertising medium occurs (e.g., four Sundays per month) or the maximum number of times BP&J recommends that the medium be used.

The decision to be made is how many times to use each medium. We begin by defining the decision variables:

$$DTV = \text{number of times daytime TV is used}$$
$$ETV = \text{number of times evening TV is used}$$
$$DN = \text{number of times daily newspaper is used}$$
$$SN = \text{number of times Sunday newspaper is used}$$
$$R = \text{number of times radio is used}$$

The data on quality of exposure in Table 4.1 show that each daytime TV (DTV) advertisement is rated at 65 exposure quality units. Thus, an advertising plan with DTV advertisements will provide a total of $65DTV$ exposure quality units. Continuing with the data in Table 4.1, we find evening TV (ETV) rated at 90 exposure quality units, daily newspaper (DN) rated at 40 exposure quality units, Sunday newspaper (SN) rated at 60 exposure quality units, and radio (R) rated at 20 exposure quality units. With the objective of maximizing the total exposure quality units for the overall media selection plan, the objective function becomes

Care must be taken to ensure the linear programming model accurately reflects the real problem. Always review your formulation thoroughly before attempting to solve the model.

$$\text{Max} \quad 65DTV + 90ETV + 40DN + 60SN + 20R \qquad \text{Exposure quality}$$

We now formulate the constraints for the model from the information given:

$$
\begin{aligned}
DTV &&&&&&&&\leq\ 15 &\quad\rbrace \\
&ETV &&&&&&&\leq\ 10 &\quad \\
&&DN &&&&&&\leq\ 25 &\quad\rbrace \text{Availability} \\
&&&SN &&&&&\leq\ \ 4 &\quad \text{of media} \\
&&&&R &\leq\ 30 &\quad\rbrace \\
1500DTV + 3000ETV +\ \ 400DN + 1000SN + 100R &\leq\ 30{,}000 &\quad \text{Budget} \\
DTV +\quad ETV &\geq\ 10 &\quad\rbrace \text{Television} \\
1500DTV + 3000ETV &\leq\ 18{,}000 &\quad\rbrace \text{restrictions} \\
1000DTV + 2000ETV + 1500DN + 2500SN + 300R &\geq\ 50{,}000 &\quad \text{Customers reached} \\
DTV, ETV, DN, SN, R &\geq\ 0 &\quad
\end{aligned}
$$

Problem 1 provides practice at formulating a similar media selection model.

The optimal solution to this five-variable, nine-constraint linear programming model is shown in Figure 4.1; a summary is presented in Table 4.2.

The optimal solution calls for advertisements to be distributed among daytime TV, daily newspaper, Sunday newspaper, and radio. The maximum number of exposure quality units is 2370, and the total number of customers reached is 61,500. The Reduced Costs column in Figure 4.1 indicates that the number of exposure quality units for evening TV would have to increase by at least 65 before this media alternative could appear in the optimal solution. Note that the budget constraint (constraint 6) has a dual value of 0.060. Therefore, a \$1.00 increase in the advertising budget will lead to an increase of 0.06 exposure quality units. The dual value of −25.000 for constraint 7 indicates that increasing the number of television commercials by 1 will decrease the exposure quality of the advertising plan by 25 units. Alternatively, decreasing the number of television commercials by 1 will increase the exposure quality of the advertising plan by 25 units. Thus,

FIGURE 4.1 THE SOLUTION FOR THE RELAX-AND-ENJOY LAKE DEVELOPMENT CORPORATION PROBLEM

WEB file

Relax

```
Optimal Objective Value =        2370.00000

    Variable              Value          Reduced Cost
  --------------      --------------      --------------
       DTV                10.00000             0.00000
       ETV                 0.00000           -65.00000
       DN                 25.00000             0.00000
       SN                  2.00000             0.00000
       R                  30.00000             0.00000


   Constraint         Slack/Surplus         Dual Value
  --------------      --------------      --------------
       1                   5.00000             0.00000
       2                  10.00000             0.00000
       3                   0.00000            16.00000
       4                   2.00000             0.00000
       5                   0.00000            14.00000
       6                   0.00000             0.06000
       7                   0.00000           -25.00000
       8                3000.00000             0.00000
       9               11500.00000             0.00000
```

Media Availability

Budget

Television Restrictions

Audience Coverage

TABLE 4.2 ADVERTISING PLAN FOR THE RELAX-AND-ENJOY LAKE DEVELOPMENT CORPORATION

Media	Frequency	Budget
Daytime TV	10	$15,000
Daily newspaper	25	10,000
Sunday newspaper	2	2,000
Radio	30	3,000
		$30,000

Exposure quality units = 2370
Total customers reached = 61,500

Relax-and-Enjoy should consider reducing the requirement of having at least 10 television commercials.

A possible shortcoming of this model is that, even if the exposure quality measure were not subject to error, it offers no guarantee that maximization of total exposure quality will lead to maximization of profit or of sales (a common surrogate for profit). However, this issue is not a shortcoming of linear programming; rather, it is a shortcoming of the use of exposure quality as a criterion. If we could directly measure the effect of an advertisement on profit, we could use total profit as the objective to be maximized.

NOTES AND COMMENTS

1. The media selection model required subjective evaluations of the exposure quality for the media alternatives. Marketing managers may have substantial data concerning exposure quality, but the final coefficients used in the objective function may also include considerations based primarily on managerial judgment. Judgment is an acceptable way of obtaining input for a linear programming model.

2. The media selection model presented in this section uses exposure quality as the objective function and places a constraint on the number of customers reached. An alternative formulation of this problem would be to use the number of customers reached as the objective function and add a constraint indicating the minimum total exposure quality required for the media plan.

Marketing Research

An organization conducts marketing research to learn about consumer characteristics, attitudes, and preferences. Marketing research firms that specialize in providing such information often do the actual research for client organizations. Typical services offered by a marketing research firm include designing the study, conducting market surveys, analyzing the data collected, and providing summary reports and recommendations for the client. In the research design phase, targets or quotas may be established for the number and types of respondents to be surveyed. The marketing research firm's objective is to conduct the survey so as to meet the client's needs at a minimum cost.

Market Survey, Inc. (MSI), specializes in evaluating consumer reaction to new products, services, and advertising campaigns. A client firm requested MSI's assistance in ascertaining consumer reaction to a recently marketed household product. During meetings with the client, MSI agreed to conduct door-to-door personal interviews to obtain responses from households with children and households without children. In addition, MSI agreed to conduct both day and evening interviews. Specifically, the client's contract called for MSI to conduct 1000 interviews under the following quota guidelines.

1. Interview at least 400 households with children.
2. Interview at least 400 households without children.
3. The total number of households interviewed during the evening must be at least as great as the number of households interviewed during the day.
4. At least 40% of the interviews for households with children must be conducted during the evening.
5. At least 60% of the interviews for households without children must be conducted during the evening.

Because the interviews for households with children take additional interviewer time and because evening interviewers are paid more than daytime interviewers, the cost varies with the type of interview. Based on previous research studies, estimates of the interview costs are as follows:

Household	Interview Cost	
	Day	**Evening**
Children	$20	$25
No children	$18	$20

420

What is the household, time-of-day interview plan that will satisfy the contract requirements at a minimum total interviewing cost?

In formulating the linear programming model for the MSI problem, we utilize the following decision-variable notation:

DC = the number of daytime interviews of households with children

EC = the number of evening interviews of households with children

DNC = the number of daytime interviews of households without children

ENC = the number of evening interviews of households without children

We begin the linear programming model formulation by using the cost-per-interview data to develop the objective function:

$$\text{Min} \quad 20DC + 25EC + 18DNC + 20ENC$$

The constraint requiring a total of 1000 interviews is

$$DC + EC + DNC + ENC = 1000$$

The five specifications concerning the types of interviews are as follows.

- Households with children:

$$DC + EC \geq 400$$

- Households without children:

$$DNC + ENC \geq 400$$

- At least as many evening interviews as day interviews:

$$EC + ENC \geq DC + DNC$$

- At least 40% of interviews of households with children during the evening:

$$EC \geq 0.4(DC + EC)$$

- At least 60% of interviews of households without children during the evening:

$$ENC \geq 0.6(DNC + ENC)$$

When we add the nonnegativity requirements, the four-variable and six-constraint linear programming model becomes

Min $20DC + 25EC + 18DNC + 20ENC$

s.t.

$DC +$	$EC +$	$DNC +$	$ENC = 1000$	Total interviews
$DC +$	EC		≥ 400	Households with children
		$DNC +$	$ENC \geq 400$	Households without children
	$EC + ENC \geq DC + DNC$			Evening interviews
	$EC \geq 0.4(DC + EC)$			Evening interviews in households with children
	$ENC \geq 0.6(DNC + ENC)$			Evening interviews in households without children

$DC, EC, DNC, ENC \geq 0$

The optimal solution to this linear program is shown in Figure 4.2. The solution reveals that the minimum cost of $20,320 occurs with the following interview schedule.

| Household | Number of Interviews | | |
	Day	Evening	Totals
Children	240	160	400
No children	240	360	600
Totals	480	520	1000

Hence, 480 interviews will be scheduled during the day and 520 during the evening. Households with children will be covered by 400 interviews, and households without children will be covered by 600 interviews.

Selected sensitivity analysis information from Figure 4.2 shows a dual value of 19.200 for constraint 1. In other words, the value of the optimal solution will increase by $19.20 if the number of interviews is increased from 1000 to 1001. Thus, $19.20 is the incremental cost of obtaining additional interviews. It also is the savings that could be realized by reducing the number of interviews from 1000 to 999.

The surplus variable, with a value of 200.000, for constraint 3 shows that 200 more households without children will be interviewed than required. Similarly, the surplus variable, with a value of 40.000, for constraint 4 shows that the number of evening interviews exceeds the number of daytime interviews by 40. The zero values for the surplus variables in constraints 5 and 6 indicate that the more expensive evening interviews are being held at a minimum. Indeed, the dual value of 5.000 for constraint 5 indicates that if one more household (with children) than the minimum requirement must be interviewed during the evening, the total interviewing cost will go up by $5.00. Similarly, constraint 6 shows that requiring one more household (without children) to be interviewed during the evening will increase costs by $2.00.

FIGURE 4.2   THE SOLUTION FOR THE MARKET SURVEY PROBLEM

Market

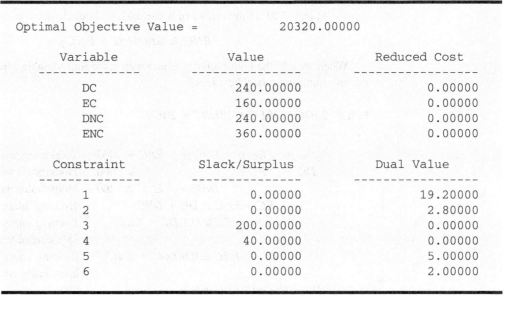

```
Optimal Objective Value =          20320.00000

        Variable              Value           Reduced Cost
     -------------        -------------       -------------
          DC               240.00000             0.00000
          EC               160.00000             0.00000
          DNC              240.00000             0.00000
          ENC              360.00000             0.00000

       Constraint        Slack/Surplus          Dual Value
     -------------        -------------       -------------
           1                 0.00000            19.20000
           2                 0.00000             2.80000
           3               200.00000             0.00000
           4                40.00000             0.00000
           5                 0.00000             5.00000
           6                 0.00000             2.00000
```

4.2 FINANCIAL APPLICATIONS

In finance, linear programming can be applied in problem situations involving capital budgeting, make-or-buy decisions, asset allocation, portfolio selection, financial planning, and many more. In this section, we describe a portfolio selection problem and a problem involving funding of an early retirement program.

Portfolio Selection

Portfolio selection problems involve situations in which a financial manager must select specific investments—for example, stocks and bonds—from a variety of investment alternatives. Managers of mutual funds, credit unions, insurance companies, and banks frequently encounter this type of problem. The objective function for portfolio selection problems usually is maximization of expected return or minimization of risk. The constraints usually take the form of restrictions on the type of permissible investments, state laws, company policy, maximum permissible risk, and so on. Problems of this type have been formulated and solved using a variety of mathematical programming techniques. In this section we formulate and solve a portfolio selection problem as a linear program.

Consider the case of Welte Mutual Funds, Inc., located in New York City. Welte just obtained $100,000 by converting industrial bonds to cash and is now looking for other investment opportunities for these funds. Based on Welte's current investments, the firm's top financial analyst recommends that all new investments be made in the oil industry, steel industry, or in government bonds. Specifically, the analyst identified five investment opportunities and projected their annual rates of return. The investments and rates of return are shown in Table 4.3.

Management of Welte imposed the following investment guidelines.

1. Neither industry (oil or steel) should receive more than $50,000.
2. Government bonds should be at least 25% of the steel industry investments.
3. The investment in Pacific Oil, the high-return but high-risk investment, cannot be more than 60% of the total oil industry investment.

What portfolio recommendations—investments and amounts—should be made for the available $100,000? Given the objective of maximizing projected return subject to the budgetary and managerially imposed constraints, we can answer this question by formulating and solving a linear programming model of the problem. The solution will provide investment recommendations for the management of Welte Mutual Funds.

TABLE 4.3   INVESTMENT OPPORTUNITIES FOR WELTE MUTUAL FUNDS

Investment	Projected Rate of Return (%)
Atlantic Oil	7.3
Pacific Oil	10.3
Midwest Steel	6.4
Huber Steel	7.5
Government bonds	4.5

Let

A = dollars invested in Atlantic Oil

P = dollars invested in Pacific Oil

M = dollars invested in Midwest Steel

H = dollars invested in Huber Steel

G = dollars invested in government bonds

Using the projected rates of return shown in Table 4.3, we write the objective function for maximizing the total return for the portfolio as

$$\text{Max} \quad 0.073A + 0.103P + 0.064M + 0.075H + 0.045G$$

The constraint specifying investment of the available $100,000 is

$$A + P + M + H + G = 100,000$$

The requirements that neither the oil nor the steel industry should receive more than $50,000 are

$$A + P \leq 50,000$$
$$M + H \leq 50,000$$

The requirement that government bonds be at least 25% of the steel industry investment is expressed as

$$G \geq 0.25(M + H)$$

Finally, the constraint that Pacific Oil cannot be more than 60% of the total oil industry investment is

$$P \leq 0.60(A + P)$$

By adding the nonnegativity restrictions, we obtain the complete linear programming model for the Welte Mutual Funds investment problem:

Max $\quad 0.073A + 0.103P + 0.064M + 0.075H + 0.045G$

s.t.

$A +$	$P +$	$M +$	$H +$	G	$=$	$100,000$	Available funds
$A +$	P				$\leq$	$50,000$	Oil industry maximum
		$M +$	H		$\leq$	$50,000$	Steel industry maximum
		$G \geq 0.25\,(M + H)$					Government bonds minimum
		$P \leq 0.60\,(A + P)$					Pacific Oil restriction

$$A, P, M, H, G \geq 0$$

The optimal solution to this linear program is shown in Figure 4.3. Table 4.4 shows how the funds are divided among the securities. Note that the optimal solution indicates that the portfolio should be diversified among all the investment opportunities except

424

FIGURE 4.3 THE SOLUTION FOR THE WELTE MUTUAL FUNDS PROBLEM

```
Optimal Objective Value =          8000.00000

        Variable            Value          Reduced Costs
        --------            -----          -------------
           A           20000.00000            0.00000
           P           30000.00000            0.00000
           M               0.00000           -0.01100
           H           40000.00000            0.00000
           G           10000.00000            0.00000


        Constraint      Slack/Surplus         Dual Value
        ----------      -------------         ----------
           1               0.00000            0.06900
           2               0.00000            0.02200
           3           10000.00000            0.00000
           4               0.00000           -0.02400
           5               0.00000            0.03000
```

WEB file

Welte

Midwest Steel. The projected annual return for this portfolio is $8000, which is an overall return of 8%.

The optimal solution shows the dual value for constraint 3 is zero. The reason is that the steel industry maximum isn't a binding constraint; increases in the steel industry limit of $50,000 will not improve the value of the optimal solution. Indeed, the slack variable for this constraint shows that the current steel industry investment is $10,000 below its limit of $50,000. The dual values for the other constraints are nonzero, indicating that these constraints are binding.

The dual value for the available funds constraint provides information on the rate of return from additional investment funds.

The dual value of 0.069 for constraint 1 shows that the value of the optimal solution can be increased by 0.069 if one more dollar can be made available for the portfolio investment. If more funds can be obtained at a cost of less than 6.9%, management should consider obtaining them. However, if a return in excess of 6.9% can be obtained by investing funds elsewhere (other than in these five securities), management should question the wisdom of investing the entire $100,000 in this portfolio.

Similar interpretations can be given to the other dual values. Note that the dual value for constraint 4 is negative at –0.024. This result indicates that increasing the value on the

TABLE 4.4 OPTIMAL PORTFOLIO SELECTION FOR WELTE MUTUAL FUNDS

Investment	Amount	Expected Annual Return
Atlantic Oil	$ 20,000	$1460
Pacific Oil	30,000	3090
Huber Steel	40,000	3000
Government bonds	10,000	450
Totals	$100,000	$8000

Expected annual return of $8000
Overall rate of return = 8%

right-hand side of the constraint by one unit can be expected to decrease the objective function value of the optimal solution by 0.024. In terms of the optimal portfolio, then, if Welte invests one more dollar in government bonds (beyond the minimum requirement), the total return will decrease by $0.024. To see why this decrease occurs, note again from the dual value for constraint 1 that the marginal return on the funds invested in the portfolio is 6.9% (the average return is 8%). The rate of return on government bonds is 4.5%. Thus, the cost of investing one more dollar in government bonds is the difference between the marginal return on the portfolio and the marginal return on government bonds: 6.9% − 4.5% = 2.4%.

Practice formulating a variation of the Welte problem by working Problem 9.

Note that the optimal solution shows that Midwest Steel should not be included in the portfolio ($M = 0$). The associated reduced cost for M of −0.011 tells us that the objective function coefficient for Midwest Steel would have to increase by 0.011 before considering the Midwest Steel investment alternative would be advisable. With such an increase the Midwest Steel return would be $0.064 + 0.011 = 0.075$, making this investment just as desirable as the currently used Huber Steel investment alternative.

Finally, a simple modification of the Welte linear programming model permits determining the fraction of available funds invested in each security. That is, we divide each of the right-hand-side values by 100,000. Then the optimal values for the variables will give the fraction of funds that should be invested in each security for a portfolio of any size.

NOTES AND COMMENTS

1. The optimal solution to the Welte Mutual Funds problem indicates that $20,000 is to be spent on the Atlantic Oil stock. If Atlantic Oil sells for $75 per share, we would have to purchase exactly 266⅔ shares in order to spend exactly $20,000. The difficulty of purchasing fractional shares can be handled by purchasing the largest possible integer number of shares with the allotted funds (e.g., 266 shares of Atlantic Oil). This approach guarantees that the budget constraint will not be violated. This approach, of course, introduces the possibility that the solution will no longer be optimal, but the danger is slight if

a large number of securities are involved. In cases where the analyst believes that the decision variables *must* have integer values, the problem must be formulated as an integer linear programming model. Integer linear programming is the topic of Chapter 7.

2. Financial portfolio theory stresses obtaining a proper balance between risk and return. In the Welte problem, we explicitly considered return in the objective function. Risk is controlled by choosing constraints that ensure diversity among oil and steel stocks and a balance between government bonds and the steel industry investment.

Financial Planning

Linear programming has been used for a variety of financial planning applications. The Management Science in Action, Optimal Lease Structuring at GE Capital, describes how linear programming is used to optimize the structure of a leveraged lease.

MANAGEMENT SCIENCE IN ACTION

OPTIMAL LEASE STRUCTURING AT GE CAPITAL*

GE Capital is a $70 billion subsidiary of General Electric. As one of the nation's largest and most diverse financial services companies, GE Capital arranges leases in both domestic and international markets, including leases for telecommunications;

data processing; construction; and fleets of cars, trucks, and commercial aircraft. To help allocate and schedule the rental and debt payments of a leveraged lease, GE Capital analysts developed an optimization model, which is available as an

426

optional component of the company's lease analysis proprietary software.

Leveraged leases are designed to provide financing for assets with economic lives of at least five years, which require large capital outlays. A leveraged lease represents an agreement among the lessor (the owner of the asset), the lessee (the user of the asset), and the lender who provides a nonrecourse loan of 50% to 80% of the lessor's purchase price. In a nonrecourse loan, the lenders cannot turn to the lessor for repayment in the event of default. As the lessor in such arrangements, GE Capital is able to claim ownership and realize income tax benefits such as depreciation and interest deductions. These deductions usually produce tax losses during the early years of the lease, which reduces the total tax liability. Approximately 85% of all financial leases in the United States are leveraged leases.

In its simplest form, the leveraged lease structuring problem can be formulated as a linear program. The linear program models the after-tax cash flow for the lessor, taking into consideration rental receipts, borrowing and repaying of the loan, and income taxes. Constraints are formulated to ensure compliance with IRS guidelines and to enable customizing of leases to meet lessee and lessor requirements. The objective function can be entered in a custom fashion or selected from a predefined list. Typically, the objective is to minimize the lessee's cost, expressed as the net present value of rental payments, or to maximize the lessor's after-tax yield.

GE Capital developed an optimization approach that could be applied to single-investor lease structuring. In a study with the department most involved with these transactions, the optimization approach yielded substantial benefits. The approach helped GE Capital win some single-investor transactions ranging in size from $1 million to $20 million.

*Based on C. J. Litty, "Optimal Lease Structuring at GE Capital," *Interfaces* (May/June 1994): 34–45.

Hewlitt Corporation established an early retirement program as part of its corporate restructuring. At the close of the voluntary sign-up period, 68 employees had elected early retirement. As a result of these early retirements, the company incurs the following obligations over the next eight years:

Year	1	2	3	4	5	6	7	8
Cash Requirement	430	210	222	231	240	195	225	255

The cash requirements (in thousands of dollars) are due at the beginning of each year.

The corporate treasurer must determine how much money must be set aside today to meet the eight yearly financial obligations as they come due. The financing plan for the retirement program includes investments in government bonds as well as savings. The investments in government bonds are limited to three choices:

Bond	Price	Rate (%)	Years to Maturity
1	$1150	8.875	5
2	1000	5.500	6
3	1350	11.750	7

The government bonds have a par value of $1000, which means that even with different prices each bond pays $1000 at maturity. The rates shown are based on the par value. For purposes of planning, the treasurer assumed that any funds not invested in bonds will be placed in savings and earn interest at an annual rate of 4%.

We define the decision variables as follows:

F = total dollars required to meet the retirement plan's eight-year obligation

B_1 = units of bond 1 purchased at the beginning of year 1

B_2 = units of bond 2 purchased at the beginning of year 1

B_3 = units of bond 3 purchased at the beginning of year 1

S_i = amount placed in savings at the beginning of year i for $i = 1, \ldots, 8$

The objective function is to minimize the total dollars needed to meet the retirement plan's eight-year obligation, or

$$\text{Min} \quad F$$

A key feature of this type of financial planning problem is that a constraint must be formulated for each year of the planning horizon. In general, each constraint takes the form:

$$\begin{pmatrix} \text{Funds available at} \\ \text{the beginning of the year} \end{pmatrix} - \begin{pmatrix} \text{Funds invested in bonds} \\ \text{and placed in savings} \end{pmatrix} = \begin{pmatrix} \text{Cash obligation for} \\ \text{the current year} \end{pmatrix}$$

The funds available at the beginning of year 1 are given by F. With a current price of $1150 for bond 1 and investments expressed in thousands of dollars, the total investment for B_1 units of bond 1 would be $1.15B_1$. Similarly, the total investment in bonds 2 and 3 would be $1B_2$ and $1.35B_3$, respectively. The investment in savings for year 1 is S_1. Using these results and the first-year obligation of 430, we obtain the constraint for year 1:

$$F - 1.15B_1 - 1B_2 - 1.35B_3 - S_1 = 430 \quad \text{Year 1}$$

We do not consider future investments in bonds because the future price of bonds depends on interest rates and cannot be known in advance.

Investments in bonds can take place only in this first year, and the bonds will be held until maturity.

The funds available at the beginning of year 2 include the investment returns of 8.875% on the par value of bond 1, 5.5% on the par value of bond 2, 11.75% on the par value of bond 3, and 4% on savings. The new amount to be invested in savings for year 2 is S_2. With an obligation of 210, the constraint for year 2 is

$$0.08875B_1 + 0.055B_2 + 0.1175B_3 + 1.04S_1 - S_2 = 210 \quad \text{Year 2}$$

Similarly, the constraints for years 3 to 8 are

$$0.08875B_1 + 0.055B_2 + 0.1175B_3 + 1.04S_2 - S_3 = 222 \quad \text{Year 3}$$
$$0.08875B_1 + 0.055B_2 + 0.1175B_3 + 1.04S_3 - S_4 = 231 \quad \text{Year 4}$$
$$0.08875B_1 + 0.055B_2 + 0.1175B_3 + 1.04S_4 - S_5 = 240 \quad \text{Year 5}$$
$$1.08875B_1 + 0.055B_2 + 0.1175B_3 + 1.04S_5 - S_6 = 195 \quad \text{Year 6}$$
$$1.055B_2 + 0.1175B_3 + 1.04S_6 - S_7 = 225 \quad \text{Year 7}$$
$$1.1175B_3 + 1.04S_7 - S_8 = 255 \quad \text{Year 8}$$

Note that the constraint for year 6 shows that funds available from bond 1 are $1.08875B_1$. The coefficient of 1.08875 reflects the fact that bond 1 matures at the end of year 5. As a result, the par value plus the interest from bond 1 during year 5 is available at the beginning of year 6. Also, because bond 1 matures in year 5 and becomes available for use at the beginning of year 6, the variable B_1 does not appear in the constraints for years 7 and 8. Note the similar interpretation for bond 2, which matures at the end of year 6 and has the par value plus interest available at the beginning of year 7. In addition, bond 3 matures at the end of year 7 and has the par value plus interest available at the beginning of year 8.

Finally, note that a variable S_8 appears in the constraint for year 8. The retirement fund obligation will be completed at the beginning of year 8, so we anticipate that S_8 will be zero and no funds will be put into savings. However, the formulation includes S_8 in the event that the bond income plus interest from the savings in year 7 exceed the 255 cash requirement for year 8. Thus, S_8 is a surplus variable that shows any funds remaining after the eight-year cash requirements have been satisfied.

The optimal solution to this 12-variable, 8-constraint linear program is shown in Figure 4.4. With an objective function value of 1728.79385, the total investment required to meet the retirement plan's eight-year obligation is $1,728,794. Using the current prices of $1150, $1000, and $1350 for each of the bonds, respectively, we can summarize the initial investments in the three bonds as follows:

Bond	Units Purchased	Investment Amount
1	$B_1 = 144.988$	$1150(144.988) = $166,736
2	$B_2 = 187.856$	$1000(187.856) = $187,856
3	$B_3 = 228.188$	$1350(228.188) = $308,054

FIGURE 4.4 THE SOLUTION FOR THE HEWLITT CORPORATION CASH REQUIREMENTS PROBLEM

WEB file

Hewlitt

```
Optimal Objective Value =              1728.79385

       Variable              Value            Reduced Cost
    --------------       --------------      --------------
         F                 1728.79385             0.00000
         B1                 144.98815             0.00000
         B2                 187.85585             0.00000
         B3                 228.18792             0.00000
         S1                 636.14794             0.00000
         S2                 501.60571             0.00000
         S3                 349.68179             0.00000
         S4                 182.68091             0.00000
         S5                   0.00000             0.06403
         S6                   0.00000             0.01261
         S7                   0.00000             0.02132
         S8                   0.00000             0.67084


      Constraint         Slack/Surplus          Dual Value
    --------------       --------------      --------------
          1                   0.00000             1.00000
          2                   0.00000             0.96154
          3                   0.00000             0.92456
          4                   0.00000             0.88900
          5                   0.00000             0.85480
          6                   0.00000             0.76036
          7                   0.00000             0.71899
          8                   0.00000             0.67084
```

The solution also shows that $636,148 (see S_1) will be placed in savings at the beginning of the first year. By starting with $1,728,794, the company can make the specified bond and savings investments and have enough left over to meet the retirement program's first-year cash requirement of $430,000.

The optimal solution in Figure 4.4 shows that the decision variables S_1, S_2, S_3, and S_4 all are greater than zero, indicating investments in savings are required in each of the first four years. However, interest from the bonds plus the bond maturity incomes will be sufficient to cover the retirement program's cash requirements in years 5 through 8.

In this application, the dual value can be thought of as the present value of each dollar in the cash requirement. For example, each dollar that must be paid in year 8 has a present value of $0.67084.

The dual values have an interesting interpretation in this application. Each right-hand-side value corresponds to the payment that must be made in that year. Note that the dual values are positive, indicating that increasing the required payment in any year by $1,000 would *increase* the total funds required for the retirement program's obligation by $1,000 times the dual value. Also note that the dual values show that increases in required payments in the early years have the largest impact. This makes sense in that there is little time to build up investment income in the early years versus the subsequent years. This suggests that if Hewlitt faces increases in required payments it would benefit by deferring those increases to later years if possible.

NOTES AND COMMENTS

1. The optimal solution for the Hewlitt Corporation problem shows fractional numbers of government bonds at 144.988, 187.856, and 228.188 units, respectively. However, fractional bond units usually are not available. If we were conservative and rounded up to 145, 188, and 229 units, respectively, the total funds required for the eight-year retirement program obligation would be approximately $1254 more than the total funds indicated by the objective function. Because of the magnitude of the funds involved, rounding up probably would provide a workable solution. If an optimal integer solution were required, the methods of integer linear programming covered in Chapter 7 would have to be used.

2. We implicitly assumed that interest from the government bonds is paid annually. Investments such as treasury notes actually provide interest payments every six months. In such cases, the model can be reformulated with six-month periods, with interest and/or cash payments occurring every six months.

4.3 OPERATIONS MANAGEMENT APPLICATIONS

Linear programming applications developed for production and operations management include scheduling, staffing, inventory control, and capacity planning. In this section we describe examples with make-or-buy decisions, production scheduling, and workforce assignments.

A Make-or-Buy Decision

We illustrate the use of a linear programming model to determine how much of each of several component parts a company should manufacture and how much it should purchase from an outside supplier. Such a decision is referred to as a make-or-buy decision.

The Janders Company markets various business and engineering products. Currently, Janders is preparing to introduce two new calculators: one for the business market called the Financial Manager and one for the engineering market called the Technician. Each calculator has three components: a base, an electronic cartridge, and a faceplate or top. The same base is used for both calculators, but the cartridges and tops are different. All components can be manufactured by the company or purchased from outside suppliers. The manufacturing costs and purchase prices for the components are summarized in Table 4.5.

TABLE 4.5 MANUFACTURING COSTS AND PURCHASE PRICES FOR JANDERS
CALCULATOR COMPONENTS

	Cost per Unit	
Component	Manufacture (regular time)	Purchase
Base	$0.50	$0.60
Financial cartridge	$3.75	$4.00
Technician cartridge	$3.30	$3.90
Financial top	$0.60	$0.65
Technician top	$0.75	$0.78

Company forecasters indicate that 3000 Financial Manager calculators and 2000 Technician calculators will be needed. However, manufacturing capacity is limited. The company has 200 hours of regular manufacturing time and 50 hours of overtime that can be scheduled for the calculators. Overtime involves a premium at the additional cost of $9 per hour. Table 4.6 shows manufacturing times (in minutes) for the components.

The problem for Janders is to determine how many units of each component to manufacture and how many units of each component to purchase. We define the decision variables as follows:

$$BM = \text{number of bases manufactured}$$
$$BP = \text{number of bases purchased}$$
$$FCM = \text{number of Financial cartridges manufactured}$$
$$FCP = \text{number of Financial cartridges purchased}$$
$$TCM = \text{number of Technician cartridges manufactured}$$
$$TCP = \text{number of Technician cartridges purchased}$$
$$FTM = \text{number of Financial tops manufactured}$$
$$FTP = \text{number of Financial tops purchased}$$
$$TTM = \text{number of Technician tops manufactured}$$
$$TTP = \text{number of Technician tops purchased}$$

One additional decision variable is needed to determine the hours of overtime that must be scheduled:

$$OT = \text{number of hours of overtime to be scheduled}$$

TABLE 4.6 MANUFACTURING TIMES IN MINUTES PER UNIT FOR JANDERS
CALCULATOR COMPONENTS

Component	Manufacturing Time
Base	1.0
Financial cartridge	3.0
Technician cartridge	2.5
Financial top	1.0
Technician top	1.5

The objective function is to minimize the total cost, including manufacturing costs, purchase costs, and overtime costs. Using the cost-per-unit data in Table 4.5 and the overtime premium cost rate of $9 per hour, we write the objective function as

$$\text{Min} \quad 0.5BM + 0.6BP + 3.75FCM + 4FCP + 3.3TCM + 3.9TCP + 0.6FTM$$
$$+ 0.65FTP + 0.75TTM + 0.78TTP + 9OT$$

The first five constraints specify the number of each component needed to satisfy the demand for 3000 Financial Manager calculators and 2000 Technician calculators. A total of 5000 base components are needed, with the number of other components depending on the demand for the particular calculator. The five demand constraints are

$$BM + BP = 5000 \quad \text{Bases}$$
$$FCM + FCP = 3000 \quad \text{Financial cartridges}$$
$$TCM + TCP = 2000 \quad \text{Technician cartridges}$$
$$FTM + FTP = 3000 \quad \text{Financial tops}$$
$$TTM + TTP = 2000 \quad \text{Technician tops}$$

Two constraints are needed to guarantee that manufacturing capacities for regular time and overtime cannot be exceeded. The first constraint limits overtime capacity to 50 hours, or

$$OT \leq 50$$

The same units of measure must be used for both the left-hand side and right-hand side of the constraint. In this case, minutes are used.

The second constraint states that the total manufacturing time required for all components must be less than or equal to the total manufacturing capacity, including regular time plus overtime. The manufacturing times for the components are expressed in minutes, so we state the total manufacturing capacity constraint in minutes, with the 200 hours of regular time capacity becoming $60(200) = 12,000$ minutes. The actual overtime required is unknown at this point, so we write the overtime as $60OT$ minutes. Using the manufacturing times from Table 4.6, we have

$$BM + 3FCM + 2.5TCM + FTM + 1.5TTM \leq 12,000 + 60OT$$

The complete formulation of the Janders make-or-buy problem with all decision variables greater than or equal to zero is

$$\text{Min} \quad 0.5BM + 0.6BP + 3.75FCM + 4FCP + 3.3TCM + 3.9TCP$$
$$+ 0.6FTM + 0.65FTP + 0.75TTM + 0.78TTP + 9OT$$

s.t.

BM				$+ \ BP =$	5000	Bases
	FCM			$+ \ FCP =$	3000	Financial cartridges
		TCM		$+ \ TCP =$	2000	Technician cartridges
			FTM	$+ \ FTP =$	3000	Financial tops
			$TTM +$	$TTP =$	2000	Technician tops
				$OT \leq$	50	Overtime hours
$BM + 3FCM + 2.5TCM + FTM + 1.5TTM$				$\leq \ 12,000 + 60OT$		Manufacturing capacity

The optimal solution to this 11-variable, 7-constraint linear program is shown in Figure 4.5. The optimal solution indicates that all 5000 bases (*BM*), 667 Financial Manager cartridges (*FCM*), and 2000 Technician cartridges (*TCM*) should be manufactured. The remaining 2333 Financial Manager cartridges (*FCP*), all the Financial Manager tops (*FTP*),

FIGURE 4.5 THE SOLUTION FOR THE JANDERS MAKE-OR-BUY PROBLEM

```
Optimal Objective Value =          24443.33333

        Variable              Value           Reduced Cost
     --------------      --------------      -----------------
          BM              5000.00000              0.00000
          BP                 0.00000              0.01667
          FCM              666.66667              0.00000
          FCP             2333.33333              0.00000
          TCM             2000.00000              0.00000
          TCP                0.00000              0.39167
          FTM                0.00000              0.03333
          FTP             3000.00000              0.00000
          TTM                0.00000              0.09500
          TTP             2000.00000              0.00000
          OT                 0.00000              4.00000

       Constraint        Slack/Surplus          Dual Value
     --------------      --------------      -----------------
           1                 0.00000              0.58333
           2                 0.00000              4.00000
           3                 0.00000              3.50833
           4                 0.00000              0.65000
           5                 0.00000              0.78000
           6                50.00000              0.00000
           7                 0.00000             -0.08333

                         Objective        Allowable        Allowable
        Variable        Coefficient        Increase         Decrease
     ----------        ------------       ----------       ----------
          BM             0.50000           0.01667           Infinite
          BP             0.60000           Infinite          0.01667
          FCM            3.75000           0.10000           0.05000
          FCP            4.00000           0.05000           0.10000
          TCM            3.30000           0.39167           Infinite
          TCP            3.90000           Infinite          0.39167
          FTM            0.60000           Infinite          0.03333
          FTP            0.65000           0.03333           Infinite
          TTM            0.75000           Infinite          0.09500
          TTP            0.78000           0.09500           Infinite
          OT             9.00000           Infinite          4.00000

                            RHS          Allowable        Allowable
       Constraint          Value          Increase         Decrease
     ----------        ------------       ----------       ----------
           1           5000.00000        2000.00000        5000.00000
           2           3000.00000         Infinite         2333.33333
           3           2000.00000         800.00000        2000.00000
           4           3000.00000         Infinite         3000.00000
           5           2000.00000         Infinite         2000.00000
           6             50.00000         Infinite           50.00000
           7          12000.00000        7000.00000        2000.00000
```

Janders

and all Technician tops (*TTP*) should be purchased. No overtime manufacturing is necessary, and the total cost associated with the optimal make-or-buy plan is $24,443.33.

Sensitivity analysis provides some additional information about the unused overtime capacity. The Reduced Costs column shows that the overtime (*OT*) premium would have to decrease by $4 per hour before overtime production should be considered. That is, if the overtime premium is $9 − $4 = $5 or less, Janders may want to replace some of the purchased components with components manufactured on overtime.

The dual value for the manufacturing capacity constraint 7 is −0.083. This value indicates that an additional hour of manufacturing capacity is worth $0.083 per minute or ($0.083)(60) = $5 per hour. The right-hand-side range for constraint 7 shows that this conclusion is valid until the amount of regular time increases to 19,000 minutes, or 316.7 hours.

Sensitivity analysis also indicates that a change in prices charged by the outside suppliers can affect the optimal solution. For instance, the objective coefficient range for *BP* is 0.583 (0.600 − 0.017) to no upper limit. If the purchase price for bases remains at $0.583 or more, the number of bases purchased (*BP*) will remain at zero. However, if the purchase price drops below $0.583, Janders should begin to purchase rather than manufacture the base component. Similar sensitivity analysis conclusions about the purchase price ranges can be drawn for the other components.

NOTES AND COMMENTS

The proper interpretation of the dual value for manufacturing capacity (constraint 7) in the Janders problem is that an additional hour of manufacturing capacity is worth ($0.083)(60) = $5 per hour. Thus, the company should be willing to pay a premium of $5 per hour over and above the current regular time cost per hour, which is already included in the manufacturing cost of the product. Thus, if the regular time cost is $18 per hour, Janders should be willing to pay up to $18 + $5 = $23 per hour to obtain additional labor capacity.

Production Scheduling

One of the most important applications of linear programming deals with multiperiod planning such as production scheduling. The solution to a production scheduling problem enables the manager to establish an efficient low-cost production schedule for one or more products over several time periods (weeks or months). Essentially, a production scheduling problem can be viewed as a product-mix problem for each of several periods in the future. The manager must determine the production levels that will allow the company to meet product demand requirements, given limitations on production capacity, labor capacity, and storage space, while minimizing total production costs.

One advantage of using linear programming for production scheduling problems is that they recur. A production schedule must be established for the current month, then again for the next month, for the month after that, and so on. When looking at the problem each month, the production manager will find that, although demand for the products has changed, production times, production capacities, storage space limitations, and so on are roughly the same. Thus, the production manager is basically re-solving the same problem handled in previous months, and a general linear programming model of the production scheduling procedure may be applied frequently. Once the model has been formulated, the manager can simply supply the data—demand, capacities, and so on—for the given production period and use the linear programming model repeatedly to develop the production schedule. The Management Science in Action, Optimizing Production of Flight Manuals at

TABLE 4.7   THREE-MONTH DEMAND SCHEDULE FOR BOLLINGER ELECTRONICS COMPANY

Component	April	May	June
322A	1000	3000	5000
802B	1000	500	3000

Jeppesen Sanderson, Inc., describes how linear programming is used to minimize the cost of producing weekly revisions to flight manuals.

Let us consider the case of the Bollinger Electronics Company, which produces two different electronic components for a major airplane engine manufacturer. The airplane engine manufacturer notifies the Bollinger sales office each quarter of its monthly requirements for components for each of the next three months. The monthly requirements for the components may vary considerably, depending on the type of engine the airplane engine manufacturer is producing. The order shown in Table 4.7 has just been received for the next three-month period.

After the order is processed, a demand statement is sent to the production control department. The production control department must then develop a three-month production plan for the components. In arriving at the desired schedule, the production manager will want to identify the following:

1. Total production cost
2. Inventory holding cost
3. Change-in-production-level costs

In the remainder of this section, we show how to formulate a linear programming model of the production and inventory process for Bollinger Electronics to minimize the total cost.

MANAGEMENT SCIENCE IN ACTION

OPTIMIZING PRODUCTION OF FLIGHT MANUALS AT JEPPESEN SANDERSON, INC.*

Jeppesen Sanderson, Inc., manufactures and distributes flight manuals that contain safety information to more than 300,000 pilots and 4000 airlines. Every week Jeppesen mails between 5 and 30 million pages of chart revisions to 200,000 customers worldwide, and the company receives about 1500 new orders each week. In the late 1990s, its customer service deteriorated as its existing production and supporting systems failed to keep up with this level of activity. To meet customer service goals, Jeppesen turned to optimization-based decision support tools for production planning.

Jeppesen developed a large-scale linear program called Scheduler to minimize the cost of producing the weekly revisions. Model constraints included capacity constraints and numerous internal business rules. The model includes 250,000

variables, and 40,000 to 50,000 constraints. Immediately after introducing the model, Jeppesen established a new record for the number of consecutive weeks with 100% on-time revisions. Scheduler decreased tardiness of revisions from approximately 9% to 3% and dramatically improved customer satisfaction. Even more importantly, Scheduler provided a model of the production system for Jeppesen to use in strategic economic analysis. Overall, the use of optimization techniques at Jeppesen resulted in cost reductions of nearly 10% and a 24% increase in profit.

*Based on E. Katok, W. Tarantino, and R. Tiedman, "Improving Performance and Flexibility at Jeppesen: The World's Leading Aviation-Information Company," *Interfaces* (January/February 2001): 7–29.

435

To develop the model, we let x_{im} denote the production volume in units for product i in month m. Here $i = 1, 2$, and $m = 1, 2, 3$; $i = 1$ refers to component 322A, $i = 2$ refers to component 802B, $m = 1$ refers to April, $m = 2$ refers to May, and $m = 3$ refers to June. The purpose of the double subscript is to provide a more descriptive notation. We could simply use x_6 to represent the number of units of product 2 produced in month 3, but x_{23} is more descriptive, identifying directly the product and month represented by the variable.

If component 322A costs \$20 per unit produced and component 802B costs \$10 per unit produced, the total production cost part of the objective function is

$$\text{Total production cost} = 20x_{11} + 20x_{12} + 20x_{13} + 10x_{21} + 10x_{22} + 10x_{23}$$

Because the production cost per unit is the same each month, we don't need to include the production costs in the objective function; that is, regardless of the production schedule selected, the total production cost will remain the same. In other words, production costs are not relevant costs for the production scheduling decision under consideration. In cases in which the production cost per unit is expected to change each month, the variable production costs per unit per month must be included in the objective function. The solution for the Bollinger Electronics problem will be the same regardless of whether these costs are included; therefore, we included them so that the value of the linear programming objective function will include all the costs associated with the problem.

To incorporate the relevant inventory holding costs into the model, we let s_{im} denote the inventory level for product i at the end of month m. Bollinger determined that on a monthly basis inventory holding costs are 1.5% of the cost of the product; that is, $(0.015)(\$20) = \$0.30$ per unit for component 322A and $(0.015)(\$10) = \$0.15$ per unit for component 802B. A common assumption made in using the linear programming approach to production scheduling is that monthly ending inventories are an acceptable approximation to the average inventory levels throughout the month. Making this assumption, we write the inventory holding cost portion of the objective function as

$$\text{Inventory holding cost} = 0.30s_{11} + 0.30s_{12} + 0.30s_{13} + 0.15s_{21} + 0.15s_{22} + 0.15s_{23}$$

To incorporate the costs of fluctuations in production levels from month to month, we need to define two additional variables:

$$I_m = \text{increase in the total production level necessary during month } m$$
$$D_m = \text{decrease in the total production level necessary during month } m$$

After estimating the effects of employee layoffs, turnovers, reassignment training costs, and other costs associated with fluctuating production levels, Bollinger estimates that the cost associated with increasing the production level for any month is \$0.50 per unit increase. A similar cost associated with decreasing the production level for any month is \$0.20 per unit. Thus, we write the third portion of the objective function as

$$\text{Change-in-production-level costs} = 0.50I_1 + 0.50I_2 + 0.50I_3$$
$$+ 0.20D_1 + 0.20D_2 + 0.20D_3$$

Note that the cost associated with changes in production level is a function of the change in the total number of units produced in month m compared to the total number of units produced in month $m - 1$. In other production scheduling applications, fluctuations in production level might be measured in terms of machine hours or labor-hours required rather than in terms of the total number of units produced.

Combining all three costs, the complete objective function becomes

$$\text{Min} \quad 20x_{11} + 20x_{12} + 20x_{13} + 10x_{21} + 10x_{22} + 10x_{23} + 0.30s_{11}$$
$$+ 0.30s_{12} + 0.30s_{13} + 0.15s_{21} + 0.15s_{22} + 0.15s_{23} + 0.50I_1$$
$$+ 0.50I_2 + 0.50I_3 + 0.20D_1 + 0.20D_2 + 0.20D_3$$

We now consider the constraints. First, we must guarantee that the schedule meets customer demand. Because the units shipped can come from the current month's production or from inventory carried over from previous months, the demand requirement takes the form

$$\begin{pmatrix} \text{Ending} \\ \text{inventory} \\ \text{from previous} \\ \text{month} \end{pmatrix} + \begin{pmatrix} \text{Current} \\ \text{production} \end{pmatrix} - \begin{pmatrix} \text{Ending} \\ \text{inventory} \\ \text{for this} \\ \text{month} \end{pmatrix} = \begin{pmatrix} \text{This month's} \\ \text{demand} \end{pmatrix}$$

Suppose that the inventories at the beginning of the three-month scheduling period were 500 units for component 322A and 200 units for component 802B. The demand for both products in the first month (April) was 1000 units, so the constraints for meeting demand in the first month become

$$500 + x_{11} - s_{11} = 1000$$
$$200 + x_{21} - s_{21} = 1000$$

Moving the constants to the right-hand side, we have

$$x_{11} - s_{11} = 500$$
$$x_{21} - s_{21} = 800$$

Similarly, we need demand constraints for both products in the second and third months. We write them as follows:

Month 2

$$s_{11} + x_{12} - s_{12} = 3000$$
$$s_{21} + x_{22} - s_{22} = 500$$

Month 3

$$s_{12} + x_{13} - s_{13} = 5000$$
$$s_{22} + x_{23} - s_{23} = 3000$$

If the company specifies a minimum inventory level at the end of the three-month period of at least 400 units of component 322A and at least 200 units of component 802B, we can add the constraints

$$s_{13} \geq 400$$
$$s_{23} \geq 200$$

TABLE 4.8 MACHINE, LABOR, AND STORAGE CAPACITIES
FOR BOLLINGER ELECTRONICS

Month	Machine Capacity (hours)	Labor Capacity (hours)	Storage Capacity (square feet)
April	400	300	10,000
May	500	300	10,000
June	600	300	10,000

TABLE 4.9 MACHINE, LABOR, AND STORAGE REQUIREMENTS FOR COMPONENTS
322A AND 802B

Component	Machine (hours/unit)	Labor (hours/unit)	Storage (square feet/unit)
322A	0.10	0.05	2
802B	0.08	0.07	3

Suppose that we have the additional information on machine, labor, and storage capacity shown in Table 4.8. Machine, labor, and storage space requirements are given in Table 4.9. To reflect these limitations, the following constraints are necessary:

Machine Capacity

$$0.10x_{11} + 0.08x_{21} \leq 400 \quad \text{Month 1}$$
$$0.10x_{12} + 0.08x_{22} \leq 500 \quad \text{Month 2}$$
$$0.10x_{13} + 0.08x_{23} \leq 600 \quad \text{Month 3}$$

Labor Capacity

$$0.05x_{11} + 0.07x_{21} \leq 300 \quad \text{Month 1}$$
$$0.05x_{12} + 0.07x_{22} \leq 300 \quad \text{Month 2}$$
$$0.05x_{13} + 0.07x_{23} \leq 300 \quad \text{Month 3}$$

Storage Capacity

$$2s_{11} + 3s_{21} \leq 10,000 \quad \text{Month 1}$$
$$2s_{12} + 3s_{22} \leq 10,000 \quad \text{Month 2}$$
$$2s_{13} + 3s_{23} \leq 10,000 \quad \text{Month 3}$$

One final set of constraints must be added to guarantee that I_m and D_m will reflect the increase or decrease in the total production level for month m. Suppose that the production levels for March, the month before the start of the current production scheduling period, had been 1500 units of component 322A and 1000 units of component 802B for a total production level of $1500 + 1000 = 2500$ units. We can find the amount of the change in production for April from the relationship

$$\text{April production} - \text{March production} = \text{Change}$$

Using the April production variables, x_{11} and x_{21}, and the March production of 2500 units, we have

$$(x_{11} + x_{21}) - 2500 = \text{Change}$$

Note that the change can be positive or negative. A positive change reflects an increase in the total production level, and a negative change reflects a decrease in the total production level. We can use the increase in production for April, I_1, and the decrease in production for April, D_1, to specify the constraint for the change in total production for the month of April:

$$(x_{11} + x_{21}) - 2500 = I_1 - D_1$$

Of course, we cannot have an increase in production and a decrease in production during the same one-month period; thus, either, I_1 or D_1 will be zero. If April requires 3000 units of production, $I_1 = 500$ and $D_1 = 0$. If April requires 2200 units of production, $I_1 = 0$ and $D_1 = 300$. This approach of denoting the change in production level as the difference between two nonnegative variables, I_1 and D_1, permits both positive and negative changes in the total production level. If a single variable (say, c_m) had been used to represent the change in production level, only positive changes would be possible because of the nonnegativity requirement.

Using the same approach in May and June (always subtracting the previous month's total production from the current month's total production), we obtain the constraints for the second and third months of the production scheduling period:

$$(x_{12} + x_{22}) - (x_{11} + x_{21}) = I_2 - D_2$$
$$(x_{13} + x_{23}) - (x_{12} + x_{22}) = I_3 - D_3$$

Linear programming models for production scheduling are often very large. Thousands of decision variables and constraints are necessary when the problem involves numerous products, machines, and time periods. Data collection for large-scale models can be more time-consuming than either the formulation of the model or the development of the computer solution.

The initially rather small, two-product, three-month scheduling problem has now developed into an 18-variable, 20-constraint linear programming problem. Note that in this problem we were concerned only with one type of machine process, one type of labor, and one type of storage area. Actual production scheduling problems usually involve several machine types, several labor grades, and/or several storage areas, requiring large-scale linear programs. For instance, a problem involving 100 products over a 12-month period could have more than 1000 variables and constraints.

Figure 4.6 shows the optimal solution to the Bollinger Electronics production scheduling problem. Table 4.10 contains a portion of the managerial report based on the optimal solution.

Consider the monthly variation in the production and inventory schedule shown in Table 4.10. Recall that the inventory cost for component 802B is one-half the inventory cost for component 322A. Therefore, as might be expected, component 802B is produced heavily in the first month (April) and then held in inventory for the demand that will occur in future months. Component 322A tends to be produced when needed, and only small amounts are carried in inventory.

439

FIGURE 4.6   THE SOLUTION FOR THE BOLLINGER ELECTRONICS PROBLEM

WEB file

Bollinger

```
Optimal Objective Value =        225295.00000

       Variable             Value           Reduced Cost
    --------------      --------------      --------------
        X11               500.00000            0.00000
        X12              3200.00000            0.00000
        X13              5200.00000            0.00000
        S11                 0.00000            0.17222
        S12               200.00000            0.00000
        S12               400.00000            0.00000
        X21              2500.00000            0.00000
        X22              2000.00000            0.00000
        X23                 0.00000            0.12778
        S21              1700.00000            0.00000
        S22              3200.00000            0.00000
        S23               200.00000            0.00000
        I1                500.00000            0.00000
        I2               2200.00000            0.00000
        I3                  0.00000            0.07222
        D1                  0.00000            0.70000
        D2                  0.00000            0.70000
        D3                  0.00000            0.62778


      Constraint       Slack/Surplus          Dual Value
    --------------      --------------      ------------------
         1                  0.00000           20.00000
         2                  0.00000           10.00000
         3                  0.00000           20.12778
         4                  0.00000           10.15000
         5                  0.00000           20.42778
         6                  0.00000           10.30000
         7                  0.00000           20.72778
         8                  0.00000           10.45000
         9                150.00000            0.00000
        10                 20.00000            0.00000
        11                 80.00000            0.00000
        12                100.00000            0.00000
        13                  0.00000           -1.11111
        14                 40.00000            0.00000
        15               4900.00000            0.00000
        16                  0.00000            0.00000
        17               8600.00000            0.00000
        18                  0.00000           -0.50000
        19                  0.00000           -0.50000
        20                  0.00000           -0.42778
```

TABLE 4.10 MINIMUM COST PRODUCTION SCHEDULE INFORMATION FOR THE BOLLINGER ELECTRONICS PROBLEM

Activity	April	May	June
Production			
Component 322A	500	3200	5200
Component 802B	2500	2000	0
Totals	3000	5200	5200
Ending inventory			
Component 322A	0	200	400
Component 802B	1700	3200	200
Machine usage			
Scheduled hours	250	480	520
Slack capacity hours	150	20	80
Labor usage			
Scheduled hours	200	300	260
Slack capacity hours	100	0	40
Storage usage			
Scheduled storage	5100	10,000	1400
Slack capacity	4900	0	8600

Total production, inventory, and production-smoothing cost = $225,295

The costs of increasing and decreasing the total production volume tend to smooth the monthly variations. In fact, the minimum-cost schedule calls for a 500-unit increase in total production in April and a 2200-unit increase in total production in May. The May production level of 5200 units is then maintained during June.

The machine usage section of the report shows ample machine capacity in all three months. However, labor capacity is at full utilization (slack = 0 for constraint 13 in Figure 4.6) in the month of May. The dual value shows that an additional hour of labor capacity in May will decrease total cost by approximately $1.11.

A linear programming model of a two-product, three-month production system can provide valuable information in terms of identifying a minimum-cost production schedule. In larger production systems, where the number of variables and constraints is too large to track manually, linear programming models can provide a significant advantage in developing cost-saving production schedules. The Management Science in Action, Optimizing Production, Inventory, and Distribution at the Kellogg Company, illustrates the use of a large-scale multiperiod linear program for production planning and distribution.

Workforce Assignment

Workforce assignment problems frequently occur when production managers must make decisions involving staffing requirements for a given planning period. Workforce assignments often have some flexibility, and at least some personnel can be assigned to more than one department or work center. Such is the case when employees have been cross-trained on two or more jobs or, for instance, when sales personnel can be transferred between stores. In the following application, we show how linear programming

OPTIMIZING PRODUCTION, INVENTORY, AND DISTRIBUTION
AT THE KELLOGG COMPANY*

The Kellogg Company is the largest cereal producer in the world and a leading producer of convenience foods, such as Kellogg's Pop-Tarts and Nutri-Grain cereal bars. Kellogg produces more than 40 different cereals at plants in 19 countries, on six continents. The company markets its products in more than 160 countries and employs more than 15,600 people in its worldwide organization. In the cereal business alone, Kellogg coordinates the production of about 80 products using a total of approximately 90 production lines and 180 packaging lines.

Kellogg has a long history of using linear programming for production planning and distribution. The Kellogg Planning System (KPS) is a large-scale, multiperiod linear program. The operational version of KPS makes production, packaging, inventory, and distribution decisions on a weekly basis. The primary objective of the system is to minimize the total cost of meeting estimated demand; constraints involve processing line capacities, packaging line capacities, and satisfying safety stock requirements.

A tactical version of KPS helps to establish plant budgets and make capacity-expansion and consolidation decisions on a monthly basis. The tactical version was recently used to guide a consolidation of production capacity that resulted in projected savings of $35 to $40 million per year. Because of the success Kellogg has had using KPS in their North American operations, the company is now introducing KPS into Latin America, and is studying the development of a global KPS model.

*Based on G. Brown, J. Keegan, B. Vigus, and K. Wood, "The Kellogg Company Optimizes Production, Inventory, and Distribution," *Interfaces* (November/December 2001): 1–15.

can be used to determine not only an optimal product mix, but also an optimal workforce assignment.

McCormick Manufacturing Company produces two products with contributions to profit per unit of $10 and $9, respectively. The labor requirements per unit produced and the total hours of labor available from personnel assigned to each of four departments are shown in Table 4.11. Assuming that the number of hours available in each department is fixed, we can formulate McCormick's problem as a standard product-mix linear program with the following decision variables:

$$P_1 = \text{units of product 1}$$
$$P_2 = \text{units of product 2}$$

TABLE 4.11 DEPARTMENTAL LABOR-HOURS PER UNIT AND TOTAL HOURS
AVAILABLE FOR THE McCORMICK MANUFACTURING COMPANY

	Labor-Hours per Unit		
Department	Product 1	Product 2	Total Hours Available
1	0.65	0.95	6500
2	0.45	0.85	6000
3	1.00	0.70	7000
4	0.15	0.30	1400

The linear program is

$$\text{Max} \quad 10P_1 + 9P_2$$

s.t.

$$0.65P_1 + 0.95P_2 \leq 6500$$
$$0.45P_1 + 0.85P_2 \leq 6000$$
$$1.00P_1 + 0.70P_2 \leq 7000$$
$$0.15P_1 + 0.30P_2 \leq 1400$$
$$P_1, P_2 \geq 0$$

The optimal solution to the linear programming model is shown in Figure 4.7. After rounding, it calls for 5744 units of product 1, 1795 units of product 2, and a total profit of $73,590. With this optimal solution, departments 3 and 4 are operating at capacity, and departments 1 and 2 have a slack of approximately 1062 and 1890 hours, respectively. We would anticipate that the product mix would change and that the total profit would increase if the workforce assignment could be revised so that the slack, or unused hours, in departments 1 and 2 could be transferred to the departments currently working at capacity. However, the production manager may be uncertain as to how the workforce should be reallocated among the four departments. Let us expand the linear programming model to include decision variables that will help determine the optimal workforce assignment in addition to the profit-maximizing product mix.

Suppose that McCormick has a cross-training program that enables some employees to be transferred between departments. By taking advantage of the cross-training skills, a limited number of employees and labor-hours may be transferred from one department to another. For example, suppose that the cross-training permits transfers as shown in Table 4.12. Row 1 of this table shows that some employees assigned to department 1 have cross-training skills that permit them to be transferred to department 2 or 3. The right-hand column shows that, for the current production planning period, a maximum of 400 hours can be transferred from department 1. Similar cross-training transfer capabilities and capacities are shown for departments 2, 3, and 4.

FIGURE 4.7 THE SOLUTION FOR THE McCORMICK MANUFACTURING COMPANY PROBLEM WITH NO WORKFORCE TRANSFERS PERMITTED

WEB file

McCormick

```
Optimal Objective Value =              73589.74359

       Variable              Value          Reduced Cost
    ---------------      ---------------    ---------------
          1                5743.58974           0.00000
          2                1794.87179           0.00000

      Constraint         Slack/Surplus        Dual Value
    ---------------      ---------------    ---------------
          1                1061.53846           0.00000
          2                1889.74359           0.00000
          3                   0.00000           8.46154
          4                   0.00000          10.25641
```

TABLE 4.12   CROSS-TRAINING ABILITY AND CAPACITY INFORMATION

From Department	Cross-Training Transfers Permitted to Department				Maximum Hours Transferable
	1	**2**	**3**	**4**	
1	—	yes	yes	—	400
2	—	—	yes	yes	800
3	—	—	—	yes	100
4	yes	yes	—	—	200

When workforce assignments are flexible, we do not automatically know how many hours of labor should be assigned to or be transferred from each department. We need to add decision variables to the linear programming model to account for such changes.

b_i = the labor-hours allocated to department i for $i = 1, 2, 3,$ and 4

t_{ij} = the labor-hours transferred from department i to department j

The right-hand sides are now treated as decision variables.

With the addition of decision variables $b_1, b_2, b_3,$ and b_4, we write the capacity restrictions for the four departments as follows:

$$0.65P_1 + 0.95P_2 \leq b_1$$
$$0.45P_1 + 0.85P_2 \leq b_2$$
$$1.00P_1 + 0.70P_2 \leq b_3$$
$$0.15P_1 + 0.30P_2 \leq b_4$$

The labor-hours ultimately allocated to each department must be determined by a series of labor balance equations, or constraints, that include the number of hours initially assigned to each department plus the number of hours transferred into the department minus the number of hours transferred out of the department. Using department 1 as an example, we determine the workforce allocation as follows:

$$b_1 = \begin{pmatrix} \text{Hours} \\ \text{initially in} \\ \text{department 1} \end{pmatrix} + \begin{pmatrix} \text{Hours} \\ \text{transferred into} \\ \text{department 1} \end{pmatrix} - \begin{pmatrix} \text{Hours} \\ \text{transferred out of} \\ \text{department 1} \end{pmatrix}$$

Table 4.11 shows 6500 hours initially assigned to department 1. We use the transfer decision variables t_{i1} to denote transfers into department 1 and t_{1j} to denote transfers from department 1. Table 4.12 shows that the cross-training capabilities involving department 1 are restricted to transfers from department 4 (variable t_{41}) and transfers to either department 2 or department 3 (variables t_{12} and t_{13}). Thus, we can express the total workforce allocation for department 1 as

$$b_1 = 6500 + t_{41} - t_{12} - t_{13}$$

Moving the decision variables for the workforce transfers to the left-hand side, we have the labor balance equation or constraint

$$b_1 - t_{41} + t_{12} + t_{13} = 6500$$

This form of constraint will be needed for each of the four departments. Thus, the following labor balance constraints for departments 2, 3, and 4 would be added to the model.

$$b_2 - t_{12} - t_{42} + t_{23} + t_{24} = 6000$$
$$b_3 - t_{13} - t_{23} + t_{34} = 7000$$
$$b_4 - t_{24} - t_{34} + t_{41} + t_{42} = 1400$$

Finally, Table 4.12 shows the number of hours that may be transferred from each department is limited, indicating that a transfer capacity constraint must be added for each of the four departments. The additional constraints are

$$t_{12} + t_{13} \le 400$$
$$t_{23} + t_{24} \le 800$$
$$t_{34} \le 100$$
$$t_{41} + t_{42} \le 200$$

The complete linear programming model has two product decision variables (P_1 and P_2), four department workforce assignment variables (b_1, b_2, b_3, and b_4), seven transfer variables (t_{12}, t_{13}, t_{23}, t_{24}, t_{34}, t_{41}, and t_{42}), and 12 constraints. Figure 4.8 shows the optimal solution to this linear program.

Variations in the workforce assignment model could be used in situations such as allocating raw material resources to products, allocating machine time to products, and allocating salesforce time to stores or sales territories.

McCormick's profit can be increased by $84,011 - $73,590 = $10,421 by taking advantage of cross-training and workforce transfers. The optimal product mix of 6825 units of product 1 and 1751 units of product 2 can be achieved if $t_{13} = 400$ hours are transferred from department 1 to department 3; $t_{23} = 651$ hours are transferred from department 2 to department 3; and $t_{24} = 149$ hours are transferred from department 2 to department 4. The resulting workforce assignments for departments 1 through 4 would provide 6100, 5200, 8051, and 1549 hours, respectively.

If a manager has the flexibility to assign personnel to different departments, reduced workforce idle time, improved workforce utilization, and improved profit should result. The linear programming model in this section automatically assigns employees and labor-hours to the departments in the most profitable manner.

Blending Problems

Blending problems arise whenever a manager must decide how to blend two or more resources to produce one or more products. In these situations, the resources contain one or more essential ingredients that must be blended into final products that will contain specific percentages of each. In most of these applications, then, management must decide how much of each resource to purchase to satisfy product specifications and product demands at minimum cost.

Blending problems occur frequently in the petroleum industry (e.g., blending crude oil to produce different octane gasolines), chemical industry (e.g., blending chemicals to produce fertilizers and weed killers), and food industry (e.g., blending ingredients to produce soft drinks and soups). In this section we illustrate how to apply linear programming to a blending problem in the petroleum industry.

The Grand Strand Oil Company produces regular and premium gasoline for independent service stations in the southeastern United States. The Grand Strand refinery manufactures the gasoline products by blending three petroleum components. The gasolines are sold at different prices, and the petroleum components have different costs. The firm wants

FIGURE 4.8   THE SOLUTION FOR THE McCORMICK MANUFACTURING
COMPANY PROBLEM

```
Optimal Objective Value =           84011.29945

     Variable            Value              Reduced Cost
   -------------      ---------------      ----------------
        P1             6824.85900              0.00000
        P2             1751.41200              0.00000
        B1             6100.00000              0.00000
        B2             5200.00000              0.00000
        B3             8050.84700              0.00000
        B4             1549.15300              0.00000
        T41               0.00000              7.45763
        T12               0.00000              8.24859
        T13             400.00000              0.00000
        T42               0.00000              8.24859
        T23             650.84750              0.00000
        T24             149.15250              0.00000
        T34               0.00000              0.00000


    Constraint        Slack/Surplus           Dual Value
   -------------      ---------------      ------------------
        1                 0.00000              0.79096
        2               640.11300              0.00000
        3                 0.00000              8.24859
        4                 0.00000              8.24859
        5                 0.00000              0.79096
        6                 0.00000              0.00000
        7                 0.00000              8.24859
        8                 0.00000              8.24859
        9                 0.00000              7.45763
        10                0.00000              8.24859
        11              100.00000              0.00000
        12              200.00000              0.00000
```

to determine how to mix or blend the three components into the two gasoline products and maximize profits.

Data available show that regular gasoline can be sold for $2.90 per gallon and premium gasoline for $3.00 per gallon. For the current production planning period, Grand Strand can obtain the three petroleum components at the cost per gallon and in the quantities shown in Table 4.13.

Product specifications for the regular and premium gasolines restrict the amounts of each component that can be used in each gasoline product. Table 4.14 lists the product specifications. Current commitments to distributors require Grand Strand to produce at least 10,000 gallons of regular gasoline.

The Grand Strand blending problem is to determine how many gallons of each component should be used in the regular gasoline blend and how many should be used in the

TABLE 4.13 PETROLEUM COST AND SUPPLY FOR THE GRAND STRAND
BLENDING PROBLEM

Petroleum Component	Cost/Gallon	Maximum Available
1	$2.50	5,000 gallons
2	$2.60	10,000 gallons
3	$2.84	10,000 gallons

TABLE 4.14 PRODUCT SPECIFICATIONS FOR THE GRAND STRAND
BLENDING PROBLEM

Product	Specifications
Regular gasoline	At most 30% component 1
	At least 40% component 2
	At most 20% component 3
Premium gasoline	At least 25% component 1
	At most 45% component 2
	At least 30% component 3

premium gasoline blend. The optimal blending solution should maximize the firm's profit, subject to the constraints on the available petroleum supplies shown in Table 4.13, the product specifications shown in Table 4.14, and the required 10,000 gallons of regular gasoline.

We define the decision variables as

$$x_{ij} = \text{gallons of component } i \text{ used in gasoline } j,$$
$$\text{where } i = 1, 2, \text{ or } 3 \text{ for components } 1, 2, \text{ or } 3,$$
$$\text{and } j = r \text{ if regular or } j = p \text{ if premium}$$

The six decision variables are

$$x_{1r} = \text{gallons of component 1 in regular gasoline}$$
$$x_{2r} = \text{gallons of component 2 in regular gasoline}$$
$$x_{3r} = \text{gallons of component 3 in regular gasoline}$$
$$x_{1p} = \text{gallons of component 1 in premium gasoline}$$
$$x_{2p} = \text{gallons of component 2 in premium gasoline}$$
$$x_{3p} = \text{gallons of component 3 in premium gasoline}$$

The total number of gallons of each type of gasoline produced is the sum of the number of gallons produced using each of the three petroleum components.

Total Gallons Produced

$$\text{Regular gasoline} = x_{1r} + x_{2r} + x_{3r}$$
$$\text{Premium gasoline} = x_{1p} + x_{2p} + x_{3p}$$

447

The total gallons of each petroleum component are computed in a similar fashion.

Total Petroleum Component Use

$$\text{Component } 1 = x_{1r} + x_{1p}$$
$$\text{Component } 2 = x_{2r} + x_{2p}$$
$$\text{Component } 3 = x_{3r} + x_{3p}$$

We develop the objective function of maximizing the profit contribution by identifying the difference between the total revenue from both gasolines and the total cost of the three petroleum components. By multiplying the \$2.90 per gallon price by the total gallons of regular gasoline, the \$3.00 per gallon price by the total gallons of premium gasoline, and the component cost per gallon figures in Table 4.13 by the total gallons of each component used, we obtain the objective function:

$$\text{Max} \quad 2.90(x_{1r} + x_{2r} + x_{3r}) + 3.00(x_{1p} + x_{2p} + x_{3p})$$
$$- 2.50(x_{1r} + x_{1p}) - 2.60(x_{2r} + x_{2p}) - 2.84(x_{3r} + x_{3p})$$

When we combine terms, the objective function becomes

$$\text{Max} \quad 0.40x_{1r} + 0.30x_{2r} + 0.06x_{3r} + 0.50x_{1p} + 0.40x_{2p} + 0.16x_{3p}$$

The limitations on the availability of the three petroleum components are

$$x_{1r} + x_{1p} \leq 5{,}000 \quad \text{Component 1}$$
$$x_{2r} + x_{2p} \leq 10{,}000 \quad \text{Component 2}$$
$$x_{3r} + x_{3p} \leq 10{,}000 \quad \text{Component 3}$$

Six constraints are now required to meet the product specifications stated in Table 4.14. The first specification states that component 1 can account for no more than 30% of the total gallons of regular gasoline produced. That is,

$$x_{1r} \leq 0.30(x_{1r} + x_{2r} + x_{3r})$$

The second product specification listed in Table 4.14 becomes

$$x_{2r} \geq 0.40(x_{1r} + x_{2r} + x_{3r})$$

Similarly, we write the four remaining blending specifications listed in Table 4.14 as

$$x_{3r} \leq 0.20(x_{1r} + x_{2r} + x_{3r})$$
$$x_{1p} \geq 0.25(x_{1p} + x_{2p} + x_{3p})$$
$$x_{2p} \leq 0.45(x_{1p} + x_{2p} + x_{3p})$$
$$x_{3p} \geq 0.30(x_{1p} + x_{2p} + x_{3p})$$

The constraint for at least 10,000 gallons of regular gasoline is

$$x_{1r} + x_{2r} + x_{3r} \geq 10{,}000$$

The complete linear programming model with six decision variables and 10 constraints is

Max $\quad 0.40x_{1r} + 0.30x_{2r} + 0.06x_{3r} + 0.50x_{1p} + 0.40x_{2p} + 0.16x_{3p}$

s.t.

$$
\begin{array}{lll}
x_{1r} + x_{1p} & \leq 5{,}000 \\
x_{2r} + x_{2p} & \leq 10{,}000 \\
x_{3r} + x_{3p} & \leq 10{,}000 \\
x_{1r} & \leq 0.30(x_{1r} + x_{2r} + x_{3r}) \\
x_{2r} & \geq 0.40(x_{1r} + x_{2r} + x_{3r}) \\
x_{3r} & \leq 0.20(x_{1r} + x_{2r} + x_{3r}) \\
x_{1p} & \geq 0.25(x_{1p} + x_{2p} + x_{3p}) \\
x_{2p} & \leq 0.45(x_{1p} + x_{2p} + x_{3p}) \\
x_{3p} & \geq 0.30(x_{1p} + x_{2p} + x_{3p}) \\
x_{1r} + x_{2r} + x_{2r} & \geq 10{,}000 \\
x_{1r}, x_{2r}, x_{3r}, x_{1p}, x_{2p}, x_{3p} \geq 0
\end{array}
$$

Try Problem 15 as another example of a blending model.

The optimal solution to the Grand Strand blending problem is shown in Figure 4.9. The optimal solution, which provides a profit of $7100, is summarized in Table 4.15. The optimal blending strategy shows that 10,000 gallons of regular gasoline should be produced. The regular gasoline will be manufactured as a blend of 1250 gallons of component 1, 6750 gallons of component 2, and 2000 gallons of component 3. The 15,000 gallons of premium gasoline will be manufactured as a blend of 3750 gallons of component 1, 3250 gallons of component 2, and 8000 gallons of component 3.

FIGURE 4.9 THE SOLUTION FOR THE GRAND STRAND BLENDING PROBLEM

WEB file

Grand

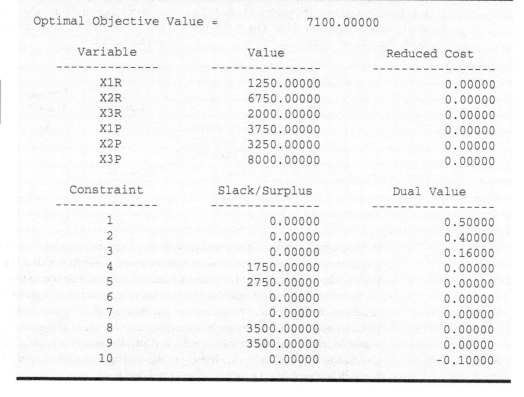

```
Optimal Objective Value =              7100.00000

        Variable              Value          Reduced Cost
     --------------      ----------------    ------------------

          X1R             1250.00000              0.00000
          X2R             6750.00000              0.00000
          X3R             2000.00000              0.00000
          X1P             3750.00000              0.00000
          X2P             3250.00000              0.00000
          X3P             8000.00000              0.00000


       Constraint         Slack/Surplus          Dual Value
     --------------      ----------------      ------------------

           1                 0.00000              0.50000
           2                 0.00000              0.40000
           3                 0.00000              0.16000
           4              1750.00000              0.00000
           5              2750.00000              0.00000
           6                 0.00000              0.00000
           7                 0.00000              0.00000
           8              3500.00000              0.00000
           9              3500.00000              0.00000
          10                 0.00000             -0.10000
```

TABLE 4.15   GRAND STRAND GASOLINE BLENDING SOLUTION

Gasoline	Component 1	Component 2	Component 3	Total
	Gallons of Component (percentage)			
Regular	1250 (12.5%)	6750 (67.5%)	2000 (20%)	10,000
Premium	3750 (25%)	3250 (21⅔%)	8000 (53⅓%)	15,000

The interpretation of the slack and surplus variables associated with the product specification constraints (constraints 4–9) in Figure 4.9 needs some clarification. If the constraint is a ≤ constraint, the value of the slack variable can be interpreted as the gallons of component use below the maximum amount of the component use specified by the constraint. For example, the slack of 1750.000 for constraint 4 shows that component 1 use is 1750 gallons below the maximum amount of component 1 that could have been used in the production of 10,000 gallons of regular gasoline. If the product specification constraint is a ≥ constraint, a surplus variable shows the gallons of component use above the minimum amount of component use specified by the blending constraint. For example, the surplus of 2750.000 for constraint 5 shows that component 2 use is 2750 gallons above the minimum amount of component 2 that must be used in the production of 10,000 gallons of regular gasoline.

NOTES AND COMMENTS

A convenient way to define the decision variables in a blending problem is to use a matrix in which the rows correspond to the raw materials and the columns correspond to the final products. For example, in the Grand Strand blending problem, we define the decision variables as follows:

This approach has two advantages: (1) it provides a systematic way to define the decision variables for any blending problem; and (2) it provides a visual image of the decision variables in terms of how they are related to the raw materials, products, and each other.

		Regular Gasoline	Premium Gasoline
		Final Products	
Raw Materials	Component 1	x_{1r}	x_{1p}
	Component 2	x_{2r}	x_{2p}
	Component 3	x_{3r}	x_{3p}

SUMMARY

In this chapter we presented a broad range of applications that demonstrate how to use linear programming to assist in the decision-making process. We formulated and solved problems from marketing, finance, and operations management, and interpreted the computer output.

Many of the illustrations presented in this chapter are scaled-down versions of actual situations in which linear programming has been applied. In real-world applications, the problem may not be so concisely stated, the data for the problem may not be as readily available, and the problem most likely will involve numerous decision variables and/or constraints. However, a thorough study of the applications in this chapter is a good place to begin in applying linear programming to real problems.

PROBLEMS

Note: The following problems have been designed to give you an understanding and appreciation of the broad range of problems that can be formulated as linear programs. You should be able to formulate a linear programming model for each of the problems. However, you will need access to a linear programming computer package to develop the solutions and make the requested interpretations.

1. The Westchester Chamber of Commerce periodically sponsors public service seminars and programs. Currently, promotional plans are under way for this year's program. Advertising alternatives include television, radio, and newspaper. Audience estimates, costs, and maximum media usage limitations are as shown.

Constraint	Television	Radio	Newspaper
Audience per advertisement	100,000	18,000	40,000
Cost per advertisement	$2000	$300	$600
Maximum media usage	10	20	10

To ensure a balanced use of advertising media, radio advertisements must not exceed 50% of the total number of advertisements authorized. In addition, television should account for at least 10% of the total number of advertisements authorized.

 a. If the promotional budget is limited to $18,200, how many commercial messages should be run on each medium to maximize total audience contact? What is the allocation of the budget among the three media, and what is the total audience reached?

 b. By how much would audience contact increase if an extra $100 were allocated to the promotional budget?

2. The management of Hartman Company is trying to determine the amount of each of two products to produce over the coming planning period. The following information concerns labor availability, labor utilization, and product profitability.

Department	Product (hours/unit) 1	2	Labor-Hours Available
A	1.00	0.35	100
B	0.30	0.20	36
C	0.20	0.50	50
Profit contribution/unit	$30.00	$15.00	

 a. Develop a linear programming model of the Hartman Company problem. Solve the model to determine the optimal production quantities of products 1 and 2.

 b. In computing the profit contribution per unit, management doesn't deduct labor costs because they are considered fixed for the upcoming planning period. However, suppose that overtime can be scheduled in some of the departments. Which departments would you recommend scheduling for overtime? How much would you be willing to pay per hour of overtime in each department?

 c. Suppose that 10, 6, and 8 hours of overtime may be scheduled in departments A, B, and C, respectively. The cost per hour of overtime is $18 in department A, $22.50 in department B, and $12 in department C. Formulate a linear programming model that can be used to determine the optimal production quantities if overtime is made available. What are the optimal production quantities, and what is the revised total contribution to profit? How much overtime do you recommend using in each department? What is the increase in the total contribution to profit if overtime is used?

3. The employee credit union at State University is planning the allocation of funds for the coming year. The credit union makes four types of loans to its members. In addition, the credit union invests in risk-free securities to stabilize income. The various revenue-producing investments together with annual rates of return are as follows:

Type of Loan/Investment	Annual Rate of Return (%)
Automobile loans	8
Furniture loans	10
Other secured loans	11
Signature loans	12
Risk-free securities	9

The credit union will have $2 million available for investment during the coming year. State laws and credit union policies impose the following restrictions on the composition of the loans and investments.

- Risk-free securities may not exceed 30% of the total funds available for investment.
- Signature loans may not exceed 10% of the funds invested in all loans (automobile, furniture, other secured, and signature loans).
- Furniture loans plus other secured loans may not exceed the automobile loans.
- Other secured loans plus signature loans may not exceed the funds invested in risk-free securities.

How should the $2 million be allocated to each of the loan/investment alternatives to maximize total annual return? What is the projected total annual return?

4. Hilltop Coffee manufactures a coffee product by blending three types of coffee beans. The cost per pound and the available pounds of each bean are as follows:

Bean	Cost per Pound	Available Pounds
1	$0.50	500
2	$0.70	600
3	$0.45	400

Consumer tests with coffee products were used to provide ratings on a scale of 0–100, with higher ratings indicating higher quality. Product quality standards for the blended coffee require a consumer rating for aroma to be at least 75 and a consumer rating for taste to be at least 80. The individual ratings of the aroma and taste for coffee made from 100% of each bean are as follows.

Bean	Aroma Rating	Taste Rating
1	75	86
2	85	88
3	60	75

Assume that the aroma and taste attributes of the coffee blend will be a weighted average of the attributes of the beans used in the blend.

a. What is the minimum-cost blend that will meet the quality standards and provide 1000 pounds of the blended coffee product?

b. What is the cost per pound for the coffee blend?

c. Determine the aroma and taste ratings for the coffee blend.

d. If additional coffee were to be produced, what would be the expected cost per pound?

5. Ajax Fuels, Inc., is developing a new additive for airplane fuels. The additive is a mixture of three ingredients: A, B, and C. For proper performance, the total amount of additive (amount of A + amount of B + amount of C) must be at least 10 ounces per gallon of fuel. However, because of safety reasons, the amount of additive must not exceed 15 ounces per gallon of fuel. The mix or blend of the three ingredients is critical. At least 1 ounce of ingredient A must be used for every ounce of ingredient B. The amount of ingredient C must be at least one-half the amount of ingredient A. If the costs per ounce for ingredients A, B, and C are $0.10, $0.03, and $0.09, respectively, find the minimum-cost mixture of A, B, and C for each gallon of airplane fuel.

6. G. Kunz and Sons, Inc., manufactures two products used in the heavy equipment industry. Both products require manufacturing operations in two departments. The following are the production time (in hours) and profit contribution figures for the two products.

| Product | Profit per Unit | Labor-Hours | |
		Dept. A	Dept. B
1	$25	6	12
2	$20	8	10

For the coming production period, Kunz has available a total of 900 hours of labor that can be allocated to either of the two departments. Find the production plan and labor allocation (hours assigned in each department) that will maximize the total contribution to profit.

7. As part of the settlement for a class action lawsuit, Hoxworth Corporation must provide sufficient cash to make the following annual payments (in thousands of dollars).

Year	1	2	3	4	5	6
Payment	190	215	240	285	315	460

The annual payments must be made at the beginning of each year. The judge will approve an amount that, along with earnings on its investment, will cover the annual payments. Investment of the funds will be limited to savings (at 4% annually) and government securities, at prices and rates currently quoted in *The Wall Street Journal*.

Hoxworth wants to develop a plan for making the annual payments by investing in the following securities (par value = $1000). Funds not invested in these securities will be placed in savings.

Security	Current Price	Rate (%)	Years to Maturity
1	$1055	6.750	3
2	$1000	5.125	4

Assume that interest is paid annually. The plan will be submitted to the judge and, if approved, Hoxworth will be required to pay a trustee the amount that will be required to fund the plan.

a. Use linear programming to find the minimum cash settlement necessary to fund the annual payments.

b. Use the dual value to determine how much more Hoxworth should be willing to pay now to reduce the payment at the beginning of year 6 to $400,000.

c. Use the dual value to determine how much more Hoxworth should be willing to pay to reduce the year 1 payment to $150,000.

d. Suppose that the annual payments are to be made at the end of each year. Reformulate the model to accommodate this change. How much would Hoxworth save if this change could be negotiated?

8. The Clark County Sheriff's Department schedules police officers for 8-hour shifts. The beginning times for the shifts are 8:00 A.M., noon, 4:00 P.M., 8:00 P.M., midnight, and 4:00 A.M. An officer beginning a shift at one of these times works for the next 8 hours. During normal weekday operations, the number of officers needed varies depending on the time of day. The department staffing guidelines require the following minimum number of officers on duty:

Time of Day	Minimum Officers on Duty
8:00 A.M.–Noon	5
Noon–4:00 P.M.	6
4:00 P.M.–8:00 P.M.	10
8:00 P.M.–Midnight	7
Midnight–4:00 A.M.	4
4:00 A.M.–8:00 A.M.	6

Determine the number of police officers that should be scheduled to begin the 8-hour shifts at each of the six times (8:00 A.M., noon, 4:00 P.M., 8:00 P.M., midnight, and 4:00 A.M.) to minimize the total number of officers required. (*Hint:* Let x_1 = the number of officers beginning work at 8:00 A.M., x_2 = the number of officers beginning work at noon, and so on.)

9. Reconsider the Welte Mutual Funds problem from Section 4.2. Define your decision variables as the fraction of funds invested in each security. Also, modify the constraints limiting investments in the oil and steel industries as follows: No more than 50% of the total funds invested in stock (oil and steel) may be invested in the oil industry, and no more than 50% of the funds invested in stock (oil and steel) may be invested in the steel industry.

a. Solve the revised linear programming model. What fraction of the portfolio should be invested in each type of security?

b. How much should be invested in each type of security?

c. What are the total earnings for the portfolio?

d. What is the marginal rate of return on the portfolio? That is, how much more could be earned by investing one more dollar in the portfolio?

10. An investment advisor at Shore Financial Services wants to develop a model that can be used to allocate investment funds among four alternatives: stocks, bonds, mutual funds, and cash. For the coming investment period, the company developed estimates of the annual rate of return and the associated risk for each alternative. Risk is measured using an index between 0 and 1, with higher risk values denoting more volatility and thus more uncertainty.

Investment	Annual Rate of Return (%)	Risk
Stocks	10	0.8
Bonds	3	0.2
Mutual funds	4	0.3
Cash	1	0.0

Because cash is held in a money market fund, the annual return is lower, but it carries essentially no risk. The objective is to determine the portion of funds allocated to each investment alternative in order to maximize the total annual return for the portfolio subject to the risk level the client is willing to tolerate.

Total risk is the sum of the risk for all investment alternatives. For instance, if 40% of a client's funds are invested in stocks, 30% in bonds, 20% in mutual funds, and 10% in cash, the total risk for the portfolio would be $0.40(0.8) + 0.30(0.2) + 0.20(0.3) + 0.10(0.0) = 0.44$. An investment advisor will meet with each client to discuss the client's investment objectives and to determine a maximum total risk value for the client. A maximum total risk value of less than 0.3 would be assigned to a conservative investor; a maximum total risk value of between 0.3 and 0.5 would be assigned to a moderate tolerance to risk; and a maximum total risk value greater than 0.5 would be assigned to a more aggressive investor.

Shore Financial Services specified additional guidelines that must be applied to all clients. The guidelines are as follows:

- No more than 75% of the total investment may be in stocks.
- The amount invested in mutual funds must be at least as much as invested in bonds.
- The amount of cash must be at least 10%, but no more than 30% of the total investment funds.

a. Suppose the maximum risk value for a particular client is 0.4. What is the optimal allocation of investment funds among stocks, bonds, mutual funds, and cash? What is the annual rate of return and the total risk for the optimal portfolio?

b. Suppose the maximum risk value for a more conservative client is 0.18. What is the optimal allocation of investment funds for this client? What is the annual rate of return and the total risk for the optimal portfolio?

c. Another more aggressive client has a maximum risk value of 0.7. What is the optimal allocation of investment funds for this client? What is the annual rate of return and the total risk for the optimal portfolio?

d. Refer to the solution for the more aggressive client in part (c). Would this client be interested in having the investment advisor increase the maximum percentage allowed in stocks or decrease the requirement that the amount of cash must be at least 10% of the funds invested? Explain.

e. What is the advantage of defining the decision variables as is done in this model rather than stating the amount to be invested and expressing the decision variables directly in dollar amounts?

11. Edwards Manufacturing Company purchases two component parts from three different suppliers. The suppliers have limited capacity, and no one supplier can meet all the company's needs. In addition, the suppliers charge different prices for the components. Component price data (in price per unit) are as follows:

Component	Supplier		
	1	2	3
1	$12	$13	$14
2	$10	$11	$10

Each supplier has a limited capacity in terms of the total number of components it can supply. However, as long as Edwards provides sufficient advance orders, each supplier can devote its capacity to component 1, component 2, or any combination of the two components, if the total number of units ordered is within its capacity. Supplier capacities are as follows:

Supplier	1	2	3
Capacity	600	1000	800

If the Edwards production plan for the next period includes 1000 units of component 1 and 800 units of component 2, what purchases do you recommend? That is, how many units of each component should be ordered from each supplier? What is the total purchase cost for the components?

12. The Atlantic Seafood Company (ASC) is a buyer and distributor of seafood products that are sold to restaurants and specialty seafood outlets throughout the Northeast. ASC has a frozen storage facility in New York City that serves as the primary distribution point for all products. One of the ASC products is frozen large black tiger shrimp, which are sized at 16–20 pieces per pound. Each Saturday ASC can purchase more tiger shrimp or sell the tiger shrimp at the existing New York City warehouse market price. The ASC goal is to buy tiger shrimp at a low weekly price and sell it later at a higher price. ASC currently has 20,000 pounds of tiger shrimp in storage. Space is available to store a maximum of 100,000 pounds of tiger shrimp each week. In addition, ASC developed the following estimates of tiger shrimp prices for the next four weeks:

Week	Price/lb.
1	$6.00
2	$6.20
3	$6.65
4	$5.55

ASC would like to determine the optimal buying-storing-selling strategy for the next four weeks. The cost to store a pound of shrimp for one week is $0.15, and to account for unforeseen changes in supply or demand, management also indicated that 25,000 pounds of tiger shrimp must be in storage at the end of week 4. Determine the optimal buying-storing-selling strategy for ASC. What is the projected four-week profit?

13. Romans Food Market, located in Saratoga, New York, carries a variety of specialty foods from around the world. Two of the store's leading products use the Romans Food Market name: Romans Regular Coffee and Romans DeCaf Coffee. These coffees are blends of Brazilian Natural and Colombian Mild coffee beans, which are purchased from a distributor located in New York City. Because Romans purchases large quantities, the coffee beans may be purchased on an as-needed basis for a price 10% higher than the market price the distributor pays for the beans. The current market price is $0.47 per pound for Brazilian Natural and $0.62 per pound for Colombian Mild. The compositions of each coffee blend are as follows:

Bean	Blend	
	Regular	DeCaf
Brazilian Natural	75%	40%
Colombian Mild	25%	60%

Romans sells the Regular blend for $3.60 per pound and the DeCaf blend for $4.40 per pound. Romans would like to place an order for the Brazilian and Colombian coffee beans that will enable the production of 1000 pounds of Romans Regular coffee and 500 pounds of Romans DeCaf coffee. The production cost is $0.80 per pound for the Regular blend. Because of the extra steps required to produce DeCaf, the production cost for the DeCaf blend is $1.05 per pound. Packaging costs for both products are $0.25 per pound. Formulate a linear programming model that can be used to determine the pounds of Brazilian Natural and Colombian Mild that will maximize the total contribution to profit. What is the optimal solution and what is the contribution to profit?

14. The production manager for the Classic Boat Corporation must determine how many units of the Classic 21 model to produce over the next four quarters. The company has a beginning inventory of 100 Classic 21 boats, and demand for the four quarters is 2000 units in quarter 1, 4000 units in quarter 2, 3000 units in quarter 3, and 1500 units in quarter 4. The firm has limited production capacity in each quarter. That is, up to 4000 units can be produced in quarter 1, 3000 units in quarter 2, 2000 units in quarter 3, and 4000 units in quarter 4. Each boat held in inventory in quarters 1 and 2 incurs an inventory holding cost of $250 per unit; the holding cost for quarters 3 and 4 is $300 per unit. The production costs for the first quarter are $10,000 per unit; these costs are expected to increase by 10% each quarter because of increases in labor and material costs. Management specified that the ending inventory for quarter 4 must be at least 500 boats.

   a. Formulate a linear programming model that can be used to determine the production schedule that will minimize the total cost of meeting demand in each quarter subject to the production capacities in each quarter and also to the required ending inventory in quarter 4.

   b. Solve the linear program formulated in part (a). Then develop a table that will show for each quarter the number of units to manufacture, the ending inventory, and the costs incurred.

   c. Interpret each of the dual values corresponding to the constraints developed to meet demand in each quarter. Based on these dual values, what advice would you give the production manager?

   d. Interpret each of the dual values corresponding to the production capacity in each quarter. Based on each of these dual values, what advice would you give the production manager?

15. Seastrand Oil Company produces two grades of gasoline: regular and high octane. Both gasolines are produced by blending two types of crude oil. Although both types of crude oil contain the two important ingredients required to produce both gasolines, the percentage of important ingredients in each type of crude oil differs, as does the cost per gallon. The percentage of ingredients A and B in each type of crude oil and the cost per gallon are shown.

Crude Oil	Cost	Ingredient A	Ingredient B	
1	$0.10	20%	60%	Crude oil 1 is 60% ingredient B
2	$0.15	50%	30%	

Each gallon of regular gasoline must contain at least 40% of ingredient A, whereas each gallon of high octane can contain at most 50% of ingredient B. Daily demand for regular and high-octane gasoline is 800,000 and 500,000 gallons, respectively. How many gallons of each type of crude oil should be used in the two gasolines to satisfy daily demand at a minimum cost?

16. The Ferguson Paper Company produces rolls of paper for use in adding machines, desk calculators, and cash registers. The rolls, which are 200 feet long, are produced in widths of $1\frac{1}{2}$, $2\frac{1}{2}$, and $3\frac{1}{2}$ inches. The production process provides 200-foot rolls in 10-inch widths only. The firm must therefore cut the rolls to the desired final product sizes. The seven cutting alternatives and the amount of waste generated by each are as follows:

Cutting Alternative	Number of Rolls			Waste (inches)
	$1\frac{1}{2}$ in.	$2\frac{1}{2}$ in.	$3\frac{1}{2}$ in.	
1	6	0	0	1
2	0	4	0	0
3	2	0	2	0
4	0	1	2	$\frac{1}{2}$
5	1	3	0	1
6	1	2	1	0
7	4	0	1	$\frac{1}{2}$

The minimum requirements for the three products are

Roll Width (inches)	$1\frac{1}{2}$	$2\frac{1}{2}$	$3\frac{1}{2}$
Units	1000	2000	4000

a. If the company wants to minimize the number of 10-inch rolls that must be manufactured, how many 10-inch rolls will be processed on each cutting alternative? How many rolls are required, and what is the total waste (inches)?

b. If the company wants to minimize the waste generated, how many 10-inch rolls will be processed on each cutting alternative? How many rolls are required, and what is the total waste (inches)?

c. What are the differences in parts (a) and (b) to this problem? In this case, which objective do you prefer? Explain. What types of situations would make the other objective more desirable?

17. Frandec Company manufactures, assembles, and rebuilds material handling equipment used in warehouses and distribution centers. One product, called a Liftmaster, is assembled from four components: a frame, a motor, two supports, and a metal strap. Frandec's production schedule calls for 5000 Liftmasters to be made next month. Frandec purchases the motors from an outside supplier, but the frames, supports, and straps may be either manufactured by the company or purchased from an outside supplier. Manufacturing and purchase costs per unit are shown.

Component	Manufacturing Cost	Purchase Cost
Frame	$38.00	$51.00
Support	$11.50	$15.00
Strap	$ 6.50	$ 7.50

Three departments are involved in the production of these components. The time (in minutes per unit) required to process each component in each department and the available capacity (in hours) for the three departments are as follows:

458

Component	Department		
	Cutting	**Milling**	**Shaping**
Frame	3.5	2.2	3.1
Support	1.3	1.7	2.6
Strap	0.8	—	1.7
Capacity (hours)	350	420	680

a. Formulate and solve a linear programming model for this make-or-buy application. How many of each component should be manufactured and how many should be purchased?

b. What is the total cost of the manufacturing and purchasing plan?

c. How many hours of production time are used in each department?

d. How much should Frandec be willing to pay for an additional hour of time in the shaping department?

e. Another manufacturer has offered to sell frames to Frandec for $45 each. Could Frandec improve its position by pursuing this opportunity? Why or why not?

18. The Two-Rivers Oil Company near Pittsburgh transports gasoline to its distributors by truck. The company recently contracted to supply gasoline distributors in southern Ohio, and it has $600,000 available to spend on the necessary expansion of its fleet of gasoline tank trucks. Three models of gasoline tank trucks are available.

Truck Model	Capacity (gallons)	Purchase Cost	Monthly Operating Cost, Including Depreciation
Super Tanker	5000	$67,000	$550
Regular Line	2500	$55,000	$425
Econo-Tanker	1000	$46,000	$350

The company estimates that the monthly demand for the region will be 550,000 gallons of gasoline. Because of the size and speed differences of the trucks, the number of deliveries or round trips possible per month for each truck model will vary. Trip capacities are estimated at 15 trips per month for the Super Tanker, 20 trips per month for the Regular Line, and 25 trips per month for the Econo-Tanker. Based on maintenance and driver availability, the firm does not want to add more than 15 new vehicles to its fleet. In addition, the company has decided to purchase at least three of the new Econo-Tankers for use on short-run, low-demand routes. As a final constraint, the company does not want more than half the new models to be Super Tankers.

a. If the company wishes to satisfy the gasoline demand with a minimum monthly operating expense, how many models of each truck should be purchased?

b. If the company did not require at least three Econo-Tankers and did not limit the number of Super Tankers to at most half the new models, how many models of each truck should be purchased?

19. The Silver Star Bicycle Company will be manufacturing both men's and women's models for its Easy-Pedal 10-speed bicycles during the next two months. Management wants to develop a production schedule indicating how many bicycles of each model should be produced in each month. Current demand forecasts call for 150 men's and 125 women's

models to be shipped during the first month and 200 men's and 150 women's models to be shipped during the second month. Additional data are shown:

Model	Production Costs	Labor Requirements (hours) Manufacturing	Assembly	Current Inventory
Men's	$120	2.0	1.5	20
Women's	$ 90	1.6	1.0	30

Last month the company used a total of 1000 hours of labor. The company's labor relations policy will not allow the combined total hours of labor (manufacturing plus assembly) to increase or decrease by more than 100 hours from month to month. In addition, the company charges monthly inventory at the rate of 2% of the production cost based on the inventory levels at the end of the month. The company would like to have at least 25 units of each model in inventory at the end of the two months.

a. Establish a production schedule that minimizes production and inventory costs and satisfies the labor-smoothing, demand, and inventory requirements. What inventories will be maintained and what are the monthly labor requirements?

b. If the company changed the constraints so that monthly labor increases and decreases could not exceed 50 hours, what would happen to the production schedule? How much will the cost increase? What would you recommend?

20. Filtron Corporation produces filtration containers used in water treatment systems. Although business has been growing, the demand each month varies considerably. As a result, the company utilizes a mix of part-time and full-time employees to meet production demands. Although this approach provides Filtron with great flexibility, it has resulted in increased costs and morale problems among employees. For instance, if Filtron needs to increase production from one month to the next, additional part-time employees have to be hired and trained, and costs go up. If Filtron has to decrease production, the workforce has to be reduced and Filtron incurs additional costs in terms of unemployment benefits and decreased morale. Best estimates are that increasing the number of units produced from one month to the next will increase production costs by $1.25 per unit, and that decreasing the number of units produced will increase production costs by $1.00 per unit. In February Filtron produced 10,000 filtration containers but only sold 7500 units; 2500 units are currently in inventory. The sales forecasts for March, April, and May are for 12,000 units, 8000 units, and 15,000 units, respectively. In addition, Filtron has the capacity to store up to 3000 filtration containers at the end of any month. Management would like to determine the number of units to be produced in March, April, and May that will minimize the total cost of the monthly production increases and decreases.

21. Greenville Cabinets received a contract to produce speaker cabinets for a major speaker manufacturer. The contract calls for the production of 3300 bookshelf speakers and 4100 floor speakers over the next two months, with the following delivery schedule:

Model	Month 1	Month 2
Bookshelf	2100	1200
Floor	1500	2600

Greenville estimates that the production time for each bookshelf model is 0.7 hour and the production time for each floor model is 1 hour. The raw material costs are $10 for each

460

bookshelf model and $12 for each floor model. Labor costs are $22 per hour using regular production time and $33 using overtime. Greenville has up to 2400 hours of regular production time available each month and up to 1000 additional hours of overtime available each month. If production for either cabinet exceeds demand in month 1, the cabinets can be stored at a cost of $5 per cabinet. For each product, determine the number of units that should be manufactured each month on regular time and on overtime to minimize total production and storage costs.

22. TriCity Manufacturing (TCM) makes Styrofoam cups, plates, and sandwich and meal containers. Next week's schedule calls for the production of 80,000 small sandwich containers, 80,000 large sandwich containers, and 65,000 meal containers. To make these containers, Styrofoam sheets are melted and formed into final products using three machines: M1, M2, and M3. Machine M1 can process Styrofoam sheets with a maximum width of 12 inches. The width capacity of machine M2 is 16 inches, and the width capacity of machine M3 is 20 inches. The small sandwich containers require 10-inch-wide Styrofoam sheets; thus, these containers can be produced on each of the three machines. The large sandwich containers require 12-inch-wide sheets; thus, these containers can also be produced on each of the three machines. However, the meal containers require 16-inch-wide Styrofoam sheets, so the meal containers cannot be produced on machine M1. Waste is incurred in the production of all three containers because Styrofoam is lost in the heating and forming process as well as in the final trimming of the product. The amount of waste generated varies depending upon the container produced and the machine used. The following table shows the waste in square inches for each machine and product combination. The waste material is recycled for future use.

Machine	Small Sandwich	Large Sandwich	Meal
M1	20	15	—
M2	24	28	18
M3	32	35	36

Production rates also depend upon the container produced and the machine used. The following table shows the production rates in units per minute for each machine and product combination. Machine capacities are limited for the next week. Time available is 35 hours for machine M1, 35 hours for machine M2, and 40 hours for machine M3.

Machine	Small Sandwich	Large Sandwich	Meal
M1	30	25	—
M2	45	40	30
M3	60	52	44

a. Costs associated with reprocessing the waste material have been increasing. Thus, TCM would like to minimize the amount of waste generated in meeting next week's production schedule. Formulate a linear programming model that can be used to determine the best production schedule.

b. Solve the linear program formulated in part (a) to determine the production schedule. How much waste is generated? Which machines, if any, have idle capacity?

461

23. EZ-Windows, Inc., manufactures replacement windows for the home remodeling business. In January, the company produced 15,000 windows and ended the month with 9000 windows in inventory. EZ-Windows' management team would like to develop a production schedule for the next three months. A smooth production schedule is obviously desirable because it maintains the current workforce and provides a similar month-to-month operation. However, given the sales forecasts, the production capacities, and the storage capabilities as shown, the management team does not think a smooth production schedule with the same production quantity each month possible.

	February	March	April
Sales forecast	15,000	16,500	20,000
Production capacity	14,000	14,000	18,000
Storage capacity	6,000	6,000	6,000

The company's cost accounting department estimates that increasing production by one window from one month to the next will increase total costs by $1.00 for each unit increase in the production level. In addition, decreasing production by one unit from one month to the next will increase total costs by $0.65 for each unit decrease in the production level. Ignoring production and inventory carrying costs, formulate and solve a linear programming model that will minimize the cost of changing production levels while still satisfying the monthly sales forecasts.

24. Morton Financial must decide on the percentage of available funds to commit to each of two investments, referred to as A and B, over the next four periods. The following table shows the amount of new funds available for each of the four periods, as well as the cash expenditure required for each investment (negative values) or the cash income from the investment (positive values). The data shown (in thousands of dollars) reflect the amount of expenditure or income if 100% of the funds available in any period are invested in either A or B. For example, if Morton decides to invest 100% of the funds available in any period in investment A, it will incur cash expenditures of $1000 in period 1, $800 in period 2, $200 in period 3, and income of $200 in period 4. Note, however, if Morton made the decision to invest 80% in investment A, the cash expenditures or income would be 80% of the values shown.

Period	New Investment Funds Available	Investment A	Investment B
1	1500	-1000	-800
2	400	-800	-500
3	500	-200	-300
4	100	200	300

The amount of funds available in any period is the sum of the new investment funds for the period, the new loan funds, the savings from the previous period, the cash income from investment A, and the cash income from investment B. The funds available in any period can be used to pay the loan and interest from the previous period, placed in savings, used to pay the cash expenditures for investment A, or used to pay the cash expenditures for investment B.

Assume an interest rate of 10% per period for savings and an interest rate of 18% per period on borrowed funds. Let

$$S(t) = \text{the savings for period } t$$
$$L(t) = \text{the new loan funds for period } t$$

Then, in any period t, the savings income from the previous period is $1.1S(t-1)$, and the loan and interest expenditure from the previous period is $1.18L(t-1)$.

At the end of period 4, investment A is expected to have a cash value of $3200 (assuming a 100% investment in A), and investment B is expected to have a cash value of $2500 (assuming a 100% investment in B). Additional income and expenses at the end of period 4 will be income from savings in period 4 less the repayment of the period 4 loan plus interest.

Suppose that the decision variables are defined as

$$x_1 = \text{the proportion of investment A undertaken}$$
$$x_2 = \text{the proportion of investment B undertaken}$$

For example, if $x_1 = 0.5$, $500 would be invested in investment A during the first period, and all remaining cash flows and ending investment A values would be multiplied by 0.5. The same holds for investment B. The model must include constraints $x_1 \leq 1$ and $x_2 \leq 1$ to make sure that no more than 100% of the investments can be undertaken.

If no more than $200 can be borrowed in any period, determine the proportions of investments A and B and the amount of savings and borrowing in each period that will maximize the cash value for the firm at the end of the four periods.

25. Western Family Steakhouse offers a variety of low-cost meals and quick service. Other than management, the steakhouse operates with two full-time employees who work 8 hours per day. The rest of the employees are part-time employees who are scheduled for 4-hour shifts during peak meal times. On Saturdays the steakhouse is open from 11:00 A.M. to 10:00 P.M. Management wants to develop a schedule for part-time employees that will minimize labor costs and still provide excellent customer service. The average wage rate for the part-time employees is $7.60 per hour. The total number of full-time and part-time employees needed varies with the time of day as shown.

Time	Total Number of Employees Needed
11:00 A.M.–Noon	9
Noon–1:00 P.M.	9
1:00 P.M.–2:00 P.M.	9
2:00 P.M.–3:00 P.M.	3
3:00 P.M.–4:00 P.M.	3
4:00 P.M.–5:00 P.M.	3
5:00 P.M.–6:00 P.M.	6
6:00 P.M.–7:00 P.M.	12
7:00 P.M.–8:00 P.M.	12
8:00 P.M.–9:00 P.M.	7
9:00 P.M.–10:00 P.M.	7

One full-time employee comes on duty at 11:00 A.M., works 4 hours, takes an hour off, and returns for another 4 hours. The other full-time employee comes to work at 1:00 P.M. and works the same 4-hours-on, 1-hour-off, 4-hours-on pattern.

   a. Develop a minimum-cost schedule for part-time employees.

   b. What is the total payroll for the part-time employees? How many part-time shifts are needed? Use the surplus variables to comment on the desirability of scheduling at least some of the part-time employees for 3-hour shifts.

   c. Assume that part-time employees can be assigned either a 3-hour or a 4-hour shift. Develop a minimum-cost schedule for the part-time employees. How many part-time shifts are needed, and what is the cost savings compared to the previous schedule?

Case Problem 1   PLANNING AN ADVERTISING CAMPAIGN

The Flamingo Grill is an upscale restaurant located in St. Petersburg, Florida. To help plan an advertising campaign for the coming season, Flamingo's management team hired the advertising firm of Haskell & Johnson (HJ). The management team requested HJ's recommendation concerning how the advertising budget should be distributed across television, radio, and newspaper advertisements. The budget has been set at $279,000.

In a meeting with Flamingo's management team, HJ consultants provided the following information about the industry exposure effectiveness rating per ad, their estimate of the number of potential new customers reached per ad, and the cost for each ad.

Advertising Media	Exposure Rating per Ad	New Customers per Ad	Cost per Ad
Television	90	4000	$10,000
Radio	25	2000	$ 3,000
Newspaper	10	1000	$ 1,000

The exposure rating is viewed as a measure of the value of the ad to both existing customers and potential new customers. It is a function of such things as image, message recall, visual and audio appeal, and so on. As expected, the more expensive television advertisement has the highest exposure effectiveness rating along with the greatest potential for reaching new customers.

At this point, the HJ consultants pointed out that the data concerning exposure and reach were only applicable to the first few ads in each medium. For television, HJ stated that the exposure rating of 90 and the 4000 new customers reached per ad were reliable for the first 10 television ads. After 10 ads, the benefit is expected to decline. For planning purposes, HJ recommended reducing the exposure rating to 55 and the estimate of the potential new customers reached to 1500 for any television ads beyond 10. For radio ads, the preceding data are reliable up to a maximum of 15 ads. Beyond 15 ads, the exposure rating declines to 20 and the number of new customers reached declines to 1200 per ad. Similarly, for newspaper ads, the preceding data are reliable up to a maximum of 20; the exposure rating declines to 5 and the potential number of new customers reached declines to 800 for additional ads.

Flamingo's management team accepted maximizing the total exposure rating, across all media, as the objective of the advertising campaign. Because of management's concern with attracting new customers, management stated that the advertising campaign must reach at least 100,000 new customers. To balance the advertising campaign and make use of all advertising media, Flamingo's management team also adopted the following guidelines.

   • Use at least twice as many radio advertisements as television advertisements.

   • Use no more than 20 television advertisements.

- The television budget should be at least $140,000.
- The radio advertising budget is restricted to a maximum of $99,000.
- The newspaper budget is to be at least $30,000.

HJ agreed to work with these guidelines and provide a recommendation as to how the $279,000 advertising budget should be allocated among television, radio, and newspaper advertising.

Managerial Report

Develop a model that can be used to determine the advertising budget allocation for the Flamingo Grill. Include a discussion of the following in your report.

1. A schedule showing the recommended number of television, radio, and newspaper advertisements and the budget allocation for each medium. Show the total exposure and indicate the total number of potential new customers reached.
2. How would the total exposure change if an additional $10,000 were added to the advertising budget?
3. A discussion of the ranges for the objective function coefficients. What do the ranges indicate about how sensitive the recommended solution is to HJ's exposure rating coefficients?
4. After reviewing HJ's recommendation, the Flamingo's management team asked how the recommendation would change if the objective of the advertising campaign was to maximize the number of potential new customers reached. Develop the media schedule under this objective.
5. Compare the recommendations from parts 1 and 4. What is your recommendation for the Flamingo Grill's advertising campaign?

Case Problem 2   PHOENIX COMPUTER

Phoenix Computer manufactures and sells personal computers directly to customers. Orders are accepted by phone and through the company's website. Phoenix will be introducing several new laptop models over the next few months and management recognizes a need to develop technical support personnel to specialize in the new laptop systems. One option being considered is to hire new employees and put them through a three-month training program. Another option is to put current customer service specialists through a two-month training program on the new laptop models. Phoenix estimates that the need for laptop specialists will grow from 0 to 100 during the months of May through September as follows: May—20; June—30; July—85; August—85; and September—100. After September, Phoenix expects that maintaining a staff of 100 laptop specialists will be sufficient.

The annual salary for a new employee is estimated to be $27,000 whether the person is hired to enter the training program or to replace a current employee who is entering the training program. The annual salary for the current Phoenix employees who are being considered for the training program is approximately $36,000. The cost of the three-month training program is $1500 per person, and the cost of the two-month training program is $1000 per person. Note that the length of the training program means that a lag will occur between the time when a new person is hired and the time a new laptop specialist is available. The number of current employees who will be available for training is limited. Phoenix estimates that the following numbers can be made available in the coming months: March—15; April—20; May—0; June—5; and July—10. The training center has the capacity to start new three-month and two-month training classes each month; however, the total number of students (new and current employees) that begin training each month cannot exceed 25.

Phoenix needs to determine the number of new hires that should begin the three-month training program each month and the number of current employees that should begin the two-month training program each month. The objective is to satisfy staffing needs during May through September at the lowest possible total cost; that is, minimize the incremental salary cost and the total training cost.

It is currently January, and Phoenix Computer would like to develop a plan for hiring new employees and determining the mix of new hires and current employees to place in the training program.

Managerial Report

Perform an analysis of the Phoenix Computer problem and prepare a report that summarizes your findings. Be sure to include information on and analysis of the following items:

1. The incremental salary and training cost associated with hiring a new employee and training him/her to be a laptop specialist.
2. The incremental salary and training cost associated with putting a current employee through the training program. (Don't forget that a replacement must be hired when the current employee enters the program.)
3. Recommendations regarding the hiring and training plan that will minimize the salary and training costs over the February through August period as well as answers to these questions: What is the total cost of providing technical support for the new laptop models? How much higher will monthly payroll costs be in September than in January?

Case Problem 3   TEXTILE MILL SCHEDULING

The Scottsville Textile Mill* produces five different fabrics. Each fabric can be woven on one or more of the mill's 38 looms. The sales department's forecast of demand for the next month is shown in Table 4.16, along with data on the selling price per yard, variable cost per yard, and purchase price per yard. The mill operates 24 hours a day and is scheduled for 30 days during the coming month.

TABLE 4.16   MONTHLY DEMAND, SELLING PRICE, VARIABLE COST, AND PURCHASE PRICE DATA FOR SCOTTSVILLE TEXTILE MILL FABRICS

Fabric	Demand (yards)	Selling Price ($/yard)	Variable Cost ($/yard)	Purchase Price ($/yard)
1	16,500	0.99	0.66	0.80
2	22,000	0.86	0.55	0.70
3	62,000	1.10	0.49	0.60
4	7,500	1.24	0.51	0.70
5	62,000	0.70	0.50	0.70

*This case is based on the Calhoun Textile Mill Case by Jeffrey D. Camm, P. M. Dearing, and Suresh K. Tadisnia, 1987.

TABLE 4.17 LOOM PRODUCTION RATES FOR THE SCOTTSVILLE TEXTILE MILL

	Loom Rate (yards/hour)	
Fabric	Dobbie	Regular
1	4.63	—
2	4.63	—
3	5.23	5.23
4	5.23	5.23
5	4.17	4.17

Note: Fabrics 1 and 2 can be manufactured only on the dobbie loom.

The mill has two types of looms: dobbie and regular. The dobbie looms are more versatile and can be used for all five fabrics. The regular looms can produce only three of the fabrics. The mill has a total of 38 looms: 8 are dobbie and 30 are regular. The rate of production for each fabric on each type of loom is given in Table 4.17. The time required to change over from producing one fabric to another is negligible and does not have to be considered.

The Scottsville Textile Mill satisfies all demand with either its own fabric or fabric purchased from another mill. Fabrics that cannot be woven at the Scottsville Mill because of limited loom capacity will be purchased from another mill. The purchase price of each fabric is also shown in Table 4.16.

Managerial Report

Develop a model that can be used to schedule production for the Scottsville Textile Mill, and at the same time, determine how many yards of each fabric must be purchased from another mill. Include a discussion and analysis of the following items in your report:

1. The final production schedule and loom assignments for each fabric.
2. The projected total contribution to profit.
3. A discussion of the value of additional loom time. (The mill is considering purchasing a ninth dobbie loom. What is your estimate of the monthly profit contribution of this additional loom?)
4. A discussion of the objective coefficients' ranges.
5. A discussion of how the objective of minimizing total costs would provide a different model than the objective of maximizing total profit contribution. (How would the interpretation of the objective coefficients' ranges differ for these two models?)

Case Problem 4 WORKFORCE SCHEDULING

Davis Instruments has two manufacturing plants located in Atlanta, Georgia. Product demand varies considerably from month to month, causing Davis extreme difficulty in workforce scheduling. Recently Davis started hiring temporary workers supplied by WorkForce Unlimited, a company that specializes in providing temporary employees for firms in the greater Atlanta area. WorkForce Unlimited offered to provide temporary employees under three contract options that differ in terms of the length of employment and the cost. The three options are summarized:

Option	Length of Employment	Cost
1	One month	$2000
2	Two months	$4800
3	Three months	$7500

The longer contract periods are more expensive because WorkForce Unlimited experiences greater difficulty finding temporary workers who are willing to commit to longer work assignments.

Over the next six months, Davis projects the following needs for additional employees:

Month	January	February	March	April	May	June
Employees Needed	10	23	19	26	20	14

Each month, Davis can hire as many temporary employees as needed under each of the three options. For instance, if Davis hires five employees in January under Option 2, WorkForce Unlimited will supply Davis with five temporary workers who will work two months: January and February. For these workers, Davis will have to pay 5($4800) = $24,000. Because of some merger negotiations under way, Davis does not want to commit to any contractual obligations for temporary employees that extend beyond June.

Davis's quality control program requires each temporary employee to receive training at the time of hire. The training program is required even if the person worked for Davis Instruments in the past. Davis estimates that the cost of training is $875 each time a temporary employee is hired. Thus, if a temporary employee is hired for one month, Davis will incur a training cost of $875, but will incur no additional training cost if the employee is on a two- or three-month contract.

Managerial Report

Develop a model that can be used to determine the number of temporary employees Davis should hire each month under each contract plan in order to meet the projected needs at a minimum total cost. Include the following items in your report:

1. A schedule that shows the number of temporary employees that Davis should hire each month for each contract option.
2. A summary table that shows the number of temporary employees that Davis should hire under each contract option, the associated contract cost for each option, and the associated training cost for each option. Provide summary totals showing the total number of temporary employees hired, total contract costs, and total training costs.
3. If the cost to train each temporary employee could be reduced to $700 per month, what effect would this change have on the hiring plan? Explain. Discuss the implications that this effect on the hiring plan has for identifying methods for reducing training costs. How much of a reduction in training costs would be required to change the hiring plan based on a training cost of $875 per temporary employee?

468

4. Suppose that Davis hired 10 full-time employees at the beginning of January in order to satisfy part of the labor requirements over the next six months. If Davis can hire full-time employees for $16.50 per hour, including fringe benefits, what effect would it have on total labor and training costs over the six-month period as compared to hiring only temporary employees? Assume that full-time and temporary employees both work approximately 160 hours per month. Provide a recommendation regarding the decision to hire additional full-time employees.

Case Problem 5 DUKE ENERGY COAL ALLOCATION*

Duke Energy manufactures and distributes electricity to customers in the United States and Latin America. Duke recently purchased Cinergy Corporation, which has generating facilities and energy customers in Indiana, Kentucky, and Ohio. For these customers Cinergy has been spending $725 to $750 million each year for the fuel needed to operate its coal-fired and gas-fired power plants; 92% to 95% of the fuel used is coal. In this region, Duke Energy uses 10 coal-burning generating plants: five located inland and five located on the Ohio River. Some plants have more than one generating unit. Duke Energy uses 28–29 million tons of coal per year at a cost of approximately $2 million every day in this region.

The company purchases coal using fixed-tonnage or variable-tonnage contracts from mines in Indiana (49%), West Virginia (20%), Ohio (12%), Kentucky (11%), Illinois (5%), and Pennsylvania (3%). The company must purchase all of the coal contracted for on fixed-tonnage contracts, but on variable-tonnage contracts it can purchase varying amounts up to the limit specified in the contract. The coal is shipped from the mines to Duke Energy's generating facilities in Ohio, Kentucky, and Indiana. The cost of coal varies from $19 to $35 per ton and transportation/delivery charges range from $1.50 to $5.00 per ton.

A model is used to determine the megawatt-hours (mWh) of electricity that each generating unit is expected to produce and to provide a measure of each generating unit's efficiency, referred to as the heat rate. The heat rate is the total BTUs required to produce 1 kilowatt-hour (kWh) of electrical power.

Coal Allocation Model

Duke Energy uses a linear programming model, called the coal allocation model, to allocate coal to its generating facilities. The objective of the coal allocation model is to determine the lowest-cost method for purchasing and distributing coal to the generating units. The supply/availability of the coal is determined by the contracts with the various mines, and the demand for coal at the generating units is determined indirectly by the megawatt-hours of electricity each unit must produce.

The cost to process coal, called the add-on cost, depends upon the characteristics of the coal (moisture content, ash content, BTU content, sulfur content, and grindability) and the efficiency of the generating unit. The add-on cost plus the transportation cost are added to the purchase cost of the coal to determine the total cost to purchase and use the coal.

---

*The authors are indebted to Thomas Mason and David Bossee of Duke Energy Corporation, formerly Cinergy Corp., for their contribution to this case problem.

Current Problem

Duke Energy signed three fixed-tonnage contracts and four variable-tonnage contracts. The company would like to determine the least-cost way to allocate the coal available through these contracts to five generating units. The relevant data for the three fixed-tonnage contracts are as follows:

Supplier	Number of Tons Contracted For	Cost ($/ton)	BTUs/lb
RAG	350,000	22	13,000
Peabody Coal Sales	300,000	26	13,300
American Coal Sales	275,000	22	12,600

For example, the contract signed with RAG requires Duke Energy to purchase 350,000 tons of coal at a price of $22 per ton; each pound of this particular coal provides 13,000 BTUs.

The data for the four variable-tonnage contracts follow:

Supplier	Number of Tons Available	Cost ($/ton)	BTUs/lb
Consol, Inc.	200,000	32	12,250
Cyprus Amax	175,000	35	12,000
Addington Mining	200,000	31	12,000
Waterloo	180,000	33	11,300

For example, the contract with Consol, Inc., enables Duke Energy to purchase up to 200,000 tons of coal at a cost of $32 per ton; each pound of this coal provides 12,250 BTUs.

The number of megawatt-hours of electricity that each generating unit must produce and the heat rate provided are as follows:

Generating Unit	Electricity Produced (mWh)	Heat Rate (BTUs per kWh)
Miami Fort Unit 5	550,000	10,500
Miami Fort Unit 7	500,000	10,200
Beckjord Unit 1	650,000	10,100
East Bend Unit 2	750,000	10,000
Zimmer Unit 1	1,100,000	10,000

For example, Miami Fort Unit 5 must produce 550,000 megawatt-hours of electricity, and 10,500 BTUs are needed to produce each kilowatt-hour.

The transportation cost and the add-on cost in dollars per ton are shown here:

	Transportation Cost ($/ton)				
Supplier	Miami Fort Unit 5	Miami Fort Unit 7	Beckjord Unit 1	East Bend Unit 2	Zimmer Unit 1
RAG	5.00	5.00	4.75	5.00	4.75
Peabody	3.75	3.75	3.50	3.75	3.50
American	3.00	3.00	2.75	3.00	2.75
Consol	3.25	3.25	2.85	3.25	2.85
Cyprus	5.00	5.00	4.75	5.00	4.75
Addington	2.25	2.25	2.00	2.25	2.00
Waterloo	2.00	2.00	1.60	2.00	1.60

	Add-On Cost ($/ton)				
Supplier	Miami Fort Unit 5	Miami Fort Unit 7	Beckjord Unit 1	East Bend Unit 2	Zimmer Unit 1
RAG	10.00	10.00	10.00	5.00	6.00
Peabody	10.00	10.00	11.00	6.00	7.00
American	13.00	13.00	15.00	9.00	9.00
Consol	10.00	10.00	11.00	7.00	7.00
Cyprus	10.00	10.00	10.00	5.00	6.00
Addington	5.00	5.00	6.00	4.00	4.00
Waterloo	11.00	11.00	11.00	7.00	9.00

Managerial Report

Prepare a report that summarizes your recommendations regarding Duke Energy's coal allocation problem. Be sure to include information and analysis for the following issues:

1. Determine how much coal to purchase from each of the mining companies and how it should be allocated to the generating units. What is the cost to purchase, deliver, and process the coal?
2. Compute the average cost of coal in cents per million BTUs for each generating unit (a measure of the cost of fuel for the generating units).
3. Compute the average number of BTUs per pound of coal received at each generating unit (a measure of the energy efficiency of the coal received at each unit).
4. Suppose that Duke Energy can purchase an additional 80,000 tons of coal from American Coal Sales as an "all or nothing deal" for $30 per ton. Should Duke Energy purchase the additional 80,000 tons of coal?
5. Suppose that Duke Energy learns that the energy content of the coal from Cyprus Amax is actually 13,000 BTUs per pound. Should Duke Energy revise its procurement plan?
6. Duke Energy has learned from its trading group that Duke Energy can sell 50,000 megawatt-hours of electricity over the grid (to other electricity suppliers) at a price of $30 per megawatt-hour. Should Duke Energy sell the electricity? If so, which generating units should produce the additional electricity?

Appendix 4.1 EXCEL SOLUTION OF HEWLITT CORPORATION FINANCIAL PLANNING PROBLEM

In Appendix 2.2 we showed how Excel could be used to solve the Par, Inc., linear programming problem. To illustrate the use of Excel in solving a more complex linear programming problem, we show the solution to the Hewlitt Corporation financial planning problem presented in Section 4.2.

The spreadsheet formulation and solution of the Hewlitt Corporation problem are shown in Figure 4.10. As described in Appendix 2.2, our practice is to put the data required for the problem in the top part of the worksheet and build the model in the bottom part of the worksheet. The model consists of a set of cells for the decision variables, a cell for the objective function, a set of cells for the left-hand-side functions, and a set of cells for the right-hand sides of the constraints. The cells for each of these model components are screened; the cells for the decision variables are also enclosed by a boldface line. Descriptive labels are used to make the spreadsheet easy to read.

Formulation

The data and descriptive labels are contained in cells A1:G12. The screened cells in the bottom portion of the spreadsheet contain the key elements of the model required by the Excel Solver.

WEB file

Hewlitt

FIGURE 4.10 EXCEL SOLUTION FOR THE HEWLITT CORPORATION PROBLEM

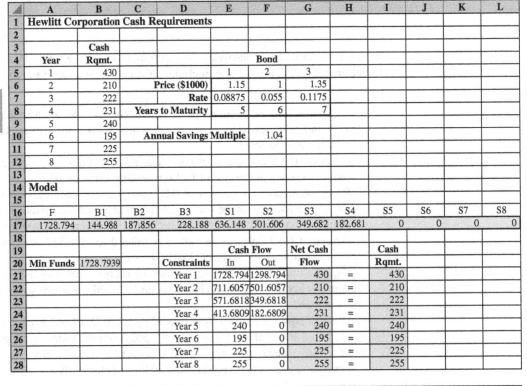

Decision Variables	Cells A17:L17 are reserved for the decision variables. The optimal values (rounded to three places), are shown to be $F = 1728.794$, $B_1 = 144.988$, $B_2 = 187.856$, $B_3 = 228.188$, $S_1 = 636.148$, $S_2 = 501.606$, $S_3 = 349.682$, $S_4 = 182.681$, and $S_5 = S_6 = S_7 = S_8 = 0$.
Objective Function	The formula =A17 has been placed into cell B20 to reflect the total funds required. It is simply the value of the decision variable, F. The total funds required by the optimal solution is shown to be $1,728,794.
Left-Hand Sides	The left-hand sides for the eight constraints represent the annual net cash flow. They are placed into cells G21:G28. Cell G21 = E21 − F21 (Copy to G22:G28)

For this problem, some of the left-hand-side cells reference other cells that contain formulas. These referenced cells provide Hewlitt's cash flow in and cash flow out for each of the eight years.* The cells and their formulas are as follows:

Cell E21 = A17

Cell E22 = SUMPRODUCT($E$7:$G$7,$B$17:$D$17)+$F$10*E17

Cell E23 = SUMPRODUCT($E$7:$G$7,$B$17:$D$17)+$F$10*F17

Cell E24 = SUMPRODUCT($E$7:$G$7,$B$17:$D$17)+$F$10*G17

Cell E25 = SUMPRODUCT($E$7:$G$7,$B$17:$D$17)+$F$10*H17

Cell E26 = (1+E7)*B17+F7*C17+G7*D17+F10*I17

Cell E27 = (1+F7)*C17+G7*D17+F10*J17

Cell E28 = (1+G7)*D17+F10*K17

Cell F21 = SUMPRODUCT(E6:G6,B17:D17)+E17

Cell F22 = F17

Cell F23 = G17

Cell F24 = H17

Cell F25 = I17

Cell F26 = J17

Cell F27 = K17

Cell F28 = L17

Right-Hand Sides	The right-hand sides for the eight constraints represent the annual cash requirements. They are placed into cells I21:I28. Cell I21 = B5 (Copy to I22:I28)

Excel Solution

We are now ready to use the information in the worksheet to determine the optimal solution to the Hewlitt Corporation problem. The following steps describe how to use Excel to obtain the optimal solution.

*The cash flow in is the sum of the positive terms in each constraint equation in the mathematical model, and the cash flow out is the sum of the negative terms in each constraint equation.

FIGURE 4.11 SOLVER PARAMETERS DIALOG BOX FOR THE HEWLITT
CORPORATION PROBLEM

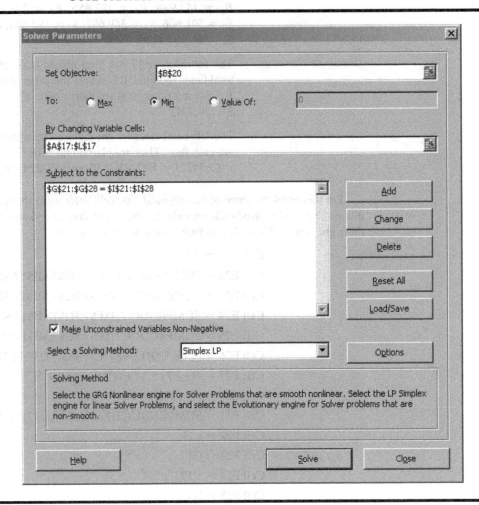

Step 1. Select the **Data** tab
Step 2. Select **Solver** from the **Analysis** group
Step 3. When the **Solver Parameters** dialog box appears (see Figure 4.11):
        Enter B20 in the **Set Objective** box
        Select the **To: Min** option
        Enter A17:L17 in the **By Changing Variable Cells** box
Step 4. Choose **Add**
        When the **Add Constraint** dialog box appears:
        Enter G21:G28 in the left-hand box of the **Cell Reference** area
        Select = from the middle drop-down button
        Enter I21:I28 in the **Constraint** area
        Click **OK**
Step 5. When the **Solver Parameters** dialog box reappears (see Figure 4.11):
        Select **Make Unconstrained Variables Non-Negative**

Step 6. Select the **Select a Solving Method** drop-down button
Select **Simplex LP**
Step 7. Choose **Solve**
Step 8. When the **Solver Results** dialog box appears:
Select **Keep Solver Solution**
Select **Sensitivity** in the **Reports** box
Click **OK**

The Solver Parameters dialog box is shown in Figure 4.11. The optimal solution is shown in Figure 4.10; the accompanying sensitivity report is shown in Figure 4.12.

Discussion

Figures 4.10 and 4.12 contain essentially the same information as that provided in Figure 4.4. Recall that the Excel sensitivity report uses the term *shadow price* to describe the *change* in value of the solution per unit increase in the right-hand side of a constraint. This is the same as the Dual Value in Figure 4.4.

FIGURE 4.12 EXCEL'S SENSITIVITY REPORT FOR THE HEWLITT CORPORATION PROBLEM

Variable Cells

Cell	Name	Final Value	Reduced Cost	Objective Coefficient	Allowable Increase	Allowable Decrease
$A$17	F	1728.793855	0	1	1E + 30	1
$B$17	B1	144.9881496	0	0	0.067026339	0.013026775
$C$17	B2	187.8558478	0	0	0.012795531	0.020273774
$D$17	B3	228.1879195	0	0	0.022906851	0.749663022
$E$17	S1	636.1479438	0	0	0.109559907	0.05507386
$F$17	S2	501.605712	0	0	0.143307365	0.056948823
$G$17	S3	349.681791	0	0	0.210854199	0.059039182
$H$17	S4	182.680913	0	0	0.413598622	0.061382404
$I$17	S5	0	0.064025159	0	1E + 30	0.064025159
$J$17	S6	0	0.012613604	0	1E + 30	0.012613604
$K$17	S7	0	0.021318233	0	1E + 30	0.021318233
$L$17	S8	0	0.670839393	0	1E + 30	0.670839393

Constraints

Cell	Name	Final Value	Shadow Price	Constraint R.H. Side	Allowable Increase	Allowable Decrease
$G$21	Year 1 Flow	430	1	430	1E + 30	1728.793855
$G$22	Year 2 Flow	210	0.961538462	210	1E + 30	661.5938616
$G$23	Year 3 Flow	222	0.924556213	222	1E + 30	521.6699405
$G$24	Year 4 Flow	231	0.888996359	231	1E + 30	363.6690626
$G$25	Year 5 Flow	240	0.854804191	240	1E + 30	189.9881496
$G$26	Year 6 Flow	195	0.760364454	195	2149.927647	157.8558478
$G$27	Year 7 Flow	225	0.718991202	225	3027.962172	198.1879195
$G$28	Year 8 Flow	255	0.670839393	255	1583.881915	255

References and Bibliography

Ahuja, R. K., T. L. Magnanti, and J. B. Orlin. *Network Flows, Theory, Algorithms, and Applications.* Prentice Hall, 1993.

Bazarra, M. S., J. J. Jarvis, and H. D. Sherali. *Linear Programming and Network Flows,* 2d ed. Wiley, 1990.

Carino, H. F., and C. H. Le Noir, Jr. "Optimizing Wood Procurement in Cabinet Manufacturing," *Interfaces* (March/April 1988): 10–19.

Dantzig, G. B. *Linear Programming and Extensions.* Princeton University Press, 1963.

Davis, Morton D. *Game Theory: A Nontechnical Introduction.* Dover, 1997.

Evans, J. R., and E. Minieka. *Optimization Algorithms for Networks and Graphs,* 2d ed. Marcel Dekker, 1992.

Ford, L. R., and D. R. Fulkerson. *Flows and Networks.* Princeton University Press, 1962.

Geoffrion, A., and G. Graves. "Better Distribution Planning with Computer Models," *Harvard Business Review* (July/August 1976).

Greenberg, H. J. "How to Analyze the Results of Linear Programs—Part 1: Preliminaries," *Interfaces* 23, no. 4 (July/August 1993): 56–67.

Greenberg, H. J. "How to Analyze the Results of Linear Programs—Part 2: Price Interpretation," *Interfaces* 23, no. 5 (September/October 1993): 97–114.

Greenberg, H. J. "How to Analyze the Results of Linear Programs—Part 3: Infeasibility Diagnosis," *Interfaces* 23, no. 6 (November/December 1993): 120–139.

Lillien, G., and A. Rangaswamy. *Marketing Engineering: Computer-Assisted Marketing Analysis and Planning.* Addison-Wesley, 1998.

Martin, R. K. *Large Scale Linear and Integer Optimization: A Unified Approach.* Kluwer Academic Publishers, 1999.

McMillian, John. *Games, Strategies, and Managers.* Oxford University Press, 1992.

Myerson, Roger B. *Game Theory: Analysis of Conflict.* Harvard University Press, 1997.

Nemhauser, G. L., and L. A. Wolsey. *Integer and Combinatorial Optimization.* Wiley, 1999.

Osborne, Martin J. *An Introduction to Game Theory.* Oxford University Press, 2004.

Schrage, Linus. *Optimization Modeling with LINDO,* 4th ed. LINDO Systems Inc., 2000.

Sherman, H. D. "Hospital Efficiency Measurement and Evaluation," *Medical Care* 22, no. 10 (October 1984): 922–938.

Winston, W. L., and S. C. Albright. *Practical Management Science,* 2d ed. Duxbury Press, 2001.

Self-Test Solutions and Answers to Even-Numbered Problems

1. a. Let T = number of television advertisements
   R = number of radio advertisements
   N = number of newspaper advertisements

   Max $100{,}000T + 18{,}000R + 40{,}000N$
   s.t.

$2000T +$	$300R +$	$600N \leq$	$18{,}200$	Budget
T		$\leq$	10	Max TV
	R	$\leq$	20	Max radio
		$N \leq$	10	Max news
$-0.5T +$	$0.5R -$	$0.5N \leq$	0	Max 50% radio
$0.9T -$	$0.1R -$	$0.1N \geq$	0	Min 10% TV
$T, R, N \geq 0$				

		Budget \$
Solution:	$T = 4$	\$ 8000
	$R = 14$	4200
	$N = 10$	6000
		\$18,200

   Audience = 1,052,000

   b. The dual value for the budget constraint is 51.30, meaning a \$100 increase in the budget should provide an increase in audience coverage of approximately 5130; the right-hand-side range for the budget constraint will show that this interpretation is correct.

2. a. $x_1 = 77.89$, $x_2 = 63.16$, \$3284.21
   b. Department A \$15.79; Department B \$47.37
   c. $x_1 = 87.21$, $x_2 = 65.12$, \$3341.34
   Department A 10 hours; Department B 3.2 hours

4. a. $x_1 = 500$, $x_2 = 300$, $x_3 = 200$, \$550
   b. \$0.55
   c. Aroma, 75; Taste 84.4
   d. $-\$0.60$

6. 50 units of product 1; 0 units of product 2; 300 hours department A; 600 hours department B

8. Schedule 19 officers as follows:
   3 begin at 8:00 A.M.; 3 begin at noon; 7 begin at 4:00 P.M.; 4 begin at midnight, 2 begin at 4:00 A.M.

9. a. Decision variables A, P, M, H, and G represent the fraction or proportion of the total investment in each alternative.

   Max $0.073A + 0.103P + 0.064M + 0.075H + 0.045G$
   s.t.

$A +$	$P +$	$M +$	$H +$	$G = 1$	
$0.5A +$	$0.5P -$	$0.5M -$	$0.5H$		≤ 0
$-0.5A -$	$0.5P +$	$0.5M +$	$0.5H$		≤ 0
		$- 0.25M -$	$0.25H +$	$G \geq 0$	
$-0.6A +$	$0.4P$				≤ 0
$A, P, M, H, G \geq 0$					

   Objective function = 0.079; $A = 0.178$; $P = 0.267$; $M = 0.000$; $H = 0.444$; $G = 0.111$

   b. Multiplying A, P, M, H, and G by the \$100,000 invested provides the following:

Atlantic Oil	\$ 17,800
Pacific Oil	26,700
Huber Steel	44,400
Government bonds	11,100
	\$100,000

   c. $0.079(\$100{,}000) = \$7900$
   d. The marginal rate of return is 0.079.

10. a. 40.9%, 14.5%, 14.5%, 30.0%
    Annual return = 5.4%
    b. 0.0%, 36.0%, 36.0%, 28.0%
    Annual return = 2.52%
    c. 75.0%, 0.0%, 15.0%, 10.0%
    Annual return = 8.2%
    d. Yes

12.

Week	Buy	Sell	Store
1	80,000	0	100,000
2	0	0	100,000
3	0	100,000	0
4	25,000	0	25,000

14. b.

Quarter	Production	Ending Inventory
1	4000	2100
2	3000	1100
3	2000	100
4	1900	500

15. Let x_{11} = gallons of crude 1 used to produce regular
    x_{12} = gallons of crude 1 used to produce high octane
    x_{21} = gallons of crude 2 used to produce regular
    x_{22} = gallons of crude 2 used to produce high octane

    Min $0.10x_{11} + 0.10x_{12} + 0.15x_{21} + 0.15x_{22}$
    s.t.

    Each gallon of regular must have at least 40% A.

    $x_{11} + x_{21}$ = amount of regular produced
    $0.4(x_{11} + x_{21})$ = amount of A required for regular
    $0.2x_{11} + 0.50x_{21}$ = amount of A in $(x_{11} + x_{21})$ gallons of regular gas
    $\therefore 0.2x_{11} + 0.50x_{21} \geq 0.4x_{11} + 0.40x_{21}$
    $\therefore -0.2x_{11} + 0.10x_{21} \geq 0$

    Each gallon of high octane can have at most 50% B.

    $x_{12} + x_{22}$ = amount high octane
    $0.5(x_{12} + x_{22})$ = amount of B required for high octane

477

$0.60x_{12} + 0.30x_{22}$ = amount of B in $(x_{12} + x_{22})$ gallons of high octane

$$\therefore 0.60x_{12} + 0.30x_{22} \le 0.5x_{12} + 0.5x_{22}$$

$$\therefore 0.1x_{12} - 0.2x_{22} \le 0$$

$$x_{11} + x_{21} \ge 800,000$$

$$x_{12} + x_{22} \ge 500,000$$

$$x_{11}, x_{12}, x_{21}, x_{22} \ge 0$$

Optimal solution: $x_{11} = 266,667$, $x_{12} = 333,333$, $x_{21} = 533,333$, $x_{22} = 166,667$

Cost = \$165,000

16. x_i = number of 10-inch rolls processed by cutting alternative i

   a. $x_1 = 0$, $x_2 = 125$, $x_3 = 500$, $x_4 = 1500$, $x_5 = 0$, $x_6 = 0$, $x_7 = 0$; 2125 rolls with waste of 750 inches

   b. 2500 rolls with no waste; however, $1\frac{1}{2}$-inch size is overproduced by 3000 units

18. a. 5 Super, 2 Regular, and 3 Econo-Tankers
   Total cost \$583,000; monthly operating cost \$4650

19. a. Let x_{11} = amount of men's model in month 1

   x_{21} = amount of women's model in month 1

   x_{12} = amount of men's model in month 2

   x_{22} = amount of women's model in month 2

   s_{11} = inventory of men's model at end of month 1

   s_{21} = inventory of women's model at end of month 1

   s_{12} = inventory of men's model at end of month 2

   s_{22} = inventory of women's model at end of month 2

Min $120x_{11} + 90x_{21} + 120x_{12} + 90x_{22} + 2.4s_{11} + 1.8s_{21} + 2.4s_{12} + 1.8s_{22}$

s.t.

$$\left. \begin{array}{l} x_{11} - \quad s_{11} \qquad\qquad\qquad = 130 \\ x_{21} - \quad s_{21} \qquad\qquad\qquad = 95 \\ s_{11} + \quad x_{12} - \quad s_{12} \qquad = 200 \\ s_{21} + \quad x_{22} - \quad s_{22} = 150 \end{array} \right\} \text{Satisfy demand}$$

$$\left. \begin{array}{l} s_{12} \ge 25 \\ s_{22} \ge 25 \end{array} \right\} \text{Ending inventory requirement}$$

Labor-hours: Men's $2.0 + 1.5 = 3.5$

Women's $1.6 + 1.0 = 2.6$

$$\left. \begin{array}{l} 3.5x_{11} + 2.6x_{21} \qquad\qquad\qquad\qquad \ge \quad 900 \\ 3.5x_{11} + 2.6x_{21} \qquad\qquad\qquad\qquad \le 1100 \\ 3.5x_{11} + 2.6x_{21} - 3.5x_{12} - 2.6x_{22} \le \quad 100 \\ -3.5x_{11} - 2.6x_{21} + 3.5x_{12} + 2.6x_{22} \le \quad 100 \end{array} \right\} \text{Labor smoothing}$$

$x_{11}, x_{12}, x_{21}, x_{22}, s_{11}, s_{12}, s_{21}, s_{22} \ge 0$

Solution: $x_{11} = 193$; $x_{21} = 95$; $x_{12} = 162$; $x_{22} = 175$

Total cost = \$67,156

Inventory levels: $s_{11} = 63$; $s_{12} = 25$; $s_{21} = 0$; $s_{22} = 25$

Labor levels: Previous   1000 hours

Month 1   922.25 hours

Month 2   1022.25 hours

   b. To accommodate the new policy, the right-hand sides of the four labor-smoothing constraints must be changed to 950, 1050, 50, and 50, respectively; the new total cost is \$67,175.

20. Produce 10,250 units in March, 10,250 units in April, and 12,000 units in May.

22. b. 5, 515, 887 sq. in. of waste
   Machine 3: 492 minutes

24. Investment strategy: 45.8% of A and 100% of B
   Objective function = \$4340.40
   Savings/Loan schedule

	Period			
	1	**2**	**3**	**4**
Savings	242.11	—	—	341.04
Funds from loan	—	200.00	127.58	—

8

Advanced Linear Programming Applications

CONTENTS

This chapter continues the study of linear programming applications. Four new applications of linear programming are introduced. We begin with data envelopment analysis (DEA), which is an application of linear programming used to measure the relative efficiency of operating units with the same goals and objectives. We illustrate how this technique is used to evaluate the performance of hospitals. In Section 5.2, we introduce the topic of revenue management. Revenue management involves managing the short-term demand for a fixed perishable inventory in order to maximize the revenue potential for an organization. Revenue management is critically important in the airline industry, and we illustrate the concept by determining the optimal full-fare and discount-fare seat allocations for flights among five cities.

Management science has a major impact in finance. Section 5.3 shows how linear programming is used to design portfolios that are consistent with a client's risk preferences. In Section 5.4, we introduce game theory, which is the study of how two or more decision makers (players) can compete against each other in an optimal fashion. We illustrate with a linear programming model for two firms competing against each other by trying to gain market share.

5.1 DATA ENVELOPMENT ANALYSIS

Data envelopment analysis (DEA) is an application of linear programming used to measure the relative efficiency of operating units with the same goals and objectives. For example, DEA has been used within individual fast-food outlets in the same chain. In this case, the goal of DEA was to identify the inefficient outlets that should be targeted for further study and, if necessary, corrective action. Other applications of DEA have measured the relative efficiencies of hospitals, banks, courts, schools, and so on. In these applications, the performance of each institution or organization was measured relative to the performance of all operating units in the same system. The Management Science in Action, Efficiency of Bank Branches, describes how a large nationally known bank used DEA to determine which branches were operating inefficiently.

MANAGEMENT SCIENCE IN ACTION

EFFICIENCY OF BANK BRANCHES*

Management of a large, nationally known bank wanted to improve operations at the branch level. A total of 182 branch banks located in four major cities were selected for the study. Data envelopment analysis (DEA) was used to determine which branches were operating inefficiently.

The DEA model compared the actual operating results of each branch with those of all other branches. A less-productive branch was one that required more resources to produce the same output as the best-performing branches. The best-performing branches are identified by a DEA efficiency rating of 100% ($E = 100$). The inefficient or less-productive branches are identified by an efficiency rating less than 100% ($E < 1.00$)

The inputs used for each branch were the number of teller full-time equivalents, the number of nonteller personnel full-time equivalents, the number of parking spaces, the number of ATMs, and the advertising expense per customer. The outputs were the amount of loans (direct, indirect, commercial, and equity), the amount of deposits (checking, savings, and CDs), the average number of accounts per customer, and the customer satisfaction score based on a quarterly customer survey. Data were collected over six consecutive quarters to determine how the branches were operating over time.

(continued)

The solution to the DEA linear programming model showed that 92 of the 182 branches were fully efficient. Only five branches fell below the 70% efficiency level, and approximately 25% of the branches had efficiency ratings between 80% and 89%. DEA identified the specific branches that were relatively inefficient and provided insights as to how these branches could improve productivity. Focusing on the less-productive branches, the bank was able to identify ways to reduce the input resources required without significantly reducing the volume and quality of service. In addition, the DEA analysis provided management with a better understanding of the factors that contribute most to the efficiency of the branch banks.

*Based on B. Golany and J. E. Storbeck, "A Data Envelopment Analysis of the Operational Efficiency of Bank Branches," *Interfaces* (May/June 1999): 14–26.

The operating units of most organizations have multiple inputs such as staff size, salaries, hours of operation, and advertising budget, as well as multiple outputs such as profit, market share, and growth rate. In these situations, it is often difficult for a manager to determine which operating units are inefficient in converting their multiple inputs into multiple outputs. This particular area is where data envelopment analysis has proven to be a helpful managerial tool. We illustrate the application of data envelopment analysis by evaluating the performance of a group of four hospitals.

Evaluating the Performance of Hospitals

The hospital administrators at General Hospital, University Hospital, County Hospital, and State Hospital have been meeting to discuss ways in which they can help one another improve the performance at each of their hospitals. A consultant suggested that they consider using DEA to measure the performance of each hospital relative to the performance of all four hospitals. In discussing how this evaluation could be done, the following three input measures and four output measures were identified:

Input Measures

1. The number of full-time equivalent (FTE) nonphysician personnel
2. The amount spent on supplies
3. The number of bed-days available

Output Measures

Problem 1 asks you to formulate and solve a linear program to assess the relative efficiency of General Hospital.

1. Patient-days of service under Medicare
2. Patient-days of service not under Medicare
3. Number of nurses trained
4. Number of interns trained

Summaries of the input and output measures for a one-year period at each of the four hospitals are shown in Tables 5.1 and 5.2. Let us show how DEA can use these data to identify relatively inefficient hospitals.

Overview of the DEA Approach

In this application of DEA, a linear programming model is developed for each hospital whose efficiency is to be evaluated. To illustrate the modeling process, we formulate a linear program that can be used to determine the relative efficiency of County Hospital.

First, using a linear programming model, we construct a **hypothetical composite,** in this case a composite hospital, based on the outputs and inputs for all operating units with

TABLE 5.1   ANNUAL RESOURCES CONSUMED (INPUTS) BY THE FOUR HOSPITALS

	Hospital			
Input Measure	General	University	County	State
Full-time equivalent nonphysicians	285.20	162.30	275.70	210.40
Supply expense ($1000s)	123.80	128.70	348.50	154.10
Bed-days available (1000s)	106.72	64.21	104.10	104.04

the same goals. For each of the four hospitals' output measures, the output for the composite hospital is determined by computing a weighted average of the corresponding outputs for all four hospitals. For each of the three input measures, the input for the composite hospital is determined by using the same weights to compute a weighted average of the corresponding inputs for all four hospitals. Constraints in the linear programming model require all outputs for the composite hospital to be *greater than or equal to* the outputs of County Hospital, the hospital being evaluated. If the inputs for the composite unit can be shown to be *less than* the inputs for County Hospital, the composite hospital is shown to have the same, or more, output for *less input*. In this case, the model shows that the composite hospital is more efficient than County Hospital. In other words, the hospital being evaluated is *less efficient* than the composite hospital. Because the composite hospital is based on all four hospitals, the hospital being evaluated can be judged *relatively inefficient* when compared to the other hospitals in the group.

DEA Linear Programming Model

To determine the weight that each hospital will have in computing the outputs and inputs for the composite hospital, we use the following decision variables:

wg = weight applied to inputs and outputs for General Hospital
wu = weight applied to inputs and outputs for University Hospital
wc = weight applied to inputs and outputs for County Hospital
ws = weight applied to inputs and outputs for State Hospital

The DEA approach requires that the sum of these weights equal 1. Thus, the first constraint is

$$wg + wu + wc + ws = 1$$

TABLE 5.2   ANNUAL SERVICES PROVIDED (OUTPUTS) BY THE FOUR HOSPITALS

	Hospital			
Output Measure	General	University	County	State
Medicare patient-days (1000s)	48.14	34.62	36.72	33.16
Non-Medicare patient-days (1000s)	43.10	27.11	45.98	56.46
Nurses trained	253	148	175	160
Interns trained	41	27	23	84

In general, every DEA linear programming model will include a constraint that requires the weights for the operating units to sum to 1.

As we stated previously, for each output measure, the output for the composite hospital is determined by computing a weighted average of the corresponding outputs for all four hospitals. For instance, for output measure 1, the number of patient days of service under Medicare, the output for the composite hospital is

$$\begin{array}{l}\text{Medicare patient-days} \\ \text{for Composite Hospital}\end{array} = \left(\begin{array}{l}\text{Medicare patient-days} \\ \text{for General Hospital}\end{array}\right)wg + \left(\begin{array}{l}\text{Medicare patient-days} \\ \text{for University Hospital}\end{array}\right)wu$$

$$+ \left(\begin{array}{l}\text{Medicare patient-days} \\ \text{for County Hospital}\end{array}\right)wc + \left(\begin{array}{l}\text{Medicare patient-days} \\ \text{for State Hospital}\end{array}\right)ws$$

Substituting the number of Medicare patient-days for each hospital as shown in Table 5.2, we obtain the following expression:

$$\begin{array}{l}\text{Medicare patient-days} \\ \text{for Composite Hospital}\end{array} = 48.14wg + 34.62wu + 36.72wc + 33.16ws$$

The other output measures for the composite hospital are computed in a similar fashion. Figure 5.1 provides a summary of the results.

For each of the four output measures, we need to write a constraint that requires the output for the composite hospital to be greater than or equal to the output for County Hospital. Thus, the general form of the output constraints is

$$\begin{array}{l}\text{Output for the} \\ \text{Composite Hospital}\end{array} \geq \begin{array}{l}\text{Output for} \\ \text{County Hospital}\end{array}$$

FIGURE 5.1   RELATIONSHIP BETWEEN THE OUTPUT MEASURES FOR THE FOUR HOSPITALS AND THE OUTPUT MEASURES FOR THE COMPOSITE HOSPITAL

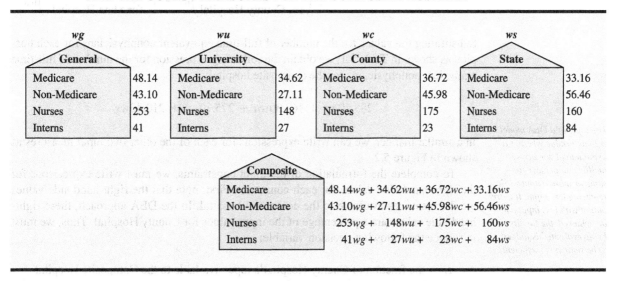

Because the number of Medicare patient-days for County Hospital is 36.72, the output constraint corresponding to the number of Medicare patient-days is

$$48.14wg + 34.62wu + 36.72wc + 33.16ws \geq 36.72$$

In a similar fashion, we formulated a constraint for each of the other three output measures, with the results as shown:

$$43.10wg + 27.11wu + 45.98wc + 56.46ws \geq 45.98 \quad \text{Non-Medicare}$$
$$253wg + 148wu + 175wc + 160ws \geq 175 \quad \text{Nurses}$$
$$41wg + 27wu + 23wc + 84ws \geq 23 \quad \text{Interns}$$

The four output constraints require the linear programming solution to provide weights that will make each output measure for the composite hospital greater than or equal to the corresponding output measure for County Hospital. Thus, if a solution satisfying the output constraints can be found, the composite hospital will have produced at least as much of each output as County Hospital.

Next, we need to consider the constraints needed to model the relationship between the inputs for the composite hospital and the resources available to the composite hospital. A constraint is required for each of the three input measures. The general form for the input constraints is as follows:

$$\begin{matrix} \text{Input for the} \\ \text{Composite Hospital} \end{matrix} \leq \begin{matrix} \text{Resources available to} \\ \text{the Composite Hospital} \end{matrix}$$

For each input measure, the input for the composite hospital is a weighted average of the corresponding input for each of the four hospitals. Thus, for input measure 1, the number of full-time equivalent nonphysicians, the input for the composite hospital is

$$\begin{matrix} \text{FTE nonphysicians} \\ \text{for Composite Hospital} \end{matrix} = \left(\begin{matrix} \text{FTE nonphysicians} \\ \text{for General Hospital} \end{matrix} \right) wg + \left(\begin{matrix} \text{FTE nonphysicians} \\ \text{for University Hospital} \end{matrix} \right) wu$$
$$+ \left(\begin{matrix} \text{FTE nonphysicians} \\ \text{for County Hospital} \end{matrix} \right) wc + \left(\begin{matrix} \text{FTE nonphysicians} \\ \text{for State Hospital} \end{matrix} \right) ws$$

Substituting the values for the number of full-time equivalent nonphysicians for each hospital as shown in Table 5.1, we obtain the following expression for the number of full-time equivalent nonphysicians for the composite hospital:

$$285.20wg + 162.30wu + 275.70wc + 210.40ws$$

The logic of a DEA model is to determine whether a hypothetical composite facility can achieve the same or more output while requiring less input. If more output with less input can be achieved, the facility being evaluated is judged to be relatively inefficient.

In a similar manner, we can write expressions for each of the other two input measures as shown in Figure 5.2.

To complete the formulation of the input constraints, we must write expressions for the right-hand-side values for each constraint. First, note that the right-hand-side values are the resources available to the composite hospital. In the DEA approach, these right-hand-side values are a percentage of the input values for County Hospital. Thus, we must introduce the following decision variable:

$$E = \text{the fraction of County Hospital's input available to the Composite Hospital}$$

FIGURE 5.2   RELATIONSHIP BETWEEN THE INPUT MEASURES FOR THE FOUR HOSPITALS AND THE INPUT MEASURES FOR THE COMPOSITE HOSPITAL

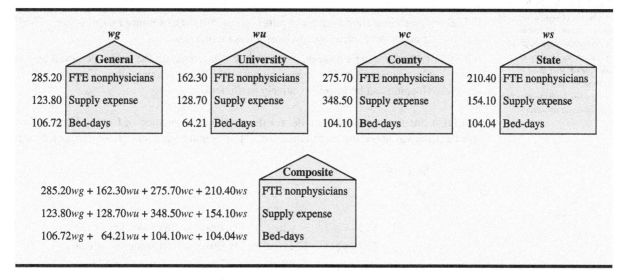

To illustrate the important role that E plays in the DEA approach, we show how to write the expression for the number of FTE nonphysicians available to the composite hospital. Table 5.1 shows that the number of FTE nonphysicians used by County Hospital was 275.70; thus, 275.70E is the number of FTE nonphysicians available to the composite hospital. If $E = 1$, the number of FTE nonphysicians available to the composite hospital is 275.70, the same as the number of FTE nonphysicians used by County Hospital. However, if E is greater than 1, the composite hospital would have available proportionally more nonphysicians, whereas if E is less than 1, the composite hospital would have available proportionally fewer FTE nonphysicians. Because of the effect that E has in determining the resources available to the composite hospital, E is referred to as the **efficiency index.**

We can now write the input constraint corresponding to the number of FTE nonphysicians available to the composite hospital:

$$285.50wg + 162.30wu + 275.70wc + 210.40ws \leq 275.70E$$

In a similar manner, we can write the input constraints for the supplies and bed-days available to the composite hospital. First, using the data in Table 5.1, we note that for each of these resources, the amount that is available to the composite hospital is 348.50E and 104.10E, respectively. Thus, the input constraints for the supplies and bed-days are written as follows:

$$123.80wg + 128.70wu + 348.50wc + 154.10ws \leq 348.50E \quad \text{Supplies}$$
$$106.72wg + 64.21wu + 104.10wc + 104.04ws \leq 104.10E \quad \text{Bed-days}$$

If a solution with $E < 1$ can be found, the composite hospital does not need as many resources as County Hospital needs to produce the same level of output.

The objective function for the DEA model is to minimize the value of E, which is equivalent to minimizing the input resources available to the composite hospital. Thus, the objective function is written as

$$\text{Min } E$$

The objective function in a DEA model is always Min E. The facility being evaluated (County Hospital in this example) can be judged relatively inefficient if the optimal solution provides E less than 1, indicating that the composite facility requires less in input resources.

The DEA efficiency conclusion is based on the optimal objective function value for E. The decision rule is as follows:

If $E = 1$, the composite hospital requires *as much input* as County Hospital does. There is no evidence that County Hospital is inefficient.

If $E < 1$, the composite hospital requires *less input* to obtain the output achieved by County Hospital. The composite hospital is more efficient; thus, County Hospital can be judged relatively inefficient.

The DEA linear programming model for the efficiency evaluation of County Hospital has five decision variables and eight constraints. The complete model is rewritten as follows:

$$
\begin{aligned}
\text{Min} \quad & E \\
\text{s.t.} \quad & \\
wg + wu + wc + ws &= 1 \\
48.14wg + 34.62wu + 36.72wc + 33.16ws &\geq 36.72 \\
43.10wg + 27.11wu + 45.98wc + 56.46ws &\geq 45.98 \\
253wg + 148wu + 175wc + 160ws &\geq 175 \\
41wg + 27wu + 23wc + 84ws &\geq 23 \\
285.20wg + 162.30wu + 275.70wc + 210.40ws &\leq 275.70E \\
123.80wg + 128.70wu + 348.50wc + 154.10ws &\leq 348.50E \\
106.72wg + 64.21wu + 104.10wc + 104.04ws &\leq 104.10E \\
E, wg, wu, wc, ws &\geq 0
\end{aligned}
$$

The optimal solution is shown in Figure 5.3. We first note that the value of the objective function shows that the efficiency score for County Hospital is 0.905. This score tells us that the composite hospital can obtain at least the level of each output that County Hospital obtains by having available no more than 90.5% of the input resources required by County Hospital. Thus, the composite hospital is more efficient, and the DEA analysis identified County Hospital as being relatively inefficient.

From the solution in Figure 5.3, we see that the composite hospital is formed from the weighted average of General Hospital ($wg = 0.212$), University Hospital ($wu = 0.260$), and State Hospital ($ws = 0.527$). Each input and output of the composite hospital is determined by the same weighted average of the inputs and outputs of these three hospitals.

The Slack/Surplus column provides some additional information about the efficiency of County Hospital compared to the composite hospital. Specifically, the composite hospital has at least as much of each output as County Hospital has (constraints 2–5) and provides 1.6 more nurses trained (surplus for constraint 4) and 37 more interns trained (surplus for constraint 5). The slack of zero from constraint 8 shows that the composite hospital uses approximately 90.5% of the bed-days used by County Hospital. The slack values for constraints 6 and 7 show that less than 90.5% of the FTE nonphysician and the supplies expense resources used at County Hospital are used by the composite hospital.

Clearly, the composite hospital is more efficient than County Hospital, and we are justified in concluding that County Hospital is relatively inefficient compared to the other hospitals in the group. Given the results of the DEA analysis, hospital administrators should examine operations to determine how County Hospital resources can be more effectively utilized.

FIGURE 5.3   THE SOLUTION FOR THE COUNTY HOSPITAL DATA ENVELOPMENT ANALYSIS PROBLEM

Optimal Objective Value =   0.90524

Variable	Value	Reduced Cost
wg	0.21227	0.00000
wu	0.26045	0.00000
wc	0.00000	0.09476
ws	0.52729	0.00000
E	0.90524	0.00000

Constraint	Slack/Surplus	Dual Value
1	0.00000	-0.23889
2	0.00000	0.01396
3	0.00000	0.01373
4	1.61539	0.00000
5	37.02707	0.00000
6	35.82408	0.00000
7	174.42242	0.00000
8	0.00000	-0.00961

Variable	Objective Coefficient	Allowable Increase	Allowable Decrease
wg	0.00000	0.44643	0.19991
wu	0.00000	0.36384	Infinite
wc	0.00000	Infinite	0.09476
ws	0.00000	0.17972	0.42671
E	1.00000	Infinite	1.00000

Constraint	RHS Value	Allowable Increase	Allowable Decrease
1	1.00000	0.01462	0.08491
2	36.72000	8.19078	0.23486
3	45.98000	7.30499	2.15097
4	175.00000	1.61539	Infinite
5	23.00000	37.02707	Infinite
6	0.00000	Infinite	35.82408
7	0.00000	Infinite	174.42242
8	0.00000	13.52661	Infinite

Summary of the DEA Approach

To use data envelopment analysis to measure the relative efficiency of County Hospital, we used a linear programming model to construct a hypothetical composite hospital based on the outputs and inputs for the four hospitals in the problem. The approach to solving other types of problems using DEA is similar. For each operating unit that we want to measure the efficiency of, we must formulate and solve a linear programming model similar to the linear program we solved to measure the relative efficiency of County Hospital. The following step-by-step procedure should help you in formulating a linear programming model for other types of DEA applications. Note that the operating unit that we want to measure the relative efficiency of is referred to as the *j*th operating unit.

Step 1. Define decision variables or weights (one for each operating unit) that can be used to determine the inputs and outputs for the composite operating unit.

Step 2. Write a constraint that requires the weights to sum to 1.

Step 3. For each output measure, write a constraint that requires the output for the composite operating unit to be greater than or equal to the corresponding output for the *j*th operating unit.

Step 4. Define a decision variable, E, which determines the fraction of the *j*th operating unit's input available to the composite operating unit.

Step 5. For each input measure, write a constraint that requires the input for the composite operating unit to be less than or equal to the resources available to the composite operating unit.

Step 6. Write the objective function as Min E.

NOTES AND COMMENTS

1. Remember that the goal of data envelopment analysis is to identify operating units that are relatively inefficient. The method *does not* necessarily identify the operating units that are *relatively efficient*. Just because the efficiency index is $E = 1$, we cannot conclude that the unit being analyzed is relatively efficient. Indeed, any unit that has the largest output on any one of the output measures cannot be judged relatively inefficient.

2. It is possible for DEA to show all but one unit to be relatively inefficient. Such would be the case if a unit producing the most of every output also consumes the least of every input. Such cases are extremely rare in practice.

3. In applying data envelopment analysis to problems involving a large group of operating units, practitioners have found that roughly 50% of the operating units can be identified as inefficient. Comparing each relatively inefficient unit to the units contributing to the composite unit may be helpful in understanding how the operation of each relatively inefficient unit can be improved.

5.2 REVENUE MANAGEMENT

Revenue management involves managing the short-term demand for a fixed perishable inventory in order to maximize the revenue potential for an organization. The methodology, originally developed for American Airlines, was first used to determine how many airline flight seats to sell at an early reservation discount fare and how many airline flight seats to sell at a full fare. By making the optimal decision for the number of discount-fare seats and the number of full-fare seats on each flight, the airline is able to increase its average number of passengers per flight and maximize the total revenue generated by the combined sale of discount-fare and full-fare seats. Today, all major airlines use some form of revenue management.

Given the success of revenue management in the airline industry, it was not long before other industries began using this approach. Revenue management systems often include pricing strategies, overbooking policies, short-term supply decisions, and the management of nonperishable assets. Application areas now include hotels, apartment rentals, car rentals, cruise lines, and golf courses. The Management Science in Action, Revenue Management at National Car Rental, discusses how National implemented revenue management.

MANAGEMENT SCIENCE IN ACTION

REVENUE MANAGEMENT AT NATIONAL CAR RENTAL*

During its recovery from a near liquidation in the mid-1990s, National Car Rental developed a revenue management system that uses linear programming and other analytical models to help manage rental car capacity, pricing, and reservations. The goal of the revenue management system is to develop procedures that identify unrealized revenue opportunities, improve utilization, and ultimately increase revenue for the company.

Management science models play a key role in revenue management at National. For instance, a linear programming model is used for length-of-rent control. An overbooking model identifies optimal overbooking levels subject to service level constraints, and a planned upgrade algorithm allows cars in a higher-priced class to be used to satisfy excess demand for cars in a lower-priced class.

Another model generates length-of-rent categories for each arrival day, which maximizes revenue. Pricing models are used to manage revenue by segmenting the market between business and leisure travel. For example, fares are adjusted to account for the fact that leisure travelers are willing to commit further in advance than business travelers and are willing to stay over a weekend.

The implementation of the revenue management system is credited with returning National Car Rental to profitability. In the first year of use, revenue management resulted in increased revenues of $56 million.

*Based on M. K. Geraghty and Ernest Johnson, "Revenue Management Saves National Car Rental," *Interfaces* 27, no. 1 (January/February 1997): 107–127.

The development of a revenue management system can be expensive and time-consuming, but the potential payoffs may be substantial. For instance, the revenue management system used at American Airlines generates nearly $1 billion in annual incremental revenue. To illustrate the fundamentals of revenue management, we will use a linear programming model to develop a revenue management plan for Leisure Air, a regional airline that provides service for Pittsburgh, Newark, Charlotte, Myrtle Beach, and Orlando.

Leisure Air has two Boeing 737-400 airplanes, one based in Pittsburgh and the other in Newark. Both airplanes have a coach section with a 132-seat capacity. Each morning the Pittsburgh-based plane flies to Orlando with a stopover in Charlotte, and the Newark-based plane flies to Myrtle Beach, also with a stopover in Charlotte. At the end of the day, both planes return to their home bases. To keep the size of the problem reasonable, we restrict our attention to the Pittsburgh–Charlotte, Charlotte–Orlando, Newark–Charlotte, and Charlotte–Myrtle Beach flight legs for the morning flights. Figure 5.4 illustrates the logistics of the Leisure Air problem situation.

Leisure Air uses two fare classes: a discount-fare Q class and a full-fare Y class. Reservations using the discount-fare Q class must be made 14 days in advance and must include a Saturday night stay in the destination city. Reservations using the full-fare Y class may be made anytime, with no penalty for changing the reservation at a later date. To determine the itinerary and fare alternatives that Leisure Air can offer its customers, we must consider not only the origin and the destination of each flight, but also the fare class. For instance, possible products include Pittsburgh to Charlotte using Q class, Newark to Orlando using Q class, Charlotte to Myrtle Beach using Y class, and so on. Each product is referred to as an origin-destination-itinerary fare (ODIF). For May 5, Leisure Air established fares and developed forecasts of customer demand for each of 16 ODIFs. These data are shown in Table 5.3.

Suppose that on April 4 a customer calls the Leisure Air reservation office and requests a Q class seat on the May 5 flight from Pittsburgh to Myrtle Beach. Should Leisure Air

FIGURE 5.4   LOGISTICS OF THE LEISURE AIR PROBLEM

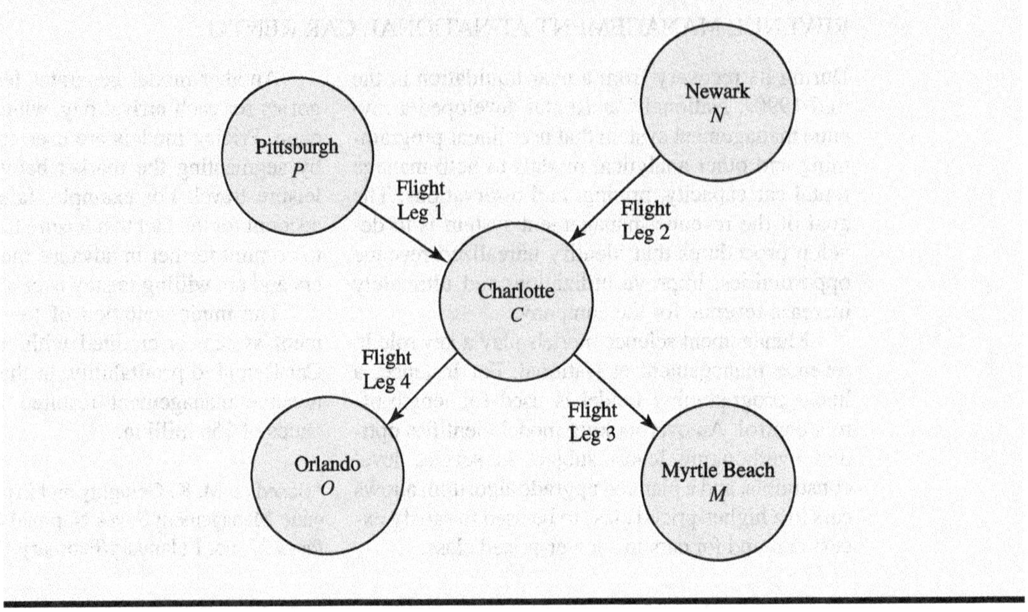

Pittsburgh
P

Newark
N

Flight Leg 1

Flight Leg 2

Charlotte
C

Flight Leg 4

Flight Leg 3

Orlando
O

Myrtle Beach
M

TABLE 5.3   FARE AND DEMAND DATA FOR 16 LEISURE AIR
ORIGIN-DESTINATION-ITINERARY FARES (ODIFs)

ODIF	Origin	Destination	Fare Class	ODIF Code	Fare	Forecasted Demand
1	Pittsburgh	Charlotte	Q	PCQ	$178	33
2	Pittsburgh	Myrtle Beach	Q	PMQ	268	44
3	Pittsburgh	Orlando	Q	POQ	228	45
4	Pittsburgh	Charlotte	Y	PCY	380	16
5	Pittsburgh	Myrtle Beach	Y	PMY	456	6
6	Pittsburgh	Orlando	Y	POY	560	11
7	Newark	Charlotte	Q	NCQ	199	26
8	Newark	Myrtle Beach	Q	NMQ	249	56
9	Newark	Orlando	Q	NOQ	349	39
10	Newark	Charlotte	Y	NCY	385	15
11	Newark	Myrtle Beach	Y	NMY	444	7
12	Newark	Orlando	Y	NOY	580	9
13	Charlotte	Myrtle Beach	Q	CMQ	179	64
14	Charlotte	Myrtle Beach	Y	CMY	380	8
15	Charlotte	Orlando	Q	COQ	224	46
16	Charlotte	Orlando	Y	COY	582	10

accept the reservation? The difficulty in making this decision is that even though Leisure Air may have seats available, the company may not want to accept this reservation at the Q class fare of $268, especially if it is possible to sell the same reservation later at the Y class fare of $456. Thus, determining how many Q and Y class seats to make available are important decisions that Leisure Air must make in order to operate its reservation system.

To develop a linear programming model that can be used to determine how many seats Leisure Air should allocate to each fare class, we need to define 16 decision variables, one for each origin-destination-itinerary fare alternative. Using P for Pittsburgh, N for Newark, C for Charlotte, M for Myrtle Beach, and O for Orlando, the decision variables take the following form:

PCQ = number of seats allocated to Pittsburgh–Charlotte Q class

PMQ = number of seats allocated to Pittsburgh–Myrtle Beach Q class

POQ = number of seats allocated to Pittsburgh–Orlando Q class

PCY = number of seats allocated to Pittsburgh–Charlotte Y class
$\vdots$

NCQ = number of seats allocated to Newark–Charlotte Q class
$\vdots$

COY = number of seats allocated to Charlotte–Orlando Y class

The objective is to maximize total revenue. Using the fares shown in Table 5.3, we can write the objective function for the linear programming model as follows:

$$\text{Max} \quad 178PCQ + 268PMQ + 228POQ + 380PCY + 456PMY + 560POY$$
$$+ 199NCQ + 249NMQ + 349NOQ + 385NCY + 444NMY$$
$$+ 580NOY + 179CMQ + 380CMY + 224COQ + 582COY$$

Next, we must write the constraints. We need two types of constraints: capacity and demand. We begin with the capacity constraints.

Consider the Pittsburgh–Charlotte flight leg in Figure 5.4. The Boeing 737-400 airplane has a 132-seat capacity. Three possible final destinations for passengers on this flight (Charlotte, Myrtle Beach, or Orlando) and two fare classes (Q and Y) provide six ODIF alternatives: (1) Pittsburgh–Charlotte Q class, (2) Pittsburgh–Myrtle Beach Q class, (3) Pittsburgh–Orlando Q class, (4) Pittsburgh–Charlotte Y class, (5) Pittsburgh–Myrtle Beach Y class, and (6) Pittsburgh–Orlando Y class. Thus, the number of seats allocated to the Pittsburgh–Charlotte flight leg is $PCQ + PMQ + POQ + PCY + PMY + POY$. With the capacity of 132 seats, the capacity constraint is as follows:

$$PCQ + PMQ + POQ + PCY + PMY + POY \leq 132 \quad \text{Pittsburgh–Charlotte}$$

The capacity constraints for the Newark–Charlotte, Charlotte–Myrtle Beach, and Charlotte–Orlando flight legs are developed in a similar manner. These three constraints are as follows:

$$NCQ + NMQ + NOQ + NCY + NMY + NOY \leq 132 \quad \text{Newark–Charlotte}$$
$$PMQ + PMY + NMQ + NMY + CMQ + CMY \leq 132 \quad \text{Charlotte–Myrtle Beach}$$
$$POQ + POY + NOQ + NOY + COQ + COY \leq 132 \quad \text{Charlotte–Orlando}$$

The demand constraints limit the number of seats for each ODIF based on the forecasted demand. Using the demand forecasts in Table 5.3, 16 demand constraints must be added to the model. The first four demand constraints are as follows:

$$PCQ \leq 33 \quad \text{Pittsburgh–Charlotte Q class}$$
$$PMQ \leq 44 \quad \text{Pittsburgh–Myrtle Beach Q class}$$
$$POQ \leq 45 \quad \text{Pittsburgh–Orlando Q class}$$
$$PCY \leq 16 \quad \text{Pittsburgh–Charlotte Y class}$$

The complete linear programming model with 16 decision variables, 4 capacity constraints, and 16 demand constraints is as follows:

$$\text{Max} \quad 178PCQ + 268PMQ + 228POQ + 380PCY + 456PMY + 560POY$$
$$+ 199NCQ + 249NMQ + 349NOQ + 385NCY + 444NMY$$
$$+ 580NOY + 179CMQ + 380CMY + 224COQ + 582COY$$

s.t.

$$PCQ + PMQ + POQ + PCY + PMY + POY \leq 132 \quad \text{Pittsburgh–Charlotte}$$
$$NCQ + NMQ + NOQ + NCY + NMY + NOY \leq 132 \quad \text{Newark–Charlotte}$$
$$PMQ + PMY + NMQ + NMY + CMQ + CMY \leq 132 \quad \text{Charlotte–Myrtle Beach}$$
$$POQ + POY + NOQ + NOY + COQ + COY \leq 132 \quad \text{Charlotte–Orlando}$$

$$
\left.
\begin{aligned}
PCQ &\leq 33 \\
PMQ &\leq 44 \\
POQ &\leq 45 \\
PCY &\leq 16 \\
PMY &\leq 6 \\
POY &\leq 11 \\
NCQ &\leq 26 \\
NMQ &\leq 56 \\
NOQ &\leq 39 \\
NCY &\leq 15 \\
NMY &\leq 7 \\
NOY &\leq 9 \\
CMQ &\leq 64 \\
CMY &\leq 8 \\
COQ &\leq 46 \\
COY &\leq 10
\end{aligned}
\right\} \quad \text{Demand Constraints}
$$

$$PCQ, PMQ, POQ, PCY, \dots, COY \geq 0$$

The optimal solution to the Leisure Air revenue management problem is shown in Figure 5.5. The value of the optimal solution is $103,103. The optimal solution shows that $PCQ = 33$, $PMQ = 44$, $POQ = 22$, $PCY = 16$, and so on. Thus, to maximize revenue, Leisure Air should allocate 33 Q class seats to Pittsburgh–Charlotte, 44 Q class seats to Pittsburgh–Myrtle Beach, 22 Q class seats to Pittsburgh–Orlando, 16 Y class seats to Pittsburgh–Charlotte, and so on.

Over time, reservations will come into the system and the number of remaining seats available for each ODIF will decrease. For example, the optimal solution allocated 44 Q class seats to Pittsburgh–Myrtle Beach. Suppose that two weeks prior to the departure date of May 5, all 44 seats have been sold. Now, suppose that a new customer calls the Leisure Air reservation office and requests a Q class seat for the Pittsburgh–Myrtle Beach flight. Should Leisure Air accept the new reservation even though it exceeds the original 44-seat allocation? The dual value for the Pittsburgh–Myrtle Beach Q class demand constraint will provide information that will help a Leisure Air reservation agent make this decision.

Constraint 6, $PMQ \leq 44$, restricts the number of Q class seats that can be allocated to Pittsburgh–Myrtle Beach to 44 seats. In Figure 5.5 we see that the dual value for constraint 6 is $85. The dual value tells us that if one more Q class seat were available from Pittsburgh

Dual values tell reservation agents the additional revenue associated with overbooking each ODIF.

FIGURE 5.5 THE SOLUTION FOR THE LEISURE AIR REVENUE MANAGEMENT PROBLEM

Optimal Objective Value =   103103.00000

Variable	Value	Reduced Cost
PCQ	33.00000	0.00000
PMQ	44.00000	0.00000
POQ	22.00000	0.00000
PCY	16.00000	0.00000
PMY	6.00000	0.00000
POY	11.00000	0.00000
NCQ	26.00000	0.00000
NMQ	36.00000	0.00000
NOQ	39.00000	0.00000
NCY	15.00000	0.00000
NMY	7.00000	0.00000
NOY	9.00000	0.00000
CMQ	31.00000	0.00000
CMY	8.00000	0.00000
COQ	41.00000	0.00000
COY	10.00000	0.00000

Constraint	Slack/Surplus	Dual Value
1	0.00000	4.00000
2	0.00000	70.00000
3	0.00000	179.00000
4	0.00000	224.00000
5	0.00000	174.00000
6	0.00000	85.00000
7	23.00000	0.00000
8	0.00000	376.00000
9	0.00000	273.00000
10	0.00000	332.00000
11	0.00000	129.00000
12	20.00000	0.00000
13	0.00000	55.00000
14	0.00000	315.00000
15	0.00000	195.00000
16	0.00000	286.00000
17	33.00000	0.00000
18	0.00000	201.00000
19	5.00000	0.00000
20	0.00000	358.00000

WEB file

Leisure

to Myrtle Beach, revenue would increase by $85. This increase in revenue is referred to as the bid price for this origin-destination-itinerary fare. In general, the bid price for an ODIF tells a Leisure Air reservation agent the value of one additional reservation once a particular ODIF has been sold out.

By looking at the dual values for the demand constraints in Figure 5.5, we see that the highest dual value (bid price) is $376 for constraint 8, $PCY \leq 16$. This constraint corresponds to the Pittsburgh–Charlotte Y class itinerary. Thus, if all 16 seats allocated to this itinerary have been sold, accepting another reservation will provide additional revenue of $376. Given this revenue contribution, a reservation agent would most likely accept the additional reservation even if it resulted in an overbooking of the flight. Other dual values for the demand constraints show a value of $358 for constraint 20 ($COY$) and a value of $332 for constraint 10 ($POY$). Thus, accepting additional reservations for the Charlotte–Orlando Y class and the Pittsburgh–Orlando Y class itineraries is a good choice for increasing revenue.

A revenue management system like the one at Leisure Air must be flexible and adjust to the ever-changing reservation status. Conceptually, each time a reservation is accepted for an origin-destination-itinerary fare that is at its capacity, the linear programming model should be updated and re-solved to obtain new seat allocations along with the revised bid price information. In practice, updating the allocations on a real-time basis is not practical because of the large number of itineraries involved. However, the bid prices from a current solution and some simple decision rules enable reservation agents to make decisions that improve the revenue for the firm. Then, on a periodic basis such as once a day or once a week, the entire linear programming model can be updated and re-solved to generate new seat allocations and revised bid price information.

5.3 PORTFOLIO MODELS AND ASSET ALLOCATION

In 1952 Harry Markowitz showed how to develop a portfolio that optimized the trade-off between risk and return. His work earned him a share of the 1990 Nobel Prize in Economics.

Asset allocation refers to the process of determining how to allocate investment funds across a variety of asset classes such as stocks, bonds, mutual funds, real estate, and cash. Portfolio models are used to determine the percentage of the investment funds that should be made in each asset class. The goal is to create a portfolio that provides the best balance between risk and return. In this section we show how linear programming models can be developed to determine an optimal portfolio involving a mix of mutual funds. The first model is designed for conservative investors who are strongly averse to risk. The second model is designed for investors with a variety of risk tolerances.

A Portfolio of Mutual Funds

Hauck Investment Services designs annuities, IRAs, 401(k) plans, and other investment vehicles for investors with a variety of risk tolerances. Hauck would like to develop a portfolio model that can be used to determine an optimal portfolio involving a mix of six mutual funds. A variety of measures can be used to indicate risk, but for portfolios of financial assets all are related to variability in return. Table 5.4 shows the annual return (%) for five 1-year periods for the six mutual funds. Year 1 represents a year in which the annual returns are good for all the mutual funds. Year 2 is also a good year for most of the mutual funds. But year 3 is a bad year for the small-cap value fund; year 4 is a bad year for the intermediate-term bond fund; and year 5 is a bad year for four of the six mutual funds.

It is not possible to predict exactly the returns for any of the funds over the next 12 months, but the portfolio managers at Hauck Financial Services think that the returns for the five years shown in Table 5.4 are scenarios that can be used to represent the possibilities for the next year. For the purpose of building portfolios for their clients, Hauck's portfolio

TABLE 5.4   MUTUAL FUND PERFORMANCE IN FIVE SELECTED YEARS (USED AS PLANNING SCENARIOS FOR THE NEXT 12 MONTHS)

Mutual Fund	Annual Return (%)				
	Year 1	Year 2	Year 3	Year 4	Year 5
Foreign Stock	10.06	13.12	13.47	45.42	−21.93
Intermediate-Term Bond	17.64	3.25	7.51	−1.33	7.36
Large-Cap Growth	32.41	18.71	33.28	41.46	−23.26
Large-Cap Value	32.36	20.61	12.93	7.06	−5.37
Small-Cap Growth	33.44	19.40	3.85	58.68	−9.02
Small-Cap Value	24.56	25.32	−6.70	5.43	17.31

managers will choose a mix of these six mutual funds and assume that one of the five possible scenarios will describe the return over the next 12 months.

Conservative Portfolio

One of Hauck's portfolio managers has been asked to develop a portfolio for the firm's conservative clients who express a strong aversion to risk. The manager's task is to determine the proportion of the portfolio to invest in each of the six mutual funds so that the portfolio provides the best return possible with a minimum risk. Let us see how linear programming can be used to develop a portfolio for these clients.

In portfolio models, risk is minimized by diversification. To see the value of diversification, suppose we first consider investing the entire portfolio in just one of the six mutual funds. Assuming the data in Table 5.4 represent the possible outcomes over the next 12 months, the clients run the risk of losing 21.93% over the next 12 months if the entire portfolio is invested in the foreign stock mutual fund. Similarly, if the entire portfolio is invested in any one of the other five mutual funds, the clients will also run the risk of losing money; that is, the possible losses are 1.33% for the intermediate-term bond fund, 23.26% for the large-cap growth fund, 5.37% for the large-cap value fund, 9.02% for the small-cap growth fund, and 6.70% for the small-cap value fund. Let us now see how we can construct a diversified portfolio of these mutual funds that minimizes the risk of a loss.

To determine the proportion of the portfolio that will be invested in each of the mutual funds we use the following decision variables:

FS = proportion of portfolio invested in the foreign stock mutual fund

IB = proportion of portfolio invested in the intermediate-term bond fund

LG = proportion of portfolio invested in the large-cap growth fund

LV = proportion of portfolio invested in the large-cap value fund

SG = proportion of portfolio invested in the small-cap growth fund

SV = proportion of portfolio invested in the small-cap value fund

Because the sum of these proportions must equal 1, we need the following constraint:

$$FS + IB + LG + LV + SG + SV = 1$$

The other constraints are concerned with the return that the portfolio will earn under each of the planning scenarios in Table 5.4.

The portfolio return over the next 12 months depends on which of the possible scenarios (years 1 through 5) in Table 5.4 occurs. Let $R1$ denote the portfolio return if the scenario represented by year 1 occurs, $R2$ denote the portfolio return if the scenario represented by year 2 occurs, and so on. The portfolio returns for the five planning scenarios are as follows:

Scenario 1 return:

$$R1 = 10.06FS + 17.64IB + 32.41LG + 32.36LV + 33.44SG + 24.56SV$$

Scenario 2 return:

$$R2 = 13.12FS + 3.25IB + 18.71LG + 20.61LV + 19.40SG + 25.32SV$$

Scenario 3 return:

$$R3 = 13.47FS + 7.51IB + 33.28LG + 12.93LV + 3.85SG - 6.70SV$$

Scenario 4 return:

$$R4 = 45.42FS - 1.33IB + 41.46LG + 7.06LV + 58.68SG + 5.43SV$$

Scenario 5 return:

$$R5 = -21.93FS + 7.36IB - 23.26LG - 5.37LV - 9.02SG + 17.31SV$$

Let us now introduce a variable M to represent the minimum return for the portfolio. As we have already shown, one of the five possible scenarios in Table 5.4 will determine the portfolio return. Thus, the minimum possible return for the portfolio will be determined by the scenario which provides the worst case return. But we don't know which of the scenarios will turn out to represent what happens over the next 12 months. To ensure that the return under each scenario is at least as large as the minimum return M, we must add the following minimum-return constraints:

$R1 \geq M$	Scenario 1 minimum return
$R2 \geq M$	Scenario 2 minimum return
$R3 \geq M$	Scenario 3 minimum return
$R4 \geq M$	Scenario 4 minimum return
$R5 \geq M$	Scenario 5 minimum return

Substituting the values shown previously for $R1$, $R2$, and so on, provides the following five minimum-return constraints:

$10.06FS + 17.64IB + 32.41LG + 32.36LV + 33.44SG + 24.56SV \geq M$	Scenario 1
$13.12FS + 3.25IB + 18.71LG + 20.61LV + 19.40SG + 25.32SV \geq M$	Scenario 2
$13.47FS + 7.51IB + 33.28LG + 12.93LV + 3.85SG - 6.70SV \geq M$	Scenario 3
$45.42FS + 1.33IB + 41.46LG + 7.06LV + 58.68SG + 5.43SV \geq M$	Scenario 4
$-21.93FS + 7.36IB - 23.26LG - 5.37LV - 9.02SG + 17.31SV \geq M$	Scenario 5

To develop a portfolio that provides the best return possible with a minimum risk, we need to maximize the minimum return for the portfolio. Thus, the objective function is simple:

$$\text{Max } M$$

With the five minimum-return constraints present, the optimal value of M will equal the value of the minimum return scenario. The objective is to maximize the value of the minimum return scenario.

Because the linear programming model was designed to maximize the minimum return over all the scenarios considered, we refer to it as the *maximin* model. The complete maximin model for the problem of choosing a portfolio of mutual funds for a conservative, risk-averse investor involves seven variables and six constraints. The complete maximin model is written as follows:

Max M

s.t.

$$10.06FS + 17.64IB + 32.41LG + 32.36LV + 33.44SG + 24.56SV \geq M$$
$$13.12FS + 3.25IB + 18.71LG + 20.61LV + 19.40SG + 25.32SV \geq M$$
$$13.47FS + 7.51IB + 33.28LG + 12.93LV + 3.85SG - 6.70SV \geq M$$
$$45.42FS + 1.33IB + 41.46LG + 7.06LV + 58.68SG + 5.43SV \geq M$$
$$-21.93FS + 7.36IB - 23.26LG - 5.37LV - 9.02SG + 17.31SV \geq M$$
$$FS + IB + LG + LV + SG + SV = 1$$
$$M, FS, IB, LG, LV, SG, SV \geq 0$$

Note that we have written the constraint that requires the sum of the proportion of the portfolio invested in each mutual fund as the last constraint in the model. In this way, when we interpret the computer solution of the model, constraint 1 will correspond to planning scenario 1, constraint 2 will correspond to planning scenario 2, and so on.

The optimal solution to the Hauck maximin model is shown in Figure 5.6. The optimal value of the objective function is 6.445; thus, the optimal portfolio will earn 6.445% in the worst-case scenario. The optimal solution calls for 55.4% of the portfolio to be invested in the intermediate-term bond fund, 13.2% of the portfolio to be invested in the large-cap growth fund, and 31.4% of the portfolio to be invested in the small-cap value fund.

Because we do not know at the time of solving the model which of the five possible scenarios will occur, we cannot say for sure that the portfolio return will be 6.445%. However, using the surplus variables, we can learn what the portfolio return will be under each of the scenarios. Constraints 3, 4, and 5 correspond to scenarios 3, 4, and 5 (years 3, 4, and 5 in Table 5.4). The surplus variables for these constraints are zero to indicate that the portfolio return will be $M = 6.445\%$ if any of these three scenarios occur. The surplus variable for constraint 1 is 15.321, indicating that the portfolio return will exceed $M = 6.445$ by 15.321 if scenario 1 occurs. So, if scenario 1 occurs, the portfolio return will be 6.445% + 15.321% = 21.766%. Referring to the surplus variable for constraint 2, we see that the portfolio return will be 6.445% + 5.785% = 12.230% if scenario 2 occurs.

We must also keep in mind that in order to develop the portfolio model, Hauck made the assumption that over the next 12 months one of the five possible scenarios in Table 5.4 will occur. But we also recognize that the actual scenario that occurs over the next 12 months may be different from the scenarios Hauck considered. Thus, Hauck's experience and judgment in selecting representative scenarios plays a key part in determining how valuable the model recommendations will be for the client.

Moderate Risk Portfolio

Hauck's portfolio manager would like to also construct a portfolio for clients who are willing to accept a moderate amount of risk in order to attempt to achieve better returns. Suppose

FIGURE 5.6 THE SOLUTION FOR THE HAUCK MAXIMIN PORTFOLIO MODEL

```
Optimal Objective Value =              6.44516

    Variable              Value          Reduced Cost
  --------------      --------------    ----------------
        FS              0.00000             -6.76838
        IB              0.55357              0.00000
        LG              0.13204              0.00000
        LV              0.00000             -3.15571
        SG              0.00000             -2.76428
        SV              0.31439              0.00000
        M               6.44516              0.00000


   Constraint         Slack/Surplus         Dual Value
  --------------      --------------    ----------------
        1               15.32060             0.00000
        2                5.78469             0.00000
        3                0.00000            -0.39703
        4                0.00000            -0.11213
        5                0.00000            -0.49084
        6                0.00000             6.44516
```

that clients in this risk category are willing to accept some risk but do not want the annual return for the portfolio to drop below 2%. By setting $M = 2$ in the minimum-return constraints in the maximin model, we can constrain the model to provide a solution with an annual return of at least 2%. The minimum-return constraints needed to provide an annual return of at least 2% are as follows:

$R1 \geq 2$ Scenario 1 minimum return
$R2 \geq 2$ Scenario 2 minimum return
$R3 \geq 2$ Scenario 3 minimum return
$R4 \geq 2$ Scenario 4 minimum return
$R5 \geq 2$ Scenario 5 minimum return

In addition to these five minimum-return constraints, we still need the constraint that requires that the sum of the proportions invested in the separate mutual funds is 1.

$$FS + IB + LG + LV + SG + SV = 1$$

A different objective is needed for this portfolio optimization problem. A common approach is to maximize the expected value of the return for the portfolio. For instance, if we assume that the planning scenarios are equally likely, we would assign a probability of 0.20 to each scenario. In this case, the objective function is to maximize

Expected value of the return $= 0.2R1 + 0.2R2 + 0.2R3 + 0.2R4 + 0.2R5$

Because the objective is to maximize the expected value of the return, we write Hauck's objective as follows:

$$\text{Max} \quad 0.2R1 + 0.2R2 + 0.2R3 + 0.2R4 + 0.2R5$$

The complete linear programming formulation for this version of the portfolio optimization problem involves 11 variables and 11 constraints.

$$\text{Max} \quad 0.2R1 + 0.2R2 + 0.2R3 + 0.2R4 + 0.2R5 \tag{5.1}$$

s.t.

$$10.06FS + 17.64IB + 32.41LG + 32.36LV + 33.44SG + 24.56SV = R1 \tag{5.2}$$
$$13.12FS + 3.25IB + 18.71LG + 20.61LV + 19.40SG + 25.32SV = R2 \tag{5.3}$$
$$13.47FS + 7.51IB + 33.28LG + 12.93LV + 3.85SG + 6.70SV = R3 \tag{5.4}$$
$$45.42FS - 1.33IB + 41.46LG + 7.06LV + 58.68SG - 5.43SV = R4 \tag{5.5}$$
$$-21.93FS + 7.36IB + 23.26LG - 5.37LV + 9.02SG + 17.31SV = R5 \tag{5.6}$$

$$R1 \geq 2 \tag{5.7}$$
$$R2 \geq 2 \tag{5.8}$$
$$R3 \geq 2 \tag{5.9}$$
$$R4 \geq 2 \tag{5.10}$$
$$R5 \geq 2 \tag{5.11}$$

$$FS + IB + LG + LV + SG + SV = 1 \tag{5.12}$$

$$FS, IB, LG, LV, SG, SV \geq 0 \tag{5.13}$$

NOTES AND COMMENTS

1. In this formulation, unlike in the previous maximin model, we keep the variables $R1$, $R2$, $R3$, $R4$, $R5$ in the model. The variables $R1$, $R2$, $R3$, $R4$, and $R5$ defined in constraints (5.2)–(5.6) are often called *definitional variables* (a variable that is defined in terms of other variables). These variables could be substituted out of the formulation, resulting in a smaller model. However, we believe that when formulating a model, clarity is of utmost importance and definitional variables often make the model easier to read and understand. Furthermore, stating the model as we have eliminates the need for the user to do the arithmetic calculations necessary to simplify the model. These calculations can lead to error and are best left to the software.

2. Most optimization codes have *preprocessing routines* that will eliminate and substitute out the definitional variables in constraints (5.2)–(5.6). Indeed, the optimization model actually solved by the solver may differ considerably from the actual model formulation. This is why we recommend the user focus on clarity when model building.

3. When building a model such as (5.1)–(5.13) in Excel, we recommend defining adjustable cells for only investment variables, that is, FS, IB, LG, LV, SG, and SV. There will be cells with formulas that calculate the returns given in (5.2)–(5.6), but they need not be adjustable. The Excel Solver model should have only six adjustable cells. See the Excel Web file Moderate Risk that illustrates this point.

The optimal solution is shown in Figure 5.7. The optimal allocation is to invest 10.8% of the portfolio in a large-cap growth mutual fund, 41.5% in a small-cap growth mutual fund, and 47.7% in a small-cap value mutual fund. The objective function value shows that this allocation provides a maximum expected return of 17.33%. From the surplus variables, we see that

FIGURE 5.7   THE SOLUTION FOR THE MODERATE RISK PORTFOLIO MODEL

Optimal Objective Value =   17.33172

Variable	Value	Reduced Cost
R1	29.09269	0.00000
R2	22.14934	0.00000
R3	2.00000	0.00000
R4	31.41658	0.00000
R5	2.00000	0.00000
FS	0.00000	12.24634
IB	0.00000	7.14602
LG	0.10814	0.00000
LV	0.00000	4.35448
SG	0.41484	0.00000
SV	0.47702	0.00000

Constraint	Slack/Surplus	Dual Value
1	0.00000	-0.20000
2	0.00000	-0.20000
3	0.00000	-0.41594
4	0.00000	-0.20000
5	0.00000	-0.59363
6	27.09269	0.00000
7	20.14934	0.00000
8	0.00000	-0.21594
9	29.41658	0.00000
10	0.00000	-0.39363
11	0.00000	18.55087

WEB file

Moderate Risk

the portfolio return will only be 2% if scenarios 3 or 5 occur (constraints 8 and 10 are binding). The returns will be excellent if scenarios 1, 2, or 4 occur: The portfolio return will be 29.093% if scenario 1 occurs, 22.149% if scenario 2 occurs, and 31.417% if scenario 4 occurs.

The moderate risk portfolio exposes Hauck's clients to more risk than the maximin portfolio developed for a conservative investor. With the maximin portfolio, the worst-case scenario provided a return of 6.44%. With this moderate risk portfolio, the worst-case scenarios (scenarios 3 and 5) only provide a return of 2%, but the portfolio also provides the possibility of higher returns.

The formulation we have developed for a moderate risk portfolio can be modified to account for other risk tolerances. If an investor can tolerate the risk of no return, the right-hand sides of the minimum-return constraints would be set to 0. If an investor can tolerate a *loss* of 3%, the right-hand side of the minimum-return constraints would be set equal to –3. In practice, we would expect Hauck to provide the client with a sensitivity analysis that gives the expected return as a function of minimum risk. Linear programming models can be solved quickly, so it is certainly practical to solve a series of linear programs where the minimum return is varied from, for example, –5% to 15% in increments of 1%, and the optimal expected return is calculated for each value of minimum return. Clients can then select an expected value and minimum return combination that they feel is most consistent with their risk preference.

ASSET ALLOCATION AND VARIABLE ANNUITIES*

Insurance companies use portfolio models for asset allocation to structure a portfolio for their clients who purchase variable annuities. A variable annuity is an insurance contract that involves an accumulation phase and a distribution phase. In the accumulation phase the individual either makes a lump sum contribution or contributes to the annuity over a period of time. In the distribution phase the investor receives payments either in a lump sum or over a period of time. The distribution phase usually occurs at retirement, but because a variable annuity is an insurance product, a benefit is paid to a beneficiary should the annuitant die before or during the distribution period.

Most insurance companies selling variable annuities offer their clients the benefit of an asset allocation model to help them decide how to allocate their investment among a family of mutual funds. Usually the client fills out a questionnaire to assess his or her level of risk tolerance. Then, given that risk tolerance, the insurance company's asset allocation model recommends how the client's investment should be allocated over a family of mutual funds. American Skandia, a Prudential Financial Company, markets variable annuities that provide the types of services mentioned. A questionnaire is used to assess the client's risk tolerance, and the Morningstar Asset Allocator is used to develop portfolios for five levels of risk tolerance. Clients with low levels of risk tolerance are guided to portfolios consisting of bond funds and T-bills, and the most risk-tolerant investors are guided to portfolios consisting of a large proportion of growth stock mutual funds. Investors with intermediate, or moderate, risk tolerances are guided to portfolios that may consist of suitable mixtures of value and growth stock funds as well as some bond funds.

*Based on information provided by James R. Martin of the Martin Company, a financial services company.

5.4 GAME THEORY

In **game theory,** two or more decision makers, called players, compete against each other. Each player selects one of several strategies without knowing in advance the strategy selected by the other player or players. The combination of the competing strategies provides the value of the game to the players. Game theory applications have been developed for situations in which the competing players are teams, companies, political candidates, and contract bidders.

In this section, we describe **two-person, zero-sum games.** *Two-person* means that two players participate in the game. *Zero-sum* means that the gain (or loss) for one player is equal to the loss (or gain) for the other player. As a result, the gain and loss balance out (resulting in a zero-sum) for the game. What one player wins, the other player loses. Let us demonstrate a two-person, zero-sum game and its solution by considering two companies competing for market share.

Competing for Market Share

Suppose that two companies are the only manufacturers of a particular product; they compete against each other for market share. In planning a marketing strategy for the coming year, each company will select one of three strategies designed to take market share from the other company. The three strategies, which are assumed to be the same for both companies, are as follows:

Strategy 1: Increase advertising.

Strategy 2: Provide quantity discounts.

Strategy 3: Extend warranty.

TABLE 5.5 PAYOFF TABLE SHOWING THE PERCENTAGE GAIN IN MARKET SHARE FOR COMPANY A

		Company B		
		Increase Advertising b_1	Quantity Discounts b_2	Extend Warranty b_3
	Increase Advertising a_1	4	3	2
Company A	Quantity Discounts a_2	−1	4	1
	Extend Warranty a_3	5	−2	0

A payoff table showing the percentage gain in the market share for Company A for each combination of strategies is shown in Table 5.5. Because it is a zero-sum game, any gain in market share for Company A is a loss in market share for Company B.

In interpreting the entries in the table, we see that if Company A increases advertising (a_1) and Company B increases advertising (b_1), Company A will come out ahead with an increase in market share of 4%, while Company B will have a decrease in market share of 4%. On the other hand, if Company A provides quantity discounts (a_2) and Company B increases advertising (b_1), Company A will lose 1% of market share, while Company B will gain 1% of market share. Therefore, Company A wants to maximize the payoff that is its increase in market share. Company B wants to minimize the payoff because the increase in market share for Company A is the decrease in market share for Company B.

This market-share game meets the requirements of a two-person, zero-sum game. The two companies are the two players, and the zero-sum occurs because the gain (or loss) in market share for Company A is the same as the loss (or gain) in market share for Company B. Each company will select one of its three alternative strategies. Because of the planning horizon, each company will have to select its strategy before knowing the other company's strategy. What is the optimal strategy for each company?

The logic of game theory assumes that each player has the same information and will select a strategy that provides the best possible payoff from its point of view. Suppose Company A selects strategy a_1. Market share increases of 4%, 3%, or 2% are possible depending upon Company B's strategy. At this point, Company A assumes that Company B will select the strategy that is best for it. Thus, if Company A selects strategy a_1, Company A assumes Company B will select its best strategy b_3, which will limit Company A's increase in market share to 2%. Continuing with this logic, Company A analyzes the game by protecting itself against the strategy that may be taken by Company B. Doing so, Company A identifies the minimum payoff for each of its strategies, which is the minimum value in each row of the payoff table. These row minimums are shown in Table 5.6.

The player seeking to maximize the value of the game selects a maximin strategy.

Considering the entries in the Row Minimum column, we see that Company A can be guaranteed an increase in market share of at least 2% by selecting strategy a_1. Strategy a_2 could result in a decrease in market share of 1% and strategy a_3 could result in a decrease in market share of 2%. After comparing the row minimum values, Company A selects the strategy that provides the *maximum* of the row *minimum* values. This is called a **maximin** strategy. Thus, Company A selects strategy a_1 as its optimal strategy; an increase in market share of at least 2% is guaranteed.

Let us now look at the payoff table from the point of view of the other player, Company B. The entries in the payoff table represent gains in market share for Company A, which

TABLE 5.6 PAYOFF TABLE WITH ROW MINIMUMS

		Company B			
		Increase Advertising b_1	Quantity Discounts b_2	Extend Warranty b_3	Row Minimum
	Increase Advertising a_1	4	3	2	② ←Maximum
Company A	Quantity Discounts a_2	−1	4	1	−1
	Extend Warranty a_3	5	−2	0	−2

correspond to losses in market share for Company B. Consider what happens if Company B selects strategy b_1. Company B market share decreases of 4%, –1%, and 5% are possible. Under the assumption that Company A will select the strategy that is best for it, Company B assumes Company A will select strategy a_3, resulting in a gain in market share of 5% for Company A and a loss in market share of 5% for Company B. At this point, Company B analyzes the game by protecting itself against the strategy taken by Company A. Doing so, Company B identifies the maximum payoff to Company A for each of its strategies b_1, b_2, and b_3. This payoff value is the maximum value in each column of the payoff table. These column maximums are shown in Table 5.7.

The player seeking to minimize the value of the game selects a minimax strategy.

Considering the entries in the Column Maximum row, Company B can be guaranteed a decrease in market share of no more than 2% by selecting the strategy b_3. Strategy b_1 could result in a decrease in market share of 5% and strategy b_2 could result in a decrease in market share of 4%. After comparing the column maximum values, Company B selects the strategy that provides the *minimum* of the column *maximum* values. This is called a **minimax** strategy. Thus, Company B selects b_3 as its optimal strategy. Company B has guaranteed that Company A cannot gain more than 2% in market share.

Identifying a Pure Strategy Solution

If it is optimal for both players to select one strategy and stay with that strategy regardless of what the other player does, the game has a **pure strategy** solution. Whenever the maximum of the row minimums *equals* the minimum of the column maximums, the players cannot improve their payoff by changing to a different strategy. The game is said to have a

TABLE 5.7 PAYOFF TABLE WITH COLUMN MAXIMUMS

		Company B			
		Increase Advertising b_1	Quantity Discounts b_2	Extend Warranty b_3	Row Minimum
	Increase Advertising a_1	4	3	2	② ←Maximum
Company A	Quantity Discounts a_2	−1	4	1	−1
	Extend Warranty a_3	5	−2	0	−2
	Column Maximum	5	4	② ←Minimum	

saddle point, or an equilibrium point. Thus, a pure strategy is the optimal strategy for the players. The requirement for a pure strategy solution is as follows:

A Game Has a Pure Strategy Solution If:

Maximum (Row minimums) = Minimum (Column maximums)

Because this equality is the case in our example, the solution to the game is for Company A to increase advertising (strategy a_1) and for Company B to extend the warranty (strategy b_3). Company A's market share will increase by 2% and Company B's market share will decrease by 2%.

With Company A selecting its pure strategy a_1, let us see what happens if Company B tries to change from its pure strategy b_3. Company A's market share will increase 4% if b_1 is selected or will increase 3% if b_2 is selected. Company B must stay with its pure strategy b_3 to limit Company A to a 2% increase in market share. Similarly, with Company B selecting its pure strategy b_3, let us see what happens if Company A tries to change from its pure strategy a_1. Company A's market share will increase only 1% if a_2 is selected or will not increase at all if a_3 is selected. Company A must stay with its pure strategy a_1 in order to keep its 2% increase in market share. Thus, even if one of the companies discovers its opponent's pure strategy in advance, neither company can gain any advantage by switching from its pure strategy.

If a pure strategy solution exists, it is the optimal solution to the game. The following steps can be used to determine when a game has a pure strategy solution and to identify the optimal pure strategy for each player:

Analyze a two-person, zero-sum game by first checking to see whether a pure strategy solution exists.

Step 1. Compute the minimum payoff for each row (Player A).
Step 2. For Player A, select the strategy that provides the maximum of the row minimums.
Step 3. Compute the maximum payoff for each column (Player B).
Step 4. For Player B, select the strategy that provides the minimum of the column maximums.
Step 5. If the maximum of the row minimums is equal to the minimum of the column maximums, this value is the value of the game and a pure strategy solution exists. The optimal pure strategy for Player A is identified in Step 2, and the optimal pure strategy for Player B is identified in Step 4.

If the maximum of the row minimums *does not equal* the minimum of the column maximums, a pure strategy solution does not exist. In this case, a mixed strategy solution becomes optimal. In the following discussion, we define a mixed strategy solution and show how linear programming can be used to identify the optimal mixed strategy for each player.

Identifying a Mixed Strategy Solution

Let us continue with the two-company market-share game and consider a slight modification in the payoff table as shown in Table 5.8. Only one payoff has changed. If both Company A and Company B choose the extended warranty strategy, the payoff to Company A is now a 5% increase in market share rather than the previous 0%. The row minimums do not change, but the column maximums do. Note that the column maximum for strategy b_3 is 5% instead of the previous 2%.

504

TABLE 5.8 MODIFIED PAYOFF TABLE SHOWING THE PERCENTAGE GAIN IN MARKET SHARE FOR COMPANY A

| | | Company B | | | |
		Increase Advertising b_1	Quantity Discounts b_2	Extend Warranty b_3	Row Minimum
Company A	Increase Advertising a_1	4	3	2	② ←Maximum
	Quantity Discounts a_2	−1	4	1	−1
	Extend Warranty a_3	5	−2	5	−2
	Column Maximum	5	④	5	

↑
Minimum

In analyzing the game to determine whether a pure strategy solution exists, we find that the maximum of the row minimums is 2% while the minimum of the row maximums is 4%. Because these values are not equal, a pure strategy solution does not exist. In this case, it is not optimal for each company to be predictable and select a pure strategy regardless of what the other company does. The optimal solution is for both players to adopt a mixed strategy.

With a **mixed strategy,** each player selects its strategy according to a probability distribution. In the market share example, each company will first determine an optimal probability distribution for selecting whether to increase advertising, provide quantity discounts, or extend warranty. Then, when the game is played, each company will use its probability distribution to randomly select one of its three strategies.

First, consider the game from the point of view of Company A. Company A will select one of its three strategies based on the following probabilities:

$PA1$ = the probability that Company A selects strategy a_1

$PA2$ = the probability that Company A selects strategy a_2

$PA3$ = the probability that Company A selects strategy a_3

The expected value, computed by multiplying each payoff by its probability and summing, can be interpreted as a long-run average payoff for a mixed strategy.

Using these probabilities for Company A's mixed strategy, what happens if Company B selects strategy b_1? Using the payoffs in the b_1 column of Table 5.8, we see Company A will experience an increase in market share of 4% with probability $PA1$, a decrease in market share of 1% with probability $PA2$, and an increase in market share of 5% with probability $PA3$. Weighting each payoff by its probability and summing provides the **expected value** of the increase in market share for Company A. If Company B selects strategy b_1, this expected value, referred to as the *expected gain* if strategy b_1 is selected, can be written as follows:

$$EG(b_1) = 4PA1 - 1PA2 = 5PA3$$

The expression for the expected gain in market share for Company A for each Company B strategy is provided in Table 5.9.

TABLE 5.9   EXPECTED GAIN IN MARKET SHARE FOR COMPANY A FOR EACH
COMPANY B STRATEGY

Company B Strategy	Expected Gain for Company A
b_1	$EG(b_1) = 4PA1 - 1PA2 + 5PA3$
b_2	$EG(b_2) = 3PA1 + 4PA2 - 2PA3$
b_3	$EG(b_3) = 2PA1 + 1PA2 + 5PA3$

For example, if Company A uses a mixed strategy with equal probabilities ($PA1 = \frac{1}{3}$, $PA2 = \frac{1}{3}$, and $PA3 = \frac{1}{3}$), Company A's expected gain in market share for each Company B strategy is as follows:

$$EG(b_1) = 4PA1 - 1PA2 + 5PA3 = 4(\tfrac{1}{3}) - 1(\tfrac{1}{3}) + 5(\tfrac{1}{3}) = \tfrac{8}{3} = 2.67$$

$$EG(b_2) = 3PA1 + 4PA2 - 2PA3 = 3(\tfrac{1}{3}) + 4(\tfrac{1}{3}) - 2(\tfrac{1}{3}) = \tfrac{5}{3} = 1.67$$

$$EG(b_3) = 2PA1 + 1PA2 + 5PA3 = 2(\tfrac{1}{3}) + 1(\tfrac{1}{3}) + 5(\tfrac{1}{3}) = \tfrac{8}{3} = 2.67$$

The logic of game theory assumes that if Company A uses a mixed strategy, Company B will select the strategy that will minimize Company A's expected gain. Using these results, Company A assumes Company B will select strategy b_2 and limit Company A's expected gain in market share to 1.67%. Because Company A's pure strategy a_1 provides a 2% increase in market share, the mixed strategy with equal probabilities, $PA1 = \frac{1}{3}$, $PA2 = \frac{1}{3}$, and $PA3 = \frac{1}{3}$, is not the optimal strategy for Company A.

Let us show how Company A can use linear programming to find its optimal mixed strategy. Our goal is to find probabilities, $PA1$, $PA2$, and $PA3$, that maximize the expected gain in market share for Company A regardless of the strategy selected by Company B. In effect, Company A will protect itself against any strategy selected by Company B by being sure its expected gain in market share is as large as possible even if Company B selects its own optimal strategy.

Given the probabilities $PA1$, $PA2$, and $PA3$ and the expected gain expressions in Table 5.9, game theory assumes that Company B will select a strategy that provides the minimum expected gain for Company A. Thus, Company B will select b_1, b_2, or b_3 based on

$$\text{Min } \{EG(b_1), EG(b_2), EG(b_3)\}$$

The player seeking to maximize the value of the game selects a maximin strategy by maximizing the minimum expected gain.

When Company B selects its strategy, the value of the game will be the minimum expected gain. This strategy will minimize Company A's expected gain in market share.

Company A will select its optimal mixed strategy using a *maximin* strategy, which will maximize the minimum expected gain. This objective is written as follows:

$$\text{Max } [\text{Min } \{EG(b_1), EG(b_2), EG(b_3)\}]$$

Company A seeks to maximize the minimum *EG* Company B can obtain

Company B will select a strategy to minimize the *EG* for Company A

Define *GAINA* to be the optimal expected gain in market share for Company A. Because Company B will select a strategy that minimizes this expected gain, we know *GAINA* is equal to Min $\{EG(b_1), EG(b_2), EG(b_3)\}$. Thus, the individual expected gains, $EG(b_1)$, $EG(b_2)$, and $EG(b_3)$, must all be *greater than or equal to GAINA*. If Company B selects strategy b_1, we know

$$EG(b_1) \geq GAINA$$

Using the probabilities $PA1$, $PA2$, and $PA3$ and the expected gain expression in Table 5.9, this condition can be written as follows:

$$4PA1 - 1PA2 + 5PA3 \geq GAINA$$

Similarly, for Company B strategies b_2 and b_3, the fact that both $EG(b_2) \geq GAINA$ and $EG(b_3) \geq GAINA$ provides the following two expressions:

$$3PA1 + 4PA2 - 2PA3 \geq GAINA$$
$$2PA1 + 1PA2 + 5PA3 \geq GAINA$$

In addition, we know that the sum of the Company A's mixed strategy probabilities must equal 1.

$$PA1 + PA2 + PA3 = 1$$

Finally, realizing that the objective of Company A is to maximize its expected gain, $GAINA$, we have the following linear programming model. Solving this linear program will provide Company A's optimal mixed strategy.

Max	$GAINA$	
s.t.		Company B strategy
	$4PA1 - 1PA2 + 5PA3 \geq GAINA$	(Strategy b_1)
	$3PA1 + 4PA2 - 2PA3 \geq GAINA$	(Strategy b_2)
	$2PA1 + 1PA2 + 5PA3 \geq GAINA$	(Strategy b_3)
	$PA1 + PA2 + PA3 \quad\quad = 1$	
	$PA1, PA2, PA3, GAINA \geq 0$	

The solution of Company A's linear program is shown in Figure 5.8.

From Figure 5.8, we see Company A's optimal mixed strategy is to increase advertising (a_1) with a probability of 0.875 and extend warranty (a_3) with a probability of 0.125. Company A should never provide quantity discounts (a_2) because $PA2 = 0$. The expected value of this mixed strategy is a 2.375% increase in market share for Company A.

Let us show what happens to the expected gain if Company A uses this optimal mixed strategy. Company A's expected gain for each Company B strategy follows:

$$EG(b_1) = 4PA1 - 1PA2 + 5PA3 = 4(0.875) - 1(0) + 5(0.125) = 4.125$$
$$EG(b_2) = 3PA1 + 4PA2 - 2PA3 = 3(0.875) + 4(0) - 2(0.125) = 2.375$$
$$EG(b_3) = 2PA1 + 1PA2 + 5PA3 = 2(0.875) + 1(0) + 5(0.125) = 2.375$$

Company B will minimize Company A's expected gain by selecting either strategy b_2 or b_3. However, Company A has selected its optimal mixed strategy by maximizing this

FIGURE 5.8   THE SOLUTION FOR COMPANY A'S OPTIMAL MIXED STRATEGY

```
Optimal Objective Value =                    2.37500

      Variable              Value              Reduced Costs
   --------------        --------------        --------------
       PA1                 0.87500                0.00000
       PA2                 0.00000               -0.25000
       PA3                 0.12500                0.00000
       GAINA               2.37500                0.00000

    Constraint           Slack/Surplus           Dual Value
   --------------        --------------        --------------
        1                  1.75000                0.00000
        2                  0.00000               -0.37500
        3                  0.00000               -0.62500
        4                  0.00000                2.37500
```

minimum expected gain. Thus, Company A obtains an expected gain in market share of 2.375% regardless of the strategy selected by Company B. The mixed strategy with $PA1 = 0.875$, $PA2 = 0.0$, and $PA3 = 0.125$ is the optimal strategy for Company A. The expected gain of 2.375% is better than Company A's best pure strategy (a_1), which provides a 2% increase in market share.

Now consider the game from the point of view of Company B. Company B will select one of its strategies based on the following probabilities:

$PB1 =$ the probability that Company B selects strategy b_1

$PB2 =$ the probability that Company B selects strategy b_2

$PB3 =$ the probability that Company B selects strategy b_3

Based on these probabilities for Company B's mixed strategy, what happens if Company A selects strategy a_1? Using the payoffs in the a_1 row of Table 5.8, Company B will experience a decrease in market share of 4% with probability $PB1$, a decrease in market share of 3% with probability $PB2$, and a decrease in market share of 2% with probability $PB3$. If Company A selects strategy a_1, the expected value, referred to as Company B's *expected loss* if strategy a_1 is selected, can be written as follows:

$$EL(a_1) = 4PB1 + 3PB2 + 2PB3$$

The expression for the expected loss in market share for Company B for each Company A strategy is provided in Table 5.10.

Let us show how Company B can use linear programming to find its optimal mixed strategy. Our goal is to find the probabilities, $PB1$, $PB2$, and $PB3$, that minimize the expected loss in market share to Company B regardless of the strategy selected by Company A. In effect, Company B will protect itself from any strategy selected by Company A by being sure its expected loss in market share is as small as possible even if Company A selects its own optimal strategy.

TABLE 5.10   EXPECTED LOSS IN MARKET SHARE FOR COMPANY B FOR EACH COMPANY A STRATEGY

Company A Strategy	Expected Loss for Company B
a_1	$4PB1 + 3PB2 + 2PB3$
a_2	$-1PB1 + 4PB2 + 1PB3$
a_3	$5PB1 - 2PB2 + 5PB3$

Given the probabilities $PB1$, $PB2$, and $PB3$ and the expected loss expressions in Table 5.10, game theory assumes that Company A will select a strategy that provides the maximum expected loss for Company B. Thus, Company A will select a_1, a_2, or a_3 based on

$$\text{Max } \{EL(a_1), EL(a_2), EL(a_3)\}$$

When Company A selects its strategy, the value of the game will be the expected loss, which will maximize Company B's expected loss in market share.

Company B will select its optimal mixed strategy using a *minimax* strategy to minimize the maximum expected loss. This objective is written as follows:

The player seeking to minimize the value of the game selects a minimax strategy by minimizing the maximum expected loss.

$$\text{Min } [\text{Max } \{EL(a_1), EL(a_2), EL(a_3)\}]$$

Company B seeks to maximize the minimum EL Company A can obtain

Company A will select a strategy to minimize the EL for Company B

Define $LOSSB$ to be the optimal expected loss in market share for Company B. Because Company A will select a strategy that maximizes this expected loss, we know $LOSSB$ is equal to Max $\{EL(a_1), EL(a_2), EL(a_3)\}$. Thus, the individual expected losses, $EL(a_1)$, $EL(a_2)$, and $EL(a_3)$, must all be *less than or equal to LOSSB*. If Company A selects strategy, a_1, we know

$$EL(a_1) \le LOSSB$$

Using the probabilities $PB1$, $PB2$, and $PB3$ and the expected loss expression for $EL(a_1)$ in Table 5.10, this condition can be written as follows:

$$4PB1 + 3PB2 + 2PB3 \le LOSSB$$

Similarly, for Company A strategies a_2 and a_3, the fact that both $EL(a_2) \le LOSSB$ and $EL(a_3) \le LOSSB$ provides the following two expressions:

$$-1PB1 + 4PB2 + 1PB3 \le LOSSB$$
$$5PB1 - 2PB2 + 5PB3 \le LOSSB$$

In addition, we know that the sum of the Company B's mixed strategy probabilities must equal 1.

$$PB1 + PB2 + PB3 = 1$$

FIGURE 5.9   THE SOLUTION FOR COMPANY B'S OPTIMAL MIXED STRATEGY

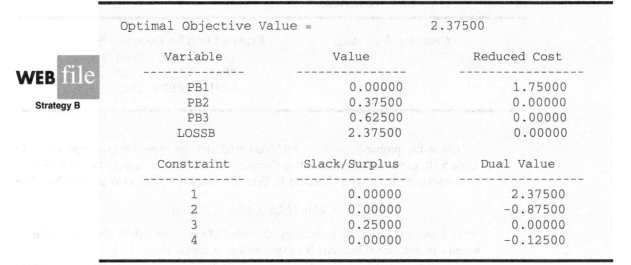

```
Optimal Objective Value =                    2.37500

        Variable              Value            Reduced Cost
     --------------       --------------      ----------------
           PB1               0.00000              1.75000
           PB2               0.37500              0.00000
           PB3               0.62500              0.00000
           LOSSB             2.37500              0.00000

        Constraint        Slack/Surplus          Dual Value
     --------------       --------------      ----------------
            1                0.00000              2.37500
            2                0.00000             -0.87500
            3                0.25000              0.00000
            4                0.00000             -0.12500
```

WEB file

Strategy B

Finally, realizing that the objective of Company B is to minimize its expected loss, *LOSSB*, we have the following linear programming model. Solving this linear program will provide Company B's optimal mixed strategy.

Min   *LOSSB*

s.t.   Company A strategy

$$4PB1 + 3PB2 + 2PB3 \leq LOSSB \quad \text{(Strategy } a_1)$$

$$-1PB1 + 4PB2 + 1PB3 \leq LOSSB \quad \text{(Strategy } a_2)$$

$$5PB1 - 2PB2 + 5PB3 \leq LOSSB \quad \text{(Strategy } a_3)$$

$$PB1 + PB2 + PB3 \qquad = 1$$

$$PB1, PB2, PB3, LOSSB \geq 0$$

The solution of Company B's linear program is shown in Figure 5.9.

From Figure 5.9, we see Company B's optimal mixed strategy is to provide quantity discounts (b_2) with a probability of 0.375 and extend warranty (b_3) with a probability of 0.625. Company B should not increase advertising (b_1), because $PB1 = 0$. The expected value or expected loss of this mixed strategy is 2.375%. Note that the expected loss of 2.375% of the market share for Company B is the same as the expected gain in market share for Company A. The mixed strategy solution shows the zero-sum for the expected payoffs.

Let us show what happens to the expected loss if Company B uses this optimal mixed strategy. Company B's expected loss for each Company A strategy follows:

$$EL(a_1) = 4PB1 + 3PB2 + 2PB3 = 4(0) + 3(0.375) + 2(0.625) = 2.375$$

$$EL(a_2) = -1PB1 + 4PB2 + 1PB3 = -1(0) + 4(0.375) + 1(0.625) = 2.125$$

$$EL(a_3) = 5PB1 - 2PB2 + 5PB3 = 5(0) - 2(0.375) + 5(0.625) = 2.375$$

Company A will maximize Company B's expected loss by selecting either strategy a_1 or a_3. However, Company B has selected its optimal mixed strategy by minimizing this maximum expected loss. Thus, Company B obtains an expected loss in market share of 2.375% regardless of the strategy selected by Company A. The mixed strategy with $PB1 = 0.0$, $PB2 = 0.375$, and $PB3 = 0.625$ is the optimal strategy for Company B. The expected loss of 2.375% is better than Company B's best pure strategy (b_2), which provides a 4% loss in market share.

The optimal mixed strategy solution with a value of 2.375% is an equilibrium solution. Given Company A's mixed strategy probabilities, Company B cannot improve the value of the game by changing $PB1$, $PB2$, or $PB3$. Likewise, given Company B's mixed strategy probabilities, Company A cannot improve the value of the game by changing $PA1$, $PA2$, or $PA3$. In general, the solution to the linear program will provide an equilibrium optimal mixed strategy solution for the game.

With a mixed strategy game, only solve the linear program for one of the players. Provided the value of the game is greater than zero, the absolute value of the dual values provides the optimal mixed strategy solution for the other player.

Let us conclude this linear programming application by making some observations and suggestions about using linear programming to solve mixed strategy two-person, zero-sum games. First of all, consider the dual value for constraint 2 in the solution of the Company A linear program in Figure 5.8. This dual value is –0.375. Recall that constraint 2 provides Company A's expected gain if Company B selects strategy b_2. The *absolute value* of the dual value is Company B's optimal probability for this strategy. Thus, we know $PB2 = 0.375$ without having to solve the Company B linear program. Using the absolute value of the dual values for the Company A linear program in Figure 5.8, we know that the optimal mixed strategy solution for Company B is $PB1 = 0.0$, $PB2 = 0.375$, and $PB3 = 0.625$. Therefore, when a two-person, zero-sum game has a mixed strategy, we only need to solve the linear program for one of the players. The optimal mixed strategy for the other player can be found by using the absolute value of the dual values.

Finally, note that a nonnegativity constraint in the linear program for Company A requires the value of the game, *GAINA*, to be greater than or equal to 0. A similar nonnegativity constraint in the linear program for Company B requires the value of the game, *LOSSB*, to be greater than or equal to 0. Because the value of the game in our example was 2.375%, we met these nonnegativity requirements. However, consider a two-person, zero-sum game where the payoff table contains several negative payoffs for player A. It may turn out that when player A selects an optimal mixed strategy, a negative value of the game is the best the player can do. In this case *GAINA* and *LOSSB* would be negative, which causes the linear program to have an infeasible solution.

If this condition exists or may exist, the following strategy can be used to modify the game and ensure that the linear program has a feasible solution. Define a constant c as follows:

If the value of a mixed strategy game may be negative, this procedure will guarantee that the linear program used to determine the optimal mixed strategy will have a feasible solution.

$$c = \text{the absolute value of the largest negative payoff for player A}$$

A revised payoff table can be created by adding c to each payoff, turning it into an equivalent two-person, zero-sum game. Because the revised payoff table contains no negative payoffs, the nonnegativity constraint for the value of the game will be satisfied and a feasible solution will exist for the linear program. More importantly, the optimal mixed strategy using the revised payoffs *will be the same* as the optimal mixed strategy for the original game. By subtracting c from the optimal objective function value for the game with the revised payoffs, you will obtain the objective function value for the original game.

NOTES AND COMMENTS

1. The analysis of a two-person, zero-sum game begins with checking to see whether a pure strategy solution exists. If the maximum of the row minimums for player A, V_A, is not equal to the minimum the column maximums for player B, V_B, a pure strategy solution does not exist. At this point, we can also conclude that a mixed strategy solution is optimal and that the value of the game will be *between* V_A and V_B. For example, in our mixed strategy market-share game, the maximum of the row minimums was 2% and the minimum of the column maximums was 4%. Thus, we can conclude that a mixed strategy solution exists and that the value of the game is between 2% and 4%. We would know this result before solving the mixed strategy linear program.

   If the maximum of the row minimums, V_A, is positive and the minimum of the column maximums, V_B, is positive, we know that the value of the mixed strategy game will be positive. In this case, it is not necessary to revise the payoff table by the constant c to obtain a feasible linear programming solution. However, if one or both V_A and V_B are negative, the value of the mixed strategy game can be negative. In this case, it is desirable to revise the payoff table by adding the constant c to all payoffs prior to solving the linear program.

2. The linear programming formulation presented in this section used nonnegativity constraints $GAINA \geq 0$ and $LOSSB \geq 0$ so that the two-person, mixed strategy game could be solved with traditional linear programming software. If you are using software such as LINGO or Excel, these variables do not have to be nonnegative. In this case, eliminate the nonnegative requirements and make $GAINA$ and $LOSSB$ unrestricted in sign. This treatment guarantees that the linear program will have a feasible solution and eliminates the need to add a constant to the payoffs in situations where $GAINA$ and $LOSSB$ may be negative.

SUMMARY

In this chapter we presented selected advanced linear programming applications. In particular, we applied linear programming to evaluating the performance of hospitals, maximizing revenue for airlines, constructing mutual fund portfolios, and competing for market share. In practice, most of the modeling effort in these types of linear programming applications involves clearly understanding the problem, stating the problem mathematically, and then finding reliable data in the format required by the model.

GLOSSARY

Data envelopment analysis (DEA) A linear programming application used to measure the relative efficiency of operating units with the same goals and objectives.

Hypothetical composite A weighted average of outputs and inputs of all operating units with similar goals.

Efficiency index Percentage of an individual operating unit's resources that are available to the composite operating unit.

Game theory A decision-making situation in which two or more decision makers compete by each selecting one of several strategies. The combination of the competing strategies provides the value of the game to the players.

Two-person, zero-sum game A game with two players in which the gain to one player is equal to the loss to the other player.

Maximin strategy   A strategy where the player seeking to maximize the value of the game selects the strategy that maximizes the minimum payoff obtainable by the other player.

Minimax strategy   A strategy where the player seeking to minimize the value of the game selects the strategy that minimizes the maximum payoff obtainable by the other player.

Pure strategy   When one of the available strategies is optimal and the player always selects this strategy regardless of the strategy selected by the other player.

Saddle point   A condition that exists when pure strategies are optimal for both players. Neither player can improve the value of the game by changing from the optimal pure strategy.

Mixed strategy   When a player randomly selects its strategy based on a probability distribution. The strategy selected can vary each time the game is played.

Expected value   In a mixed strategy game, a value computed by multiplying each payoff by its probability and summing. It can be interpreted as the long-run average payoff for the mixed strategy.

PROBLEMS

Note: The following problems have been designed to give you an understanding and appreciation of the broad range of problems that can be formulated as linear programs. You should be able to formulate a linear programming model for each of the problems. However, you will need access to a linear programming computer package to develop the solutions and make the requested interpretations.

1. In Section 5.1 data envelopment analysis was used to evaluate the relative efficiencies of four hospitals. Data for three input measures and four output measures were provided in Tables 5.1 and 5.2.
   a. Use these data to develop a linear programming model that could be used to evaluate the performance of General Hospital.
   b. The following solution is optimal. Does the solution indicate that General Hospital is relatively inefficient?

Objective Function Value = 1.000

Variable	Value	Reduced Costs
E	1.000	0.000
WG	1.000	0.000
WU	0.000	0.000
WC	0.000	0.331
WS	0.000	0.215

   c. Explain which hospital or hospitals make up the composite unit used to evaluate General Hospital and why.

2. Data envelopment analysis can measure the relative efficiency of a group of hospitals. The following data from a particular study involving seven teaching hospitals include three input measures and four output measures:
   a. Formulate a linear programming model so that data envelopment analysis can be used to evaluate the performance of hospital D.

b. Solve the model.

c. Is hospital D relatively inefficient? What is the interpretation of the value of the objective function?

Hospital	Input Measures		
	Full-Time Equivalent Nonphysicians	Supply Expense (1000s)	Bed-Days Available (1000s)
A	310.0	134.60	116.00
B	278.5	114.30	106.80
C	165.6	131.30	65.52
D	250.0	316.00	94.40
E	206.4	151.20	102.10
F	384.0	217.00	153.70
G	530.1	770.80	215.00

Hospital	Output Measures			
	Patient-Days (65 or older) (1000s)	Patient-Days (under 65) (1000s)	Nurses Trained	Interns Trained
A	55.31	49.52	291	47
B	37.64	55.63	156	3
C	32.91	25.77	141	26
D	33.53	41.99	160	21
E	32.48	55.30	157	82
F	48.78	81.92	285	92
G	58.41	119.70	111	89

d. How many patient-days of each type are produced by the composite hospital?

e. Which hospitals would you recommend hospital D consider emulating to improve the efficiency of its operation?

3. Refer again to the data presented in Problem 2.

a. Formulate a linear programming model that can be used to perform data envelopment analysis for hospital E.

b. Solve the model.

c. Is hospital E relatively inefficient? What is the interpretation of the value of the objective function?

d. Which hospitals are involved in making up the composite hospital? Can you make a general statement about which hospitals will make up the composite unit associated with a unit that is not inefficient?

4. The Ranch House, Inc., operates five fast-food restaurants. Input measures for the restaurants include weekly hours of operation, full-time equivalent staff, and weekly supply expenses. Output measures of performance include average weekly contribution to profit,

514

market share, and annual growth rate. Data for the input and output measures are shown in the following tables:

	Input Measures		
Restaurant	Hours of Operation	FTE Staff	Supplies ($)
Bardstown	96	16	850
Clarksville	110	22	1400
Jeffersonville	100	18	1200
New Albany	125	25	1500
St. Matthews	120	24	1600

	Output Measures		
Restaurant	Weekly Profit	Market Share (%)	Growth Rate (%)
Bardstown	$3800	25	8.0
Clarksville	$4600	32	8.5
Jeffersonville	$4400	35	8.0
New Albany	$6500	30	10.0
St. Matthews	$6000	28	9.0

   a. Develop a linear programming model that can be used to evaluate the performance of the Clarksville Ranch House restaurant.

   b. Solve the model.

   c. Is the Clarksville Ranch House restaurant relatively inefficient? Discuss.

   d. Where does the composite restaurant have more output than the Clarksville restaurant? How much less of each input resource does the composite restaurant require when compared to the Clarksville restaurant?

   e. What other restaurants should be studied to find suggested ways for the Clarksville restaurant to improve its efficiency?

5. Reconsider the Leisure Airlines problem from Section 5.2. The demand forecasts shown in Table 5.3 represent Leisure Air's best estimates of demand. But because demand cannot be forecasted perfectly, the number of seats actually sold for each origin-destination-itinerary fare (ODIF) may turn out to be smaller or larger than forecasted. Suppose that Leisure Air believes that economic conditions have improved and that their original forecast may be too low. To account for this possibility, Leisure Air is considering switching the Boeing 737-400 airplanes that are based in Pittsburgh and Newark with Boeing 757-200 airplanes that Leisure Air has available in other markets. The Boeing 757-200 airplane has a seating capacity of 158 in the coach section.

   a. Because of scheduling conflicts in other markets, suppose that Leisure Air is only able to obtain one Boeing 757-200. Should the larger plane be based in Pittsburgh or in Newark? Explain.

   b. Based upon your answer in part (a), determine a new allocation for the ODIFs. Briefly summarize the major differences between the new allocation using one Boeing 757-200 and the original allocation summarized in Figure 5.5.

   c. Suppose that two Boeing 757-200 airplanes are available. Determine a new allocation for the ODIFs using the two larger airplanes. Briefly summarize the major differences between the new allocation using two Boeing 757-200 airplanes and the original allocation shown in Figure 5.5.

   d. Consider the new solution obtained in part (b). Which ODIF has the highest bid price? What is the interpretation for this bid price?

6. Reconsider the Leisure Airlines problem from Section 5.2. Suppose that as of May 1 the following number of seats have been sold:

ODIF	1	2	3	4	5	6	7	8	9	10	11	12	13	14	15	16
Seats Sold	25	44	18	12	5	9	20	33	37	11	5	8	27	6	35	7

a. Determine how many seats are still available for sale on each flight leg.
b. Using the original demand forecasted for each ODIF, determine the remaining demand for each ODIF.
c. Revise the linear programming model presented in Section 5.2 to account for the number of seats currently sold and a demand of one additional seat for the Pittsburgh–Myrtle Beach Q class ODIF. Resolve the linear programming model to determine a new allocation schedule for the ODIFs.

7. Hanson Inn is a 96-room hotel located near the airport and convention center in Louisville, Kentucky. When a convention or a special event is in town, Hanson increases its normal room rates and takes reservations based on a revenue management system. The Classic Corvette Owners Association scheduled its annual convention in Louisville for the first weekend in June. Hanson Inn agreed to make at least 50% of its rooms available for convention attendees at a special convention rate in order to be listed as a recommended hotel for the convention. Although the majority of attendees at the annual meeting typically request a Friday and Saturday two-night package, some attendees may select a Friday night only or a Saturday night only reservation. Customers not attending the convention may also request a Friday and Saturday two-night package, or make a Friday night only or Saturday night only reservation. Thus, six types of reservations are possible: Convention customers/two-night package; convention customers/Friday night only; convention customers/Saturday night only; regular customers/two-night package; regular customers/Friday night only; and regular customers/Saturday night only. The cost for each type of reservation is shown here:

	Two-Night Package	Friday Night Only	Saturday Night Only
Convention	$225	$123	$130
Regular	$295	$146	$152

The anticipated demand for each type of reservation is as follows:

	Two-Night Package	Friday Night Only	Saturday Night Only
Convention	40	20	15
Regular	20	30	25

Hanson Inn would like to determine how many rooms to make available for each type of reservation in order to maximize total revenue.

a. Define the decision variables and state the objective function.
b. Formulate a linear programming model for this revenue management application.
c. What are the optimal allocation and the anticipated total revenue?
d. Suppose that one week before the convention, the number of regular customers/Saturday night only rooms that were made available sell out. If another nonconvention customer calls and requests a Saturday night only room, what is the value of accepting this additional reservation?

TABLE 5.11 RETURNS OVER FIVE 1-YEAR PERIODS FOR SIX MUTUAL FUNDS

| | Planning Scenarios for Next 12 Months | | | | |
Mutual Funds	Year 1	Year 2	Year 3	Year 4	Year 5
Large-Cap Stock	35.3	20.0	28.3	10.4	−9.3
Mid-Cap Stock	32.3	23.2	−0.9	49.3	−22.8
Small-Cap Stock	20.8	22.5	6.0	33.3	6.1
Energy/Resources Sector	25.3	33.9	−20.5	20.9	−2.5
Health Sector	49.1	5.5	29.7	77.7	−24.9
Technology Sector	46.2	21.7	45.7	93.1	−20.1
Real Estate Sector	20.5	44.0	−21.1	2.6	5.1

8. In the latter part of Section 5.3 we developed a moderate risk portfolio model for Hauck Investment Services. Modify the model given so that it can be used to construct a portfolio for more aggressive investors. In particular, do the following:

   a. Develop a portfolio model for investors who are willing to risk a portfolio with a return as low as 0%.

   b. What is the recommended allocation for this type of investor?

   c. How would you modify your recommendation in part (b) for an investor who also wants to have at least 10% of his or her portfolio invested in the foreign stock mutual fund? How does requiring at least 10% of the portfolio be invested in the foreign stock fund affect the expected return?

9. Table 5.11 shows data on the returns over five 1-year periods for six mutual funds. A firm's portfolio managers will assume that one of these scenarios will accurately reflect the investing climate over the next 12 months. The probabilities of each of the scenarios occurring are 0.1, 0.3, 0.1, 0.1, and 0.4 for years 1 to 5, respectively.

   a. Develop a portfolio model for investors who are willing to risk a portfolio with a return no lower than 2%.

   b. Solve the model in part (a) and recommend a portfolio allocation for the investor with this risk tolerance.

   c. Modify the portfolio model in part (a) and solve it to develop a portfolio for an investor with a risk tolerance of 0%.

   d. Is the expected return higher for investors following the portfolio recommendations in part (c) as compared to the returns for the portfolio in part (b)? If so, do you believe the returns are enough higher to justify investing in that portfolio?

10. Consider the following two-person, zero-sum game. Payoffs are the winnings for Player A. Identify the pure strategy solution. What is the value of the game?

		Player B		
		b_1	b_2	b_3
Player A	a_1	8	5	7
	a_2	2	4	10

11. Assume that a two-person, zero-sum game has a pure strategy solution. If this game were solved using a linear programming formulation, how would you know from the linear programming solution that the game had a pure strategy solution?

12. Consider the payoff table below that shows the percentage increase in market share for Company A for each combination of Company A and Company B strategies. Assume that Company B implements a mixed strategy by using strategy b_2 with probability 0.5 and strategy b_3 with probability 0.5. Company B decides never to use strategy b_1. What is the expected payoff to Company A under each of its three strategies? If Company B were to always use the stated mixed strategy probabilities, what would the optimal strategy for Company A be?

		Company B		
		Increase Advertising b_1	Quantity Discounts b_2	Extend Warranty b_3
	Increase Advertising a_1	4	3	2
Company A	Quantity Discounts a_2	−1	4	1
	Extend Warranty a_3	5	−2	5

13. Two television stations compete with each other for viewing audience. Local programming options for the 5:00 P.M. weekday time slot include a sitcom rerun, an early news program, or a home improvement show. Each station has the same programming options and must make its preseason program selection before knowing what the other television station will do. The viewing audience gains in thousands of viewers for Station A are shown in the payoff table.

		Station B		
		Sitcom Rerun b_1	News Program b_2	Home Improvement b_3
	Sitcom Rerun a_1	10	−5	3
Station A	News Program a_2	8	7	6
	Home Improvement a_3	4	8	7

Determine the optimal strategy for each station. What is the value of the game?

14. Two Indiana state senate candidates must decide which city to visit the day before the November election. The same four cities—Indianapolis, Evansville, Fort Wayne, and South Bend—are available for both candidates. Travel plans must be made in advance, so the candidates must decide which city to visit prior to knowing the city the other candidate will visit. Values in the payoff table show thousands of voters gained by the Republican candidate based on the strategies selected by the two candidates. Which city should each candidate visit and what is the value of the game?

		Democratic Candidate			
		Indianapolis b_1	Evansville b_2	Fort Wayne b_3	South Bend b_4
	Indianapolis a_1	0	−15	−8	20
Republican	Evansville a_2	30	−5	5	−10
Candidate	Fort Wayne a_3	10	−25	0	20
	South Bend a_4	20	20	10	15

518

15. Consider a game in which each player selects one of three colored poker chips: red, white, or blue. The players must select a chip without knowing the color of the chip selected by the other player. The players then reveal their chips. Payoffs to Player A in dollars are as follows:

		Player B		
		Red b_1	**White** b_2	**Blue** b_3
	Red a_1	0	−1	2
Player A	**White** a_2	5	4	−3
	Blue a_3	2	3	−4

   a. What is the optimal strategy for each player?
   b. What is the value of the game?
   c. Would you prefer to be Player A or Player B? Why?

16. Two companies compete for a share of the soft drink market. Each has worked with an advertising agency to develop alternative advertising strategies for the coming year. A variety of television advertisements, newspaper advertisements, product promotions, and in-store displays have provided four different strategies for each company. The payoff table summarizes the gain in market share for Company A projected for the various combinations of Company A and Company B strategies. What is the optimal strategy for each company? What is the value of the game?

	Company B			
	b_1	b_2	b_3	b_4
a_1	3	0	2	4
a_2	2	−2	1	0
a_3	4	2	5	6
a_4	−2	6	−1	0

Company A is labeled to the left of rows a_2 and a_3.

17. The offensive coordinator for the Chicago Bears professional football team is preparing a game plan for the upcoming game against the Green Bay Packers. A review of game tapes from previous Bears–Packers games provides data on the yardage gained for run plays and pass plays. Data show that when the Bears run against the Packers' run defense, the Bears gain an average of 2 yards. However, when the Bears run against the Packers' pass defense, the Bears gain an average of 6 yards. A similar analysis of pass plays reveals that if the Bears pass against the Packers' run defense, the Bears gain an average of 11 yards. However, if the Bears pass against the Packers' pass defense, the Bears average a loss of 1 yard. This loss, or negative gain of −1, includes the lost yardage due to quarterback sacks and interceptions. Develop a payoff table that shows the Bears' average yardage gain for each combination of the Bears' offensive strategy to run or pass and the Packers' strategy of using a run defense or a pass defense. What is the optimal strategy for the Chicago Bears during the upcoming game against the Green Bay Packers? What is the expected value of this strategy?

References and Bibliography

Ahuja, R. K., T. L. Magnanti, and J. B. Orlin. *Network Flows, Theory, Algorithms, and Applications.* Prentice Hall, 1993.

Bazarra, M. S., J. J. Jarvis, and H. D. Sherali. *Linear Programming and Network Flows,* 2d ed. Wiley, 1990.

Carino, H. F., and C. H. Le Noir, Jr. "Optimizing Wood Procurement in Cabinet Manufacturing," *Interfaces* (March/April 1988): 10–19.

Dantzig, G. B. *Linear Programming and Extensions.* Princeton University Press, 1963.

Davis, Morton D. *Game Theory: A Nontechnical Introduction.* Dover, 1997.

Evans, J. R., and E. Minieka. *Optimization Algorithms for Networks and Graphs,* 2d ed. Marcel Dekker, 1992.

Ford, L. R., and D. R. Fulkerson. *Flows and Networks.* Princeton University Press, 1962.

Geoffrion, A., and G. Graves. "Better Distribution Planning with Computer Models," *Harvard Business Review* (July/August 1976).

Greenberg, H. J. "How to Analyze the Results of Linear Programs—Part 1: Preliminaries," *Interfaces* 23, no. 4 (July/August 1993): 56–67.

Greenberg, H. J. "How to Analyze the Results of Linear Programs—Part 2: Price Interpretation," *Interfaces* 23, no. 5 (September/October 1993): 97–114.

Greenberg, H. J. "How to Analyze the Results of Linear Programs—Part 3: Infeasibility Diagnosis," *Interfaces* 23, no. 6 (November/December 1993): 120–139.

Lillien, G., and A. Rangaswamy. *Marketing Engineering: Computer-Assisted Marketing Analysis and Planning.* Addison-Wesley, 1998.

Martin, R. K. *Large Scale Linear and Integer Optimization: A Unified Approach.* Kluwer Academic Publishers, 1999.

McMillian, John. *Games, Strategies, and Managers.* Oxford University Press, 1992.

Myerson, Roger B. *Game Theory: Analysis of Conflict.* Harvard University Press, 1997.

Nemhauser, G. L., and L. A. Wolsey. *Integer and Combinatorial Optimization.* Wiley, 1999.

Osborne, Martin J. *An Introduction to Game Theory.* Oxford University Press, 2004.

Schrage, Linus. *Optimization Modeling with LINDO,* 4th ed. LINDO Systems Inc., 2000.

Sherman, H. D. "Hospital Efficiency Measurement and Evaluation," *Medical Care* 22, no. 10 (October 1984): 922–938.

Winston, W. L., and S. C. Albright. *Practical Management Science,* 2d ed. Duxbury Press, 2001.

Self-Test Solutions and Answers to Even-Numbered Problems

2. b. $E = 0.924$
   $wa = 0.074$
   $wc = 0.436$
   $we = 0.489$
   c. D is relatively inefficient.
   Composite requires 92.4 of D's resources.
   d. 34.37 patient days (65 or older)
   41.99 patient days (under 65)
   e. Hospitals A, C, and E

4. b. $E = 0.960$
   $wb = 0.074$
   $wc = 0.000$
   $wj = 0.436$
   $wn = 0.489$
   $ws = 0.000$
   c. Yes; $E = 0.960$
   d. More: $220 profit per week
   Less: Hours of Operation 4.4 hours
   FTE Staff 2.6
   Supply Expense $185.61
   d. Bardstown, Jeffersonville, and New Albany

6. a. 19, 18, 12, 18

   b. | PCQ $= 8$ | PMQ $= 0$ | POQ $= 27$ |
      |---|---|---|
      | PCY $= 4$ | PMY $= 1$ | POY $= 2$ |
      | NCQ $= 6$ | NMQ $= 23$ | NOQ $= 2$ |
      | NCY $= 4$ | NMY $= 2$ | NOY $= 1$ |
      | CMQ $= 37$ | CMY $= 2$ | |
      | COQ $= 11$ | COY $= 3$ | |

   c. | PCQ $= 8$ | PMQ $= 1$ | POQ $= 3$ |
      |---|---|---|
      | PCY $= 4$ | PMY $= 1$ | POY $= 2$ |
      | NCQ $= 6$ | NMQ $= 3$ | NOQ $= 2$ |
      | NCY $= 4$ | NMY $= 2$ | NOY $= 1$ |
      | CMQ $= 3$ | CMY $= 2$ | |
      | COQ $= 7$ | COY $= 3$ | |

8. b. 65.7% small-cap growth fund
   34.3% of the portfolio in a small-cap value
   Expected return $= 18.5\%$
   c. 10% foreign stock
   50.8% small-cap growth fund
   39.2% of the portfolio in a small-cap value
   Expected return $= 17.178\%$

10.

		Player B			
		b_1	b_2	b_3	Minimum
Player A	a_1	8	5	7	⑤
	a_2	2	4	10	4
	Maximum	8	⑤	7	

Minimum ↑   Maximum →

The game has a pure strategy: Player A strategy a_1; Player B strategy b_2; and value of game $= 5$.

12. 2.5, 2.5, 1.5
    Strategy a_1 or a_2
    Expected payoff $= 2.5$

14. Pure strategies a_4 and b_3
    Value $= 10$

15. a. The maximum of the row minimums is not equal to the minimum of the column maximums, so a mixed strategy exists.
    Linear program for Player A:

    Max   *GAINA*
    s.t.   Player B strategy
    $$5PA2 + 2PA3 - GAINA \geq 0 \quad \text{(red chip)}$$
    $$-PA1 + 4PA2 + 3PA3 - GAINA \geq 0 \quad \text{(white chip)}$$
    $$2PA1 - 3PA2 - 4PA3 - GAINA \geq 0 \quad \text{(blue chip)}$$
    $$PA1 + PA2 + PA3 = 1$$
    $$PA1, PA2, PA3 \geq 0$$

    Player A: $P(\text{red}) = 0.7$, $P(\text{white}) = 0.3$, $P(\text{blue}) = 0.0$
    From dual values:
    Player B: $P(\text{red}) = 0.0$, $P(\text{white}) = 0.5$, $P(\text{blue}) = 0.5$
    b. The value of the game is a 50-cent expected gain for Player A.
    c. Player A

16. Company A: 0.0, 0.0, 0.8, 0.2
    Company B: 0.4, 0.6, 0.0, 0.0
    Expected gain for A $= 2.8$

9

Distribution and Network Models

CONTENTS

The models discussed in this chapter belong to a special class of linear programming problems called *network flow* problems. Five different problems are considered:

- Transportation problem
- Assignment problem
- Transshipment problem
- Shortest-route problem
- Maximal flow problem

A separate chapter is devoted to these problems because of the similarity in the problem structure and solution procedure. In each case, we will present a graphical representation of the problem in the form of a *network*. We will then show how the problem can be formulated and solved as a linear program. In the last section of the chapter we present a production and inventory problem that is an interesting application of the transshipment problem.

6.1 TRANSPORTATION PROBLEM

The **transportation problem** arises frequently in planning for the distribution of goods and services from several supply locations to several demand locations. Typically, the quantity of goods available at each supply location (origin) is limited, and the quantity of goods needed at each of several demand locations (destinations) is known. The usual objective in a transportation problem is to minimize the cost of shipping goods from the origins to the destinations.

Let us illustrate by considering a transportation problem faced by Foster Generators. This problem involves the transportation of a product from three plants to four distribution centers. Foster Generators operates plants in Cleveland, Ohio; Bedford, Indiana; and York, Pennsylvania. Production capacities over the next three-month planning period for one particular type of generator are as follows:

Origin	Plant	Three-Month Production Capacity (units)
1	Cleveland	5,000
2	Bedford	6,000
3	York	2,500
	Total	13,500

The firm distributes its generators through four regional distribution centers located in Boston, Chicago, St. Louis, and Lexington; the three-month forecast of demand for the distribution centers is as follows:

Destination	Distribution Center	Three-Month Demand Forecast (units)
1	Boston	6,000
2	Chicago	4,000
3	St. Louis	2,000
4	Lexington	1,500
	Total	13,500

FIGURE 6.1 THE NETWORK REPRESENTATION OF THE FOSTER GENERATORS
TRANSPORTATION PROBLEM

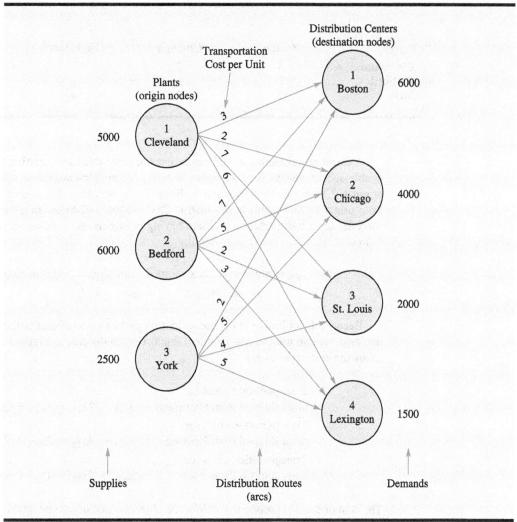

Management would like to determine how much of its production should be shipped from each plant to each distribution center. Figure 6.1 shows graphically the 12 distribution routes Foster can use. Such a graph is called a **network;** the circles are referred to as **nodes** and the lines connecting the nodes as **arcs.** Each origin and destination is represented by a node, and each possible shipping route is represented by an arc. The amount of the supply is written next to each origin node, and the amount of the demand is written next to each destination node. The goods shipped from the origins to the destinations represent the flow in the network. Note that the direction of flow (from origin to destination) is indicated by the arrows.

Try Problem 1 for practice in developing a network model of a transportation problem.

For Foster's transportation problem, the objective is to determine the routes to be used and the quantity to be shipped via each route that will provide the minimum total transportation cost. The cost for each unit shipped on each route is given in Table 6.1 and is shown on each arc in Figure 6.1.

The first subscript identifies the "from" node of the corresponding arc and the second subscript identifies the "to" node of the arc.

TABLE 6.1   TRANSPORTATION COST PER UNIT FOR THE FOSTER GENERATORS TRANSPORTATION PROBLEM

Origin	Destination			
	Boston	Chicago	St. Louis	Lexington
Cleveland	3	2	7	6
Bedford	7	5	2	3
York	2	5	4	5

A linear programming model can be used to solve this transportation problem. We use double-subscripted decision variables, with x_{11} denoting the number of units shipped from origin 1 (Cleveland) to destination 1 (Boston), x_{12} denoting the number of units shipped from origin 1 (Cleveland) to destination 2 (Chicago), and so on. In general, the decision variables for a transportation problem having m origins and n destinations are written as follows:

$$x_{ij} = \text{number of units shipped from origin } i \text{ to destination } j,$$
$$\text{where } i = 1, 2, \ldots, m \text{ and } j = 1, 2, \ldots, n$$

Because the objective of the transportation problem is to minimize the total transportation cost, we can use the cost data in Table 6.1 or on the arcs in Figure 6.1 to develop the following cost expressions:

Transportation costs for
units shipped from Cleveland $= 3x_{11} + 2x_{12} + 7x_{13} + 6x_{14}$

Transportation costs for
units shipped from Bedford $\quad = 7x_{21} + 5x_{22} + 2x_{23} + 3x_{24}$

Transportation costs for
units shipped from York $\quad\;\; = 2x_{31} + 5x_{32} + 4x_{33} + 5x_{34}$

The sum of these expressions provides the objective function showing the total transportation cost for Foster Generators.

Transportation problems need constraints because each origin has a limited supply and each destination has a demand requirement. We consider the supply constraints first. The capacity at the Cleveland plant is 5000 units. With the total number of units shipped from the Cleveland plant expressed as $x_{11} + x_{12} + x_{13} + x_{14}$, the supply constraint for the Cleveland plant is

$$x_{11} + x_{12} + x_{13} + x_{14} \leq 5000 \quad \text{Cleveland supply}$$

With three origins (plants), the Foster transportation problem has three supply constraints. Given the capacity of 6000 units at the Bedford plant and 2500 units at the York plant, the two additional supply constraints are

$$x_{21} + x_{22} + x_{23} + x_{24} \leq 6000 \quad \text{Bedford supply}$$
$$x_{31} + x_{32} + x_{33} + x_{34} \leq 2500 \quad \text{York supply}$$

With the four distribution centers as the destinations, four demand constraints are needed to ensure that destination demands will be satisfied:

$$x_{11} + x_{21} + x_{31} = 6000 \quad \text{Boston demand}$$
$$x_{12} + x_{22} + x_{32} = 4000 \quad \text{Chicago demand}$$
$$x_{13} + x_{23} + x_{33} = 2000 \quad \text{St. Louis demand}$$
$$x_{14} + x_{24} + x_{34} = 1500 \quad \text{Lexington demand}$$

To obtain a feasible solution, the total supply must be greater than or equal to the total demand.

Combining the objective function and constraints into one model provides a 12-variable, 7-constraint linear programming formulation of the Foster Generators transportation problem:

$$\text{Min} \quad 3x_{11} + 2x_{12} + 7x_{13} + 6x_{14} + 7x_{21} + 5x_{22} + 2x_{23} + 3x_{24} + 2x_{31} + 5x_{32} + 4x_{33} + 5x_{34}$$

s.t.

$$
\begin{array}{llllllll}
x_{11} + & x_{12} + & x_{13} + & x_{14} & & & & \leq 5000 \\
& & & x_{21} + & x_{22} + & x_{23} + & x_{24} & \leq 6000 \\
& & & & & & x_{31} + x_{32} + x_{33} + x_{34} \leq 2500 \\
x_{11} & & & + x_{21} & & + x_{31} & & = 6000 \\
& x_{12} & & + x_{22} & & + x_{32} & & = 4000 \\
& & x_{13} & + x_{23} & & + x_{33} & & = 2000 \\
& & x_{14} & + x_{24} & & + x_{34} & & = 1500
\end{array}
$$

$$x_{ij} \geq 0 \quad \text{for } i = 1, 2, 3 \text{ and } j = 1, 2, 3, 4$$

Comparing the linear programming formulation to the network in Figure 6.1 leads to several observations. All the information needed for the linear programming formulation is on the network. Each node has one constraint, and each arc has one variable. The sum of the variables corresponding to arcs from an origin node must be less than or equal to the origin's supply, and the sum of the variables corresponding to the arcs into a destination node must be equal to the destination's demand.

Can you now use the computer to solve a linear programming model of a transportation problem? Try Problem 2.

The solution to the Foster Generators problem (see Figure 6.2) shows that the minimum total transportation cost is $39,500. The values for the decision variables show the

FIGURE 6.2   THE SOLUTION FOR THE FOSTER GENERATORS TRANSPORTATION PROBLEM

WEB file

Foster

```
Optimal Objective Value = 39500.00000

       Variable              Value              Reduced Costs
    --------------        --------------        --------------
         X11              3500.00000               0.00000
         X12              1500.00000               0.00000
         X13                 0.00000               8.00000
         X14                 0.00000               6.00000
         X21                 0.00000               1.00000
         X22              2500.00000               0.00000
         X23              2000.00000               0.00000
         X24              1500.00000               0.00000
         X31              2500.00000               0.00000
         X32                 0.00000               4.00000
         X33                 0.00000               6.00000
         X34                 0.00000               6.00000
```

TABLE 6.2 OPTIMAL SOLUTION TO THE FOSTER GENERATORS
TRANSPORTATION PROBLEM

Route		Units	Cost	Total
From	**To**	Shipped	per Unit	Cost
Cleveland	Boston	3500	$3	$10,500
Cleveland	Chicago	1500	$2	3,000
Bedford	Chicago	2500	$5	12,500
Bedford	St. Louis	2000	$2	4,000
Bedford	Lexington	1500	$3	4,500
York	Boston	2500	$2	5,000
				$39,500

optimal amounts to ship over each route. For example, with $x_{11} = 3500$, 3500 units should be shipped from Cleveland to Boston, and with $x_{12} = 1500$, 1500 units should be shipped from Cleveland to Chicago. Other values of the decision variables indicate the remaining shipping quantities and routes. Table 6.2 shows the minimum cost transportation schedule and Figure 6.3 summarizes the optimal solution on the network.

Problem Variations

The Foster Generators problem illustrates use of the basic transportation model. Variations of the basic transportation model may involve one or more of the following situations:

1. Total supply not equal to total demand
2. Maximization objective function
3. Route capacities or route minimums
4. Unacceptable routes

With slight modifications in the linear programming model, we can easily accommodate these situations.

Total Supply Not Equal to Total Demand Often *the total supply is not equal to the total demand.* If total supply exceeds total demand, no modification in the linear programming formulation is necessary. Excess supply will appear as slack in the linear programming solution. Slack for any particular origin can be interpreted as the unused supply or amount not shipped from the origin.

Whenever total supply is less than total demand, the model does not determine how the unsatisfied demand is handled (e.g., backorders). The manager must handle this aspect of the problem.

If total supply is less than total demand, the linear programming model of a transportation problem will not have a feasible solution. In this case, we modify the network representation by adding a **dummy origin** with a supply equal to the difference between the total demand and the total supply. With the addition of the dummy origin, and an arc from the dummy origin to each destination, the linear programming model will have a feasible solution. A zero cost per unit is assigned to each arc leaving the dummy origin so that the value of the optimal solution for the revised problem will represent the shipping cost for the units actually shipped (no shipments actually will be made from the dummy origin). When the optimal solution is implemented, the destinations showing shipments being received from the dummy origin will be the destinations experiencing a shortfall, or unsatisfied demand.

FIGURE 6.3 OPTIMAL SOLUTION TO THE FOSTER GENERATORS TRANSPORTATION PROBLEM

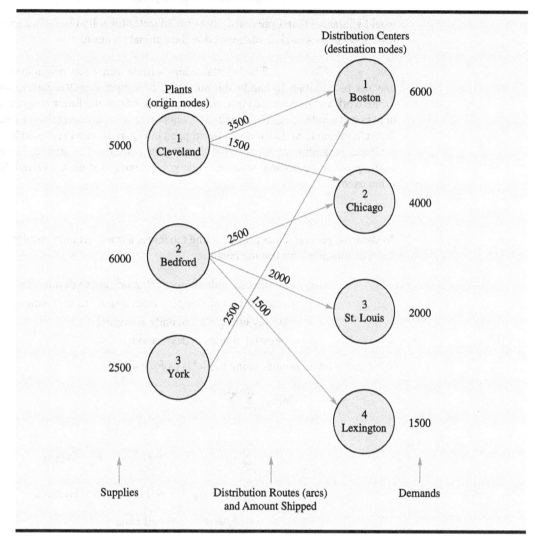

Try Problem 6 for practice with a case in which demand is greater than supply with a maximization objective.

Maximization Objective Function In some transportation problems, the objective is to find a solution that maximizes profit or revenue. Using the values for profit or revenue per unit as coefficients in the objective function, we simply solve a maximization rather than a minimization linear program. This change does not affect the constraints.

Route Capacities or Route Minimums The linear programming formulation of the transportation problem also can accommodate capacities or minimum quantities for one or more of the routes. For example, suppose that in the Foster Generators problem the York–Boston route (origin 3 to destination 1) had a capacity of 1000 units because of limited space availability on its normal mode of transportation. With x_{31} denoting the amount shipped from York to Boston, the route capacity constraint for the York–Boston route would be

$$x_{31} \leq 1000$$

Similarly, route minimums can be specified. For example,

$$x_{22} \geq 2000$$

would guarantee that a previously committed order for a Bedford–Chicago delivery of at least 2000 units would be maintained in the optimal solution.

Unacceptable Routes Finally, establishing a route from every origin to every destination may not be possible. To handle this situation, we simply drop the corresponding arc from the network and remove the corresponding variable from the linear programming formulation. For example, if the Cleveland–St. Louis route were unacceptable or unusable, the arc from Cleveland to St. Louis could be dropped in Figure 6.1, and x_{13} could be removed from the linear programming formulation. Solving the resulting 11-variable, 7-constraint model would provide the optimal solution while guaranteeing that the Cleveland–St. Louis route is not used.

A General Linear Programming Model

To show the general linear programming model for a transportation problem with m origins and n destinations, we use the notation:

$$x_{ij} = \text{number of units shipped from origin } i \text{ to destination } j$$
$$c_{ij} = \text{cost per unit of shipping from origin } i \text{ to destination } j$$
$$s_i = \text{supply or capacity in units at origin } i$$
$$d_j = \text{demand in units at destination } j$$

The general linear programming model is as follows:

$$\text{Min} \quad \sum_{i=1}^{m} \sum_{j=1}^{n} c_{ij} x_{ij}$$

s.t.

$$\sum_{j=1}^{n} x_{ij} \leq s_i \quad i = 1, 2, \ldots, m \quad \text{Supply}$$
$$\sum_{i=1}^{m} x_{ij} = d_j \quad j = 1, 2, \ldots, n \quad \text{Demand}$$
$$x_{ij} \geq 0 \quad \text{for all } i \text{ and } j$$

NOTES AND COMMENTS

1. Transportation problems encountered in practice usually lead to large linear programs. Transportation problems with 100 origins and 100 destinations are not unusual. Such a problem would involve $(100)(100) = 10,000$ variables.

2. To handle a situation in which some routes may be unacceptable, we stated that you could drop the corresponding arc from the network and remove the corresponding variable from the linear programming formulation. Another approach often used is to assign an extremely large objective function cost coefficient to any unacceptable arc. If the problem has already been formulated, another option is to add a constraint to the formulation that sets the variable you want to remove equal to zero.

3. The optimal solution to a transportation model will consist of integer values for the decision variables as long as all supply and demand values are integers. The reason is the special mathematical structure of the linear programming model. Each variable appears in exactly one supply and one demand constraint, and all coefficients in the constraint equations are 1 or 0.

EMPTY FREIGHT CAR ASSIGNMENT AT UNION PACIFIC RAILROAD*

Union Pacific Railroad is the largest railroad in North America. The company owns over 32,000 miles of railroad track and has 50,000 employees. It deploys over 8,000 locomotives and over 100,000 freight cars to move goods for its customers.

When goods are delivered to a location, the freight car is left at the customer site to be unloaded. Therefore, at any particular point in time, empty freight cars are located throughout the North American network of tracks. At the same time, Union Pacific's customers require empty freight cars so they may be loaded for shipments. A critical decision for Union Pacific is how to assign empty freight cars to its customers who are in need of cars. That is, given the location of the empty cars and the demand for empty cars at other locations, which cars should be sent to which demand points? The decision is further complicated by the fact that supply of freight cars is usually smaller than the demand, there are a variety of types of freight cars (for example, box cars, auto transport cars, etc.) and service time expectations must be met while also controlling costs.

Prior to the development of an optimization model for freight car assignment, car managers assigned cars to customers from pools of a particular type of car. These managers had no tool to assess how the assignments they were making impacted the overall rail network.

Union Pacific, working with faculty from Purdue University, developed a transportation model similar to the one discussed in this section. The model minimizes a linear weighted cost objective subject to supply and demand constraints. The objective function is a weighted combination of transportation costs, car-substitution costs (a penalty for assigning a feasible but different type of car than was demanded), penalties for deviating from the delivery schedule, customer priority, and corridor efficiency. The model was successfully implemented and resulted in 35% return on investment.

*Based on A.K. Narisetty, J. P. Richard, D. Ramcharan, D. Murphy, G. Minks, and J. Fuller, "An Optimization Model for Empty Freight Car Assignment at Union Pacific Railroad," *Interfaces* (March/April: 2008): 89–102.

As mentioned previously, we can add constraints of the form $x_{ij} \leq L_{ij}$ if the route from origin i to destination j has capacity L_{ij}. A transportation problem that includes constraints of this type is called a **capacitated transportation problem.** Similarly, we can add route minimum constraints of the form $x_{ij} \geq M_{ij}$ if the route from origin i to destination j must handle at least M_{ij} units.

6.2 ASSIGNMENT PROBLEM

The **assignment problem** arises in a variety of decision-making situations; typical assignment problems involve assigning jobs to machines, agents to tasks, sales personnel to sales territories, contracts to bidders, and so on. A distinguishing feature of the assignment problem is that *one* agent is assigned to *one and only one* task. Specifically, we look for the set of assignments that will optimize a stated objective, such as minimize cost, minimize time, or maximize profits.

To illustrate the assignment problem, let us consider the case of Fowle Marketing Research, which has just received requests for market research studies from three new clients. The company faces the task of assigning a project leader (agent) to each client (task). Currently, three individuals have no other commitments and are available for the project leader assignments. Fowle's management realizes, however, that the time required to complete each study will depend on the experience and ability of the project leader assigned. The three projects have approximately the same priority, and management wants to assign project leaders to minimize the total number of days required to complete all three projects. If a project leader is to be assigned to one client only, what assignments should be made?

To answer the assignment question, Fowle's management must first consider all possible project leader–client assignments and then estimate the corresponding project completion times. With three project leaders and three clients, nine assignment alternatives are possible. The alternatives and the estimated project completion times in days are summarized in Table 6.3.

Try Problem 9 (part a) for practice in developing a network model for an assignment problem.

Figure 6.4 shows the network representation of Fowle's assignment problem. The nodes correspond to the project leaders and clients, and the arcs represent the possible assignments of project leaders to clients. The supply at each origin node and the demand at

TABLE 6.3 ESTIMATED PROJECT COMPLETION TIMES (DAYS) FOR THE FOWLE MARKETING RESEARCH ASSIGNMENT PROBLEM

	Client		
Project Leader	1	2	3
1. Terry	10	15	9
2. Carle	9	18	5
3. McClymonds	6	14	3

FIGURE 6.4 A NETWORK MODEL OF THE FOWLE MARKETING RESEARCH ASSIGNMENT PROBLEM

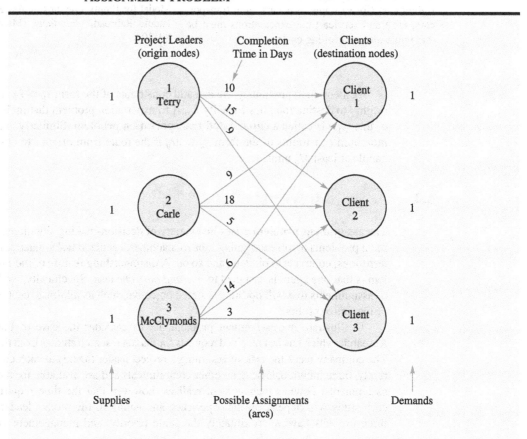

532

The assignment problem is a special case of the transportation problem.

each destination node are 1; the cost of assigning a project leader to a client is the time it takes that project leader to complete the client's task. Note the similarity between the network models of the assignment problem (Figure 6.4) and the transportation problem (Figure 6.1). The assignment problem is a special case of the transportation problem in which all supply and demand values equal 1, and the amount shipped over each arc is either 0 or 1.

Because the assignment problem is a special case of the transportation problem, a linear programming formulation can be developed. Again, we need a constraint for each node and a variable for each arc. As in the transportation problem, we use double-subscripted decision variables, with x_{11} denoting the assignment of project leader 1 (Terry) to client 1, x_{12} denoting the assignment of project leader 1 (Terry) to client 2, and so on. Thus, we define the decision variables for Fowle's assignment problem as

$$x_{ij} = \begin{cases} 1 & \text{if project leader } i \text{ is assigned to client } j \\ 0 & \text{otherwise} \end{cases}$$

where $i = 1, 2, 3$, and $j = 1, 2, 3$

Using this notation and the completion time data in Table 6.3, we develop completion time expressions:

Days required for Terry's assignment	$= 10x_{11} + 15x_{12} + 9x_{13}$
Days required for Carle's assignment	$= 9x_{21} + 18x_{22} + 5x_{23}$
Days required for McClymonds's assignment	$= 6x_{31} + 14x_{32} + 3x_{33}$

Because the number of project leaders equals the number of clients, all the constraints could be written as equalities. But when the number of project leaders exceeds the number of clients, less-than-or-equal-to constraints must be used for the project leader constraints.

The sum of the completion times for the three project leaders will provide the total days required to complete the three assignments. Thus, the objective function is

$$\text{Min} \quad 10x_{11} + 15x_{12} + 9x_{13} + 9x_{21} + 18x_{22} + 5x_{23} + 6x_{31} + 14x_{32} + 3x_{33}$$

The constraints for the assignment problem reflect the conditions that each project leader can be assigned to at most one client and that each client must have one assigned project leader. These constraints are written as follows:

$$\begin{array}{ll} x_{11} + x_{12} + x_{13} \leq 1 & \text{Terry's assignment} \\ x_{21} + x_{22} + x_{23} \leq 1 & \text{Carle's assignment} \\ x_{31} + x_{32} + x_{33} \leq 1 & \text{McClymonds's assignment} \\ x_{11} + x_{21} + x_{31} = 1 & \text{Client 1} \\ x_{12} + x_{22} + x_{32} = 1 & \text{Client 2} \\ x_{13} + x_{23} + x_{33} = 1 & \text{Client 3} \end{array}$$

Note that each node in Figure 6.4 has one constraint.

Try Problem 9 (part b) for practice in formulating and solving a linear programming model for an assignment problem on the computer.

Combining the objective function and constraints into one model provides the following 9-variable, 6-constraint linear programming model of the Fowle Marketing Research assignment problem:

$$\text{Min} \quad 10x_{11} + 15x_{12} + 9x_{13} + 9x_{21} + 18x_{22} + 5x_{23} + 6x_{31} + 14x_{32} + 3x_{33}$$
s.t.
$$\begin{array}{ccccccccc} x_{11} + & x_{12} + & x_{13} & & & & & & \leq 1 \\ & & & x_{21} + & x_{22} + & x_{23} & & & \leq 1 \\ & & & & & & x_{31} + & x_{32} + & x_{33} \leq 1 \\ x_{11} & & & + x_{21} & & & + x_{31} & & = 1 \\ & x_{12} & & & + x_{22} & & & + x_{32} & = 1 \\ & & x_{13} & & & + x_{23} & & & + x_{33} = 1 \end{array}$$
$$x_{ij} \geq 0 \quad \text{for } i = 1, 2, 3; j = 1, 2, 3$$

FIGURE 6.5   THE SOLUTION FOR THE FOWLE MARKETING RESEARCH ASSIGNMENT PROBLEM

WEB file

Fowle

```
Optimal Objective Value = 26.00000

        Variable              Value              Reduced Costs
     ---------------      ---------------      ---------------
         X11                 0.00000               0.00000
         X12                 1.00000               0.00000
         X13                 0.00000               2.00000
         X21                 0.00000               1.00000
         X22                 0.00000               5.00000
         X23                 1.00000               0.00000
         X31                 1.00000               0.00000
         X32                 0.00000               3.00000
         X33                 0.00000               0.00000
```

TABLE 6.4   OPTIMAL PROJECT LEADER ASSIGNMENTS FOR THE FOWLE MARKETING RESEARCH ASSIGNMENT PROBLEM

Project Leader	Assigned Client	Days
Terry	2	15
Carle	3	5
McClymonds	1	6
	Total	26

Figure 6.5 shows the computer solution for this model. Terry is assigned to client 2 ($x_{12} = 1$), Carle is assigned to client 3 ($x_{23} = 1$), and McClymonds is assigned to client 1 ($x_{31} = 1$). The total completion time required is 26 days. This solution is summarized in Table 6.4.

Problem Variations

Because the assignment problem can be viewed as a special case of the transportation problem, the problem variations that may arise in an assignment problem parallel those for the transportation problem. Specifically, we can handle the following issues:

1. Total number of agents (supply) not equal to the total number of tasks (demand)
2. A maximization objective function
3. Unacceptable assignments

In the linear programming formulation of a problem with five clients and only three project leaders, we could get by with one dummy project leader by placing a 2 on the right-hand side of the constraint for the dummy project leader.

The situation in which the number of agents does not equal the number of tasks is analogous to total supply not equaling total demand in a transportation problem. If the number of agents exceeds the number of tasks, the extra agents simply remain unassigned in the linear programming solution. If the number of tasks exceeds the number of agents, the linear programming model will not have a feasible solution. In this situation, a simple modification is to add enough dummy agents to equalize the number of agents and the number of tasks. For instance, in the Fowle problem we might have had five clients (tasks) and only three project leaders (agents). By adding two dummy project leaders, we can create a new assignment problem with the number of project leaders equal to the number of clients. The objective function coefficients for the assignment of dummy project leaders would be zero so that the value of the optimal solution would represent the total number of days required by the assignments actually made (no assignments will actually be made to the clients receiving dummy project leaders).

If the assignment alternatives are evaluated in terms of revenue or profit rather than time or cost, the linear programming formulation can be solved as a maximization rather than a minimization problem. In addition, if one or more assignments are unacceptable, the corresponding decision variable can be removed from the linear programming formulation. This situation could happen, for example, if an agent did not have the experience necessary for one or more of the tasks.

A General Linear Programming Model

To show the general linear programming model for an assignment problem with m agents and n tasks, we use the notation:

$$x_{ij} = \begin{cases} 1 & \text{if agent } i \text{ is assigned to task } j \\ 0 & \text{otherwise} \end{cases}$$

$$c_{ij} = \text{the cost of assigning agent } i \text{ to task } j$$

The general linear programming model is as follows:

$$\text{Min} \quad \sum_{i=1}^{m} \sum_{j=1}^{n} c_{ij} x_{ij}$$

s.t.

$$\sum_{j=1}^{n} x_{ij} \leq 1 \quad i = 1, 2, \ldots, m \quad \text{Agents}$$

$$\sum_{i=1}^{m} x_{ij} = 1 \quad j = 1, 2, \ldots, n \quad \text{Tasks}$$

$$x_{ij} \geq 0 \quad \text{for all } i \text{ and } j$$

NOTES AND COMMENTS

1. As noted, the assignment model is a special case of the transportation model. We stated in the notes and comments at the end of the preceding section that the optimal solution to the transportation problem will consist of integer values for the decision variables as long as the supplies and demands are integers. For the assignment problem, all supplies and demands equal 1; thus, the optimal solution must be integer valued and the integer values must be 0 or 1.

2. Combining the method for handling multiple assignments with the notion of a dummy agent provides another means of dealing with situations when the number of tasks exceeds the number of agents. That is, we add one dummy agent, but provide the dummy agent with the capability to handle multiple tasks. The number of tasks the dummy agent can handle is equal to the difference between the number of tasks and the number of agents.

3. The Management Science in Action, Assigning Project Managers at Heery International, describes how managers are assigned to construction projects. The application involves multiple assignments.

ASSIGNING PROJECT MANAGERS AT HEERY INTERNATIONAL*

Heery International contracts with the State of Tennessee and others for a variety of construction projects including higher education facilities, hotels, and park facilities. At any particular time, Heery typically has more than 100 ongoing projects. Each of these projects must be assigned a single manager. With seven managers available, it means that there are 7(100) = 700 assignment variables. Assisted by an outside consultant, Heery International developed a mathematical model for assigning construction managers to projects.

The assignment problem developed by Heery uses 0-1 decision variables for each manager/project pair, just as in the assignment problem discussed previously. The goal in assigning managers is to balance the workload among managers and, at the same time, to minimize travel cost from the manager's home to the construction site. Thus, an objective function coefficient for each possible assignment was developed that combined project intensity (a function of the size of the project budget) with the travel distance from the manager's home to the construction site. The objective function calls for minimizing the sum over all possible assignments of the product of these coefficients with the assignment variables.

With more construction projects than managers, it was necessary to consider a variation of the standard assignment problem involving multiple assignments. Of the two sets of constraints, one set enforces the requirement that each project receive one and only one manager. The other set of constraints limits the number of assignments each manager can accept by placing an upper bound on the total intensity that is acceptable over all projects assigned.

Heery International implemented this assignment model with considerable success. According to Emory F. Redden, a Heery vice president, "The optimization model . . . has been very helpful for assigning managers to projects. . . . We have been satisfied with the assignments chosen at the Nashville office. . . . We look forward to using the model in our Atlanta office and elsewhere in the Heery organization."

*Based on Larry J. LeBlanc, Dale Randels, Jr., and T. K. Swann, "Heery International's Spreadsheet Optimization Model for Assigning Managers to Construction Projects," *Interfaces* (November/December 2000): 95–106.

At the beginning of this section, we indicated that a distinguishing feature of the assignment problem is that *one* agent is assigned to *one and only one* task. In generalizations of the assignment problem where one agent can be assigned to two or more tasks, the linear programming formulation of the problem can be easily modified. For example, let us assume that in the Fowle Marketing Research problem Terry could be assigned up to two clients; in this case, the constraint representing Terry's assignment would be $x_{11} + x_{12} + x_{13} \leq 2$. In general, if a_i denotes the upper limit for the number of tasks to which agent i can be assigned, we write the agent constraints as

$$\sum_{j=1}^{n} x_{ij} \leq a_i \qquad i = 1, 2, \ldots, m$$

If some tasks require more than one agent, the linear programming formulation can also accommodate the situation. Use the number of agents required as the right-hand side of the appropriate task constraint.

6.3 TRANSSHIPMENT PROBLEM

The **transshipment problem** is an extension of the transportation problem in which intermediate nodes, referred to as *transshipment nodes,* are added to account for locations such as warehouses. In this more general type of distribution problem, shipments may be made between any pair of the three general types of nodes: origin nodes, transshipment nodes, and destination nodes. For example, the transshipment problem permits shipments of goods from origins to intermediate nodes and on to destinations, from one origin to another origin, from one intermediate location to another, from one destination location to another, and directly from origins to destinations.

As was true for the transportation problem, the supply available at each origin is limited, and the demand at each destination is specified. The objective in the transshipment problem is to determine how many units should be shipped over each arc in the network so that all destination demands are satisfied with the minimum possible transportation cost.

Try Problem 17 (part a) for practice in developing a network representation of a transshipment problem.

Let us consider the transshipment problem faced by Ryan Electronics. Ryan is an electronics company with production facilities in Denver and Atlanta. Components produced at either facility may be shipped to either of the firm's regional warehouses, which are located in Kansas City and Louisville. From the regional warehouses, the firm supplies retail outlets in Detroit, Miami, Dallas, and New Orleans. The key features of the problem are shown in the network model depicted in Figure 6.6. Note that the supply at

FIGURE 6.6   NETWORK REPRESENTATION OF THE RYAN ELECTRONICS TRANSSHIPMENT PROBLEM

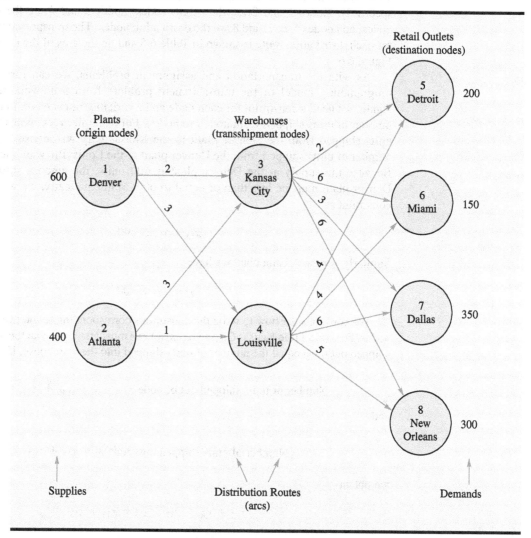

TABLE 6.5   TRANSPORTATION COST PER UNIT FOR THE RYAN ELECTRONICS TRANSSHIPMENT PROBLEM

	Warehouse	
Plant	**Kansas City**	**Louisville**
Denver	2	3
Atlanta	3	1

	Retail Outlet			
Warehouse	**Detroit**	**Miami**	**Dallas**	**New Orleans**
Kansas City	2	6	3	6
Louisville	4	4	6	5

each origin and demand at each destination are shown in the left and right margins, respectively. Nodes 1 and 2 are the origin nodes; nodes 3 and 4 are the transshipment nodes; and nodes 5, 6, 7, and 8 are the destination nodes. The transportation cost per unit for each distribution route is shown in Table 6.5 and on the arcs of the network model in Figure 6.6.

As with the transportation and assignment problems, we can formulate a linear programming model of the transshipment problem from a network representation. Again, we need a constraint for each node and a variable for each arc. Let x_{ij} denote the number of units shipped from node i to node j. For example, x_{13} denotes the number of units shipped from the Denver plant to the Kansas City warehouse, x_{14} denotes the number of units shipped from the Denver plant to the Louisville warehouse, and so on. Because the supply at the Denver plant is 600 units, the amount shipped from the Denver plant must be less than or equal to 600. Mathematically, we write this supply constraint as

$$x_{13} + x_{14} \leq 600$$

Similarly, for the Atlanta plant we have

$$x_{23} + x_{24} \leq 400$$

We now consider how to write the constraints corresponding to the two transshipment nodes. For node 3 (the Kansas City warehouse), we must guarantee that the number of units shipped out must equal the number of units shipped into the warehouse. If

$$\text{Number of units shipped out of node 3} = x_{35} + x_{36} + x_{37} + x_{38}$$

and

$$\text{Number of units shipped into node 3} = x_{13} + x_{23}$$

we obtain

$$x_{35} + x_{36} + x_{37} + x_{38} = x_{13} + x_{23}$$

FIGURE 6.7 LINEAR PROGRAMMING FORMULATION OF THE RYAN ELECTRONICS
TRANSSHIPMENT PROBLEM

$$\text{Min } 2x_{13} + 3x_{14} + 3x_{23} + 1x_{24} + 2x_{35} + 6x_{36} + 3x_{37} + 6x_{38} + 4x_{45} + 4x_{46} + 6x_{47} + 5x_{48}$$

s.t.

$$
\begin{array}{llll}
x_{13} + x_{14} & & \leq 600 & \left.\vphantom{\begin{array}{c}a\\b\end{array}}\right\} \text{ Origin node} \\
\quad\quad x_{23} + x_{24} & & \leq 400 & \text{constraints} \\
-x_{13} \quad\quad - x_{23} \quad\quad + x_{35} + x_{36} + x_{37} + x_{38} & & = 0 & \left.\vphantom{\begin{array}{c}a\\b\end{array}}\right\} \text{ Transshipment node} \\
\quad\quad - x_{14} \quad\quad - x_{24} \quad\quad\quad\quad\quad + x_{45} + x_{46} + x_{47} + x_{48} & = 0 & & \text{constraints} \\
x_{35} \quad\quad\quad\quad\quad + x_{45} & & = 200 & \left.\vphantom{\begin{array}{c}a\\b\\c\\d\end{array}}\right\} \\
x_{36} \quad\quad\quad\quad\quad + x_{46} & & = 150 & \text{Destination node} \\
x_{37} \quad\quad\quad\quad\quad + x_{47} & & = 350 & \text{constraints} \\
x_{38} \quad\quad\quad\quad\quad + x_{48} & = 300 & &
\end{array}
$$

$$x_{ij} \geq 0 \quad \text{for all } i \text{ and } j$$

Similarly, the constraint corresponding to node 4 is

$$x_{45} + x_{46} + x_{47} + x_{48} = x_{14} + x_{24}$$

To develop the constraints associated with the destination nodes, we recognize that for each node the amount shipped to the destination must equal the demand. For example, to satisfy the demand for 200 units at node 5 (the Detroit retail outlet), we write

$$x_{35} + x_{45} = 200$$

Similarly, for nodes 6, 7, and 8, we have

$$x_{36} + x_{46} = 150$$
$$x_{37} + x_{47} = 350$$
$$x_{38} + x_{48} = 300$$

Try Problem 17 (parts b and c) for practice in developing the linear programming model and in solving a transshipment problem on the computer.

As usual, the objective function reflects the total shipping cost over the 12 shipping routes. Combining the objective function and constraints leads to a 12-variable, 8-constraint linear programming model of the Ryan Electronics transshipment problem (see Figure 6.7). Figure 6.8 shows the solution to the Ryan Electronics problem and Table 6.6 summarizes the optimal solution.

As mentioned at the beginning of this section, in the transshipment problem, arcs may connect any pair of nodes. All such shipping patterns are possible in a transshipment problem. We still require only one constraint per node, but the constraint must include a variable for every arc entering or leaving the node. For origin nodes, the sum of the shipments out minus the sum of the shipments in must be less than or equal to the origin supply. For destination nodes, the sum of the shipments in minus the sum of the shipments out must equal demand. For transshipment nodes, the sum of the shipments out must equal the sum of the shipments in, as before.

For an illustration of this more general type of transshipment problem, let us modify the Ryan Electronics problem. Suppose that it is possible to ship directly from Atlanta to New Orleans at $4 per unit and from Dallas to New Orleans at $1 per unit. The network

FIGURE 6.8   THE SOLUTION FOR THE RYAN ELECTRONICS TRANSSHIPMENT
             PROBLEM

WEB file

Ryan

```
Optimal Objective Value = 5200.00000

      Variable              Value           Reduced Costs
   ---------------     ---------------     -----------------
        X13               550.00000             0.00000
        X14                50.00000             0.00000
        X23                 0.00000             3.00000
        X24               400.00000             0.00000
        X35               200.00000             0.00000
        X36                 0.00000             1.00000
        X37               350.00000             0.00000
        X38                 0.00000             0.00000
        X45                 0.00000             3.00000
        X46               150.00000             0.00000
        X47                 0.00000             4.00000
        X48               300.00000             0.00000
```

TABLE 6.6   OPTIMAL SOLUTION TO THE RYAN ELECTRONICS
            TRANSSHIPMENT PROBLEM

Route		Units Shipped	Cost per Unit	Total Cost
From	**To**			
Denver	Kansas City	550	$2	$1100
Denver	Louisville	50	$3	150
Atlanta	Louisville	400	$1	400
Kansas City	Detroit	200	$2	400
Kansas City	Dallas	350	$3	1050
Louisville	Miami	150	$4	600
Louisville	New Orleans	300	$5	1500
				$5200

model corresponding to this modified Ryan Electronics problem is shown in Figure 6.9, the linear programming formulation is shown in Figure 6.10, and the computer solution is shown in Figure 6.11.

Try Problem 18 for practice working with transshipment problems with this more general structure.

In Figure 6.9 we added two new arcs to the network model. Thus, two new variables are necessary in the linear programming formulation. Figure 6.10 shows that the new variables x_{28} and x_{78} appear in the objective function and in the constraints corresponding to the nodes to which the new arcs are connected. Figure 6.11 shows that the value of the optimal solution has been reduced $600 by adding the two new shipping routes; $x_{28} = 250$ units are being shipped directly from Atlanta to New Orleans, and $x_{78} = 50$ units are being shipped from Dallas to New Orleans.

FIGURE 6.9 NETWORK REPRESENTATION OF THE MODIFIED RYAN ELECTRONICS TRANSSHIPMENT PROBLEM

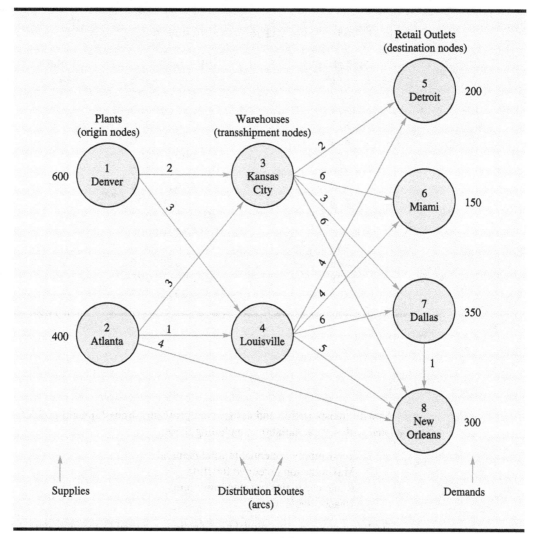

FIGURE 6.10 LINEAR PROGRAMMING FORMULATION OF THE MODIFIED RYAN ELECTRONICS TRANSSHIPMENT PROBLEM

Min $\quad 2x_{13} + 3x_{14} + 3x_{23} + 1x_{24} + 2x_{35} + 6x_{36} + 3x_{37} + 6x_{38} + 4x_{45} + 4x_{46} + 6x_{47} + 5x_{48} + 4x_{28} + 1x_{78}$

s.t.

$$
\begin{array}{llll}
x_{13} + x_{14} & & \leq 600 & \left.\right\} \text{Origin node} \\
\phantom{x_{13}} x_{23} + x_{24} & + x_{28} & \leq 400 & \left.\right\} \text{constraints} \\
-x_{13} - x_{23} + x_{35} + x_{36} + x_{37} + x_{38} & & = 0 & \left.\right\} \text{Transshipment node} \\
x_{14} - x_{24} + x_{45} + x_{46} + x_{47} + x_{48} & & = 0 & \left.\right\} \text{constraints} \\
\phantom{-x_{13}} x_{35} + x_{45} & & = 200 & \left.\right\} \\
\phantom{-x_{13}} x_{36} + x_{46} & & = 150 & \left.\right\} \text{Destination node} \\
\phantom{-x_{13}} x_{37} + x_{47} - x_{78} & & = 350 & \left.\right\} \text{constraints} \\
\phantom{-x_{13}} x_{38} + x_{48} + x_{28} + x_{78} & & = 300 & \left.\right\} \\
\end{array}
$$

$x_{ij} \geq 0$ for all i and j

FIGURE 6.11   THE SOLUTION FOR THE MODIFIED RYAN ELECTRONICS
TRANSSHIPMENT PROBLEM

```
Optimal Objective Value = 4600.00000

      Variable              Value              Reduced Costs
   --------------       --------------        ----------------
        X13              600.00000                0.00000
        X14                0.00000                0.00000
        X23                0.00000                3.00000
        X24              150.00000                0.00000
        X35              200.00000                0.00000
        X36                0.00000                1.00000
        X37              400.00000                0.00000
        X38                0.00000                2.00000
        X45                0.00000                3.00000
        X46              150.00000                0.00000
        X47                0.00000                4.00000
        X48                0.00000                2.00000
        X28              250.00000                0.00000
        X78               50.00000                0.00000
```

Problem Variations

As with transportation and assignment problems, transshipment problems may be formulated with several variations, including these:

1. Total supply not equal to total demand
2. Maximization objective function
3. Route capacities or route minimums
4. Unacceptable routes

The linear programming model modifications required to accommodate these variations are identical to the modifications required for the transportation problem described in Section 6.1. When we add one or more constraints of the form $x_{ij} \leq L_{ij}$ to show that the route from node i to node j has capacity L_{ij}, we refer to the transshipment problem as a **capacitated transshipment problem.**

A General Linear Programming Model

To show the general linear programming model for the transshipment problem, we use the notation:

$$x_{ij} = \text{number of units shipped from the node } i \text{ to node } j$$
$$c_{ij} = \text{cost per unit of shipping from node } i \text{ to node } j$$
$$s_i = \text{supply at origin node } i$$
$$d_j = \text{demand at destination node } j$$

542

The general linear programming model for the transshipment problem is as follows:

$$\text{Min} \quad \sum_{\text{all arcs}} c_{ij} x_{ij}$$

s.t.

$$\sum_{\text{arcs out}} x_{ij} - \sum_{\text{arcs in}} x_{ij} \leq s_i \quad \text{Origin node } i$$

$$\sum_{\text{arcs out}} x_{ij} = \sum_{\text{arcs in}} x_{ij} \quad \text{Transshipment nodes}$$

$$\sum_{\text{arcs in}} x_{ij} - \sum_{\text{arcs out}} x_{ij} = d_j \quad \text{Destination node } j$$

$$x_{ij} \geq 0 \text{ for all } i \text{ and } j$$

NOTES AND COMMENTS

1. The Management Science in Action, Product Sourcing Heuristic at Procter & Gamble, describes how Procter & Gamble used a transshipment model to redesign its North American distribution system.

2. In more advanced treatments of linear programming and network flow problems, the capacitated transshipment problem is called the *pure network flow problem*. Efficient special-purpose solution procedures are available for network flow problems and their special cases.

3. In the general linear programming formulation of the transshipment problem, the constraints for the destination nodes are often written as

$$\sum_{\text{arcs out}} x_{ij} - \sum_{\text{arcs in}} x_{ij} = -d_j$$

The advantage of writing the constraints this way is that the left-hand side of each constraint then represents the flow out of the node minus the flow in. But such constraints would then have to be multiplied by –1 to obtain nonnegative right-hand sides before solving the problem by many linear programming codes.

MANAGEMENT SCIENCE IN ACTION

PRODUCT SOURCING HEURISTIC AT PROCTER & GAMBLE*

A few years ago Procter & Gamble (P&G) embarked on a major strategic planning initiative called the North American Product Sourcing Study. P&G wanted to consolidate its product sources and optimize its distribution system design throughout North America. A decision support system used to aid in this project was called the Product Sourcing Heuristic (PSH) and was based on a transshipment model much like the ones described in this chapter.

In a preprocessing phase, the many P&G products were aggregated into groups that shared the same technology and could be made at the same plant. The PSH employing the transshipment model was then used by product strategy teams responsible for developing product sourcing options for these product groups. The various plants that could produce the product group were the source nodes, the company's regional distribution centers were the transshipment nodes, and P&G's customer zones were the destinations. Direct shipments to customer zones as well as shipments through distribution centers were employed.

The product strategy teams used the heuristic interactively to explore a variety of questions concerning product sourcing and distribution. For instance, the team might be interested in the impact of closing two of five plants and consolidating production in the three remaining plants. The product sourcing heuristic would then delete the source nodes corresponding to the two closed plants,

(continued)

make any capacity modifications necessary to the sources corresponding to the remaining three plants, and re-solve the transshipment problem. The product strategy team could then examine the new solution, make some more modifications, solve again, and so on.

The Product Sourcing Heuristic was viewed as a valuable decision support system by all who used

it. When P&G implemented the results of the study, it realized annual savings in the $200-million range. The PSH proved so successful in North America that P&G used it in other markets around the world.

*Based on information provided by Franz Dill and Tom Chorman of Procter & Gamble.

6.4 SHORTEST-ROUTE PROBLEM

In this section we consider a problem in which the objective is to determine the **shortest route,** or *path,* between two nodes in a network. We will demonstrate the shortest-route problem by considering the situation facing the Gorman Construction Company. Gorman has several construction sites located throughout a three-county area. With multiple daily trips carrying personnel, equipment, and supplies from Gorman's office to the construction sites, the costs associated with transportation activities are substantial. The travel alternatives between Gorman's office and each construction site can be described by the road network shown in Figure 6.12. The road distances in miles between the nodes are shown above the corresponding arcs. In this application, Gorman would like to determine the route that will minimize the total travel distance between Gorman's office (located at node 1) and the construction site located at node 6.

A key to developing a model for the shortest-route problem is to understand that the problem is a special case of the transshipment problem. Specifically, the Gorman shortest-route problem can be viewed as a transshipment problem with one origin node (node 1), one destination node (node 6), and four transshipment nodes (nodes 2, 3, 4, and 5). The

FIGURE 6.12 ROAD NETWORK FOR THE GORMAN COMPANY SHORTEST-ROUTE PROBLEM

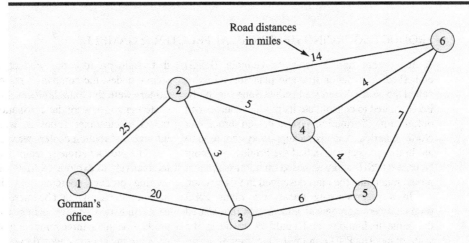

Note: (1) The length of each arc is not necessarily proportional to the travel distance it represents.

(2) All roads are two-way; thus, flow may be in either direction.

FIGURE 6.13 TRANSSHIPMENT NETWORK FOR THE GORMAN SHORTEST-ROUTE PROBLEM

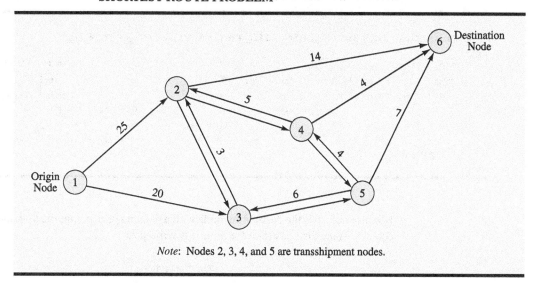

Note: Nodes 2, 3, 4, and 5 are transshipment nodes.

transshipment network for the Gorman shortest-route problem is shown in Figure 6.13. Arrows added to the arcs show the direction of flow, which is always *out* of the origin node and *into* the destination node. Note also that two directed arcs are shown between the pairs of transshipment nodes. For example, one arc going from node 2 to node 3 indicates that the shortest route may go from node 2 to node 3, and one arc going from node 3 to node 2 indicates that the shortest route may go from node 3 to node 2. The distance between two transshipment nodes is the same in either direction.

To find the shortest route between node 1 and node 6, think of node 1 as having a supply of 1 unit and node 6 as having a demand of 1 unit. Let x_{ij} denote the number of units that flow or are shipped from node i to node j. Because only 1 unit will be shipped from node 1 to node 6, the value of x_{ij} will be either 1 or 0. Thus, if $x_{ij} = 1$, the arc from node i to node j is on the shortest route from node 1 to node 6; if $x_{ij} = 0$, the arc from node i to node j is not on the shortest route. Because we are looking for the shortest route between node 1 and node 6, the objective function for the Gorman problem is

$$\text{Min } 25x_{12} + 20x_{13} + 3x_{23} + 3x_{32} + 5x_{24} + 5x_{42} + 14x_{26} + 6x_{35} + 6x_{53}$$
$$+ 4x_{45} + 4x_{54} + 4x_{46} + 7x_{56}$$

To develop the constraints for the model, we begin with node 1. Because the supply at node 1 is 1 unit, the flow out of node 1 must equal 1. Thus, the constraint for node 1 is written

$$x_{12} + x_{13} = 1$$

For transshipment nodes 2, 3, 4, and 5, the flow out of each node must equal the flow into each node; thus, the flow out minus the flow in must be 0. The constraints for the four transshipment nodes are as follows:

	Flow Out		**Flow In**
Node 2	$x_{23} + x_{24} + x_{26}$	$=$	$x_{12} + x_{32} + x_{42}$
Node 3	$x_{32} + x_{35}$	$=$	$x_{13} + x_{23} + x_{53}$
Node 4	$x_{42} + x_{45} + x_{46}$	$=$	$x_{24} + x_{54}$
Node 5	$x_{53} + x_{54} + x_{56}$	$=$	$x_{35} + x_{45}$

FIGURE 6.14 LINEAR PROGRAMMING FORMULATION OF THE GORMAN SHORTEST-ROUTE PROBLEM

$$\text{Min } 25x_{12} + 20x_{13} + 3x_{23} + 3x_{32} + 5x_{24} + 5x_{42} + 14x_{26} + 6x_{35} + 6x_{53} + 4x_{45} + 4x_{54} + 4x_{46} + 7x_{56}$$

s.t.

$$
\begin{array}{llll}
x_{12} + x_{13} & = 1 & \text{Origin node} \\
-x_{12} + x_{23} - x_{32} + x_{24} - x_{42} + x_{26} & = 0 \\
- x_{13} - x_{23} + x_{32} + x_{35} - x_{53} & = 0 \\
- x_{24} + x_{42} + x_{45} - x_{54} + x_{46} & = 0 \\
- x_{35} + x_{53} - x_{45} + x_{54} + x_{56} & = 0 \\
x_{26} + x_{46} + x_{56} & = 1 & \text{Destination node}
\end{array}
$$

Transshipment nodes

$x_{ij} \geq 0$ for all i and j

Because node 6 is the destination node with a demand of one unit, the flow into node 6 must equal 1. Thus, the constraint for node 6 is written as

$$x_{26} + x_{46} + x_{56} = 1$$

Including the negative constraints $x_{ij} \geq 0$ for all i and j, the linear programming model for the Gorman shortest-route problem is shown in Figure 6.14.

Try Problem 22 to practice solving a shortest-route problem.

The solution to the Gorman shortest-route problem is shown in Figure 6.15. The objective function value of 32 indicates that the shortest route between Gorman's office located at node 1 to the construction site located at node 6 is 32 miles. With $x_{13} = 1$, $x_{32} = 1$, $x_{24} = 1$, and $x_{46} = 1$, the shortest-route from node 1 to node 6 is 1–3–2–4–6; in other words, the shortest route takes us from node 1 to node 3; then from node 3 to node 2; then from node 2 to node 4; and finally from node 4 to node 6.

FIGURE 6.15 THE SOLUTION OF THE GORMAN SHORTEST-ROUTE PROBLEM

Optimal Objective Value = 32.00000

Variable	Value	Reduced Cost
X12	0.00000	2.00000
X13	1.00000	0.00000
X23	0.00000	6.00000
X32	1.00000	0.00000
X24	1.00000	0.00000
X42	0.00000	10.00000
X26	0.00000	5.00000
X35	0.00000	0.00000
X53	0.00000	12.00000
X45	0.00000	7.00000
X54	0.00000	1.00000
X46	1.00000	0.00000
X56	0.00000	0.00000

WEB file

Gorman

A General Linear Programming Model

To show the general linear programming model for the shortest-route problem we use the notation:

$$x_{ij} = \begin{cases} 1 & \text{if the arc from node } i \text{ to node } j \text{ is on the shortest route} \\ 0 & \text{otherwise} \end{cases}$$

$c_{ij} =$ the distance, time, or cost associated with the arc from node i to node j

The general linear programming model for the shortest-route problem is as follows:

$$\text{Min} \quad \sum_{\text{all arcs}} c_{ij} x_{ij}$$

s.t.

$$\sum_{\text{arcs out}} x_{ij} = 1 \qquad \text{Origin node } i$$

$$\sum_{\text{arcs out}} x_{ij} = \sum_{\text{arcs in}} x_{ij} \quad \text{Transshipment nodes}$$

$$\sum_{\text{arcs in}} x_{ij} = 1 \qquad \text{Destination node } j$$

NOTES AND COMMENTS

In the Gorman problem, we assumed that all roads in the network are two-way. As a result, the road connecting nodes 2 and 3 in the road network resulted in the creation of two corresponding arcs in the transshipment network. Two decision variables, x_{23} and x_{32}, were required to show that the shortest route might go from node 2 to node 3 or from node 3 to node 2. If the road connecting nodes 2 and 3 had been a one-way road allowing flow only from node 2 to node 3, decision variable x_{32} would not have been included in the model.

6.5 MAXIMAL FLOW PROBLEM

The objective in a **maximal flow** problem is to determine the maximum amount of flow (vehicles, messages, fluid, etc.) that can enter and exit a network system in a given period of time. In this problem, we attempt to transmit flow through all arcs of the network as efficiently as possible. The amount of flow is limited due to capacity restrictions on the various arcs of the network. For example, highway types limit vehicle flow in a transportation system, whereas pipe sizes limit oil flow in an oil distribution system. The maximum or upper limit on the flow in an arc is referred to as the **flow capacity** of the arc. Even though we do not specify capacities for the nodes, we do assume that the flow out of a node is equal to the flow into the node.

As an example of the maximal flow problem, consider the north–south interstate highway system passing through Cincinnati, Ohio. The north–south vehicle flow reaches a level of 15,000 vehicles per hour at peak times. Due to a summer highway maintenance program, which calls for the temporary closing of lanes and lower speed limits, a network of alternate routes through Cincinnati has been proposed by a transportation planning committee. The alternate routes include other highways as well as city streets. Because of differences in speed limits and traffic patterns, flow capacities vary, depending on the

FIGURE 6.16   NETWORK OF HIGHWAY SYSTEM AND FLOW CAPACITIES
(1000s/HOUR) FOR CINCINNATI

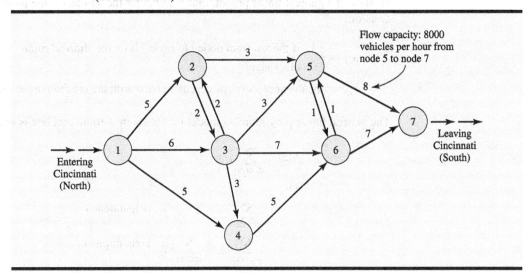

particular streets and roads used. The proposed network with arc flow capacities is shown
in Figure 6.16.

The direction of flow for each arc is indicated, and the arc capacity is shown next to
each arc. Note that most of the streets are one-way. However, a two-way street can be found
between nodes 2 and 3 and between nodes 5 and 6. In both cases, the capacity is the same
in each direction.

We will show how to develop a capacitated transshipment model for the maximal flow
problem. First, we will add an arc from node 7 back to node 1 to represent the total flow
through the highway system. Figure 6.17 shows the modified network. The newly added

FIGURE 6.17   FLOW OVER ARC FROM NODE 7 TO NODE 1 TO REPRESENT TOTAL
FLOW THROUGH THE CINCINNATI HIGHWAY SYSTEM

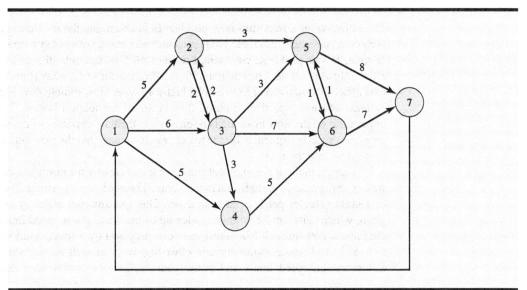

arc shows no capacity; indeed, we will want to maximize the flow over that arc. Maximizing the flow over the arc from node 7 to node 1 is equivalent to maximizing the number of cars that can get through the north–south highway system passing through Cincinnati.

The decision variables are as follows:

$$x_{ij} = \text{amount of traffic flow from node } i \text{ to node } j$$

The objective function that maximizes the flow over the highway system is

$$\text{Max } x_{71}$$

As with all transshipment problems, each arc generates a variable and each node generates a constraint. For each node, a conservation of flow constraint represents the requirement that the flow out must equal the flow in. For node 1, the flow out is $x_{12} + x_{13} + x_{14}$, and the flow in is x_{71}. Therefore, the constraint for node 1 is

$$x_{12} + x_{13} + x_{14} = x_{71}$$

The conservation of flow constraints for the other six nodes are developed in a similar fashion:

	Flow Out		**Flow In**
Node 2	$x_{23} + x_{25}$	$=$	$x_{12} + x_{32}$
Node 3	$x_{32} + x_{34} + x_{35} + x_{36}$	$=$	$x_{13} + x_{23}$
Node 4	x_{46}	$=$	$x_{14} + x_{34}$
Node 5	$x_{56} + x_{57}$	$=$	$x_{25} + x_{35} + x_{65}$
Node 6	$x_{65} + x_{67}$	$=$	$x_{36} + x_{46} + x_{56}$
Node 7	x_{71}	$=$	$x_{57} + x_{67}$

Additional constraints are needed to enforce the capacities on the arcs. These 14 simple upper-bound constraints are given:

$$x_{12} \leq 5 \quad x_{13} \leq 6 \quad x_{14} \leq 5$$
$$x_{23} \leq 2 \quad x_{25} \leq 3$$
$$x_{32} \leq 2 \quad x_{34} \leq 3 \quad x_{35} \leq 3 \quad x_{36} \leq 7$$
$$x_{46} \leq 5$$
$$x_{56} \leq 1 \quad x_{57} \leq 8$$
$$x_{65} \leq 1 \quad x_{67} \leq 7$$

Note that the only arc without a capacity is the one we added from node 7 to node 1.

The solution to this 15-variable, 21-constraint linear programming problem is shown in Figure 6.18. We note that the value of the optimal solution is 14. This result implies that the maximal flow over the highway system is 14,000 vehicles. Figure 6.19 shows how the vehicle flow is routed through the original highway network. We note, for instance, that 5000 vehicles per hour are routed between nodes 1 and 2, 2000 vehicles per hour are routed between nodes 2 and 3, and so on.

The results of the maximal flow analysis indicate that the planned highway network system will not handle the peak flow of 15,000 vehicles per hour. The transportation

Try Problem 29 for practice in solving a maximal flow problem.

FIGURE 6.18   THE SOLUTION TO THE CINCINNATI HIGHWAY SYSTEM MAXIMAL
FLOW PROBLEM

```
Optimal Objective Value =  14.00000

        Variable            Value          Reduced Cost
     --------------    --------------    --------------
          X12             5.00000            0.00000
          X13             6.00000            0.00000
          X14             3.00000            0.00000
          X23             2.00000            0.00000
          X25             3.00000            0.00000
          X34             0.00000            0.00000
          X35             3.00000            0.00000
          X36             5.00000            0.00000
          X32             0.00000            0.00000
          X46             3.00000            0.00000
          X56             0.00000            1.00000
          X57             7.00000            0.00000
          X65             1.00000            0.00000
          X67             7.00000            0.00000
          X71            14.00000            0.00000
```

FIGURE 6.19   MAXIMAL FLOW PATTERN FOR THE CINCINNATI HIGHWAY
SYSTEM NETWORK

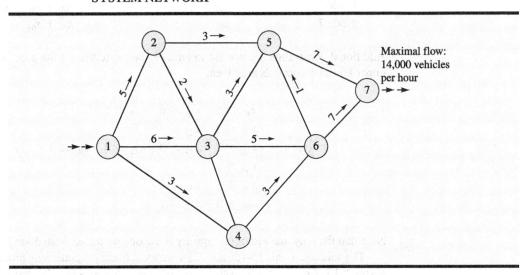

planners will have to expand the highway network, increase current arc flow capacities, or
be prepared for serious traffic problems. If the network is extended or modified, another
maximal flow analysis will determine the extent of any improved flow. The Management
Science in Action, Optimizing Restoration Capacity at AT&T, notes that AT&T solved
shortest-route and maximal flow problems in designing a transmission network.

1. The maximal flow problem of this section can also be solved with a slightly different formulation if the extra arc between nodes 7 and 1 is not used. The alternate approach is to maximize the flow into node 7 ($x_{57} + x_{67}$) and drop the conservation of flow constraints for nodes 1 and 7. However, the formulation used in this section is most common in practice.

2. Network models can be used to describe a variety of management science problems. Unfortunately, no one network solution algorithm can be used to solve every network problem. It is important to recognize the specific type of problem being modeled in order to select the correct specialized solution algorithm.

MANAGEMENT SCIENCE IN ACTION

OPTIMIZING RESTORATION CAPACITY AT AT&T*

AT&T is a global telecommunications company that provides long-distance voice and data, video, wireless, satellite, and Internet services. The company uses state-of-the-art switching and transmission equipment to provide service to more than 80 million customers. In the continental United States, AT&T's transmission network consists of more than 40,000 miles of fiber-optic cable. On peak days AT&T handles as many as 290 million calls of various types.

Power outages, natural disasters, cable cuts, and other events can disable a portion of the transmission network. When such events occur, spare capacity comprising the restoration network must be immediately employed so that service is not disrupted. Critical issues with respect to the restoration network are: How much capacity is necessary? and Where should it be located? In 1997, AT&T assembled a RestNet team to address these issues.

To optimize restoration capacity, the RestNet team developed a large-scale linear programming model. One subproblem in their model involves determining the shortest route connecting an origin and destination whenever a failure occurs in a span of the transmission network. Another subproblem solves a maximal flow problem to find the best restoration paths from each switch to a disaster recovery switch.

The RestNet team was successful, and their work is an example of how valuable management science methodology is to companies. According to C. Michael Armstrong, chair and CEO, "Last year the work of the RestNet team allowed us to reduce capital spending by tens of millions of dollars."

*Based on Ken Ambs, Sebastian Cwilich, Mei Deng, David J. Houck, David F. Lynch, and Dicky Yan, "Optimizing Restoration Capacity in the AT&T Network," *Interfaces* (January/February 2000): 26–44.

6.6 A PRODUCTION AND INVENTORY APPLICATION

The introduction to the transportation and transshipment problems in Sections 6.1 and 6.3 involved applications for the shipment of goods from several supply locations or origins to several demand sites or destinations. Although the shipment of goods is the subject of many transportation and transshipment problems, transportation or transshipment models can be developed for applications that have nothing to do with the physical shipment of goods from origins to destinations. In this section we show how to use a transshipment model to solve a production and inventory problem.

Contois Carpets is a small manufacturer of carpeting for home and office installations. Production capacity, demand, production cost per square yard, and inventory holding cost per square yard for the next four quarters are shown in Table 6.7. Note that production

TABLE 6.7 PRODUCTION, DEMAND, AND COST ESTIMATES FOR CONTOIS CARPETS

Quarter	Production Capacity (square yards)	Demand (square yards)	Production Cost ($/square yard)	Inventory Cost ($/square yard)
1	600	400	2	0.25
2	300	500	5	0.25
3	500	400	3	0.25
4	400	400	3	0.25

capacity, demand, and production costs vary by quarter, whereas the cost of carrying inventory from one quarter to the next is constant at $0.25 per yard. Contois wants to determine how many yards of carpeting to manufacture each quarter to minimize the total production and inventory cost for the four-quarter period.

The network flows into and out of demand nodes are what make the model a transshipment model.

We begin by developing a network representation of the problem. First, we create four nodes corresponding to the production in each quarter and four nodes corresponding to the demand in each quarter. Each production node is connected by an outgoing arc to the demand node for the same period. The flow on the arc represents the number of square yards of carpet manufactured for the period. For each demand node, an outgoing arc represents the amount of inventory (square yards of carpet) carried over to the demand node for the next period. Figure 6.20 shows the network model. Note that nodes 1–4 represent the production for each quarter and that nodes 5–8 represent the demand for each quarter. The quarterly production capacities are shown in the left margin, and the quarterly demands are shown in the right margin.

The objective is to determine a production scheduling and inventory policy that will minimize the total production and inventory cost for the four quarters. Constraints involve production capacity and demand in each quarter. As usual, a linear programming model can be developed from the network by establishing a constraint for each node and a variable for each arc.

Let x_{15} denote the number of square yards of carpet manufactured in quarter 1. The capacity of the facility is 600 square yards in quarter 1, so the production capacity constraint is

$$x_{15} \leq 600$$

Using similar decision variables, we obtain the production capacities for quarters 2–4:

$$x_{26} \leq 300$$
$$x_{37} \leq 500$$
$$x_{48} \leq 400$$

We now consider the development of the constraints for each of the demand nodes. For node 5, one arc enters the node, which represents the number of square yards of carpet produced in quarter 1, and one arc leaves the node, which represents the number of square yards of carpet that will not be sold in quarter 1 and will be carried over for possible sale in quarter 2. In general, for each quarter the beginning inventory plus the production minus the ending inventory must equal demand. However, because quarter 1 has no beginning inventory, the constraint for node 5 is

$$x_{15} - x_{56} = 400$$

FIGURE 6.20   NETWORK REPRESENTATION OF THE CONTOIS CARPETS PROBLEM

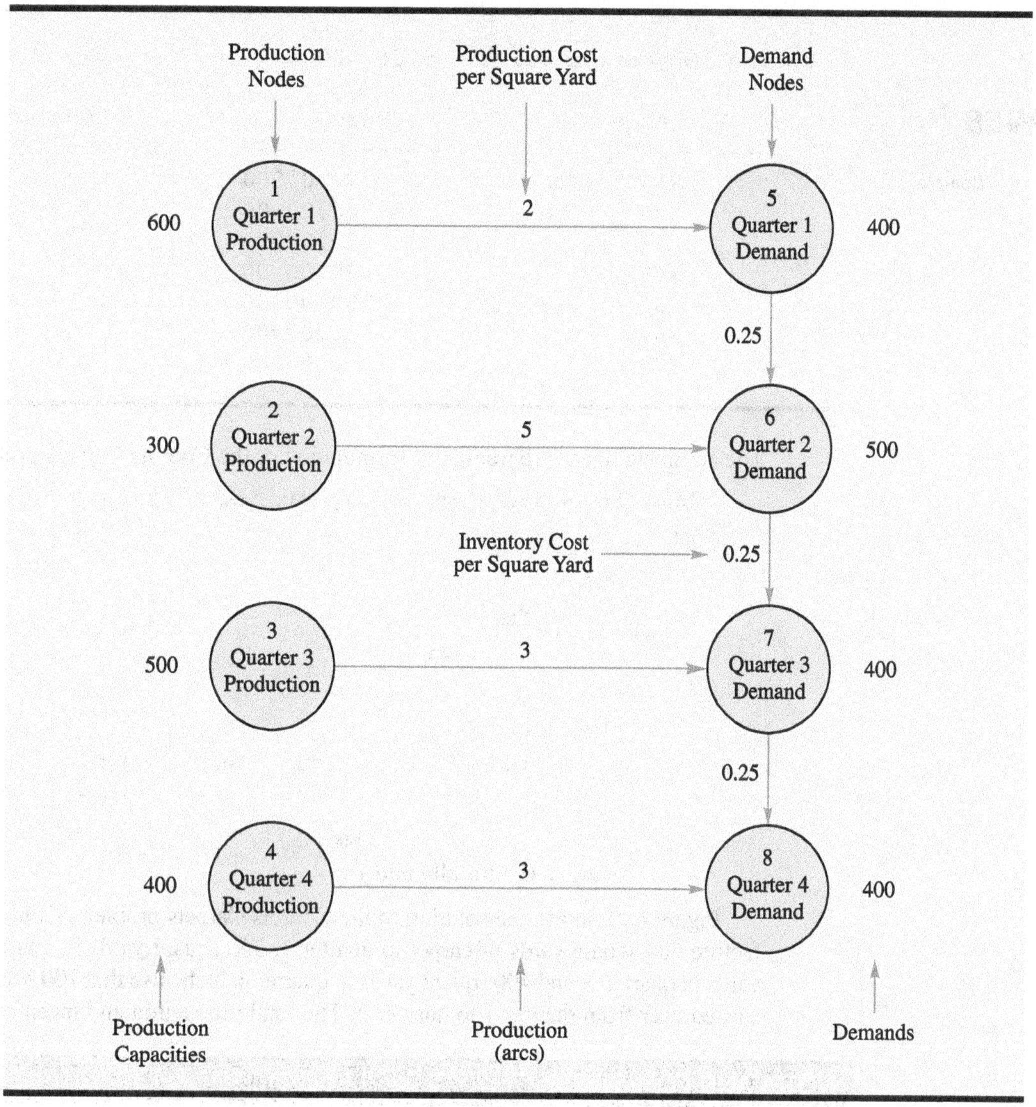

The constraints associated with the demand nodes in quarters 2, 3, and 4 are

$$x_{56} + x_{26} - x_{67} = 500$$
$$x_{67} + x_{37} - x_{78} = 400$$
$$x_{78} + x_{48} = 400$$

Note that the constraint for node 8 (fourth-quarter demand) involves only two variables because no provision is made for holding inventory for a fifth quarter.

The objective is to minimize total production and inventory cost, so we write the objective function as

$$\text{Min} \quad 2x_{15} + 5x_{26} + 3x_{37} + 3x_{48} + 0.25x_{56} + 0.25x_{67} + 0.25x_{78}$$

FIGURE 6.21 THE SOLUTION FOR THE CONTOIS CARPETS PROBLEM

Contois

```
Optimal Objective Value = 5150.00000

     Variable              Value              Reduced Cost
   --------------      --------------       ----------------
       X15               600.00000              0.00000
       X26               300.00000              0.00000
       X37               400.00000              0.00000
       X48               400.00000              0.00000
       X56               200.00000              0.00000
       X67                 0.00000              2.25000
       X78                 0.00000              0.00000
```

The complete linear programming formulation of the Contois Carpets problem is

$$\text{Min} \quad 2x_{15} + 5x_{26} + 3x_{37} + 3x_{48} + 0.25x_{56} + 0.25x_{67} + 0.25x_{78}$$

s.t.

$$
\begin{aligned}
x_{15} & & & & & & & \le 600 \\
& x_{26} & & & & & & \le 300 \\
& & x_{37} & & & & & \le 500 \\
& & & x_{48} & & & & \le 400 \\
x_{15} & & & & - \; x_{56} & & & = 400 \\
& x_{26} & & & + \; x_{56} & - \; x_{67} & & = 500 \\
& & x_{37} & & & + \; x_{67} & - \; x_{78} & = 400 \\
& & & x_{48} & & & + \; x_{78} & = 400
\end{aligned}
$$

$$x_{ij} \ge 0 \quad \text{for all } i \text{ and } j$$

Figure 6.21 shows the solution to the Contois Carpets problem. Contois should manufacture 600 square yards of carpet in quarter 1, 300 square yards in quarter 2, 400 square yards in quarter 3, and 400 square yards in quarter 4. Note also that 200 square yards will be carried over from quarter 1 to quarter 2. The total production and inventory cost is $5150.

NOTES AND COMMENTS

For the network models presented in this chapter, the amount leaving the starting node for an arc is always equal to the amount entering the ending node for that arc. An extension of such a network model is the case where a gain or a loss occurs as an arc is traversed. The amount entering the destination node may be greater or smaller than the amount leaving the origin node. For instance, if cash is the commodity flowing across an arc, the cash earns interest from one period to the next. Thus, the amount of cash entering the next period is greater than the amount leaving the previous period by the amount of interest earned. Networks with gains or losses are treated in more advanced texts on network flow programming.

SUMMARY

In this chapter we introduced transportation, assignment, transshipment, shortest-route, and maximal flow problems. All five types of problems belong to the special category of linear programs called *network flow problems*. In general, the network model for these problems consists of nodes representing origins, destinations, and if necessary, transshipment points in the network system. Arcs are used to represent the routes for shipment, travel, or flow between the various nodes.

The general transportation problem has m origins and n destinations. Given the supply at each origin, the demand at each destination, and unit shipping cost between each origin and each destination, the transportation model determines the optimal amounts to ship from each origin to each destination.

The assignment problem is a special case of the transportation problem in which all supply and all demand values are 1. We represent each agent as an origin node and each task as a destination node. The assignment model determines the minimum cost or maximum profit assignment of agents to tasks.

The transshipment problem is an extension of the transportation problem involving transfer points referred to as transshipment nodes. In this more general model, we allow arcs between any pair of nodes in the network. If desired, capacities can be specified for arcs, which makes it a capacitated transshipment problem.

The shortest-route problem finds the shortest route or path between two nodes of a network. Distance, time, and cost are often the criteria used for this model. The shortest-route problem can be expressed as a transshipment problem with one origin and one destination. By shipping one unit from the origin to the destination, the solution will determine the shortest route through the network.

The maximal flow problem can be used to allocate flow to the arcs of the network so that flow through the network system is maximized. Arc capacities determine the maximum amount of flow for each arc. With these flow capacity constraints, the maximal flow problem is expressed as a capacitated transshipment problem.

In the last section of the chapter, we showed how a variation of the transshipment problem could be used to solve a production and inventory problem. In the chapter appendix we show how to use Excel to solve three of the distribution and network problems presented in the chapter.

GLOSSARY

Transportation problem A network flow problem that often involves minimizing the cost of shipping goods from a set of origins to a set of destinations; it can be formulated and solved as a linear program by including a variable for each arc and a constraint for each node.

Network A graphical representation of a problem consisting of numbered circles (nodes) interconnected by a series of lines (arcs); arrowheads on the arcs show the direction of flow. Transportation, assignment, and transshipment problems are network flow problems.

Nodes The intersection or junction points of a network.

Arcs The lines connecting the nodes in a network.

Dummy origin An origin added to a transportation problem to make the total supply equal to the total demand. The supply assigned to the dummy origin is the difference between the total demand and the total supply.

Capacitated transportation problem A variation of the basic transportation problem in which some or all of the arcs are subject to capacity restrictions.

Assignment problem A network flow problem that often involves the assignment of agents to tasks; it can be formulated as a linear program and is a special case of the transportation problem.

Transshipment problem An extension of the transportation problem to distribution problems involving transfer points and possible shipments between any pair of nodes.

Capacitated transshipment problem   A variation of the transshipment problem in which some or all of the arcs are subject to capacity restrictions.

Shortest route   Shortest path between two nodes in a network.

Maximal flow   The maximum amount of flow that can enter and exit a network system during a given period of time.

Flow capacity   The maximum flow for an arc of the network. The flow capacity in one direction may not equal the flow capacity in the reverse direction.

PROBLEMS

1. A company imports goods at two ports: Philadelphia and New Orleans. Shipments of one product are made to customers in Atlanta, Dallas, Columbus, and Boston. For the next planning period, the supplies at each port, customer demands, and shipping costs per case from each port to each customer are as follows:

Port	Customers				Port Supply
	Atlanta	**Dallas**	**Columbus**	**Boston**	
Philadelphia	2	6	6	2	5000
New Orleans	1	2	5	7	3000
Demand	1400	3200	2000	1400	

Develop a network representation of the distribution system (transportation problem).

2. Consider the following network representation of a transportation problem:

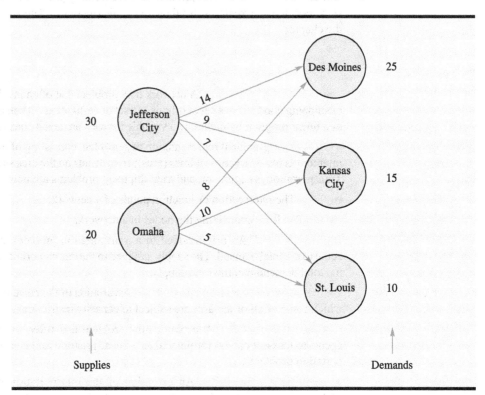

The supplies, demands, and transportation costs per unit are shown on the network.

a. Develop a linear programming model for this problem; be sure to define the variables in your model.

b. Solve the linear program to determine the optimal solution.

3. Tri-County Utilities, Inc., supplies natural gas to customers in a three-county area. The company purchases natural gas from two companies: Southern Gas and Northwest Gas. Demand forecasts for the coming winter season are Hamilton County, 400 units; Butler County, 200 units; and Clermont County, 300 units. Contracts to provide the following quantities have been written: Southern Gas, 500 units; and Northwest Gas, 400 units. Distribution costs for the counties vary, depending upon the location of the suppliers. The distribution costs per unit (in thousands of dollars) are as follows:

From	Hamilton	Butler	Clermont
Southern Gas	10	20	15
Northwest Gas	12	15	18

a. Develop a network representation of this problem.

b. Develop a linear programming model that can be used to determine the plan that will minimize total distribution costs.

c. Describe the distribution plan and show the total distribution cost.

d. Recent residential and industrial growth in Butler County has the potential for increasing demand by as much as 100 units. Which supplier should Tri-County contract with to supply the additional capacity?

4. Arnoff Enterprises manufactures the central processing unit (CPU) for a line of personal computers. The CPUs are manufactured in Seattle, Columbus, and New York and shipped to warehouses in Pittsburgh, Mobile, Denver, Los Angeles, and Washington, D.C., for further distribution. The following table shows the number of CPUs available at each plant, the number of CPUs required by each warehouse, and the shipping costs (dollars per unit):

Plant	Pittsburgh	Mobile	Denver	Los Angeles	Washington	CPUs Available
Seattle	10	20	5	9	10	9000
Columbus	2	10	8	30	6	4000
New York	1	20	7	10	4	8000
CPUs Required	3000	5000	4000	6000	3000	21,000

a. Develop a network representation of this problem.

b. Determine the amount that should be shipped from each plant to each warehouse to minimize the total shipping cost.

c. The Pittsburgh warehouse just increased its order by 1000 units, and Arnoff authorized the Columbus plant to increase its production by 1000 units. Will this production increase lead to an increase or decrease in total shipping costs? Solve for the new optimal solution.

557

5. Premier Consulting's two consultants, Avery and Baker, can be scheduled to work for clients up to a maximum of 160 hours each over the next four weeks. A third consultant, Campbell, has some administrative assignments already planned and is available for clients up to a maximum of 140 hours over the next four weeks. The company has four clients with projects in process. The estimated hourly requirements for each of the clients over the four-week period are

Client	Hours
A	180
B	75
C	100
D	85

Hourly rates vary for the consultant–client combination and are based on several factors, including project type and the consultant's experience. The rates (dollars per hour) for each consultant–client combination are as follows:

	Client			
Consultant	A	B	C	D
Avery	100	125	115	100
Baker	120	135	115	120
Campbell	155	150	140	130

a. Develop a network representation of the problem.
b. Formulate the problem as a linear program, with the optimal solution providing the hours each consultant should be scheduled for each client to maximize the consulting firm's billings. What is the schedule and what is the total billing?
c. New information shows that Avery doesn't have the experience to be scheduled for client B. If this consulting assignment is not permitted, what impact does it have on total billings? What is the revised schedule?

6. Klein Chemicals, Inc., produces a special oil-based material that is currently in short supply. Four of Klein's customers have already placed orders that together exceed the combined capacity of Klein's two plants. Klein's management faces the problem of deciding how many units it should supply to each customer. Because the four customers are in different industries, different prices can be charged because of the various industry pricing structures. However, slightly different production costs at the two plants and varying transportation costs between the plants and customers make a "sell to the highest bidder" strategy unacceptable. After considering price, production costs, and transportation costs, Klein established the following profit per unit for each plant–customer alternative:

	Customer			
Plant	D_1	D_2	D_3	D_4
Clifton Springs	$32	$34	$32	$40
Danville	$34	$30	$28	$38

The plant capacities and customer orders are as follows:

Plant Capacity (units)		Distributor Orders (units)	
Clifton Springs	5000	D_1	2000
		D_2	5000
Danville	3000	D_3	3000
		D_4	2000

How many units should each plant produce for each customer in order to maximize profits? Which customer demands will not be met? Show your network model and linear programming formulation.

7. Forbelt Corporation has a one-year contract to supply motors for all refrigerators produced by the Ice Age Corporation. Ice Age manufactures the refrigerators at four locations around the country: Boston, Dallas, Los Angeles, and St. Paul. Plans call for the following number (in thousands) of refrigerators to be produced at each location:

Boston	50
Dallas	70
Los Angeles	60
St. Paul	80

Forbelt's three plants are capable of producing the motors. The plants and production capacities (in thousands) are

Denver	100
Atlanta	100
Chicago	150

Because of varying production and transportation costs, the profit that Forbelt earns on each lot of 1000 units depends on which plant produced the lot and which destination it was shipped to. The following table gives the accounting department estimates of the profit per unit (shipments will be made in lots of 1000 units):

	Shipped To			
Produced At	Boston	Dallas	Los Angeles	St. Paul
Denver	7	11	8	13
Atlanta	20	17	12	10
Chicago	8	18	13	16

With profit maximization as a criterion, Forbelt's management wants to determine how many motors should be produced at each plant and how many motors should be shipped from each plant to each destination.

a. Develop a network representation of this problem.
b. Find the optimal solution.

8. The Ace Manufacturing Company has orders for three similar products:

Product	Orders (units)
A	2000
B	500
C	1200

Three machines are available for the manufacturing operations. All three machines can produce all the products at the same production rate. However, due to varying defect percentages of each product on each machine, the unit costs of the products vary depending on the machine used. Machine capacities for the next week, and the unit costs, are as follows:

Machine	Capacity (units)
1	1500
2	1500
3	1000

	Product		
Machine	A	B	C
1	$1.00	$1.20	$0.90
2	$1.30	$1.40	$1.20
3	$1.10	$1.00	$1.20

Use the transportation model to develop the minimum cost production schedule for the products and machines. Show the linear programming formulation.

9. Scott and Associates, Inc., is an accounting firm that has three new clients. Project leaders will be assigned to the three clients. Based on the different backgrounds and experiences of the leaders, the various leader–client assignments differ in terms of projected completion times. The possible assignments and the estimated completion times in days are as follows:

	Client		
Project Leader	1	2	3
Jackson	10	16	32
Ellis	14	22	40
Smith	22	24	34

a. Develop a network representation of this problem.
b. Formulate the problem as a linear program, and solve. What is the total time required?

10. CarpetPlus sells and installs floor covering for commercial buildings. Brad Sweeney, a CarpetPlus account executive, was just awarded the contract for five jobs. Brad must now assign a CarpetPlus installation crew to each of the five jobs. Because the commission Brad will earn depends on the profit CarpetPlus makes, Brad would like to determine an assignment that will minimize total installation costs. Currently, five installation crews are available for assignment. Each crew is identified by a color code, which aids in tracking of

job progress on a large white board. The following table shows the costs (in hundreds of dollars) for each crew to complete each of the five jobs:

				Job		
		1	**2**	**3**	**4**	**5**
	Red	30	44	38	47	31
	White	25	32	45	44	25
Crew	**Blue**	23	40	37	39	29
	Green	26	38	37	45	28
	Brown	26	34	44	43	28

a. Develop a network representation of the problem.
b. Formulate and solve a linear programming model to determine the minimum cost assignment.

11. A local television station plans to drop four Friday evening programs at the end of the season. Steve Botuchis, the station manager, developed a list of six potential replacement programs. Estimates of the advertising revenue (in dollars) that can be expected for each of the new programs in the four vacated time slots are as follows. Mr. Botuchis asked you to find the assignment of programs to time slots that will maximize total advertising revenue.

	5:00– 5:30 P.M.	5:30– 6:00 P.M.	7:00– 7:30 P.M.	8:00– 8:30 P.M.
Home Improvement	5000	3000	6000	4000
World News	7500	8000	7000	5500
NASCAR Live	8500	5000	6500	8000
Wall Street Today	7000	6000	6500	5000
Hollywood Briefings	7000	8000	3000	6000
Ramundo & Son	6000	4000	4500	7000

12. The U.S. Cable Company uses a distribution system with five distribution centers and eight customer zones. Each customer zone is assigned a sole source supplier; each customer zone receives all of its cable products from the same distribution center. In an effort to balance demand and workload at the distribution centers, the company's vice president of logistics specified that distribution centers may not be assigned more than three customer zones. The following table shows the five distribution centers and cost of supplying each customer zone (in thousands of dollars):

Distribution Centers	Customer Zones							
	Los Angeles	Chicago	Columbus	Atlanta	Newark	Kansas City	Denver	Dallas
Plano	70	47	22	53	98	21	27	13
Nashville	75	38	19	58	90	34	40	26
Flagstaff	15	78	37	82	111	40	29	32
Springfield	60	23	8	39	82	36	32	45
Boulder	45	40	29	75	86	25	11	37

a. Determine the assignment of customer zones to distribution centers that will minimize cost.
b. Which distribution centers, if any, are not used?
c. Suppose that each distribution center is limited to a maximum of two customer zones. How does this constraint change the assignment and the cost of supplying customer zones?

13. United Express Service (UES) uses large quantities of packaging materials at its four distribution hubs. After screening potential suppliers, UES identified six vendors that can provide packaging materials that will satisfy its quality standards. UES asked each of the six vendors to submit bids to satisfy annual demand at each of its four distribution hubs over the next year. The following table lists the bids received (in thousands of dollars). UES wants to ensure that each of the distribution hubs is serviced by a different vendor. Which bids should UES accept, and which vendors should UES select to supply each distribution hub?

	Distribution Hub			
Bidder	1	2	3	4
Martin Products	190	175	125	230
Schmidt Materials	150	235	155	220
Miller Containers	210	225	135	260
D&J Burns	170	185	190	280
Larbes Furnishings	220	190	140	240
Lawler Depot	270	200	130	260

14. The quantitative methods department head at a major midwestern university will be scheduling faculty to teach courses during the coming autumn term. Four core courses need to be covered. The four courses are at the UG, MBA, MS, and Ph.D. levels. Four professors will be assigned to the courses, with each professor receiving one of the courses. Student evaluations of professors are available from previous terms. Based on a rating scale of 4 (excellent), 3 (very good), 2 (average), 1 (fair), and 0 (poor), the average student evaluations for each professor are shown. Professor D does not have a Ph.D. and cannot be assigned to teach the Ph.D.-level course. If the department head makes teaching assignments based on maximizing the student evaluation ratings over all four courses, what staffing assignments should be made?

	Course			
Professor	UG	MBA	MS	Ph.D.
A	2.8	2.2	3.3	3.0
B	3.2	3.0	3.6	3.6
C	3.3	3.2	3.5	3.5
D	3.2	2.8	2.5	—

15. A market research firm's three clients each requested that the firm conduct a sample survey. Four available statisticians can be assigned to these three projects; however, all four statisticians are busy, and therefore each can handle only one client. The following data

show the number of hours required for each statistician to complete each job; the differences in time are based on experience and ability of the statisticians.

| | Client | | |
Statistician	A	B	C
1	150	210	270
2	170	230	220
3	180	230	225
4	160	240	230

a. Formulate and solve a linear programming model for this problem.
b. Suppose that the time statistician 4 needs to complete the job for client A is increased from 160 to 165 hours. What effect will this change have on the solution?
c. Suppose that the time statistician 4 needs to complete the job for client A is decreased to 140 hours. What effect will this change have on the solution?
d. Suppose that the time statistician 3 needs to complete the job for client B increases to 250 hours. What effect will this change have on the solution?

16. Hatcher Enterprises uses a chemical called Rbase in production operations at five divisions. Only six suppliers of Rbase meet Hatcher's quality control standards. All six suppliers can produce Rbase in sufficient quantities to accommodate the needs of each division. The quantity of Rbase needed by each Hatcher division and the price per gallon charged by each supplier are as follows:

Division	Demand (1000s of gallons)	Supplier	Price per Gallon ($)
1	40	1	12.60
2	45	2	14.00
3	50	3	10.20
4	35	4	14.20
5	45	5	12.00
		6	13.00

The cost per gallon (in dollars) for shipping from each supplier to each division is provided in the following table:

| | Supplier | | | | | |
Division	1	2	3	4	5	6
1	2.75	2.50	3.15	2.80	2.75	2.75
2	0.80	0.20	5.40	1.20	3.40	1.00
3	4.70	2.60	5.30	2.80	6.00	5.60
4	2.60	1.80	4.40	2.40	5.00	2.80
5	3.40	0.40	5.00	1.20	2.60	3.60

Hatcher believes in spreading its business among suppliers so that the company will be less affected by supplier problems (e.g., labor strikes or resource availability). Company policy requires that each division have a separate supplier.

a. For each supplier–division combination, compute the total cost of supplying the division's demand.

b. Determine the optimal assignment of suppliers to divisions.

SELF test

17. The distribution system for the Herman Company consists of three plants, two warehouses, and four customers. Plant capacities and shipping costs per unit (in dollars) from each plant to each warehouse are as follows:

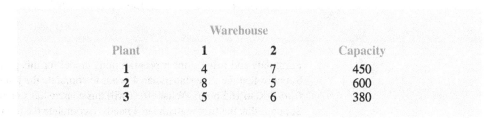

	Warehouse		
Plant	1	2	Capacity
1	4	7	450
2	8	5	600
3	5	6	380

Customer demand and shipping costs per unit (in dollars) from each warehouse to each customer are

	Customer			
Warehouse	1	2	3	4
1	6	4	8	4
2	3	6	7	7
Demand	300	300	300	400

a. Develop a network representation of this problem.

b. Formulate a linear programming model of the problem.

c. Solve the linear program to determine the optimal shipping plan.

18. Refer to Problem 17. Suppose that shipments between the two warehouses are permitted at $2 per unit and that direct shipments can be made from plant 3 to customer 4 at a cost of $7 per unit.

a. Develop a network representation of this problem.

b. Formulate a linear programming model of this problem.

c. Solve the linear program to determine the optimal shipping plan.

19. Adirondack Paper Mills, Inc., operates paper plants in Augusta, Maine, and Tupper Lake, New York. Warehouse facilities are located in Albany, New York, and Portsmouth, New Hampshire. Distributors are located in Boston, New York, and Philadelphia. The plant capacities and distributor demands for the next month are as follows:

Plant	Capacity (units)
Augusta	300
Tupper Lake	100

Distributor	Demand (units)
Boston	150
New York	100
Philadelphia	150

564

The unit transportation costs (in dollars) for shipments from the two plants to the two warehouses and from the two warehouses to the three distributors are as follows:

	Warehouse	
Plant	Albany	Portsmouth
Augusta	7	5
Tupper Lake	3	4

	Distributor		
Warehouse	Boston	New York	Philadelphia
Albany	8	5	7
Portsmouth	5	6	10

   a. Draw the network representation of the Adirondack Paper Mills problem.

   b. Formulate the Adirondack Paper Mills problem as a linear programming problem.

   c. Solve the linear program to determine the minimum cost shipping schedule for the problem.

20. The Moore & Harman Company is in the business of buying and selling grain. An important aspect of the company's business is arranging for the purchased grain to be shipped to customers. If the company can keep freight costs low, profitability will improve.

     The company recently purchased three rail cars of grain at Muncie, Indiana; six rail cars at Brazil, Indiana; and five rail cars at Xenia, Ohio. Twelve carloads of grain have been sold. The locations and the amount sold at each location are as follows:

Location	Number of Rail Car Loads
Macon, GA	2
Greenwood, SC	4
Concord, SC	3
Chatham, NC	3

All shipments must be routed through either Louisville or Cincinnati. Shown are the shipping costs per bushel (in cents) from the origins to Louisville and Cincinnati and the costs per bushel to ship from Louisville and Cincinnati to the destinations.

	To	
From	Louisville	Cincinnati
Muncie	8	6 ← Cost per bushel
Brazil	3	8 from Muncie to
Xenia	9	3 Cincinnati is 6¢

		To		
From	**Macon**	**Greenwood**	**Concord**	**Chatham**
Louisville	44	34	34	32
Cincinnati	57	35	28	24

Cost per bushel from
Cincinnati to Greenwood is 35¢

Determine a shipping schedule that will minimize the freight costs necessary to satisfy demand. Which (if any) rail cars of grain must be held at the origin until buyers can be found?

21. The following linear programming formulation is for a transshipment problem:

$$\text{Min} \quad 11x_{13} + 12x_{14} + 10x_{21} + 8x_{34} + 10x_{35} + 11x_{42} + 9x_{45} + 12x_{52}$$

s.t.

$$
\begin{aligned}
x_{13} + x_{14} - x_{21} & & & & & \leq 5 \\
x_{21} & - x_{42} & - x_{52} & \leq 3 \\
x_{13} & - x_{34} - x_{35} & & = 6 \\
- x_{14} & - x_{34} & + x_{42} + x_{45} & \leq 2 \\
& x_{35} & + x_{45} - x_{52} & = 4
\end{aligned}
$$

$$x_{ij} \geq 0 \quad \text{for all } i, j$$

Show the network representation of this problem.

22. A rental car company has an imbalance of cars at seven of its locations. The following network shows the locations of concern (the nodes) and the cost to move a car between locations. A positive number by a node indicates an excess supply at the node, and a negative number indicates an excess demand.

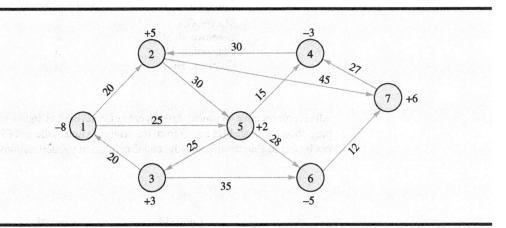

a. Develop a linear programming model of this problem.
b. Solve the model formulated in part (a) to determine how the cars should be redistributed among the locations.

23. Find the shortest route from node 1 to node 7 in the network shown.

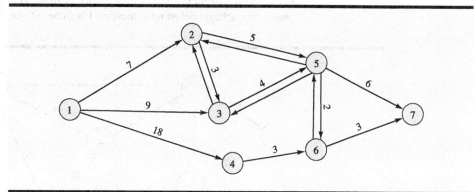

24. In the original Gorman Construction Company problem, we found the shortest distance from the office (node 1) to the construction site located at node 6. Because some of the roads are highways and others are city streets, the shortest-distance routes between the office and the construction site may not necessarily provide the quickest or shortest-time route. Shown here is the Gorman road network with travel time rather than distance. Find the shortest route from Gorman's office to the construction site at node 6 if the objective is to minimize travel time rather than distance.

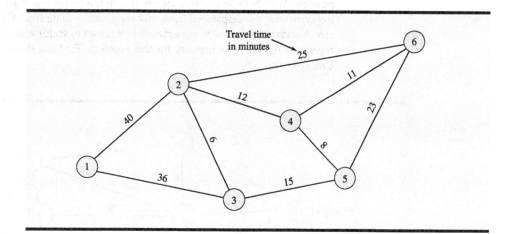

25. CARD, Cleveland Area Rapid Delivery, operates a delivery service in the Cleveland metropolitan area. Most of CARD's business involves rapid delivery of documents and parcels between offices during the business day. CARD promotes its ability to make fast and on-time deliveries anywhere in the metropolitan area. When a customer calls with a delivery request, CARD quotes a guaranteed delivery time. The following network shows the street routes available. The numbers above each arc indicate the travel time in minutes between the two locations.

    a. Develop a linear programming model that can be used to find the minimum time required to make a delivery from location 1 to location 6.
    b. How long does it take to make a delivery from location 1 to location 6?

c. Assume that it is now 1:00 P.M. CARD just received a request for a pickup at location 1, and the closest CARD courier is 8 minutes away from location 1. If CARD provides a 20% safety margin in guaranteeing a delivery time, what is the guaranteed delivery time if the package picked up at location 1 is to be delivered to location 6?

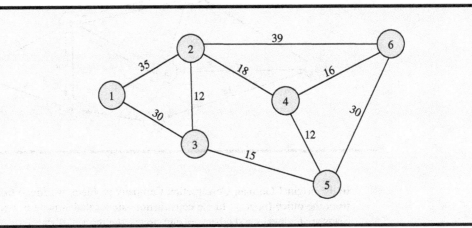

26. Morgan Trucking Company operates a special pickup and delivery service between Chicago and six other cities located in a four-state area. When Morgan receives a request for service, it dispatches a truck from Chicago to the city requesting service as soon as possible. With both fast service and minimum travel costs as objectives for Morgan, it is important that the dispatched truck take the shortest route from Chicago to the specified city. Assume that the following network (not drawn to scale) with distances given in miles represents the highway network for this problem. Find the shortest-route distance from Chicago to node 6.

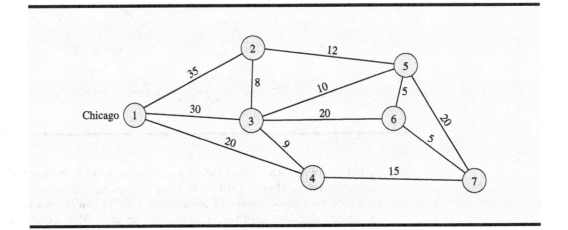

27. City Cab Company identified 10 primary pickup and drop locations for cab riders in New York City. In an effort to minimize travel time and improve customer service and the utilization of the company's fleet of cabs, management would like the cab drivers to take the shortest route between locations whenever possible. Using the following network of roads

and streets, what is the route a driver beginning at location 1 should take to reach location 10? The travel times in minutes are shown on the arcs of the network. Note that there are two one-way streets with the direction shown by the arrows.

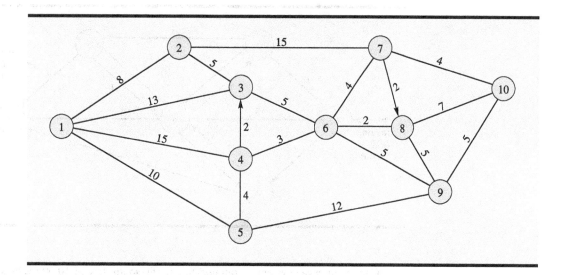

28. The five nodes in the following network represent points one year apart over a four-year period. Each node indicates a time when a decision is made to keep or replace a firm's computer equipment. If a decision is made to replace the equipment, a decision must also be made as to how long the new equipment will be used. The arc from node 0 to node 1 represents the decision to keep the current equipment one year and replace it at the end of the year. The arc from node 0 to node 2 represents the decision to keep the current equipment two years and replace it at the end of year 2. The numbers above the arcs indicate the total cost associated with the equipment replacement decisions. These costs include discounted purchase price, trade-in value, operating costs, and maintenance costs. Use a shortest-route model to determine the minimum cost equipment replacement policy for the four-year period.

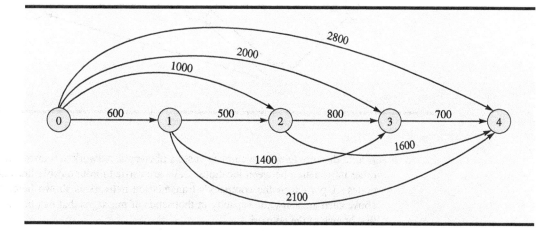

29. The north–south highway system passing through Albany, New York, can accommodate the capacities shown:

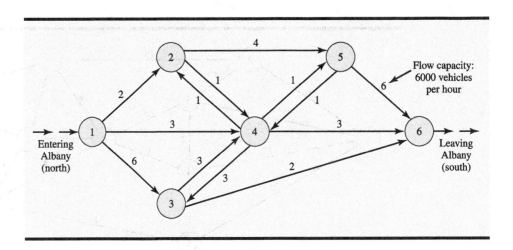

Can the highway system accommodate a north–south flow of 10,000 vehicles per hour?

30. If the Albany highway system described in Problem 29 has revised flow capacities as shown in the following network, what is the maximal flow in vehicles per hour through the system? How many vehicles per hour must travel over each road (arc) to obtain this maximal flow?

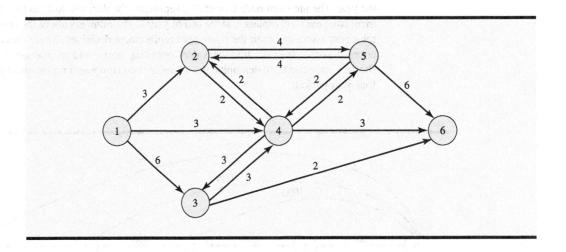

31. A long-distance telephone company uses a fiber-optic network to transmit phone calls and other information between locations. Calls are carried through cable lines and switching nodes. A portion of the company's transmission network is shown here. The numbers above each arc show the capacity in thousands of messages that can be transmitted over that branch of the network.

570

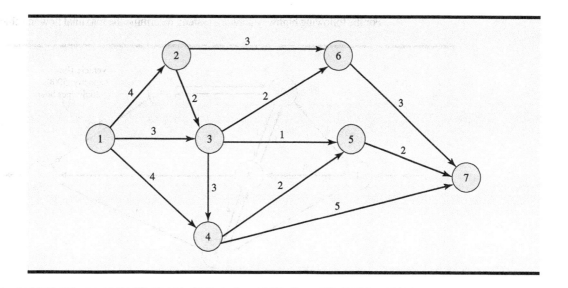

To keep up with the volume of information transmitted between origin and destination points, use the network to determine the maximum number of messages that may be sent from a city located at node 1 to a city located at node 7.

32. The High-Price Oil Company owns a pipeline network that is used to convey oil from its source to several storage locations. A portion of the network is as follows:

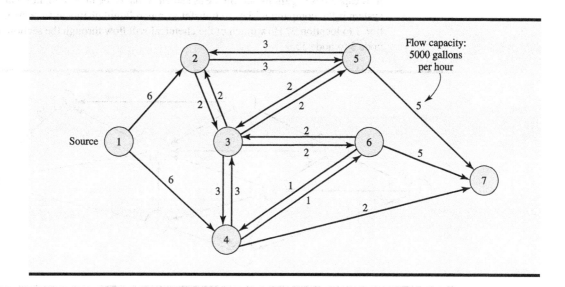

Due to the varying pipe sizes, the flow capacities vary. By selectively opening and closing sections of the pipeline network, the firm can supply any of the storage locations.

a. If the firm wants to fully utilize the system capacity to supply storage location 7, how long will it take to satisfy a location 7 demand of 100,000 gallons? What is the maximal flow for this pipeline system?

b. If a break occurs on line 2–3 and it is closed down, what is the maximal flow for the system? How long will it take to transmit 100,000 gallons to location 7?

33. For the following highway network system, determine the maximal flow in vehicles per hour.

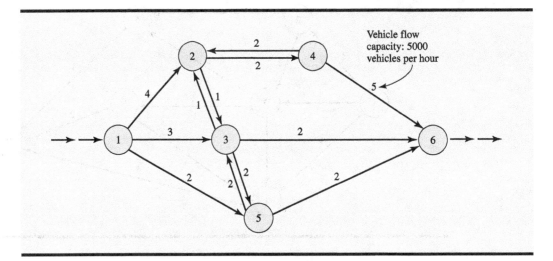

The highway commission is considering adding highway section 3–4 to permit a flow of 2000 vehicles per hour or, at an additional cost, a flow of 3000 vehicles per hour. What is your recommendation for the 3–4 arc of the network?

34. A chemical processing plant has a network of pipes that are used to transfer liquid chemical products from one part of the plant to another. The following pipe network has pipe flow capacities in gallons per minute as shown. What is the maximum flow capacity for the system if the company wishes to transfer as much liquid chemical as possible from location 1 to location 9? How much of the chemical will flow through the section of pipe from node 3 to node 5?

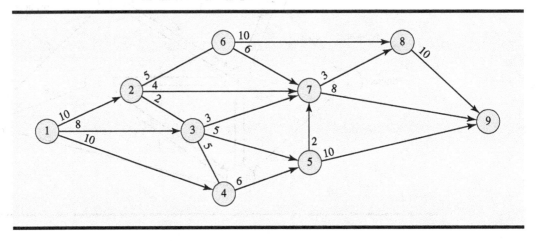

35. Refer to the Contois Carpets problem for which the network representation is shown in Figure 6.20. Suppose that Contois has a beginning inventory of 50 yards of carpet and requires an inventory of 100 yards at the end of quarter 4.
   a. Develop a network representation of this modified problem.
   b. Develop a linear programming model and solve for the optimal solution.

36. Sanders Fishing Supply of Naples, Florida, manufactures a variety of fishing equipment that it sells throughout the United States. For the next three months, Sanders estimates demand for a particular product at 150, 250, and 300 units, respectively. Sanders can supply

this demand by producing on regular time or overtime. Because of other commitments and anticipated cost increases in month 3, the production capacities in units and the production costs per unit are as follows:

Production	Capacity (units)	Cost per Unit
Month 1—Regular	275	$ 50
Month 1—Overtime	100	80
Month 2—Regular	200	50
Month 2—Overtime	50	80
Month 3—Regular	100	60
Month 3—Overtime	50	100

Inventory may be carried from one month to the next, but the cost is $20 per unit per month. For example, regular production from month 1 used to meet demand in month 2 would cost Sanders $50 + $20 = $70 per unit. This same month 1 production used to meet demand in month 3 would cost Sanders $50 + 2($20) = $90 per unit.

a. Develop a network representation of this production scheduling problem as a transportation problem. (*Hint:* Use six origin nodes; the supply for origin node 1 is the maximum that can be produced in month 1 on regular time, and so on.)

b. Develop a linear programming model that can be used to schedule regular and overtime production for each of the three months.

c. What is the production schedule, how many units are carried in inventory each month, and what is the total cost?

d. Is there any unused production capacity? If so, where?

Case Problem 1   SOLUTIONS PLUS

Solutions Plus is an industrial chemicals company that produces specialized cleaning fluids and solvents for a wide variety of applications. Solutions Plus just received an invitation to submit a bid to supply Great North American railroad with a cleaning fluid for locomotives. Great North American needs the cleaning fluid at 11 locations (railway stations); it provided the following information to Solutions Plus regarding the number of gallons of cleaning fluid required at each location (see Table 6.8):

Solutions Plus can produce the cleaning fluid at its Cincinnati plant for $1.20 per gallon. Even though the Cincinnati location is its only plant, Solutions Plus has negotiated with an industrial chemicals company located in Oakland, California, to produce and ship up to 50,000 gallons of the locomotive cleaning fluid to selected Solutions Plus customer locations. The Oakland company will charge Solutions Plus $1.65 per gallon to produce the cleaning fluid, but Solutions Plus thinks that the lower shipping costs from Oakland to some customer locations may offset the added cost to produce the product.

TABLE 6.8   GALLONS OF CLEANING FLUID REQUIRED AT EACH LOCATION

Location	Gallons Required	Location	Gallons Required
Santa Ana	22,418	Glendale	33,689
El Paso	6,800	Jacksonville	68,486
Pendleton	80,290	Little Rock	148,586
Houston	100,447	Bridgeport	111,475
Kansas City	241,570	Sacramento	112,000
Los Angeles	64,761		

TABLE 6.9   FREIGHT COST ($ PER GALLON)

	Cincinnati	Oakland
Santa Ana	—	0.22
El Paso	0.84	0.74
Pendleton	0.83	0.49
Houston	0.45	—
Kansas City	0.36	—
Los Angeles	—	0.22
Glendale	—	0.22
Jacksonville	0.34	—
Little Rock	0.34	—
Bridgeport	0.34	—
Sacramento	—	0.15

The president of Solutions Plus, Charlie Weaver, contacted several trucking companies to negotiate shipping rates between the two production facilities (Cincinnati and Oakland) and the locations where the railroad locomotives are cleaned. Table 6.9 shows the quotes received in terms of dollars per gallon. The — entries in Table 6.9 identify shipping routes that will not be considered because of the large distances involved. These quotes for shipping rates are guaranteed for one year.

To submit a bid to the railroad company, Solutions Plus must determine the price per gallon they will charge. Solutions Plus usually sells its cleaning fluids for 15% more than its cost to produce and deliver the product. For this big contract, however, Fred Roedel, the director of marketing, suggested that maybe the company should consider a smaller profit margin. In addition, to ensure that if Solutions Plus wins the bid, they will have adequate capacity to satisfy existing orders as well as accept orders for other new business, the management team decided to limit the number of gallons of the locomotive cleaning fluid produced in the Cincinnati plant to 500,000 gallons at most.

Managerial Report

You are asked to make recommendations that will help Solutions Plus prepare a bid. Your report should address, but not be limited to, the following issues:

1. If Solutions Plus wins the bid, which production facility (Cincinnati or Oakland) should supply the cleaning fluid to the locations where the railroad locomotives are cleaned? How much should be shipped from each facility to each location?
2. What is the breakeven point for Solutions Plus? That is, how low can the company go on its bid without losing money?
3. If Solutions Plus wants to use its standard 15% markup, how much should it bid?
4. Freight costs are significantly affected by the price of oil. The contract on which Solutions Plus is bidding is for two years. Discuss how fluctuation in freight costs might affect the bid Solutions Plus submits.

Case Problem 2   DISTRIBUTION SYSTEM DESIGN

The Darby Company manufactures and distributes meters used to measure electric power consumption. The company started with a small production plant in El Paso and gradually built a customer base throughout Texas. A distribution center was established in Fort

TABLE 6.10   SHIPPING COST PER UNIT FROM PRODUCTION PLANTS TO
DISTRIBUTION CENTERS (IN $)

	Distribution Center		
Plant	Fort Worth	Santa Fe	Las Vegas
El Paso	3.20	2.20	4.20
San Bernardino	—	3.90	1.20

Worth, Texas, and later, as business expanded, a second distribution center was established in Santa Fe, New Mexico.

The El Paso plant was expanded when the company began marketing its meters in Arizona, California, Nevada, and Utah. With the growth of the West Coast business, the Darby Company opened a third distribution center in Las Vegas and just two years ago opened a second production plant in San Bernardino, California.

Manufacturing costs differ between the company's production plants. The cost of each meter produced at the El Paso plant is $10.50. The San Bernardino plant utilizes newer and more efficient equipment; as a result, manufacturing costs are $0.50 per meter less than at the El Paso plant.

Due to the company's rapid growth, not much attention had been paid to the efficiency of the distribution system, but Darby's management decided that it is time to address this issue. The cost of shipping a meter from each of the two plants to each of the three distribution centers is shown in Table 6.10.

The quarterly production capacity is 30,000 meters at the older El Paso plant and 20,000 meters at the San Bernardino plant. Note that no shipments are allowed from the San Bernardino plant to the Fort Worth distribution center.

The company serves nine customer zones from the three distribution centers. The forecast of the number of meters needed in each customer zone for the next quarter is shown in Table 6.11.

The cost per unit of shipping from each distribution center to each customer zone is given in Table 6.12; note that some distribution centers cannot serve certain customer zones.

In the current distribution system, demand at the Dallas, San Antonio, Wichita, and Kansas City customer zones is satisfied by shipments from the Fort Worth distribution center. In a similar manner, the Denver, Salt Lake City, and Phoenix customer zones are served by the Santa Fe distribution center, and the Los Angeles and San Diego customer zones are

TABLE 6.11   QUARTERLY DEMAND FORECAST

Customer Zone	Demand (meters)
Dallas	6300
San Antonio	4880
Wichita	2130
Kansas City	1210
Denver	6120
Salt Lake City	4830
Phoenix	2750
Los Angeles	8580
San Diego	4460

TABLE 6.12   SHIPPING COST FROM THE DISTRIBUTION CENTERS TO THE CUSTOMER ZONES

Distribution Center	Dallas	San Antonio	Wichita	Kansas City	Denver	Salt Lake City	Phoenix	Los Angeles	San Diego
					Customer Zone				
Fort Worth	0.3	2.1	3.1	4.4	6.0	—	—	—	—
Santa Fe	5.2	5.4	4.5	6.0	2.7	4.7	3.4	3.3	2.7
Las Vegas	—	—	—	—	5.4	3.3	2.4	2.1	2.5

served by the Las Vegas distribution center. To determine how many units to ship from each plant, the quarterly customer demand forecasts are aggregated at the distribution centers, and a transportation model is used to minimize the cost of shipping from the production plants to the distribution centers.

Managerial Report

You are asked to make recommendations for improving the distribution system. Your report should address, but not be limited to, the following issues:

1. If the company does not change its current distribution strategy, what will its distribution costs be for the following quarter?
2. Suppose that the company is willing to consider dropping the distribution center limitations; that is, customers could be served by any of the distribution centers for which costs are available. Can costs be reduced? By how much?
3. The company wants to explore the possibility of satisfying some of the customer demand directly from the production plants. In particular, the shipping cost is $0.30 per unit from San Bernardino to Los Angeles and $0.70 from San Bernardino to San Diego. The cost for direct shipments from El Paso to San Antonio is $3.50 per unit. Can distribution costs be further reduced by considering these direct plant-to-customer shipments?
4. Over the next five years, Darby is anticipating moderate growth (5000 meters) to the North and West. Would you recommend that they consider plant expansion at this time?

Appendix 6.1   EXCEL SOLUTION OF TRANSPORTATION, ASSIGNMENT, AND TRANSSHIPMENT PROBLEMS

In this appendix we will use an Excel Worksheet to solve transportation, assignment, and transshipment problems. We start with the Foster Generators transportation problem (see Section 6.1).

TRANSPORTATION PROBLEM

The first step is to enter the data for the transportation costs, the origin supplies, and the destination demands in the top portion of the worksheet. Then the linear programming model is developed in the bottom portion of the worksheet. As with all linear programs, the worksheet model has four key elements: the decision variables, the objective function, the constraint left-hand sides, and the constraint right-hand sides. For a transportation problem, the decision variables are the amounts shipped from each origin to each destination; the

FIGURE 6.22 EXCEL SOLUTION OF THE FOSTER GENERATORS PROBLEM

WEB file

Foster

	A	B	C	D	E	F	G	H
1	**Foster Generators**							
2								
3			**Destination**					
4	Origin	Boston	Chicago	St. Louis	Lexington	Supply		
5	Cleveland	3	2	7	6	5000		
6	Bedford	7	5	2	3	6000		
7	York	2	5	4	5	2500		
8	**Demand**	6000	4000	2000	1500			
9								
10								
11	**Model**							
12								
13		**Min Cost**	39500					
14								
15			**Destination**					
16	Origin	Boston	Chicago	St. Louis	Lexington	Total		
17	Cleveland	3500	1500	0	0	5000	<=	5000
18	Bedford	0	2500	2000	1500	6000	<=	6000
19	York	2500	0	0	0	2500	<=	2500
20	**Total**	6000	4000	2000	1500			
21		=	=	=	=			
22		6000	4000	2000	1500			

objective function is the total transportation cost; the left-hand sides are the number of units shipped from each origin and the number of units shipped into each destination; and the right-hand sides are the origin supplies and the destination demands.

The formulation and solution of the Foster Generators problem are shown in Figure 6.22. The data are in the top portion of the worksheet. The model appears in the bottom portion of the worksheet; the key elements are screened.

Formulation

The data and descriptive labels are contained in cells A1:F8. The transportation costs are in cells B5:E7. The origin supplies are in cells F5:F7, and the destination demands are in cells B8:E8. The key elements of the model required by the Excel Solver are the decision variables, the objective function, the constraint left-hand sides, and the constraint right-hand sides. These cells are screened in the bottom portion of the worksheet.

Decision Variables — Cells B17:E19 are reserved for the decision variables. The optimal values are shown to be $x_{11} = 3500$, $x_{12} = 1500$, $x_{22} = 2500$, $x_{23} = 2000$, $x_{24} = 1500$, and $x_{41} = 2500$. All other decision variables equal zero, indicating nothing will be shipped over the corresponding routes.

Objective Function — The formula=SUMPRODUCT(B5:E7,B17:E19) has been placed into cell C13 to compute the cost of the solution. The minimum cost solution is shown to have a value of \$39,500.

Left-Hand Sides — Cells F17:F19 contain the left-hand sides for the supply constraints, and cells B20:E20 contain the left-hand sides for the demand constraints.

    Cell F17 = SUM(B17:E17) (Copy to F18:F19)
    Cell B20 = SUM(B17:B19) (Copy to C20:E20)

FIGURE 6.23   SOLVER PARAMETERS DIALOG BOX FOR THE FOSTER
                GENERATORS PROBLEM

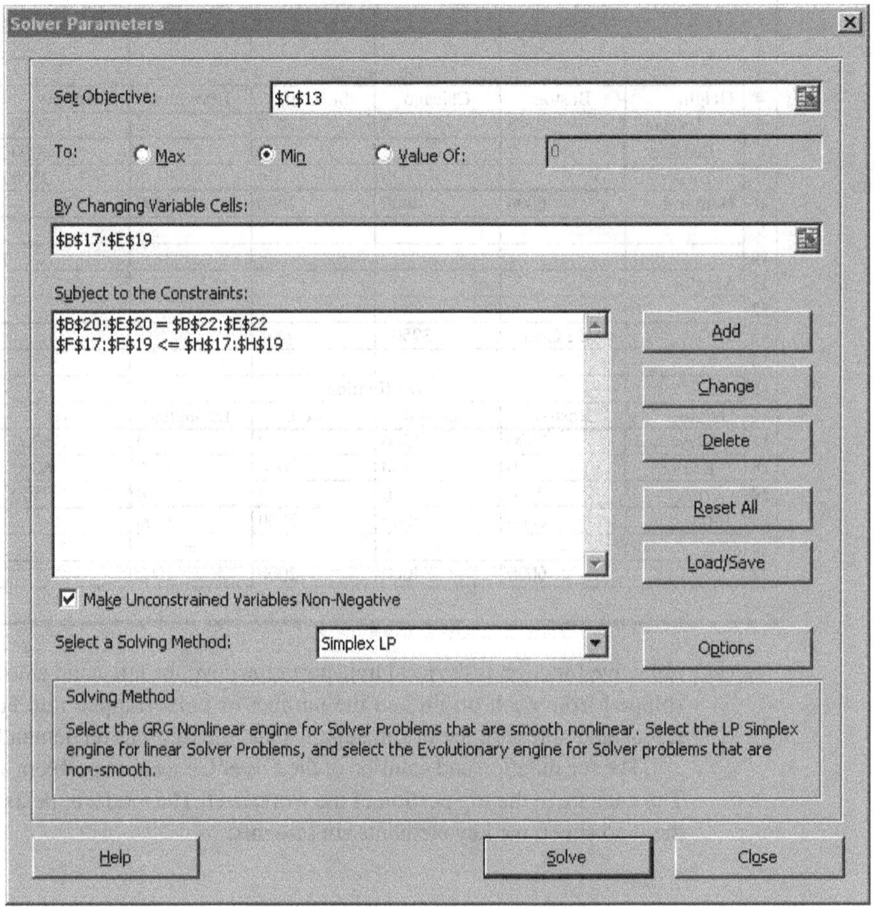

Right-Hand Sides   Cells H17:H19 contain the right-hand sides for the supply con-
                    straints and Cells B22:E22 contain the right-hand sides for the
                    demand constraints.
                        Cell H17 = F5 (Copy to H18:H19)
                        Cell B22 = B8 (Copy to C22:E22)

Excel Solution

The solution shown in Figure 6.22 can be obtained by selecting **Solver** from the **Analysis**
group under the **Data** tab, entering the proper values into the **Solver Parameters** dialog
box, selecting the **Make Unconstrained Variables Non-Negative** checkbox, and selecting
Simplex LP from the **Select a Solving Method** drop-down box. Then click **Solve.** The information entered into the **Solver Parameters** dialog box is shown in Figure 6.23.

FIGURE 6.24 EXCEL SOLUTION OF THE FOWLE MARKETING RESEARCH PROBLEM

WEB file

Fowle

	A	B	C	D	E	F	G
1	**Fowle Marketing Research**						
2							
3			**Client**				
4	**Project Leader**	1	2	3			
5	Terry	10	15	9			
6	Carle	9	18	5			
7	McClymonds	6	14	3			
8							
9							
10	**Model**						
11							
12		**Min Time**	26				
13							
14			**Client**				
15	**Project Leader**	1	2	3	**Total**		
16	Terry	0	1	0	1	<=	1
17	Carle	0	0	1	1	<=	1
18	McClymonds	1	0	0	1	<=	1
19	**Total**	1	1	1			
20		=	=	=			
21		1	1	1			

ASSIGNMENT PROBLEM

The first step is to enter the data for the assignment costs in the top portion of the work-sheet. Even though the assignment model is a special case of the transportation model, it is not necessary to enter values for origin supplies and destination demands because they are always equal to one.

The linear programming model is developed in the bottom portion of the worksheet. As with all linear programs the model has four key elements: the decision variables, the objective function, the constraint left-hand sides, and the constraint right-hand sides. For an assignment problem, the decision variables indicate whether an agent is assigned to a task (with a 1 for yes or 0 for no); the objective function is the total cost of all assignments; the constraint left-hand sides are the number of tasks that are assigned to each agent and the number of agents that are assigned to each task; and the right-hand sides are the number of tasks each agent can handle (1) and the number of agents each task requires (1). The work-sheet formulation and solution for the Fowle Marketing Research Problem are shown in Figure 6.24.

Formulation

The data and descriptive labels are contained in cells A1:D7. Note that we have not inserted supply and demand values because they are always equal to 1 in an assignment problem. The model appears in the bottom portion of the worksheet with the key elements screened.

Decision Variables	Cells B16:D18 are reserved for the decision variables. The optimal values are shown to be $x_{12} = 1$, $x_{23} = 1$, and $x_{31} = 1$ with all other variables $= 0$.
Objective Function	The formula =SUMPRODUCT(B5:D7,B16:D18) has been placed into cell C12 to compute the number of days required to complete all the jobs. The minimum time solution has a value of 26 days.
Left-Hand Sides	Cells E16:E18 contain the left-hand sides of the constraints for the number of clients each project leader can handle. Cells B19:D19 contain the left-hand sides of the constraints requiring that each client must be assigned a project leader.
	Cell E16 = SUM(B16:D16) (Copy to E17:E18)
	Cell B19 = SUM(B16:B18) (Copy to C19:D19)
Right-Hand Sides	Cells G16:G18 contain the right-hand sides for the project leader constraints and cells B21:D21 contain the right-hand sides for the client constraints. All right-hand side cell values are 1.

FIGURE 6.25 SOLVER PARAMETERS DIALOG BOX FOR THE FOWLE MARKETING RESEARCH PROBLEM

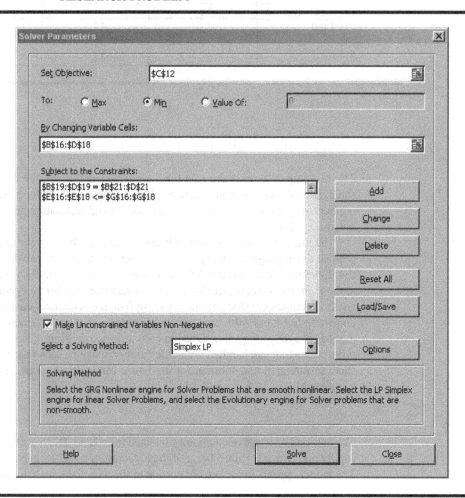

Excel Solution

The solution shown in Figure 6.24 can be obtained by selecting **Solver** from the **Analysis** group under the **Data** tab, entering the proper values into the **Solver Parameters** dialog box, selecting the **Make Unconstrained Variables Non-Negative** checkbox, and selecting **Simplex LP** from the **Select a Solving Method** drop-down box. Then click **Solve.** The information entered into the **Solver Parameters** dialog box is shown in Figure 6.25.

TRANSSHIPMENT PROBLEM

The worksheet model we present for the transshipment problem can be used for all the network flow problems (transportation, assignment, and transshipment) in this chapter. We organize the worksheet into two sections: an arc section and a node section. Let us illustrate by showing the worksheet formulation and solution of the Ryan Electronics transshipment problem. Refer to Figure 6.26 as we describe the steps involved. The key elements are screened.

Formulation

The arc section uses cells A3:D16. For each arc, the start node and end node are identified in cells A5:B16. The arc costs are identified in cells C5:C16, and cells D5:D16 are reserved for the values of the decision variables (the amount shipped over the arcs).

The node section uses cells F5:K14. Each of the nodes is identified in cells F7:F14. The following formulas are entered into cells G7:H14 to represent the flow out and the flow in for each node:

Units shipped in:	Cell G9	=D5+D7
	Cell G10	=D6+D8
	Cell G11	=D9+D13
	Cell G12	=D10+D14
	Cell G13	=D11+D15
	Cell G14	=D12+D16

FIGURE 6.26   EXCEL SOLUTION FOR THE RYAN ELECTRONICS PROBLEM

	A	B	C	D	E	F	G	H	I	J	K
1	**Ryan Electronics Transshipment**										
2											
3		**Arc**		**Units**							
4	Start Node	End Node	Cost	Shipped							
5	Denver	Kansas City	2	550			**Units Shipped**		**Net**		
6	Denver	Louisville	3	50		**Node**	**In**	**Out**	**Shipments**		**Supply**
7	Atlanta	Kansas City	3	0		Denver		600	600	<=	600
8	Atlanta	Louisville	1	400		Atlanta		400	400	<=	400
9	Kansas City	Detroit	2	200		Kansas City	550	550	0	=	0
10	Kansas City	Miami	6	0		Louisville	450	450	0	=	0
11	Kansas City	Dallas	3	350		Detroit	200		-200	=	-200
12	Kansas City	New Orleans	6	0		Miami	150		-150	=	-150
13	Louisville	Detroit	4	0		Dallas	350		-350	=	-350
14	Louisville	Miami	4	150		New Orleans	300		-300	=	-300
15	Louisville	Dallas	6	0							
16	Louisville	New Orleans	5	300							
17											
18								**Total Cost**	5200		

Units shipped out:	Cell H7	=SUM(D5:D6)
	Cell H8	=SUM(D7:D8)
	Cell H9	=SUM(D9:D12)
	Cell H10	=SUM(D13:D16)

The net shipments in cells I7:I14 are the flows out minus the flows in for each node. For supply nodes, the flow out will exceed the flow in, resulting in positive net shipments. For demand nodes, the flow out will be less than the flow in, resulting in negative net shipments. The "net" supply appears in cells K7:K14. Note that the net supply is negative for demand nodes.

As in previous worksheet formulations, we screened the key elements required by the Excel Solver.

FIGURE 6.27 SOLVER PARAMETERS DIALOG BOX FOR THE RYAN ELECTRONICS PROBLEM

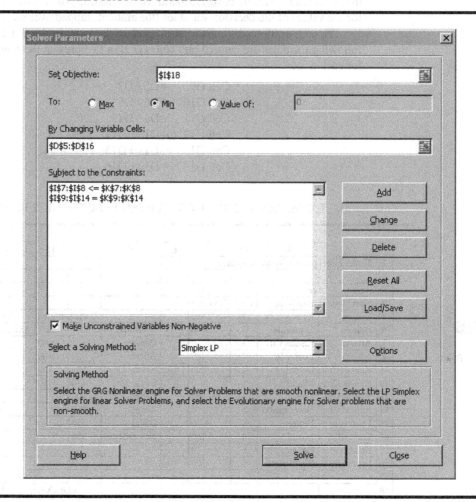

Decision Variables	Cells D5:D16 are reserved for the decision variables. The optimal number of units to ship over each arc is shown.
Objective Function	The formula =SUMPRODUCT(C5:C16,D5:D16) is placed into cell I18 to show the total cost associated with the solution. As shown, the minimum total cost is $5200.
Left-Hand Sides	The left-hand sides of the constraints represent the net shipments for each node. Cells I7:I14 are reserved for these constraints. Cell I7 = H7-G7 (Copy to I8:I14)
Right-Hand Sides	The right-hand sides of the constraints represent the supply at each node. Cells K7:K14 are reserved for these values. (Note the negative supply at the four demand nodes.)

Excel Solution

The solution can be obtained by selecting **Solver** from the **Analysis** group under the **Data** tab, entering the proper values into the **Solver Parameters** dialog box, selecting the **Make Unconstrained Variables Non-Negative** checkbox, and selecting **Simplex LP** from the **Select a Solving Method** drop-down box. Then click **Solve.** The information entered into the **Solver Parameters** dialog box is shown in Figure 6.27.

References and Bibliography

Ahuja, R. K., T. L. Magnanti, and J. B. Orlin. *Network Flows, Theory, Algorithms, and Applications.* Prentice Hall, 1993.

Bazarra, M. S., J. J. Jarvis, and H. D. Sherali. *Linear Programming and Network Flows,* 2d ed. Wiley, 1990.

Carino, H. F., and C. H. Le Noir, Jr. "Optimizing Wood Procurement in Cabinet Manufacturing," *Interfaces* (March/April 1988): 10–19.

Dantzig, G. B. *Linear Programming and Extensions.* Princeton University Press, 1963.

Davis, Morton D. *Game Theory: A Nontechnical Introduction.* Dover, 1997.

Evans, J. R., and E. Minieka. *Optimization Algorithms for Networks and Graphs,* 2d ed. Marcel Dekker, 1992.

Ford, L. R., and D. R. Fulkerson. *Flows and Networks.* Princeton University Press, 1962.

Geoffrion, A., and G. Graves. "Better Distribution Planning with Computer Models," *Harvard Business Review* (July/August 1976).

Greenberg, H. J. "How to Analyze the Results of Linear Programs—Part 1: Preliminaries," *Interfaces* 23, no. 4 (July/August 1993): 56–67.

Greenberg, H. J. "How to Analyze the Results of Linear Programs—Part 2: Price Interpretation," *Interfaces* 23, no. 5 (September/October 1993): 97–114.

Greenberg, H. J. "How to Analyze the Results of Linear Programs—Part 3: Infeasibility Diagnosis," *Interfaces* 23, no. 6 (November/December 1993): 120–139.

Lillien, G., and A. Rangaswamy. *Marketing Engineering: Computer-Assisted Marketing Analysis and Planning.* Addison-Wesley, 1998.

Martin, R. K. *Large Scale Linear and Integer Optimization: A Unified Approach.* Kluwer Academic Publishers, 1999.

McMillian, John. *Games, Strategies, and Managers.* Oxford University Press, 1992.

Myerson, Roger B. *Game Theory: Analysis of Conflict.* Harvard University Press, 1997.

Nemhauser, G. L., and L. A. Wolsey. *Integer and Combinatorial Optimization.* Wiley, 1999.

Osborne, Martin J. *An Introduction to Game Theory.* Oxford University Press, 2004.

Schrage, Linus. *Optimization Modeling with LINDO,* 4th ed. LINDO Systems Inc., 2000.

Sherman, H. D. "Hospital Efficiency Measurement and Evaluation," *Medical Care* 22, no. 10 (October 1984): 922–938.

Winston, W. L., and S. C. Albright. *Practical Management Science,* 2d ed. Duxbury Press, 2001.

Self-Test Solutions and Answers to Even-Numbered Problems

1.

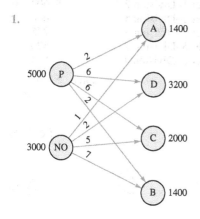

2. a. Let x_{11} = amount shipped from Jefferson City to Des Moines

   x_{12} = amount shipped from Jefferson City to Kansas City

   .
   .
   .

   x_{23} = amount shipped from Omaha to St. Louis

   Min $14x_{11} + 9x_{12} + 7x_{13} + 8x_{21} + 10x_{22} + 5x_{23}$
   s.t.

   $$
   \begin{aligned}
   x_{11} + x_{12} + x_{13} &&&\leq 30 \\
   x_{21} + x_{22} + x_{23} &&&\leq 20 \\
   x_{11} \quad\quad + x_{21} &&&= 25 \\
   x_{12} \quad\quad + x_{22} &&&= 15 \\
   x_{13} \quad\quad + x_{23} &&&= 10
   \end{aligned}
   $$

   $x_{11}, x_{12}, x_{13}, x_{21}, x_{22}, x_{23} \geq 0$

b.

Optimal Solution	Amount	Cost
Jefferson City–Des Moines	5	70
Jefferson City–Kansas City	15	135
Jefferson City–St. Louis	10	70
Omaha–Des Moines	20	160
	Total	435

4. b.

Seattle–Denver	4000	Seattle–Los Angeles	5000
Columbus–Mobile	4000	New York–Pittsburgh	3000
New York–Mobile	1000	New York–Los Angeles	1000
New York–Washington	3000		

   Cost = $150,000

c.

Seattle–Denver	4000	Seattle–Los Angeles	5000
Columbus–Mobile	5000	New York–Pittsburgh	4000
New York–Los Angeles	1000	New York–Washington	3000

   Cost actually decreases by $9000

6. The network model, the linear programming formulation, and the optimal solution are shown. Note that the third constraint corresponds to the dummy origin; the variables

$x_{31}, x_{32}, x_{33},$ and x_{34} are the amounts shipped out of the dummy origin and do not appear in the objective function because they are given a coefficient of zero.

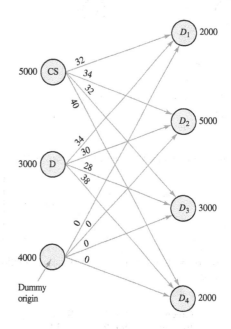

Max $32x_{11} + 34x_{12} + 32x_{13} + 40x_{14} + 34x_{21} + 30x_{22} + 28x_{23} + 38x_{24}$
s.t.

$$
\begin{aligned}
x_{11} + x_{12} + x_{13} + x_{14} &&&\leq 5000 \\
x_{21} + x_{22} + x_{23} + x_{24} &&&\leq 3000 \\
x_{31} + x_{32} + x_{33} + x_{34} &&&\leq 4000 \\
x_{11} \quad + x_{21} \quad + x_{31} &&&= 2000 \\
x_{12} \quad + x_{22} \quad + x_{32} &&&= 5000 \\
x_{13} \quad + x_{23} \quad + x_{33} &&&= 3000 \\
x_{14} \quad + x_{24} \quad + x_{34} &&&= 2000
\end{aligned}
$$

$x_{ij} \geq 0$ for all i, j

Optimal Solution	Units	Cost
Clifton Springs-D_2	4,000	$136,000
Clifton Springs-D_4	1,000	40,000
Danville-D_1	2,000	68,000
Danville-D_4	1,000	38,000
	Total	$282,000

Customer 2 demand has a shortfall of 1000; customer 3 demand of 3000 is not satisfied.

8. 1–A 300; 1–C 1200; 2–A 1200; 3–A 500; 3–B 500

9. a.

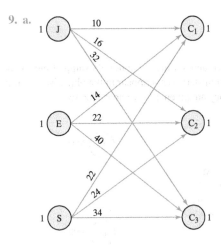

b.

Min $10x_{12} + 16x_{12} + 32x_{13} + 14x_{21} + 22x_{22} + 40x_{23} + 22x_{31} + 24x_{32} + 34x_{33}$
s.t.

$$x_{11} + x_{12} + x_{13} \leq 1$$
$$x_{21} + x_{22} + x_{23} \leq 1$$
$$x_{31} + x_{32} + x_{33} \leq 1$$
$$x_{11} + x_{21} + x_{31} = 1$$
$$x_{12} + x_{22} + x_{32} = 1$$
$$x_{13} + x_{23} + x_{33} = 1$$
$$x_{ij} \geq 0 \quad \text{for all } i, j$$

Solution $x_{12} = 1$, $x_{21} = 1$, $x_{33} = 1$; total completion time = 64

10. b.

Green:	Job 1	$ 26
Brown:	Job 2	34
Red:	Job 3	38
Blue:	Job 4	39
White:	Job 5	25
	Total Cost	$162

12. a. Plano: Kansas City and Dallas
Flagstaff: Los Angeles
Springfield: Chicago, Columbus, and Atlanta
Boulder: Newark and Denver
Cost = $216,000

b. Nashville

c. Columbus is switched from Springfield to Nashville.
Cost = $227,000

14. A to MS, B to Ph.D., C to MBA, D to undergrad
Maximum total rating = 13.3

16. a.

			Supplier			
Division	**1**	**2**	**3**	**4**	**5**	**6**
1	614	660	534	680	590	630
2	603	639	702	693	693	630
3	865	830	775	850	900	930
4	532	553	511	581	595	553
5	720	648	684	693	657	747

b. Optimal solution:

Supplier 1–Division 2	$ 603
Supplier 2–Division 5	648
Supplier 3–Division 3	775
Supplier 5–Division 1	590
Supplier 6–Division 4	553
Total	$3169

17. a.

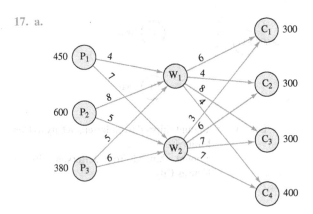

b.

Min $4x_{14} + 7x_{15} + 8x_{24} + 5x_{25} + 5x_{34} + 6x_{35} + 6x_{46} + 4x_{47} + 8x_{48} + 4x_{49} + 3x_{56} + 6x_{57} + 7x_{58} + 7x_{59}$
s.t.

$$x_{14} + x_{15} \leq 450$$
$$x_{24} + x_{25} \leq 600$$
$$x_{34} + x_{35} \leq 380$$
$$-x_{14} - x_{24} - x_{34} + x_{46} + x_{47} + x_{48} + x_{49} = 0$$
$$-x_{15} - x_{25} - x_{35} + x_{56} + x_{57} + x_{58} + x_{59} = 0$$
$$x_{46} + x_{56} = 300$$
$$x_{47} + x_{57} = 300$$
$$x_{48} + x_{58} = 300$$
$$x_{49} + x_{59} = 400$$

c.

	Warehouse	
Plant	**1**	**2**
1	450	—
2	—	600
3	250	—

Total cost = $11,850

	Customer			
Warehouse	**1**	**2**	**3**	**4**
1	—	300	—	400
2	300	—	300	—

18. c. $x_{14} = 320$, $x_{25} = 600$, $x_{47} = 300$, $x_{49} = 20$, $x_{56} = 300$, $x_{58} = 300$, $x_{39} = 380$
Cost = $11,220

20.

Optimal Solution	Units Shipped	Cost
Muncie–Cincinnati	1	6
Cincinnati–Concord	3	84
Brazil–Louisville	6	18
Louisville–Macon	2	88
Louisville–Greenwood	4	136
Xenia–Cincinnati	5	15
Cincinnati–Chatham	3	72
	Total	419

Two rail cars must be held at Muncie until a buyer is found.

22. b. $x_{25} = 8$, $x_{31} = 8$, $x_{42} = 3$, $x_{53} = 5$, $x_{56} = 5$, $x_{74} = 6$, $x_{56} = 5$
Total cost = $917

23. Min $7x_{12} + 9x_{13} + 18x_{14} + 3x_{23} + 5x_{25} + 3x_{32} + 4x_{35}$
$+ 3x_{46} + 5x_{52} + 4x_{53} + 2x_{56} + 6x_{57} + 2x_{65} + 3x_{67}$
s.t.

	Flow Out	Flow In		
Node 1	$x_{12} + x_{13} + x_{14}$		=	1
Node 2	$x_{23} + x_{25}$	$-x_{12} - x_{32} - x_{52}$	=	0
Node 3	$x_{32} + x_{35}$	$-x_{13} - x_{23} - x_{53}$	=	0
Node 4	x_{46}	$-x_{14}$	=	0
Node 5	$x_{52} + x_{53} + x_{56} + x_{57}$	$-x_{25} - x_{35} - x_{65}$	=	0
Node 6	$x_{65} + x_{67}$	$-x_{46} - x_{56}$	=	0
Node 7		$+x_{57} + x_{67}$	=	1

$x_{ij} \geq 0$ for all i and j

Optimal solution: $x_{12} = 1$, $x_{25} = 1$, $x_{56} = 1$, and $x_{67} = 1$
Shortest route 1–2–5–6–7
Length = 17

24. Route: 1–2–4–6
Travel time = 63 minutes

26. Route: 1–4–7–6
Distance = 40 miles

28. Replace years 2, 3, and 4
Total cost = $2500

29. The capacitated transshipment problem to solve is given:

Max x_{61}
s.t.

$x_{12} + x_{13} + x_{14} - x_{61} = 0$
$x_{24} + x_{25} - x_{12} - x_{42} = 0$
$x_{34} + x_{36} - x_{13} - x_{43} = 0$
$x_{42} + x_{43} + x_{45} + x_{46} - x_{14} - x_{24} - x_{34} - x_{54} = 0$
$x_{54} + x_{56} - x_{25} - x_{45} = 0$
$x_{61} - x_{36} + x_{46} - x_{56} = 0$
$x_{12} \leq 2$ $x_{13} \leq 6$ $x_{14} \leq 3$
$x_{24} \leq 1$ $x_{25} \leq 4$
$x_{34} \leq 3$ $x_{36} \leq 2$
$x_{42} \leq 1$ $x_{43} \leq 3$ $x_{45} \leq 1$ $x_{46} \leq 3$
$x_{54} \leq 1$ $x_{56} \leq 6$
$x_{ij} \geq 0$ for all i, j

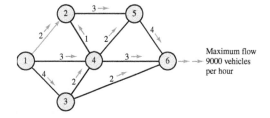

Maximum flow 9000 vehicles per hour

30. Maximal flow = 11,000 vehicles per hour

32. a. 10 hours; 10,000 gallons per hour
b. 11.1 hours; flow reduced to 9000 gallons per hour

34. Maximal flow = 23 gallons/minute
The total flow from 3 to 5 must be 5 gallons/minute.

36. c. Regular month 1: 275; overtime month 1: 25; inventory at end of month 1: 150
Regular month 2: 200; overtime month 2: 50; inventory at end of month 2: 150
Regular month 3: 100; overtime month 3: 50; inventory at end of month 3: 0

Integer Linear Programming

CONTENTS

In this chapter we discuss a class of problems that are modeled as linear programs with the additional requirement that one or more variables must be integer. Such problems are called **integer linear programs.** If all variables must be integer, we have an all-integer linear program. If some, but not all, variables must be integer, we have a mixed-integer linear program. In many applications of integer linear programming, one or more integer variables are required to equal either 0 or 1. Such variables are called 0-1 or *binary variables.* If all variables are 0-1 variables, we have a 0-1 integer linear program.

Integer variables—especially 0-1 variables—provide substantial modeling flexibility. As a result, the number of applications that can be addressed with linear programming methodology is expanded. For instance, the Management Science in Action, Crew Scheduling at Air New Zealand, describes how that airline company employs 0-1 integer programming models to schedule its pilots and flight attendants. Later Management Science in Actions describe how Valley Metal Containers uses a mixed-integer program for scheduling aluminum can production for Coors beer, and how the modeling flexibility provided by 0-1 variables helped Ketron build a customer order allocation model for a sporting goods company. Many other applications of integer programming are described throughout the chapter.

The objective of this chapter is to provide an applications-oriented introduction to integer linear programming. First, we discuss the different types of integer linear programming models. Then we show the formulation, graphical solution, and computer solution of an all-integer linear program. In Section 7.3 we discuss five applications of integer linear programming that make use of 0-1 variables: capital budgeting, fixed cost, distribution system design, bank location, and market share optimization problems. In Section 7.4 we provide additional illustrations of the modeling flexibility provided by 0-1 variables. Chapter appendices illustrate the use of Excel and LINGO for solving integer programs.

Information about open-source software can be found at the COIN-OR foundation website.

The cost of the added modeling flexibility provided by integer programming is that problems involving integer variables are often much more difficult to solve. A linear programming problem with several thousand continuous variables can be solved with any of several commercial linear programming solvers. However, an all-integer linear programming problem with fewer than 100 variables can be extremely difficult to solve. Experienced management scientists can help identify the types of integer linear programs that are easy, or at least reasonable, to solve. Commercial computer software packages, such as LINGO, CPLEX, Xpress-MP, and the commercial version of Solver have extensive integer programming capability, and very robust open-source software packages for integer programming are also available.

MANAGEMENT SCIENCE IN ACTION

CREW SCHEDULING AT AIR NEW ZEALAND*

As noted in Chapter 1, airlines make extensive use of management science (see Management Science in Action, Revenue Management at American Airlines). Air New Zealand is the largest national and international airline based in New Zealand. Over the past 15 years, Air New Zealand developed integer programming models for crew scheduling.

Air New Zealand finalizes flight schedules at least 12 weeks in advance of when the flights are to take place. At that point the process of assigning crews to implement the flight schedule begins. The

crew-scheduling problem involves staffing the flight schedule with pilots and flight attendants. It is solved in two phases. In the first phase, tours of duty (ToD) are generated that will permit constructing sequences of flights for pilots and flight attendants that will allow the airline's flight schedule to be implemented. A tour of duty is a one-day or multiday alternating sequence of duty periods (flight legs, training, etc.) and rest periods (layovers). In the ToD problem, no consideration is given to which individual crew members will perform the tours of duty. In the second phase, individual crew members are assigned to the tours of duty, which is called the rostering problem.

Air New Zealand employs integer programming models to solve both the ToD problem and the rostering problem. In the integer programming model of the ToD problem, each variable is a 0-1 variable that corresponds to a possible tour of duty that could be flown by a crew member (e.g., pilot or flight attendant). Each constraint corresponds to a particular flight and ensures that the flight is included in exactly one tour of duty. The cost of variable j reflects the cost of operating the jth tour of duty, and the objective is to minimize total cost. Air New Zealand solves a separate ToD problem for each crew type (pilot type or flight attendant type).

In the rostering problem, the tours of duty from the solution to the ToD problem are used to construct lines of work (LoW) for each crew member. In the integer programming model of the rostering problem, a 0-1 variable represents the possible LoWs for each crew member. A separate constraint for each crew member guarantees that

each will be assigned a single LoW. Other constraints correspond to the ToDs that must be covered by any feasible solution to the rostering problem.

The crew-scheduling optimizers developed by Air New Zealand showed a significant impact on profitability. Over the 15 years it took to develop these systems, the estimated development costs were approximately NZ$2 million. The estimated savings are NZ$15.6 million per year. In 1999 the savings from employing these integer programming models represented 11% of Air New Zealand's net operating profit. In addition to the direct dollar savings, the optimization systems provided many intangible benefits such as higher-quality solutions in less time, less dependence on a small number of highly skilled schedulers, flexibility to accommodate small changes in the schedule, and a guarantee that the airline satisfies legislative and contractual rules.

*Based on E. Rod Butchers et al., "Optimized Crew Scheduling at Air New Zealand," *Interfaces* (January/February 2001): 30–56.

NOTES AND COMMENTS

1. Because integer linear programs are harder to solve than linear programs, one should not try to solve a problem as an integer program if simply rounding the linear programming solution is adequate. In many linear programming problems, such as those in previous chapters, rounding has little economic consequence on the objective function, and feasibility is not an issue. But, in problems such as determining how many jet engines to manufacture, the consequences of rounding can be substantial and integer programming methodology should be employed.
2. Some linear programming problems have a special structure, which guarantees that the

variables will have integer values. The assignment, transportation, and transshipment problems of Chapter 6 have such structures. If the supply and the demand for transportation and transshipment problems are integer, the optimal linear programming solution will provide integer amounts shipped. For the assignment problem, the optimal linear programming solution will consist of 0s and 1s. So, for these specially structured problems, linear programming methodology can be used to find optimal integer solutions. Integer linear programming algorithms are not necessary.

7.1 TYPES OF INTEGER LINEAR PROGRAMMING MODELS

The only difference between the problems studied in this chapter and the ones studied in earlier chapters on linear programming is that one or more variables are required to be integer. If all variables are required to be integer, we have an **all-integer linear program.** The following is a two-variable, all-integer linear programming model:

$$\text{Max} \quad 2x_1 + 3x_2$$
$$\text{s.t.}$$
$$3x_1 + 3x_2 \leq 12$$
$$\tfrac{2}{3}x_1 + 1x_2 \leq 4$$
$$1x_1 + 2x_2 \leq 6$$
$$x_1, x_2 \geq 0 \text{ and integer}$$

If we drop the phrase "and integer" from the last line of this model, we have the familiar two-variable linear program. The linear program that results from dropping the integer requirements is called the **LP Relaxation** of the integer linear program.

If some, but not necessarily all, variables are required to be integer, we have a **mixed-integer linear program.** The following is a two-variable, mixed-integer linear program:

$$\text{Max} \quad 3x_1 + 4x_2$$
$$\text{s.t.}$$
$$-1x_1 + 2x_2 \leq 8$$
$$1x_1 + 2x_2 \leq 12$$
$$2x_1 + 1x_2 \leq 16$$
$$x_1, x_2 \geq 0 \text{ and } x_2 \text{ integer}$$

We obtain the LP Relaxation of this mixed-integer linear program by dropping the requirement that x_2 be integer.

In some applications, the integer variables may only take on the values 0 or 1. Then we have a **0-1 linear integer program.** As we see later in the chapter, 0-1 variables provide additional modeling capability. The Management Science in Action, Aluminum Can Production at Valley Metal Container, describes how a mixed-integer linear program involving 0-1 integer variables is used to schedule production of aluminum beer cans for Coors breweries. The 0-1 variables are used to model production line changeovers; the continuous variables model production quantities.

MANAGEMENT SCIENCE IN ACTION

ALUMINUM CAN PRODUCTION AT VALLEY METAL CONTAINER*

Valley Metal Container (VMC) produces cans for the seven brands of beer produced by the Coors breweries: Coors Extra Gold, Coors Light, Coors Original, Keystone Ale, Keystone Ice, Keystone Light, and Keystone Premium. VMC produces these cans on six production lines and stores them in three separate inventory storage areas from which they are shipped on to the Coors breweries in Golden, Colorado; Memphis, Tennessee; and Shenandoah, Virginia.

Two important issues face production scheduling at the VMC facility. First, each time a production line must be changed over from producing one type of can to another (label change), it takes time to get the color just right for the new label. As a result, downtime is incurred and scrap is generated.

Second, proper scheduling can reduce the amount of inventory that must be transferred from long-term to short-term storage. Thus, two costs are critical in determining the best production schedule at the VMC facility: the label-change cost and the cost of transferring inventory from one type of storage to another. To determine a production schedule that will minimize these two costs, VMC developed a mixed-integer linear programming model of its production process.

The model's objective function calls for minimizing the sum of the weekly cost of changing labels and the cost of transferring inventory from long-term to short-term storage. Binary (0-1) variables are used to represent a label change in the production process. Continuous variables are used to represent the size of the production run for each type of label on each line during each shift; analogous variables are used to represent inventories for each type of can produced. Additional continuous variables are used to represent the amount of inventory transferred to short-term storage during the week.

The VMC production scheduling problem is solved weekly using a personal computer. Excel worksheets are used for input data preparation and for storing the output report. The GAMS mathe- matical programming system is used to solve the mixed-integer linear program. Susan Schultz, man- ager of Logistics for Coors Container Operations, reports that using the system resulted in docu- mented annual savings of $169,230.

*Based on Elena Katok and Dennis Ott, "Using Mixed- Integer Programming to Reduce Label Changes in the Coors Aluminum Can Plant," *Interfaces* (March/April 2000): 1–12.

7.2 GRAPHICAL AND COMPUTER SOLUTIONS FOR AN ALL-INTEGER LINEAR PROGRAM

Eastborne Realty has $2 million available for the purchase of new rental property. After an initial screening, Eastborne reduced the investment alternatives to townhouses and apart- ment buildings. Each townhouse can be purchased for $282,000, and five are available. Each apartment building can be purchased for $400,000, and the developer will construct as many buildings as Eastborne wants to purchase.

Eastborne's property manager can devote up to 140 hours per month to these new prop- erties; each townhouse is expected to require 4 hours per month, and each apartment building is expected to require 40 hours per month. The annual cash flow, after deducting mortgage payments and operating expenses, is estimated to be $10,000 per townhouse and $15,000 per apartment building. Eastborne's owner would like to determine the number of townhouses and the number of apartment buildings to purchase to maximize annual cash flow.

We begin by defining the decision variables as follows:

$$T = \text{number of townhouses}$$
$$A = \text{number of apartment buildings}$$

The objective function for cash flow ($1000s) is

$$\text{Max} \quad 10T + 15A$$

Three constraints must be satisfied:

$$282T + 400A \leq 2000 \quad \text{Funds available (\$1000s)}$$
$$4T + 40A \leq 140 \quad \text{Manager's time (hours)}$$
$$T \quad\quad\quad \leq 5 \quad \text{Townhouses available}$$

The variables T and A must be nonnegative. In addition, the purchase of a fractional num- ber of townhouses and/or a fractional number of apartment buildings is unacceptable. Thus, T and A must be integer. The model for the Eastborne Realty problem is the follow- ing all-integer linear program:

$$\text{Max} \quad 10T + 15A$$
$$\text{s.t.}$$
$$282T + 400A \leq 2000$$
$$4T + 40A \leq 140$$
$$T \quad\quad\quad \leq 5$$
$$T, A \geq 0 \text{ and integer}$$

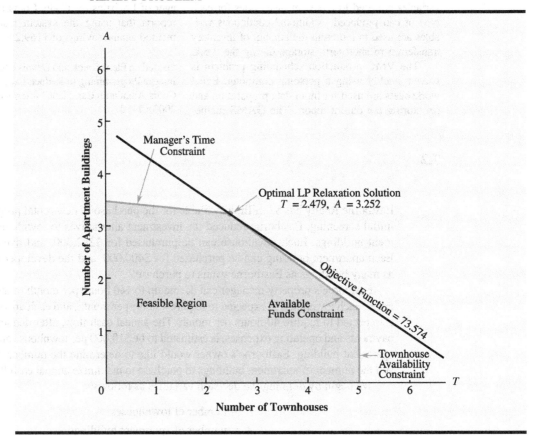

Graphical Solution of the LP Relaxation

Suppose that we drop the integer requirements for T and A and solve the LP Relaxation of the Eastborne Realty problem. Using the graphical solution procedure, as presented in Chapter 2, the optimal linear programming solution is shown in Figure 7.1. It is $T = 2.479$ townhouses and $A = 3.252$ apartment buildings. The optimal value of the objective function is 73.574, which indicates an annual cash flow of $73,574. Unfortunately, Eastborne cannot purchase fractional numbers of townhouses and apartment buildings; further analysis is necessary.

Rounding to Obtain an Integer Solution

In many cases, a noninteger solution can be rounded to obtain an acceptable integer solution. For instance, a linear programming solution to a production scheduling problem might call for the production of 15,132.4 cases of breakfast cereal. The rounded integer solution of 15,132 cases would probably have minimal impact on the value of the objective function and the feasibility of the solution. Rounding would be a sensible approach. Indeed, whenever rounding has a minimal impact on the objective function and constraints, most managers find it acceptable. A near-optimal solution is fine.

However, rounding may not always be a good strategy. When the decision variables take on small values that have a major impact on the value of the objective function or feasibility, an optimal integer solution is needed. Let us return to the Eastborne Realty problem and examine the impact of rounding. The optimal solution to the LP Relaxation for Eastborne Realty resulted in $T = 2.479$ townhouses and $A = 3.252$ apartment buildings. Because each townhouse costs \$282,000 and each apartment building costs \$400,000, rounding to an integer solution can be expected to have a significant economic impact on the problem.

If a problem has only less-than-or-equal-to constraints with nonnegative coefficients for the variables, rounding down will always provide a feasible integer solution.

Suppose that we round the solution to the LP Relaxation to obtain the integer solution $T = 2$ and $A = 3$, with an objective function value of $10(2) + 15(3) = 65$. The annual cash flow of \$65,000 is substantially less than the annual cash flow of \$73,574 provided by the solution to the LP Relaxation. Do other rounding possibilities exist? Exploring other rounding alternatives shows that the integer solution $T = 3$ and $A = 3$ is infeasible because it requires more funds than the \$2,000,000 Eastborne has available. The rounded solution of $T = 2$ and $A = 4$ is also infeasible for the same reason. At this point, rounding has led to two townhouses and three apartment buildings with an annual cash flow of \$65,000 as the best feasible integer solution to the problem. Unfortunately, we don't know whether this solution is the best integer solution to the problem.

Rounding to an integer solution is a trial-and-error approach. Each rounded solution must be evaluated for feasibility as well as for its impact on the value of the objective function. Even in cases where a rounded solution is feasible, we do not have a guarantee that we have found the optimal integer solution. We will see shortly that the rounded solution ($T = 2$ and $A = 3$) is not optimal for Eastborne Realty.

Graphical Solution of the All-Integer Problem

Try Problem 2 for practice with the graphical solution of an integer program.

Figure 7.2 shows the changes in the linear programming graphical solution procedure required to solve the Eastborne Realty integer linear programming problem. First, the graph of the feasible region is drawn exactly as in the LP Relaxation of the problem. Then, because the optimal solution must have integer values, we identify the feasible integer solutions with the dots shown in Figure 7.2. Finally, instead of moving the objective function line to the best extreme point in the feasible region, we move it in an improving direction as far as possible until reaching the dot (feasible integer point) providing the best value for the objective function. Viewing Figure 7.2, we see that the optimal integer solution occurs at $T = 4$ townhouses and $A = 2$ apartment buildings. The objective function value is $10(4) + 15(2) = 70$, providing an annual cash flow of \$70,000. This solution is significantly better than the best solution found by rounding: $T = 2$, $A = 3$, with an annual cash flow of \$65,000. Thus, we see that rounding would not have been the best strategy for Eastborne Realty.

Using the LP Relaxation to Establish Bounds

An important observation can be made from the analysis of the Eastborne Realty problem. It has to do with the relationship between the value of the optimal integer solution and the value of the optimal solution to the LP Relaxation.

For integer linear programs involving maximization, the value of the optimal solution to the LP Relaxation provides an upper bound on the value of the optimal integer solution. For integer linear programs involving minimization, the value of the optimal solution to the LP Relaxation provides a lower bound on the value of the optimal integer solution.

FIGURE 7.2   GRAPHICAL SOLUTION OF THE EASTBORNE REALTY INTEGER PROBLEM

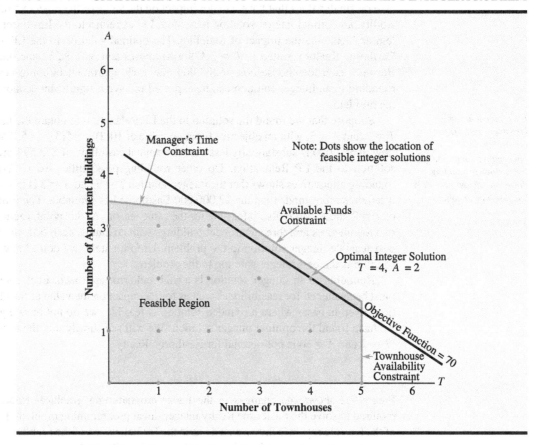

This observation is valid for the Eastborne Realty problem. The value of the optimal integer solution is $70,000, and the value of the optimal solution to the LP Relaxation is $73,574. Thus, we know from the LP Relaxation solution that the upper bound for the value of the objective function is $73,574.

Try Problem 5 for the graphical solution of a mixed-integer program.

The bounding property of the LP Relaxation allows us to conclude that if, by chance, the solution to an LP Relaxation turns out to be an integer solution, it is also optimal for the integer linear program. This bounding property can also be helpful in determining whether a rounded solution is "good enough." If a rounded LP Relaxation solution is feasible and provides a value of the objective function that is "almost as good as" the value of the objective function for the LP Relaxation, we know the rounded solution is a near-optimal integer solution. In this case, we can avoid having to solve the problem as an integer linear program.

Computer Solution

LINGO or Frontline Systems' Solver can be used to solve most of the integer linear programs in this chapter. In the appendices at the end of this chapter, we discuss how to solve integer linear programs using Solver and LINGO.

Specifying both T and A as integers provides the optimal integer solution shown in Figure 7.3. The solution of $T = 4$ townhouses and $A = 2$ apartment buildings has a maximum

FIGURE 7.3   THE SOLUTION FOR THE EASTBORNE REALTY PROBLEM

WEB file

Eastborne

```
        Optimal Objective Value =  70.00000

           Variable                     Value
        --------------            ---------------
              T                        4.00000
              A                        2.00000

          Constraint              Slack/Surplus
        --------------            ---------------
              1                       72.00000
              2                       44.00000
              3                        1.00000
```

annual cash flow of $70,000. The values of the slack variables tell us that the optimal solution has $72,000 of available funds unused, 44 hours of the manager's time still available, and 1 of the available townhouses not purchased.

NOTES AND COMMENTS

The computer output we show in this chapter for integer programs does not include reduced costs, dual values, or sensitivity ranges because these are not meaningful for integer programs.

7.3   APPLICATIONS INVOLVING 0-1 VARIABLES

Much of the modeling flexibility provided by integer linear programming is due to the use of 0-1 variables. In many applications, 0-1 variables provide selections or choices with the value of the variable equal to 1 if a corresponding activity is undertaken and equal to 0 if the corresponding activity is not undertaken. The capital budgeting, fixed cost, distribution system design, bank location, and product design/market share applications presented in this section make use of 0-1 variables.

Capital Budgeting

The Ice-Cold Refrigerator Company is considering investing in several projects that have varying capital requirements over the next four years. Faced with limited capital each year, management would like to select the most profitable projects. The estimated net present value for each project,[1] the capital requirements, and the available capital over the four-year period are shown in Table 7.1.

------

[1]The estimated net present value is the net cash flow discounted back to the beginning of year 1.

TABLE 7.1 PROJECT NET PRESENT VALUE, CAPITAL REQUIREMENTS, AND AVAILABLE CAPITAL FOR THE ICE-COLD REFRIGERATOR COMPANY

| | Project | | | | |
	Plant Expansion	Warehouse Expansion	New Machinery	New Product Research	Total Capital Available
Present Value	$90,000	$40,000	$10,000	$37,000	
Year 1 Cap Rqmt	$15,000	$10,000	$10,000	$15,000	$40,000
Year 2 Cap Rqmt	$20,000	$15,000		$10,000	$50,000
Year 3 Cap Rqmt	$20,000	$20,000		$10,000	$40,000
Year 4 Cap Rqmt	$15,000	$ 5,000	$ 4,000	$10,000	$35,000

The four 0-1 decision variables are as follows:

$P = 1$ if the plant expansion project is accepted; 0 if rejected

$W = 1$ if the warehouse expansion project is accepted; 0 if rejected

$M = 1$ if the new machinery project is accepted; 0 if rejected

$R = 1$ if the new product research project is accepted; 0 if rejected

In a **capital budgeting problem,** the company's objective function is to maximize the net present value of the capital budgeting projects. This problem has four constraints: one for the funds available in each of the next four years.

A 0-1 integer linear programming model with dollars in thousands is as follows:

$$\text{Max} \quad 90P + 40W + 10M + 37R$$

s.t.

$$15P + 10W + 10M + 15R \leq 40 \quad \text{(Year 1 capital available)}$$
$$20P + 15W \qquad\quad + 10R \leq 50 \quad \text{(Year 2 capital available)}$$
$$20P + 20W \qquad\quad + 10R \leq 40 \quad \text{(Year 3 capital available)}$$
$$15P + \;5W + \;4M + 10R \leq 35 \quad \text{(Year 4 capital available)}$$
$$P, W, M, R = 0, 1$$

The integer programming solution is shown in Figure 7.4. The optimal solution is $P = 1$, $W = 1$, $M = 1$, $R = 0$, with a total estimated net present value of $140,000. Thus, the company should fund the plant expansion, the warehouse expansion, and the new machinery projects. The new product research project should be put on hold unless additional capital funds become available. The values of the slack variables (see Figure 7.4) show that the company will have $5,000 remaining in year 1, $15,000 remaining in year 2, and $11,000 remaining in year 4. Checking the capital requirements for the new product research project, we see that enough funds are available for this project in year 2 and year 4. However, the company would have to find additional capital funds of $10,000 in year 1 and $10,000 in year 3 to fund the new product research project.

Fixed Cost

In many applications, the cost of production has two components: a setup cost, which is a fixed cost, and a variable cost, which is directly related to the production quantity. The use of 0-1 variables makes including the setup cost possible in a model for a production application.

FIGURE 7.4 THE SOLUTION FOR THE ICE-COLD REFRIGERATOR COMPANY PROBLEM

WEB file

Ice-Cold

```
         Optimal Objective Value = 140.00000

             Variable              Value
             --------              -----

                P                 1.00000
                W                 1.00000
                M                 1.00000
                R                 0.00000


            Constraint         Slack/Surplus
            ----------         -------------

                1                 5.00000
                2                15.00000
                3                 0.00000
                4                11.00000
```

As an example of a **fixed cost problem,** consider the RMC problem. Three raw materials are used to produce three products: a fuel additive, a solvent base, and a carpet cleaning fluid. The following decision variables are used:

$$F = \text{tons of fuel additive produced}$$
$$S = \text{tons of solvent base produced}$$
$$C = \text{tons of carpet cleaning fluid produced}$$

The profit contributions are $40 per ton for the fuel additive, $30 per ton for the solvent base, and $50 per ton for the carpet cleaning fluid. Each ton of fuel additive is a blend of 0.4 tons of material 1 and 0.6 tons of material 3. Each ton of solvent base requires 0.5 tons of material 1, 0.2 tons of material 2, and 0.3 tons of material 3. Each ton of carpet cleaning fluid is a blend of 0.6 tons of material 1, 0.1 tons of material 2, and 0.3 tons of material 3. RMC has 20 tons of material 1, 5 tons of material 2, and 21 tons of material 3 and is interested in determining the optimal production quantities for the upcoming planning period. A linear programming model of the RMC problem is shown:

$$\text{Max} \quad 40F + 30S + 50C$$

s.t.

$$0.4F + 0.5S + 0.6C \leq 20 \quad \text{Material 1}$$
$$0.2S + 0.1C \leq 5 \quad \text{Material 2}$$
$$0.6F + 0.3S + 0.3C \leq 21 \quad \text{Material 3}$$
$$F, S, C \geq 0$$

The optimal solution consists of 27.5 tons of fuel additive, 0 tons of solvent base, and 15 tons of carpet cleaning fluid, with a value of $1850, as shown in Figure 7.5.

This linear programming formulation of the RMC problem does not include a fixed cost for production setup of the products. Suppose that the following data are available

FIGURE 7.5 THE SOLUTION TO THE RMC PROBLEM

WEB file
RMC

```
Optimal Objective Value = 1850.00000

    Variable              Value              Reduced Costs
  --------------      ---------------      ------------------
       F                 27.50000                0.00000
       S                  0.00000              -12.50000
       C                 15.00000                0.00000
```

concerning the setup cost and the maximum production quantity for each of the three products:

Product	Setup Cost	Maximum Production
Fuel additive	$200	50 tons
Solvent base	$ 50	25 tons
Carpet cleaning fluid	$400	40 tons

The modeling flexibility provided by 0-1 variables can now be used to incorporate the fixed setup costs into the production model. The 0-1 variables are defined as follows:

$$SF = 1 \text{ if the fuel additive is produced; 0 if not}$$
$$SS = 1 \text{ if the solvent base is produced; 0 if not}$$
$$SC = 1 \text{ if the carpet cleaning fluid is produced; 0 if not}$$

Using these setup variables, the total setup cost is

$$200SF + 50SS + 400SC$$

We can now rewrite the objective function to include the setup cost. Thus, the net profit objective function becomes

$$\text{Max} \quad 40F + 30S + 50C - 200SF - 50SS - 400SC$$

Next, we must write production capacity constraints so that if a setup variable equals 0, production of the corresponding product is not permitted and, if a setup variable equals 1, production is permitted up to the maximum quantity. For the fuel additive, we do so by adding the following constraint:

$$F \le 50SF$$

Note that, with this constraint present, production of the fuel additive is not permitted when $SF = 0$. When $SF = 1$, production of up to 50 tons of fuel additive is permitted. We can think of the setup variable as a switch. When it is off ($SF = 0$), production is not permitted; when it is on ($SF = 1$), production is permitted.

FIGURE 7.6 THE SOLUTION TO THE RMC PROBLEM WITH SETUP COSTS

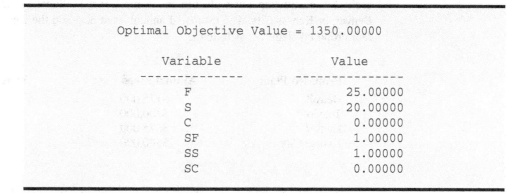

WEB file

RMC Setup

```
Optimal Objective Value = 1350.00000

       Variable                    Value
    ---------------            ---------------
          F                        25.00000
          S                        20.00000
          C                         0.00000
          SF                        1.00000
          SS                        1.00000
          SC                        0.00000
```

Similar production capacity constraints, using 0-1 variables, are added for the solvent base and carpet cleaning products:

$$S \leq 25SS$$
$$C \leq 40SC$$

We have then the following fixed cost model for the RMC problem:

Max $40F + 30S + 50C - 200SF - 50SS - 400SC$

s.t.

$0.4F + 0.5S + 0.6C$	$\leq \quad 20$	Material 1
$0.2S + 0.1C$	$\leq \quad 5$	Material 2
$0.6F + 0.3S + 0.3C$	$\leq \quad 21$	Material 3
F	$\leq 50SF$	Maximum F
S	$\leq 25SS$	Maximum S
C	$\leq 40SC$	Maximum C

$$F, S, C \geq 0; SF, SS, SC = 0, 1$$

The solution to the RMC problem with setup costs is shown in Figure 7.6. The optimal solution shows 25 tons of fuel additive and 20 tons of solvent base. The value of the objective function after deducting the setup cost is $1350. The setup cost for the fuel additive and the solvent base is $200 + $50 = $250. The optimal solution shows $SC = 0$, which indicates that the more expensive $400 setup cost for the carpet cleaning fluid should be avoided. Thus, the carpet cleaning fluid is not produced.

The Management Science in Action, Aluminum Can Production at Valley Metal Containers (see Section 7.1), employs 0-1 fixed cost variables for production line changeovers.

The key to developing a fixed cost model is the introduction of a 0-1 variable for each fixed cost and the specification of an upper bound for the corresponding production variable. For a production quantity x, a constraint of the form $x \leq My$ can then be used to allow production when the setup variable $y = 1$ and not to allow production when the setup variable $y = 0$. The value of the maximum production quantity M should be large enough to allow for all reasonable levels of production. But research has shown that choosing values of M excessively large will slow the solution procedure.

Distribution System Design

The Martin-Beck Company operates a plant in St. Louis with an annual capacity of 30,000 units. Product is shipped to regional distribution centers located in Boston, Atlanta, and

Houston. Because of an anticipated increase in demand, Martin-Beck plans to increase capacity by constructing a new plant in one or more of the following cities: Detroit, Toledo, Denver, or Kansas City. The estimated annual fixed cost and the annual capacity for the four proposed plants are as follows:

Proposed Plant	Annual Fixed Cost	Annual Capacity
Detroit	$175,000	10,000
Toledo	$300,000	20,000
Denver	$375,000	30,000
Kansas City	$500,000	40,000

The company's long-range planning group developed forecasts of the anticipated annual demand at the distribution centers as follows:

Distribution Center	Annual Demand
Boston	30,000
Atlanta	20,000
Houston	20,000

The shipping cost per unit from each plant to each distribution center is shown in Table 7.2. A network representation of the potential Martin-Beck distribution system is shown in Figure 7.7. Each potential plant location is shown; capacities and demands are shown in thousands of units. This network representation is for a transportation problem with a plant at St. Louis and at all four proposed sites. However, the decision has not yet been made as to which new plant or plants will be constructed.

Let us now show how 0-1 variables can be used in this **distribution system design problem** to develop a model for choosing the best plant locations and for determining how much to ship from each plant to each distribution center. We can use the following 0-1 variables to represent the plant construction decision:

y_1 = 1 if a plant is constructed in Detroit; 0 if not
y_2 = 1 if a plant is constructed in Toledo; 0 if not
y_3 = 1 if a plant is constructed in Denver; 0 if not
y_4 = 1 if a plant is constructed in Kansas City; 0 if not

TABLE 7.2   SHIPPING COST PER UNIT FOR THE MARTIN-BECK DISTRIBUTION SYSTEM

Plant Site	Distribution Centers		
	Boston	Atlanta	Houston
Detroit	5	2	3
Toledo	4	3	4
Denver	9	7	5
Kansas City	10	4	2
St. Louis	8	4	3

FIGURE 7.7 THE NETWORK REPRESENTATION OF THE MARTIN-BECK COMPANY DISTRIBUTION SYSTEM PROBLEM

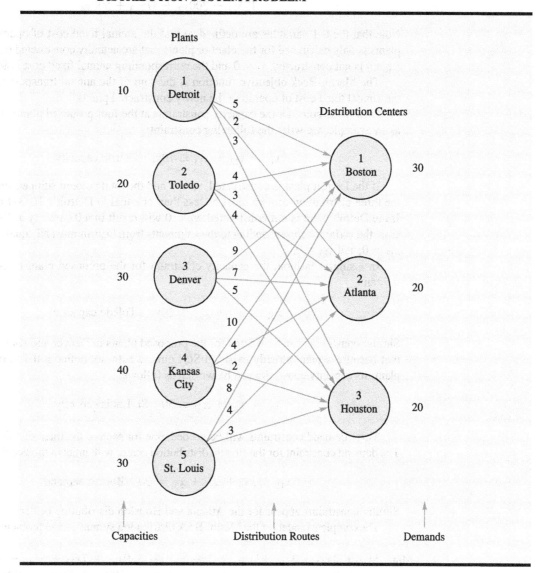

The variables representing the amount shipped from each plant site to each distribution center are defined just as for a transportation problem.

x_{ij} = the units shipped in thousands from plant i to distribution center j

$$i = 1, 2, 3, 4, 5 \quad \text{and} \quad j = 1, 2, 3$$

Using the shipping cost data in Table 7.2, the annual transportation cost in thousands of dollars is written

$$5x_{11} + 2x_{12} + 3x_{13} + 4x_{21} + 3x_{22} + 4x_{23} + 9x_{31} + 7x_{32} + 5x_{33}$$
$$+ 10x_{41} + 4x_{42} + 2x_{43} + 8x_{51} + 4x_{52} + 3x_{53}$$

The annual fixed cost of operating the new plant or plants in thousands of dollars is written as

$$175y_1 + 300y_2 + 375y_3 + 500y_4$$

Note that the 0-1 variables are defined so that the annual fixed cost of operating the new plants is only calculated for the plant or plants that are actually constructed (i.e., $y_i = 1$). If a plant is not constructed, $y_i = 0$ and the corresponding annual fixed cost is $0.

The Martin-Beck objective function is the sum of the annual transportation cost plus the annual fixed cost of operating the newly constructed plants.

Now let us consider the capacity constraints at the four proposed plants. Using Detroit as an example, we write the following constraint:

$$x_{11} + x_{12} + x_{13} \leq 10y_1 \quad \text{Detroit capacity}$$

If the Detroit plant is constructed, $y_1 = 1$ and the total amount shipped from Detroit to the three distribution centers must be less than or equal to Detroit's 10,000-unit capacity. If the Detroit plant is not constructed, $y_1 = 0$ will result in a 0 capacity at Detroit. In this case, the variables corresponding to the shipments from Detroit must all equal zero: $x_{11} = 0$, $x_{12} = 0$, and $x_{13} = 0$.

In a similar fashion, the capacity constraint for the proposed plant in Toledo can be written

$$x_{21} + x_{22} + x_{23} \leq 20y_2 \quad \text{Toledo capacity}$$

Similar constraints can be written for the proposed plants in Denver and Kansas City. Note that because a plant already exists in St. Louis, we do not define a 0-1 variable for this plant. Its capacity constraint can be written as follows:

$$x_{51} + x_{52} + x_{53} \leq 30 \quad \text{St. Louis capacity}$$

Three demand constraints will be needed, one for each of the three distribution centers. The demand constraint for the Boston distribution center with units in thousands is written as

$$x_{11} + x_{21} + x_{31} + x_{51} = 30 \quad \text{Boston demand}$$

Similar constraints appear for the Atlanta and Houston distribution centers.

The complete model for the Martin-Beck distribution system design problem is as follows:

Min $5x_{11} + 2x_{12} + 3x_{13} + 4x_{21} + 3x_{22} + 4x_{23} + 9x_{31} + 7x_{32} + 5x_{33} + 10x_{41} + 4x_{42}$
$+ 2x_{43} + 8x_{51} + 4x_{52} + 3x_{53} + 175y_1 + 300y_2 + 375y_3 + 500y_4$

s.t.

$x_{11} + x_{12} + x_{13}$	$\leq 10y_1$	Detroit capacity
$x_{21} + x_{22} + x_{23}$	$\leq 20y_2$	Toledo capacity
$x_{31} + x_{32} + x_{33}$	$\leq 30y_3$	Denver capacity
$x_{41} + x_{42} + x_{43}$	$\leq 40y_4$	Kansas City capacity
$x_{51} + x_{52} + x_{53}$	≤ 30	St. Louis capacity
$x_{11} + x_{21} + x_{31} + x_{41} + x_{51}$	$= 30$	Boston demand
$x_{12} + x_{22} + x_{32} + x_{42} + x_{52}$	$= 20$	Atlanta demand
$x_{13} + x_{23} + x_{33} + x_{43} + x_{53}$	$= 20$	Houston demand

$x_{ij} \geq 0$ for all i and j; $y_1, y_2, y_3, y_4 = 0, 1$

FIGURE 7.8   THE SOLUTION FOR THE MARTIN-BECK COMPANY DISTRIBUTION
SYSTEM PROBLEM

WEB file

Martin-Beck

```
Optimal Objective Value = 860.00000

      Variable                    Value
  ---------------           ---------------
        X11                     0.00000
        X12                     0.00000
        X13                     0.00000
        X21                     0.00000
        X22                     0.00000
        X23                     0.00000
        X31                     0.00000
        X32                     0.00000
        X33                     0.00000
        X41                     0.00000
        X42                    20.00000
        X43                    20.00000
        X51                    30.00000
        X52                     0.00000
        X53                     0.00000
        Y1                      0.00000
        Y2                      0.00000
        Y3                      0.00000
        Y4                      1.00000


      Constraint                Slack/Surplus
  ---------------           ---------------
         1                      0.00000
         2                      0.00000
         3                      0.00000
         4                      0.00000
         5                      0.00000
         6                      0.00000
         7                      0.00000
         8                      0.00000
```

The solution for the Martin-Beck problem is shown in Figure 7.8. The optimal solution calls for the construction of a plant in Kansas City ($y_4 = 1$); 20,000 units will be shipped from Kansas City to Atlanta ($x_{42} = 20$), 20,000 units will be shipped from Kansas City to Houston ($x_{43} = 20$), and 30,000 units will be shipped from St. Louis to Boston ($x_{51} = 30$). Note that the total cost of this solution including the fixed cost of $500,000 for the plant in Kansas City is $860,000.

This basic model can be expanded to accommodate distribution systems involving direct shipments from plants to warehouses, from plants to retail outlets, and multiple

605

products.[2] Using the special properties of 0-1 variables, the model can also be expanded to accommodate a variety of configuration constraints on the plant locations. For example, suppose in another problem, site 1 were in Dallas and site 2 were in Fort Worth. A company might not want to locate plants in both Dallas and Fort Worth because the cities are so close together. To prevent this result from happening, the following constraint can be added to the model:

Problem 13, which is based on the Martin-Beck distribution system problem, provides additional practice involving 0-1 variables.

$$y_1 + y_2 \leq 1$$

This constraint allows either y_1 or y_2 to equal 1, but not both. If we had written the constraints as an equality, it would require that a plant be located in either Dallas or Fort Worth.

Bank Location

The long-range planning department for the Ohio Trust Company is considering expanding its operation into a 20-county region in northeastern Ohio (see Figure 7.9). Currently, Ohio

FIGURE 7.9   THE 20-COUNTY REGION IN NORTHEASTERN OHIO

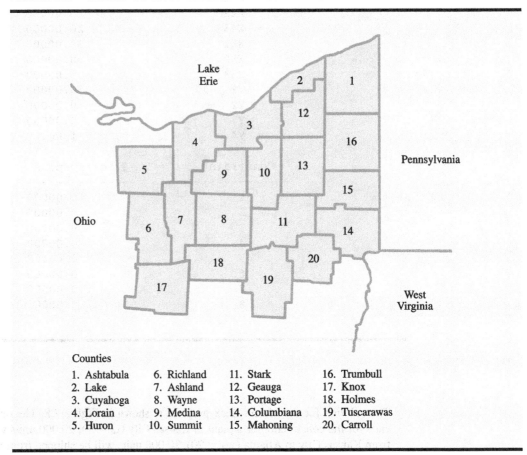

Counties

1. Ashtabula
2. Lake
3. Cuyahoga
4. Lorain
5. Huron
6. Richland
7. Ashland
8. Wayne
9. Medina
10. Summit
11. Stark
12. Geauga
13. Portage
14. Columbiana
15. Mahoning
16. Trumbull
17. Knox
18. Holmes
19. Tuscarawas
20. Carroll

---

[2]For computational reasons, it is usually preferable to replace the *m* plant capacity constraints with *mn* shipping route capacity constraints of the form $x_{ij} \leq \text{Min } \{s_i, d_j\} \, y_i$ for $i = 1, \ldots, m$, and $j = 1, \ldots, n$. The coefficient for y_i in each of these constraints is the smaller of the origin capacity (s_i) or the destination demand (d_j). These additional constraints often cause the solution of the LP Relaxation to be integer.

TABLE 7.3 COUNTIES IN THE OHIO TRUST EXPANSION REGION

Counties Under Consideration	Adjacent Counties (by Number)
1. Ashtabula	2, 12, 16
2. Lake	1, 3, 12
3. Cuyahoga	2, 4, 9, 10, 12, 13
4. Lorain	3, 5, 7, 9
5. Huron	4, 6, 7
6. Richland	5, 7, 17
7. Ashland	4, 5, 6, 8, 9, 17, 18
8. Wayne	7, 9, 10, 11, 18
9. Medina	3, 4, 7, 8, 10
10. Summit	3, 8, 9, 11, 12, 13
11. Stark	8, 10, 13, 14, 15, 18, 19, 20
12. Geauga	1, 2, 3, 10, 13, 16
13. Portage	3, 10, 11, 12, 15, 16
14. Columbiana	11, 15, 20
15. Mahoning	11, 13, 14, 16
16. Trumbull	1, 12, 13, 15
17. Knox	6, 7, 18
18. Holmes	7, 8, 11, 17, 19
19. Tuscarawas	11, 18, 20
20. Carroll	11, 14, 19

Trust does not have a principal place of business in any of the 20 counties. According to the banking laws in Ohio, if a bank establishes a principal place of business (PPB) in any county, branch banks can be established in that county and in any adjacent county. However, to establish a new principal place of business, Ohio Trust must either obtain approval for a new bank from the state's superintendent of banks or purchase an existing bank.

Table 7.3 lists the 20 counties in the region and adjacent counties. For example, Ashtabula County is adjacent to Lake, Geauga, and Trumbull counties; Lake County is adjacent to Ashtabula, Cuyahoga, and Geauga counties; and so on.

As an initial step in its planning, Ohio Trust would like to determine the minimum number of PPBs necessary to do business throughout the 20-county region. A 0-1 integer programming model can be used to solve this **location problem** for Ohio Trust. We define the variables as

$$x_i = 1 \text{ if a PPB is established in county } i; 0 \text{ otherwise}$$

To minimize the number of PPBs needed, we write the objective function as

$$\text{Min} \quad x_1 + x_2 + \cdots + x_{20}$$

The bank may locate branches in a county if the county contains a PPB or is adjacent to another county with a PPB. Thus, the linear program will need one constraint for each county. For example, the constraint for Ashtabula County is

$$x_1 + x_2 + x_{12} + x_{16} \geq 1 \quad \text{Ashtabula}$$

Note that satisfaction of this constraint ensures that a PPB will be placed in Ashtabula County *or* in one or more of the adjacent counties. This constraint thus guarantees that Ohio Trust will be able to place branch banks in Ashtabula County.

The complete statement of the bank location problem is

$$\text{Min} \quad x_1 + x_2 + \quad \cdots \quad + x_{20}$$

s.t.

$$
\begin{array}{llll}
x_1 + x_2 & + x_{12} + x_{16} & \geq 1 & \text{Ashtabula} \\
x_1 + x_2 + x_3 & + x_{12} & \geq 1 & \text{Lake}
\end{array}
$$

.

.

.

$$x_{11} + x_{14} + x_{19} + x_{20} \geq 1 \quad \text{Carroll}$$

$$x_i = 0, 1 \quad i = 1, 2, \ldots, 20$$

In Figure 7.10 we show the solution to the Ohio Trust problem. Using the output, we see that the optimal solution calls for principal places of business in Ashland, Stark, and Geauga counties. With PPBs in these three counties, Ohio Trust can place branch banks in all 20 counties (see Figure 7.11). All other decision variables have an optimal value of zero, indicating that a PPB should not be placed in these counties. Clearly the integer

FIGURE 7.10   THE SOLUTION FOR THE OHIO TRUST PPB LOCATION PROBLEM

WEB file

Ohio Trust

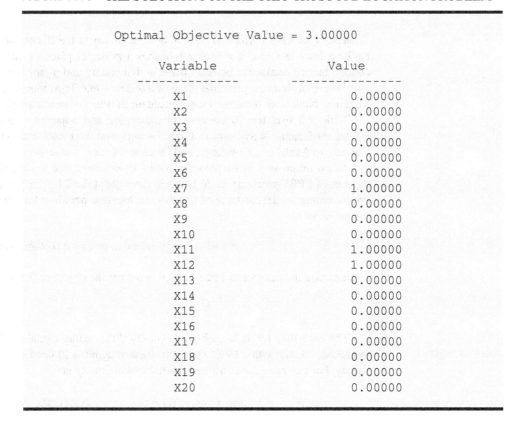

```
              Optimal Objective Value = 3.00000

              Variable                     Value
              ------------                 ----------
                  X1                        0.00000
                  X2                        0.00000
                  X3                        0.00000
                  X4                        0.00000
                  X5                        0.00000
                  X6                        0.00000
                  X7                        1.00000
                  X8                        0.00000
                  X9                        0.00000
                  X10                       0.00000
                  X11                       1.00000
                  X12                       1.00000
                  X13                       0.00000
                  X14                       0.00000
                  X15                       0.00000
                  X16                       0.00000
                  X17                       0.00000
                  X18                       0.00000
                  X19                       0.00000
                  X20                       0.00000
```

FIGURE 7.11   PRINCIPAL PLACE OF BUSINESS COUNTIES FOR OHIO TRUST

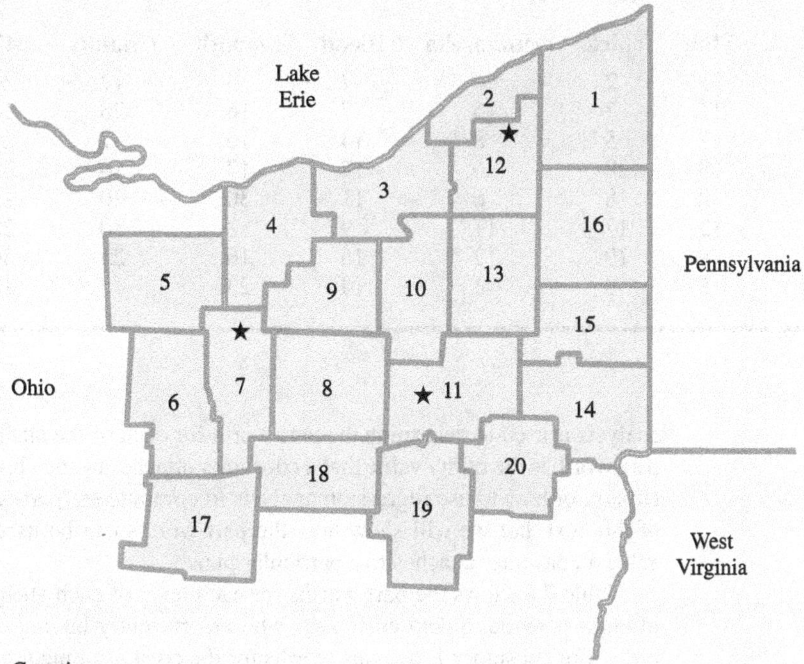

Counties

1. Ashtabula	6. Richland	11. Stark	16. Trumbull	★ A principal place
2. Lake	7. Ashland	12. Geauga	17. Knox	of business
3. Cuyahoga	8. Wayne	13. Portage	18. Holmes	should be located
4. Lorain	9. Medina	14. Columbiana	19. Tuscarawas	in these counties.
5. Huron	10. Summit	15. Mahoning	20. Carroll	

programming model could be enlarged to allow for expansion into a larger area or throughout the entire state.

Product Design and Market Share Optimization

Conjoint analysis is a market research technique that can be used to learn how prospective buyers of a product value the product's attributes. In this section we will show how the results of conjoint analysis can be used in an integer programming model of a **product design and market share optimization problem.** We illustrate the approach by considering a problem facing Salem Foods, a major producer of frozen foods.

Salem Foods is planning to enter the frozen pizza market. Currently, two existing brands, Antonio's and King's, have the major share of the market. In trying to develop a sausage pizza that will capture a significant share of the market, Salem determined that the four most important attributes when consumers purchase a frozen sausage pizza are crust, cheese, sauce, and sausage flavor. The crust attribute has two levels (thin and thick); the cheese attribute has two levels (mozzarella and blend); the sauce attribute has two levels (smooth and chunky); and the sausage flavor attribute has three levels (mild, medium, and hot).

In a typical conjoint analysis, a sample of consumers is asked to express their preference for specially prepared pizzas with chosen levels for the attributes. Then regression

TABLE 7.4   PART-WORTHS FOR THE SALEM FOODS PROBLEM

	Crust		Cheese		Sauce		Sausage Flavor		
Consumer	Thin	Thick	Mozzarella	Blend	Smooth	Chunky	Mild	Medium	Hot
1	11	2	6	7	3	17	26	27	8
2	11	7	15	17	16	26	14	1	10
3	7	5	8	14	16	7	29	16	19
4	13	20	20	17	17	14	25	29	10
5	2	8	6	11	30	20	15	5	12
6	12	17	11	9	2	30	22	12	20
7	9	19	12	16	16	25	30	23	19
8	5	9	4	14	23	16	16	30	3

analysis is used to determine the part-worth for each of the attribute levels. In essence, the part-worth is the utility value that a consumer attaches to each level of each attribute. A discussion of how to use regression analysis to compute the part-worths is beyond the scope of this text, but we will show how the part-worths can be used to determine the overall value a consumer attaches to a particular pizza.

Table 7.4 shows the part-worths for each level of each attribute provided by a sample of eight potential Salem customers who are currently buying either King's or Antonio's pizza. For consumer 1, the part-worths for the crust attribute are 11 for thin crust and 2 for thick crust, indicating a preference for thin crust. For the cheese attribute, the part-worths are 6 for the mozzarella cheese and 7 for the cheese blend; thus, consumer 1 has a slight preference for the cheese blend. From the other part-worths, we see that consumer 1 shows a strong preference for the chunky sauce over the smooth sauce (17 to 3) and has a slight preference for the medium-flavored sausage. Note that consumer 2 shows a preference for the thin crust, the cheese blend, the chunky sauce, and mild-flavored sausage. The part-worths for the other consumers are interpreted in a similar manner.

The part-worths can be used to determine the overall value (utility) each consumer attaches to a particular type of pizza. For instance, consumer 1's current favorite pizza is the Antonio's brand, which has a thick crust, mozzarella cheese, chunky sauce, and medium-flavored sausage. We can determine consumer 1's utility for this particular type of pizza using the part-worths in Table 7.4. For consumer 1, the part-worths are 2 for thick crust, 6 for mozzarella cheese, 17 for chunky sauce, and 27 for medium-flavored sausage. Thus, consumer 1's utility for the Antonio's brand pizza is 2 + 6 + 17 + 27 = 52. We can compute consumer 1's utility for a King's brand pizza in a similar manner. The King's brand pizza has a thin crust, a cheese blend, smooth sauce, and mild-flavored sausage. Because the part-worths for consumer 1 are 11 for thin crust, 7 for cheese blend, 3 for smooth sauce, and 26 for mild-flavored sausage, consumer 1's utility for the King's brand pizza is 11 + 7 + 3 + 26 = 47. In general, each consumer's utility for a particular type of pizza is just the sum of the appropriate part-worths.

In order to be successful with its brand, Salem Foods realizes that it must entice consumers in the marketplace to switch from their current favorite brand of pizza to the Salem product. That is, Salem must design a pizza (choose the type of crust, cheese, sauce, and sausage flavor) that will have the highest utility for enough people to ensure sufficient sales to justify making the product. Assuming the sample of eight consumers in the current study is representative of the marketplace for frozen sausage pizza, we can formulate and solve an integer programming model that can help Salem come up with such a design. In marketing literature, the problem being solved is called the *share of choices* problem.

The decision variables are defined as follows:

$$l_{ij} = 1 \text{ if Salem chooses level } i \text{ for attribute } j; 0 \text{ otherwise}$$
$$y_k = 1 \text{ if consumer } k \text{ chooses the Salem brand}; 0 \text{ otherwise}$$

The objective is to choose the levels of each attribute that will maximize the number of consumers preferring the Salem brand pizza. Because the number of customers preferring the Salem brand pizza is just the sum of the y_k variables, the objective function is

$$\text{Max} \quad y_1 + y_2 + \cdots + y_8$$

One constraint is needed for each consumer in the sample. To illustrate how the constraints are formulated, let us consider the constraint corresponding to consumer 1. For consumer 1, the utility of a particular type of pizza can be expressed as the sum of the part-worths:

$$\text{Utility for Consumer 1} = 11l_{11} + 2l_{21} + 6l_{12} + 7l_{22} + 3l_{13} + 17l_{23}$$
$$+ 26l_{14} + 27l_{24} + 8l_{34}$$

In order for consumer 1 to prefer the Salem pizza, the utility for the Salem pizza must be greater than the utility for consumer 1's current favorite. Recall that consumer 1's current favorite brand of pizza is Antonio's, with a utility of 52. Thus, consumer 1 will only purchase the Salem brand if the levels of the attributes for the Salem brand are chosen such that

$$11l_{11} + 2l_{21} + 6l_{12} + 7l_{22} + 3l_{13} + 17l_{23} + 26l_{14} + 27l_{24} + 8l_{34} > 52$$

Given the definitions of the y_k decision variables, we want $y_1 = 1$ when the consumer prefers the Salem brand and $y_1 = 0$ when the consumer does not prefer the Salem brand. Thus, we write the constraint for consumer 1 as follows:

$$11l_{11} + 2l_{21} + 6l_{12} + 7l_{22} + 3l_{13} + 17l_{23} + 26l_{14} + 27l_{24} + 8l_{34} \geq 1 + 52y_1$$

With this constraint, y_1 cannot equal 1 unless the utility for the Salem design (the left-hand side of the constraint) exceeds the utility for consumer 1's current favorite by at least 1. Because the objective function is to maximize the sum of the y_k variables, the optimization will seek a product design that will allow as many y_k as possible to equal 1.

A similar constraint is written for each consumer in the sample. The coefficients for the l_{ij} variables in the utility functions are taken from Table 7.4 and the coefficients for the y_k variables are obtained by computing the overall utility of the consumer's current favorite brand of pizza. The following constraints correspond to the eight consumers in the study:

Antonio's brand is the current favorite pizza for consumers 1, 4, 6, 7, and 8. King's brand is the current favorite pizza for consumers 2, 3, and 5.

$$11l_{11} + 2l_{21} + 6l_{12} + 7l_{22} + 3l_{13} + 17l_{23} + 26l_{14} + 27l_{24} + 8l_{34} \geq 1 + 52y_1$$
$$11l_{11} + 7l_{21} + 15l_{12} + 17l_{22} + 16l_{13} + 26l_{23} + 14l_{14} + 1l_{24} + 10l_{34} \geq 1 + 58y_2$$
$$7l_{11} + 5l_{21} + 8l_{12} + 14l_{22} + 16l_{13} + 7l_{23} + 29l_{14} + 16l_{24} + 19l_{34} \geq 1 + 66y_3$$
$$13l_{11} + 20l_{21} + 20l_{12} + 17l_{22} + 17l_{13} + 14l_{23} + 25l_{14} + 29l_{24} + 10l_{34} \geq 1 + 83y_4$$
$$2l_{11} + 8l_{21} + 6l_{12} + 11l_{22} + 30l_{13} + 20l_{23} + 15l_{14} + 5l_{24} + 12l_{34} \geq 1 + 58y_5$$
$$12l_{11} + 17l_{21} + 11l_{12} + 9l_{22} + 2l_{13} + 30l_{23} + 22l_{14} + 12l_{24} + 20l_{34} \geq 1 + 70y_6$$
$$9l_{11} + 19l_{21} + 12l_{12} + 16l_{22} + 16l_{13} + 25l_{23} + 30l_{14} + 23l_{24} + 19l_{34} \geq 1 + 79y_7$$
$$5l_{11} + 9l_{21} + 4l_{12} + 14l_{22} + 23l_{13} + 16l_{23} + 16l_{14} + 30l_{24} + 3l_{34} \geq 1 + 59y_8$$

Four more constraints must be added, one for each attribute. These constraints are necessary to ensure that one and only one level is selected for each attribute. For attribute 1 (crust), we must add the constraint

$$l_{11} + l_{21} = 1$$

Because l_{11} and l_{21} are both 0-1 variables, this constraint requires that one of the two variables equals 1 and the other equals 0. The following three constraints ensure that one and only one level is selected for each of the other three attributes:

$$l_{12} + l_{22} = 1$$
$$l_{13} + l_{23} = 1$$
$$l_{14} + l_{24} + l_{34} = 1$$

Salem

The optimal solution to this integer linear program is $l_{11} = l_{22} = l_{23} = l_{14} = 1$ and $y_1 = y_2 = y_6 = y_7 = 1$. The value of the optimal solution is 4, indicating that if Salem makes this type of pizza it will be preferable to the current favorite for four of the eight consumers. With $l_{11} = l_{22} = l_{23} = l_{14} = 1$, the pizza design that obtains the largest market share for Salem has a thin crust, a cheese blend, a chunky sauce, and mild-flavored sausage. Note also that with $y_1 = y_2 = y_6 = y_7 = 1$, consumers 1, 2, 6, and 7 will prefer the Salem pizza. With this information Salem may choose to market this type of pizza.

NOTES AND COMMENTS

1. Most practical applications of integer linear programming involve only 0-1 integer variables. Indeed, some mixed-integer computer codes are designed to handle only integer variables with binary values. However, if a clever mathematical trick is employed, these codes can still be used for problems involving general integer variables. The trick is called *binary expansion* and requires that an upper bound be established for each integer variable. More advanced texts on integer programming show how it can be done.

2. The Management Science in Action, Volunteer Scheduling for the Edmonton Folk Festival, describes how a series of three integer programming models was used to schedule volunteers. Two of the models employ 0-1 variables.

3. General-purpose mixed-integer linear programming codes and some spreadsheet packages can be used for linear programming problems, all-integer problems, and problems involving some continuous and some integer variables. General-purpose codes are seldom the fastest for solving problems with special structure (such as the transportation, assignment, and transshipment problems); however, unless the problems are very large, speed is usually not a critical issue. Thus, most practitioners prefer to use one general-purpose computer package that can be used on a variety of problems rather than to maintain a variety of computer programs designed for special problems.

MANAGEMENT SCIENCE IN ACTION

VOLUNTEER SCHEDULING FOR THE EDMONTON FOLK FESTIVAL*

The Edmonton Folk Festival is a four-day outdoor event that is run almost entirely by volunteers. In 2002, 1800 volunteers worked on 35 different crews and contributed more than 50,000 volunteer hours. With this many volunteers, coordination requires a major effort. For instance, in 2002, two volunteer coordinators used a trial-and-error procedure to develop schedules for the volunteers in the two gate crews. However, developing these schedules proved to be time consuming and frustrating; the coordinators spent as much time scheduling as they did supervising volunteers during the festival. To reduce the time spent on gate-crew scheduling, one of the coordinators asked the Centre for Excellence in Operations at the University of Alberta School of Business for help in automating the scheduling process. The Centre agreed to help.

The scheduling system developed consists of three integer programming models. Model 1 is used to determine daily shift schedules. This model determines the length of each shift (number of hours) and how many volunteers are needed for each shift to meet the peaks and valleys in demand. Model 2 is a binary integer program used to assign

volunteers to shifts. The objective is to maximize volunteer preferences subject to several constraints, such as number of hours worked, balance between morning and afternoon shifts, a mix of experienced and inexperienced volunteers on each shift, no conflicting shifts, and so on. Model 3 is used to allocate volunteers between the two gates.

The coordinators of the gate crews were pleased with the results provided by the models and learned to use them effectively. Vicki Fannon, the manager of volunteers for the festival, now has plans to expand the use of the integer programming models to the scheduling of other crews in the future.

*Based on L. Gordon and E. Erkut, "Improving Volunteer Scheduling for the Edmonton Folk Festival," *Interfaces* (September/October 2004): 367–376.

7.4 MODELING FLEXIBILITY PROVIDED BY 0-1 INTEGER VARIABLES

In Section 7.3 we presented four applications involving 0-1 integer variables. In this section we continue the discussion of the use of 0-1 integer variables in modeling. First, we show how 0-1 integer variables can be used to model multiple-choice and mutually exclusive constraints. Then, we show how 0-1 integer variables can be used to model situations in which k projects out of a set of n projects must be selected, as well as situations in which the acceptance of one project is conditional on the acceptance of another. We close the section with a cautionary note on the role of sensitivity analysis in integer linear programming.

Multiple-Choice and Mutually Exclusive Constraints

Recall the Ice-Cold Refrigerator capital budgeting problem introduced in Section 7.3. The decision variables were defined as

$P = 1$ if the plant expansion project is accepted; 0 if rejected

$W = 1$ if the warehouse expansion project is accepted; 0 if rejected

$M = 1$ if the new machinery project is accepted; 0 if rejected

$R = 1$ if the new product research project is accepted; 0 if rejected

Suppose that, instead of one warehouse expansion project, the Ice-Cold Refrigerator Company actually has three warehouse expansion projects under consideration. One of the warehouses *must* be expanded because of increasing product demand, but new demand isn't sufficient to make expansion of more than one warehouse necessary. The following variable definitions and **multiple-choice constraint** could be incorporated into the previous 0-1 integer linear programming model to reflect this situation. Let

$W_1 = 1$ if the original warehouse expansion project is accepted; 0 if rejected

$W_2 = 1$ if the second warehouse expansion project is accepted; 0 if rejected

$W_3 = 1$ if the third warehouse expansion project is accepted; 0 if rejected

The following multiple-choice constraint reflects the requirement that exactly one of these projects must be selected:

$$W_1 + W_2 + W_3 = 1$$

If W_1, W_2, and W_3 are allowed to assume only the values 0 or 1, then one and only one of these projects will be selected from among the three choices.

If the requirement that one warehouse must be expanded did not exist, the multiple-choice constraint could be modified as follows:

$$W_1 + W_2 + W_3 \leq 1$$

This modification allows for the case of no warehouse expansion ($W_1 = W_2 = W_3 = 0$) but does not permit more than one warehouse to be expanded. This type of constraint is often called a **mutually exclusive constraint.**

k out of n Alternatives Constraint

An extension of the notion of a multiple-choice constraint can be used to model situations in which k *out of a set of n* projects must be selected—a **k out of n alternatives constraint.** Suppose that W_1, W_2, W_3, W_4, and W_5 represent five potential warehouse expansion projects and that two of the five projects must be accepted. The constraint that satisfies this new requirement is

$$W_1 + W_2 + W_3 + W_4 + W_5 = 2$$

If no more than two of the projects are to be selected, we would use the following less-than-or-equal-to constraint:

$$W_1 + W_2 + W_3 + W_4 + W_5 \leq 2$$

Again, each of these variables must be restricted to 0-1 values.

Conditional and Corequisite Constraints

Sometimes the acceptance of one project is conditional on the acceptance of another. For example, suppose for the Ice-Cold Refrigerator Company that the warehouse expansion project was conditional on the plant expansion project. That is, management will not consider expanding the warehouse unless the plant is expanded. With P representing plant expansion and W representing warehouse expansion, a **conditional constraint** could be introduced to enforce this requirement:

$$W \leq P$$

Both P and W must be 0 or 1; whenever P is 0, W will be forced to 0. When P is 1, W is also allowed to be 1; thus, both the plant and the warehouse can be expanded. However, we note that the preceding constraint does not force the warehouse expansion project (W) to be accepted if the plant expansion project (P) is accepted.

If the warehouse expansion project had to be accepted whenever the plant expansion project was, and vice versa, we would say that P and W represented **corequisite constraint** projects. To model such a situation, we simply write the preceding constraint as an equality:

$$W = P$$

The constraint forces P and W to take on the same value.

Try Problem 7 for practice with the modeling flexibility provided by 0-1 variables.

The Management Science in Action, Customer Order Allocation Model at Ketron, describes how the modeling flexibility provided by 0-1 variables helped Ketron build a customer order allocation model for a sporting goods company.

CUSTOMER ORDER ALLOCATION MODEL AT KETRON*

Ketron Management Science provides consulting services for the design and implementation of mathematical programming applications. One such application involved the development of a mixed-integer programming model of the customer order allocation problem for a major sporting goods company. The sporting goods company markets approximately 300 products and has about 30 sources of supply (factory and warehouse locations). The problem is to determine how best to allocate customer orders to the various sources of supply such that the total manufacturing cost for the products ordered is minimized. Figure 7.12 provides a graphical representation of this problem. Note in the figure that each customer can receive shipments from only a few of the various sources of supply. For example, we see that customer 1 may be supplied by source A or B, customer 2 may be supplied only by source A, and so on.

The sporting equipment company classifies each customer order as either a "guaranteed" or "secondary" order. Guaranteed orders are single-source orders in that they must be filled by a single supplier to ensure that the complete order will be delivered to the customer at one time. This single-

source requirement necessitates the use of 0-1 integer variables in the model. Approximately 80% of the company's orders are guaranteed orders. Secondary orders can be split among the various sources of supply. These orders are made by customers restocking inventory, and receiving partial shipments from different sources at different times is not a problem. The 0-1 variables are used to represent the assignment of a guaranteed order to a supplier and continuous variables are used to represent the secondary orders.

Constraints for the problem involve raw material capacities, manufacturing capacities, and individual product capacities. A fairly typical problem has about 800 constraints, 2000 0-1 assignment variables, and 500 continuous variables associated with the secondary orders. The customer order allocation problem is solved periodically as orders are received. In a typical period, between 20 and 40 customers are to be supplied. Because most customers require several products, usually between 600 and 800 orders must be assigned to the sources of supply.

*Based on information provided by J. A. Tomlin of Ketron Management Science.

FIGURE 7.12   GRAPHICAL REPRESENTATION OF THE CUSTOMER ORDER ALLOCATION PROBLEM

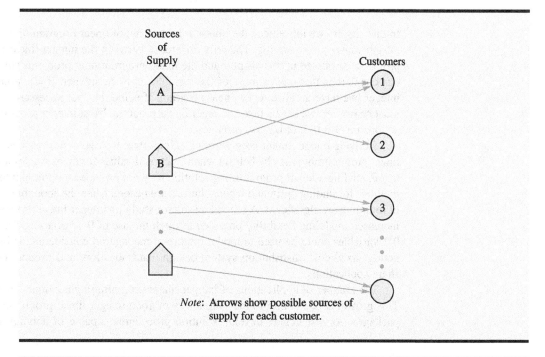

Note: Arrows show possible sources of supply for each customer.

A Cautionary Note About Sensitivity Analysis

Sensitivity analysis often is more crucial for integer linear programming problems than for linear programming problems. A small change in one of the coefficients in the constraints can cause a relatively large change in the value of the optimal solution. To understand why, consider the following integer programming model of a simple capital budgeting problem involving four projects and a budgetary constraint for a single time period:

$$\text{Max} \quad 40x_1 + 60x_2 + 70x_3 + 160x_4$$
$$\text{s.t.}$$
$$16x_1 + 35x_2 + 45x_3 + 85x_4 \leq 100$$
$$x_1, x_2, x_3, x_4 = 0, 1$$

We can obtain the optimal solution to this problem by enumerating the alternatives. It is $x_1 = 1$, $x_2 = 1$, $x_3 = 1$, and $x_4 = 0$, with an objective function value of $170. However, note that if the budget available is increased by $1 (from $100 to $101), the optimal solution changes to $x_1 = 1$, $x_2 = 0$, $x_3 = 0$, and $x_4 = 1$, with an objective function value of $200. That is, one additional dollar in the budget would lead to a $30 increase in the return. Surely management, when faced with such a situation, would increase the budget by $1. Because of the extreme sensitivity of the value of the optimal solution to the constraint coefficients, practitioners usually recommend re-solving the integer linear program several times with slight variations in the coefficients before attempting to choose the best solution for implementation.

SUMMARY

In this chapter we introduced the important extension of linear programming referred to as *integer linear programming*. The only difference between the integer linear programming problems discussed in this chapter and the linear programming problems studied in previous chapters is that one or more of the variables must be integer. If all variables must be integer, we have an all-integer linear program. If some, but not necessarily all, variables must be integer, we have a mixed-integer linear program. Most integer programming applications involve 0-1, or binary, variables.

Studying integer linear programming is important for two major reasons. First, integer linear programming may be helpful when fractional values for the variables are not permitted. Rounding a linear programming solution may not provide an optimal integer solution; methods for finding optimal integer solutions are needed when the economic consequences of rounding are significant. A second reason for studying integer linear programming is the increased modeling flexibility provided through the use of 0-1 variables. We showed how 0-1 variables could be used to model important managerial considerations in capital budgeting, fixed cost, distribution system design, bank location, and product design/market share applications.

The number of applications of integer linear programming continues to grow rapidly. This growth is due in part to the availability of good integer linear programming software packages. As researchers develop solution procedures capable of solving larger integer linear programs and as computer speed increases, a continuation of the growth of integer programming applications is expected.

GLOSSARY

Integer linear program A linear program with the additional requirement that one or more of the variables must be integer.

All-integer linear program An integer linear program in which all variables are required to be integer.

LP Relaxation The linear program that results from dropping the integer requirements for the variables in an integer linear program.

Mixed-integer linear program An integer linear program in which some, but not necessarily all, variables are required to be integer.

0-1 integer linear program An all-integer or mixed-integer linear program in which the integer variables are only permitted to assume the values 0 or 1. Also called *binary integer program*.

Capital budgeting problem A 0-1 integer programming problem that involves choosing which projects or activities provide the best investment return.

Fixed cost problem A 0-1 mixed-integer programming problem in which the binary variables represent whether an activity, such as a production run, is undertaken (variable = 1) or not (variable = 0).

Distribution system design problem A mixed-integer linear program in which the binary integer variables usually represent sites selected for warehouses or plants and continuous variables represent the amount shipped over arcs in the distribution network.

Location problem A 0-1 integer programming problem in which the objective is to select the best locations to meet a stated objective. Variations of this problem (see the bank location problem in Section 7.3) are known as covering problems.

Product design and market share optimization problem Sometimes called the share of choices problem, it involves choosing a product design that maximizes the number of consumers preferring it.

Multiple-choice constraint A constraint requiring that the sum of two or more 0-1 variables equal 1. Thus, any feasible solution makes a choice of which variable to set equal to 1.

Mutually exclusive constraint A constraint requiring that the sum of two or more 0-1 variables be less than or equal to 1. Thus, if one of the variables equals 1, the others must equal 0. However, all variables could equal 0.

k out of n alternatives constraint An extension of the multiple-choice constraint. This constraint requires that the sum of n 0-1 variables equal k.

Conditional constraint A constraint involving 0-1 variables that does not allow certain variables to equal 1 unless certain other variables are equal to 1.

Corequisite constraint A constraint requiring that two 0-1 variables be equal. Thus, they are both in or out of solution together.

PROBLEMS

1. Indicate which of the following is an all-integer linear program and which is a mixed-integer linear program. Write the LP Relaxation for the problem but do not attempt to solve.

   a. Max $30x_1 + 25x_2$

   s.t.

   $$3x_1 + 1.5x_2 \leq 400$$
   $$1.5x_1 + 2x_2 \leq 250$$
   $$1x_1 + 1x_2 \leq 150$$
   $$x_1, x_2 \geq 0 \text{ and } x_2 \text{ integer}$$

   b. Min $3x_1 + 4x_2$

   s.t.

   $$2x_1 + 4x_2 \geq 8$$
   $$2x_1 + 6x_2 \geq 12$$
   $$x_1, x_2 \geq 0 \text{ and integer}$$

SELF test 2. Consider the following all-integer linear program:

$$\text{Max} \quad 5x_1 + 8x_2$$

s.t.

$$6x_1 + 5x_2 \leq 30$$
$$9x_1 + 4x_2 \leq 36$$
$$1x_1 + 2x_2 \leq 10$$
$$x_1, x_2 \geq 0 \text{ and integer}$$

   a. Graph the constraints for this problem. Use dots to indicate all feasible integer solutions.
   b. Find the optimal solution to the LP Relaxation. Round down to find a feasible integer solution.
   c. Find the optimal integer solution. Is it the same as the solution obtained in part (b) by rounding down?

3. Consider the following all-integer linear program:

$$\text{Max} \quad 1x_1 + 1x_2$$

s.t.

$$4x_1 + 6x_2 \leq 22$$
$$1x_1 + 5x_2 \leq 15$$
$$2x_1 + 1x_2 \leq 9$$
$$x_1, x_2 \geq 0 \text{ and integer}$$

   a. Graph the constraints for this problem. Use dots to indicate all feasible integer solutions.
   b. Solve the LP Relaxation of this problem.
   c. Find the optimal integer solution.

4. Consider the following all-integer linear program:

$$\text{Max} \quad 10x_1 + 3x_2$$

s.t.

$$6x_1 + 7x_2 \leq 40$$
$$3x_1 + 1x_2 \leq 11$$
$$x_1, x_2 \geq 0 \text{ and integer}$$

618

a. Formulate and solve the LP Relaxation of the problem. Solve it graphically, and round down to find a feasible solution. Specify an upper bound on the value of the optimal solution.

b. Solve the integer linear program graphically. Compare the value of this solution with the solution obtained in part (a).

c. Suppose the objective function changes to Max $3x_1 + 6x_2$. Repeat parts (a) and (b).

5. Consider the following mixed-integer linear program:

$$\text{Max} \quad 2x_1 + 3x_2$$

s.t.

$$4x_1 + 9x_2 \leq 36$$
$$7x_1 + 5x_2 \leq 35$$
$$x_1, x_2 \geq 0 \text{ and } x_1 \text{ integer}$$

a. Graph the constraints for this problem. Indicate on your graph all feasible mixed-integer solutions.

b. Find the optimal solution to the LP Relaxation. Round the value of x_1 down to find a feasible mixed-integer solution. Is this solution optimal? Why or why not?

c. Find the optimal solution for the mixed-integer linear program.

6. Consider the following mixed-integer linear program:

$$\text{Max} \quad 1x_1 + 1x_2$$

s.t.

$$7x_1 + 9x_2 \leq 63$$
$$9x_1 + 5x_2 \leq 45$$
$$3x_1 + 1x_2 \leq 12$$
$$x_1, x_2 \geq 0 \text{ and } x_2 \text{ integer}$$

a. Graph the constraints for this problem. Indicate on your graph all feasible mixed-integer solutions.

b. Find the optimal solution to the LP Relaxation. Round the value of x_2 down to find a feasible mixed-integer solution. Specify upper and lower bounds on the value of the optimal solution to the mixed-integer linear program.

c. Find the optimal solution to the mixed-integer linear program.

7. The following questions refer to a capital budgeting problem with six projects represented by 0-1 variables $x_1, x_2, x_3, x_4, x_5,$ and x_6:

a. Write a constraint modeling a situation in which two of the projects 1, 3, 5, and 6 must be undertaken.

b. Write a constraint modeling a situation in which, if projects 3 and 5 must be undertaken, they must be undertaken simultaneously.

c. Write a constraint modeling a situation in which project 1 or 4 must be undertaken, but not both.

d. Write constraints modeling a situation where project 4 cannot be undertaken unless projects 1 and 3 also are undertaken.

e. In addition to the requirement in part (d), assume that when projects 1 and 3 are undertaken, project 4 also must be undertaken.

8. Spencer Enterprises must choose among a series of new investment alternatives. The potential investment alternatives, the net present value of the future stream of returns,

the capital requirements, and the available capital funds over the next three years are summarized as follows:

Alternative	Net Present Value ($)	Capital Requirements ($)		
		Year 1	Year 2	Year 3
Limited warehouse expansion	4,000	3,000	1,000	4,000
Extensive warehouse expansion	6,000	2,500	3,500	3,500
Test market new product	10,500	6,000	4,000	5,000
Advertising campaign	4,000	2,000	1,500	1,800
Basic research	8,000	5,000	1,000	4,000
Purchase new equipment	3,000	1,000	500	900
Capital funds available		10,500	7,000	8,750

a. Develop and solve an integer programming model for maximizing the net present value.

b. Assume that only one of the warehouse expansion projects can be implemented. Modify your model of part (a).

c. Suppose that, if test marketing of the new product is carried out, the advertising campaign also must be conducted. Modify your formulation of part (b) to reflect this new situation.

9. Hawkins Manufacturing Company produces connecting rods for 4- and 6-cylinder automobile engines using the same production line. The cost required to set up the production line to produce the 4-cylinder connecting rods is $2000, and the cost required to set up the production line for the 6-cylinder connecting rods is $3500. Manufacturing costs are $15 for each 4-cylinder connecting rod and $18 for each 6-cylinder connecting rod. Hawkins makes a decision at the end of each week as to which product will be manufactured the following week. If a production changeover is necessary from one week to the next, the weekend is used to reconfigure the production line. Once the line has been set up, the weekly production capacities are 6000 6-cylinder connecting rods and 8000 4-cylinder connecting rods. Let

x_4 = the number of 4-cylinder connecting rods produced next week

x_6 = the number of 6-cylinder connecting rods produced next week

s_4 = 1 if the production line is set up to produce the 4-cylinder connecting rods;
  0 if otherwise

s_6 = 1 if the production line is set up to produce the 6-cylinder connecting rods;
  0 if otherwise

a. Using the decision variables x_4 and s_4, write a constraint that limits next week's production of the 4-cylinder connecting rods to either 0 or 8000 units.

b. Using the decision variables x_6 and s_6, write a constraint that limits next week's production of the 6-cylinder connecting rods to either 0 or 6000 units.

c. Write three constraints that, taken together, limit the production of connecting rods for next week.

d. Write an objective function for minimizing the cost of production for next week.

10. Grave City is considering the relocation of several police substations to obtain better enforcement in high-crime areas. The locations under consideration together

with the areas that can be covered from these locations are given in the following table:

Potential Locations for Substations	Areas Covered
A	1, 5, 7
B	1, 2, 5, 7
C	1, 3, 5
D	2, 4, 5
E	3, 4, 6
F	4, 5, 6
G	1, 5, 6, 7

a. Formulate an integer programming model that could be used to find the minimum number of locations necessary to provide coverage to all areas.

b. Solve the problem in part (a).

11. Hart Manufacturing makes three products. Each product requires manufacturing operations in three departments: A, B, and C. The labor-hour requirements, by department, are as follows:

Department	Product 1	Product 2	Product 3
A	1.50	3.00	2.00
B	2.00	1.00	2.50
C	0.25	0.25	0.25

During the next production period, the labor-hours available are 450 in department A, 350 in department B, and 50 in department C. The profit contributions per unit are $25 for product 1, $28 for product 2, and $30 for product 3.

a. Formulate a linear programming model for maximizing total profit contribution.

b. Solve the linear program formulated in part (a). How much of each product should be produced, and what is the projected total profit contribution?

c. After evaluating the solution obtained in part (b), one of the production supervisors noted that production setup costs had not been taken into account. She noted that setup costs are $400 for product 1, $550 for product 2, and $600 for product 3. If the solution developed in part (b) is to be used, what is the total profit contribution after taking into account the setup costs?

d. Management realized that the optimal product mix, taking setup costs into account, might be different from the one recommended in part (b). Formulate a mixed-integer linear program that takes setup costs into account. Management also stated that we should not consider making more than 175 units of product 1, 150 units of product 2, or 140 units of product 3.

e. Solve the mixed-integer linear program formulated in part (d). How much of each product should be produced, and what is the projected total profit contribution? Compare this profit contribution to that obtained in part (c).

12. Yates Company supplies road salt to county highway departments. The company has three trucks, and the dispatcher is trying to schedule tomorrow's deliveries to Polk, Dallas, and Jasper counties. Two trucks have 15-ton capacities, and the third truck has a 30-ton capacity. Based on these truck capacities, two counties will receive 15 tons and the third will

receive 30 tons of road salt. The dispatcher wants to determine how much to ship to each county. Let

$$P = \text{amount shipped to Polk County}$$
$$D = \text{amount shipped to Dallas County}$$
$$J = \text{amount shipped to Jasper County}$$

and

$$Y_i = \begin{cases} 1 & \text{if the 30-ton truck is assigned to county } i \\ 0 & \text{otherwise} \end{cases}$$

a. Use these variable definitions and write constraints that appropriately restrict the amount shipped to each county.

b. The cost of assigning the 30-ton truck to the three counties is $100 to Polk, $85 to Dallas, and $50 to Jasper. Formulate and solve a mixed-integer linear program to determine how much to ship to each county.

13. Recall the Martin-Beck Company distribution system problem in Section 7.3.

a. Modify the formulation shown in Section 7.3 to account for the policy restriction that one plant, but not two, must be located either in Detroit or in Toledo.

b. Modify the formulation shown in Section 7.3 to account for the policy restriction that no more than two plants can be located in Denver, Kansas City, and St. Louis.

14. An automobile manufacturer has five outdated plants: one each in Michigan, Ohio, and California and two in New York. Management is considering modernizing these plants to manufacture engine blocks and transmissions for a new model car. The cost to modernize each plant and the manufacturing capacity after modernization are as follows:

Plant	Cost ($ millions)	Engine Blocks (1000s)	Transmissions (1000s)
Michigan	25	500	300
New York	35	800	400
New York	35	400	800
Ohio	40	900	600
California	20	200	300

The projected needs are for total capacities of 900,000 engine blocks and 900,000 transmissions. Management wants to determine which plants to modernize to meet projected manufacturing needs and, at the same time, minimize the total cost of modernization.

a. Develop a table that lists every possible option available to management. As part of your table, indicate the total engine block capacity and transmission capacity for each possible option, whether the option is feasible based on the projected needs, and the total modernization cost for each option.

b. Based on your analysis in part (a), what recommendation would you provide management?

c. Formulate a 0-1 integer programming model that could be used to determine the optimal solution to the modernization question facing management.

d. Solve the model formulated in part (c) to provide a recommendation for management.

15. CHB, Inc., is a bank holding company that is evaluating the potential for expanding into a 13-county region in the southwestern part of the state. State law permits establishing branches in any county that is adjacent to a county in which a PPB (principal place of business) is located. The following map shows the 13-county region with the population of each county indicated.

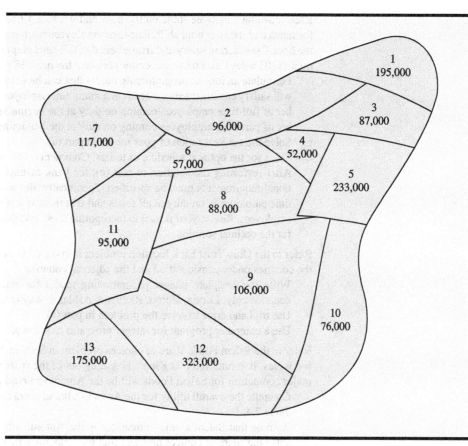

a. Assume that only one PPB can be established in the region. Where should it be located to maximize the population served? (*Hint:* Review the Ohio Trust formulation in Section 7.3. Consider minimizing the population not served, and introduce variable $y_i = 1$ if it is not possible to establish a branch in county i, and $y_i = 0$ otherwise.)

b. Suppose that two PPBs can be established in the region. Where should they be located to maximize the population served?

c. Management learned that a bank located in county 5 is considering selling. If CHB purchases this bank, the requisite PPB will be established in county 5, and a base for beginning expansion in the region will also be established. What advice would you give the management of CHB?

16. The Northshore Bank is working to develop an efficient work schedule for full-time and part-time tellers. The schedule must provide for efficient operation of the bank including adequate customer service, employee breaks, and so on. On Fridays the bank is open from 9:00 A.M. to 7:00 P.M. The number of tellers necessary to provide adequate customer service during each hour of operation is summarized here.

Time	Number of Tellers	Time	Number of Tellers
9:00 A.M.–10:00 A.M.	6	2:00 P.M.–3:00 P.M.	6
10:00 A.M.–11:00 A.M.	4	3:00 P.M.–4:00 P.M.	4
11:00 A.M.–Noon	8	4:00 P.M.–5:00 P.M.	7
Noon–1:00 P.M.	10	5:00 P.M.–6:00 P.M.	6
1:00 P.M.–2:00 P.M.	9	6:00 P.M.–7:00 P.M.	6

Each full-time employee starts on the hour and works a 4-hour shift, followed by 1 hour for lunch and then a 3-hour shift. Part-time employees work one 4-hour shift beginning on the hour. Considering salary and fringe benefits, full-time employees cost the bank $15 per hour ($105 a day), and part-time employees cost the bank $8 per hour ($32 per day).

a. Formulate an integer programming model that can be used to develop a schedule that will satisfy customer service needs at a minimum employee cost. (*Hint:* Let x_i = number of full-time employees coming on duty at the beginning of hour i and y_i = number of part-time employees coming on duty at the beginning of hour i.)

b. Solve the LP Relaxation of your model in part (a).

c. Solve for the optimal schedule of tellers. Comment on the solution.

d. After reviewing the solution to part (c), the bank manager realized that some additional requirements must be specified. Specifically, she wants to ensure that one full-time employee is on duty at all times and that there is a staff of at least five full-time employees. Revise your model to incorporate these additional requirements and solve for the optimal solution.

17. Refer to the Ohio Trust bank location problem introduced in Section 7.3. Table 7.3 shows the counties under consideration and the adjacent counties.

a. Write the complete integer programming model for expansion into the following counties only: Lorain, Huron, Richland, Ashland, Wayne, Medina, and Knox.

b. Use trial and error to solve the problem in part (a).

c. Use a computer program for integer programs to solve the problem.

18. Refer to the Salem Foods share of choices problem in Section 7.3 and address the following issues. It is rumored that King's is getting out of the frozen pizza business. If so, the major competitor for Salem Foods will be the Antonio's brand pizza.

a. Compute the overall utility for the Antonio's brand pizza for each of the consumers in Table 7.4.

b. Assume that Salem's only competitor is the Antonio's brand pizza. Formulate and solve the share of choices problem that will maximize market share. What is the best product design and what share of the market can be expected?

19. Burnside Marketing Research conducted a study for Barker Foods on some designs for a new dry cereal. Three attributes were found to be most influential in determining which cereal had the best taste: ratio of wheat to corn in the cereal flake, type of sweetener (sugar, honey, or artificial), and the presence or absence of flavor bits. Seven children participated in taste tests and provided the following part-worths for the attributes:

	Wheat/Corn		Sweetener			Flavor Bits	
Child	Low	High	Sugar	Honey	Artificial	Present	Absent
1	15	35	30	40	25	15	9
2	30	20	40	35	35	8	11
3	40	25	20	40	10	7	14
4	35	30	25	20	30	15	18
5	25	40	40	20	35	18	14
6	20	25	20	35	30	9	16
7	30	15	25	40	40	20	11

a. Suppose the overall utility (sum of part-worths) of the current favorite cereal is 75 for each child. What is the product design that will maximize the share of choices for the seven children in the sample?

b. Assume the overall utility of the current favorite cereal for the first four children in the group is 70, and the overall utility of the current favorite cereal for the last three children

624

in the group is 80. What is the product design that will maximize the share of choices for the seven children in the sample?

20. Refer to Problem 14. Suppose that management determined that its cost estimates to modernize the New York plants were too low. Specifically, suppose that the actual cost is $40 million to modernize each plant.

   a. What changes in your previous 0-1 integer linear programming model are needed to incorporate these changes in costs?

   b. For these cost changes, what recommendations would you now provide management regarding the modernization plan?

   c. Reconsider the solution obtained using the revised cost figures. Suppose that management decides that closing two plants in the same state is not acceptable. How could this policy restriction be added to your 0-1 integer programming model?

   d. Based on the cost revision and the policy restriction presented in part (c), what recommendations would you now provide management regarding the modernization plan?

21. The Bayside Art Gallery is considering installing a video camera security system to reduce its insurance premiums. A diagram of the eight display rooms that Bayside uses for exhibitions is shown in Figure 7.13; the openings between the rooms are numbered 1 through 13. A security firm proposed that two-way cameras be installed at some room openings. Each camera has the ability to monitor the two rooms between which the camera is located. For example, if a camera were located at opening number 4, rooms 1 and 4 would be covered; if a camera were located at opening 11, rooms 7 and 8 would be covered; and so on. Management decided not to locate a camera system at the entrance to the display rooms. The objective is to provide security coverage for all eight rooms using the minimum number of two-way cameras.

   a. Formulate a 0-1 integer linear programming model that will enable Bayside's management to determine the locations for the camera systems.

   b. Solve the model formulated in part (a) to determine how many two-way cameras to purchase and where they should be located.

   c. Suppose that management wants to provide additional security coverage for room 7. Specifically, management wants room 7 to be covered by two cameras. How would your model formulated in part (a) have to change to accommodate this policy restriction?

   d. With the policy restriction specified in part (c), determine how many two-way camera systems will need to be purchased and where they will be located.

22. The Delta Group is a management consulting firm specializing in the health care industry. A team is being formed to study possible new markets, and a linear programming model has been developed for selecting team members. However, one constraint the president imposed is a team size of three, five, or seven members. The staff cannot figure out how to incorporate this requirement in the model. The current model requires that team members be selected from three departments and uses the following variable definitions:

$$x_1 = \text{the number of employees selected from department 1}$$
$$x_2 = \text{the number of employees selected from department 2}$$
$$x_3 = \text{the number of employees selected from department 3}$$

Show the staff how to write constraints that will ensure that the team will consist of three, five, or seven employees. The following integer variables should be helpful:

$$y_1 = \begin{cases} 1 & \text{if team size is 3} \\ 0 & \text{otherwise} \end{cases}$$

$$y_2 = \begin{cases} 1 & \text{if team size is 5} \\ 0 & \text{otherwise} \end{cases}$$

$$y_3 = \begin{cases} 1 & \text{if team size is 7} \\ 0 & \text{otherwise} \end{cases}$$

FIGURE 7.13   DIAGRAM OF DISPLAY ROOMS FOR BAYSIDE ART GALLERY

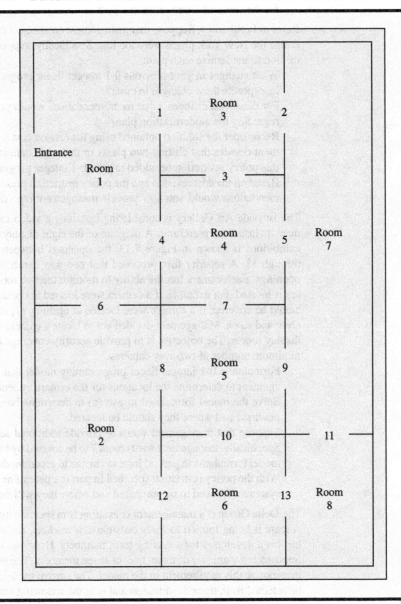

23. Roedel Electronics produces a variety of electrical components, including a remote controller for televisions and a remote controller for VCRs. Each controller consists of three subassemblies that are manufactured by Roedel: a base, a cartridge, and a keypad. Both controllers use the same base subassembly, but different cartridge and keypad subassemblies.

Roedel's sales forecast indicates that 7000 TV controllers and 5000 VCR controllers will be needed to satisfy demand during the upcoming Christmas season. Because only 500 hours of in-house manufacturing time are available, Roedel is considering purchasing some, or all, of the subassemblies from outside suppliers. If Roedel manufactures a subassembly in-house, it incurs a fixed setup cost as well as a variable manufacturing cost. The following table shows the setup cost, the manufacturing time per subassembly, the manufacturing cost per subassembly, and the cost to purchase each of the subassemblies from an outside supplier:

Subassembly	Setup Cost ($)	Manufacturing Time per Unit (min.)	Manufacturing Cost per Unit ($)	Purchase Cost per Unit ($)
Base	1000	0.9	0.40	0.65
TV cartridge	1200	2.2	2.90	3.45
VCR cartridge	1900	3.0	3.15	3.70
TV keypad	1500	0.8	0.30	0.50
VCR keypad	1500	1.0	0.55	0.70

a. Determine how many units of each subassembly Roedel should manufacture and how many units Roedel should purchase. What is the total manufacturing and purchase cost associated with your recommendation?

b. Suppose Roedel is considering purchasing new machinery to produce VCR cartridges. For the new machinery, the setup cost is $3000; the manufacturing time is 2.5 minutes per cartridge, and the manufacturing cost is $2.60 per cartridge. Assuming that the new machinery is purchased, determine how many units of each subassembly Roedel should manufacture and how many units of each subassembly Roedel should purchase. What is the total manufacturing and purchase cost associated with your recommendation? Do you think the new machinery should be purchased? Explain.

24. A mathematical programming system named SilverScreener uses a 0-1 integer programming model to help theater managers decide which movies to show on a weekly basis in a multiple-screen theater (*Interfaces,* May/June 2001). Suppose that management of Valley Cinemas would like to investigate the potential of using a similar scheduling system for their chain of multiple-screen theaters. Valley selected a small two-screen movie theater for the pilot testing and would like to develop an integer programming model to help schedule movies for the next four weeks. Six movies are available. The first week each movie is available, the last week each movie can be shown, and the maximum number of weeks that each movie can run are shown here:

Movie	First Week Available	Last Week Available	Max. Run (weeks)
1	1	2	2
2	1	3	2
3	1	1	2
4	2	4	2
5	3	6	3
6	3	5	3

The overall viewing schedule for the theater is composed of the individual schedules for each of the six movies. For each movie, a schedule must be developed that specifies the week the movie starts and the number of consecutive weeks it will run. For instance, one possible schedule for movie 2 is for it to start in week 1 and run for two weeks. Theater policy requires that once a movie is started it must be shown in consecutive weeks. It cannot be stopped and restarted again. To represent the schedule possibilities for each movie, the following decision variables were developed:

$$x_{ijw} = \begin{cases} 1 & \text{if movie } i \text{ is scheduled to start in week } j \text{ and run for } w \text{ weeks} \\ 0 & \text{otherwise} \end{cases}$$

For example, $x_{532} = 1$ means that the schedule selected for movie 5 is to begin in week 3 and run for two weeks. For each movie, a separate variable is given for each possible schedule.

a. Three schedules are associated with movie 1. List the variables that represent these schedules.

b. Write a constraint requiring that only one schedule be selected for movie 1.

c. Write a constraint requiring that only one schedule be selected for movie 5.

d. What restricts the number of movies that can be shown in week 1? Write a constraint that restricts the number of movies selected for viewing in week 1.

e. Write a constraint that restricts the number of movies selected for viewing in week 3.

25. East Coast Trucking provides service from Boston to Miami using regional offices located in Boston, New York, Philadelphia, Baltimore, Washington, Richmond, Raleigh, Florence, Savannah, Jacksonville, and Tampa. The number of miles between each of the regional offices is provided in the following table:

	New York	Philadelphia	Baltimore	Washington	Richmond	Raleigh	Florence	Savannah	Jacksonville	Tampa	Miami
Boston	211	320	424	459	565	713	884	1056	1196	1399	1669
New York		109	213	248	354	502	673	845	985	1188	1458
Philadelphia			104	139	245	393	564	736	876	1079	1349
Baltimore				35	141	289	460	632	772	975	1245
Washington					106	254	425	597	737	940	1210
Richmond						148	319	491	631	834	1104
Raleigh							171	343	483	686	956
Florence								172	312	515	785
Savannah									140	343	613
Jacksonville										203	473
Tampa											270

The company's expansion plans involve constructing service facilities in some of the cities where a regional office is located. Each regional office must be within 400 miles of a service facility. For instance, if a service facility is constructed in Richmond, it can provide service to regional offices located in New York, Philadelphia, Baltimore, Washington, Richmond, Raleigh, and Florence. Management would like to determine the minimum number of service facilities needed and where they should be located.

a. Formulate an integer linear program that can be used to determine the minimum number of service facilities needed and their location.

b. Solve the linear program formulated in part (a). How many service facilities are required, and where should they be located?

c. Suppose that each service facility can only provide service to regional offices within 300 miles. How many service facilities are required, and where should they be located?

Case Problem 1 TEXTBOOK PUBLISHING

ASW Publishing, Inc., a small publisher of college textbooks, must make a decision regarding which books to publish next year. The books under consideration are listed in the following table, along with the projected three-year sales expected from each book:

Book Subject	Type of Book	Projected Sales ($1000s)
Business calculus	New	20
Finite mathematics	Revision	30
General statistics	New	15
Mathematical statistics	New	10
Business statistics	Revision	25
Finance	New	18
Financial accounting	New	25
Managerial accounting	Revision	50
English literature	New	20
German	New	30

The books listed as revisions are texts that ASW already has under contract; these texts are being considered for publication as new editions. The books that are listed as new have been reviewed by the company, but contracts have not yet been signed.

Three individuals in the company can be assigned to these projects, all of whom have varying amounts of time available; John has 60 days available, and Susan and Monica both have 40 days available. The days required by each person to complete each project are shown in the following table. For instance, if the business calculus book is published, it will require 30 days of John's time and 40 days of Susan's time. An "X" indicates that the person will not be used on the project. Note that at least two staff members will be assigned to each project except the finance book.

Book Subject	John	Susan	Monica
Business calculus	30	40	X
Finite mathematics	16	24	X
General statistics	24	X	30
Mathematical statistics	20	X	24
Business statistics	10	X	16
Finance	X	X	14
Financial accounting	X	24	26
Managerial accounting	X	28	30
English literature	40	34	30
German	X	50	36

ASW will not publish more than two statistics books or more than one accounting text in a single year. In addition, management decided that one of the mathematics books (business calculus or finite math) must be published, but not both.

Managerial Report

Prepare a report for the managing editor of ASW that describes your findings and recommendations regarding the best publication strategy for next year. In carrying out your analysis, assume that the fixed costs and the sales revenues per unit are approximately equal for all books; management is interested primarily in maximizing the total unit sales volume.

The managing editor also asked that you include recommendations regarding the following possible changes:

1. If it would be advantageous to do so, Susan can be moved off another project to allow her to work 12 more days.
2. If it would be advantageous to do so, Monica can also be made available for another 10 days.
3. If one or more of the revisions could be postponed for another year, should they be? Clearly the company will risk losing market share by postponing a revision.

Include details of your analysis in an appendix to your report.

Case Problem 2   YEAGER NATIONAL BANK

Using aggressive mail promotion with low introductory interest rates, Yeager National Bank (YNB) built a large base of credit card customers throughout the continental United States. Currently, all customers send their regular payments to the bank's corporate office located in Charlotte, North Carolina. Daily collections from customers making their regular payments are substantial, with an average of approximately $600,000. YNB estimates that it makes about 15 percent on its funds and would like to ensure that customer payments are credited to the bank's account as soon as possible. For instance, if it takes five days for a customer's payment to be sent through the mail, processed, and credited to the bank's account, YNB has potentially lost five days' worth of interest income. Although the time needed for this collection process cannot be completely eliminated, reducing it can be beneficial given the large amounts of money involved.

Instead of having all its credit card customers send their payments to Charlotte, YNB is considering having customers send their payments to one or more regional collection centers, referred to in the banking industry as lockboxes. Four lockbox locations have been proposed: Phoenix, Salt Lake City, Atlanta, and Boston. To determine which lockboxes to open and where lockbox customers should send their payments, YNB divided its customer base into five geographical regions: Northwest, Southwest, Central, Northeast, and Southeast. Every customer in the same region will be instructed to send his or her payment to the same lockbox. The following table shows the average number of days it takes before a customer's payment is credited to the bank's account when the payment is sent from each of the regions to each of the potential lockboxes:

Customer Zone	Location of Lockbox				Daily Collection ($1000s)
	Phoenix	**Salt Lake City**	**Atlanta**	**Boston**	
Northwest	4	2	4	4	80
Southwest	2	3	4	6	90
Central	5	3	3	4	150
Northeast	5	4	3	2	180
Southeast	4	6	2	3	100

Managerial Report

Dave Wolff, the vice president for cash management, asked you to prepare a report containing your recommendations for the number of lockboxes and the best lockbox locations. Mr. Wolff is primarily concerned with minimizing lost interest income, but he wants you to also consider the effect of an annual fee charged for maintaining a lockbox at any location. Although the amount of the fee is unknown at this time, we can assume that the fees will be in the range of $20,000 to $30,000 per location. Once good potential locations have been selected, Mr. Wolff will inquire as to the annual fees.

Case Problem 3 PRODUCTION SCHEDULING WITH CHANGEOVER COSTS

Buckeye Manufacturing produces heads for engines used in the manufacture of trucks. The production line is highly complex, and it measures 900 feet in length. Two types of engine heads are produced on this line: the P-Head and the H-Head. The P-Head is used in heavy-duty trucks and the H-Head is used in smaller trucks. Because only one type of head can be produced at a time, the line is set up to manufacture either the P-Head or the H-Head, but not both. Changeovers are made over a weekend; costs are $500 in going from a setup for the P-Head to a setup for the H-Head, and vice versa. When set up for the P-Head, the maximum production rate is 100 units per week and when set up for the H-Head, the maximum production rate is 80 units per week.

Buckeye just shut down for the week after using the line to produce the P-Head. The manager wants to plan production and changeovers for the next eight weeks. Currently, Buckeye's inventory consists of 125 P-Heads and 143 H-Heads. Inventory carrying costs are charged at an annual rate of 19.5 percent of the value of inventory. The production cost for the P-Head is $225, and the production cost for the H-Head is $310. The objective in developing a production schedule is to minimize the sum of production cost, plus inventory carrying cost, plus changeover cost.

Buckeye received the following requirements schedule from its customer (an engine assembly plant) for the next nine weeks:

	Product Demand	
Week	P-Head	H-Head
1	55	38
2	55	38
3	44	30
4	0	0
5	45	48
6	45	48
7	36	58
8	35	57
9	35	58

Safety stock requirements are such that week-ending inventory must provide for at least 80 percent of the next week's demand.

631

Managerial Report

Prepare a report for Buckeye's management with a production and changeover schedule for the next eight weeks. Be sure to note how much of the total cost is due to production, how much is due to inventory, and how much is due to changeover.

Appendix 7.1 EXCEL SOLUTION OF INTEGER LINEAR PROGRAMS

Worksheet formulation and solution for integer linear programs are similar to that for linear programming problems. Actually the worksheet formulation is exactly the same, but additional information must be provided when setting up the **Solver Parameters** dialog box. In the **Solver Parameters** dialog box it is necessary to identify the integer variables. The user should also be aware of settings related to integer linear programming in the **Solver Options** dialog box.

Let us demonstrate the Excel solution of an integer linear program by showing how Excel can be used to solve the Eastborne Realty problem. The worksheet with the optimal solution is shown in Figure 7.14. We will describe the key elements of the worksheet and how to obtain the solution, and then interpret the solution.

Formulation

The data and descriptive labels appear in cells A1:G7 of the worksheet in Figure 7.14. The screened cells in the lower portion of the worksheet contain the information required by the

FIGURE 7.14 EXCEL SOLUTION FOR THE EASTBORNE REALTY PROBLEM

WEB file

Eastborne

	A	B	C	D	E	F	G	H
1	**Eastborne Realty Problem**							
2								
3		Townhouse	Apt. Bldg.					
4	**Price($1000s)**	282	400		**Funds Avl.($1000s)**		2000	
5	**Mgr. Time**	4	40		**Mgr. Time Avl.**		140	
6					**Townhouses Avl.**		5	
7	**Ann. Cash Flow ($1000s)**	10	15					
8								
9								
10	**Model**							
11								
12								
13	**Max Cash Flow**	70						
14					**Constraints**	**LHS**		**RHS**
15		**Number of**			Funds	1928	<=	2000
16		Townhouses	Apt. Bldgs.		Time	96	<=	140
17	**Purchase Plan**	4	2		Townhouses	4	<=	5
18								

Excel Solver (decision variables, objective function, constraint left-hand sides, and constraint right-hand sides).

Decision Variables — Cells B17:C17 are reserved for the decision variables. The optimal solution is to purchase four townhouses and two apartment buildings.

Objective Function — The formula =SUMPRODUCT(B7:C7,B17:C17) has been placed into cell B13 to reflect the annual cash flow associated with the solution. The optimal solution provides an annual cash flow of $70,000.

Left-Hand Sides — The left-hand sides for the three constraints are placed into cells F15:F17.

> Cell F15 =SUMPRODUCT(B4:C4,$B$17:$C$17)
>> (Copy to sell F16)
> Cell F17 =B17

Right-Hand Sides — The right-hand sides for the three constraints are placed into cells H15:H17.

> Cell H15 =G4 (Copy to cells H16:H17)

Excel Solution

Begin the solution procedure by selecting the Data tab and Solver from the Analysis group, and entering the proper values into the **Solver Parameters** dialog box as shown in Figure 7.15. The first constraint shown is $B$17:$C$17 = integer. This constraint tells Solver that the decision variables in cell B17 and cell C17 must be integer. The integer requirement is created by using the **Add-Constraint** procedure. $B$17:$C17 is entered in the left-hand box of the **Cell Reference** area and **"int"** rather than $<=$, =, or $=>$ is selected as the form of the constraint. When **"int"** is selected, the term integer automatically appears as the right-hand side of the constraint. Figure 7.15 shows the additional information required to complete the **Solver Parameters** dialog box. Note that the checkbox Make **Unconstrained Variables Non-Negative** is selected.

0-1 variables are identified with the "bin" designation in the Solver Parameters dialog box.

If binary variables are present in an integer linear programming problem, you must select the designation **"bin"** instead of **"int"** when setting up the constraints in the **Solver Parameters** dialog box.

To ensure you will find the optimal solution to an integer program using Excel Solver, be sure that the Integer Optimality percentage is 0% and that the Ignore Integer Constraints checkbox is not checked.

Next select the **Options** button. The **Solver** options are shown in Figure 7.16. When solving an integer linear program make sure that the **Ignore Integer Constraints** checkbox is not selected. Also, the time required to obtain an optimal solution can be highly variable for integer linear programs. As shown in Figure 7.16, **Integer Optimality** (%) is set to 0 by default. This means that an optimal integer solution will be found. For larger problems it may be necessary to make this option positive. For example, if this option value were set to 5, then **Solver** will stop its search when it can guarantee that the best solution it has found so far is within 5% of the optimal solution in terms of objective function value.

Clicking **OK** in the **Solver Options** dialog box and selecting **Solve** in the **Solver Parameters** dialog box will instruct **Solver** to compute the optimal integer solution. The worksheet in Figure 7.14 shows that the optimal solution is to purchase four townhouses and two apartment buildings. The annual cash flow is $70,000.

Appendix 7.2 LINGO SOLUTION OF INTEGER LINEAR PROGRAMS

LINGO may be used to solve linear integer programs. An integer linear model is entered into LINGO exactly as described in Appendix 7.2, but with additional statements for

FIGURE 7.15   SOLVER PARAMETERS DIALOG BOX FOR THE EASTBORNE
              REALTY PROBLEM

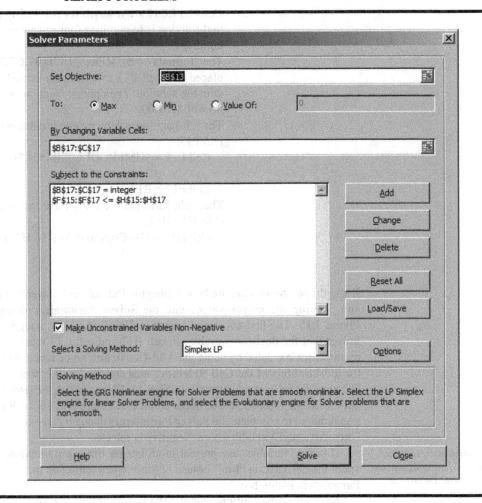

declaring variables as either general integer or binary. For example, to declare a variable x integer, you need to include the following statement:

@GIN(x) ;

Note the use of the semicolon to end the statement. GIN stands for "general integer." Likewise to declare a variable y a binary variable, the following statement is required:

@BIN(y) ;

BIN stands for "binary."

To illustrate the use of integer variables, the following statements are used to model the Eastborne Reality problem discussed in this chapter:

First, we enter the following:

MODEL:
TITLE   EASTBORNE REALTY;

FIGURE 7.16   SOLVER OPTIONS DIALOG BOX FOR THE EASTBORNE REALTY PROBLEM

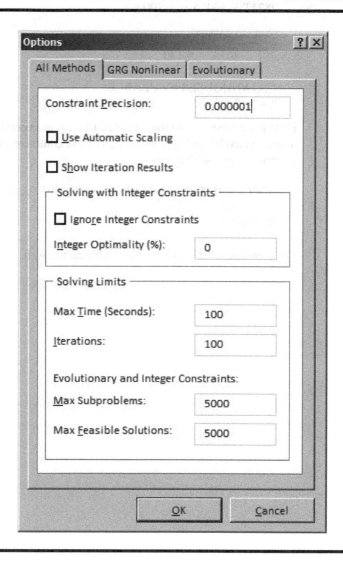

This statement gives the LINGO model the title Eastborne Realty.

Next, we enter the following two lines to document the definition of our decision variables (recall that ! denotes a comment, and each comment ends with a semicolon).

!	T = NUMBER OF TOWNHOUSES PURCHASED;
!	A = NUMBER OF APARTMENT BUILDINGS PURCHASED;

Next, we enter the objective function and constraints, each with a descriptive comment.

!	MAXIMIZE THE CASH FLOW;
MAX = 10*T + 15*A;

! FUNDS AVAILABLE ($1000);
282*T + 400*A <= 2000;

! TIME AVAILABLILITY;
4*T + 40*A <= 140;

! TOWNHOUSES AVAILABLE;
T <= 5;

Finally, we must declare the variables T and A as general integer variables. Again, to document the model we begin with a descriptive comment and then declare each variable as a general integer variable:

! DECLARE THE VARIABLES TO BE GENERAL INTEGER VARIABLES;
@GIN(T);
@GIN(A);

The complete LINGO model is available on the Web.

References and Bibliography

Ahuja, R. K., T. L. Magnanti, and J. B. Orlin. *Network Flows, Theory, Algorithms, and Applications.* Prentice Hall, 1993.

Bazarra, M. S., J. J. Jarvis, and H. D. Sherali. *Linear Programming and Network Flows,* 2d ed. Wiley, 1990.

Carino, H. F., and C. H. Le Noir, Jr. "Optimizing Wood Procurement in Cabinet Manufacturing," *Interfaces* (March/April 1988): 10–19.

Dantzig, G. B. *Linear Programming and Extensions.* Princeton University Press, 1963.

Davis, Morton D. *Game Theory: A Nontechnical Introduction.* Dover, 1997.

Evans, J. R., and E. Minieka. *Optimization Algorithms for Networks and Graphs,* 2d ed. Marcel Dekker, 1992.

Ford, L. R., and D. R. Fulkerson. *Flows and Networks.* Princeton University Press, 1962.

Geoffrion, A., and G. Graves. "Better Distribution Planning with Computer Models," *Harvard Business Review* (July/August 1976).

Greenberg, H. J. "How to Analyze the Results of Linear Programs—Part 1: Preliminaries," *Interfaces* 23, no. 4 (July/August 1993): 56–67.

Greenberg, H. J. "How to Analyze the Results of Linear Programs—Part 2: Price Interpretation," *Interfaces* 23, no. 5 (September/October 1993): 97–114.

Greenberg, H. J. "How to Analyze the Results of Linear Programs—Part 3: Infeasibility Diagnosis," *Interfaces* 23, no. 6 (November/December 1993): 120–139.

Lillien, G., and A. Rangaswamy. *Marketing Engineering: Computer-Assisted Marketing Analysis and Planning.* Addison-Wesley, 1998.

Martin, R. K. *Large Scale Linear and Integer Optimization: A Unified Approach.* Kluwer Academic Publishers, 1999.

McMillian, John. *Games, Strategies, and Managers.* Oxford University Press, 1992.

Myerson, Roger B. *Game Theory: Analysis of Conflict.* Harvard University Press, 1997.

Nemhauser, G. L., and L. A. Wolsey. *Integer and Combinatorial Optimization.* Wiley, 1999.

Osborne, Martin J. *An Introduction to Game Theory.* Oxford University Press, 2004.

Schrage, Linus. *Optimization Modeling with LINDO,* 4th ed. LINDO Systems Inc., 2000.

Sherman, H. D. "Hospital Efficiency Measurement and Evaluation," *Medical Care* 22, no. 10 (October 1984): 922–938.

Winston, W. L., and S. C. Albright. *Practical Management Science,* 2d ed. Duxbury Press, 2001.

Self-Test Solutions and Answers to Even-Numbered Problems

2. a.

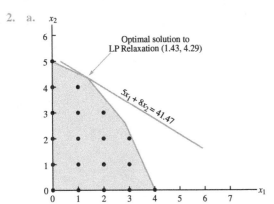

Optimal solution to LP Relaxation (1.43, 4.29)

$5x_1 + 8x_2 = 41.47$

b. The optimal solution to the LP Relaxation is given by $x_1 = 1.43$, $x_2 = 4.29$, with an objective function value of 41.47. Rounding down gives the feasible integer solution $x_1 = 1$, $x_2 = 4$; its value is 37.

c.

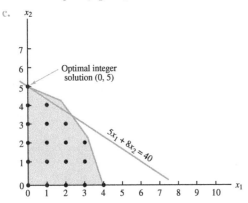

Optimal integer solution (0, 5)

$5x_1 + 8x_2 = 40$

The optimal solution is given by $x_1 = 0$, $x_2 = 5$; its value is 40. It is not the same solution as found by rounding down; it provides a 3-unit increase in the value of the objective function.

4. a. $x_1 = 3.67$, $x_2 = 0$; Value = 36.7
   Rounded: $x_1 = 3$, $x_2 = 0$; Value = 30
   Lower bound = 30; Upper bound = 36.7
   b. $x_1 = 3$, $x_2 = 2$; Value = 36
   c. Alternative optimal solutions: $x_1 = 0$, $x_2 = 5$
   $\qquad\qquad\qquad\qquad\qquad\qquad x_1 = 2$, $x_2 = 4$

5. a. The feasible mixed-integer solutions are indicated by the boldface vertical lines in the graph.

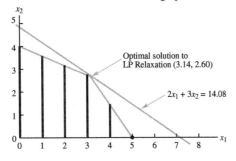

Optimal solution to LP Relaxation (3.14, 2.60)

$2x_1 + 3x_2 = 14.08$

b. The optimal solution to the LP Relaxation is given by $x_1 = 3.14$, $x_2 = 2.60$; its value is 14.08.
   Rounding down the value of x_1 to find a feasible mixed-integer solution yields $x_1 = 3$, $x_2 = 2.60$ with a value of 13.8; this solution is clearly not optimal; with $x_1 = 3$, x_2 can be made larger without violating the constraints.
   c. The optimal solution to the MILP is given by $x_1 = 3$, $x_2 = 2.67$; its value is 14, as shown in the following figure:

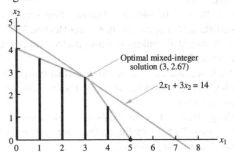

Optimal mixed-integer solution (3, 2.67)

$2x_1 + 3x_2 = 14$

6. b. $x_1 = 1.96$, $x_2 = 5.48$; Value = 7.44
   Rounded: $x_1 = 1.96$, $x_2 = 5$; Value = 6.96
   Lower bound = 6.96; Upper bound = 7.44
   c. $x_1 = 1.29$, $x_2 = 6$; Value = 7.29

7. a. $x_1 + x_3 + x_5 + x_6 = 2$
   b. $x_3 - x_5 = 0$
   c. $x_1 + x_4 = 1$
   d. $x_4 \leq x_1$
      $x_4 \leq x_3$
   e. $x_4 \leq x_1$
      $x_4 \leq x_3$
      $x_4 \geq x_1 + x_3 - 1$

8. a. $x_3 = 1$, $x_4 = 1$, $x_6 = 1$; Value = 17,500
   b. Add $x_1 + x_2 \leq 1$
   c. Add $x_3 - x_4 = 0$

10. b. Choose locations B and E.

12. a. $P \leq 15 + 15Y_P$
    $D \leq 15 + 15Y_D$
    $J \leq 15 + 15Y_J$
    $Y_P + Y_D + Y_J \leq 1$
    b. $P = 15$, $D = 15$, $J = 30$
    $Y_P = 0$, $Y_D = 0$, $Y_J = 1$; Value = 50

13. a. Add the following multiple-choice constraint to the problem:
    $y_1 + y_2 = 1$
    New optimal solution: $y_1 = 1$, $y_3 = 1$, $x_{12} = 10$, $x_{31} = 30$, $x_{52} = 10$, $x_{53} = 20$
    Value = 940
    b. Because one plant is already located in St. Louis, it is only necessary to add the following constraint to the model:
    $y_3 = y_4 \leq 1$

New optimal solution: $y_4 = 1$, $x_{42} = 20$, $x_{43} = 20$, $x_{51} = 30$

Value $= 860$

14. b. Modernize plants 1 and 3 or plants 4 and 5.

 d. Modernize plants 1 and 3.

16. b. Use all part-time employees.

 Bring on as follows: 9:00 A.M.–6, 11:00 A.M.–2, 12:00 noon–6, 1:00 P.M.–1, 3:00 P.M.–6

 Cost $= \$672$

 c. Same as in part (b)

 d. New solution is to bring on 1 full-time employee at 9:00 A.M., 4 more at 11:00 A.M., and part-time employees as follows:

 9:00 A.M.–5, 12:00 noon–5, and 3:00 P.M.–2

18. a. 52, 49, 36, 83, 39, 70, 79, 59

 b. Thick crust, cheese blend, chunky sauce, medium sausage: Six of eight consumers will prefer this pizza (75%).

20. a. New objective function: Min $25x_1 + 40x_2 + 40x_3 + 40x_4 + 25x_5$

 b. $x_4 = x_5 = 1$; modernize the Ohio and California plants.

 c. Add the constraint $x_2 + x_3 = 1$.

 d. $x_1 = x_3 = 1$

22. $x_1 + x_2 + x_3 = 3y_1 + 5y_2 + 7y_3$

 $y_1 + y_2 + y_3 = 1$

24. a. $x_{111}, x_{112}, x_{121}$

 b. $x_{111} + x_{112} + x_{121} \leq 1$

 c. $x_{531} + x_{532} + x_{533} + x_{541} + x_{542} + x_{543} + x_{551} + x_{552} + x_{561} \leq 1$

 d. Only two screens are available.

 e. $x_{222} + x_{231} + x_{422} + x_{431} + x_{531} + x_{531} + x_{532} + x_{533} + x_{631} + x_{632} + x_{633} \leq 2$

Nonlinear Optimization Models

CONTENTS

Many business processes behave in a nonlinear manner. For example, the price of a bond is a nonlinear function of interest rates, and the price of a stock option is a nonlinear function of the price of the underlying stock. The marginal cost of production often decreases with the quantity produced, and the quantity demanded for a product is usually a nonlinear function of the price. These and many other nonlinear relationships are present in many business applications.

A **nonlinear optimization problem** is any optimization problem in which at least one term in the objective function or a constraint is nonlinear. We begin our study of nonlinear applications by considering a production problem in which the objective function is a nonlinear function of the decision variables. In Section 8.2 we develop a nonlinear application that involves designing a portfolio of securities to track a stock market index. We extend our treatment of portfolio models in Section 8.3 by presenting the Nobel Prize–winning Markowitz model for managing the trade-off between risk and return. Section 8.4 provides a nonlinear application of the linear programming blending model introduced in Chapter 4. In Section 8.5, we present a well-known and successful model used in forecasting sales or adoptions of a new product. As further illustrations of the use of nonlinear optimization in practice, the Management Science in Action, Pricing for Environmental Compliance in the Auto Industry, discusses how General Motors uses a mathematical model for coordinating pricing and production while satisfying government regulations on the gas mileage average of the car fleet. The Management Science in Action, Scheduling Flights and Crews for Bombardier Flexjet, discusses how Flexjet uses nonlinear optimization to assign aircraft and crews to flights.

Chapter appendices describe how to solve nonlinear programs using LINGO and Excel Solver.

MANAGEMENT SCIENCE IN ACTION

SCHEDULING FLIGHTS AND CREWS FOR BOMBARDIER FLEXJET*

Bombardier Flexjet is a leading company in the fast-growing fractional aircraft industry. Flexjet sells shares of business jets in share sizes equal to 50 hours of flying per year. A firm with fractional ownership is guaranteed 24-hour access to an aircraft with as little as a 4-hour lead time. Companies with a fractional share pay monthly management and usage fees. In exchange for the management fee, Flexjet provides hangar facilities, maintenance, and flight crews.

Because of the flexibility provided in the fractional aircraft business, the problem of scheduling crews and flights is even more complicated than in the commercial airline industry. Initially, Flexjet attempted to schedule flights by hand. However, this task quickly proved to be infeasible. Indeed, the inadequate manual scheduling resulted in Flexjet maintaining extra business jets and crews. The cost of the extra jets and crews was estimated at several hundred dollars per flight hour. A scheduling system using optimization was clearly required.

The scheduling system developed for Flexjet includes a large nonlinear optimization model that is integrated with a graphical user interface (GUI) used by Flexjet personnel. The model includes "hard" constraints based on Federal Aviation Administration (FAA) regulations, company rules, and aircraft performance characteristics. It also includes "soft constraints" that involve cost trade-offs. The model is used to assign aircraft and crews to flights.

The resulting model is too large to solve directly with commercial optimization software. Models with too many variables to solve directly are often solved using *decomposition* methods. Decomposition methods work with a *master problem* that includes only a small fraction of the total number of variables. Variables that are good candidates to be part of the optimal solution are identified through the solution of a *subproblem*. In the Flexjet model, the subproblem is a nonlinear integer program. The heart of the nonlinearity is the product of a binary variable that is 1 if a particular pair of flight legs is used and a continuous variable that is used to impose a time window on flight times. The subproblem is optimized using a technique called dynamic programming.

The optimization model was a big success. The model initially saved Flexjet $54 million, with a projected annual savings of $27 million. Much of this cost saving is the result of reducing crew levels by 20% and aircraft inventory by 40%. Aircraft utilization also increased by 10%.

*Based on Richard Hicks et al., "Bombardier Flexjet Significantly Improves Its Fractional Aircraft Ownership Operations," *Interfaces* 35, no. 1 (January/ February 2005): 49–60.

8.1 A PRODUCTION APPLICATION—PAR, INC., REVISITED

We introduce constrained and unconstrained nonlinear optimization problems by considering an extension of the Par, Inc., linear program introduced in Chapter 2. We first consider the case in which the relationship between price and quantity sold causes the objective function to become nonlinear. The resulting unconstrained nonlinear program is then solved, and we observe that the unconstrained optimal solution does not satisfy the production constraints. Adding the production constraints back into the problem allows us to show the formulation and solution of a constrained nonlinear program. The section closes with a discussion of local and global optima.

An Unconstrained Problem

Let us consider a revision of the Par, Inc., problem from Chapter 2. Recall that Par, Inc., decided to manufacture standard and deluxe golf bags. In formulating the linear programming model for the Par, Inc., problem, we assumed that it could sell all of the standard and deluxe bags it could produce. However, depending on the price of the golf bags, this assumption may not hold. An inverse relationship usually exists between price and demand. As price goes up, the quantity demanded goes down. Let P_S denote the price Par, Inc., charges for each standard bag and P_D denote the price for each deluxe bag. Assume that the demand for standard bags S and the demand for deluxe bags D are given by

$$S = 2250 - 15P_S \tag{8.1}$$
$$D = 1500 - 5P_D \tag{8.2}$$

The revenue generated from standard bags is the price of each standard bag P_S times the number of standard bags sold S. If the cost to produce a standard bag is $70, the cost to produce S standard bags is 70 S. Thus the profit contribution for producing and selling S standard bags (revenue – cost) is

$$P_S S - 70S \tag{8.3}$$

We can solve equation (8.1) for P_S to show how the price of a standard bag is related to the number of standard bags sold. It is $P_S = 150 - \frac{1}{15}S$. Substituting $150 - \frac{1}{15}S$ for P_S in equation (8.3), the profit contribution for standard bags is

$$P_S S - 70S = (150 - \tfrac{1}{15}S)S - 70S = 80S - \tfrac{1}{15}S^2 \tag{8.4}$$

Suppose that the cost to produce each deluxe golf bag is \$150. Using the same logic we used to develop equation (8.4), the profit contribution for deluxe bags is

$$P_D D - 150D = (300 - \tfrac{1}{5}D)D - 150D = 150D - \tfrac{1}{5}D^2$$

Total profit contribution is the sum of the profit contribution for standard bags and the profit contribution for deluxe bags. Thus, total profit contribution is written as

$$\text{Total profit contribution} = 80S - \tfrac{1}{15}S^2 + 150D - \tfrac{1}{5}D^2 \qquad (8.5)$$

Note that the two linear demand functions, equations (8.1) and (8.2), give a nonlinear total profit contribution function, equation (8.5). This function is an example of a *quadratic function* because the nonlinear terms have a power of 2.

Using LINGO (see Appendix 8.1), we find that the values of S and D that maximize the profit contribution function are $S = 600$ and $D = 375$. The corresponding prices are \$110 for standard bags and \$225 for deluxe bags, and the profit contribution is \$52,125. These values provide the optimal solution for Par, Inc., if all production constraints are also satisfied.

A Constrained Problem

Unfortunately, Par, Inc., cannot make the profit contribution associated with the optimal solution to the unconstrained problem because the constraints defining the feasible region are violated. For instance, the cutting and dyeing constraint is

$$\tfrac{7}{10}S + D \leq 630$$

A production quantity of 600 standard bags and 375 deluxe bags will require $\tfrac{7}{10}(600) + 1(375) = 795$ hours, which exceeds the limit of 630 hours by 165 hours. The feasible region for the original Par, Inc., problem along with the unconstrained optimal solution point (600, 375) are shown in Figure 8.1. The unconstrained optimum of (600, 375) is obviously outside the feasible region.

Clearly, the problem that Par, Inc., must solve is to maximize the total profit contribution

$$80S - \tfrac{1}{15}S^2 + 150D - \tfrac{1}{5}D^2$$

subject to all of the departmental labor hour constraints that were given in Chapter 2. The complete mathematical model for the Par, Inc., constrained nonlinear maximization problem follows:

$$\text{Max} \quad 80S - \tfrac{1}{15}S^2 + 150D - \tfrac{1}{5}D^2$$

s.t.

$\tfrac{7}{10}S +$	$D \leq 630$	Cutting and dyeing
$\tfrac{1}{2}S + \tfrac{5}{6}D \leq 600$		Sewing
$S + \tfrac{2}{3}D \leq 708$		Finishing
$\tfrac{1}{10}S + \tfrac{1}{4}D \leq 135$		Inspection and packaging
$S, D \geq 0$		

WEB file

ParNonlinear

FIGURE 8.1   THE PAR, INC., FEASIBLE REGION AND THE OPTIMAL SOLUTION FOR THE UNCONSTRAINED OPTIMIZATION PROBLEM

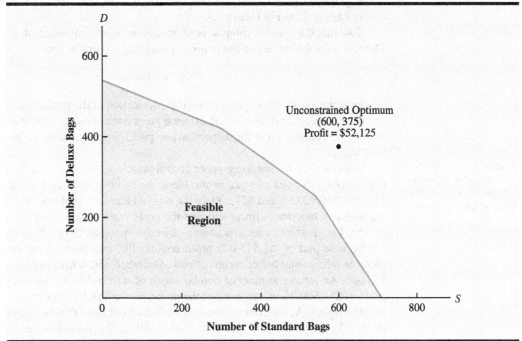

This maximization problem is exactly the same as the Par, Inc., problem in Chapter 2 except for the nonlinear objective function. The solution to this constrained nonlinear maximization problem is shown in Figure 8.2.

The optimal value of the objective function is $49,920.55. The Variable section shows that the optimal solution is to produce 459.7166 standard bags and 308.1984 deluxe bags. In the Constraint section, in the Slack/Surplus column, the value of 0 in Constraint 1 means that

FIGURE 8.2   SOLUTION FOR THE NONLINEAR PAR, INC., PROBLEM

```
Optimal Objective value = 49920.54655

      Variable              Value            Reduced Cost
    ------------        ---------------      ---------------
         S                 459.71660            0.00000
         D                 308.19838            0.00000

      Constraint          Slack/Surplus          Dual Value
    ------------        ---------------      ---------------
         1                   0.00000             26.72059
         2                 113.31074             0.00000
         3                  42.81679             0.00000
         4                  11.97875             0.00000
```

the optimal solution uses all the labor hours in the cutting and dyeing department; but the nonzero values in rows 2–4 indicate that slack hours are available in the other departments.

A graphical view of the optimal solution of 459.7166 standard bags and 308.1984 deluxe bags is shown in Figure 8.3.

Note that the optimal solution is no longer at an extreme point of the feasible region. The optimal solution lies on the cutting and dyeing constraint line

$$\tfrac{7}{10}S + D = 630$$

but *not* at the extreme point formed by the intersection of the cutting and dyeing constraint and the finishing constraint, or the extreme point formed by the intersection of the cutting and dyeing constraint and the inspection and packaging constraint. To understand why, we look at Figure 8.3.

Figure 8.3 shows that the profit contribution contour lines for the nonlinear Par, Inc., problem are ellipses.

In Figure 8.3 we see three profit contribution *contour lines*. Each point on the same contour line is a point of equal profit. Here, the contour lines show profit contributions of $45,000, $49,920.55, and $51,500. In the original Par, Inc., problem described in Chapter 2 the objective function is linear and thus the profit contours are straight lines. However, for the Par, Inc., problem with a quadratic objective function, the profit contours are ellipses.

Because part of the $45,000 profit contour line cuts through the feasible region, we know an infinite number of combinations of standard and deluxe bags will yield a profit of $45,000. An infinite number of combinations of standard and deluxe bags also provide a profit of $51,500. However, none of the points on the $51,500 contour profit line are in the feasible region. As the contour lines move further out from the unconstrained optimum of (600, 375), the profit contribution associated with each contour line decreases. The contour

FIGURE 8.3   THE PAR, INC., FEASIBLE REGION WITH OBJECTIVE FUNCTION CONTOUR LINES

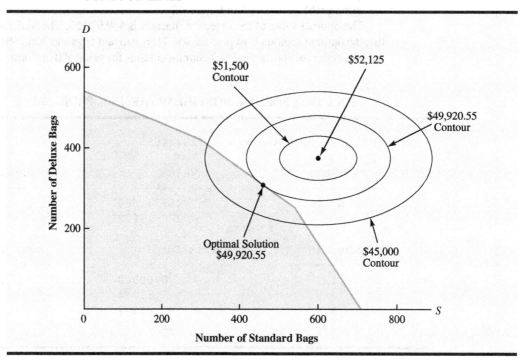

line representing a profit of $49,920.55 intersects the feasible region at a single point. This solution provides the maximum possible profit. No contour line that has a profit contribution greater than $49,920.55 will intersect the feasible region. Because the contour lines are nonlinear, the contour line with the highest profit can touch the boundary of the feasible region at any point, not just an extreme point. In the Par, Inc., case the optimal solution is on the cutting and dyeing constraint line part way between two extreme points.

It is also possible for the optimal solution to a nonlinear optimization problem to lie in the interior of the feasible region. For instance, if the right-hand sides of the constraints in the Par, Inc., problem were all increased by a sufficient amount, the feasible region would expand so that the optimal unconstrained solution point of (600, 375) in Figure 8.3 would be in the interior of the feasible region. Many linear programming algorithms (e.g., the simplex method) optimize by examining only the extreme points and selecting the extreme point that gives the best solution value. As the solution to the constrained Par, Inc., nonlinear problem illustrates, such a method will not work in the nonlinear case because the optimal solution is generally not an extreme point solution. Hence, nonlinear programming algorithms are more complex than linear programming algorithms, and the details are beyond the scope of this text. Fortunately, we don't need to know how nonlinear algorithms work; we just need to know how to use them. Computer software such as LINGO and Excel Solver are available to solve nonlinear programming problems, and we describe how to use these software packages in the chapter appendices.

Local and Global Optima

A feasible solution is a **local optimum** if no other feasible solutions with a better objective function value are found in the immediate neighborhood. For example, for the constrained Par problem, the local optimum corresponds to a **local maximum;** a point is a local maximum if no other feasible solutions with a larger objective function value are in the immediate neighborhood. Similarly, for a minimization problem, a point is a **local minimum** if no other feasible solutions with a smaller objective function value are in the immediate neighborhood.

Nonlinear optimization problems can have multiple local optimal solutions, which means we are concerned with finding the best of the local optimal solutions. A feasible solution is a **global optimum** if no other feasible points with a better objective function value are found in the feasible region. In the case of a maximization problem, the global optimum corresponds to a global maximum. A point is a **global maximum** if no other points in the feasible region give a strictly larger objective function value. For a minimization problem, a point is a **global minimum** if no other feasible points with a strictly smaller objective function value are in the feasible region. Obviously a global maximum is also a local maximum, and a global minimum is also a local minimum.

Nonlinear problems with multiple local optima are difficult to solve. But in many nonlinear applications, a single local optimal solution is also the global optimal solution. For such problems, we only need to find a local optimal solution. We will now present some of the more common classes of nonlinear problems of this type.

Consider the function $f(X, Y) = -X^2 - Y^2$. The shape of this function is illustrated in Figure 8.4. A function that is bowl-shaped down is called a **concave function.** The maximum value for this particular function is 0, and the point (0, 0) gives the optimal value of 0. The point (0, 0) is a local maximum; but it is also a *global maximum* because no point gives a larger function value. In other words, no values of X or Y result in an objective function value greater than 0. Functions that are concave, such as $f(X, Y) = -X^2 - Y^2$, have a single local maximum that is also a global maximum. This type of nonlinear problem is relatively easy to maximize.

FIGURE 8.4 A CONCAVE FUNCTION $f(X, Y) = -X^2 - Y^2$

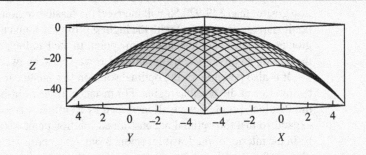

The objective function for the nonlinear Par, Inc., problem is another example of a concave function.

$$80S - \tfrac{1}{15} S^2 + 150D - \tfrac{1}{5} D^2$$

In general, if all of the squared terms in a quadratic function have a negative coefficient and there are no cross-product terms, such as xy, then the function is a concave quadratic function. Thus, for the Par, Inc., problem, we are assured that the local maximum identified by LINGO in Figure 8.2 is the global maximum.

Let us now consider another type of function with a single local optimum that is also a global optimum. Consider the function $f(X, Y) = X^2 + Y^2$. The shape of this function is illustrated in Figure 8.5. It is bowl-shaped up and called a **convex function.** The minimum value for this particular function is 0, and the point (0, 0) gives the minimum value of 0. The point (0, 0) is a local minimum and a global minimum because no values of X or Y give an objective function value less than 0. Functions that are convex, such as $f(X, Y) = X^2 + Y^2$, have a single local minimum and are relatively easy to minimize.

For a concave function, we can be assured that if our computer software finds a local maximum, it is a global maximum. Similarly, for a convex function, we know that if our computer software finds a local minimum, it is a global minimum. Concave and convex functions are well behaved. However, some nonlinear functions have multiple local optima. For example, Figure 8.6 shows the graph of the following function:[1]

$$f(X, Y) = 3(1 - X)^2 e^{-X^2 - (Y+1)^2} - 10(X/5 - X^3 - Y^5)e^{-X^2 - Y^2} - e^{-(X+1)^2 - Y^2}/3.$$

FIGURE 8.5 A CONVEX FUNCTION $f(X, Y) = X^2 + Y^2$

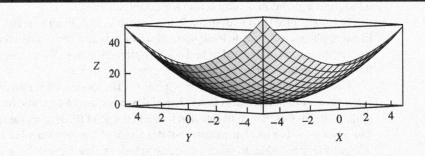

---

[1] This example is taken from the LINDO API manual available at www.lindo.com.

FIGURE 8.6   A FUNCTION WITH LOCAL MAXIMUMS AND MINIMUMS

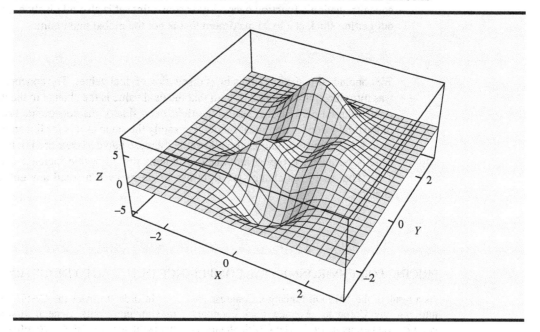

The hills and valleys in this graph show that this function has several local maximums and local minimums. These concepts are further illustrated in Figure 8.7, which is the same function as in Figure 8.6 but from a different viewpoint. It indicates two local minimums and three local maximums. One of the local minimums is also the global minimum, and one of the local maximums is also the global maximum.

Note that the output we use in this chapter for nonlinear optimization uses the label Optimal Objective Value. However, the solution may be either a local or a global optimum, depending on the problem characteristics.

From a technical standpoint, functions with multiple local optima pose a serious challenge for optimization software; most nonlinear optimization software methods can get "stuck" and terminate at a local optimum. Unfortunately, many applications can be nonlinear, and there is a severe penalty for finding a local optimum that is not a global optimum. Developing algorithms capable of finding the global optimum is currently an active research area. But the problem of minimizing a convex quadratic function over a linear constraint set is relatively easy, and for problems of this type there is no danger in getting stuck

FIGURE 8.7   ANOTHER VIEWPOINT OF A FUNCTION WITH LOCAL MAXIMUMS
AND MINIMUMS

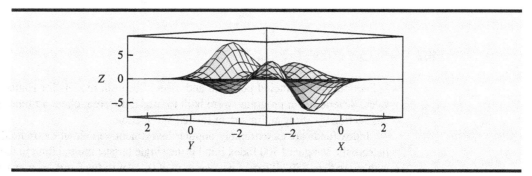

at a local minimum that is not a global minimum. Similarly, the problem of maximizing a concave quadratic function over a linear constraint set is also relatively easy to solve without getting stuck at a local maximum that is not the global maximum.

Dual Values

We conclude this section with a brief discussion of dual values. The concept of a dual value was introduced in Chapter 3. Recall that the dual value is the change in the value of the optimal solution per unit increase in the right-hand side of the constraint. The interpretation of the dual value for nonlinear models is exactly the same as it is for linear programs. However, for nonlinear problems the allowable increase and decrease are not usually reported. This is because for typical nonlinear problems the allowable increase and decrease are zero. That is, if you change the right-hand side by even a small amount, the dual value changes.

MANAGEMENT SCIENCE IN ACTION

PRICING FOR ENVIRONMENTAL COMPLIANCE IN THE AUTO INDUSTRY*

As a result of the 1973 Oil Embargo, Congress put into law the Corporate Average Fuel Economy (CAFE) regulations in 1975. The CAFE standards are designed to promote the sale of fuel-efficient automobiles and light trucks, thus reducing dependence on oil. The CAFE standards were modified when President Bush signed into law the Clean Energy Act of 2007. This law requires that automakers boost fleet gas mileage average to 35 MPG by the year 2020. Although polls reveal strong support for such regulatory action, actual consumer behavior runs counter to supporting the purchase of fuel-efficient cars. Indeed, car manufacturers are faced with the problem of influencing consumers to purchase more fuel-efficient cars in order for the manufacturer to meet the CAFE mandated standard. One way to influence consumer purchase behavior is through price. Lowering the price of fuel-efficient cars is one way to shift demand to this market. Of course, this should be done in a way to keep profits as large as possible subject to the CAFE constraints.

In order to meet the CAFE constraints while maximizing profits, General Motors (GM) used a mathematical model for coordinated pricing and production called Visual CAFE. This was built into an Excel spreadsheet with data input from Microsoft Access. The objective function for this model is much like the objective function for the nonlinear version of Par, Inc., that we develop in this section. In both cases the objective is to maximize profit, and the profit function is the product of quantity sold times the contribution margin of each product. The quantity sold is based on a linear demand function. A key constraint is the CAFE constraint, which is a constraint on the average miles per gallon for the GM fleet of cars. In addition, there are constraints on assembly, engine, and transmission capacity.

*Based on Stephan Biller and Julie Swan, "Pricing for Environmental Compliance in the Auto Industry," *Interfaces* 36, no. 2 (March/April 2007): 118–125.

8.2   CONSTRUCTING AN INDEX FUND

In Section 5.4 we studied portfolio and asset allocation models for Hauck Financial Services. Several linear programs were built to model different client attitudes toward risk. In this section we study an important related application.

Index funds are an extremely popular investment vehicle in the mutual fund industry. Indeed, the Vanguard 500 Index Fund is the single largest mutual fund in the United States, with more than \$89 billion in net assets in 2009. An **index fund** is an example of passive

TABLE 8.1   ONE-YEAR RETURNS FOR FOUR VANGUARD INDEX FUNDS

Vanguard Fund	Vanguard Fund Return	Market Index	Market Index Return
500 Index Fund	4.77%	S&P 500	4.91%
Total Stock Index	5.98%	MSCI Broad Market	6.08%
REIT Index	11.90%	MSCI REIT	12.13%
Short-Term Bond	1.31%	Lehman 1-5 Index	1.44%

asset management. The key idea behind an index fund is to construct a portfolio of stocks, mutual funds, or other securities that matches as closely as possible the performance of a broad market index such as the S&P 500.

Table 8.1 shows the one-year returns for four Vanguard Index Funds[2] and the returns for the corresponding market indexes. Several interesting issues are illustrated in this table. First, Vanguard has index funds for numerous types of investments. For example, the first two index funds are stock funds: the S&P 500 Index Fund and the MSCI Broad Market fund. The MSCI REIT fund is an investment in the real estate market, and the Short-Term Bond (Lehman 1-5) fund is an investment in the corporate bond market. Second, notice that even though the returns show considerable variation between the funds, the index funds do a good job of matching the return of the corresponding market index.

Why are index funds so popular? Behind the popularity of index funds is a substantial amount of research in finance that basically says, "You can't beat the market." In fact, the vast majority of mutual fund managers actually underperform leading market indexes such as the S&P 500. Therefore, many investors are satisfied with investments that provide a return that more closely matches the market return.

Now, let's revisit the Hauck Financial Services example from Chapter 5. Assume that Hauck has a substantial number of clients who wish to own a mutual fund portfolio with the characteristic that the portfolio, as a whole, closely matches the performance of the S&P 500 stock index. What percentage of the portfolio should be invested in each mutual fund in order to most closely mimic the performance of the entire S&P 500 index?

In Table 8.2 we reproduce Table 5.4 (see Chapter 5), with an additional row that gives the S&P 500 return for each planning scenario. Recall that the columns show the actual percentage return that was earned by each mutual fund in that year. These five columns represent the most likely scenarios for the coming year.

The variables used in the model presented in Section 5.4 represented the proportion of the portfolio invested in each mutual fund.

FS = proportion of portfolio invested in a foreign stock mutual fund

IB = proportion of portfolio invested in an intermediate-term bond fund

LG = proportion of portfolio invested in a large-cap growth fund

LV = proportion of portfolio invested in a large-cap value fund

SG = proportion of portfolio invested in a small-cap growth fund

SV = proportion of portfolio invested in a small-cap value fund

---

[2] These data were taken from www.vanguard.com and are for the one-year period ending December 31, 2005.

TABLE 8.2   MUTUAL FUND PERFORMANCE IN FIVE SELECTED YEARS USED AS PLANNING SCENARIOS FOR THE NEXT 12 MONTHS

	Planning Scenarios				
Mutual Fund	Year 1	Year 2	Year 3	Year 4	Year 5
Foreign Stock	10.06	13.12	13.47	45.42	−21.93
Intermediate-Term Bond	17.64	3.25	7.51	−1.33	7.36
Large-Cap Growth	32.41	18.71	33.28	41.46	−23.26
Large-Cap Value	32.36	20.61	12.93	7.06	−5.37
Small-Cap Growth	33.44	19.40	3.85	58.68	−9.02
Small-Cap Value	24.56	25.32	−6.70	5.43	17.31
S&P 500 Return	**25.00**	**20.00**	**8.00**	**30.00**	**−10.00**

The portfolio models presented in Section 5.4 chose the proportion of the portfolio to invest in each mutual fund in order to maximize return subject to constraints on the portfolio risk. Here we wish to choose the proportion of the portfolio to invest in each mutual fund in order to track as closely as possible the S&P 500 return.

For clarity of model exposition, we introduce variables $R1$, $R2$, $R3$, $R4$, and $R5$, which measure the portfolio return for each scenario. Consider, for example, variable $R1$. If the scenario represented by year 1 reflects what happens over the next 12 months, the portfolio return under scenario 1 is

$$10.06FS + 17.64IB + 32.41LG + 32.36LV + 33.44SG + 24.56SV = R1$$

Similarly, if scenarios 2–5 reflect the returns obtained over the next 12 months, the portfolio returns under scenarios 2–5 are as follows:

Scenario 2 return:

$$13.12FS + 3.25IB + 18.71LG + 20.61LV + 19.40SG + 25.32SV = R2$$

Scenario 3 return:

$$13.47FS + 7.51IB + 33.28LG + 12.93LV + 3.85SG - 6.70SV = R3$$

Scenario 4 return:

$$45.42FS - 1.33IB + 41.46LG + 7.06LV + 58.68SG + 5.43SV = R4$$

Scenario 5 return:

$$-21.93FS + 7.36IB - 23.26LG - 5.37LV - 9.02SG + 17.31SV = R5$$

Next, for each scenario we compute the deviation between the return for the scenario and the S&P 500 return. Based on the last row of Table 8.2, the deviations are

$$R1 - 25, \quad R2 - 20, \quad R3 - 8, \quad R4 - 30, \quad R5 - (-10) \qquad (8.6)$$

The objective is for the portfolio returns to match as closely as possible the S&P 500 returns. To do so, we might try minimizing the sum of the deviations given in equation (8.6) as follows:

$$\text{Min } (R1 - 25) + (R2 - 20) + (R3 - 8) + (R4 - 30) + (R5 - [-10]) \quad (8.7)$$

Unfortunately, if we use expression (8.7), positive and negative deviations will cancel each other out, so a portfolio that has a small value for expression (8.7) might actually behave quite differently than the target index. Also, because we want to get as close to the target returns as possible, it makes sense to assign a higher marginal penalty cost for large deviations than for small deviations. A function that achieves this goal is

$$\text{Min } (R1 - 25)^2 + (R2 - 20)^2 + (R3 - 8)^2 + (R4 - 30)^2 + (R5 - [-10])^2$$

When we square each term, positive and negative deviations do not cancel each other out, and the marginal penalty cost for deviations increases as the deviation gets larger. The complete mathematical model we have developed involves 11 variables and 6 constraints (excluding the nonnegativity constraints).

HauckIndex

$$\text{Min } (R1 - 25)^2 + (R2 - 20)^2 + (R3 - 8)^2 + (R4 - 30)^2 + (R5 - [-10])^2$$
s.t.
$$10.06FS + 17.64IB + 32.41LG + 32.36LV + 33.44SG + 24.56SV = R1$$
$$13.12FS + 3.25IB + 18.71LG + 20.61LV + 19.40SG + 25.32SV = R2$$
$$13.47FS + 7.51IB + 33.28LG + 12.93LV + 3.85SG - 6.70SV = R3$$
$$45.42FS - 1.33IB + 41.46LG + 7.06LV + 58.68SG + 5.43SV = R4$$
$$-21.93FS + 7.36IB - 23.26LG - 5.37LV - 9.02SG + 17.31SV = R5$$
$$FS + IB + LG + LV + SG + SV = 1$$
$$FS, IB, LG, LV, SG, SV \geq 0$$

This minimization problem is nonlinear because of the quadratic terms that appear in the objective function. For example, in the term $(R1 - 25)^2$ the variable $R1$ is raised to a power of 2 and is therefore nonlinear. However, because the coefficient of each squared term is positive, and there are no cross-product terms, the objective function is a convex function. Therefore, we are guaranteed that any local minimum is also a global minimum.

The solution for the Hauck Financial Services problem is given in Figure 8.8. The optimal value of the objective function is 4.42689, the sum of the squares of the return deviations. The portfolio calls for approximately 30% of the funds to be invested in the foreign stock fund ($FS = 0.30334$), 36% of the funds to be invested in the large-cap value fund ($LV = 0.36498$), 23% of the funds to be invested in the small-cap growth fund ($SG = 0.22655$), and 11% of the funds to be invested in the small-cap value fund ($SV = 0.10513$).

Table 8.3 shows a comparison of the portfolio return (see $R1$, $R2$, $R3$, $R4$, and $R5$ in Figure 8.8) to the S&P 500 return for each scenario. Notice how closely the portfolio returns match the S&P 500 returns. Based on historical data, a portfolio with this mix of Hauck mutual funds will indeed closely match the returns for the S&P 500 stock index.

We just illustrated an important application of nonlinear programming in finance. In the next section we show how the Markowitz model can be used to construct a portfolio that minimizes risk subject to a constraint requiring a minimum level of return.

FIGURE 8.8   SOLUTION FOR THE HAUCK FINANCIAL SERVICES PROBLEM

```
Optimal Objective Value = 4.42689

        Variable              Value           Reduced Cost
     --------------       --------------      --------------
            FS                0.30334            0.00000
            IB                0.00000           64.84640
            LG                0.00000           18.51296
            LV                0.36498            0.00000
            SG                0.22655            0.00000
            SV                0.10513            0.00000
            R1               25.02024            0.00000
            R2               18.55903            0.00000
            R3                8.97303            0.00000
            R4               30.21926            0.00000
            R5               -8.83586            0.00000

       Constraint         Slack/Surplus          Dual Value
     --------------      -----------------      --------------
            1                 0.00000            0.04047
            2                 0.00000           -2.88192
            3                 0.00000            1.94607
            4                 0.00000            0.43855
            5                 0.00000            2.32829
            6                 0.00000          -42.33078
```

TABLE 8.3   PORTFOLIO RETURN VERSUS S&P 500 RETURN

Scenario	Portfolio Return	S&P 500 Return
1	25.02	25
2	18.56	20
3	8.97	8
4	30.22	30
5	−8.84	−10

NOTES AND COMMENTS

1. The returns for the planning scenarios in Table 8.2 are the actual returns for five years in the past. They were chosen as the past data most likely to represent what could happen over the next year. By using actual past data, the correlation among the mutual funds is automatically incorporated into the model.

2. Notice that the return variables $(R1, R2, \ldots, R5)$ in the Hauck model are not restricted to be ≥ 0. This is because it might be that the best investment strategy results in a negative return in a given year. From Figure 8.8 you can see that the optimal value of $R5$ is −8.84, a return of −8.84%. A variable may be designated in LINGO as a free variable using the statement @FREE. For example, @FREE(R1); would designate R1 as a free variable. For an Excel model with some variables restricted to be nonnegative and others unrestricted, do not check **Make Unconstrained Variables Non-Negative** and add any nonnegativity constraints in the constraint section of the **Solver Dialog** box.

3. While we used variables $R1$, $R2$, . . . , $R5$ for model clarity in the Hauck model, they are not needed to solve the problem. They do, however, make the model simpler to read and interpret. Also, a model user is likely to be interested in the investment return in each year and these variables provide this information. The use of extra variables for clarity exposes an interesting difference between LINGO models and Excel models. In a LINGO model these quantities must be designated decision variables. In an Excel model the returns can simply be calculated in a cell used in the model and do not have to be designated as adjustable cells (because they are functions of adjustable cells).

4. It would not be practical for an individual investor who desires to receive the same return as the S&P 500 to purchase all the S&P 500 stocks. The index fund we have constructed permits such an investor to approximate the S&P 500 return.

5. In this section we constructed an index fund from among mutual funds. The investment alternatives used to develop the index fund could also be individual stocks that are part of the S&P 500.

8.3   MARKOWITZ PORTFOLIO MODEL

Harry Markowitz received the 1990 Nobel Prize for his path-breaking work in portfolio optimization. The Markowitz mean-variance portfolio model is a classic application of nonlinear programming. In this section we present the **Markowitz mean-variance portfolio model.** Numerous variations of this basic model are used by money management firms throughout the world.

A key trade-off in most portfolio optimization models must be made between risk and return. In order to get greater returns, the investor must also face greater risk. The index fund model of the previous section managed the trade-off passively. An investor in the index fund we constructed must be satisfied with the risk/return characteristics of the S&P 500. Other portfolio models explicitly quantify the trade-off between risk and return. In most portfolio optimization models, the return used is the expected return (or average) of the possible outcomes.

Consider the Hauck Financial Services example developed in the previous section. Five scenarios represented the possible outcomes over a one-year planning horizon. The return under each scenario was defined by the variables $R1$, $R2$, $R3$, $R4$, and $R5$, respectively. If p_s is the probability of scenario s among n possible scenarios, then the *expected return* for the portfolio $\overline{R}$ is

$$\overline{R} = \sum_{s=1}^{n} p_s R_s \tag{8.8}$$

If we assume that the five planning scenarios in the Hauck Financial Services model are equally likely, then

$$\overline{R} = \sum_{s=1}^{5} \tfrac{1}{5} R_s = \tfrac{1}{5} \sum_{s=1}^{5} R_s$$

Measuring risk is a bit more difficult. Entire books are devoted to the topic. The measure of risk most often associated with the Markowitz portfolio model is the variance of the portfolio. If the expected return is defined by equation (8.8), the portfolio *variance* is

$$Var = \sum_{s=1}^{n} p_s (R_s - \overline{R})^2 \tag{8.9}$$

For the Hauck Financial Services example, the five planning scenarios are equally likely. Thus,

$$Var = \sum_{s=1}^{5} \frac{1}{5}(R_s - \overline{R})^2 = \frac{1}{5}\sum_{s=1}^{5}(R_s - \overline{R})^2$$

The portfolio variance is the average of the sum of the squares of the deviations from the mean value under each scenario. The larger this number, the more widely dispersed the scenario returns are about their average value. If the portfolio variance were equal to zero, then every scenario return R_i would be equal.

Two basic ways to formulate the Markowitz model are (1) minimize the variance of the portfolio subject to a constraint on the expected return of the portfolio; and (2) maximize the expected return of the portfolio subject to a constraint on variance. Consider the first case. Assume that Hauck clients would like to construct a portfolio from the six mutual funds listed in Table 8.2 that will minimize their risk as measured by the portfolio variance. However, the clients also require the expected portfolio return to be at least 10%. In our notation, the objective function is

$$\text{Min } \frac{1}{5}\sum_{s=1}^{5}(R_s - \overline{R})^2$$

The constraint on expected portfolio return is $\overline{R} \geq 10$. The complete Markowitz model involves 12 variables and 8 constraints (excluding the nonnegativity constraints).

WEB file

HauckMarkowitz

$$\text{Min } \frac{1}{5}\sum_{s=1}^{5}(R_s - \overline{R})^2 \qquad (8.10)$$

s.t.

$$10.06FS + 17.64IB + 32.41LG + 32.36LV + 33.44SG + 24.56SV = R1 \quad (8.11)$$

$$13.12FS + 3.25IB + 18.71LG + 20.61LV + 19.40SG + 25.32SV = R2 \quad (8.12)$$

$$13.47FS + 7.51IB + 33.28LG + 12.93LV + 3.85SG - 6.70SV = R3 \quad (8.13)$$

$$45.42FS - 1.33IB + 41.46LG + 7.06LV + 58.68SG + 5.43SV = R4 \quad (8.14)$$

$$-21.93FS + 7.36IB - 23.26LG - 5.37LV - 9.02SG + 17.31SV = R5 \quad (8.15)$$

$$FS + IB + LG + LV + SG + SV = 1 \quad (8.16)$$

$$\frac{1}{5}\sum_{s=1}^{5}R_s = \overline{R} \quad (8.17)$$

$$\overline{R} \geq 10 \quad (8.18)$$

$$FS, IB, LG, LV, SG, SV \geq 0 \quad (8.19)$$

The objective for the Markowitz model is to minimize portfolio variance. Note that equations (8.11) through (8.15) were present in the index fund model presented in Section 8.2. These equations define the return for each scenario. Equation (8.16), which was also present in the index fund model, requires all of the money to be invested in the mutual funds; this constraint is often called the *unity constraint*. Equation (8.17) defines $\overline{R}$, which is the expected return of the portfolio. Equation (8.18) requires the portfolio return to be at least 10%. Finally, expression (8.19) requires a nonnegative investment in each Hauck mutual fund.

A portion of the solution for this model using a required return of at least 10% appears in Figure 8.9. The minimum value for the portfolio variance is 27.13615. This solution

FIGURE 8.9 SOLUTION FOR THE HAUCK MINIMUM VARIANCE PORTFOLIO WITH A REQUIRED RETURN OF AT LEAST 10%

```
Optimal Objective Value = 27.13615

        Variable             Value          Reduced Cost
     --------------     ----------------    ------------------
           FS               0.15841             0.00000
           IB               0.52548             0.00000
           LG               0.04207             0.00000
           LV               0.00000            41.64139
           SG               0.00000            15.60953
           SV               0.27405             0.00000
           R1              18.95698             0.00000
           R2              11.51205             0.00000
           R3               5.64390             0.00000
           R4               9.72807             0.00000
           R5               4.15899             0.00000
           RBAR            10.00000             0.00000
```

implies that the clients will get an expected return of 10% (RBAR = 10.00000) and minimize their risk as measured by portfolio variance by investing approximately 16% of the portfolio in the foreign stock fund ($FS = 0.15841$), 53% in the intermediate bond fund ($IB = 0.52548$), 4% in the large-cap growth fund ($LG = 0.04207$), and 27% in the small-cap value fund ($SV = 0.27405$).

The Markowitz portfolio model provides a convenient way for an investor to trade off risk versus return. In practice, this model is typically solved iteratively for different values of return. Figure 8.10 graphs these minimum portfolio variances versus required expected returns as required expected return is varied from 8% to 12% in increments of 1%. In finance this graph is called the *efficient frontier.* Each point on the efficient frontier is the minimum possible risk (measured by portfolio variance) for the given return. By looking at the graph of the efficient frontier an investor can pick the mean-variance trade-off that he or she is most comfortable with.

FIGURE 8.10 AN EFFICIENT FRONTIER FOR THE MARKOWITZ PORTFOLIO MODEL

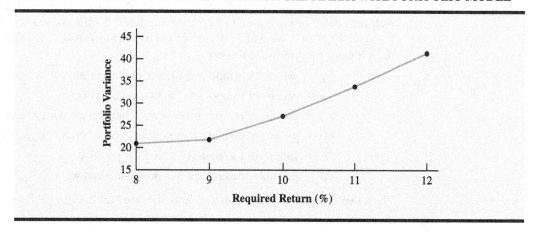

NOTES AND COMMENTS

1. Upper and lower bounds on the amount of an asset type in the portfolio can be easily modeled. Notice that the solution given in Figure 8.9 has more than 50% of the portfolio invested in the intermediate-term bond fund. It may be unwise to let one asset contribute so heavily to the portfolio. Hence upper bounds are often placed on the percentage of the portfolio invested in a single asset. Likewise, it might be undesirable to include an extremely small quantity of an asset in the portfolio. Thus, there may be constraints that require nonzero amounts of an asset to be at least a minimum percentage of the portfolio.

2. In the Hauck example, 100% of the available portfolio was invested in mutual funds. However, risk-averse investors often prefer to have some of their money in a "risk-free" asset such as U.S. Treasury bills. Thus, many portfolio optimization models allow funds to be invested in a risk-free asset.

3. In this section portfolio variance was used to measure risk. However, variance as it is defined counts deviations both above and below the mean. Most investors are happy with returns above the mean but wish to avoid returns below the mean. Hence, numerous portfolio models allow for flexible risk measures.

4. In practice, both brokers and mutual fund companies readjust portfolios as new information becomes available. However, constantly readjusting a portfolio may lead to large transaction costs. Case Problem 1 requires the student to develop a modification of the Markowitz portfolio selection problem in order to account for transaction costs.

8.4 BLENDING: THE POOLING PROBLEM

In Chapter 4 we showed how to use linear programming to solve the Grand Strand Oil Company blending problem. Recall that the Grand Strand refinery wanted to refine three petroleum components into regular and premium gasoline in order to maximize profit. In the Grand Strand model presented in Chapter 4 we assumed that all three petroleum components have separate storage tanks; as a result, components were not mixed together prior to producing gasoline. However, in practice it is often the case that at a blending site the number of storage facilities that hold the blending components is less than the number of components. In this case the components must share a storage tank or storage facility. Similarly, when transporting the components, the components often must share a pipeline or transportation container. Components that share a storage facility or pipeline are called *pooled* components. This pooling is illustrated in Figure 8.11.

Consider Figure 8.11. Components 1 and 2 are pooled in a single storage tank and component 3 has its own storage tank. Regular and premium gasoline are made from blending the pooled components and component 3. Two types of decisions must be made. First, what percentages of component 1 and component 2 should be used in the pooled mixture? Second, how much of the mixture of components 1 and 2 from the pooling tank are to be blended with component 3 to make regular and premium gasoline? These decisions require the following six decision variables:

$$y_1 = \text{gallons of component 1 in the pooling tank}$$
$$y_2 = \text{gallons of component 2 in the pooling tank}$$
$$x_{pr} = \text{gallons of pooled components 1 and 2 in regular gasoline}$$
$$x_{pp} = \text{gallons of pooled components 1 and 2 in premium gasoline}$$
$$x_{3r} = \text{gallons of component 3 in regular gasoline}$$
$$x_{3p} = \text{gallons of component 3 in premium gasoline}$$

These decision variables are shown as flows over the arcs in Figure 8.11.

FIGURE 8.11 THE GRAND STRAND OIL COMPANY POOLING PROBLEM

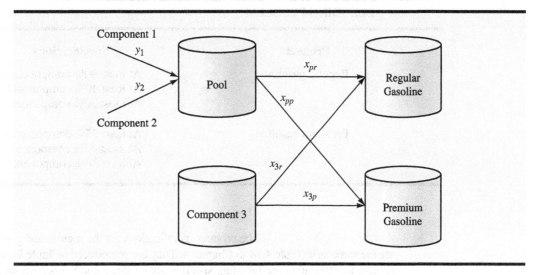

The constraints for the Grand Strand Oil Company pooling problem are similar to the constraints for the original Grand Strand blending problem in Chapter 4. First, we need expressions for the total amount of regular and premium gasoline produced.

Total Gallons Produced Because the gasoline produced is a blend of the input components, the total number of gallons of each type of gasoline produced is the sum of the pooled components and component 3.

$$\text{Regular gasoline} = x_{pr} + x_{3r}$$
$$\text{Premium gasoline} = x_{pp} + x_{3p}$$

Total Petroleum Component Use The total gallons of components 1 and 2 consumed are the amount of the pooled mixture used in making regular and premium gasoline. The total gallons of component 3 consumed is the amount of component 3 used in regular gasoline plus the amount used in premium gasoline.

Components 1 and 2 consumed: $\quad y_1 + y_2 = x_{pr} + x_{pp}$
Component 3 consumed: $\quad x_{3r} + x_{3p}$

The equation involving components 1 and 2 is referred to as a *conservation equation;* this equation shows that the total amount of components 1 and 2 consumed must equal the amount of the pooled mixture used to make regular and premium gasoline.

Component Availability For the current production planning period, the maximum number of gallons available for the three components are 5000, 10,000, and 10,000, respectively. Thus, the three constraints that limit the availability of the three components are

Component 1 $\quad y_1 \leq 5000$
Component 2 $\quad y_2 \leq 10,000$
Component 3 $\quad x_{3r} + x_{3p} \leq 10,000$

TABLE 8.4   PRODUCT SPECIFICATIONS FOR THE GRAND STRAND
BLENDING PROBLEM

Product	Specifications
Regular gasoline	At most 30% component 1
	At least 40% component 2
	At most 20% component 3
Premium gasoline	At least 25% component 1
	At most 45% component 2
	At least 30% component 3

Product Specifications   The product specifications for the regular and premium gasoline are the same as in Table 4.14 in Chapter 4. They are reproduced in Table 8.4 for ease of reference. Incorporating the blending specifications from Table 8.4 is a bit more difficult for the pooling problem because the amount of components 1 and 2 that go into the regular and premium gasoline depend on the proportion of these components in the pooled tank. For example, consider the constraint that component 1 can account for no more than 30% of the total gallons of regular gasoline produced. If x_{pr} gallons of the pooled components are blended with component 3 to make regular gasoline, it is necessary to know the percentage of component 1 in x_{pr}. The total gallons of components 1 and 2 in the pooled tank are $y_1 + y_2$; therefore, the fraction of component 1 in the pooled tank is

$$\left(\frac{y_1}{y_1 + y_2} \right)$$

As a result,

$$\left(\frac{y_1}{y_1 + y_2} \right) x_{pr}$$

is the number of gallons of component 1 used to blend regular gasoline. The total number of gallons of regular gasoline is $x_{pr} + x_{3r}$. So the constraint that the number of gallons of component 1 can account for no more than 30% of the total gallons of regular gasoline produced is

$$\left(\frac{y_1}{y_1 + y_2} \right) x_{pr} \leq .3(x_{pr} + x_{3r})$$

This expression is nonlinear because it involves the ratio of variables multiplied by another variable. The logic is similar for the other constraints required to implement the product specifications given in Table 8.4.

As in Section 4.4, the objective is to maximize the total profit contribution. Thus, we want to develop the objective function by maximizing the difference between the total revenue from both gasolines and the total cost of the three petroleum components. Recall that the price per gallon of the regular gasoline is $2.90 and the price per gallon of premium gasoline is $3.00. The cost of components 1, 2, and 3 is $2.50, $2.60, and $2.84, respectively. Finally, at least 10,000 gallons of regular gasoline must be produced.

The complete nonlinear model for the Grand Strand pooling problem, containing 6 decision variables and 11 constraints (excluding nonnegativity), follows:

$$\text{Max} \quad 2.9\,(x_{pr} + x_{3r}) + 3.00(x_{pp} + x_{3p}) - 2.5y_1 - 2.6y_2 - 2.84(x_{3r} + x_{3p})$$

s.t.

$$y_1 + y_2 = x_{pr} + x_{pp}$$

$$\left(\frac{y_1}{y_1 + y_2}\right)x_{pr} \le .3(x_{pr} + x_{3r})$$

$$\left(\frac{y_2}{y_1 + y_2}\right)x_{pr} \ge .4(x_{pr} + x_{3r})$$

$$x_{3r} \le .2(x_{pr} + x_{3r})$$

$$\left(\frac{y_1}{y_1 + y_2}\right)x_{pp} \ge .25(x_{pp} + x_{3p})$$

$$\left(\frac{y_2}{y_1 + y_2}\right)x_{pp} \le .45(x_{pp} + x_{3p})$$

$$x_{3p} \ge .3(x_{pp} + x_{3p})$$

$$y_1 \le 5000$$

$$y_2 \le 10{,}000$$

$$x_{3r} + x_{3p} \le 10{,}000$$

$$x_{pr} + x_{3r} \ge 10{,}000$$

$$x_{pr}, x_{pp}, x_{3r}, x_{3p}, y_1, y_2 \ge 0$$

WEB file

GrandPooling

The optimal solution to the Grand Strand pooling problem is shown in Figure 8.12. The number of gallons of each component used and the percentage in regular and premium gasoline are shown in Table 8.5. For example, the 10,000 gallons of regular gasoline contain 2857.143 gallons of component 1. The number 2857.143 does not appear directly in the solution in Figure 8.12. It must be calculated. In the solution, $y_1 = 5000$, $y_2 = 9000$, and $x_{pr} = 8000$, which means that the number of gallons of component 1 in regular gasoline is

$$\left(\frac{y_1}{y_1 + y_2}\right)x_{pr} = \left(\frac{5000}{5000 + 9000}\right)8000 = 2857.143$$

In Figure 8.12 the objective value of 5831.429 corresponds to a total profit contribution of $5831.43. In Section 4.4 we found that the value of the optimal solution to the original Grand Strand blending problem is $7100. Why is the total profit contribution smaller for the model where components 1 and 2 are pooled? Note that any feasible solution to the problem with pooled components is feasible to the problem with no pooling. However, the converse is not true. For example, Figure 8.12 shows that the ratio of the number of gallons of component 1 to the number of gallons of component 2 in both regular and premium gasoline is constant. That is,

$$\frac{2857.143}{5142.857} = .5556 = \frac{2142.857}{3857.143}$$

FIGURE 8.12 SOLUTION TO THE GRAND STRAND POOLING PROBLEM

```
Optimal Objective Value = 5831.42857

        Variable              Value            Reduced Cost
    --------------      ---------------    ------------------
          XPR              8000.00000             0.00000
          X3R              2000.00000             0.00000
          XPP              6000.00000             0.00000
          X3P              2571.42857             0.00000
          Y1               5000.00000             0.00000
          Y2               9000.00000             0.00000

       Constraint        Slack/Surplus           Dual Value
    --------------      ---------------    ------------------
           1                0.00000              1.41200
           2             1000.00000              0.00000
           3             5428.57143              0.00000
           4                0.00000             -3.06134
           5              142.85714              0.00000
           6             1142.85714              0.00000
           7                0.00000              0.22857
           8                0.00000             -2.19657
           9                0.00000              0.86476
          10                0.00000              0.00000
          11                0.00000             -0.12286
```

TABLE 8.5 GRAND STRAND POOLING SOLUTION

| Gasoline | Gallons of Component (percentage) | | | |
	Component 1	Component 2	Component 3	Total
Regular	2857.143 (28.57%)	5142.857 (51.43%)	2000 (20%)	10,000
Premium	2142.857 (25%)	3857.143 (45%)	2571.429 (30%)	8571.429

This must be the case because this ratio is y_1/y_2, the ratio of component 1 to component 2 in the pooled mixture. Table 8.6 shows the solution to the original Grand Strand problem without pooling (this table also appears in Section 4.4). The ratio of component 1 to component 2 in regular gasoline is $1250/6750 = 0.1852$, and the ratio of component 1 to component 2 in premium gasoline is $3750/3250 = 1.1538$, which is a large difference. By forcing us to use the same ratio of component 1 to component 2 in the pooling model, we lose flexibility and must spend more on the petroleum components used to make the gasoline.

The lack of enough storage tanks for all the components reduces the number of blending feasible solutions, which in turn leads to a lower profit. Indeed, one use of this model is to provide management with a good estimate of the profit loss due to a shortage of storage tanks. Management would then be able to assess the profitability of purchasing additional storage tanks.

TABLE 8.6   SOLUTION TO THE GRAND STRAND PROBLEM WITHOUT POOLING

| Gasoline | Gallons of Component (percentage) | | | Total |
	Component 1	Component 2	Component 3	
Regular	1250 (12.50%)	6750 (67.50%)	2000 (20%)	10,000
Premium	3750 (25%)	3250 (21.67%)	8000 (53.33%)	15,000

8.5   FORECASTING ADOPTION OF A NEW PRODUCT

Forecasting new adoptions after a product introduction is an important marketing problem. In this section we introduce a forecasting model developed by Frank Bass that has proven to be particularly effective in forecasting the adoption of innovative and new technologies in the market place.[3] Nonlinear programming is used to estimate the parameters of the Bass forecasting model. The model has three parameters that must be estimated.

m = the number of people estimated to eventually adopt the new product

A company introducing a new product is obviously interested in the value of this parameter.

q = the coefficient of imitation

This parameter measures the likelihood of adoption due to a potential adopter being influenced by someone who has already adopted the product. It measures the "word-of-mouth" effect influencing purchases.

p = the coefficient of innovation

This parameter measures the likelihood of adoption, assuming no influence from someone who has already purchased (adopted) the product. It is the likelihood of someone adopting the product due to her or his own interest in the innovation.

Using these parameters, let us now develop the forecasting model. Let C_{t-1} denote the number of people who have adopted the product through time $t - 1$. Because m is the number of people estimated to eventually adopt the product, $m - C_{t-1}$ is the number of potential adopters remaining at time $t - 1$. We refer to the time interval between time $t - 1$ and time t as time period t. During period t, some percentage of the remaining number of potential adopters, $m - C_{t-1}$, will adopt the product. This value depends upon the likelihood of a new adoption.

Loosely speaking, the likelihood of a new adoption is the likelihood of adoption due to imitation plus the likelihood of adoption due to innovation. The likelihood of adoption due to imitation is a function of the number of people that have already adopted the product. The larger the current pool of adopters, the greater their influence through word of mouth. Because C_{t-1}/m is the fraction of the number of people estimated to adopt the product by time $t - 1$, the likelihood of adoption due to imitation is computed by multiplying this fraction by q, the coefficient of imitation. Thus, the likelihood of adoption due to imitation is

$$q(C_{t-1}/m)$$

---

[3]See Frank M. Bass, "A New Product Growth for Model Consumer Durables," *Management Science* 15 (1969).

The likelihood of adoption due to innovation is simply p, the coefficient of innovation. Thus, the likelihood of adoption is

$$p + q(C_{t-1}/m)$$

Using the likelihood of adoption, we can develop a forecast of the remaining number of potential customers that will adopt the product during time period t. Thus, F_t, the forecast of the number of new adopters during time period t, is

$$F_t = (p + q[C_{t-1}/m])(m - C_{t-1}) \qquad (8.20)$$

The Bass forecasting model given in equation (8.20) can be rigorously derived from statistical principles. Rather than providing such a derivation, we have emphasized the intuitive aspects of the model. In developing a forecast of new adoptions in period t using the Bass model, the value of C_{t-1} will be known from past sales data. But we also need to know the values of the parameters to use in the model. Let us now see how nonlinear programming is used to estimate the parameter values m, p, and q.

Consider Figure 8.13. This figure shows the graph of box office revenues (in $ millions) for the films *The Doctor* and *Terminator 3* over the first 12 weeks after release.[4] Strictly speaking, box office revenues for time period t are not the same as the number of adopters during time period t. But the number of repeat customers is usually small and box office revenues are a multiple of the number of movie goers. The Bass forecasting model seems appropriate here.

These two films illustrate drastically different adoption patterns. Note that revenues for *The Doctor* grow until they peak in week 4 and then they decline. For this film, much of the revenue is obviously due to word-of-mouth influence. In terms of the Bass model the imitation factor dominates the innovation factor, and we expect $q > p$. However, for

FIGURE 8.13   WEEKLY BOX OFFICE REVENUES FOR *THE DOCTOR* AND *TERMINATOR 3*

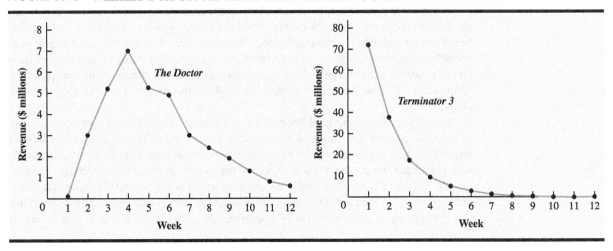

---

[4]The data for *The Doctor* are from Gary Lilien and Arvind Rangaswamy, *Marketing Engineering* (Victoria, BC: Trafford Publishing, 2004). The data for *Terminator 3* came from www.rottentomatoes.com/m/terminator_3_rise_of_the_machines/numbers.php.

the film *Terminator 3*, revenues peak in week 1 and drop sharply afterward. The innovation factor dominates the imitation factor, and we expect $q < p$.

The forecasting model, equation (8.20), can be incorporated into a nonlinear optimization problem to find the values of p, q, and m that give the best forecasts for a set of data. Assume that N periods of data are available. Let S_t denote the actual number of adopters (or a multiple of that number, such as sales) in period t for $t = 1, \ldots, N$. Then the forecast in each period and the corresponding forecast error E_t is defined by

$$F_t = (p + q[C_{t-1}/m])(m - C_{t-1})$$

$$E_t = F_t - S_t$$

Notice that the forecast error is the difference between the forecast value F_t and the actual value, S_t. It is common statistical practice to estimate parameters by minimizing the sum of errors squared.

Doing so for the Bass forecasting model leads to the follow nonlinear optimization problem:

WEB file

BassDoctor

$$\text{Min} \sum_{t=1}^{N} E_t^2 \tag{8.21}$$

s.t.

$$F_t = (p + q[C_{t-1}/m])(m - C_{t-1}), \quad t = 1, \ldots, N \tag{8.22}$$

$$E_t = F_t - S_t, \quad t = 1, \ldots, N \tag{8.23}$$

Because equations (8.21) and (8.22) both contain nonlinear terms, this model is a nonlinear minimization problem.

The data in Table 8.7 provide the revenue and cumulative revenues for *The Doctor* in weeks 1–12. Using these data, the nonlinear model to estimate the parameters of the Bass forecasting model for *The Doctor* follows:

$$\begin{aligned}
\text{Min} \quad & E_1^2 + E_2^2 + \cdots + E_{12}^2 \\
\text{s.t.} \quad & F_1 = (p)m \\
& F_2 = [p + q(0.10/m)](m - 0.10) \\
& F_3 = [p + q(3.10/m)](m - 3.10) \\
& \qquad \cdot \\
& \qquad \cdot \\
& \qquad \cdot \\
& F_{12} = [p + q(34.85/m)](m - 34.85) \\
& E_1 = F_1 - 0.10 \\
& E_2 = F_2 - 3.00 \\
& \qquad \cdot \\
& \qquad \cdot \\
& \qquad \cdot \\
& E_{12} = F_{12} - 0.60
\end{aligned}$$

665

TABLE 8.7 BOX OFFICE REVENUES AND CUMULATIVE REVENUES IN $ MILLIONS FOR *THE DOCTOR*

Week	Revenues S_t	Cumulative Revenues C_t
1	0.10	0.10
2	3.00	3.10
3	5.20	8.30
4	7.00	15.30
5	5.25	20.55
6	4.90	25.45
7	3.00	28.45
8	2.40	30.85
9	1.90	32.75
10	1.30	34.05
11	0.80	34.85
12	0.60	35.45

Problem 21 asks you to formulate and solve a nonlinear model for Terminator 3.

The solution to this nonlinear program and the solution to a similar nonlinear program for *Terminator 3* are given in Table 8.8.

The optimal forecasting parameter values given in Table 8.8 are intuitively appealing and consistent with Figure 8.13. For the film *The Doctor,* which has the largest revenues in week 4, the value of the imitation parameter q is 0.49; this value is substantially larger than the innovation parameter $p = 0.074$. The film picks up momentum over time due to favorable word of mouth. After week 4 revenues decline as more and more of the potential market for the film has already seen it. Contrast these data with those for *Terminator 3*, which has a negative value of –0.018 for the imitation parameter and an innovation parameter of 0.49. The greatest number of adoptions are in week 1, and new adoptions decline afterward. Obviously the word-of-mouth influence was not favorable.

In Figure 8.14 we show the forecast values based on the parameters in Table 8.8 and the observed values in the same graph. The forecast values are denoted by a ■. The Bass forecasting model does a good job of tracking revenue for *The Doctor.* For *Terminator 3*, the Bass model does an outstanding job; it is virtually impossible to distinguish the forecast line from the actual adoption line.

You may wonder what good a forecasting model is if we must wait until after the adoption cycle is complete to estimate the parameters. One way to use the Bass forecasting

TABLE 8.8 OPTIMAL FORECAST PARAMETERS FOR *THE DOCTOR* AND *TERMINATOR 3*

Parameter	*The Doctor*	*Terminator*
p	0.074	.49
q	0.49	−.018
m	34.85	149.54

FIGURE 8.14 FORECAST AND ACTUAL WEEKLY BOX OFFICE REVENUES FOR *THE DOCTOR* AND *TERMINATOR 3*

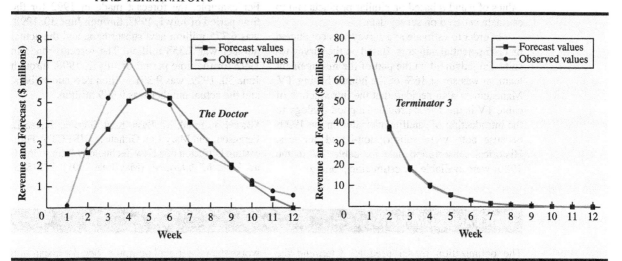

model for a new product is to assume that sales of the new product will behave in a way that is similar to a previous product for which p and q have been calculated and to subjectively estimate m, the potential market for the new product. For example, one might assume that sales of DVD players will be similar to sales of VCRs. Then the p and q used for the DVD forecasts would be the p and q values calculated from the actual sales of VCRs. The Management Science in Action, Forecasting Adoption of Satellite Television, describes how this approach was used to forecast sales of satellite TV, using p and q values from the adoption history of cable television.

A second approach is to wait until several periods of data for the new product are available. For example, if five periods of data are available, the sales data for these five periods could be used to forecast demand for period 6. Then, after six periods of sales are observed, a forecast for period 7 is made. This method is often called a rolling-horizon approach. (See the related discussion in the Management Science in Action just mentioned.)

MANAGEMENT SCIENCE IN ACTION

FORECASTING ADOPTION OF SATELLITE TELEVISION*

DIRECTV was founded in 1991. The goal of this company was to bring to market a direct-broadcast-satellite television service to compete with cable television. Much like cable television, the DIRECTV adoption model was based on new monthly subscription fees. Obviously, a forecast was needed by management to estimate future adoptions. Unfortunately, because it was a completely new product, no historical data were available.

In particular, management wanted to forecast (1) how many television owners in the United States would subscribe to a satellite television service; and (2) the rate at which they would subscribe to this service. DIRECTV, working in conjunction with the SMART (Strategic Marketing And Research Techniques) consulting firm, developed the required forecast. It was decided to use the Bass forecasting model because of its success in forecasting the adoption and diffusion of new products.

The parameters required to use the Bass model are p, the coefficient of innovation; q, the coefficient of imitation; and m, the estimate of the

(continued)

number of subscribers or adopters. Because no historical data were available it was decided to select values of p and q based on similar products and to estimate m based on survey data.

In order to estimate m a survey was conducted of 1145 potential adopters. Based on the survey results and judgment on the part of the management team, m was set at 16% of the homes having TV. Management also decided that the introduction of cable TV in the 1980s provided a good analogy to the introduction of satellite television in the 1990s because both were subscription-based services. Historical subscription data for cable TV in the 1980s were available for estimating p and q.

The forecasts generated using these parameter values with the Bass model were remarkably good. For example, the forecast made in 1992 for the time period of July 1, 1997, through June 30, 1998, was 6.775 million new subscribers, and the actual number was 7.358 million. The forecast made in 1992 for the time period of July 1, 1998, through June 30, 1999, was 9.391 million new subscribers, and the actual number was 9.989 million.

*Based on Frank M. Bass, Kent Gordon, Teresa L. Ferguson, and Mary Lou Githens, "DIRECTV: Forecasting Diffusion of a New Technology Prior to Product Launch," *Interfaces* (May/June 2001): S82–S93.

NOTES AND COMMENTS

The optimization model used to determine the parameter values for the Bass forecasting model is an example of a hard nonlinear optimization problem. It is neither convex nor concave. For such models, local optima may give values that are much worse than the global optimum. See the discussion in Appendix 8.1 and Appendix 8.2 on how to use the LINGO and Solver software to find a global optimum.

SUMMARY

In this chapter we introduced nonlinear optimization models. A nonlinear optimization model is a model with a least one nonlinear term in either a constraint or the objective function. Because so many processes in business and nature behave in a nonlinear fashion, allowing nonlinear terms greatly increases the number of important applications that can be modeled as an optimization problem. Numerous problems in portfolio optimization, pricing options, blending, economics, facility location, forecasting, and scheduling lend themselves to nonlinear models.

Unfortunately, nonlinear optimization models are not as easy to solve as linear optimization models, or even linear integer optimization models. As a rule of thumb, if a problem can be modeled realistically as a linear or linear integer problem, then it is probably best to do so. Many nonlinear formulations have local optima that are not globally optimal. Because most nonlinear optimization codes will terminate with a local optimum, the solution returned by the code may not be the best solution available. However, as pointed out in this chapter, numerous important classes of optimization problems, such as the Markowitz portfolio model, are convex optimization problems. For a convex optimization problem, a local optimum is also the global optimum. Additionally, the development of nonlinear optimization codes that do find globally optimal solutions is proceeding at a rapid rate.

GLOSSARY

Nonlinear optimization problem An optimization problem that contains at least one nonlinear term in the objective function or a constraint.

Local optimum A feasible solution is a local optimum if there are no other feasible solutions with a better objective function value in the immediate neighborhood. A local optimum may be either a local maximum or a local minimum.

Local maximum A feasible solution is a local maximum if there are no other feasible solutions with a larger objective function value in the immediate neighborhood.

Local minimum A feasible solution is a local minimum if there are no other feasible solutions with a smaller objective function value in the immediate neighborhood.

Global optimum A feasible solution is a global optimum if there are no other feasible points with a better objective function value in the entire feasible region. A global optimum may be either a global maximum or a global minimum.

Global maximum A feasible solution is a global maximum if there are no other feasible points with a larger objective function value in the entire feasible region. A global maximum is also a local maximum.

Global minimum A feasible solution is a global minimum if there are no other feasible points with a smaller objective function value in the entire feasible region. A global minimum is also a local minimum.

Concave function A function that is bowl-shaped down: For example, the functions $f(x) = -5x^2 - 5x$ and $f(x, y) = -x^2 - 11y^2$ are concave functions.

Convex function A function that is bowl-shaped up: For example, the functions $f(x) = x^2 - 5x$ and $f(x, y) = x^2 + 5y^2$ are convex functions.

Index fund A portfolio of stocks, mutual funds, or other securities that matches as closely as possible the performance of a broad market index such as the S&P 500.

Markowitz portfolio model A portfolio optimization model used to construct a portfolio that minimizes risk subject to a constraint requiring a minimum level of return.

PROBLEMS

1. The purpose of this exercise is to provide practice using the LINGO or Excel solvers. Find the values of X and Y that minimize the function

$$\text{Min} \quad X^2 - 4X + Y^2 + 8Y + 20$$

Do not assume nonnegativity of the X and Y variables. Recall that by default LINGO assumes nonnegative variables. In order to allow the variables to take on negative values you can add

@FREE(X);   @FREE(Y);

Alternatively, if you want LINGO to allow for negative values by default, in the LINGO menu select **Options** and then click **General Solver,** and then uncheck the **Variables assumed nonnegative** tab.

2. Consider the problem

$$\text{Min} \quad 2X^2 - 20X + 2XY + Y^2 - 14Y + 58$$
$$\text{s.t.} \quad X + 4Y \leq 8$$

a. Find the minimum solution to this problem.
b. If the right-hand side of the constraint is increased from 8 to 9, how much do you expect the objective function to change?
c. Resolve the problem with a new right-hand side of 9. How does the actual change compare with your estimate?

3. The Macon Psychiatric Institute is interested in redesigning its mental health care delivery system in order to maximize the number of people who can benefit from its services.

669

Unfortunately, having a large number of patients in residence places a burden on the staff and lengthens patient recovery times. Based on patient records and recovery time estimates by the clinic's staff members, the following mathematical relationship has been developed to describe how the number of patients in residence affects the patient recovery time.

$$T = \frac{45}{180 - P}$$

where

T = average patient recovery time in years
P = number of patients in residence

In answering the following questions, think of P as the equilibrium number of patients in residence. We admit a new patient every time we discharge a cured patient in order to keep the number of patients in residence fixed at P.

a. Suppose patients are admitted at a rate that maintains 150 patients in residence at the clinic. What is the average recovery time per patient, and how many patients will recover per year?

b. Using the formula for average patient recovery time, develop an expression for N, which is equal to the number of patients that recover per year as a function of P.

c. Determine the optimal number of patients for the clinic to have in residence if it is interested in maximizing the number of patients that recover per year.

4. Lawn King manufactures two types of riding lawn mowers. One is a low-cost mower sold primarily to residential home owners; the other is an industrial model sold to landscaping and lawn service companies. The company is interested in establishing a pricing policy for the two mowers that will maximize the gross profit for the product line. A study of the relationships between sales prices and quantities sold of the two mowers has validated the following price-quantity relationships.

$$q_1 = 950 - 1.5p_1 + 0.7p_2$$
$$q_2 = 2500 + 0.3p_1 - 0.5p_2$$

where

q_1 = number of residential mowers sold
q_2 = number of industrial mowers sold
p_1 = selling price of the residential mower in dollars
p_2 = selling price of the industrial mower in dollars

The accounting department developed cost information on the fixed and variable cost of producing the two mowers. The fixed cost of production for the residential mower is $10,000 and the variable cost is $1500 per mower. The fixed cost of production for the industrial mower is $30,000 and the variable cost is $4000 per mower.

a. Lawn King traditionally priced the lawn mowers at $2000 and $6000 for the residential and industrial mowers, respectively. Gross profit is computed as the sales revenue minus production cost. How many mowers will be sold, and what is the gross profit with this pricing policy?

b. Following the approach of Section 8.1, develop an expression for gross profit as a function of the selling prices for the two mowers.

c. What are the optimal prices for Lawn King to charge? How many units of each mower will be sold at these prices and what will the gross profit be?

d. Try a different formulation for this problem. Write the objective function as

$$\text{Max} \quad p_1q_1 + p_2q_2 - c_1 - c_2$$

where c_1 and c_2 represent the production costs for the two mowers. Then add four constraints to the problem, two based on the price-quantity relationships and two based on the cost functions. Solve this new constrained optimization problem to see whether you get the same answer. What are the advantages of this formulation, if any?

SELF test

5. GreenLawns provides a lawn fertilizer and weed control service. The company is adding a special aeration treatment as a low-cost extra service option, which it hopes will help attract new customers. Management is planning to promote this new service in two media: radio and direct-mail advertising. A media budget of $3000 is available for this promotional campaign. Based on past experience in promoting its other services, GreenLawns obtained the following estimate of the relationship between sales and the amount spent on promotion in these two media:

$$S = -2R^2 - 10M^2 - 8RM + 18R + 34M$$

where

S = total sales in thousands of dollars
R = thousands of dollars spent on radio advertising
M = thousands of dollars spent on direct-mail advertising

GreenLawns would like to develop a promotional strategy that will lead to maximum sales subject to the restriction provided by the media budget.

   a. What is the value of sales if $2000 is spent on radio advertising and $1000 is spent on direct-mail advertising?

   b. Formulate an optimization problem that can be solved to maximize sales subject to the media budget.

   c. Determine the optimal amount to spend on radio and direct-mail advertising. How much money will be generated in sales?

You may also use Excel Solver to solve this problem. However, you must put bounds on the variables (for example, lower and upper bounds of -10 and 10) on both X and Y and use the Multistart option as described in Appendix 8.2.

6. The function

$$f(X, Y) = 3(1 - X)^2 e^{(-X^2 - (Y+1)^2)} - 10(X/5 - X^3 - Y^5) e^{(-X^2 - Y^2)} - e^{(-(X+1)^2 - Y^2)}/3$$

was used to generate Figures 8.6 and 8.7 in order to illustrate the concept of local optima versus global optima.

   a. Minimize this function using LINGO. (*Warning:* Make sure you use the unary minus sign correctly. In other words, rewrite a term such as $-X^2$ as $-(X)^2$. See Appendix 8.1.)

   b. Now minimize this function using LINGO with the Global Solver option turned on.

7. The Cobb-Douglas production function is a classic model from economics used to model output as a function of capital and labor. It has the form

$$f(L, C) = c_0 L^{c_1} C^{c_2}$$

where c_0, c_1, and c_2 are constants. The variable L represents the units of input of labor and the variable C represents the units of input of capital.

   a. In this example, assume $c_0 = 5$, $c_1 = 0.25$, and $c_2 = 0.75$. Assume each unit of labor costs $25 and each unit of capital costs $75. With $75,000 available in the budget, develop an optimization model for determining how the budgeted amount should be allocated between capital and labor in order to maximize output.

   b. Find the optimal solution to the model you formulated in part (a). *Hint:* Put bound constraints on the variables based on the budget constraint. Use $L \leq 3000$ and $C \leq 1000$ and use the Multistart option as described in Appendix 8.2.

8. Let S represent the amount of steel produced (in tons). Steel production is related to the amount of labor used (L) and the amount of capital used (C) by the following function:

$$S = 20L^{0.30}C^{0.70}$$

In this formula L represents the units of labor input and C the units of capital input. Each unit of labor costs \$50, and each unit of capital costs \$100.

a. Formulate an optimization problem that will determine how much labor and capital are needed in order to produce 50,000 tons of steel at minimum cost.

b. Solve the optimization problem you formulated in part (a). *Hint:* Use the Multistart option as described in Appendix 8.2. Add lower and upper bound constraints of 0 and 5000 for both L and C before solving.

9. The profit function for two products is

$$Profit = -3x_1^2 + 42x_1 - 3x_2^2 + 48x_2 + 700$$

where x_1 represents units of production of product 1 and x_2 represents units of production of product 2. Producing one unit of product 1 requires 4 labor-hours and producing one unit of product 2 requires 6 labor-hours. Currently, 24 labor-hours are available. The cost of labor-hours is already factored into the profit function. However, it is possible to schedule overtime at a premium of \$5 per hour.

a. Formulate an optimization problem that can be used to find the optimal production quantity of products 1 and the optimal number of overtime hours to schedule.

b. Solve the optimization model you formulated in part (a). How much should be produced and how many overtime hours should be scheduled?

10. Heller Manufacturing has two production facilities that manufacture baseball gloves. Production costs at the two facilities differ because of varying labor rates, local property taxes, type of equipment, capacity, and so on. The Dayton plant has weekly costs that can be expressed as a function of the number of gloves produced:

$$TCD(X) = X^2 - X + 5$$

where X is the weekly production volume in thousands of units and $TCD(X)$ is the cost in thousands of dollars. The Hamilton plant's weekly production costs are given by

$$TCH(Y) = Y^2 + 2Y + 3$$

where Y is the weekly production volume in thousands of units and $TCH(Y)$ is the cost in thousands of dollars. Heller Manufacturing would like to produce 8000 gloves per week at the lowest possible cost.

a. Formulate a mathematical model that can be used to determine the optimal number of gloves to produce each week at each facility.

b. Use LINGO or Excel Solver to find the solution to your mathematical model to determine the optimal number of gloves to produce at each facility.

11. In the Markowitz portfolio optimization model defined in equations (8.10) through (8.19), the decision variables represent the percentage of the portfolio invested in each of the mutual funds. For example, $FS = 0.25$ in the solution means that 25% of the money in the portfolio is invested in the foreign stock mutual fund. It is possible to define the decision variables to represent the actual dollar amount invested in each mutual fund or stock. Redefine the decision variables so that now each variable represents the dollar amount invested in the mutual fund. Assume an investor has \$50,000 to invest and wants to minimize the variance of his or her portfolio subject to a constraint that the portfolio returns a minimum of 10%. Reformulate the model given by (8.10) through (8.19) based on the new definition of the decision variables. Solve the revised model with LINGO or Excel Solver.

12. Many forecasting models use parameters that are estimated using nonlinear optimization. A good example is the Bass model introduced in this chapter. Another example is the exponential smoothing forecasting model. The exponential smoothing model is common in

TABLE 8.9   EXPONENTIAL SMOOTHING MODEL FOR $\alpha = 0.3$

Week (t)	Observed Value (Y_t)	Forecast (F_t)	Forecast Error ($Y_t - F_t$)	Squared Forecast Error $(Y_t - F_t)^2$
1	17	17.00	0.00	0.00
2	21	17.00	4.00	16.00
3	19	18.20	0.80	0.64
4	23	18.44	4.56	20.79
5	18	19.81	−1.81	3.27
6	16	19.27	−3.27	10.66
7	20	18.29	1.71	2.94
8	18	18.80	−0.80	0.64
9	22	18.56	3.44	11.83
10	20	19.59	0.41	0.17
11	15	19.71	−4.71	22.23
12	22	18.30	3.70	13.69
				SUM = 102.86

practice and is described in further detail in Chapter 15. For instance, the basic exponential smoothing model for forecasting sales is

$$F_{t+1} = \alpha Y_t + (1 - \alpha)F_t$$

where

$$F_{t+1} = \text{forecast of sales for period } t + 1$$
$$Y_t = \text{actual value of sales for period } t$$
$$F_t = \text{forecast of sales for period } t$$
$$\alpha = \text{smoothing constant } 0 \le \alpha \le 1$$

This model is used recursively; the forecast for time period $t + 1$ is based on the forecast for period t, F_t, the observed value of sales in period t, Y_t, and the smoothing parameter α. The use of this model to forecast sales for 12 months is illustrated in Table 8.9 with the smoothing constant $\alpha = 0.3$. The forecast errors, $Y_t - F_t$, are calculated in the fourth column. The value of α is often chosen by minimizing the sum of squared forecast errors, commonly referred to as the mean squared error (MSE). The last column of Table 8.9 shows the square of the forecast error and the sum of squared forecast errors.

In using exponential smoothing models one tries to choose the value of α that provides the best forecasts. Build an Excel Solver or LINGO optimization model that will find the smoothing parameter, α, that minimizes the sum of forecast errors squared. You may find it easiest to put Table 8.9 into an Excel spreadsheet and then use Solver to find the optimal value of α.

13. The purpose of this exercise is to learn how to calculate stock returns for portfolio models using actual stock price data. First, it is necessary to obtain stock price data. One source (of many) is Yahoo! Go to the link http://finance.yahoo.com and type in a ticker symbol such as AAPL (for Apple Computer). Then on the left-hand side of the page, select Historical Data.

These data are easily downloaded to a spreadsheet by clicking on the link Download to Spreadsheet at the bottom of the page. For Apple Computer (AAPL), Advanced Micro Devices (AMD), and Oracle Corporation (ORCL), download the monthly price data for

FIGURE 8.15 YEARLY RETURNS FOR AAPL, AMD, AND ORCL

StockReturns

Date	AAPL Adj. Close	AMD Adj. Close	ORCL Adj. Close	AAPL Return	AMD Return	ORCL Return
2-Jan-97	4.16	17.57	4.32	0.0962	−0.5537	−0.1074
2-Jan-98	4.58	10.1	3.88	0.8104	0.1272	0.8666
4-Jan-99	10.3	11.47	9.23	0.9236	0.4506	0.9956
3-Jan-00	25.94	18	24.98	−0.8753	0.3124	0.1533
2-Jan-01	10.81	24.6	29.12	0.1340	−0.4270	−0.5230
2-Jan-02	12.36	16.05	17.26	−0.5432	−1.1194	−0.3610
2-Jan-03	7.18	5.24	12.03	0.4517	1.0424	0.1416
2-Jan-04	11.28	14.86	13.86	1.2263	0.0613	−0.0065
3-Jan-05	38.45	15.8	13.77	0.6749	0.9729	−0.0912
3-Jan-06	75.51	41.8	12.57			

Data Source: CSI
Web site: http://www.csidata.com

January 1997 through January 2006. These data contain closing prices that are adjusted for stock dividends and splits.

You now have stock prices for 10 years and the objective is to calculate the annual returns for each stock for the years 1997 through 2005. Returns are often calculated using continuous compounding. If the stock prices are adjusted for splits and stock dividends, then the price of stock i in period $t + 1$, $P_{i,t+1}$, is given by

$$p_{i,t+1} = p_t e^{r_{it}}$$

where p_{it} is the price of stock i in period t and r_{it} is the return on stock i in period t. This calculation assumes no cash dividends were paid, which is true of Apple Computer, Advanced Micro Devices, and Oracle Corporation. Solving the equation $p_{i,t+1} = p_t e^{r_{it}}$ for the return on stock i in period t gives

$$r_{it} = \ln\left(\frac{p_{i,t+1}}{p_t}\right)$$

For example, the Apple Computer adjusted closing price in January 2005 was 38.45. The closing price in January 2006 was 75.51. Thus, the continuously compounded return for Apple Computer from January 2005 to January 2006 is

$$\ln(75.51/38.45) = 0.6749064$$

We use this calculation as our estimate of the annual return for Apple Computer for the year 2005.

Take the closing stock prices that you have downloaded and calculate the annual returns for 1997–2005 for AAPL, AMD, and ORCL using $r_{it} = \ln(p_{i,t+1}/p_t)$. If you calculate the returns properly, your results should appear as in Figure 8.15.

14. Formulate and solve the Markowitz portfolio optimization model that was defined in equations (8.10) through (8.19) using the data from Problem 13. In this case, nine scenarios correspond to the yearly returns from 1997–2005, inclusive. Treat each scenario as being equally likely and use the scenario returns that were calculated in Problem 13.

15. Using the data obtained in Problem 13, construct a portfolio from Apple, AMD, and Oracle that matches the Information Technology S&P index as closely as possible. Use the return data for the Information Technology S&P index given in the following table. The model for constructing the portfolio should be similar to the one developed for Hauck Financial Services in Section 8.2.

Year	Return
1997	28.54%
1998	78.14
1999	78.74
2000	−40.90
2001	−25.87
2002	−37.41
2003	48.40
2004	2.56
2005	0.99

16. Most investors are happy when their returns are "above average," but not so happy when they are "below average." In the Markowitz portfolio optimization problem given by equations (8.10) through (8.19), the objective function is to minimize variance, which is given by

$$\text{Min } \frac{1}{5} \sum_{s=1}^{5} (R_s - \overline{R})^2$$

where R_s is the portfolio return under scenario s and $\overline{R}$ is the expected or average return of the portfolio.

With this objective function, we are choosing a portfolio that minimizes deviations both above and below the average, $\overline{R}$. However, most investors are happy when $R_s > \overline{R}$), but unhappy when $R_s < R$. With this preference in mind, an alternative to the variance measure in the objective function for the Markowitz model is the *semivariance*. The semivariance is calculated by only considering deviations below $\overline{R}$.

Let $D_{sp} - D_{sn} = R_s - \overline{R}$, and restrict D_{sp} and D_{sn} to be nonnegative. Then D_{sp} measures the positive deviation from the mean return in scenario s (i.e., $D_{sp} = R_s - \overline{R}$ when $R_s > \overline{R}$). In the case where the scenario return is below the average return, $R_s < \overline{R}$, we have $-D_{sn} = R_s - \overline{R}$. Using these new variables, we can reformulate the Markowitz model to minimize only the square of negative deviations below the average return. By doing so, we will use the semivariance rather than the variance in the objective function.

Reformulate the Markowitz portfolio optimization model given in equations (8.10) through (8.19) to use semivariance in the objective function. Solve the model using either Excel Solver or LINGO. *Hint:* When using Excel Solver, put an upper bound of 1 on each proportion variable and use the Multistart option as described in Appendix 8.2.

17. This problem requires a basic understanding of the normal probability distribution. Investors are often interested in knowing the probabilities of poor returns. For example, for what cutoff return will the probability of the actual return falling below this cutoff value be at most 1%?

Consider the solution to the Markowitz portfolio problem given in Figure 8.9. The mean return of the portfolio is 10% and the standard deviation (calculated by taking the square root of the variance, which is the objective function value) is

$$\sigma = \sqrt{27.13615} = 5.209237$$

Assume that the portfolio scenario returns are normally distributed about the mean return. From the normal probability table, we see that less than 1% of the returns fall more than 2.33 standard deviations below the mean. This result implies a probability of 1% or less that a portfolio return will fall below

$$10 - (2.33)(5.209237) = -2.1375$$

Stated another way, if the initial value of the portfolio is $1, then the investor faces a probability of 1% of incurring a loss of 2.1375 cents or more. The value at risk is 2.1375 cents at 1%. This measure of risk is called the *value at risk,* or VaR. It was popularized by JPMorgan Chase & Co. in the early 1990s (then, just JP Morgan).

A table of normal probabilities appears in Appendix B, but they are also easily calculated in LINGO and Excel. In LINGO the function @PSN(Z) and the equivalent function NORMDIST in Excel provide the probability that a standard normal random variables is less than Z.

a. Consider the Markowitz portfolio problem given in equations (8.10) through (8.19). Delete the required return constraint (8.18), and reformulate this problem to minimize the VaR at 1%.

b. Is minimizing the VaR the same as minimizing the variances of the portfolio? Answer Yes or No, and justify.

c. For a fixed return, is minimizing the VaR the same as minimizing the variances of the portfolio? Answer Yes or No, and justify.

18. Options are popular instruments in the world of finance. A *call option* on a stock gives the owner the right to buy the stock at a predetermined price before the expiration date of the option. For example, on Friday, August 25, 2006, call options were selling for Procter & Gamble stock that gave the owner of the option the right to buy a share of stock for $60 on or before September 15, 2006. The asking price on the option was $1.45 at the market close. How are options priced? A pricing formula for options was developed by Fischer Black and Myron Scholes and published in 1973. Scholes was later awarded the Nobel Prize for this work in 1997 (Black was deceased). The Black-Scholes pricing model is widely used today by hedge funds and traders. The Black-Scholes formula for the price of a call option is

$$C = S\left[PSN(Z)\right] - Xe^{-rT}\left[PSN(Z - \sigma\sqrt{T}\,)\right]$$

where

C = market price of the call option
X = strike or exercise price of the stock
S = current price of the stock
r = annual risk-free interest rate
T = time to maturity of the option
σ = yearly standard deviation

In the Black-Scholes formula, $Z = [(r + \sigma^2/2)T + \ln(S/X)]/(\sigma\sqrt{T}\,)$ and $PSN(Z)$ is the probability of an observation of Z or less for a normal distribution with mean 0 and variance 1.

The purpose of this exercise is to price a Procter & Gamble call option offered on August 25, 2006. The option expires September 15, 2006, which includes 21 days between the market close on August 25, 2006, and the expiration of the option on September 15, 2006. Use the yield on three-month Treasury bills as the risk-free interest rate. As of August 25, 2006, this yield was 0.0494. The strike price on the option is $60 and at the market close on August 25, 2006, the stock was trading at $60.87. In order to use the

Black-Scholes formula, the yearly standard deviation, σ is required. One way to obtain this number is to estimate the weekly variance of Procter & Gamble, multiply the weekly variance by 52, and then take the square root to get the annual standard deviation. For this problem, use a weekly variance of 0.000479376. Use these data to calculate the option price using the Black-Scholes formula. For Friday, August 25, 2006, the actual bid on this option was $1.35 and actual ask was $1.45.

19. The port of Lajitas has three loading docks. The distance (in meters) between the loading docks is given in the following table:

	1	2	3
1	0	100	150
2	100	0	50
3	150	50	0

Three tankers currently at sea are coming into Lajitas. It is necessary to assign a dock for each tanker. Also, only one tanker can anchor in a given dock. Currently, ships 2 and 3 are empty and have no cargo. However, ship 1 has cargo that must be loaded onto the other two ships. The number of tons that must be transferred are as follows:

		To		
		1	2	3
From	1	0	60	80

Formulate and solve with Excel Solver or LINGO an optimization problem with binary decision variables (where 1 means an assignment and 0 means no assignment) that will assign ships to docks so that the product of tonnage moved times distance is minimized. (*Hints:* This problem is an extension of the assignment problem introduced in Chapter 6. Also, be careful with the objective function. Only include the nonzero terms. Each of the 12 nonzero terms in the objective function is a quadratic term, or the product of two variables.) There are 12 nonzero terms in the objective function.

This problem formulation is an example of a *quadratic assignment problem*. The quadratic assignment problem is a powerful model. It is used in a number of facility location problems and components on circuit boards. It is also used to assign jets to gates at airports to minimize product of passengers and distance walked.

20. Andalus Furniture Company has two manufacturing plants, one at Aynor and another at Spartanburg. The cost of producing Q_1 kitchen chairs at Aynor is:

$$75Q_1 + 5Q_1^2 + 100$$

and the cost of producing Q_2 kitchen chairs at Spartanburg is

$$25Q_2 + 2.5Q_2^2 + 150$$

Andalus needs to manufacture a total of 40 kitchen chairs to meet an order just received. How many chairs should be made at Aynor and how many should be made at Spartanburg in order to minimize total production cost?

21. The weekly box office revenues (in $ millions) for *Terminator 3* are given here. Use these data in the Bass forecasting model given by equations (8.21) through (8.23) to estimate the

parameters p, q, and m. Solve the model using Solver and see whether you can duplicate the results in Table 8.8.

Week	*Terminator 3*
1	72.39
2	37.93
3	17.58
4	9.57
5	5.39
6	3.13
7	1.62
8	0.87
9	0.61
10	0.26
11	0.19
12	0.35

The Bass forecasting model is a good example of a "hard" nonlinear program and the answer you get may be a local optimum that is not nearly as good as the result given in Table 8.8. If you find your results do not match those in Table 8.8, use the Multistart option as described in Appendix 8.2. Use a lower bound of -1 and an upper bound of 1 on both p and q. Use a lower bound of 100 and an upper bound of 1000 on m.

Case Problem 1 PORTFOLIO OPTIMIZATION WITH TRANSACTION COSTS[5]

Hauck Financial Services has a number of passive, buy-and-hold clients. For these clients, Hauck offers an investment account whereby clients agree to put their money into a portfolio of mutual funds that is rebalanced once a year. When the rebalancing occurs, Hauck determines the mix of mutual funds in each investor's portfolio by solving an extension of the Markowitz portfolio model that incorporates transaction costs. Investors are charged a small transaction cost for the annual rebalancing of their portfolio. For simplicity, assume the following:

- At the beginning of the time period (in this case one year), the portfolio is rebalanced by buying and selling Hauck mutual funds.
- The transaction costs associated with buying and selling mutual funds are paid at the beginning of the period when the portfolio is rebalanced, which, in effect, reduces the amount of money available to reinvest.
- No further transactions are made until the end of the time period, at which point the new value of the portfolio is observed.
- The transaction cost is a linear function of the dollar amount of mutual funds bought or sold.

---

[5]The authors appreciate helpful input from Linus Schrage on this case.

Jean Delgado is one of Hauck's buy-and-hold clients. We briefly describe the model as it is used by Hauck for rebalancing her portfolio. The mix of mutual funds that are being considered for her portfolio are a foreign stock fund (*FS*), an intermediate-term bond fund (*IB*), a large-cap growth fund (*LG*), a large-cap value fund (*LV*), a small-cap growth fund (*SG*), and a small-cap value fund (*SV*). In the traditional Markowitz model, the variables are usually interpreted as the *proportion* of the portfolio invested in the asset represented by the variable. For example, *FS* is the proportion of the portfolio invested in the foreign stock fund. However, it is equally correct to interpret *FS* as the dollar amount invested in the foreign stock fund. Then *FS* = 25,000 implies $25,000 is invested in the foreign stock fund. Based on these assumptions, the initial portfolio value must equal the amount of money spent on transaction costs plus the amount invested in all the assets after rebalancing. That is,

Initial portfolio value = Amount invested in all assets after rebalancing +
Transaction costs

The extension of the Markowitz model that Hauck uses for rebalancing portfolios requires a balance constraint for each mutual fund. This balance constraint is

Amount invested in fund *i* = Initial holding of fund *i* +
Amount of fund *i* purchased − Amount of fund *i* sold

Using this balance constraint requires three additional variables for each fund: one for the amount invested prior to rebalancing, one for the amount sold, and one for the amount purchased. For instance, the balance constraint for the foreign stock fund is

$$FS = FS\_START + FS\_BUY - FS\_SELL$$

Jean Delgado has $100,000 in her account prior to the annual rebalancing, and she has specified a minimum acceptable return of 10%. Hauck plans to use the following model to rebalance Ms. Delgado's portfolio. The complete model with transaction costs is

$$\text{Min } \tfrac{1}{5} \sum_{s=1}^{5} (R_s - \overline{R})^2$$

s.t.

$$0.1006FS + 0.1764IB + 0.3241LG + 0.3236LV + 0.3344SG + 0.2456SV = R1$$
$$0.1312FS + 3.25IB + 0.1871LG + 0.2061LV + 0.1940SG + 0.2532SV = R2$$
$$0.1347FS + 0.0751IB + 0.3328LG + 0.1293LV + 0.385SG - 0.0670SV = R3$$
$$0.4542FS - 0.0133IB + 0.4146LG + 0.0706LV + 0.5868SG + 0.0543SV = R4$$
$$-0.2193FS + 0.0736IB - 0.2326LG - 0.0537LV - 0.0902SG + 0.1731SV = R5$$

$$\tfrac{1}{5} \sum_{s=1}^{5} R_s = \overline{R}$$

$$\overline{R} \geq 10,000$$

$$FS + IB + LG + LV + SG + SV + TRANS\_COST = 100,000$$
$$FS\_START + FS\_BUY - FS\_SELL = FS$$
$$IB\_START + IB\_BUY - IB\_SELL = IB$$
$$LG\_START + LG\_BUY - LG\_SELL = LG$$
$$LV\_START + LV\_BUY - LV\_SELL = LV$$
$$SG\_START + SG\_BUY - SG\_SELL = SG$$
$$SV\_START + SV\_BUY - SV\_SELL = SV$$

$$TRANS\_FEE * (FS\_BUY + FS\_SELL + IB\_BUY + IB\_SELL +$$
$$LG\_BUY + LG\_SELL + LV\_BUY + LV\_SELL + SG\_BUY + SG\_SELL +$$
$$SV\_BUY + SV\_SELL) = TRANS\_COST$$
$$FS\_START = 10,000$$
$$IB\_START = 10,000$$
$$LG\_START = 10,000$$
$$LV\_START = 40,000$$
$$SG\_START = 10,000$$
$$SV\_START = 20,000$$
$$TRANS\_FEE = 0.01$$
$$FS, IB, LG, LV, SG, SV \geq 0$$

Notice that the transaction fee is set at 1% in the model (the last constraint) and that the transaction cost for buying and selling shares of the mutual funds is a linear function of the amount bought and sold. With this model, the transactions costs are deducted from the client's account at the time of rebalancing and thus reduce the amount of money invested. The LINGO solution for Ms. Delgado's rebalancing problem is shown in Figure 8.16.

Managerial Report

Assume you are a newly employed quantitative analyst hired by Hauck Financial Services. One of your first tasks is to review the portfolio rebalancing model in order to help resolve a dispute with Jean Delgado. Ms. Delgado has had one of the Hauck passively managed portfolios for the last five years and has complained that she is not getting the rate of return of 10% that she specified. After a review of her annual statements for the last five years, she feels that she is actually getting less than 10% on average.

1. According to the model solution in Figure 8.16, $IB\_BUY = \$41,268.51$. How much transaction cost did Ms. Delgado pay for purchasing additional shares of the intermediate-term bond fund?
2. Based on the model solution given in Figure 8.16, what is the total transaction cost associated with rebalancing Ms. Delgado's portfolio?
3. After paying transactions costs, how much did Ms. Delgado have invested in mutual funds after her portfolio was rebalanced?
4. According to the model solution in Figure 8.16, $IB = \$51,268.51$. How much can Ms. Delgado expect to have in the intermediate-term bond fund at the end of the year?
5. According to the model solution in Figure 8.16, the expected return of the portfolio is $10,000. What is the expected dollar amount in Ms. Delgado's portfolio at the end of the year? Can she expect to earn 10% on the $100,000 she had at the beginning of the year?
6. It is now time to prepare a report to management to explain why Ms. Delgado did not earn 10% each year on her investment. Make a recommendation in terms of a revised portfolio model that can be used so that Jean Delgado can have an expected portfolio balance of $110,000 at the end of next year. Prepare a report that includes a modified optimization model that will give an expected return of 10% on the amount of money available at the beginning of the year before paying the transaction costs. Explain why the current model does not do this.
7. Solve the formulation in part (6) for Jean Delgado. How does the portfolio composition differ from that shown in Figure 8.16?

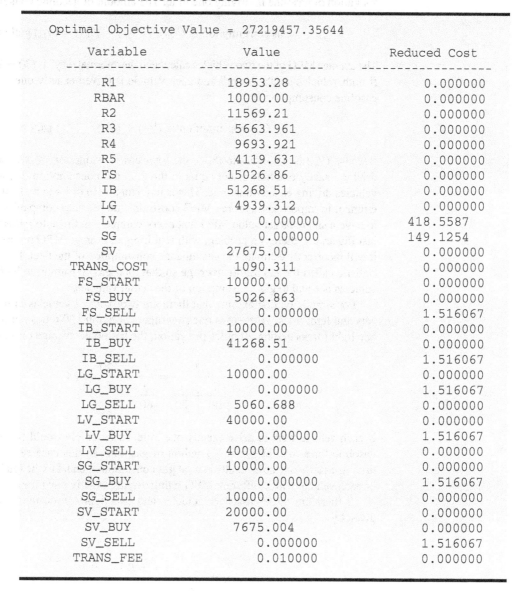

FIGURE 8.16   SOLUTION TO HAUCK MINIMUM VARIANCE PORTFOLIO WITH TRANSACTION COSTS

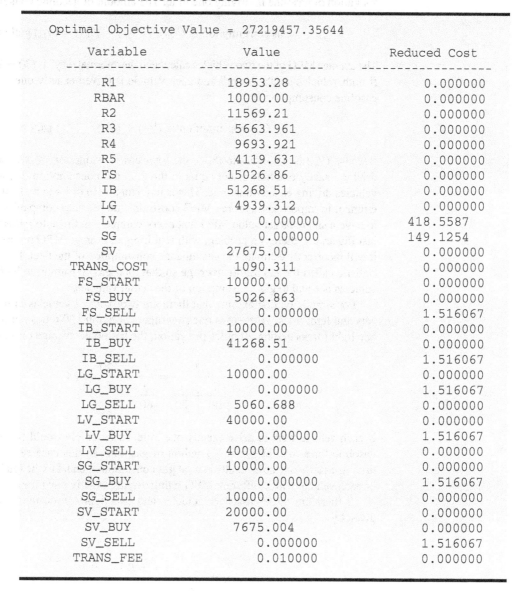

WEB file

HauckCase

```
Optimal Objective Value = 27219457.35644

         Variable              Value           Reduced Cost
       --------------    ------------------    --------------
             R1             18953.28              0.000000
            RBAR            10000.00              0.000000
             R2             11569.21              0.000000
             R3              5663.961             0.000000
             R4              9693.921             0.000000
             R5              4119.631             0.000000
             FS             15026.86              0.000000
             IB             51268.51              0.000000
             LG              4939.312             0.000000
             LV              0.000000            418.5587
             SG              0.000000            149.1254
             SV             27675.00              0.000000
         TRANS_COST          1090.311             0.000000
         FS_START          10000.00              0.000000
          FS_BUY            5026.863             0.000000
          FS_SELL           0.000000             1.516067
         IB_START          10000.00              0.000000
          IB_BUY           41268.51              0.000000
          IB_SELL           0.000000             1.516067
         LG_START          10000.00              0.000000
          LG_BUY            0.000000             1.516067
          LG_SELL           5060.688             0.000000
         LV_START          40000.00              0.000000
          LV_BUY            0.000000             1.516067
          LV_SELL          40000.00              0.000000
         SG_START          10000.00              0.000000
          SG_BUY            0.000000             1.516067
          SG_SELL          10000.00              0.000000
         SV_START          20000.00              0.000000
          SV_BUY            7675.004             0.000000
          SV_SELL           0.000000             1.516067
         TRANS_FEE          0.010000             0.000000
```

Case Problem 2   CAFE COMPLIANCE IN THE AUTO INDUSTRY

This case is based on the Management Science in Action, Pricing for Environmental Compliance in the Auto Industry. In this case we build a model similar to the one built for General Motors. The CAFE requirement on fleet miles per gallon is based on an average. The **harmonic average** is used to calculate the CAFE requirement on average miles per gallon.

In order to understand the harmonic average, assume that there is a passenger car and a light truck. The passenger car gets 30 miles per gallon (MPG) and the light truck gets 20 miles per gallon (MPG). Assume each vehicle is driven exactly one mile. Then the passenger car consumes $\frac{1}{30}$ gallon of gasoline in driving one mile and the light truck consumes $\frac{1}{20}$ gallon of gasoline in driving one mile. The amount of gasoline consumed in total is

$$\text{Gas consumption} = (\tfrac{1}{30}) + (\tfrac{1}{20}) = (\tfrac{5}{60}) = (\tfrac{1}{12}) \text{ gallon}$$

The average MPG of the two vehicles calculated the "normal way" is $(30 + 20)/2 = 25$ MPG. If both vehicles are "average," and each vehicle is driven exactly one mile, then the total gasoline consumption is

$$\text{Gas consumption} = (\tfrac{1}{25}) + (\tfrac{1}{25}) = (\tfrac{2}{25}) \text{ gallon}$$

Because $(\tfrac{2}{25})$ is not equal to $(\tfrac{5}{60})$, the total gas consumption of two "average vehicles" driving exactly one mile is not equal to the total gas consumption of each of the original vehicles driving exactly one mile. This is unfortunate. In order to make it easy for the government to impose and enforce MPG constraints on the auto companies, it would be nice to have a single target value MPG that every company in the auto industry must meet. As just illustrated, there is a problem with requiring an average MPG on the industry because it will incorrectly estimate the gas mileage consumption of the fleet. Fortunately, there is a statistic called the **harmonic average** so that total gas consumption by harmonic average vehicles is equal to gas consumption of the actual vehicles.

For simplicity, first assume that there are two types of vehicles in the fleet, passenger cars and light trucks. If there is one passenger car getting 30 miles per gallon and there is one light trucks getting 20 miles per gallon, the harmonic average of these two vehicles is

$$\frac{2}{\dfrac{1}{30} + \dfrac{1}{20}} = \frac{2}{\dfrac{5}{60}} = \frac{120}{5} = 24$$

If each vehicle were to drive exactly one mile, each vehicle would consume $\frac{1}{24}$ gallon of gasoline for a total of $\frac{2}{24} = \frac{1}{12}$ gallon of gasoline. In this case each "average" vehicle driving exactly one mile results in total gas consumption equal to the total gas consumption of each vehicle with a different MPG rating driving exactly one mile.

If there are three passenger vehicles and two light trucks, the harmonic average is given by

$$\frac{5}{\dfrac{3}{30} + \dfrac{2}{20}} = \frac{5}{0.1 + 0.1} = \frac{5}{0.2} = 25$$

In general, when calculating the harmonic average, the numerator is the total number of vehicles. The denominator is the sum of two terms. Each term is the ratio of the number of vehicles in that class to the MPG of cars in that class. For example, the first ratio in the denominator is $\frac{3}{30}$ because there are 3 cars (the numerator) each getting 30 MPG (the denominator). These calculations are illustrated in Figure 8.17.

Based on Figure 8.17, if each of the 5 cars is average and drives exactly one mile, $(\frac{5}{25}) = (\frac{1}{5})$ gallon of gas is consumed. If three cars getting 30 MPG drive exactly one mile each and two cars getting 20 MPG drive exactly one mile, then $(\frac{3}{30}) + (\frac{2}{20}) = (\frac{2}{10}) = (\frac{1}{5})$ gallon is consumed. Thus, the average cars exactly duplicate the gas consumption of the fleet with varying MPG.

FIGURE 8.17   AN EXCEL SPREADSHEET WITH A CAFÉ CALCULATION

	A	B	C	D
1			Number	
2		MPG	of Vehicles	Café Weight
3	Passenger Cars	30	3	0.1000
4	Light Trucks	20	3	0.1000
5			5	0.2000
6				
7	Café Average	25		

Now assume that the demand function for passenger cars is

$$\text{Demand} = 750 - P_C \qquad (8.24)$$

where P_C is the price of a passenger car. Similarly, the demand function for light trucks is

$$\text{Demand} = 830 - P_T \qquad (8.25)$$

where P_T is the price of a light truck.

Managerial Report

1. Using the formulas given in (8.24) and (8.25), develop an expression for the total profit contribution as a function of the price of cars and the price of light trucks.
2. Using Excel Solver or LINGO, find the price for each car so that the total profit contribution is maximized.
3. Given the prices determined in Question 2, calculate the number of passenger cars sold and the number of light trucks sold.
4. Duplicate the spreadsheet in Figure 8.17. Your spreadsheet should have formulas in cells D3:D5 and B7 and be able to calculate the harmonic (CAFE) average for any MPG rating and any number of vehicles in each category.
5. Again, assume that passenger cars get 30 MPG and light trucks get 20 MPG; calculate the CAFE average for the fleet size from part (3).
6. If you do the calculation in part (5) correctly, the CAFE average of the fleet is 23.57. Add a constraint that the fleet average must be 25 MPG and resolve the model to get the maximum total profit contribution subject to meeting the CAFE constraint.

Appendix 8.1 SOLVING NONLINEAR PROBLEMS WITH LINGO

Appendix 2.1 shows how to use LINGO to solve linear programs.

Solving a nonlinear optimization problem in LINGO is no different from solving a linear optimization problem in LINGO. Simply type in the formulation, select the **LINGO** menu and choose the **Solve** option. Just remember that LINGO uses the ^ sign for exponentiation and the / sign for division. Also note that an asterisk (*) must be used to indicate multiplication.

We show how the unconstrained Par, Inc., problem from Section 8.1 is solved using LINGO. After starting LINGO, we type in the problem formulation in the model window as follows:

$$\text{MAX} = 80*S - (1/15)*S^2 + 150*D - (1/5)*D^2;$$

The solution obtained is shown in Figure 8.18. To solve the problem, select the **Solve** command from the **LINGO** menu or press the **Solve** button on the toolbar. Note that the value of the objective function is 52125.00, $S = 600$, and $D = 375$.

Now solve the constrained Par, Inc., problem from Section 8.1 using LINGO. The only difference from the constrained problem is that four lines must be added to the formulation to account for the production constraints. After starting LINGO, we type in the problem formulation in the model window as follows.

$$\text{MAX} = 80*S - (1/15)*S^2 + 150*D - (1/5)*D^2;$$
$$(7/10)*S + D < 630;$$
$$(1/2)*S + (5/6)*D < 600;$$
$$S + (2/3)*D < 708;$$
$$(1/10)*S + (1/4)*D < 135;$$

Note that at the end of the objective function and each constraint a semicolon is used. After selecting the **Solve** command from the **LINGO** menu, the solution shown in Figure 8.2 is obtained.

In the Par, Inc., problem, all the variables are constrained to be nonnegative. If some of the variables may assume negative values, extra lines must be added to the LINGO formulation and the @FREE command must be used. For instance, the Hauck index fund model

FIGURE 8.18 THE LINGO OPTIMAL SOLUTION FOR THE UNCONSTRAINED PAR, INC., PROBLEM

```
Local optimal solution found.
   Objective value:                      52125.00
   Extended solver steps:                       5
   Total solver iterations:                    40

      Variable              Value          Reduced Cost
   --------------    ---------------     ----------------
             S            600.0000             0.000000
             D            375.0000             0.000000

           Row      Slack or Surplus           Dual Price
   --------------    ---------------     ----------------
             1            52125.00             1.000000
```

shown in Section 8.2 did not contain nonnegativity constraints for variables $R1, R2, R3, R4,$ and $R5$ because these variables are allowed to assume negative values. Thus, after entering the objective function and constraints, the following five lines must be added to the LINGO model to produce the solution shown in Figure 8.8.

$$\text{@FREE}(R1);$$
$$\text{@FREE}(R2);$$
$$\text{@FREE}(R3);$$
$$\text{@FREE}(R4);$$
$$\text{@FREE}(R5);$$

LINGO also provides the user with a wide variety of nonlinear functions that are useful in finance, inventory management, statistics, and other applications. To get a list of these functions, use the online LINGO User's Manual that is available under the Help menu. In the User's Manual you will find a chapter entitled "LINGO's Operators and Functions." This chapter contains a list of the available functions. When using a LINGO function you must precede the function name with the @ sign. For example, if you wanted to take the natural logarithm of X you would write @LOG(X).

The demo LINGO provided on the website accompanying this text allows only five variables for problems that use the global solver.

We have discussed the concept of global versus local optimum. By default, LINGO finds a local optimum and the global solver is turned off. In order to turn on the global solver, select **Options** from the **LINGO** menu. When the Options dialog box appears, select the **Global Solver** tab and check the **Use Global Solver** box.

When using LINGO one must exercise care in how the minus sign is used. When used in an expression such as $y - x^2$, the minus sign is a binary operator because it connects two terms y and x^2. By convention, exponentiation has higher "precedence" than the minus; so if $y = 2$ and $x = -1$, the expression $y - x^2$ evaluates to

$$y - x^2 = 2 - (-1)^2 = 2 - 1 = 1$$

However, in the expression $-x^2 + y$, the minus sign is a unary operator because it does not combine terms. LINGO, by default, assigns the unary minus sign higher precedence than exponentiation. Thus, if $y = 2$ and $x = -1$ the expression $-x^2 + y$ evaluates to

$$-x^2 + y = (-x)^2 + y = 1^2 + 2 = 3$$

This is a potential source of confusion. In this text we, like many authors, expect $-x^2$ to be interpreted as $-(x^2)$, not $(-x)^2$. Excel also treats the unary minus sign in this fashion.

Appendix 8.2 SOLVING NONLINEAR PROBLEMS WITH EXCEL SOLVER

Excel Solver can be used for nonlinear optimization. The Excel formulation of the nonlinear version of the Par, Inc., problem developed in Section 8.1 is shown in Figure 8.19. A worksheet model is constructed just as in the linear case. The formula in cell B18 is the objective function. The formulas in cells B21:B24 are the left-hand sides of constraint inequalities. And the formulas in cells D21:D24 provide the right-hand sides for the constraint inequalities.

Note how the nonlinearity comes into the model. The formula in cell B18, the objective function cell, is

$$=\text{B27*B16} + \text{B28*C16} - \text{B9*B16} - \text{C9*C16}$$

FIGURE 8.19   THE MODIFIED PAR, INC., PROBLEM IN EXCEL SOLVER

ParNonlinear

	A	B	C	D
1	Par, Inc.			
2				
3		Production Time		
4	Operation	Standard	Deluxe	Time Available
5	Cutting and Dyeing	0.7	1	630
6	Sewing	0.5	0.83333	600
7	Finishing	1	0.66667	708
8	Inspection and Packaging	0.1	0.25	135
9	Marginal Cost	70	150	
10				
11				
12	Model			
13				
14		Decision Variables		
15		Standard	Deluxe	
16	Bags Produced			
17				
18	Maximize Total Profit	=B27*B16+B28*C16-B9*B16-C9*C16		
19				
20	Constraints	Hours Used (LHS)		Hours Available (RHS)
21	Cutting and Dyeing	=B5*B16+C5*C16	<=	=D5
22	Sewing	=B6*B16+C6*C16	<=	=D6
23	Finishing	=B7*B16+C7*C16	<=	=D7
24	Inspection and Packaging	=B8*B16+C8*C16	<=	=D8
25				
26				
27	Standard Bag Price Function	=150-(1/15)*SB$16		
28	Deluxe Bag Price Function	=300-(1/15)*SC$16		

This formula takes the product of the variable cell B16 corresponding to the number of standard bags produced and multiplies it by cell B27 which is the price function for standard bags. But cell B27 also contains the standard bag variable cell B16 in the formula. This creates a nonlinear term and means Excel cannot solve using the standard LP Simplex Solver engine.

Refer to Figure 8.20, which is the **Solver Parameters** dialog box. To solve nonlinear models with Excel Solver, select **GRG Nonlinear** from the **Select a Solving Method** drop-down button. Solver uses a nonlinear algorithm known as the Generalized Reduced Gradient (GRG) technique. GRG uses a tool from calculus called the gradient. The gradient essentially calculates a direction of improvement for the objective function based on contour lines.

In Section 8.1, we discussed the difficulties associated with functions that have local optima. Excel Solver has an option that is helpful in overcoming local optimal solutions to find the globally optimal solution. The **Multistart** option is found by selecting the **Options** button from the **Solver Parameters** dialog box, selecting the **GRG Nonlinear** tab and selecting the **Multistart** checkbox from the **Multistart** section. This option works best when

FIGURE 8.20 THE MODIFIED PAR, INC., PROBLEM WITH SOLVER OPTIONS

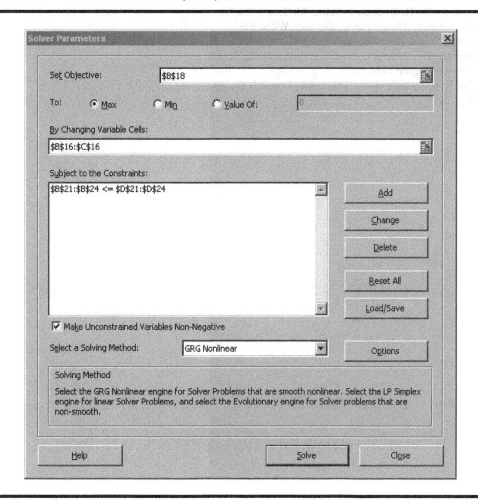

you can specify reasonable lower and upper bounds on each variable. In this case you should also select the **Require Bounds on Variables** checkbox in the **Multistart** section.

When using Excel, one must exercise care in how the minus sign is used. When used in a cell formula such as =A1 – B1^2, the minus sign is a binary operator because it connects two terms, A1 and B1^2. By convention, exponentiation has higher "precedence" than the minus, so if cell A1 contains 2 and cell B1 contains –1, the expression =A1 – B1^2 evaluates to

$$=A1 - B1^2 = 2 - (-1)^2 = 2 - 1 = 1$$

However, in the expression –B1^2 + A1, the minus sign is a unary operator because it does not combine terms. Excel, by default, assigns the unary minus sign higher precedence than exponentiation. Thus, if cell A1 contains 2 and cell B1 contains –1, the expression –B1^2 + A1 evaluates to

$$-B1^2 + A1 = (-B1)^2 + A1 + 1^2 + 2 = 3$$

LINGO also treats the unary minus sign in this fashion. This is a potential source of confusion. In this text we, like many authors, expect $-x^2$ to be interpreted as $-(x^2)$, not $(-x)^2$.

References and Bibliography

Bazarra, M. S., H. D. Sherali, and C. M. Shetty. *Nonlinear Programming Theory and Applications.* Wiley, 1993.

Benninga, Simon. *Financial Modeling.* MIT Press, 2000.

Luenberger, D. *Linear and Nonlinear Programming,* 2d ed. Addison-Wesley, 1984.

Rardin, R. L. *Optimization in Operations Research.* Prentice Hall, 1998.

Chapter 8

2. a. $X = 4.32$ and $Y = 0.92$, for an optimal solution value of 4.84.

   b. The dual value on the constraint $X + 4Y \leq 8$ is 0.88, which is the decrease in the optimal objective function value if we increase the right-hand-side from 8 to 9.

   c. The new optimal objective function value is 4.0, so the actual decrease is only 0.84 rather than 0.88.

4. a. $q_1 = 2150$
   $q_2 = 100$
   Gross profit = $1,235,000

   b. $G = -1.5p_1^2 - 0.5p_2^2 + p_1p_2 + 2000p_1 + 3450p_2 - 11,465,000$

   c. $p_1 = \$2725$ and $p_2 = \$6175$; $q_1 = 1185$ and $q_2 = 230$; $G = \$1,911,875$

   d. Max $p_1q_1 + p_2q_2 - c_1 - c_2$
   s.t.
   $c_1 = 10000 + 1500q_1$
   $c_2 = 30000 + 4000q_2$
   $q_1 = 950 - 1.5p_1 + 0.7p_2$
   $q_2 = 2500 + 0.3p_1 - 0.5p_2$

5. a. If $1000 is spent on radio and $1000 is spent on direct mail, simply substitute those values into the sales function:

   $$S = -2R^2 - 10M^2 - 8RM + 18R + 34M$$
   $$= -2(2^2) - 10(1^2) - 8(2)(1) + 18(2) + 34(1)$$
   $$= 18$$
   Sales = $18,000

   b. Max $-2R^2 - 10M^2 - 8RM + 18R + 34M$
   s.t.
   $R + M \leq 3$

   c. The optimal solution is Radio = $2500 and Direct mail = $500
   Total sales = $37,000

6. a. Without the global solver option turned on, LINGO returns $X = 4.978$ and $Y = 1.402$ for a value of 0.3088137E-08, which is a local minimum.

   b. With the global solver option turned on, the optimal solution (which is a global minimum) is $X = 0.228$ and $Y = -1.626$ for an objective function value of -6.551.

8. b. $L = 2244.281$ and $C = 2618.328$; Optimal solution = $374,046.9 (If Excel Solver is used for this problem, we recommend starting with an initial solution that has $L > 0$ and $C > 0$.)

10. a. Min $X^2 - X^2 + 5 + Y^2 + 2Y + 3$
    s.t.
    $X + Y = 8$
    $X, Y \geq 0$

    b. $X = 4.75$ and $Y = 3.25$; Optimal objective value = 42.875

11. The LINGO formulation:
    Min = (1/5)*((R1 − RBAR)^2 + (R2 − RBAR)^2 + (R3 − RBAR)^2 + (R4 − RBAR)^2 + (R5 − RBAR)^2;

.1006*FS + .1764*IB + .3241*LG + .3236*LV + .3344*SG + .2456*SV = R1;
.1312*FS + .0325*IB + .1871*LG + .2061*LV + .1940*SG + .2532*SV = R2;
.1347*FS + .0751*IB + .3328*LG + .1293*LV + .0385*SG + .0670*SV = R3;
.4542*FS + .0133*IB + .4146*LG + .0706*LV + .5868*SG + .0543*SV = R4;
−.2193*FS + .0736*IB + .2326*LG + .0537*LV + .0902*SG + .1731*SV = R5;

FS + IB + LG + LV + SG + SV = 50000;

(1/5)*(R1 + R2 + R3 + R4 + R5) = RBAR;

RBAR > RMIN;
RMIN = 5000;
@FREE(R1);
@FREE(R2);
@FREE(R3);
@FREE(R4);
@FREE(R5);

Optimal solution:

```
Local optimal solution found.
   Objective value:        6784038
   Total solver iterations:     19

Model Title: MARKOWITZ
   Variable          Value       Reduced Cost
      R1          9478.492         0.000000
     RBAR         5000.000         0.000000
      R2          5756.023         0.000000
      R3          2821.951         0.000000
      R4          4864.037         0.000000
      R5          2079.496         0.000000
      FS          7920.372         0.000000
      IB          26273.98         0.000000
      LG          2103.251         0.000000
      LV          0.000000         208.2068
      SG          0.000000         78.04764
      SV          13702.40         0.000000
     RMIN         5000.000         0.000000
```

(Excel Solver will produce the same optimal solution.)

12. Optimal value of $\alpha = 0.1743882$
    Sum of squared errors = 98.56

14. Optimal solution:

```
Local optimal solution found.
   Objective value:       0.1990478
   Total solver iterations:     12
   Model Title: MARKOWITZ

   Variable          Value       Reduced Cost
      R1          -0.1457056        0.000000
     RBAR          0.1518649        0.000000
      R2           0.7316081        0.000000
      R3           0.8905417        0.000000
      R4          -0.6823468E-02    0.000000
      R5          -0.3873745        0.000000
      R6          -0.5221017        0.000000
      R7           0.3499810        0.000000
      R8           0.2290317        0.000000
      R9           0.2276271        0.000000
     AAPL          0.1817734        0.000000
     AMD           0.1687534        0.000000
     ORCL          0.6494732        0.000000
```

15.

```
MODEL TITLE: MARKOWITZ;
! MINIMIZE VARIANCE OF THE PORTFOLIO;
MIN = (1/9) * ((R1 − RBAR)^2 + (R2 − RBAR)^2 + (R3 − RBAR)^2 +
(R4 − RBAR)^2 + (R5 − RBAR)^2 + (R6 − RBAR)^2 + (R7 − RBAR)^2 +
(R8 − RBAR)^2 + (R9 − RBAR)^2);

! SCENARIO 1 RETURN;
0.0962*AAPL − 0.5537*AMD − 0.1074*ORCL = R1;
! SCENARIO 2 RETURN;
0.8104*AAPL + 0.1272*AMD + 0.8666*ORCL = R2;
! SCENARIO 3 RETURN;
0.9236*AAPL + 0.4506*AMD + 0.9956*ORCL = R3;
! SCENARIO 4 RETURN;
−0.8753*AAPL + 0.3124*AMD + 0.1533*ORCL = R4;
! SCENARIO 5 RETURN;
0.1340*AAPL − 0.4270*AMD − 0.5230*ORCL = R5;
! SCENARIO 6 RETURN;
−0.5432*AAPL − 1.1194*AMD − 0.3610*ORCL = R6;
! SCENARIO 7 RETURN;
0.4517*AAPL + 1.0424*AMD + 0.1416*ORCL = R7;
! SCENARIO 8 RETURN;
1.2263*AAPL + 0.0613*AMD − 0.0065*ORCL = R8;
! SCENARIO 9 RETURN;
0.6749*AAPL + 0.9729*AMD − 0.0912*ORCL = R9;
! MUST BE FULLY INVESTED IN THE MUTUAL FUNDS;
AAPL + AMD + ORCL = 1;
! DEFINE THE MEAN RETURN;
(1/9) * (R1 + R2 + R3 + R4 + R5 + R6 + R7 + R8 + R9) = RBAR;
! THE MEAN RETURN MUST BE AT LEAST 10 PERCENT;
RBAR > 0.12;
! SCENARIO RETURNS MAY BE NEGATIVE;
@FREE(R1);
@FREE(R2);
@FREE(R3);
@FREE(R4);
@FREE(R5);
@FREE(R6);
@FREE(R7);
@FREE(R8);
@FREE(R9);
END
```

Optimal solution:

```
Local optimal solution found.
   Objective value:      0.4120213
   Total solver iterations:    8

   Model Title: MATCHING S&P INFO TECH
   RETURNS

      Variable       Value      Reduced Cost
        R1       −0.5266475E-01    0.000000
        R2        0.8458175        0.000000
        R3        0.9716207        0.000000
        R4       −0.1370104        0.000000
        R5       −0.3362695        0.000000
        R6       −0.4175977        0.000000
        R7        0.2353628        0.000000
        R8        0.3431437        0.000000
        R9        0.1328016        0.000000
       AAPL       0.2832558        0.000000
       AMD        0.6577707E-02    0.000000
       ORCL       0.7101665        0.000000
```

(Excel Solver produces the same return.)

16. Optimal solution:

```
Local optimal solution found.
   Objective value:      7.503540
   Total solver iterations:    18

Model Title: MARKOWITZ WITH SEMIVARIANCE

      Variable       Value      Reduced Cost
        D1N       0.000000        0.000000
        D2N       0.8595142       0.000000
        D3N       3.412762        0.000000
        D4N       2.343876        0.000000
        D5N       4.431505        0.000000
        FS        0.000000        6.491646
        IB        0.6908001       0.000000
        LG        0.6408726E-01   0.000000
        LV        0.000000        14.14185
        SG        0.8613837E-01   0.000000
        SV        0.1589743       0.000000
        R1        21.04766        0.000000
        R2        9.140486        0.000000
        R3        6.587238        0.000000
        R4        7.656124        0.000000
        R5        5.568495        0.000000
        RBAR      10.00000        0.000000
        RMIN      10.00000        0.000000
        D1P       11.04766        0.000000
        D2P       0.000000        0.3438057
        D3P       0.000000        1.365105
        D4P       0.000000        0.9375505
        D5P       0.000000        1.772602
```

The solution calls for investing 69.1% of the portfolio in the intermediate-term bond fund, 6.4% in the large-cap growth fund, 8.6% in the small-cap growth fund, and 15.9% in the small-cap value fund.

(Excel Solver may have trouble with this problem, depending upon the starting solution that is used; a starting solution of each fund at 0.167 will produce the optimal value.)

18. Call option price for Friday, August 25, 2006, is approximately $C = \$1.524709$.

20. Optimal solution: Produce 10 chairs at Aynor, cost = $1350; 30 chairs at Spartanburg, cost = $3150; Total cost = $4500

Project Scheduling: PERT/CPM

CONTENTS

In many situations, managers are responsible for planning, scheduling, and controlling projects that consist of numerous separate jobs or tasks performed by a variety of departments and individuals. Often these projects are so large or complex that the manager cannot possibly remember all the information pertaining to the plan, schedule, and progress of the project. In these situations the **program evaluation and review technique (PERT)** and the **critical path method (CPM)** have proven to be extremely valuable.

PERT and CPM can be used to plan, schedule, and control a wide variety of projects:

Henry L. Gantt developed the Gantt Chart as a graphical aid to scheduling jobs on machines in 1918. This application was the first of what has become known as project scheduling techniques.

1. Research and development of new products and processes
2. Construction of plants, buildings, and highways
3. Maintenance of large and complex equipment
4. Design and installation of new systems

In these types of projects, project managers must schedule and coordinate the various jobs or **activities** so that the entire project is completed on time. A complicating factor in carrying out this task is the interdependence of the activities; for example, some activities depend on the completion of other activities before they can be started. Because projects may have as many as several thousand activities, project managers look for procedures that will help them answer questions such as the following:

1. What is the total time to complete the project?
2. What are the scheduled start and finish dates for each specific activity?
3. Which activities are "critical" and must be completed *exactly* as scheduled to keep the project on schedule?
4. How long can "noncritical" activities be delayed before they cause an increase in the total project completion time?

PERT and CPM can help answer these questions.

PERT (Navy) and CPM (DuPont and Remington Rand) differ because they were developed by different people working on different projects. Today, the best aspects of each have been combined to provide a valuable project scheduling technique.

Although PERT and CPM have the same general purpose and utilize much of the same terminology, the techniques were developed independently. PERT was developed in the late 1950s specifically for the Polaris missile project. Many activities associated with this project had never been attempted previously, so PERT was developed to handle uncertain activity times. CPM was developed primarily for industrial projects for which activity times were known. CPM offered the option of reducing activity times by adding more workers and/or resources, usually at an increased cost. Thus, a distinguishing feature of CPM was that it identified trade-offs between time and cost for various project activities.

Today's computerized versions of PERT and CPM combine the best features of both approaches. Thus, the distinction between the two techniques is no longer necessary. As a result, we refer to the project scheduling procedures covered in this chapter as PERT/CPM. We begin the discussion of PERT/CPM by considering a project for the expansion of the Western Hills Shopping Center. At the end of the section we describe how the investment securities firm of Seasongood & Mayer used PERT/CPM to schedule a $31 million hospital revenue bond project.

9.1 PROJECT SCHEDULING WITH KNOWN ACTIVITY TIMES

The owner of the Western Hills Shopping Center is planning to modernize and expand the current 32-business shopping center complex. The project is expected to provide room for 8 to 10 new businesses. Financing has been arranged through a private investor. All that remains is for the owner of the shopping center to plan, schedule, and complete the expansion project. Let us show how PERT/CPM can help.

TABLE 9.1   LIST OF ACTIVITIES FOR THE WESTERN HILLS SHOPPING CENTER PROJECT

Activity	Activity Description	Immediate Predecessor	Activity Time
A	Prepare architectural drawings	—	5
B	Identify potential new tenants	—	6
C	Develop prospectus for tenants	A	4
D	Select contractor	A	3
E	Prepare building permits	A	1
F	Obtain approval for building permits	E	4
G	Perform construction	D, F	14
H	Finalize contracts with tenants	B, C	12
I	Tenants move in	G, H	2
		Total	51

The effort that goes into identifying activities, determining interrelationships among activities, and estimating activity times is crucial to the success of PERT/CPM. A significant amount of time may be needed to complete this initial phase of the project scheduling process.

Immediate predecessor information determines whether activities can be completed in parallel (worked on simultaneously) or in series (one completed before another begins). Generally, the more series relationships present in a project, the more time will be required to complete the project.

A project network is extremely helpful in visualizing the interrelationships among the activities. No rules guide the conversion of a list of activities and immediate predecessor information into a project network. The process of constructing a project network generally improves with practice and experience.

The first step in the PERT/CPM scheduling process is to develop a list of the activities that make up the project. Table 9.1 shows the list of activities for the Western Hills Shopping Center expansion project. Nine activities are described and denoted A through I for later reference. Table 9.1 also shows the immediate predecessor(s) and the activity time (in weeks) for each activity. For a given activity, the **immediate predecessor** column identifies the activities that must be completed *immediately prior* to the start of that activity. Activities A and B do not have immediate predecessors and can be started as soon as the project begins; thus, a dash is written in the immediate predecessor column for these activities. The other entries in the immediate predecessor column show that activities C, D, and E cannot be started until activity A has been completed; activity F cannot be started until activity E has been completed; activity G cannot be started until both activities D and F have been completed; activity H cannot be started until both activities B and C have been completed; and, finally, activity I cannot be started until both activities G and H have been completed. The project is finished when activity I is completed.

The last column in Table 9.1 shows the number of weeks required to complete each activity. For example, activity A takes 5 weeks, activity B takes 6 weeks, and so on. The sum of activity times is 51. As a result, you may think that the total time required to complete the project is 51 weeks. However, as we show, two or more activities often may be scheduled concurrently, thus shortening the completion time for the project. Ultimately, PERT/CPM will provide a detailed activity schedule for completing the project in the shortest time possible.

Using the immediate predecessor information in Table 9.1, we can construct a graphical representation of the project, or the **project network.** Figure 9.1 depicts the project network for Western Hills Shopping Center. The activities correspond to the *nodes* of the network (drawn as rectangles), and the *arcs* (the lines with arrows) show the precedence relationships among the activities. In addition, nodes have been added to the network to denote the start and the finish of the project. A project network will help a manager visualize the activity relationships and provide a basis for carrying out the PERT/CPM computations.

The Concept of a Critical Path

To facilitate the PERT/CPM computations, we modified the project network as shown in Figure 9.2. Note that the upper left-hand corner of each node contains the corresponding activity letter. The activity time appears immediately below the letter.

FIGURE 9.1   PROJECT NETWORK FOR THE WESTERN HILLS SHOPPING CENTER

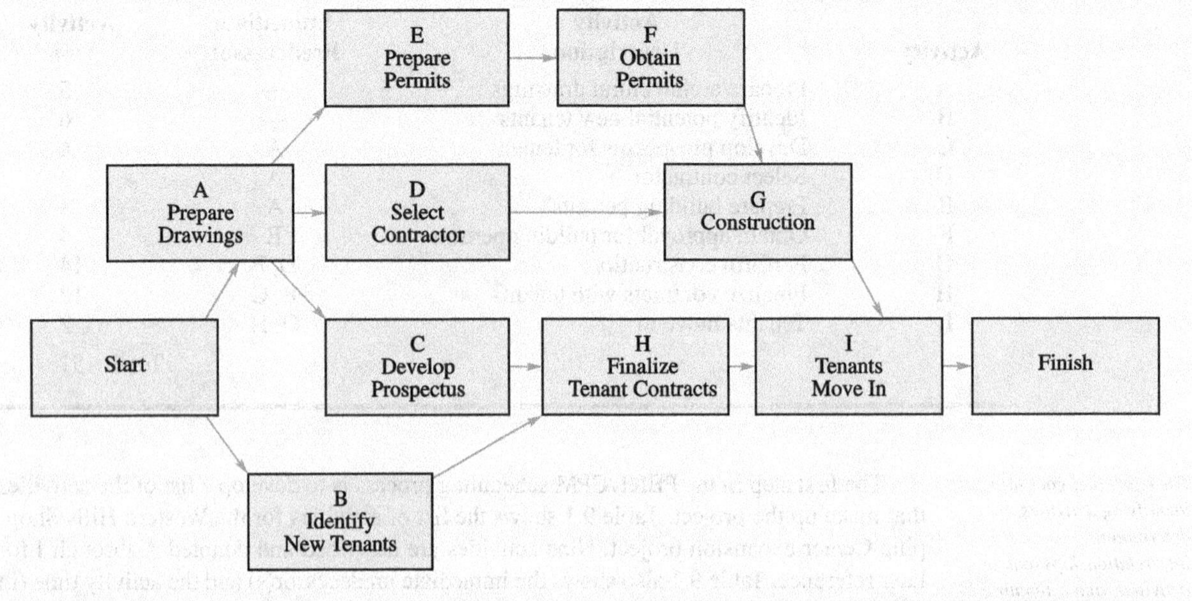

FIGURE 9.2   WESTERN HILLS SHOPPING CENTER PROJECT NETWORK WITH ACTIVITY TIMES

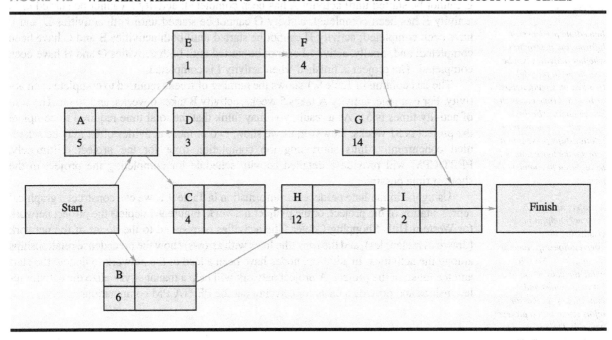

Problem 3 provides the immediate predecessor information for a project with seven activities and asks you to develop the project network.

For convenience, we use the convention of referencing activities with letters. Generally, we assign the letters in approximate order as we move from left to right through the project network.

To determine the project completion time, we have to analyze the network and identify what is called the **critical path** for the network. However, before doing so, we need to define the concept of a path through the network. A **path** is a sequence of connected nodes that leads from the Start node to the Finish node. For instance, one path for the network in Figure 9.2 is defined by the sequence of nodes A–E–F–G–I. By inspection, we see that other paths are possible, such as A–D–G–I, A–C–H–I, and B–H–I. All paths in the network must be traversed in order to complete the project, so we will look for the path that requires the most time. Because all other paths are shorter in duration, this *longest* path determines the total time required to complete the project. If activities on the longest path are delayed, the entire project will be delayed. Thus, the longest path is the *critical path*. Activities on the critical path are referred to as the **critical activities** for the project. The following discussion presents a step-by-step algorithm for finding the critical path in a project network.

Determining the Critical Path

We begin by finding the **earliest start time** and a **latest start time** for all activities in the network. Let

$$ES = \text{earliest start time for an activity}$$
$$EF = \text{earliest finish time for an activity}$$
$$t = \text{activity time}$$

The **earliest finish time** for any activity is

$$EF = ES + t \tag{9.1}$$

Activity A can start as soon as the project starts, so we set the earliest start time for activity A equal to 0. With an activity time of 5 weeks, the earliest finish time for activity A is $EF = ES + t = 0 + 5 = 5$.

We will write the earliest start and earliest finish times in the node to the right of the activity letter. Using activity A as an example, we have

Because an activity cannot be started until *all* immediately preceding activities have been finished, the following rule can be used to determine the earliest start time for each activity:

The earliest start time for an activity is equal to the *largest* of the earliest finish times for all its immediate predecessors.

Let us apply the earliest start time rule to the portion of the network involving nodes A, B, C, and H, as shown in Figure 9.3. With an earliest start time of 0 and an activity time of 6 for activity B, we show $ES = 0$ and $EF = ES + t = 0 + 6 = 6$ in the node for activity B. Looking at node C, we note that activity A is the only immediate predecessor for activity C.

695

FIGURE 9.3 A PORTION OF THE WESTERN HILLS SHOPPING CENTER PROJECT
NETWORK, SHOWING ACTIVITIES A, B, C, AND H

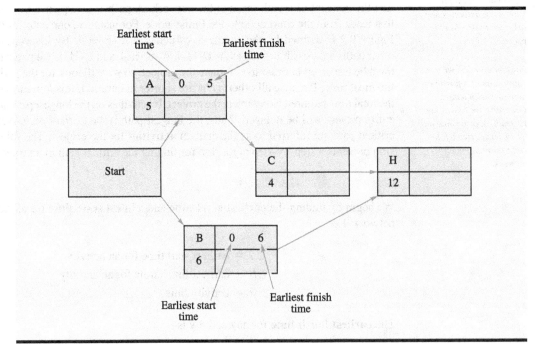

The earliest finish time for activity A is 5, so the earliest start time for activity C must be $ES = 5$. Thus, with an activity time of 4, the earliest finish time for activity C is $EF = ES + t = 5 + 4 = 9$. Both the earliest start time and the earliest finish time can be shown in the node for activity C (see Figure 9.4).

Continuing with Figure 9.4, we move on to activity H and apply the earliest start time rule for this activity. With both activities B and C as immediate predecessors, the earliest start time for activity H must be equal to the largest of the earliest finish times for activities B and C. Thus, with $EF = 6$ for activity B and $EF = 9$ for activity C, we select the largest value, 9, as the earliest start time for activity H ($ES = 9$). With an activity time of 12, as shown in the node for activity H, the earliest finish time is $EF = ES + t = 9 + 12 = 21$. The $ES = 9$ and $EF = 21$ values can now be entered in the node for activity H in Figure 9.4.

Continuing with this **forward pass** through the network, we can establish the earliest start times and the earliest finish times for all activities in the network. Figure 9.5 shows the Western Hills Shopping Center project network with the ES and EF values for each activity. Note that the earliest finish time for activity I, the last activity in the project, is 26 weeks. Therefore, we now know that the total completion time for the project is 26 weeks.

We now continue the algorithm for finding the critical path by making a **backward pass** through the network. Because the total completion time for the project is 26 weeks, we begin the backward pass with a **latest finish time** of 26 for activity I. Once the latest finish time for an activity is known, the *latest start time* for an activity can be computed as follows. Let

LS = latest start time for an activity

LF = latest finish time for an activity

Then

$$LS = LF - t \qquad (9.2)$$

696

FIGURE 9.4 DETERMINING THE EARLIEST START TIME FOR ACTIVITY H

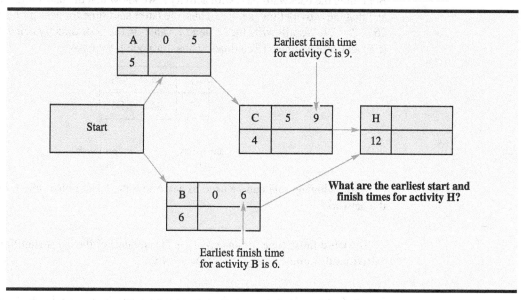

FIGURE 9.5 WESTERN HILLS SHOPPING CENTER PROJECT NETWORK WITH EARLIEST START AND EARLIEST FINISH TIMES SHOWN FOR ALL ACTIVITIES

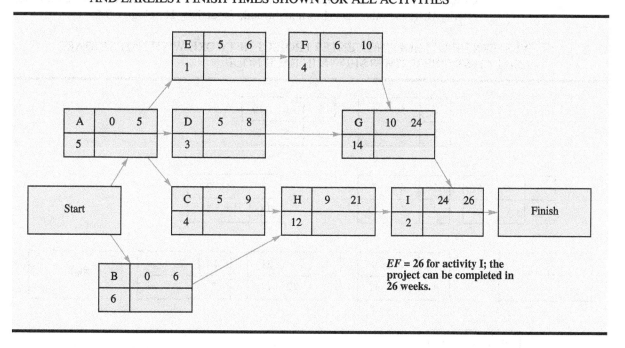

Beginning the backward pass with activity I, we know that the latest finish time is $LF = 26$ and that the activity time is $t = 2$. Thus, the latest start time for activity I is $LS = LF - t = 26 - 2 = 24$. We will write the LS and LF values in the node directly below the earliest start (ES) and earliest finish (EF) times. Thus, for node I, we have

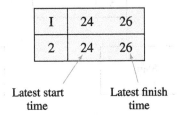

Latest start   Latest finish
time   time

The following rule can be used to determine the latest finish time for each activity in the network:

> The latest finish time for an activity is the smallest of the latest start times for all activities that immediately follow the activity.

Logically, this rule states that the latest time an activity can be finished equals the earliest (smallest) value for the latest start time of the following activities. Figure 9.6 shows the complete project network with the LS and LF backward pass results. We can use the latest finish time rule to verify the LS and LF values shown for activity H. The latest finish time for activity H must be the latest start time for activity I. Thus, we set $LF = 24$ for activity H. Using equation (9.2), we find that $LS = LF - t = 24 - 12 = 12$ as the latest start time for activity H. These values are shown in the node for activity H in Figure 9.6.

FIGURE 9.6   WESTERN HILLS SHOPPING CENTER PROJECT NETWORK WITH LATEST START AND LATEST FINISH TIMES SHOWN IN EACH NODE

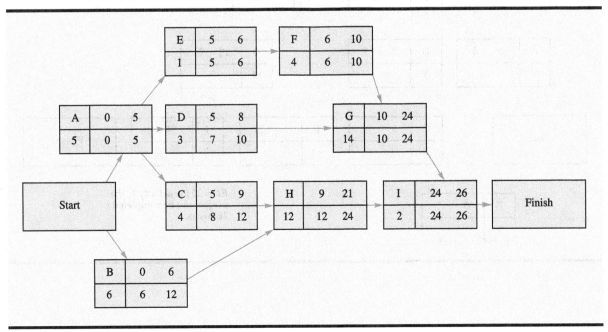

Activity A requires a more involved application of the latest start time rule. First, note that three activities (C, D, and E) immediately follow activity A. Figure 9.6 shows that the latest start times for activities C, D, and E are $LS = 8$, $LS = 7$, and $LS = 5$, respectively. The latest finish time rule for activity A states that the LF for activity A is the smallest of the latest start times for activities C, D, and E. With the smallest value being 5 for activity E, we set the latest finish time for activity A to $LF = 5$. Verify this result and the other latest start times and latest finish times shown in the nodes in Figure 9.6.

The slack for each activity indicates the length of time the activity can be delayed without increasing the project completion time.

After we complete the forward and backward passes, we can determine the amount of slack associated with each activity. **Slack** is the length of time an activity can be delayed without increasing the project completion time. The amount of slack for an activity is computed as follows:

$$\text{Slack} = LS - ES = LF - EF \qquad (9.3)$$

For example, the slack associated with activity C is $LS - ES = 8 - 5 = 3$ weeks. Hence, activity C can be delayed up to 3 weeks, and the entire project can still be completed in 26 weeks. In this sense, activity C is not critical to the completion of the entire project in 26 weeks. Next, we consider activity E. Using the information in Figure 9.6, we find that the slack is $LS - ES = 5 - 5 = 0$. Thus, activity E has zero, or no, slack. Thus, this activity cannot be delayed without increasing the completion time for the entire project. In other words, completing activity E exactly as scheduled is critical in terms of keeping the project on schedule. Thus, activity E is a critical activity. In general, the *critical activities* are the activities with zero slack.

One of the primary contributions of PERT/CPM is the identification of the critical activities. The project manager will want to monitor critical activities closely because a delay in any one of these activities will lengthen the project completion time.

The start and finish times shown in Figure 9.6 can be used to develop a detailed start time and finish time schedule for all activities. Putting this information in tabular form provides the activity schedule shown in Table 9.2. Note that the slack column shows that activities A, E, F, G, and I have zero slack. Hence, these activities are the critical activities for the project. The path formed by nodes A–E–F–G–I is the *critical path* in the Western Hills Shopping Center project network. The detailed schedule shown in Table 9.2 indicates the slack or delay that can be tolerated for the noncritical activities before these activities will increase project completion time.

The critical path algorithm is essentially a longest path algorithm. From the start node to the finish node, the critical path identifies the path that requires the most time.

Contributions of PERT/CPM

If the total time required to complete the project is too long, judgment about where and how to shorten the time of critical activities must be exercised. If any activity times are altered, the critical path calculations should be repeated to determine the impact on the activity schedule and the impact on total project completion time. In Section 9.3 we show how to use linear programming to find the least-cost way to shorten the project completion time.

Previously, we stated that project managers look for procedures that will help answer important questions regarding the planning, scheduling, and controlling of projects. Let us reconsider these questions in light of the information that the critical path calculations have given us.

1. How long will the project take to complete?
   Answer: The project can be completed in 26 weeks if each activity is completed on schedule.
2. What are the scheduled start and completion times for each activity?
   Answer: The activity schedule (see Table 9.2) shows the earliest start, latest start, earliest finish, and latest finish times for each activity.
3. Which activities are critical and must be completed *exactly* as scheduled to keep the project on schedule?
   Answer: A, E, F, G, and I are the critical activities.
4. How long can noncritical activities be delayed before they cause an increase in the completion time for the project?
   Answer: The activity schedule (see Table 9.2) shows the slack associated with each activity.

TABLE 9.2 ACTIVITY SCHEDULE FOR THE WESTERN HILLS SHOPPING
CENTER PROJECT

Activity	Earliest Start (ES)	Latest Start (LS)	Earliest Finish (EF)	Latest Finish (LF)	Slack (LS − ES)	Critical Path?
A	0	0	5	5	0	Yes
B	0	6	6	12	6	
C	5	8	9	12	3	
D	5	7	8	10	2	
E	5	5	6	6	0	Yes
F	6	6	10	10	0	Yes
G	10	10	24	24	0	Yes
H	9	12	21	24	3	
I	24	24	26	26	0	Yes

Software packages such as Microsoft Office Project perform the critical path calculations quickly and efficiently. The project manager can modify any aspect of the project and quickly determine how the modification affects the activity schedule and the total time required to complete the project.

Such information is valuable in managing any project. Although larger projects usually increase the effort required to develop the immediate predecessor relationships and the activity time estimates, the procedure and contribution of PERT/CPM to larger projects are identical to those shown for the shopping center expansion project. The Management Science in Action, Hospital Revenue Bond at Seasongood & Mayer, describes a 23-activity project that introduced a $31-million hospital revenue bond. PERT/CPM identified the critical activities, the expected project completion time of 29 weeks, and the activity start times and finish times necessary to keep the entire project on schedule.

Finally, computer packages may be used to carry out the steps of the PERT/CPM procedure. Figure 9.7 shows the activity schedule for the shopping center expansion project produced by Microsoft Office Project. Input to the program included the activities, their immediate predecessors, and the expected activity times. Microsoft Office Project automatically generates the critical path and activity schedule. More details are provided in Appendix 9.1.

Summary of the PERT/CPM Critical Path Procedure

Before leaving this section, let us summarize the PERT/CPM critical path procedure.
Step 1. Develop a list of the activities that make up the project.
Step 2. Determine the immediate predecessor(s) for each activity in the project.
Step 3. Estimate the completion time for each activity.

FIGURE 9.7 MICROSOFT OFFICE PROJECT ACTIVITY SCHEDULE FOR THE WESTERN HILLS
SHOPPING CENTER PROJECT

Step 4. Draw a project network depicting the activities and immediate predecessors listed in steps 1 and 2.

Step 5. Use the project network and the activity time estimates to determine the earliest start and the earliest finish time for each activity by making a forward pass through the network. The earliest finish time for the last activity in the project identifies the total time required to complete the project.

Step 6. Use the project completion time identified in step 5 as the latest finish time for the last activity and make a backward pass through the network to identify the latest start and latest finish time for each activity.

Step 7. Use the difference between the latest start time and the earliest start time for each activity to determine the slack for each activity.

Step 8. Find the activities with zero slack; these are the critical activities.

Step 9. Use the information from steps 5 and 6 to develop the activity schedule for the project.

MANAGEMENT SCIENCE IN ACTION

HOSPITAL REVENUE BOND AT SEASONGOOD & MAYER

Seasongood & Mayer is an investment securities firm located in Cincinnati, Ohio. The firm engages in municipal financing, including the underwriting of new issues of municipal bonds, acting as a market maker for previously issued bonds, and performing other investment banking services.

Seasongood & Mayer provided the underwriting for a $31-million issue of hospital facilities revenue bonds for Providence Hospital in Hamilton County, Ohio. The project of underwriting this municipal bond issue began with activities such as drafting the legal documents, drafting a description of the existing hospital facilities, and completing a feasibility study. A total of 23 activities defined the project that would be completed when the hospital signed the construction contract and then made the bond proceeds available. The immediate predecessor relationships for the activities and the activity times were developed by a project management team.

PERT/CPM analysis of the project network identified the 10 critical path activities. The analysis also provided the expected completion time of 29 weeks, or approximately seven months. The activity schedule showed the start time and finish time for each activity and provided the information necessary to monitor the project and keep it on schedule. PERT/CPM was instrumental in helping Seasongood & Mayer obtain the financing for the project within the time specified in the construction bid.

NOTES AND COMMENTS

Suppose that, after analyzing a PERT/CPM network, the project manager finds that the project completion time is unacceptable (i.e., the project is going to take too long). In this case, the manager must take one or both of the following steps. First, review the original PERT/CPM network to see whether any immediate predecessor relationships can be modified so that at least some of the critical path activities can be done simultaneously. Second, consider adding resources to critical path activities in an attempt to shorten the critical path; we discuss this alternative, referred to as *crashing*, in Section 9.3.

9.2 PROJECT SCHEDULING WITH UNCERTAIN ACTIVITY TIMES

In this section we consider the details of project scheduling for a problem involving new-product research and development. Because many of the activities in this project have never been attempted, the project manager wants to account for uncertainties in the activity times. Let us show how project scheduling can be conducted with uncertain activity times.

The Daugherty Porta-Vac Project

Accurate activity time estimates are important in the development of an activity schedule. When activity times are uncertain, the three time estimates—optimistic, most probable, and pessimistic—allow the project manager to take uncertainty into consideration in determining the critical path and the activity schedule. This approach was developed by the designers of PERT.

The H. S. Daugherty Company has manufactured industrial vacuum cleaning systems for many years. Recently, a member of the company's new-product research team submitted a report suggesting that the company consider manufacturing a cordless vacuum cleaner. The new product, referred to as Porta-Vac, could contribute to Daugherty's expansion into the household market. Management hopes that it can be manufactured at a reasonable cost and that its portability and no-cord convenience will make it extremely attractive.

Daugherty's management wants to study the feasibility of manufacturing the Porta-Vac product. The feasibility study will recommend the action to be taken. To complete this study, information must be obtained from the firm's research and development (R&D), product testing, manufacturing, cost estimating, and market research groups. How long will this feasibility study take? In the following discussion, we show how to answer this question and provide an activity schedule for the project.

Again, the first step in the project scheduling process is to identify all activities that make up the project and then determine the immediate predecessor(s) for each activity. Table 9.3 shows these data for the Porta-Vac project.

The Porta-Vac project network is shown in Figure 9.8. Verify that the network does in fact maintain the immediate predecessor relationships shown in Table 9.3.

Uncertain Activity Times

Once we develop the project network, we will need information on the time required to complete each activity. This information is used in the calculation of the total time required to complete the project and in the scheduling of specific activities. For repeat projects, such as construction and maintenance projects, managers may have the experience and historical data necessary to provide accurate activity time estimates. However, for new or unique projects, estimating the time for each activity may be quite difficult. In fact, in many cases activity times are uncertain and are best described by a range of possible values rather than by one specific time estimate. In these instances, the uncertain activity times are treated as random variables with associated probability distributions. As a result, probability statements will be provided about the ability to meet a specific project completion date.

TABLE 9.3   ACTIVITY LIST FOR THE PORTA-VAC PROJECT

Activity	Description	Immediate Predecessor
A	Develop product design	—
B	Plan market research	—
C	Prepare routing (manufacturing engineering)	A
D	Build prototype model	A
E	Prepare marketing brochure	A
F	Prepare cost estimates (industrial engineering)	C
G	Do preliminary product testing	D
H	Complete market survey	B, E
I	Prepare pricing and forecast report	H
J	Prepare final report	F, G, I

FIGURE 9.8   PORTA-VAC CORDLESS VACUUM CLEANER PROJECT NETWORK

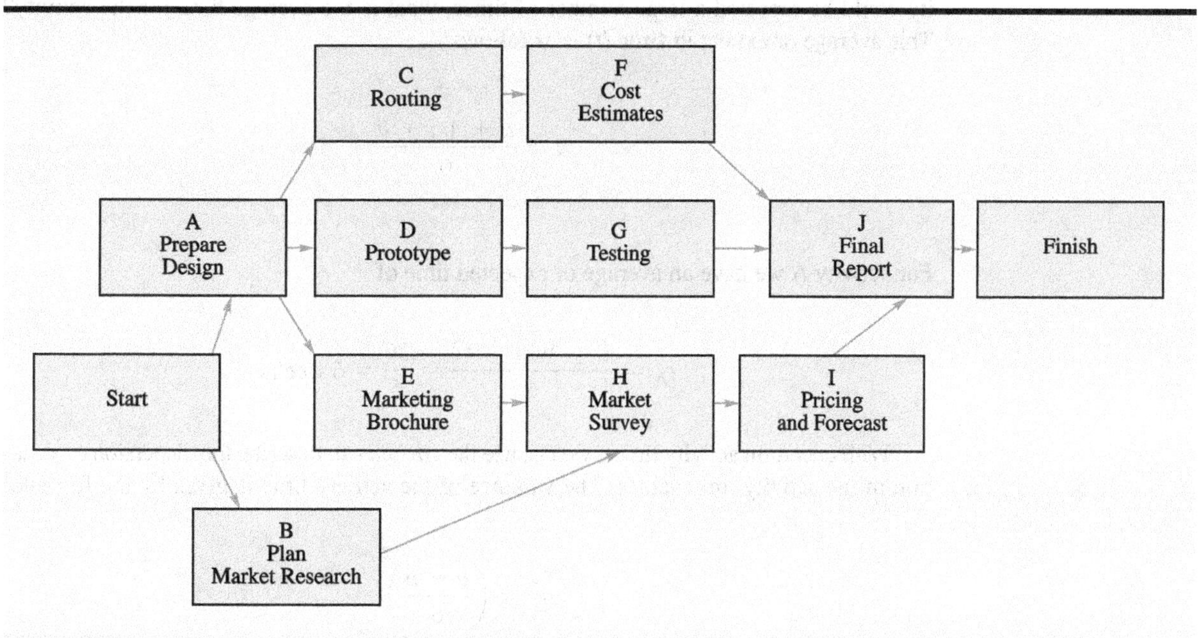

To incorporate uncertain activity times into the analysis, we need to obtain three time estimates for each activity:

Optimistic time a = the minimum activity time if everything progresses ideally
Most probable time m = the most probable activity time under normal conditions
Pessimistic time b = the maximum activity time if significant delays are encountered

To illustrate the PERT/CPM procedure with uncertain activity times, let us consider the optimistic, most probable, and pessimistic time estimates for the Porta-Vac activities as presented in Table 9.4. Using activity A as an example, we see that the most probable time

TABLE 9.4   OPTIMISTIC, MOST PROBABLE, AND PESSIMISTIC ACTIVITY TIME ESTIMATES (IN WEEKS) FOR THE PORTA-VAC PROJECT

Activity	Optimistic (*a*)	Most Probable (*m*)	Pessimistic (*b*)
A	4	5	12
B	1	1.5	5
C	2	3	4
D	3	4	11
E	2	3	4
F	1.5	2	2.5
G	1.5	3	4.5
H	2.5	3.5	7.5
I	1.5	2	2.5
J	1	2	3

is 5 weeks, with a range from 4 weeks (optimistic) to 12 weeks (pessimistic). If the activity could be repeated a large number of times, what is the average time for the activity? This average or **expected time** (t) is as follows:

$$t = \frac{a + 4m + b}{6} \tag{9.4}$$

For activity A we have an average or expected time of

$$t_A = \frac{4 + 4(5) + 12}{6} = \frac{36}{6} = 6 \text{ weeks}$$

With uncertain activity times, we can use the *variance* to describe the dispersion or variation in the activity time values. The variance of the activity time is given by the formula[1]

$$\sigma^2 = \left(\frac{b - a}{6}\right)^2 \tag{9.5}$$

The difference between the pessimistic (b) and optimistic (a) time estimates greatly affects the value of the variance. Large differences in these two values reflect a high degree of uncertainty in the activity time. Using equation (9.5), we obtain the measure of uncertainty—that is, the variance—of activity A, denoted σ_A^2:

$$\sigma_A^2 = \left(\frac{12 - 4}{6}\right)^2 = \left(\frac{8}{6}\right)^2 = 1.78$$

Equations (9.4) and (9.5) are based on the assumption that the activity time distribution can be described by a **beta probability distribution.**[2] With this assumption, the probability distribution for the time to complete activity A is as shown in Figure 9.9. Using equations (9.4) and (9.5) and the data in Table 9.4, we calculated the expected times and variances for all Porta-Vac activities; the results are summarized in Table 9.5. The Porta-Vac project network with expected activity times is shown in Figure 9.10.

The Critical Path

When we have the project network and the expected activity times, we are ready to proceed with the critical path calculations necessary to determine the expected time required to complete the project and determine the activity schedule. In these calculations, we treat the

---

[1]The variance equation is based on the notion that a standard deviation is approximately ⅙ of the difference between the extreme values of the distribution: $(b - a)/6$. The variance is the square of the standard deviation.

[2]The equations for t and σ^2 require additional assumptions about the parameters of the beta probability distribution. However, even when these additional assumptions are not made, the equations still provide good approximations of t and σ^2.

FIGURE 9.9 ACTIVITY TIME DISTRIBUTION FOR PRODUCT DESIGN (ACTIVITY A) FOR THE PORTA-VAC PROJECT

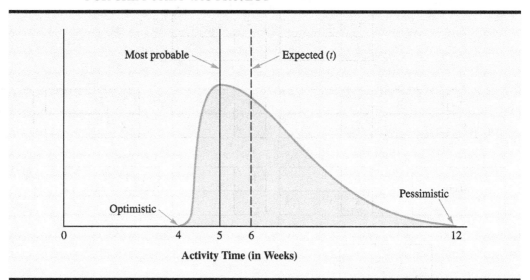

Activity Time (in Weeks)

When uncertain activity times are used, the critical path calculations will determine only the expected or average time to complete the project. The actual time required to complete the project may differ. However, for planning purposes, the expected time should be valuable information for the project manager.

expected activity times (Table 9.5) as the fixed length or known duration of each activity. As a result, we can use the critical path procedure introduced in Section 9.1 to find the critical path for the Porta-Vac project. After the critical activities and the expected time to complete the project have been determined, we analyze the effect of the activity time variability.

Proceeding with a forward pass through the network shown in Figure 9.10, we can establish the earliest start (*ES*) and earliest finish (*EF*) times for each activity. Figure 9.11 shows the project network with the *ES* and *EF* values. Note that the earliest finish time for activity J, the last activity, is 17 weeks. Thus, the expected completion time for the project

TABLE 9.5 EXPECTED TIMES AND VARIANCES FOR THE PORTA-VAC PROJECT ACTIVITIES

Activities that have larger variances show a greater degree of uncertainty. The project manager should monitor the progress of any activity with a large variance even if the expected time does not identify the activity as a critical activity.

Activity	Expected Time (weeks)	Variance
A	6	1.78
B	2	0.44
C	3	0.11
D	5	1.78
E	3	0.11
F	2	0.03
G	3	0.25
H	4	0.69
I	2	0.03
J	2	0.11
Total	32	

FIGURE 9.10   PORTA-VAC PROJECT NETWORK WITH EXPECTED ACTIVITY TIMES

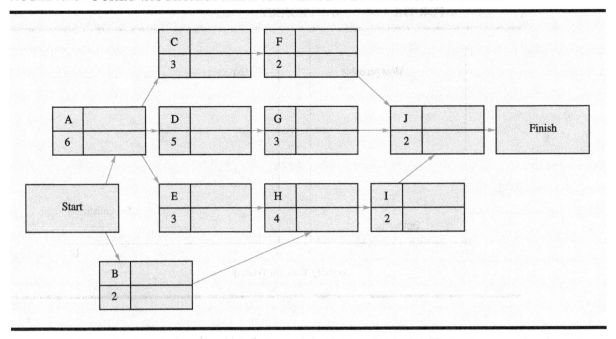

FIGURE 9.11   PORTA-VAC PROJECT NETWORK WITH EARLIEST START AND EARLIEST FINISH TIMES

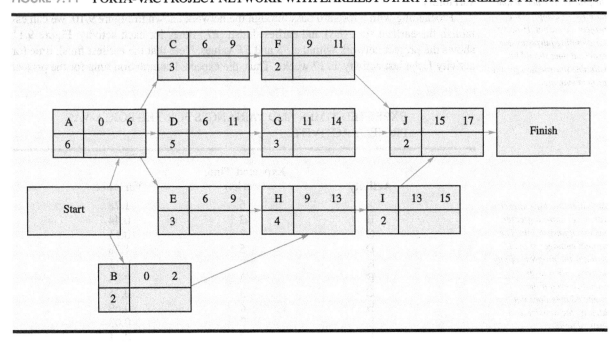

FIGURE 9.12 PORTA-VAC PROJECT NETWORK WITH LATEST START AND LATEST FINISH TIMES

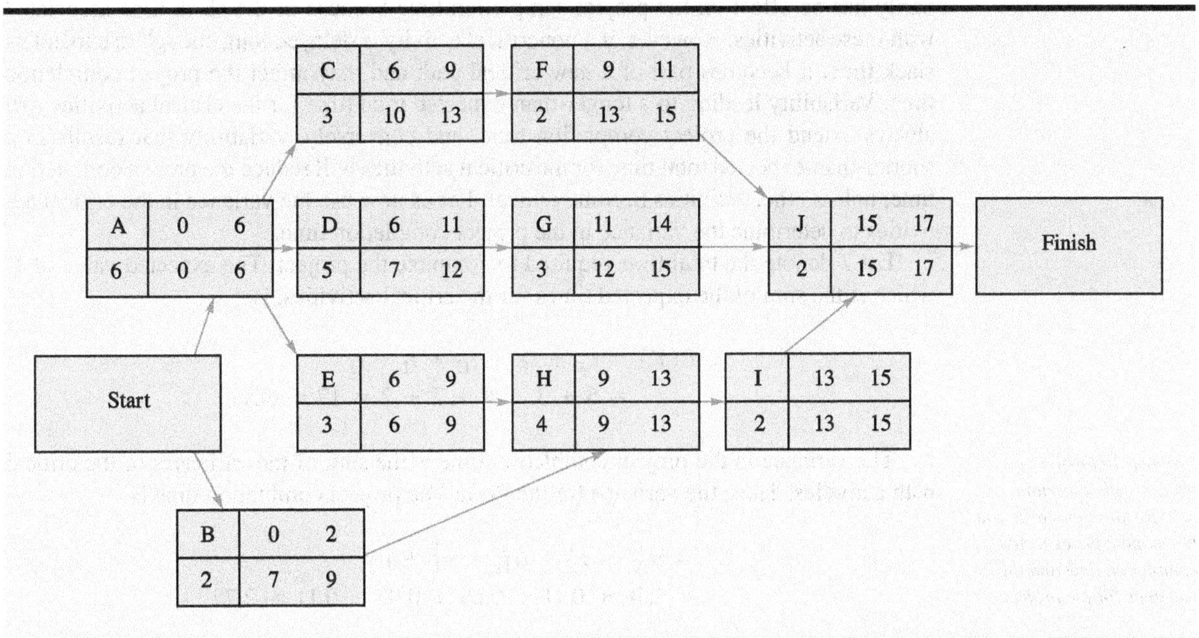

is 17 weeks. Next, we make a backward pass through the network. The backward pass provides the latest start (*LS*) and latest finish (*LF*) times shown in Figure 9.12.

The activity schedule for the Porta-Vac project is shown in Table 9.6. Note that the slack time (*LS* − *ES*) is also shown for each activity. The activities with zero slack (A, E, H, I, and J) form the critical path for the Porta-Vac project network.

Variability in Project Completion Time

We know that for the Porta-Vac project the critical path of A–E–H–I–J resulted in an expected total project completion time of 17 weeks. However, variation in critical activities

TABLE 9.6 ACTIVITY SCHEDULE FOR THE PORTA-VAC PROJECT

Activity	Earliest Start (*ES*)	Latest Start (*LS*)	Earliest Finish (*EF*)	Latest Finish (*LF*)	Slack (*LS* − *ES*)	Critical Path?
A	0	0	6	6	0	Yes
B	0	7	2	9	7	
C	6	10	9	13	4	
D	6	7	11	12	1	
E	6	6	9	9	0	Yes
F	9	13	11	15	4	
G	11	12	14	15	1	
H	9	9	13	13	0	Yes
I	13	13	15	15	0	Yes
J	15	15	17	17	0	Yes

can cause variation in the project completion time. Variation in noncritical activities ordinarily has no effect on the project completion time because of the slack time associated with these activities. However, if a noncritical activity is delayed long enough to expend its slack time, it becomes part of a new critical path and may affect the project completion time. Variability leading to a longer-than-expected total time for the critical activities will always extend the project completion time, and conversely, variability that results in a shorter-than-expected total time for the critical activities will reduce the project completion time, unless other activities become critical. Let us now use the variance in the critical activities to determine the variance in the project completion time.

Let T denote the total time required to complete the project. The expected value of T, which is the sum of the expected times for the critical activities, is

$$E(T) = t_A + t_E + t_H + t_I + t_J$$
$$= 6 + 3 + 4 + 2 + 2 = 17 \text{ weeks}$$

Problem 10 involves a project with uncertain activity times and asks you to compute the expected completion time and the variance for the project.

The variance in the project completion time is the sum of the variances of the critical path activities. Thus, the variance for the Porta-Vac project completion time is

$$\sigma^2 = \sigma_A^2 + \sigma_E^2 + \sigma_H^2 + \sigma_I^2 + \sigma_J^2$$
$$= 1.78 + 0.11 + 0.69 + 0.03 + 0.11 = 2.72$$

where σ_A^2, σ_E^2, σ_H^2, σ_I^2, and σ_J^2 are the variances of the critical activities.

The formula for σ^2 is based on the assumption that the activity times are independent. If two or more activities are dependent, the formula provides only an approximation of the variance of the project completion time. The closer the activities are to being independent, the better the approximation.

Knowing that the standard deviation is the square root of the variance, we compute the standard deviation σ for the Porta-Vac project completion time as

$$\sigma = \sqrt{\sigma^2} = \sqrt{2.72} = 1.65$$

The normal distribution tends to be a better approximation of the distribution of total time for larger projects where the critical path has many activities.

Assuming that the distribution of the project completion time T follows a normal, or bell-shaped, distribution[3] allows us to draw the distribution shown in Figure 9.13. With this distribution, we can compute the probability of meeting a specified project completion date. For example, suppose that management allotted 20 weeks for the Porta-Vac project. What is the probability that we will meet the 20-week deadline? Using the normal probability distribution shown in Figure 9.14, we are asking for the probability that $T \leq 20$; this probability is shown graphically as the shaded area in the figure. The z value for the normal probability distribution at $T = 20$ is

$$z = \frac{20 - 17}{1.65} = 1.82$$

Using $z = 1.82$ and the table for the cumulative standard normal distribution (see Appendix B), we find that the probability of the project meeting the 20-week deadline is 0.9656. Thus,

---

[3]Use of the normal distribution as an approximation is based on the central limit theorem, which indicates that the sum of independent random variables (activity times) follows a normal distribution as the number of random variables becomes large.

FIGURE 9.13 NORMAL DISTRIBUTION OF THE PROJECT COMPLETION TIME
FOR THE PORTA-VAC PROJECT

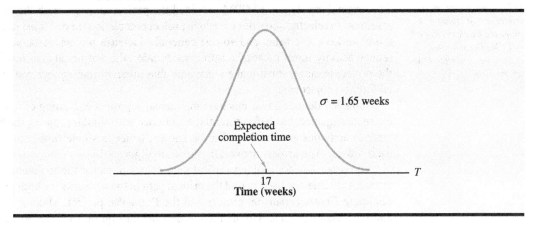

FIGURE 9.14 PROBABILITY THE PORTA-VAC PROJECT WILL MEET
THE 20-WEEK DEADLINE

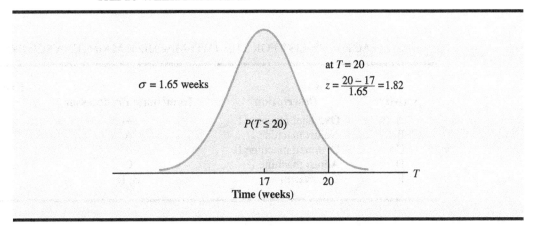

even though activity time variability may cause the completion time to exceed 17 weeks, calculations indicate an excellent chance that the project will be completed before the 20-week deadline. Similar probability calculations can be made for other project deadline alternatives.

NOTES AND COMMENTS

For projects involving uncertain activity times, the probability that the project can be completed within a specified amount of time is helpful managerial information. However, remember that this probability estimate is based *only* on the critical activities. When uncertain activity times exist, longer-than-expected completion times for one or more noncritical activities may cause an original noncritical activity to become critical and hence increase the time required to complete the project. By frequently monitoring the progress of the project to make sure all activities are on schedule, the project manager will be better prepared to take corrective action if a noncritical activity begins to lengthen the duration of the project.

9.3 CONSIDERING TIME-COST TRADE-OFFS

The original developers of CPM provided the project manager with the option of adding resources to selected activities to reduce project completion time. Added resources (such as more workers, overtime, and so on) generally increase project costs, so the decision to reduce activity times must take into consideration the additional cost involved. In effect, the project manager must make a decision that involves trading reduced activity time for additional project cost.

Table 9.7 defines a two-machine maintenance project consisting of five activities. Because management has had substantial experience with similar projects, the times for maintenance activities are considered to be known; hence, a single time estimate is given for each activity. The project network is shown in Figure 9.15.

The procedure for making critical path calculations for the maintenance project network is the same one used to find the critical path in the networks for both the Western Hills Shopping Center expansion project and the Porta-Vac project. Making the forward pass and backward pass calculations for the network in Figure 9.15, we obtained the activity schedule shown in Table 9.8. The zero slack times, and thus the critical path, are associated with activities A–B–E. The length of the critical path, and thus the total time required to complete the project, is 12 days.

TABLE 9.7   ACTIVITY LIST FOR THE TWO-MACHINE MAINTENANCE PROJECT

Activity	Description	Immediate Predecessor	Expected Time (days)
A	Overhaul machine I	—	7
B	Adjust machine I	A	3
C	Overhaul machine II	—	6
D	Adjust machine II	C	3
E	Test system	B, D	2

FIGURE 9.15   TWO-MACHINE MAINTENANCE PROJECT NETWORK

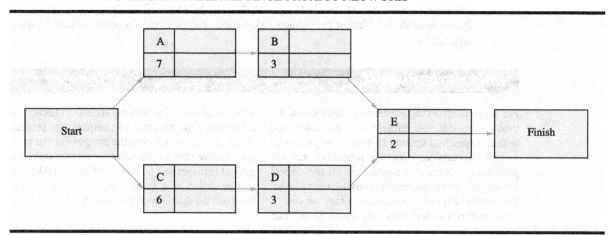

TABLE 9.8   ACTIVITY SCHEDULE FOR THE TWO-MACHINE MAINTENANCE PROJECT

Activity	Earliest Start (ES)	Latest Start (LS)	Earliest Finish (EF)	Latest Finish (LF)	Slack (LS − ES)	Critical Path?
A	0	0	7	7	0	Yes
B	7	7	10	10	0	Yes
C	0	1	6	7	1	
D	6	7	9	10	1	
E	10	10	12	12	0	Yes

Crashing Activity Times

Now suppose that current production levels make completing the maintenance project within 10 days imperative. By looking at the length of the critical path of the network (12 days), we realize that meeting the desired project completion time is impossible unless we can shorten selected activity times. This shortening of activity times, which usually can be achieved by adding resources, is referred to as **crashing**. However, the added resources associated with crashing activity times usually result in added project costs, so we will want to identify the activities that cost the least to crash and then crash those activities only the amount necessary to meet the desired project completion time.

To determine just where and how much to crash activity times, we need information on how much each activity can be crashed and how much the crashing process costs. Hence, we must ask for the following information:

1. Activity cost under the normal or expected activity time
2. Time to complete the activity under maximum crashing (i.e., the shortest possible activity time)
3. Activity cost under maximum crashing

Let

τ_i = expected time for activity i

τ_i' = time for activity i under maximum crashing

M_i = maximum possible reduction in time for activity i due to crashing

Given τ_i and τ_i', we can compute M_i:

$$M_i = \tau_i - \tau_i' \qquad (9.6)$$

Next, let C_i denote the cost for activity i under the normal or expected activity time and C_i' denote the cost for activity i under maximum crashing. Thus, per unit of time (e.g., per day), the crashing cost K_i for each activity is given by

$$K_i = \frac{C_i' - C_i}{M_i} \qquad (9.7)$$

711

For example, if the normal or expected time for activity A is 7 days at a cost of $C_A = \$500$ and the time under maximum crashing is 4 days at a cost of $C'_A = \$800$, equations (9.6) and (9.7) show that the maximum possible reduction in time for activity A is

$$M_A = 7 - 4 = 3 \text{ days}$$

with a crashing cost of

$$K_A = \frac{C'_A - C_A}{M_A} = \frac{800 - 500}{3} = \frac{300}{3} = \$100 \text{ per day}$$

We make the assumption that any portion or fraction of the activity crash time can be achieved for a corresponding portion of the activity crashing cost. For example, if we decided to crash activity A by only 1½ days, the added cost would be 1½ ($100) = $150, which results in a total activity cost of $500 + $150 = $650. Figure 9.16 shows the graph of the time-cost relationship for activity A. The complete normal and crash activity data for the two-machine maintenance project are given in Table 9.9.

Which activities should be crashed—and by how much—to meet the 10-day project completion deadline at minimum cost? Your first reaction to this question may be to consider crashing the critical activities—A, B, or E. Activity A has the lowest crashing cost per day of the three, and crashing this activity by 2 days will reduce the A–B–E path to the desired 10 days. Keep in mind, however, that as you crash the current critical activities, other paths may become critical. Thus, you will need to check the critical path in the revised network and perhaps either identify additional activities to crash or modify your initial crashing decision. For a small network, this trial-and-error approach can be used to make crashing decisions; in larger networks, however, a mathematical procedure is required to determine the optimal crashing decisions.

FIGURE 9.16   TIME-COST RELATIONSHIP FOR ACTIVITY A

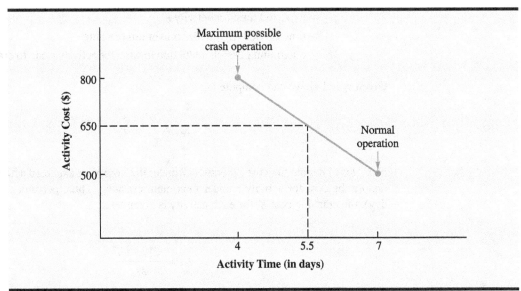

TABLE 9.9 NORMAL AND CRASH ACTIVITY DATA FOR THE TWO-MACHINE MAINTENANCE PROJECT

| Activity | Time (days) | | Total Cost | | Maximum Reduction in Time (M_i) | Crash Cost per Day $\left(K_i = \dfrac{C_i' - C_i}{M_i} \right)$ |
	Normal	Crash	Normal (C_i)	Crash (C_i')		
A	7	4	$ 500	$ 800	3	$100
B	3	2	200	350	1	150
C	6	4	500	900	2	200
D	3	1	200	500	2	150
E	2	1	300	550	1	250
			$1700	$3100		

Linear Programming Model for Crashing

Let us describe how linear programming can be used to solve the network crashing problem. With PERT/CPM, we know that when an activity starts at its earliest start time, then

$$\text{Finish time} = \text{Earliest start time} + \text{Activity time}$$

However, if slack time is associated with an activity, then the activity need not start at its earliest start time. In this case, we may have

$$\text{Finish time} > \text{Earliest start time} + \text{Activity time}$$

Because we do not know ahead of time whether an activity will start at its earliest start time, we use the following inequality to show the general relationship among finish time, earliest start time, and activity time for each activity:

$$\text{Finish time} \geq \text{Earliest start time} + \text{Activity time}$$

Consider activity A, which has an expected time of 7 days. Let x_A = finish time for activity A, and y_A = amount of time activity A is crashed. If we assume that the project begins at time 0, the earliest start time for activity A is 0. Because the time for activity A is reduced by the amount of time that activity A is crashed, the finish time for activity A must satisfy the relationship

$$x_A \geq 0 + (7 - y_A)$$

Moving y_A to the left side,

$$x_A + y_A \geq 7$$

In general, let

$$x_i = \text{the finish time for activity } i \qquad i = \text{A, B, C, D, E}$$
$$y_i = \text{the amount of time activity } i \text{ is crashed} \quad i = \text{A, B, C, D, E}$$

If we follow the same approach that we used for activity A, the constraint corresponding to the finish time for activity C (expected time = 6 days) is

$$x_C \geq 0 + (6 - y_C) \quad \text{or} \quad x_C + y_C \geq 6$$

Continuing with the forward pass of the PERT/CPM procedure, we see that the earliest start time for activity B is x_A, the finish time for activity A. Thus, the constraint corresponding to the finish time for activity B is

$$x_B \geq x_A + (3 - y_B) \quad \text{or} \quad x_B + y_B - x_A \geq 3$$

Similarly, we obtain the constraint for the finish time for activity D:

$$x_D \geq x_C + (3 - y_D) \quad \text{or} \quad x_D + y_D - x_C \geq 3$$

Finally, we consider activity E. The earliest start time for activity E equals the *largest* of the finish times for activities B and D. Because the finish times for both activities B and D will be determined by the crashing procedure, we must write two constraints for activity E, one based on the finish time for activity B and one based upon the finish time for activity D:

$$x_E + y_E - x_B \geq 2 \quad \text{and} \quad x_E + y_E - x_D \geq 2$$

Recall that current production levels made completing the maintenance project within 10 days imperative. Thus, the constraint for the finish time for activity E is

$$x_E \leq 10$$

In addition, we must add the following five constraints corresponding to the maximum allowable crashing time for each activity:

$$x_A \leq 3, \quad y_B \leq 1, \quad y_C \leq 2, \quad y_D \leq 2, \quad \text{and} \quad y_E \leq 1$$

As with all linear programs, we add the usual nonnegativity requirements for the decision variables.

All that remains is to develop an objective function for the model. Because the total project cost for a normal completion time is fixed at $1700 (see Table 9.9), we can minimize the total project cost (normal cost plus crashing cost) by minimizing the total crashing costs. Thus, the linear programming objective function becomes

$$\text{Min} \quad 100y_A + 150y_B + 200y_C + 150y_D + 250y_E$$

Thus, to determine the optimal crashing for each of the activities, we must solve a 10-variable, 12-constraint linear programming model. The linear programming solution from either LINGO or Excel Solver provides the optimal solution of crashing activity A by 1 day and activity E by 1 day, with a total crashing cost of $100 + $250 = $350. With the minimum cost crashing solution, the activity times are as follows:

Activity	Time in Days	
A	6	(Crash 1 day)
B	3	
C	6	
D	3	
E	1	(Crash 1 day)

The linear programming solution provided the revised activity times, but not the revised earliest start time, latest start time, and slack information. The revised activity times and the usual PERT/CPM procedure must be used to develop the activity schedule for the project.

NOTES AND COMMENTS

Note that the two-machine maintenance project network for the crashing illustration (see Figure 9.15) has only one activity, activity E, leading directly to the Finish node. As a result, the project completion time is equal to the completion time for activity E. Thus, the linear programming constraint requiring the project completion in 10 days or less could be written $x_E \leq 10$.

If two or more activities lead directly to the Finish node of a project network, a slight modification is required in the linear programming model for crashing. Consider the portion of the project network shown here. In this case, we suggest creating an additional variable, x_{FIN}, which indicates the finish or completion time for the entire project. The fact that the project cannot be finished until both activities E and G are completed can be modeled by the two constraints

$$x_{FIN} \geq x_E \quad \text{or} \quad x_{FIN} - x_E \geq 0$$
$$x_{FIN} \geq x_G \quad \text{or} \quad x_{FIN} - x_G \geq 0$$

The constraint that the project must be finished by time T can be added as $x_{FIN} \leq T$. Problem 22 gives you practice with this type of project network.

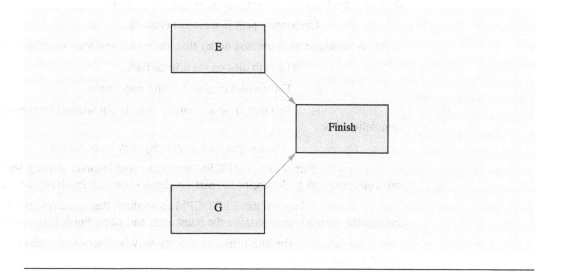

SUMMARY

In this chapter we showed how PERT/CPM can be used to plan, schedule, and control a wide variety of projects. The key to this approach to project scheduling is the development of a PERT/CPM project network that depicts the activities and their precedence relationships. From this project network and activity time estimates, the critical path for the network and the associated critical activities can be identified. In the process, an activity schedule showing the earliest start and earliest finish times, the latest start and latest finish times, and the slack for each activity can be identified.

We showed how we can include capabilities for handling variable or uncertain activity times and how to use this information to provide a probability statement about the chances the project can be completed in a specified period of time. We introduced crashing as a procedure for reducing activity times to meet project completion deadlines, and showed how a linear programming model can be used to determine the crashing decisions that will minimize the cost of reducing the project completion time.

GLOSSARY

Program evaluation and review technique (PERT)   A network-based project scheduling procedure.

Critical path method (CPM)   A network-based project scheduling procedure.

Activities   Specific jobs or tasks that are components of a project. Activities are represented by nodes in a project network.

Immediate predecessors   The activities that must be completed immediately prior to the start of a given activity.

Project network   A graphical representation of a project that depicts the activities and shows the predecessor relationships among the activities.

Critical path   The longest path in a project network.

Path   A sequence of connected nodes that leads from the Start node to the Finish node.

Critical activities   The activities on the critical path.

Earliest start time   The earliest time an activity may begin.

Latest start time   The latest time an activity may begin without increasing the project completion time.

Earliest finish time   The earliest time an activity may be completed.

Forward pass   Part of the PERT/CPM procedure that involves moving forward through the project network to determine the earliest start and earliest finish times for each activity.

Backward pass   Part of the PERT/CPM procedure that involves moving backward through the network to determine the latest start and latest finish times for each activity.

Latest finish time   The latest time an activity may be completed without increasing the project completion time.

Slack   The length of time an activity can be delayed without affecting the project completion time.

Optimistic time   The minimum activity time if everything progresses ideally.

Most probable time   The most probable activity time under normal conditions.

Pessimistic time   The maximum activity time if significant delays are encountered.

Expected time   The average activity time.

Beta probability distribution   A probability distribution used to describe activity times.

Crashing   The shortening of activity times by adding resources and hence usually increasing cost.

PROBLEMS

1. The Mohawk Discount Store is designing a management training program for individuals at its corporate headquarters. The company wants to design the program so that trainees can complete it as quickly as possible. Important precedence relationships must be maintained between assignments or activities in the program. For example, a trainee cannot serve as an assistant to the store manager until the trainee has obtained experience in the credit department and at least one sales department. The following activities are the assignments that must be completed by each trainee in the program. Construct a project network for this problem. Do not perform any further analysis.

Activity	A	B	C	D	E	F	G	H
Immediate Predecessor	—	—	A	A, B	A, B	C	D, F	E, G

2. Bridge City Developers is coordinating the construction of an office complex. As part of the planning process, the company generated the following activity list. Draw a project network that can be used to assist in the scheduling of the project activities.

Activity	A	B	C	D	E	F	G	H	I	J
Immediate Predecessor	—	—	—	A, B	A, B	D	E	C	C	F, G, H, I

3. Construct a project network for the following project. The project is completed when activities F and G are both complete.

Activity	A	B	C	D	E	F	G
Immediate Predecessor	—	—	A	A	C, B	C, B	D, E

4. Assume that the project in Problem 3 has the following activity times (in months):

Activity	A	B	C	D	E	F	G
Time	4	6	2	6	3	3	5

a. Find the critical path.
b. The project must be completed in 1½ years. Do you anticipate difficulty in meeting the deadline? Explain.

5. Management Decision Systems (MDS) is a consulting company that specializes in the development of decision support systems. MDS obtained a contract to develop a computer system to assist the management of a large company in formulating its capital expenditure plan. The project leader developed the following list of activities and immediate predecessors. Construct a project network for this problem.

Activity	A	B	C	D	E	F	G	H	I	J
Immediate Predecessor	—	—	—	B	A	B	C, D	B, E	F, G	H

717

6. Consider the following project network and activity times (in weeks):

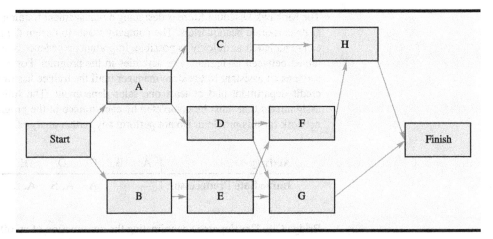

Activity	A	B	C	D	E	F	G	H
Time	5	3	7	6	7	3	10	8

a. Identify the critical path.
b. How much time will be needed to complete this project?
c. Can activity D be delayed without delaying the entire project? If so, by how many weeks?
d. Can activity C be delayed without delaying the entire project? If so, by how many weeks?
e. What is the schedule for activity E?

7. Embassy Club Condominium, located on the west coast of Florida, is undertaking a summer renovation of its main building. The project is scheduled to begin May 1, and a September 1 (17-week) completion date is desired. The condominium manager identified the following renovation activities and their estimated times:

Activity	Immediate Predecessor	Time
A	—	3
B	—	1
C	—	2
D	A, B, C	4
E	C, D	5
F	A	3
G	D, F	6
H	E	4

a. Draw a project network.
b. What are the critical activities?
c. What activity has the most slack time?
d. Will the project be completed by September 1?

718

8. Colonial State College is considering building a new multipurpose athletic complex on campus. The complex would provide a new gymnasium for intercollegiate basketball games, expanded office space, classrooms, and intramural facilities. The following activities would have to be undertaken before construction can begin:

Activity	Description	Immediate Predecessor	Time (weeks)
A	Survey building site	—	6
B	Develop initial design	—	8
C	Obtain board approval	A, B	12
D	Select architect	C	4
E	Establish budget	C	6
F	Finalize design	D, E	15
G	Obtain financing	E	12
H	Hire contractor	F, G	8

a. Draw a project network.
b. Identify the critical path.
c. Develop the activity schedule for the project.
d. Does it appear reasonable that construction of the athletic complex could begin one year after the decision to begin the project with the site survey and initial design plans? What is the expected completion time for the project?

9. Hamilton County Parks is planning to develop a new park and recreational area on a recently purchased 100-acre tract. Project development activities include clearing playground and picnic areas, constructing roads, constructing a shelter house, purchasing picnic equipment, and so on. The following network and activity times (in weeks) are being used in the planning, scheduling, and controlling of this project:

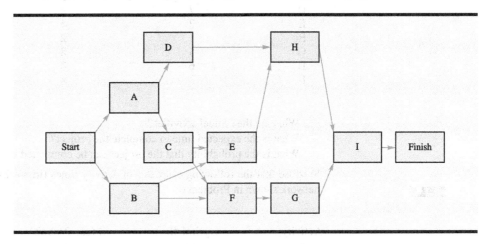

Activity	A	B	C	D	E	F	G	H	I
Time	9	6	6	3	0	3	2	6	3

a. What is the critical path for this network?
b. Show the activity schedule for this project.
c. The park commissioner would like to open the park to the public within six months from the time the work on the project is started. Does this opening date appear to be feasible? Explain.

10. The following estimates of activity times (in days) are available for a small project:

Activity	Optimistic	Most Probable	Pessimistic
A	4	5.0	6
B	8	9.0	10
C	7	7.5	11
D	7	9.0	10
E	6	7.0	9
F	5	6.0	7

a. Compute the expected activity completion times and the variance for each activity.
b. An analyst determined that the critical path consists of activities B–D–F. Compute the expected project completion time and the variance.

11. Building a backyard swimming pool consists of nine major activities. The activities and their immediate predecessors are shown. Develop the project network.

Activity	A	B	C	D	E	F	G	H	I
Immediate Predecessor	—	—	A, B	A, B	B	C	D	D, F	E, G, H

12. Assume that the activity time estimates (in days) for the swimming pool construction project in Problem 11 are as follows:

Activity	Optimistic	Most Probable	Pessimistic
A	3	5	6
B	2	4	6
C	5	6	7
D	7	9	10
E	2	4	6
F	1	2	3
G	5	8	10
H	6	8	10
I	3	4	5

a. What are the critical activities?
b. What is the expected time to complete the project?
c. What is the probability that the project can be completed in 25 or fewer days?

13. Suppose that the following estimates of activity times (in weeks) were provided for the network shown in Problem 6:

Activity	Optimistic	Most Probable	Pessimistic
A	4.0	5.0	6.0
B	2.5	3.0	3.5
C	6.0	7.0	8.0
D	5.0	5.5	9.0
E	5.0	7.0	9.0
F	2.0	3.0	4.0
G	8.0	10.0	12.0
H	6.0	7.0	14.0

What is the probability that the project will be completed
a. Within 21 weeks?
b. Within 22 weeks?
c. Within 25 weeks?

14. Davison Construction Company is building a luxury lakefront home in the Finger Lakes region of New York. Coordination of the architect and subcontractors will require a major effort to meet the 44-week (approximately 10-month) completion date requested by the owner. The Davison project manager prepared the following project network:

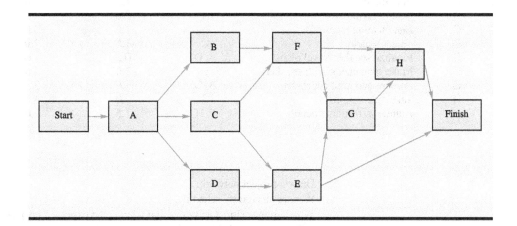

Estimates of the optimistic, most probable, and pessimistic times (in weeks) for the activities are as follows:

Activity	Optimistic	Most Probable	Pessimistic
A	4	8	12
B	6	7	8
C	6	12	18
D	3	5	7
E	6	9	18
F	5	8	17
G	10	15	20
H	5	6	13

a. Find the critical path.
b. What is the expected project completion time?
c. What is the probability the project can be completed in the 44 weeks as requested by the owner?
d. What is the probability the building project could run more than 3 months late? Use 57 weeks for this calculation.
e. What should the construction company tell the owner?

15. Doug Casey is in charge of planning and coordinating next spring's sales management training program for his company. Doug listed the following activity information for this project:

Activity	Description	Immediate Predecessor	Optimistic	Most Probable	Pessimistic
A	Plan topic	—	1.5	2.0	2.5
B	Obtain speakers	A	2.0	2.5	6.0
C	List meeting locations	—	1.0	2.0	3.0
D	Select location	C	1.5	2.0	2.5
E	Finalize speaker travel plans	B, D	0.5	1.0	1.5
F	Make final check with speakers	E	1.0	2.0	3.0
G	Prepare and mail brochure	B, D	3.0	3.5	7.0
H	Take reservations	G	3.0	4.0	5.0
I	Handle last-minute details	F, H	1.5	2.0	2.5

The header "Time (weeks)" spans the Optimistic, Most Probable, and Pessimistic columns.

a. Draw a project network.
b. Prepare an activity schedule.
c. What are the critical activities and what is the expected project completion time?
d. If Doug wants a 0.99 probability of completing the project on time, how far ahead of the scheduled meeting date should he begin working on the project?

16. The Daugherty Porta-Vac project discussed in Section 9.2 has an expected project completion time of 17 weeks. The probability that the project could be completed in 20 weeks or less is 0.9656. The noncritical paths in the Porta-Vac project network are

$$A–D–G–J$$
$$A–C–F–J$$
$$B–H–I–J$$

a. Use the information in Table 9.5 to compute the expected time and variance for each path shown.
b. Compute the probability that each path will be completed in the desired 20-week period.
c. Why is the computation of the probability of completing a project on time based on the analysis of the critical path? In what case, if any, would making the probability computation for a noncritical path be desirable?

17. The Porsche Shop, founded in 1985 by Dale Jensen, specializes in the restoration of vintage Porsche automobiles. One of Jensen's regular customers asked him to prepare an estimate for the restoration of a 1964 model 356SC Porsche. To estimate the time and cost to perform such a restoration, Jensen broke the restoration process into four separate activities: disassembly and initial preparation work (A), body restoration (B), engine restoration (C), and final assembly (D). Once activity A has been completed, activities B and C can be performed independently of each other; however, activity D can be started only if

both activities B and C have been completed. Based on his inspection of the car, Jensen believes that the following time estimates (in days) are applicable:

Activity	Optimistic	Most Probable	Pessimistic
A	3	4	8
B	5	8	11
C	2	4	6
D	4	5	12

Jensen estimates that the parts needed to restore the body will cost $3000 and that the parts needed to restore the engine will cost $5000. His current labor costs are $400 a day.

a. Develop a project network.
b. What is the expected project completion time?
c. Jensen's business philosophy is based on making decisions using a best- and worst-case scenario. Develop cost estimates for completing the restoration based on both a best- and worst-case analysis. Assume that the total restoration cost is the sum of the labor cost plus the material cost.
d. If Jensen obtains the job with a bid that is based on the costs associated with an expected completion time, what is the probability that he will lose money on the job?
e. If Jensen obtains the job based on a bid of $16,800, what is the probability that he will lose money on the job?

18. The manager of the Oak Hills Swimming Club is planning the club's swimming team program. The first team practice is scheduled for May 1. The activities, their immediate predecessors, and the activity time estimates (in weeks) are as follows:

Activity	Description	Immediate Predecessor	Optimistic	Most Probable	Pessimistic
A	Meet with board	—	1	1	2
B	Hire coaches	A	4	6	8
C	Reserve pool	A	2	4	6
D	Announce program	B, C	1	2	3
E	Meet with coaches	B	2	3	4
F	Order team suits	A	1	2	3
G	Register swimmers	D	1	2	3
H	Collect fees	G	1	2	3
I	Plan first practice	E, H, F	1	1	1

a. Draw a project network.
b. Develop an activity schedule.
c. What are the critical activities, and what is the expected project completion time?
d. If the club manager plans to start the project on February 1, what is the probability the swimming program will be ready by the scheduled May 1 date (13 weeks)? Should the manager begin planning the swimming program before February 1?

19. The product development group at Landon Corporation has been working on a new computer software product that has the potential to capture a large market share. Through outside sources, Landon's management learned that a competitor is working to introduce a similar product. As a result, Landon's top management increased its pressure on the product development group. The group's leader turned to PERT/CPM as an aid to scheduling

the activities remaining before the new product can be brought to the market. The project network is as follows:

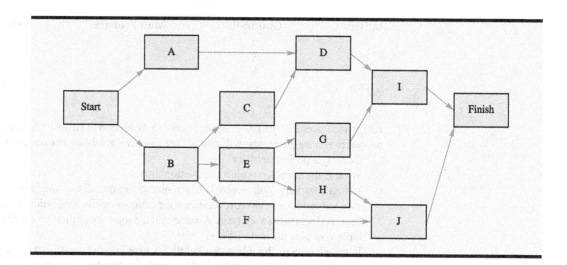

The activity time estimates (in weeks) are

Activity	Optimistic	Most Probable	Pessimistic
A	3.0	4.0	5.0
B	3.0	3.5	7.0
C	4.0	5.0	6.0
D	2.0	3.0	4.0
E	6.0	10.0	14.0
F	7.5	8.5	12.5
G	4.5	6.0	7.5
H	5.0	6.0	13.0
I	2.0	2.5	6.0
J	4.0	5.0	6.0

a. Develop an activity schedule for this project and identify the critical path activities.
b. What is the probability that the project will be completed so that Landon Corporation may introduce the new product within 25 weeks? Within 30 weeks?

20. Norton Industries is installing a new computer system. The activities, the activity times, and the project network are as follows:

Activity	Time	Activity	Time
A	3	E	4
B	6	F	3
C	2	G	9
D	5	H	3

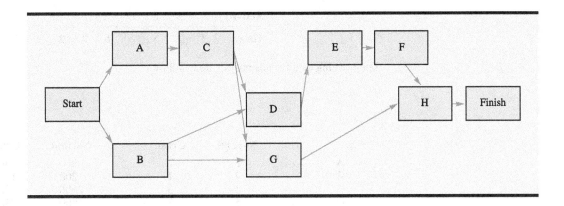

The critical path calculation shows B–D–E–F–H is the critical path, and the expected project completion time is 21 weeks. After viewing this information, management requested overtime be used to complete the project in 16 weeks. Thus, crashing of the project is necessary. The following information is relevant:

	Time (weeks)		Cost ($)	
Activity	Normal	Crash	Normal	Crash
A	3	1	900	1700
B	6	3	2000	4000
C	2	1	500	1000
D	5	3	1800	2400
E	4	3	1500	1850
F	3	1	3000	3900
G	9	4	8000	9800
H	3	2	1000	2000

a. Formulate a linear programming model that can be used to make the crashing decisions for this project.
b. Solve the linear programming model and make the minimum cost crashing decisions. What is the added cost of meeting the 16-week completion time?
c. Develop a complete activity schedule based on the crashed activity times.

21. Consider the following project network and activity times (in days):

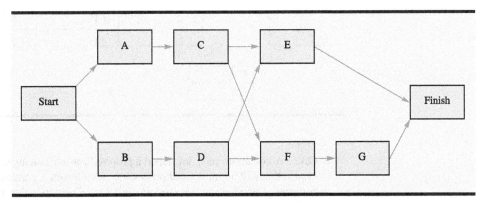

Activity	A	B	C	D	E	F	G
Time	3	2	5	5	6	2	2

The crashing data for this project are as follows:

Activity	Time (days) Normal	Crash	Cost ($) Normal	Crash
A	3	2	800	1400
B	2	1	1200	1900
C	5	3	2000	2800
D	5	3	1500	2300
E	6	4	1800	2800
F	2	1	600	1000
G	2	1	500	1000

a. Find the critical path and the expected project completion time.

b. What is the total project cost using the normal times?

22. Refer to Problem 21. Assume that management desires a 12-day project completion time.

a. Formulate a linear programming model that can be used to assist with the crashing decisions.

b. What activities should be crashed?

c. What is the total project cost for the 12-day completion time?

23. Consider the following project network. Note that the normal or expected activity times are denoted τ_i, $i =$ A, B, . . . , I. Let $x_i =$ the earliest finish time for activity i. Formulate a linear programming model that can be used to determine the length of the critical path.

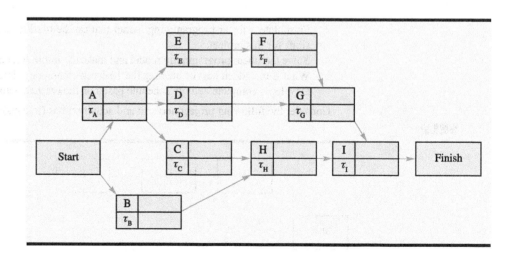

24. Office Automation, Inc., developed a proposal for introducing a new computerized office system that will improve word processing and interoffice communications for a particular company. Contained in the proposal is a list of activities that must be accomplished to

complete the new office system project. Use the following relevant information about the activities:

Activity	Description	Immediate Predecessor	Time (weeks)		Cost ($1000s)	
			Normal	Crash	Normal	Crash
A	Plan needs	—	10	8	30	70
B	Order equipment	A	8	6	120	150
C	Install equipment	B	10	7	100	160
D	Set up training lab	A	7	6	40	50
E	Conduct training course	D	10	8	50	75
F	Test system	C, E	3	3	60	—

a. Develop a project network.
b. Develop an activity schedule.
c. What are the critical activities, and what is the expected project completion time?
d. Assume that the company wants to complete the project in six months or 26 weeks. What crashing decisions do you recommend to meet the desired completion time at the least possible cost? Work through the network and attempt to make the crashing decisions by inspection.
e. Develop an activity schedule for the crashed project.
f. What added project cost is required to meet the six-month completion time?

25. Because Landon Corporation (see Problem 19) is being pressured to complete the product development project at the earliest possible date, the project leader requested that the possibility of crashing the project be evaluated.
a. Formulate a linear programming model that could be used in making the crashing decisions.
b. What information would have to be provided before the linear programming model could be implemented?

Case Problem R. C. COLEMAN

R. C. Coleman distributes a variety of food products that are sold through grocery store and supermarket outlets. The company receives orders directly from the individual outlets, with a typical order requesting the delivery of several cases of anywhere from 20 to 50 different products. Under the company's current warehouse operation, warehouse clerks dispatch order-picking personnel to fill each order and have the goods moved to the warehouse shipping area. Because of the high labor costs and relatively low productivity of hand order-picking, management has decided to automate the warehouse operation by installing a computer-controlled order-picking system along with a conveyor system for moving goods from storage to the warehouse shipping area.

R. C. Coleman's director of material management has been named the project manager in charge of the automated warehouse system. After consulting with members of the engineering staff and warehouse management personnel, the director compiled a list of activities associated with the project. The optimistic, most probable, and pessimistic times (in weeks) have also been provided for each activity.

Activity	Description	Immediate Predecessor
A	Determine equipment needs	—
B	Obtain vendor proposals	—
C	Select vendor	A, B
D	Order system	C
E	Design new warehouse layout	C
F	Design warehouse	E
G	Design computer interface	C
H	Interface computer	D, F, G
I	Install system	D, F
J	Train system operators	H
K	Test system	I, J

Activity	Time		
	Optimistic	Most Probable	Pessimistic
A	4	6	8
B	6	8	16
C	2	4	6
D	8	10	24
E	7	10	13
F	4	6	8
G	4	6	20
H	4	6	8
I	4	6	14
J	3	4	5
K	2	4	6

Managerial Report

Develop a report that presents the activity schedule and expected project completion time for the warehouse expansion project. Include a project network in the report. In addition, take into consideration the following issues:

1. R. C. Coleman's top management established a required 40-week completion time for the project. Can this completion time be achieved? Include probability information in your discussion. What recommendations do you have if the 40-week completion time is required?

2. Suppose that management requests that activity times be shortened to provide an 80% chance of meeting the 40-week completion time. If the variance in the project completion time is the same as you found in part (1), how much should the expected project completion time be shortened to achieve the goal of an 80% chance of completion within 40 weeks?

3. Using the expected activity times as the normal times and the following crashing information, determine the activity crashing decisions and revised activity schedule for the warehouse expansion project:

Activity	Crashed Activity Time (weeks)	Cost ($) Normal	Cost ($) Crashed
A	4	1,000	1,900
B	7	1,000	1,800
C	2	1,500	2,700
D	8	2,000	3,200
E	7	5,000	8,000
F	4	3,000	4,100
G	5	8,000	10,250
H	4	5,000	6,400
I	4	10,000	12,400
J	3	4,000	4,400
K	3	5,000	5,500

Appendix 9.1 USING MICROSOFT OFFICE PROJECT

In this appendix we provide a brief introduction to Microsoft Office Project. A trial version of this software is provided on the CD that is packaged with this book. Microsoft Office Project is software designed to manage and control a project. This software can be used for critical path calculations.

If Microsoft Office Project is properly installed, it will be listed under All Programs in the Start menu along with the other members of the Microsoft Office Family. After starting Microsoft Office Project, you will see what is displayed in Figure 9.17. This is an empty

FIGURE 9.17   MICROSOFT OFFICE PROJECT NETWORK EMPTY PROJECT

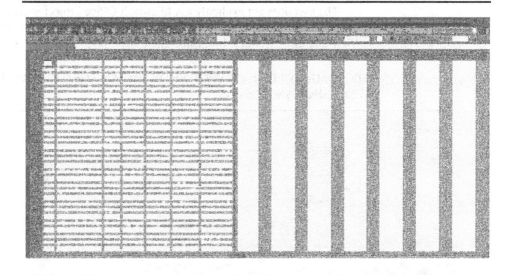

FIGURE 9.18 MICROSOFT OFFICE PROJECT ACTIVITY LIST AND GANTT CHART FOR WESTERN HILLS SHOPPING CENTER

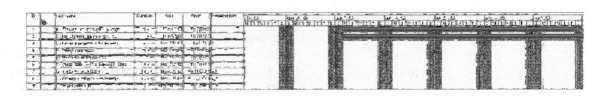

project. Refer back to the list of activities in Table 9.1 for the Western Hills Shopping Center project. Begin entering these activity data. Notice the area of the screen that is much like a spreadsheet. Start in the first row under the column Task Name and type "A - Prepare architectural drawings" and hit return. Next, put the cursor in the column named Duration and type "5 weeks." Note that the default time unit is days, which is why it is important to type "5 weeks" rather than "5 days." Microsoft Office Project will assume that this activity begins on the first available workday. This can be adjusted as well as the number of work days per week, and so on. Enter all of the activities in Table 9.1.

When entering the activities, make sure to enter the appropriate predecessor activities. In Table 9.1 we identified each activity with a letter. However, Microsoft Office Project identifies each activity uniquely with an integer. When entering a predecessor activity use the unique integer identifying it.

In Figure 9.18 we see the result of entering all of the activities in Table 9.1. As mentioned, Microsoft Office Project uses integers to identify activities. In Figure 9.18 we actually started the name of each activity with corresponding letter from Table 9.1 in order to make the correspondence with Table 9.1 more clear. Notice also the second column in Figure 9.18. This is the Indicators column. Double clicking on this column brings up a list of useful possibilities such as % complete.

Notice that the screen in Figure 9.18 is divided into two parts. On the left we see the list of activities, the earliest they can start, and the earliest they can finish. On the right we see the corresponding **Gantt Chart**. This chart has the times superimposed on a calendar. This provides a very useful graphic of when projects can start and end.

The user does not explicitly ask Microsoft Office Project to calculate the critical path. This is automatically done in the background. In order to get the network graphic, select **View** and then **Network Diagram.** The critical path is outlined in red (see Figure 9.19).

FIGURE 9.19 MICROSOFT OFFICE PROJECT NETWORK AND CRITICAL PATH FOR WESTERN HILLS SHOPPING CENTER

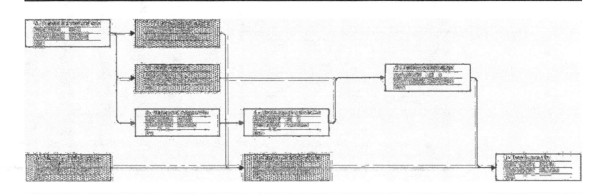

FIGURE 9.20 MICROSOFT OFFICE PROJECT ACTIVITY LIST MODIFIED TO GIVE EARLIEST AND LATEST START, EARLIEST AND LATEST FINISH, AND SLACK

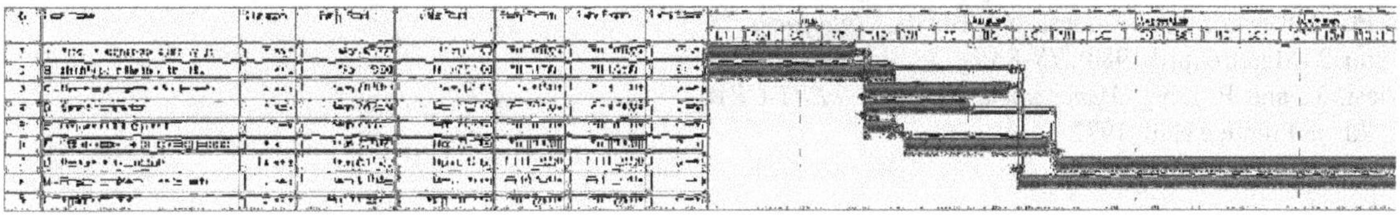

In Figure 9.20 we list the earliest start and finish, latest start and finish, and total slack for each activity. Total slack is the Microsoft Office Project terminology for what we are calling slack. We can access these columns by right-clicking on the column bar and selecting the column heading we wish.

References and Bibliography

Moder, J. J., C. R. Phillips, and E. W. Davis. *Project Management with CPM, PERT and Precedence Diagramming,* 3d ed. Blitz, 1995.

Wasil, E. A., and A. A. Assad. "Project Management on the PC: Software, Applications, and Trends," *Interfaces* 18, no. 2 (March/April 1988): 75–84.

Wiest, J., and F. Levy. *Management Guide to PERT-CPM,* 2d ed. Prentice Hall, 1977.

Self-Test Solutions and Answers to Even-Numbered Problems

2.

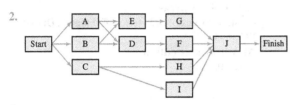

3.

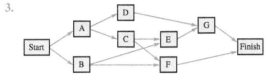

4. a. A–D–G

   b. No; Time = 15 months

6. a. Critical path: A–D–F–H

   b. 22 weeks

   c. No, it is a critical activity.

   d. Yes, 2 weeks

   e. Schedule for activity E:

Earliest start	3
Latest start	4
Earliest finish	10
Latest finish	11

8. b. B–C–E–F–H

   d. Yes, time = 49 weeks

10. a.

Activity	Optimistic	Most Probable	Pessimistic	Expected Times	Variance
A	4	5.0	6	5.00	0.11
B	8	9.0	10	9.00	0.11
C	7	7.5	11	8.00	0.44
D	7	9.0	10	8.83	0.25
E	6	7.0	9	7.17	0.25
F	5	6.0	7	6.00	0.11

   b. Critical activities: B–D–F

   Expected project completion time: $9.00 + 8.83 + 6.00 = 23.83$

   Variance of projection completion time: $0.11 + 0.25 + 0.11 = 0.47$

12. a. A–D–H–I

   b. 25.66 days

   c. 0.2578

13.

Activity	Expected Time	Variance
A	5	0.11
B	3	0.03
C	7	0.11
D	6	0.44
E	7	0.44
F	3	0.11
G	10	0.44
H	8	1.78

From Problem 6, A–D–F–H is the critical path, so $E(T) = 5 + 6 + 3 + 8 = 22.$

$\sigma^2 = 0.11 + 0.44 + 0.11 + 1.78 = 2.44$

$$z = \frac{\text{Time} - E(T)}{\sigma} = \frac{\text{Time} - 22}{\sqrt{2.44}}$$

   a. Time = 21: $z = -0.64$

   Cumulative Probability = 0.2611

   P(21 weeks) = 0.2611

   b. Time = 22: $z = 0$

   Cumulative Probability = 0.5000

   P(22 weeks) = 0.5000

   c. Time = 25: $z = +1.92$

   Cumulative Probability = 0.9726

   P(25 weeks) = 0.9726

14. a. A–C–E–G–H

   b. 52 weeks (1 year)

   c. 0.0174

   d. 0.0934

   e. 10 month doubtful

   13 month very likely

   Estimate 12 months (1 year)

16. a.

$E(T)$	Variance
16	3.92
13	2.03
10	1.27

   b. 0.9783, approximately 1.00, approximately 1.00

18. c. A–B–D–G–H–I, 14.17 weeks

   d. 0.0951, yes

20. b. Crash B(1 week), D(2 weeks), E(1 week), F(1 week), G(1 week)

   Total cost = $2427

   c. All activities are critical.

21. a.

Activity	Earliest Start	Latest Start	Earliest Finish	Latest Finish	Slack	Critical Activity
A	0	0	3	3	0	Yes
B	0	1	2	3	1	
C	3	3	8	8	0	Yes
D	2	3	7	8	1	
E	8	8	14	14	0	Yes
F	8	10	10	12	2	
G	10	12	12	14	2	

Critical path: A–C–E

Project completion time $= t_A + t_C + t_E = 3 + 5 + 6 = 14$ days

b. Total cost $= \$8400$

22. a.

Activity	Max Crash Days	Crash Cost/Day
A	1	600
B	1	700
C	2	400
D	2	400
E	2	500
F	1	400
G	1	500

Min $600Y_A + 700Y_B + 400Y_C + 400Y_D + 500Y_E + 400Y_F + 400Y_G$

s.t.

$$X_A + Y_A \geq 3$$
$$X_B + Y_B \geq 2$$
$$-X_A + X_C + Y_C \geq 5$$
$$-X_B + X_D + Y_D \geq 5$$
$$-X_C + X_E + Y_E \geq 6$$
$$-X_D + X_E + Y_E \geq 6$$
$$-X_C + X_F + Y_F \geq 2$$
$$-X_D + X_F + Y_F \geq 2$$
$$-X_F + X_G + Y_G \geq 2$$
$$-X_E + X_{FIN} \geq 0$$
$$-X_G + X_{FIN} \geq 0$$
$$X_{FIN} \leq 12$$
$$Y_A \leq 1$$
$$Y_B \leq 1$$
$$Y_C \leq 2$$
$$Y_D \leq 2$$
$$Y_E \leq 2$$
$$Y_F \leq 1$$
$$Y_G \leq 1$$

All $X, Y \geq 0$

b. Solution of the linear programming model in part (a) shows

Activity	Crash	Crashing Cost
C	1 day	$400
E	1 day	500
	Total	$900

c. Total cost = Normal cost + Crashing cost
$= \$8400 + \$900 = \$9300$

24. c. A–B–C–F, 31 weeks

d. Crash A(2 weeks), B(2 weeks), C(1 week), D(1 week), E(1 week)

e. All activities are critical.

f. $112,500

734

Inventory Models

CONTENTS

Inventory refers to idle goods or materials held by an organization for use sometime in the future. Items carried in inventory include raw materials, purchased parts, components, subassemblies, work-in-process, finished goods, and supplies. Some reasons organizations maintain inventory include the difficulties in precisely predicting sales levels, production times, demand, and usage needs. Thus, inventory serves as a buffer against uncertain and fluctuating usage and keeps a supply of items available in case the items are needed by the organization or its customers. Even though inventory serves an important and essential role, the expense associated with financing and maintaining inventories is a substantial part of the cost of doing business. In large organizations, the cost associated with inventory can run into millions of dollars.

In applications involving inventory, managers must answer two important questions:

1. *How much* should be ordered when the inventory is replenished?
2. *When* should the inventory be replenished?

Virtually every business uses some sort of inventory management model or system to address the preceding questions. Hewlett-Packard works with its retailers to help determine the retailer's inventory replenishment strategies for printers and other HP products. IBM developed inventory management policies for a range of microelectronic parts that are used in IBM plants as well as sold to a number of outside customers. The Management Science in Action, Inventory Management at CVS Corporation, describes an inventory system used to determine order quantities in the drugstore industry.

The purpose of this chapter is to show how quantitative models can assist in making the how-much-to-order and when-to-order inventory decisions. We will first consider *deterministic* inventory models in which we assume that the rate of demand for the item is constant or nearly constant. Later we will consider *probabilistic* inventory models in which the demand for the item fluctuates and can be described only in probabilistic terms.

MANAGEMENT SCIENCE IN ACTION

INVENTORY MANAGEMENT AT CVS CORPORATION*

The inventory procedure described for the drugstore industry is discussed in detail in Section 10.7.

CVS is the largest drugstore chain in the United States with 4100 stores in 25 states. The primary inventory management area in the drugstore involves the numerous basic products that are carried in inventory on an everyday basis. For these items, the most important issue is the replenishment quantity or order size each time an order is placed. In most drugstore chains, basic products are ordered under a periodic review inventory system, with the review period being one week.

The weekly review system uses electronic ordering equipment that scans an order label affixed to the shelf directly below each item. Among other information on the label is the item's replenishment level, or order-to-quantity. The store employee placing the order determines the weekly order quantity by counting the number of units of the product on the shelf and subtracting this quantity from the replenishment level. A computer program determines the replenishment quantity for each item in each individual store, based on each store's movement, rather than on the company movement. To minimize stockouts the replenishment quantity is set equal to the store's three-week demand, or movement, for the product.

*Based on information provided by Bob Carver. (The inventory system described was originally implemented in the CVS stores formerly known as SupeRx.)

10.1 ECONOMIC ORDER QUANTITY (EOQ) MODEL

The **economic order quantity (EOQ)** model is applicable when the demand for an item shows a constant, or nearly constant, rate and when the entire quantity ordered arrives in inventory at one point in time. The **constant demand rate** assumption means that the same number of units is taken from inventory each period of time, such as 5 units every day, 25 units every week, 100 units every four-week period, and so on.

To illustrate the EOQ model, let us consider the situation faced by the R&B Beverage Company. R&B Beverage is a distributor of beer, wine, and soft drink products. From a main warehouse located in Columbus, Ohio, R&B supplies nearly 1000 retail stores with beverage products. The beer inventory, which constitutes about 40% of the company's total inventory, averages approximately 50,000 cases. With an average cost per case of approximately $8, R&B estimates the value of its beer inventory to be $400,000.

The warehouse manager decided to conduct a detailed study of the inventory costs associated with Bub Beer, the number one selling R&B beer. The purpose of the study is to establish the how-much-to-order and the when-to-order decisions for Bub Beer that will result in the lowest possible total cost. As the first step in the study, the warehouse manager obtained the following demand data for the past 10 weeks:

Week	Demand (cases)
1	2000
2	2025
3	1950
4	2000
5	2100
6	2050
7	2000
8	1975
9	1900
10	2000
Total cases	20,000
Average cases per week	2000

One of the most criticized assumptions of the EOQ model is the constant demand rate. Obviously, the model would be inappropriate for items with widely fluctuating and variable demand rates. However, as this example shows, the EOQ model can provide a realistic approximation of the optimal order quantity when demand is relatively stable and occurs at a nearly constant rate.

Strictly speaking, these weekly demand figures do not show a constant demand rate. However, given the relatively low variability exhibited by the weekly demand, inventory planning with a constant demand rate of 2000 cases per week appears acceptable. In practice, you will find that the actual inventory situation seldom, if ever, satisfies the assumptions of the model exactly. Thus, in any particular application, the manager must determine whether the model assumptions are close enough to reality for the model to be useful. In this situation, because demand varies from a low of 1900 cases to a high of 2100 cases, the assumption of constant demand of 2000 cases per week appears to be a reasonable approximation.

The how-much-to-order decision involves selecting an order quantity that draws a compromise between (1) keeping small inventories and ordering frequently, and (2) keeping large inventories and ordering infrequently. The first alternative can result in undesirably high ordering costs, whereas the second alternative can result in undesirably high inventory holding costs. To find an optimal compromise between these conflicting alternatives, let us consider a mathematical model that shows the total cost as the sum of the holding cost and the ordering cost.[1]

---

[1] Even though analysts typically refer to "total cost" models for inventory systems, often these models describe only the total variable or total relevant costs for the decision being considered. Costs that are not affected by the how-much-to-order decision are considered fixed or constant and are not included in the model.

As with other quantitative models, accurate estimates of cost parameters are critical. In the EOQ model, estimates of both the inventory holding cost and the ordering cost are needed. Also see footnote 1, which refers to relevant costs.

Holding costs are the costs associated with maintaining or carrying a given level of inventory; these costs depend on the size of the inventory. The first holding cost to consider is the cost of financing the inventory investment. When a firm borrows money, it incurs an interest charge. If the firm uses its own money, it experiences an opportunity cost associated with not being able to use the money for other investments. In either case, an interest cost exists for the capital tied up in inventory. This **cost of capital** is usually expressed as a percentage of the amount invested. R&B estimates its cost of capital at an annual rate of 18%.

A number of other holding costs such as insurance, taxes, breakage, pilferage, and warehouse overhead also depend on the value of the inventory. R&B estimates these other costs at an annual rate of approximately 7% of the value of its inventory. Thus, the total holding cost for the R&B beer inventory is 18% + 7% = 25% of the value of the inventory. The cost of one case of Bub Beer is $8. With an annual holding cost rate of 25%, the cost of holding one case of Bub Beer in inventory for 1 year is 0.25($8) = $2.00.

The next step in the inventory analysis is to determine the **ordering cost.** This cost, which is considered fixed regardless of the order quantity, covers the preparation of the voucher, the processing of the order including payment, postage, telephone, transportation, invoice verification, receiving, and so on. For R&B Beverage, the largest portion of the ordering cost involves the salaries of the purchasers. An analysis of the purchasing process showed that a purchaser spends approximately 45 minutes preparing and processing an order for Bub Beer. With a wage rate and fringe benefit cost for purchasers of $20 per hour, the labor portion of the ordering cost is $15. Making allowances for paper, postage, telephone, transportation, and receiving costs at $17 per order, the manager estimates that the ordering cost is $32 per order. That is, R&B is paying $32 per order regardless of the quantity requested in the order.

The holding cost, ordering cost, and demand information are the three data items that must be known prior to the use of the EOQ model. After developing these data for the R&B problem, we can look at how they are used to develop a total cost model. We begin by defining Q as the order quantity. Thus, the how-much-to-order decision involves finding the value of Q that will minimize the sum of holding and ordering costs.

The inventory for Bub Beer will have a maximum value of Q units when an order of size Q is received from the supplier. R&B will then satisfy customer demand from inventory until the inventory is depleted, at which time another shipment of Q units will be received. Thus, assuming a constant demand, the graph of the inventory for Bub Beer is as shown in Figure 10.1. Note that the graph indicates an average inventory of $\frac{1}{2}Q$ for the period in question. This level should appear reasonable because the maximum inventory is Q, the minimum is zero, and the inventory declines at a constant rate over the period.

Figure 10.1 shows the inventory pattern during one order cycle of length T. As time goes on, this pattern will repeat. The complete inventory pattern is shown in Figure 10.2. If the average inventory during each cycle is $\frac{1}{2}Q$, the average inventory over any number of cycles is also $\frac{1}{2}Q$.

Most inventory cost models use an annual cost. Thus, demand should be expressed in units per year and inventory holding cost should be based on an annual rate.

The holding cost can be calculated using the average inventory. That is, we can calculate the holding cost by multiplying the average inventory by the cost of carrying one unit in inventory for the stated period. The period selected for the model is up to you; it could be one week, one month, one year, or more. However, because the holding cost for many industries and businesses is expressed as an *annual* percentage, most inventory models are developed on an *annual* cost basis.

FIGURE 10.1 INVENTORY FOR BUB BEER

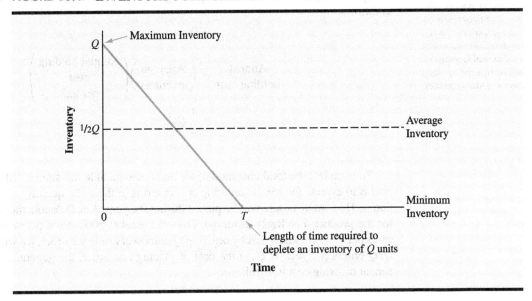

Let

$$I = \text{annual holding cost rate}$$
$$C = \text{unit cost of the inventory item}$$
$$C_h = \text{annual cost of holding one unit in inventory}$$

The annual cost of holding one unit in inventory is

$$C_h = IC \tag{10.1}$$

FIGURE 10.2 INVENTORY PATTERN FOR THE EOQ INVENTORY MODEL

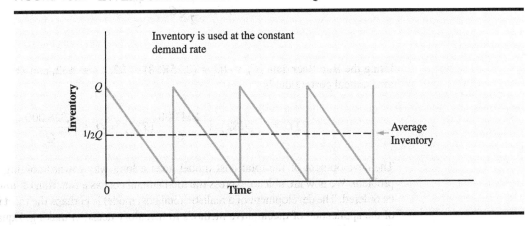

C_h is the cost of holding one unit in inventory for one year. Because smaller order quantities Q will result in lower inventory, total annual holding cost can be reduced by using smaller order quantities.

The general equation for the annual holding cost for the average inventory of $\frac{1}{2}Q$ units is as follows:

$$\begin{pmatrix} \text{Annual} \\ \text{holding cost} \end{pmatrix} = \begin{pmatrix} \text{Average} \\ \text{inventory} \end{pmatrix} \begin{pmatrix} \text{Annual holding} \\ \text{cost} \\ \text{per unit} \end{pmatrix}$$

$$= \frac{1}{2}QC_h \qquad (10.2)$$

To complete the total cost model, we must now include the annual ordering cost. The goal is to express the annual ordering cost in terms of the order quantity Q. The first question is, How many orders will be placed during the year? Let D denote the annual demand for the product. For R&B Beverage, $D = $ (52 weeks)(2000 cases per week) $= 104,000$ cases per year. We know that by ordering Q units every time we order, we will have to place D/Q orders per year. If C_o is the cost of placing one order, the general equation for the annual ordering cost is as follows:

C_o, the fixed cost per order, is independent of the amount ordered. For a given annual demand of D units, the total annual ordering cost can be reduced by using larger order quantities.

$$\begin{pmatrix} \text{Annual} \\ \text{ordering cost} \end{pmatrix} = \begin{pmatrix} \text{Number of} \\ \text{orders} \\ \text{per year} \end{pmatrix} \begin{pmatrix} \text{Cost} \\ \text{per} \\ \text{order} \end{pmatrix}$$

$$= \left(\frac{D}{Q} \right) C_o \qquad (10.3)$$

Thus, the total annual cost, denoted TC, can be expressed as follows:

$$\begin{pmatrix} \text{Total} \\ \text{annual} = \\ \text{cost} \end{pmatrix} \begin{pmatrix} \text{Annual} \\ \text{holding} \\ \text{cost} \end{pmatrix} \begin{pmatrix} \text{Annual} \\ \text{ordering} \\ \text{cost} \end{pmatrix}$$

$$TC = \frac{1}{2}QC_h + \frac{D}{Q}C_o \qquad (10.4)$$

Using the Bub Beer data [$C_h = IC = (0.25)(\$8) = \$2$, $C_o = \$32$, and $D = 104,000$], the total annual cost model is

$$TC = \frac{1}{2}Q(\$2) + \frac{104,000}{Q}(\$32) = Q + \frac{3,328,000}{Q}$$

The development of the total cost model goes a long way toward solving the inventory problem. We now are able to express the total annual cost as a function of *how much* should be ordered. The development of a realistic total cost model is perhaps the most important part of the application of quantitative methods to inventory decision making. Equation (10.4) is the general total cost equation for inventory situations in which the assumptions of the economic order quantity model are valid.

The How-Much-to-Order Decision

The next step is to find the order quantity Q that will minimize the total annual cost for Bub Beer. Using a trial-and-error approach, we can compute the total annual cost for several possible order quantities. As a starting point, let us consider $Q = 8000$. The total annual cost for Bub Beer is

$$TC = Q + \frac{3{,}328{,}000}{Q}$$

$$= 8000 + \frac{3{,}328{,}000}{8000} = \$8416$$

A trial order quantity of 5000 gives

$$TC = 5000 + \frac{3{,}328{,}000}{5000} = \$5666$$

The results of several other trial order quantities are shown in Table 10.1. It shows the lowest-cost solution to be about 2000 cases. Graphs of the annual holding and ordering costs and total annual costs are shown in Figure 10.3.

The advantage of the trial-and-error approach is that it is rather easy to do and provides the total annual cost for a number of possible order quantity decisions. In this case, the minimum cost order quantity appears to be approximately 2000 cases. The disadvantage of this approach, however, is that it does not provide the exact minimum cost order quantity.

Refer to Figure 10.3. The minimum total cost order quantity is denoted by an order size of Q^*. By using differential calculus, it can be shown (see Appendix 10.1) that the value of Q^* that minimizes the total annual cost is given by the formula

The EOQ formula determines the optimal order quantity by balancing the annual holding cost and the annual ordering cost.

In 1915 F. W. Harris derived the mathematical formula for the economic order quantity. It was the first application of quantitative methods to the area of inventory management.

$$Q^* = \sqrt{\frac{2DC_o}{C_h}} \tag{10.5}$$

This formula is referred to as the *economic order quantity (EOQ) formula*.

TABLE 10.1 ANNUAL HOLDING, ORDERING, AND TOTAL COSTS FOR VARIOUS ORDER QUANTITIES OF BUB BEER

Order Quantity	Annual Cost		
	Holding	**Ordering**	**Total**
5000	$5000	$ 666	$5666
4000	$4000	$ 832	$4832
3000	$3000	$1109	$4109
2000	$2000	$1664	$3664
1000	$1000	$3328	$4328

FIGURE 10.3   ANNUAL HOLDING, ORDERING, AND TOTAL COSTS FOR BUB BEER

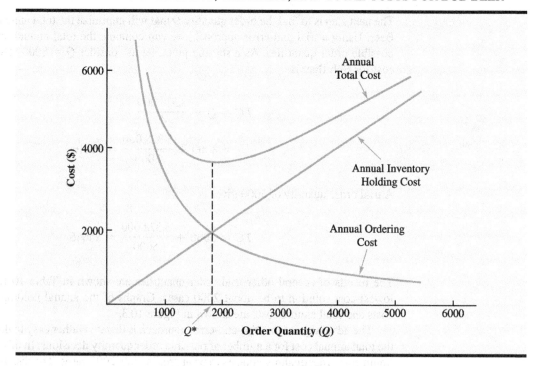

Using equation (10.5), the minimum total annual cost order quantity for Bub Beer is

$$Q^* = \sqrt{\frac{2(104,000)32}{2}} = 1824 \text{ cases}$$

Problem 2 at the end of the chapter asks you to show that equal holding and ordering costs is a property of the EOQ model.

The use of an order quantity of 1824 in equation (10.4) shows that the minimum cost inventory policy for Bub Beer has a total annual cost of \$3649. Note that $Q^* = 1824$ balances the holding and ordering costs. Check for yourself to see that these costs are equal.[2]

The When-to-Order Decision

The reorder point is expressed in terms of inventory position, the amount of inventory on hand plus the amount on order. Some people think that the reorder point is expressed in terms of inventory on hand. With short lead times, inventory position is usually the same as the inventory on hand. However, with long lead times, inventory position may be larger than inventory on hand.

Now that we know how much to order, we want to address the question of *when* to order. To answer this question, we need to introduce the concept of inventory position. The **inventory position** is defined as the amount of inventory on hand plus the amount of inventory on order. The when-to-order decision is expressed in terms of a **reorder point**—the inventory position at which a new order should be placed.

The manufacturer of Bub Beer guarantees a two-day delivery on any order placed by R&B Beverage. Hence, assuming R&B Beverage operates 250 days per year, the annual demand of 104,000 cases implies a daily demand of $104,000/250 = 416$ cases. Thus, we expect (2 days)(416 cases per day) = 832 cases of Bub to be sold during the two days it takes a new order to reach the R&B warehouse. In inventory terminology, the two-day

[2]Actually, Q^* from equation (10.5) is 1824.28, but because we cannot order fractional cases of beer, a Q^* of 1824 is shown. This value of Q^* may cause a few cents deviation between the two costs. If Q^* is used at its exact value, the holding and ordering costs will be exactly the same.

delivery period is referred to as the **lead time** for a new order, and the 832-case demand anticipated during this period is referred to as the **lead-time demand.** Thus, R&B should order a new shipment of Bub Beer from the manufacturer when the inventory reaches 832 cases. For inventory systems using the constant demand rate assumption and a fixed lead time, the reorder point is the same as the lead-time demand. For these systems, the general expression for the reorder point is as follows:

$$r = dm \qquad (10.6)$$

where

$$r = \text{reorder point}$$
$$d = \text{demand per day}$$
$$m = \text{lead time for a new order in days}$$

The question of how frequently the order will be placed can now be answered. The period between orders is referred to as the **cycle time.** Previously in equation (10.2), we defined D/Q as the number of orders that will be placed in a year. Thus, $D/Q^* = 104{,}000/1824 = 57$ is the number of orders R&B Beverage will place for Bub Beer each year. If R&B places 57 orders over 250 working days, it will order approximately every $250/57 = 4.39$ working days. Thus, the cycle time is 4.39 working days. The general expression for a cycle time[3] of T days is given by

$$T = \frac{250}{D/Q^*} = \frac{250Q^*}{D} \qquad (10.7)$$

Sensitivity Analysis for the EOQ Model

Even though substantial time may have been spent in arriving at the cost per order ($32) and the holding cost rate (25%), we should realize that these figures are at best good estimates. Thus, we may want to consider how much the recommended order quantity would change with different estimated ordering and holding costs. To determine the effects of various cost scenarios, we can calculate the recommended order quantity under several different cost conditions. Table 10.2 shows the minimum total cost order quantity for several cost possibilities. As you can see from the table, the value of Q^* appears relatively stable, even with some variations in the cost estimates. Based on these results, the best order quantity for Bub Beer is in the range of 1700–2000 cases. If operated properly, the total cost for the Bub Beer inventory system should be close to $3400 to $3800 per year. We also note that little risk is associated with implementing the calculated order quantity of 1824. For example, if holding cost rate = 24%, $C_o = \$34$, and the true optimal order quantity $Q^* = 1919$, R&B experiences only a $5 increase in the total annual cost; that is, $3690 − $3685 = 5, with $Q = 1824$.

From the preceding analysis, we would say that this EOQ model is insensitive to small variations or errors in the cost estimates. This insensitivity is a property of EOQ models in

[3]This general expression for cycle time is based on 250 working days per year. If the firm operated 300 working days per year and wanted to express cycle time in terms of working days, the cycle time would be given by $T = 300Q^*/D$.

TABLE 10.2 OPTIMAL ORDER QUANTITIES FOR SEVERAL COST POSSIBILITIES

Possible Inventory Holding Cost (%)	Possible Cost per Order	Optimal Order Quantity (Q^*)	Projected Total Annual Cost	
			Using Q^*	Using $Q = 1824$
24	$30	1803	$3461	$3462
24	34	1919	3685	3690
26	30	1732	3603	3607
26	34	1844	3835	3836

general, which indicates that if we have at least reasonable estimates of ordering cost and holding cost, we can expect to obtain a good approximation of the true minimum cost order quantity.

Excel Solution of the EOQ Model

Inventory models such as the EOQ model are easily implemented with the aid of worksheets. The Excel EOQ worksheet for Bub Beer is shown in Figure 10.4. The formula worksheet is in the background; the value worksheet is in the foreground. Data on annual

FIGURE 10.4 WORKSHEET FOR THE BUB BEER EOQ INVENTORY MODEL

WEB file

EOQ

	A	B	C
1	**Economic Order Quantity**		
2			
3	Annual Demand	104,000	
4	Ordering Cost	$32.00	
5	Annual Inventory Holding Rate %	25	
6	Cost per Unit	$8.00	
7	Working Days per Year	250	
8	Lead Time (Days)	2	
9			
10			
11	**Optimal Inventory Policy**		
12			
13	Economic Order Quantity	=SQRT(2*B3*B4/(B5/100*B6))	
14	Annual Inventory Holding Cost	=(1/2)*B13*(B5/100*B6)	
15	Annual Ordering Cost	=(B3/B13)*B4	
16	Total Annual Cost	=B14+B15	
17	Maximum Inventory Level	=B13	
18	Average Inventory Level	=B17/2	
19	Reorder Point	=(B3/B7)*B8	
20	Number of Orders per Year	=B3/B13	
21	Cycle Time (Days)	=B7/B20	

	A	B
1	**Economic Order Quantity**	
2		
3	Annual Demand	104,000
4	Ordering Cost	$32.00
5	Annual Inventory Holding Rate %	25
6	Cost per Unit	$8.00
7	Working Days per Year	250
8	Lead Time (Days)	2
9		
10		
11	**Optimal Inventory Policy**	
12		
13	Economic Order Quantity	1824.28
14	Annual Inventory Holding Cost	$1,824.28
15	Annual Ordering Cost	$1,824.28
16	Total Annual Cost	$3,648.56
17	Maximum Inventory Level	1824.28
18	Average Inventory Level	912.14
19	Reorder Point	832.00
20	Number of Orders per Year	57.01
21	Cycle Time (Days)	4.39

demand, ordering cost, annual inventory holding cost rate, cost per unit, working days per year, and lead time in days are input in cells B3 to B8. The appropriate EOQ model formulas, which determine the optimal inventory policy, are placed in cells B13 to B21. The value worksheet in the foreground shows the optimal economic order quantity 1824.28, the total annual cost \$3,648.56, and a variety of additional information. If sensitivity analysis is desired, one or more of the input data values can be modified. The impact of any change or changes on the optimal inventory policy will then appear in the worksheet.

The Excel worksheet in Figure 10.4 is a template that can be used for the EOQ model. This worksheet and similar Excel worksheets for the other inventory models presented in this chapter are available on the website that accompanies this text.

Summary of the EOQ Model Assumptions

You should carefully review the assumptions of the inventory model before applying it in an actual situation. Several inventory models discussed later in this chapter alter one or more of the assumptions of the EOQ model.

To use the optimal order quantity and reorder point model described in this section, an analyst must make assumptions about how the inventory system operates. The EOQ model with its economic order quantity formula is based on some specific assumptions about the R&B inventory system. A summary of the assumptions for this model is provided in Table 10.3. Before using the EOQ formula, carefully review these assumptions to ensure that they are applicable to the inventory system being analyzed. If the assumptions are not reasonable, seek a different inventory model.

Various types of inventory systems are used in practice, and the inventory models presented in the following sections alter one or more of the EOQ model assumptions shown in Table 10.3. When the assumptions change, a different inventory model with different optimal operating policies becomes necessary.

TABLE 10.3   THE EOQ MODEL ASSUMPTIONS

1. Demand D is deterministic and occurs at a constant rate.
2. The order quantity Q is the same for each order. The inventory level increases by Q units each time an order is received.
3. The cost per order, C_o, is constant and does not depend on the quantity ordered.
4. The purchase cost per unit, C, is constant and does not depend on the quantity ordered.
5. The inventory holding cost per unit per time period, C_h, is constant. The total inventory holding cost depends on both C_h and the size of the inventory.
6. Shortages such as stockouts or backorders are not permitted.
7. The lead time for an order is constant.
8. The inventory position is reviewed continuously. As a result, an order is placed as soon as the inventory position reaches the reorder point.

NOTES AND COMMENTS

With relatively long lead times, the lead-time demand and the resulting reorder point r, determined by equation (10.6), may exceed Q^*. If this condition occurs, at least one order will be outstanding when a new order is placed. For example, assume that Bub Beer has a lead time of $m = 6$ days. With a daily demand of $d = 432$ cases, equation (10.6) shows that the reorder point would be $r = dm = 6$ $\times$ 432 = 2592 cases. Thus, a new order for Bub Beer should be placed whenever the inventory position (the amount of inventory on hand plus the amount of inventory on order) reaches 2592. With an order quantity of $Q = 2000$ cases, the inventory position of 2592 cases occurs when one order of 2000 cases is outstanding and 2592 − 2000 = 592 cases are on hand.

10.2 ECONOMIC PRODUCTION LOT SIZE MODEL

The inventory model in this section alters assumption 2 of the EOQ model (see Table 10.3). The assumption concerning the arrival of Q units each time an order is received is changed to a constant production supply rate.

The inventory model presented in this section is similar to the EOQ model in that we are attempting to determine *how much* we should order and *when* the order should be placed. We again assume a constant demand rate. However, instead of assuming that the order arrives in a shipment of size Q^*, as in the EOQ model, we assume that units are supplied to inventory at a constant rate over several days or several weeks. The **constant supply rate** assumption implies that the same number of units is supplied to inventory each period of time (e.g., 10 units every day or 50 units every week). This model is designed for production situations in which, once an order is placed, production begins and a constant number of units is added to inventory each day until the production run has been completed.

If we have a production system that produces 50 units per day and we decide to schedule 10 days of production, we have a $50(10) = 500$-unit production lot size. The **lot size** is the number of units in an order. In general, if we let Q indicate the production lot size, the approach to the inventory decisions is similar to the EOQ model; that is, we build a holding and ordering cost model that expresses the total cost as a function of the production lot size. Then we attempt to find the production lot size that minimizes the total cost.

One other condition that should be mentioned at this time is that the model only applies to situations where the production rate is greater than the demand rate; the production system must be able to satisfy demand. For instance, if the constant demand rate is 400 units per day, the production rate must be at least 400 units per day to satisfy demand.

During the production run, demand reduces the inventory while production adds to inventory. Because we assume that the production rate exceeds the demand rate, each day during a production run we produce more units than are demanded. Thus, the excess production causes a gradual inventory buildup during the production period. When the production run is completed, the continuing demand causes the inventory to gradually decline until a new production run is started. The inventory pattern for this system is shown in Figure 10.5.

This model differs from the EOQ model in that a setup cost replaces the ordering cost and the sawtooth inventory pattern shown in Figure 10.5 differs from the inventory pattern shown in Figure 10.2.

As in the EOQ model, we are now dealing with two costs, the holding cost and the ordering cost. Here the holding cost is identical to the definition in the EOQ model, but the interpretation of the ordering cost is slightly different. In fact, in a production situation the ordering cost is more correctly referred to as the production **setup cost.** This cost, which includes labor, material, and lost production costs incurred while preparing the production system for operation, is a fixed cost that occurs for every production run regardless of the production lot size.

FIGURE 10.5 INVENTORY PATTERN FOR THE PRODUCTION LOT SIZE INVENTORY MODEL

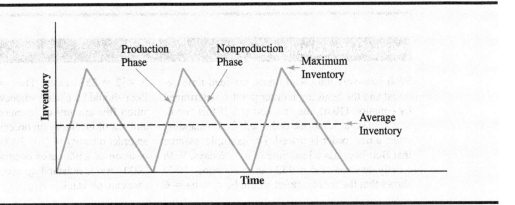

Total Cost Model

Let us begin building the production lot size model by writing the holding cost in terms of the production lot size Q. Again, the approach is to develop an expression for average inventory and then establish the holding costs associated with the average inventory. We use a one-year time period and an annual cost for the model.

In the EOQ model the average inventory is one-half the maximum inventory or $\frac{1}{2}Q$. Figure 10.5 shows that for a production lot size model a constant inventory buildup rate occurs during the production run and a constant inventory depletion rate occurs during the nonproduction period; thus, the average inventory will be one-half the maximum inventory. However, in this inventory system the production lot size Q does not go into inventory at one point in time, and thus the inventory never reaches a level of Q units.

To show how we can compute the maximum inventory, let

$$d = \text{daily demand rate}$$
$$p = \text{daily production rate}$$
$$t = \text{number of days for a production run}$$

At this point, the logic of the production lot size model is easier to follow using a daily demand rate d and a daily production rate p. However, when the total annual cost model is eventually developed, we recommend that inputs to the model be expressed in terms of the annual demand rate D and the annual production rate P.

Because we are assuming that p will be larger than d, the daily inventory buildup rate during the production phase is $p - d$. If we run production for t days and place $p - d$ units in inventory each day, the inventory at the end of the production run will be $(p - d)t$. From Figure 10.5 we can see that the inventory at the end of the production run is also the maximum inventory. Thus,

$$\text{Maximum inventory} = (p - d)t \tag{10.8}$$

If we know we are producing a production lot size of Q units at a daily production rate of p units, then $Q = pt$, and the length of the production run t must be

$$t = \frac{Q}{p} \text{ days} \tag{10.9}$$

Thus,

$$\text{Maximum inventory} = (p - d)t = (p - d)\left(\frac{Q}{p}\right)$$
$$= \left(1 - \frac{d}{p}\right)Q \tag{10.10}$$

The average inventory, which is one-half the maximum inventory, is given by

$$\text{Average inventory} = \frac{1}{2}\left(1 - \frac{d}{p}\right)Q \tag{10.11}$$

With an annual per unit holding cost of C_h, the general equation for annual holding cost is as follows:

$$\begin{pmatrix} \text{Annual} \\ \text{holding cost} \end{pmatrix} = \begin{pmatrix} \text{Average} \\ \text{inventory} \end{pmatrix} \begin{pmatrix} \text{Annual} \\ \text{cost} \\ \text{per unit} \end{pmatrix}$$

$$= \frac{1}{2}\left(1 - \frac{d}{p}\right)QC_h \qquad\qquad (10.12)$$

If D is the annual demand for the product and C_o is the setup cost for a production run, then the annual setup cost, which takes the place of the annual ordering cost in the EOQ model, is as follows:

$$\text{Annual setup cost} = \begin{pmatrix} \text{Number of production} \\ \text{runs per year} \end{pmatrix} \begin{pmatrix} \text{Setup cost} \\ \text{per run} \end{pmatrix}$$

$$= \frac{D}{Q}C_o \qquad\qquad (10.13)$$

Thus, the total annual cost (TC) model is

$$TC = \frac{1}{2}\left(1 - \frac{d}{p}\right)QC_h + \frac{D}{Q}C_o \qquad\qquad (10.14)$$

Suppose that a production facility operates 250 days per year. Then we can write daily demand d in terms of annual demand D as follows:

$$d = \frac{D}{250}$$

Now let P denote the annual production for the product if the product were produced every day. Then

$$P = 250p \qquad \text{and} \qquad p = \frac{P}{250}$$

Thus,[4]

$$\frac{d}{p} = \frac{D/250}{P/250} = \frac{D}{P}$$

---

[4]The ratio $d/p = D/P$ holds regardless of the number of days of operation; 250 days is used here merely as an illustration.

748

Therefore, we can write the total annual cost model as follows:

$$TC = \frac{1}{2}\left(1 - \frac{D}{P}\right)QC_h + \frac{D}{Q}C_o \qquad (10.15)$$

Equations (10.14) and (10.15) are equivalent. However, equation (10.15) may be used more frequently because an *annual* cost model tends to make the analyst think in terms of collecting *annual* demand data (*D*) and *annual* production data (*P*) rather than daily data.

Economic Production Lot Size

Given estimates of the holding cost (C_h), setup cost (C_o), annual demand rate (*D*), and annual production rate (*P*), we could use a trial-and-error approach to compute the total annual cost for various production lot sizes (*Q*). However, trial and error is not necessary; we can use the minimum cost formula for *Q** that has been developed using differential calculus (see Appendix 10.2). The equation is as follows:

$$Q^* = \sqrt{\frac{2DC_o}{(1 - D/P)C_h}} \qquad (10.16)$$

As the production rate P approaches infinity, D/P approaches zero. In this case, equation (10.16) is equivalent to the EOQ model in equation (10.5).

An Example   Beauty Bar Soap is produced on a production line that has an annual capacity of 60,000 cases. The annual demand is estimated at 26,000 cases, with the demand rate essentially constant throughout the year. The cleaning, preparation, and setup of the production line cost approximately $135. The manufacturing cost per case is $4.50, and the annual holding cost is figured at a 24% rate. Thus, $C_h = IC = 0.24(\$4.50) = \$1.08$. What is the recommended production lot size?

Using equation (10.16), we have

$$Q^* = \sqrt{\frac{2(26,000)(135)}{(1 - 26,000/60,000)(1.08)}} = 3387$$

WEB file

Lot Size

The total annual cost using equation (10.15) and $Q^* = 3387$ is $2073.

Work Problem 13 as an example of an economic production lot size model.

Other relevant data include a five-day lead time to schedule and set up a production run and 250 working days per year. Thus, the lead-time demand of $(26,000/250)(5) = 520$ cases is the reorder point. The cycle time is the time between production runs. Using equation (10.7), the cycle time is $T = 250Q^*/D = [(250)(3387)]/26,000$, or 33 working days. Thus, we should plan a production run of 3387 units every 33 working days.

10.3   INVENTORY MODEL WITH PLANNED SHORTAGES

A **shortage,** or **stockout,** is a demand that cannot be supplied. In many situations, shortages are undesirable and should be avoided if at all possible. However, in other cases it may be desirable—from an economic point of view—to plan for and allow shortages. In practice, these types of situations are most commonly found where the value of the inventory per unit is high and hence the holding cost is high. An example of this type of situation is

The assumptions of the EOQ model in Table 10.3 apply to this inventory model, with the exception that shortages, referred to as backorders, are now permitted.

a new car dealer's inventory. Often a specific car that a customer wants is not in stock. However, if the customer is willing to wait a few weeks, the dealer is usually able to order the car.

The model developed in this section takes into account a type of shortage known as a **backorder.** In a backorder situation, we assume that when a customer places an order and discovers that the supplier is out of stock, the customer waits until the new shipment arrives, and then the order is filled. Frequently, the waiting period in backorder situations is relatively short. Thus, by promising the customer top priority and immediate delivery when the goods become available, companies may be able to convince the customer to wait until the order arrives. In these cases, the backorder assumption is valid.

The backorder model that we develop is an extension of the EOQ model presented in Section 10.1. We use the EOQ model in which all goods arrive in inventory at one time and are subject to a constant demand rate. If we let S indicate the number of backorders that are accumulated when a new shipment of size Q is received, then the inventory system for the backorder case has the following characteristics:

- If S backorders exist when a new shipment of size Q arrives, then S backorders are shipped to the appropriate customers, and the remaining $Q - S$ units are placed in inventory. Therefore, $Q - S$ is the maximum inventory.
- The inventory cycle of T days is divided into two distinct phases: t_1 days when inventory is on hand and orders are filled as they occur, and t_2 days when stockouts occur and all new orders are placed on backorder.

The inventory pattern for the inventory model with backorders, where negative inventory represents the number of backorders, is shown in Figure 10.6.

With the inventory pattern now defined, we can proceed with the basic step of all inventory models—namely, the development of a total cost model. For the inventory model with backorders, we encounter the usual holding costs and ordering costs. We also incur a backorder cost in terms of the labor and special delivery costs directly associated with the handling of the backorders. Another portion of the backorder cost accounts for the loss of goodwill because some customers will have to wait for their orders. Because the **goodwill cost** depends on how long a customer has to wait, it is customary to adopt the convention of expressing backorder cost in terms of the cost of having a unit on backorder for a stated period of time. This method of costing backorders on a time basis is similar to the method

FIGURE 10.6   INVENTORY PATTERN FOR AN INVENTORY MODEL WITH BACKORDERS

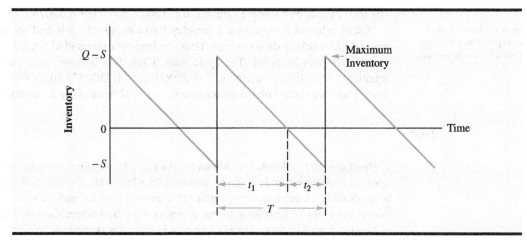

used to compute the inventory holding cost, and we can use it to compute a total annual cost of backorders once the average backorder level and the backorder cost per unit per period are known.

Let us begin the development of a total cost model by calculating the average inventory for a hypothetical problem. If we have an average inventory of two units for three days and no inventory on the fourth day, what is the average inventory over the four-day period? It is

$$\frac{2 \text{ units } (3 \text{ days}) + 0 \text{ units } (1 \text{ day})}{4 \text{ days}} = \frac{6}{4} = 1.5 \text{ units}$$

Refer to Figure 10.6. You can see that this situation is what happens in the backorder model. With a maximum inventory of $Q - S$ units, the t_1 days we have inventory on hand will have an average inventory of $(Q - S)/2$. No inventory is carried for the t_2 days in which we experience backorders. Thus, over the total cycle time of $T = t_1 + t_2$ days, we can compute the average inventory as follows:

$$\text{Average inventory} = \frac{\frac{1}{2}(Q - S)t_1 + 0t_2}{t_1 + t_2} = \frac{\frac{1}{2}(Q - S)t_1}{T} \qquad (10.17)$$

Can we find other ways of expressing t_1 and T? Because we know that the maximum inventory is $Q - S$ and that d represents the constant daily demand, we have

$$t_1 = \frac{Q - S}{d} \text{ days} \qquad (10.18)$$

That is, the maximum inventory of $Q - S$ units will be used up in $(Q - S)/d$ days. Because Q units are ordered each cycle, we know the length of a cycle must be

$$T = \frac{Q}{d} \text{ days} \qquad (10.19)$$

Combining equations (10.18) and (10.19) with equation (10.17), we can compute the average inventory as follows:

$$\text{Average inventory} = \frac{\frac{1}{2}(Q - S)[(Q - S)/d]}{Q/d} = \frac{(Q - S)^2}{2Q} \qquad (10.20)$$

Thus, the average inventory is expressed in terms of two inventory decisions: how much we will order (Q) and the maximum number of backorders (S).

The formula for the annual number of orders placed using this model is identical to that for the EOQ model. With D representing the annual demand, we have

$$\text{Annual number of orders} = \frac{D}{Q} \qquad (10.21)$$

The next step is to develop an expression for the average backorder level. Because we know the maximum for backorders is S, we can use the same logic we used to establish average inventory in finding the average number of backorders. We have an average number of backorders during the period t_2 of $\frac{1}{2}$ the maximum number of backorders, or $\frac{1}{2}S$. We do not have any backorders during the t_1 days we have inventory; therefore, we can calculate the average backorders in a manner similar to equation (10.17). Using this approach, we have

$$\text{Average backorders} = \frac{0t_1 + (S/2)t_2}{T} = \frac{(S/2)t_2}{T} \qquad (10.22)$$

When we let the maximum number of backorders reach an amount S at a daily rate of d, the length of the backorder portion of the inventory cycle is

$$t_2 = \frac{S}{d} \qquad (10.23)$$

Using equations (10.23) and (10.19) in equation (10.22), we have

$$\text{Average backorders} = \frac{(S/2)(S/d)}{Q/d} = \frac{S^2}{2Q} \qquad (10.24)$$

Let

C_h = cost to maintain one unit in inventory for one year
C_o = cost per order
C_b = cost to maintain one unit on backorder for one year

The total annual cost (TC) for the inventory model with backorders becomes

$$TC = \frac{(Q - S)^2}{2Q} C_h + \frac{D}{Q} C_o + \frac{S^2}{2Q} C_b \qquad (10.25)$$

Given C_h, C_o, and C_b and the annual demand D, differential calculus can be used to show that the minimum cost values for the order quantity Q^* and the planned backorders S^* are as follows:

$$Q^* = \sqrt{\frac{2DC_o}{C_h}\left(\frac{C_h + C_b}{C_b}\right)} \tag{10.26}$$

$$S^* = Q^*\left(\frac{C_h}{C_h + C_b}\right) \tag{10.27}$$

Shortage

An inventory situation that incorporates backorder costs is considered in Problem 15.

The backorder cost C_b is one of the most difficult costs to estimate in inventory models. The reason is that it attempts to measure the cost associated with the loss of goodwill when a customer must wait for an order. Expressing this cost on an annual basis adds to the difficulty.

If backorders can be tolerated, the total cost including the backorder cost will be less than the total cost of the EOQ model. Some people think the model with backorders will have a greater cost because it includes a backorder cost in addition to the usual inventory holding and ordering costs. You can point out the fallacy in this thinking by noting that the backorder model leads to lower inventory and hence lower inventory holding costs.

An Example Suppose that the Higley Radio Components Company has a product for which the assumptions of the inventory model with backorders are valid. Information obtained by the company is as follows:

$$D = 2000 \text{ units per year}$$
$$I = 20\%$$
$$C = \$50 \text{ per unit}$$
$$C_h = IC = (0.20)(\$50) = \$10 \text{ per unit per year}$$
$$C_o = \$25 \text{ per order}$$

The company is considering the possibility of allowing some backorders to occur for the product. The annual backorder cost is estimated to be $30 per unit per year. Using equations (10.26) and (10.27), we have

$$Q^* = \sqrt{\frac{2(2000)(25)}{10}\left(\frac{10 + 30}{20}\right)} = 115.47$$

and

$$S^* = 115\left(\frac{10}{10 + 30}\right) = 28.87$$

If this solution is implemented, the system will operate with the following properties:

$$\text{Maximum inventory} = Q - S = 115.47 - 28.87 = 86.6$$

$$\text{Cycle time} = T = \frac{Q}{D}(250) = \frac{115.47}{2000}(250) = 14.43 \text{ working days}$$

The total annual cost is

$$\text{Holding cost} = \frac{(86.6)^2}{2(115.47)}(10) = \$325$$

$$\text{Ordering cost} = \frac{2000}{115.47}(25) = \$433$$

$$\text{Backorder cost} = \frac{(28.87)^2}{2(115.47)}(30) = \$108$$

$$\text{Total cost} = \$866$$

If the company chooses to prohibit backorders and adopts the regular EOQ model, the recommended inventory decision would be

$$Q^* = \sqrt{\frac{2(2000)(25)}{10}} = \sqrt{10,000} = 100$$

This order quantity would result in a holding cost and an ordering cost of $500 each, or a total annual cost of $1000. Thus, in this problem, allowing backorders is projecting a $1000 − $866 = $134 or 13.4% savings in cost from the no-stockout EOQ model. The preceding comparison and conclusion are based on the assumption that the backorder model with an annual cost per backordered unit of $30 is a valid model for the actual inventory situation. If the company is concerned that stockouts might lead to lost sales, then the savings might not be enough to warrant switching to an inventory policy that allowed for planned shortages.

NOTES AND COMMENTS

Equation (10.27) shows that the optimal number of planned backorders S^* is proportional to the ratio $C_h/(C_h + C_b)$, where C_h is the annual holding cost per unit and C_b is the annual backorder cost per unit. Whenever C_h increases, this ratio becomes larger, and the number of planned backorders increases. This relationship explains why items that have a high per-unit cost and a correspondingly high annual holding cost are more economically handled on a backorder basis. On the other hand, whenever the backorder cost C_b increases, the ratio becomes smaller, and the number of planned backorders decreases. Thus, the model provides the intuitive result that items with high backorder costs will be handled with few backorders. In fact, with high backorder costs, the backorder model and the EOQ model with no backordering allowed provide similar inventory policies.

10.4 QUANTITY DISCOUNTS FOR THE EOQ MODEL

In the quantity discount model, assumption 4 of the EOQ model in Table 10.3 is altered. The cost per unit varies depending on the quantity ordered.

Quantity discounts occur in numerous situations in which suppliers provide an incentive for large order quantities by offering a lower purchase cost when items are ordered in larger quantities. In this section we show how the EOQ model can be used when quantity discounts are available.

Assume that we have a product in which the basic EOQ model (see Table 10.3) is applicable. Instead of a fixed unit cost, the supplier quotes the following discount schedule:

Discount Category	Order Size	Discount (%)	Unit Cost
1	0 to 999	0	$5.00
2	1000 to 2499	3	4.85
3	2500 and over	5	4.75

The 5% discount for the 2500-unit minimum order quantity looks tempting. However, realizing that higher order quantities result in higher inventory holding costs, we should prepare a thorough cost analysis before making a final ordering and inventory policy recommendation.

Suppose that the data and cost analyses show an annual holding cost rate of 20%, an ordering cost of \$49 per order, and an annual demand of 5000 units; what order quantity should we select? The following three-step procedure shows the calculations necessary to make this decision. In the preliminary calculations, we use Q_1 to indicate the order quantity for discount category 1, Q_2 for discount category 2, and Q_3 for discount category 3.

Step 1. For each discount category, compute a Q^* using the EOQ formula based on the unit cost associated with the discount category.

Recall that the EOQ model provides $Q^* = \sqrt{2DC_o/C_h}$, where $C_h = IC = (0.20)C$. With three discount categories providing three different unit costs C, we obtain

WEB file

Discount

$$Q_1^* = \sqrt{\frac{2(5000)49}{(0.20)(5.00)}} = 700$$

$$Q_2^* = \sqrt{\frac{2(5000)49}{(0.20)(4.85)}} = 711$$

$$Q_3^* = \sqrt{\frac{2(5000)49}{(0.20)(4.75)}} = 718$$

Because the only differences in the EOQ formulas come from slight differences in the holding cost, the economic order quantities resulting from this step will be approximately the same. However, these order quantities will usually not all be of the size necessary to qualify for the discount price assumed. In the preceding case, both Q_2^* and Q_3^* are insufficient order quantities to obtain their assumed discounted costs of \$4.85 and \$4.75, respectively. For those order quantities for which the assumed price cannot be obtained, the following procedure must be used:

Step 2. For the Q^* that is too small to qualify for the assumed discount price, adjust the order quantity upward to the nearest order quantity that will allow the product to be purchased at the assumed price.

In our example, this adjustment causes us to set

$$Q_2^* = 1000$$

and

$$Q_3^* = 2500$$

Problem 23 at the end of the chapter asks you to show that this property is true.

If a calculated Q^* for a given discount price is large enough to qualify for a bigger discount, that value of Q^* cannot lead to an optimal solution. Although the reason may not be obvious, it does turn out to be a property of the EOQ quantity discount model.

In the EOQ model with quantity discounts, the annual purchase cost must be included because purchase cost depends on the order quantity. Thus, it is a relevant cost.

In the previous inventory models considered, the annual purchase cost of the item was not included because it was constant and never affected by the inventory order policy decision. However, in the quantity discount model, the annual purchase cost depends on the order quantity and the associated unit cost. Thus, annual purchase cost (annual demand $D \times$ unit cost C) is included in the equation for total cost, as shown here:

$$TC = \frac{Q}{2}C_h + \frac{D}{Q}C_o + DC \qquad (10.28)$$

TABLE 10.4 TOTAL ANNUAL COST CALCULATIONS FOR THE EOQ MODEL
WITH QUANTITY DISCOUNTS

Discount Category	Unit Cost	Order Quantity	Annual Cost			
			Holding	**Ordering**	**Purchase**	**Total**
1	$5.00	700	$ 350	$350	$25,000	$25,700
2	4.85	1000	$ 485	$245	$24,250	$24,980
3	4.75	2500	$1188	$ 98	$23,750	$25,036

Using this total cost equation, we can determine the optimal order quantity for the EOQ discount model in step 3.

Step 3. For each order quantity resulting from steps 1 and 2, compute the total annual cost using the unit price from the appropriate discount category and equation (10.28). The order quantity yielding the minimum total annual cost is the optimal order quantity.

Problem 21 will give you practice in applying the EOQ model to situations with quantity discounts.

The step 3 calculations for the example problem are summarized in Table 10.4. As you can see, a decision to order 1000 units at the 3% discount rate yields the minimum cost solution. Even though the 2500-unit order quantity would result in a 5% discount, its excessive holding cost makes it the second-best solution. Figure 10.7 shows the total cost curve for each of the three discount categories. Note that $Q^* = 1000$ provides the minimum cost order quantity.

10.5   SINGLE-PERIOD INVENTORY MODEL WITH PROBABILISTIC DEMAND

This inventory model is the first in the chapter that explicitly treats probabilistic demand. Unlike the EOQ model, it is for a single period with unused inventory not carried over to future periods.

The inventory models discussed thus far were based on the assumption that the demand rate is constant and **deterministic** throughout the year. We developed minimum cost order quantity and reorder point policies based on this assumption. In situations in which the demand rate is not deterministic, other models treat demand as **probabilistic** and best described by a probability distribution. In this section we consider a **single-period inventory model** with probabilistic demand.

The single-period inventory model refers to inventory situations in which *one* order is placed for the product; at the end of the period, the product has either sold out or a surplus of unsold items will be sold for a salvage value. The single-period inventory model is applicable in situations involving seasonal or perishable items that cannot be carried in inventory and sold in future periods. Seasonal clothing (such as bathing suits and winter coats) is typically handled in a single-period manner. In these situations, a buyer places one pre-season order for each item and then experiences a stockout or holds a clearance sale on the surplus stock at the end of the season. No items are carried in inventory and sold the following year. Newspapers are another example of a product that is ordered one time and is either sold or not sold during the single period. Although newspapers are ordered daily, they cannot be carried in inventory and sold in later periods. Thus, newspaper orders may be treated as a sequence of single-period models; that is, each day or period is separate, and a single-period inventory decision must be made each period (day). Because we order only once for the period, the only inventory decision we must make is *how much* of the product to order at the start of the period.

FIGURE 10.7 TOTAL COST CURVES FOR THE THREE DISCOUNT CATEGORIES

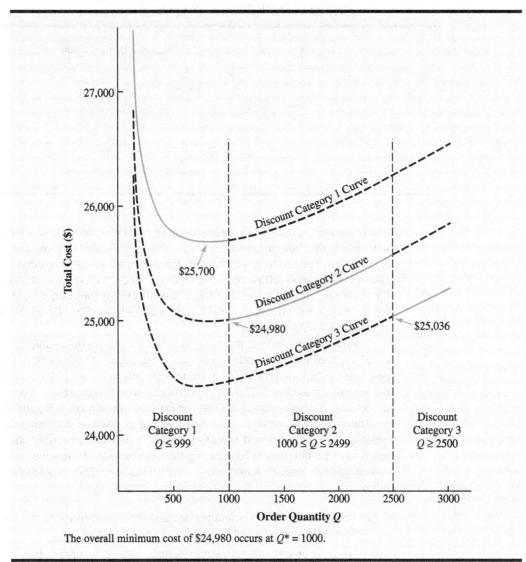

The overall minimum cost of $24,980 occurs at $Q^* = 1000$.

Obviously, if the demand were known for a single-period inventory situation, the solution would be easy; we would simply order the amount we knew would be demanded. However, in most single-period models, the exact demand is not known. In fact, forecasts may show that demand can have a wide variety of values. If we are going to analyze this type of inventory problem in a quantitative manner, we need information about the probabilities associated with the various demand values. Thus, the single-period model presented in this section is based on probabilistic demand.

Johnson Shoe Company

Let us consider a single-period inventory model that could be used to make a how-much-to-order decision for the Johnson Shoe Company. The buyer for the Johnson Shoe Company decided to order a men's shoe shown at a buyers' meeting in New York City. The shoe

FIGURE 10.8 UNIFORM PROBABILITY DISTRIBUTION OF DEMAND FOR THE JOHNSON SHOE COMPANY PROBLEM

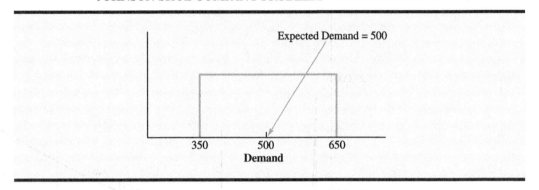

will be part of the company's spring–summer promotion and will be sold through nine retail stores in the Chicago area. Because the shoe is designed for spring and summer months, it cannot be expected to sell in the fall. Johnson plans to hold a special August clearance sale in an attempt to sell all shoes not sold by July 31. The shoes cost $40 a pair and retail for $60 a pair. At the sale price of $30 a pair, all surplus shoes can be expected to sell during the August sale. If you were the buyer for the Johnson Shoe Company, how many pairs of the shoes would you order?

An obvious question at this time is, What are the possible values of demand for the shoe? We need this information to answer the question of how much to order. Let us suppose that the uniform probability distribution shown in Figure 10.8 can be used to describe the demand for the size 10D shoes. In particular, note that the range of demand is from 350 to 650 pairs of shoes, with an average, or expected, demand of 500 pairs of shoes.

Incremental analysis is a method that can be used to determine the optimal order quantity for a single-period inventory model. Incremental analysis addresses the how-much-to-order question by comparing the cost or loss of *ordering one additional unit* with the cost or loss of *not ordering one additional unit*. The costs involved are defined as follows:

c_o = cost per unit of *overestimating* demand. This cost represents the loss of ordering one additional unit and finding that it cannot be sold.

c_u = cost per unit of *underestimating* demand. This cost represents the opportunity loss of not ordering one additional unit and finding that it could have been sold.

The cost of underestimating demand is usually harder to determine than the cost of overestimating demand. The reason is that the cost of underestimating demand includes a lost profit and may include a customer goodwill cost because the customer is unable to purchase the item when desired.

In the Johnson Shoe Company problem, the company will incur the cost of overestimating demand whenever it orders too much and has to sell the extra shoes during the August sale. Thus, the cost per unit of overestimating demand is equal to the purchase cost per unit minus the August sales price per unit; that is, $c_o = \$40 - \$30 = \$10$. Therefore, Johnson will lose $10 for each pair of shoes that it orders over the quantity demanded. The cost of underestimating demand is the lost profit because a pair of shoes that could have been sold was not available in inventory. Thus, the per-unit cost of underestimating demand is the difference between the regular selling price per unit and the purchase cost per unit; that is, $c_u = \$60 - \$40 = \$20$.

Because the exact level of demand for the size 10D shoes is unknown, we have to consider the probability of demand and thus the probability of obtaining the associated costs or losses. For example, let us assume that Johnson Shoe Company management wishes to

758

consider an order quantity equal to the average or expected demand for 500 pairs of shoes. In incremental analysis, we consider the possible losses associated with an order quantity of 501 (ordering one additional unit) and an order quantity of 500 (not ordering one additional unit). The order quantity alternatives and the possible losses are summarized here:

Order Quantity Alternatives	Loss Occurs If	Possible Loss	Probability Loss Occurs
$Q = 501$	Demand overestimated; the additional unit *cannot* be sold	$c_o = \$10$	$P(\text{demand} \leq 500)$
$Q = 500$	Demand underestimated; an additional unit *could have* been sold	$c_u = \$20$	$P(\text{demand} > 500)$

By looking at the demand probability distribution in Figure 10.8, we see that $P(\text{demand} \leq 500) = 0.50$ and that $P(\text{demand} > 500) = 0.50$. By multiplying the possible losses, $c_o = \$10$ and $c_u = \$20$, by the probability of obtaining the loss, we can compute the expected value of the loss, or simply the *expected loss* (EL), associated with the order quantity alternatives. Thus,

$$\text{EL}(Q = 501) = c_o P(\text{demand} \leq 500) = \$10(0.50) = \$5$$
$$\text{EL}(Q = 500) = c_u P(\text{demand} > 500) = \$20(0.50) = \$10$$

Based on these expected losses, do you prefer an order quantity of 501 or 500 pairs of shoes? Because the expected loss is greater for $Q = 500$ and because we want to avoid this higher cost or loss, we should make $Q = 501$ the preferred decision. We could now consider incrementing the order quantity one additional unit to $Q = 502$ and repeating the expected loss calculations.

Although we could continue this unit-by-unit analysis, it would be time-consuming and cumbersome. We would have to evaluate $Q = 502$, $Q = 503$, $Q = 504$, and so on, until we found the value of Q where the expected loss of ordering one incremental unit is equal to the expected loss of not ordering one incremental unit; that is, the optimal order quantity Q^* occurs when the incremental analysis shows that

$$\text{EL}(Q^* + 1) = \text{EL}(Q^*) \tag{10.29}$$

When this relationship holds, increasing the order quantity by one additional unit has no economic advantage. Using the logic with which we computed the expected losses for the order quantities of 501 and 500, the general expressions for $\text{EL}(Q^* + 1)$ and $\text{EL}(Q^*)$ can be written

$$\text{EL}(Q^* + 1) = c_o P(\text{demand} \leq Q^*) \tag{10.30}$$
$$\text{EL}(Q^*) = c_u P(\text{demand} > Q^*) \tag{10.31}$$

Because we know from basic probability that

$$P(\text{demand} \le Q^*) + P(\text{demand} > Q^*) = 1 \qquad (10.32)$$

we can write

$$P(\text{demand} > Q^*) = 1 - P(\text{demand} \le Q^*) \qquad (10.33)$$

Using this expression, equation (10.31) can be rewritten as

$$\text{EL}(Q^*) = c_u[1 - P(\text{demand} \le Q^*)] \qquad (10.34)$$

Equations (10.30) and (10.34) can be used to show that $\text{EL}(Q^* + 1) = \text{EL}(Q^*)$ whenever

$$c_o P(\text{demand} \le Q^*) = c_u[1 - P(\text{demand} \le Q^*)] \qquad (10.35)$$

Solving for $P(\text{demand} \le Q^*)$, we have

$$P(\text{demand} \le Q^*) = \frac{c_u}{c_u + c_o} \qquad (10.36)$$

This expression provides the general condition for the optimal order quantity Q^* in the single-period inventory model.

In the Johnson Shoe Company problem $c_o = \$10$ and $c_u = \$20$. Thus, equation (10.36) shows that the optimal order size for Johnson shoes must satisfy the following condition:

$$P(\text{demand} \le Q^*) = \frac{c_u}{c_u + c_o} = \frac{20}{20 + 10} = \frac{20}{30} = \frac{2}{3}$$

We can find the optimal order quantity Q^* by referring to the probability distribution shown in Figure 10.8 and finding the value of Q that will provide $P(\text{demand} \le Q^*) = \frac{2}{3}$. To find this solution, we note that in the uniform distribution the probability is evenly distributed over the entire range of 350 to 650 pairs of shoes. Thus, we can satisfy the expression for Q^* by moving two-thirds of the way from 350 to 650. Because this range is $650 - 350 = 300$, we move 200 units from 350 toward 650. Doing so provides the optimal order quantity of 550 pairs of shoes.

In summary, the key to establishing an optimal order quantity for single-period inventory models is to identify the probability distribution that describes the demand for the item and the costs of overestimation and underestimation. Then, using the information for the costs of overestimation and underestimation, equation (10.36) can be used to find the location of Q^* in the probability distribution.

Nationwide Car Rental

As another example of a single-period inventory model with probabilistic demand, consider the situation faced by Nationwide Car Rental. Nationwide must decide how many automobiles to have available at each car rental location at specific points in time throughout the year. Using the Myrtle Beach, South Carolina, location as an example, management would like to know the number of full-sized automobiles to have available for the Labor Day weekend. Based on previous experience, customer demand for full-sized automobiles for the Labor Day weekend has a normal distribution with a mean of 150 automobiles and a standard deviation of 14 automobiles.

The Nationwide Car Rental situation can benefit from use of a single-period inventory model. The company must establish the number of full-sized automobiles to have available prior to the weekend. Customer demand over the weekend will then result in either a stock-out or a surplus. Let us denote the number of full-sized automobiles available by Q. If Q is greater than customer demand, Nationwide will have a surplus of cars. The cost of a surplus is the cost of overestimating demand. This cost is set at $80 per car, which reflects, in part, the opportunity cost of not having the car available for rent elsewhere.

If Q is less than customer demand, Nationwide will rent all available cars and experience a stockout, or shortage. A shortage results in an underestimation cost of $200 per car. This figure reflects the cost due to lost profit and the lost goodwill of not having a car available for a customer. Given this information, how many full-sized automobiles should Nationwide make available for the Labor Day weekend?

Using the cost of underestimation, $c_u = \$200$, and the cost of overestimation, $c_o = \$80$, equation (10.36) indicates that the optimal order quantity must satisfy the following condition:

$$P(\text{demand} \leq Q^*) = \frac{c_u}{(c_u + c_o)} = \frac{200}{200 + 80} = 0.7143$$

We can use the normal probability distribution for demand, as shown in Figure 10.9, to find the order quantity that satisfies the condition that $P(\text{demand} \leq Q^*) = 0.7143$. Using the cumulative probabilities for the normal distribution (see Appendix B), the cumulative

---

FIGURE 10.9   PROBABILITY DISTRIBUTION OF DEMAND FOR THE NATIONWIDE
CAR RENTAL PROBLEM SHOWING THE LOCATION OF Q^*

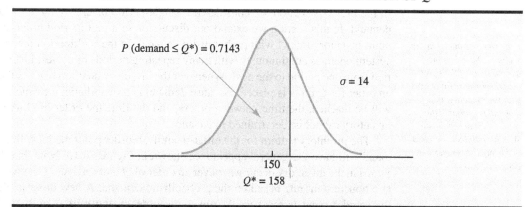

probability closest to 0.7143 occurs at $z = 0.57$. Thus, the optimal order quantity occurs at 0.57 standard deviations above the mean. With a mean demand of $\mu = 150$ automobiles and a standard deviation of $\sigma = 14$ automobiles, we have

$$Q^* = \mu + 0.57\sigma$$
$$= 150 + 0.57(14) = 158$$

An example of a single-period inventory model with probabilistic demand described by a normal probability distribution is considered in Problem 25.

Thus, Nationwide Car Rental should plan to have 158 full-sized automobiles available in Myrtle Beach for the Labor Day weekend. Note that in this case the cost of overestimation is less than the cost of underestimation. Thus, Nationwide is willing to risk a higher probability of overestimating demand and hence a higher probability of a surplus. In fact, Nationwide's optimal order quantity has a 0.7143 probability of a surplus and a $1 - 0.7143 = 0.2857$ probability of a stockout. As a result, the probability is 0.2857 that all 158 full-sized automobiles will be rented during the Labor Day weekend.

NOTES AND COMMENTS

1. In any probabilistic inventory model, the assumption about the probability distribution for demand is critical and can affect the recommended inventory decision. In the problems presented in this section, we used the uniform and the normal probability distributions to describe demand. In some situations, other probability distributions may be more appropriate. In using probabilistic inventory models, we must exercise care in selecting the probability distribution that most realistically describes demand.

2. In the single-period inventory model, the value of $c_u/(c_u + c_o)$ plays a critical role in selecting the order quantity the ratio [see equation (10.36)]. Whenever $c_u = c_o$, the ratio $(c_u/(c_u + c_o)) = 0.50$;

in this case, we should select an order quantity corresponding to the median demand. With this choice, a stockout is just as likely as a surplus because the two costs are equal. However, whenever $c_u < c_o$, a smaller order quantity will be recommended. In this case, the smaller order quantity will provide a higher probability of a stockout; however, the more expensive cost of overestimating demand and having a surplus will tend to be avoided. Finally, whenever $c_u > c_o$, a larger order quantity will be recommended. In this case, the larger order quantity provides a lower probability of a stockout in an attempt to avoid the more expensive cost of underestimating demand and experiencing a stockout.

10.6 ORDER-QUANTITY, REORDER POINT MODEL WITH PROBABILISTIC DEMAND

The inventory model in this section is based on the assumptions of the EOQ model shown in Table 10.3, with the exception that demand is probabilistic rather than deterministic. With probabilistic demand, occasional shortages may occur.

In the previous section we considered a single-period inventory model with probabilistic demand. In this section we extend our discussion to a multiperiod order-quantity, reorder point inventory model with probabilistic demand. In the multiperiod model, the inventory system operates continuously with many repeating periods or cycles; inventory can be carried from one period to the next. Whenever the inventory position reaches the reorder point, an order for Q units is placed. Because demand is probabilistic, the time the reorder point will be reached, the time between orders, and the time the order of Q units will arrive in inventory cannot be determined in advance.

The inventory pattern for the order-quantity, reorder point model with probabilistic demand will have the general appearance shown in Figure 10.10. Note that the increases or jumps in the inventory occur whenever an order of Q units arrives. The inventory decreases at a nonconstant rate based on the probabilistic demand. A new order is placed whenever the reorder point is reached. At times, the order quantity of Q units will arrive before

FIGURE 10.10   INVENTORY PATTERN FOR AN ORDER-QUANTITY, REORDER POINT MODEL WITH PROBABILISTIC DEMAND

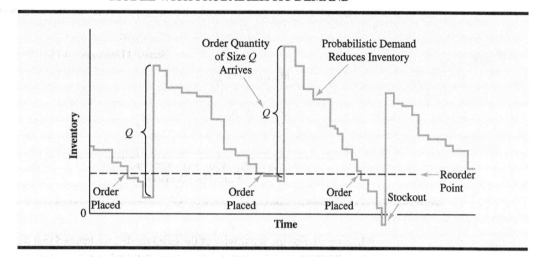

inventory reaches zero. However, at other times, higher demand will cause a stockout before a new order is received. As with other order-quantity, reorder point models, the manager must determine the order quantity Q and the reorder point r for the inventory system.

The exact mathematical formulation of an order-quantity, reorder point inventory model with probabilistic demand is beyond the scope of this text. However, we present a procedure that can be used to obtain good, workable order quantity and reorder point inventory policies. The solution procedure can be expected to provide only an approximation of the optimal solution, but it can yield good solutions in many practical situations.

Let us consider the inventory problem of Dabco Industrial Lighting Distributors. Dabco purchases a special high-intensity lightbulb for industrial lighting systems from a well-known lightbulb manufacturer. Dabco would like a recommendation on how much to order and when to order so that a low-cost inventory policy can be maintained. Pertinent facts are that the ordering cost is $12 per order, one bulb costs $6, and Dabco uses a 20% annual holding cost rate for its inventory ($C_h = IC = 0.20 \times \$6 = \$1.20$). Dabco, which has more than 1000 customers, experiences a probabilistic demand; in fact, the number of units demanded varies considerably from day to day and from week to week. The lead time for a new order of lightbulbs is one week. Historical sales data indicate that demand during a one-week lead time can be described by a normal probability distribution with a mean of 154 lightbulbs and a standard deviation of 25 lightbulbs. The normal distribution of demand during the lead time is shown in Figure 10.11. Because the mean demand during one week is 154 units, Dabco can anticipate a mean or expected annual demand of 154 units per week = 52 weeks per year = 8008 units per year.

The How-Much-to-Order Decision

Although we are in a probabilistic demand situation, we have an estimate of the expected annual demand of 8008 units. We can apply the EOQ model from Section 10.1 as an approximation of the best order quantity, with the expected annual demand used for D. In Dabco's case

Q Prob

$$Q^* = \sqrt{\frac{2DC_o}{C_h}} = \sqrt{\frac{2(8008)(12)}{(1.20)}} = 400 \text{ units}$$

FIGURE 10.11 LEAD-TIME DEMAND PROBABILITY DISTRIBUTION
FOR DABCO LIGHTBULBS

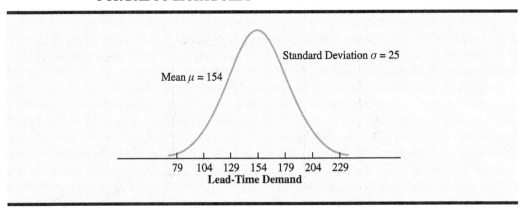

When we studied the sensitivity of the EOQ model, we learned that the total cost of operating an inventory system was relatively insensitive to order quantities that were in the neighborhood of Q^*. Using this knowledge, we expect 400 units per order to be a good approximation of the optimal order quantity. Even if annual demand were as low as 7000 units or as high as 9000 units, an order quantity of 400 units should be a relatively good low-cost order size. Thus, given our best estimate of annual demand at 8008 units, we will use $Q^* = 400$.

We have established the 400-unit order quantity by ignoring the fact that demand is probabilistic. Using $Q^* = 400$, Dabco can anticipate placing approximately $D/Q^* = 8008/400 = 20$ orders per year with an average of approximately $250/20 = 12.5$ working days between orders.

The When-to-Order Decision

We now want to establish a when-to-order decision rule or reorder point that will trigger the ordering process. With a mean lead-time demand of 154 units, you might first suggest a 154-unit reorder point. However, considering the probability of demand now becomes extremely important. If 154 is the mean lead-time demand, and if demand is symmetrically distributed about 154, then the lead-time demand will be more than 154 units roughly 50% of the time. When the demand during the one-week lead time exceeds 154 units, Dabco will experience a shortage, or stockout. Thus, using a reorder point of 154 units, approximately 50% of the time (10 of the 20 orders a year) Dabco will be short of bulbs before the new supply arrives. This shortage rate would most likely be viewed as unacceptable.

The probability of a stockout during any one inventory cycle is easiest to estimate by first determining the number of orders that are expected during the year. The inventory manager can usually state a willingness to allow perhaps one, two, or three stockouts during the year. The allowable stockouts per year divided by the number of orders per year will provide the desired probability of a stockout.

Refer to the **lead-time demand distribution** shown in Figure 10.11. Given this distribution, we can now determine how the reorder point r affects the probability of a stockout. Because stockouts occur whenever the demand during the lead time exceeds the reorder point, we can find the probability of a stockout by using the lead-time demand distribution to compute the probability that demand will exceed r.

We could now approach the when-to-order problem by defining a cost per stockout and then attempting to include this cost in a total cost equation. Alternatively, we can ask management to specify the average number of stockouts that can be tolerated per year. If demand for a product is probabilistic, a manager who will never tolerate a stockout is being somewhat unrealistic because attempting to avoid stockouts completely will require high reorder points, high inventory, and an associated high holding cost.

FIGURE 10.12   REORDER POINT *r* THAT ALLOWS A 5% CHANCE OF A STOCKOUT FOR DABCO LIGHTBULBS

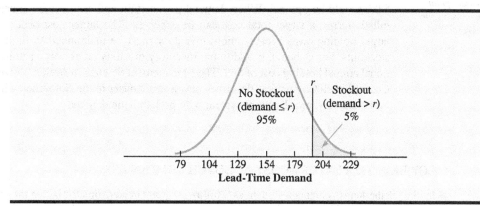

Suppose in this case that Dabco management is willing to tolerate an average of one stockout per year. Because Dabco places 20 orders per year, this decision implies that management is willing to allow demand during lead time to exceed the reorder point one time in 20, or 5% of the time. The reorder point *r* can be found by using the lead-time demand distribution to find the value of *r*, with a 5% chance of having a lead-time demand that will exceed it. This situation is shown graphically in Figure 10.12.

We can now use the cumulative probabilities for the standard normal distribution (see Appendix B) to determine the reorder point *r*. In Figure 10.12, the 5% chance of a stockout occurs with the cumulative probability of no stockout being $1.00 - 0.05 = 0.95$. From Appendix B, we see that the cumulative probability of 0.95 occurs at $z = 1.645$ standard deviations above the mean. Therefore, for the assumed normal distribution for lead-time demand with $\mu = 154$ and $\sigma = 25$, the reorder point *r* is

$$r = 154 + 1.645(25) = 195$$

If a normal distribution is used for lead-time demand, the general equation for *r* is

$$r = \mu + z\sigma \qquad (10.37)$$

where *z* is the number of standard deviations necessary to obtain the acceptable stockout probability.

Thus, the recommended inventory decision is to order 400 units whenever the inventory reaches the reorder point of 195. Because the mean or expected demand during the lead time is 154 units, the $195 - 154 = 41$ units serve as a **safety stock,** which absorbs higher than usual demand during the lead time. Roughly 95% of the time, the 195 units will be able to satisfy demand during the lead time. The anticipated annual cost for this system is as follows:

Holding cost, normal inventory $(Q/2)C_h =$	$(400/2)(1.20)$	$= \$240$
Holding cost, safety stock $(41)C_h =$	$41(1.20)$	$= \$ 49$
Ordering cost $(D/Q)C_o =$	$(8008/400)12$	$= \$240$
	Total	$\$529$

Try Problem 29 as an example of an order-quantity, reorder point model with probabilistic demand.

If Dabco could assume that a known, constant demand rate of 8008 units per year existed for the lightbulbs, then $Q^* = 400$, $r = 154$, and a total annual cost of $240 + $240 = $480 would be optimal. When demand is uncertain and can only be expressed in probabilistic terms, a larger total cost can be expected. The larger cost occurs in the form of larger holding costs because more inventory must be maintained to limit the number of stockouts. For Dabco, this additional inventory or safety stock was 41 units, with an additional annual holding cost of $49. The Management Science in Action, Lowering Inventory Cost at Dutch Companies, describes how a warehouser in the Netherlands implemented an order-quantity, reorder point system with probabilistic demand.

MANAGEMENT SCIENCE IN ACTION

LOWERING INVENTORY COST AT DUTCH COMPANIES*

In the Netherlands, companies such as Philips, Rank Xerox, and Fokker have followed the trend of developing closer relations between the firm and its suppliers. As teamwork, coordination, and information sharing improve, opportunities are available for better cost control in the operation of inventory systems.

One Dutch public warehouser has a contract with its supplier under which the supplier routinely provides information regarding the status and schedule of upcoming production runs. The warehouser's inventory system operates as an order-quantity, reorder point system with probabilistic demand. When the order quantity Q has been determined, the warehouser selects the desired reorder point for the product. The distribution of the lead-time demand is essential in determining the reorder point. Usually, the lead-time demand distribution is

approximated directly, taking into account both the probabilistic demand and the probabilistic length of the lead-time period.

The supplier's information concerning scheduled production runs provides the warehouser with a better understanding of the lead time involved for a product and the resulting lead-time demand distribution. With this information, the warehouse can modify the reorder point accordingly. Information sharing by the supplier thus enables the order-quantity, reorder point system to operate with a lower inventory holding cost.

*Based on F. A. van der Duyn Schouten, M. J. G. van Eijs, and R. M. J. Heuts, "The Value of Supplier Information to Improve Management of a Retailer's Inventory," *Decision Sciences* 25, no. 1 (January/February 1994): 1–14.

NOTES AND COMMENTS

The Dabco reorder point was based on a 5% probability of a stockout during the lead-time period. Thus, on 95% of all order cycles Dabco will be able to satisfy customer demand without experiencing a stockout. Defining *service level* as the percentage of all order cycles that do not experience a stockout, we would say that Dabco has a 95%

service level. However, other definitions of service level may include the percentage of all customer demand that can be satisfied from inventory. Thus, when an inventory manager expresses a desired service level, it is a good idea to clarify exactly what the manager means by the term *service level*.

10.7 PERIODIC REVIEW MODEL WITH PROBABILISTIC DEMAND

The order-quantity, reorder point inventory models previously discussed require a **continuous review inventory system.** In a continuous review inventory system, the inventory position is monitored continuously so that an order can be placed whenever the reorder point is reached. Computerized inventory systems can easily provide the continuous review required by the order-quantity, reorder point models.

Up to this point, we have assumed that the inventory position is reviewed continuously so that an order can be placed as soon as the inventory position reaches the reorder point. The inventory model in this section assumes probabilistic demand and a periodic review of the inventory position.

An alternative to the continuous review system is the **periodic review inventory system.** With a periodic review system, the inventory is checked and reordering is done only at specified points in time. For example, inventory may be checked and orders placed on a weekly, biweekly, monthly, or some other periodic basis. When a firm or business handles multiple products, the periodic review system offers the advantage of requiring that orders for several items be placed at the same preset periodic review time. With this type of inventory system, the shipping and receiving of orders for multiple products are easily coordinated. Under the previously discussed order-quantity, reorder point systems, the reorder points for various products can be encountered at substantially different points in time, making the coordination of orders for multiple products more difficult.

To illustrate this system, let us consider Dollar Discounts, a firm with several retail stores that carry a wide variety of products for household use. The company operates its inventory system with a two-week periodic review. Under this system, a retail store manager may order any number of units of any product from the Dollar Discounts central warehouse every two weeks. Orders for all products going to a particular store are combined into one shipment. When making the order quantity decision for each product at a given review period, the store manager knows that a reorder for the product cannot be made until the next review period.

Assuming that the lead time is less than the length of the review period, an order placed at a review period will be received prior to the next review period. In this case, the how-much-to-order decision at any review period is determined using the following:

$$Q = M - H \tag{10.38}$$

where

Q = order quantity

M = replenishment level

H = inventory on hand at the review period

Because the demand is probabilistic, the inventory on hand at the review period, H, will vary. Thus, the order quantity that must be sufficient to bring the inventory position back to its maximum or replenishment level M can be expected to vary each period. For example, if the replenishment level for a particular product is 50 units, and the inventory on hand at the review period is $H = 12$ units, an order of $Q = M - H = 50 - 12 = 38$ units should be made. Thus, under the periodic review model, enough units are ordered each review period to bring the inventory position back up to the replenishment level.

A typical inventory pattern for a periodic review system with probabilistic demand is shown in Figure 10.13. Note that the time between periodic reviews is predetermined and fixed. The order quantity Q at each review period can vary and is shown to be the difference between the replenishment level and the inventory on hand. Finally, as with other probabilistic models, an unusually high demand can result in an occasional stockout.

The decision variable in the periodic review model is the replenishment level M. To determine M, we could begin by developing a total cost model, including holding, ordering, and stockout costs. Instead, we describe an approach that is often used in practice. In this approach, the objective is to determine a replenishment level that will meet a desired performance level, such as a reasonably low probability of stockout or a reasonably low number of stockouts per year.

FIGURE 10.13   INVENTORY PATTERN FOR PERIODIC REVIEW MODEL WITH PROBABILISTIC DEMAND

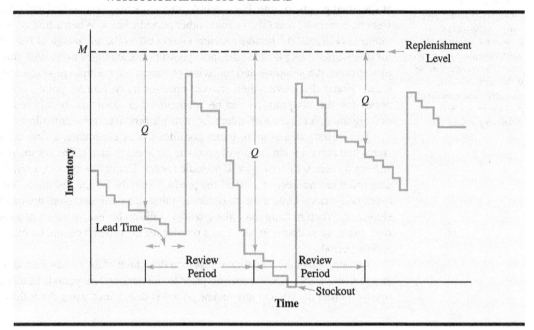

In the Dollar Discounts problem, we assume that management's objective is to determine the replenishment level with only a 0.01 probability of a stockout. In the periodic review model, the order quantity at each review period must be sufficient to cover demand for the *review period plus the demand for the following lead time.* That is, the order quantity that brings the inventory position up to the replenishment level M must last until the order made at the next review period is received in inventory. The length of this time is equal to the review period plus the lead time. Figure 10.14 shows the normal probability distribution of demand during the review period plus the lead-time period for one of the Dollar Discounts products. The mean demand is 250 units, and the standard deviation of demand is 45 units. Given this situation, the logic used to establish M is similar to the logic used to

FIGURE 10.14   PROBABILITY DISTRIBUTION OF DEMAND DURING THE REVIEW PERIOD AND LEAD TIME FOR THE DOLLAR DISCOUNTS PROBLEM

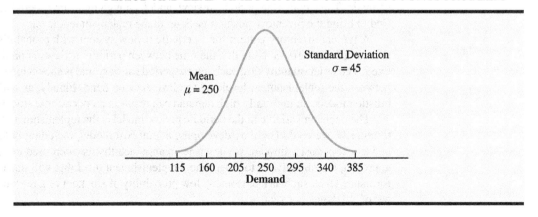

FIGURE 10.15 REPLENISHMENT LEVEL *M* THAT ALLOWS A 1% CHANCE
OF A STOCKOUT FOR THE DOLLAR DISCOUNTS PROBLEM

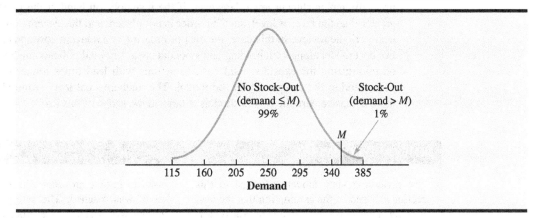

Periodic

*Problem 33 gives you
practice in computing the
replenishment level for a
periodic review model with
probabilistic demand.*

establish the reorder point in Section 10.6. Figure 10.15 shows the replenishment level *M*
with a 0.01 probability of a stockout due to demand exceeding the replenishment level.
This means that there will be a 0.99 probability of no stockout. Using the cumulative probability 0.99 and the cumulative probability table for the standard normal distribution (Appendix B), we see that the value of *M* must be $z = 2.33$ standard deviations above the mean.
Thus, for the given probability distribution, the replenishment level that allows a 0.01 probability of stockout is

$$M = 250 = 2.33(45) = 355$$

Although other probability distributions can be used to express the demand during the
review period plus the lead-time period, if the normal probability distribution is used,
the general expression for *M* is

$$M = \mu + z\sigma \qquad (10.39)$$

where *z* is the number of standard deviations necessary to obtain the acceptable stockout
probability.

*Periodic review systems
provide advantages of
coordinated orders for
multiple items. However,
periodic review systems
require larger safety stock
levels than corresponding
continuous review systems.*

If demand had been deterministic rather than probabilistic, the replenishment level
would have been the demand during the review period plus the demand during the lead-time
period. In this case, the replenishment level would have been 250 units, and no stockout
would have occurred. However, with the probabilistic demand, we have seen that higher inventory is necessary to allow for uncertain demand and to control the probability of a stockout. In the Dollar Discounts problem, $355 - 250 = 105$ is the safety stock that is necessary
to absorb any higher than usual demand during the review period plus the demand during the
lead-time period. This safety stock limits the probability of a stockout to 1%.

More Complex Periodic Review Models

The periodic review model just discussed is one approach to determining a replenishment
level for the periodic review inventory system with probabilistic demand. More complex versions of the periodic review model incorporate a reorder point as another decision variable;

that is, instead of ordering at every periodic review, a reorder point is established. If the inventory on hand at the periodic review is at or below the reorder point, a decision is made to order up to the replenishment level. However, if the inventory on hand at the periodic review is greater than the reorder level, such an order is not placed, and the system continues until the next periodic review. In this case, the cost of ordering is a relevant cost and can be included in a cost model along with holding and stockout costs. Optimal policies can be reached based on minimizing the expected total cost. Situations with lead times longer than the review period add to the complexity of the model. The mathematical level required to treat these more extensive periodic review models is beyond the scope of this text.

NOTES AND COMMENTS

1. The periodic review model presented in this section is based on the assumption that the lead time for an order is less than the periodic review period. Most periodic review systems operate under this condition. However, the case in which the lead time is longer than the review period can be handled by defining H in equation (10.38) as the inventory position, where H includes the inventory on hand plus the inventory on order. In this case, the order quantity at any review period is the amount needed for the inventory on hand plus *all* outstanding orders needed to reach the replenishment level.

2. In the order-quantity, reorder point model discussed in Section 10.6, a continuous review was used to initiate an order whenever the reorder point was reached. The safety stock for this model was based on the probabilistic demand during the lead time. The periodic review model presented in this section also determined a recommended safety stock. However, because the inventory review was only periodic, the safety stock was based on the probabilistic demand during the *review period plus the lead-time period*. This longer period for the safety stock computation means that periodic review systems tend to require a larger safety stock than do continuous review systems.

SUMMARY

In this chapter we presented some of the approaches management scientists use to assist managers in establishing low-cost inventory policies. We first considered cases in which the demand rate for the product is constant. In analyzing these inventory systems, total cost models were developed, which included ordering costs, holding costs, and, in some cases, backorder costs. Then minimum cost formulas for the order quantity Q were presented. A reorder point r can be established by considering the lead-time demand.

In addition, we discussed inventory models in which a deterministic and constant rate could not be assumed, and thus demand was described by a probability distribution. A critical issue with these probabilistic inventory models is obtaining a probability distribution that most realistically approximates the demand distribution. We first described a single-period model where only one order is placed for the product and, at the end of the period, either the product has sold out or a surplus remains of unsold products that will be sold for a salvage value. Solution procedures were then presented for multiperiod models based on either an order-quantity, reorder point, continuous review system or a replenishment-level, periodic review system.

In closing this chapter we reemphasize that inventory and inventory systems can be an expensive phase of a firm's operation. It is important for managers to be aware of the cost of inventory systems and to make the best possible operating policy decisions for the inventory system. Inventory models, as presented in this chapter, can help managers to develop good inventory policies. The Management Science in Action, Multistage Inventory Planning at Deere & Company, provides another example of how computer-based inventory models can be used to provide optimal inventory policies and cost reductions.

MULTISTAGE INVENTORY PLANNING AT DEERE & COMPANY*

Deere & Company's Commercial & Consumer Equipment (C&CE) Division, located in Raleigh, North Carolina, produces seasonal products such as lawn mowers and snow blowers. The seasonal aspect of demand requires the products to be built in advance. Because many of the products involve impulse purchases, the products must be available at dealerships when the customers walk in. Historically, high inventory levels resulted in high inventory costs and an unacceptable return on assets. As a result, management concluded that C&CE needed an inventory planning system that would reduce the average finished goods inventory levels in company warehouses and dealer locations, and at the same time would ensure that stockouts would not cause a negative impact on sales.

In order to optimize inventory levels, Deere moved from an aggregate inventory planning model to a series of individual product inventory models. This approach enabled Deere to determine optimal inventory levels for each product at each dealer, as well as optimal levels for each product at each plant and warehouse. The computerized system developed, known as SmartOps Multistage Inventory Planning and Optimization (MIPO), manages inventory for four C&CE Division plants, 21 dealers, and 150 products. Easily updated, MIPO provides target inventory levels for each product on a weekly basis. In addition, the system provides information about how optimal inventory levels are affected by lead times, forecast errors, and target service levels.

The inventory optimization system enabled the C&CE Division to meet its inventory reduction goals. C&CE management estimates that the company will continue to achieve annual cost savings from lower inventory carrying costs. Meanwhile, the dealers also benefit from lower warehouse expenses, as well as lower interest and insurance costs.

*Based on "Deere's New Software Achieves Inventory Reduction Goals," *Inventory Management Report* (March 2003): 2.

GLOSSARY

Economic order quantity (EOQ) The order quantity that minimizes the annual holding cost plus the annual ordering cost.

Constant demand rate An assumption of many inventory models that states that the same number of units are taken from inventory each period of time.

Holding cost The cost associated with maintaining an inventory investment, including the cost of the capital investment in the inventory, insurance, taxes, warehouse overhead, and so on. This cost may be stated as a percentage of the inventory investment or as a cost per unit.

Cost of capital The cost a firm incurs to obtain capital for investment. It may be stated as an annual percentage rate, and it is part of the holding cost associated with maintaining inventory.

Ordering cost The fixed cost (salaries, paper, transportation, etc.) associated with placing an order for an item.

Inventory position The inventory on hand plus the inventory on order.

Reorder point The inventory position at which a new order should be placed.

Lead time The time between the placing of an order and its receipt in the inventory system.

Lead-time demand The number of units demanded during the lead-time period.

Cycle time The length of time between the placing of two consecutive orders.

Constant supply rate A situation in which the inventory is built up at a constant rate over a period of time.

Lot size The order quantity in the production inventory model.

Setup cost The fixed cost (labor, materials, lost production) associated with preparing for a new production run.

Shortage, or stockout Demand that cannot be supplied from inventory.

Backorder The receipt of an order for a product when no units are in inventory. These backorders become shortages, which are eventually satisfied when a new supply of the product becomes available.

Goodwill cost A cost associated with a backorder, a lost sale, or any form of stockout or unsatisfied demand. This cost may be used to reflect the loss of future profits because a customer experienced an unsatisfied demand.

Quantity discounts Discounts or lower unit costs offered by the manufacturer when a customer purchases larger quantities of the product.

Deterministic inventory model A model where demand is considered known and not subject to uncertainty.

Probabilistic inventory model A model where demand is not known exactly; probabilities must be associated with the possible values for demand.

Single-period inventory model An inventory model in which only one order is placed for the product, and at the end of the period either the item has sold out, or a surplus of unsold items will be sold for a salvage value.

Incremental analysis A method used to determine an optimal order quantity by comparing the cost of ordering an additional unit with the cost of not ordering an additional unit.

Lead-time demand distribution The distribution of demand that occurs during the lead-time period.

Safety stock Inventory maintained in order to reduce the number of stockouts resulting from higher than expected demand.

Continuous review inventory system A system in which the inventory position is monitored or reviewed on a continuous basis so that a new order can be placed as soon as the reorder point is reached.

Periodic review inventory system A system in which the inventory position is checked or reviewed at predetermined periodic points in time. Reorders are placed only at periodic review points.

PROBLEMS

1. Suppose that the R&B Beverage Company has a soft drink product that shows a constant annual demand rate of 3600 cases. A case of the soft drink costs R&B $3. Ordering costs are $20 per order and holding costs are 25% of the value of the inventory. R&B has 250 working days per year, and the lead time is 5 days. Identify the following aspects of the inventory policy:
   a. Economic order quantity
   b. Reorder point
   c. Cycle time
   d. Total annual cost

2. A general property of the EOQ inventory model is that total inventory holding and total ordering costs are equal at the optimal solution. Use the data in Problem 1 to show that this result is true. Use equations (10.2), (10.3), and (10.5) to show that, in general, total holding costs and total ordering costs are equal whenever Q^* is used.

3. The reorder point [see equation (10.6)] is defined as the lead-time demand for an item. In cases of long lead times, the lead-time demand and thus the reorder point may exceed the economic order quantity Q^*. In such cases, the inventory position will not equal the inventory on hand when an order is placed, and the reorder point may be expressed in terms of either the inventory position or the inventory on hand. Consider the economic order quantity model with $D = 5000$, $C_o = \$32$, $C_h = \$2$, and 250 working days per year. Identify the reorder point in terms of the inventory position and in terms of the inventory on hand for each of the following lead times:
   a. 5 days
   b. 15 days
   c. 25 days
   d. 45 days

4. Westside Auto purchases a component used in the manufacture of automobile generators directly from the supplier. Westside's generator production operation, which is operated at a constant rate, will require 1000 components per month throughout the year (12,000 units annually). Assume that the ordering costs are $25 per order, the unit cost is $2.50 per component, and annual holding costs are 20% of the value of the inventory. Westside has 250 working days per year and a lead time of 5 days. Answer the following inventory policy questions:
   a. What is the EOQ for this component?
   b. What is the reorder point?
   c. What is the cycle time?
   d. What are the total annual holding and ordering costs associated with your recommended EOQ?

5. Suppose that Westside's management in Problem 4 likes the operational efficiency of ordering once each month and in quantities of 1000 units. How much more expensive would this policy be than your EOQ recommendation? Would you recommend in favor of the 1000-unit order quantity? Explain. What would the reorder point be if the 1000-unit quantity were acceptable?

6. Tele-Reco is a new specialty store that sells television sets, videotape recorders, video games, and other television-related products. A new Japanese-manufactured videotape recorder costs Tele-Reco $600 per unit. Tele-Reco's annual holding cost rate is 22%. Ordering costs are estimated to be $70 per order.
   a. If demand for the new videotape recorder is expected to be constant with a rate of 20 units per month, what is the recommended order quantity for the videotape recorder?

773

   b. What are the estimated annual inventory holding and ordering costs associated with this product?

   c. How many orders will be placed per year?

   d. With 250 working days per year, what is the cycle time for this product?

7. A large distributor of oil-well drilling equipment operated over the past two years with EOQ policies based on an annual holding cost rate of 22%. Under the EOQ policy, a particular product has been ordered with a $Q^* = 80$. A recent evaluation of holding costs shows that because of an increase in the interest rate associated with bank loans, the annual holding cost rate should be 27%.

   a. What is the new economic order quantity for the product?

   b. Develop a general expression showing how the economic order quantity changes when the annual holding cost rate is changed from I to I'.

8. Nation-Wide Bus Lines is proud of its six-week bus driver training program that it conducts for all new Nation-Wide drivers. As long as the class size remains less than or equal to 35, a six-week training program costs Nation-Wide $22,000 for instructors, equipment, and so on. The Nation-Wide training program must provide the company with approximately five new drivers per month. After completing the training program, new drivers are paid $1600 per month but do not work until a full-time driver position is open. Nation-Wide views the $1600 per month paid to each idle new driver as a holding cost necessary to maintain a supply of newly trained drivers available for immediate service. Viewing new drivers as inventory-type units, how large should the training classes be to minimize Nation-Wide's total annual training and new driver idle-time costs? How many training classes should the company hold each year? What is the total annual cost associated with your recommendation?

9. Cress Electronic Products manufactures components used in the automotive industry. Cress purchases parts for use in its manufacturing operation from a variety of different suppliers. One particular supplier provides a part where the assumptions of the EOQ model are realistic. The annual demand is 5000 units, the ordering cost is $80 per order, and the annual holding cost rate is 25%.

   a. If the cost of the part is $20 per unit, what is the economic order quantity?

   b. Assume 250 days of operation per year. If the lead time for an order is 12 days, what is the reorder point?

   c. If the lead time for the part is seven weeks (35 days), what is the reorder point?

   d. What is the reorder point for part (c) if the reorder point is expressed in terms of the inventory on hand rather than the inventory position?

10. All-Star Bat Manufacturing, Inc., supplies baseball bats to major and minor league baseball teams. After an initial order in January, demand over the six-month baseball season is approximately constant at 1000 bats per month. Assuming that the bat production process can handle up to 4000 bats per month, the bat production setup costs are $150 per setup, the production cost is $10 per bat, and the holding costs have a monthly rate of 2%, what production lot size would you recommend to meet the demand during the baseball season? If All-Star operates 20 days per month, how often will the production process operate, and what is the length of a production run?

11. Assume that a production line operates such that the production lot size model of Section 10.2 is applicable. Given $D = 6400$ units per year, $C_o = \$100$, and $C_h = \$2$ per unit per year, compute the minimum cost production lot size for each of the following production rates:

   a. 8000 units per year

   b. 10,000 units per year

   c. 32,000 units per year

   d. 100,000 units per year

Compute the EOQ recommended lot size using equation (10.5). What two observations can you make about the relationship between the EOQ model and the production lot size model?

12. Assume that you are reviewing the production lot size decision associated with a production operation where $P = 8000$ units per year, $D = 2000$ units per year, $C_o = \$300$, and $C_h = \$1.60$ per unit per year. Also assume that current practice calls for production runs of 500 units every three months. Would you recommend changing the current production lot size? Why or why not? How much could be saved by converting to your production lot size recommendation?

13. Wilson Publishing Company produces books for the retail market. Demand for a current book is expected to occur at a constant annual rate of 7200 copies. The cost of one copy of the book is $14.50. The holding cost is based on an 18% annual rate, and production setup costs are $150 per setup. The equipment on which the book is produced has an annual production volume of 25,000 copies. Wilson has 250 working days per year, and the lead time for a production run is 15 days. Use the production lot size model to compute the following values:
   a. Minimum cost production lot size
   b. Number of production runs per year
   c. Cycle time
   d. Length of a production run
   e. Maximum inventory
   f. Total annual cost
   g. Reorder point

14. A well-known manufacturer of several brands of toothpaste uses the production lot size model to determine production quantities for its various products. The product known as Extra White is currently being produced in production lot sizes of 5000 units. The length of the production run for this quantity is 10 days. Because of a recent shortage of a particular raw material, the supplier of the material announced that a cost increase will be passed along to the manufacturer of Extra White. Current estimates are that the new raw material cost will increase the manufacturing cost of the toothpaste products by 23% per unit. What will be the effect of this price increase on the production lot sizes for Extra White?

15. Suppose that Westside Auto of Problem 4, with $D = 12,000$ units per year, $C_h = (2.50)(0.20) = \$0.50$, and $C_o = \$25$, decided to operate with a backorder inventory policy. Backorder costs are estimated to be $5 per unit per year. Identify the following:
   a. Minimum cost order quantity
   b. Maximum number of backorders
   c. Maximum inventory
   d. Cycle time
   e. Total annual cost

16. Assuming 250 days of operation per year and a lead time of 5 days, what is the reorder point for Westside Auto in Problem 15? Show the general formula for the reorder point for the EOQ model with backorders. In general, is the reorder point when backorders are allowed greater than or less than the reorder point when backorders are not allowed? Explain.

17. A manager of an inventory system believes that inventory models are important decision-making aids. Even though often using an EOQ policy, the manager never considered a backorder model because of the assumption that backorders were "bad" and should be avoided. However, with upper management's continued pressure for cost reduction, you have been asked to analyze the economics of a backorder policy for some products that can possibly be backordered. For a specific product with $D = 800$ units per year,

C_o = $150, C_h = $3, and C_b = $20, what is the difference in total annual cost between the EOQ model and the planned shortage or backorder model? If the manager adds constraints that no more than 25% of the units can be backordered and that no customer will have to wait more than 15 days for an order, should the backorder inventory policy be adopted? Assume 250 working days per year.

18. If the lead time for new orders is 20 days for the inventory system discussed in Problem 17, find the reorder point for both the EOQ and the backorder models.

19. The A&M Hobby Shop carries a line of radio-controlled model racing cars. Demand for the cars is assumed to be constant at a rate of 40 cars per month. The cars cost $60 each, and ordering costs are approximately $15 per order, regardless of the order size. The annual holding cost rate is 20%.

   a. Determine the economic order quantity and total annual cost under the assumption that no backorders are permitted.

   b. Using a $45 per-unit per-year backorder cost, determine the minimum cost inventory policy and total annual cost for the model racing cars.

   c. What is the maximum number of days a customer would have to wait for a backorder under the policy in part (b)? Assume that the Hobby Shop is open for business 300 days per year.

   d. Would you recommend a no-backorder or a backorder inventory policy for this product? Explain.

   e. If the lead time is six days, what is the reorder point for both the no-backorder and backorder inventory policies?

20. Assume that the following quantity discount schedule is appropriate. If annual demand is 120 units, ordering costs are $20 per order, and the annual holding cost rate is 25%, what order quantity would you recommend?

Order Size	Discount (%)	Unit Cost
0 to 49	0	$30.00
50 to 99	5	$28.50
100 or more	10	$27.00

21. Apply the EOQ model to the following quantity discount situation in which D = 500 units per year, C_o = $40, and the annual holding cost rate is 20%. What order quantity do you recommend?

Discount Category	Order Size	Discount (%)	Unit Cost
1	0 to 99	0	$10.00
2	100 or more	3	$ 9.70

22. Keith Shoe Stores carries a basic black men's dress shoe that sells at an approximate constant rate of 500 pairs of shoes every three months. Keith's current buying policy is to order 500 pairs each time an order is placed. It costs Keith $30 to place an order. The annual holding cost rate is 20%. With the order quantity of 500, Keith obtains the shoes at the lowest possible unit cost of $28 per pair. Other quantity discounts offered by the manufacturer are as follows. What is the minimum cost order quantity for the shoes? What are the annual savings of your inventory policy over the policy currently being used by Keith?

776

Order Quantity	Price per Pair
0–99	$36
100–199	$32
200–299	$30
300 or more	$28

23. In the EOQ model with quantity discounts, we stated that if the Q^* for a price category is larger than necessary to qualify for the category price, the category cannot be optimal. Use the two discount categories in Problem 21 to show that this statement is true. That is, plot total cost curves for the two categories and show that if the category 2 minimum cost Q is an acceptable solution, we do not have to consider category 1.

24. The J&B Card Shop sells calendars depicting a different Colonial scene each month. The once-a-year order for each year's calendar arrives in September. From past experience, the September-to-July demand for the calendars can be approximated by a normal probability distribution with $\mu = 500$ and $\sigma = 120$. The calendars cost $1.50 each, and J&B sells them for $3 each.
    a. If J&B throws out all unsold calendars at the end of July (i.e., salvage value is zero), how many calendars should be ordered?
    b. If J&B reduces the calendar price to $1 at the end of July and can sell all surplus calendars at this price, how many calendars should be ordered?

25. The Gilbert Air-Conditioning Company is considering the purchase of a special shipment of portable air conditioners manufactured in Japan. Each unit will cost Gilbert $80, and it will be sold for $125. Gilbert does not want to carry surplus air conditioners over until the following year. Thus, all surplus air conditioners will be sold to a wholesaler for $50 per unit. Assume that the air conditioner demand follows a normal probability distribution with $\mu = 20$ and $\sigma = 8$.
    a. What is the recommended order quantity?
    b. What is the probability that Gilbert will sell all units it orders?

26. The Bridgeport city manager and the chief of police agreed on the size of the police force necessary for normal daily operations. However, they need assistance in determining the number of additional police officers needed to cover daily absences due to injuries, sickness, vacations, and personal leave. Records over the past three years show that the daily demand for additional police officers is normally distributed with a mean of 50 officers and a standard deviation of 10 officers. The cost of an additional police officer is based on the average pay rate of $150 per day. If the daily demand for additional police officers exceeds the number of additional officers available, the excess demand will be covered by overtime at the pay rate of $240 per day for each overtime officer.
    a. If the number of additional police officers available is greater than demand, the city will have to pay for more additional police officers than needed. What is the cost of overestimating demand?
    b. If the number of additional police officers available is less than demand, the city will have to use overtime to meet the demand. What is the cost of underestimating demand?
    c. What is the optimal number of additional police officers that should be included in the police force?
    d. On a typical day, what is the probability that overtime will be necessary?

27. A perishable dairy product is ordered daily at a particular supermarket. The product, which costs $1.19 per unit, sells for $1.65 per unit. If units are unsold at the end of the day,

the supplier takes them back at a rebate of $1 per unit. Assume that daily demand is approximately normally distributed with $\mu = 150$ and $\sigma = 30$.

a. What is your recommended daily order quantity for the supermarket?

b. What is the probability that the supermarket will sell all the units it orders?

c. In problems such as these, why would the supplier offer a rebate as high as $1? For example, why not offer a nominal rebate of, say, 25¢ per unit? What happens to the supermarket order quantity as the rebate is reduced?

28. A retail outlet sells a seasonal product for $10 per unit. The cost of the product is $8 per unit. All units not sold during the regular season are sold for half the retail price in an end-of-season clearance sale. Assume that demand for the product is uniformly distributed between 200 and 800.

a. What is the recommended order quantity?

b. What is the probability that at least some customers will ask to purchase the product after the outlet is sold out? That is, what is the probability of a stockout using your order quantity in part (a)?

c. To keep customers happy and returning to the store later, the owner feels that stock-outs should be avoided if at all possible. What is your recommended order quantity if the owner is willing to tolerate a 0.15 probability of a stockout?

d. Using your answer to part (c), what is the goodwill cost you are assigning to a stockout?

29. Floyd Distributors, Inc., provides a variety of auto parts to small local garages. Floyd purchases parts from manufacturers according to the EOQ model and then ships the parts from a regional warehouse direct to its customers. For a particular type of muffler, Floyd's EOQ analysis recommends orders with $Q^* = 25$ to satisfy an annual demand of 200 mufflers. Floyd's has 250 working days per year, and the lead time averages 15 days.

a. What is the reorder point if Floyd assumes a constant demand rate?

b. Suppose that an analysis of Floyd's muffler demand shows that the lead-time demand follows a normal probability distribution with $\mu = 12$ and $\sigma = 2.5$. If Floyd's management can tolerate one stockout per year, what is the revised reorder point?

c. What is the safety stock for part (b)? If $C_h = \$5/\text{unit/year}$, what is the extra cost due to the uncertainty of demand?

30. For Floyd Distributors in Problem 29, we were given $Q^* = 25$, $D = 200$, $C_h = \$5$, and a normal lead-time demand distribution with $\mu = 12$ and $\sigma = 2.5$.

a. What is Floyd's reorder point if the firm is willing to tolerate two stockouts during the year?

b. What is Floyd's reorder point if the firm wants to restrict the probability of a stockout on any one cycle to at most 1%?

c. What are the safety stock levels and the annual safety stock costs for the reorder points found in parts (a) and (b)?

31. A product with an annual demand of 1000 units has $C_o = \$25.50$ and $C_h = \$8$. The demand exhibits some variability such that the lead-time demand follows a normal probability distribution with $\mu = 25$ and $\sigma = 5$.

a. What is the recommended order quantity?

b. What are the reorder point and safety stock if the firm desires at most a 2% probability of stockout on any given order cycle?

c. If a manager sets the reorder point at 30, what is the probability of a stockout on any given order cycle? How many times would you expect a stockout during the year if this reorder point were used?

32. The B&S Novelty and Craft Shop in Bennington, Vermont, sells a variety of quality hand-made items to tourists. B&S will sell 300 hand-carved miniature replicas of a Colonial

soldier each year, but the demand pattern during the year is uncertain. The replicas sell for $20 each, and B&S uses a 15% annual inventory holding cost rate. Ordering costs are $5 per order, and demand during the lead time follows a normal probability distribution with $\mu = 15$ and $\sigma = 6$.

a. What is the recommended order quantity?

b. If B&S is willing to accept a stockout roughly twice a year, what reorder point would you recommend? What is the probability that B&S will have a stockout in any one order cycle?

c. What are the safety stock and annual safety stock costs for this product?

33. A firm uses a one-week periodic review inventory system. A two-day lead time is needed for any order, and the firm is willing to tolerate an average of one stockout per year.

a. Using the firm's service guideline, what is the probability of a stockout associated with each replenishment decision?

b. What is the replenishment level if demand during the review period plus lead-time period is normally distributed with a mean of 60 units and a standard deviation of 12 units?

c. What is the replenishment level if demand during the review period plus lead-time period is uniformly distributed between 35 and 85 units?

34. Foster Drugs, Inc., handles a variety of health and beauty aid products. A particular hair conditioner product costs Foster Drugs $2.95 per unit. The annual holding cost rate is 20%. An order-quantity, reorder point inventory model recommends an order quantity of 300 units per order.

a. Lead time is one week and the lead-time demand is normally distributed with a mean of 150 units and a standard deviation of 40 units. What is the reorder point if the firm is willing to tolerate a 1% chance of stockout on any one cycle?

b. What safety stock and annual safety stock costs are associated with your recommendation in part (a)?

c. The order-quantity, reorder point model requires a continuous review system. Management is considering making a transition to a periodic review system in an attempt to coordinate ordering for many of its products. The demand during the proposed two-week review period and the one-week lead-time period is normally distributed with a mean of 450 units and a standard deviation of 70 units. What is the recommended replenishment level for this periodic review system if the firm is willing to tolerate the same 1% chance of stockout associated with any replenishment decision?

d. What safety stock and annual safety stock costs are associated with your recommendation in part (c)?

e. Compare your answers to parts (b) and (d). The company is seriously considering the periodic review system. Would you support this decision? Explain.

f. Would you tend to favor the continuous review system for more expensive items? For example, assume that the product in the preceding example sold for $295 per unit. Explain.

35. Statewide Auto Parts uses a four-week periodic review system to reorder parts for its inventory stock. A one-week lead time is required to fill the order. Demand for one particular part during the five-week replenishment period is normally distributed with a mean of 18 units and a standard deviation of 6 units.

a. At a particular periodic review, 8 units are in inventory. The parts manager places an order for 16 units. What is the probability that this part will have a stockout before an order that is placed at the next four-week review period arrives?

b. Assume that the company is willing to tolerate a 2.5% chance of a stockout associated with a replenishment decision. How many parts should the manager have ordered in part (a)? What is the replenishment level for the four-week periodic review system?

36. Rose Office Supplies, Inc., which is open six days a week, uses a two-week periodic review for its store inventory. On alternating Monday mornings, the store manager fills out an order sheet requiring a shipment of various items from the company's warehouse. A particular three-ring notebook sells at an average rate of 16 notebooks per week. The standard deviation in sales is 5 notebooks per week. The lead time for a new shipment is three days. The mean lead-time demand is 8 notebooks with a standard deviation of 3.5.

    a. What is the mean or expected demand during the review period plus the lead-time period?

    b. Under the assumption of independent demand from week to week, the variances in demands are additive. Thus, the variance of the demand during the review period plus the lead-time period is equal to the variance of demand during the first week plus the variance of demand during the second week plus the variance of demand during the lead-time period. What is the variance of demand during the review period plus the lead-time period? What is the standard deviation of demand during the review period plus the lead-time period?

    c. Assuming that demand has a normal probability distribution, what is the replenishment level that will provide an expected stockout rate of one per year?

    d. On Monday, March 22, 18 notebooks remain in inventory at the store. How many notebooks should the store manager order?

Case Problem 1   WAGNER FABRICATING COMPANY

Managers at Wagner Fabricating Company are reviewing the economic feasibility of manufacturing a part that it currently purchases from a supplier. Forecasted annual demand for the part is 3200 units. Wagner operates 250 days per year.

Wagner's financial analysts established a cost of capital of 14% for the use of funds for investments within the company. In addition, over the past year $600,000 was the average investment in the company's inventory. Accounting information shows that a total of $24,000 was spent on taxes and insurance related to the company's inventory. In addition, an estimated $9000 was lost due to inventory shrinkage, which included damaged goods as well as pilferage. A remaining $15,000 was spent on warehouse overhead, including utility expenses for heating and lighting.

An analysis of the purchasing operation shows that approximately two hours are required to process and coordinate an order for the part regardless of the quantity ordered. Purchasing salaries average $28 per hour, including employee benefits. In addition, a detailed analysis of 125 orders showed that $2375 was spent on telephone, paper, and postage directly related to the ordering process.

A one-week lead time is required to obtain the part from the supplier. An analysis of demand during the lead time shows it is approximately normally distributed with a mean of 64 units and a standard deviation of 10 units. Service level guidelines indicate that one stockout per year is acceptable.

Currently, the company has a contract to purchase the part from a supplier at a cost of $18 per unit. However, over the past few months, the company's production capacity has been expanded. As a result, excess capacity is now available in certain production departments, and the company is considering the alternative of producing the parts itself.

Forecasted utilization of equipment shows that production capacity will be available for the part being considered. The production capacity is available at the rate of 1000 units per month, with up to five months of production time available. Management believes that with a two-week lead time, schedules can be arranged so that the part can be produced whenever needed. The demand during the two-week lead time is approximately normally distributed, with a mean of 128 units and a standard deviation of 20 units. Production costs are expected to be $17 per part.

A concern of management is that setup costs will be significant. The total cost of labor and lost production time is estimated to be $50 per hour, and a full eight-hour shift will be needed to set up the equipment for producing the part.

Managerial Report

Develop a report for management of Wagner Fabricating that will address the question of whether the company should continue to purchase the part from the supplier or begin to produce the part itself. Include the following factors in your report:

1. An analysis of the holding costs, including the appropriate annual holding cost rate
2. An analysis of ordering costs, including the appropriate cost per order from the supplier
3. An analysis of setup costs for the production operation
4. A development of the inventory policy for the following two alternatives:
   a. Ordering a fixed quantity Q from the supplier
   b. Ordering a fixed quantity Q from in-plant production
5. Include the following in the policies of parts 4(a) and 4(b):
   a. Optimal quantity $Q*$
   b. Number of order or production runs per year
   c. Cycle time
   d. Reorder point
   e. Amount of safety stock
   f. Expected maximum inventory
   g. Average inventory
   h. Annual holding cost
   i. Annual ordering cost
   j. Annual cost of the units purchased or manufactured
   k. Total annual cost of the purchase policy and the total annual cost of the production policy
6. Make a recommendation as to whether the company should purchase or manufacture the part. What savings are associated with your recommendation as compared with the other alternative?

Case Problem 2   RIVER CITY FIRE DEPARTMENT

The River City Fire Department (RCFD) fights fires and provides a variety of rescue operations in the River City metropolitan area. The RCFD staffs 13 ladder companies, 26 pumper companies, and several rescue units and ambulances. Normal staffing requires 186 firefighters to be on duty every day.

RCFD is organized with three firefighting units. Each unit works a full 24-hour day and then has two days (48 hours) off. For example, Unit 1 covers Monday, Unit 2 covers Tuesday, and Unit 3 covers Wednesday. Then Unit 1 returns on Thursday, and so on. Over a three-week (21-day) scheduling period, each unit will be scheduled for seven days. On a rotational basis, firefighters within each unit are given one of the seven regularly scheduled days off. This day off is referred to as a Kelley day. Thus, over a three-week scheduling period, each firefighter in a unit works six of the seven scheduled unit days and gets one Kelley day off.

Determining the number of firefighters to be assigned to each unit includes the 186 fire-fighters who must be on duty plus the number of firefighters in the unit who are off for a Kelley day. Furthermore, each unit needs additional staffing to cover firefighter absences due to injury, sick leave, vacations, or personal time. This additional staffing involves finding the best mix of adding full-time firefighters to each unit and the selective use of overtime. If the number of absences on a particular day brings the number of available firefighters below the required 186, firefighters who are currently off (e.g., on a Kelley day) must be scheduled to work overtime. Overtime is compensated at 1.55 times the regular pay rate.

Analysis of the records maintained over the last several years concerning the number of daily absences shows a normal probability distribution. A mean of 20 and a standard deviation of 5 provide a good approximation of the probability distribution for the number of daily absences.

Managerial Report

Develop a report that will enable Fire Chief O. E. Smith to determine the necessary num-bers for the Fire Department. Include, at a minimum, the following items in your report:

1. Assuming no daily absences and taking into account the need to staff Kelley days, determine the base number of firefighters needed by each unit.
2. Using a minimum cost criterion, how many additional firefighters should be added to each unit in order to cover the daily absences? These extra daily needs will be filled by the additional firefighters and, when necessary, the more expensive use of overtime by off-duty firefighters.
3. On a given day, what is the probability that Kelley-day firefighters will be called in to work overtime?
4. Based on the three-unit organization, how many firefighters should be assigned to each unit? What is the total number of full-time firefighters required for the River City Fire Department?

Appendix 10.1 DEVELOPMENT OF THE OPTIMAL ORDER QUANTITY ($Q*$) FORMULA FOR THE EOQ MODEL

Given equation (10.4) as the total annual cost for the EOQ model,

$$TC = \frac{1}{2}QC_h + \frac{D}{Q}C_o \tag{10.4}$$

we can find the order quantity Q that minimizes the total cost by setting the derivative, dTC/dQ, equal to zero and solving for $Q*$.

$$\frac{dTC}{dQ} = \frac{1}{2}C_h - \frac{D}{Q^2}C_o = 0$$

$$\frac{1}{2}C_h = \frac{D}{Q^2}C_o$$

$$C_hQ^2 = 2DC_o$$

$$Q^2 = \frac{2DC_o}{C_h}$$

782

Hence,

$$Q^* = \sqrt{\frac{2DC_o}{C_h}} \qquad (10.5)$$

The second derivative is

$$\frac{d^2TC}{dQ^2} = \frac{2D}{Q^3} C_o$$

Because the value of the second derivative is greater than zero, Q^* from equation (10.5) is the minimum cost solution.

Appendix 10.2 DEVELOPMENT OF THE OPTIMAL LOT SIZE (Q^*) FORMULA FOR THE PRODUCTION LOT SIZE MODEL

Given equation (10.15) as the total annual cost for the production lot size model,

$$TC = \frac{1}{2}\left(1 - \frac{D}{P}\right)QC_h + \frac{D}{Q}C_o \qquad (10.15)$$

we can find the order quantity Q that minimizes the total cost by setting the derivative, dTC/dQ, equal to zero and solving for Q^*.

$$\frac{dTC}{dQ} = \frac{1}{2}\left(1 - \frac{D}{P}\right)C_h - \frac{D}{Q^2} C_o = 0$$

Solving for Q^*, we have

$$\frac{1}{2}\left(1 - \frac{D}{P}\right)C_h = \frac{D}{Q^2} C_o$$

$$\left(1 - \frac{D}{P}\right)C_h Q^2 = 2DC_o$$

$$Q^2 = \frac{2DC_o}{(1 - D/P)C_h}$$

Hence,

$$Q^* = \sqrt{\frac{2DC_o}{(1 - D/P)C_h}} \qquad (10.16)$$

The second derivative is

$$\frac{d^2TC}{dQ^2} = \frac{2DC_o}{Q^3}$$

Because the value of the second derivative is greater than zero, Q^* from equation (10.16) is a minimum cost solution.

References and Bibliography

Fogarty, D. W., J. H. Blackstone, and T. R. Hoffman. *Production and Inventory Management,* 2d ed. South-Western, 1990.

Hillier, F., and G. J. Lieberman. *Introduction to Operations Research,* 7th ed. McGraw-Hill, 2000.

Narasimhan, S. L., D. W. McLeavey, and P. B. Lington. *Production Planning and Inventory Control,* 2d ed. Prentice Hall, 1995.

Orlicky, J., and G. W. Plossi. *Orlicky's Material Requirements Planning.* McGraw-Hill, 1994.

Vollmann, T. E., W. L. Berry, and D. C. Whybark. *Manufacturing Planning and Control Systems,* 4th ed. McGraw-Hill, 1997.

Zipkin, P. H. *Foundations of Inventory Management.* McGraw-Hill/Irwin, 2000.

Self-Test Solutions and Answers to Even-Numbered Problems

1. a. $Q^* = \sqrt{\dfrac{2DC_o}{C_h}} = \sqrt{\dfrac{2(3600)(20)}{0.25(3)}} = 438.18$

    b. $r = dm = \dfrac{3600}{250}(5) = 72$

    c. $T = \dfrac{250Q^*}{D} = \dfrac{250(438.18)}{3600} = 30.43$ days

    d. $TC = \dfrac{1}{2}QC_h + \dfrac{D}{Q}C_o$

    $= \dfrac{1}{2}(438.18)(0.25)(3) + \dfrac{3600}{438.18}(20) = \$328.63$

2. \$164.32 for each; Total cost = \$328.64

4. a. 1095.45
    b. 240
    c. 22.82 days
    d. \$273.86 for each; Total cost = \$547.72

6. a. 15.95
    b. \$2106
    c. 15.04
    d. 16.62 days

8. $Q^* = 11.73$; use 12
    5 classes per year
    \$225,200

10. $Q^* = 1414.21$
    $T = 28.28$ days
    Production runs of 7.07 days

12. $Q^* = 1000$; Total cost = \$1200
    Yes, the change saves \$300 per year.

13. a. $Q^* = \sqrt{\dfrac{2DC_o}{(1 - D/P)C_h}}$

    $= \sqrt{\dfrac{2(7200)(150)}{(1 - 7200/25,000)(0.18)(14.50)}} = 1078.12$

    b. Number of production runs $= \dfrac{D}{Q^*} = \dfrac{7200}{1078.12} = 6.68$

    c. $T = \dfrac{250Q}{D} = \dfrac{250(1078.12)}{7200} = 37.43$ days

    d. Production run length $= \dfrac{Q}{P/250}$

    $= \dfrac{1078.12}{25,000/250} = 10.78$ days

    e. Maximum inventory $= \left(1 - \dfrac{D}{P}\right)Q$

    $= \left(1 - \dfrac{7200}{25,000}\right)(1078.12)$

    $= 767.62$

    f. Holiday cost $= \dfrac{1}{2}\left(a - \dfrac{D}{P}\right)QC_h$

    $= \dfrac{1}{2}\left(1 - \dfrac{7200}{25,000}\right)(1078.12)(0.18)(14.50)$

    $= \$1001.74$

    Ordering cost $= \dfrac{D}{Q}C_o = \dfrac{7200}{1078.12}(150) = \$1001.74$

    Total cost = \$2003.48

    g. $r = dm = \left(\dfrac{D}{250}\right)m = \dfrac{7200}{250}(15) = 432$

14. New $Q^* = 4509$

15. a. $Q^* = \sqrt{\dfrac{2DC_o}{C_h}\left(\dfrac{C_h + C_b}{C_b}\right)}$

    $= \sqrt{\dfrac{2(12,000)(25)}{0.50}\left(\dfrac{0.50 + 5}{0.50}\right)} = 1148.91$

    b. $S^* = Q^*\left(\dfrac{C_h}{C_h + C_b}\right) = 1148.91\left(\dfrac{0.50}{0.50 + 5}\right) = 104.45$

    c. Max inventory $= Q^* - S^* = 1044.46$

    d. $T = \dfrac{250Q^*}{D} = \dfrac{250(1148.91)}{12,000} = 23.94$ days

    e. Holding $= \dfrac{(Q - S)^2}{2Q}C_h = \$237.38$

    Ordering $= \dfrac{D}{Q}C_o = \$261.12$

    Backorder $= \dfrac{S^2}{2Q}C_b = \$23.74$

    Total cost = \$522.24
    The total cost for the EOQ model in Problem 4 was \$547.72; allowing backorders reduces the total cost.

16. 135.55; $r = dm - S$; less than

18. 64, 24.44

20. $Q^* = 100$; Total cost = \$3601.50

21. $Q = \sqrt{\dfrac{2DC_o}{C_h}}$

    $Q_1 = \sqrt{\dfrac{2(500)(40)}{0.20(10)}} = 141.42$

    $Q_2 = \sqrt{\dfrac{2(500)(40)}{0.20(9.7)}} = 143.59$

    Because Q_1 is over its limit of 99 units, Q_1 cannot be optimal (see Problem 23); use $Q_2 = 143.59$ as the optimal order quantity.

Total cost $= \frac{1}{2}QC_h + \frac{D}{Q}C_o + DC$

$= 139.28 + 139.28 + 4850.00 = \$5128.56$

22. $Q^* = 300$; Savings $= \$480$

24. a. 500
    b. 580.4

25. a.
$$c_o = 80 - 50 = 30$$
$$c_u = 125 - 80 = 45$$
$$P(D \leq Q^*) = \frac{c_u}{c_u + c_o} = \frac{45}{45 + 30} = 0.60$$

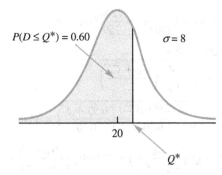

$P(D \leq Q^*) = 0.60$ $\sigma = 8$

20

Q^*

For the cumulative standard normal probability 0.60, $z = 0.25$.
$Q^* = 20 + 0.25(8) = 22$
    b. $P(\text{Sell all}) = P(D \geq Q^*) = 1 - 0.60 = 0.40$

26. a. \$150
    b. $\$240 - \$150 = \$90$
    c. 47
    d. 0.625

28. a. 440
    b. 0.60
    c. 710
    d. $c_u = \$17$

29. a. $r = dm = (200/250)15 = 12$
    b. $\frac{D}{Q} = \frac{200}{25} = 8$ orders/year

    The limit of 1 stockout per year means that
    $P(\text{Stockout/cycle}) = 1/8 = 0.125$.

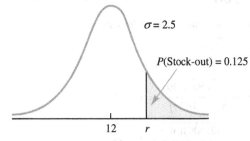

$\sigma = 2.5$

$P(\text{Stock-out}) = 0.125$

12   r

$P(\text{No Stockout/cycle}) = 1 - 0.125 = 0.875$
For cumulative probability 0.875, $z = 1.15$

Thus, $z = \frac{r - 12}{2.5} = 1.15$

$r = 12 + 1.15(2.5) = 14.875$ Use 15.
    c. Safety stock $= 3$ units
       Added cost $= 3(\$5) = \$15$/year

30. a. 13.68 (14)
    b. 17.83 (18)
    c. 2, \$10; 6, \$30

32. a. 31.62
    b. 19.86 (20); 0.2108
    c. 5, \$15

33. a. $1/52 = 0.0192$
    b. $P(\text{No Stockout}) = 1 - 0.0192 = 0.9808$
       For cumulative probability 0.9808, $z = 2.07$

       Thus, $z = \frac{M - 60}{12} = 2.07$

       $M = \mu + z\,\sigma = 60 + 2.07(12) = 85$
    c. $M = 35 + (0.9808)(85 - 35) = 84$

34. a. 243
    b. 93, \$54.87
    c. 613
    d. 163, \$96.17
    e. Yes, added cost would only be \$41.30 per year.
    f. Yes, added cost would be \$4130 per year.

36. a. 40
    b. 62.25; 7.9
    c. 54
    d. 36

14

Simulation

CONTENTS

Simulation is one of the most widely used quantitative approaches to decision making. It is a method for learning about a real system by experimenting with a model that represents the system. The simulation model contains the mathematical expressions and logical relationships that describe how to compute the value of the outputs given the values of the inputs. Any simulation model has two inputs: controllable inputs and probabilistic inputs. Figure 12.1 shows a conceptual diagram of a simulation model.

In conducting a **simulation experiment,** an analyst selects the value, or values, for the **controllable inputs.** Then values for the **probabilistic inputs** are randomly generated. The simulation model uses the values of the controllable inputs and the values of the probabilistic inputs to compute the value, or values, of the output. By conducting a series of experiments using a variety of values for the controllable inputs, the analyst learns how values of the controllable inputs affect or change the output of the simulation model. After reviewing the simulation results, the analyst is often able to make decision recommendations for the controllable inputs that will provide the desired output for the real system.

Simulation has been successfully applied in a variety of applications. The following examples are typical:

1. *New product development.* The objective of this simulation is to determine the probability that a new product will be profitable. A model is developed relating profit (the output measure) to various probabilistic inputs such as demand, parts cost, and labor cost. The only controllable input is whether to introduce the product. A variety of possible values will be generated for the probabilistic inputs, and the resulting profit will be computed. We develop a simulation model for this type of application in Section 12.1.

2. *Airline overbooking.* The objective of this simulation is to determine the number of reservations an airline should accept for a particular flight. A simulation model is developed relating profit for the flight to a probabilistic input, the number of passengers with a reservation who show up and use their reservation, and a controllable input, the number of reservations accepted for the flight. For each selected value for the controllable input, a variety of possible values will be generated for the number of passengers who show up, and the resulting profit can be computed. Similar simulation models are applicable for hotel and car rental reservation systems.

3. *Inventory policy.* The objective of this simulation is to choose an inventory policy that will provide good customer service at a reasonable cost. A model is developed relating two output measures, total inventory cost and the service level, to probabilistic inputs, such as product demand and delivery lead time from vendors, and controllable inputs, such as the order quantity and the reorder point. For each setting of the controllable inputs, a variety of possible values would be generated for the probabilistic inputs, and the resulting cost and service levels would be computed.

FIGURE 12.1   DIAGRAM OF A SIMULATION MODEL

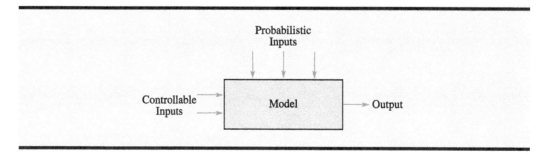

4. *Traffic flow.* The objective of this simulation is to determine the effect of installing a left turn signal on the flow of traffic through a busy intersection. A model is developed relating waiting time for vehicles to get through the intersection to probabilistic inputs such as the number of vehicle arrivals and the fraction that want to make a left turn, and controllable inputs such as the length of time the left turn signal is on. For each setting of the controllable inputs, values would be generated for the probabilistic inputs, and the resulting vehicle waiting times would be computed.

5. *Waiting lines.* The objective of this simulation is to determine the waiting times for customers at a bank's automated teller machine (ATM). A model is developed relating customer waiting times to probabilistic inputs such as customer arrivals and service times, and a controllable input, the number of ATM machines installed. For each value of the controllable input (the number of ATM machines), a variety of values would be generated for the probabilistic inputs, and the customer waiting times would be computed. The Management Science in Action, Call Center Design, describes how simulation of a waiting line system at a call center helped the company balance the service to its customers with the cost of agents providing the service.

Simulation is not an optimization technique. It is a method that can be used to describe or predict how a system will operate given certain choices for the controllable inputs and randomly generated values for the probabilistic inputs. Management scientists often use simulation to determine values for the controllable inputs that are likely to lead to desirable system outputs. In this sense, simulation can be an effective tool in designing a system to provide good performance.

MANAGEMENT SCIENCE IN ACTION

CALL CENTER DESIGN*

A call center is a place where large volumes of calls are made to or received from current or potential customers. More than 60,000 call centers operate in the United States. Saltzman and Mehrotra describe how a simulation model helped make a strategic change in the design of the technical support call center for a major software company. The application used a waiting line simulation model to balance the service to customers calling for assistance with the cost of agents providing the service.

Historically, the software company provided free phone-in technical support, but over time service requests grew to the point where 80% of the callers were waiting between 5 and 10 minutes and abandonment rates were too high. On some days 40% of the callers hung up before receiving service. This service level was unacceptable. As a result, management considered instituting a Rapid Program in which customers would pay a fee for service, but would be guaranteed to receive service within one minute, or the service would be free. Nonpaying customers would continue receiving service but without a guarantee of short service times.

A simulation model was developed to help understand the impact of this new program on the waiting line characteristics of the call center. Data available were used to develop the arrival distribution, the service time distribution, and the probability distribution for abandonment. The key design variables considered were the number of agents (channels) and the percentage of callers subscribing to the Rapid Program. The model was developed using the Arena simulation package.

The simulation results helped the company decide to go ahead with the Rapid Program. Under most of the scenarios considered, the simulation model showed that 95% of the callers in the Rapid Program would receive service within one minute and that free service to the remaining customers could be maintained within acceptable limits. Within nine months, 10% of the software company's customers subscribed to the Rapid Program, generating $2 million in incremental revenue. The company viewed the simulation model as a vehicle for mitigating risk. The model helped evaluate the likely impact of the Rapid Program without experimenting with actual customers.

*Based on Robert M. Saltzman and Vijay Mehrotra, "A Call Center Uses Simulation to Drive Strategic Change," *Interfaces* (May/June 2001): 87–101.

In this chapter we begin by showing how simulation can be used to study the financial risks associated with the development of a new product. We continue with illustrations showing how simulation can be used to establish an effective inventory policy and how simulation can be used to design waiting line systems. Other issues, such as verifying the simulation program, validating the model, and selecting a simulation software package, are discussed in Section 12.4.

12.1 RISK ANALYSIS

Risk analysis is the process of predicting the outcome of a decision in the face of uncertainty. In this section, we describe a problem that involves considerable uncertainty: the development of a new product. We first show how risk analysis can be conducted without using simulation; then we show how a more comprehensive risk analysis can be conducted with the aid of simulation.

PortaCom Project

PortaCom manufactures personal computers and related equipment. PortaCom's product design group developed a prototype for a new high-quality portable printer. The new printer features an innovative design and has the potential to capture a significant share of the portable printer market. Preliminary marketing and financial analyses provided the following selling price, first-year administrative cost, and first-year advertising cost:

$$\text{Selling price} = \$249 \text{ per unit}$$
$$\text{Administrative cost} = \$400,000$$
$$\text{Advertising cost} = \$600,000$$

In the simulation model for the PortaCom project, the preceding values are constants and are referred to as **parameters** of the model.

The cost of direct labor, the cost of parts, and the first-year demand for the printer are not known with certainty and are considered probabilistic inputs. At this stage of the planning process, PortaCom's best estimates of these inputs are $45 per unit for the direct labor cost, $90 per unit for the parts cost, and 15,000 units for the first-year demand. PortaCom would like an analysis of the first-year profit potential for the printer. Because of PortaCom's tight cash flow situation, management is particularly concerned about the potential for a loss.

What-If Analysis

One approach to risk analysis is called **what-if analysis.** A what-if analysis involves generating values for the probabilistic inputs (direct labor cost, parts cost, and first-year demand) and computing the resulting value for the output (profit). With a selling price of $249 per unit and administrative plus advertising costs equal to $400,000 + $600,000 = $1,000,000, the PortaCom profit model is

Profit = ($249 – Direct labor cost per unit – Parts cost per unit) (Demand) – $1,000,000

Letting

$$c_1 = \text{direct labor cost per unit}$$
$$c_2 = \text{parts cost per unit}$$
$$x = \text{first-year demand}$$

the profit model for the first year can be written as follows:

$$\text{Profit} = (249 - c_1 - c_2)x - 1{,}000{,}000 \qquad (12.1)$$

The PortaCom profit model can be depicted as shown in Figure 12.2.

Recall that PortaCom's best estimates of the direct labor cost per unit, the parts cost per unit, and first-year demand are \$45, \$90, and 15,000 units, respectively. These values constitute the **base-case scenario** for PortaCom. Substituting these values into equation (12.1) yields the following profit projection:

$$\text{Profit} = (249 - 45 - 90)(15{,}000) - 1{,}000{,}000 = 710{,}000$$

Thus, the base-case scenario leads to an anticipated profit of \$710,000.

In risk analysis we are concerned with both the probability of a loss and the magnitude of a loss. Although the base-case scenario looks appealing, PortaCom might be interested in what happens if the estimates of the direct labor cost per unit, parts cost per unit, and first-year demand do not turn out to be as expected under the base-case scenario. For instance, suppose that PortaCom believes that direct labor costs could range from \$43 to \$47 per unit, parts cost could range from \$80 to \$100 per unit, and first-year demand could range from 1500 to 28,500 units. Using these ranges, what-if analysis can be used to evaluate a **worst-case scenario** and a **best-case scenario.**

The worst-case value for the direct labor cost is \$47 (the highest value), the worst-case value for the parts cost is \$100 (the highest value), and the worst-case value for demand is 1500 units (the lowest value). Thus, in the worst-case scenario, $c_1 = 47$, $c_2 = 100$, and $x = 1500$. Substituting these values into equation (12.1) leads to the following profit projection:

$$\text{Profit} = (249 - 47 - 100)(1500) - 1{,}000{,}000 = -847{,}000$$

The worst-case scenario leads to a projected loss of \$847,000.

The best-case value for the direct labor cost is \$43 (the lowest value), the best-case value for the parts cost is \$80 (the lowest value), and the best-case value for demand is 28,500 units (the highest value). Substituting these values into equation (12.1) leads to the following profit projection:

Problem 2 will give you practice using what-if analysis.

$$\text{Profit} = (249 - 43 - 80)(28{,}500) - 1{,}000{,}000 = 2{,}591{,}000$$

The best-case scenario leads to a projected profit of \$2,591,000.

FIGURE 12.2 PORTACOM PROFIT MODEL

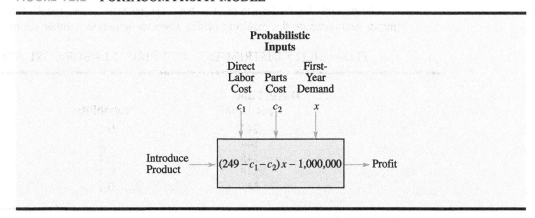

At this point the what-if analysis provides the conclusion that profits can range from a loss of $847,000 to a profit of $2,591,000 with a base-case profit of $710,000. Although the base-case profit of $710,000 is possible, the what-if analysis indicates that either a substantial loss or a substantial profit is possible. Other scenarios that PortaCom might want to consider can also be evaluated. However, the difficulty with what-if analysis is that it does not indicate the likelihood of the various profit or loss values. In particular, we do not know anything about the *probability* of a loss.

Simulation

Using simulation to perform risk analysis for the PortaCom project is like playing out many what-if scenarios by randomly generating values for the probabilistic inputs. The advantage of simulation is that it allows us to assess the probability of a profit and the probability of a loss.

Using the what-if approach to risk analysis, we selected values for the probabilistic inputs [direct labor cost per unit (c_1), parts cost per unit (c_2), and first-year demand (x)], and then computed the resulting profit. Applying simulation to the PortaCom project requires generating values for the probabilistic inputs that are representative of what we might observe in practice. To generate such values, we must know the probability distribution for each probabilistic input. Further analysis by PortaCom led to the following probability distributions for the direct labor cost per unit, the parts cost per unit, and first-year demand:

One advantage of simulation is the ability to use probability distributions that are unique to the system being studied.

Direct Labor Cost   PortaCom believes that the direct labor cost will range from $43 to $47 per unit and is described by the discrete probability distribution shown in Table 12.1. Thus, we see a 0.1 probability that the direct labor cost will be $43 per unit, a 0.2 probability that the direct labor cost will be $44 per unit, and so on. The highest probability of 0.4 is associated with a direct labor cost of $45 per unit.

Parts Cost   This cost depends upon the general economy, the overall demand for parts, and the pricing policy of PortaCom's parts suppliers. PortaCom believes that the parts cost will range from $80 to $100 per unit and is described by the uniform probability distribution shown in Figure 12.3. Costs per unit between $80 and $100 are equally likely.

First-Year Demand   PortaCom believes that first-year demand is described by the normal probability distribution shown in Figure 12.4. The mean or expected value of first-year demand is 15,000 units. The standard deviation of 4500 units describes the variability in the first-year demand.

To simulate the PortaCom project, we must generate values for the three probabilistic inputs and compute the resulting profit. Then we generate another set of values for the

TABLE 12.1   PROBABILITY DISTRIBUTION FOR DIRECT LABOR COST PER UNIT

Direct Labor Cost per Unit	Probability
$43	0.1
$44	0.2
$45	0.4
$46	0.2
$47	0.1

FIGURE 12.3   UNIFORM PROBABILITY DISTRIBUTION FOR THE PARTS
              COST PER UNIT

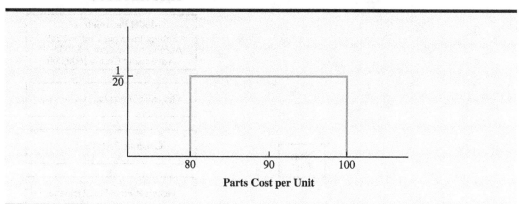

A flowchart provides a graphical representation that helps describe the logic of the simulation model.

probabilistic inputs, compute a second value for profit, and so on. We continue this process until we are satisfied that enough trials have been conducted to describe the probability distribution for profit. This process of generating probabilistic inputs and computing the value of the output is called *simulation*. The sequence of logical and mathematical operations required to conduct a simulation can be depicted with a flowchart. A flowchart for the PortaCom simulation is shown in Figure 12.5.

Following the logic described by the flowchart, we see that the model parameters—selling price, administrative cost, and advertising cost—are $249, $400,000, and $600,000, respectively. These values will remain fixed throughout the simulation.

The next three blocks depict the generation of values for the probabilistic inputs. First, a value for the direct labor cost (c_1) is generated. Then a value for the parts cost (c_2) is generated, followed by a value for the first-year demand (x). These probabilistic input values are combined using the profit model given by equation (12.1).

$$\text{Profit} = (249 - c_1 - c_2)x - 1{,}000{,}000$$

The computation of profit completes one trial of the simulation. We then return to the block where we generated the direct labor cost and begin another trial. This process is repeated until a satisfactory number of trials has been generated.

FIGURE 12.4   NORMAL PROBABILITY DISTRIBUTION OF FIRST-YEAR DEMAND

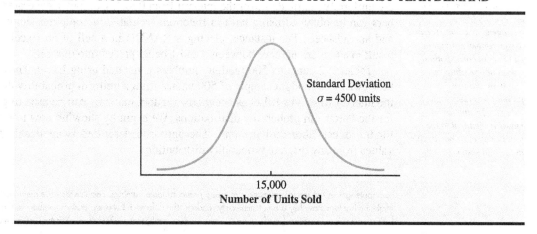

FIGURE 12.5   FLOWCHART FOR THE PORTACOM SIMULATION

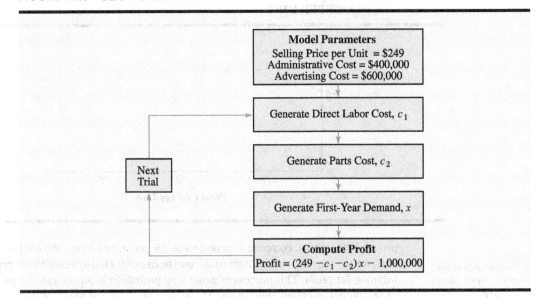

At the end of the simulation, output measures of interest can be developed. For example, we will be interested in computing the average profit and the probability of a loss. For the output measures to be meaningful, the values of the probabilistic inputs must be representative of what is likely to happen when the PortaCom printer is introduced into the market. An essential part of the simulation procedure is the ability to generate representative values for the probabilistic inputs. We now discuss how to generate these values.

Random Numbers and Generating Probabilistic Input Values   In the PortaCom simulation, representative values must be generated for the direct labor cost per unit (c_1), the parts cost per unit (c_2), and the first-year demand (x). Random numbers and the probability distributions associated with each probabilistic input are used to generate representative values. To illustrate how to generate these values, we need to introduce the concept of *computer-generated random numbers*.

Computer-generated random numbers[1] are randomly selected decimal numbers from 0 up to, but not including, 1. The computer-generated random numbers are equally likely and are uniformly distributed over the interval from 0 to 1. Computer-generated random numbers can be obtained using built-in functions available in computer simulation packages and spreadsheets. For instance, placing =RAND() in a cell of an Excel worksheet will result in a random number between 0 and 1 being placed into that cell.

Table 12.2 contains 500 random numbers generated using Excel. These numbers can be viewed as a random sample of 500 values from a uniform probability distribution over the interval from 0 to 1. Let us show how random numbers can be used to generate values for the PortaCom probability distributions. We begin by showing how to generate a value for the direct labor cost per unit. The approach described is applicable for generating values from any discrete probability distribution.

Because random numbers are equally likely, management scientists can assign ranges of random numbers to corresponding values of probabilistic inputs so that the probability of any input value to the simulation model is identical to the probability of its occurrence in the real system.

---

[1]Computer-generated random numbers are called *pseudorandom numbers*. Because they are generated through the use of mathematical formulas, they are not technically random. The difference between random numbers and pseudorandom numbers is primarily philosophical, and we use the term *random numbers* regardless of whether they are generated by a computer.

TABLE 12.2   500 COMPUTER-GENERATED RANDOM NUMBERS

0.6953	0.5247	0.1368	0.9850	0.7467	0.3813	0.5827	0.7893	0.7169	0.8166
0.0082	0.9925	0.6874	0.2122	0.6885	0.2159	0.4299	0.3467	0.2186	0.1033
0.6799	0.1241	0.3056	0.5590	0.0423	0.6515	0.2750	0.8156	0.2871	0.4680
0.8898	0.1514	0.1826	0.0004	0.5259	0.2425	0.8421	0.9248	0.9155	0.9518
0.6515	0.5027	0.9290	0.5177	0.3134	0.9177	0.2605	0.6668	0.1167	0.7870
0.3976	0.7790	0.0035	0.0064	0.0441	0.3437	0.1248	0.5442	0.9800	0.1857
0.0642	0.4086	0.6078	0.2044	0.0484	0.4691	0.7058	0.8552	0.5029	0.3288
0.0377	0.5250	0.7774	0.2390	0.9121	0.5345	0.8178	0.8443	0.4154	0.2526
0.5739	0.5181	0.0234	0.7305	0.0376	0.5169	0.5679	0.5495	0.7872	0.5321
0.5827	0.0341	0.7482	0.6351	0.9146	0.4700	0.7869	0.1337	0.0702	0.4219
0.0508	0.7905	0.2932	0.4971	0.0225	0.4466	0.5118	0.1200	0.0200	0.5445
0.4757	0.1399	0.5668	0.9569	0.7255	0.4650	0.4084	0.3701	0.9446	0.8064
0.6805	0.9931	0.4166	0.1091	0.7730	0.0691	0.9411	0.3468	0.0014	0.7379
0.2603	0.7507	0.6414	0.9907	0.2699	0.4571	0.9254	0.2371	0.8664	0.9553
0.8143	0.7625	0.1708	0.1900	0.2781	0.2830	0.6877	0.0488	0.8635	0.3155
0.5681	0.7854	0.5016	0.9403	0.1078	0.5255	0.8727	0.3815	0.5541	0.9833
0.1501	0.9363	0.3858	0.3545	0.5448	0.0643	0.3167	0.6732	0.6283	0.2631
0.8806	0.7989	0.7484	0.8083	0.2701	0.5039	0.9439	0.1027	0.9677	0.4597
0.4582	0.7590	0.4393	0.4704	0.6903	0.3732	0.6587	0.8675	0.2905	0.3058
0.0785	0.1467	0.3880	0.5274	0.8723	0.7517	0.9905	0.8904	0.8177	0.6660
0.1158	0.6635	0.4992	0.9070	0.2975	0.5686	0.8495	0.1652	0.2039	0.2553
0.2762	0.7018	0.6782	0.4013	0.2224	0.4672	0.5753	0.6219	0.6871	0.9255
0.9382	0.6411	0.7984	0.0608	0.5945	0.3977	0.4570	0.9924	0.8398	0.8361
0.5102	0.7021	0.4353	0.3398	0.8038	0.2260	0.1250	0.1884	0.3432	0.1192
0.2354	0.7410	0.7089	0.2579	0.1358	0.8446	0.1648	0.3889	0.5620	0.6555
0.9082	0.7906	0.7589	0.8870	0.1189	0.7125	0.6324	0.1096	0.5155	0.3449
0.6936	0.0702	0.9716	0.0374	0.0683	0.2397	0.7753	0.2029	0.1464	0.8000
0.4042	0.8158	0.3623	0.6614	0.7954	0.7516	0.6518	0.3638	0.3107	0.2718
0.9410	0.2201	0.6348	0.0367	0.0311	0.0688	0.2346	0.3927	0.7327	0.9994
0.0917	0.2504	0.2878	0.1735	0.3872	0.6816	0.2731	0.3846	0.6621	0.8983
0.8532	0.4869	0.2685	0.6349	0.9364	0.3451	0.4998	0.2842	0.0643	0.6656
0.8980	0.0455	0.8314	0.8189	0.6783	0.8086	0.1386	0.4442	0.9941	0.6812
0.8412	0.8792	0.2025	0.9320	0.7656	0.3815	0.5302	0.8744	0.4584	0.3585
0.5688	0.8633	0.5818	0.0692	0.2543	0.5453	0.9955	0.1237	0.7535	0.5993
0.5006	0.1215	0.8102	0.1026	0.9251	0.6851	0.1559	0.1214	0.2628	0.9374
0.5748	0.4164	0.3427	0.2809	0.8064	0.5855	0.2229	0.2805	0.9139	0.9013
0.1100	0.0873	0.9407	0.8747	0.0496	0.4380	0.5847	0.4183	0.5929	0.4863
0.5802	0.7747	0.1285	0.0074	0.6252	0.7747	0.0112	0.3958	0.3285	0.5389
0.1019	0.6628	0.8998	0.1334	0.2798	0.7351	0.7330	0.6723	0.6924	0.3963
0.9909	0.8991	0.2298	0.2603	0.6921	0.5573	0.8191	0.0384	0.2954	0.0636
0.6292	0.4923	0.0276	0.6734	0.6562	0.4231	0.1980	0.6551	0.3716	0.0507
0.9430	0.2579	0.7933	0.0945	0.3192	0.3195	0.7772	0.4672	0.7070	0.5925
0.9938	0.7098	0.7964	0.7952	0.8947	0.1214	0.8454	0.8294	0.5394	0.9413
0.4690	0.1395	0.0930	0.3189	0.6972	0.7291	0.8513	0.9256	0.7478	0.8124
0.2028	0.3774	0.0485	0.7718	0.9656	0.2444	0.0304	0.1395	0.1577	0.8625
0.6141	0.4131	0.2006	0.2329	0.6182	0.5151	0.6300	0.9311	0.3837	0.7828
0.2757	0.8479	0.7880	0.8492	0.6859	0.8947	0.6246	0.1574	0.4936	0.8077
0.0561	0.0126	0.6531	0.0378	0.4975	0.1133	0.3572	0.0071	0.4555	0.7563
0.1419	0.4308	0.8073	0.4681	0.0481	0.2918	0.2975	0.0685	0.6384	0.0812
0.3125	0.0053	0.9209	0.9768	0.3584	0.0390	0.2161	0.6333	0.4391	0.6991

TABLE 12.3 RANDOM NUMBER INTERVALS FOR GENERATING VALUES OF DIRECT
LABOR COST PER UNIT

Direct Labor Cost per Unit	Probability	Interval of Random Numbers
$43	0.1	0.0 but less than 0.1
$44	0.2	0.1 but less than 0.3
$45	0.4	0.3 but less than 0.7
$46	0.2	0.7 but less than 0.9
$47	0.1	0.9 but less than 1.0

An interval of random numbers is assigned to each possible value of the direct labor cost
in such a fashion that the probability of generating a random number in the interval is equal to
the probability of the corresponding direct labor cost. Table 12.3 shows how this process is
done. The interval of random numbers greater than or equal to 0.0 but less than 0.1 is associated with a direct labor cost of $43, the interval of random numbers greater than or equal to 0.1
but less than 0.3 is associated with a direct labor cost of $44, and so on. With this assignment
of random number intervals to the possible values of the direct labor cost, the probability of
generating a random number in any interval is equal to the probability of obtaining the corresponding value for the direct labor cost. Thus, to select a value for the direct labor cost, we generate a random number between 0 and 1. If the random number is greater than or equal to 0.0
but less than 0.1, we set the direct labor cost equal to $43. If the random number is greater than
or equal to 0.1 but less than 0.3, we set the direct labor cost equal to $44, and so on.

*Try Problem 5 for an
opportunity to establish
intervals of random
numbers and simulate
demand from a discrete
probability distribution.*

Each trial of the simulation requires a value for the direct labor cost. Suppose that on
the first trial the random number is 0.9109. From Table 12.3, the simulated value for the
direct labor cost is $47 per unit. Suppose that on the second trial the random number is
0.2841. From Table 12.3, the simulated value for the direct labor cost is $44 per unit.
Table 12.4 shows the results obtained for the first 10 simulation trials.

Each trial in the simulation requires a value of the direct labor cost, parts cost, and first-
year demand. Let us now turn to the issue of generating values for the parts cost. The probability distribution for the parts cost per unit is the uniform distribution shown in Figure 12.3.
Because this random variable has a different probability distribution than direct labor cost,
we use random numbers in a slightly different way to generate values for parts cost. With a

TABLE 12.4 RANDOM GENERATION OF 10 VALUES FOR THE DIRECT LABOR COST
PER UNIT

Trial	Random Number	Direct Labor Cost ($)
1	0.9109	47
2	0.2841	44
3	0.6531	45
4	0.0367	43
5	0.3451	45
6	0.2757	44
7	0.6859	45
8	0.6246	45
9	0.4936	45
10	0.8077	46

uniform probability distribution, the following relationship between the random number and the associated value of the parts cost is used:

$$\text{Parts cost} = a + r(b - a) \qquad (12.2)$$

where

r = random number between 0 and 1
a = smallest value for parts cost
b = largest value for parts cost

For PortaCom, the smallest value for the parts cost is $80, and the largest value is $100. Applying equation (12.2) with $a = 80$ and $b = 100$ leads to the following formula for generating the parts cost given a random number, r:

$$\text{Parts cost} = 80 + r(100 - 80) = 80 + r20 \qquad (12.3)$$

Equation (12.3) generates a value for the parts cost. Suppose that a random number of 0.2680 is obtained. The value for the parts cost is

$$\text{Parts cost} = 80 + 0.2680(20) = 85.36 \text{ per unit}$$

Spreadsheet packages such as Excel have built-in functions that make simulations based on probability distributions such as the normal probability distribution relatively easy.

Suppose that a random number of 0.5842 is generated on the next trial. The value for the parts cost is

$$\text{Parts cost} = 80 + 0.5842(20) = 91.68 \text{ per unit}$$

With appropriate choices of a and b, equation (12.2) can be used to generate values for any uniform probability distribution. Table 12.5 shows the generation of 10 values for the parts cost per unit.

Finally, we need a random number procedure for generating the first-year demand. Because first-year demand is normally distributed with a mean of 15,000 units and a standard deviation of 4500 units (see Figure 12.4), we need a procedure for generating random

TABLE 12.5   RANDOM GENERATION OF 10 VALUES FOR THE PARTS COST PER UNIT

Trial	Random Number	Parts Cost ($)
1	0.2680	85.36
2	0.5842	91.68
3	0.6675	93.35
4	0.9280	98.56
5	0.4180	88.36
6	0.7342	94.68
7	0.4325	88.65
8	0.1186	82.37
9	0.6944	93.89
10	0.7869	95.74

values from a normal probability distribution. Because of the mathematical complexity, a detailed discussion of the procedure for generating random values from a normal probability distribution is omitted. However, computer simulation packages and spreadsheets include a built-in function that provides randomly generated values from a normal probability distribution. In most cases the user only needs to provide the mean and standard deviation of the normal distribution. For example, using Excel the following formula can be placed into a cell to obtain a value for a probabilistic input that is normally distributed:

$$= \text{NORMINV(RAND(),Mean,Standard Deviation)}$$

Because the mean for the first-year demand in the PortaCom problem is 15,000 and the standard deviation is 4500, the Excel statement

$$= \text{NORMINV(RAND(),15000,4500)} \tag{12.4}$$

will provide a normally distributed value for first-year demand. For example, if Excel's RAND() function generates the random number 0.7005, the Excel function shown in equation (12.4) will provide a first-year demand of 17,366 units. If RAND() generates the random number 0.3204, equation (12.4) will provide a first-year demand of 12,900. Table 12.6 shows the results for the first 10 randomly generated values for demand. Note that random numbers less than 0.5 generate first-year demand values below the mean and that random numbers greater than 0.5 generate first-year demand values greater than the mean.

Running the Simulation Model Running the simulation model means implementing the sequence of logical and mathematical operations described in the flowchart in Figure 12.5. The model parameters are $249 per unit for the selling price, $400,000 for the administrative cost, and $600,000 for the advertising cost. Each trial in the simulation involves randomly generating values for the probabilistic inputs (direct labor cost, parts cost, and first-year demand) and computing profit. The simulation is complete when a satisfactory number of trials have been conducted.

Let us compute the profit for the first trial assuming the following probabilistic inputs:

Direct labor cost: $C_1 = 47$
Parts cost: $C_2 = 85.36$
First-year demand: $x = 17,366$

TABLE 12.6   RANDOM GENERATION OF 10 VALUES FOR FIRST-YEAR DEMAND

Trial	Random Number	Demand
1	0.7005	17,366
2	0.3204	12,900
3	0.8968	20,686
4	0.1804	10,888
5	0.4346	14,259
6	0.9605	22,904
7	0.5646	15,732
8	0.7334	17,804
9	0.0216	5,902
10	0.3218	12,918

TABLE 12.7 PORTACOM SIMULATION RESULTS FOR 10 TRIALS

Trial	Direct Labor Cost per Unit ($)	Parts Cost per Unit ($)	Units Sold	Profit ($)
1	47	85.36	17,366	1,025,570
2	44	91.68	12,900	461,828
3	45	93.35	20,686	1,288,906
4	43	98.56	10,888	169,807
5	45	88.36	14,259	648,911
6	44	94.68	22,904	1,526,769
7	45	88.65	15,732	814,686
8	45	82.37	17,804	1,165,501
9	45	93.89	5,902	−350,131
10	46	95.74	12,918	385,585
Total	449	912.64	151,359	7,137,432
Average	$44.90	$91.26	15,136	$713,743

Referring to the flowchart in Figure 12.5, we see that the profit obtained is

$$\text{Profit} = (249 - c_1 - c_2)x - 1{,}000{,}000$$
$$= (249 - 47 - 85.36)17{,}366 - 1{,}000{,}000 = 1{,}025{,}570$$

The first row of Table 12.7 shows the result of this trial of the PortaCom simulation.

The simulated profit for the PortaCom printer if the direct labor cost is $47 per unit, the parts cost is $85.36 per unit, and first-year demand is 17,366 units is $1,025,570. Of course, one simulation trial does not provide a complete understanding of the possible profit and loss. Because other values are possible for the probabilistic inputs, we can benefit from additional simulation trials.

Suppose that on a second simulation trial, random numbers of 0.2841, 0.5842, and 0.3204 are generated for the direct labor cost, the parts cost, and first-year demand, respectively. These random numbers will provide the probabilistic inputs of $44 for the direct labor cost, $91.68 for the parts cost, and 12,900 for first-year demand. These values provide a simulated profit of $461,828 on the second simulation trial (see the second row of Table 12.7).

Repetition of the simulation process with different values for the probabilistic inputs is an essential part of any simulation. Through the repeated trials, management will begin to understand what might happen when the product is introduced into the real world. We have shown the results of 10 simulation trials in Table 12.7. For these 10 cases, we find a profit as high as $1,526,769 for the 6th trial and a loss of $350,131 for the 9th trial. Thus, we see both the possibility of a profit and of a loss. Averages for the 10 trials are presented at the bottom of the table. We see that the average profit for the 10 trials is $713,743. The probability of a loss is 0.10, because one of the 10 trials (the 9th) resulted in a loss. We note also that the average values for labor cost, parts cost, and first-year demand are fairly close to their means of $45, $90, and 15,000, respectively.

Simulation of the PortaCom Project

Using an Excel worksheet, we simulated the PortaCom project 500 times. The worksheet used to carry out the simulation is shown in Figure 12.6. Note that the simulation results for trials 6 through 495 have been hidden so that the results can be shown in a reasonably sized

FIGURE 12.6 EXCEL WORKSHEET SIMULATION FOR THE PORTACOM PROJECT

	A	B	C	D	E	F
1	**PortaCom Risk Analysis**					
2						
3	Selling Price per Unit		$249			
4	Administrative Cost		$400,000			
5	Advertising Cost		$600,000			
6						
7	**Direct Labor Cost**			**Parts Cost (Uniform Distribution)**		
8	Lower	Upper		Smallest Value	$80	
9	Random No.	Random No.	Cost per Unit	Largest Value	$100	
10	0.0	0.1	$43			
11	0.1	0.3	$44			
12	0.3	0.7	$45	**Demand (Normal Distribution)**		
13	0.7	0.9	$46	Mean	15000	
14	0.9	1.0	$47	Std Deviation	4500	
15						
16						
17	**Simulation Trials**					
18						
19		Direct Labor	Parts	First-Year		
20	Trial	Cost per Unit	Cost per Unit	Demand	Profit	
21	1	47	$85.36	17,366	$1,025,570	
22	2	44	$91.68	12,900	$461,828	
23	3	45	$93.35	20,686	$1,288,906	
24	4	43	$98.56	10,888	$169,807	
25	5	45	$88.36	14,259	$648,911	
516	496	44	$98.67	8,730	($71,739)	
517	497	45	$94.38	19,257	$1,110,952	
518	498	44	$90.85	14,920	$703,118	
519	499	43	$90.37	13,471	$557,652	
520	500	46	$92.50	18,614	$1,056,847	
521						
522			**Summary Statistics**			
523			Mean Profit		$698,457	
524			Standard Deviation		$520,485	
525			Minimum Profit		($785,234)	
526			Maximum Profit		$2,367,058	
527			Number of Losses		51	
528			Probability of Loss		0.1020	

WEB file

PortaCom

Excel worksheets for all simulations presented in this chapter are available on the website that accompanies this text.

figure. If desired, the rows for these trials can be shown and the simulation results displayed for all 500 trials. The details of the Excel worksheet that provided the PortaCom simulation are described in Appendix 12.1.

The simulation summary statistics in Figure 12.6 provide information about the risk associated with PortaCom's new printer. The worst result obtained in a simulation of 500 trials is a loss of $785,234, and the best result is a profit of $2,367,058. The mean profit is

$698,457. Fifty-one of the trials resulted in a loss; thus, the estimated probability of a loss is 51/500 = 0.1020.

Simulation studies enable an objective estimate of the probability of a loss, which is an important aspect of risk analysis.

A histogram of simulated profit values is shown in Figure 12.7. We note that the distribution of profit values is fairly symmetric with a large number of values in the range of $250,000 to $1,250,000. The probability of a large loss or a large gain is small. Only three trials resulted in a loss of more than $500,000, and only three trials resulted in a profit greater than $2,000,000. However, the probability of a loss is significant. Forty-eight of the 500 trials resulted in a loss in the $0 to $500,000 range—almost 10%. The modal category, the one with the largest number of values, is the range of profits between $750,000 and $1,000,000.

In comparing the simulation approach to risk analysis to the what-if approach, we see that much more information is obtained by using simulation. With the what-if analysis, we learned that the base-case scenario projected a profit of $710,000. The worst-case scenario projected a loss of $847,000, and the best-case scenario projected a profit of $2,591,000. From the 500 trials of the simulation run, we see that the worst- and best-case scenarios, although possible, are unlikely. None of the 500 trials provided a loss as low as the worst-case or a profit as high as the best-case. Indeed, the advantage of simulation for risk analysis is the information it provides on the likely values of the output. We now know the probability of a loss, how the profit values are distributed over their range, and what profit values are most likely.

For practice working through a simulation problem, try Problems 9 and 14.

The simulation results help PortaCom's management better understand the profit/loss potential of the PortaCom portable printer. The 0.1020 probability of a loss may be acceptable to management given a probability of almost 0.80 (see Figure 12.7) that profit will exceed $250,000. On the other hand, PortaCom might want to conduct further market research before deciding whether to introduce the product. In any case, the simulation results should be helpful in reaching an appropriate decision. The Management Science in Action, Meeting Demand Levels at Pfizer, describes how a simulation model helped find ways to meet increasing demand for a product.

FIGURE 12.7   HISTOGRAM OF SIMULATED PROFIT FOR 500 TRIALS OF THE PORTACOM SIMULATION

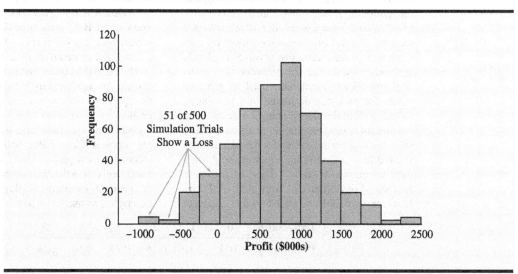

MEETING DEMAND LEVELS AT PFIZER*

Pharmacia & Upjohn's merger with Pfizer created one of the world's largest pharmaceutical firms. Demand for one of Pharmacia & Upjohn's long-standing products remained stable for several years at a level easily satisfied by the company's manufacturing facility. However, changes in market conditions caused an increase in demand to a level beyond the current capacity. A simulation model of the production process was developed to explore ways to increase production to meet the new level of demand in a cost-effective manner.

Simulation results were used to help answer the following questions:

- What is the maximum throughput of the existing facility?
- How can the existing production process be modified to increase throughput?
- How much equipment must be added to the existing facility to meet the increased demand?

- What is the desired size and configuration of the new production process?

The simulation model was able to demonstrate that the existing facilities, with some operating policy improvements, were large enough to satisfy the increased demand for the next several years. Expansion to a new production facility was not necessary. The simulation model also helped determine the number of operators required as the production level increased in the future. This result helped ensure that the proper number of operators would be trained by the time they were needed. The simulation model also provided a way reprocessed material could be used to replace fresh raw materials, resulting in a savings of approximately $3 million per year.

*Based on information provided by David B. Magerlein, James M. Magerlein, and Michael J. Goodrich.

Appendix 12.2 shows how to perform a simulation of the PortaCom project using Crystal Ball.

1. The PortaCom simulation model is based on independent trials in which the results for one trial do not affect what happens in subsequent trials. Historically, this type of simulation study was referred to as a *Monte Carlo simulation*. The term *Monte Carlo simulation* was used because early practitioners of simulation saw similarities between the models they were developing and the gambling games played in the casinos of Monte Carlo. Today, many individuals interpret the term *Monte Carlo simulation* more broadly to mean any simulation that involves randomly generating values for the probabilistic inputs.

2. The probability distribution used to generate values for probabilistic inputs in a simulation model is often developed using historical data. For instance, suppose that an analysis of daily sales at a new car dealership for the past 50 days showed that on 2 days no cars were sold, on 5 days one car was sold, on 9 days two cars were sold, on 24 days three cars were sold, on 7 days four cars were sold, and on 3 days five cars were

sold. We can estimate the probability distribution of daily demand using the relative frequencies for the observed data. An estimate of the probability that no cars are sold on a given day is $2/50 = 0.04$, an estimate of the probability that one car is sold is $5/50 = 0.10$, and so on. The estimated probability distribution of daily demand is shown in the table below.

3. Spreadsheet add-in packages such as @RISK® and Crystal Ball® have been developed to make spreadsheet simulation easier. For instance, using Crystal Ball we could simulate the PortaCom new product introduction by first entering the formulas showing the relationships between the probabilistic inputs and the output measure, profit. Then, a probability distribution type is selected for each probabilistic input from among a number of available choices. Crystal Ball will generate random values for each probabilistic input, compute the profit, and repeat the simulation for as many trials as specified. Graphical displays and a variety of descriptive statistics can be easily obtained.

Daily Sales	0	1	2	3	4	5
Probability	0.04	0.10	0.18	0.48	0.14	0.06

In this section we describe how simulation can be used to establish an inventory policy for a product that has an uncertain demand. The product is a home ventilation fan distributed by the Butler Electrical Supply Company. Each fan costs Butler $75 and sells for $125. Thus Butler realizes a gross profit of $125 − $75 = $50 for each fan sold. Monthly demand for the fan is described by a normal probability distribution with a mean of 100 units and a standard deviation of 20 units.

Butler receives monthly deliveries from its supplier and replenishes its inventory to a level of Q at the beginning of each month. This beginning inventory level is referred to as the replenishment level. If monthly demand is less than the replenishment level, an inventory holding cost of $15 is charged for each unit that is not sold. However, if monthly demand is greater than the replenishment level, a stockout occurs and a shortage cost is incurred. Because Butler assigns a goodwill cost of $30 for each customer turned away, a shortage cost of $30 is charged for each unit of demand that cannot be satisfied. Management would like to use a simulation model to determine the average monthly net profit resulting from using a particular replenishment level. Management would also like information on the percentage of total demand that will be satisfied. This percentage is referred to as the *service level*.

The controllable input to the Butler simulation model is the replenishment level, Q. The probabilistic input is the monthly demand, D. The two output measures are the average monthly net profit and the service level. Computation of the service level requires that we keep track of the number of fans sold each month and the total demand for fans for each month. The service level will be computed at the end of the simulation run as the ratio of total units sold to total demand. A diagram of the relationship between the inputs and the outputs is shown in Figure 12.8.

When demand is less than or equal to the replenishment level ($D \leq Q$), D units are sold, and an inventory holding cost of $15 is incurred for each of the $Q - D$ units that remain in inventory. Net profit for this case is computed as follows:

Case 1: $D \leq Q$

Gross profit $= \$50D$

Holding cost $= \$15(Q - D)$ (12.5)

    Net profit $=$ Gross profit $-$ Holding cost $= \$50D - \$15(Q - D)$

When demand is greater than the replenishment level ($D > Q$), Q fans are sold, and a shortage cost of $30 is imposed for each of the $D - Q$ units of demand not satisfied. Net profit for this case is computed as follows:

Case 2: $D > Q$

Gross profit $= \$50Q$

Shortage cost $= \$30(D - Q)$ (12.6)

    Net profit $=$ Gross profit $-$ Shortage cost $= \$50Q - \$30(D - Q)$

Figure 12.9 shows a flowchart that defines the sequence of logical and mathematical operations required to simulate the Butler inventory system. Each trial in the simulation

FIGURE 12.8   BUTLER INVENTORY SIMULATION MODEL

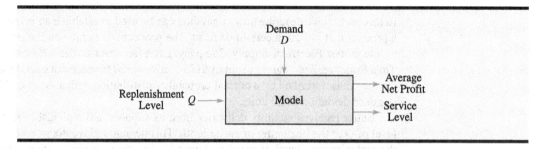

FIGURE 12.9   FLOWCHART FOR THE BUTLER INVENTORY SIMULATION

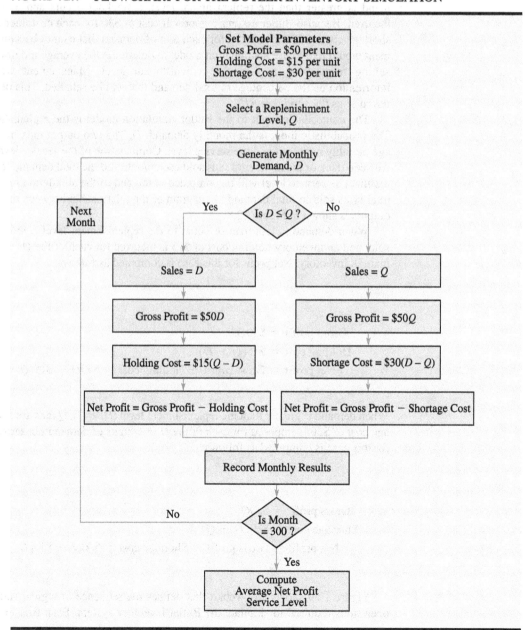

represents one month of operation. The simulation is run for 300 months using a given replenishment level, Q. Then the average profit and service level output measures are computed. Let us describe the steps involved in the simulation by illustrating the results for the first two months of a simulation run using a replenishment level of $Q = 100$.

The first block of the flowchart in Figure 12.9 sets the values of the model parameters: gross profit = \$50 per unit, holding cost = \$15 per unit, and shortage cost = \$30 per unit. The next block shows that a replenishment level of Q is selected; in our illustration, $Q = 100$. Then a value for monthly demand is generated. Because monthly demand is normally distributed with a mean of 100 units and a standard deviation of 20 units, we can use the Excel function =NORMINV(RAND(),100,20), as described in Section 12.1, to generate a value for monthly demand. Suppose that a value of $D = 79$ is generated on the first trial. This value of demand is then compared with the replenishment level, Q. With the replenishment level set at $Q = 100$, demand is less than the replenishment level, and the left branch of the flowchart is followed. Sales are set equal to demand (79), and gross profit, holding cost, and net profit are computed as follows:

$$\text{Gross profit} = 50D = 50(79) = 3950$$
$$\text{Holding cost} = 15(Q - D) = 15(100 - 79) = 315$$
$$\text{Net profit} = \text{Gross profit} - \text{Holding cost} = 3950 - 315 = 3635$$

The values of demand, sales, gross profit, holding cost, and net profit are recorded for the first month. The first row of Table 12.8 summarizes the information for this first trial.

For the second month, suppose that a value of 111 is generated for monthly demand. Because demand is greater than the replenishment level, the right branch of the flowchart is followed. Sales are set equal to the replenishment level (100), and gross profit, shortage cost, and net profit are computed as follows:

$$\text{Gross profit} = 50Q = 50(100) = 5000$$
$$\text{Shortage cost} = 30(D - Q) = 30(111 - 100) = 330$$
$$\text{Net profit} = \text{Gross profit} - \text{Shortage cost} = 5000 - 330 = 4670$$

The values of demand, sales, gross profit, holding cost, shortage cost, and net profit are recorded for the second month. The second row of Table 12.8 summarizes the information generated in the second trial.

Results for the first five months of the simulation are shown in Table 12.8. The totals show an accumulated total net profit of \$22,310, which is an average monthly net profit of

TABLE 12.8 BUTLER INVENTORY SIMULATION RESULTS FOR FIVE TRIALS WITH $Q = 100$

Month	Demand	Sales	Gross Profit (\$)	Holding Cost (\$)	Shortage Cost (\$)	Net Profit (\$)
1	79	79	3,950	315	0	3,635
2	111	100	5,000	0	330	4,670
3	93	93	4,650	105	0	4,545
4	100	100	5,000	0	0	5,000
5	118	100	5,000	0	540	4,460
Totals	501	472	23,600	420	870	22,310
Average	100	94	\$4,720	\$ 84	\$174	\$4,462

$22,310/5 = \$4462$. Total unit sales are 472, and total demand is 501. Thus, the service level is $472/501 = 0.942$, indicating Butler has been able to satisfy 94.2% of demand during the five-month period.

Butler Inventory Simulation

Using Excel, we simulated the Butler inventory operation for 300 months. The worksheet used to carry out the simulation is shown in Figure 12.10. Note that the simulation results for months 6 through 295 have been hidden so that the results can be shown in a reasonably sized figure. If desired, the rows for these months can be shown and the simulation results displayed for all 300 months.

FIGURE 12.10 EXCEL WORKSHEET FOR THE BUTLER INVENTORY SIMULATION

WEB file

Butler

	A	B	C	D	E	F	G	H
1	**Butler Inventory**							
2								
3	Gross Profit per Unit		$50					
4	Holding Cost per Unit		$15					
5	Shortage Cost per Unit		$30					
6								
7	**Replenishment Level**		100					
8								
9	**Demand (Normal Distribution)**							
10	Mean	100						
11	Std Deviation	20						
12								
13								
14	**Simulation**							
15								
16	Month	Demand	Sales	Gross Profit	Holding Cost	Shortage Cost	Net Profit	
17	1	79	79	$3,950	$315	$0	$3,635	
18	2	111	100	$5,000	$0	$330	$4,670	
19	3	93	93	$4,650	$105	$0	$4,545	
20	4	100	100	$5,000	$0	$0	$5,000	
21	5	118	100	$5,000	$0	$540	$4,460	
312	296	89	89	$4,450	$165	$0	$4,285	
313	297	91	91	$4,550	$135	$0	$4,415	
314	298	122	100	$5,000	$0	$660	$4,340	
315	299	93	93	$4,650	$105	$0	$4,545	
316	300	126	100	$5,000	$0	$780	$4,220	
317								
318	Totals	30,181	27,917		**Summary Statistics**			
319					Mean Profit		$4,293	
320					Standard Deviation		$658	
321					Minimum Profit		($206)	
322					Maximum Profit		$5,000	
323					Service Level		92.5%	

TABLE 12.9   BUTLER INVENTORY SIMULATION RESULTS FOR 300 TRIALS

Replenishment Level	Average Net Profit ($)	Service Level (%)
100	4293	92.5
110	4524	96.5
120	4575	98.6
130	4519	99.6
140	4399	99.9

Simulation allows the user to consider different operating policies and changes to model parameters and then to observe the impact of the changes on output measures such as profit or service level.

The summary statistics in Figure 12.10 show what can be anticipated over 300 months if Butler operates its inventory system using a replenishment level of 100. The average net profit is $4293 per month. Because 27,917 units of the total demand of 30,181 units were satisfied, the service level is 27,917/30,181 = 92.5%. We are now ready to use the simulation model to consider other replenishment levels that may improve the net profit and the service level.

At this point, we conducted a series of simulation experiments by repeating the Butler inventory simulation with replenishment levels of 110, 120, 130, and 140 units. The average monthly net profits and the service levels are shown in Table 12.9. The highest monthly net profit of $4575 occurs with a replenishment level of $Q = 120$. The associated service level is 98.6%. On the basis of these results, Butler selected a replenishment level of $Q = 120$.

Experimental simulation studies, such as this one for Butler's inventory policy, can help identify good operating policies and decisions. Butler's management used simulation to choose a replenishment level of 120 for its home ventilation fan. With the simulation model in place, management can also explore the sensitivity of this decision to some of the model parameters. For instance, we assigned a shortage cost of $30 for any customer demand not met. With this shortage cost, the replenishment level was $Q = 120$ and the service level was 98.6%. If management felt a more appropriate shortage cost was $10 per unit, running the simulation again using $10 as the shortage cost would be a simple matter.

Problem 18 gives you a chance to develop a different simulation model.

We mentioned earlier that simulation is not an optimization technique. Even though we used simulation to choose a replenishment level, it does not guarantee that this choice is optimal. All possible replenishment levels were not tested. Perhaps a manager would like to consider additional simulation runs with replenishment levels of $Q = 115$ and $Q = 125$ to search for an even better inventory policy. Also, we have no guarantee that with another set of 300 randomly generated demand values the replenishment level with the highest profit would not change. However, with a large number of simulation trials, we should find a good and, at least, near optimal solution. The Management Science in Action, Petroleum Distribution in the Gulf of Mexico, describes a simulation application for 15 petroleum companies in the state of Florida.

MANAGEMENT SCIENCE IN ACTION

PETROLEUM DISTRIBUTION IN THE GULF OF MEXICO*

Domestic suppliers who operate oil refineries along the Gulf Coast are helping to satisfy Florida's increasing demand for refined petroleum products. Barge fleets, operated either by independent shipping companies or by the petroleum companies themselves, are used to transport more than 20 different petroleum products to 15 Florida petroleum companies. The petroleum products are loaded at refineries in Texas, Louisiana, and Mississippi and are discharged at tank terminals concentrated in Tampa, Port Everglades, and Jacksonville.

Barges operate under three types of contracts between the fleet operator and the client petroleum company:

- The client assumes total control of a barge and uses it for trips between its own refinery and one or more discharging ports.
- The client is guaranteed a certain volume will be moved during the contract period. Schedules vary considerably depending upon the customer's needs and the fleet operator's capabilities.
- The client hires a barge for a single trip.

A simulation model was developed to analyze the complex process of operating barge fleets in the Gulf of Mexico. An appropriate probability distribution was used to simulate requests for shipments by the petroleum companies. Additional probability distributions were used to simulate the travel times depending upon the size and type of barge. Using this information, the simulation model was used to track barge loading times, barge discharge times, barge utilization, and total cost.

Analysts used simulation runs with a variety of what-if scenarios to answer questions about the petroleum distribution system and to make recommendations for improving the efficiency of the operation. Simulation helped determine the following:

- The optimal trade-off between fleet utilization and on-time delivery
- The recommended fleet size
- The recommended barge capacities
- The best service contract structure to balance the trade-off between customer service and delivery cost

Implementation of the simulation-based recommendations demonstrated a significant improvement in the operation and a significant lowering of petroleum distribution costs.

*Based on E. D. Chajakis, "Sophisticated Crude Transportation," *OR/MS Today* (December 1997): 30–34.

12.3 WAITING LINE SIMULATION

The simulation models discussed thus far have been based on independent trials in which the results for one trial do not affect what happens in subsequent trials. In this sense, the system being modeled does not change or evolve over time. Simulation models such as these are referred to as **static simulation models.** In this section we develop a simulation model of a waiting line system where the state of the system, including the number of customers in the waiting line and whether the service facility is busy or idle, changes or evolves over time. To incorporate time into the simulation model, we use a simulation clock to record the time that each customer arrives for service as well as the time that each customer completes service. Simulation models that must take into account how the system changes or evolves over time are referred to as **dynamic simulation models.** In situations where the arrivals and departures of customers are **events** that occur at *discrete* points in time, the simulation model is also referred to as a **discrete-event simulation model.**

In Chapter 11 we presented formulas that could be used to compute the steady-state operating characteristics of a waiting line, including the average waiting time, the average number of units in the waiting line, the probability of waiting, and so on. In most cases, the waiting line formulas were based on specific assumptions about the probability distribution for arrivals, the probability distribution for service times, the queue discipline, and so on. Simulation, as an alternative for studying waiting lines, is more flexible. In applications where the assumptions required by the waiting line formulas are not reasonable, simulation may be the only feasible approach to studying the waiting line system. In this section we discuss the simulation of the waiting line for the Hammondsport Savings Bank automated teller machine (ATM).

Hammondsport Savings Bank ATM Waiting Line

Hammondsport Savings Bank will open several new branch banks during the coming year. Each new branch is designed to have one automated teller machine (ATM). A concern is that during busy periods several customers may have to wait to use the ATM. This concern prompted the bank to undertake a study of the ATM waiting line system. The bank's vice president wants to determine whether one ATM will be sufficient. The bank established service guidelines for its ATM system stating that the average customer waiting time for an ATM should be one minute or less. Let us show how a simulation model can be used to study the ATM waiting line at a particular branch.

Customer Arrival Times

One probabilistic input to the ATM simulation model is the arrival times of customers who use the ATM. In waiting line simulations, arrival times are determined by randomly generating the time between two successive arrivals, referred to as the *interarrival time*. For the branch bank being studied, the customer interarrival times are assumed to be uniformly distributed between 0 and 5 minutes, as shown in Figure 12.11. With r denoting a random number between 0 and 1, an interarrival time for two successive customers can be simulated by using the formula for generating values from a uniform probability distribution.

$$\text{Interarrival time} = a + r(b - a) \qquad (12.7)$$

where

$$r = \text{random number between 0 and 1}$$
$$a = \text{minimum interarrival time}$$
$$b = \text{maximum interarrival time}$$

A uniform probability distribution of interarrival times is used here to illustrate the simulation computations. Actually, any interarrival time probability distribution can be assumed, and the logic of the waiting line simulation model will not change.

For the Hammondsport ATM system, the minimum interarrival time is $a = 0$ minutes, and the maximum interarrival time is $b = 5$ minutes; therefore, the formula for generating an interarrival time is

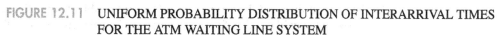

$$\text{Interarrival time} = 0 + r(5 - 0) = 5r \qquad (12.8)$$

Assume that the simulation run begins at time $= 0$. A random number of $r = 0.2804$ generates an interarrival time of $5(0.2804) = 1.4$ minutes for customer 1. Thus, customer 1 arrives 1.4 minutes after the simulation run begins. A second random number of $r = 0.2598$

FIGURE 12.11   UNIFORM PROBABILITY DISTRIBUTION OF INTERARRIVAL TIMES FOR THE ATM WAITING LINE SYSTEM

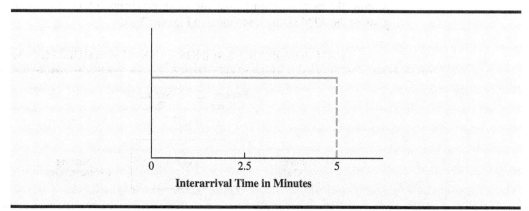

Interarrival Time in Minutes

FIGURE 12.12   NORMAL PROBABILITY DISTRIBUTION OF SERVICE TIMES
FOR THE ATM WAITING LINE SYSTEM

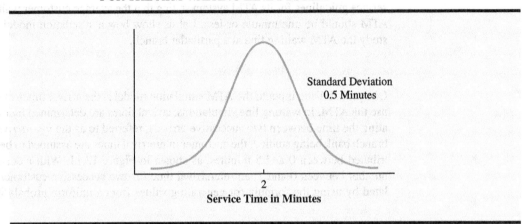

generates an interarrival time of 5(0.2598) = 1.3 minutes, indicating that customer 2 arrives 1.3 minutes after customer 1. Thus, customer 2 arrives 1.4 + 1.3 = 2.7 minutes after the simulation begins. Continuing, a third random number of $r = 0.9802$ indicates that customer 3 arrives 4.9 minutes after customer 2, which is 7.6 minutes after the simulation begins.

Customer Service Times

Another probabilistic input in the ATM simulation model is the service time, which is the time a customer spends using the ATM machine. Past data from similar ATMs indicate that a normal probability distribution with a mean of 2 minutes and a standard deviation of 0.5 minutes, as shown in Figure 12.12, can be used to describe service times. As discussed in Sections 12.1 and 12.2, values from a normal probability distribution with mean 2 and standard deviation 0.5 can be generated using the Excel function =NORMINV(RAND(),2,0.5). For example, the random number of 0.7257 generates a customer service time of 2.3 minutes.

Simulation Model

The probabilistic inputs to the Hammondsport Savings Bank ATM simulation model are the interarrival time and the service time. The controllable input is the number of ATMs used. The output will consist of various operating characteristics such as the probability of waiting, the average waiting time, the maximum waiting time, and so on. We show a diagram of the ATM simulation model in Figure 12.13.

FIGURE 12.13   HAMMONDSPORT SAVINGS BANK ATM SIMULATION MODEL

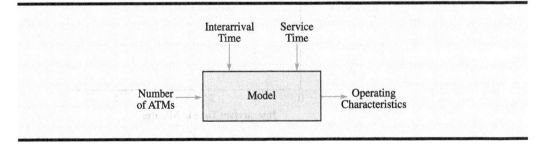

Figure 12.14 shows a flowchart that defines the sequence of logical and mathematical operations required to simulate the Hammondsport ATM system. The flowchart uses the following notation:

$$IAT = \text{interarrival time generated}$$

Arrival time (i) = time at which customer i arrives

Start time (i) = time at which customer I service

Wait time (i) = waiting time for customer i

$$ST = \text{service time generated}$$

Completion time (i) = time at which customer i completes service

System time (i) = system time for customer i (completion time − arrival time)

FIGURE 12.14   FLOWCHART OF THE HAMMONDSPORT SAVINGS BANK ATM WAITING LINE SIMULATION

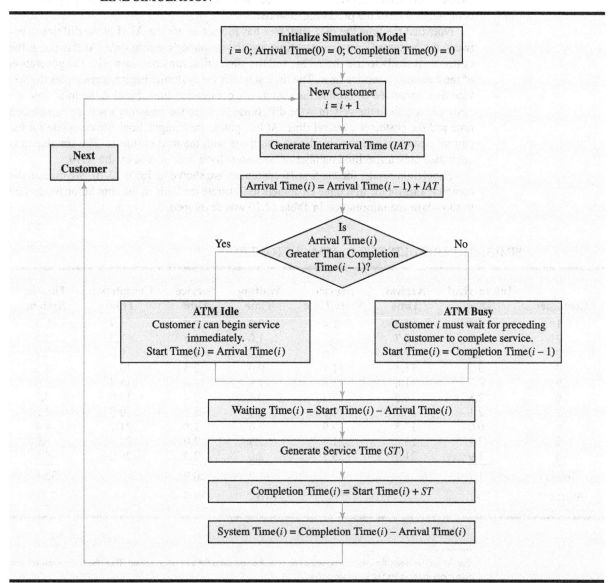

Referring to Figure 12.14, we see that the simulation is initialized in the first block of the flowchart. Then a new customer is created. An interarrival time is generated to determine the time since the preceding customer arrived.[2] The arrival time for the new customer is then computed by adding the interarrival time to the arrival time of the preceding customer.

The decision rule for deciding whether the ATM is idle or busy is the most difficult aspect of the logic in a waiting line simulation model.

The arrival time for the new customer must be compared to the completion time of the preceding customer to determine whether the ATM is idle or busy. If the arrival time of the new customer is greater than the completion time of the preceding customer, the preceding customer will have finished service prior to the arrival of the new customer. In this case, the ATM will be idle, and the new customer can begin service immediately. The service start time for the new customer is equal to the arrival time of the new customer. However, if the arrival time for the new customer is not greater than the completion time of the preceding customer, the new customer arrived before the preceding customer finished service. In this case, the ATM is busy; the new customer must wait to use the ATM until the preceding customer completes service. The service start time for the new customer is equal to the completion time of the preceding customer.

Note that the time the new customer has to wait to use the ATM is the difference between the customer's service start time and the customer's arrival time. At this point, the customer is ready to use the ATM, and the simulation run continues with the generation of the customer's service time. The time at which the customer begins service plus the service time generated determine the customer's completion time. Finally, the total time the customer spends in the system is the difference between the customer's service completion time and the customer's arrival time. At this point, the computations are complete for the current customer, and the simulation continues with the next customer. The simulation is continued until a specified number of customers have been served by the ATM.

Simulation results for the first 10 customers are shown in Table 12.10. We discuss the computations for the first three customers to illustrate the logic of the simulation model and to show how the information in Table 12.10 was developed.

TABLE 12.10   SIMULATION RESULTS FOR 10 ATM CUSTOMERS

Customer	Interarrival Time	Arrival Time	Service Start Time	Waiting Time	Service Time	Completion Time	Time in System
1	1.4	1.4	1.4	0.0	2.3	3.7	2.3
2	1.3	2.7	3.7	1.0	1.5	5.2	2.5
3	4.9	7.6	7.6	0.0	2.2	9.8	2.2
4	3.5	11.1	11.1	0.0	2.5	13.6	2.5
5	0.7	11.8	13.6	1.8	1.8	15.4	3.6
6	2.8	14.6	15.4	0.8	2.4	17.8	3.2
7	2.1	16.7	17.8	1.1	2.1	19.9	3.2
8	0.6	17.3	19.9	2.6	1.8	21.7	4.4
9	2.5	19.8	21.7	1.9	2.0	23.7	3.9
10	1.9	21.7	23.7	2.0	2.3	26.0	4.3
Totals	21.7			11.2	20.9		32.1
Averages	2.17			1.12	2.09		3.21

---

[2]For the first customer, the interarrival time determines the time since the simulation started. Thus, the first interarrival time determines the time the first customer arrives.

Customer 1

- An interarrival time of $IAT = 1.4$ minutes is generated.
- Because the simulation run begins at time 0, the arrival time for customer 1 is $0 + 1.4 = 1.4$ minutes.
- Customer 1 may begin service immediately with a start time of 1.4 minutes.
- The waiting time for customer 1 is the start time minus the arrival time: $1.4 - 1.4 = 0$ minutes.
- A service time of $ST = 2.3$ minutes is generated for customer 1.
- The completion time for customer 1 is the start time plus the service time: $1.4 + 2.3 = 3.7$ minutes.
- The time in the system for customer 1 is the completion time minus the arrival time: $3.7 - 1.4 = 2.3$ minutes.

Customer 2

- An interarrival time of $IAT = 1.3$ minutes is generated.
- Because the arrival time of customer 1 is 1.4, the arrival time for customer 2 is $1.4 + 1.3 = 2.7$ minutes.
- Because the completion time of customer 1 is 3.7 minutes, the arrival time of customer 2 is not greater than the completion time of customer 1; thus, the ATM is busy when customer 2 arrives.
- Customer 2 must wait for customer 1 to complete service before beginning service. Customer 1 completes service at 3.7 minutes, which becomes the start time for customer 2.
- The waiting time for customer 2 is the start time minus the arrival time: $3.7 - 2.7 = 1$ minute.
- A service time of $ST = 1.5$ minutes is generated for customer 2.
- The completion time for customer 2 is the start time plus the service time: $3.7 = 1.5 = 5.2$ minutes.
- The time in the system for customer 2 is the completion time minus the arrival time: $5.2 - 2.7 = 2.5$ minutes.

Customer 3

- An interarrival time of $IAT = 4.9$ minutes is generated.
- Because the arrival time of customer 2 was 2.7 minutes, the arrival time for customer 3 is $2.7 + 4.9 = 7.6$ minutes.
- The completion time of customer 2 is 5.2 minutes, so the arrival time for customer 3 is greater than the completion time of customer 2. Thus, the ATM is idle when customer 3 arrives.
- Customer 3 begins service immediately with a start time of 7.6 minutes.
- The waiting time for customer 3 is the start time minus the arrival time: $7.6 - 7.6 = 0$ minutes.
- A service time of $ST = 2.2$ minutes is generated for customer 3.
- The completion time for customer 3 is the start time plus the service time: $7.6 + 2.2 = 9.8$ minutes.
- The time in the system for customer 3 is the completion time minus the arrival time: $9.8 - 7.6 = 2.2$ minutes.

Using the totals in Table 12.10, we can compute an average waiting time for the 10 customers of $11.2/10 = 1.12$ minutes, and an average time in the system of $32.1/10 = 3.21$ minutes. Table 12.10 shows that seven of the 10 customers had to wait. The total time for the

813

10-customer simulation is given by the completion time of the 10th customer: 26.0 minutes. However, at this point, we realize that a simulation for 10 customers is much too short a period to draw any firm conclusions about the operation of the waiting line.

Hammondsport Savings Bank ATM Simulation

Using an Excel worksheet, we simulated the operation of the Hammondsport ATM waiting line system for 1000 customers. The worksheet used to carry out the simulation is shown in Figure 12.15. Note that the simulation results for customers 6 through 995 have been hidden so that the results can be shown in a reasonably sized figure. If desired, the rows for these customers can be shown and the simulation results displayed for all 1000 customers.

FIGURE 12.15   EXCEL WORKSHEET FOR THE HAMMONDSPORT SAVINGS BANK WITH ONE ATM

WEB file

Hammondsport1

	A	B	C	D	E	F	G	H	I
1	**Hammondsport Savings Bank with One ATM**								
2									
3	**Interarrival Times (Uniform Distribution)**								
4	Smallest Value	0							
5	Largest Value	5							
6									
7	**Service Times (Normal Distribution)**								
8	Mean	2							
9	Std Deviation	0.5							
10									
11									
12	**Simulation**								
13									
14		Interarrival	Arrival	Service	Waiting	Service	Completion	Time	
15	Customer	Time	Time	Start Time	Time	Time	Time	in System	
16	1	1.4	1.4	1.4	0.0	2.3	3.7	2.3	
17	2	1.3	2.7	3.7	1.0	1.5	5.2	2.5	
18	3	4.9	7.6	7.6	0.0	2.2	9.8	2.2	
19	4	3.5	11.1	11.1	0.0	2.5	13.6	2.5	
20	5	0.7	11.8	13.6	1.8	1.8	15.4	3.6	
1011	996	0.5	2496.8	2498.1	1.3	0.6	2498.7	1.9	
1012	997	0.2	2497.0	2498.7	1.7	2.0	2500.7	3.7	
1013	998	2.7	2499.7	2500.7	1.0	1.8	2502.5	2.8	
1014	999	3.7	2503.4	2503.4	0.0	2.4	2505.8	2.4	
1015	1000	4.0	2507.4	2507.4	0.0	1.9	2509.3	1.9	
1016									
1017		**Summary Statistics**							
1018		Number Waiting			549				
1019		Probability of Waiting			0.6100				
1020		Average Waiting Time			1.59				
1021		Maximum Waiting Time			13.5				
1022		Utilization of ATM			0.7860				
1023		Number Waiting > 1 Min			393				
1024		Probability of Waiting > 1 Min			0.4367				

FIGURE 12.16   HISTOGRAM SHOWING THE WAITING TIME FOR 900 ATM CUSTOMERS

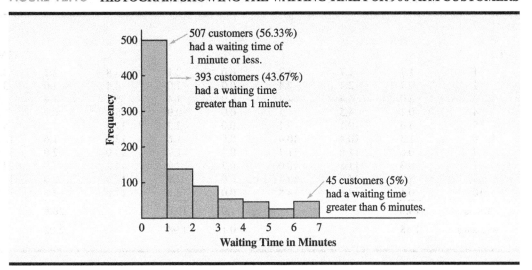

Ultimately, summary statistics will be collected in order to describe the results of 1000 customers. Before collecting the summary statistics, let us point out that most simulation studies of dynamic systems focus on the operation of the system during its long-run or steady-state operation. To ensure that the effects of start-up conditions are not included in the steady-state calculations, a dynamic simulation model is usually run for a specified period without collecting any data about the operation of the system. The length of the start-up period can vary depending on the application. For the Hammondsport Savings Bank ATM simulation, we treated the results for the first 100 customers as the start-up period. Thus, the summary statistics shown in Figure 12.15 are for the 900 customers arriving during the steady-state period.

The summary statistics show that 549 of the 900 Hammondsport customers had to wait. This result provides a 549/900 = 0.61 probability that a customer will have to wait for service. In other words, approximately 61% of the customers will have to wait because the ATM is in use. The average waiting time is 1.59 minutes per customer with at least one customer waiting the maximum time of 13.5 minutes. The utilization rate of 0.7860 indicates that the ATM is in use 78.6% of the time. Finally, 393 of the 900 customers had to wait more than 1 minute (43.67% of all customers). A histogram of waiting times for the 900 customers is shown in Figure 12.16. This figure shows that 45 customers (5%) had a waiting time greater than 6 minutes.

The simulation supports the conclusion that the branch will have a busy ATM system. With an average customer wait time of 1.59 minutes, the branch does not satisfy the bank's customer service guideline. This branch is a good candidate for installation of a second ATM.

Simulation with Two ATMs

We extended the simulation model to the case of two ATMs. For the second ATM we also assume that the service time is normally distributed with a mean of 2 minutes and a standard deviation of 0.5 minutes. Table 12.11 shows the simulation results for the first 10 customers. In comparing the two-ATM system results in Table 12.11 with the single ATM simulation results shown in Table 12.10, we see that two additional columns are needed. These two columns show when each ATM becomes available for customer service. We assume that, when a new customer arrives, the customer will be served by the ATM that frees up first. When the simulation begins, the first customer is assigned to ATM 1.

815

TABLE 12.11   SIMULATION RESULTS FOR 10 CUSTOMERS FOR A TWO-ATM SYSTEM

Customer	Interarrival Time	Arrival Time	Service Start Time	Waiting Time	Service Time	Completion Time	Time in System	Time Available ATM 1	Time Available ATM 2
1	1.7	1.7	1.7	0.0	2.1	3.8	2.1	3.8	0.0
2	0.7	2.4	2.4	0.0	2.0	4.4	2.0	3.8	4.4
3	2.0	4.4	4.4	0.0	1.4	5.8	1.4	5.8	4.4
4	0.1	4.5	4.5	0.0	0.9	5.4	0.9	5.8	5.4
5	4.6	9.1	9.1	0.0	2.2	11.3	2.2	5.8	11.3
6	1.3	10.4	10.4	0.0	1.6	12.0	1.6	12.0	11.3
7	0.6	11.0	11.3	0.3	1.7	13.0	2.0	12.0	13.0
8	0.3	11.3	12.0	0.7	2.2	14.2	2.9	14.2	13.0
9	3.4	14.7	14.7	0.0	2.9	17.6	2.9	14.2	17.6
10	0.1	14.8	14.8	0.0	2.8	17.6	2.8	17.6	17.6
Totals	14.8			1.0	19.8		20.8		
Averages	1.48			0.1	1.98		2.08		

Table 12.11 shows that customer 7 is the first customer who has to wait to use an ATM. We describe how customers 6, 7, and 8 are processed to show how the logic of the simulation run for two ATMs differs from that with a single ATM.

Customer 6

- An interarrival time of 1.3 minutes is generated, and customer 6 arrives $9.1 + 1.3 = 10.4$ minutes into the simulation.
- From the customer 5 row, we see that ATM 1 frees up at 5.8 minutes, and ATM 2 will free up at 11.3 minutes into the simulation. Because ATM 1 is free, customer 6 does not wait and begins service on ATM 1 at the arrival time of 10.4 minutes.
- A service time of 1.6 minutes is generated for customer 6. So customer 6 has a completion time of $10.4 + 1.6 = 12.0$ minutes.
- The time ATM 1 will next become available is set at 12.0 minutes; the time available for ATM 2 remains 11.3 minutes.

Customer 7

- An interarrival time of 0.6 minute is generated, and customer 7 arrives $10.4 + 0.6 = 11.0$ minutes into the simulation.
- From the previous row, we see that ATM 1 will not be available until 12.0 minutes, and ATM 2 will not be available until 11.3 minutes. So customer 7 must wait to use an ATM. Because ATM 2 will free up first, customer 7 begins service on that machine at a start time of 11.3 minutes. With an arrival time of 11.0 and a service start time of 11.3, customer 7 experiences a waiting time of $11.3 - 11.0 = 0.3$ minute.
- A service time of 1.7 minutes is generated, leading to a completion time of $11.3 + 1.7 = 13.0$ minutes.
- The time available for ATM 2 is updated to 13.0 minutes, and the time available for ATM 1 remains at 12.0 minutes.

Customer 8

- An interarrival time of 0.3 minute is generated, and customer 8 arrives $11.0 + 0.3 = 11.3$ minutes into the simulation.
- From the previous row, we see that ATM 1 will be the first available. Thus, customer 8 starts service on ATM 1 at 12.0 minutes resulting in a waiting time of $12.0 - 11.3 = 0.7$ minute.

816

- A service time of 2.2 minutes is generated, resulting in a completion time of 12.0 + 2.2 = 14.2 minutes and a system time of 0.7 + 2.2 = 2.9 minutes.
- The time available for ATM 1 is updated to 14.2 minutes, and the time available for ATM 2 remains at 13.0 minutes.

From the totals in Table 12.11, we see that the average waiting time for these 10 customers is only 1.0/10 = 0.1 minute. Of course, a much longer simulation will be necessary before any conclusions can be drawn.

Simulation Results with Two ATMs

Worksheets for the Hammondsport one-ATM and two-ATM systems are available on the website that accompanies this text.

The Excel worksheet that we used to conduct a simulation for 1000 customers using two ATMs is shown in Figure 12.17. Results for the first 100 customers were discarded to account for the start-up period. With two ATMs, the number of customers who had to wait was reduced from 549 to 78. This reduction provides a 78/900 = 0.0867 probability that a customer will have to wait for service when two ATMs are used. The two-ATM system also reduced the

FIGURE 12.17 EXCEL WORKSHEET FOR THE HAMMONDSPORT SAVINGS BANK WITH TWO ATMs

WEB file

Hammondsport2

	A	B	C	D	E	F	G	H	I	J	K
1	Hammondsport Savings Bank with Two ATMs										
2											
3	Interarrival Times (Uniform Distribution)										
4	Smallest Value	0									
5	Largest Value	5									
6											
7	Service Times (Normal Distribution)										
8	Mean	2									
9	Std Deviation	0.5									
10											
11											
12	Simulation										
13											
14		Interarrival	Arrival	Service	Waiting	Service	Completion	Time	Time Available		
15	Customer	Time	Time	Start Time	Time	Time	Time	in System	ATM 1	ATM 2	
16	1	1.7	1.7	1.7	0.0	2.1	3.8	2.1	3.8	0.0	
17	2	0.7	2.4	2.4	0.0	2.0	4.4	2.0	3.8	4.4	
18	3	2.0	4.4	4.4	0.0	1.4	5.8	1.4	5.8	4.4	
19	4	0.1	4.5	4.5	0.0	0.9	5.4	0.9	5.8	5.4	
20	5	4.6	9.1	9.1	0.0	2.2	11.3	2.2	5.8	11.3	
1011	996	3.3	2483.2	2483.2	0.0	2.2	2485.4	2.2	2485.4	2482.1	
1012	997	4.5	2487.7	2487.7	0.0	1.9	2489.6	1.9	2485.4	2489.6	
1013	998	3.8	2491.5	2491.5	0.0	3.2	2494.7	3.2	2494.7	2489.6	
1014	999	0.0	2491.5	2491.5	0.0	2.4	2493.9	2.4	2494.7	2493.9	
1015	1000	2.6	2494.1	2494.1	0.0	2.8	2496.9	2.8	2494.7	2496.9	
1016											
1017		Summary Statistics									
1018		Number Waiting			78						
1019		Probability of Waiting			0.0867						
1020		Average Waiting Time			0.07						
1021		Maximum Waiting Time			2.9						
1022		Utilization of ATMs			0.4084						
1023		Number Waiting > 1 Min			23						
1024		Probability of Waiting > 1 Min			0.0256						

average waiting time to 0.07 minute (4.2 seconds) per customer. The maximum waiting time was reduced from 13.5 to 2.9 minutes, and each ATM was in use 40.84% of the time. Finally, only 23 of the 900 customers had to wait more than 1 minute for an ATM to become available. Thus, only 2.56% of customers had to wait more than 1 minute. The simulation results provide evidence that Hammondsport Savings Bank needs to expand to the two-ATM system.

The simulation models that we developed can now be used to study the ATM operation at other branch banks. In each case, assumptions must be made about the appropriate interarrival time and service time probability distributions. However, once appropriate assumptions have been made, the same simulation models can be used to determine the operating characteristics of the ATM waiting line system. The Management Science in Action, Preboard Screening at Vancouver International Airport, describes another use of simulation for a queueing system.

MANAGEMENT SCIENCE IN ACTION

PREBOARD SCREENING AT VANCOUVER INTERNATIONAL AIRPORT*

Following the September 11, 2001, terrorist attacks in the United States, long lines at airport security checkpoints became commonplace. In order to reduce passenger waiting time, the Vancouver International Airport Authority teamed up with students and faculty at the University of British Columbia's Centre for Operations Excellence (COE) to build a simulation model of the airport's preboard screening security checkpoints. The goal was to use the simulation model to help achieve acceptable service standards.

Prior to building the simulation model, students from the COE observed the flow of passengers through the screening process and collected data on the service time at each process step. In addition to service time data, passenger demand data provided input to the simulation model. Two triangular probability distributions were used to simulate passenger arrivals at the preboarding facilities. For flights to Canadian destinations a 90-40-20 triangle was used.

This distribution assumes that, for each flight, the first passenger will arrive at the screening checkpoint 90 minutes before departure, the last passenger will arrive 20 minutes before departure, and the most likely arrival time is 40 minutes before departure. For international flights a 150-80-20 triangle was used.

Output statistics from the simulation model provided information concerning resource utilization, waiting line lengths, and the time passengers spend in the system. The simulation model provided information concerning the number of personnel needed to process 90% of the passengers with a waiting time of 10 minutes or less. Ultimately, the airport authority was able to design and staff the preboarding checkpoints in such a fashion that waiting times for 90% of the passengers were a maximum of 10 minutes.

*Based on Derek Atkins et al., "Right on Queue," *OR/MS Today* (April 2003): 26–29.

NOTES AND COMMENTS

1. The ATM waiting line model was based on uniformly distributed interarrival times and normally distributed service times. One advantage of simulation is its flexibility in accommodating a variety of different probability distributions. For instance, if we believe an exponential distribution is more appropriate for interarrival times, the ATM simulation could be repeated by simply changing the way the interarrival times are generated.

2. At the beginning of this section, we defined *discrete-event simulation* as involving a dynamic system that evolves over time. The simulation computations focus on the sequence of events as they occur at discrete points in time. In the ATM waiting line example, customer arrivals and the customer service completions were the discrete events. Referring to the arrival times and completion times in Table 12.10, we see

(continued)

that the first five discrete events for the ATM waiting line simulation were as follows:

Event	Time
Customer 1 arrives	1.4
Customer 2 arrives	2.7
Customer 1 finished	3.7
Customer 2 finished	5.2
Customer 3 arrives	7.6

3. We did not keep track of the number of customers in the ATM waiting line as we carried out the ATM simulation computations on a customer-by-customer basis. However, we can determine the average number of customers in the waiting line from other information in the simulation output. The following relationship is valid for any waiting line system:

$$\frac{\text{Average number}}{\text{in waiting line}} = \frac{\text{Total waiting time}}{\text{Total time of simulation}}$$

For the system with one ATM, the 100th customer completed service at 247.8 minutes into the simulation. Thus, the total time of the simulation for the next 900 customers was $2509.3 - 247.8 = 2261.5$ minutes. The average waiting time was 1.59 minutes. During the simulation, the 900 customers had a total waiting time of $900(1.59) = 1431$ minutes. Therefore, the average number of customers in the waiting line is

$$\begin{aligned} \text{Average number} \\ \text{in waiting line} \end{aligned} = 1431/2261.5$$
$$= 0.63 \text{ customer}$$

12.4 OTHER SIMULATION ISSUES

Because simulation is one of the most widely used quantitative analysis techniques, various software tools have been developed to help analysts implement a simulation model on a computer. In this section we comment on the software available and discuss some issues involved in verifying and validating a simulation model. We close the section with a discussion of some of the advantages and disadvantages of using simulation to study a real system.

Computer Implementation

The use of spreadsheets for simulation has grown rapidly in recent years, and third-party software vendors have developed spreadsheet add-ins that make building simulation models on a spreadsheet much easier. These add-in packages provide an easy facility for generating random values from a variety of probability distributions and provide a rich array of statistics describing the simulation output. Two popular spreadsheet add-ins are Crystal Ball from Oracle Corporation and @RISK from Palisade Corporation. Although spreadsheets can be a valuable tool for some simulation studies, they are generally limited to smaller, less complex systems.

With the growth of simulation applications, both users of simulation and software developers began to realize that computer simulations have many common features: model development, generating values from probability distributions, maintaining a record of what happens during the simulation, and recording and summarizing the simulation output. A variety of special-purpose simulation packages are available, including GPSS®, SIMSCRIPT®, SLAM®, and Arena®. These packages have built-in simulation clocks, simplified methods for generating probabilistic inputs, and procedures for collecting and summarizing the simulation output. Special-purpose simulation packages enable quantitative analysts to simplify the process of developing and implementing the simulation model. Indeed, Arena 6.0 was used to develop the simulation model described in the Management Science in Action, Preboard Screening at Vancouver International Airport.

Simulation models can also be developed using general-purpose computer programming languages such as BASIC, FORTRAN, PASCAL, C, and C++. The disadvantage of using these languages is that special simulation procedures are not built in. One command in a special-purpose simulation package often performs the computations and record-keeping

The computational and record-keeping aspects of simulation models are assisted by special simulation software packages. The packages ease the tasks of developing a computer simulation model.

tasks that would require several BASIC, FORTRAN, PASCAL, C, or C++ statements to duplicate. The advantage of using a general-purpose programming language is that they offer greater flexibility in terms of being able to model more complex systems.

To decide which software to use, an analyst will have to consider the relative merits of a spreadsheet, a special-purpose simulation package, and a general-purpose computer programming language. The goal is to select the method that is easy to use while still providing an adequate representation of the system being studied.

Verification and Validation

An important aspect of any simulation study involves confirming that the simulation model accurately describes the real system. Inaccurate simulation models cannot be expected to provide worthwhile information. Thus, before using simulation results to draw conclusions about a real system, one must take steps to verify and validate the simulation model.

Verification is the process of determining that the computer procedure that performs the simulation calculations is logically correct. Verification is largely a debugging task to make sure that no errors are in the computer procedure that implements the simulation. In some cases, an analyst may compare computer results for a limited number of events with independent hand calculations. In other cases, tests may be performed to verify that the probabilistic inputs are being generated correctly and that the output from the simulation model seems reasonable. The verification step is not complete until the user develops a high degree of confidence that the computer procedure is error free.

Validation is the process of ensuring that the simulation model provides an accurate representation of a real system. Validation requires an agreement among analysts and managers that the logic and the assumptions used in the design of the simulation model accurately reflect how the real system operates. The first phase of the validation process is done prior to, or in conjunction with, the development of the computer procedure for the simulation process. Validation continues after the computer program has been developed, with the analyst reviewing the simulation output to see whether the simulation results closely approximate the performance of the real system. If possible, the output of the simulation model is compared to the output of an existing real system to make sure that the simulation output closely approximates the performance of the real system. If this form of validation is not possible, an analyst can experiment with the simulation model and have one or more individuals experienced with the operation of the real system review the simulation output to determine whether it is a reasonable approximation of what would be obtained with the real system under similar conditions.

Verification and validation are not tasks to be taken lightly. They are key steps in any simulation study and are necessary to ensure that decisions and conclusions based on the simulation results are appropriate for the real system.

Advantages and Disadvantages of Using Simulation

Using simulation, we can ask what-if questions and project how the real system will behave. Although simulation does not guarantee optimality, it will usually provide near-optimal solutions. In addition, simulation models often warn against poor decision strategies by projecting disastrous outcomes such as system failures, large financial losses, and so on.

The primary advantages of simulation are that it is easy to understand and that the methodology can be used to model and learn about the behavior of complex systems that would be difficult, if not impossible, to deal with analytically. Simulation models are flexible; they can be used to describe systems without requiring the assumptions that are often required by mathematical models. In general, the larger the number of probabilistic inputs a system has, the more likely that a simulation model will provide the best approach for studying the system. Another advantage of simulation is that a simulation model provides a convenient experimental laboratory for the real system. Changing assumptions or operating policies in the simulation model and rerunning it can provide results that help predict how such changes will affect the operation of the real system. Experimenting directly with a real system is often not feasible.

Simulation is not without some disadvantages. For complex systems, the process of developing, verifying, and validating a simulation model can be time-consuming and expensive. In addition, each simulation run provides only a sample of how the real system will operate. As such, the summary of the simulation data provides only estimates or approximations about the real system. Consequently, simulation does not guarantee an optimal solution. Nonetheless, the danger of obtaining poor solutions is slight if the analyst exercises good judgment in developing the simulation model and if the simulation process is run long enough under a wide variety of conditions so that the analyst has sufficient data to predict how the real system will operate.

SUMMARY

Simulation is a method for learning about a real system by experimenting with a model that represents the system. Some of the reasons simulation is frequently used are listed here:

1. It can be used for a wide variety of practical problems.
2. The simulation approach is relatively easy to explain and understand. As a result, management confidence is increased, and acceptance of the results is more easily obtained.
3. Spreadsheet packages now provide another alternative for model implementation, and third-party vendors have developed add-ins that expand the capabilities of the spreadsheet packages.
4. Computer software developers have produced simulation packages that make it easier to develop and implement simulation models for more complex problems.

We first showed how simulation can be used for risk analysis by analyzing a situation involving the development of a new product: the PortaCom printer. We then showed how simulation can be used to select an inventory replenishment level that would provide both a good profit and a good customer service level. Finally, we developed a simulation model for the Hammondsport Savings Bank ATM waiting line system. This model is an example of a dynamic simulation model in which the state of the system changes or evolves over time.

Our approach was to develop a simulation model that contained both controllable inputs and probabilistic inputs. Procedures were developed for randomly generating values for the probabilistic inputs, and a flowchart was developed to show the sequence of logical and mathematical operations that describe the steps of the simulation process. Simulation results obtained by running the simulation for a suitable number of trials or length of time provided the basis for conclusions drawn about the operation of the real system.

The Management Science in Action, Netherlands Company Improves Warehouse Order-Picking Efficiency, describes how a simulation model determined the warehouse storage location for 18,000 products and the sequence in which products were retrieved by order-picking personnel.

NETHERLANDS COMPANY IMPROVES WAREHOUSE ORDER-PICKING EFFICIENCY*

As a wholesaler of tools, hardware, and garden equipment, Ankor, based in The Netherlands, warehouses more than 18,000 different products for customers who are primarily retail store chains, do-it-yourself businesses, and garden centers. Warehouse managers store the fastest-moving products on the ends of the aisles on the ground floor, the medium-moving products in the middle section of the aisles on the ground floor, and the slow-moving products on the mezzanine.

When a new order is received, a warehouse order-picker travels to each product location and selects the requested number of units. An average order includes 25 different products, which requires the order-picker to travel to 25 different locations in the warehouse. In order to minimize damage to the products, heavier products are picked first and breakable products are picked last. Order-picking is typically one of the most time-consuming and expensive aspects of operating the warehouse. The company is under continuous pressure to improve the efficiency of this operation.

To increase efficiency, researchers developed a simulation model of the warehouse order-picking system. Using a sequence of 1098 orders received for 27,790 products over a seven-week period, the researchers used the model to simulate the required order-picking times. The researchers, with the help of the model, varied the assignment of products to storage locations and the sequence in which products were retrieved from the storage locations. The model simulated order-picking times for a variety of product storage location alternatives and four different routing policies that determined the sequence in which products were picked.

Analysis of the simulation results provided a new storage assignment policy for the warehouse as well as new routing rules for the sequence in which to retrieve products from storage. Implementation of the new storage and routing procedures reduced the average route length of the order-picking operation by 31%. Due to the increased efficiency of the operation, the number of order pickers was reduced by more than 25%, saving the company an estimated €140,00 per year.

*Based on R. Dekker, M. B. M. de Koster, K. J. Roodbergen, and H. van Kalleveen, "Improving Order-Picking Response Time at Ankor's Warehouse," *Interfaces* (July/August 2004): 303–313.

GLOSSARY

Simulation A method for learning about a real system by experimenting with a model that represents the system.

Simulation experiment The generation of a sample of values for the probabilistic inputs of a simulation model and computing the resulting values of the model outputs.

Controllable input Input to a simulation model that is selected by the decision maker.

Probabilistic input Input to a simulation model that is subject to uncertainty. A probabilistic input is described by a probability distribution.

Risk analysis The process of predicting the outcome of a decision in the face of uncertainty.

Parameters Numerical values that appear in the mathematical relationships of a model. Parameters are considered known and remain constant over all trials of a simulation.

What-if analysis A trial-and-error approach to learning about the range of possible outputs for a model. Trial values are chosen for the model inputs (these are the what-ifs) and the value of the output(s) is computed.

Base-case scenario Determining the output given the most likely values for the probabilistic inputs of a model.

Worst-case scenario Determining the output given the worst values that can be expected for the probabilistic inputs of a model.

Best-case scenario Determining the output given the best values that can be expected for the probabilistic inputs of a model.

Static simulation model A simulation model used in situations where the state of the system at one point in time does not affect the state of the system at future points in time. Each trial of the simulation is independent.

Dynamic simulation model A simulation model used in situations where the state of the system affects how the system changes or evolves over time.

Event An instantaneous occurrence that changes the state of the system in a simulation model.

Discrete-event simulation model A simulation model that describes how a system evolves over time by using events that occur at discrete points in time.

Verification The process of determining that a computer program implements a simulation model as it is intended.

Validation The process of determining that a simulation model provides an accurate representation of a real system.

PROBLEMS

Note: Problems 1–12 are designed to give you practice in setting up a simulation model and demonstrating how random numbers can be used to generate values for the probabilistic inputs. These problems, which ask you to provide a small number of simulation trials, can be done with hand calculations. This approach should give you a good understanding of the simulation process, but the simulation results will not be sufficient for you to draw final conclusions or make decisions about the situation. Problems 13–24 are more realistic in that they ask you to generate simulation output(s) for a large number of trials and use the results to draw conclusions about the behavior of the system being studied. These problems require the use of a computer to carry out the simulation computations. The ability to use Excel will be necessary when you attempt Problems 13–24.

1. Consider the PortaCom project discussed in Section 12.1.
   a. An engineer on the product development team believes that first-year sales for the new printer will be 20,000 units. Using estimates of $45 per unit for the direct labor cost and $90 per unit for the parts cost, what is the first-year profit using the engineer's sales estimate?
   b. The financial analyst on the product development team is more conservative, indicating that parts cost may well be $100 per unit. In addition, the analyst suggests that a sales volume of 10,000 units is more realistic. Using the most likely value of $45 per unit for the direct labor cost, what is the first-year profit using the financial analyst's estimates?
   c. Why is the simulation approach to risk analysis preferable to generating a variety of what-if scenarios such as those suggested by the engineer and the financial analyst?

2. The management of Madeira Manufacturing Company is considering the introduction of a new product. The fixed cost to begin the production of the product is $30,000. The variable cost for the product is expected to be between $16 and $24 with a most likely value of $20 per unit. The product will sell for $50 per unit. Demand for the product is expected to range from 300 to 2100 units, with 1200 units the most likely demand.
   a. Develop the profit model for this product.
   b. Provide the base-case, worst-case, and best-case analyses.
   c. Discuss why simulation would be desirable.

3. Use the random numbers 0.3753, 0.9218, 0.0336, 0.5145, and 0.7000 to generate five simulated values for the PortaCom direct labor cost per unit.

4. To generate leads for new business, Gustin Investment Services offers free financial planning seminars at major hotels in Southwest Florida. Attendance is limited to 25 individuals per seminar. Each seminar costs Gustin $3500, and the average first-year commission for each new account opened is $5000. Historical data collected over the past four years show that the number of new accounts opened at a seminar varies from no accounts opened to a maximum of six accounts opened according to the following probability distribution:

Number of New Accounts Opened	Probability
0	0.01
1	0.04
2	0.10
3	0.25
4	0.40
5	0.15
6	0.05

a. Set up intervals of random numbers that can be used to simulate the number of new accounts opened at a seminar.
b. Using the first 10 random numbers in column 9 of Table 12.2, simulate the number of new accounts opened for 10 seminars.
c. Would you recommend that Gustin continue running the seminars?

5. The price of a share of a particular stock listed on the New York Stock Exchange is currently $39. The following probability distribution shows how the price per share is expected to change over a three-month period:

Stock Price Change ($)	Probability
−2	0.05
−1	0.10
0	0.25
+1	0.20
+2	0.20
+3	0.10
+4	0.10

a. Set up intervals of random numbers that can be used to generate the change in stock price over a three-month period.
b. With the current price of $39 per share and the random numbers 0.1091, 0.9407, 0.1941, and 0.8083, simulate the price per share for the next four 3-month periods. What is the ending simulated price per share?

6. The Statewide Auto Insurance Company developed the following probability distribution for automobile collision claims paid during the past year:

Payment($)	Probability
0	0.83
500	0.06
1,000	0.05
2,000	0.02
5,000	0.02
8,000	0.01
10,000	0.01

a. Set up intervals of random numbers that can be used to generate automobile collision claim payments.

b. Using the first 20 random numbers in column 4 of Table 12.2, simulate the payments for 20 policyholders. How many claims are paid and what is the total amount paid to the policyholders?

7. A variety of routine maintenance checks are made on commercial airplanes prior to each takeoff. A particular maintenance check of an airplane's landing gear requires between 10 and 18 minutes of a maintenance engineer's time. In fact, the exact time required is uniformly distributed over this interval. As part of a larger simulation model designed to determine total on-ground maintenance time for an airplane, we will need to simulate the actual time required to perform this maintenance check on the airplane's landing gear. Using random numbers of 0.1567, 0.9823, 0.3419, 0.5572, and 0.7758, compute the time required for each of five simulated maintenance checks of the airplane's landing gear.

8. Baseball's World Series is a maximum of seven games, with the winner being the first team to win four games. Assume that the Atlanta Braves are in the World Series and that the first two games are to be played in Atlanta, the next three games at the opponent's ball park, and the last two games, if necessary, back in Atlanta. Taking into account the projected starting pitchers for each game and the homefield advantage, the probabilities of Atlanta winning each game are as follows:

Game	1	2	3	4	5	6	7
Probability of Win	0.60	0.55	0.48	0.45	0.48	0.55	0.50

a. Set up random number intervals that can be used to determine the winner of each game. Let the smaller random numbers indicate that Atlanta wins the game. For example, the random number interval "0.00 but less than 0.60" corresponds to Atlanta winning game 1.

b. Use the random numbers in column 6 of Table 12.2 beginning with 0.3813 to simulate the playing of the World Series. Do the Atlanta Braves win the series? How many games are played?

c. Discuss how repeated simulation trials could be used to estimate the overall probability of Atlanta winning the series as well as the most likely number of games in the series.

9. A project has four activities (A, B, C, and D) that must be performed sequentially. The probability distributions for the time required to complete each of the activities are as follows:

Activity	Activity Time (weeks)	Probability
A	5	0.25
	6	0.35
	7	0.25
	8	0.15
B	3	0.20
	5	0.55
	7	0.25
C	10	0.10
	12	0.25
	14	0.40
	16	0.20
	18	0.05
D	8	0.60
	10	0.40

a. Provide the base-case, worst-case, and best-case calculations for the time to complete the project.

b. Use the random numbers 0.1778, 0.9617, 0.6849, and 0.4503 to simulate the completion time of the project in weeks.

c. Discuss how simulation could be used to estimate the probability the project can be completed in 35 weeks or less.

10. Blackjack, or 21, is a popular casino game that begins with each player and the dealer being dealt two cards. The value of each hand is determined by the point total of the cards in the hand. Face cards and 10s count 10 points; aces can be counted as either 1 or 11 points; and all other cards count at their face value. For instance, the value of a hand consisting of a jack and an 8 is 18; the value of a hand consisting of an ace and a two is either 3 or 13 depending on whether the ace is counted as 1 or 11 points. The goal is to obtain a hand with a value of 21, or as close to it as possible without exceeding 21. After the initial deal, each player and the dealer may draw additional cards (called taking a "hit") in order to improve their hand. If a player or the dealer takes a hit and the value of their hand exceeds 21, that person "goes broke" and loses. The dealer's advantage is that each player must decide whether to take a hit before the dealer. If a player takes a hit and goes over 21, the player loses even if the dealer later takes a hit and goes over 21. For this reason, players will often decide not to take a hit when the value of their hand is 12 or greater.

The dealer's hand is dealt with one card up and one card down. The player then decides whether to take a hit based on knowledge of the dealer's up card. A gambling professional determined that when the dealer's up card is a 6, the following probabilities describe the ending value of the dealer's hand:

Value of Hand	17	18	19	20	21	Broke
Probability	0.1654	0.1063	0.1063	0.1017	0.0972	0.4231

a. Set up intervals of random numbers that can be used to simulate the ending value of the dealer's hand when the dealer has a 6 as the up card.

b. Use the random numbers in column 4 of Table 12.2 to simulate the ending value of the dealer's hand for 20 plays of the game.

c. Suppose you are playing blackjack and your hand has a value of 16 for the two cards initially dealt. If you decide to take a hit, the following cards will improve your hand: ace, 2, 3, 4, and 5. Any card with a point count greater than 5 will result in you going broke. Suppose you have a hand with a value of 16 and decide to take a hit. The following probabilities describe the ending value of your hand:

Value of Hand	17	18	19	20	21	Broke
Probability	0.0769	0.0769	0.0769	0.0769	0.0769	0.6155

Use the random numbers in column 5 of Table 12.2 to simulate the ending value of your hand after taking a hit for 20 plays of the game.

d. Use the results of parts (b) and (c) to simulate the result of 20 blackjack hands when the dealer has a 6 up and the player chooses to take a hit with a hand that has a value of 16. How many hands result in the dealer winning, a push (a tie), and the player winning?

e. If the player has a hand with a value of 16 and doesn't take a hit, the only way the player can win is if the dealer goes broke. How many of the hands in part (b) result in the player winning without taking a hit? On the basis of this result and the results in part (d), would you recommend the player take a hit if the player has a hand with a value of 16 and the dealer has a 6 up?

11. Over a five-year period, the quarterly change in the price per share of common stock for a major oil company ranged from –8% to +12%. A financial analyst wants to learn what can be expected for price appreciation of this stock over the next two years. Using the five-year history as a basis, the analyst is willing to assume the change in price for each quarter is uniformly distributed between –8% and 12%. Use simulation to provide information about the price per share for the stock over the coming two-year period (eight quarters).
    a. Use two-digit random numbers from column 2 of Table 12.2, beginning with 0.52, 0.99, and so on, to simulate the quarterly price change for each of the eight quarters.
    b. If the current price per share is $80, what is the simulated price per share at the end of the two-year period?
    c. Discuss how risk analysis would be helpful in identifying the risk associated with a two-year investment in this stock.

12. The management of Brinkley Corporation is interested in using simulation to estimate the profit per unit for a new product. Probability distributions for the purchase cost, the labor cost, and the transportation cost are as follows:

Purchase Cost ($)	Probability	Labor Cost ($)	Probability	Transportation Cost ($)	Probability
10	0.25	20	0.10	3	0.75
11	0.45	22	0.25	5	0.25
12	0.30	24	0.35		
		25	0.30		

Assume that these are the only costs and that the selling price for the product will be $45 per unit.
    a. Provide the base-case, worst-case, and best-case calculations for the profit per unit.
    b. Set up intervals of random numbers that can be used to randomly generate the three cost components.
    c. Using the random numbers 0.3726, 0.5839, and 0.8275, calculate the profit per unit.
    d. Using the random numbers 0.1862, 0.7466, and 0.6171, calculate the profit per unit.
    e. Management believes the project may not be profitable if the profit per unit is less than $5. Explain how simulation can be used to estimate the probability the profit per unit will be less than $5.

13. Using the PortaCom Risk Analysis worksheet in Figure 12.6 and on the website accompanying the text, develop your own worksheet for the PortaCom simulation model.
    a. Compute the mean profit, the minimum profit, and the maximum profit.
    b. What is your estimate of the probability of a loss?

14. The management of Madeira Manufacturing Company is considering the introduction of a new product. The fixed cost to begin the production of the product is $30,000. The variable cost for the product is uniformly distributed between $16 and $24 per unit. The product will sell for $50 per unit. Demand for the product is best described by a normal probability distribution with a mean of 1200 units and a standard deviation of 300 units. Develop a spreadsheet simulation similar to Figure 12.6. Use 500 simulation trials to answer the following questions:
    a. What is the mean profit for the simulation?
    b. What is the probability the project will result in a loss?
    c. What is your recommendation concerning the introduction of the product?

15. Use a worksheet to simulate the rolling of dice. Use the VLOOKUP function as described in Appendix 12.1 to select the outcome for each die. Place the number for the first die in column B and the number for the second die in column C. Show the sum in column D.

Repeat the simulation for 1000 rolls of the dice. What is your simulation estimate of the probability of rolling a 7?

16. Strassel Investors buys real estate, develops it, and resells it for a profit. A new property is available, and Bud Strassel, the president and owner of Strassel Investors, believes it can be sold for $160,000. The current property owner asked for bids and stated that the property will be sold for the highest bid in excess of $100,000. Two competitors will be submitting bids for the property. Strassel does not know what the competitors will bid, but he assumes for planning purposes that the amount bid by each competitor will be uniformly distributed between $100,000 and $150,000.

   a. Develop a worksheet that can be used to simulate the bids made by the two competitors. Strassel is considering a bid of $130,000 for the property. Using a simulation of 1000 trials, what is the estimate of the probability Strassel will be able to obtain the property using a bid of $130,000?

   b. How much does Strassel need to bid to be assured of obtaining the property? What is the profit associated with this bid?

   c. Use the simulation model to compute the profit for each trial of the simulation run. With maximization of profit as Strassel's objective, use simulation to evaluate Strassel's bid alternatives of $130,000, $140,000, or $150,000. What is the recommended bid, and what is the expected profit?

17. Grear Tire Company has produced a new tire with an estimated mean lifetime mileage of 36,500 miles. Management also believes that the standard deviation is 5000 miles and that tire mileage is normally distributed. Use a worksheet to simulate the miles obtained for a sample of 500 tires.

   a. Use the Excel COUNTIF function to determine the number of tires that last longer than 40,000 miles. What is your estimate of the percentage of tires that will exceed 40,000 miles?

   b. Use COUNTIF to find the number of tires that obtain mileage less than 32,000 miles. Then, find the number with less than 30,000 miles and the number with less than 28,000 miles.

   c. If management would like to advertise a tire mileage guarantee such that approximately no more than 10% of the tires would obtain mileage low enough to qualify for the guarantee, what tire mileage considered in part (b) would you recommend for the guarantee?

18. A building contractor is preparing a bid on a new construction project. Two other contractors will be submitting bids for the same project. Based on past bidding practices, bids from the other contractors can be described by the following probability distributions:

Contractor	Probability Distribution of Bid
A	Uniform probability distribution between $600,000 and $800,000
B	Normal probability distribution with a mean bid of $700,000 and a standard deviation of $50,000

   a. If the building contractor submits a bid of $650,000, what is the probability that the contractor submits the lowest bid and wins the contract for the new construction project? Use a worksheet to simulate 1000 trials of the contract bidding process.

   b. The building contractor is also considering bids of $625,000 and $615,000. If the building contractor would like to bid such that the probability of winning the bid is about 0.80, what bid would you recommend? Repeat the simulation process with bids of $625,000 and $615,000 to justify your recommendation.

19. Develop your own worksheet for the Butler inventory simulation model shown in Figure 12.10. Suppose that management prefers not to charge for loss of goodwill. Run the

Butler inventory simulation model with replenishment levels of 110, 115, 120, and 125. What is your recommendation?

20. In preparing for the upcoming holiday season, Mandrell Toy Company designated a new doll called Freddy. The fixed cost to produce the doll is $100,000. The variable cost, which includes material, labor, and shipping costs, is $34 per doll. During the holiday selling season, Mandrell will sell the dolls for $42 each. If Mandrell overproduces the dolls, the excess dolls will be sold in January through a distributor who has agreed to pay Mandrell $10 per doll. Demand for new toys during the holiday selling season is extremely uncertain. Forecasts are for expected sales of 60,000 dolls with a standard deviation of 15,000. The normal probability distribution is assumed to be a good description of the demand.

   a. Create a worksheet similar to the inventory worksheet in Figure 12.10. Include columns showing demand, sales, revenue from sales, amount of surplus, revenue from sales of surplus, total cost, and net profit. Use your worksheet to simulate the sales of the Freddy doll using a production quantity of 60,000 units. Using 500 simulation trials, what is the estimate of the mean profit associated with the production quantity of 60,000 dolls?

   b. Before making a final decision on the production quantity, management wants an analysis of a more aggressive 70,000 unit production quantity and a more conservative 50,000 unit production quantity. Run your simulation with these two production quantities. What is the mean profit associated with each? What is your recommendation on the production of the Freddy doll?

   c. Assuming that Mandrell's management adopts your recommendation, what is the probability of a stockout and a shortage of the Freddy dolls during the holiday season?

21. South Central Airlines operates a commuter flight between Atlanta and Charlotte. The plane holds 30 passengers, and the airline makes a $100 profit on each passenger on the flight. When South Central takes 30 reservations for the flight, experience has shown that on average, two passengers do not show up. As a result, with 30 reservations, South Central is averaging 28 passengers with a profit of 28(100) = $2800 per flight. The airline operations office has asked for an evaluation of an overbooking strategy where they would accept 32 reservations even though the airplane holds only 30 passengers. The probability distribution for the number of passengers showing up when 32 reservations are accepted is as follows:

Passengers Showing Up	Probability
28	0.05
29	0.25
30	0.50
31	0.15
32	0.05

The airline will receive a profit of $100 for each passenger on the flight up to the capacity of 30 passengers. The airline will incur a cost for any passenger denied seating on the flight. This cost covers added expenses of rescheduling the passenger as well as loss of goodwill, estimated to be $150 per passenger. Develop a worksheet model that will simulate the performance of the overbooking system. Simulate the number of passengers showing up for each of 500 flights by using the VLOOKUP function. Use the results to compute the profit for each flight.

   a. Does your simulation recommend the overbooking strategy? What is the mean profit per flight if overbooking is implemented?

   b. Explain how your simulation model could be used to evaluate other overbooking levels such as 31, 33, or 34 and for recommending a best overbooking strategy.

22. Develop your own waiting line simulation model for the Hammondsport Savings Bank problem (see Figure 12.14). Assume that a new branch is expected to open with interarrival times uniformly distributed between 0 and 4 minutes. The service times at this branch are anticipated to be normal with a mean of 2 minutes and a standard deviation of 0.5 minute. Simulate the operation of this system for 600 customers using one ATM. What is your assessment of the ability to operate this branch with one ATM? What happens to the average waiting time for customers near the end of the simulation period?

23. The Burger Dome waiting line model in Section 11.2 studies the waiting time of customers at its fast-food restaurant. Burger Dome's single-channel waiting line system has an arrival rate of 0.75 customers per minute and a service rate of 1 customer per minute.

    a. Use a worksheet based on Figure 12.15 to simulate the operation of this waiting line. Assuming that customer arrivals follow a Poisson probability distribution, the interarrival times can be simulated with the cell formula $-(1/\lambda)*LN(RAND())$, where $\lambda = 0.75$. Assuming that the service time follows an exponential probability distribution, the service times can be simulated with the cell formula $-\mu*LN(RAND())$, where $\mu = 1$. Run the Burger Dome simulation for 500 customers. The analytical model in Chapter 11 indicates an average waiting time of 3 minutes per customer. What average waiting time does your simulation model show?

    b. One advantage of using simulation is that a simulation model can be altered easily to reflect other assumptions about the probabilistic inputs. Assume that the service time is more accurately described by a normal probability distribution with a mean of 1 minute and a standard deviation of 0.2 minute. This distribution has less service time variability than the exponential probability distribution used in part (a). What is the impact of this change on the average waiting time?

24. Telephone calls come into an airline reservations office randomly at the mean rate of 15 calls per hour. The time between calls follows an exponential distribution with a mean of 4 minutes. When the two reservation agents are busy, a telephone message tells the caller that the call is important and to please wait on the line until the next reservation agent becomes available. The service time for each reservation agent is normally distributed with a mean of 4 minutes and a standard deviation of 1 minute. Use a two-channel waiting line simulation model to evaluate this waiting line system. Use the worksheet design shown in Figure 12.17. The cell formula $=-4*LN(RAND())$ can be used to generate the interarrival times. Simulate the operation of the telephone reservation system for 600 customers. Discard the first 100 customers, and collect data over the next 500 customers.

    a. Compute the mean interarrival time and the mean service time. If your simulation model is operating correctly, both of these should have means of approximately 4 minutes.

    b. What is the mean customer waiting time for this system?

    c. Use the =COUNTIF function to determine the number of customers who have to wait for a reservation agent. What percentage of the customers have to wait?

Case Problem 1 TRI-STATE CORPORATION

What will your portfolio be worth in 10 years? In 20 years? When you stop working? The Human Resources Department at Tri-State Corporation was asked to develop a financial planning model that would help employees address these questions. Tom Gifford was asked to lead this effort and decided to begin by developing a financial plan for himself. Tom has a degree in business and, at the age of 25, is making $34,000 per year. After two years of contributions to his company's retirement program and the receipt of a small inheritance, Tom has accumulated a portfolio valued at $14,500. Tom plans to work 30 more years and hopes to accumulate a portfolio valued at $1 million. Can he do it?

Tom began with a few assumptions about his future salary, his new investment contributions, and his portfolio growth rate. He assumed 5% annual salary growth rate as reasonable and wanted to make new investment contributions at 4% of his salary. After some research on historical stock market performance, Tom decided that a 10% annual portfolio growth rate was reasonable. Using these assumptions, Tom developed the Excel worksheet shown in Figure 12.18. Tom's specific situation and his assumptions are in the top portion of the worksheet (cells D3:D8). The worksheet provides a financial plan for the next five years. In computing the portfolio earnings for a given year, Tom assumed that his new investment contribution would occur evenly throughout the year and thus half of the new investment could be included in the computation of the portfolio earnings for the year. Using Figure 12.18, we see that at age 29, Tom is projected to have a portfolio valued at $32,898.

Tom's plan was to use this worksheet as a template to develop financial plans for the company's employees. The assumptions in cells D3:D8 would be different for each employee, and rows would be added to the worksheet to reflect the number of years appropriate for each employee. After adding another 25 rows to the worksheet, Tom found that he could expect to have a portfolio of $627,937 after 30 years. Tom then took his results to show his boss, Kate Riegle.

Although Kate was pleased with Tom's progress, she voiced several criticisms. One of the criticisms was the assumption of a constant annual salary growth rate. She noted that most employees experience some variation in the annual salary growth rate from year to year. In addition, she pointed out that the constant annual portfolio growth rate was unrealistic and that the actual growth rate would vary considerably from year to year. She further suggested that a simulation model for the portfolio projection might allow Tom to account for the random variability in the salary growth rate and the portfolio growth rate.

After some research, Tom and Kate decided to assume that the annual salary growth rate would vary from 0% to 10% and that a uniform probability distribution would provide a realistic approximation. Tri-State's accounting firm suggested that the annual portfolio growth rate could be approximated by a normal probability distribution with a mean of 10% and a standard deviation of 5%. With this information, Tom set off to develop a simulation model that could be used by the company's employees for financial planning.

FIGURE 12.18 FINANCIAL PLANNING WORKSHEET FOR TOM GIFFORD

	A	B	C	D	E	F	G	H
1	Financial Analysis - Portfolio Projection							
2								
3	Age			25				
4	Current Salary			$34,000				
5	Current Portfolio			$14,500				
6	Annual Salary Growth Rate			5%				
7	Annual Investment Rate			4%				
8	Annual Portfolio Growth Rate			10%				
9								
10			Beginning		New	Portfolio	Ending	
11	Year	Age	Portfolio	Salary	Investment	Earnings	Portfolio	
12	1	25	14,500	34,000	1,360	1,518	17,378	
13	2	26	17,378	35,700	1,428	1,809	20,615	
14	3	27	20,615	37,485	1,499	2,136	24,251	
15	4	28	24,251	39,359	1,574	2,504	28,329	
16	5	29	28,329	41,327	1,653	2,916	32,898	

Managerial Report

Play the role of Tom Gifford and develop a simulation model for financial planning. Write a report for Tom's boss and, at a minimum, include the following:

1. Without considering the random variability in growth rates, extend the worksheet in Figure 12.18 to 30 years. Confirm that by using the constant annual salary growth rate and the constant annual portfolio growth rate, Tom can expect to have a 30-year portfolio of $627,937. What would Tom's annual investment rate have to increase to in order for his portfolio to reach a 30-year, $1 million goal?

2. Incorporate the random variability of the annual salary growth rate and the annual portfolio growth rate into a simulation model. Assume that Tom is willing to use the annual investment rate that predicted a 30-year, $1 million portfolio in part 1. Show how to simulate Tom's 30-year financial plan. Use results from the simulation model to comment on the uncertainty associated with Tom reaching the 30-year, $1 million goal. Discuss the advantages of repeating the simulation numerous times.

3. What recommendations do you have for employees with a current profile similar to Tom's after seeing the impact of the uncertainty in the annual salary growth rate and the annual portfolio growth rate?

4. Assume that Tom is willing to consider working 35 years instead of 30 years. What is your assessment of this strategy if Tom's goal is to have a portfolio worth $1 million?

5. Discuss how the financial planning model developed for Tom Gifford can be used as a template to develop a financial plan for any of the company's employees.

Case Problem 2   HARBOR DUNES GOLF COURSE

Harbor Dunes Golf Course was recently honored as one of the top public golf courses in South Carolina. The course, situated on land that was once a rice plantation, offers some of the best views of saltwater marshes available in the Carolinas. Harbor Dunes targets the upper end of the golf market and in the peak spring golfing season, charges green fees of $160 per person and golf cart fees of $20 per person.

Harbor Dunes takes reservations for tee times for groups of four players (foursome) starting at 7:30 each morning. Foursomes start at the same time on both the front nine and the back nine of the course, with a new group teeing off every nine minutes. The process continues with new foursomes starting play on both the front and back nine at noon. To enable all players to complete 18 holes before darkness, the last two afternoon foursomes start their rounds at 1:21 P.M. Under this plan, Harbor Dunes can sell a maximum of 20 afternoon tee times.

Last year Harbor Dunes was able to sell every morning tee time available for every day of the spring golf season. The same result is anticipated for the coming year. Afternoon tee times, however, are generally more difficult to sell. An analysis of the sales data for last year enabled Harbor Dunes to develop the probability distribution of sales for the afternoon tee times as shown in Table 12.12. For the season, Harbor Dunes averaged selling approximately 14 of the 20 available afternoon tee times. The average income from afternoon green fees and cart fees has been $10,240. However, the average of six unused tee times per day resulted in lost revenue.

In an effort to increase the sale of afternoon tee times, Harbor Dunes is considering an idea popular at other golf courses. These courses offer foursomes that play in the morning the option to play another round of golf in the afternoon by paying a reduced fee for the afternoon round. Harbor Dunes is considering two replay options: (1) a green fee of $25

TABLE 12.12 PROBABILITY DISTRIBUTION OF SALES FOR THE AFTERNOON TEE TIMES

Number of Tee Times Sold	Probability
8	0.01
9	0.04
10	0.06
11	0.08
12	0.10
13	0.11
14	0.12
15	0.15
16	0.10
17	0.09
18	0.07
19	0.05
20	0.02

per player plus a cart fee of $20 per player; (2) a green fee of $50 per player plus a cart fee of $20 per player. For option 1, each foursome will generate additional revenues of $180; for option 2, each foursome will generate additional revenues of $280. The key in making a decision as to what option is best depends upon the number of groups that find the option attractive enough to take the replay offer. Working with a consultant who has expertise in statistics and the golf industry, Harbor Dunes developed probability distributions for the number of foursomes requesting a replay for each of the two options. These probability distributions are shown in Table 12.13.

In offering these replay options, Harbor Dunes' first priority will be to sell full-price afternoon advance reservations. If the demand for replay tee times exceeds the number of afternoon tee times available, Harbor Dunes will post a notice that the course is full. In this case, any excess replay requests will not be accepted.

TABLE 12.13 PROBABILITY DISTRIBUTIONS FOR THE NUMBER OF GROUPS
REQUESTING A REPLAY

Option 1: $25 per Person + Cart Fee		Option 2: $50 per Person + Cart Fee	
Number of Foursomes Requesting a Replay	Probability	Number of Foursomes Requesting a Replay	Probability
0	0.01	0	0.06
1	0.03	1	0.09
2	0.05	2	0.12
3	0.05	3	0.17
4	0.11	4	0.20
5	0.15	5	0.13
6	0.17	6	0.11
7	0.15	7	0.07
8	0.13	8	0.05
9	0.09		
10	0.06		

Managerial Report

Develop simulation models for both replay options using Crystal Ball. Run each simulation for 5000 trials. Prepare a report that will help management of Harbor Dunes Golf Course decide which replay option to implement for the upcoming spring golf season. In preparing your report be sure to include the following:

1. Statistical summaries of the revenue expected under each replay option.
2. Your recommendation as to the best replay option.
3. Assuming a 90-day spring golf season, what is the estimate of the added revenue using your recommendation?
4. Discuss any other recommendations you have that might improve the income for Harbor Dunes.

Case Problem 3   COUNTY BEVERAGE DRIVE-THRU

County Beverage Drive-Thru, Inc., operates a chain of beverage supply stores in Northern Illinois. Each store has a single service lane; cars enter at one end of the store and exit at the other end. Customers pick up soft drinks, beer, snacks, and party supplies without getting out of their cars. When a new customer arrives at the store, the customer waits until the preceding customer's order is complete and then drives into the store for service.

Typically, three employees operate each store during peak periods; two clerks take and fill orders, and a third clerk serves as cashier and store supervisor. County Beverage is considering a revised store design in which computerized order-taking and payment are integrated with specialized warehousing equipment. Management hopes that the new design will permit operating each store with one clerk. To determine whether the new design is beneficial, management decided to build a new store using the revised design.

County Beverage's new store will be located near a major shopping center. Based on experience at other locations, management believes that during the peak late afternoon and evening hours, the time between arrivals follows an exponential probability distribution with a mean of six minutes. These peak hours are the most critical time period for the company; most of their profit is generated during these peak hours.

An extensive study of times required to fill orders with a single clerk led to the following probability distribution of service times:

Service Time (minutes)	Probability
2	0.24
3	0.20
4	0.15
5	0.14
6	0.12
7	0.08
8	0.05
9	0.02
Total	1.00

In case customer waiting times prove too long with just a single clerk, County Beverage's management is considering two alternatives: add a second clerk to help with bagging, taking orders, and related tasks, or enlarge the drive-thru area so that two cars can be served at once (a two-channel system). With either of these options, two clerks will be needed. With the two-channel option, service times are expected to be the same for each channel.

With the second clerk helping with a single channel, service times will be reduced. The following probability distribution describes service times given that option:

Service Time (minutes)	Probability
1	0.20
2	0.35
3	0.30
4	0.10
5	0.05
Total	1.00

County Beverage's management would like you to develop a spreadsheet simulation model of the new system and use it to compare the operation of the system using the following three designs:

Design
A   One channel, one clerk
B   One channel, two clerks
C   Two channels, each with one clerk

Management is especially concerned with how long customers have to wait for service. Research has shown that 30% of the customers will wait no longer than 6 minutes and that 90% will wait no longer than 10 minutes. As a guideline, management requires the average waiting time to be less than 1.5 minutes.

Managerial Report

Prepare a report that discusses the general development of the spreadsheet simulation model, and make any recommendations that you have regarding the best store design and staffing plan for County Beverage. One additional consideration is that the design allowing for a two-channel system will cost an additional $10,000 to build.

1. List the information the spreadsheet simulation model should generate so that a decision can be made on the store design and the desired number of clerks.
2. Run the simulation for 1000 customers for each alternative considered. You may want to consider making more than one run with each alternative. [*Note:* Values from an exponential probability distribution with mean μ can be generated in Excel using the following function: $=-\mu*LN(RAND())$.]
3. Be sure to note the number of customers County Beverage is likely to lose due to long customer waiting times with each design alternative.

Appendix 12.1   SIMULATION WITH EXCEL

Excel enables small and moderate-sized simulation models to be implemented relatively easily and quickly. In this appendix we show the Excel worksheets for the three simulation models presented in the chapter.

The PortaCom Simulation Model

We simulated the PortaCom problem 500 times. The worksheet used to carry out the simulation is shown again in Figure 12.19. Note that the simulation results for trials 6 through 495

FIGURE 12.19   WORKSHEET FOR THE PORTACOM PROBLEM

	A	B	C	D	E	F
1	**PortaCom Risk Analysis**					
2						
3	Selling Price per Unit		$249			
4	Administrative Cost		$400,000			
5	Advertising Cost		$600,000			
6						
7	**Direct Labor Cost**			**Parts Cost (Uniform Distribution)**		
8	Lower	Upper		Smallest Value	$80	
9	Random No.	Random No.	Cost per Unit	Largest Value	$100	
10	0.0	0.1	$43			
11	0.1	0.3	$44			
12	0.3	0.7	$45	**Demand (Normal Distribution)**		
13	0.7	0.9	$46	Mean	15000	
14	0.9	1.0	$47	Std Deviation	4500	
15						
16						
17	**Simulation Trials**					
18						
19		Direct Labor	Parts	First-Year		
20	Trial	Cost per Unit	Cost per Unit	Demand	Profit	
21	1	47	$85.36	17,366	$1,025,570	
22	2	44	$91.68	12,900	$461,828	
23	3	45	$93.35	20,686	$1,288,906	
24	4	43	$98.56	10,888	$169,807	
25	5	45	$88.36	14,259	$648,911	
516	496	44	$98.67	8,730	($71,739)	
517	497	45	$94.38	19,257	$1,110,952	
518	498	44	$90.85	14,920	$703,118	
519	499	43	$90.37	13,471	$557,652	
520	500	46	$92.50	18,614	$1,056,847	
521						
522			**Summary Statistics**			
523			Mean Profit		$698,457	
524			Standard Deviation		$520,485	
525			Minimum Profit		($785,234)	
526			Maximum Profit		$2,367,058	
527			Number of Losses		51	
528			Probability of Loss		0.1020	

have been hidden so that the results can be shown in a reasonably sized figure. If desired, the rows for these trials can be shown and the simulation results displayed for all 500 trials. Let us describe the details of the Excel worksheet that provided the PortaCom simulation.

First, the PortaCom data are presented in the first 14 rows of the worksheet. The selling price per unit, administrative cost, and advertising cost parameters are entered directly into cells C3, C4, and C5. The discrete probability distribution for the direct labor cost per unit is shown in a tabular format. Note that the random number intervals are entered first, followed by the corresponding cost per unit. For example, 0.0 in cell A10 and 0.1 in cell B10 show that a cost of $43 per unit will be assigned if the random number is in the interval 0.0 but less than 0.1. Thus, approximately 10% of the simulated direct labor costs will be $43 per unit. The uniform probability distribution with a smallest value of $80 in cell E8 and a largest value of $100 in cell E9 describes the parts cost per unit. Finally, a normal probability distribution with a mean of 15,000 units in cell E13 and a standard deviation of 4500 units in cell E14 describes the first-year demand distribution for the product. At this point we are ready to insert the Excel formulas that will carry out each simulation trial.

Simulation information for the first trial appears in row 21 of the worksheet. The cell formulas for row 21 are as follows:

Cell A21   Enter 1 for the first simulation trial

Cell B21   Simulate the direct labor cost per unit*
            =VLOOKUP(RAND(),$A$10:$C$14,3)

Cell C21   Simulate the parts cost per unit (uniform distribution)
            =$E$8+($E$9–$E$8)*RAND()

Cell D21   Simulate the first-year demand (normal distribution)
            =NORMINV(RAND(),$E$13,$E$14)

Cell E21   The profit obtained for the first trial
            =($C$3–B21–C21)*D21–$C$4–$C$5

Cells A21:E21 can be copied to A520:E520 in order to provide the 500 simulation trials.

Ultimately, summary statistics will be collected in order to describe the results of the 500 simulated trials. Using the standard Excel functions, the following summary statistics are computed for the 500 simulated profits appearing in cells E21 to E520:

Cell E523   The mean profit per trial = AVERAGE(E21:E520)

Cell E524   The standard deviation of profit = STDEV(E21:E520)

Cell E525   The minimum profit = MIN(E21:E520)

Cell E526   The maximum profit = MAX(E21:E520)

Cell E527   The count of the number of trials where a loss occurred
             (i.e., profit < $0) = COUNTIF(E21:E520,"<0")

Cell E528   The percentage or probability of a loss based on the 500 trials
             = E527/500

The F9 key can be used to perform another complete simulation of PortaCom. In this case, the entire worksheet will be recalculated and a set of new simulation results will be provided. Any data summaries, measures, or functions that have been built into the worksheet earlier will be updated automatically.

The Butler Inventory Simulation Model

We simulated the Butler inventory operation for 300 months. The worksheet used to carry out the simulation is shown again in Figure 12.20. Note that the simulation results for

---

*The VLOOKUP function generates a random number using the RAND() function. Then, using the table defined by the region from cells $A$10 to $C$14, the function identifies the row containing the RAND() random number and assigns the corresponding direct labor cost per unit shown in column C.

FIGURE 12.20   WORKSHEET FOR THE BUTLER INVENTORY PROBLEM

	A	B	C	D	E	F	G	H
1	**Butler Inventory**							
2								
3	Gross Profit per Unit		$50					
4	Holding Cost per Unit		$15					
5	Shortage Cost per Unit		$30					
6								
7	**Replenishment Level**		100					
8								
9	**Demand (Normal Distribution)**							
10	Mean	100						
11	Std Deviation	20						
12								
13								
14	**Simulation**							
15								
16	Month	Demand	Sales	Gross Profit	Holding Cost	Shortage Cost	Net Profit	
17	1	79	79	$3,950	$315	$0	$3,635	
18	2	111	100	$5,000	$0	$330	$4,670	
19	3	93	93	$4,650	$105	$0	$4,545	
20	4	100	100	$5,000	$0	$0	$5,000	
21	5	118	100	$5,000	$0	$540	$4,460	
312	296	89	89	$4,450	$165	$0	$4,285	
313	297	91	91	$4,550	$135	$0	$4,415	
314	298	122	100	$5,000	$0	$660	$4,340	
315	299	93	93	$4,650	$105	$0	$4,545	
316	300	126	100	$5,000	$0	$780	$4,220	
317								
318	Totals	30,181	27,917		**Summary Statistics**			
319					Mean Profit		$4,293	
320					Standard Deviation		$658	
321					Minimum Profit		($206)	
322					Maximum Profit		$5,000	
323					Service Level		92.5%	

months 6 through 295 have been hidden so that the results can be shown in a reasonably sized figure. If desired, the rows for these months can be shown and the simulation results displayed for all 300 months. Let us describe the details of the Excel worksheet that provided the Butler inventory simulation.

First, the Butler inventory data are presented in the first 11 rows of the worksheet. The gross profit per unit, holding cost per unit, and shortage cost per unit data are entered directly into cells C3, C4, and C5. The replenishment level is entered into cell C7, and the mean and standard deviation of the normal probability distribution for demand are entered into cells B10 and B11. At this point we are ready to insert Excel formulas that will carry out each simulation month or trial.

Simulation information for the first month or trial appears in row 17 of the worksheet. The cell formulas for row 17 are as follows:

Cell A17   Enter 1 for the first simulation month
Cell B17   Simulate demand (normal distribution)
           =NORMINV(RAND(),$B$10,$B$11)

Next compute the sales, which is equal to demand (cell B17) if demand is less than or equal to the replenishment level, or is equal to the replenishment level (cell C7) if demand is greater than the replenishment level.

Cell C17   Compute sales =IF(B17<=$C$7,B17,$C$7)
Cell D17   Calculate gross profit =$C$3*C17
Cell E17   Calculate the holding cost if demand is less than or equal
           to the replenishment level
           =IF(B17<=$C$7,$C$4*($C$7–B17),0)
Cell F17   Calculate the shortage cost if demand is greater than the replenishment level
           =IF(B17>$C$7,$C$5*(B17–$C$7),0)
Cell G17   Calculate net profit =D17–E17–F17

Cells A17:G17 can be copied to cells A316:G316 in order to provide the 300 simulation months.

Finally, summary statistics will be collected in order to describe the results of the 300 simulated trials. Using the standard Excel functions, the following totals and summary statistics are computed for the 300 months:

Cell B318   Total demand =SUM(B17:B316)
Cell C319   Total sales =SUM(C17:C316)
Cell G319   The mean profit per month =AVERAGE(G17:G316)
Cell G320   The standard deviation of net profit =STDEV(G17:G316)
Cell G321   The minimum net profit =MIN(G17:G316)
Cell G322   The maximum net profit =MAX(G17:G316)
Cell G323   The service level =C318/B318

The Hammondsport ATM Simulation Model

We simulated the operation of the Hammondsport ATM waiting line system for 1000 customers. The worksheet used to carry out the simulation is shown again in Figure 12.21. Note that the simulation results for customers 6 through 995 have been hidden so that the results can be shown in a reasonably sized figure. If desired, the rows for these customers can be shown and the simulation results displayed for all 1000 customers. Let us describe the details of the Excel worksheet that provided the Hammondsport ATM simulation.

The data are presented in the first 9 rows of the worksheet. The interarrival times are described by a uniform distribution with a smallest time of 0 minutes (cell B4) and a largest time of 5 minutes (cell B5). A normal probability distribution with a mean of 2 minutes (cell B8) and a standard deviation of 0.5 minute (cell B9) describes the service time distribution.

FIGURE 12.21   WORKSHEET FOR THE HAMMONDSPORT SAVINGS BANK WITH ONE ATM

WEB file

Hammondsport1

	A	B	C	D	E	F	G	H	I
1	**Hammondsport Savings Bank with One ATM**								
2									
3	**Interarrival Times (Uniform Distribution)**								
4	Smallest Value	0							
5	Largest Value	5							
6									
7	**Service Times (Normal Distribution)**								
8	Mean	2							
9	Std Deviation	0.5							
10									
11									
12	**Simulation**								
13									
14		Interarrival	Arrival	Service	Waiting	Service	Completion	Time	
15	Customer	Time	Time	Start Time	Time	Time	Time	in System	
16	1	1.4	1.4	1.4	0.0	2.3	3.7	2.3	
17	2	1.3	2.7	3.7	1.0	1.5	5.2	2.5	
18	3	4.9	7.6	7.6	0.0	2.2	9.8	2.2	
19	4	3.5	11.1	11.1	0.0	2.5	13.6	2.5	
20	5	0.7	11.8	13.6	1.8	1.8	15.4	3.6	
1011	996	0.5	2496.8	2498.1	1.3	0.6	2498.7	1.9	
1012	997	0.2	2497.0	2498.7	1.7	2.0	2500.7	3.7	
1013	998	2.7	2499.7	2500.7	1.0	1.8	2502.5	2.8	
1014	999	3.7	2503.4	2503.4	0.0	2.4	2505.8	2.4	
1015	1000	4.0	2507.4	2507.4	0.0	1.9	2509.3	1.9	
1016									
1017		**Summary Statistics**							
1018		Number Waiting			549				
1019		Probability of Waiting			0.6100				
1020		Average Waiting Time			1.59				
1021		Maximum Waiting Time			13.5				
1022		Utilization of ATM			0.7860				
1023		Number Waiting > 1 Min			393				
1024		Probability of Waiting > 1 Min			0.4367				

Simulation information for the first customer appears in row 16 of the worksheet. The cell formulas for row 16 are as follows:

Cell A16   Enter 1 for the first customer

Cell B16   Simulate the interarrival time for customer 1 (uniform distribution)
=$B$4+RAND()*($B$5–$B$4)

Cell C16   Compute the arrival time for customer 1 =B16

Cell D16   Compute the start time for customer 1 =C16

Cell E16   Compute the waiting time for customer 1 =D1–C16

Cell F16   Simulate the service time for customer 1 (normal distribution)
           =NORMINV(RAND(),$B$8,$B$9)

Cell G16   Compute the completion time for customer 1 =D16+F16

Cell H16   Compute the time in the system for customer 1 =G16–C16

Simulation information for the second customer appears in row 17 of the worksheet. The cell formulas for row 17 are as follows:

Cell A17   Enter 2 for the second customer

Cell B17   Simulate the interarrival time for customer 2 (uniform distribution)
           =$B$4+RAND()*($B$5–$B$4)

Cell C17   Compute the arrival time for customer 2 =C16+B17

Cell D17   Compute the start time for customer 2 =IF(C17>G16,C17,G16)

Cell E17   Compute the waiting time for customer 2 =D17–C17

Cell F17   Simulate the service time for customer 2 (normal distribution)
           =NORMINV(RAND(),$B$8,$B$9)

Cell G17   Compute the completion time for customer 2 =D17+F17

Cell H17   Compute the time in the system for customer 2 =G17–C17

Cells A17:H17 can be copied to cells A1015:H1015 in order to provide the 1000-customer simulation.

Ultimately, summary statistics will be collected in order to describe the results of 1000 customers. Before collecting the summary statistics, let us point out that most simulation studies of dynamic systems focus on the operation of the system during its long-run or steady-state operation. To ensure that the effects of start-up conditions are not included in the steady-state calculations, a dynamic simulation model is usually run for a specified period without collecting any data about the operation of the system. The length of the start-up period can vary depending on the application. For the Hammondsport Savings Bank ATM simulation, we treated the results for the first 100 customers as the start-up period. The simulation information for customer 100 appears in row 115 of the spreadsheet. Cell G115 shows that the completion time for the 100th customer is 247.8. Thus the length of the start-up period is 247.8 minutes.

Summary statistics are collected for the next 900 customers corresponding to rows 116 to 1015 of the worksheet. The following Excel formulas provided the summary statistics:

Cell E1018   Number of customers who had to wait (i.e., waiting time > 0)
             =COUNTIF(E116:E1015,">0")

Cell E1019   Probability of waiting =E1018/900

Cell E1020   The average waiting time =AVERAGE(E116:E1015)

Cell E1021   The maximum waiting time =MAX(E116:E1015)

Cell E1022   The utilization of the ATM* =SUM(F116:F1015)/(G1015–G115)

---

*The proportion of time the ATM is in use is equal to the sum of the 900 customer service times in column F divided by the total elapsed time required for the 900 customers to complete service. This total elapsed time is the difference between the completion time of customer 1000 and the completion time of customer 100.

Cell E1023   The number of customers who had to wait more than 1 minute
=COUNTIF(E116:E1015, ">1")

Cell E1024   Probability of waiting more than 1 minute =E1023/900

Appendix 12.2   SIMULATION USING CRYSTAL BALL

In Section 12.1 we used simulation to perform risk analysis for the PortaCom problem, and in Appendix 12.1 we showed how to construct the Excel worksheet that provided the simulation results. Developing the worksheet simulation for the PortaCom problem using the basic Excel package was relatively easy. The use of add-ins enables larger and more complex simulation problems to be easily analyzed using spreadsheets. In this appendix, we show how Crystal Ball, an add-in package, can be used to perform the PortaCom simulation. We will run the simulation for 1000 trials here. Instructions for installing and starting Crystal Ball are included with the Crystal Ball software.

Formulating a Crystal Ball Model

We begin by entering the problem data into the top portion of the worksheet. For the PortaCom problem, we must enter the following data: selling price, administrative cost, advertising cost, probability distribution for the direct labor cost per unit, smallest and largest values for the parts cost per unit (uniform distribution), and the mean and standard deviation for first-year demand (normal distribution). These data with appropriate descriptive labels are shown in cells A1:E13 of Figure 12.22.

For the PortaCom problem, the Crystal Ball model contains the following two components: (1) cells for the probabilistic inputs (direct labor cost, parts cost, first-year demand), and (2) a cell containing a formula for computing the value of the simulation model output (profit). In Crystal Ball the cells that contain the values of the probabilistic inputs are called *assumption cells*, and the cells that contain the formulas for the model outputs are referred to as *forecast cells*. The PortaCom problem requires only one output (profit), and thus the Crystal Ball model only contains one forecast cell. In more complex simulation problems more than one forecast cell may be necessary.

The assumption cells may only contain simple numeric values. In this model-building stage, we entered PortaCom's best estimates of the direct labor cost ($45), the parts cost ($90), and the first-year demand (15,000) into cells C21:C23, respectively. The forecast cells in a Crystal Ball model contain formulas that refer to one or more of the assumption cells. Because only one forecast cell in the PortaCom problem corresponds to profit, we entered the following formula into cell C27:

$$=(C3-C21-C22)*C23-C4-C5$$

The resulting value of $710,000 is the profit corresponding to the base-case scenario discussed in Section 12.1.

Defining and Entering Assumptions

We are now ready to define the probability distributions corresponding to each of the assumption cells. We begin by defining the probability distribution for the direct labor cost.

Step 1.   Select the Crystal Ball tab
Step 2.   Select cell C21

FIGURE 12.22 CRYSTAL BALL WORKSHEET FOR THE PORTACOM PROBLEM

	A	B	C	D	E	F
1	**PortaCom Risk Analysis**					
2						
3	Selling Price per Unit		$249			
4	Administrative Cost		$400,000			
5	Advertising Cost		$600,000			
6						
7		**Direct Labor**		**Parts Cost (Uniform Distribution)**		
8		Cost per Unit	Probability	Smallest Value	$80	
9		$43	0.1	Largest Value	$100	
10		$44	0.2			
11		$45	0.4	**Demand (Normal Distribution)**		
12		$46	0.2	Mean	15,000	
13		$47	0.1	Standard Dev	4,500	
14						
15						
16						
17	**Crystal Ball Model**					
18						
19			**Assumption**			
20			**Cells**			
21		**Direct Labor Cost**	$45			
22		**Parts Cost**	$90			
23		**Demand**	15,000			
24						
25			**Forecast**			
26			**Cell**			
27		**Profit**	$710,000			

Step 3. Choose **Define Assumption** from the **Define** group of the **Crystal Ball** ribbon.

Step 4. When the **Distribution Gallery: Cell 21** dialog box appears:
Choose **Custom*** (Use the scroll bar to see all possible distributions.)
Click **OK**

Step 5. When the **Define Assumption: Cell C21** dialog box appears:
If the ⌄ button is to the right of the **Name** box, proceed to step 6

If the ⌃ button is to the right of the **Name** box, click the ⌃ button to

obtain the ⌄ button

Step 6. Choose **Load Data**
Enter B9:C13 in the **Location of data** box
Click **Keep Linked to Spreadsheet**
Click **OK** to terminate the data entry process
Click **OK**

*You may have to click **All** and use the scroll bar to see all possible distributions.

The procedure for defining the probability distribution for the parts cost is similar.

Step 1. Select cell C22
Step 2. Choose **Define Assumption** from the **Define** group of the **Crystal Ball** ribbon.
Step 3. When the **Distribution Gallery: Cell C22** dialog box appears:
    Choose **Uniform** (Use the scroll bar to see all possible distributions.)
    Click **OK**
Step 4. When the **Define Assumption: Cell C22** dialog box appears:
    Enter =E8 in the **Minimum** box
    Enter =E9 in the **Maximum** box
    Click **Enter**
    Click **OK**

Finally, we perform the following steps to define the probability distribution for first-year demand:

Step 1. Select cell C23
Step 2. Choose **Define Assumption** from the **Define** group of the **Crystal Ball** ribbon.
Step 3. When the **Distribution Gallery: Cell 23** dialog box appears:
    Choose **Normal** (Use the scroll bar to see all possible distributions.)
    Click **OK**
Step 4. When the **Define Assumption: Cell C23** dialog box appears:
    Enter =E12 in the **Mean** box
    Enter =E13 in the **Std. Dev.** box
    Click **Enter**
    Click **OK**

Defining Forecasts

After defining the assumption cells, we are ready to define the forecast cells. The following steps show this process for cell C27, which is the profit forecast cell for the PortaCom project:

Step 1. Select cell C27
Step 2. Choose **Define Forecast** from the **Define** group of the **Crystal Ball** ribbon.
Step 3. When the **Define Forecast: Cell C27** dialog box appears:
    Profit will appear in the **Name** box
    Click **OK**

Setting Run Preferences

We must now make the choices that determine how Crystal Ball runs the simulation. For the PortaCom simulation, we only need to specify the number of trials.

Step 1. Choose **Run Preferences** from the **Run** group of the **Crystal Ball** ribbon.
Step 2. When the **Run Preferences** dialog box appears:
    Make sure the **Trials** tab has been selected
    Enter 1000 in the **Number of trials to run:** box
    Click **OK**

Running the Simulation

Crystal Ball repeats three steps on each of the 1000 trials of the PortaCom simulation.

1. Values are generated for the three assumption cells according to the defined probability distributions.
2. A new simulated profit (forecast cell) is computed based on the new values in the three assumption cells.
3. The new simulated profit is recorded.

The simulation is started by selecting the **Start** button 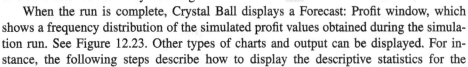 .

When the run is complete, Crystal Ball displays a Forecast: Profit window, which shows a frequency distribution of the simulated profit values obtained during the simulation run. See Figure 12.23. Other types of charts and output can be displayed. For instance, the following steps describe how to display the descriptive statistics for the simulation run:

Step 1. Select the **View** menu in the **Forecast: Profit** window
Step 2. Choose **Statistics**

FIGURE 12.23   CRYSTAL BALL FREQUENCY CHART FOR THE PORTACOM SIMULATION

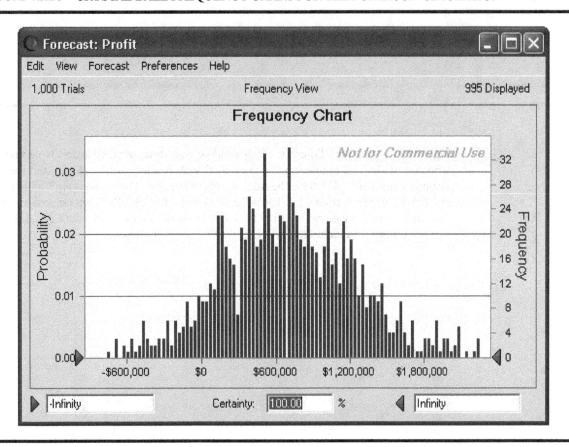

FIGURE 12.24   CRYSTAL BALL STATISTICS FOR THE PORTACOM SIMULATION

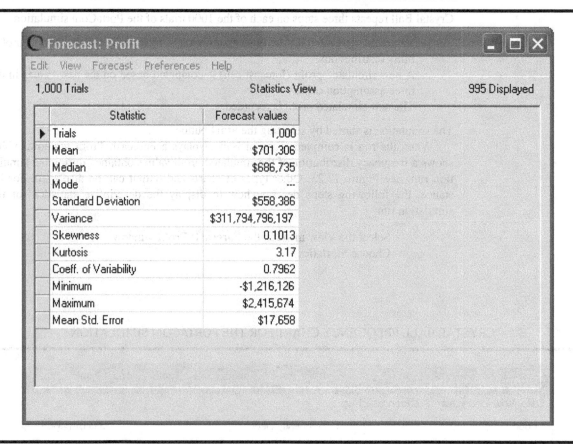

Figure 12.24 shows the Forecast: Profit window with descriptive statistics. Note that the worst result obtained in this simulation of 1000 trials is a loss of $1,216,126, and the best result is a profit of $2,415,674. The mean profit is $701,306. These values are similar to the results obtained in Section 12.1. The differences result from the different random numbers used in the two simulations and from the fact that we used 1000 trials with Crystal Ball. If you perform another simulation, your results will differ slightly.

References and Bibliography

Banks, J., J. S. Carson, and B. L. Nelson. *Discrete-Event System Simulation,* 2d ed. Prentice Hall, 1995.

Fishwick, P. A. *Simulation Model Design and Execution: Building Digital Worlds.* Prentice Hall, 1995.

Harrell, C. R., and K. Tumau. *Simulation Made Easy: A Manager's Guide.* Institute of Industrial Engineers, 1996.

Kelton, W. D., R. P. Sadowski, and D. A. Sadowski. *Simulation with Arena,* 4th ed. McGraw-Hill, 2007.

Law, A. M., and W. D. Kelton. *Simulation Modeling and Analysis,* 3d ed. McGraw-Hill, 1999.

Pidd, M. *Computer Simulation in Management Science,* 4th ed. Wiley, 1998.

Thesen, A., and L. E. Travis. *Simulation for Decision Making.* Wadsworth, 1992.

Self-Test Solutions and Answers to Even-Numbered Problems

Chapter 14: Simulation

2. a. c = variable cost per unit
   x = demand
   Profit = $(50 - c)x - 30,000$

   b. Base: Profit = $(50 - 20)1200 - 30,000 = 6,000$
   Worst: Profit = $(50 - 24)300 - 30,000 = -22,200$
   Best: Profit = $(50 - 16)2100 - 30,000 = 41,400$

   c. Simulation will be helpful in estimating the probability of a loss.

4. a.

Number of New Accounts	Interval
0	0.00 but less than 0.01
1	0.01 but less than 0.05
2	0.05 but less than 0.15
3	0.15 but less than 0.40
4	0.40 but less than 0.80
5	0.80 but less than 0.95
6	0.95 but less than 1.00

   b. 4, 3, 3, 5, 2, 6, 4, 4, 4, 2
   37 new accounts

   c. First-year commission = $185,000
   Cost of 10 seminars = $35,000
   Yes

5. a.

Stock Price Change	Interval
−2	0.00 but less than 0.05
−1	0.05 but less than 0.15
0	0.15 but less than 0.40
+1	0.40 but less than 0.60
+2	0.60 but less than 0.80
+3	0.80 but less than 0.90
+4	0.90 but less than 1.00

   b. Beginning price $39
   0.1091 indicates −1 change; $38

0.9407 indicates +4 change; $42
0.1941 indicates 0 change; $42
0.8083 indicates +3 change; $45 (ending price)

6. a. 0.00–0.83, 0.83–0.89, 0.89–0.94, 0.94–0.96, 0.96–0.98, 0.98–0.99, 0.99–1.00

   b. 4 claims paid; Total = $22,000

8. a. Atlanta wins each game if random number is in interval 0.00–0.60, 0.00–0.55, 0.00–0.48, 0.00–0.45, 0.00–0.48, 0.00–0.55, 0.00–0.50.

   b. Atlanta wins games 1, 2, 4, and 6.
   Atlanta wins series 4 to 2.

   c. Repeat many times; record % of Atlanta wins.

9. a. Base-case based on most likely;
   Time = $6 + 5 + 14 + 8 = 33$ weeks
   Worst: Time = $8 + 7 + 18 + 10 = 43$ weeks
   Best: Time = $5 + 3 + 10 + 8 = 26$ weeks

   b. 0.1778 for A: 5 weeks
   0.9617 for B: 7 weeks
   0.6849 for C: 14 weeks
   0.4503 for D: 8 weeks; Total = 34 weeks

   c. Simulation will provide an estimate of the probability of 35 weeks or less.

10. a.

Hand Value	Interval
17	0.0000 but less than 0.1654
18	0.1654 but less than 0.2717
19	0.2717 but less than 0.3780
20	0.3780 but less than 0.4797
21	0.4797 but less than 0.5769
e. Broke	0.5769 but less than 1.0000

   b, c, & d. Dealer wins 13 hands, Player wins 5, 2 pushes. Player wins 7, dealer wins 13.

FIGURE E12.14 WORKSHEET FOR THE MADEIRA MANUFACTURING SIMULATION

	A	B	C	D	E	F	G	H
1	Madeira Manufacturing Company							
2								
3	Selling Price per Unit		$50					
4	Fixed Cost		$30,000					
5								
6	Variable Cost (Uniform Distribution)				Demand (Normal Distribution)			
7	Smallest Value		$16		Mean		1200	
8	Largest Value		$24		Standard Deviation		300	
9								
10	Simulation trials							
11		Variable						
12	Trial	Cost per Unit	Demand	Profit				
13	1	$17.81	788	($4,681)				
14	2	$18.86	1078	$3,580				
15								

12. a. $7, $3, $12
    b. Purchase: 0.00–0.25, 0.25–0.70, 0.70–1.00
       Labor: 0.00–0.10, 0.10–0.35, 0.35–0.70, 0.70–1.00
       Transportation: 0.00–0.75, 0.75–1.00
    c. $5
    d. $7
    e. Provide probability profit less than $5/unit.

14. Selected cell formulas for the worksheet shown in Figure E12.14 are as follows:

Cell	Formula
B13	=$C$7+RAND()*($C$8−$C$7)
C13	=NORMINV(RAND(),$G$7,$G$8)
D13	=($C$3−B13)*C13−$C$4

   a. The mean profit should be approximately $6000; simulation results will vary, with most simulations having a mean profit between $5500 and $6500.
   b. 120 to 150 of the 500 simulation trials should show a loss; thus, the probability of a loss should be between 0.24 and 0.30.
   c. This project appears too risky.

16. a. About 36% of simulation runs will show $130,000 as the winning bid.
    b. $150,000; $10,000
    c. Recommended $140,000

18. Selected cell formulas for the worksheet shown in Figure E12.18 are as follows:

Cell	Formula
B11	=$C$4+RAND()*($C$5−$C$4)
C11	=NORMINV(RAND(),$H$4,$H$5)
D11	=MIN(B11:C11)
G11	=COUNTIF($D$11:$D$1010,">650")
H11	=G11/COUNT($D$11:$D$1010)

   a. $650,000 should win roughly 600 to 650 of the 1000 times; the probability of winning the bid should be between 0.60 and 0.65.
   b. The probability of $625,000 winning should be roughly 0.82, and the probability of $615,000 winning should be roughly 0.88; a contractor's bid of $625,000 is recommended.

20. a. Results vary with each simulation run.
       Approximate results: 50,000 provided $230,000
                            60,000 provided $190,000
                            70,000 less than $100,000
    b. Recommend 50,000 units.
    c. Roughly 0.75

22. Very poor operation; some customers wait 30 minutes or more.

24. b. Waiting time is approximately 0.8 minutes.
    c. 30% to 35% of customers have to wait.

FIGURE E12.18   WORKSHEET FOR THE CONTRACTOR BIDDING SIMULATION

	A	B	C	D	E	F	G	H	I
1	Contractor Bidding								
2									
3	Contractor A (Uniform Distribution)					Contractor B (Normal Distribution)			
4	Smallest Value		$600			Mean		$700	
5	Largest Value		$800			Standard Deviation		$50	
6									
7									
8	Simulation					Results			
9		Contractor	Contractor	Lowest		Contractor's	Number	Probability	
10	Trial	A's Bid	B's Bid	Bid		Bid	of Wins	of Winning	
11	1	$673	$720	$673		$650	628	0.628	
12	2	$757	$655	$655		$625	812	0.812	
13	3	$706	$791	$706		$615	875	0.875	
14	4	$638	$677	$638					
15									

15

Decision Analysis

CONTENTS

Decision analysis can be used to develop an optimal strategy when a decision maker is faced with several decision alternatives and an uncertain or risk-filled pattern of future events. For example, Ohio Edison used decision analysis to choose the best type of particulate control equipment for coal-fired generating units when it faced future uncertainties concerning sulfur content requirements, construction costs, and so on. The State of North Carolina used decision analysis in evaluating whether to implement a medical screening test to detect metabolic disorders in newborns. Thus, decision analysis repeatedly proves its value in decision making. The Management Science in Action, Decision Analysis at Eastman Kodak, describes how the use of decision analysis added approximately $1 billion in value.

Even when a careful decision analysis has been conducted, uncertain future events make the final consequence uncertain. In some cases, the selected decision alternative may provide good or excellent results. In other cases, a relatively unlikely future event may occur, causing the selected decision alternative to provide only fair or even poor results. The risk associated with any decision alternative is a direct result of the uncertainty associated with the final consequence. A good decision analysis includes risk analysis. Through risk analysis, the decision maker is provided with probability information about favorable as well as unfavorable consequences that may occur.

MANAGEMENT SCIENCE IN ACTION

DECISION ANALYSIS AT EASTMAN KODAK*

Clemen and Kwit conducted a study to determine the value of decision analysis at the Eastman Kodak Company. The study involved an analysis of 178 decision analysis projects over a 10-year period. The projects involved a variety of applications including strategy development, vendor selection, process analysis, new-product brainstorming, product-portfolio selection, and emission-reduction analysis. These projects required 14,372 hours of analyst time and the involvement of many other individuals at Kodak over the 10-year period. The shortest projects took less than 20 hours, and the longest projects took almost a year to complete.

Most decision analysis projects are one-time activities, which makes it difficult to measure the value added to the corporation. Clemen and Kwit used detailed records that were available and some innovative approaches to develop estimates of the incremental dollar value generated by the decision analysis projects. Their conservative estimate of the average value per project was $6.65 million, and their optimistic estimate of the average value per project was $16.35 million. Their analysis led to the conclusion that all projects taken together added more than $1 billion in value to Eastman Kodak. Using these estimates, Clemen and Kwit concluded that decision analysis returned substan-

tial value to the company. Indeed, they concluded that the value added by the projects was at least 185 times the cost of the analysts' time.

In addition to the monetary benefits, the authors point out that decision analysis adds value by facilitating discussion among stakeholders, promoting careful thinking about strategies, providing a common language for discussing the elements of a decision problem, and speeding implementation by helping to build consensus among decision makers. In commenting on the value of decision analysis at Eastman Kodak, Nancy L. S. Sousa said, "As General Manager, New Businesses, VP Health Imaging, Eastman Kodak, I encourage all of the business planners to use the decision and risk principles and processes as part of evaluating new business opportunities. The processes have clearly led to better decisions about entry and exit of businesses."

Although measuring the value of a particular decision analysis project can be difficult, it would be hard to dispute the success that decision analysis had at Kodak.

*Based on Robert T. Clemen and Robert C. Kwit, "The Value of Decision Analysis at Eastman Kodak Company," *Interfaces* (September/October 2001): 74–92.

We begin the study of decision analysis by considering problems that involve reasonably few decision alternatives and reasonably few possible future events. Influence diagrams and payoff tables are introduced to provide a structure for the decision problem and to illustrate the fundamentals of decision analysis. We then introduce decision trees to show the sequential nature of decision problems. Decision trees are used to analyze more complex problems and to identify an optimal sequence of decisions, referred to as an optimal decision strategy. Sensitivity analysis shows how changes in various aspects of the problem affect the recommended decision alternative.

13.1 PROBLEM FORMULATION

The first step in the decision analysis process is problem formulation. We begin with a verbal statement of the problem. We then identify the **decision alternatives,** the uncertain future events, referred to as **chance events,** and the **consequences** associated with each decision alternative and each chance event outcome. Let us begin by considering a construction project of the Pittsburgh Development Corporation.

Pittsburgh Development Corporation (PDC) purchased land that will be the site of a new luxury condominium complex. The location provides a spectacular view of downtown Pittsburgh and the Golden Triangle where the Allegheny and Monongahela Rivers meet to form the Ohio River. PDC plans to price the individual condominium units between $300,000 and $1,400,000.

PDC commissioned preliminary architectural drawings for three different projects: one with 30 condominiums, one with 60 condominiums, and one with 90 condominiums. The financial success of the project depends upon the size of the condominium complex and the chance event concerning the demand for the condominiums. The statement of the PDC decision problem is to select the size of the new luxury condominium project that will lead to the largest profit given the uncertainty concerning the demand for the condominiums.

Given the statement of the problem, it is clear that the decision is to select the best size for the condominium complex. PDC has the following three decision alternatives:

$$d_1 = \text{a small complex with 30 condominiums}$$
$$d_2 = \text{a medium complex with 60 condominiums}$$
$$d_3 = \text{a large complex with 90 condominiums}$$

A factor in selecting the best decision alternative is the uncertainty associated with the chance event concerning the demand for the condominiums. When asked about the possible demand for the condominiums, PDC's president acknowledged a wide range of possibilities but decided that it would be adequate to consider two possible chance event outcomes: a strong demand and a weak demand.

In decision analysis, the possible outcomes for a chance event are referred to as the **states of nature.** The states of nature are defined so that one, and only one, of the possible states of nature will occur. For the PDC problem, the chance event concerning the demand for the condominiums has two states of nature:

$$s_1 = \text{strong demand for the condominiums}$$
$$s_2 = \text{weak demand for the condominiums}$$

Management must first select a decision alternative (complex size); then a state of nature follows (demand for the condominiums); and finally a consequence will occur. In this case, the consequence is PDC's profit.

Influence Diagrams

An **influence diagram** is a graphical device that shows the relationships among the decisions, the chance events, and the consequences for a decision problem. The **nodes** in an influence diagram represent the decisions, chance events, and consequences. Rectangles or squares depict **decision nodes**, circles or ovals depict **chance nodes**, and diamonds depict **consequence nodes.** The lines connecting the nodes, referred to as *arcs,* show the direction of influence that the nodes have on one another. Figure 13.1 shows the influence diagram for the PDC problem. The complex size is the decision node, demand is the chance node, and profit is the consequence node. The arcs connecting the nodes show that both the complex size and the demand influence PDC's profit.

Payoff Tables

Given the three decision alternatives and the two states of nature, which complex size should PDC choose? To answer this question, PDC will need to know the consequence associated with each decision alternative and each state of nature. In decision analysis, we refer to the consequence resulting from a specific combination of a decision alternative and a state of nature as a **payoff.** A table showing payoffs for all combinations of decision alternatives and states of nature is a **payoff table.**

Payoffs can be expressed in terms of profit, cost, time, distance, or any other measure appropriate for the decision problem being analyzed.

Because PDC wants to select the complex size that provides the largest profit, profit is used as the consequence. The payoff table with profits expressed in millions of dollars is shown in Table 13.1. Note, for example, that if a medium complex is built and demand turns out to be strong, a profit of $14 million will be realized. We will use the notation V_{ij} to denote the payoff associated with decision alternative i and state of nature j. Using Table 13.1, $V_{31} = 20$ indicates a payoff of $20 million occurs if the decision is to build a large complex (d_3) and the strong demand state of nature (s_1) occurs. Similarly, $V_{32} = -9$ indicates a loss of $9 million if the decision is to build a large complex (d_3) and the weak demand state of nature (s_2) occurs.

FIGURE 13.1   INFLUENCE DIAGRAM FOR THE PDC PROJECT

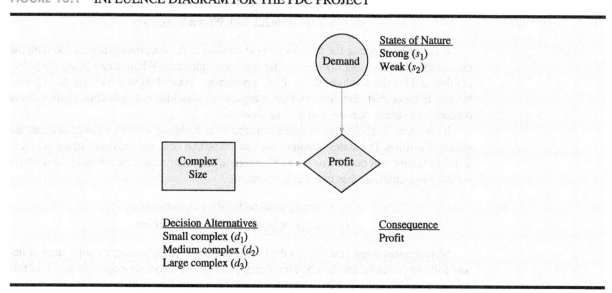

TABLE 13.1 PAYOFF TABLE FOR THE PDC CONDOMINIUM PROJECT (PAYOFFS IN $ MILLIONS)

Decision Alternative	State of Nature	
	Strong Demand s_1	Weak Demand s_2
Small complex, d_1	8	7
Medium complex, d_2	14	5
Large complex, d_3	20	−9

Decision Trees

A **decision tree** provides a graphical representation of the decision-making process. Figure 13.2 presents a decision tree for the PDC problem. Note that the decision tree shows the natural or logical progression that will occur over time. First, PDC must make a decision regarding the size of the condominium complex (d_1, d_2, or d_3). Then, after the decision is implemented, either state of nature s_1 or s_2 will occur. The number at each end point of the tree indicates the payoff associated with a particular sequence. For example, the topmost payoff of 8 indicates that an $8 million profit is anticipated if PDC constructs a small condominium complex (d_1) and demand turns out to be strong (s_1). The next payoff of 7 indicates an anticipated profit of $7 million if PDC constructs a small condominium complex (d_1) and demand turns out to be weak (s_2). Thus, the decision tree shows graphically the sequences of decision alternatives and states of nature that provide the six possible payoffs for PDC.

FIGURE 13.2 DECISION TREE FOR THE PDC CONDOMINIUM PROJECT (PAYOFFS IN $ MILLIONS)

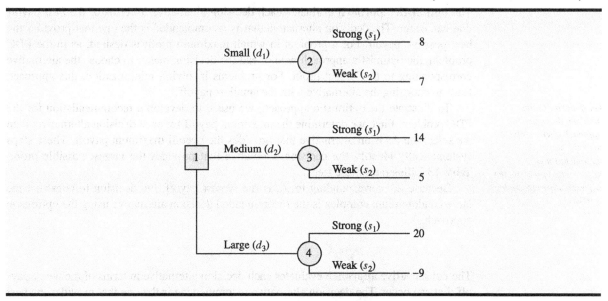

If you have a payoff table, you can develop a decision tree. Try Problem 1(a).

The decision tree in Figure 13.2 shows four nodes, numbered 1–4. Squares are used to depict decision nodes and circles are used to depict chance nodes. Thus, node 1 is a decision node, and nodes 2, 3, and 4 are chance nodes. The **branches** connect the nodes; those leaving the decision node correspond to the decision alternatives. The branches leaving each chance node correspond to the states of nature. The payoffs are shown at the end of the states-of-nature branches. We now turn to the question: How can the decision maker use the information in the payoff table or the decision tree to select the best decision alternative? Several approaches may be used.

NOTES AND COMMENTS

1. Experts in problem solving agree that the first step in solving a complex problem is to decompose it into a series of smaller subproblems. Decision trees provide a useful way to show how a problem can be decomposed and the sequential nature of the decision process.

2. People often view the same problem from different perspectives. Thus, the discussion regarding the development of a decision tree may provide additional insight about the problem.

13.2 DECISION MAKING WITHOUT PROBABILITIES

Many people think of a good decision as one in which the consequence is good. However, in some instances, a good, well-thought-out decision may still lead to a bad or undesirable consequence.

In this section we consider approaches to decision making that do not require knowledge of the probabilities of the states of nature. These approaches are appropriate in situations in which the decision maker has little confidence in his or her ability to assess the probabilities, or in which a simple best-case and worst-case analysis is desirable. Because different approaches sometimes lead to different decision recommendations, the decision maker should understand the approaches available and then select the specific approach that, according to the decision maker's judgment, is the most appropriate.

Optimistic Approach

The **optimistic approach** evaluates each decision alternative in terms of the *best* payoff that can occur. The decision alternative that is recommended is the one that provides the best possible payoff. For a problem in which maximum profit is desired, as in the PDC problem, the optimistic approach would lead the decision maker to choose the alternative corresponding to the largest profit. For problems involving minimization, this approach leads to choosing the alternative with the smallest payoff.

For a maximization problem, the optimistic approach often is referred to as the maximax approach; for a minimization problem, the corresponding terminology is minimin.

To illustrate the optimistic approach, we use it to develop a recommendation for the PDC problem. First, we determine the maximum payoff for each decision alternative; then we select the decision alternative that provides the overall maximum payoff. These steps systematically identify the decision alternative that provides the largest possible profit. Table 13.2 illustrates these steps.

Because 20, corresponding to d_3, is the largest payoff, the decision to construct the large condominium complex is the recommended decision alternative using the optimistic approach.

Conservative Approach

The **conservative approach** evaluates each decision alternative in terms of the *worst* payoff that can occur. The decision alternative recommended is the one that provides the best

TABLE 13.2   MAXIMUM PAYOFF FOR EACH PDC DECISION ALTERNATIVE

Decision Alternative	Maximum Payoff	
Small complex, d_1	8	
Medium complex, d_2	14	
Large complex, d_3	20 ←	Maximum of the maximum payoff values

of the worst possible payoffs. For a problem in which the output measure is profit, as in the PDC problem, the conservative approach would lead the decision maker to choose the alternative that maximizes the minimum possible profit that could be obtained. For problems involving minimization, this approach identifies the alternative that will minimize the maximum payoff.

For a maximization problem, the conservative approach often is referred to as the maximax approach; for a minimization problem, the corresponding terminology is minimax.

To illustrate the conservative approach, we use it to develop a recommendation for the PDC problem. First, we identify the minimum payoff for each of the decision alternatives; then we select the decision alternative that maximizes the minimum payoff. Table 13.3 illustrates these steps for the PDC problem.

Because 7, corresponding to d_1, yields the maximum of the minimum payoffs, the decision alternative of a small condominium complex is recommended. This decision approach is considered conservative because it identifies the worst possible payoffs and then recommends the decision alternative that avoids the possibility of extremely "bad" payoffs. In the conservative approach, PDC is guaranteed a profit of at least $7 million. Although PDC may make more, it *cannot* make less than $7 million.

Minimax Regret Approach

The **minimax regret approach** to decision making is neither purely optimistic nor purely conservative. Let us illustrate the minimax regret approach by showing how it can be used to select a decision alternative for the PDC problem.

Suppose that PDC constructs a small condominium complex (d_1) and demand turns out to be strong (s_1). Table 13.1 showed that the resulting profit for PDC would be $8 million. However, given that the strong demand state of nature (s_1) has occurred, we realize that the decision to construct a large condominium complex (d_3), yielding a profit of $20 million, would have been the best decision. The difference between the payoff for the best decision alternative ($20 million) and the payoff for the decision to construct a small condominium complex ($8 million) is the **opportunity loss,** or **regret,** associated with decision alternative d_1 when state of nature s_1 occurs; thus, for this case, the opportunity loss or regret is $20 million − $8 million = $12 million. Similarly, if PDC makes the decision to construct a medium condominium complex (d_2) and the strong demand state of nature (s_1) occurs, the opportunity loss, or regret, associated with d_2 would be $20 million − $14 million = $6 million.

TABLE 13.3   MINIMUM PAYOFF FOR EACH PDC DECISION ALTERNATIVE

Decision Alternative	Minimum Payoff	
Small complex, d_1	7 ←	Maximum of the minimum payoff values
Medium complex, d_2	5	
Large complex, d_3	−9	

In general, the following expression represents the opportunity loss, or regret:

$$R_{ij} = |V_j^* - V_{ij}| \qquad (13.1)$$

where

R_{ij} = the regret associated with decision alternative d_i and state of nature s_j
V_j^* = the payoff value[1] corresponding to the best decision for the state of nature s_j
V_{ij} = the payoff corresponding to decision alternative d_i and state of nature s_j

Note the role of the absolute value in equation (13.1). For minimization problems, the best payoff, V_j^*, is the smallest entry in column j. Because this value always is less than or equal to V_{ij}, the absolute value of the difference between V_j^* and V_{ij} ensures that the regret is always the magnitude of the difference.

Using equation (4.1) and the payoffs in Table 13.1, we can compute the regret associated with each combination of decision alternative d_i and state of nature s_j. Because the PDC problem is a maximization problem, V_j^* will be the largest entry in column j of the payoff table. Thus, to compute the regret, we simply subtract each entry in a column from the largest entry in the column. Table 13.4 shows the opportunity loss, or regret, table for the PDC problem.

The next step in applying the minimax regret approach is to list the maximum regret for each decision alternative; Table 13.5 shows the results for the PDC problem. Selecting the decision alternative with the *minimum* of the *maximum* regret values—hence, the name *minimax regret*—yields the minimax regret decision. For the PDC problem, the alternative to construct the medium condominium complex, with a corresponding maximum regret of $6 million, is the recommended minimax regret decision.

For practice in developing a decision recommendation using the optimistic, conservative, and minimax regret approaches, try Problem 1 (part b).

Note that the three approaches discussed in this section provide different recommendations, which in itself isn't bad. It simply reflects the difference in decision-making philosophies that underlie the various approaches. Ultimately, the decision maker will have to choose the most appropriate approach and then make the final decision accordingly. The main criticism of the approaches discussed in this section is that they do not consider any information about the probabilities of the various states of nature. In the next section we discuss an approach that utilizes probability information in selecting a decision alternative.

TABLE 13.4 OPPORTUNITY LOSS, OR REGRET, TABLE FOR THE PDC CONDOMINIUM PROJECT ($ MILLIONS)

	State of Nature	
Decision Alternative	**Strong Demand s_1**	**Weak Demand s_2**
Small complex, d_1	12	0
Medium complex, d_2	6	2
Large complex, d_3	0	16

---

[1]In maximization problems, V_j^* will be the largest entry in column j of the payoff table. In minimization problems, V_j^* will be the smallest entry in column j of the payoff table.

TABLE 13.5 MAXIMUM REGRET FOR EACH PDC DECISION ALTERNATIVE

Decision Alternative	Maximum Regret	
Small complex, d_1	12	
Medium complex, d_2	6 ← Minimum of the maximum regret
Large complex, d_3	16	

13.3 DECISION MAKING WITH PROBABILITIES

In many decision-making situations, we can obtain probability assessments for the states of nature. When such probabilities are available, we use the **expected value approach** to identify the best decision alternative. Let us first define the expected value of a decision alternative and then apply it to the PDC problem.

Let

$$N = \text{the number of states of nature}$$
$$P(s_j) = \text{the probability of state of nature } s_j$$

Because one and only one of the N states of nature can occur, the probabilities must satisfy two conditions:

$$P(s_j) \geq 0 \qquad \text{for all states of nature} \qquad (13.2)$$

$$\sum_{j=1}^{N} P(s_j) = P(s_1) + P(s_2) + \cdots + P(s_N) = 1 \qquad (13.3)$$

The **expected value (EV)** of decision alternative d_i is defined as follows:

$$\text{EV}(d_i) = \sum_{j=1}^{N} P(s_j)V_{ij} \qquad (13.4)$$

In words, the expected value of a decision alternative is the sum of weighted payoffs for the decision alternative. The weight for a payoff is the probability of the associated state of nature and therefore the probability that the payoff will occur. Let us return to the PDC problem to see how the expected value approach can be applied.

PDC is optimistic about the potential for the luxury high-rise condominium complex. Suppose that this optimism leads to an initial subjective probability assessment of 0.8 that demand will be strong (s_1) and a corresponding probability of 0.2 that demand will be weak (s_2). Thus, $P(s_1) = 0.8$ and $P(s_2) = 0.2$. Using the payoff values in Table 13.1 and equation

(13.4), we compute the expected value for each of the three decision alternatives as follows:

$$EV(d_1) = 0.8(8) + 0.2(7) = 7.8$$
$$EV(d_2) = 0.8(14) + 0.2(5) = 12.2$$
$$EV(d_3) = 0.8(20) + 0.2(-9) = 14.2$$

Thus, using the expected value approach, we find that the large condominium complex, with an expected value of $14.2 million, is the recommended decision.

Can you now use the expected value approach to develop a decision recommendation? Try Problem 4.

The calculations required to identify the decision alternative with the best expected value can be conveniently carried out on a decision tree. Figure 13.3 shows the decision tree for the PDC problem with state-of-nature branch probabilities. Working backward through the decision tree, we first compute the expected value at each chance node. That is, at each chance node, we weight each possible payoff by its probability of occurrence. By doing so, we obtain the expected values for nodes 2, 3, and 4, as shown in Figure 13.4.

Because the decision maker controls the branch leaving decision node 1 and because we are trying to maximize the expected profit, the best decision alternative at node 1 is d_3. Thus, the decision tree analysis leads to a recommendation of d_3, with an expected value of $14.2 million. Note that this recommendation is also obtained with the expected value approach in conjunction with the payoff table.

Computer software packages are available to help in constructing more complex decision trees. See Appendix 13.1.

Other decision problems may be substantially more complex than the PDC problem, but if a reasonable number of decision alternatives and states of nature are present, you can use the decision tree approach outlined here. First, draw a decision tree consisting of decision nodes, chance nodes, and branches that describe the sequential nature of the problem. If you use the expected value approach, the next step is to determine the probabilities for each of the states of nature and compute the expected value at each chance node. Then select the decision branch leading to the chance node with the best expected value. The decision alternative associated with this branch is the recommended decision.

FIGURE 13.3 PDC DECISION TREE WITH STATE-OF-NATURE BRANCH PROBABILITIES

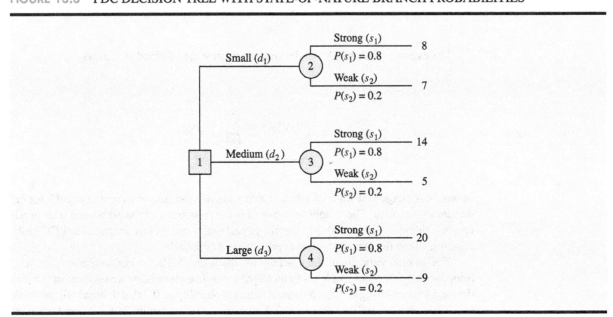

FIGURE 13.4 APPLYING THE EXPECTED VALUE APPROACH USING A DECISION TREE

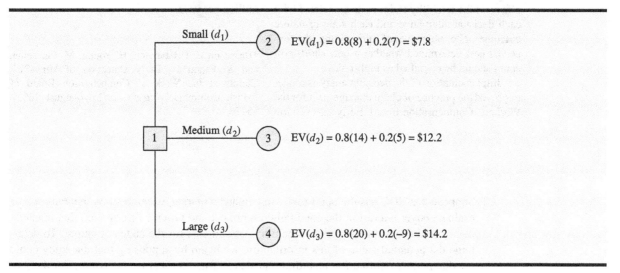

The Management Science in Action, Early Detection of High-Risk Worker Disability Claims, describes how the Workers' Compensation Board of British Columbia used a decision tree and expected cost to help determine whether a short-term disability claim should be considered a high-risk or a low-risk claim.

EARLY DETECTION OF HIGH-RISK WORKER DISABILITY CLAIMS*

The Workers' Compensation Board of British Columbia (WCB) helps workers and employers maintain safe workplaces and helps injured workers obtain disability income and return to work safely. The funds used to make the disability compensation payments are obtained from assessments levied on employers. In return, employers receive protection from lawsuits arising from work-related injuries. In recent years, the WCB spent more than $1 billion on worker compensation and rehabilitation.

A short-term disability claim occurs when a worker suffers an injury or illness that results in temporary absence from work. Whenever a worker fails to recover completely from a short-term disability, the claim is reclassified as a long-term disability claim and more expensive long-term benefits are paid.

The WCB wanted a systematic way to identify short-term disability claims that posed a high financial risk of being converted to the more expensive long-term disability claims. If a short-term disability claim could be classified as high risk early in the process, a WCB management team could intervene and monitor the claim and the recovery process more closely. As a result, WCB could improve the management of the high-risk claims and reduce the cost of any subsequent long-term disability claims.

The WCB used a decision analysis approach to classify each new short-term disability claim as being either a high-risk claim or a low-risk claim. A decision tree consisting of two decision nodes and two states-of-nature nodes was developed. The two decision alternatives were: (1) Classify the new short-term claim as high-risk and intervene. (2) Classify the new short-term claim as low-risk and do not intervene. The two states of nature were: (1) The short-term claim converts to a long-term claim. (2) The short-term claim does not convert to a long-term claim. The characteristics of each new short-term claim were used to determine the probabilities for the states of nature. The payoffs were the disability claim costs associated with each decision alternative and each state-of-nature outcome. The objective of minimizing the expected cost determined whether a new short-term claim should be classified as high-risk.

Implementation of the decision analysis model improved the practice of claim management for the Workers' Compensation Board. Early intervention

on the high-risk claims saved an estimated $4.7 million per year.

*Based on E. Urbanovich, E. Young, M. Puterman, and S. Fattedad, "Early Detection of High-Risk Claims at the Workers' Compensation Board of British Columbia," *Interfaces* (July/August 2003): 15–26.

Expected Value of Perfect Information

Suppose that PDC has the opportunity to conduct a market research study that would help evaluate buyer interest in the condominium project and provide information that management could use to improve the probability assessments for the states of nature. To determine the potential value of this information, we begin by supposing that the study could provide *perfect information* regarding the states of nature; that is, we assume for the moment that PDC could determine with certainty, prior to making a decision, which state of nature is going to occur. To make use of this perfect information, we will develop a decision strategy that PDC should follow once it knows which state of nature will occur. A decision strategy is simply a decision rule that specifies the decision alternative to be selected after new information becomes available.

To help determine the decision strategy for PDC, we reproduced PDC's payoff table as Table 13.6. Note that, if PDC knew for sure that state of nature s_1 would occur, the best decision alternative would be d_3, with a payoff of $20 million. Similarly, if PDC knew for sure that state of nature s_2 would occur, the best decision alternative would be d_1, with a payoff of $7 million. Thus, we can state PDC's optimal decision strategy when the perfect information becomes available as follows:

If s_1, select d_3 and receive a payoff of $20 million.

If s_2, select d_1 and receive a payoff of $7 million.

What is the expected value for this decision strategy? To compute the expected value with perfect information, we return to the original probabilities for the states of nature: $P(s_1) = 0.8$ and $P(s_2) = 0.2$. Thus, there is a 0.8 probability that the perfect information will indicate state of nature s_1 and the resulting decision alternative d_3 will provide a $20 million profit. Similarly, with a 0.2 probability for state of nature s_2, the optimal decision alternative d_1 will provide a $7 million profit. Thus, from equation (13.4), the expected value of the decision strategy that uses perfect information is

$$0.8(20) + 0.2(7) = 17.4$$

We refer to the expected value of $17.4 million as the *expected value with perfect information* (EVwPI).

Earlier in this section we showed that the recommended decision using the expected value approach is decision alternative d_3, with an expected value of $14.2 million. Because this decision recommendation and expected value computation were made without the benefit of perfect information, $14.2 million is referred to as the *expected value without perfect information* (EVwoPI).

TABLE 13.6 PAYOFF TABLE FOR THE PDC CONDOMINIUM PROJECT ($ MILLIONS)

	State of Nature	
Decision Alternative	Strong Demand s_1	Weak Demand s_2
Small complex, d_1	8	7
Medium complex, d_2	14	5
Large complex, d_3	20	−9

It would be worth $3.2 million for PDC to learn the level of market acceptance before selecting a decision alternative.

The expected value with perfect information is $17.4 million, and the expected value without perfect information is $14.2; therefore, the expected value of the perfect information (EVPI) is $17.4 − $14.2 = $3.2 million. In other words, $3.2 million represents the additional expected value that can be obtained if perfect information were available about the states of nature.

Generally speaking, a market research study will not provide "perfect" information; however, if the market research study is a good one, the information gathered might be worth a sizable portion of the $3.2 million. Given the EVPI of $3.2 million, PDC might seriously consider a market survey as a way to obtain more information about the states of nature.

In general, the **expected value of perfect information (EVPI)** is computed as follows:

$$EVPI = |EVwPI - EVwoPI| \qquad (13.5)$$

where

EVPI = expected value of perfect information

EVwPI = expected value *with* perfect information about the states of nature

EVwoPI = expected value *without* perfect information about the states of nature

For practice in determining the expected value of perfect information, try Problem 14.

Note the role of the absolute value in equation (13.5). For minimization problems the expected value with perfect information is always less than or equal to the expected value without perfect information. In this case, EVPI is the magnitude of the difference between EVwPI and EVwoPI, or the absolute value of the difference as shown in equation (13.5).

NOTES AND COMMENTS

We restate the *opportunity loss,* or *regret,* table for the PDC problem (see Table 13.4) as follows.

	State of Nature	
	Strong Demand	Weak Demand
Decision Alternative	s_1	s_2
Small complex, d_1	12	0
Medium complex, d_2	6	2
Large complex, d_3	0	16

Using $P(s_1)$, $P(s_2)$, and the opportunity loss values, we can compute the *expected opportunity loss* (EOL) for each decision alternative. With $P(s_1) = 0.8$ and $P(s_2) = 0.2$, the expected opportunity loss for each of the three decision alternatives is

$$EOL(d_1) = 0.8(12) + 0.2(0) = 9.6$$
$$EOL(d_2) = 0.8(6) + 0.2(2) = 5.2$$
$$EOL(d_3) = 0.8(0) + 0.2(16) = 3.2$$

Regardless of whether the decision analysis involves maximization or minimization, the *minimum* expected opportunity loss always provides the best decision alternative. Thus, with EOL(d_3) = 3.2, d_3 is the recommended decision. In addition, the minimum expected opportunity loss always is *equal to* *the expected value of perfect information.* That is, EOL(best decision) = EVPI; for the PDC problem, this value is $3.2 million.

13.4 RISK ANALYSIS AND SENSITIVITY ANALYSIS

Risk analysis helps the decision maker recognize the difference between the expected value of a decision alternative and the payoff that may actually occur. **Sensitivity analysis** also helps the decision maker by describing how changes in the state-of-nature probabilities and/or changes in the payoffs affect the recommended decision alternative.

Risk Analysis

A decision alternative and a state of nature combine to generate the payoff associated with a decision. The **risk profile** for a decision alternative shows the possible payoffs along with their associated probabilities.

Let us demonstrate risk analysis and the construction of a risk profile by returning to the PDC condominium construction project. Using the expected value approach, we identified the large condominium complex (d_3) as the best decision alternative. The expected value of $14.2 million for d_3 is based on a 0.8 probability of obtaining a $20 million profit and a 0.2 probability of obtaining a $9 million loss. The 0.8 probability for the $20 million payoff and the 0.2 probability for the $-$9 million payoff provide the risk profile for the large complex decision alternative. This risk profile is shown graphically in Figure 13.5.

Sometimes a review of the risk profile associated with an optimal decision alternative may cause the decision maker to choose another decision alternative even though the expected value of the other decision alternative is not as good. For example, the risk profile for the medium complex decision alternative (d_2) shows a 0.8 probability for a $14 million

FIGURE 13.5 RISK PROFILE FOR THE LARGE COMPLEX DECISION ALTERNATIVE FOR THE PDC CONDOMINIUM PROJECT

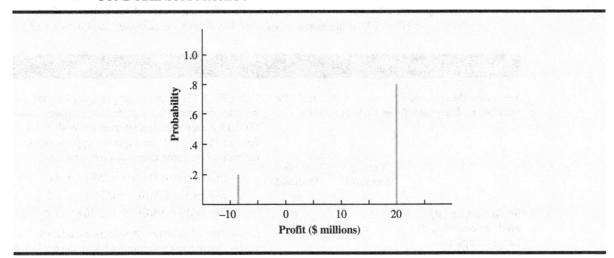

payoff and a 0.2 probability for a $5 million payoff. Because no probability of a loss is associated with decision alternative d_2, the medium complex decision alternative would be judged less risky than the large complex decision alternative. As a result, a decision maker might prefer the less-risky medium complex decision alternative even though it has an expected value of $2 million less than the large complex decision alternative.

Sensitivity Analysis

Sensitivity analysis can be used to determine how changes in the probabilities for the states of nature or changes in the payoffs affect the recommended decision alternative. In many cases, the probabilities for the states of nature and the payoffs are based on subjective assessments. Sensitivity analysis helps the decision maker understand which of these inputs are critical to the choice of the best decision alternative. If a small change in the value of one of the inputs causes a change in the recommended decision alternative, the solution to the decision analysis problem is sensitive to that particular input. Extra effort and care should be taken to make sure the input value is as accurate as possible. On the other hand, if a modest to large change in the value of one of the inputs does not cause a change in the recommended decision alternative, the solution to the decision analysis problem is not sensitive to that particular input. No extra time or effort would be needed to refine the estimated input value.

One approach to sensitivity analysis is to select different values for the probabilities of the states of nature and the payoffs and then re-solve the decision analysis problem. If the recommended decision alternative changes, we know that the solution is sensitive to the changes made. For example, suppose that in the PDC problem the probability for a strong demand is revised to 0.2 and the probability for a weak demand is revised to 0.8. Would the recommended decision alternative change? Using $P(s_1) = 0.2$, $P(s_2) = 0.8$, and equation (13.4), the revised expected values for the three decision alternatives are

$$
\begin{aligned}
EV(d_1) &= 0.2(8) & + 0.8(7) & = & 7.2 \\
EV(d_2) &= 0.2(14) & + 0.8(5) & = & 6.8 \\
EV(d_3) &= 0.2(20) & + 0.8(-9) & = & -3.2
\end{aligned}
$$

With these probability assessments the recommended decision alternative is to construct a small condominium complex (d_1), with an expected value of $7.2 million. The probability of strong demand is only 0.2, so constructing the large condominium complex (d_3) is the least preferred alternative, with an expected value of −$3.2 million (a loss).

Computer software packages for decision analysis make it easy to calculate these revised scenarios.

Thus, when the probability of strong demand is large, PDC should build the large complex; when the probability of strong demand is small, PDC should build the small complex. Obviously, we could continue to modify the probabilities of the states of nature and learn even more about how changes in the probabilities affect the recommended decision alternative. The drawback to this approach is the numerous calculations required to evaluate the effect of several possible changes in the state-of-nature probabilities.

For the special case of two states of nature, a graphical procedure can be used to determine how changes for the probabilities of the states of nature affect the recommended decision alternative. To demonstrate this procedure, we let p denote the probability of state of nature s_1; that is, $P(s_1) = p$. With only two states of nature in the PDC problem, the probability of state of nature s_2 is

$$
P(s_2) = 1 - P(s_1) = 1 - p
$$

Using equation (13.4) and the payoff values in Table 13.1, we determine the expected value for decision alternative d_1 as follows:

$$
\begin{aligned}
\text{EV}(d_1) &= P(s_1)(8) + P(s_2)(7) \\
&= p(8) + (1 - p)(7) \\
&= 8p + 7 - 7p = p + 7
\end{aligned}
\tag{13.6}
$$

Repeating the expected value computations for decision alternatives d_2 and d_3, we obtain expressions for the expected value of each decision alternative as a function of p:

$$
\text{EV}(d_2) = 9p + 5
\tag{13.7}
$$

$$
\text{EV}(d_3) = 29p - 9
\tag{13.8}
$$

Thus, we have developed three equations that show the expected value of the three decision alternatives as a function of the probability of state of nature s_1.

We continue by developing a graph with values of p on the horizontal axis and the associated EVs on the vertical axis. Because equations (13.6), (13.7), and (13.8) are linear equations, the graph of each equation is a straight line. For each equation, we can obtain the line by identifying two points that satisfy the equation and drawing a line through the points. For instance, if we let $p = 0$ in equation (13.6), $\text{EV}(d_1) = 7$. Then, letting $p = 1$, $\text{EV}(d_1) = 8$. Connecting these two points, $(0, 7)$ and $(1, 8)$, provides the line labeled $\text{EV}(d_1)$ in Figure 13.6. Similarly, we obtain the lines labeled $\text{EV}(d_2)$ and $\text{EV}(d_3)$; these lines are the graphs of equations (13.7) and (13.8), respectively.

Figure 13.6 shows how the recommended decision changes as p, the probability of the strong demand state of nature (s_1), changes. Note that for small values of p, decision alternative d_1 (small complex) provides the largest expected value and is thus the recommended decision. When the value of p increases to a certain point, decision alternative d_2 (medium complex) provides the largest expected value and is the recommended decision. Finally, for large values of p, decision alternative d_3 (large complex) becomes the recommended decision.

The value of p for which the expected values of d_1 and d_2 are equal is the value of p corresponding to the intersection of the $\text{EV}(d_1)$ and the $\text{EV}(d_2)$ lines. To determine this value, we set $\text{EV}(d_1) = \text{EV}(d_2)$ and solve for the value of p:

$$
\begin{aligned}
p + 7 &= 9p + 5 \\
8p &= 2 \\
p &= \frac{2}{8} = 0.25
\end{aligned}
$$

Graphical sensitivity analysis shows how changes in the probabilities for the states of nature affect the recommended decision alternative. Try Problem 8.

Hence, when $p = 0.25$, decision alternatives d_1 and d_2 provide the same expected value. Repeating this calculation for the value of p corresponding to the intersection of the $\text{EV}(d_2)$ and $\text{EV}(d_3)$ lines, we obtain $p = 0.70$.

Using Figure 13.6, we can conclude that decision alternative d_1 provides the largest expected value for $p \leq 0.25$, decision alternative d_2 provides the largest expected value for

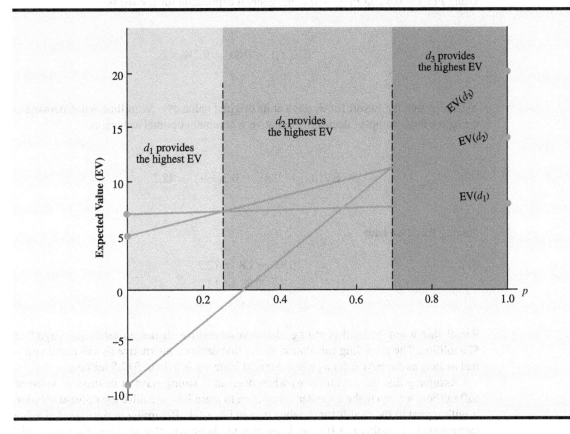

$0.25 \leq p \leq 0.70$, and decision alternative d_3 provides the largest expected value for $p \geq 0.70$. Because p is the probability of state of nature s_1 and $(1 - p)$ is the probability of state of nature s_2, we now have the sensitivity analysis information that tells us how changes in the state-of-nature probabilities affect the recommended decision alternative.

Sensitivity analysis calculations can also be made for the values of the payoffs. In the original PDC problem, the expected values for the three decision alternatives were as follows: $EV(d_1) = 7.8$, $EV(d_2) = 12.2$, and $EV(d_3) = 14.2$. Decision alternative d_3 (large complex) was recommended. Note that decision alternative d_2 with $EV(d_2) = 12.2$ was the second best decision alternative. Decision alternative d_3 will remain the optimal decision alternative as long as $EV(d_3)$ is greater than or equal to the expected value of the second best decision alternative. Thus, decision alternative d_3 will remain the optimal decision alternative as long as

$$EV(d_3) \geq 12.2 \qquad\qquad (13.9)$$

Let

S = the payoff of decision alternative d_3 when demand is strong

W = the payoff of decision alternative d_3 when demand is weak

Using $P(s_1) = 0.8$ and $P(s_2) = 0.2$, the general expression for EV(d_3) is

$$EV(d_3) = 0.8S + 0.2W \qquad (13.10)$$

Assuming that the payoff for d_3 stays at its original value of $-\$9$ million when demand is weak, the large complex decision alternative will remain optimal as long as

$$EV(d_3) = 0.8S + 0.2(-9) \geq 12.2 \qquad (13.11)$$

Solving for S, we have

$$0.8S - 1.8 \geq 12.2$$
$$0.8S \geq 14$$
$$S \geq 17.5$$

Recall that when demand is strong, decision alternative d_3 has an estimated payoff of $20 million. The preceding calculation shows that decision alternative d_3 will remain optimal as long as the payoff for d_3 when demand is strong is at least $17.5 million.

Assuming that the payoff for d_3 when demand is strong stays at its original value of $20 million, we can make a similar calculation to learn how sensitive the optimal solution is with regard to the payoff for d_3 when demand is weak. Returning to the expected value calculation of equation (13.10), we know that the large complex decision alternative will remain optimal as long as

$$EV(d_3) = 0.8(20) + 0.2W \geq 12.2 \qquad (13.12)$$

Solving for W, we have

$$16 + 0.2W \geq 12.2$$
$$0.2W \geq -3.8$$
$$W \geq -19$$

Recall that when demand is weak, decision alternative d_3 has an estimated payoff of $-\$9$ million. The preceding calculation shows that decision alternative d_3 will remain optimal as long as the payoff for d_3 when demand is weak is at least $-\$19$ million.

Based on this sensitivity analysis, we conclude that the payoffs for the large complex decision alternative (d_3) could vary considerably, and d_3 would remain the recommended decision alternative. Thus, we conclude that the optimal solution for the PDC decision problem is not particularly sensitive to the payoffs for the large complex decision alternative. We note, however, that this sensitivity analysis has been conducted based on only one change at a time. That is, only one payoff was changed and the probabilities for the states

Sensitivity analysis can assist management in deciding whether more time and effort should be spent obtaining better estimates of payoffs and probabilities.

of nature remained $P(s_1) = 0.8$ and $P(s_2) = 0.2$. Note that similar sensitivity analysis calculations can be made for the payoffs associated with the small complex decision alternative d_1 and the medium complex decision alternative d_2. However, in these cases, decision alternative d_3 remains optimal only if the changes in the payoffs for decision alternatives d_1 and d_2 meet the requirements that $EV(d_1) \leq 14.2$ and $EV(d_2) \leq 14.2$.

NOTES AND COMMENTS

1. Some decision analysis software automatically provides the risk profiles for the optimal decision alternative. These packages also allow the user to obtain the risk profiles for other decision alternatives. After comparing the risk profiles, a decision maker may decide to select a decision alternative with a good risk profile even though the expected value of the decision alternative is not as good as the optimal decision alternative.
2. A *tornado diagram,* a graphical display, is particularly helpful when several inputs combine

to determine the value of the optimal solution. By varying each input over its range of values, we obtain information about how each input affects the value of the optimal solution. To display this information, a bar is constructed for the input with the width of the bar showing how the input affects the value of the optimal solution. The widest bar corresponds to the input that is most sensitive. The bars are arranged in a graph with the widest bar at the top, resulting in a graph that has the appearance of a tornado.

13.5 DECISION ANALYSIS WITH SAMPLE INFORMATION

In applying the expected value approach, we showed how probability information about the states of nature affects the expected value calculations and thus the decision recommendation. Frequently, decision makers have preliminary or **prior probability** assessments for the states of nature that are the best probability values available at that time. However, to make the best possible decision, the decision maker may want to seek additional information about the states of nature. This new information can be used to revise or update the prior probabilities so that the final decision is based on more accurate probabilities for the states of nature. Most often, additional information is obtained through experiments designed to provide **sample information** about the states of nature. Raw material sampling, product testing, and market research studies are examples of experiments (or studies) that may enable management to revise or update the state-of-nature probabilities. These revised probabilities are called **posterior probabilities.**

Let us return to the PDC problem and assume that management is considering a six-month market research study designed to learn more about potential market acceptance of the PDC condominium project. Management anticipates that the market research study will provide one of the following two results:

1. Favorable report: A significant number of the individuals contacted express interest in purchasing a PDC condominium.
2. Unfavorable report: Very few of the individuals contacted express interest in purchasing a PDC condominium.

Influence Diagram

By introducing the possibility of conducting a market research study, the PDC problem becomes more complex. The influence diagram for the expanded PDC problem is shown in Figure 13.7. Note that the two decision nodes correspond to the research study and the

FIGURE 13.7   INFLUENCE DIAGRAM FOR THE PDC PROBLEM WITH SAMPLE INFORMATION

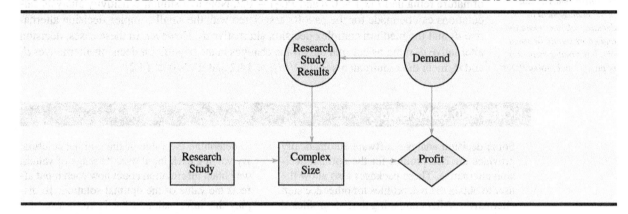

complex-size decisions. The two chance nodes correspond to the research study results and demand for the condominiums. Finally, the consequence node is the profit. From the arcs of the influence diagram, we see that demand influences both the research study results and profit. Although demand is currently unknown to PDC, some level of demand for the condominiums already exists in the Pittsburgh area. If existing demand is strong, the research study is likely to find a significant number of individuals who express an interest in purchasing a condominium. However, if the existing demand is weak, the research study is more likely to find a significant number of individuals who express little interest in purchasing a condominium. In this sense, existing demand for the condominiums will influence the research study results, and clearly, demand will have an influence upon PDC's profit.

The arc from the research study decision node to the complex-size decision node indicates that the research study decision precedes the complex-size decision. No arc spans from the research study decision node to the research study results node, because the decision to conduct the research study does not actually influence the research study results. The decision to conduct the research study makes the research study results available, but it does not influence the results of the research study. Finally, the complex-size node and the demand node both influence profit. Note that if a stated cost to conduct the research study were given, the decision to conduct the research study would also influence profit. In such a case, we would need to add an arc from the research study decision node to the profit node to show the influence that the research study cost would have on profit.

Decision Tree

The decision tree for the PDC problem with sample information shows the logical sequence for the decisions and the chance events in Figure 13.8.

First, PDC's management must decide whether the market research should be conducted. If it is conducted, PDC's management must be prepared to make a decision about the size of the condominium project if the market research report is favorable and, possibly, a different decision about the size of the condominium project if the market research report is unfavorable. In Figure 13.8, the squares are decision nodes and the circles are chance nodes. At each decision node, the branch of the tree that is taken is based on the decision made. At each chance node, the branch of the tree that is taken is based on probability or chance. For example, decision node 1 shows that PDC must first make the decision

870

FIGURE 13.8 THE PDC DECISION TREE INCLUDING THE MARKET RESEARCH STUDY

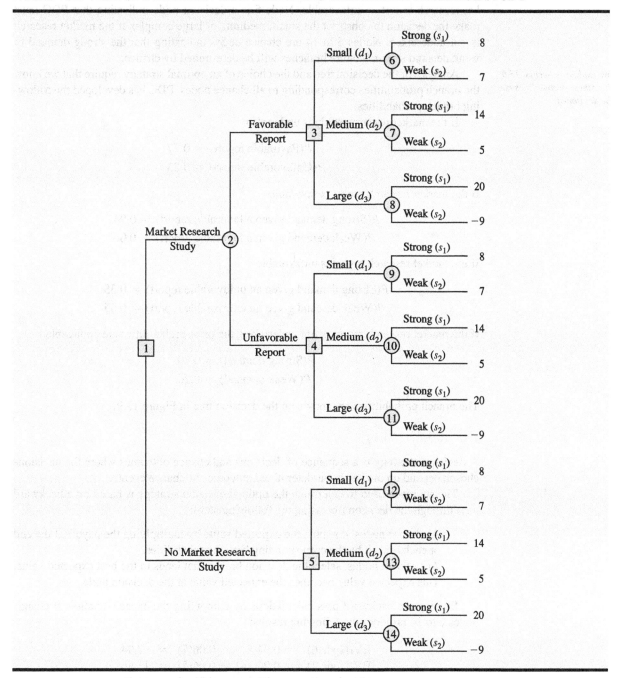

of whether to conduct the market research study. If the market research study is undertaken, chance node 2 indicates that both the favorable report branch and the unfavorable report branch are not under PDC's control and will be determined by chance. Node 3 is a decision node, indicating that PDC must make the decision to construct the small, medium, or large complex if the market research report is favorable. Node 4 is a decision node showing that

PDC must make the decision to construct the small, medium, or large complex if the market research report is unfavorable. Node 5 is a decision node indicating that PDC must make the decision to construct the small, medium, or large complex if the market research is not undertaken. Nodes 6 to 14 are chance nodes indicating that the strong demand or weak demand state-of-nature branches will be determined by chance.

Analysis of the decision tree and the choice of an optimal strategy require that we know the branch probabilities corresponding to all chance nodes. PDC has developed the following branch probabilities:

We explain in Section 13.6 how these probabilities can be developed.

If the market research study is undertaken

$$P(\text{Favorable report}) = 0.77$$
$$P(\text{Unfavorable report}) = 0.23$$

If the market research report is favorable

$$P(\text{Strong demand given a favorable report}) = 0.94$$
$$P(\text{Weak demand given a favorable report}) = 0.06$$

If the market research report is unfavorable

$$P(\text{Strong demand given an unfavorable report}) = 0.35$$
$$P(\text{Weak demand given an unfavorable report}) = 0.65$$

If the market research report is not undertaken, the prior probabilities are applicable.

$$P(\text{Strong demand}) = 0.80$$
$$P(\text{Weak demand}) = 0.20$$

The branch probabilities are shown on the decision tree in Figure 13.9.

Decision Strategy

A **decision strategy** is a sequence of decisions and chance outcomes where the decisions chosen depend on the yet-to-be-determined outcomes of chance events.

The approach used to determine the optimal decision strategy is based on a backward pass through the decision tree using the following steps:

1. At chance nodes, compute the expected value by multiplying the payoff at the end of each branch by the corresponding branch probabilities.
2. At decision nodes, select the decision branch that leads to the best expected value. This expected value becomes the expected value at the decision node.

Starting the backward pass calculations by computing the expected values at chance nodes 6 to 14 provides the following results:

$$
\begin{aligned}
\text{EV(Node 6)} &= 0.94(8) + 0.06(7) = 7.94 \\
\text{EV(Node 7)} &= 0.94(14) + 0.06(5) = 13.46 \\
\text{EV(Node 8)} &= 0.94(20) + 0.06(-9) = 18.26 \\
\text{EV(Node 9)} &= 0.35(8) + 0.65(7) = 7.35 \\
\text{EV(Node 10)} &= 0.35(14) + 0.65(5) = 8.15 \\
\text{EV(Node 11)} &= 0.35(20) + 0.65(-9) = 1.15 \\
\text{EV(Node 12)} &= 0.80(8) + 0.20(7) = 7.80 \\
\text{EV(Node 13)} &= 0.80(14) + 0.20(5) = 12.20 \\
\text{EV(Node 14)} &= 0.80(20) + 0.20(-9) = 14.20
\end{aligned}
$$

FIGURE 13.9   THE PDC DECISION TREE WITH BRANCH PROBABILITIES

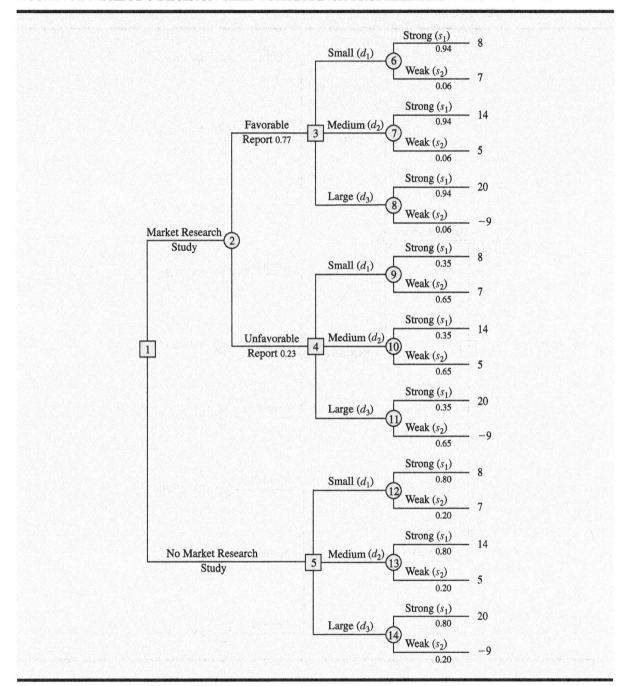

Figure 13.10 shows the reduced decision tree after computing expected values at these chance nodes.

Next, move to decision nodes 3, 4, and 5. For each of these nodes, we select the decision alternative branch that leads to the best expected value. For example, at node 3 we have the choice of the small complex branch with EV(Node 6) = 7.94, the medium complex branch with EV(Node 7) = 13.46, and the large complex branch with EV(Node 8) = 18.26. Thus,

FIGURE 13.10   PDC DECISION TREE AFTER COMPUTING EXPECTED VALUES AT CHANCE
NODES 6 TO 14

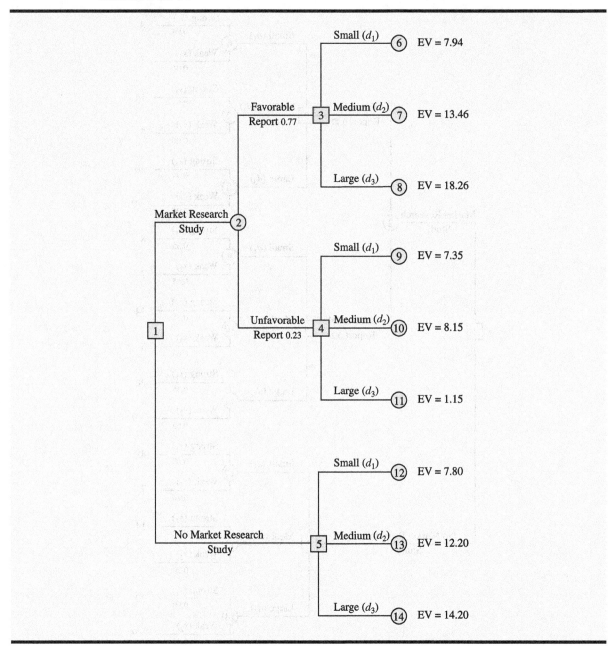

we select the large complex decision alternative branch and the expected value at node 3
becomes EV(Node 3) = 18.26.

For node 4, we select the best expected value from nodes 9, 10, and 11. The best decision alternative is the medium complex branch that provides EV(Node 4) = 8.15. For node
5, we select the best expected value from nodes 12, 13, and 14. The best decision alternative is the large complex branch that provides EV(Node 5) = 14.20. Figure 13.11 shows the
reduced decision tree after choosing the best decisions at nodes 3, 4, and 5.

FIGURE 13.11   PDC DECISION TREE AFTER CHOOSING BEST DECISIONS AT NODES 3, 4, AND 5

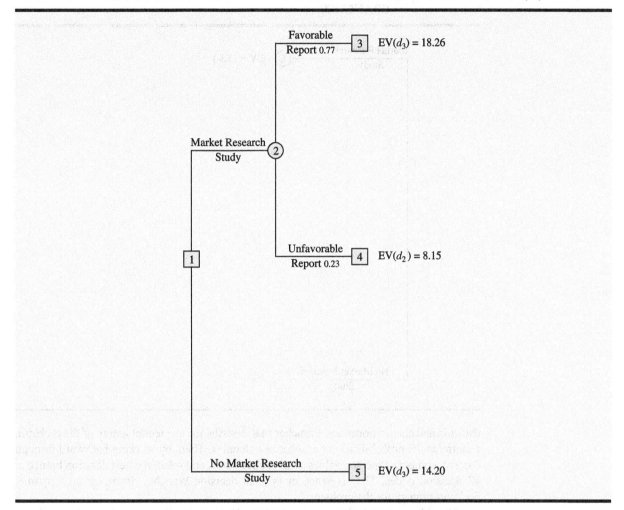

The expected value at chance node 2 can now be computed as follows:

$$EV(\text{Node } 2) = 0.77EV(\text{Node } 3) + 0.23EV(\text{Node } 4)$$
$$= 0.77(18.26) + 0.23(8.15) = 15.93$$

This calculation reduces the decision tree to one involving only the two decision branches from node 1 (see Figure 13.12).

Finally, the decision can be made at decision node 1 by selecting the best expected values from nodes 2 and 5. This action leads to the decision alternative to conduct the market research study, which provides an overall expected value of 15.93.

The optimal decision for PDC is to conduct the market research study and then carry out the following decision strategy:

If the market research is favorable, construct the large condominium complex.

If the market research is unfavorable, construct the medium condominium complex.

Problem 16 will test your ability to develop an optimal decision strategy.

The analysis of the PDC decision tree describes the methods that can be used to analyze more complex sequential decision problems. First, draw a decision tree consisting of

FIGURE 13.12 PDC DECISION TREE REDUCED TO TWO DECISION BRANCHES

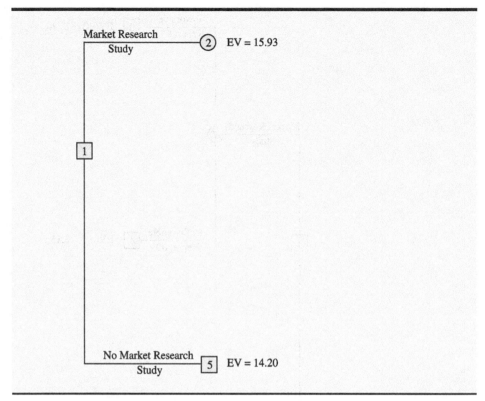

decision and chance nodes and branches that describe the sequential nature of the problem. Determine the probabilities for all chance outcomes. Then, by working backward through the tree, compute expected values at all chance nodes and select the best decision branch at all decision nodes. The sequence of optimal decision branches determines the optimal decision strategy for the problem.

The Management Science in Action, New Drug Decision Analysis at Bayer Pharmaceuticals, describes how an extension of the decision analysis principles presented in this section enabled Bayer to make decisions about the development and marketing of a new drug.

Risk Profile

Figure 13.13 provides a reduced decision tree showing only the sequence of decision alternatives and chance events for the PDC optimal decision strategy. By implementing the optimal decision strategy, PDC will obtain one of the four payoffs shown at the terminal branches of the decision tree. Recall that a risk profile shows the possible payoffs with their associated probabilities. Thus, in order to construct a risk profile for the optimal decision strategy, we will need to compute the probability for each of the four payoffs.

Note that each payoff results from a sequence of branches leading from node 1 to the payoff. For instance, the payoff of $20 million is obtained by following the upper branch from node 1, the upper branch from node 2, the lower branch from node 3, and the upper branch from node 8. The probability of following that sequence of branches can be found by multiplying the probabilities for the branches from the chance nodes in the sequence.

FIGURE 13.13   PDC DECISION TREE SHOWING ONLY BRANCHES ASSOCIATED WITH OPTIMAL
DECISION STRATEGY

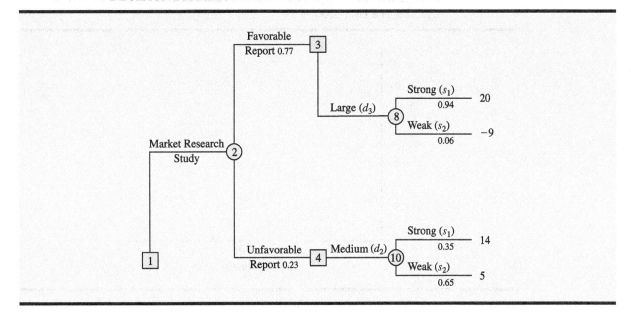

Thus, the probability of the $20 million payoff is (0.77)(0.94) = 0.72. Similarly, the probabilities for each of the other payoffs are obtained by multiplying the probabilities for the branches from the chance nodes leading to the payoffs. Doing so, we find the probability of the –$9 million payoff is (0.77)(0.06) = 0.05; the probability of the $14 million payoff is (0.23)(0.35) = 0.08; and the probability of the $5 million payoff is (0.23)(0.65) = 0.15. The following table showing the probability distribution for the payoffs for the PDC optimal decision strategy is the tabular representation of the risk profile for the optimal decision strategy.

Payoff ($ millions)	Probability
−9	0.05
5	0.15
14	0.08
20	0.72
	1.00

Figure 13.14 provides a graphical representation of the risk profile. Comparing Figures 13.5 and 13.14, we see that the PDC risk profile is changed by the strategy to conduct the market research study. In fact, the use of the market research study lowered the probability of the $9 million loss from 0.20 to 0.05. PDC's management would most likely view that change as a significant reduction in the risk associated with the condominium project.

FIGURE 13.14 RISK PROFILE FOR PDC CONDOMINIUM PROJECT WITH SAMPLE INFORMATION SHOWING PAYOFFS ASSOCIATED WITH OPTIMAL DECISION STRATEGY

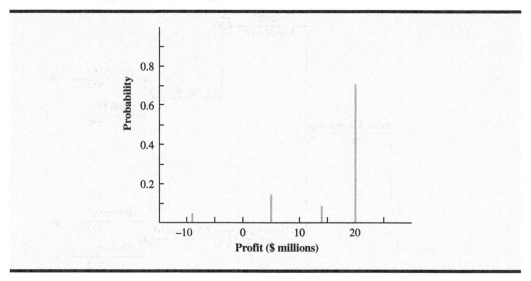

NEW DRUG DECISION ANALYSIS AT BAYER PHARMACEUTICALS*

Drug development in the United States requires substantial investment and is very risky. It takes nearly 15 years to research and develop a new drug. The Bayer Biological Products (BP) group used decision analysis to evaluate the potential for a new blood clot–busting drug. An influence diagram was used to describe the complex structure of the decision analysis process. Six key yes-or-no decision nodes were identified: (1) begin preclinical development; (2) begin testing in humans; (3) continue development into phase 3; (4) continue development into phase 4; (5) file a license application with the FDA; and (6) launch the new drug into the marketplace. More than 50 chance nodes appeared in the influence diagram. The chance nodes showed how uncertainties—related to factors such as direct labor costs, process development costs, market share, tax rate, and pricing—affected the outcome. Net present value provided the consequence and the decision-making criterion.

Probability assessments were made concerning both the technical risk and market risk at each stage of the process. The resulting sequential decision tree had 1955 possible paths that led to different net present value outcomes. Cost inputs, judgments of potential outcomes, and the assignment of probabilities helped evaluate the project's potential contribution. Sensitivity analysis was used to identify key variables that would require special attention by the project team and management during the drug development process. Application of decision analysis principles allowed Bayer to make good decisions about how to develop and market the new drug.

*Based on Jeffrey S. Stonebraker, "How Bayer Makes Decisions to Develop New Drugs," *Interfaces,* no. 6 (November/December 2002): 77–90.

The EVSI = $1.73 million suggests PDC should be willing to pay up to $1.73 million to conduct the market research study.

Expected Value of Sample Information

In the PDC problem, the market research study is the sample information used to determine the optimal decision strategy. The expected value associated with the market research study is $15.93. In Section 13.3 we showed that the best expected value if the market research study is *not* undertaken is $14.20. Thus, we can conclude that the difference, $15.93 − $14.20 = $1.73, is the **expected value of sample information (EVSI)**. In other words, conducting the market research study adds $1.73 million to the PDC expected value. In general, the expected value of sample information is as follows:

$$EVSI = |EVwSI − EVwoSI| \qquad (13.13)$$

where

$\quad$ EVSI = expected value of sample information

$\quad$ EVwSI = expected value *with* sample information about the states of nature

$\quad$ EVwoSI = expected value *without* sample information about the states of nature

Note the role of the absolute value in equation (13.13). For minimization problems the expected value with sample information is always less than or equal to the expected value without sample information. In this case, EVSI is the magnitude of the difference between EVwSI and EVwoSI; thus, by taking the absolute value of the difference as shown in equation (13.13), we can handle both the maximization and minimization cases with one equation.

Efficiency of Sample Information

In Section 13.3 we showed that the expected value of perfect information (EVPI) for the PDC problem is $3.2 million. We never anticipated that the market research report would obtain perfect information, but we can use an **efficiency** measure to express the value of the market research information. With perfect information having an efficiency rating of 100%, the efficiency rating E for sample information is computed as follows:

$$E = \frac{EVSI}{EVPI} \times 100 \qquad (13.14)$$

For the PDC problem,

$$E = \frac{1.73}{3.2} \times 100 = 54.1\%$$

In other words, the information from the market research study is 54.1% as efficient as perfect information.

Low efficiency ratings for sample information might lead the decision maker to look for other types of information. However, high efficiency ratings indicate that the sample information is almost as good as perfect information and that additional sources of information would not yield significantly better results.

13.6 COMPUTING BRANCH PROBABILITIES

In Section 13.5 the branch probabilities for the PDC decision tree chance nodes were specified in the problem description. No computations were required to determine these probabilities. In this section we show how **Bayes' theorem** can be used to compute branch probabilities for decision trees.

879

FIGURE 13.15   THE PDC DECISION TREE

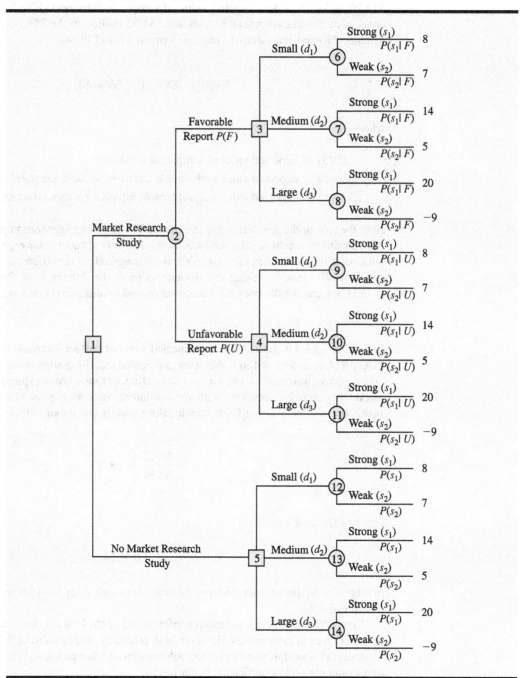

The PDC decision tree is shown again in Figure 13.15. Let

F = Favorable market research report

U = Unfavorable market research report

s_1 = Strong demand (state of nature 1)

s_2 = Weak demand (state of nature 2)

At chance node 2, we need to know the branch probabilities $P(F)$ and $P(U)$. At chance nodes 6, 7, and 8, we need to know the branch probabilities $P(s_1 \mid F)$, the probability of state of nature 1 given a favorable market research report, and $P(s_2 \mid F)$, the probability of state of nature 2 given a favorable market research report. $P(s_1 \mid F)$ and $P(s_2 \mid F)$ are referred to as *posterior probabilities* because they are conditional probabilities based on the outcome of the sample information. At chance nodes 9, 10, and 11, we need to know the branch probabilities $P(s_1 \mid U)$ and $P(s_2 \mid U)$; note that these are also posterior probabilities, denoting the probabilities of the two states of nature *given* that the market research report is unfavorable. Finally, at chance nodes 12, 13, and 14, we need the probabilities for the states of nature, $P(s_1)$ and $P(s_2)$, if the market research study is not undertaken.

In making the probability computations, we need to know PDC's assessment of the probabilities for the two states of nature, $P(s_1)$ and $P(s_2)$, which are the prior probabilities as discussed earlier. In addition, we must know the **conditional probability** of the market research outcomes (the sample information) *given* each state of nature. For example, we need to know the conditional probability of a favorable market research report given that the state of nature is strong demand for the PDC project; note that this conditional probability of F given state of nature s_1 is written $P(F \mid s_1)$. To carry out the probability calculations, we will need conditional probabilities for all sample outcomes given all states of nature, that is, $P(F \mid s_1)$, $P(F \mid s_2)$, $P(U \mid s_1)$, and $P(U \mid s_2)$. In the PDC problem we assume that the following assessments are available for these conditional probabilities:

	Market Research	
State of Nature	Favorable, F	Unfavorable, U
Strong demand, s_1	$P(F \mid s_1) = 0.90$	$P(U \mid s_1) = 0.10$
Weak demand, s_2	$P(F \mid s_2) = 0.25$	$P(U \mid s_2) = 0.75$

Note that the preceding probability assessments provide a reasonable degree of confidence in the market research study. If the true state of nature is s_1, the probability of a favorable market research report is 0.90, and the probability of an unfavorable market research report is 0.10. If the true state of nature is s_2, the probability of a favorable market research report is 0.25, and the probability of an unfavorable market research report is 0.75. The reason for a 0.25 probability of a potentially misleading favorable market research report for state of nature s_2 is that when some potential buyers first hear about the new condominium project, their enthusiasm may lead them to overstate their real interest in it. A potential buyer's initial favorable response can change quickly to a "no thank you" when later faced with the reality of signing a purchase contract and making a down payment.

In the following discussion we present a tabular approach as a convenient method for carrying out the probability computations. The computations for the PDC problem based on a favorable market research report (F) are summarized in Table 13.7. The steps used to develop this table are as follows:

Step 1. In column 1 enter the states of nature. In column 2 enter the *prior probabilities* for the states of nature. In column 3 enter the *conditional probabilities* of a favorable market research report (F) given each state of nature.

Step 2. In column 4 compute the **joint probabilities** by multiplying the prior probability values in column 2 by the corresponding conditional probability values in column 3.

TABLE 13.7 BRANCH PROBABILITIES FOR THE PDC CONDOMINIUM PROJECT BASED ON A FAVORABLE MARKET RESEARCH REPORT

States of Nature s_j	Prior Probabilities $P(s_j)$	Conditional Probabilities $P(F \mid s_j)$	Joint Probabilities $P(F > s_j)$	Posterior Probabilities $P(s_j \mid F)$
s_1	0.8	0.90	0.72	0.94
s_2	0.2	0.25	0.05	0.06
	1.0		$P(F) = 0.77$	1.00

Step 3. Sum the joint probabilities in column 4 to obtain the probability of a favorable market research report, $P(F)$.

Step 4. Divide each joint probability in column 4 by $P(F) = 0.77$ to obtain the revised or *posterior probabilities*, $P(s_1 \mid F)$ and $P(s_2 \mid F)$.

Table 13.7 shows that the probability of obtaining a favorable market research report is $P(F) = 0.77$. In addition, $P(s_1 \mid F) = 0.94$ and $P(s_2 \mid F) = 0.06$. In particular, note that a favorable market research report will prompt a revised or posterior probability of 0.94 that the market demand of the condominium will be strong, s_1.

The tabular probability computation procedure must be repeated for each possible sample information outcome. Thus, Table 13.8 shows the computations of the branch probabilities of the PDC problem based on an unfavorable market research report. Note that the probability of obtaining an unfavorable market research report is $P(U) = 0.23$. If an unfavorable report is obtained, the posterior probability of a strong market demand, s_1, is 0.35 and of a weak market demand, s_2, is 0.65. The branch probabilities from Tables 13.7 and 13.8 were shown on the PDC decision tree in Figure 13.9.

Problem 23 asks you to compute the posterior probabilities.

The discussion in this section shows an underlying relationship between the probabilities on the various branches in a decision tree. To assume different prior probabilities, $P(s_1)$ and $P(s_2)$, without determining how these changes would alter $P(F)$ and $P(U)$, as well as the posterior probabilities $P(s_1 \mid F)$, $P(s_2 \mid F)$, $P(s_1 \mid U)$, and $P(s_2 \mid U)$, would be inappropriate.

The Management Science in Action, Medical Screening Test at Duke University Medical Center, shows how posterior probability information and decision analysis helped management understand the risks and costs associated with a new screening procedure.

TABLE 13.8 BRANCH PROBABILITIES FOR THE PDC CONDOMINIUM PROJECT BASED ON AN UNFAVORABLE MARKET RESEARCH REPORT

States of Nature s_j	Prior Probabilities $P(s_j)$	Conditional Probabilities $P(U \mid s_j)$	Joint Probabilities $P(U > s_j)$	Posterior Probabilities $P(s_j \mid U)$
s_1	0.8	0.10	0.08	0.35
s_2	0.2	0.75	0.15	0.65
	1.0		$P(U) = 0.23$	1.00

MEDICAL SCREENING TEST AT DUKE UNIVERSITY MEDICAL CENTER*

A medical screening test developed at the Duke University Medical Center involved using blood samples from newborns to screen for metabolic disorders. A positive test result indicated that a deficiency was present, while a negative test result indicated that a deficiency was not present. However, it was understood that the screening test was not a perfect predictor; that is, false-positive test results as well as false-negative test results were possible. A false-positive test result meant that the test detected a deficiency when in fact no deficiency was present. This case resulted in unnecessary further testing as well as unnecessary worry for the parents of the newborn. A false-negative test result meant that the test did not detect the presence of an existing deficiency. Using probability and decision analysis, a research team analyzed the role and value of the screening test.

A decision tree with six nodes, 13 branches, and eight outcomes was used to model the screening test procedure. A decision node with the decision branches Test and No Test was placed at the start of the decision tree. Chance nodes and branches were used to describe the possible sequences of a positive test result, a negative test result, a deficiency present, and a deficiency not present.

The particular deficiency in question was rare, occurring at a rate of one case for every 250,000

newborns. Thus, the prior probability of a deficiency was $1/250,000 = 0.000004$. Based on judgments about the probabilities of false-positive and false-negative test results, Bayes' theorem was used to calculate the posterior probability that a newborn with a positive test result actually had a deficiency. This posterior probability was 0.074. Thus, while a positive test result increased the probability the newborn had a deficiency from 0.000004 to 0.074, the probability that the newborn had a deficiency was still relatively low (0.074).

The probability information was helpful to doctors in reassuring worried parents that even though further testing was recommended, the chances were greater than 90% that a deficiency was not present. After the assignment of costs to the eight possible outcomes, decision analysis showed that the decision alternative to conduct the test provided the optimal decision strategy. The expected cost criterion established the expected cost to be approximately $6 per test. Decision analysis helped provide a realistic understanding of the risks and costs associated with the screening test.

*Based on James E. Smith and Robert L. Winkler, "Casey's Problem: Interpreting and Evaluating a New Test," *Interfaces* 29, no. 3 (May/June 1999): 63–76.

SUMMARY

Decision analysis can be used to determine a recommended decision alternative or an optimal decision strategy when a decision maker is faced with an uncertain and risk-filled pattern of future events. The goal of decision analysis is to identify the best decision alternative or the optimal decision strategy given information about the uncertain events and the possible consequences or payoffs. The uncertain future events are called chance events and the outcomes of the chance events are called states of nature.

We showed how influence diagrams, payoff tables, and decision trees could be used to structure a decision problem and describe the relationships among the decisions, the chance events, and the consequences. We presented three approaches to decision making without probabilities: the optimistic approach, the conservative approach, and the minimax regret approach. When probability assessments are provided for the states of nature, the expected value approach can be used to identify the recommended decision alternative or decision strategy.

In cases where sample information about the chance events is available, a sequence of decisions has to be made. First we must decide whether to obtain the sample information.

If the answer to this decision is yes, an optimal decision strategy based on the specific sample information must be developed. In this situation, decision trees and the expected value approach can be used to determine the optimal decision strategy.

Even though the expected value approach can be used to obtain a recommended decision alternative or optimal decision strategy, the payoff that actually occurs will usually have a value different from the expected value. A risk profile provides a probability distribution for the possible payoffs and can assist the decision maker in assessing the risks associated with different decision alternatives. Finally, sensitivity analysis can be conducted to determine the effect changes in the probabilities for the states of nature and changes in the values of the payoffs have on the recommended decision alternative.

Decision analysis has been widely used in practice. The Management Science in Action, Investing in a Transmission System at Oglethorpe Power, describes the use of decision analysis to decide whether to invest in a major transmission system between Georgia and Florida.

MANAGEMENT SCIENCE IN ACTION

INVESTING IN A TRANSMISSION SYSTEM AT OGLETHORPE POWER*

Oglethorpe Power Corporation (OPC) provides wholesale electrical power to consumer-owned cooperatives in the state of Georgia. Florida Power Corporation proposed that OPC join in the building of a major transmission line from Georgia to Florida. Deciding whether to become involved in the building of the transmission line was a major decision for OPC because it would involve the commitment of substantial OPC resources. OPC worked with Applied Decision Analysis, Inc., to conduct a comprehensive decision analysis of the problem.

In the problem formulation step, three decisions were identified: (1) build a transmission line from Georgia to Florida; (2) upgrade existing transmission facilities; and (3) who would control the new facilities. Oglethorpe was faced with five chance events: (1) construction costs, (2) competition, (3) demand in Florida, (4) OPC's share of the operation, and (5) pricing. The consequence or payoff was measured in terms of dollars saved. The influence diagram for the problem had three decision nodes, five chance nodes, a consequence node, and several intermediate nodes that described

intermediate calculations. The decision tree for the problem had more than 8000 paths from the starting node to the terminal branches.

An expected value analysis of the decision tree provided an optimal decision strategy for OPC. However, the risk profile for the optimal decision strategy showed that the recommended strategy was very risky and had a significant probability of increasing OPC's cost rather than providing a savings. The risk analysis led to the conclusion that more information about the competition was needed in order to reduce OPC's risk. Sensitivity analysis involving various probabilities and payoffs showed that the value of the optimal decision strategy was stable over a reasonable range of input values. The final recommendation from the decision analysis was that OPC should begin negotiations with Florida Power Corporation concerning the building of the new transmission line.

*Based on Adam Borison, "Oglethorpe Power Corporation Decides About Investing in a Major Transmission System," *Interfaces* (March/April 1995): 25–36.

GLOSSARY

Decision alternatives Options available to the decision maker.

Chance event An uncertain future event affecting the consequence, or payoff, associated with a decision.

Consequence The result obtained when a decision alternative is chosen and a chance event occurs. A measure of the consequence is often called a payoff.

States of nature   The possible outcomes for chance events that affect the payoff associated with a decision alternative.

Influence diagram   A graphical device that shows the relationship among decisions, chance events, and consequences for a decision problem.

Node   An intersection or junction point of an influence diagram or a decision tree.

Decision nodes   Nodes indicating points where a decision is made.

Chance nodes   Nodes indicating points where an uncertain event will occur.

Consequence nodes   Nodes of an influence diagram indicating points where a payoff will occur.

Payoff   A measure of the consequence of a decision such as profit, cost, or time. Each combination of a decision alternative and a state of nature has an associated payoff (consequence).

Payoff table   A tabular representation of the payoffs for a decision problem.

Decision tree   A graphical representation of the decision problem that shows the sequential nature of the decision-making process.

Branch   Lines showing the alternatives from decision nodes and the outcomes from chance nodes.

Optimistic approach   An approach to choosing a decision alternative without using probabilities. For a maximization problem, it leads to choosing the decision alternative corresponding to the largest payoff; for a minimization problem, it leads to choosing the decision alternative corresponding to the smallest payoff.

Conservative approach   An approach to choosing a decision alternative without using probabilities. For a maximization problem, it leads to choosing the decision alternative that maximizes the minimum payoff; for a minimization problem, it leads to choosing the decision alternative that minimizes the maximum payoff.

Minimax regret approach   An approach to choosing a decision alternative without using probabilities. For each alternative, the maximum regret is computed, which leads to choosing the decision alternative that minimizes the maximum regret.

Opportunity loss, or regret   The amount of loss (lower profit or higher cost) from not making the best decision for each state of nature.

Expected value approach   An approach to choosing a decision alternative based on the expected value of each decision alternative. The recommended decision alternative is the one that provides the best expected value.

Expected value (EV)   For a chance node, it is the weighted average of the payoffs. The weights are the state-of-nature probabilities.

Expected value of perfect information (EVPI)   The expected value of information that would tell the decision maker exactly which state of nature is going to occur (i.e., perfect information).

Risk analysis   The study of the possible payoffs and probabilities associated with a decision alternative or a decision strategy.

Sensitivity analysis   The study of how changes in the probability assessments for the states of nature or changes in the payoffs affect the recommended decision alternative.

Risk profile   The probability distribution of the possible payoffs associated with a decision alternative or decision strategy.

Prior probabilities   The probabilities of the states of nature prior to obtaining sample information.

Sample information   New information obtained through research or experimentation that enables an updating or revision of the state-of-nature probabilities.

Posterior (revised) probabilities   The probabilities of the states of nature after revising the prior probabilities based on sample information.

Decision strategy   A strategy involving a sequence of decisions and chance outcomes to provide the optimal solution to a decision problem.

Expected value of sample information (EVSI)   The difference between the expected value of an optimal strategy based on sample information and the "best" expected value without any sample information.

Efficiency   The ratio of EVSI to EVPI as a percentage; perfect information is 100% efficient.

Bayes' theorem   A theorem that enables the use of sample information to revise prior probabilities.

Conditional probability   The probability of one event given the known outcome of a (possibly) related event.

Joint probabilities   The probabilities of both sample information and a particular state of nature occurring simultaneously.

PROBLEMS

1. The following payoff table shows profit for a decision analysis problem with two decision alternatives and three states of nature:

	State of Nature		
Decision Alternative	s_1	s_2	s_3
d_1	250	100	25
d_2	100	100	75

a. Construct a decision tree for this problem.
b. If the decision maker knows nothing about the probabilities of the three states of nature, what is the recommended decision using the optimistic, conservative, and minimax regret approaches?

2. Suppose that a decision maker faced with four decision alternatives and four states of nature develops the following profit payoff table:

	State of Nature			
Decision Alternative	s_1	s_2	s_3	s_4
d_1	14	9	10	5
d_2	11	10	8	7
d_3	9	10	10	11
d_4	8	10	11	13

a. If the decision maker knows nothing about the probabilities of the four states of nature, what is the recommended decision using the optimistic, conservative, and minimax regret approaches?

b. Which approach do you prefer? Explain. Is establishing the most appropriate approach before analyzing the problem important for the decision maker? Explain.

c. Assume that the payoff table provides *cost* rather than profit payoffs. What is the recommended decision using the optimistic, conservative, and minimax regret approaches?

3. Southland Corporation's decision to produce a new line of recreational products resulted in the need to construct either a small plant or a large plant. The best selection of plant size depends on how the marketplace reacts to the new product line. To conduct an analysis, marketing management has decided to view the possible long-run demand as low, medium, or high. The following payoff table shows the projected profit in millions of dollars:

	Long-Run Demand		
Plant Size	Low	Medium	High
Small	150	200	200
Large	50	200	500

a. What is the decision to be made, and what is the chance event for Southland's problem?
b. Construct an influence diagram.
c. Construct a decision tree.
d. Recommend a decision based on the use of the optimistic, conservative, and minimax regret approaches.

4. The following profit payoff table was presented in Problem 1. Suppose that the decision maker obtained the probability assessments $P(s_1) = 0.65$, $P(s_2) = 0.15$, and $P(s_3) = 0.20$. Use the expected value approach to determine the optimal decision.

	State of Nature		
Decision Alternative	s_1	s_2	s_3
d_1	250	100	25
d_2	100	100	75

5. An investor wants to select one of seven mutual funds for the coming year. Data showing the percentage annual return for each fund during five typical one-year periods are shown here. The assumption is that one of these five-year periods will occur again during the coming year. Thus, years A, B, C, D, and E are the states of nature for the mutual fund decision.

	State of Nature				
Mutual Fund	Year A	Year B	Year C	Year D	Year E
Large-Cap Stock	35.3	20.0	28.3	10.4	−9.3
Mid-Cap Stock	32.3	23.2	−0.9	49.3	−22.8
Small-Cap Stock	20.8	22.5	6.0	33.3	6.1
Energy/Resources Sector	25.3	33.9	−20.5	20.9	−2.5
Health Sector	49.1	5.5	29.7	77.7	−24.9
Technology Sector	46.2	21.7	45.7	93.1	−20.1
Real Estate Sector	20.5	44.0	−21.1	2.6	5.1

a. Assume that the investor is conservative. What is the recommended mutual fund? Using this mutual fund, what are the minimum and maximum annual returns?

b. Suppose that an experienced financial analyst reviews the five states of nature and provides the following probabilities: 0.1, 0.3, 0.1, 0.1, and 0.4. Using the expected value, what is the recommended mutual fund? What is the expected annual return? Using this mutual fund, what are the minimum and maximum annual returns?

c. What is the expected annual return for the mutual fund recommended in part (a)? How much of an increase in the expected annual return can be obtained by following the recommendation in part (b)?

d. Which of the two mutual funds appears to have more risk? Why? Is the expected annual return greater for the mutual fund with more risk?

e. What mutual fund would you recommend to the investor? Explain.

6. Amy Lloyd is interested in leasing a new Saab and has contacted three automobile dealers for pricing information. Each dealer offered Amy a closed-end 36-month lease with no down payment due at the time of signing. Each lease includes a monthly charge and a mileage allowance. Additional miles receive a surcharge on a per-mile basis. The monthly lease cost, the mileage allowance, and the cost for additional miles follow:

Dealer	Monthly Cost	Mileage Allowance	Cost per Additional Mile
Forno Saab	$299	36,000	$0.15
Midtown Motors	$310	45,000	$0.20
Hopkins Automotive	$325	54,000	$0.15

Amy decided to choose the lease option that will minimize her total 36-month cost. The difficulty is that Amy is not sure how many miles she will drive over the next three years. For purposes of this decision she believes it is reasonable to assume that she will drive 12,000 miles per year, 15,000 miles per year, or 18,000 miles per year. With this assumption Amy estimated her total costs for the three lease options. For example, she figures that the Forno Saab lease will cost her $10,764 if she drives 12,000 miles per year, $12,114 if she drives 15,000 miles per year, or $13,464 if she drives 18,000 miles per year.

a. What is the decision, and what is the chance event?

b. Construct a payoff table for Amy's problem.

c. If Amy has no idea which of the three mileage assumptions is most appropriate, what is the recommended decision (leasing option) using the optimistic, conservative, and minimax regret approaches?

d. Suppose that the probabilities that Amy drives 12,000, 15,000, and 18,000 miles per year are 0.5, 0.4, and 0.1, respectively. What option should Amy choose using the expected value approach?

e. Develop a risk profile for the decision selected in part (d). What is the most likely cost, and what is its probability?

f. Suppose that after further consideration Amy concludes that the probabilities that she will drive 12,000, 15,000, and 18,000 miles per year are 0.3, 0.4, and 0.3, respectively. What decision should Amy make using the expected value approach?

7. Hudson Corporation is considering three options for managing its data processing operation: continuing with its own staff, hiring an outside vendor to do the managing (referred to as *outsourcing*), or using a combination of its own staff and an outside vendor. The cost

of the operation depends on future demand. The annual cost of each option (in thousands of dollars) depends on demand as follows:

		Demand	
Staffing Options	**High**	**Medium**	**Low**
Own staff	650	650	600
Outside vendor	900	600	300
Combination	800	650	500

a. If the demand probabilities are 0.2, 0.5, and 0.3, which decision alternative will minimize the expected cost of the data processing operation? What is the expected annual cost associated with that recommendation?

b. Construct a risk profile for the optimal decision in part (a). What is the probability of the cost exceeding $700,000?

8. The following payoff table shows the profit for a decision problem with two states of nature and two decision alternatives:

	State of Nature	
Decision Alternative	s_1	s_2
d_1	10	1
d_2	4	3

a. Use graphical sensitivity analysis to determine the range of probabilities of state of nature s_1 for which each of the decision alternatives has the largest expected value.

b. Suppose $P(s_1) = 0.2$ and $P(s_2) = 0.8$. What is the best decision using the expected value approach?

c. Perform sensitivity analysis on the payoffs for decision alternative d_1. Assume the probabilities are as given in part (b) and find the range of payoffs under states of nature s_1 and s_2 that will keep the solution found in part (b) optimal. Is the solution more sensitive to the payoff under state of nature s_1 or s_2?

9. Myrtle Air Express decided to offer direct service from Cleveland to Myrtle Beach. Management must decide between a full-price service using the company's new fleet of jet aircraft and a discount service using smaller capacity commuter planes. It is clear that the best choice depends on the market reaction to the service Myrtle Air offers. Management developed estimates of the contribution to profit for each type of service based upon two possible levels of demand for service to Myrtle Beach: strong and weak. The following table shows the estimated quarterly profits (in thousands of dollars):

	Demand for Service	
Service	**Strong**	**Weak**
Full price	$960	−$490
Discount	$670	$320

a. What is the decision to be made, what is the chance event, and what is the consequence for this problem? How many decision alternatives are there? How many outcomes are there for the chance event?

b. If nothing is known about the probabilities of the chance outcomes, what is the recommended decision using the optimistic, conservative, and minimax regret approaches?

c. Suppose that management of Myrtle Air Express believes that the probability of strong demand is 0.7 and the probability of weak demand is 0.3. Use the expected value approach to determine an optimal decision.

d. Suppose that the probability of strong demand is 0.8 and the probability of weak demand is 0.2. What is the optimal decision using the expected value approach?

e. Use graphical sensitivity analysis to determine the range of demand probabilities for which each of the decision alternatives has the largest expected value.

10. Video Tech is considering marketing one of two new video games for the coming holiday season: Battle Pacific or Space Pirates. Battle Pacific is a unique game and appears to have no competition. Estimated profits (in thousands of dollars) under high, medium, and low demand are as follows:

| Battle Pacific | Demand | | |
	High	Medium	Low
Profit	$1000	$700	$300
Probability	0.2	0.5	0.3

Video Tech is optimistic about its Space Pirates game. However, the concern is that profitability will be affected by a competitor's introduction of a video game viewed as similar to Space Pirates. Estimated profits (in thousands of dollars) with and without competition are as follows:

| Space Pirates with Competition | Demand | | |
	High	Medium	Low
Profit	$800	$400	$200
Probability	0.3	0.4	0.3

| Space Pirates without Competition | Demand | | |
	High	Medium	Low
Profit	$1600	$800	$400
Probability	0.5	0.3	0.2

a. Develop a decision tree for the Video Tech problem.

b. For planning purposes, Video Tech believes there is a 0.6 probability that its competitor will produce a new game similar to Space Pirates. Given this probability of competition, the director of planning recommends marketing the Battle Pacific video game. Using expected value, what is your recommended decision?

c. Show a risk profile for your recommended decision.

d. Use sensitivity analysis to determine what the probability of competition for Space Pirates would have to be for you to change your recommended decision alternative.

11. For the Pittsburgh Development Corporation problem in Section 13.3, the decision alternative to build the large condominium complex was found to be optimal using the expected value approach. In Section 13.4 we conducted a sensitivity analysis for the payoffs associated with this decision alternative. We found that the large complex remained optimal as long as the payoff for the strong demand was greater than or equal to $17.5 million and as long as the payoff for the weak demand was greater than or equal to –$19 million.

    a. Consider the medium complex decision. How much could the payoff under strong demand increase and still keep decision alternative d_3 the optimal solution?

    b. Consider the small complex decision. How much could the payoff under strong demand increase and still keep decision alternative d_3 the optimal solution?

12. The distance from Potsdam to larger markets and limited air service have hindered the town in attracting new industry. Air Express, a major overnight delivery service, is considering establishing a regional distribution center in Potsdam. However, Air Express will not establish the center unless the length of the runway at the local airport is increased. Another candidate for new development is Diagnostic Research, Inc. (DRI), a leading producer of medical testing equipment. DRI is considering building a new manufacturing plant. Increasing the length of the runway is not a requirement for DRI, but the planning commission feels that doing so will help convince DRI to locate their new plant in Potsdam. Assuming that the town lengthens the runway, the Potsdam planning commission believes that the probabilities shown in the following table are applicable:

	DRI Plant	No DRI Plant
Air Express Center	0.30	0.10
No Air Express Center	0.40	0.20

For instance, the probability that Air Express will establish a distribution center and DRI will build a plant is 0.30.

The estimated annual revenue to the town, after deducting the cost of lengthening the runway, is as follows:

	DRI Plant	No DRI Plant
Air Express Center	$600,000	$150,000
No Air Express Center	$250,000	–$200,000

If the runway expansion project is not conducted, the planning commission assesses the probability DRI will locate their new plant in Potsdam at 0.6; in this case, the estimated annual revenue to the town will be $450,000. If the runway expansion project is not conducted and DRI does not locate in Potsdam, the annual revenue will be $0 because no cost will have been incurred and no revenues will be forthcoming.

    a. What is the decision to be made, what is the chance event, and what is the consequence?

    b. Compute the expected annual revenue associated with the decision alternative to lengthen the runway.

    c. Compute the expected annual revenue associated with the decision alternative not to lengthen the runway.

d. Should the town elect to lengthen the runway? Explain.

e. Suppose that the probabilities associated with lengthening the runway were as follows:

	DRI Plant	No DRI Plant
Air Express Center	0.40	0.10
No Air Express Center	0.30	0.20

What effect, if any, would this change in the probabilities have on the recommended decision?

13. Seneca Hill Winery recently purchased land for the purpose of establishing a new vineyard. Management is considering two varieties of white grapes for the new vineyard: Chardonnay and Riesling. The Chardonnay grapes would be used to produce a dry Chardonnay wine, and the Riesling grapes would be used to produce a semidry Riesling wine. It takes approximately four years from the time of planting before new grapes can be harvested. This length of time creates a great deal of uncertainty about future demand and makes the decision concerning the type of grapes to plant difficult. Three possibilities are being considered: Chardonnay grapes only; Riesling grapes only; and both Chardonnay and Riesling grapes. Seneca management decided that for planning purposes it would be adequate to consider only two demand possibilities for each type of wine: strong or weak. With two possibilities for each type of wine it was necessary to assess four probabilities. With the help of some forecasts in industry publications management made the following probability assessments:

	Riesling Demand	
Chardonnay Demand	Weak	Strong
Weak	0.05	0.50
Strong	0.25	0.20

Revenue projections show an annual contribution to profit of $20,000 if Seneca Hill only plants Chardonnay grapes and demand is weak for Chardonnay wine, and $70,000 if they only plant Chardonnay grapes and demand is strong for Chardonnay wine. If they only plant Riesling grapes, the annual profit projection is $25,000 if demand is weak for Riesling grapes and $45,000 if demand is strong for Riesling grapes. If Seneca plants both types of grapes, the annual profit projections are shown in the following table:

	Riesling Demand	
Chardonnay Demand	Weak	Strong
Weak	$22,000	$40,000
Strong	$26,000	$60,000

a. What is the decision to be made, what is the chance event, and what is the consequence? Identify the alternatives for the decisions and the possible outcomes for the chance events.

b. Develop a decision tree.

c. Use the expected value approach to recommend which alternative Seneca Hill Winery should follow in order to maximize expected annual profit.

d. Suppose management is concerned about the probability assessments when demand for Chardonnay wine is strong. Some believe it is likely for Riesling demand to also be strong in this case. Suppose the probability of strong demand for Chardonnay and weak demand for Riesling is 0.05 and that the probability of strong demand for Chardonnay and strong demand for Riesling is 0.40. How does this change the recommended decision? Assume that the probabilities when Chardonnay demand is weak are still 0.05 and 0.50.

e. Other members of the management team expect the Chardonnay market to become saturated at some point in the future, causing a fall in prices. Suppose that the annual profit projections fall to $50,000 when demand for Chardonnay is strong and Chardonnay grapes only are planted. Using the original probability assessments, determine how this change would affect the optimal decision.

14. The following profit payoff table was presented in Problems 1 and 4:

Decision Alternative	State of Nature		
	s_1	s_2	s_3
d_1	250	100	25
d_2	100	100	75

The probabilities for the states of nature are $P(s_1) = 0.65$, $P(s_2) = 0.15$, and $P(s_3) = 0.20$.

a. What is the optimal decision strategy if perfect information were available?

b. What is the expected value for the decision strategy developed in part (a)?

c. Using the expected value approach, what is the recommended decision without perfect information? What is its expected value?

d. What is the expected value of perfect information?

15. The Lake Placid Town Council decided to build a new community center to be used for conventions, concerts, and other public events, but considerable controversy surrounds the appropriate size. Many influential citizens want a large center that would be a showcase for the area. But the mayor feels that if demand does not support such a center, the community will lose a large amount of money. To provide structure for the decision process, the council narrowed the building alternatives to three sizes: small, medium, and large. Everybody agreed that the critical factor in choosing the best size is the number of people who will want to use the new facility. A regional planning consultant provided demand estimates under three scenarios: worst case, base case, and best case. The worst-case scenario corresponds to a situation in which tourism drops significantly; the base-case scenario corresponds to a situation in which Lake Placid continues to attract visitors at current levels; and the best-case scenario corresponds to a significant increase in tourism. The consultant has provided probability assessments of 0.10, 0.60, and 0.30 for the worst-case, base-case, and best-case scenarios, respectively.

The town council suggested using net cash flow over a five-year planning horizon as the criterion for deciding on the best size. The following projections of net cash flow (in thousands of dollars) for a five-year planning horizon have been developed. All costs, including the consultant's fee, have been included.

	Demand Scenario		
Center Size	Worst Case	Base Case	Best Case
Small	400	500	660
Medium	−250	650	800
Large	−400	580	990

a. What decision should Lake Placid make using the expected value approach?

b. Construct risk profiles for the medium and large alternatives. Given the mayor's concern over the possibility of losing money and the result of part (a), which alternative would you recommend?

c. Compute the expected value of perfect information. Do you think it would be worth trying to obtain additional information concerning which scenario is likely to occur?

d. Suppose the probability of the worst-case scenario increases to 0.2, the probability of the base-case scenario decreases to 0.5, and the probability of the best-case scenario remains at 0.3. What effect, if any, would these changes have on the decision recommendation?

e. The consultant has suggested that an expenditure of $150,000 on a promotional campaign over the planning horizon will effectively reduce the probability of the worst-case scenario to zero. If the campaign can be expected to also increase the probability of the best-case scenario to 0.4, is it a good investment?

16. Consider a variation of the PDC decision tree shown in Figure 13.9. The company must first decide whether to undertake the market research study. If the market research study is conducted, the outcome will either be favorable (F) or unfavorable (U). Assume there are only two decision alternatives d_1 and d_2 and two states of nature s_1 and s_2. The payoff table showing profit is as follows:

	State of Nature	
Decision Alternative	s_1	s_2
d_1	100	300
d_2	400	200

a. Show the decision tree.

b. Using the following probabilities, what is the optimal decision strategy?

$$P(F) = 0.56 \quad P(s_1 \mid F) = 0.57 \quad P(s_1 \mid U) = 0.18 \quad P(s_1) = 0.40$$
$$P(U) = 0.44 \quad P(s_2 \mid F) = 0.43 \quad P(s_2 \mid U) = 0.82 \quad P(s_2) = 0.60$$

17. Hemmingway, Inc., is considering a $5 million research and development (R&D) project. Profit projections appear promising, but Hemmingway's president is concerned because the probability that the R&D project will be successful is only 0.50. Secondly, the president knows that even if the project is successful, it will require that the company build a new production facility at a cost of $20 million in order to manufacture the product. If the facility is built, uncertainty remains about the demand and thus uncertainty about the profit

FIGURE 13.16 DECISION TREE FOR HEMMINGWAY, INC.

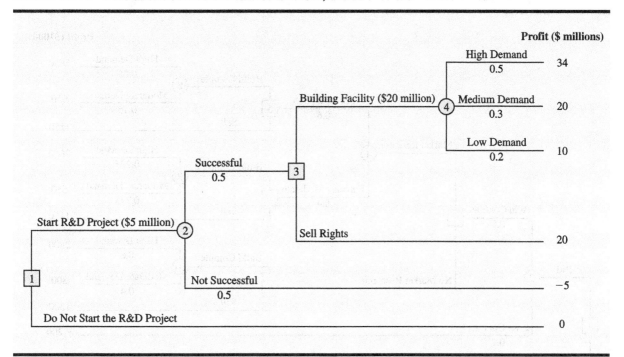

that will be realized. Another option is that if the R&D project is successful, the company could sell the rights to the product for an estimated $25 million. Under this option, the company would not build the $20 million production facility.

The decision tree is shown in Figure 13.16. The profit projection for each outcome is shown at the end of the branches. For example, the revenue projection for the high demand outcome is $59 million. However, the cost of the R&D project ($5 million) and the cost of the production facility ($20 million) show the profit of this outcome to be $59 − $5 − $20 = $34 million. Branch probabilities are also shown for the chance events.

a. Analyze the decision tree to determine whether the company should undertake the R&D project. If it does, and if the R&D project is successful, what should the company do? What is the expected value of your strategy?

b. What must the selling price be for the company to consider selling the rights to the product?

c. Develop a risk profile for the optimal strategy.

18. Dante Development Corporation is considering bidding on a contract for a new office building complex. Figure 13.17 shows the decision tree prepared by one of Dante's analysts. At node 1, the company must decide whether to bid on the contract. The cost of preparing the bid is $200,000. The upper branch from node 2 shows that the company has a 0.8 probability of winning the contract if it submits a bid. If the company wins the bid, it will have to pay $2,000,000 to become a partner in the project. Node 3 shows that the company will then consider doing a market research study to forecast demand for the office units prior to beginning construction. The cost of this study is $150,000. Node 4 is a chance node showing the possible outcomes of the market research study.

Nodes 5, 6, and 7 are similar in that they are the decision nodes for Dante to either build the office complex or sell the rights in the project to another developer. The decision to build the complex will result in an income of $5,000,000 if demand is high and

FIGURE 13.17   DECISION TREE FOR THE DANTE DEVELOPMENT CORPORATION

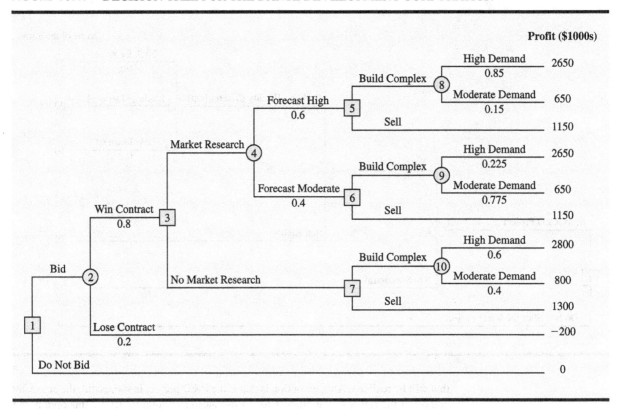

$3,000,000 if demand is moderate. If Dante chooses to sell its rights in the project to another developer, income from the sale is estimated to be $3,500,000. The probabilities shown at nodes 4, 8, and 9 are based on the projected outcomes of the market research study.

a. Verify Dante's profit projections shown at the ending branches of the decision tree by calculating the payoffs of $2,650,000 and $650,000 for first two outcomes.
b. What is the optimal decision strategy for Dante, and what is the expected profit for this project?
c. What would the cost of the market research study have to be before Dante would change its decision about the market research study?
d. Develop a risk profile for Dante.

19. Hale's TV Productions is considering producing a pilot for a comedy series in the hope of selling it to a major television network. The network may decide to reject the series, but it may also decide to purchase the rights to the series for either one or two years. At this point in time, Hale may either produce the pilot and wait for the network's decision or transfer the rights for the pilot and series to a competitor for $100,000. Hale's decision alternatives and profits (in thousands of dollars) are as follows:

	State of Nature		
Decision Alternative	Reject, s_1	1 Year, s_2	2 Years, s_3
Produce pilot, d_1	−100	50	150
Sell to competitor, d_2	100	100	100

The probabilities for the states of nature are $P(s_1) = 0.20$, $P(s_2) = 0.30$, and $P(s_3) = 0.50$. For a consulting fee of $5000, an agency will review the plans for the comedy series and indicate the overall chances of a favorable network reaction to the series. Assume that the agency review will result in a favorable (F) or an unfavorable (U) review and that the following probabilities are relevant:

$$P(F) = 0.69 \qquad P(s_1 \mid F) = 0.09 \qquad P(s_1 \mid U) = 0.45$$
$$P(U) = 0.31 \qquad P(s_2 \mid F) = 0.26 \qquad P(s_2 \mid U) = 0.39$$
$$P(s_3 \mid F) = 0.65 \qquad P(s_3 \mid U) = 0.16$$

a. Construct a decision tree for this problem.
b. What is the recommended decision if the agency opinion is not used? What is the expected value?
c. What is the expected value of perfect information?
d. What is Hale's optimal decision strategy assuming the agency's information is used?
e. What is the expected value of the agency's information?
f. Is the agency's information worth the $5000 fee? What is the maximum that Hale should be willing to pay for the information?
g. What is the recommended decision?

20. Embassy Publishing Company received a six-chapter manuscript for a new college textbook. The editor of the college division is familiar with the manuscript and estimated a 0.65 probability that the textbook will be successful. If successful, a profit of $750,000 will be realized. If the company decides to publish the textbook and it is unsuccessful, a loss of $250,000 will occur.

Before making the decision to accept or reject the manuscript, the editor is considering sending the manuscript out for review. A review process provides either a favorable (F) or unfavorable (U) evaluation of the manuscript. Past experience with the review process suggests probabilities $P(F) = 0.7$ and $P(U) = 0.3$ apply. Let $s_1 =$ the textbook is successful, and $s_2 =$ the textbook is unsuccessful. The editor's initial probabilities of s_1 and s_2 will be revised based on whether the review is favorable or unfavorable. The revised probabilities are as follows:

$$P(s_1 \mid F) = 0.75 \qquad P(s_1 \mid U) = 0.417$$
$$P(s_2 \mid F) = 0.25 \qquad P(s_2 \mid U) = 0.583$$

a. Construct a decision tree assuming that the company will first make the decision of whether to send the manuscript out for review and then make the decision to accept or reject the manuscript.
b. Analyze the decision tree to determine the optimal decision strategy for the publishing company.
c. If the manuscript review costs $5000, what is your recommendation?
d. What is the expected value of perfect information? What does this EVPI suggest for the company?

21. A real estate investor has the opportunity to purchase land currently zoned residential. If the county board approves a request to rezone the property as commercial within the next year, the investor will be able to lease the land to a large discount firm that wants to open a new store on the property. However, if the zoning change is not approved, the investor

will have to sell the property at a loss. Profits (in thousands of dollars) are shown in the following payoff table:

	State of Nature	
	Rezoning Approved	**Rezoning Not Approved**
Decision Alternative	s_1	s_2
Purchase, d_1	600	-200
Do not purchase, d_2	0	0

a. If the probability that the rezoning will be approved is 0.5, what decision is recommended? What is the expected profit?

b. The investor can purchase an option to buy the land. Under the option, the investor maintains the rights to purchase the land anytime during the next three months while learning more about possible resistance to the rezoning proposal from area residents. Probabilities are as follows:

Let H = High resistance to rezoning

L = Low resistance to rezoning

$$P(H) = 0.55 \qquad P(s_1 \mid H) = 0.18 \qquad P(s_2 \mid H) = 0.82$$
$$P(L) = 0.45 \qquad P(s_1 \mid L) = 0.89 \qquad P(s_2 \mid L) = 0.11$$

What is the optimal decision strategy if the investor uses the option period to learn more about the resistance from area residents before making the purchase decision?

c. If the option will cost the investor an additional $10,000, should the investor purchase the option? Why or why not? What is the maximum that the investor should be willing to pay for the option?

22. Lawson's Department Store faces a buying decision for a seasonal product for which demand can be high, medium, or low. The purchaser for Lawson's can order 1, 2, or 3 lots of the product before the season begins but cannot reorder later. Profit projections (in thousands of dollars) are shown.

	State of Nature		
	High Demand	**Medium Demand**	**Low Demand**
Decision Alternative	s_1	s_2	s_3
Order 1 lot, d_1	60	60	50
Order 2 lots, d_2	80	80	30
Order 3 lots, d_3	100	70	10

a. If the prior probabilities for the three states of nature are 0.3, 0.3, and 0.4, respectively, what is the recommended order quantity?

b. At each preseason sales meeting, the vice president of sales provides a personal opinion regarding potential demand for this product. Because of the vice president's enthusiasm and optimistic nature, the predictions of market conditions have always been either "excellent" (E) or "very good" (V). Probabilities are as follows:

$$P(E) = 0.70 \qquad P(s_1 \mid E) = 0.34 \qquad P(s_1 \mid V) = 0.20$$
$$P(V) = 0.30 \qquad P(s_2 \mid E) = 0.32 \qquad P(s_2 \mid V) = 0.26$$
$$\qquad\qquad\qquad P(s_3 \mid E) = 0.34 \qquad P(s_3 \mid V) = 0.54$$

What is the optimal decision strategy?

c. Use the efficiency of sample information and discuss whether the firm should consider a consulting expert who could provide independent forecasts of market conditions for the product.

23. Suppose that you are given a decision situation with three possible states of nature: s_1, s_2, and s_3. The prior probabilities are $P(s_1) = 0.2$, $P(s_2) = 0.5$, and $P(s_3) = 0.3$. With sample information I, $P(I \mid s_1) = 0.1$, $P(I \mid s_2) = 0.05$, and $P(I \mid s_3) = 0.2$. Compute the revised or posterior probabilities: $P(s_1 \mid I)$, $P(s_2 \mid I)$, and $P(s_3 \mid I)$.

24. To save on expenses, Rona and Jerry agreed to form a carpool for traveling to and from work. Rona preferred to use the somewhat longer but more consistent Queen City Avenue. Although Jerry preferred the quicker expressway, he agreed with Rona that they should take Queen City Avenue if the expressway had a traffic jam. The following payoff table provides the one-way time estimate in minutes for traveling to or from work:

	State of Nature	
	Expressway Open	Expressway Jammed
Decision Alternative	s_1	s_2
Queen City Avenue, d_1	30	30
Expressway, d_2	25	45

Based on their experience with traffic problems, Rona and Jerry agreed on a 0.15 probability that the expressway would be jammed.

In addition, they agreed that weather seemed to affect the traffic conditions on the expressway. Let

$$C = \text{clear}$$
$$O = \text{overcast}$$
$$R = \text{rain}$$

The following conditional probabilities apply:

$$P(C \mid s_1) = 0.8 \quad P(O \mid s_1) = 0.2 \quad P(R \mid s_1) = 0.0$$
$$P(C \mid s_2) = 0.1 \quad P(O \mid s_2) = 0.3 \quad P(R \mid s_2) = 0.6$$

a. Use Bayes' theorem for probability revision to compute the probability of each weather condition and the conditional probability of the expressway open s_1 or jammed s_2 given each weather condition.
b. Show the decision tree for this problem.
c. What is the optimal decision strategy, and what is the expected travel time?

25. The Gorman Manufacturing Company must decide whether to manufacture a component part at its Milan, Michigan, plant or purchase the component part from a supplier. The resulting profit is dependent upon the demand for the product. The following payoff table shows the projected profit (in thousands of dollars):

	State of Nature		
	Low Demand	Medium Demand	High Demand
Decision Alternative	s_1	s_2	s_3
Manufacture, d_1	−20	40	100
Purchase, d_2	10	45	70

The state-of-nature probabilities are $P(s_1) = 0.35$, $P(s_2) = 0.35$, and $P(s_3) = 0.30$.

a.   Use a decision tree to recommend a decision.

b.   Use EVPI to determine whether Gorman should attempt to obtain a better estimate of demand.

c.   A test market study of the potential demand for the product is expected to report either a favorable (F) or unfavorable (U) condition. The relevant conditional probabilities are as follows:

$$P(F \mid s_1) = 0.10 \qquad P(U \mid s_1) = 0.90$$
$$P(F \mid s_2) = 0.40 \qquad P(U \mid s_2) = 0.60$$
$$P(F \mid s_3) = 0.60 \qquad P(U \mid s_3) = 0.40$$

What is the probability that the market research report will be favorable?

d.   What is Gorman's optimal decision strategy?

e.   What is the expected value of the market research information?

f.   What is the efficiency of the information?

Case Problem 1   PROPERTY PURCHASE STRATEGY

Glenn Foreman, president of Oceanview Development Corporation, is considering submitting a bid to purchase property that will be sold by sealed bid at a county tax foreclosure. Glenn's initial judgment is to submit a bid of $5 million. Based on his experience, Glenn estimates that a bid of $5 million will have a 0.2 probability of being the highest bid and securing the property for Oceanview. The current date is June 1. Sealed bids for the property must be submitted by August 15. The winning bid will be announced on September 1.

If Oceanview submits the highest bid and obtains the property, the firm plans to build and sell a complex of luxury condominiums. However, a complicating factor is that the property is currently zoned for single-family residences only. Glenn believes that a referendum could be placed on the voting ballot in time for the November election. Passage of the referendum would change the zoning of the property and permit construction of the condominiums.

The sealed-bid procedure requires the bid to be submitted with a certified check for 10% of the amount bid. If the bid is rejected, the deposit is refunded. If the bid is accepted, the deposit is the down payment for the property. However, if the bid is accepted and the bidder does not follow through with the purchase and meet the remainder of the financial obligation within six months, the deposit will be forfeited. In this case, the county will offer the property to the next highest bidder.

To determine whether Oceanview should submit the $5 million bid, Glenn conducted some preliminary analysis. This preliminary work provided an assessment of 0.3 for the probability that the referendum for a zoning change will be approved and resulted in the following estimates of the costs and revenues that will be incurred if the condominiums are built:

Cost and Revenue Estimates

Revenue from condominium sales	$15,000,000
Cost	
Property	$5,000,000
Construction expenses	$8,000,000

If Oceanview obtains the property and the zoning change is rejected in November, Glenn believes that the best option would be for the firm not to complete the purchase of the property. In this case, Oceanview would forfeit the 10% deposit that accompanied the bid.

Because the likelihood that the zoning referendum will be approved is such an important factor in the decision process, Glenn suggested that the firm hire a market research service to conduct a survey of voters. The survey would provide a better estimate of the likelihood that the referendum for a zoning change would be approved. The market research firm that Oceanview Development has worked with in the past has agreed to do the study for $15,000. The results of the study will be available August 1, so that Oceanview will have this information before the August 15 bid deadline. The results of the survey will be either a prediction that the zoning change will be approved or a prediction that the zoning change will be rejected. After considering the record of the market research service in previous studies conducted for Oceanview, Glenn developed the following probability estimates concerning the accuracy of the market research information:

$$P(A \mid s_1) = 0.9 \quad P(N \mid s_1) = 0.1$$
$$P(A \mid s_2) = 0.2 \quad P(N \mid s_2) = 0.8$$

where

A = prediction of zoning change approval
N = prediction that zoning change will not be approved
s_1 = the zoning change is approved by the voters
s_2 = the zoning change is rejected by the voters

Managerial Report

Perform an analysis of the problem facing the Oceanview Development Corporation, and prepare a report that summarizes your findings and recommendations. Include the following items in your report:

1. A decision tree that shows the logical sequence of the decision problem
2. A recommendation regarding what Oceanview should do if the market research information is not available
3. A decision strategy that Oceanview should follow if the market research is conducted
4. A recommendation as to whether Oceanview should employ the market research firm, along with the value of the information provided by the market research firm

Include the details of your analysis as an appendix to your report.

Case Problem 2 LAWSUIT DEFENSE STRATEGY

John Campbell, an employee of Manhattan Construction Company, claims to have injured his back as a result of a fall while repairing the roof at one of the Eastview apartment buildings. He filed a lawsuit against Doug Reynolds, the owner of Eastview Apartments, asking for damages of $1,500,000. John claims that the roof had rotten sections and that his fall could have been prevented if Mr. Reynolds had told Manhattan Construction about the problem. Mr. Reynolds notified his insurance company, Allied Insurance, of the lawsuit. Allied must defend Mr. Reynolds and decide what action to take regarding the lawsuit.

Some depositions and a series of discussions took place between both sides. As a result, John Campbell offered to accept a settlement of $750,000. Thus, one option is for Allied to pay John $750,000 to settle the claim. Allied is also considering making John a counteroffer of $400,000 in the hope that he will accept a lesser amount to avoid the time and cost of going to trial. Allied's preliminary investigation shows that John's case is strong; Allied is concerned that John may reject their counteroffer and request a jury trial. Allied's lawyers spent some time exploring John's likely reaction if they make a counteroffer of $400,000.

The lawyers concluded that it is adequate to consider three possible outcomes to represent John's possible reaction to a counteroffer of $400,000: (1) John will accept the counteroffer and the case will be closed; (2) John will reject the counteroffer and elect to have a jury decide the settlement amount; or (3) John will make a counteroffer to Allied of $600,000. If John does make a counteroffer, Allied has decided that they will not make additional counteroffers. They will either accept John's counteroffer of $600,000 or go to trial.

If the case goes to a jury trial, Allied considers three outcomes possible: (1) the jury may reject John's claim and Allied will not be required to pay any damages; (2) the jury will find in favor of John and award him $750,000 in damages; or (3) the jury will conclude that John has a strong case and award him the full amount of $1,500,000.

Key considerations as Allied develops its strategy for disposing of the case are the probabilities associated with John's response to an Allied counteroffer of $400,000 and the probabilities associated with the three possible trial outcomes. Allied's lawyers believe the probability that John will accept a counteroffer of $400,000 is 0.10, the probability that John will reject a counteroffer of $400,000 is 0.40, and the probability that John will, himself, make a counteroffer to Allied of $600,000 is 0.50. If the case goes to court, they believe that the probability the jury will award John damages of $1,500,000 is 0.30, the probability that the jury will award John damages of $750,000 is 0.50, and the probability that the jury will award John nothing is 0.20.

Managerial Report

Perform an analysis of the problem facing Allied Insurance and prepare a report that summarizes your findings and recommendations. Be sure to include the following items:

1. A decision tree
2. A recommendation regarding whether Allied should accept John's initial offer to settle the claim for $750,000
3. A decision strategy that Allied should follow if they decide to make John a counteroffer of $400,000
4. A risk profile for your recommended strategy

Appendix 13.1 DECISION ANALYSIS WITH TREEPLAN

TreePlan* is an Excel add-in that can be used to develop decision trees for decision analysis problems. The software package is provided at the website that accompanies this text. Instructions for installing TreePlan are included with the software. A manual containing additional information on starting and using TreePlan is also at the website. In this

---

*TreePlan was developed by Professor Michael R. Middleton at the University of San Francisco and modified for use by Professor James E. Smith at Duke University. The TreePlan website is www.treeplan.com.

FIGURE 13.18   PDC DECISION TREE

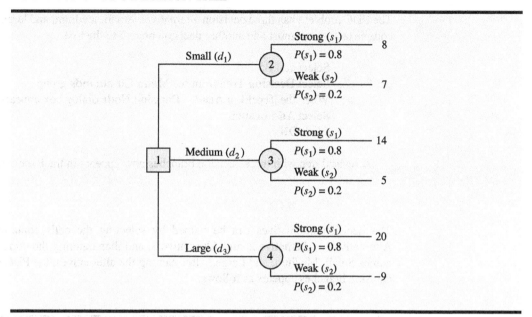

appendix we show how to use TreePlan to build a decision tree and solve the PDC problem presented in Section 13.3. The decision tree for the PDC problem is shown in Figure 13.18.

Getting Started: An Initial Decision Tree

We begin by assuming that TreePlan has been installed and an Excel worksheet is open. To build a TreePlan version of the PDC decision tree, proceed as follows:

Step 1. Select cell A1
Step 2. Select the **Add-Ins** tab and choose **Decision Tree** from the **Menu Commands** group
Step 3. When the **TreePlan Acad. - New Tree** dialog box appears:
Click **New Tree**

A decision tree with one decision node and two branches appears as follows:

	A	B	C	D	E	F	G
1	TreePlan Academic Version Only For Academic Use						
2				Alternative 1			
3						◁	0
4				0		0	
5			1				
6		0					
7				Alternative 2			
8						◁	0
9				0		0	

Adding a Branch

The PDC problem has three decision alternatives (small, medium, and large condominium complexes), so we must add another decision branch to the tree.

Step 1. Select cell B5
Step 2. Select **Decision Tree** from the **Menu Commands** group
Step 3. When the **TreePlan Acad. - Decision Node** dialog box appears:
Select **Add branch**
Click **OK**

A revised tree with three decision branches now appears in the Excel worksheet.

Naming the Decision Alternatives

The decision alternatives can be named by selecting the cells containing the labels Alternative 1, Alternative 2, and Alternative 3, and then entering the corresponding PDC names Small, Medium, and Large. After naming the alternatives, the PDC tree with three decision branches appears as follows:

	A	B	C	D	E	F	G
1	TreePlan Academic Version Only For Academic Use						
2				Small			
3							0
4				0	0		
5							
6							
7				Medium			
8		1					0
9	0			0	0		
10							
11							
12				Large			
13							0
14				0	0		

Adding Chance Nodes

The chance event for the PDC problem is the demand for the condominiums, which may be either strong or weak. Thus, a chance node with two branches must be added at the end of each decision alternative branch.

Step 1. Select cell F3
Step 2. Select **Decision Tree** from the **Menu Commands** group
Step 3. When the **TreePlan Acad. - Terminal Node** dialog box appears:
Select **Change to event node**
Select **Two** in the **Branches** section
Click **OK**

The tree now appears as follows:

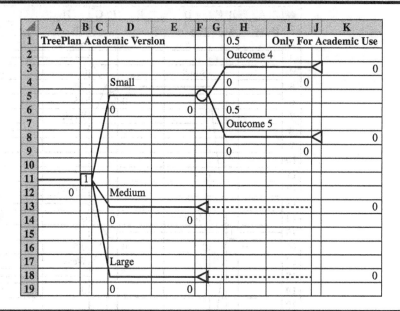

	A	B	C	D	E	F	G	H	I	J	K
1	TreePlan Academic Version							0.5		Only For Academic Use	
2								Outcome 4			
3											0
4				Small				0	0		
5											
6				0		0		0.5			
7								Outcome 5			
8											0
9								0	0		
10											
11			1								
12	0			Medium							
13											0
14				0		0					
15											
16											
17				Large							
18											0
19				0		0					

We next select the cells containing Outcome 4 and Outcome 5 and rename them Strong and Weak to provide the proper names for the PDC states of nature. After doing so we can copy the subtree for the chance node in cell F5 to the other two decision branches to complete the structure of the PDC decision tree.

Step 1. Select cell F5
Step 2. Select **Decision Tree** from the **Menu Commands** group
Step 3. When the **TreePlan Acad. - Event Node** dialog box appears:
Select **Copy subtree**
Click **OK**
Step 4. Select cell F13
Step 5. Select **Decision Tree** from the **Menu Commands** group
Step 6. When the **TreePlan Acad. - Terminal Node** dialog box appears:
Select **Paste subtree**
Click **OK**

This copy/paste procedure places a chance node at the end of the Medium decision branch. Repeating the same copy/paste procedure for the Large decision branch completes the structure of the PDC decision tree as shown in Figure 13.19.

Inserting Probabilities and Payoffs

TreePlan provides the capability of inserting probabilities and payoffs into the decision tree. In Figure 13.19 we see that TreePlan automatically assigned an equal probability 0.5 to each of the chance outcomes. For PDC, the probability of strong demand is 0.8 and the probability of weak demand is 0.2. We can select cells H1, H6, H11, H16, H21, and H26 and insert the appropriate probabilities. The payoffs for the chance outcomes are inserted in cells H4, H9, H14, H19, H24, and H29. After inserting the PDC probabilities and payoffs, the PDC decision tree appears as shown in Figure 13.20.

FIGURE 13.19   THE PDC DECISION TREE DEVELOPED BY TREEPLAN

	A	B	C	D	E	F	G	H	I	J	K
1	TreePlan Academic Version							0.5		Only For Academic Use	
2								Strong			
3											0
4				Small				0		0	
5											
6				0		0		0.5			
7								Weak			
8											0
9								0		0	
10											
11								0.5			
12								Strong			
13											0
14				Medium				0		0	
15			1								
16	0			0		0		0.5			
17								Weak			
18											0
19								0		0	
20											
21								0.5			
22								Strong			
23											0
24				Large				0		0	
25											
26				0		0		0.5			
27								Weak			
28											0
29								0		0	

Note that the payoffs also appear in the right-hand margin of the decision tree. The payoffs in the right margin are computed by a formula that adds the payoffs on all of the branches leading to the associated terminal node. For the PDC problem, no payoffs are associated with the decision alternatives branches so we leave the default values of zero in cells D6, D16, and D24. The PDC decision tree is now complete.

Interpreting the Result

When probabilities and payoffs are inserted, TreePlan automatically makes the backward pass computations necessary to determine the optimal solution. Optimal decisions are identified by the number in the corresponding decision node. In the PDC decision tree in Figure 13.20, cell B15 contains the decision node. Note that a 3 appears in this node, which tells us that decision alternative branch 3 provides the optimal decision. Thus, decision analysis recommends PDC construct the Large condominium complex. The expected value of this decision appears at the beginning of the tree in cell A16. Thus, we see the optimal expected value is $14.2 million. The expected values of the other decision alternatives are displayed at the end of the corresponding decision branch. Thus, referring to cells E6 and E16, we see that the expected value of the Small complex is $7.8 million and the expected value of the Medium complex is $12.2 million.

FIGURE 13.20   THE PDC DECISION TREE WITH BRANCH PROBABILITIES AND PAYOFFS

PDC Tree

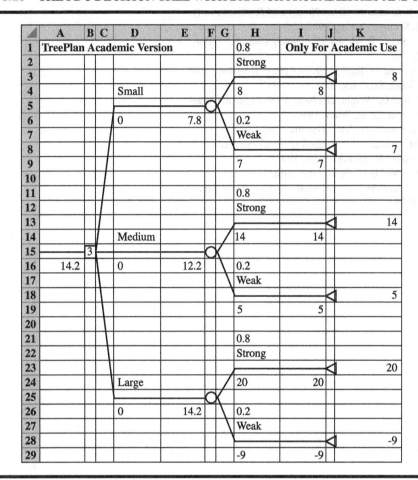

	A	B	C	D	E	F	G	H	I	J	K
1	TreePlan Academic Version							0.8	Only For Academic Use		
2								Strong			
3											8
4				Small				8	8		
5											
6				0	7.8			0.2			
7								Weak			
8											7
9								7	7		
10											
11								0.8			
12								Strong			
13											14
14				Medium				14	14		
15			3								
16	14.2			0	12.2			0.2			
17								Weak			
18											5
19								5	5		
20											
21								0.8			
22								Strong			
23											20
24				Large				20	20		
25											
26				0	14.2			0.2			
27								Weak			
28											-9
29								-9	-9		

Other Options

TreePlan defaults to a maximization objective. If you would like a minimization objective, follow these steps:

Step 1. Select **Decision Tree** from the **Menu Commands** group
Step 2. Select **Options**
Step 3. Choose **Minimize (costs)**
         Click **OK**

In using a TreePlan decision tree, we can modify probabilities and payoffs and quickly observe the impact of the changes on the optimal solution. Using this "what-if" type of sensitivity analysis, we can identify changes in probabilities and payoffs that would change the optimal decision. Also, because TreePlan is an Excel add-in, most of Excel's capabilities are available. For instance, we could use boldface to highlight the name of the optimal decision alternative on the final decision tree solution. A variety of other options TreePlan provides are contained in the TreePlan manual at the website that accompanies this text. Computer software packages such as TreePlan make it easier to do a thorough analysis of a decision problem.

References and Bibliography

Berger, J. O. *Statistical Decision Theory and Bayesian Analysis,* 2d ed. Springer-Verlag, 1985.

Chernoff, H., and L. E. Moses. *Elementary Decision Theory.* Dover, 1987.

Clemen, R. T., and T. Reilly. *Making Hard Decisions with Decision Tools.* Duxbury, 2001.

Goodwin, P., and G. Wright. *Decision Analysis for Management Judgment,* 2d ed. Wiley, 1999.

Gregory, G. *Decision Analysis.* Plenum, 1988.

Pratt, J. W., H. Raiffa, and R. Schlaifer. *Introduction to Statistical Decision Theory.* MIT Press, 1995.

Raiffa, H. *Decision Analysis.* McGraw-Hill, 1997.

Schlaifer, R. *Analysis of Decisions Under Uncertainty.* Krieger, 1978.

Self-Test Solutions and Answers to Even-Numbered Problems

1. a.

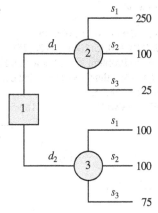

b. Influence diagram:

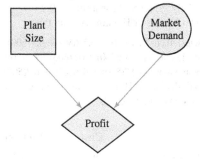

b.

Decision	Maximum Profit	Minimum Profit
d_1	250	25
d_2	100	75

Optimistic approach: Select d_1
Conservative approach: Select d_2
Regret or opportunity loss table:

Decision	s_1	s_2	s_3
d_1	0	0	50
d_2	150	0	0

Maximum regret: 50 for d_1 and 150 for d_2; select d_1

2. a. Optimistic: d_1
Conservative: d_3
Minimax regret: d_3
c. Optimistic: d_1
Conservative: d_2 or d_3
Minimax regret: d_2

3. a. Decision: Choose the best plant size from the two alternatives—a small plant and a large plant.
　　Chance event: market demand for the new product line with three possible outcomes (states of nature)—low, medium, and high

c.

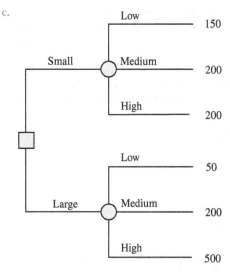

d.

Decision	Maximum Profit	Minimum Profit	Maximum Regret
Small	200	150	300
Large	500	50	100

Optimistic approach: Large plant
Conservative approach: Small plant
Minimax regret: Large plant

4. $EV(d_1) = 0.65(250) + 0.15(100) + 0.20(25) = 182.5$
$EV(d_2) = 0.65(100) + 0.15(100) + 0.20(75) = 95$
The optimal decision is d_1.

6. a. Decision: Which lease option to choose
Chance event: Miles driven

b.

	Annual Miles Driven		
	12,000	15,000	18,000
Forno	10,764	12,114	13,464
Midtown	11,160	11,160	12,960
Hopkins	11,700	11,700	11,700

c. Optimistic: Forno Saab
Conservative: Hopkins Automotive
Minimax: Hopkins Automotive

d. Midtown Motors

e. Most likely: $11,160; Probability = 0.9

f. Midtown Motors or Hopkins Automotive

7. a. EV(own staff) = 0.2(650) + 0.5(650) + 0.3(600) = 635
EV(outside vendor) = 0.2(900) + 0.5(600) + 0.3(300) = 570
EV(combination) = 0.2(800) + 0.5(650) + 0.3(500) = 635
Optimal decision: Hire an outside vendor with an expected cost of $570,000.

b.

	Cost	Probability
Own staff	300	0.3
Outside vendor	600	0.5
Combination	900	0.2
		1.0

8. a. $EV(d_1) = p(10) + (1 - p)(1) = 9p + 1$
$EV(d_2) = p(4) + (1 - p)(3) = 1p + 3$

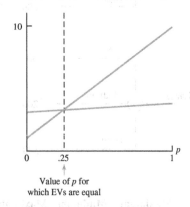

Value of p for which EVs are equal

$9p + 1 = 1p + 3$ and hence $p = 0.25$
d_2 is optimal for $p \leq 0.25$, d_1 is optimal for $p \geq 0.25$

b. d_2

c. As long as the payoff for $s_1 \geq 2$, then d_2 is optimal.

10. b. Space Pirates
EV = $724,000
$84,000 better than Battle Pacific

c. $200   0.18
$400   0.32
$800   0.30
$1600   0.20

d. $P(\text{Competition}) > 0.7273$

12. a. Decision: Whether to lengthen the runway
Chance event: The location decisions of Air Express and DRI
Consequence: Annual revenue

b. $255,000

c. $270,000

d. No

e. Lengthen the runway.

14. a. If s_1, then d_1; if s_2, then d_1 or d_2; if s_3, then d_2

b. EVwPI = 0.65(250) + 0.15(100) + 0.20(75) = 192.5

c. From the solution to Problem 4, we know that EV(d_1) = 182.5 and EV(d_2) = 95; thus, recommended decision is d_1; hence, EVwoPI = 182.5.

d. EVPI = EVwPI − EVwoPI = 192.5 − 182.5 = 10

16. a.

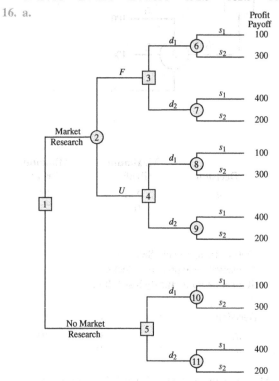

b. EV (node 6) = 0.57(100) + 0.43(300) = 186
EV (node 7) = 0.57(400) + 0.43(200) = 314
EV (node 8) = 0.18(100) + 0.82(300) = 264
EV (node 9) = 0.18(400) + 0.82(200) = 236
EV (node 10) = 0.40(100) + 0.60(300) = 220
EV (node 11) = 0.40(400) + 0.60(200) = 280

EV (node 3) = Max(186,314) = 314 d_2
EV (node 4) = Max(264,236) = 264 d_1
EV (node 5) = Max(220,280) = 280 d_2

EV (node 2) = 0.56(314) + 0.44(264) = 292
EV (node 1) = Max(292,280) = 292

∴ Market research
If favorable, decision d_2
If unfavorable, decision d_1

18. a. $5000 - 200 - 2000 - 150 = 2650$
      $3000 - 200 - 2000 - 150 = 650$

    b. Expected values at nodes:

8: 2350	5: 2350	9: 1100
6: 1150	10: 2000	7: 2000
4: 1870	3: 2000	2: 1560
1: 1560		

    c. Cost would have to decrease by at least $130,000.

    d.

Payoff (in millions)	Probability
−$200	0.20
800	0.32
2800	0.48
	1.00

20. b. If Do Not Review, Accept
       If Review and F, Accept
       If Review and U, Accept
       Always Accept

    c. Do not review; EVSI = $0

    d. $87,500; better method of predicting success

22. a. Order 2 lots; $60,000

    b. If E, order 2 lots
       If V, order 1 lot
       EV = $60,500

    c. EVPI = $14,000
       EVSI = $500
       Efficiency = 3.6%
       Yes, use consultant.

23.

State of Nature	$P(s_j)$	$P(I/s_j)$	$P(I \cap s_j)$	$P(s_j/I)$
s_1	0.2	0.10	0.020	0.1905
s_2	0.5	0.05	0.025	0.2381
s_3	0.3	0.20	0.060	0.5714
	1.0		$P(I) = 0.105$	1.0000

24. a. 0.695, 0.215, 0.090
       0.98, 0.02
       0.79, 0.21
       0.00, 1.00

    c. If C, Expressway
       If O, Expressway
       If R, Queen City
       26.6 minutes

Appendix   Building Spreadsheet Models

The purpose of this appendix is twofold. First, we provide an overview of Excel and discuss the basic operations needed to work with Excel workbooks and worksheets. Second, we provide an introduction to building mathematical models using Excel, including a discussion of how to find and use particular Excel functions, how to design and build good spreadsheet models, and how to ensure that these models are free of errors.

OVERVIEW OF MICROSOFT EXCEL

When using Excel for modeling, the data and the model are displayed in workbooks, each of which contains a series of worksheets. Figure A.1 shows the layout of a blank workbook created each time Excel is opened. The workbook is named Book1 and consists of three worksheets named Sheet1, Sheet2, and Sheet3. Excel highlights the worksheet currently displayed (Sheet1) by setting the name on the worksheet tab in bold. To select a different worksheet, simply click on the corresponding tab. Note that cell A1 is initially selected.

A workbook is a file containing one or more worksheets.

    The wide bar located across the top of the workbook is referred to as the Ribbon. Tabs, located at the top of the Ribbon, provide quick access to groups of related commands. There are eight tabs: Home, Insert, Page Layout, Formulas, Data, Review, View, and Add-Ins. Each tab contains several groups of related commands. Note that the Home tab is selected when Excel is opened. Four of the seven groups are displayed in Figure A.2. Under the Home tab there are seven groups of related commands: Clipboard, Font, Alignment, Number, Styles, Cells, and Editing. Commands are arranged within each group. For example, to change selected text to boldface, click the Home tab and click the Bold button in the Font group.

    Figure A.3 illustrates the location of the File tab, the Quick Access Toolbar, and the Formula Bar. When you click the File tab, Excel provides a list of workbook options such as opening, saving, and printing (worksheets). The Quick Access Toolbar allows you to quickly access these workbook options. For instance, the Quick Access Toolbar shown in Figure A.3 includes a Save button 🖫 that can be used to save files without having to first click the File tab. To add or remove features on the Quick Access Toolbar click the Customize Quick Access Toolbar button ⬍ on the Quick Access Toolbar.

    The Formula Bar contains a Name box, the Insert Function button *f*ₓ, and a Formula box. In Figure A.3, "A1" appears in the Name box because cell A1 is selected. You can select any other cell in the worksheet by using the mouse to move the cursor to another cell and clicking or by typing the new cell location in the name box and pressing the enter key. The Formula box is used to display the formula in the currently selected cell. For instance, if you had entered $=A1+A2$ into cell A3, whenever you select cell A3, the formula $=A1+A2$ will be shown in the Formula box. This feature makes it very easy to see and edit a formula in a particular cell. The Insert Function button allows you to quickly access all of the functions available in Excel. Later, we show how to find and use a particular function.

FIGURE A.1   BLANK WORKBOOK CREATED WHEN EXCEL IS STARTED

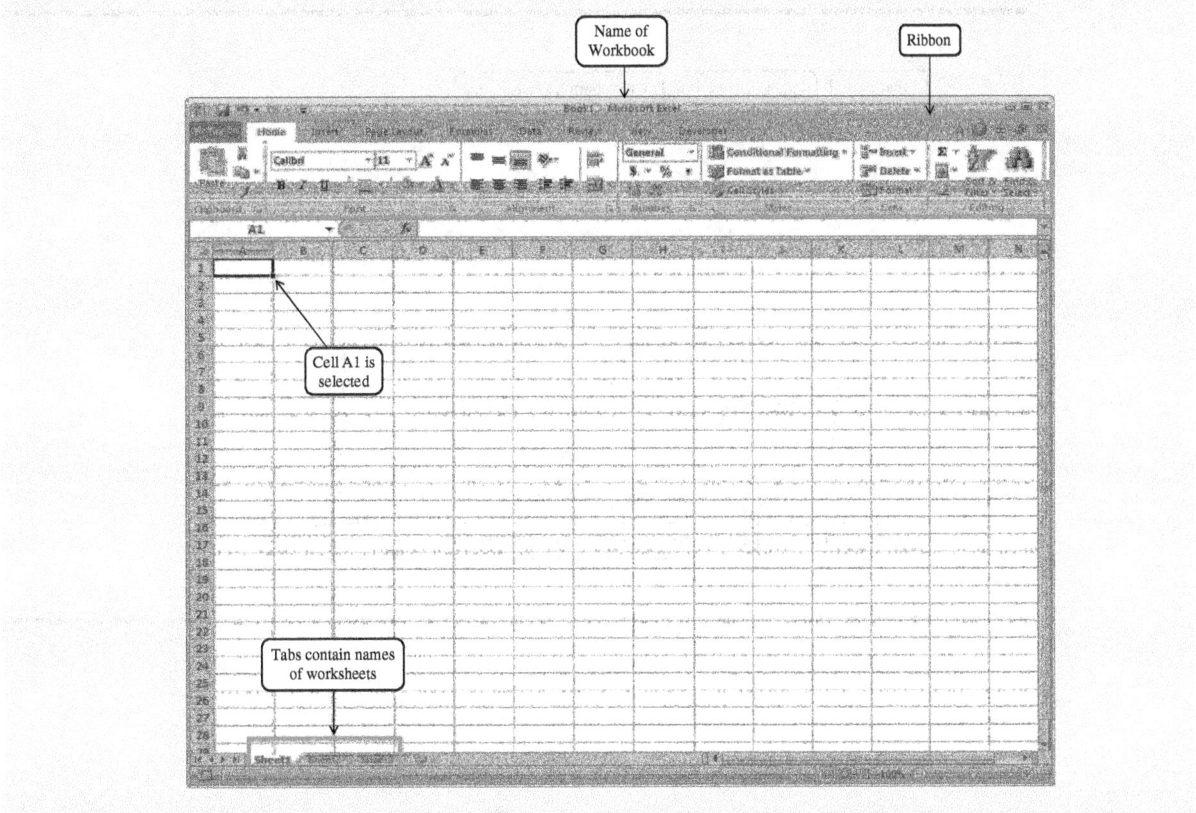

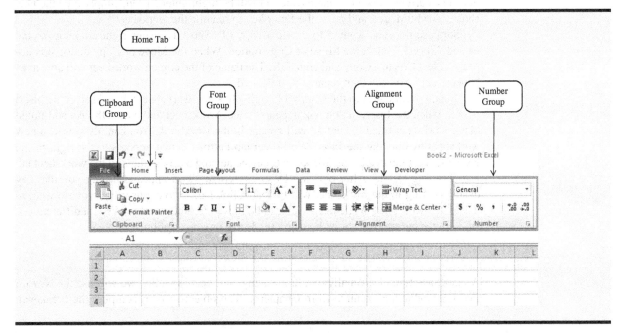

FIGURE A.2   PORTION OF THE HOME TAB

FIGURE A.3 EXCEL FILE TAB, QUICK ACCESS TOOLBAR, AND FORMULA BAR

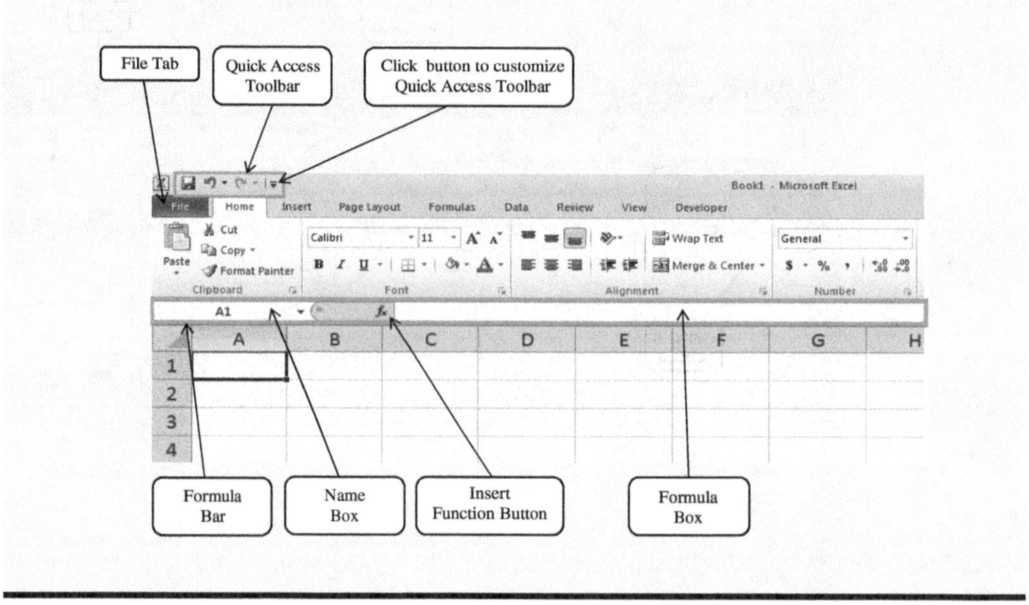

BASIC WORKBOOK OPERATIONS

Figure A.4 illustrates the worksheet options that can be performed after right clicking on a worksheet tab. For instance, to change the name of the current worksheet from "Sheet1" to "NowlinModel," right click the worksheet tab named "Sheet1" and select the Rename option. The current worksheet name (Sheet1) will be highlighted. Then, simply type the new name (NowlinModel) and press the Enter key to rename the worksheet.

Suppose that you wanted to create a copy of "Sheet 1." After right clicking the tab named "Sheet1," select the Move or Copy option. When the Move or Copy dialog box appears, select Create a Copy and click OK. The name of the copied worksheet will appear as "Sheet1 (2)." You can then rename it, if desired.

To add a worksheet to the workbook, right click any worksheet tab and select the Insert option; when the Insert dialog box appears, select Worksheet and click OK. An additional blank worksheet titled "Sheet 4" will appear in the workbook. You can also insert a new worksheet by clicking the Insert Worksheet tab button that appears to the right of the last worksheet tab displayed. Worksheets can be deleted by right clicking the worksheet tab and choosing Delete. After clicking Delete, a window will appear warning you that any data appearing in the worksheet will be lost. Click Delete to confirm that you do want to delete the worksheet. Worksheets can also be moved to other workbooks or a different position in the current workbook by using the Move or Copy option.

Creating, Saving, and Opening Files

As an illustration of manually entering, saving, and opening a file, we will use the Nowlin Plastics production example from Chapter 1. The objective is to compute the breakeven

FIGURE A.4   WORKSHEET OPTIONS OBTAINED AFTER RIGHT CLICKING ON A
WORKSHEET TAB

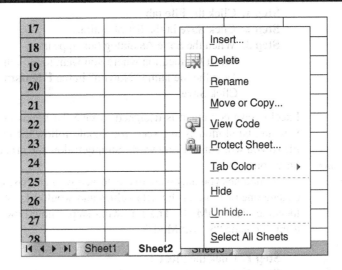

point for a product that has a fixed cost of $3000, a variable cost per unit of $2, and a selling price per unit of $5. We begin by creating a worksheet containing the problem data.

If you have just opened Excel, a blank workbook containing three worksheets will be displayed. The Nowlin data can now be entered manually by simply typing the fixed cost of $3000, the variable cost of $2, and the selling price of $5 into one of the worksheets. If Excel is currently running and no blank workbook is displayed, you can create a new blank workbook using the following steps:

Step 1. Click the **File** tab
Step 2. Click **New** in the list of options
Step 3. When the New Workbook dialog box appears:
Double click **Blank Workbook**

A new workbook containing three worksheets labeled Sheet1, Sheet2, and Sheet3 will appear.

We will place the data for the Nowlin example in the top portion of Sheet1 of the new workbook. First, we enter the label "Nowlin Plastics" into cell A1. To identify each of the three data values we enter the label "Fixed Cost" into cell A3, the label "Variable Cost Per Unit" into cell A5, and the label "Selling Price Per Unit" into cell A7. Next, we enter the actual cost and price data into the corresponding cells in column B: the value of $3000 in cell B3; the value of $2 in cell B5; and the value of $5 into cell B7. Finally, we will change the name of the worksheet from "Sheet1" to "NowlinModel" using the procedure described previously. Figure A.5 shows a portion of the worksheet we have just developed.

Before we begin the development of the model portion of the worksheet, we recommend that you first save the current file; this will prevent you from having to reenter the data in case something happens that causes Excel to close. To save the workbook using the filename "Nowlin," we perform the following steps:

Step 1. Click the **File** tab

Step 2. Click **Save** in the list of options

Step 3. When the **Save As** dialog box appears:
Select the location where you want to save the file
Type the file name "Nowlin" in the **File name** box
Click **Save**

Excel's Save command is designed to save the file as an Excel workbook. As you work with and build models in Excel, you should follow the practice of periodically saving the file so you will not lose any work. Simply follow the procedure described above, using the Save command.

*Keyboard shortcut: To save the file, press **CTRL S**.*

Sometimes you may want to create a copy of an existing file. For instance, suppose you change one or more of the data values and would like to save the modified file using the filename "NowlinMod." The following steps show how to save the modified workbook using filename "NowlinMod."

Step 1. Click the **File** tab

Step 2. Position the mouse pointer over **Save As**

Step 3. Click **Excel Workbook** from the list of options

Step 4. When the **Save As** dialog box appears:
In the **Save in** box select the location where you want to save the file
Type the filename "NowlinMod" in the **File name** box
Click **Save**

FIGURE A.5   NOWLIN PLASTICS DATA

	A	B
1	**Nowlin Plastics**	
2		
3	**Fixed Cost**	$3,000
4		
5	**Variable Cost Per Unit**	$2
6		
7	**Selling Price Per Unit**	$5
8		
9		
10		
11		
12		
13		
14		
15		
16		
17		
18		

Once the NowlinMod workbook has been saved, you can continue to work with the file to perform whatever type of analysis is appropriate. When you are finished working with the file, simply click the close window button ⊠ located at the top right-hand corner of the Ribbon.

You can easily access a saved file at another point in time. For example, the following steps show how to open the previously saved Nowlin workbook.

Step 1. Click the **File** tab
Step 2. Click **Open** in the list of options
Step 3. When the **Open** dialog box appears:
      Select the location where you previously saved the file
      Type the filename "Nowlin" in the **File name** box
      Click **Open**

The procedures we showed for saving or opening a workbook begin by clicking on the File tab to access the Save and Open commands. Once you have used Excel for a while, you will probably find it more convenient to add these commands to the Quick Access Toolbar.

CELLS, REFERENCES, AND FORMULAS IN EXCEL

Assume that the Nowlin workbook is open again and that we would like to develop a model that can be used to compute the profit or loss associated with a given production volume. We will use the bottom portion of the worksheet shown in Figure A.5 to develop the model. The model will contain formulas that *refer to the location of the data cells* in the upper section of the worksheet. By putting the location of the data cells in the formula, we will build a model that can be easily updated with new data. This will be discussed in more detail later in this appendix in the section Principles for Building Good Spreadsheet Models.

We enter the label "Models" into cell A10 to provide a visual reminder that the bottom portion of this worksheet will contain the model. Next, we enter the labels "Production Volume" into cell A12, "Total Cost" into cell A14, "Total Revenue" into cell A16, and "Total Profit (Loss)" into cell A18. Cell B12 is used to contain a value for the production volume. We will now enter formulas into cells B14, B16, and B18 that use the production volume in cell B12 to compute the values for total cost, total revenue, and total profit or loss.

Total cost is the sum of the fixed cost (cell B3) and the total variable cost. The total variable cost is the product of the variable cost per unit (cell B5) and production volume (cell B12). Thus, the formula for total variable cost is B5*B12 and to compute the value of total cost, we enter the formula =B3+B5*B12 into cell B14. Next, total revenue is the product of the selling price per unit (cell B7) and the number of units produced (cell B12), which we enter in cell B16 as the formula =B7*B12. Finally, the total profit or loss is the difference between the total revenue (cell B16) and the total cost (cell B14). Thus, in cell B18 we enter the formula =B16-B14. Figure A.6 shows a portion of the formula worksheet just described.

We can now compute the total profit or loss for a particular production volume by entering a value for the production volume into cell B12. Figure A.7 shows the results after entering a value of 800 into cell B12. We see that a production volume of 800 units results in a total cost of $4600, a total revenue of $4000, and a loss of $600.

FIGURE A.6 NOWLIN PLASTICS DATA AND MODEL

	A	B
1	**Nowlin Plastics**	
2		
3	**Fixed Cost**	3000
4		
5	**Variable Cost Per Unit**	2
6		
7	**Selling Price Per Unit**	5
8		
9		
10	**Models**	
11		
12	**Production Volume**	
13		
14	**Total Cost**	=B3+B5*B12
15		
16	**Total Revenue**	=B7*B12
17		
18	**Total Profit (Loss)**	=B16-B14

FIGURE A.7 NOWLIN PLASTICS RESULTS

	A	B
1	**Nowlin Plastics**	
2		
3	**Fixed Cost**	$3,000
4		
5	**Variable Cost Per Unit**	$2
6		
7	**Selling Price Per Unit**	$5
8		
9		
10	**Models**	
11		
12	**Production Volume**	800
13		
14	**Total Cost**	$4,600
15		
16	**Total Revenue**	$4,000
17		
18	**Total Profit (Loss)**	−$600

USING EXCEL FUNCTIONS

Excel provides a wealth of built-in formulas or functions for developing mathematical models. If we know which function is needed and how to use it, we can simply enter the function into the appropriate worksheet cell. However, if we are not sure which functions are available to accomplish a task or are not sure how to use a particular function, Excel can provide assistance.

Finding the Right Excel Function

To identify the functions available in Excel, click the Formulas tab on the Ribbon and then click the Insert Function button in the Function Library group. Alternatively, click the Insert Function button f_x on the formula bar. Either approach provides the Insert Function dialog box shown in Figure A.8.

The Search for a function box at the top of the Insert Function dialog box enables us to type a brief description for what we want to do. After doing so and clicking Go, Excel will search for and display, in the Select a function box, the functions that may accomplish our task. In many situations, however, we may want to browse through an entire category of functions to see what is available. For this task, the Or select a category box is helpful.

It contains a dropdown list of several categories of functions provided by Excel. Figure A.8 shows that we selected the Math & Trig category. As a result, Excel's Math &

FIGURE A.8   INSERT FUNCTION DIALOG BOX

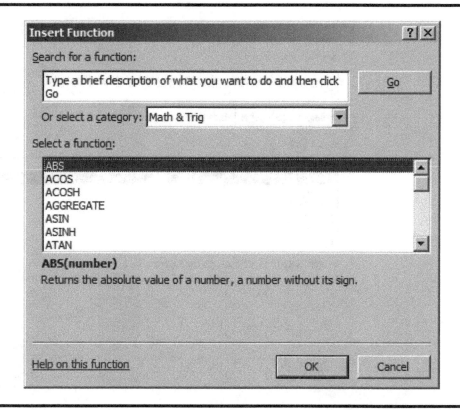

Trig functions appear in alphabetical order in the Select a function box. We see the ABS function listed first, followed by the ACOS function, and so on.

Colon Notation

Although many functions, such as the ABS function, have a single argument, some Excel functions depend on arrays. Colon notation provides an efficient way to convey arrays and matrices of cells to functions. The colon notation may be described as follows: B3:B5 means cell B1 "through" cell B5, namely the array of values stored in the locations (B1,B2,B3,B4,B5). Consider for example the following function =SUM(B1:B5). The sum function adds up the elements contained in the function's argument. Hence, =SUM(B1:B5) evaluates the following formula:

$$=B1+B2+B3+B4+B5$$

Inserting a Function into a Worksheet Cell

Through the use of an example, we will now show how to use the Insert Function and Function Arguments dialog boxes to select a function, develop its arguments, and insert

FIGURE A.9   DESCRIPTION OF THE SUMPRODUCT FUNCTION IN THE INSERT FUNCTION DIALOG BOX

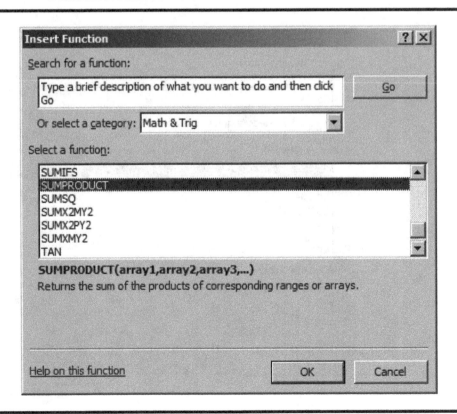

the function into a worksheet cell. We also illustrate the use of a very useful function, the SUMPRODUCT function, and how to use colon notation in the argument of a function.

The SUMPRODUCT function, as shown in Figure A.9, is used in many of the Solver examples in the textbook. Note that SUMPRODUCT is now highlighted, and that immediately below the Select a function box we see SUMPRODUCT(array1,array2,array3, . . .), which indicates that the SUMPRODUCT function contains the array arguments array1, array2, array3, ... In addition, we see that the description of the SUMPRODUCT function is "Returns the sum of the products of corresponding ranges or arrays." For example, the function =SUMPRODUCT(A1:A3, B1:B3) evaluates the formula A1*B1 + A2*B2 + A3*B3. As shown in the following example, this function can be very useful in calculations of cost, profit, and other such functions involving multiple arrays of numbers.

Figure A.10 displays an Excel worksheet for the Foster Generators Problem that appears in Chapter 6. This problem involves the transportation of a product from three plants (Cleveland, Bedford, and York) to four distribution centers (Boston, Chicago, St. Louis, and Lexington). The costs for each unit shipped from each plant to each distribution center are shown in cells B5:E7, and the values in cells B17:E19 are the number of units shipped from each plant to each distribution center. Cell B13 will contain the total transportation cost corresponding to the transportation cost values in cells B5:E7 and the values of the number of units shipped in cells B17:E19.

The following steps show how to use the SUMPRODUCT function to compute the total transportation cost for Foster Generators.

FIGURE A.10   EXCEL WORKSHEET USED TO CALCULATE TOTAL SHIPPING COSTS
FOR THE FOSTER GENERATORS TRANSPORTATION PROBLEM

WEB file

Foster Generators

	A	B	C	D	E	F	G	H
1	**Foster Generators**							
2								
3				**Destination**				
4	**Origin**	Boston	Chicago	St. Louis	Lexington	**Supply**		
5	Cleveland	3	2	7	6	5000		
6	Bedford	7	5	2	3	6000		
7	York	2	5	4	5	2500		
8	**Demand**	6000	4000	2000	1500			
9								
10								
11	**Model**							
12								
13		**Min Cost**						
14								
15				**Destination**				
16	**Origin**	Boston	Chicago	St. Louis	Lexington	**Total**		
17	Cleveland	3500	1500	0	0	5000	<=	5000
18	Bedford	0	2500	2000	1500	6000	<=	6000
19	York	2500	0	0	0	2500	<=	2500
20	**Total**	6000	4000	2000	1500			
21		=	=	=	=			
22		6000	4000	2000	1500			

FIGURE A.11 COMPLETED FUNCTION ARGUMENTS DIALOG BOX FOR THE SUMPRODUCT FUNCTION

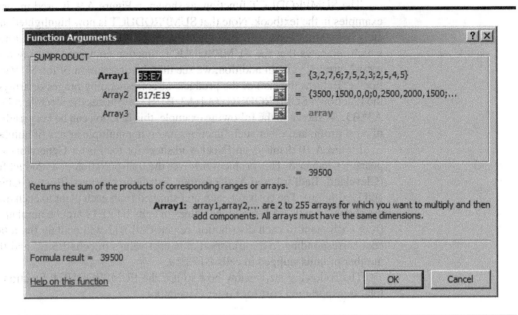

Step 1. Select **cell C13**
Step 2. Click *fx* on the formula bar
Step 3. When the **Insert Function** dialog box appears:
Select **Math & Trig** in the **Or select a category** box
Select **SUMPRODUCT** in the **Select a function** box (as shown in Figure A.9)
Click **OK**
Step 4. When the **Function Arguments** box appears (see Figure A.11):
Enter B5:E7 in the **Array1** box
Enter B17:E19 in the **Array2** box
Click **OK**

The worksheet then appears as shown in Figure A.12. The value of the total transportation cost in cell C13 is 39500, or $39,500.

We illustrated the use of Excel's capability to provide assistance in using the SUMPRODUCT function. The procedure is similar for all Excel functions. This capability is especially helpful if you do not know which function to use or forget the proper name and/or syntax for a function.

ADDITIONAL EXCEL FUNCTIONS FOR MODELING

In this section we introduce some additional Excel functions that have proven useful in modeling decision problems.

FIGURE A.12   EXCEL WORKSHEET SHOWING THE USE OF EXCEL'S SUMPRODUCT FUNCTION TO CALCULATE TOTAL SHIPPING COSTS

	A	B	C	D	E	F	G	H
1	Foster Generators							
2								
3			Destination					
4	Origin	Boston	Chicago	St. Louis	Lexington	Supply		
5	Cleveland	3	2	7	6	5000		
6	Bedford	7	5	2	3	6000		
7	York	2	5	4	5	2500		
8	Demand	6000	4000	2000	1500			
9								
10								
11	Model							
12								
13		Min Cost	39500					
14								
15			Destination					
16	Origin	Boston	Chicago	St. Louis	Lexington	Total		
17	Cleveland	3500	1500	0	0	5000	<=	5000
18	Bedford	0	2500	2000	1500	6000	<=	6000
19	York	2500	0	0	0	2500	<=	2500
20	Total	6000	4000	2000	1500			
21		=	=	=	=			
22		6000	4000	2000	1500			

IF and COUNTIF Functions

Let us consider the case of Gambrell Manufacturing. Gambrell Manufacturing produces car stereos. Stereos are composed of a variety of components that the company must carry in inventory to keep production running smoothly. However, because inventory can be a costly investment, Gambrell generally likes to keep the amount of inventory of the components it uses in manufacturing to a minimum. To help monitor and control its inventory of components, Gambrell uses an inventory policy known as an "order up to" policy. This type of inventory policy and others are discussed in detail in Chapter 14.

The "order up to policy" is as follows. Whenever the inventory on hand drops below a certain level, enough units are ordered to return the inventory to that predetermined level. If the current number of units in inventory, denoted by H, drops below M units, we order enough to get the inventory level back up to M units. M is called the Order Up to Point. Stated mathematically, if Q is the amount we order, then

$$Q = M - H$$

An inventory model for Gambrell Manufacturing appears in Figure A.13. In this worksheet, labeled "OrderQuantity" in the upper half of the worksheet, the component ID number, inventory on hand (H), order up to point (M), and cost per unit are given for each of four components. Also given in this sheet is the fixed cost per order. The fixed cost is interpreted as follows: Each time a component is ordered, it costs Gambrell $120 to process the order. The fixed cost of $120 is incurred regardless of how many units are ordered.

923

WEB file

Gambrell

	A	B	C	D	E	F
4	Component ID	570	578	741	755	
5	Inventory On-Hand	5	30	70	17	
6	Up to Order Point	100	55	70	45	
7	Cost per unit	$4.50	$12.50	$3.26	$4.15	
8						
9	Fixed Cost per Order	$120				
10						
11	**Model**					
12						
13	Component ID	570	578	741	755	
14	Order Quantity	95	25	0	28	
15	Cost of Goods	$384.75	$312.50	$0.00	$116.20	
16						
17	Total Number of Orders	3				
18						
19	Total Fixed costs	$360.00				
20	Total Cost of Goods	$813.45				
21	Total Cost	$1,173.45				
22						

The model portion of the worksheet calculates the order quantity for each component. For example, for component 570, $M = 100$ and $H = 5$, so $Q = M - H = 100 - 5 = 95$. For component 741, $M = 70$ and $H = 70$ and no units are ordered because the on-hand inventory of 70 units is equal to the order point of 70. The calculations are similar for the other two components.

Depending on the number of units ordered, Gambrell receives a discount on the cost per unit. If 50 or more units are ordered, there is a quantity discount of 10% on every unit purchased. For example, for component 741, the cost per unit is $4.50 and 95 units are ordered. Because 95 exceeds the 50-unit requirement, there is a 10% discount and the cost per unit is reduced to $4.50 - 0.1($4.50) = $4.50 - $0.45 = $4.05. Not including the fixed cost, the cost of goods purchased is then $4.05(95) = $384.75.

The Excel functions used to perform these calculations are shown in Figure A.14. The IF function is used to calculate the purchase cost of goods for each component in row 15. The general form of the IF function is

$$=IF(condition,\ result\ if\ condition\ is\ true,\ result\ if\ condition\ is\ false)$$

For example, in cell B15 we have =IF(B14>=50,0.9*B7,B7)*B14. This statement says if the order quantity (cell B14) is greater than or equal to 50, then the cost per unit is 0.9*B7 (there is a 10% discount); otherwise, there is no discount and the cost per unit is the amount given in cell B7. The purchase cost of goods for the other components are computed in a like manner.

The total cost in cell B21 is the sum of the purchase cost of goods ordered in row 15 and the fixed ordering costs. Because we place three orders (one each for components 570, 578, and 755), the fixed cost of the orders is 3*120 = $360.

	A	B	C	D	E
1					
2	**Gambrell Manufacturing**				
3					
4	Component ID	570	578	741	755
5	Inventory On-Hand	5	30	70	17
6	Up to Order Point	100	55	70	45
7	Cost per unit	4.5	12.5	3.26	4.15
8					
9	Fixed Cost per Order	120			
10					
11	**Model**				
12					
13	Component ID	=B4	=C4	=D4	=E4
14	Order Quantity	=B6-B5	=C6-C5	=D6-D5	=E6-E5
15	Cost of Goods	=IF(B14>=50,0.9*B7,B7)*B14	=IF(C14>=50, 0.9*C7,C7)*C14	=IF(D14>=50, 0.9*D7,D7)*D14	=IF(E14>=50, 0.9*E7,E7)*E14
16					
17	Total Number of Orders	=COUNTIF(B14:E14,">0")			
18					
19	Total Fixed Costs	=B17*B9			
20	Total Cost of Goods	=SUM(B15:E15)			
21	Total Cost	=SUM(B19:B20)			
22					

The COUNTIF function in cell B17 is used to count how many times we order. In particular, it counts the number of components having a positive order quantity. The general form of the COUNTIF function is

$$=\text{COUNTIF}(\textit{range, condition})$$

The *range* is the range to search for the *condition*. The condition is the test to be counted when satisfied. *Note that quotes are required for the condition with the COUNTIF function.* In the Gambrell model in Figure A.14, cell B17 counts the number of cells that are greater than zero in the range of cells B14:E14. In the model, because only cells B14, C14, and E14 are greater than zero, the COUNTIF function in cell B17 returns 3.

As we have seen, IF and COUNTIF are powerful functions that allow us to make calculations based on a condition holding (or not). There are other such conditional functions available in Excel. In the problems at the end of this appendix, we ask you to investigate one such function, the SUMIF function. Another conditional function that is extremely useful in modeling is the VLOOKUP function. We discuss the VLOOKUP function with an example in the next section.

VLOOKUP Function

Next, consider the workbook named *OM455* shown in Figure A.15. The worksheet named Grades is shown. This worksheet calculates the course grades for the course OM 455. There are 11 students in the course. Each student has a midterm exam score and a final exam score, and these are averaged in column D to get the course average. The scale given in the upper portion of the worksheet is used to determine the course grade for each student.

FIGURE A.15 OM455 GRADE SPREADSHEET

OM455

	A	B	C	D	E	F
1	OM455					
2	Section 001					
3	Course Grading Scale Based on Course Average:					
4		Lower	Upper	Course		
5		Limit	Limit	Grade		
6		0	59	F		
7		60	69	D		
8		70	79	C		
9		80	89	B		
10		90	100	A		
11						
12		Midterm	Final	Course	Course	
13	Lastname	Score	Score	Average	Grade	
14	Benson	70	56	63.0	D	
15	Chin	95	91	93.0	A	
16	Choi	82	80	81.0	B	
17	Cruz	45	78	61.5	D	
18	Doe	68	45	56.5	F	
19	Honda	91	98	94.5	A	
20	Hume	87	74	80.5	B	
21	Jones	60	80	70.0	C	
22	Miranda	80	93	86.5	B	
23	Murigami	97	98	97.5	A	
24	Ruebush	90	91	90.5	A	
25						

Consider, for example, the performance of student Choi in row 16. This student earned an 82 on the midterm, an 80 on the final, and a course average of 81. From the grading scale, this equates to a course grade of B.

The course average is simply the average of the midterm and final scores, but how do we get Excel to look in the grading scale table and automatically assign the correct course letter grade to each student? The VLOOKUP function allows us to do just that. The formulas and functions used in *OM455* are shown in Figure A.16.

The VLOOKUP function allows the user to pull a subset of data from a larger table of data based on some criterion. The general form of the VLOOKUP function is

$$=VLOOKUP(arg1,arg2,arg3,arg4)$$

where arg1 is the value to search for in the first column of the table, arg2 is the table location, arg3 is the column location in the table to be returned, and arg4 is TRUE if looking for the first partial match of arg1 and FALSE for looking for an exact match of arg1. We will explain the difference between a partial and exact match in a moment. VLOOKUP assumes that the first column of the table is sorted in ascending order.

The VLOOKUP function for student Choi in cell E16 is as follows:

$$=VLOOKUP(D16,B6:D10,3,TRUE)$$

This function uses the course average from cell D16 and searches the first column of the table defined by B6:D10. In the first column of the table (column B), Excel searches from the top until it finds a number strictly greater than the value of D16 (81). It then backs up one row (to row 9). That is, it finds the last value in the first column less than or equal to 81.

FIGURE A.16   THE FORMULAS AND FUNCTIONS USED IN OM 455

	A	B	C	D	E
1	OM 455				
2	Section 001				
3	Course Grading Scale Based on Course Average:				
4		Lower	Upper	Course	
5		Limit	Limit	Grade	
6		0	59	F	
7		60	69	D	
8		70	79	C	
9		80	89	B	
10		90	100	A	
11					
12		Midterm	Final	Course	Course
13	Lastname	Score	Score	Average	Grade
14	Benson	70	56	=AVERAGE(B14:C14)	=VLOOKUP(D14,B6:D10,3,TRUE)
15	Chin	95	91	=AVERAGE(B15:C15)	=VLOOKUP(D15,B6:D10,3,TRUE)
16	Choi	82	80	=AVERAGE(B16:C16)	=VLOOKUP(D16,B6:D10,3,TRUE)
17	Cruz	45	78	=AVERAGE(B17:C17)	=VLOOKUP(D17,B6:D10,3,TRUE)
18	Doe	68	45	=AVERAGE(B18:C18)	=VLOOKUP(D18,B6:D10,3,TRUE)
19	Honda	91	98	=AVERAGE(B19:C19)	=VLOOKUP(D19,B6:D10,3,TRUE)
20	Hume	87	74	=AVERAGE(B20:C20)	=VLOOKUP(D20,B6:D10,3,TRUE)
21	Jones	60	80	=AVERAGE(B21:C21)	=VLOOKUP(D21,B6:D10,3,TRUE)
22	Miranda	80	93	=AVERAGE(B22:C22)	=VLOOKUP(D22,B6:D10,3,TRUE)
23	Murigami	97	98	=AVERAGE(B23:C23)	=VLOOKUP(D23,B6:D10,3,TRUE)
24	Ruebush	90	91	=AVERAGE(B24:C24)	=VLOOKUP(D24,B6:D10,3,TRUE)
25					

Because there is a 3 in the third argument of the VLOOKUP function, it takes the element in row 9 in the third column of the table, which is the letter "B." In summary, the VLOOKUP takes the first argument and searches the first column of the table for the last row that is less than or equal to the first argument. It then selects from that row the element in the column number of the third argument.

Note: If the last element of the VLOOKUP function is "False," the only change is that Excel searches for an exact match of the first argument in the first column of the data. VLOOKUP is very useful when you seek subsets of a table based on a condition.

PRINCIPLES FOR BUILDING GOOD SPREADSHEET MODELS

We have covered some of the fundamentals of building spreadsheet models. There are some generally accepted guiding principles for how to build a spreadsheet so that it is more easily used by others and so that the risk of error is mitigated. In this section we discuss some of those principles.

Separate the Data from the Model

One of the first principles of good modeling is to separate the data from the model. This enables the user to update the model parameters without fear of mistakenly typing over a formula or function. For this reason, it is good practice to have a data section at the top of the spreadsheet. A separate model section should contain all calculations and in general should not be updated by a user. For a what-if model or an optimization model, there might also be a separate section for decision cells (values that are not data or calculations, but are the outputs we seek from the model).

The Nowlin model in Figure A.6 is a good example. The data section is in the upper part of the spreadsheet followed by the model section that contains the calculations. The Gambrell model in Figure A.13 does not totally employ the principle of data/model separation. A better model would have the 50-unit hurdle and the 90% cost (10% discount) as data in the upper section. Then the formulas in row 15 would simply refer to the cells in the upper section. This would allow the user to easily change the discount, for example, without having to change all four formulas in row 15.

Document the Model

A good spreadsheet model is well documented. Clear labels and proper formatting and alignment make the spreadsheet easier to navigate and understand. For example, if the values in a worksheet are cost, currency formatting should be used. No cells should be unlabeled. A new user should be able to easily understand the model and its calculations. Figure A.17 shows a better-documented version of the Foster Generators model previously discussed (Figure A.10). The tables are more explicitly labeled, and shading focuses the user on the objective and the decision cells (amount to ship). The per-unit shipping cost data and total (Min) cost have been properly formatted as currency.

FIGURE A.17 A BETTER-DOCUMENTED FOSTER GENERATORS MODEL

WEB file

Foster Rev

	A	B	C	D	E	F	G	H
1	**Foster Generators**							
2								
3	Origin to Destination—Cost per unit to ship							
4			**Destination**					
5	**Origin**	Boston	Chicago	St. Louis	Lexington	**Units Available**		
6	Cleveland	$3.00	$2.00	$7.00	$6.00	5000		
7	Bedford	$7.00	$5.00	$2.00	$3.00	6000		
8	York	$2.00	$5.00	$4.00	$5.00	2500		
9	**Units Demanded**	6000	4000	2000	1500			
10								
11								
12	**Model**							
13								
14		**Min Cost**	$39,500.00					
15								
16	Origin to Destination—Units Shipped							
17			**Destination**					
18	**Origin**	Boston	Chicago	St. Louis	Lexington	**Units Shipped**		
19	Cleveland	3500	1500	0	0	5000	<=	5000
20	Bedford	0	2500	2000	1500	6000	<=	6000
21	York	2500	0	0	0	2500	<=	2500
22	**Units Received**	6000	4000	2000	1500			
23		=	=	=	=			
24		6000	4000	2000	1500			

Use Simple Formulas and Cell Names

Clear formulas can eliminate unnecessary calculations, reduce errors, and make it easier to maintain your spreadsheet. Long and complex calculations should be divided into several cells. This makes the formula easier to understand and easier to edit. Avoid using numbers in a formula. Instead, put the number in a cell in the data section of your worksheet and refer to the cell location of the data in the formula. Building the formula in this manner avoids having to edit the formula for a simple data change.

Using cell names can make a formula much easier to understand. To assign a name to a cell, use the following steps:

Step 1. Select the cell or range of cells you would like to name
Step 2. Select the **Formulas** tab from the Ribbon
Step 3. Choose **Define Name** from the Define Names section
Step 4. The **New Name** dialog box will appear, as shown in Figure A.18
Enter the name you would like to use in the top portion of the dialog box and Click **OK**

Following this procedure and naming all cells in the *Nowlin Plastics* spreadsheet model leads to the model shown in Figure A.19. Compare this to Figure A.6 to easily understand the formulas in the model.

A name is also easily applied to range as follows. First, highlight the range of interest. Then click on the Name Box in the Formula Bar (refer back to Figure A.3) and type in the desired range name.

Use of Relative and Absolute Cell References

There are a number of ways to copy a formula from one cell to another in an Excel worksheet. One way to copy the a formula from one cell to another is presented here:

Step 1. Select the cell you would like to copy
Step 2. Right click on the mouse
Step 3. Click **Copy**
Step 4. Select the cell where you would like to put the copy
Step 5. Right click on the mouse
Step 6. Click **Paste**

When copying in Excel, one can use a relative or an absolute address. When copied, a relative address adjusts with the move of the copy, whereas an absolute address stays in its original form. Relative addresses are of the form C7. Absolute addresses have $ in front of the column and row, for example, $C$7. How you use relative and absolute addresses can have an impact on the amount of effort it takes to build a model and the opportunity for error in constructing the model.

Let us reconsider the OM455 grading spreadsheet previously discussed in this appendix and shown in Figure A.16. Recall that we used the VLOOKUP function to retrieve the appropriate letter grade for each student. The following formula is in cell E14:

$$=VLOOKUP(D14,B6:D10,3,TRUE)$$

FIGURE A.18 THE DEFINE NAME DIALOG BOX

WEB file

Nowlin Plastics

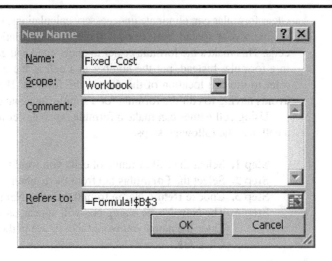

FIGURE A.19 THE NOWLIN PLASTIC MODEL FORMULAS WITH NAMED CELLS

	A	B
1	**Nowlin Plastics**	
2		
3	**Fixed Cost**	3000
4		
5	**Variable Cost Per Unit**	2
6		
7	**Selling Price Per Unit**	5
8		
9		
10	**Models**	
11		
12	**Production Volume**	800
13		
14	**Total Cost**	=Fixed_Cost+Variable_Cost*Production_Volume
15		
16	**Total Revenue**	=Selling_Price*Production_Volume
17		
18	**Total Profit (Loss)**	=Total_Revenue-Total_Cost

Note that this formula contains only relative addresses. If we copy this to cell E15, we get the following result:

=VLOOKUP(D15,B7:D11,3,TRUE)

Although the first argument has correctly changed to D15 (we want to calculate the letter grade for the student in row 15), the table in the function has also shifted to B7:D11. What we desired was for this table location to remain the same. A better approach would have been to use the following formula in cell E14:

$$=VLOOKUP(D14,\$B\$6:\$D\$10,3,TRUE)$$

Copying this formula to cell E15 results in the following formula:

$$=VLOOKUP(D15,\$B\$6:\$D\$10,3,TRUE)$$

This correctly changes the first argument to D15 and keeps the data table intact. Using absolute referencing is extremely useful if you have a function that has a reference that should not change when applied to another cell and you are copying the formula to other locations. In the case of the OM455 workbook, instead of typing the VLOOKUP for each student, we can use absolute referencing on the table and then copy from row 14 to rows 15 through 24.

In this section we have discussed guidelines for good spreadsheet model building. In the next section we discuss EXCEL tools available for checking and debugging spreadsheet models.

AUDITING EXCEL MODELS

EXCEL contains a variety of tools to assist you in the development and debugging of spreadsheet models. These tools are found in the Formula Auditing group of the Formulas Tab as shown in Figure A.20. Let us review each of the tools available in this group.

Trace Precedents and Dependents

The Trace Precedents button ![Trace Precedents] creates arrows pointing to the selected cell from cells that are part of the formula in that cell. The Trace Dependents button ![Trace Dependents] , on the other hand, shows arrows pointing from the selected cell, to cells that depend on the selected cell. Both of the tools are excellent for quickly ascertaining how parts of a model are linked.

An example of Trace Precedents is shown in Figure A.21. Here we have opened the *Foster Rev* worksheet, selected cell C14, and clicked the Trace Precedents button in the Formula Auditing Group. Recall that the cost in cell C14 is calculated as the SUMPRODUCT of the per-unit shipping cost and units shipped. In Figure A.21, to show this relationship, arrows are drawn to these respective areas of the spreadsheet to cell C14. These arrows may be removed by clicking on the Remove Arrows button in the Auditing Tools Group.

FIGURE A.20   THE FORMULA AUDITING GROUP OF THE FORMULAS TAB

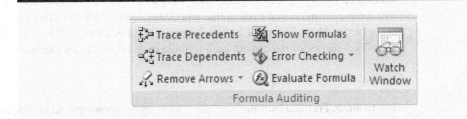

FIGURE A.21 TRACE PRECEDENTS FOR CELL C14 (COST) IN THE FOSTER GENERATORS REV MODEL

Foster Rev

| C14 | ▼ | fx | =SUMPRODUCT(B6:E8,B19:E21) | | | | |

	A	B	C	D	E	F	G	H
1	**Foster Generators**							
2								
3	Origin to Destination—Cost per unit to ship							
4			**Destination**					
5	**Origin**	Boston	Chicago	St. Louis	Lexington	**Units Available**		
6	Cleveland	$3.00	$2.00	$7.00	$6.00	5000		
7	Bedford	$7.00	$5.00	$2.00	$3.00	6000		
8	York	$2.00	$5.00	$4.00	$5.00	2500		
9	**Units Demanded**	6000	4000	2000	1500			
10								
11								
12	**Model**							
13								
14		**Min Cost**	$39,500.00					
15								
16	Origin to Destination—Units Shipped							
17			**Destination**					
18	**Origin**	Boston	Chicago	St. Louis	Lexington	**Units Shipped**		
19	Cleveland	3500	1500	0	0	5000	<=	5000
20	Bedford	0	2500	2000	1500	6000	<=	6000
21	York	2500	0	0	0	2500	<=	2500
22	**Units Received**	6000	4000	2000	1500			
23		=	=	=	=			
24		6000	4000	2000	1500			

An example of Trace Dependents is shown in Figure A.22. We have selected cell E20, the units shipped from Bedford to Lexington, and clicked on the Trace Dependents button in the Formula Auditing Group. As shown in Figure A.22, units shipped from Bedford to Lexington impacts the cost function in cell C14, the total units shipped from Bedford given in cell F20, and the total units shipped to Lexington in cell E22. These arrows may be removed by clicking on the Remove Arrows button in the Auditing Tools Group.

Trace Precedents and Trace Dependents can highlight errors in copying and formula construction by showing that incorrect sections of the worksheet are referenced.

Show Formulas

The Show Formulas button, 🔲 Show Formulas , does exactly that. To see the formulas in a worksheet, simply click on any cell in the worksheet and then click on Show Formulas. You will see the formulas that exist in that worksheet. To go back to hiding the formulas, click again on the Show Formulas button. Figure A.6 gives an example of the show formulas view. This allows you to inspect each formula in detail in its cell location.

Evaluate Formulas

The Evaluate Formula button, 🔘 Evaluate Formula , allows you to investigate the calculations of particular cell in great detail. To invoke this tool, we simply select a cell containing

FIGURE A.22   TRACE DEPENDENTS FOR CELL C14 (COST) IN THE FOSTER
GENERATORS REV MODEL

	E20	▼	●	*fx*	1500			
	A	B	C	D	E	F	G	H
12	Model							
13								
14		**Min Cost**	$39,500.00					
15								
16	Origin to Destination—Units Shipped							
17			**Destination**					
18	**Origin**	Boston	Chicago	St. Louis	Lexington	**Units Shipped**		
19	Cleveland	3500	1500	0	0	5000	<=	5000
20	Bedford	0	2500	2000	1500	6000	<=	6000
21	York	2500	0	0	0	2500	<=	2500
22	**Units Received**	6000	4000	2000	1500			
23		=	=	=	=			
24		6000	4000	2000	1500			

a formula and click on the Evaluate Formula button in the Formula Auditing Group. As an
example, we select cell B15 of the Gambrell Manufacturing model (see Figures A.13 and
A.14). Recall we are calculating cost of goods based upon whether or not there is a quantity
discount. Clicking on the Evaluate button allows you to evaluate this formula explicitly. The
Evaluate Formula dialog box appears in Figure A.23. Figure A.24 shows the result of one
click of the Evaluate button. The B14 has changed to its value of 95. Further clicks would
evaluate in order, from left to right, the remaining components of the formula. We ask the
reader to further explore this tool in an exercise at the end of this appendix.

The Evaluate Formula tool provides an excellent means of identifying the exact location of an error in a formula.

FIGURE A.23   THE EVALUATE FORMULA DIALOG BOX

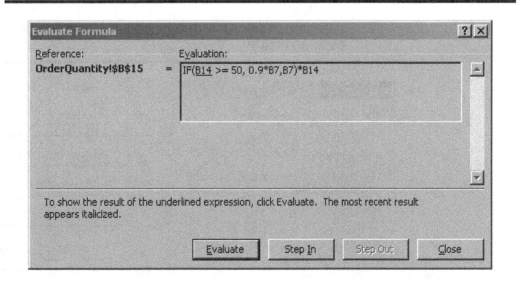

FIGURE A.24   THE EVALUATE FORMULA AFTER ONE CLICK OF THE
EVALUATE BUTTON

Evaluate Formula	? X
Reference:	Evaluation:
OrderQuantity!$B$15 =	IF(*95* >= 50, 0.9*B7,B7)*B14

To show the result of the underlined expression, click Evaluate. The most recent result
appears italicized.

| Evaluate | Step In | Step Out | Close |

Error Checking

The Error Checking Button, 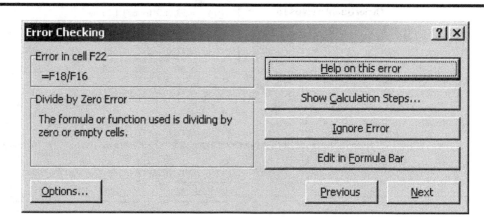, provides an automatic means of checking
for mathematical errors within formulas of a worksheet. Clicking on the Error Checking
button causes Excel to check every formula in the sheet for calculation errors. If an error is
found, the Error Checking dialog box appears. An example for a hypothetical division by
zero error is shown in Figure A.25. From this box, the formula can be edited or the calculation steps can be observed (as in the previous section on Evaluate Formulas).

FIGURE A.25   THE ERROR CHECKING DIALOG BOX FOR A DIVISION
BY ZERO ERROR

Error Checking	? X
Error in cell F22	Help on this error
=F18/F16	
Divide by Zero Error	Show Calculation Steps...
The formula or function used is dividing by zero or empty cells.	Ignore Error
	Edit in Formula Bar
Options...	Previous Next

FIGURE A.26   THE WATCH WINDOW FOR THE GAMBRELL MANUFACTURING
MODEL

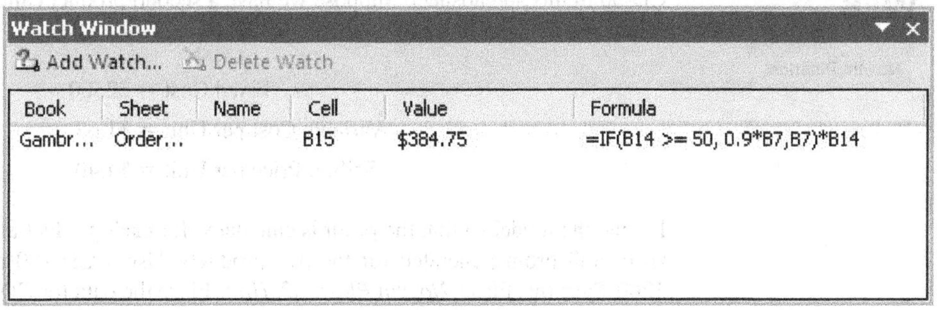

Watch Window

The Watch Window, located in the Formula Auditing Group, allows the user to observe the values of cells included in the Watch Window box list. This is useful for large models when not all the model is observable on the screen or when multiple worksheets are used. The user can monitor how the listed cells change with a change in the model without searching through the worksheet or changing from one worksheet to another.

A Watch Window for the Gambrell Manufacturing model is shown in Figure A.26. The following steps were used from the OrderQuantity worksheet to add cell B15 of the OrderQuantity worksheet to the watch list:

Step 1. Select the **Formulas** tab
Step 2. Select **Watch Window** from the Formula Auditing Group
The Watch Window will appear
Step 3. Select **Add Watch**
Step 4. Click on the cell you would like to add to the watch list (in this case B15)

As shown in Figure A.26, the list gives the workbook name, worksheet name, cell name (if used), cell location, cell value, and cell formula. To delete a cell from the watch list, select the entry from the list and then click on the Delete Watch button in the upper part of the Watch Window.

The Watch Window, as shown in Figure A.26, allows us to monitor the value of B15 as we make changes elsewhere in the worksheet. Furthermore, if we had other worksheets in this workbook, we could monitor changes to B15 of the OrderQuantity worksheet even from these other worksheets. The Watch Window is observable regardless of where we are in any worksheet of a workbook.

SUMMARY

In this appendix we have discussed how to build effective spreadsheet models using Excel. We provided an overview on workbooks and worksheets and details on useful Excel functions. We also discussed a set of principles for good modeling and tools for auditing spreadsheet models.

PROBLEMS

Nowlin Plastics

1. Open the file *Nowlin Plastics*. Recall that we have modeled total profit for the product CD-50 in this spreadsheet. Suppose we have a second product called a CD-100, with the following characteristics:

$$Fixed\ Cost = \$2500$$
$$Variable\ Cost\ per\ Unit = \$1.67$$
$$Selling\ Price\ per\ Unit = \$4.40$$

Extend the model so that the profit is calculated for each product and then totaled to give an overall profit generated for the two products. Use a CD-100 production volume of 1200. Save this file as *Nowlin Plastics2. Hint:* Place the data for CD-100 in column C and copy the formulas in rows 14, 16, and 18 to column C.

2. Assume that in an empty Excel worksheet in cell A1 you enter the formula =B1*$F$3. You now copy this formula into cell E6. What is the modified formula that appears in E6?

Foster Rev

3. Open the file *Foster Rev*. Select cells B6:E8 and name these cells Shipping_Cost. Select cells B19:E21 and name these cells Units_Shipped. Use these names in the SUMPRODUCT function in cell C14 to compute cost and verify that you obtain the same cost ($39,500).

4. Open the file *Nowlin Plastics*. Recall that we have modeled total profit for the product CD-50 in this spreadsheet. Modify the spreadsheet to take into account production capacity and forecasted demand. If forecasted demand is less than or equal to capacity, Nowlin will produce only the forecasted demand; otherwise, they will produce the full capacity. For this example, use forecasted demand of 1200 and capacity of 1500. *Hint:* Enter demand and capacity into the data section of the model. Then use an IF statement to calculate production volume.

Cox Electric

5. Cox Electric makes electronic components and has estimated the following for a new design of one of its products:

$$Fixed\ Cost = \$10,000$$
$$Revenue\ per\ unit = \$0.65$$
$$Material\ cost\ per\ unit = \$0.15$$
$$Labor\ cost\ per\ unit = \$0.10$$

These data are given in the spreadsheet *Cox Electric*. Also in the spreadsheet in row 14 is a profit model that gives the profit (or loss) for a specified volume (cell C14).

a. Use the Show Formula button in the Formula Auditing Group of the Formulas tab to see the formulas and cell references used in row 14.

b. Use the Trace Precedents tool to see how the formulas are dependent on the elements of the data section.

c. Use trial and error, by trying various values of volume in cell C14, to arrive at a breakeven volume.

6. Return to the Cox Electric spreadsheet. Build a table of profits based on different volume levels by doing the following: In cell C15, enter a volume of 20,000. Look at each formula in row 14 and decide which references should be absolute or relative for purposes of copying the formulas to row 15. Make the necessary changes to row 14 (change any references that should be absolute by putting in $). Copy cells D14:I14 to row 15. Continue this with new rows until a positive profit is found. Save your file as *Cox_Breakeven*.

OM455

7. Open the workbook *OM455*. Save the file under a new name, *OM455COUNTIF*. Suppose we wish to automatically count the number of each letter grade.

   a. Begin by putting the letters A, B, C, D, and F in cells C29:C33. Use the COUNTIF function in cells D29:D33 to count the number of each letter grade. *Hint:* Create the necessary COUNTIF function in cell D29. Use absolute referencing on the range ($E14:$E$24) and then copy the function to cells D30:D33 to count the number of each of the other letter grades.

   b. We are considering a different grading scale as follows:

Lower	Upper	Grade
0	69	F
70	76	D
77	84	C
85	92	B
93	100	A

   For the current list of students, use the COUNTIF function to determine the number of A, B, C, D, and F letter grades earned under this new system.

OM455

8. Open the workbook *OM455*. Save the file under a new name, *OM4555Revised*. Suppose we wish to use a more refined grading system, as shown below:

Lower	Upper	Grade
0	59	F
60	69	D
70	72	C−
73	76	C−
77	79	C+
80	82	B−
83	86	B
87	89	B+
90	92	A−
93	100	A

   Update the file to use this more refined grading system. How many of each letter grade are awarded under the new system? *Hint:* Build a new grading table and use VLOOKUP and an absolute reference to the table. Then use COUNTIF to count the number of each letter grade.

Newton_data

9. Newton Manufacturing produces scientific calculators. The models are N350, N450, and the N900. Newton has planned its distribution of these products around eight customer zones: Brazil, China, France, Malaysia, U.S. Northeast, U.S. Southeast, U.S. Midwest, and U.S. West. Data for the current quarter (volume to be shipped in thousands of units) for each product and each customer zone are given in the file *Newton_data*.

   Newton would like to know the total number of units going to each customer zone and also the total units of each product shipped. There are several ways to get this information from the data set. One way is to use the SUMIF function.

   The SUMIF function extends the SUM function by allowing the user to add the values of cells meeting a logical condition. This general form of the function is

   =SUMIF(*test range, condition, range to be summed*)

The *test range* is an area to search to test the *condition,* and the *range to be summed* is the position of the data to be summed. So, for example, using the *Newton_data* file, we would use the following function to get the total units sent to Malaysia:

$$=SUMIF(A3:A26,A3,C3:C26)$$

Here, A3 is Malaysia, A3:A26 is the range of customer zones, and C3:C26 are the volumes for each product for these customer zones. The SUMIF looks for matches of Malaysia in column A and, if a match is found, adds the volume to the total. Use the SUMIF function to get each total volume by zone and each total volume by product.

Williamson

10. Consider the transportation model given in the Excel file *Williamson.* It is a model that is very similar to the Foster Generators model. Williamson produces a single product and has plants in Atlanta, Lexington, Chicago, and Salt Lake City and warehouses in Portland, St. Paul, Las Vegas, Tuscon, and Cleveland. Each plant has a capacity and each warehouse has a demand. Williamson would like to find a low-cost shipping plan. Mr. Williamson has reviewed the results and notices right away that the total cost is way out of line. Use the Formula Auditing Tools under the Formulas tab in Excel to find any errors in this model. Correct the errors. *Hint:* There are two errors in this model. Be sure to check every formula.

Self-Test Solutions and Answers to Even-Numbered Problems

2. =F6*$F$3

4.

	A	B
1	**Nowlin Plastics**	
2		
3	Fixed Cost	$3,000.00
4		
5	Variable Cost Per Unit	$2.00
6		
7	Selling Price Per Unit	$5.00
8		
9	Capacity	1500
10		
11	Forecasted Demand	1200
12		
13	**Model**	
14		
15	Production Volume	1200
16		
17	Total Cost	$5,400.00
18		
19	Total Revenue	$6,000.00
20		
21	Total Profit (Loss)	$600.00
22		

	A	B
14		
15	Production Volume	=IF(B11<B9,B11,B9)
16		
17	Total Cost	=B3+B5*B15
18		
19	Total Revenue	=B7*B15
20		
21	Total Profit (Loss)	=B19-B17
22		

6.

Cell	Formula
D14	=C14*$B$3
E14	=C14*$B$7
F14	=C14*$B$9
G14	=$B$5
H14	=SUM(E14:G14)
I14	=D14-H14

	A	B	C	D	E	F	G	H	I
1	**Cox Electric Breakeven Analysis**								
2									
3	Revenue per Unit	$0.63							
4									
5	Fixed Costs	$10,000.00							
6									
7	Material Cost per Unit	$0.15							
8									
9	Labor Cost per Unit	$0.10							
10									
11									
12	**Model**								
13			Volume	Total Revenue	Material Cost	Labor Cost	Fixed Cost	Total Cost	Profit
14			10000	$6,300.00	$1,500.00	$1,000.00	$10,000.00	$12,500.00	-$6,200.00
15			20000	$12,600.00	$3,000.00	$2,000.00	$10,000.00	$15,000.00	-$2,400.00
16			30000	$18,900.00	$4,500.00	$3,000.00	$10,000.00	$17,500.00	$1,400.00
17									

8.

Grade	Count
F	1
D	2
C-	1
C-	1
C+	0
B-	2
B	1
B+	0
A-	1
A	3

10. Error in SUMPRODUCT range in cell B17
Cell A23 should be Lexington.

Appendix   Areas for the Standard Normal Distribution

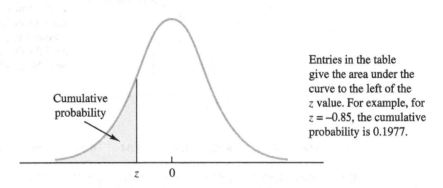

Entries in the table give the area under the curve to the left of the z value. For example, for z = –0.85, the cumulative probability is 0.1977.

z	0.00	0.01	0.02	0.03	0.04	0.05	0.06	0.07	0.08	0.09
−3.0	0.0013	0.0013	0.0013	0.0012	0.0012	0.0011	0.0011	0.0011	0.0010	0.0010
−2.9	0.0019	0.0018	0.0018	0.0017	0.0016	0.0016	0.0015	0.0015	0.0014	0.0014
−2.8	0.0026	0.0025	0.0024	0.0023	0.0023	0.0022	0.0021	0.0021	0.0020	0.0019
−2.7	0.0035	0.0034	0.0033	0.0032	0.0031	0.0030	0.0029	0.0028	0.0027	0.0026
−2.6	0.0047	0.0045	0.0044	0.0043	0.0041	0.0040	0.0039	0.0038	0.0037	0.0036
−2.5	0.0062	0.0060	0.0059	0.0057	0.0055	0.0054	0.0052	0.0051	0.0049	0.0048
−2.4	0.0082	0.0080	0.0078	0.0075	0.0073	0.0071	0.0069	0.0068	0.0066	0.0064
−2.3	0.0107	0.0104	0.0102	0.0099	0.0096	0.0094	0.0091	0.0089	0.0087	0.0084
−2.2	0.0139	0.0136	0.0132	0.0129	0.0125	0.0122	0.0119	0.0116	0.0113	0.0110
−2.1	0.0179	0.0174	0.0170	0.0166	0.0162	0.0158	0.0154	0.0150	0.0146	0.0143
−2.0	0.0228	0.0222	0.0217	0.0212	0.0207	0.0202	0.0197	0.0192	0.0188	0.0183
−1.9	0.0287	0.0281	0.0274	0.0268	0.0262	0.0256	0.0250	0.0244	0.0239	0.0233
−1.8	0.0359	0.0351	0.0344	0.0336	0.0329	0.0322	0.0314	0.0307	0.0301	0.0294
−1.7	0.0446	0.0436	0.0427	0.0418	0.0409	0.0401	0.0392	0.0384	0.0375	0.0367
−1.6	0.0548	0.0537	0.0526	0.0516	0.0505	0.0495	0.0485	0.0475	0.0465	0.0455
−1.5	0.0668	0.0655	0.0643	0.0630	0.0618	0.0606	0.0594	0.0582	0.0571	0.0559
−1.4	0.0808	0.0793	0.0778	0.0764	0.0749	0.0735	0.0721	0.0708	0.0694	0.0681
−1.3	0.0968	0.0951	0.0934	0.0918	0.0901	0.0885	0.0869	0.0853	0.0838	0.0823
−1.2	0.1151	0.1131	0.1112	0.1093	0.1075	0.1056	0.1038	0.1020	0.1003	0.0985
−1.1	0.1357	0.1335	0.1314	0.1292	0.1271	0.1251	0.1230	0.1210	0.1190	0.1170
−1.0	0.1587	0.1562	0.1539	0.1515	0.1492	0.1469	0.1446	0.1423	0.1401	0.1379
−0.9	0.1841	0.1814	0.1788	0.1762	0.1736	0.1711	0.1685	0.1660	0.1635	0.1611
−0.8	0.2119	0.2090	0.2061	0.2033	0.2005	0.1977	0.1949	0.1922	0.1894	0.1867
−0.7	0.2420	0.2389	0.2358	0.2327	0.2296	0.2266	0.2236	0.2206	0.2177	0.2148
−0.6	0.2743	0.2709	0.2676	0.2643	0.2611	0.2578	0.2546	0.2514	0.2483	0.2451
−0.5	0.3085	0.3050	0.3015	0.2981	0.2946	0.2912	0.2877	0.2843	0.2810	0.2776
−0.4	0.3446	0.3409	0.3372	0.3336	0.3300	0.3264	0.3228	0.3192	0.3156	0.3121
−0.3	0.3821	0.3783	0.3745	0.3707	0.3669	0.3632	0.3594	0.3557	0.3520	0.3483
−0.2	0.4207	0.4168	0.4129	0.4090	0.4052	0.4013	0.3974	0.3936	0.3897	0.3859
−0.1	0.4602	0.4562	0.4522	0.4483	0.4443	0.4404	0.4364	0.4325	0.4286	0.4247
−0.0	0.5000	0.4960	0.4920	0.4880	0.4840	0.4801	0.4761	0.4721	0.4681	0.4641

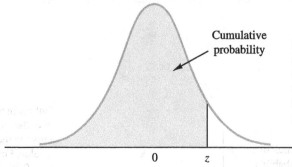

Cumulative probability

Entries in the table give the area under the curve to the left of the z value. For example, for $z = 1.25$, the cumulative probability is 0.8944.

z	0.00	0.01	0.02	0.03	0.04	0.05	0.06	0.07	0.08	0.09
0.0	0.5000	0.5040	0.5080	0.5120	0.5160	0.5199	0.5239	0.5279	0.5319	0.5359
0.1	0.5398	0.5438	0.5478	0.5517	0.5557	0.5596	0.5636	0.5675	0.5714	0.5753
0.2	0.5793	0.5832	0.5871	0.5910	0.5948	0.5987	0.6026	0.6064	0.6103	0.6141
0.3	0.6179	0.6217	0.6255	0.6293	0.6331	0.6368	0.6406	0.6443	0.6480	0.6517
0.4	0.6554	0.6591	0.6628	0.6664	0.6700	0.6736	0.6772	0.6808	0.6844	0.6879
0.5	0.6915	0.6950	0.6985	0.7019	0.7054	0.7088	0.7123	0.7157	0.7190	0.7224
0.6	0.7257	0.7291	0.7324	0.7357	0.7389	0.7422	0.7454	0.7486	0.7517	0.7549
0.7	0.7580	0.7611	0.7642	0.7673	0.7704	0.7734	0.7764	0.7794	0.7823	0.7852
0.8	0.7881	0.7910	0.7939	0.7967	0.7995	0.8023	0.8051	0.8078	0.8106	0.8133
0.9	0.8159	0.8186	0.8212	0.8238	0.8264	0.8289	0.8315	0.8340	0.8365	0.8389
1.0	0.8413	0.8438	0.8461	0.8485	0.8508	0.8531	0.8554	0.8577	0.8599	0.8621
1.1	0.8643	0.8665	0.8686	0.8708	0.8729	0.8749	0.8770	0.8790	0.8810	0.8830
1.2	0.8849	0.8869	0.8888	0.8907	0.8925	0.8944	0.8962	0.8980	0.8997	0.9015
1.3	0.9032	0.9049	0.9066	0.9082	0.9099	0.9115	0.9131	0.9147	0.9162	0.9177
1.4	0.9192	0.9207	0.9222	0.9236	0.9251	0.9265	0.9279	0.9292	0.9306	0.9319
1.5	0.9332	0.9345	0.9357	0.9370	0.9382	0.9394	0.9406	0.9418	0.9429	0.9441
1.6	0.9452	0.9463	0.9474	0.9484	0.9495	0.9505	0.9515	0.9525	0.9535	0.9545
1.7	0.9554	0.9564	0.9573	0.9582	0.9591	0.9599	0.9608	0.9616	0.9625	0.9633
1.8	0.9641	0.9649	0.9656	0.9664	0.9671	0.9678	0.9686	0.9693	0.9699	0.9706
1.9	0.9713	0.9719	0.9726	0.9732	0.9738	0.9744	0.9750	0.9756	0.9761	0.9767
2.0	0.9772	0.9778	0.9783	0.9788	0.9793	0.9798	0.9803	0.9808	0.9812	0.9817
2.1	0.9821	0.9826	0.9830	0.9834	0.9838	0.9842	0.9846	0.9850	0.9854	0.9857
2.2	0.9861	0.9864	0.9868	0.9871	0.9875	0.9878	0.9881	0.9884	0.9887	0.9890
2.3	0.9893	0.9896	0.9898	0.9901	0.9904	0.9906	0.9909	0.9911	0.9913	0.9913
2.4	0.9916	0.9920	0.9922	0.9925	0.9927	0.9929	0.9931	0.9932	0.9934	0.9936
2.5	0.9938	0.9940	0.9941	0.9943	0.9945	0.9946	0.9948	0.9949	0.9951	0.9952
2.6	0.9953	0.9955	0.9956	0.9957	0.9959	0.9960	0.9961	0.9962	0.9963	0.9964
2.7	0.9965	0.9966	0.9967	0.9968	0.9969	0.9970	0.9971	0.9972	0.9973	0.9974
2.8	0.9974	0.9975	0.9976	0.9977	0.9977	0.9978	0.9979	0.9979	0.9980	0.9981
2.9	0.9981	0.9982	0.9982	0.9983	0.9984	0.9984	0.9985	0.9985	0.9986	0.9986
3.0	0.9987	0.9987	0.9987	0.9988	0.9988	0.9989	0.9989	0.9989	0.9990	0.9990

Appendix   Values of $e^{-\lambda}$

λ	$e^{-\lambda}$	λ	$e^{-\lambda}$	λ	$e^{-\lambda}$
0.05	0.9512	2.05	0.1287	4.05	0.0174
0.10	0.9048	2.10	0.1225	4.10	0.0166
0.15	0.8607	2.15	0.1165	4.15	0.0158
0.20	0.8187	2.20	0.1108	4.20	0.0150
0.25	0.7788	2.25	0.1054	4.25	0.0143
0.30	0.7408	2.30	0.1003	4.30	0.0136
0.35	0.7047	2.35	0.0954	4.35	0.0129
0.40	0.6703	2.40	0.0907	4.40	0.0123
0.45	0.6376	2.45	0.0863	4.45	0.0117
0.50	0.6065	2.50	0.0821	4.50	0.0111
0.55	0.5769	2.55	0.0781	4.55	0.0106
0.60	0.5488	2.60	0.0743	4.60	0.0101
0.65	0.5220	2.65	0.0707	4.65	0.0096
0.70	0.4966	2.70	0.0672	4.70	0.0091
0.75	0.4724	2.75	0.0639	4.75	0.0087
0.80	0.4493	2.80	0.0608	4.80	0.0082
0.85	0.4274	2.85	0.0578	4.85	0.0078
0.90	0.4066	2.90	0.0550	4.90	0.0074
0.95	0.3867	2.95	0.0523	4.95	0.0071
1.00	0.3679	3.00	0.0498	5.00	0.0067
1.05	0.3499	3.05	0.0474	5.05	0.0064
1.10	0.3329	3.10	0.0450	5.10	0.0061
1.15	0.3166	3.15	0.0429	5.15	0.0058
1.20	0.3012	3.20	0.0408	5.20	0.0055
1.25	0.2865	3.25	0.0388	5.25	0.0052
1.30	0.2725	3.30	0.0369	5.30	0.0050
1.35	0.2592	3.35	0.0351	5.35	0.0047
1.40	0.2466	3.40	0.0334	5.40	0.0045
1.45	0.2346	3.45	0.0317	5.45	0.0043
1.50	0.2231	3.50	0.0302	5.50	0.0041
1.55	0.2122	3.55	0.0287	5.55	0.0039
1.60	0.2019	3.60	0.0273	5.60	0.0037
1.65	0.1920	3.65	0.0260	5.65	0.0035
1.70	0.1827	3.70	0.0247	5.70	0.0033
1.75	0.1738	3.75	0.0235	5.75	0.0032
1.80	0.1653	3.80	0.0224	5.80	0.0030
1.85	0.1572	3.85	0.0213	5.85	0.0029
1.90	0.1496	3.90	0.0202	5.90	0.0027
1.95	0.1423	3.95	0.0193	5.95	0.0026
2.00	0.1353	4.00	0.0183	6.00	0.0025
				7.00	0.0009
				8.00	0.000335
				9.00	0.000123
				10.00	0.000045

G